S0-AYT-119

McGRAW-HILL YEARBOOK OF SCIENCE & TECHNOLOGY

2014

McGRAW-HILL YEARBOOK OF SCIENCE & TECHNOLOGY

2014

Comprehensive coverage of recent events and research as compiled by
the staff of the McGraw-Hill Encyclopedia of Science & Technology

New York   Chicago   San Francisco   Athens   London   Madrid

Mexico City   Milan   New Delhi   Singapore   Sydney   Toronto

On the front cover
Image of the Sun made with the Atmospheric Imaging Assembly (AIA) aboard the *Solar Dynamics Observatory* (*SDO*) satellite, with extreme ultraviolet light from the spectral line at a wavelength of 19.3 nm. The image shows a mix of 1- and 10-million-kelvin plasma. (*SDO; AIA*)

503
MIAY
2014

ISBN   978-0-07-183106-2
MHID   0-07-183106-1
ISSN   0076-2016

McGRAW-HILL YEARBOOK OF SCIENCE & TECHNOLOGY
Copyright © 2014 by McGraw-Hill Education.
All rights reserved. Printed in the United States of America.
Except as permitted under the United States Copyright Act of 1976,
no part of this publication may be reproduced or distributed in any
form or by any means, or stored in a database or retrieval system,
without prior written permission of the publisher.

The following articles are excluded from McGraw-Hill Education Copyright:
Aluminum-based battery technologies; Biomarkers: key to exposure reconstruction;
Data-mining and informatics approaches for environmental contaminants; Dawn's
asteroid exploration; Evolution of asteroid 4 Vesta; Future of fungal genomics for energy
and the environment; LED roadway lighting: the Los Angeles conversion project;
Mobile search and social media modeling in the molecular sciences; Mining Internet
for epidemiology; Personal chemical exposure informatics; Strength loss in decayed
wood; The electrical nature of thunderstorms.

1 2 3 4 5 6 7 8 9 0   DOW/DOW   1 9 8 7 6 5 4 3

This book was printed on acid-free paper.

*It was set in Garamond Book and Neue Helvetica Black Condensed by
Aptara, New Delhi, India. The art was prepared by Aptara.
The book was printed and bound by RR Donnelley.*

Contents

$199.00/$195.91

FEB 12 2014

Editorial and Production

John Rennie, Editorial Director

Jonathan Weil, Senior Staff Editor

David Blumel, Senior Staff Editor

Stefan Malmoli, Senior Staff Editor

Hilary Maybaum, Senior Online Editor

Charles Wagner, Manager, Digital Content

Renee Taylor, Editorial Coordinator

Richard C. Ruzycka, Senior Production Supervisor

Frank Kotowski, Jr., Managing Editor

Consulting Editors

Prof. Vernon D. Barger. *Vilas Professor and Van Vleck Professor of Physics, University of Wisconsin-Madison.* CLASSICAL MECHANICS; ELEMENTARY PARTICLE PHYSICS; THEORETICAL PHYSICS.

Prof. Rahim F. Benekohal. *Department of Civil and Environmental Engineering, University of Illinois, Urbana-Champaign.* TRANSPORTATION ENGINEERING.

Dr. James A. Birchler. *Division of Biological Sciences, University of Missouri, Columbia.* GENETICS.

Dr. Marty K. Bradley. *The Boeing Company, Boeing Research and Technology, Huntington Beach, California.* AERONAUTICAL ENGINEERING AND PROPULSION.

Robert D. Briskman. *Technical Executive, Sirius XM Radio, New York.* TELECOMMUNICATIONS.

Dr. Mark W. Chase. *Molecular Systematics Section, Jodrell Laboratory, Royal Botanic Gardens, Kew, Richmond, Surrey, United Kingdom.* PLANT TAXONOMY.

Prof. Wai-Fah Chen. *Department of Civil and Environmental Engineering, University of Hawaii at Manoa, Honolulu, Hawaii.* CIVIL ENGINEERING.

Prof. J. John Cohen. *Department of Immunology, University of Colorado Medical School, Aurora.* IMMUNOLOGY.

Prof. Peter J. Davies. *Department of Plant Biology, Cornell University, Ithaca, New York.* PLANT PHYSIOLOGY.

Prof. Mohammed E. El-Hawary. *Associate Dean of Engineering, Dalhousie University, Halifax, Nova Scotia, Canada.* ELECTRICAL POWER ENGINEERING.

Dr. Gaithri A. Fernando. *Department of Psychology, California State University, Los Angeles.* CLINICAL PSYCHOLOGY.

Barry A. J. Fisher. *Retired; formerly, Director, Scientific Services Bureau, Los Angeles County Sheriff's Department, Los Angeles, California.* FORENSIC SCIENCE AND TECHNOLOGY.

Dr. Kenneth G. Foote. *Woods Hole Oceanographic Institution, Woods Hole, Massachusetts.* ACOUSTICS.

Dr. Margaret L. Fraiser. *Department of Geosciences, University of Wisconsin–Milwaukee.* INVERTEBRATE PALEONTOLOGY.

Dr. Richard L. Greenspan. *Retired; formerly, The Charles Stark Draper Laboratory, Cambridge, Massachusetts.* NAVIGATION.

Prof. Joseph H. Hamilton. *Landon C. Garland Distinguished Professor of Physics, Department of Physics and Astronomy, Vanderbilt University, Nashville, Tennessee.* NUCLEAR PHYSICS.

Prof. Terry Harrison. *Department of Anthropology, Paleoanthropology Laboratory, New York University, New York.* ANTHROPOLOGY AND ARCHEOLOGY.

Dr. Ralph E. Hoffman. *Yale Psychiatric Institute, Yale University School of Medicine, New Haven, Connecticut.* PSYCHIATRY.

Dr. Beat Jeckelmann. *Head of Electricity Section, Federal Office of Metrology (METAS), Bern-Wabern, Switzerland.* ELECTRICITY AND ELECTROMAGNETISM.

Dr. S. C. Jong. *Senior Staff Scientist and Program Director, Mycology and Protistology Program, American Type Culture Collection, Manassas, Virginia.* MYCOLOGY.

Prof. Robert E. Knowlton. *Department of Biological Sciences, George Washington University, Washington, DC.* INVERTEBRATE ZOOLOGY.

Prof. Chao-Jun Li. *Canada Research Chair in Green Chemistry, Department of Chemistry, McGill University, Montreal, Quebec, Canada.* ORGANIC CHEMISTRY.

Prof. Donald W. Linzey. *Department of Biology, Wytheville Community College, Wytheville, Virginia.* VERTEBRATE ZOOLOGY.

Dr. Dan Luss. *Cullen Professor of Engineering, Department of Chemical and Biomolecular Engineering, University of Houston, Texas.* CHEMICAL ENGINEERING.

Prof. Albert Marden. *School of Mathematics, University of Minnesota, Minneapolis.* MATHEMATICS.

Dr. Ramon A. Mata-Toledo. *Professor of Computer Science, James Madison University, Harrisonburg, Virginia.* COMPUTING.

Prof. Krzysztof Matyjaszewski. *J. C. Warner Professor of Natural Sciences, Department of Chemistry, Carnegie Mellon University, Pittsburgh, Pennsylvania.* POLYMER SCIENCE AND ENGINEERING.

Prof. Jay M. Pasachoff. *Director, Hopkins Observatory, and Field Memorial Professor of Astronomy, Williams College, Williamstown, Massachusetts.* ASTRONOMY.

Prof. Stanley Pau. *College of Optical Sciences, University of Arizona, Tucson.* ELECTROMAGNETIC RADIATION AND OPTICS.

Dr. William Peck, *Department of Geology, Colgate University, Hamilton, New York.* MINERALOGY AND PETROLOGY.

Dr. Marcia M. Pierce. *Department of Biological Sciences, Eastern Kentucky University, Richmond.* MICROBIOLOGY.

Dr. Donald Platt. *Micro Aerospace Solutions, Inc., Melbourne, Florida.* SPACE TECHNOLOGY.

Dr. Kenneth P. H. Pritzker. *Professor, Laboratory Medicine and Pathobiology, and Surgery, University of Toronto, and Pathology and Laboratory Medicine, Mount Sinai Hospital, Toronto, Ontario, Canada.* MEDICINE AND PATHOLOGY.

Dr. John D. Protasiewicz. *Department of Chemistry, Case Western Reserve University, Cleveland, Ohio.* INORGANIC CHEMISTRY.

Dr. Roger M. Rowell. *Professor Emeritus, Department of Biological Systems Engineering, University of Wisconsin, Madison.* FORESTRY.

Dr. Thomas C. Royer. *Department of Ocean, Earth, and Atmospheric Sciences, Old Dominion University, Norfolk, Virginia.* OCEANOGRAPHY.

Prof. Ali M. Sadegh. *Director, Center for Advanced Engineering Design and Development, Department of Mechanical Engineering, The City College of the City University of New York.* MECHANICAL ENGINEERING.

Prof. Joseph A. Schetz. *Fred D. Durham Endowed Chair Professor of Aerospace & Ocean Engineering, Virginia Polytechnic Institute and State University, Blacksburg.* FLUID MECHANICS.

Dr. Alfred S. Schlachter. *Advanced Light Source, Lawrence Berkeley National Laboratory, Berkeley, California.* ATOMIC AND MOLECULAR PHYSICS.

Prof. Ivan K. Schuller. *Department of Physics, University of California, San Diego, La Jolla.* CONDENSED-MATTER PHYSICS.

Jonathan Slutsky. *Naval Surface Warfare Center, Carderock Division, West Bethesda, Maryland.* NAVAL ARCHITECTURE AND MARINE ENGINEERING.

Dr. Arthur A. Spector. *Department of Biochemistry, University of Iowa, Iowa City.* BIOCHEMISTRY.

Dr. Anthony P. Stanton. *Teaching Professor and Director, Graphic Media Management, Tepper School of Business, Carnegie Mellon University, Pittsburgh, Pennsylvania.* GRAPHIC ARTS AND PHOTOGRAPHY.

Dr. Michael R. Stark. *Department of Physiology, Brigham Young University, Provo, Utah.* DEVELOPMENTAL BIOLOGY.

Dr. Timothy E. Valentine. *Director, Radiation Safety Information Computational Center, Leader, Nuclear Security Modeling Group, Reactor and Nuclear Systems Division, Oak Ridge National Laboratory, Oak Ridge, Tennessee.* NUCLEAR ENGINEERING.

Dr. Daniel A. Vallero. *Adjunct Professor of Engineering Ethics, Pratt School of Engineering, Duke University, Durham, North Carolina.* ENVIRONMENTAL ENGINEERING.

Prof. Pao K. Wang. *Department of Atmospheric and Oceanic Sciences, University of Wisconsin, Madison.* METEOROLOGY AND CLIMATOLOGY.

Dr. Nicole Y. Weekes. *Department of Psychology, Pomona College, Claremont, California.* NEUROPSYCHOLOGY.

Dr. Bruce White. *Department of Physics, Applied Physics and Astronomy, Binghamton University, State University of New York.* PHYSICAL ELECTRONICS.

Prof. Mary Anne White. *Department of Chemistry, Dalhousie University, Halifax, Nova Scotia, Canada.* MATERIALS SCIENCE AND METALLURGICAL ENGINEERING.

Dr. Thomas A. Wikle. *Department of Geography, Oklahoma State University, Stillwater.* PHYSICAL GEOGRAPHY.

Article Titles and Authors

Preface

Digital information technologies have followed a curious trajectory in our lives. Computers started out almost exclusively as tools for running calculations and thereby creating information. Then the digital revolution in telephony, broadcasting, and the Internet made computers important for communicating information. The invention of the Web revolutionized the ways in which people and machines could access information. And more recently, the ascent of search engines such as Google and other Web enterprises has been fueled by the importance of finding and efficiently navigating to precisely the right information.

In that sense, digital communications has grown into a function that reference volumes like this one have always served: helping people locate trustworthy answers about what they need to know. Doing so for science and technology is particularly daunting because millions of new research papers appear annually, making it all but impossible for interested nonspecialists to keep track of noteworthy discoveries in the fields they care about.

That is where the 2014 edition of the *McGraw-Hill Yearbook of Science & Technology* comes in. It continues the more than 50-year mission of this series to help keep professionals and nonspecialists alike abreast of recent key research and technological developments. It does so by offering a wide range of concise reviews invited by a distinguished panel of consulting editors and written by international leaders in science and technology.

In this edition, we report on progress in small modular nuclear reactors; the landing of NASA's Mars Science Laboratory and the Curiosity rover's first forays onto the Red Planet; the latest insights into *Homo floresiensis*, the extinct "hobbit" people who inhabited the island of Flores; quantum cascade lasers; surprises in the genomes of bonobos and kangaroos; the field of plasmonics; the devastating effects of invasive Burmese pythons on wildlife in the Everglades; the discovery of naturally occurring quasicrystals; the unexpected identification of a new spider family, the Trogloraptoridae; the exotic astronomical objects called black widow pulsars; the use of bariatric surgery to fight obesity; color electronic paper; the exploration of the asteroid Vesta by the *Dawn* space probe; the influence of the microorganisms making up the human microbiome on health; heart regeneration; a report on the construction of Masdar, the first sustainable desert city; outbreaks of hantavirus; new techniques for evaluating how planned changes to roadways will affect traffic patterns; and more than 100 other fascinating topics.

Each contribution to the Yearbook is the result of a well-informed collaboration. Our consulting editors, whose collective expertise covers a full spectrum of disciplines, select the topics with our editorial staff based on the present significance and potential applications of recent findings. One or more authorities are then invited to write concise yet thorough articles that explore the new work in each field. Through careful editing and extensive use of specially prepared graphics, McGraw-Hill Education strives to make every article as readily understandable as possible to nonspecialists.

Librarians, students, teachers, the scientific community, journalists and other communicators, and general readers continue to find in the *McGraw-Hill Yearbook of Science & Technology* the information they need to follow the rapid pace of advances in science and technology and to understand the developments in these fields that will shape the world of the twenty-first century.

John Rennie
Editorial Director

McGRAW-HILL YEARBOOK OF SCIENCE & TECHNOLOGY

2014

Access control models

In the field of computer and information security, access control is the process of managing policies that grant rights (also called privileges) to subjects in relation to objects. A policy tuple is a formal description of a policy, typically written as ⟨s,o,r⟩, where s is a subject, o is an object, and r is a right. For example, a policy may give a user named Alice, who is a member of a company's sales team, the ability to read the customer list file. In this case, the policy tuple would be written as ⟨Alice, customer list, read⟩. Another policy tuple, ⟨Bob, customer list, write⟩, may indicate that Bob, as a sales manager, has the ability to write or modify the customer list.

All of the policy tuples for an information system can be combined into a large access control matrix. In its most basic form, the access control matrix is a table that shows the mapping of rights to subjects and objects. Each row of the matrix corresponds to a single subject, while each column corresponds to a single object. The presence of a right at the intersection of a row and column indicates that the right has been granted; the absence of the right indicates that the requested access would be defined. Building on our sales team example from before, the access control matrix for that company may look something like the following **table**.

	Customer list	Alice's sales records	Dave's sales records
Alice	read	read, write	
Bob	read, write	read	read
Charlie	read		
Dave	read		read, write

Undecidability of safety in protection systems. In an influential early work in computer security, M. A. Harrison, W. L. Ruzzo, and J. D. Ullman used the access control matrix to evaluate the theoretical limits of safety in computer systems. In this limited model, called the HRU security model, subjects and objects could be created or destroyed, and rights could be entered into or deleted from the matrix. These six actions are referred to as primitive operations. These

primitive operations could then be used by commands, such as object creation or right granting. By removing all other computing abilities from consideration, the HRU model allowed the authors to focus exclusively on how much security could be guaranteed by access control systems.

The authors used the HRU model to evaluate the decidability of safety in protection systems. Given an instantaneous description of the access control matrix, also called a configuration, is it possible to create an algorithm that will determine whether a security leak can occur? In this question, a leak occurs if an arbitrary subject can acquire a particular right to an object. As such, the HRU model is determining whether or not it is possible to automatically detect system configurations that could allow leaks to occur.

Unfortunately, the authors proved that the answer, in the general case, is that it is not possible. That is, no security system that supports the primitive operations and commands of the HRU model can ever certify the security of an arbitrary configuration. Consequently, unless there are constraints placed on the creation of objects and administration of rights, the protection of sensitive information can never be wholly automated. Furthermore, the HRU model highlights the necessity of constructing more advanced mechanisms for administering privileges.

DAC, RBAC, and MAC. While the access control matrix serves as a useful foundation for theoretical analysis, storing the entire matrix is inefficient in practice. As such, computer systems typically employ a practical variant of this model. The most common variant is known as the access control list (ACL). ACLs correspond to a column of the access control matrix and are stored with the object they are protecting. For example, the ACL for Alice's sales records would denote that Alice has read and write permission, while Bob has read permission. All other requests to access that file would be denied by the system. Another less common variant is known as capabilities. In a capability-based system, each subject has an explicit list of accesses that are allowed, and the subject uses a persistent credential that attests to this authorization.

Both ACLs and capabilities are examples of discretionary access control (DAC) models. In DAC, the ability to grant or revoke access to an object is primarily reserved to the owner of the object, often the user who creates it. In some variations, the owner can grant the ability to administer privileges to other users as well. DAC approaches have the advantage that permissions can be granted or revoked in a decentralized manner, which is often very advantageous for organizations that require flexibility. DAC systems are generally identity-based, meaning that subjects correspond to human users. This feature makes DAC systems moderately easy to use.

For large enterprise settings, maintaining a system-wide DAC model would be impractical. As employees join, leave, or change positions within the organization, the access control policies must be updated accordingly. Handling this appropriately would require a great deal of coordination to ensure that system administrators are informed when policies need to be changed. In addition, policy maintenance is only one aspect of system administration, so there is no guarantee that the policies would be updated quickly. In short, handling identity-based policy updates manually is error-prone.

To streamline policy administration, while retaining some of the flexibility of DAC, many organizations adopt role-based access control (RBAC) models. In RBAC, subjects do not correspond to individual users; rather, subjects are defined to be roles, which roughly correspond to a type of job within the organization. Users are then assigned to one or more roles according to their job duties. As an example, database administrator may be one role, while software developer is another, and project manager is third. A user, Alice, may be assigned to both the database administrator and developer roles, giving her permission to act as either one, while Bob's duties may only require developer permissions.

In addition, roles can be defined to be mutually exclusive, allowing for separation of duty constraints. These constraints can be used as a means to prevent corruption or the appearance of impropriety. For example, completion of a purchase order may require approval of an office manager and project manager role. The system may enforce the requirement that no user can act in both of these roles simultaneously, thus requiring two people to sign off on the purchase.

For many organizations, the flexibility of DAC and RBAC are highly undesirable. For example, in a military or government organization, access to information is granted according to one's security clearance level. In businesses that strive to prevent conflicts of interest, access control might consider the user's prior history of accesses. Regardless of the motivation, many organizations adopt mandatory access control (MAC) models, meaning the system applies certain rules that are beyond the control of owners of individual objects.

Lattice-based MAC models. Most MAC models are based on the mathematical concept of a lattice. In a lattice, elements have a hierarchical ordering with a maximum and minimum level. All elements in the lattice are "less than" the maximum element and "greater than" the minimum. For any two arbitrary elements, it may or may not be the case that one item is less than the other. As an example, the common subset relation can be used to create a lattice. For example, if S is the set consisting of items A, B, and C (that is, S = {A,B,C}), {A} is a subset of {A,B}; however, {A,B} is not a subset of {B,C} and vice versa.

The Bell-LaPadula model is a lattice-based MAC model for confidentiality, or secrecy. The original motivation for the work was to model how information can flow in a military environment. As an example of a multilevel security system, the Bell-LaPadula model assigns objects various security levels, such as top secret, secret, confidential, or unclassified. Subjects are also assigned clearance levels that correspond to the security classifications. Any time a user starts a new process in the system, the process inherits that user's clearance level.

To ensure confidentiality, the Bell-LaPadula model employs two system-wide rules: the simple security property and the *-property (star-property). The simple security property mandates that a process cannot read data at a higher classification; a user with only confidential clearance would not be allowed to read top secret material. This property is also known as "no read up." The *-property, also called "no write down," focuses on preventing insecure writes. A process with a high clearance level cannot write to a file with a low classification level. Consequently, a process with top secret clearance (which may have read top secret material) would not be allowed to write into an unclassified file, as the system cannot guarantee that critical information would not be leaked in the process.

Variations on the Bell-LaPadula model expand on the classification system by adding compartmentation, making it a multilateral security system. In this expanded model, objects are assigned both a security level and one or more categories; the combination of the security level and categories form a lattice. For example, an object may be labeled as {secret, {nuclear}}; in that case, a process with {secret, {infantry}} clearance would be denied access, as the category does not match.

The Biba model rules work in the opposite direction of Bell-LaPadula. The goal of the Biba model is to guarantee the integrity, indicating that a piece of data is trustworthy. In this model, a new process would be considered to have high integrity. As the process interacts with additional data, such as reading data from the network, its integrity level is monotonically reduced, as if the process has become tainted.

As an inverse of the Bell-LaPadula *-property, a low-integrity process in the Biba model cannot write to a high-integrity file. That is, the system enforces "no write up." Allowing such an access would corrupt the file, possibly reducing the integrity of the whole system. However, the Biba inverse of the simple security property behaves differently than in

Bell-LaPadula. In the Biba model, a high-integrity process is allowed to read from low-integrity sources. Rather than denying the access, the system reduces the integrity classification of the process in response. As a result of this tainting procedure, the Biba model is sometimes referred to as a low watermark model; the process's current integrity level is always the lowest integrity level of all data sources that it has accessed.

The Chinese Wall model proposed by D. F. C. Brewer and M. J. Nash defines rules for preventing conflicts of interest, which is a security requirement of many businesses. The Chinese Wall model was initially defined in relation to the financial sector, but has been adapted to other enterprise settings. Objects are grouped into conflict of interest classes, and restrictions are based on these structures.

For example, an advertising company might have contracts with multiple transportation companies, multiple restaurants, and multiple retailers. If a single employee had access to the information for two competing retailers, a conflict of interest might occur. Specifically, the employee might leak information about one of the retailers to the other. The retailers would be in the same conflict of interest class. However, an employee with information about both a retailer and a transportation company would not necessarily create a conflict of interest, as these companies are not competitors. Thus, the retailer and transportation company would be in different conflict of interest classes.

In the Chinese Wall model, a company dataset refers to the collection of data related to a particular company. Once an employee has accessed data from one company dataset, the simple security property states that additional read accesses are granted under two conditions: The new object belongs to the same company dataset as a previously accessed object or the new object belongs to a different conflict of interest class. The *-property requires the simple security property hold for writes, but also adds an additional requirement that prevents writing unsanitized information. Specifically, information about one company cannot be leaked to another company, even if the companies are in different conflict of interest classes, unless the information has been disguised in some way.

Non-lattice-based MAC integrity protection. The Clark-Wilson model is noteworthy in contrast to the preceding MAC models. As with the Chinese Wall model, Clark-Wilson is focused on business, rather than military, needs. Specifically, Clark-Wilson aims to ensure the integrity of business processes, or transactions. Clark-Wilson is fundamentally different than the preceding models, as the authors showed that a lattice structure is insufficient for this goal.

In the Clark-Wilson model, protected assets are classified as either constrained data items (CDIs) or unconstrained data items (UDIs). Before a transaction on a CDI can be processed, an integrity verification procedure (IVP) tests that all relevant integrity constraints on the CDI will be upheld. If so, the system would be in a valid state. A transformation procedure (TP) would then execute to change from one valid state to another. For example, in a bank setting, account balances would be considered CDIs. Before money can be transferred from one account to another, an IVP would test that sufficient funds are present. If so, a TP would execute, atomically transferring the funds.

The Clark-Wilson model goes on to define a number of certification and enforcement rules that specify the proper behavior of the system. Protection mechanisms that implement the Clark-Wilson model provide assurance that these rules are enforced and the integrity of the transaction is sound.

For background information *see* COMPUTER SECURITY; DATABASE MANAGEMENT SYSTEM in the McGraw-Hill Encyclopedia of Science & Technology.

Michael S. Kirkpatrick

Bibliography. D. E. Bell and L. J. LaPadula, Secure computer system: Unified exposition and multics interpretation, Tech. Rep. MTR-2997, Mitre Corp., July 1975; K. J. Biba, Integrity considerations for secure computer systems, Tech. Rep. TR-3153, Mitre Corp., 1977; D. F. C. Brewer and M. J. Nash, The Chinese Wall security policy, in *Proceedings of the 1989 IEEE Symposium on Security and Privacy*, pp. 206–214, 1989, DOI:10.1109/SECPRI.1989.36295; D. D. Clark and D. R. Wilson, A comparison of commercial and military computer security policies, in *Proceedings of the 1987 IEEE Symposium on Security and Privacy*, pp. 184–195, 1987, DOI:10.1109/SP.1987.10001; D. F. Ferraiolo and D. R. Kuhn, Role-based access control, in *Proceedings of the 15th National Computer Security Conference*, pp. 554–563, October 1992; M. A. Harrison, W. L. Ruzzo, and J. D. Ullman, Protection in operating systems, *Comm. ACM*, 19(8):461–471, 1976, DOI:10.1145/360303.360333; R. S. Sandhu et al., Role-based access control models, *IEEE Computer*, 29:38–47, 1996, DOI:10.1109/2.485845.

Alternative satellite navigation systems

The satellite navigation systems GPS (the U.S.-managed Global Positioning System) and GLONASS (the Russian global navigation satellite system) have been operational in some form for decades. Other global and regional navigational satellite systems are under development, however, bringing their own capabilities to satellite-based navigation.

Galileo. The European program aiming to realize a civil global satellite navigation system, managed by the European Commission (EC), realized by the European Space Agency (ESA), and operated by ESA and the European GNSS Agency (GSA), is moving from the development phase to the deployment phase. Galileo will consist of a constellation of 30 satellites, disposed on three circular medium-altitude Earth orbits (MEOs), with an inclination of the orbital planes of 56° with respect to the equatorial plane. By the end of 2014, Galileo will start to provide early services with a gradual transition toward full services as more satellites become available. The four services that Galileo will offer are the following:

1. Open Service (OS), provided at E1 (1575.42 MHz) and E5 (1191.795 MHz) carrier frequencies. The Galileo OS also will guarantee the interoperability of the system with GPS through the E1 signal that shares the multiplexed binary offset carrier (MBOC) modulation with the new GPS L1C signal.

2. Public Regulated Service (PRS), which is an encrypted service designed to offer greater robustness and higher availability for government use, transmitted at E1 (1575.42 MHz) and E6 (1278.75 MHz).

3. Commercial Service (CS), delivering added-value features for commercial applications, such as authentication and high precision. The added-value data are transmitted in the E6 band. The CS will not be part of the early services provided from 2014 onward, but a service demonstrator will be made available by that time. An early CS service is planned to be provided from 2016.

4. Search and Rescue Service (SAR) is Europe's contribution to the Medium-altitude Earth Orbit Search and Rescue (MEOSAR) system of COSPAS-SARSAT. It also will be provided as early service during 2014.

During 2010–2012, all the contracts for manufacturing and operating the Galileo system were awarded to European industries, including the realization of 22 operational satellites. These satellites will follow the four In-Orbit Validation (IOV) satellites, which were successfully launched with two launches in October 2011 and October 2012, respectively, and also will be part of the operational constellation. Contracts for the launchers have been signed as well, and the currently contracted 22 satellites are to be placed in orbit by means of Soyuz (carrying two satellites per launch) and Ariane 5 (with four satellites at a time). The plan as of mid-2013 was to have five Soyuz launches followed by three Ariane 5 missions. The first of the five Soyuz launches was scheduled for October 2013.

The first two Galileo test satellites, *Giove-A* and *Giove-B*, were decommissioned in June and July 2012, respectively, after having reached all their planned objectives. *Giove-A* and *Giove-B* had been launched in 2005 and 2008, respectively, to secure the frequencies and test the technology in space. *Giove-B* was also carrying the first passive hydrogen maser atomic clock ever flown in space.

The IOV phase is a critical milestone for the system deployment. It has many different goals, the first being the verification of all space, ground, and user components, including their interfaces, prior to full system deployment. In mid-2013, the four IOV satellites and all the involved system components were already showing outstanding performance, and the first ever Galileo-only position fix was successfully obtained on March 12, 2013.

In recent years, several important ground installations have also been set up around the globe, including the two Galileo Control Centers in Munich, Germany and Fucino, Italy, and the new Galileo Service Center (GSC) in Madrid, Spain. The GSC will act primarily as an interface between the Galileo navigation system and user communities of the Open and Commercial Services provided by Galileo.

The ultimate goal for the Galileo deployment is to achieve full operational capability (FOC) with 30 satellites in space delivering full services by 2020.

Beidou. The Chinese system, also known as Compass, and its development and deployment are usually presented by Chinese officials as a three-step program. The first Beidou system provided radio determination satellite services (RDSS) beginning in 2000. This system consisted of two geostationary (GEO) satellites and one spare, all launched between 2000 and 2003. This service was available to civil regional users by 2004. However, it required active user terminals. This means that, together with the signal disseminated by the satellites at S-band frequencies, a return link from the user receiver was necessary to establish its position. In addition to the evident limit of an active user terminal, the system also suffered low accuracy, especially in latitudinal position, due to poor geometry of the satellite constellation. In early 2000 the Chinese authorities reviewed the development plans and during 2005–2007 they announced a two-phase project initially called Compass, providing positioning services first in the region and later globally. The two phases (regional and global, respectively) were often labeled as Compass II and Compass III, to maintain continuity with the initial Beidou system, even if the fundamental concept was completely different. To reinforce such continuity, the name Beidou is now used by Chinese officials when referring to the system and the use of the name Compass now has been almost discontinued. The new system, similar to GPS and Galileo, will consist of a constellation of MEO and GEO satellites providing passive position, velocity, and time to open and authorized users by means of two dedicated services.

Beidou will provide radio navigation satellite services (RNSS), first over China and the Asia-Pacific region, until at least 2020, at which time the services should become global. The satellite constellation in its regional version consists of 14 satellites: five GEOs, five inclined geosynchronous orbits (IGSOs), and four MEOs. Those satellites were all launched during 2009–2012, and on December 27, 2011, the system started to provide services. Exactly 1 year later, on December 27, 2012, the China Satellite Navigation Office announced the availability of the Interface Control Document (ICD), which was a fundamental step for the development of Beidou user terminals. The ICD describes characteristics of the navigation signal broadcast by the system as well as details of the navigation message, including parameters of the satellite almanacs and ephemerides that were missing from a "test version" of the ICD released in 2011.

The Chinese authorities plan to make Beidou a global system by 2020. The global constellation will consist of five GEOs, three IGSOs, and 27 MEO satellites. In its current regional version, Beidou is providing navigation signals in three different frequency bands, sharing almost the same frequency allocations as Galileo. The only difference for the moment is the carrier frequency of the B1 signal (corresponding to the Galileo E1 frequency band), that is transmitted at 1561.098 MHz. However, there is a plan to shift the carrier frequency to 1575.42 MHz (the same as Galileo and GPS), and this will be done with the deployment of the global constellation. The other frequency bands at which the Beidou signals are transmitted are B2 and B3, corresponding to the E5 and E6 frequency bands already mentioned in the case of Galileo.

Other regional systems. Together with Beidou, there are also two other regional systems that are being developed in Asia, the Japanese QZSS and the Indian IRNSS.

The Quasi-Zenith Satellite System (QZSS) is the Japanese regional satellite navigation system. It will consist of four satellites, three IGSOs, and one GEO, and is designed to guarantee that at any time at least one of its three IGSO satellites is close to the zenith over Japan. QZSS is designed to be fully interoperable with GPS. The system is intended to complement GPS, improving the positioning availability, and also to augment it, improving positioning accuracy and reliability. On top of this, QZSS also is implementing a messaging service, enabling the possibility of sending short messages such as emergency warnings.

The current plan is to have the system fully deployed and providing services by 2018. The first IGSO satellite, labeled as Michibiki, was successfully launched in 2010 and is already transmitting signals. In a recently presented plan the Japanese authorities mentioned the possibility of a future extension of the QZSS constellation to seven satellites.

The Indian Regional Navigation Satellite System (IRNSS) is a seven-satellite constellation intended to cover the Indian subcontinent. Out of these seven satellites, three GEOs and four IGSOs are planned. The launch of the first satellite as of mid-2013 was scheduled for July 1, 2013. As India is also deploying a system to augment GPS, namely GAGAN (GPS-Aided Geo-Augmented Navigation), IRNSS will transmit signals intended to provide independent open and authorized navigation services. The signals will be broadcast in both S-band and L-band.

For background information *see* ATOMIC CLOCK; SATELLITE NAVIGATION SYSTEMS in the McGraw-Hill Encyclopedia of Science & Technology.

Matteo Paonni

Bibliography. D. Hayes, *The European Satellite Navigation System (GALILEO) and the European Geostationary Navigation Overlay Service (EGNOS)*, Seventh Meeting of the International Committee on Global Navigation Satellite Systems (ICG), Beijing, China, 2012; G. W. Hein et al., Envisioning a future GNSS system of systems, Part 1, *Inside GNSS*, 2(1):58–67, January–February, 2007; Q. Huang, *Development of BeiDou Navigation Satellite System*, Seventh Meeting of the International Committee on Global Navigation Satellite Systems (ICG), Beijing, China, 2012; E. Nomura, *The Quasi-Zenith Satellite System*, Seventh Meeting of the International Committee on Global Navigation Satellite Systems (ICG), Beijing, China, 2012.

Aluminum-based battery technologies

The development of advanced energy-storage technologies, such as high-energy-density batteries, is a critical component in the development of the next generation of light- and heavy-duty transportation vehicles, with the ultimate goal of developing batteries for all-electric vehicles that have a driving range >300 mi (483 km). State-of-the-art lithium-ion batteries have a specific energy (energy per unit weight) of about 150 Wh kg^{-1} and electric vehicles with these batteries do not come close to the specific energy of vehicles powered by internal combustion engines. There is great interest and motivation for society to transition from fossil-energy-based electricity to electricity generated from renewable sources such as solar or wind. For large-scale solar- or wind-based electrical generation to be practical, the development of new electrical-energy-storage systems are critical for meeting continuous energy demands and effectively leveling the cyclic nature of these energy sources.

When considering the possibilities for increasing charge-storage density, it is apparent that the use of metals having multi-electron redox couples (reductant/oxidant; for example, Al^{3+}/Al) involving the lighter metallic elements is the most attractive option. The theoretical specific energy of a battery anode (negative electrode) scales as the battery voltage times the number of electrons divided by the atomic weight of the element. Among the lighter elements, the conversion of lithium (Li) metal to lithium ion is a one-electron process, while the corresponding reaction in magnesium (Mg) is a two-electron process. The oxidation of aluminum (Al) metal is a three-electron process, and theoretically this metal is a particularly attractive choice for the anode of an advanced battery. The maximum theoretical specific energy of Li, Al, and Mg electrodes scale as 7:9:12 (atomic weight divided by the valence of the ion), assuming the voltage of the anode is roughly the same. Lithium is the third lightest element with the most negative potential of the metallic elements, but aluminum looks more attractive when it is realized that the lithium anode of state-of-the-art batteries does not use lithium metal but rather is lithium metal intercalated into graphite with the composition LiC_6. The specific energy of this anode scales with aluminum as 9:79 Al:LiC_6, a factor of almost 9 in favor of aluminum. The earth's abundance and cost of aluminum are attractive advantages for this metal as well. The theoretical capacity, abundance,

TABLE 1. Aluminum versus other metal anodes in terms of theoretical capacity, abundance, and price

Metal	Metal equivalent, mAh/g	Metal equivalent, mAh/cm^3	Abundance in earth*	Price,[†] $/kg
Al	2980	8040	0.2	1.86
Li	3860	2060	0.0002	64.34
Mg	2200	3830	0.03	3.33
Zn	820	5850	0.0001	1.83

*Relative abundance to silicon as 1.0.
[†] http://www.metalprices.com, accessed May 31, 2013.

and cost of some metals that have been used or suggested as battery anodes are listed in **Table 1**.

As a battery anode, aluminum features a trivalent electrochemical redox reaction, with a theoretical specific capacity of 2980 mAh/g and volumetric capacity of 8040 mAh/cm^3, values that are close to and four times those of lithium, respectively. Compared with other energy carriers (hydrogen, lithium, and other alkali metals), aluminum is also advantageous in terms of safety of material handling and device operation.

Aluminum-battery technology. The development and commercialization of aluminum batteries has been noted as a desirable activity for many years. The earliest research can be tracked back to the 1800s when aluminum was first used as a battery electrode. Since then, many aluminum battery chemistries have been investigated, such as Al-air, Al-MnO$_2$, Al-AgO, Al-H$_2$O$_2$, Al-S, Al-I$_2$, Al-K$_3$Fe(CN)$_6$, Al-NiOOH, and Al-KMnO$_4$, mainly as primary batteries in aqueous electrolytes. However, these aluminum-anode batteries have not been commercialized, except for some Al-air battery products on the market. A start-up company (Phinergy) has recently announced the introduction of an Al-air battery for vehicle use. The limitation of these batteries comes from the voltage loss and voltage delay due to the formation of surface oxide film and self-discharge due to Al corrosion in aqueous electrolytes. These aqueous electrolyte aluminum batteries are primary (single-use) batteries that cannot be recharged.

Inspiration for the development of rechargeable aluminum-anode batteries comes from the extensive literature of electrolytic aluminum deposition and dissolution. Most aluminum is produced by the electrolysis of alumina (Al$_2$O$_3$) in a fluoride-containing molten salt. This raw aluminum can be further purified by electrolytic dissolution and deposition in an organic electrolyte. For the electrolytic deposition of aluminum there are various types of aprotic organic electrolytes which can be distinguished by their aluminum source:

1. AlX$_3$ (aluminum trihalides, especially AlCl$_3$, AlBr$_3$, their complexes with alkali metals) in which the electrolysis is conducted in a melt or an aromatic solvent.

2. AlH$_3$ (aluminum hydrides as mixtures of Li [A1H$_4$] and AlCl$_3$) in ethers such as tetrahydrofuran.

3. AlR$_3$ (aluminum trialkyls and their complexes with alkali metals or tetraalkylammonium halides,

especially fluorides) in aromatic solvents or as melts. This process is among the most acceptable from a technical point of view.

Rechargeable Al battery. The emergence of ionic liquids (low-temperature molten salts) has given rise to new hopes for Al batteries, because aluminum does not form an oxide film in these non-aqueous electrolytes. More importantly, it was found that aluminum can be reversibly dissolved and deposited in some ionic liquids (for example, acidic chloroaluminate-based ionic liquids). This might make a rechargeable Al battery possible. As a result, some rechargeable Al-battery chemistries, such as Al-Cl$_2$ and Al-FeCl$_3$, have been studied in ionic-liquid electrolytes. However, the performance of these batteries was limited by the difficulty associated with chlorine storage, and the solubility of metal chlorides in acidic chloroaluminate-based ionic liquids. In a recent patent application, a rechargeable MnO$_2$-Al battery was reported by G. M. Brown and coworkers. This battery concept uses an electrolyte of lithium chloroaluminate in 1-ethyl-3-methyl imidazolium chloroaluminate. The battery was reported to have an average discharge voltage of 2.0 V, rechargeable capacity with tens of cycles, and good stability without self-discharge. This concept of a hybrid aluminum-lithium-ion battery increases the feasibility of using aluminum as the active electrode material for cheaper and safer rechargeable batteries. However, rechargeable Al batteries still remain as a challenge to be a viable battery system.

Single-use recyclable Al-air battery. The future for rechargeable aluminum anode batteries with an aprotic electrolyte is uncertain, but the well-developed technology for aluminum deposition and dissolution is cause for hope. Aluminum-air batteries based on an aqueous electrolyte have a murky future as well, but thermodynamics is clearly on the side of further development. **Table 2** lists the free energy content with respect to complete reaction with oxygen of a series of liquid fuels in use for internal combustion engines or under consideration for fuel cells along with aluminum metal. It is hard to beat gasoline for specific energy, but aluminum is competitive with ethanol and superior to methanol. In reality, the situation is less rosy than the numbers indicate because the formation of dense Al$_2$O$_3$ on the surface of an Al anode would inhibit its performance. Internal combustion engines have modest efficiencies (25%), so an aluminum-air battery that

TABLE 2. Energy content of various materials used as fuels compared to aluminum

Material	Specific energy, MJ/kg
Gasoline	44
Diesel fuel	43
Aluminum	29
Ethanol	28
Methanol	21

Data from R. A. Huggins, Reversible chemical reactions, chap. 4, in *Energy Storage*, Springer, New York, NY, 2010

is used once and then recycled would not need to have great efficiency to be economically viable. With the price of aluminum metal at $2/kg ($0.92/lb), it can be shown that this is equivalent to gasoline at roughly $4/gal ($1.06/L). Thus the barrier to a use once and recycle Al-air battery is the distribution system for swapping discharged Al-air batteries for fresh ones.

For background information *see* ALUMINUM; ALUMINUM METALLURGY; BATTERY; ELECTRIC VEHICLE; ELECTROLYTE; ENERGY STORAGE; INTERNAL COMBUSTION ENGINE; FREE ENERGY; IONIC LIQUIDS; OXIDATION-REDUCTION; PERIODIC TABLE in the McGraw-Hill Encyclopedia of Science & Technology.

Gilbert M. Brown

Bibliography. G. M. Brown et al., High Energy Density Aluminum Battery, U.S. Patent Application no. 20120082905, filed September 28, 2011; H. Lehmkuhl, K. Mehler, and U. Landau, The principles and techniques of electrolytic aluminum deposition and dissolution, in H. Gerischer and C. W. Tobias (eds.), *Advances in Electrochemical Science and Engineering*, vol. 3, Wiley-VCH Verlag GmbH, Weinheim, Germany, 2008, DOI:10.1002/9783527616770.ch4; Q. Li and N. J. Bjerrum, Aluminium as anode for energy storage and conversion: A review, *J. Power Sources*, 110:1–10, 2002, DOI:10.1016/S0378-7753(01)01014-X.

Ancient lethal hothouse

Earth's current climate is relatively "cold" in comparison to most intervals of geological time, with permanent ice caps at the poles. However, for most of its history, our planet was ice-free and is considered to have been in a greenhouse state. Conditions of exceptional warmth are thought to have occurred in the Early Triassic, Middle Cretaceous, and Early Eocene, with the first of these intervals, the Early Triassic, recently having been recognized as one of the hottest of all hothouse intervals.

Early Triassic world. The Early Triassic interval [approximately 250 million years ago (MYA); **Fig. 1**] came at the end of an interval of major climatic change and immediately after the greatest mass extinction found in the fossil record: the end-Permian mass extinction (252 MYA). The Carboniferous–Permian interval saw major and prolonged glacia-

tions in the southern polar latitudes, but this ice age had terminated by the end of the Early Permian. Small mountain glaciers may have persisted a little longer, but there were few (if any) glaciers left after the Middle Permian. The ocean at this time was dominated by diverse and abundant organisms, including ammonoids (extinct marine cephalopods), brachiopods, corals, foraminiferans, and radiolarians. On land, the dominant animals of the Late Permian were the herbivorous pareiasaurs (extinct anapsid reptiles with turtle-like features), and the top predators were the carnivorous gorgonopsids (extinct mammal-like reptiles). They lived in a terrestrial ecosystem with vegetation that was dominated by seed-bearing gymnosperms. Most of these marine and terrestrial organisms were lost in the end-Permian mass extinction and were replaced by the low-diversity and monotonous assemblages in the Early Triassic: A shrub-like tree fern (*Dicroidium*) and a pig-sized herbivorous reptile (*Lystrosaurus*) dominated on land, whereas mollusks (notably, the bivalve *Claraia*) appeared in great numbers in the ocean. The Early Triassic world took an unusually long time to recover from the end-Permian mass extinction, and diversity in most ecosystems remained low for 5 million years. The interval was characterized by a global absence of coal burial, the formation of deep-sea radiolarian chert (a hard, dense sedimentary rock composed of fine-grained silica) and metazoan reefs (that is, reefs formed from calcified multicellular animals), and the prevalence of small and dwarfed animals. Conditions must have been harsh at this time, and new Mesozoic marine communities were only gradually established in the Middle Triassic.

Temperature reconstructions. Calculating the temperature changes during this period of extinction has proved difficult. Calcite-based fossils are often used as "thermometers" to determine paleotemperatures. However, because organisms such as brachiopods, which create calcite-based fossils, suffered great losses in the end-Permian mass extinction, they are very rare in the Early Triassic and cannot be used for paleotemperature determinations. Other shelled fossils, such as bivalves, mainly consisted of aragonite or high-magnesium calcite that is unreliable for reconstructing the original oxygen isotopic composition that is used to infer paleotemperatures. Fortunately, conodonts (an extinct group of primitive eel-like vertebrates) produced tiny bladed teeth made of bone. The conodont bone (bioapatite) is very resistant to postdepositional (sediment into rock) changes and is ideal for temperature reconstructions in deep time (**Fig. 2**). Equally fortunate, conodonts suffered minimal loss in the mass extinction. Hence, they are able to provide a continuous temperature record across this extinction period.

Conodont oxygen isotope ratios suggest that the equatorial sea surface temperatures of the latest Permian were around 25°C (77°F), which is very similar to those of today [the annual mean value of the equatorial sea surface temperature is roughly in the range

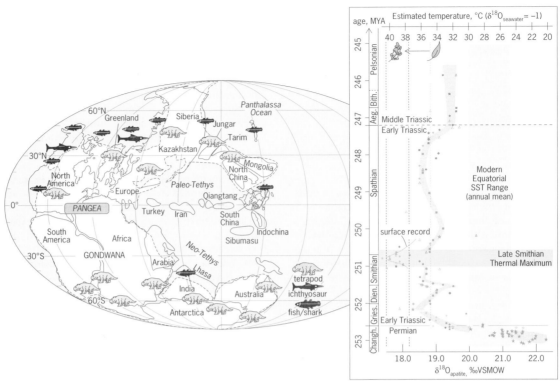

Fig. 1. Paleogeography reconstruction of the Early Triassic world (*left panel*), showing that fishes and ichthyosaurs vacated the equator during the Smithian, with tetrapods exclusively occurring in the northern and southern middle to high latitudes throughout the Early Triassic (approximately 252–247 MYA). The gray band (*right panel*) represents the temperature record of the upper water column [water depth: approximately 70 m (230 ft)]. Leaf icons and the arrow represent, respectively, the marine and land C3 plants and the temperatures at which photorespiration dominates over photosynthesis. Abbreviations of stages: **Changh.**, Changhsingian; **Gries.**, Griesbachian; **Dien.**, Dienerian; **Aeg.**, Aegean; **Bith.**, Bithynian.

of 25–30°C (77–86°F)]. The temperatures quickly increased to 32°C (89.6°F) at the beginning of the Early Triassic and continued to increase, reaching a thermal maximum within the Griesbachian (the first substage of the Early Triassic). Many Permian survivors, such as the conodont *Hindeodus* and the ammonoid

Fig. 2. A scanning electron microscope image of the Early Triassic conodont *Neospathodus*, which is used for temperature reconstruction in this study.

Otoceras, went extinct at the end of the Griesbachian, and these losses may have been caused by the Late Griesbachian Thermal Maximum. The following substage, the Dienerian, saw a temperature decrease of 3–4°C (5.4–7.2°F), which coincides with a transient recovery pulse in which several groups began to diversify. The early and middle parts of the Smithian (the third substage of the Early Triassic) represent a relatively stable high-temperature plateau, but the Late Smithian saw a further temperature increase of 2°C (3.6°F) that produced sea surface temperatures that exceeded 40°C (104°F). This was the hottest interval in the Early Triassic and one of the hottest intervals ever recorded. The final substage, the Spathian, saw an initial cooling trend followed by relatively stable temperatures in the middle part, further cooling at the end of this stage, and then stabilization of temperatures.

Effects on biodiversity. The Early Triassic record shows temperatures that are consistently in excess of modern equatorial values. Such high temperatures would be expected to have major effects on biodiversity, particularly of marine organisms. Temperatures above 45°C (113°F) cause protein denaturation (protein unfolding, which disrupts protein structure and function) for most animals, and their response (the production of heat-shock proteins) can delay death for only a short interval. However, for marine animals, the thermal limit is even lower; this occurs because aerobic metabolic demands increase with temperature, whereas oxygen solubility in seawater and bodily fluids decreases as the temperature increases. Thus, most marine organisms cannot long survive when temperatures exceed 35°C (95°F). This is most clearly observed for creatures with high performance and consequently high oxygen demand, including ammonoid cephalopods and fishes. The former group suffered a major diversity decline in the Late Smithian Thermal Maximum that was similar to its great losses during the end-Permian mass extinction. Nektonic (swimming) vertebrates, such as fishes and ichthyosaurs, show both high mobility and low oxygen-dependent thermal tolerance. They could vacate the equator and migrate to more comfortable areas when the temperatures increased. This is clearly shown in the fossil record. In the Late Permian, fishes were globally distributed. They became rare in equatorial waters during the Griesbachian and Dienerian and became very scarce in low latitudes during the Smithian. In contrast, at higher latitudes, in places such as Spitsbergen (Norway) and British Columbia (Canada), the fish fossil record during the Smithian is exceptional, with abundant and diverse faunas present. Interestingly, ichthyosaurs first appeared in northern high latitudes during the Smithian, and yet they did not appear in low-latitude waters until the Late Spathian, about several million years later. Fishes and ichthyosaurs returned to the equator during the Late Spathian to Early Anisian (Middle Triassic) and showed a globally distributed pattern that had not been seen since the Late Permian.

The active migration of vertebrates with temperature oscillations also can be examined on land. Most abundant and fairly diverse Early Triassic tetrapod fossil assemblages are known from high latitudes, such as South Africa and Antarctica in the south and Russia in the north. In contrast, Early Triassic terrestrial strata from low latitudes are widespread (for example, the Buntsandstein of central Europe) and have been studied intensively for 200 years, and yet vertebrate remains are exceptionally rare; only in the Spathian and Middle Triassic do they start to become common. Again, the prohibitively high equatorial temperatures at this time can explain this pattern: Life in the tropics was unsustainable because of the heat.

The high-temperature scenario for the Early Triassic also helps to explain the cause of the delayed recovery on land after the end-Permian mass extinction. Sea surface temperatures at or near 35°C (95°F) are likely to correspond to continental temperatures of 40–45°C (104–113°F). Such high temperatures would have been inimical (harmful) to most plants and animals. This is because photorespiration (light-dependent carbon dioxide release and oxygen uptake) dominates over photosynthesis in the majority of plants (C3 plants, which produce the three-

carbon compound phosphoglyceric acid as the first stage of photosynthesis) when temperatures exceed 35°C (95°F), whereas the upper thermal tolerance of ectotherms (animals that obtain most of their heat from the environment and thus have a body temperature very close to that of their environment) is below 45°C (113°F). Furthermore, high temperatures enhance the activities of decomposers (for example, bacteria and fungi). The low plant mass and the high decomposition rate under high-temperature conditions were probably responsible for the suspension of global peat formation in the Early Triassic. Gymnosperm forests and peat formation first returned at high latitudes in the Late Spathian to Anisian, whereas this return was much later in equatorial regions. In equatorial South China, peat-forming conditions were not restored until the Late Triassic, about 15 million years after their disappearance.

The Early Triassic low latitudes, both on land and in the ocean, were dominated by small species; this phenomenon has been called the "Lilliput effect." The prevalence of small size can be explained by the observation that many organisms decrease their body size as temperatures increase. When this is combined with increased juvenile mortalities, hothouse environments will produce fossil records that are dominated by small species. Similar size reductions among mammals are also observed during the Paleocene–Eocene transition, which is another hothouse interval occurring about 55 MYA.

Finally, another common feature observed in all greenhouse intervals is the prevalence of exceptionally warm poles. The fairly diverse reptiles and amphibians and humus-poor "rainforest"-type paleosols (fossil soils) in Antarctica during the Early Triassic all indirectly suggest warm climatic conditions; this is a probable scenario because ectotherms cannot cope with cold temperatures, whereas humus-poor paleosols are frequently associated with the enhanced decomposing activities found in warm and wet conditions. Indeed, conditions seem to have been especially favorable to polar life at this time, being warm but not excessively so; the world's hothouse was lethal only in equatorial locations. Thus, one of the clear features of the Early Triassic high latitudes was the fast recovery and explosive radiation of primitive amphibians (for example, the extinct temnospondyls) immediately after the end-Permian mass extinction. This was probably related to the warm environments, which were beneficial to these creatures in their aquatic ecosystem.

For background information *see* BIODIVERSITY; CLIMATE MODIFICATION; CONODONT; EXTINCTION (BIOLOGY); FOSSIL; GEOLOGIC TIME SCALE; GLOBAL CLIMATE CHANGE; GREENHOUSE EFFECT; PALEOECOLOGY; PALEOSOL; TAPHONOMY; TEMPERATURE; TRIASSIC in the McGraw-Hill Encyclopedia of Science & Technology.   Yadong Sun; Paul B. Wignall

Bibliography. W. C. Clyde and P. D. Gingerich, Mammalian community response to the latest Paleocene thermal maximum: An isotaphonomic study in the northern Bighorn Basin, Wyoming, *Geology*, 26(11):1011–1014, 1998, DOI:10.1130/0091-7613(1998)026<1011:MCRTTL>2.3.CO.2; M. Daufresne, K. Lengfellner, and U. Sommer, Global warming benefits the small in aquatic ecosystems, *Proc. Natl. Acad. Sci. USA*, 106(31):12788–12793, 2009, DOI:10.1073/pnas.0902080106; A. Hallam, Major bio-events in the Triassic and Jurassic, pp. 265–283, in O. H. Walliser (ed.), *Global Events and Event Stratigraphy in the Phanerozoic*, Springer-Verlag, Berlin, 1995; M. M. Joachimski et al., Climate warming in the latest Permian and the Permian–Triassic mass extinction, *Geology*, 40(3):195–198, 2012, DOI:10.1130/G32707.1; G. J. Retallack and E. S. Krull, Landscape ecological shift at the Permian–Triassic boundary in Antarctica, *Aust. J. Earth Sci.*, 46:785–812, 1999, DOI:10.1046/j.1440-0952.1999.00745.x; Y. Sun et al., Lethally hot temperatures during the Early Triassic greenhouse, *Science*, 338(6105):366–370, 2012, DOI:10.1126/science.1224126.

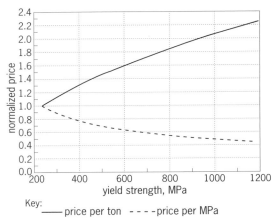

Fig. 1. Comparison of normalized price among different steel grades. (*From P. Collin and B. Johansson, Bridges in High Strength Steel, Responding to Tomorrow's Challenges in Structural Engineering: IABSE Symposium Budapest 2006, International Association for Bridge and Structural Engineering, 2006*)

Application and research of high-strength constructional steel

High-strength steel refers to a family of constructional steels with minimum yield strengths of 460 MPa. The yield strength is the stress required to produce a specified inelastic strain (permanent deformation). Compared to conventional mild (<0.3% carbon) steels with yield strengths in the range of 235–355 MPa, high-strength steels are higher in strength and lighter in weight. Moreover, an optimized balance of strength, weldability, ductility, toughness, corrosion resistance, and formability can guarantee the performance of high-strength steel, which is also known as high-performance steel.

Cost efficiency. The price of high-strength steel is usually higher than the price of ordinary-strength steel. However, the increase in steel price is lower than the increase in steel strength. Thus, when provided with the same strength, the cost of high-strength steel is actually lower than the cost of ordinary-strength steel, as shown in **Fig. 1**. If its strength can be fully utilized, it is economical to use high-strength steel in structures. Therefore, the most economical and efficient use of high-strength steel is in tension members, where buckling is not a problem. According to research and economic analysis of high-strength steels, tension members show weight savings of up to 67%, and corresponding material cost savings are as high as 32% for fabricated tension members. High-strength steel is similarly very effective for long-span bridges. Depending on the bridge type and span length, high-performance steel may provide cost savings of up to 18% and weight savings of up to 28% when compared to conventional steel materials used in bridge design. For compression members, stocky columns near the base of high-rise buildings can be designed more efficiently with high-strength steels. For these high-strength stocky columns, typical mass reductions are about 38% and cost reductions are about 18% when compared with ordinary-strength (350 MPa) steels.

Reduced pollution. Global steel production is directly and indirectly dependent on coal. According to the World Coal Association, 70% of the steel is produced in basic oxygen furnaces. Coking coal is a vital ingredient in this steel-making process. A further 29% of steel is produced in electric-arc furnaces. Much of the electricity used in this process is generated from coal-fired power stations. World crude steel production was 1.5 billion tons in 2011 and around 761 million tons of coking coal was used in the production of steel. The use of coal for steel production has been inevitably associated with a number of environmental challenges primarily associated with greenhouse-gas and particulate emissions.

Because of global warming and regional climate change, as well as the effect of particle pollution on public health and safety, there is now a growing requirement that technology developments have to be part of the solution to climate change and environmental pollution. This is particularly true for steel because its use is significantly growing in so many large economies, including the largest and fastest growing countries such as China. By using high-strength steel, fewer resources are needed for fulfilling a given function, which will result in reduced environmental impact.

Architectural and structural advantages. The application of high-strength steel in construction can reduce member size and structure weight and provide a rational structural design for large and complicated structures. The advantages to be derived from the application of high-strength steels are summarized as follows. (1) In lieu of conventional mild carbon steels, adopting high-strength steels can reduce plate thickness and member size because of

Fig. 2. China Central Television Headquarters. (*Photo courtesy China Construction Steel Corp. Ltd.*)

Fig. 3. The Chinese National Stadium.

its increased design stresses. (2) Consequently, the usable floor area of the structures can be increased and the overall weight of the structures can be reduced. Also, special architectural forms lead to many difficulties in structural design, so lightweight and slim members are usually desirable. (3) As a result of the reduction in plate thickness and member size, difficulties in welding thick plates and the amount of welding are reduced. (4) Owing to the lighter weight structures, savings may be made in transportation and erection, and smaller foundations can be constructed. (5) Mass-dependent dynamic forces, such as from earthquake actions, are reduced.

Application in China. High-strength steels have been available in the United States and Japan since the 1960s. However, early high-strength steels did not find extensive application in building and bridge structures until the 1990s because of difficulties

in weldability and inadequate ductility. With recent developments of metallurgical technology and advances in quenching and tempering processes, newly developed high-strength steels can be produced with significantly enhanced ductility, weldability, and fracture toughness. These new types of high-strength and high-performance steels have been used in the design and construction of building and bridge structures.

The China Central Television Headquarters is a 234 m, 44-story skyscraper located in the Beijing central business district. Owing to its striking style, the construction of the building was considered to be a structural challenge, especially because it is located in a seismic zone. The two L-shaped high-rise towers linked at the top result in considerably high stresses in the connection location between the mega-cantilevered steel truss and the perimeter steel

Fig. 4. Landmark Tower in Yokohama, Japan. (*Photo by Rs1421, available under a Creative Commons Attribution-Share Alike 3.0 Unported license*)

frames (**Fig. 2**). A total of 750 tons of high-strength steel Q460E (yield strength 460 MPa) was used in this project to increase the design stresses of the critical joint zones.

The Chinese National Stadium (**Fig. 3**), which is affectionately known as the Bird's Nest, has become an icon for China and the city of Beijing. This stadium was designed for the 2008 Olympic Games, with a gross floor area of 254,600 m² and seating capacity of 91,000, including 11,000 temporary seats. Twenty-four trussed columns encase the inner bowl, each weighing more than 1000 tons. The plate thickness of the columns was reduced from 220 mm to 110 mm by using Q460E high-strength steel instead of ordinary-strength steel. As a result, difficulties in thick-plate welding, transportation, and erection were reduced or eliminated.

Applications outside of China. Projects using high-strength steel worldwide include the Landmark Tower in Yokohama (**Fig. 4**), NTV Tower in Tokyo (**Fig. 5**), Sony Center in Berlin (**Fig. 6**), and Star City (**Fig. 7**) and Latitude Tower (**Fig. 8**) in Sydney. In the United States, high-performance steel (HPS345, HPS485, and HPS690) has been used in more than 400 bridges in 43 states.

Current situation. There was a 68% increase in steel production worldwide between 2000 and 2010, with China experiencing an increase of 396% for the same period (**Fig. 9**). Similarly, global use of steel increased 69% from 2000 to 2010, while the use of steel in China increased more than 400% for the same period. Because of rapid industrialization and urban-

ization, China accounted for approximately 45% of the global steel production in 2010 (**Fig. 10**), with more than half of that devoted to construction. Even for developed countries, construction steel has the greatest market share. For example, 42% of the total U.S. steel was used in construction in 2010, as shown in **Fig. 11**. Because of architectural and structural advantages, high-strength steels have been increasingly used in high-rise buildings, large-span buildings, and bridges in the past two decades. However, high-strength steel still only makes up a small fraction of construction steel. According to the 2010 China Steel Construction Society annual report, the most used steel is Q345, which accounts for 62% of the total steel consumption, but Q460 HSS is only 1% of the total steel consumption, as shown in **Fig. 12**.

Limits. With the recent development of high-strength steel and advances in metallurgical technology, high-strength steel can be produced at

Fig. 5. Nippon Television Tower (headquarters) in Minato, Tokyo, Japan. (*Photo by Kure, available under a Creative Commons Attribution-Share Alike 3.0 Unported license*)

Fig. 6. Sony Center in Berlin. (*Photo: Copyright Sony Center am Potsdamer Platz*)

a reasonable cost and preferable performance, including Chinese steel grades of Q460–Q690 (yield strength 460–690 MPa), European steel grades of S690–S960 (yield strength 690–960 MPa), and U.S. high-performance steel HPS70 (yield strength 485 MPa). However, the use of such improved steels is limited by current design codes. The Chinese code for the design of steel structures, GB 50017-2003, limits steel grades up to Q420. European and U.S. specifications for steel structures allow the use of high-strength steel up to grades S700 (700 MPa) and ASTM A514 (690 MPa), but the current specifications are established on the available experimental and analytical studies of mild carbon steels usually

Fig. 7. Star City Casino, in Sydney, Australia. (*Photo by Saberwyn, available under a Creative Commons Attribution-Share Alike 3.0 Unported license*)

Fig. 8. Latitude (Ernst & Young) Tower in Sydney, Australia. (*Photo by Randwicked, available under a Creative Commons Attribution-Share Alike 2.5 Generic license*)

with nominal yield strengths from 235–345 MPa. Consequently, more work must be done to investigate whether the members fabricated from high-strength steels can be designed according to the

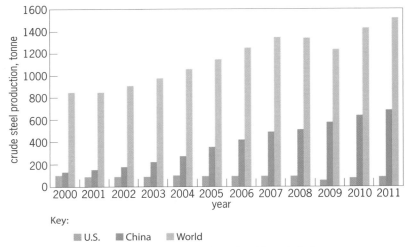

Fig. 9. Annual crude steel production. (*From World Steel Association*)

existing codes or whether the codes need to be modified to include high-strength steels.

Moreover, seismic design of buildings requires higher ductility of steels because of the expectation of inelastic behavior of structural elements and connections from rare earthquakes. With the increase in material strength, the yield-strength-to-tensile-strength ratio and elongation ratio of high-strength steel could hardly meet the requirements. Therefore, it is important to further determine the suitability of high-strength steels and elements fabricated from high-strength steels for use in seismic structures.

Recent research in China. The following discussion represents some of the research efforts for high-strength steel with yield strengths of 460 MPa or greater.

Material properties. The material properties of Q460 and Q690 were studied through monotonic-loading and cyclic-loading experiments, as shown in **Fig. 13***a*. It was found that, unlike mild carbon steel, no significant strain hardening occurs in high-strength steel Q460. For some tensile coupons, there was no well-defined yield plateau (Fig. 13*b*). Yield strength, tensile strength, modulus of elasticity, and stress-strain curves were obtained from tensile coupon tests. The stress-strain hysteretic curves of high-strength steel were obtained from the cyclic-loading experiment, and the hysteretic model for Q460 steel was proposed.

Residual stresses. It is well known that residual stresses exist in most structural steel members induced by welding, flame cutting, uneven cooling, or cold forming during processes of manufacture and fabrication. Although the self-equilibrium residual stresses are not detrimental to the cross-section strength of the steel members, the presence of residual stress will significantly jeopardize the stiffness of compression members and shorten the fatigue life of steel members under periodical load or dynamic load. The residual stress distributions of box and H sections fabricated from Q460 high-strength steel plates were measured. Both sectioning and hole-drilling methods were used in the measurement, as shown in **Fig. 14**. The corresponding simplified residual stress patterns were proposed for welded box and H section members of Q460 steel.

Column and beam-column. An experimental study on the buckling behavior and ultimate bearing capacity of high-strength steel columns has been carried out at Tongji University and Tsinghua University, including box-section and H-section columns fabricated from high-strength steel with yield strengths of 460–960 MPa. The compression specimens were tested to failure under concentric and eccentric loading, as illustrated in **Fig. 15**. The ultimate bearing capacities obtained from experiments were compared with current design codes and used to verify the theoretical analysis method. It was found that the numerical simulation results, which take into account the measured residual stress and

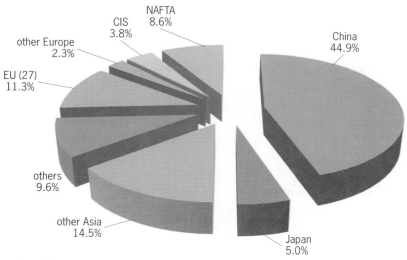

Fig. 10. Global use of steel in 2010. (*From World Coal Association*)

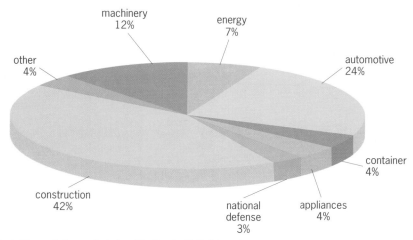

Fig. 11. U.S. steel shipments by market classification in 2010. (*From American Iron and Steel Institute*)

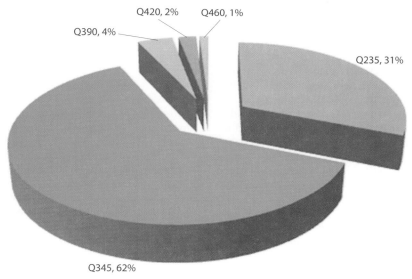

Fig. 12. The percentage of each steel grade consumed by mainland China in 2010. (*From China Steel Construction Society*)

(a)

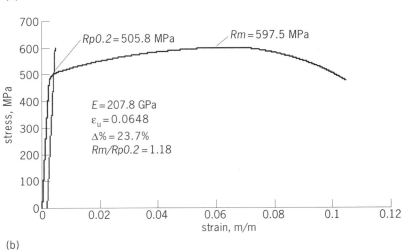

(b)

Fig. 13. Material test. (a) Tensile coupon test. (b) Stress-strain curve of Q460 steel. *Rp0.2* is the 0.2% proof stress, which is adopted as yield strength of steel plates; *Rm* is ultimate tensile stress; ε_u is the corresponding strain of ultimate stress; *E* is Young's modulus; and Δ% is the percentage of elongation after fracture.

geometrical imperfection, can accurately predict the behavior of high-strength steel columns under axial loading. Extensive numerical parametric analysis has been done to propose design recommendations for accurately predicting the ultimate bearing capacity of high-strength steel columns and beam-columns.

Hysteretic behavior. Cyclic-loading experiments were carried out to obtain the load-displacement and moment-curvature hysteretic curves of Q460 high-strength steel columns, as shown in **Fig. 16**. The cumulative plastic displacement ratio was used to study the effect of cumulative damage to high-strength steel columns. Based on experimental and finite element analysis, moment-curvature hysteretic models were proposed for

box-shaped and H-shaped high-strength steel columns.

Seismic design method. Current seismic design philosophy is based on the assumption that structural members and connections can undergo a certain plastic deformation without loss of structural bearing capacity under expected rare earthquakes. The correctness of this assumption is ensured by the specified material requirements of current seismic specifications. Accordingly, as high-strength steels may not meet the material requirements as easily as ordinary-strength steels, high-strength steel members may not be allowed to be used in seismic structures. However, the application of high-strength steel in seismic structures could be reconsidered in the level of seismic design philosophy if we give up

(a)

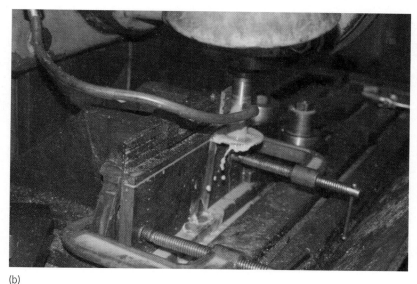

(b)

Fig. 14. Measurement of residual stresses. (*a*) Hole-drilling method. (*b*) Sectioning method.

this assumption. Consequently, two seismic design methodologies of high-strength steel structures are proposed.

Increasing earthquake-resistant design. In view of structural seismic design and performance, seismic action could be reduced in accordance with the ductility of structures, as shown in **Fig. 17**. Structures with good ductility could use reduced seismic loads in their design, so that the inelastic behavior of the structures is expected in an actual earthquake and the seismic energy could be dissipated by plastic deformation of the members and connections. Brittle structures should use higher seismic loads in their design than ductile structures to reduce the requirement of structural ductility.

Limiting yielding of structural high-strength steel components. The elastic design of steel structures under expected rare earthquakes is usually uneconomical and unrea-

sonable. Thus, seismic-resistant buildings mostly are designed as dissipative structures that allow for the formation of plastic hinges in the expected locations, such as the "strong column and weak beam" concept. However, the ductility of high-strength steel members is not guaranteed to satisfy the demands of structural plastic behavior under earthquake actions. It is important to note that the ductility of structures, in addition to the ductility of materials and members, also depends on the selection of structural systems. If an appropriate structural system is selected for high-strength structures, the plastic deformations will be isolated in the specified dissipative members to prevent the yield of high-strength steel members, as shown in **Fig. 18**. Semirigid frames could provide sufficient deformation under seismic force, and dissipative lateral force-resistant members, such as buckling-restrained braces (BRB) and buckling-restrained steel-plate shear wall (BRSW), are designed to have sufficient plastic capacity. Consequently, members with higher yield strength could be designed with sufficient overstrength (reserve strength) to not yield under earthquake actions.

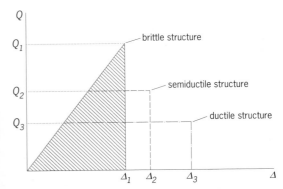

Fig. 17. The effect of ductility on the requirement of design seismic actions. Q_1, Q_2, Q_3, and Δ_1, Δ_2, Δ_3 are the design value of yield earthquake load and the corresponding required deformation capacity of brittle structure, semiductile structure, and ductile structure, respectively.

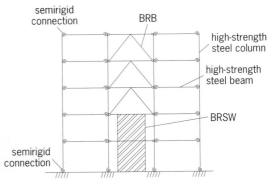

Fig. 18. Structure system limiting yielding of high-strength steel member. BRB = buckling-restrained braces. BRSW = buckling-restrained steel-plate shear wall.

(a)   (b)

Fig. 15. Axial compression test. (a) Square hollow-section column under axial concentric loading. (b) H-section column under axial eccentric loading.

Fig. 16. Test setup of cyclic loading experiment.

For background information *see* ARC HEATING; BEAM-COLUMN; COKE; COLUMN; CORROSION; EARTHQUAKE ENGINEERING; FINITE ELEMENT METHOD; METAL, MECHANICAL PROPERTIES OF; STEEL; STEEL MANUFACTURE; STRESS AND STRAIN; WELDING AND CUTTING OF MATERIALS in the McGraw-Hill Encyclopedia of Science & Technology.

Guo-Qiang Li; Yan-Bo Wang

Bibliography. R. Bjorhovde, Development and use of high performance steel, *J. Constr. Steel Res.*, 60(3–5):393–400, 2004, DOI:10.1016/S0143-974X(03)00118-4; H. V. Long et al., Field of application of high strength steel circular tubes for steel and composite columns from an economic point of view, *J. Constr. Steel Res.*, 67(6):1001–1021, 2011, DOI:10.1016/j.jcsr.2011.01.008; G. Pocock, High strength steel use in Australia, Japan and the US, *Struct. Eng.*, 84(21):27–30, 2006; Y-B Wang et al., Experimental and numerical study on the behavior of axially compressed high strength steel columns with H-section, *Eng. Struct.*, 43:149–159, 2012, DOI:10.1016/j.engstruct.2012.05.018; Y-B Wang, G-Q Li, and S-W Chen, The assessment of residual stresses in welded high strength steel box sections, *J. Constr. Steel Res.*, 76(0):93–99, 2012, DOI:10.1016/j.jcsr.2012.03.025; W. Wright, High-performance steel: Research to practice, *Public Roads*, 60(4):34–38, 1997.

Application of shape memory alloys in earthquake-resistant design

The use of shape memory alloys (SMAs) in seismic applications has been explored in structural systems such as steel braces, bridge restrainers, beam-column connections, isolation devices, and retrofitting systems. While SMAs have been shown to enhance a structure's seismic performance, their applications in civil structures are primarily focused on passive systems. Compared with active systems, passive systems have fixed properties and do not require external energy in order to function. They are therefore usually more economical, predictable, and energy efficient.

Shape memory alloys. Shape memory alloys are smart materials that exhibit unique mechanical and thermal properties. Two such properties are the shape memory effect and the superelasticity effect. Within a certain temperature range, SMAs have the ability to revert to their original shape after they have been strained in the inelastic range. This is referred to as the shape memory effect. If shape recovery occurs only upon heating, the SMAs are said to have one-way shape memory. However, if a change in shape occurs upon both heating and recooling, the SMAs are said to have two-way shape memory. At another temperature range, SMAs can exhibit the superelasticity effect, whereby they can undergo relatively large strain (up to 8%) without showing permanent deformation, and with a stress-strain curve that exhibits a distinctive plateau and a hysteresis.

In addition, certain SMAs possess other desirable mechanical properties, such as energy dissipation through hysteresis of response, good resistance to corrosion, high fatigue resistance, and high strength. All these attributes make SMAs suitable for use in many branches of engineering, including biomedical, mechanical, aerospace, and civil engineering.

Many alloys have been found to exhibit shape memory effect. Gold-cadmium (AuCd) was first noticed to exhibit reversibility of transformation as early as 1932. In 1951, similar effects were discovered in brass (copper-zinc alloy). In 1961, while working for the U.S. Naval Ordnance Laboratory, W. J. Buehler and R. C. Wiley developed a series of alloys with shape memory effect. These alloys consist of an equiatomic composition of nickel and titanium (NiTi). This type of SMA is commonly referred to as nitinol, an acronym for Nickel Titanium Naval Ordnance Laboratory. Today, more than 30 types of SMAs have been discovered. Of these alloys, NiTi and a few of the copper-based alloys have received a great deal of research and development effort because not only are they capable of recovering a substantial amount of strain, but they also can generate a rather large restoring force during strain recovery.

The shape memory and superelasticity effects of SMAs are related to their metallurgical structures. SMAs often consist of two different crystal phases. For NiTi, these two phases are martensite and

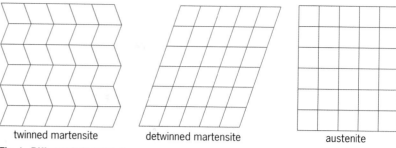

twinned martensite   detwinned martensite   austenite

Fig. 1. Different NiTi solid phases.

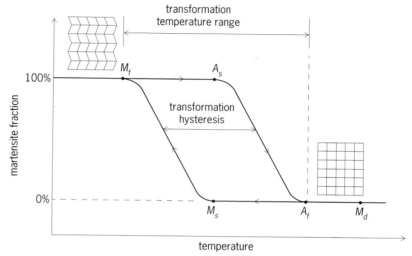

Fig. 2. Temperature-induced phase transformations of a typical SMA.

austenite. Depending on the crystal orientation direction, martensite can exist in two forms: twinned or detwinned (**Fig. 1**). Martensite is stable at low temperatures and high stresses, while austenite is stable at high temperatures and low stresses. These two phases have different mechanical properties and can be transformed into each other under different stress and thermal conditions. Therefore, SMAs exhibit versatile properties when circumstances change.

For temperature-induced solid-to-solid phase transformations, there are four characteristic temperatures at which these transformations can occur: (1) the austenite start temperature, A_s, where the material starts to transform from twinned martensite into austenite; (2) the austenite finish temperature, A_f, where the material is completely transformed into austenite; (3) the martensite start temperature, M_s, where austenite begins to transform into twinned martensite; and (4) the martensite finish temperature, M_f, where the transformation into martensite is complete (**Fig. 2**). M_d in the figure represents a critical temperature above which austenite will become stable and no solid-to-solid phase transformation is likely to occur. As shown in **Table 1**, different SMAs have different transformation temperature ranges and hystereses.

Within a given temperature range, the solid-to-solid phase transformations can occur as a result of

TABLE 1. Transformation temperature ranges and transformation hystereses of selected SMAs (Tadaki et al., 1988)

Alloy	Composition	Transformation-temperature range °C (°F)	Transformation hysteresis Δ°C (Δ°F)
Ag-Cd	44/49 atomic % Cd	−190 to −50 (−310 to −60)	≈15 (≈25)
Au-Cd	46.5/50 atomic % Cd	30 to 100 (85 to 212)	≈15 (≈25)
Cu-Al-Ni	14/14.5 weight % Al 3/4.5 weight % Ni	−140 to 100 (−220 to 212)	≈35 (≈65)
Cu-Sn	≈15 atomic % Sn	−120 to 30 (−185 to 85)	−
Cu-Zn	38.5/41.5 weight % Zn	−180 to −10 (−290 to 15)	≈10 (≈20)
Cu-Zn-X (X = Si, Sn, Al)	a few weight % X	−180 to 200 (−290 to 390)	≈10 (≈20)
In-Ti	18/23 atomic % Ti	60 to 100 (140 to 212)	≈4 (≈7)
Ni-Al	36/38 atomic % Al	−180 to 100 (−290 to 212)	≈10 (≈20)
Ni-Ti	49/51 atomic % Ni	−50 to 110 (−60 to 230)	≈30 (≈55)
Fe-Pt	≈25 atomic % Pt	≈ −130 (≈−200)	≈4 (≈7)
Mn-Cu	5/35 atomic % Cu	−250 to 180 (−420 to 355)	≈25 (≈45)
Fe-Mn-Si	32 weight % Mn, 6 weight % Si	−200 to 150 (−330 to 300)	≈100 (≈180)

an applied stress. Stress-induced phase transformation gives rise to different mechanical behavior at different temperature ranges.

When the temperature is below M_f, an SMA such as NiTi is in its twinned martensite phase. If a stress above a critical level is applied, the SMA undergoes a phase transformation to detwinned martensite and stays in this phase even upon removal of the applied load. The material can regain its initial shape only when it is heated to a temperature above A_f. Heating the SMA material above A_f not only results in shape recovery, but also leads to the formation of the austenite phase. Through subsequent cooling, the SMA transforms to its initial twinned martensite phase with little or no residual deformation. This phenomenon is referred to as the shape memory effect, that is, the ability of an SMA to recover its original shape through thermal cycling.

When the temperature is above A_f, an SMA is in its austenite phase. When a sufficiently high stress is applied, the SMA transforms into detwinned martensite. Upon removal of the load, a reverse transformation to the austenite phase takes place, with the material undergoing shape recovery and exhibiting a noticeable hysteresis loop. This phenomenon is referred to as the superelasticity effect, that is, the recovery of large strains as a result of the stress-induced phase transformations under constant temperature. If the temperature is below A_f but above M_f, there will be only a partial shape recovery after the load is removed, and the remaining strain can be recovered only via a heating and cooling cycle. When the temperature is above M_d, the SMA is stable in its austenite phase and will behave like an ordinary metal that undergoes plastic deformation when stressed beyond a certain limiting stress (**Fig. 3**).

Performance-based design. The purpose of performance-based design is to provide guidelines and methods for siting, designing, constructing, and maintaining buildings so that they have enough margin of safety to perform in a predictable manner under earthquake excitations. The basic concept of performance-based design is not new. In traditional practices, the general objectives in seismic design are to resist (1) minor earthquakes without damage, (2) moderate earthquakes with limited structural and nonstructural damage, (3) major earthquakes with limited risk to life safety, and (4) severe earthquakes without collapse, even when structural and nonstructural elements may have experienced substantial damage.

The Building Seismic Safety Council's (BSSC) National Earthquake Hazards Reduction Program (NEHRP) and the Structural Engineers Association of California's (SEAOC) Vision 2000 have set design objectives, prescribed design criteria, introduced analytical techniques for performance evaluation, and attempted to define the margin of safety inherent in buildings that conform to these provisions (**Table 2**).

For buildings to remain fully functional and operational after an earthquake, they need to have the capability to dissipate a sufficient amount of seismic energy and remain more or less damage-free (**Fig. 4**). While buildings that are designed and equipped with traditional dampers (for example, viscoelastic shear dampers, friction dampers, or metallic dampers) often have good energy-dissipation capability,

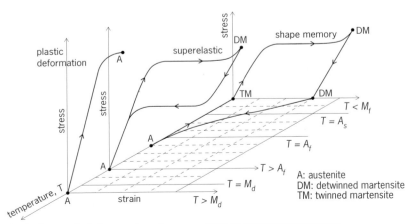

Fig. 3. Stress–strain temperature diagrams of NiTi at different temperatures.

TABLE 2. Performance-based design requirements and levels

Performance level		Description
NEHRP Guidelines	Vision 2000	
Operational	Fully functional	No significant damage has occurred to structural and nonstructural components. The building is suitable for normal intended occupancy and use.
Immediate occupancy	Operational	No significant damage has occurred to the structure, which retains nearly all of its pre-earthquake strength and stiffness. Nonstructural components are secure, and most would function if utilities are available. The building may be used for its intended purpose, albeit in an impaired mode.
Life safety	Life safe	Significant damage to structural elements, with substantial reduction in stiffness; however, a safety margin remains against collapse. Nonstructural elements are secured but may not function. Occupancy may be prevented until repairs can be instituted.
Collapse prevention	Near collapse	Substantial structural and nonstructural damage. Structural strength and stiffness substantially degraded. Little safety margin against collapse. Some falling debris hazards may have occurred.

buildings without such devices will have to rely primarily on plastic or inelastic deformations, hysteresis, and localized damage of selected structural members to absorb the seismic energy. As earthquake intensity increases, so do the inelastic deformations.

Large residual deformations are undesirable because they can dramatically affect the functionality of buildings, making them appear unsafe to occupy or impairing their structural response to subsequent aftershocks, as well as significantly increasing the cost of postseismic repairs or replacements.

Recentering, or self-centering, is defined as the ability of a building structure to resume its original configuration after a seismic event that may have caused noticeable inelastic deformations in some of the building's elements. In the event of large residual deformations, recentering capability becomes vital if a building is to remain fully functional or operational after an earthquake.

Shape memory alloys in earthquake resistant design. Certain features of SMAs make them quite desirable for meeting the requirements for performance-based seismic-resistant design. In the martensite phase, SMAs such as NiTi have good hysteresis and through thermal cycling exhibit two-way shape memory effect, which can help restore a structure to its original undeformed state after being stressed. In the austenite phase, although the hysteresis is reduced, SMAs can undergo large deformation with little or no residual strain. This superelasticity effect can be used to assist with the recentering of a structure after a seismic event. The hysteresis can also help with the structure's energy-dissipation capacity. Because the superelasticity effect is applicable over a wide temperature range, it is effective in extreme temperature conditions. For instance, the austenite finish temperature of NiTi is in the range of −50 to 0°C; a copper-based SMA, CuAlBe, exhibits superelastic behavior in the temperature range of −65 to 180°C; a newly discovered ferrous-based SMA called NCATB (FeNiCoAlTaB), has an austenite finish temperature of −62°C. Moreover, a number of SMAs have excellent fatigue and corrosion resistance and exhibit stable mechanical properties after a training process involving controlled cyclic loading and unloading of the SMA component at the expected working temperature until its mechanical properties stabilize. All these attributes make SMAs rather suitable for use in devices that enhance the performance of structures under earthquake excitations. A comparison of the mechanical properties of NiTi with steel and aluminum alloys is given in **Table 3**.

Over the years, researchers have developed constitutive models and explored material modeling and the application and design aspects of SMA-based devices in civil structures through numerical and experimental investigations. Several examples will be discussed.

SMA braces. Braces are used in concentrically or eccentrically braced frames (CBFs or EBFs) to resist lateral loads. If braces are not provided, the frames, referred to as moment-resisting frames (MRFs), will have to rely on the flexural stiffness of the columns and beams to resist the loads generated from wind and earthquakes. Braces resist lateral deflection primarily through their axial stiffness, and the addition of braces often results in a reduction in column and beam sizes.

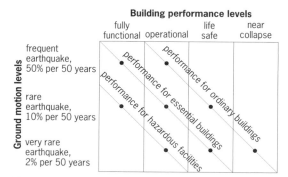

Fig. 4. SEAOC Vision 2000 performance-based seismic design levels.

TABLE 3. Comparison of NiTi shape memory alloy with steel and aluminum alloys (1 MPa = 0.145 ksi)

Property	NiTi	Steel	Aluminum alloys
Elastic modulus	8.7×10^4 MPa (Austenite) 1.4–2.8×10^4 MPa (Martensite)	200×10^3 MPa	$(70$~$73) \times 10^3$ MPa
Yield strength	200–700 MPa (Austenite) 70–140 MPa (Martensite)	250–690 MPa	230–500 MPa
Tensile strength	900 MPa (Fully annealed) 2000 MPa (Work hardened)	400–760 MPa	260–570 MPa
Recoverable elongation	8%		
Elongation at failure	25–50% (Fully annealed) 5–10% (Work hardened)	0.125–0.345% 17–21%	0.3–0.7% 11–19%

Although braced frames often have high lateral stiffness, they usually lack sufficient damping to absorb the earthquake energy. For instance, the recommended damping ratios for reinforced concrete and steel buildings are only 3 and 5%, respectively. To improve the damping capacity of these frames, supplementary energy-dissipation devices, such as frictional dampers, elasto-plastic hysteretic dampers, and viscous dampers, need to be provided. A special type of device that combines the stiffness of a brace and the energy-dissipative feature of an SMA is an SMA-equipped brace. These braces are often installed in different stories and dissipate energy through relative interstory displacements.

Because it is not economical to design and build conventional structures to resist strong earthquakes in the elastic range, an excursion into the inelastic region is often unavoidable. This results in inelastic or residual deformation, which is undesirable if the structures are to be operational or fully functional in the context of performance-based design. In addition to energy dissipation, these structures should be designed to have self-centering capability. Considering both these goals, a hybrid device incorporating energy dissipation and austenite SMA could provide an optimal solution. Examples of hybrid braces that

use frictional dampers or soft steel struts as supplementary energy-dissipating components in conjunction with SMAs are shown in **Fig. 5**. To fully utilize the superelasticity effect and to prevent buckling, SMA wires or bars should be placed in the device in such a way that they will be under tension.

Though these hybrid devices are not yet used in real construction, numerical and experimental studies have shown that when used in braced frames, they could help enhance energy-dissipation capacity and reduce residual displacements.

SMA base-isolation devices. Base-isolation techniques involve the introduction of one or more layers of energy-absorbing materials at the base of a structure to isolate the superstructure from the substructure or the foundation. The superstructure is allowed to move relative to the substructure or foundation with relatively large horizontal displacements. This decoupling effect could significantly reduce the amount of seismic energy transferred from the foundation to the superstructure. To limit the magnitude of horizontal displacements occurring in the isolator and to reduce the number of vibration cycles experienced by the structure under an excitation force, the isolation system must be provided with energy-dissipation capabilities. In terms of the technology

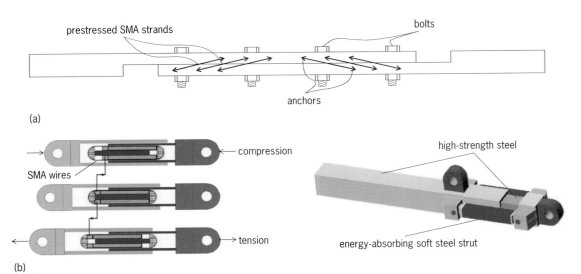

Fig. 5. Application of SMA in braces equipped with (*a*) a frictional damper (*Zhu and Zhang, 2008*) and (*b*) a soft steel damper (*reprinted from C. W. Yang, R. DesRoches, and R. T. Leon, Design and analysis of braced frames with shape memory alloy and energy-absorbing hybrid devices, Engineering Structures, 32:498–507, 2010, with permission from Elsevier, http://www.sciencedirect.com/science/journal/01410296*).

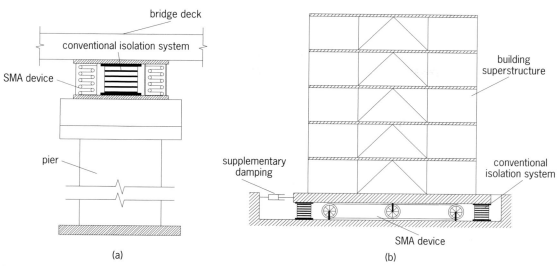

Fig. 6. Application of SMA in base-isolation system for (*a*) bridge deck (*Ozbulut and Hurlebaus, 2011*) and (*b*) building (*Qian et al., 2010*).

and materials used to achieve the decoupling and energy-dissipating effects, isolation devices can be classified as (1) rubber isolators, (2) sliding isolators, (3) rolling isolators, and (4) isolators with added energy dissipation.

It should be noted that energy dissipation by itself is a necessary but not a sufficient condition to address all problems that arise from earthquakes. To achieve a postseismic fully functional or operational level prescribed by performance-based design criteria, the residual displacements of the superstructure should also be limited. In other words, an effective isolation system should both be able to dissipate energy and be capable of assisting with the recentering of the structure. A case in point is the bridge deck isolator. The traditional isomeric and frictional isolators often used between a bridge deck and its supporting piers usually do not resume their original configurations after an intermediate-to-strong ground motion. Although these residual deformations could be manually or mechanically reduced or eliminated after a seismic event, their presence could interfere with, or prevent, the immediate use of the bridge right after the earthquake. The same is true for isolators used in buildings.

To improve the performance of base-isolation systems, many researchers have proposed and carried out numerical and experimental studies on "smart" isolation systems, in which a superelastic SMA is used in conjunction with a conventional isolation system (**Fig. 6**). One such novel base-isolation system consists of a series of laminated rubber bearings used in conjunction with an SMA device for protecting elevated highway bridges from earthquake hazards. Another system combines a flat sliding bearing with a superelastic SMA device. Though these devices are not yet available on the market, design guidelines are available for some of them, and optimal design parameters have been proposed for their applications in different earthquake design levels.

Other SMA applications. Other applications of SMAs in civil structures include beam-column connections, bridge-deck restrainers, bridge-cable vibration dampers, and SMA-reinforced concrete beams and columns. The distinctive features of SMAs, such as their superelasticity effect and damping capacity, make them ideal for use in building and bridge structures to meet the performance-based design criteria. SMAs as smart materials have shown great potential in civil-engineering applications.

Some practical concerns, such as high cost, the lack of codifications, unfamiliarity of the material, and the need for special fabrication and design requirements, have prevented the widespread use of SMAs in civil engineering applications. However, it is anticipated that their cost will be lower once SMA-based products are commercialized and new types of cost-effective SMAs are developed. For instance, the ferrous-based shape memory alloy NCATB (FeNiCoAlTaB) was discovered in 2010. It exhibits a superelastic strain of up to 15% at room temperature and has a tensile strength of more than 1 GPa, the highest of all SMAs known today. Also, because the austenite finish temperature of NCATB is $-62°C$, a superelastic SMA device made of NCATB can find application in extremely cold regions of the world. As more interest develops and additional efforts and funding are spent on research on SMAs and SMA-based devices, unified design criteria that lead to codification and commercialization will result. The use of SMAs will then become a routine process in the seismic design profession.

For background information *see* BEAM-COLUMN; BUILDINGS; EARTHQUAKE; EARTHQUAKE ENGINEERING; HYSTERESIS; PHASE TRANSITIONS; REINFORCED CONCRETE; SHAPE MEMORY ALLOYS; STRESS AND STRAIN; STRUCTURE (ENGINEERING); SUPERPLASTICITY; TWINNING (CRYSTALLOGRAPHY) in the McGraw-Hill Encyclopedia of Science & Technology.

Wenke Tang; Eric M. Lui

Bibliography. O. E. Ozbulut and S. Hurlebaus, Seismic protection of bridge structures using shape memory alloy-based isolation devices, pp. 2066–2077 in *Proceedings of the 2011 ASCE Structures Congress*, Las Vegas, NV, April 14–16, 2011, ASCE, Reston, VA, 2011; H. Qian et al., Seismic vibration control of civil structures using shape memory alloys: A review, pp. 3377–3395 in *Earth and Space 2010: Engineering, Science, Construction, and Operations in Challenging Environments*, ASCE, Reston, VA, 2010; T. Tadaki, K. Otsuka, and K. Shimizu, Shape memory alloys, *Annu. Rev. Mater. Sci.*, 18:25–45, 1988, DOI:10.1146/annurev.ms. 18.080188.000325; C. W. Yang, R. DesRoches, and R. T. Leon, Design and analysis of braced frames with shape memory alloy and energy-absorbing hybrid devices, *Eng. Struct.*, 32:498–507, 2010, DOI:10.1016/j.engstruct.2009.10.011; S. Zhu and Y. Zhang, Seismic analysis of concentrically braced frame systems with self-centering friction damping braces, *J. Struct. Eng.*, 134:121–131, 2008, DOI:0.1061/(ASCE)0733-9445(2008)134:1(121).

Atom interferometry

An atom interferometer is a device that uses the wave–particle duality of quantum mechanics: A particle—for example, an atom—can be described as a wave whose amplitude is large at places where the atom is likely to be found. In an interferometer, such a wave can simultaneously explore two or more paths. The waves that emerge from either path can add or cancel, changing the number of detected atoms in a way that depends on interactions encountered by the waves along the paths. Atom interferometers have been used to measure rotations and accelerations, including the acceleration of free fall and its position dependence. Thus, they can be applied in geology and mineral exploration as well as navigation. They have also been used to measure fundamental constants, and for some of the most stringent tests of fundamental theories of physics such as quantum mechanics and general relativity.

Two waves (for example, water waves or sound waves) can be combined to form a larger wave, or a smaller one. If the lowest point, the trough, of one wave is overlapped with the highest point, the crest, of the other, the waves cancel each other out. On the other hand, if the crests are aligned, they combine to a wave of maximum intensity. The two cases are called destructive and constructive interference. When the crests are aligned, one says that the phase difference of the waves is zero, and constructive interference takes place (**Fig. 1**). A phase difference of half a wavelength, or 180°, makes the waves cancel.

Atomic waves. A small particle such as an atom can be described by a wave in quantum mechanics. In places where the atom is likely to be, the wave is large in amplitude. An atom interferometer offers two paths for the atom-wave to travel to the same

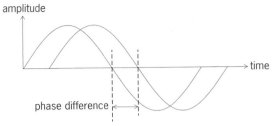

Fig. 1. Phase difference. The phase difference between two waves of equal wavelength or frequency describes the time difference between them. If they are identical, for example, the phase difference is said to be zero. If they are shifted relative to one another by half a wavelength, it is said to be 180°. A shift of a total wavelength, or 360°, is identical in its effects to one of zero.

place (**Fig. 2**). Where the paths cross, the two parts of the atom-wave combine and interfere with one another, either constructively or destructively.

Because atoms are not created or destroyed in the interferometer, each atom must emerge from output A or output B (Fig. 2). The probability that it emerges from a particular output is determined by the relative amplitude of the wave function at that output. This amplitude is a function of the relative phase difference accumulated by the wave function while propagating along the two paths.

To detect the atom, a laser brings the atom into an excited state. The atom will then decay to the ground state, emitting fluorescent light that can be observed. **Figure 3** shows the fluorescence measured in one output as a function of the phase difference in one of the most sensitive interferometers.

Analogy to waves on water. For atom waves, such a phase difference can be caused by such influences as gravity, the atom's motion, and magnetic fields. Imagine a water wave that strikes a barrier with two channels in it. On the far side of the barrier, the waves exiting the channels interfere with one another. Now consider what happens if we make one

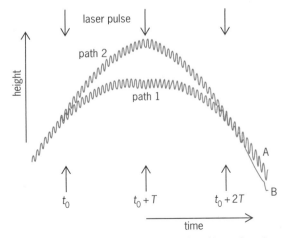

Fig. 2. Trajectories of the atom versus time. Upward- and downward-pointing arrows indicate laser pulses. The atoms' motion and the laser beams are vertical. The phase difference of the matter waves that traversed path 1 and 2 determines the probability that the atom emerges at the outputs A and B.

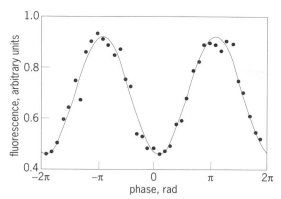

Fig. 3. Measured atom number in port B (Fig. 2) as a function of the relative phase shift.

channel longer than the other. This affects whether the two waves exiting the channels reach their crests or troughs at the same time, that is, their relative phase. This relative phase is equal to the frequency of the waves' oscillation multiplied by the time lag between the two.

For atoms, the relative phase is given by the oscillation frequency of the wave for an atom at rest times the proper time, or the time that would be recorded by a clock carried along with the atom. This proper time passes more slowly for an atom that is moving quickly than it does for one at rest, just as in the twins paradox of special relativity, and also for an atom that is deeper in a gravitational field, because of the gravitational redshift. The paths of free atoms are determined by the usual laws of mechanics. There is one additional effect on the phase: As we shall see later, the splitting of the matter waves is accomplished by laser beams. Laser beams are also (electromagnetic) waves, and can exchange their phase with the atomic wave. Whenever an atom absorbs light, this changes the phase of the matter wave by adding the phase of the laser wave at the location and time where the interaction happens. This gives rise to a "laser phase" φ_L. From these rules, the phase difference between the matter waves can be calculated. These rules also explain how atom interferometers can be used for testing relativity.

Usually, the atoms move slowly compared to the velocity of light, and gravitational fields are weak. In this case, the above rules can be simplified: One calculates the paths of the atoms and then the time-averaged kinetic energy $E_{\mathrm{kin,av}}$ and potential energy $E_{\mathrm{pot,av}}$ on these paths, and divides them by the Planck constant h (equal to 6.67×10^{-34} joules per hertz). The phase on each path is given by 2π times the difference of these quantities times the total time $2T$ during which the matter waves are split (where the time T is defined in Fig. 2), as in Eq. (1).

$$\varphi = \varphi_L + 4\pi(E_{\mathrm{kin,av}} - E_{\mathrm{pot,av}})T/h \qquad (1)$$

Atoms and lasers. Many atom interferometers start with a sample of atoms cooled to a temperature of microkelvins, very close to absolute zero, to freeze

the atoms' motion to a virtual standstill. Often, researchers toss the atoms upward and use them during the following period of free fall. Such atomic fountains typically are 0.3–1 m (1–3 ft) high, but a 10-m (30-ft) fountain has been built. This allows atoms to fall freely for up to about 2.5 s. The atoms are not close to an object or otherwise confined, so unwanted influences on the atoms will be extremely low.

A beam splitter is used to split the matter wave so that it takes the two paths shown in Fig. 2. Laser beams can be used for this purpose. Light consists of photons, and each carries a small momentum. In practice, pairs of antiparallel beams are used. The atom absorbs a photon from a first beam, and is stimulated by the second beam to reemit the photon. The atom thus receives two momentum kicks that make it move. For cesium atoms and infrared light, for example, the recoil velocity is 0.7 cm/s (about 0.25 in./s). The light is applied in flashes that are carefully calibrated to "hit" each atom with a probability of 50%, thus sending the atom-wave along the two paths simultaneously. More flashes (Fig. 2) later are used to bring the paths back together, so that they interfere. In atom interferometers using large momentum transfer, a momentum of up to 24 photons is applied to each atom in order to increase the separation between the paths and boost the sensitivity.

Applications. Some important applications of atom interferometers will now be discussed.

Inertial measurement. Atom interferometers can be used to measure the acceleration of gravity, which can be used for geology and mineral exploration. Such interferometers have reached a sensitivity of several parts per billion. Other methods have similar or better sensitivities, but atom interferometers are highly accurate and reproducible: Any two different interferometers will measure exactly the same value, just as two atomic clocks will tick at precisely the same rate without need for additional calibration.

By measuring gravity simultaneously at different places, its local variations can be studied. The sensitivity is sufficient to note the change in gravity produced by a person walking by. Atom interferometers have also been used to measure rotation. In that application, they may one day surpass the accuracy of gyroscopes and ring lasers, and thus improve inertial guidance and navigation to safely steer aircraft to their destination when all external clues (such as the global positioning system) fail.

Measurement of the fine-structure constant. The theory of relativity famously postulates mass–energy equivalence: A particle of mass m has a mass-energy $E = mc^2$, where c is the velocity of light, $c = 299{,}792{,}458$ m/s or about 670 million mi/h. The fine-structure constant α (equal to about 1/137) describes the strength of electric forces on fundamental particles in relation to their mass–energy. For example, the binding energy E_{H} of an electron in a hydrogen atom in the ground state is given by one-half its mass–energy $m_{\mathrm{e}}c^2$ times the fine-structure constant squared, $E_H = (1/2) \, m_e c^2 \alpha^2$. Measuring this energy would allow one to measure the fine-structure constant, provided that the electron's mass–energy is known.

The binding energy, however, is best measured by measuring the frequencies of light emitted by the atom. In quantum mechanics, the Planck constant h relates energy E and frequency f by the equation $E = hf$, which is closely related to Eq. (1). In particular, the frequencies emitted by transitions in hydrogen are given by $(1/n^2 - 1/m^2)f$, where n and m are the quantum numbers of the energy levels involved, and f is given by Eq. (2). This frequency f is known as

$$f = (1/2) \, \alpha^2 (m_e c^2 / h) \qquad (2)$$

the product of the Rydberg constant and the speed of light. It is known to an accuracy of 5 parts in 10^{12}, thanks to a lifelong pursuit of Nobel laureate Theodor Hänsch. Using this measurement, Eq. (2) can be solved for the fine-structure constant.

This, however, is possible only provided that the ratio $m_e c^2/h$ of the electron's mass–energy and the Planck constant are known. This ratio can be determined in turn from the electron-to-cesium-atom mass ratio, m_e/m, which is known very accurately from Penning trap measurements, and then by measuring $m_e c^2/h$, where m is the mass of a cesium atom. This latter ratio can be measured using an atom interferometer having four beam-splitter pulses, as shown in the right half of **Fig. 4**. Each beam splitter changes the motion of the atom by applying the momentum kicks provided by pho-

tons. The momentum difference p between the two paths is given by the momentum of a photon, which is the Planck constant h times the frequency f_L of the light, divided by the speed of light c: $p = hf_L/c$. According to Eq. (1), the phase of an atom interferometer is sensitive to the particle's average kinetic energy. For applying the equation, we must choose a particular frame of reference. The simplest one to use is the one in which the "unkicked" atom is at rest, having a kinetic energy of zero. The kinetic energy of the moving one is given by the particle's momentum p and its mass m according to $E_{kin} = p^2/(2m)$. In the simplest case, the laser phase φ_L is set to zero by adjusting the timing and frequency of the laser pulses. Combining all contributions, the phase is given by Eq. (3).

$$\varphi = 4\pi \, T f_L^2 / (mc^2 / h) \qquad (3)$$

Since the laser frequency and the time $2T$ during which the atoms are moving are known, the atom interferometer measures the quantity mc^2/h. This allows converting a measurement of hydrogen transition frequencies into a measurement of the fine-structure constant.

The most precise measurement of that kind has been carried out by a research group led by François Biraben in Paris. It has measured the fine-structure constant to an accuracy of 0.66 parts in 10^9, just slightly short of the most precise measurement ever of this constant, using a different method. In physics, comparing measurements based on completely different principles can confirm the consistency of the

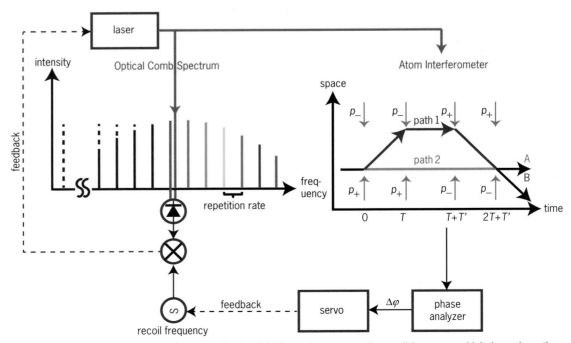

Fig. 4. Compton clock. An atom interferometer (on the right) is used to measure the recoil frequency, which depends on the laser frequency and the Compton frequency. A servo adjusts an oscillator to this measured recoil frequency using feedback. The frequency comb generator multiplies this frequency by a factor N of about 3×10^9, creating an infrared signal that is used to synchronize the laser oscillations by a second feedback loop. When both loops are closed, the recoil frequency is equal to f_0/N^2 and the setup becomes a Compton clock: a clock referenced to the mass of a particle.

Fig. 5. Atom interferometer used for measuring the fine-structure constant and for building the Compton clock.

experimental methods and fundamental theories. Comparison of the two measurements of the fine-structure constant, for example, provides one of the most precise checks of the theory of quantum electrodynamics.

Compton clock and the kilogram. Can a single particle experience the passing of time, and thus be used as a timing standard? In theory, the possibility has been long established. Relativity and quantum mechanics relate mass m to energy $E = mc^2$, and energy to frequency, $f_0 = E/h$. Again, c and h stand for the speed of light and the Planck constant, respectively. So a single particle of mass m defines a frequency $f_0 = mc^2/h$, called the Compton frequency. If the oscillations at that frequency could somehow be counted, they could be used to measure time. Alas, this frequency is unmeasurably high, about 3×10^{25} hertz, or 30 billion billion million cycles per second, for a cesium atom.

Researchers at the University of California, Berkeley, have realized that this is just the quantity measured by the atom interferometer used for measuring the fine-structure constant (previously discussed). However, the atom interferometer's phase also depends on the laser frequency. If the laser frequency could be synchronized to the atom interferometer, everything would be linked to the atom's mass. The signal measured by the atom interferometer is given by Eq. (3) and is proportional to f_L^2/f_0. This quantity is called the recoil frequency and is about 100,000 Hz, or cycles per second, whereas the laser frequency is about 3×10^{14} Hz, or 300 trillion cycles per second.

To bridge that gap, the researchers used an optical comb generator, which earned its coinventors, John Hall and Hänsch, a Nobel prize in 2005. The comb was used as a frequency multiplier, to multiply the recoil frequency by a factor of N (about 3×10^9) and stabilize the laser frequency to it (Fig. 4). The recoil frequency is now synchronized to the Compton frequency divided by N^2. The Berkeley researchers have shown that time can indeed be measured using a single massive particle as a reference (**Fig. 5**).

This also suggests a new precise way of measuring mass: If the Compton frequency of an atom is known, so is its mass—provided the Planck constant h and the speed of light c are known. The value of the speed of light is already an exactly specified number, and in the future, the Planck constant is likely to be elevated to the status of a fixed (integer or rational) number as well. Then, masses can indeed be defined by their Compton frequency. The standard kilogram, until now a platinum–iridium cylinder stored in a vault in Paris, can be retired.

Outlook. Many new ideas based on atom interferometry are currently being tested. Researchers used atom interferometers to measure Newton's constant G—which specifies how much two bodies of given mass attract each other gravitationally—though not yet with competitive accuracy. New insights into how gravity affects quantum mechanical processes might be gained by a gravitational Aharonov-Bohm experiment that is under construction. Gravitational waves, the feeble gravitational signatures of violent events in the cosmos, could perhaps be detected with atom interferometers. Measuring gravity simultaneously with different kinds of atoms can be used to test the equivalence principle—the notion that gravity affects all matter in exact proportion to its mass—which underlies general relativity. Compact interferometers under development may soon bring this technology out of the laboratory, and may enable a wide range of inertial and gravitational sensor applications.

For background information *see* AHARONOV-BOHM EFFECT; CLOCK PARADOX; EARTH, GRAVITY FIELD OF; FLUORESCENCE; FREQUENCY COMB; FUNDAMENTAL CONSTANTS; GRAVITATIONAL RADIATION; GRAVITATIONAL REDSHIFT; GRAVITY METER; INERTIAL NAVIGATION SYSTEM; INTERFERENCE OF WAVES; INTERFEROMETRY; LASER SPECTROSCOPY; LIGHT; PARTICLE TRAP; PHASE (PERIODIC PHENOMENA); PHOTON; PHYSICAL MEASUREMENT; QUANTUM ELECTRODYNAMICS; QUANTUM MECHANICS; RELATIVITY; RYDBERG CONSTANT in the McGraw-Hill Encyclopedia of Science & Technology.

Michael Hohensee; Shau-Yu Lan; Holger Müller

Bibliography. A. D. Cronin, J. Schmiedmayer, and D. E. Pritchard, Optics and interferometry with atoms and molecules, *Rev. Mod. Phys.*, 81:1051–1129, 2009, DOI:10.1103/RevModPhys.81.1051; R. P. Feynman, *QED: The Strange Theory of Light and Matter*, Princeton University Press, Princeton, NJ, 1988; S.-Y. Lan et al., A clock directly linking time to a particle's mass, *Science*, 339:554–557, 2013, DOI:10.1126/science.1230767; A. Peters, K.-Y. Chung, and S. Chu, Measurement of gravitational acceleration by dropping atoms, *Nature*, 400:849–852, 1999, DOI:10.1038/23655.

Atoms in microtraps

Nanoelectronics and information technologies have revolutionized everyday life. More recently, atoms and light quanta with engineered quantum states have opened new avenues for quantum information and measurement technologies. Is it possible to wire these systems together? Can we integrate atomic quantum systems on chips that form operational parts of integrated quantum circuits?

Trapping atoms and ions in microtraps naturally realizes a solid-state–cold-atom interface. There are well-established micro-ion traps based on miniaturized electrodes and magnetic microtraps for paramagnetic atoms based on microscopic magnets. Optical fields are also used to form versatile potentials close to surfaces. Together these give almost unlimited opportunities for potential shaping near prepared and structured surfaces. These advances involve cold-atom technologies, quantum electronic–optical device engineering, and material sciences.

Interaction with surfaces. The realization of an interface that can transfer quantum information between atoms and solids requires understanding of fundamental atom-surface interactions. Atoms held at micrometer distances from a surface are exposed to electromagnetic field fluctuations that are differ-

ent from blackbody radiation in free space. The solid body sets boundary conditions for electromagnetic fields and is the source of electromagnetic fluctuations at the same time. The power spectrum of these fluctuations depends on the conductivity, temperature, and geometry of the surface. Interestingly, heating of the atomic cloud is negligible on experimental timescales (nanoseconds to minutes), even if the temperature of the cloud is just a few nanokelvins and the surface is at room temperature. However, the response of internal atomic degrees of freedom is much more sensitive, and is manifested in dispersion forces between atoms and the surface and in the decoherence of internal quantum states (that is, in the destruction of the quantum character of these states). Thus, trapped atoms can function as ultrasensitive surface probes for electromagnetic fields and their fluctuations.

Trapping ultracold atoms on a chip. The preparation of atoms in microtraps starts with the well-established techniques of laser cooling. Almost all trapping and detection techniques that have been developed for macroscopic traps can be scaled down to a chip. It is particularly striking that a magnetic microtrap can be formed by a simple current-carrying wire and some bias and offset fields (**Fig. 1**). The trapping potential for atoms with a magnetic moment $\vec{\mu}$ derives from the Zeeman Hamiltonian, $H_z = -\vec{\mu} \cdot \vec{B}(\vec{r})$, where $\vec{B}(\vec{r})$ is the field of magnetic induction. Trapping requires a potential minimum. Now, Earnshaw's theorem states that there are no local minima or maxima of the field potential in free space, only saddle points. This rigorous

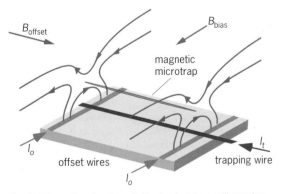

Fig. 1. Magnetic microtrap. In the basic trap configuration, the current-driven trapping wire generates a circular magnetic field that decays with the inverse of the distance from the conductor. The strong magnetic field gradients close to the wire are used to generate traps with strong confinement for paramagnetic atoms. For this, a homogeneous (uniform) bias field B_{bias} is added perpendicular to the trapping wire to generate a line of vanishing magnetic field along which paramagnetic atoms are trapped. An additional magnetic field B_{offset} is added parallel to the trapping wire by applying currents through the offset wires to provide axial confinement. Typical microtraps use a few tens of milliamps and bias and offset fields of the order of a few gauss to generate a harmonic oscillator trapping potential. (1 gauss 10⁻⁴ tesla; the magnetic field at the Earth's surface is 0.5 gauss.) The center-of-mass oscillation frequency of the atoms in such traps is typically of the order of tens to thousands of hertz.

statement seemingly prohibits magnetic trapping in static field configurations. However, the dynamics of atomic magnetic moments in a magnetic field, the Larmor precession, breaks the static picture and solves the problem. The precession of the magnetic moment around the field line keeps the magnetic moment aligned with the field while the atom is moving through space. Therefore atoms that have been trapped with a magnetic moment $\vec{\mu}$ that is antiparallel to $\vec{B}$ (a so-called low-field-seeking state) remain trapped in a local minimum of the field strength $|\vec{B}(\vec{r})|$, and it is indeed possible to form such a minimum in free space, as shown in Fig. 1. The trapping potential for low-field-seeking atoms takes the simple form $U = |\vec{\mu}||\vec{B}(\vec{r})|$.

Miniaturization boosts gradients and curvatures. The field $\vec{B}$ of a current-carrying wire decays as $1/r$ with the distance r from the wire, and the field gradient decays as $1/r^2$. For small values of r, both the field and the gradient are large, and thus the force and the potential experienced by a trapped particle are strong. This straightforward geometrical effect allows us to form traps at nanowires with extraordinarily strong confinement, even stronger than macroscopic electromagnets can achieve. Simple microtraps confine atomic clouds in a small space and provide outstanding conditions for experiments done by atomic physicists, such as Bose-Einstein condensation, degenerate Fermi gases, quantum-state control of single atoms, integrated atomic clocks, atom interferometers, and even scanning surface probes. *See* ATOM INTERFEROMETRY.

Cold atoms as surface probes. Atom clouds can be scanned above surfaces (**Figs. 2** and **3**) to probe local electromagnetic fields and their fluctuations. Gaseous "probe tips" of 10,000–100,000 atoms, at densities below 10^{14} cm^{-3}, can mimic the contact and dynamical modes of an atomic force microscope (AFM), but they also possess individual features. In particular, the quantum electronic and magnetic structure of atoms determines the response to electromagnetic fields. This makes ultracold atoms suitable for ultrasensitive mapping of dispersion forces, to detect charge distributions or polarized adatoms on surfaces, and to measure currents through nanowires.

A particularly interesting application is the spectral analysis of magnetic field fluctuations near nanostructures. These fluctuations drive Zeeman transitions between magnetic quantum states, that is, from trapped to nontrapped states. Varying the magnetic offset field in the trap shifts the Larmor frequency at which the atoms are sensitive to the fluctuations. Thus, the spectral power density of magnetic field fluctuations can be recorded by measuring atom losses from the trap. If the Zeeman transition of single atoms is detected with a state-selective single-atom detector, a quantum galvanometer for measuring quantum fluctuations of transport currents in nanowires can be realized. Quantum probes formed by Bose-Einstein condensates and nonclassical superposition states of atoms open new opportunities

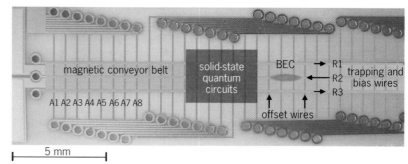

Fig. 2. Cold atoms on a chip. Complex wire structures based on the simple wire trap scheme shown in Fig.1 realize a magnetic conveyor belt (a millimeter-sized device) that is used for nanopositioning ultracold atoms and Bose-Einstein condensates (BEC) in a three-dimensional volume above the chip surface. (Arrows indicate currents in wires.) The BEC cloud has a typical diameter of 10 micrometers (μm) [it is enlarged in the figure], while thermal atom clouds can have sizes of hundreds micrometers. The conveyor belt operates as follows (see also online movie referenced in legend of Fig. 3): The current-driven trapping wire, R2, and the bias wires, R1 and R3, define the centerline of a guiding potential along R2 (compare Fig.1). One pair of the eight offset wires (A1,..., A8) patterned to the rear side of the chip is driven with current to break the translation invariance and to close the trap in the axial direction (compare Fig.1). Swapping the current from the active pair of offset wires (such as A1 and A4) to a neighboring pair (such as A2 and A5) shifts the trap center parallel to R2. The periodically repeated array of offset wires allows a smooth translation of the atom cloud along R2. At the same time, the currents in R1, R2, and R3 control the cloud-surface separation and lateral position of the cloud between R1 and R3. An atom cloud trapped on the chip can thus be translated, shifted up and down, or shifted to the side by controlling the wire currents. In this way, atoms can be interfaced with integrated solid-state quantum circuits that are installed on top of the conveyor belt.

Fig. 3. Nanopositioning atoms on chip surfaces. An atom cloud (white in this image) has been loaded into a magnetic conveyor belt formed by the wire components on a chip that has been installed upside down. The atom cloud can be transported to various positions at the chip surface by varying the current in the chip conductors. This experimental data has been taken with rubidium atoms (^{87}Rb) at microkelvin temperature. At any position the atom cloud can be cooled further to Bose-Einstein condensation and brought into interaction with nanostructures integrated on the chip surface. This image is a clip from a movie that is available at http://bcove.me/2v35bel1.

for the development of ultrasensitive surface probes, outperforming classical systems.

Cold-atom–solid-state hybrid quantum devices. Microtraps realize a versatile cold-atom–solid-state quantum interface. The experiments so far have focused on fundamental interactions between atoms and surfaces and the development of atomic manipulation techniques. Current research is considering the possibility of coherent coupling between atoms and solid-state quantum devices. What kind of useful quantum devices can we construct based on atoms and nanostructures? Integrated atomic clocks or chip-based atom interferometers? Trapped-ion quantum processors? Atomic quantum memories on superconducting chips? Cold-atom scanning-probe microscopes, quantum galvanometers, and spectrum analyzers? Research on microtraps has developed many facets and continues to expand rapidly, inspired by the exquisite quantum control of atoms, light, and solids.

For background information *see* ATOMIC FERMI GAS; ATOMIC CLOCK; ATOMIC FORCE MICROSCOPY; ATOMIC STRUCTURE AND SPECTRA; BOSE-EINSTEIN CONDENSATION; GALVANOMETER; HEAT RADIATION; INTEGRATED CIRCUITS; INTERMOLECULAR FORCES; LARMOR PRECESSION; LASER COOLING; MAGNETISM; NANOSTRUCTURES; PARTICLE TRAP; QUANTUM COMPUTATION; QUANTUM ELECTRONICS; QUANTUM MECHANICS; SPECTRUM ANALYZER; SURFACE PHYSICS; ZEEMAN EFFECT in the McGraw-Hill Encyclopedia of Science & Technology.   József Fortágh

Bibliography. J. Fortágh and C. Zimmermann, Magnetic microtraps for ultracold atoms, *Rev. Mod. Phys.*, 79:235–289, 2007, DOI:10.1103/RevModPhys.79.235; M. Gierling et al., Cold-atom scanning probe microscopy, *Nat. Nanotechnol.*, 6:446–451, 2011, DOI:10.1038/nnano.2011.80; O. Kalman et al., Quantum galvanometer by interfacing a vibrating nanowire and cold atoms, *Nano Lett.*, 12:435–439, 2012, DOI:10.1021/nl203762g; S. Seidelin et al., Microfabricated surface-electrode ion trap for scalable quantum information processing, *Phys. Rev. Lett.*, 96:253003 (4 pp.), DOI:10.1103/PhysRevLett.96.253003, 2006; M. Wallquist et al., Hybrid quantum devices and quantum engineering, *Phys. Scripta*, T137:014001 (7 pp.), DOI:10.1088/0031-8949/2009/T137/014001, 2009.

Bariatric surgery for obesity

One of the current burdens placing significant strain on the health care system in the United States, as well as worldwide, is the obesity epidemic. Obesity is defined as a body mass index (BMI, units kg/m^2) greater than 30. Those who are considered overweight have a BMI between 25 and 30, with morbid obesity considered at a BMI greater than 40. Current estimates for the prevalence of overweight and obese patients are as high as two-thirds of the United States population and up to 1.7 billion people worldwide. The preponderance of the obese population has been steadily rising in the United States since 1980 (**Fig. 1**), nearly doubling to 30% of the population. According to current projections, 44% of the worldwide population will fall into the category of obese or overweight by the year 2020.

Not only are the current numbers alarming, but the significance of this illness is rather profound. Obesity has been shown to have an increasing correlation with multiple illnesses, including heart disease, stroke, diabetes, sleep apnea, arthritis, polycystic ovarian syndrome (PCOS), biliary diseases, and multiple types of cancer (for example, breast,

prostate, colon, and endometrial cancer) [**Fig. 2**]. A BMI of greater than 30 has been shown to increase mortality by 50–100% and decrease life expectancy by 5–20 years compared to individuals of normal weight. Furthermore, this illness has taken a serious financial toll on health care in the United States, accounting for an estimated $147 billion in 2008, and representing roughly 5.7% of current national health care expenditures.

Nonsurgical treatments for obesity. Multiple treatment options for obesity exist, but controversy remains concerning what factors warrant surgical intervention and what surgical modalities are appropriate. The first step in treating this disorder is to begin with lifestyle modifications. Multiple studies have demonstrated that both dieting and increased physical activity are strongly associated with weight loss. Low-calorie diets, of 1000–1500 kcal/day, have been shown to reduce body weight, and low-fat diets have been shown to have an even greater effect on weight loss when combined with low-calorie diets. Not surprising, physical activity alone has also been shown to lead to weight loss, independent of calorie reduction. Before considering surgery, there are also some medical options that have been tried, including the use of such drugs as sibutramine, orlistat, fenfluramine, and phentermine; however, there are no published data proving significant sustained weight loss with these methods.

Surgical treatments for obesity. Bariatric surgery is a fairly new field, which has shown its merit as a useful tool in the treatment of obesity, although it is by no means meant to serve as a cure for the condition. Before a patient can be considered as a candidate for surgical intervention, he or she must meet the specific indications. According to the National Institutes of Health Consensus Panel, indications to treat include the following: BMI greater than 40; BMI greater than 35 with two or more medical comorbidities (for example, diabetes and hypertension); inability to lose weight or maintain loss with conventional therapy; having an acceptable operative risk; and being able to comply with long-term treatment and follow-up. Of note, these indications change for gastric banding (see below), as this option can be considered in patients with a BMI greater than 35 or with a BMI greater than 30 with two or more comorbidities.

Current surgical options for treatment of obesity include adjustable gastric banding, vertical gastric sleeve gastrectomy, Roux-en-Y gastric bypass, and biliopancreatic diversion with or without duodenal switch. Gastric banding is considered by many to be the least invasive of the four options. This procedure consists of placing a constrictive silicone band around the stomach that can be filled with saline through the skin via an access port (**Fig. 3**). The potential advantages include the reversible and adjustable nature of the procedure. Risks include slipping or erosion of the band, band prolapse (stomach herniation up through the band), and failed weight loss. The gastric sleeve procedure consists of

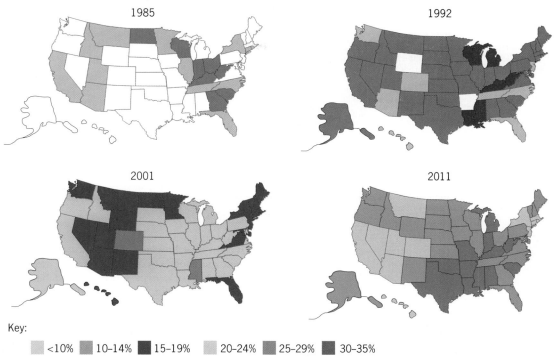

Key:

| | <10% | | 10–14% | | 15–19% | | 20–24% | | 25–29% | | 30–35% |

Fig. 1. Obesity trend among adults in the United States as demonstrated by the prevalence of BMI ≥ 30 by year.
(*Image courtesy of the Centers for Disease Control and Prevention: www.cdc.gov/obesity/data/adult.html*)

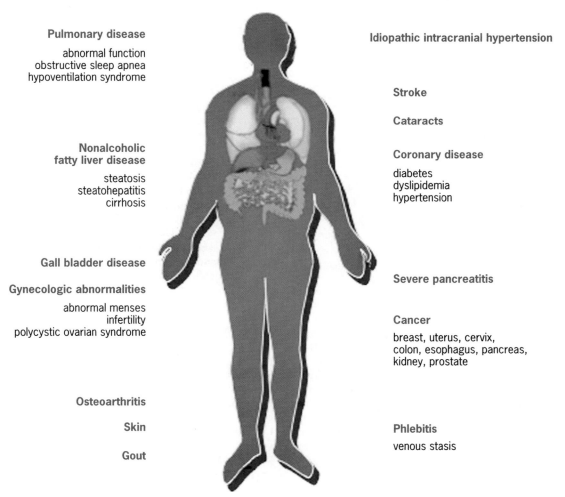

Pulmonary disease

abnormal function
obstructive sleep apnea
hypoventilation syndrome

**Nonalcoholic
fatty liver disease**

steatosis
steatohepatitis
cirrhosis

Gall bladder disease

Gynecologic abnormalities

abnormal menses
infertility
polycystic ovarian syndrome

Osteoarthritis

Skin

Gout

Idiopathic intracranial hypertension

Stroke

Cataracts

Coronary disease

diabetes
dyslipidemia
hypertension

Severe pancreatitis

Cancer

breast, uterus, cervix,
colon, esophagus, pancreas,
kidney, prostate

Phlebitis

venous stasis

Fig. 2. The wide effects of obesity can be organized according to the organ system. Obesity has been linked to multiple comorbid conditions, affecting almost every major organ system in the body.

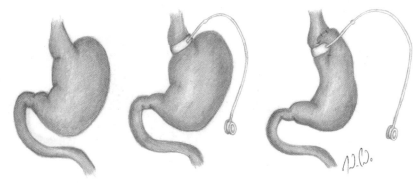

Fig. 3. Adjustable gastric banding. The band is placed around the proximal stomach and a fundoplication (a surgical procedure involving the fundus) is performed to keep the band in position. The silicone band is inflated with saline through the port, which is placed under the skin.

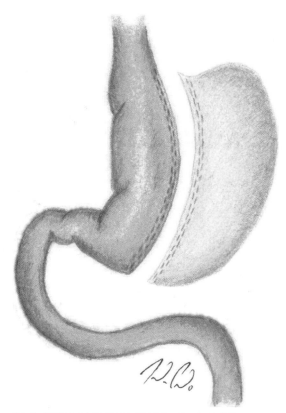

Fig. 4. Sleeve gastrectomy. The lateral aspect of the stomach (*light color*) is excluded from the rest of the stomach by a device that staples and cuts, creating a smaller stomach with an intact pylorus.

excising the fundus (the anterior portion of the stomach) and 80% of the lateral part of the stomach. This procedure leaves a smaller stomach, as well as an intact pylorus (the orifice of the stomach communicating with the small intestine) [**Fig. 4**]. This allows for early satiety, while maintaining the function of the pylorus and biliary tract (the organs and ducts involved in moving bile into the small intestine). The disadvantages of this procedure include the risk of leak from the suture line or stricture. Both gastric banding and gastric sleeve rely on gastric modification in order to help the patient achieve and maintain weight loss; however, sleeve gastrectomy also has some metabolic effects.

Roux-en-Y gastric bypass (**Fig. 5**) and biliopancreatic diversion (**Fig. 6**) are considered more invasive procedures, and both use malabsorption as well as restriction of stomach size in order to help treat obesity while resulting in positive metabolic effects. Roux-en-Y gastric bypass is the most commonly performed bariatric surgery in the United States. In this procedure, a small stomach pouch is stapled and excluded from the original stomach, and is attached to the small intestine (duodenum). The rest of the stomach and duodenum are then reconnected to the small bowel, distal to the outflow of the pouch. This procedure has been shown to have greater and longer-lasting effects than either gastric banding or gastric sleeve, but it carries small but real risks of anastomotic leak, obstruction, internal hernia, and dumping syndrome (in which undigested contents of the stomach move too rapidly into the small bowel). Biliopancreatic diversion uses a sleeve gastrectomy with a longer intestinal bypass. This method has been shown to have greater metabolic effects than gastric bypass, which may increase weight loss, but it can also cause vitamin and nutrient deficiencies.

Surgical results. The results of bariatric surgery have been well documented, and they have demonstrated repeatedly that this approach is an extremely effective means of reducing morbidity and mortality associated with obesity. The Swedish Obesity Study, a nationwide prospective controlled study of more than 4000 participants in Sweden that began in 1987, has served as one of the best indicators of the success of bariatric surgery. In this study, participants showed a mean 1- to 2-year weight loss of 32% for gastric bypass, with vertical gastric gastroplasty (stomach stapling) and gastric banding yielding weight losses of 25% and 20%, respectively. The results from 10 years after surgery showed weight losses of 25%, 16%, and 14% from baseline for bypass, vertical banding, and banding, respectively. Finally, the study demonstrated 15-year decreases from baseline of 27%, 18%, and 13% for bypass, vertical banding, and banding. These results show that multiple

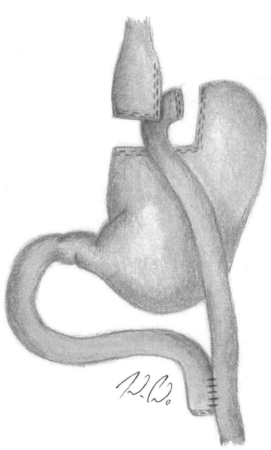

Fig. 5. Roux-en-Y gastric bypass. The stomach is divided with staples, and the small gastric pouch is anastomosed (joined) to an alimentary limb of the small bowel. Downstream, a jejunojejunostomy [a surgical opening or passage between two parts of the jejunum (the middle portion of the small intestine)] allows continuity with the biliopancreatic limb.

forms of bariatric surgery have a very high degree of efficacy, although there was some crossover in the groups and only gastric bypass was performed by a similar technique as used today. Moreover, the Swedish Obesity study shows a mortality hazard ratio of 0.76 for those undergoing bariatric surgery, when compared to controls, as well as a hazard ratio of 0.17 for the development of type 2 diabetes, demonstrating health and survival benefits to surgical management of obesity.

Other studies have provided evidence for the efficacy of bariatric surgery in treating many of the medical comorbidities that are associated with obesity. For example, a recent meta-analysis showed a resolution of diabetes in 77% of patients undergoing bariatric surgery, and a normalization of hemoglobin A1C (glycated hemoglobin) in 83% of these patients. The same study also demonstrated significant improvements in the lipid profiles of these patients, with 83%, 71%, and 82% of patients showing an improvement in hyperlipidemia, hypercholesterolemia, and hypertriglyceridemia, respectively. Of note, after bariatric surgery, the participants in this study had a drop in cholesterol of 33 mg/dL, with

a decrease in low-density lipoproteins of 29 mg/dL and triglycerides of 80 mg/dL. Other medical issues that often plague obese patients include hypertension and obstructive sleep apnea, which resolved in 62% and 86%, respectively, of the patients undergoing bariatric surgery in this study. The mortality benefit of surgery has been demonstrated in similar studies as well. In addition, when it comes to the fiscal effects of bariatric surgery, a Canadian study estimated a $3000 decrease in yearly medical costs for obese patients who chose to undergo bariatric surgery, including the cost of surgery.

Outlook. Obesity has become a pandemic with severe consequences. Not only do those who suffer from the disease face issues with increased mortality, but there are many comorbid conditions that contribute to worsening lifestyle, as well as reduced life span. Along with these issues, the prevalence of obesity has been growing for many years and will continue to grow based on current projections. The effects of this increase have not only had severe consequences for obese patients, but have driven up the cost of health care worldwide. As the medical community continues to attempt to develop solutions for the obesity pandemic, it has become quite evident that bariatric surgery can resolve comorbid diseases and add years of life expectancy for the obese patient (**Fig. 7**). It is a treatment modality that should be considered for all patients who meet the criteria for surgery.

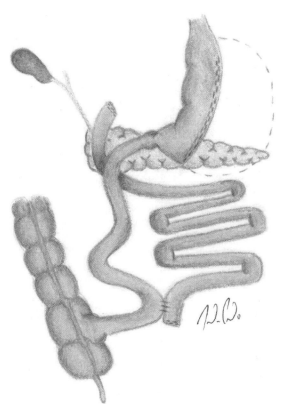

Fig. 6. Biliopancreatic diversion with duodenal switch: For this procedure, a sleeve gastrectomy is combined with a long-limb postpyloric intestinal bypass.

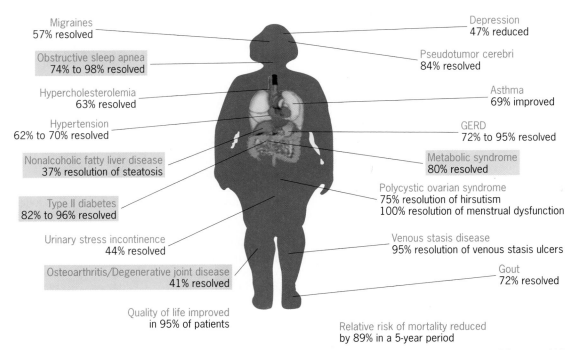

Migraines
57% resolved

Depression
47% reduced

Obstructive sleep apnea
74% to 98% resolved

Pseudotumor cerebri
84% resolved

Hypercholesterolemia
63% resolved

Asthma
69% improved

Hypertension
62% to 70% resolved

GERD
72% to 95% resolved

Nonalcoholic fatty liver disease
37% resolution of steatosis

Metabolic syndrome
80% resolved

Type II diabetes
82% to 96% resolved

Polycystic ovarian syndrome
75% resolution of hirsutism
100% resolution of menstrual dysfunction

Urinary stress incontinence
44% resolved

Venous stasis disease
95% resolution of venous stasis ulcers

Osteoarthritis/Degenerative joint disease
41% resolved

Gout
72% resolved

Quality of life improved
in 95% of patients

Relative risk of mortality reduced
by 89% in a 5-year period

Fig. 7. The many benefits of bariatric surgery. Bariatric surgery has been shown to improve or resolve many of the comorbid conditions that accompany obesity. GERD = gastroesophageal reflux disease.

For background information *see* DIABETES; HUNGER; LIPID; NUTRITION; OBESITY; PUBLIC HEALTH; STOMACH; SURGERY in the McGraw-Hill Encyclopedia of Science & Technology.

Gabriel Klein; Andrew Peredo; Aurora D. Pryor

Bibliography. H. Buchwald et al., Bariatric surgery: A systematic review and meta-analysis, *JAMA*, 292(14):1724–1737, 2004, DOI:10.1001/jama.292. 14.1724; L. M. Carlsson et al., Bariatric surgery and prevention of type 2 diabetes in Swedish obese subjects, *New Engl. J. Med.*, 367(8):695–704, 2012, DOI:10.1056/NEJMoa1112082; N. V. Christou et al., Surgery decreases long-term mortality, morbidity, and health care use in morbidly obese patients, *Ann. Surg.*, 240(3):416–424, 2004, DOI:10. 1097/01.sla.0000137343.63376.19; P. E. O'Brien, Bariatric surgery: Mechanisms, indications, and outcomes, *J. Gastroenterol. Hepatol.*, 25(8): 1358–1365, 2010, DOI:10.1111/j.1440-1746.2010. 06391.x; L. Sjöström et al., Effects of bariatric surgery on mortality in Swedish obese subjects, *New Engl. J. Med.*, 357(8):741–752, 2007, DOI:10. 1056/NEJMoa066254.

Biological relevance of metal complexes of nitric oxide

Nitric oxide (NO) is a diffusible free-radical gas. It has well-characterized reactivity with molecules such as molecular oxygen (O_2), metal ions, and thiols, but the physiological function of NO is intimately linked to its in vivo concentration. At high concentrations, NO is a potent toxin used to kill invading pathogens and tumor cells by indiscriminately reacting with cellular components. At relatively low concentrations ($\leq$ micromolar), NO typically reacts with the metal centers (usually iron) of specific metalloproteins, where it mediates cellular response to nitrosative stress. At very low concentrations ($\leq$ nanomolar), NO functions as a signaling molecule that regulates many physiological functions such as vasodilation and neurotransmission through its interaction with a selective, sensitive, and reversible sensor.

Nitric oxide synthesis. NO is synthesized by the cysteinyl thiolate-ligated protoporphyrin IX heme-containing enzyme nitric oxide synthase (NOS). NOS enzymes have been identified in a variety of organisms, but mammalian NOS is best understood (**Fig. 1**). Mammals have three NOS isoforms: neuronal (nNOS, NOS1), used in neurotransduction; inducible (iNOS, NOS2), used in the immune response; and endothelial (eNOS, NOS3), used in vasodilation.

NOS is active as a homodimer; each monomer contains an N-terminal oxidase domain and a C-terminal reductase domain. Each reductase domain has binding sites for reduced nicotinamide adenine dinucleotide phosphate (NADPH), flavin mononucleotide (FMN), flavin adenine dinucleotide (FAD), and calmodulin (CaM); each oxidase domain binds tetrahydrobiopterin (H4B) and heme, as well as cosubstrates L-arginine (L-Arg) and O_2.

NO, as well as two molecules of water and L-citrulline, is produced from L-Arg, 1.5 equivalents of NADPH, and two molecules of O_2 in a two-step, five-electron reaction regulated by calcium/CaM binding. In the first step, upon Ca^{2+}/CaM binding, two reducing equivalents are transferred from NADPH, via FMN and FAD, to the oxidase domain, resulting in the two-electron oxidation of L-Arg to

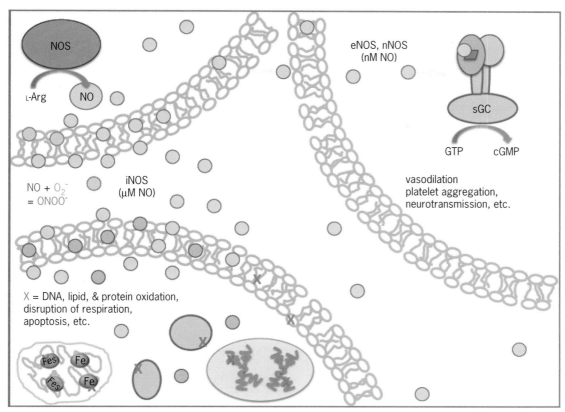

Fig. 1. Some of the roles of metal complexes of nitric oxide (NO) in eukaryotic cells. NO is synthesized by the metalloenzyme nitric oxide synthase (NOS). During an immune response, inducible NOS (iNOS) produces micromolar NO that, along with reactive oxygen species, causes nonspecific damage to cellular components. Under signaling conditions, endothelial NOS (eNOS) or neuronal NOS (nNOS) produces nanomolar NO that is detected by the heme domain of soluble guanylate cyclase (sGC), leading to regulation of important physiological events. Abbreviations: cGMP, cyclic guanosine monophosphate; GTP, guanosine triphosphate; L-Arg, L-arginine.

N-hydroxyarginine (NHA), consuming one equivalent each of NADPH and O_2. In the second step, the three-electron aerobic oxidation of NHA to NO and L-citrulline is achieved, consuming only half an equivalent of NADPH and one equivalent of O_2.

Because cytochrome P450s also use a heme-thiolate cofactor in their active sites to conduct monooxygenase chemistry, the mechanism of NOS has long been interpreted in light of the better-understood P450 oxygenase reactions. The P450 paradigm is being challenged, however, as more experimental details become available. Recently, several models have been proposed, differentiated by conflicting sources of proton and electron equivalents and a different order of events, the details of which are not discussed here.

In the last decade, proteins with significant homology to mammalian NOS have been discovered in gram-positive bacteria. Unlike their mammalian counterparts, however, bacterial NOS (bNOS) enzymes usually lack a reductase domain and therefore require the supply of reducing equivalents in trans. Nonetheless, there are significant similarities in structure, spectroscopy, and catalytic properties throughout the NOS family. In fact, experiments made possible by access to NOS homologs from thermophilic bacteria have significantly contributed

to the current debate concerning the mechanism of NOS. Current data suggest a role for bNOS in toxin biosynthesis, protection against oxidative stress, and in recovery from radiation damage.

A wide range of bacteria produce NO during denitrifying, assimilatory, and dissimilatory pathways. In the absence of O_2, facultative anaerobic bacteria can use nitrate (NO_3^-) or nitrite (NO_2^-) as alternative electron acceptors for respiration, during which NO is endogenously produced. NO can also be generated from NO_2^- by disproportionation. Bacteria enzymatically eliminate NO generated during these processes (see below), but inevitably, some of the gaseous NO remains. For example, NO is readily detected in *Escherichia coli* cultures growing in the absence of O_2 and presence of NO_3^-. These observations have led to speculation that NO produced under these conditions has a functional role and is not just a waste product of denitrification.

NO is a potent toxin. At high concentrations ($\geq$ micromolar), NO is a poisonous gas. Eukaryotes have exploited this dangerous side of NO in the innate immune response. Upon detection of invading pathogens or tumor cells, macrophages and other phagocytes activate iNOS. iNOS generates high quantities of NO, usually in an oxidative environment, which produces a burst of NO and other

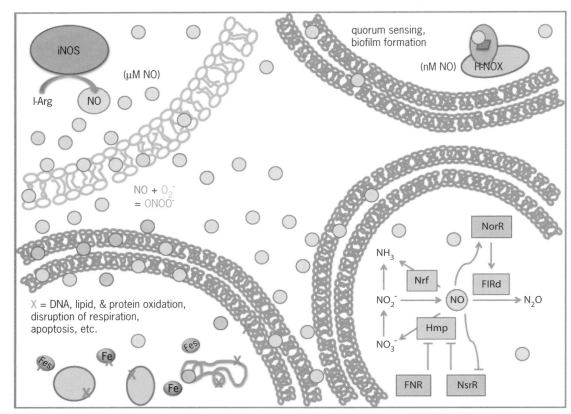

Fig. 2. Some of the roles of metal complexes of nitric oxide in bacteria. Upon detection of bacterial pathogens, eukaryotic inducible NOS (iNOS) produces micromolar nitric oxide (NO) to kill the invading cells. Bacteria have evolved nitrosative stress response mechanisms, including enzymatic modification of NO by flavohemoglobin (Hmp) or flavorubredoxin (FlRd), and transcriptional responses mediated by iron-binding transcription factors such as NorR, NsrR, and FNR. Bacteria can also produce NO with bacterial NOS enzymes (not pictured) and by reduction (Nrf) or disproportionation of nitrite (NO_2^-). Many bacteria code for H-NOX proteins, which are homologs of the eukaryotic NO receptor soluble guanylate cyclase (sGC). Bacterial H-NOX proteins are not well characterized, but early studies indicate that NO/H-NOX mediates bacterial group functions including biofilm formation. Abbreviations: L-Arg, L-arginine; NO_3^-, nitrate.

oxidative species such as peroxynitrite ($ONOO^-$). Ultimately this leads to cell toxicity through the indiscriminate oxidation and nitrosation of proteins, DNA, lipids, and other small molecules (Fig. 1 and **Fig. 2**).

Because bacteria encounter NO from various sources, including normal denitrification processes and infection of a host, they have evolved mechanisms to detoxify NO into less dangerous nitrogen oxides (Fig. 2). The best-known mechanism is the dioxygenase reaction of bacterial flavohemoglobins, such as Hmp, which converts NO into NO_3^- under aerobic conditions. Bacteria also have globin proteins that, upon generation of an oxoferryl [$Fe^{IV} = O$] species, can detoxify NO to NO_2^- and NO_3^-. Under anaerobic conditions, *E. coli* can covert NO to nitrous oxide (N_2O) by flavorubredoxin proteins (FlRd) or directly to ammonia (NH_3) by the NO_2^- reductase Nrf.

Proteins that can detect micromolar NO transcriptionally regulate some of these defense systems. Although many of these transcription factors are widely conserved in bacteria, they are best understood in *E. coli*. NsrR is a [FeS] cluster-binding repressor that regulates the expression of many different genes, including that of a flavohemoglobin, upon cluster nitrosylation by NO. Similarly, FNR is a [4Fe4S] transcription factor that is nitrosylated by NO, rendering it inactive for DNA binding and contributing to the transcriptional regulation of the flavohemoglobin Hmp. NorR is a non-heme ferrous iron protein that acts as a dedicated NO sensor, activating the transcription of a flavorubredoxin and associated oxidoreductase, under anaerobic conditions. The presence of micromolar NO results in the formation of a NorR mononitrosyl iron species [($FeNO_7$)], causing NorR to engage the σ^{54} factor and activate transcription.

There are still other transcriptional regulators that have been implicated as NO sensors, although they are not likely dedicated NO sensors. OxyR and SoxR are transcription factors that respond to oxidative stress, but there is some evidence that they also play a role in nitrosative stress responses. SoxR is a [2Fe2S] cluster protein that, in response to superoxide, activates SoxS transcription. Increased levels of SoxS turn on the *soxRS* regulon, which enhances the production of various antioxidant and repair proteins. NO has also been reported to nondestructively nitrosylate the iron-sulfur cluster of SoxR, leading to increased expression of SoxS. OxyR contains a cysteine residue that is oxidized in the presence of hydrogen peroxide, leading to activation of the *oxyR* regulon and providing resistance against higher doses of hydrogen peroxide and other oxidizing agents. NO has been reported to modify the active site cysteine of OxyR to activate transcription. Fur is an iron-dependent repressor that controls the expression of approximately 100 genes involved in the control of intracellular iron concentrations. When cellular iron levels drop, a non-heme ferrous iron atom dissociates from Fur, resulting in inactivation. The ferrous iron center of Fur can also be bound by NO to form a dinitrosyl complex, which also inactivates Fur. Fur expression is, itself, regulated by OxyR and SoxRS, therefore these mechanisms link iron metabolism to oxidative and nitrosative stress, which should minimize production of peroxynitrite and other extremely damaging reactive oxygen and nitrogen species.

NO is a powerful signaling molecule in eukaryotes. It is now well-established that at very low concentration ($\leq$ nanomolar), in eukaryotes, NO is a signaling molecule that regulates many important physiological functions, including blood vessel relaxation, insulin secretion, peristalsis, angiogenesis, myocardial function, synaptic plasticity in the brain, platelet aggregation, and egg fertilization (Fig. 1). The importance of NO as a signaling molecule is underscored by the range of diseases and disorders that result from dysfunction of the NO signaling pathway, such as high blood pressure, cardiovascular disease, gastrointestinal disorders, erectile dysfunction, and neurodegeneration.

Initially, a physiological function for NO was a surprise given its known reactivity and toxicity, but NO has many features that are ideal for signaling. NO is small and nonpolar, allowing for rapid diffusion across cell membranes. Despite being a radical, NO is fairly unreactive at low nanomolar concentrations; its primary decomposition pathway in aqueous solution is the reaction of two molecules of NO with oxygen in a slow intermolecular reaction. To function in a signaling role, however, NO requires a specific receptor. The electronic structure of NO makes it an excellent ligand for ferrous heme, and the ferrous protoporphyrin IX heme group of soluble guanylate cyclase (sGC) is a sensitive, selective, and reversible NO sensor.

Under signaling conditions, eNOS or nNOS produces a relatively low concentration of NO (1–10 nM). Once synthesized, NO quickly diffuses into neighboring tissues and binds sGC. Upon NO binding, sGC is activated several 100-fold, leading to an increase in cyclic guanosine monophosphate (cGMP) from guanosine triphosphate (GTP), which triggers downstream events through cGMP-dependent protein kinases, phosphodiesterases, and ion channels.

sGC is a heterodimeric ($\alpha 1 \beta 1$) enzyme that binds one heme per dimer. It has four distinct domains: an N-terminal heme domain, a Per/Arnt/Sim (PAS) domain, a coiled-coil domain, and a C-terminal catalytic domain. Mutagenesis and truncation experiments have localized the heme-binding domain to residues 1–194 of the $\beta 1$ subunit with histidine-105 serving as the proximal heme ligand. sGC binds NO at diffusion-limited rates (K_D estimated to be picomolar), yet there is no evidence for O_2 binding under physiologically relevant conditions. This discrimination against O_2 binding is extremely important for the fidelity of NO signaling. Since the concentration of O_2 is much higher than NO in eukaryotic cells (intracellular O_2 concentrations are about 20–40 μM), if sGC bound O_2 even weakly, this would result in nonselective formation of cGMP and/or interruption of the specific NO signal.

Interestingly, a family of bacterial heme proteins, with as much as 40% identity to the heme domain from mammalian sGC, has been identified based on genomic analysis. Cloning and spectroscopic characterization of the bacterial proteins has indicated that most members of this family, like sGC, bind NO and rigorously exclude O_2 as a ligand. Several family members from obligate anaerobes have also been spectroscopically characterized that, interestingly, form a stable O_2 complex. We have named this family H-NOX (heme-nitric oxide/oxygen binding domain), because using the same protein fold and an identical heme cofactor, some members of the family form a tight complex with O_2 whereas others bind NO while excluding O_2. A distal hydrogen-bonding network has been shown to be requisite for O_2 binding, and is used to kinetically distinguish between NO and O_2. In the absence of a hydrogen-bonding network, the O_2 dissociation rate is so fast that the O_2 complex is never formed, while the rate of NO dissociation remains unchanged, thus providing discrimination.

sGC and the H-NOX family have received considerable attention because of the importance of NO signaling in mammals. Despite this attention, the mechanism of signal transduction has not been elucidated. When NO binds the heme cofactor of sGC, the proximal histidine ligand dissociates, resulting in a five-coordinate complex, which is widely viewed as necessary for activation of sGC. Our laboratory has recently published evidence from extended x-ray absorption fine structure (EXAFS) measurements that the iron-histidine bond, although elongated, is retained upon NO-ligation, prompting the investigation of alternate mechanisms of activating sGC. Structural studies have revealed that H-NOX heme is extremely distorted from planarity. We have reported that heme flattening mimics NO binding in downstream signal transduction, and therefore we suggest that heme flattening is an essential step in signal transduction. Recent evidence also suggests that sGC is regulated by the allosteric binding of other nucleotides, and perhaps, a second molecule of NO.

Evidence for NO signaling in bacteria. With the discovery of H-NOX, fundamental questions about the role of NO signaling in bacteria are being considered. H-NOX domains have now been predicted in the genomes of hundreds of species from all subgroups of bacteria, most in close proximity to a predicted diguanylate cyclase, phosphodiesterase, or methyl-accepting chemotaxis domain—these are genomic contexts that suggest signaling. In recent years, the biological roles of several of these H-NOX proteins have been identified, revealing H-NOX to be a nanomolar NO sensor in bacterial signaling pathways affecting group behaviors such as quorum sensing (molecular signaling) and biofilm formation (Fig. 2). In *Shewanella oneidensis*, *Shewanella woodyi*, and *Legionella pneumophila*, formation of a NO-H-NOX complex has been demonstrated to regulate the intracellular concentration of cyclic-di-GMP, which is a bacterial molecule intimately involved in biofilm formation. In *Vibrio harveyi*, NO/H-NOX intersects quorum-sensing circuits, therefore contributing to the regulation of hundreds of genes involved in bacterial group behavior. The source of nanomolar NO used for these H-NOX signaling circuits has not yet been elucidated, but current evidence indicates that, like in eukaryotic systems, NO is used for cell-to-cell signal transduction in bacteria.

For background information *see* BACTERIAL PHYSIOLOGY AND METABOLISM; BIOFILM; BIOINORGANIC CHEMISTRY; CYCLIC NUCLEOTIDES; ESCHERICHIA; EXTENDED X-RAY ABSORPTION FINE STRUCTURE (EXAFS); FREE RADICAL; NICOTINAMIDE ADENINE DINUCLEOTIDE (NAD); NITRIC OXIDE; NITROGEN OXIDES; PEROXYNITRITE; SIGNAL TRANSDUCTION; TRANSCRIPTION in the McGraw-Hill Encyclopedia of Science & Technology.

Elizabeth M. Boon; Sandhya Muralidharan

Bibliography. E. M. Boon and M. A. Marletta, Ligand discrimination in soluble guanylate cyclase and the H-NOX family of heme sensor proteins, *Curr. Opin. Chem. Biol.*, 9(5):441–446, 2005, DOI:10.1016/j.cbpa.2005.08.015; E. R. Derbyshire and M. A. Marletta, Structure and regulation of soluble guanylate cyclase, *Annu. Rev. Biochem.*, 81:533–539, 2012, DOI:10.1146/annurev-biochem-050410-100030; J. Santolini, The molecular mechanism of mammalian NO-synthases: A story of electrons and protons, *J. Inorg. Biochem.*, 105(2):127–141, 2011, DOI:10.1016/j.jinorgbio.2010.10.011; S. Spiro, Nitric oxide stress in Escherichia coli and Salmonella, in *Stress Response in Pathogenic Bacteria*, pp. 48–67, CABI, Oxfordshire, UK, 2011.

Biomarkers: key to exposure reconstruction

The goal of environmental health science is to understand the interplay between the environment and humans to evaluate the effects of human activities on the public health and environment and, conversely, to evaluate the effects of various aspects of the environment on human health. When investigating the effects that exposures to chemicals have on human health, the major challenge lies in establishing the causal relationship between the magnitude of exposure to these chemicals and the incidence of adverse outcomes (such as cancer and irritation) at various biological endpoints. This causal relationship can be established only when all elements on the source–exposure–dose–effect continuum are linked (**Fig. 1**). For an adverse health outcome to occur, the chemical has to be released from a source, transported through environmental media, reach a human receptor, enter the body, and sufficiently accumulate to cause biological changes that ultimately overwhelm the adaptive mechanisms and to result in adverse health outcomes. For example, it has been established that second-hand smoke leads to an increased risk of several diseases. In this scenario, cigarette smoke is released from a source, the burning cigarette. It is transported through the environmental medium of air and reaches a human receptor, perhaps a patron in a restaurant who inhales the smoke-laden air. Cigarette smoke then enters the body through absorption in the lungs, whereupon its chemicals (for example, carcinogens and carbon monoxide) distributed to various organs and tissues, leading to an increased risk of lung cancer, asthma, pneumonia, and heart disease. Thus, to verify a causal relationship between an observed health effect and exposures to the chemical(s) of interest, exposure reconstruction is one of the necessary processes. The term exposure reconstruction is defined here as a process for identifying the specific exposure sources and routes, as well as the frequency, duration, and magnitude of the exposure.

Exposure may be reconstructed quantitatively using different approaches: (1) collecting personal monitoring data for similar exposure scenarios; (2) measuring environmental concentrations for similar exposure scenarios; (3) using computational models and available environmental measurement data to simulate plausible exposures; (4) reconstructing exposures based on biomarker data; or (5) combinations of any of the preceding approaches. As tens of thousands of biomarker measurements are now made each year as part of targeted cohort studies or recurring national surveys, there is a lot of interest in using these data to characterize exposures over a specific period of time or to correlate them to health outcomes in epidemiological studies. In addition, biomarker data can be combined with other quantitative approaches to reconstruct exposures (**Fig. 2**). Exposure reconstruction allows for better assessment of exposure sources and pathways, which not only supports better internal dose estimates for more informed human health risk assessment, but also guides and evaluates risk-mitigation efforts.

Biomarkers of exposure. A biomarker is any substance that can be measured in a biological sample and is correlated to some other metric of interest. There are disease-related biomarkers, drug-related biomarkers, biomarkers of effect, and biomarkers of susceptibility. Our focus is on biomarkers of

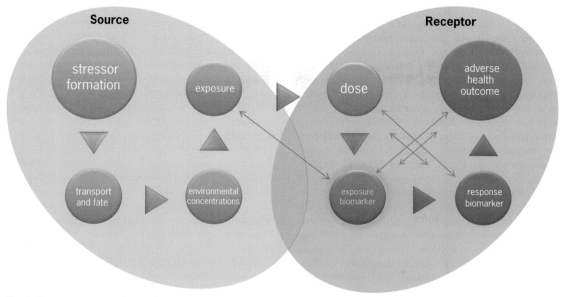

Fig. 1. Source–exposure–dose–adverse outcome continuum.

exposure, which are markers that are measured in accessible biological media (such as blood and urine) to infer exposures to exogenous chemicals. A biomarker of exposure can be the chemical itself, its metabolite, or an endogenous species that changes in response to exposure. Because biomarkers of exposure provide direct evidence of human exposure to and uptake of a chemical, they have been used to reconstruct exposures in the workplace for decades. As analytical techniques for measuring biomarker concentrations continue to advance, allowing detection of an increasing number of chemicals at ever-lower concentrations, exposure biomarkers are now being used to observe trends of exposures to environmental chemicals over time and between different populations. For example, the Centers for

Fig. 2. A visual analysis (showing 72 of 5335 terms) of 237 abstracts that contain "chemical AND exposure AND reconstruction" OR ("exposure biomarkers") using IBM's Many Eyes ⟨http://www.many-eyes.com⟩ Phrase-net analysis. (Searched on May 22, 2013.)

Disease Control and Prevention (CDC) were among the first to measure biomarkers for environmental exposures in the general population. The CDC first included exposure biomarkers in their National Health and Nutrition Examination Survey III (NHANES III: 1988–1994). To date, four national reports have been published on biomarkers measured in blood, serum, or urine, including a total of more than 300 chemicals. Illustrative classes of chemicals in the latest report include disinfection by-products, phenols, fungicides, herbicides, pesticides, metals, parabens (esters of 4-hydroxybenzoic acid; used as preservatives), perfluorinated chemicals, phthalates, polycyclic aromatic hydrocarbons (PAHs), and volatile organic compounds (VOCs).

Biomarker data may be superior to conventional exposure data collected from environmental sampling, because biomarkers reflect the actual absorbed dose from all sources and routes. These data alone, however, cannot be used to reconstruct exposures. In addition to biomarker data, the process of exposure reconstruction also requires (1) knowledge of the design and sampling procedure of the biomonitoring study; (2) exposure-related information, such as relative contributions from different routes of exposure; and (3) chemical pharmacokinetics, which describe the temporal aspects of absorption into the body, distribution to organs, tissues, and cells, metabolism to other compounds, and elimination from the body (ADME, for absorption, distribution, metabolism, and excretion).

Incorporating biomarkers in exposure reconstruction. At its foundation, exposure reconstruction from internal biomarker measurements is an inverse problem. In contrast to a forward problem that can be solved deterministically, exposure reconstruction does not, and will never have, a unique solution (regardless of future technological advances). The absence of matching exposure data for the majority of biomarker data exacerbates these problems. A wide range of exposure scenarios may result in the same biomarker measurement. In addition, the difficulty of properly reconstructing exposures increases as the biological half-life of a chemical decreases and/or the number of exposure sources increases. Especially when the available data are single spot measurements, biomarkers may reflect recent exposure, chronic exposure, or neither.

Despite these challenges, reconstructing a range of exposure scenarios is possible. The level of accuracy in exposure reconstruction depends on the availability of additional information to constrain the solution of this inverse problem. First, knowledge of the design and sampling procedure of the biomonitoring study (for example, time between exposure and biomarker sampling, sampled urine volume) allows one to select appropriate technique for exposure reconstruction. Next, exposure-related information (for example, frequency of pesticide uses in a month, duration of bath time) ensures that the reconstructed exposure scenarios reflect reality. In addition, information regarding the time-scale

variability of exposure can be extremely valuable. For example, if intra-day and intra-week variability in exposure concentrations is low, it may be possible to reconstruct an average daily dose from biomarker measurements. Besides exposure pathways, the exposure–biomarker relationship over time is also determined by the ADME processes, which can be nonlinear (for example, saturable metabolism) and are dependent on both biology and chemistry.

Data from pharmacokinetic, exposure, and biomarker measurements are often integrated using computational models, enabling the prediction of biomarkers concentrations for various exposure scenarios at different time points. In general, computational models can be used in two ways to reconstruct exposures: forward predictions and reverse predictions.

Forward predictions. First, possible exposure scenarios are simulated based on environmental concentrations (for example, chemical concentrations in vegetables), time–location human activities (for example, time of meals), and other exposure factors (for example, hand-to-mouth frequency, fraction of houses treated with pesticides). The simulated exposure concentrations are then used as inputs for pharmacokinetic models to predict biomarker concentrations. The predicted biomarker concentrations are then compared to measured data for different exposure scenarios to determine the mostly likely scenario from a range of options.

Reverse predictions. First, the mostly likely exposure scenario is selected for simulating the exposure doses and corresponding biomarker concentrations at different time points. Then, a statistical method such as Bayesian inference is used to reconstruct exposures based on these predicted exposure–biomarker relationships and measured biomarker concentrations.

Examples of computational models. Exposure models simulate the interaction between chemical concentrations in a specific environment and the amount of time an individual spends in this environment. Simple models predict an exposure concentration or an intake concentration. More complicated models can predict a time profile of exposure, including the magnitude, frequency, and duration of exposures.

Classical pharmacokinetic models use a limited number of empirically determined parameters, such as volume of distribution and systemic clearance, to predict a biomarker concentration at any given exposure/intake concentration. These models that are simple to parameterize and can be applied to many chemicals without adjusting the underlying structure of the model, but they are not necessarily correlated with any particular physical attribute of the system. For instance, the volume of distribution is calculated by taking the total amount of chemical that enters the body and dividing by the measured chemical concentration in blood (or plasma). The resulting value may be larger in magnitude than the entire volume of the human body, but because it has units of volume and gives a general sense of how concentrated or dilute the substance is, it still has a great deal of utility. When the exposure–biomarker relationship is linear, a classical pharmacokinetic model is often sufficient to reconstruct an equivalent daily dose from a steady-state biomarker concentration in blood.

Physiologically based pharmacokinetic (PBPK) models incorporate anatomical (for example, tissue volume), physiological (for example, blood flow rates), and chemical-specific (for example, partition between tissue and blood) data to predict ADME processes in the body. In the case where the exposure–biomarker relationship is nonlinear because of biochemical processes (for example, active transport), a classical pharmacokinetic model will be unable to model these accurately over a reasonable range of exposures and a PBPK model will be needed. In addition, Monte Carlo–PBPK simulations can account for uncertainty and interindividual variability in exposure patterns and pharmacokinetics. Monte Carlo methods incorporate random sampling from a specified distribution for select PBPK model parameters, with the goal of generating a distribution of model outputs, for example, biomarker concentrations. Using other statistical methods to solve the inverse problem, a distribution of reconstructed exposure concentrations can be generated based on observed biomarker concentrations.

Conclusions. Much of the uncertainty in traditional exposure studies comes from the huge variation between people, including where they spend their time, how they prepare their food, how frequently they wash their hands, whether they drink from the tap or buy bottled water, or if they have children who play outdoors or who spend all their time indoors. To reconstruct exposure to a specific chemical by tracking chemical concentrations in all possible sources from all possible activities requires a tremendous amount of resources. Biomarkers of exposure are advantageous because they are correlated to actual biological dose, which necessarily incorporates an individual's behavioral patterns, the prevalence of the chemical in the locations where the person spends time, his or her own unique physiology, and so on. However, the process of exposure reconstruction, going from biomarker concentration back to real-life exposure, is complicated by the fundamental lack of a one-to-one relationship between them.

Once a chemical has been chosen for study, the first step is to classify the exposure–biomarker relationship in general terms as either linear or nonlinear. This can be done by looking first at common sources of nonlinearity, such as active transport or saturable metabolism. If the relationship is linear, either a classic exposure model or a simple pharmacokinetic (PK) model may be sufficient to perform an accurate exposure reconstruction. If the relationship is nonlinear, a PBPK model may be required. However, if the range of exposures can be shown to be sufficiently narrow, it may still be possible to determine that the exposure–biomarker relationship is approximately linear over the range of interest.

The actual reconstruction of exposures requires a coordinated application of the models discussed above along with complementary statistical techniques, such as Bayesian inference, along with a generous helping of common sense and appropriate simplifying assumptions. All these things notwithstanding, exposure reconstruction is done every day and has proven to be of great value in furthering our understanding of the complex interactions between individuals and their environments that take place every moment of their lives.

[*Disclaimer:* The United States Environmental Protection Agency through its Office of Research and Development funded and managed the research described here. It has been subjected to Agency review and approved for publication. Mention of trade names or commercial products does not constitute endorsement or recommendation for use.]

For background information *see* BAYESIAN STATISTICS; ENVIRONMENTAL ENGINEERING; ENVIRONMENTAL TOXICOLOGY; EPIDEMIOLOGY; MODEL THEORY; MUTAGENS AND CARCINOGENS; RISK ASSESSMENT AND MANAGEMENT; TOXICOLOGY in the McGraw-Hill Encyclopedia of Science & Technology.

Yumei Tan; Martin Phillips; Jon Sobus; Daniel T. Chang; Michael-Rock Goldsmith

Bibliography. P. Georgopoulos et al., Reconstructing population exposures to environmental chemicals from biomarkers: Challenges and opportunities, *J. Exp. Sci. Environ. Epidemiol.*, 19(2):149–171, 2009, DOI:10.1038/jes.2008.9; J. Sahmel et al., The role of exposure reconstruction in occupational human health risk assessment: Current methods and a recommended framework, *Crit. Rev. Toxicol.*, 40(9):799–843, 2010, DOI:10.3109/10408444.2010.501052; Y. Tan et al., Reconstructing human exposures using biomarkers and other "clues," *J. Toxicol. Environ. Health B Crit. Rev.*, 15(1):22–38, 2012, DOI:10.1080/10937404.2012.632360.

Biosynthesis of fuels

Modern society currently depends heavily on the burning of fossil fuels to meet its ever increasing energy needs. However, unchecked use of fossil fuels from the industrial revolution to the present has greatly reduced the reservoirs of these limited resources, an urgent matter that now drives political tactics and military spending worldwide. The issue is further exacerbated by the enormous environmental impact of burning fossil fuels in the form of global warming. Studies have shown that rising levels of atmospheric carbon dioxide are anthropogenic in origin and, if allowed to continue increasing at the current rate, the resulting higher temperatures will negatively impact the well-being of the planet. In light of these pressing concerns, researchers have taken up the daunting task of finding an alternative energy source to replace fossil fuels.

Microbial fuel production. The nascent fields of metabolic engineering and synthetic biology look to overcome fuel scarcity by engineering fuel-producing microorganisms (**Fig. 1**). The use of a microbial platform would make fuel production

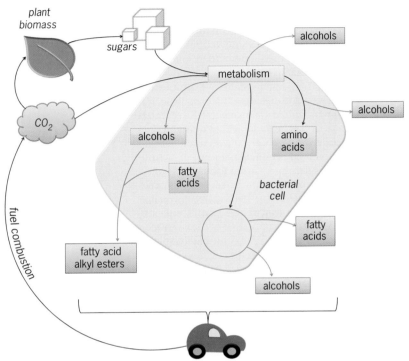

Fig. 1. Metabolic pathways within microorganisms can be modified in various ways for the production of biofuels. Black arrows indicate natural pathways for carbon uptake and use by a bacterial cell. Red arrows indicate genetically modified pathways. Bacteria will utilize plant-derived sugars as a carbon source or carbon dioxide directly in some cases.

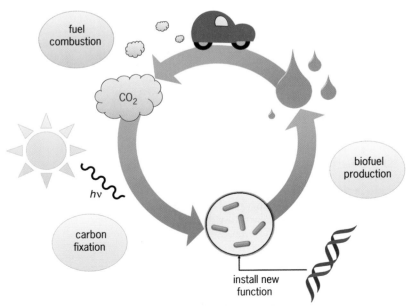

Fig. 2. The ability of cyanobacteria to utilize carbon dioxide directly streamlines the process of biofuel production by eliminating the need to obtain fermentable sugars from plants.

effectively a carbon-neutral process. Carbon dioxide released as a product of fuel combustion can be utilized by plants via photosynthesis. Sugars derived from plant biomass can then be fed to microorganisms. Engineering microorganisms that can produce fuel chemicals would then complete the carbon cycle. In such a way, fuel production could become a renewable process. Currently, microorganisms are used in the fermentation of corn-based sugars for the production of fuel-grade ethanol. However, the chemical properties of ethanol make it a non-ideal substitute for gasoline. Therefore, researchers are now manipulating the genetics of bacteria to cause them to produce other compounds that are more suitable for use as fuels. The task of engineering an organism to produce a particular organic compound in high yield and in such a way that the compound can be easily recovered is no small feat. Every living organism possesses a network of metabolic pathways by which consumed nutrients are transformed into compounds essential for that organism's survival, such as amino acids. Analysis of these compound-manipulating pathways reveals certain steps at which an enzyme can be added or removed to change a particular metabolic intermediate into a different compound than nature intended. Usually a number of different non-native enzymes are inserted to create a new metabolic pathway inside the organism. This new pathway will divert nutrients away from the organism's life-sustaining processes and toward the production of a particular chemical. Consequently, researchers must find the best way to produce fuel chemicals in high yield, while still allowing the organism to thrive. These considerations must also include the toxicity of the desired chemical to the organism, as well as the toxicity of any intermediate chemicals produced by the unnatural pathway.

Production of higher alcohols. With these considerations in mind, synthetic biologists are targeting more complex alcohols, such as 1-butanol and isobutanol, which can be readily isolated and are more energy dense than ethanol. Different pathway-engineering approaches have been explored for alcohol production in microorganisms. Fermentative pathways have long been cultivated in industry for the production of chemicals. The bacterium *Clostridium acetobutylicum* ferments starches and sugars into acetone, 1-butanol, and ethanol, by the so-called ABE fermentation. However, because of the lack of precedent for genetic manipulation and inherently slow growth of *Clostridium* species, the model organism *Escherichia coli* has been used as the host for optimizing chemical production utilizing parts of the ABE fermentative pathway. Four enzymes from *Clostridium* were introduced into *E. coli* for the production of isopropanol. The toxicity of isopropanol, however, required constant product removal to maintain chemical production. In a separate study, five enzymes from the ABE pathway were installed into *E. coli* and successfully optimized for the production of 1-butanol. Beyond traditional fermentative pathways, *E. coli* have also been engineered for the production of alcohols three to eight carbons in length via the modification of natural amino-acid biosynthetic pathways. The addition of two non-native enzymes converts the 2-ketoacid intermediates formed in amino-acid biosynthesis into alcohols. In this way, production of 1-propanol, isobutanol, 1-butanol, 2-methyl-1-butanol, 3-methyl-1-butanol, and 2-phenylethanol can be achieved, depending on the particular amino-acid pathway targeted.

Production of fatty acids. Beyond alcohols, fatty acids and alkanes are primary engineering targets as these molecules are closer structural mimics to components of fossil fuels. Because of their integral role in cellular membrane formation and energy storage, the biosynthetic pathways of fatty acids are well studied. To be used as fuel, however, fatty acids must first be converted into fatty acid alkyl esters. Currently, fatty acid alkyl esters are obtained from the chemical transformation of oils and fats obtained from plant and animal sources. Different approaches have been taken to achieve the production of fatty acid alkyl esters in *E. coli*. One strategy utilized the natural free fatty acid biosynthesis pathway. Production of free fatty acids is increased by eliminating feedback inhibition as well as by eliminating enzymes in competing metabolic pathways. Furthermore, *E. coli* can directly produce fatty acid ethyl esters via coproduction of free fatty acids and ethanol, eliminating the need for transformation of the fatty acids by chemical means. Alternatively, the fatty acid degradation pathway, known as the β-oxidation cycle, can be reversed to operate in a synthetic direction for the production of both alcohols and fatty acids.

An alternative production platform. While *E. coli* have the distinct advantage of being the most well-studied organism for genetic manipulation, the use of photosynthetic microorganisms, such as cyanobacteria, as a microbial platform for biofuel production has significant advantages. As photosynthetic organisms, cyanobacteria utilize carbon dioxide as a source of carbon and therefore do not require sugars (**Fig. 2**). This alleviates concerns of land competition between crops grown for biofuel production and those grown for food, as with corn-based bioethanol. Furthermore, the ability of cyanobacteria to fix carbon dioxide directly allows for a more carbon-neutral process by eliminating the need for processing plant biomass to generate fermentable sugars. The cyanobacterial strain *Synechococcus elongatus* has been successfully engineered to produce isobutyraldehyde as well as 2,3-butanediol via modification of the biosynthesis pathways. These two important chemical feedstocks are currently derived from petroleum. The engineering of a photosynthetic host does come with the caveat that oxygen-sensitive enzymes cannot be used in the pathway construction. Despite this drawback, cyanobacteria continue to show promise as a biofuel production platform.

Outlook. With continued improvement of biofuel production via microbial platforms, replacement of fossil fuels with fuels derived from renewable sources becomes a more realizable reality. The more we can learn about the delicately balanced networks within a biological host, the more effectively we can alter them to achieve a new state of balance with economic, political, and environmental benefits.

For background information *see* ALCOHOL; AMINO ACIDS; BACTERIA; BACTERIAL PHYSIOLOGY AND METABOLISM; BIOCHEMICAL ENGINEERING; BIOMASS; BIOSYNTHESIS; CYANOBACTERIA; ENERGY SOURCES; ENZYME; FAT AND OIL; FERMENTATION; FOSSIL FUEL; GENETIC ENGINEERING; GLOBAL CLIMATE CHANGE; PHOTOSYNTHESIS; RENEWABLE RESOURCES in the McGraw-Hill Encyclopedia of Science & Technology.   Nicole E. Nozzi; Shota Atsumi

Bibliography. S. Atsumi, T. Hanai, and J. C. Liao, Non-fermentative pathways for synthesis of branched-chain higher alcohols as biofuels, *Nature*, 451:86–89, 2008, DOI:10.1038/nature06450; S. Atsumi, W. Higashide, and J. C. Liao, Direct photosynthetic recycling of carbon dioxide to isobutyraldehyde, *Nat. Biotechnol.*, 27:1177–1180, 2009, DOI:10.1038/nbt.1586; Y. Kung, W. Runguphan, and J. D. Keasling, From fields to fuels: Recent advances in the microbial production of biofuels, *ACS Synth. Biol.*, 1, 498–513, 2012, DOI:10.1021/sb300074k; J. W. K. Oliver et al., Cyanobacterial conversion of carbon dioxide to 2,3-butanediol, *Proc. Natl. Acad. Sci. USA*, 110:1249–1254, 2013, DOI:10.1073/pnas.1213024110; C. A. Rabinovitch-Deere et al., Synthetic biology and metabolic engineering approaches to produce biofuels, *Chemical reviews*, 2013 (web), DOI:10.1021/cr300361t.

Black widow pulsars

Black widow pulsars are binary-star systems consisting of a millisecond pulsar and a very low mass stellar remnant orbiting close enough to each other for gamma rays and high-energy particles produced by the pulsar to be able to remove significant amounts of matter from the surface of its companion.

Origin and properties of neutron stars. Neutron stars are the leftover cores of very massive stars that have gone supernova. These objects contain matter in its most extreme form, with stable matter densities and magnetic fields greater than those of any other objects in the universe. They can be formed by the buildup of heavy elements through nuclear fusion at the center of stars whose mass is much greater than that of the Sun. Typically, a neutron star will form once approximately 2.8×10^{30} kg (6.2×10^{30} lb, or 1.4 times the mass of the Sun) of iron, from which energy cannot be extracted through nuclear processes, accumulates in the core of the star. At this mass, known as the Chandrasekhar mass, gravitational compression will overcome the repelling quantum-mechanical force of electrons keeping

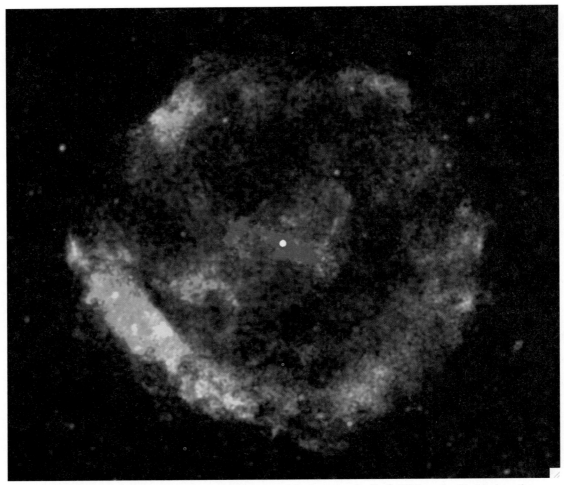

Fig. 1. **X-ray image of the young supernova remnant G11.2-0.3 (also known as the Turtle SNR) made with data from the** *Chandra X-ray Observatory.* **Red colors are low-energy x-rays, green are middle energies, and blue are higher energies. The outer ring is the blast wave from the supernova explosion that occurred approximately 2000 years ago (possibly seen by Chinese court astrologers in 386 CE). The white dot at the center is the pulsar, and the emission coming from the pulsar, seen here in blue, is due to the energetic wind generated by the central pulsar, which spins about 16 times per second.**

individual atoms separated. The result is that the electrons combine with protons in the atomic nuclei to form neutrons. This process allows all of the atomic nuclei in the core to collapse into essentially one enormous atomic nucleus approximately 20 km (12 mi) in diameter. The sudden collapse of the core of the star triggers a supernova explosion that ejects the outer layers of the star into interstellar space at supersonic speeds. This blast wave, seen as an expanding shell, is called a supernova remnant (**Fig. 1**). The bare core that is left behind is what we call a neutron star.

The center of a neutron star has densities several times those of atomic nuclei. Current nuclear theory is not able to make unique predictions about the state of matter at such densities, or even whether the material at the core remains normal nuclear matter. Some theories suggest that the core becomes a soup of strange quarks or other exotic particles. If we knew the ratio of the mass to the radius of neutron stars accurately, this would help enormously in understanding what happens to matter at greater than nuclear densities. While we can sometimes measure the mass of a neutron star accurately, the radius is much more difficult to constrain. We also do not know how great a mass a neutron star can have. We believe that at a mass somewhere around 2 to 3 times that of the Sun, gravity will overcome all resistance and the star will collapse toward a black hole state. Different supranuclear density models result in different maximum masses for neutron stars, and so finding the most massive neutron stars gives us clues about poorly understood realms of nuclear physics.

Nature and evolution of normal pulsars. When a neutron star is born, it typically has a mass close to the Chandrasekhar mass, spins 10–100 times a second, and has a magnetic field at its surface of approximately 10^8 tesla (for comparison, the Earth's magnetic field is approximately 5×10^{-5} T at the surface). When you spin a magnet fast, you have a generator that creates large electric potentials. This voltage generated by the neutron star is large enough to rip electrons and protons off the star's surface.

Many of these charged particles are trapped by the magnetic field in the region around the neutron star known as the magnetosphere. However, along field lines near the magnetic poles, there are escape paths for some of the charged particles. These escaping particles are accelerated to very high energies and emit gamma rays. This emission, in turn, produces more particles with diverse energies, resulting in the copious emission of photons at all wavelengths. Since the particles are channeled by the magnetic field, this light is preferentially emitted in certain directions (**Fig. 2**). These beams of electromagnetic radiation rotate with the star like a lighthouse. From the Earth, we see regular pulses of light in patterns that repeat with the rotation of the star. These pulses have been detected all across the electromagnetic spectrum, from radio waves to gamma rays. However, except for pulses at radio wavelengths, the data rate is usually too low for the discovery of pulsations. Neutron stars whose pulsations are visible on Earth are called pulsars.

The highly accelerated particles flow away from the pulsar at essentially the speed of light, with energies thousands of times greater than we can produce in particle accelerators such as the Large Hadron Collider (Fig. 2). This energetic wind of particles flows into the interstellar medium, creating large nebulae known as pulsar-wind nebulae (Fig. 1). The most famous of these is the Crab Nebula, the first object in Messier's catalog.

The energy for the flow of particles and the emission of light ultimately comes from the rotation of the star; hence, with time, the pulsar spins more and more slowly, and the emission becomes fainter and fainter. Eventually, after a few million years, the pulsations die off, the wind stops being generated, and the pulsar fades from sight. This fading happens when the period of rotation is approximately 5–10 s. For most of the known pulsars, which are isolated and detected primarily by their radio emission, that is the end of the story.

Rebirth of pulsars through recycling. If the neutron star is in a binary system, it can be reborn as a pulsar through a process called recycling. Matter can be stripped from the companion and fall (accrete) onto the neutron star's surface. If the matter has net angular momentum, it will transfer that momentum to the neutron star. This process has two lasting effects on the neutron star: it will suppress the magnetic field of the neutron star, and it will cause the neutron star to spin faster. The gravitation of a neutron star is very strong, and the infalling matter is heated to millions of degrees. Systems in which accretion like this is happening are called x-ray binaries, since the energy is released primarily in the form of x-ray emission.

The end result of this accretion process is determined by the mass of the companion and the initial orbital period of the system. Here we are interested in what happens when the companion is a low-mass star similar to the Sun; such systems are known as low-mass x-ray binaries. The evolution of

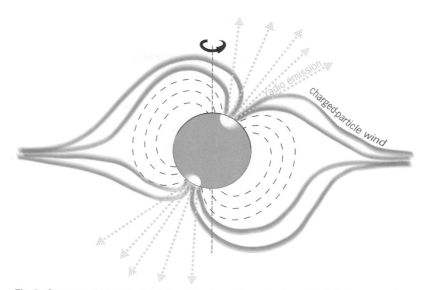

Fig. 2. Conceptual cartoon of a pulsar showing pulsar emission and wind. The magnetic field (curved broken lines) is not aligned with the rotation axis, and radio emission is produced from the magnetic poles by high-energy particles. Some of the high-energy particles escape along magnetic lines near the poles and flow equatorially out from the pulsar.

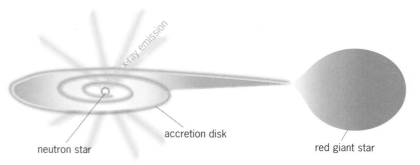

Fig. 3. Schematic of a low-mass x-ray binary, showing the process of recycling through accretion. Matter from a red giant star is being stripped away from its surface and spirals onto a neutron star, emitting x-rays from the inner edge of the accretion disk and from the surface of the neutron star. The accreting matter quenches the pulsed radio emission.

low-mass stars is slow. After billions of years as a main-sequence star burning hydrogen, the companion will start burning helium and puff up to become a red giant star, and its surface gravity will become low. The system will then remain for millions of years in a state in which matter can be transferred from the companion to the neutron star. Material stripped from the surface of the red giant will spiral toward the neutron star, forming a disk that continuously adds mass and angular momentum to the neutron star (**Fig. 3**). Low-mass x-ray binaries are the brightest sources of x-rays in the sky. In fact, the very first known cosmic x-ray source, Sco X-1, is a low-mass x-ray binary with a neutron star accreting matter from a 0.4-solar-mass companion orbiting it every 19 h.

When the companion finally loses all its outer layers and its core is exposed, which in this case is a white dwarf, the accretion may stop. This 0.1–0.3-solar-mass core is left orbiting a fully recycled "millisecond" pulsar. As the name implies, the rotation

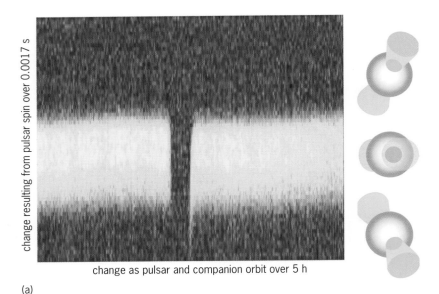

change resulting from pulsar spin over 0.0017 s

change as pulsar and companion orbit over 5 h

(a)

companion

pulsar

(b)

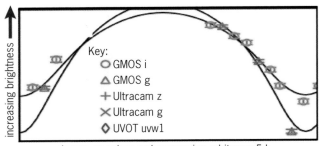

increasing brightness

Key:
○ GMOS i
△ GMOS g
+ Ultracam z
✕ Ultracam g
◇ UVOT uvw1

change as pulsar and companion orbit over 5 h

(c)

Fig. 4. Observations of the black widow pulsar PSR J1810+1744, one of the many discovered in radio by targeting gamma-ray sources detected by the Fermi mission. (*a*) Data from the Westerbork radio telescope at a frequency of 350 MHz. The vertical (*y*) axis of this plot shows the average change in brightness during one 1.7-ms spin of the pulsar. To the right of the plot is a representation of the lighthouse model, showing how changes in pulsar orientation correspond to changes in brightness. In the horizontal (*x*) direction, the radio plot shows how the brightness changes as the pulsar and its companion orbit each other every 5 h. (*Courtesy J. Hessels*) (*b*) Diagrams showing three different orientations of the binary system corresponding to the radio brightness shown in part *a* and the optical light curves shown in part *c*. If you view the system from above, the central diagram corresponds to the time the radio emission is eclipsed by the evaporated material, as in part *a*. If you view it from below, the central diagram corresponds to when the heated face of the companion is toward you, so that it looks brightest to optical telescopes, as in part *c*. (*c*) Optical data for brightness of companion from a variety of telescopes and instruments, and model light curves for two different wavelengths of light. (*Courtesy R. Breton*)

period of the neutron star is now a few milliseconds, and even though the surface magnetic field is "only" about 10^4 T, it is spinning fast enough to emit radio, x-ray, and gamma-ray pulsations again.

About 10% of the known radio pulsars, most of which are part of a binary system, are recycled. However, around 25% of millisecond pulsars appear to be isolated, with no detectable companion. The very first millisecond pulsar discovered, PSR B1937+21, which spins 641 times per second, is the most famous of these isolated recycled pulsars. What happened to the star that spun it up? While in some cases the binary orbit will shrink to under an hour during the accretion process, eventually the orbit should start getting wider again. In most plausible scenarios, accretion stops before all of the companion is consumed, and some remnant is left, even if it is only a few hundredths of a solar mass.

Original black widow pulsar. In 1988, a pulsar was discovered that provided a possible answer to the isolated-millisecond-pulsar enigma. PSR B1957+20 is one of the fastest-spinning radio pulsars known, and it orbits a companion, whose mass is approximately 2% that of the Sun, every 9 h. The radio emission from this pulsar is regularly eclipsed for about an hour each orbit, too long for the pulsar signal to be simply blocked by the companion. Multiple lines of evidence show that the eclipse is caused by extra gas in the system that scatters the radio emission. This gas is being blasted off the companion by the high-energy particle wind and gamma rays coming from the pulsar (**Fig. 4**). Because it is now obliterating the companion that gave it new life, it was nicknamed the black widow pulsar, after the North American spider species whose females are infamous for killing their mates.

This wind from the black widow pulsar heats the side of the companion facing it, making it bright in visible light (Fig. 4). This allows the companion's orbit and the inclination of the orbital plane to be determined with optical telescopes. Combined with precise information about the pulsar's motion deduced from the changes in its radio pulse period as it orbits the companion, these optical observations can be used to obtain a measurement of the individual masses of the two stars. Since the pulsar has spent millions of years accreting matter from its companion, it would be expected to have much more mass than when it was born, and systems like it can be used to constrain the maximum mass of a neutron star.

While the pulsar wind ablating the companion is a possible mechanism for destroying it completely, it is unclear whether the process is generally efficient. In fact, the original black widow is not removing matter from its companion fast enough to make it disappear within the age of the universe. In addition, for many years it appeared that systems of the black widow type were rare, perhaps too rare to explain the number of isolated millisecond pulsars.

There are technical difficulties, both computational and observational, in finding black widow systems. Advances in radio telescopes, computers, and pulse search algorithms are now able to overcome many of these difficulties. Still, it is possible for a black widow pulsar to be completely enshrouded by the gas from its companion, scattering away all radio pulsations. Gamma rays, however, can penetrate through this gas. Black widow pulsars should always be detectable as gamma-ray sources as long as the gamma-ray beam shines in our direction.

Discovery of black widow pulsars with Fermi. Between the discovery of the original black widow pulsar in 1988 and the launch of the *Fermi Gamma-ray Space Telescope* in 2008, only two other similar systems were found in our region of the Milky Way Galaxy for which we could be confident that the current companion is the one responsible for recycling the pulsar. The Large-Area Telescope on the *Fermi* satellite is roughly 10 times more sensitive to high-energy gamma rays than any previous instrument. The number of gamma rays detected from these systems is very low, making the direct detection of pulsations in the gamma-ray data extremely difficult even with *Fermi*. However, gamma-ray sources can be localized well enough for deep observations with radio telescopes to be made. If a radio pulse is detected, then an extended campaign (typically 1–2 years long) to track the radio pulsations allows us to make very precise determinations of the location, orbit, and long-term change in pulse period of the pulsar. It is then possible to go back to the *Fermi* data and use this information to detect pulsations in the gamma-ray data. Radio searches of several hundred unidentified gamma-ray sources have led to the discovery of 10 new black widow pulsars in just a few years time. Including pulsars discovered by other methods, there are now 15 known gamma-ray-emitting black widow pulsars.

The ability to localize a gamma-ray source also makes practical the search for stars whose variations in optical light may indicate that they are orbiting a black widow pulsar. The position and orbital parameters of such stars can be determined fairly precisely using optical data. Then, for the brightest sources and with a lot of computing power, it becomes feasible to directly search for pulsations in the gamma-ray data without having to already know the pulsation period from radio observations. In February 2012, an optical candidate was found with the WIYN 3.6-m (142-in.) telescope, positionally coincident with the *Fermi*-discovered gamma-ray source 2FGL J1311.7–3429. Observations of this source using a range of optical filters showed it to be strongly heated by an unseen companion that it orbits every 1.6 h. Using this information, the *Fermi* team searched 4 years of gamma-ray data using a supercomputer, and discovered 2.5-ms pulsations. This finding proves that it is possible to discover pulsars of the black widow type that are completely hidden at radio wavelengths. As it turns out, this particular source, now called PSR J1311-3430, is not completely hidden from the view of radio telescopes. Intense searches found that it

is detectable about 10% of the time at radio wavelengths.

Among the known black widows, PSR J1311-3430 has the shortest orbit with the lightest companion, less than 1% of the mass of the Sun. Further optical studies have allowed a preliminary determination of the mass of the pulsar. While there are several systematic uncertainties in the modeling of this system, the best-fit mass is 2.7 times the mass of the Sun. It is almost certainly larger than 2.1 solar masses. If this mass determination turns out to be correct, it will rule out most current models of neutron star interiors and give some of the strongest experimental constraints on nuclear matter at high densities.

Thanks largely to the *Fermi Gamma-ray Space Telescope*, there is now a fair-sized population of known black widow pulsars to study. It has also been demonstrated that black widow pulsars can be discovered even when the radio pulsations are completely hidden by gas in the system. Optical, x-ray, radio, and gamma-ray observations of these systems, currently underway, promise to shed light on several longstanding problems in astrophysics and nuclear physics. Along with many more scientific questions that were not discussed here, the new black widow pulsars are helping to clarify the full evolutionary picture of millisecond pulsars, and are addressing fundamental questions concerning the physics of matter at supra-nuclear densities.

For background information *see* ARANEAE; ASTROPHYSICS, HIGH-ENERGY; BINARY STAR; BLACK HOLE; CRAB NEBULA; GAMMA-RAY ASTRONOMY; GRAVITATIONAL COLLAPSE; NEUTRON STAR; PULSAR; RADIO ASTRONOMY; STELLAR EVOLUTION; SUPERNOVA; TELESCOPE; X-RAY ASTRONOMY in the McGraw-Hill Encyclopedia of Science & Technology.

Mallory S. E. Roberts

Bibliography. D. R. Lorimer, Binary and millisecond pulsars, *Living Rev. Relat.*, 11:8 (90 pp.), 2008, DOI:10.12942/lrr-2008-8; D. R. Lorimer and M. Kramer, *Handbook of Pulsar Astronomy*, Cambridge University Press, Cambridge, UK, 2005, paper 2012; M. S. E. Roberts, Surrounded by spiders! New black widows and redbacks in the galactic field, *Proc. Int. Astron. Union*, 291:127–132, 2013, DOI:10.1017/S174392131202337X; R. W. Romani et al., PSR J1311-3430: A heavyweight neutron star with a flyweight helium companion, *Astrophys. J. Lett.*, 760:L36 (6 pp.), 2012, DOI:10.1088/2041-8205/760/2/L36.

Body area networks for health care

Imagine knowing your overall health condition all the time, or even knowing that someone or something continuously monitors your health condition. This objective is now realizable thanks to recent advances in sensor node and network technologies. Small sensor nodes that are attached to the human body (commonly known as body sensors) and connected to the Internet, and that are able to collect

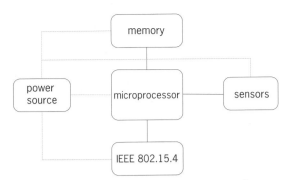

Fig. 1. Generic architecture of a wireless sensor node.

physical or biological parameters, are now a reality. These sensor nodes are used to monitor overall human health. Close control over the data collected by these sensor nodes can help detect abnormal health situations. The application of these technologies to health care represents an added value in improving the health control of patients in health-care facilities. Small body sensor nodes can be placed all over a patient's body, providing continuous and remote monitoring of certain health parameters. Thus, if an abnormal situation is detected, the system can alert the medical staff immediately, thereby reducing the time required for rapid assistance.

To connect the sensor nodes carried by patients to the Internet and make them accessible all the time requires a network infrastructure. These infrastructures are called wireless sensor networks,

and when applied in health-care facilities they can be called health-care wireless sensor networks (HWSNs).

Sensor nodes. The sensor nodes used to collect patients' health parameters are tiny devices with limited resources. However, they have some important features that enable them to operate in these scenarios. These features include wireless connectivity and the capability to collect sensorial data, potentially running programs and processing the collected data. The sensor nodes must be able to operate in stand-alone mode for long periods. Therefore, the generic constitution of these sensor nodes comprises the following modules:

1. Processor module. This is the main component of the sensor node. It allows the execution of the sensor node applications and processes all the collected data.

2. Memory module. This component allows the sensor node to store collected data.

3. Transition transceiver. This element gives the sensor node the ability to communicate wirelessly with the outside world. The sensor node's communication module typically is compliant with the standards IEEE 802.15.4 or Bluetooth.

4. Sensor module. This is a component that allows the sensor node to collect the health parameters.

5. Power module. When the sensor nodes must operate in stand-alone mode, they are powered by batteries.

Figure 1 depicts the connection of all the modules that constitutes the sensor node's architecture.

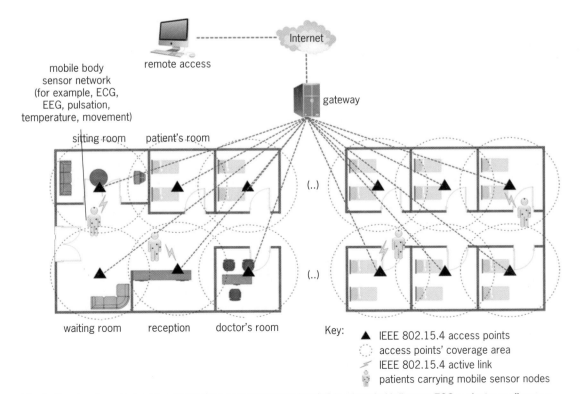

Fig. 2. Construction of a health-care wireless sensor network (HWSN) in a hospital infirmary. ECG = electrocardiogram; EEG = electroencephalogram.

In HWSNs, sensor nodes act as terminal network nodes. They send and receive data to and from the network. As already mentioned, these sensor nodes must operate in a stand-alone mode, and thus they should incorporate their own power sources, typically, small batteries. These batteries have limited lifetimes and, in most cases, depending on their location, the density of the sensor nodes, and the inconvenience of removing them, they cannot be recharged frequently or even be recharged at all. Thus, it is very important to use low-power components in the construction of the sensor nodes in order to minimize their energy consumption and thereby conserve their batteries. The optimization of software algorithms that run in the sensor nodes also can contribute greatly to reducing their energy consumption.

HWSN construction. Monitoring hospitalized patients is a daily routine in infirmaries. Nowadays, this task is usually performed by medical staff that periodically gathers the values collected by body sensors close to the patients. The use of new technologies can improve the access to this data remotely, in real time, and in a continuous way. As previously mentioned, this continuous access also allows more effective monitoring of these patients and a more rapid response in case of abnormal situations. The HWSNs comprise several body sensor nodes that collect the monitored parameters. Several access points (compliant with the standard IEEE 802.15.4, for instance) allow network connectivity to those sensor nodes within their coverage areas. A gateway acts as a bridge between the HWSN and the Internet (**Fig. 2**).

HWSNs present several special features that distinguish them from other wireless sensor networks:

1. Real-time monitoring. In HWSNs, it is important that sensor nodes remain accessible all the time without interruption. Only with this feature can one guarantee close control over a patient's health state.

2. Several access points should be used. Because the coverage area of IEEE 802.15.4 standard access points is about 10 m (33 ft) for indoor applications, the use of several devices to cover larger areas is mandatory.

3. Random and continuous mobility of the sensor nodes. This is an important feature in HWSNs. Because of the nature of the monitored "object" (a human being), mobility is an intrinsic characteristic. Also, it is important to let hospitalized patients move around, if they can, to improve their quality of life. The HWSNs should support continuous connection to the sensor nodes even in mobility.

Supporting the mobility of sensor nodes is a new challenge in HWSNs, and it can contribute to the construction of ubiquitous health-care environments. This problem will now be discussed.

Providing ubiquity in health-care scenarios. Because of the limited coverage area of IEEE 802.15.4 access points in indoor environments, it is necessary to use several access points to cover a large monitoring area, such as a hospital infirmary. In these scenarios, the HWSNs must support changes in the attached access points to each sensor node. This need arises whenever a sensor node comes close to losing connection to an access point because it is near the limit of the coverage area. If the sensor node moves out of this coverage area, it loses the connection to the

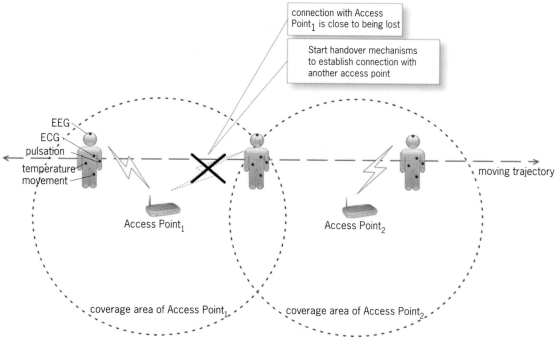

Fig. 3. Illustration of the operating principles of a handover mechanism. ECG = electrocardiogram; EEG = electroencephalogram.

network and therefore it becomes inaccessible. So, before it moves out of the coverage area, the sensor node should find a new access point to which it can attach itself, and thereby avoid becoming inaccessible. The mechanism for deciding the moment to change and the act of changing the attachment from one access point to another is called handover. In HWSNs, where continuous access to nodes is the topmost priority, the handover mechanism should have the following features:

1. Fast and seamless. The handover mechanism should prevent the sensor nodes from becoming inaccessible.

2. To decide whether a handover is needed, the access points and the sensor nodes must exchange messages. The number of messages exchanged should be minimal in order to reduce the expenditure of energy in the sensor node.

3. After a sensor node performs a handover, this information should be dispersed by the network very quickly to inform the entire network that a new access point now reaches this sensor node.

The decision to perform a handover by the sensor nodes should be transparent to the patient. Patients should be able to move freely around the monitored area knowing that they are always monitored. An HWSN and specifically the handover mechanisms should guarantee continuous access to the sensor nodes even when they travel across the coverage areas of several access points. These mechanisms are able to promote the ubiquitous vision in health-care facilities. **Figure 3** presents an illustration of this scenario and indicates the point when the handover process should be performed by the sensor nodes.

Bringing mobility support of sensor nodes to HWSNs can promote a better quality of life for patients, allowing them to move freely in the monitored region. With this feature, several new challenges arise in the HWSN area. One of the most challenging tasks in HWSN design with mobile support is the optimization of handover procedures. This optimization should take into account the limitations of the sensor nodes. Therefore, the handover process should be restrained in energy expenditure but also should guarantee continuous connectivity to the body sensor nodes. Several efforts now are in progress to achieve this objective.

For background information *see* BIOELECTRONICS; BIOSENSOR; INTERNET; MICROPROCESSOR; MICROSENSOR; MOBILE COMMUNICATIONS; TELEMETERING in the McGraw-Hill Encyclopedia of Science & Technology.   João M. L. P. Caldeira; Joel J. P. C. Rodrigues

Bibliography. H. Alemdar and C. Ersoy, Wireless sensor networks for healthcare: A survey, *Comput. Network.*, 54:2688–2710, 2010, DOI:10.1016/j.comnet.2010.05.003; J. M. L. P. Caldeira et al., A new wireless biosensor for intra-vaginal temperature monitoring, *Sensors*, 10:10314–10327, 2010, DOI:10.3390/s101110314; J. M. L. P. Caldeira et al., Intra-mobility handover enhancement in healthcare wireless sensor networks, pp. 261–266, in Institute of Electrical and Electronics Engineers, *Proceedings of the 14th International Conference on E-Health Networking, Applications and Services* (IEEE Healthcom 2012), Beijing, China, October 10–13, 2012, IEEE, Piscataway, NJ, 2012, DOI:10.1109/HealthCom.2012.6379418; J. M. L. P. Caldeira, J. J. P. C. Rodrigues, and P. Lorenz, MAC layer handover mechanism for continuous communication support in healthcare mobile wireless sensor networks, *Telecommun. Syst.*, in press; J. M. L. P. Caldeira, J. J. P. C. Rodrigues, and P. Lorenz, Toward ubiquitous mobility solutions for body sensor networks on healthcare, *IEEE Commun. Mag.*, 50(5):108–115, May 2012, DOI:10.1109/MCOM.2012.6194390; M. Chen et al., Body area networks: A survey, *Mobile Network Appl.*, 16:171–193, 2010, DOI:10.1007/s11036-010-0260-8; J. J. P. C. Rodrigues, O. R. E. Pereira, and P. A. C. S. Neves, Biofeedback data visualization for body sensor networks, *J. Net. Comput. Appl.*, 34:151–158, 2011, DOI:10.1016/j.jnca.2010.08.005.

Bonobo genome

Bonobos (*Pan paniscus*) are among the closest living relatives of the human species. Along with chimpanzees (*Pan troglodytes*), bonobos shared a common ancestor with human beings approximately 6 million years ago (MYA). The two species of *Pan* shared a much more recent common ancestor approximately 2 MYA (**Fig. 1**). The first draft version of the *Pan troglodytes* genome was published in 2005, and the first bonobo genome was published in 2012.

Bonobos are of great interest to students of primate and human evolution because of the close evolutionary affinities that they share with the human species. Bonobos are known to exhibit intriguing behavioral characteristics. For example, they have been observed practicing a great deal of affiliative behaviors (that is, behaviors that promote social cohesion) in the wild, and bonobos are generally considered to be a much more peaceful species than chimpanzees or humans. Bonobos, especially females, have also been known to frequently engage in homosexual activity. Bonobos are intelligent, and some bonobos have been taught the rudiments of human language. The most famous bonobo with this ability is Kanzi, a bonobo living in captivity in Iowa, who has a vocabulary of hundreds of words (**Fig. 2**). Because bonobos cannot produce the complex vocalizations uttered by humans, Kanzi communicates through the use of a lexigram, which is a symbolic keypad that enables him to "talk." Moreover, bonobos, like chimpanzees and humans, have been shown to make and use tools.

Today, wild bonobos are found only in the Democratic Republic of Congo in Africa. They are the least common ape species found in captivity, and they are the most recently described great ape species. There is less known about the behavior and ecology of bonobos compared to the behavior and ecology of other ape species, and they are in danger of extinction in the wild.

Bonobo genome sequence. The process of sequencing the first bonobo genome began in 2001, when blood was isolated from an 8-year-old individual bonobo. Thereafter, the DNA was isolated from lymphocytes, and the sequencing was completed using next-generation sequencing technology.

The assembled genome sequence of the bonobo was derived from a captive female individual named Ulindi. Ulindi is housed in a zoo in Leipzig, Germany. The genome was sequenced using a pyrosequencing method, or "sequencing by synthesis." The assembled genome has 26-fold coverage, meaning each nucleotide base in the genome was sequenced 26 times, on average. Approximately 2.7 billion base pairs of the DNA sequence were assembled into contigs or scaffolds. This result is consistent with an average mammalian genome size of 3 billion base pairs.

There are approximately 80 million base pairs in the bonobo genome that are the result of segmental duplication events that have occurred during the last 6 million years, since the time bonobos last shared a common ancestor with humans. Approximately 80–85% of these duplicated base pairs were duplicated before the chimpanzees and bonobos diverged from each other. The remaining base pairs were recently duplicated on the chimpanzee lineage (5.2 million base pairs) and bonobo lineage (4.9 million base pairs). Researchers have been able to experimentally validate 704,000 base pairs of these duplicated regions, including regions containing known genes.

The mitochondrial genome of Ulindi was also compared with the mitochondrial genomes of other chimpanzees and bonobos. As expected, all bonobo sequences were more similar to one another than they were to the chimpanzee mitochondrial DNA sequences. This finding suggests that chimpanzees and bonobos are each monophyletic species. (Note that a taxon is monophyletic if it contains all descendants of the group's most recent common ancestor.)

A large component of the genome consists of transposable elements. Transposable elements usually account for about half of the DNA in a given mammalian genome. Transposable elements are classified in several families, including *Alu*, L1 line elements, and endogenous retroviruses. There are 1590 transposable elements that are unique to the bonobo genome, meaning they are not present in either the human or chimpanzee genome. In comparison, there are 1079 and 6641 elements unique to the chimpanzee genome and human genome, respectively.

Evolution of bonobo and chimpanzee phenotypes. In order to identify interesting aspects of the bonobo genome that may be related to phenotype (the observable characteristics of an organism), genomic researchers conducted tests for evidence of adaptive evolution in the bonobo. Using computational methods, it is possible to identify those regions of

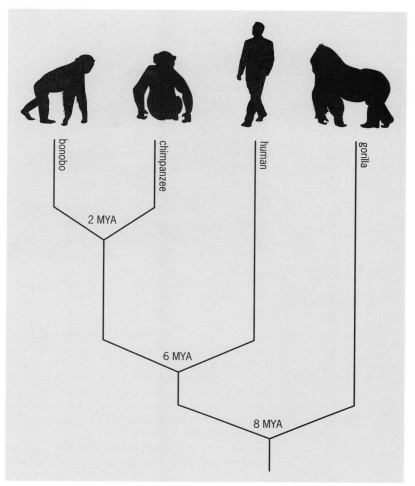

Fig. 1. Evolutionary relationships and divergence dates among bonobos, chimpanzees, humans, and gorillas (MYA = million years ago).

the bonobo genome that appear to have evolved excessively rapidly, and these regions are considered to have undergone positive selection. Not surprisingly, genomic regions near key components of the chimpanzee immune system, particularly near the major histocompatibility complex (a family of genes that encode cell surface glycoproteins that regulate interactions among cells of the immune system), were shown to have evidence for adaptive evolution. These adaptations could be a response to pathogens that ancestors of chimpanzees and bonobos faced.

When comparing the bonobo and chimpanzee genomes to each other, it was found that on average 99.6% of the DNA of the two species was identical. This is in contrast to the 98.7% identical bases found in comparisons of the bonobo and chimpanzee genomes to the human genome. There is evidence for hybridization between species in many primates, but the analyses of the bonobo and chimpanzee genomes found no evidence of interspecies gene flow. This finding is consistent with the idea that the Congo River (which formed approximately 1.5–2.5 MYA) was a strong barrier that prevented gene flow between the bonobo and chimpanzee ancestors.

Fig. 2. Kanzi, a member of the bonobo (*Pan paniscus*) species. (*Photo courtesy of the Iowa Primate Learning Sanctuary, Des Moines, IA*)

The divergence between the bonobo and chimpanzee lineages began relatively recently, with most estimates being between 1 and 3 MYA. This is only a few million years after the divergence between the *Homo* and *Pan* lineages. The pattern of inheritance of genetic variants is thus complicated by a phenomenon called incomplete lineage sorting. Incomplete lineage sorting is apparent when gene genealogies do not match species phylogenies (evolutionary histories). This means that some bonobo DNA is more closely related to human DNA than it is to chimpanzee DNA. Likewise, some chimpanzee DNA is more similar to human DNA than it is to bonobo DNA. An analysis of the nonrepetitive DNA in these genomes revealed that approximately 1.6% of the bonobo genome is more closely related to the human genome than to the chimpanzee genome. Similarly, 1.7% of the chimpanzee genome is more closely related to the human genome than to the bonobo genome. Genomic researchers have speculated that these gene regions may influence the traits that humans share with one *Pan* species but not the other.

For background information *see* ANIMAL EVOLUTION; APES; DEOXYRIBONUCLEIC ACID (DNA); FOSSIL APES; GENE; GENETIC MAPPING; GENOMICS; HUMAN GENOME; MOLECULAR ANTHROPOLOGY; PHYLOGENY; PRIMATES; TRANSPOSABLE ELEMENTS in the McGraw-Hill Encyclopedia of Science & Technology.
Derek E. Wildman

Bibliography. The Chimpanzee Sequencing and Analysis Consortium, Initial sequence of the chimpanzee genome and comparison with the human genome, *Nature*, 437(7055):69–87, 2005, DOI:10.1038/nature04072; F. de Waal, *Bonobo: The Forgotten Ape*, University of California Press, Berkeley, CA, 1997; K. Prüfer et al., The bonobo genome compared with the chimpanzee and human genomes, *Nature*, 486(7404):527–531, 2012, DOI:10.1038/nature11128; I. Roffman et al., Stone tool production and utilization by bonobo-chimpanzees (*Pan paniscus*), *Proc. Natl. Acad. Sci. USA*, 109(36):14500–14503, 2012, DOI:10.1073/pnas.1212855109; S. Savage-Rumbaugh and R. Lewin, *Kanzi: The Ape at the Brink of the Human Mind*, Wiley, New York, 1994.

Broadly neutralizing antibodies

Broadly neutralizing antibodies are immune proteins that inhibit or abolish the biological activity of a wide range of antigenically diverse viruses. Recently, broadly neutralizing antibodies have been identified for human immunodeficiency virus (HIV) and influenza virus infections, and these antibodies are capable of neutralizing many or all viral variants. The antigenic determinants (epitopes) identified by these antibodies are therefore exciting targets for vaccine design if certain biological problems can be surmounted.

Background. Antibodies, which also are known as immunoglobulin (Ig) proteins, are a critical component of the human body's immune defense against infectious agents. Antibodies typically act by blocking or interfering with the entry of pathogens into a cell. All current vaccines used in medicine exploit this property by eliciting antibodies capable of efficiently neutralizing specific pathogens. Although vaccines have achieved undoubted success in reducing and abolishing certain infectious diseases, standard vaccine approaches have thus far failed to protect against HIV or pandemic influenza infections; therefore, these viruses remain a global health concern and burden.

Both HIV and influenza are enveloped RNA viruses that rely on viral envelope proteins, glycoprotein 120 (gp120) and hemagglutinin (HA), respectively, to attach and enter cells. The HIV gp120 envelope protein binds to the CD4 receptor on T cells (T lymphocytes), and the influenza HA protein binds to a glycan (polysaccharide), sialic acid, on cell surface proteins. The polymerases (enzymes that link nucleotides together to form polynucleotide chains) that replicate the viral RNA during the viral life cycle are highly prone to error, leading to a remarkable variability in both gp120 and HA at regions to which the antibodies are often directed. This effectively leads to a race between the antibody response and viral replication in which the virus evades the current antibody response that is directed against a previous version (or versions) of the virus. However, the specific regions of gp120 and HA that bind to surface receptors on the target cells sustain less variability because they are required for cell entry and thus remain vulnerable antibody targets. Over the last several years and as a result of technological advances, a number of new broadly neutralizing antibodies have been isolated from individuals infected with either HIV or influenza. The major impetus facilitating the isolation of these new antibodies has been the ability to not only identify and isolate single B cells (B lymphocytes) from virally infected individuals, but also to clone and produce the Ig proteins that these cells express. This new approach, together with advances in high-throughput screening, has played an important role in the identification and characterization of these new protective antibodies. The ongoing characterizations of these protective antibodies and their target epitopes on HIV and influenza viruses have provided fresh insights into vaccine strategies that may be capable of eliciting protective humoral (antibody-mediated) immunity to HIV and pandemic influenza.

HIV broadly neutralizing antibodies. In the first three decades after the identification of HIV as the etiological agent of AIDS, a handful of HIV broadly neutralizing antibodies were identified and characterized. The specific HIV sites targeted by these antibodies were determined to be the gp120 CD4 binding site, a carbohydrate motif, and a membrane-proximal external region on gp41, which anchors gp120 to the viral membrane. Although these antibodies are limited by breadth or potency, passive transfer of these antibodies provided immune protection to primates, suggesting that humoral immunity could provide sufficient protection against HIV infection. In exciting developments over the last few years, investigators have successfully isolated and characterized a number of novel HIV broadly neutralizing antibodies that display significantly elevated potency and breadth. These new-generation broadly neutralizing antibodies are directed to HIV targets that include similar regions targeted by the first generation of broadly neutralizing antibodies, but they also reveal new sites of apparent viral vulnerability.

From these multiple and ongoing analyses, several new features of HIV broadly neutralizing antibodies have emerged. Specifically, these antibodies harbor considerable mutations, suggesting that the B cells from which they arise have been participating in an ongoing antibody response. Despite these mutations, broadly neutralizing antibodies that recognize the same HIV target often originate from the same germline Ig (*IGHV*) gene; this occurs even when the antibodies are isolated from different individuals, indicating that protective HIV antibodies are often derived from specific Ig genes. The two major HIV targets to emerge from structural studies of the newly identified broadly neutralizing antibodies are (1) the glycan interaction with the gp120 variable loops, characterized as the PG and PGT series of broadly neutralizing antibodies, and (2) the CD4 binding site on gp120 that is required for cell entry and for which VRC01 is the prototype. Together, these new findings indicate that a neutralizing antibody response to HIV can be mounted, although apparently after a long process of selection. The challenge going forward will be to elicit an antibody response with similar characteristics using newly identified immunogens (substances that provide an immune response and stimulate the production of specific antibodies).

Influenza broadly neutralizing antibodies. Influenza A is a highly adaptable pathogen that circulates in different host species. As mentioned previously, the success of this virus in evading the host antibody response can be partially attributed to the error-prone viral machinery that leads to a high mutation rate and a high degree of variability. Moreover, because of its segmented genome, rearrangements can quickly lead to new viral variants. These variants, if exposed to a population with inadequate immunity, could lead to another influenza pandemic. The major target for antibody-mediated neutralization of the influenza virus is the HA surface glycoprotein that is responsible for the viral binding and release of the genetic material inside the target cell. HA can be further divided into subunits. The "head" is termed HA1, whereas HA2 is the "stalk" or "stem." HA1 initiates infection of the host cell by binding sialic acid. The binding pocket for the sialic acid is relatively small, so the rest of the HA head is permissive to variability. After the virus is brought into the cell, the HA2 stem acts to fuse the viral and host membranes to release the viral genome into the host cell for translation and viral replication. This fusion mechanism requires a higher level of conservation in the stem than in the head.

HA is tightly packed on the surface of a virion (the complete, mature virus particle). As such, the stem is less accessible to neutralizing antibodies than the head. Anti-head antibodies are more potent neutralizers than anti-stem antibodies, possibly because of this issue of accessibility. However, the higher degree of variability in the head leads to a greater ability to avoid neutralization and a more restricted breadth of recognition. The stem region is more conserved across influenza subtypes, allowing for broader reactivity of the neutralizing antibodies. The majority of the anti-HA antibodies are directed against the head, but these antibodies are type-specific and thus not broadly neutralizing. In contrast, the use of new methods for isolating neutralizing antibodies, similar to those methods used to identify the novel HIV broadly neutralizing antibodies, has led to the characterization of a set of influenza broadly neutralizing antibodies that are directed to the HA2 stem region rather than the HA1 head region. The importance of stem-reactive antibodies has likely been underestimated because the HA inhibition assay historically used to assess immune responsiveness does not detect antibodies directed against HA2. The identification of broadly neutralizing epitopes in the HA2 stem region provides new immunogens to incorporate into a pan-influenza vaccine in the future.

New strategies for inducing viral broadly neutralizing antibodies. The identification of a number of broadly neutralizing antibodies with new and confirmed targets of HIV and influenza vulnerability has invigorated the challenge of generating protective vaccines against these viruses. Going forward, vaccine studies designed to elicit broadly neutralizing antibodies should also exploit the recent advances in other relevant areas, such as immunogen design, possibly through the use of nanoengineering (engineering applications on the scale of 1–100 nanometers) to optimally present new immunogens to B cells. Progress has also been made recently in understanding how antibodies respond physiologically to different types of antigens and specifically with regard to how antigens (and potential vaccines) are delivered to different immune sites. In addition, there is a growing appreciation for how different B cell subpopulations cooperate together to best provide humoral immunity.

A notable feature to come from the recent characterization of broadly neutralizing antibodies against either HIV or influenza is that, despite being isolated from different infected individuals, subsets of these protective antibodies are found repeatedly to originate from a specific Ig gene (out of more than 100 that are available). Specifically, broadly neutralizing antibodies against HIV that recognize the gp120 CD4 binding site often are encoded by the *IGHV-02* germline gene, and those that neutralize influenza by binding the HA stem region often derive from the *IGHV1-69* germline gene. This suggests that the Ig genes carried in human DNA have evolved to encode antibodies with specificities for common viral structures. Furthermore, it has been demonstrated that these *IGHV* genes may be differentially expressed by different B cell subsets; if so, this would suggest that vaccines tailored to elicit antibody responses from specific B cell subsets may lead to more effective humoral immunity.

The relatively large and growing numbers of broadly neutralizing antibodies that have been identified and characterized are revealing new vulnerable targets to combat HIV and influenza, and the administration of these protective antibodies has already been suggested as a possible therapeutic avenue. Relying on the increasing understanding of how vaccines can be targeted to different immune sites and how B cell subsets normally cooperate to fight infection will lead to more effective and rational vaccine designs.

For background information *see* ACQUIRED IMMUNE DEFICIENCY SYNDROME (AIDS); ANTIBODY; ANTIGEN; ANTIGEN-ANTIBODY REACTION; CELLULAR IMMUNOLOGY; CLINICAL IMMUNOLOGY; IMMUNITY; IMMUNOLOGY; INFECTION; INFLUENZA; MONOCLONAL ANTIBODIES; MUTATION; NEUTRALIZATION REACTION (IMMUNOLOGY); NEUTRALIZING ANTIBODY; VACCINATION; VIRUS; VIRUS CLASSIFICATION in the McGraw-Hill Encyclopedia of Science & Technology.   Raul M. Torres; Lindsey Pujanauski

Bibliography. D. R. Burton et al., A blueprint for HIV vaccine discovery, *Cell Host Microbe*, 12(4):396–407, 2012, DOI:10.1016/j.chom.2012. 09.008; D. R. Burton et al., Broadly neutralizing antibodies present new prospects to counter highly antigenically diverse viruses, *Science*, 337(6091):183–186, 2012, DOI:10.1126/science. 1225416; D. Corti and A. Lanzavecchia, Broadly neutralizing antiviral antibodies, *Annu. Rev. Immunol.*, 31:705–742, 2013, DOI:10.1146/annurev-immunol-032712-095916; D. C. Ekiert and I. A. Wilson, Broadly neutralizing antibodies against influenza virus and prospects for universal therapies, *Curr. Opin. Virol.*, 2(2):134–141, 2012, DOI:10.1016/ j.coviro.2012.02.005; P. D. Kwong and J. R. Mascola, Human antibodies that neutralize HIV-1: Identification, structures, and B cell ontogenies, *Immunity*, 37(3):412–425, 2012, DOI:10.1016/ j.immuni.2012.08.012.

Carnivorous demosponge biology

An unusual group of sponges, belonging to the class Demospongiae in the phylum Porifera, with a lie-and-wait mode of predation has been shown to be unique among multicellular taxa and has a body plan that defies the general description for this phylum. In a description of the sponge *Cladorhiza abyssicola* dating to the late 1880s, it was observed that "due to a lack of an aquiferous system the sponge must have some other means of obtaining nutrients." However, not until 1995 did direct observations confirm that carnivory (carnivorousness) was indeed present in this group of demosponges.

Description. A population of deep-water sponges (family Cladorhizidae) that had been found in a shallow, marine cave in the Mediterranean allowed researchers to collect specimens and observe their behavior, verifying, for the first time, carnivory in sponges. In addition, a new species of carnivorous sponge, *Asbestopluma hypogea*, was described. It was determined that the prey was captured by small filaments with hook-shaped spicules, and no toxins were used; therefore, the sponge was not paralyzing the prey. Once captured, rapid morphogenetic activity occurred, and the prey was enveloped by cells and digested within a few days.

Typical sponges have a system of channels and canals directing the water flow through their bodies, and they feed by filtering bacteria and other extremely small organisms from the flowing water. The current is created by the constant beating of choanocyte (collar cell) flagella and is energetically expensive. To accomplish this in food-poor environments, like the deep sea, is near futile. Defying the general description of the phylum Porifera, most carnivorous sponges lack both the choanocyte flagella and the aquiferous system, and instead feed by using hooklike spicules to capture small zooplankton prey. Carnivorous sponges have been found in food-poor ocean environments around the world at depths of 100–8840 m (328–29,000 ft). Thus, carnivorous sponges have evolved carnivory to minimize their energetic expenditures in the food-poor habitats where they are found. Common features among the carnivorous sponges (**Fig. 1***a–f*) include a shape that is symmetrical and often stipitate [possessing or borne on the end of a stipe (stalk)].

Shortly after the initial discovery of carnivory, a symbiosis between a carnivorous sponge species and methane-oxidizing bacteria at mud volcanoes

Fig. 1. Representative in situ images of carnivorous demosponges observed by remotely operated vehicles (ROVs) from the Monterey Bay Aquarium Research Institute (MBARI): (*a*) *Chondrocladia* sp.; (*b*) *Asbestopluma* sp.; (*c*) *Cladorhiza pteron*; (*d*) *Lollipocladia tiburoni*; (*e*) *Chondrocladia lyra* with two-vane morphology; (*f*) *Chondrocladia lyra* with five-vane morphology.

in the deep sea near Barbados was described. The analysis revealed two or three bacterial symbiont morphologies with a low, patchy density within the sponge tissue. Evidence of bacteria being digested by the sponge was found using stable isotope analysis. A close examination of the sponge also showed evidence of carnivory, indicated by small crustaceans that were found in various states of decay. Dense bushes of this sponge species were thought to thrive as a result of the enhanced nutrition provided by the methane-oxidizing symbionts.

Classification. Since the 1995 discovery and description of carnivory, 40 additional species have been described within the family Cladorhizidae; thus, there are 124 total species and 7 genera in this family. In addition, several species from the Guitarridae and Esperiopsidae are also thought to be carnivorous. Monophyly (development from a single common ancestral form) was demonstrated for the Cladorhizidae using molecular analysis of the *CO1* gene region; however, specimens from the two other suspected carnivorous families were not

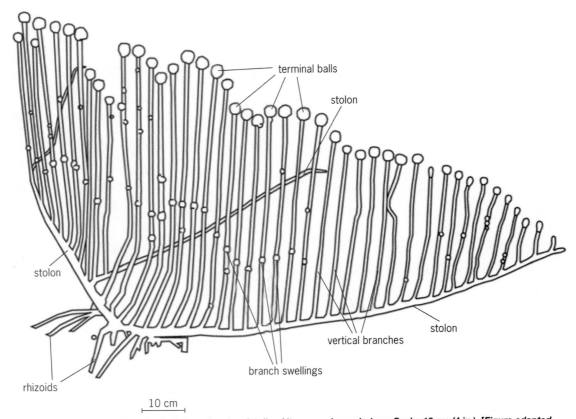

Fig. 2. Line drawing of *Chondrocladia lyra* showing details of its general morphology. Scale: 10 cm (4 in.). [*Figure adapted from W. L. Lee et al., An extraordinary new carnivorous sponge, Chondrocladia lyra, in the new subgenus Symmetrocladia (Demospongiae, Cladorhizidae), from off of northern California, USA, Invertebr. Biol., 131(4):259–284, 2012, DOI:10.1111/ivb.12001*]

available for analysis. Based on this evidence, a revised subordinal classification within the Poecilosclerida, the order that includes these three families, may be needed. It is likely that a suborder within the Poecilosclerida will be erected to include the carnivorous families of Cladorhizidae, Guitarridae, and Esperiopsidae.

Harp sponge. Recently, a new and very unusual species of *Chondrocladia* has been identified. Two specimens of *Chondrocladia lyra*, the harp sponge, were collected and 10 additional specimens were observed during dives of remotely operated vehicles (ROVs) off central and northern California at depths of 3316–3503 m (10,900–11,500 ft). These dives were conducted by the Monterey Bay Aquarium Research Institute (MBARI) as part of an ongoing study of deep-sea habitats in the northeast Pacific Ocean. The ROVs are equipped with studio-quality digital video cameras, digital still cameras, and a variety of sensors and sampling gear. Observations of *C. lyra* were recorded on digital videotape and were analyzed later using the Video Annotation and Reference System (VARS), which is a software system and database that contains more than 4 million observations of organisms, geologic features, and equipment deployed during the many years of MBARI's deep-sea research. For each observation

of *C. lyra*, the associated fauna, habitat type, and other ecological parameters were annotated within the VARS database. These observations were merged with physical data collected by the ROVs so that the position, depth, and water chemistry are known for each specimen collected or observed. Parallel red lasers (640 nm), spaced 29 cm (11.4 in.) apart, were used to estimate the organism size.

The harp sponge has numerous, evenly spaced, upright branches emanating from a horizontal stolon (a horizontal stemlike extension). The stolon and branches, which together superficially resemble a harp or lyre, have been termed a vane (Fig. 1*e,f*; **Fig. 2**). Multiple vanes radiate from the organism's center. Vanes can reach approximately 36 cm (14.2 in.) in length, and organisms have been observed with two to six vanes. Midbranch swellings were found to be the locations of oocyte maturation. Like other species of the genus *Chondrocladia*, *C. lyra* does have an aquiferous system and it is used primarily for the inflation of ball-like spheres, which appear to be sites of prey capture and the production and release of spermatophores (sperm bundles or packages). Small crustacean prey, mostly copepods, were observed in various states of digestion and provide direct evidence of carnivory. *Chondrocladia lyra* was found living anchored to soft abyssal sediments by means of a rootlike or clawlike structure, called a rhizoid. The harplike structure of the vanes maximizes the surface area for feeding and spermatophore capture.

Future outlook. Since 2000, 16 new species of carnivorous sponges have been described and countless others are probably awaiting description. In fact, several undescribed species have been collected at sampling stations in the northeast Pacific Ocean. As a result of their diversity of morphologies and habitats, and especially because their unique carnivorous behavior was only recently described, these sponges are truly interesting. Future contributions to the study of this group should focus on descriptions of feeding, reproduction, and global distribution. In addition, molecular analysis of a broader swath of species will further our understanding of the phylogenetic relationships among the Porifera, helping us to better understand the evolution of the earliest form of metazoan life on Earth.

For background information *see* DEEP-SEA FAUNA; DEMOSPONGIAE; ECOLOGICAL COMMUNITIES; MARINE BIOLOGICAL SAMPLING; MARINE ECOLOGY; OCEANOGRAPHY; PARAZOA; PORIFERA; PREDATOR-PREY INTERACTIONS; UNDERWATER VEHICLES in the McGraw-Hill Encyclopedia of Science & Technology.

Lonny Lundsten

Bibliography. W. L. Lee et al., An extraordinary new carnivorous sponge, *Chondrocladia lyra*, in the new subgenus *Symmetrocladia* (Demospongiae, Cladorhizidae), from off of northern California, USA, *Invertebr. Biol.*, 131(4):259–284, 2012, DOI:10.1111/ivb.12001; S. O. Ridley and A. Dendy, Report on the Monaxonida collected by H.M.S. 'Challenger' during the years 1873–1876, *Rep. Sci. Res. Voy. Challenger Zool.*, 20(59):1–275, 1887; B. Schlining and N. Jacobsen Stout, MBARI's video annotation and reference system, pp. 1–5, in *Oceans 2006: Proceedings of the Marine Technology Society/ Institute of Electrical and Electronics Engineers Oceans Conference*, Boston, 2006; J. Vacelet, Deep-sea sponges in a Mediterranean cave, pp. 299–312, in F. Uiblein, J. Ott, and M. Stachowitsch (eds.), *Deep-Sea and Extreme Shallow Water Habitats: Affinities and Adaptations*, Austrian Acad. Sci., Vienna, 1996; J. Vacelet, Diversity and evolution of deep-sea carnivorous sponges, pp. 107–115, in M. R. Custódio et al. (eds.), *Porifera Research: Biodiversity, Innovation and Sustainability*, Museu Nacional, Rio de Janeiro, 2007; J. Vacelet and N. Boury-Esnault, Carnivorous sponges, *Nature (London)*, 373:333–335, 1995, DOI:10.1038/373333a0; R. W. M. Van Soest et al., Global diversity of sponges (Porifera), *PLoS ONE*, 7(4):e35105, 2012, DOI:10.1371/journal.pone.0035105; S. Vargas et al., Molecular phylogeny of *Abyssocladia* (Cladorhizidae: Poecilosclerida) and *Phelloderma* (Phellodermidae: Poecilosclerida) suggests a diversification of chelae microscleres in cladorhizid sponges, *Zool. Scr.*, 42:106–116, 2012, DOI:10.1111/j.1463-6409.2012.00560.x.

Channel equalization

In digital communications systems, data is transmitted from the transmitter to the receiver over a channel, which may be a cable or a wireless medium. Every physical channel adds some random noise to the transmitted signal, and so the received signal is a noisy version of the transmitted signal. In addition, the transmitted signal will be distorted if the frequency response of the channel is not flat and its phase response is not linear. The term channel equalization stems from the requirement that the amplitude response of the channel must be flat, that is, the same for all frequencies of the channel. If the amplitude response is not flat, it must be equalized using an appropriate device at the receiver, which is called an equalizer.

Channel equalization has been an important topic in digital communications since the 1960s. The first major application was in voice-band modems for transmitting digital data on the twisted-pair telephone lines serving virtually all homes and businesses. Channel equalization made it possible to use spectrally efficient modulations and increase the transmitted data rate on these lines. The next major development was the introduction of high-capacity digital microwave radios in the early 1980s in the backbone of telecommunications networks, particularly in those areas where it is not economical to install fiber optics links. Unlike telephone lines, whose frequency response is essentially static, the channel characteristics in microwave radio links (and in all wireless systems) depend on frequency-dependent propagation conditions and are time-varying. Therefore, adaptive algorithms are essential in this type of system to track the strong and rapid time variations. Subsequently, digital cellular systems were developed and introduced in the 1990s, and this field witnessed very rapid development with the introduction of third-generation (3G) systems in the 2000s, and more recently with the introduction of beyond-3G (B3G) and fourth-generation (4G) systems, like Mobile WiMAX and the Long-Term Evolution (LTE) standard of the 3G Partnership Project (3GPP). With the introduction of these networks, adaptive equalization has become more sophisticated and an inseparable part of any modem. Also, even before the birth of digital cellular communications, digital audio broadcasting (DAB) and digital video broadcasting (DVB) were very hot topics in the 1980s and early 1990s, and terrestrial DAB and DVB applications opted for use of the orthogonal frequency-division multiplexing (OFDM) technology. Frequency-domain processing became popular, not only for OFDM systems themselves, but also for use in conventional single-carrier transmission.

This article will review channel equalization starting with the basics, the classical equalizer structures and adaptation algorithms, and continuing with fast equalizers, blind equalizers, and maximum-likelihood equalizers. After the description of these time-domain concepts, originally developed for single-carrier transmission, frequency-domain equalization (FDE) will be described, which was developed more recently for systems based on OFDM as well as for single-carrier transmission.

Equalizer structures. To introduce the principle of channel equalization and the classical equalizer structures, we consider the digital communications system depicted in **Fig. 1**. The input signal is given by Eq. (1), where the a_k's are the transmitted symbols,

$$a(t) = \sum_k a_k \delta(t - kT) \qquad (1)$$

T is the symbol period ($1/T$ is the transmission rate), and δ is the Dirac delta function, defined as $\delta(0) = 1$ and $\delta(t) = 0$ for $t \neq 0$. This signal enters the transmit filter of impulse response $f(t)$, and the resulting transmitted signal is given by Eq. (2).

$$s(t) = \sum_k a_k f(t - kT) \qquad (2)$$

The channel is modeled as a linear filter whose impulse response is $h_c(t)$, followed by the addition of white Gaussian noise $b(t)$. The received signal $r(t)$ enters the receive filter of impulse response $g(t)$, whose output can be written as Eq. (3), where $h(t)$

$$x(t) = \sum_k a_k h(t - kT) + w(t) \qquad (3)$$

is the overall impulse response obtained by the convolution of $f(t)$, $h_c(t)$, and $g(t)$, and $w(t)$ is the noise filtered by the receive filter. The signal $x(t)$ is sampled at the symbol rate $1/T$, and the resulting samples

are passed to a threshold detector to make decisions on the transmitted symbols. The sampler output at time nT can be written as Eq. (4).

$$x_n = \sum_k h_k a_{n-k} + w_n \qquad (4)$$

Digital communications systems are usually designed so as to satisfy the Nyquist criterion, which avoids interference between the transmitted data symbols when the channel is ideal. Referring to Eq. (4), the Nyquist criterion requires that all h_k's except h_0 are zero, and x_n is a function only of a_n, without any interference from the previous and the future symbols. When the signal is transmitted on a channel whose frequency response is not flat or whose phase response is not linear, the Nyquist property is destroyed and intersymbol interference (ISI) appears between the transmitted symbols.

Channel equalization was introduced in the 1960s to compensate for the nonideal channel response. The first equalizers consisted of a linear filter whose frequency response was the inverse of the channel response, so that the combined channel and equalizer had a flat frequency response and a linear phase. However, this description is too ideal, and perfect equalization of the channel cannot be achieved in practice using finite-complexity equalizers. Practical linear equalizers take the form of a transversal filter with N taps followed by a threshold detector (**Fig. 2**). The transversal filter consists of a delay line in which the individual delays have a value of T seconds (identical to the symbol period), the signal after each delay is multiplied by a complex coefficient (called tap gain), and all of these signals are added together. The transversal filter output can be expressed as Eq. (5).

$$y_n = \sum_{k=0}^{N-1} c_k x_{n-k} \qquad (5)$$

The two classical criteria used to optimize the equalizer tap gains are the zero-forcing (ZF) criterion and the minimum mean-square error (MMSE) criterion. In the ZF criterion, each tap of the equalizer except the center one cancels one sample of the ISI, and so the $N-1$ main samples of the discrete impulse response of the equalized channel will be cancelled using an N-tap equalizer. The ZF approach is efficient if the additive noise of the channel is small, but because it attempts to invert the channel transfer function, it leads to excessive noise enhancement at frequencies where the channel response has strong attenuation. In the MMSE approach, the equalizer minimizes the combined effect of ISI and additive noise. More specifically, the equalizer minimizes the mean value of the squared output error defined as the difference between the instantaneous equalizer output and the transmitted symbol at that instant. Referring to Fig. 2, this criterion minimizes the MMSE function in Eq. (6). The $E(.)$ operator in Eq. (6)

$$J = E(|y_n - a_n|^2) \qquad (6)$$

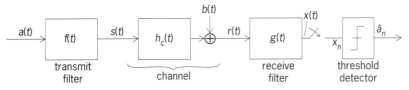

Fig. 1. Communication system block diagram.

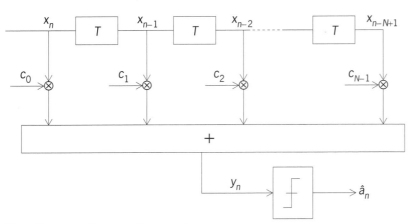

Fig. 2. Transversal linear equalizer structure.

involves ensemble averaging over data symbols and the additive noise.

Another classic equalizer structure is the so-called decision-feedback equalizer (DFE) structure, depicted in **Fig. 3**. It consists of a transversal filter operating on the received signal samples and of a second transversal filter operating on the previously detected symbols. Assuming that the feedforward filter has N_1 taps and the feedback filter has N_2 taps, the DFE output can be expressed as Eq. (7), where

$$y_n = \sum_{k=0}^{N_1-1} c_k x_{n-k} - \sum_{k=1}^{N_2} d_k \hat{a}_{n-k} \qquad (7)$$

$\hat{a}_k$ stands for the decision made by the threshold detector for symbol a_k for all integers k. The DFE theory is based on the assumption that past decisions are correct, that is, at time n, $\hat{a}_{n-k} = a_{n-k}$ for all $k \geq 1$. Simply stated, the task of the feedforward filter with coefficients c_k, $k = 0, 1, \ldots, N_1 - 1$, is to reduce precursor ISI (the ISI from future symbols), and that of the feedback filter with coefficients d_k, $k = 1, 2, \ldots, N_2$, is to cancel postcursor ISI (the ISI from previous symbols). As in linear equalizers, optimization of the DFE coefficients is usually performed using the ZF criterion or the MMSE criterion. In principle, the DFEs provide better performance than linear equalizers, but, as is well known, they suffer from error propagation, because a decision error propagates and increases the error probability on future decisions.

Fast algorithms. To introduce fast algorithms, we restrict our presentation to linear equalizers and the MMSE criterion. The conventional adaptation of the equalizer coefficients is based on the least mean-squares (LMS) algorithm, which can be written as Eq. (8), where C_k is the N-dimensional vector whose

$$C_{k+1} = C_k - \alpha X_k^* e_k \qquad (8)$$

components are the equalizer coefficients at time k, X_k is the vector whose components are the input signal samples that are present in the equalizer at that time, and e_k is the instantaneous error, defined as the difference between the equalizer output and the transmitted symbol (assumed to be known to the receiver). The asterisk in this equation as well as in subsequent equations denotes complex conjugate. This algorithm converges to the MMSE solution provided that the step-size parameter α is sufficiently small. This parameter determines the convergence speed of the LMS algorithm and also the steady-state error after convergence. A small α leads to a small steady-state error, but also to slow convergence. Conversely, a large α leads to fast convergence, but also to a large steady-state error. A mathematical analysis shows that, for a given α, convergence of the algorithm is dependent on the eigenvalue distribution of the input signal correlation matrix A, given by Eq. (9), where the superscript T

$$A = E(X_k^* X_k^T) \qquad (9)$$

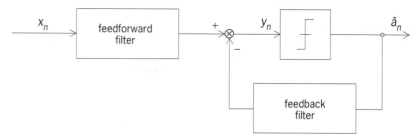

Fig. 3. Decision-feedback equalizer structure.

denotes transposition for vectors and matrices. On channels with a large eigenvalue distribution, the LMS algorithm has slow convergence, and this motivated the development of so-called fast algorithms, which are insensitive to eigenvalue distribution. The basic idea behind these algorithms is to multiply the step-size parameter α by the inverse of the signal correlation matrix A or by some estimate of its inverse. Assuming this matrix is known, the algorithm can be written as Eq. (10). The matrix multiplica-

$$C_{k+1} = C_k - \alpha A^{-1} X_k^* e_k \qquad (10)$$

tion in this equation essentially makes the algorithm insensitive to dispersion of the eigenvalues, which increases with the selectivity of the channel transfer function. In practice, the matrix A is not known, and it is constructed in a recursive manner, improving the estimate from iteration to iteration. This is known as the self-orthogonalizing algorithm, and it is closely related to the recursive least-squares (RLS) algorithm, which is the optimum solution for equalizer adaptation.

Blind algorithms. All of the theory above assumes that the transmitted data is available at the receiver, and thus the receiver can compute the error signal e_k, which is the difference between the equalizer output and the transmitted symbol. This is possible only if an initial training sequence is transmitted, which is known to the receiver. In those applications where such a sequence is unavailable, the equalizer must converge using its own decisions instead of the transmitted data symbols. Equalizers with this type of capability are called self-recovering equalizers or blind equalizers.

There are different approaches to blind equalization: A first approach consists of simply using the equalizer decisions instead of the transmitted symbols in conventional algorithms. Referring back to the LMS algorithm given by Eq. (8), the corresponding blind algorithm is given by Eq. (11), with

$$C_{k+1} = C_k - \alpha X_k^* \hat{e}_k \qquad (11)$$

$\hat{e}_k = y_k - \hat{a}_k$, where $\hat{a}_k$ is the equalizer decision corresponding to symbol a_k. A second approach consists of replacing the function J in Eq. (6) by the function J' in Eq. (12), where p is some integer, typically

$$J' = E(|y_n|^p - |a_n|^p) \qquad (12)$$

$p = 1$ or $p = 2$. This criterion makes the equalizer insensitive to phase errors in the receiver synchronization mechanism. Focusing on the phase-shift keying (PSK) signal constellations in which the constellation points are on a circle, $|a_n|^p$ is a constant that does not depend on the transmitted symbol value, and the resulting algorithm is blind. To derive a blind algorithm for the more popular quadrature amplitude modulation (QAM) constellations, $|a_n|^p$ is usually replaced by a constant.

Maximum-likelihood equalizers. In the previous sections, we reviewed adaptive linear and decision-feedback equalization that have been used as the field has developed since the 1960s. But the optimum approach to receivers on ISI channels consists of using maximum-likelihood detection. To describe this technique, let us revisit Eq. (4), which gives the expression of the signal samples at the receive filter output. The noise samples that appear here are correlated because they result from filtering the additive white Gaussian noise (AWGN) of the channel. A whitening filter can be inserted in the receiver so as to have uncorrelated noise samples at its output. Inserting such a whitening filter, we obtain an overall discrete channel whose output samples are of the form given by Eq. (13), where the H_k's represent

$$z_n = \sum_{k=0}^{L} H_k a_{n-k} + v_n \qquad (13)$$

sent the symbol-rate samples of the overall impulse response, which includes the whitening filter. In this expression, we have truncated the number of samples of this impulse response to $L+1$, where L is sufficiently large to assume that all other samples are negligible. These samples include the present sample H_0 and L postcursor samples, $H_1, H_2, \ldots, H_L$. Maximum-likelihood detection using an exhaustive search consists of computing the Euclidian metric from all possible signal sequences and selecting the sequence that is closest to the received sequence in terms of this distance. Suppose we transmit J symbols selected from an alphabet of size M. Since the symbols are random, the number of possible sequences is M^J. This number increases exponentially with the sequence length J, and obviously an exhaustive search is not manageable in practice.

The Viterbi algorithm is a well-known technique to determine the maximum-likelihood estimate of a transmitted sequence without exhaustively searching among all possible sequences. It is based on the trellis diagram, which is inherent to sequential machines with controlled state transitions. Examining Eq. (13) reveals that the z_n samples indeed can be viewed as the outputs of a sequential machine with M^L states, where M denotes the size of the signal constellation. In the trellis diagram, each state receives transitions from M previous states and it sends transitions to M future states. Using this trellis diagram, the Viterbi algorithm determines at each instant the optimum path converging to each state by computing the metrics of the M paths converging to it and

selecting the one that corresponds to the minimum metric, called the survivor path. The metric of a path is the Euclidean distance between the received signal sequence and the noiseless sequential machine output sequence corresponding to that path. Next, the survivor path converging to each state at time n is extended to M states at time $n + 1$, and the metric computation and comparison steps are repeated at each sampling instant. At the end, a number of predetermined symbols are included in the transmitted signal to terminate the trellis in a predetermined state and make a final decision on the transmitted symbol sequence. The complexity of the maximum-likelihood receiver using the Viterbi algorithm is proportional to M^L, which is much smaller than the complexity of an exhaustive search for long sequences. However, this complexity may be still excessive if the channel memory L or the alphabet size M is large, and for this reason linear equalizers and DFEs are often used in practice.

The maximum-likelihood sequence estimation (MLSE) receiver requires knowledge of the overall channel impulse response samples H_i, $i = 0$, 1, 2, ..., L. Because those samples are not known in practice, they must be estimated, and the estimates must be updated as the channel varies in time.

OFDM and frequency-domain equalization. OFDM is today used in several recently developed wireless communications standards. In this technique, the serial input data stream is converted into N parallel streams and these streams are multiplexed in frequency. That is, the original channel bandwidth is split in N different subbands, and the N parallel symbols are transmitted in different subbands, which are very narrow compared to the original channel bandwidth if N is large. The idea is to transmit each symbol in a narrow channel whose frequency response is nonselective. OFDM signals are generated using an inverse discrete Fourier transform (DFT) at the transmitter. After the DFT, a cyclic prefix is inserted between consecutive OFDM symbols to avoid interference. On the receiver side, the cyclic prefix is removed, and then the resulting signal is passed to a forward DFT operator followed by a threshold detector. Channel equalization in OFDM systems consists of placing a complex multiplier bank at the DFT output, which compensates for channel attenuation and phase response at each frequency bin. The coefficients are optimized so as to have a constant frequency response and a linear phase across the channel.

OFDM signals have the undesirable feature of high peak-to-average power ratio (PAPR) compared to conventional single-carrier transmission. An alternative technique is single-carrier transmission with frequency-domain equalization (SC-FDE). In SC-FDE, the symbols selected from the signal alphabet are transmitted without any transformation. On the receiver side, the received signal is equalized using a frequency-domain equalizer, which consists of a forward DFT that takes the signal to the frequency domain, followed by a multiplier bank, and an inverse

DFT that takes the signal back to the time domain. This is a simple description of linear FDE. As in the time-domain approach, a feedback filter operating on the receiver decisions can be included to derive a decision-feedback frequency-domain equalizer. Frequency-domain equalizers are known to handle channels with long impulse responses at considerably smaller complexity levels than time-domain equalizers.

For background information *see* ADAPTIVE SIGNAL PROCESSING; DELAY LINE; DIGITAL FILTER; DISTORTION (ELECTRONIC CIRCUITS); ELECTRICAL NOISE; EQUALIZER; FOURIER SERIES AND TRANSFORMS; INFORMATION THEORY; MATRIX THEORY; MOBILE COMMUNICATIONS; MODEM; MODULATION; MULTIPLEXING AND MULTIPLE ACCESS; WIMAX BROADBAND WIRELESS COMMUNICATIONS in the McGraw-Hill Encyclopedia of Science & Technology.　　　　Hikmet Sari

Bibliography. S. Haykin, *Adaptive Filter Theory*, 5th ed., Pearson, Boston, 2013; C. R. Johnson, Jr. et al., Blind equalization using the constant modulus criterion: A review, *Proc. IEEE*, 86:1927–1950, 1998, DOI:10.1109/5.720246; J. G. Proakis and M. Salehi, *Digital Communications*, 5th ed., McGraw-Hill, Boston, 2008; H. Sari, G. Karam, and I. Jeanclaude, Transmission techniques for digital terrestrial TV broadcasting, *IEEE Comm. Mag.*, 33(2):100–109, February 1995, DOI:10.1109/35.350382.

Chromothripsis

Chromothripsis is a phenomenon in which chromosomal rearrangements occur in a single, catastrophic event that involves the breakage of one or more chromosomes into pieces that are subsequently reshuffled and stitched back together.

Gradualism (the constant accumulation of little changes over time) has been extensively used in cancer biology to explain the accumulation of mutations that are needed to generate a malignant tumor. However, the recent description of the phenomenon that is termed chromothripsis has challenged this idea and has opened the possibility of a cataclysmic model to explain the formation and evolution of cancer cells.

Genomic instability in cancer. A common trait of all cancer cells is the accumulation of mutations that lead to genomic instability. In addition, cancer genomes usually show the gain and loss of chromosomes (aneuploidy), as well as chromosomal aberrations ranging from duplications and deletions of big chromosomal fragments to translocations of parts of one chromosome onto another. These kinds of genomic alterations usually lead to two well-known features of cancer genomes: loss of heterozygosity (LOH) and high variability in the number of copies (copy number state) of any given part of the genome present in the cell. Because human somatic cells are diploid [that is, they contain two copies (one paternal and one maternal) of the genome], their normal copy number state is two. Any form of aneuploidy will increase (by multiplication) or decrease (by deletion) the number of copy number states throughout the genome. Carrying two copies of the genome also means that human somatic cells are heterozygotes. The change from two versions of a gene to only one, by either chromosome loss or somatic recombination, will result in LOH.

The development of powerful DNA sequencing techniques has reduced the cost of sequencing a whole human genome from millions of dollars to just a few thousand dollars. This has important implications for personalized medicine, and many institutions all over the world are focusing on sequencing genomes from individuals who are suffering diverse diseases in order to find genomic clues that could help improve their treatments. For obvious reasons, a large effort has been made in sequencing cancer genomes. Notably, in the course of sequencing the genome of a patient suffering chronic lymphocytic leukemia, a research group led by Peter J. Campbell at the Sanger Institute in Cambridge, United Kingdom, found patterns of chromosomal rearrangements that were difficult to explain assuming a model of gradual accumulation of mutations. Instead, they proposed that all rearrangements occurred in a single, catastrophic event involving the breakage of one or more chromosomes into pieces that were subsequently reshuffled and stitched back. This phenomenon was named chromothripsis from the Greek words for "chromosome" (*chromo*) and "shattering into pieces" (*thripsis*).

Defining chromothripsis. Chromothripsis is defined by three main features: the occurrence of remarkable numbers of rearrangements in localized chromosomal regions; a low number of copy number states (generally between one and two) across the rearranged region; and chromothriptic areas with alternating regions of heterozygosity and regions presenting LOH. These features have important implications for understanding how and when chromothripsis arises. First, the concentration of rearrangements in a single chromosome, chromosome arm, or chromosomal region suggests that chromothripsis is most likely to occur when chromosomes are largely condensed, such as during the time of cell division (mitosis). Second, the low number of copy number states across the chromothriptic region strongly implies that such rearrangements probably occurred within a relatively short time period. If the accumulation of rearrangements had occurred progressively, the number of states would invariably increase with the number of detected break points, and this has not been observed (that is, chromothriptic events with 40, 90, or 250 break points all show a general oscillation between one and two in the amount of copy number states). Third, in chromothriptic regions, the alternation of segments retaining heterozygosity with others presenting LOH suggests that the rearrangements took place early in cancer cell development, at a time when both parental copies of the chromosome were present before the LOH. The retention of heterozygosity in patches throughout a chromothriptic region is difficult to explain by progressive rearrangement mechanisms, especially because heterozygosity cannot usually be regained after it is lost. This observation adds support to the idea that chromothripsis generally occurs in a single, catastrophic event. In line with this, analyses of primary and relapsed cancer samples suggest that chromothripsis is not an ongoing process.

Repairing shattered chromosomes. Genome rearrangements, including the ones observed in chromothripsis, invariably involve the generation and repair of DNA double-strand breaks (DSBs). Eukaryotic cells rely on two major DNA repair mechanisms in response to breaks involving both DNA strands: homologous recombination (HR) and nonhomologous end joining (NHEJ). HR is an error-free mechanism that requires the use of a sister chromatid as a template (note that a sister chromatid is one of the two iden-

tical daughter strands of a chromosome after it has duplicated). Accordingly, HR only operates when the DNA of a cell has been replicated, that is, during the synthesis (S) and gap-2 (G2) phases of the cell cycle. On the other hand, NHEJ operates throughout the cell cycle as it simply rejoins double-stranded DNA ends regardless of any sequence homology. For this reason, it can be an error-prone repair mechanism (**Fig. 1**). The complexities of the rearrangements observed in chromothriptic regions, together with the fact that sequencing analyses indicate that very little or no sequence homology is usually required to join the chromosomal fragments, point towards NHEJ as being the preferred mechanism to stitch broken chromosomes back together (**Fig. 2**).

Generation of chromothripsis. How does chromothripsis take place? As defined previously, the clustering of the rearrangements strongly suggests that chromothripsis occurs when the chromosomes are highly compacted, which is a characteristic of chromosomes at the time of cell division. One of the features of cancer cells is aneuploidy, which can be generated through the incorrect segregation of genetic material during mitosis: When chromosomes aligned at the metaphase plate (an imaginary plane perpendicular to the spindle fibers of a dividing cell) are pulled toward each of the daughter cells, any lagging chromosome has the potential to be incorrectly segregated. When this happens, the delayed chromosome may not be able to segregate in time to join the rest of the genome in the newly generated nuclear compartment; thus, it may instead get trapped in a micronucleus, which is a subcellular structure that is characteristic of cultured cancer cells. In addition, the chromosomes that are contained in the micronuclei can get pulverized during mitosis and then reincorporated into the main nucleus, offering a possible explanation for the generation of chromothriptic chromosomes.

Chromothripsis and cancer. Do chromothriptic events cause cancer or are they the consequences of cancer? The micronucleus model of chromothripsis generation requires aneuploidy (and the subsequent formation of micronuclei) as a prerequisite for chromosome shattering. Aneuploidy is not generally allowed in cells, and thus micronuclei are a good marker of genome instability. Mutations in proteins that ensure the correct chromosome segregation, such as proteins involved in the spindle assembly checkpoint or proteins involved in the cellular response to DNA damage (which either activate the DNA damage checkpoint response or are important for DNA repair), have been shown to cause genome instability and micronuclei formation. The tumor suppressor p53 is a key protein in preventing the proliferation of aneuploid cells: A cell that is exiting mitosis with an incorrect number of chromosomes gets arrested in the subsequent G1 phase in a p53-dependent manner. This arrest will become permanent (cellular senescence) or the cell will undergo apoptosis (programmed cell death). Accordingly, a high incidence of chromothripsis has been

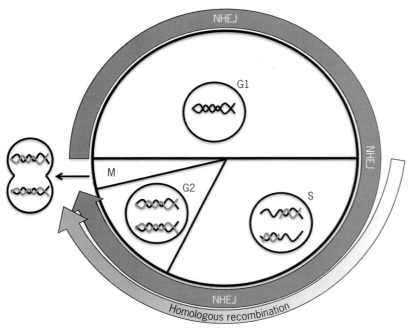

Fig. 1. DNA double-strand break (DSB) repair mechanisms throughout the cell cycle. Nonhomologous end joining (NHEJ) operates in all cell cycle phases, and it is the only DSB repair mechanism available in G1 or noncycling cells. Homologous recombination can only operate when a sister chromatid is present, that is, during replication (in the S phase) or after replication and before the cell enters mitosis (in the G2 phase). No DSB repair mechanisms operate during mitosis (M).

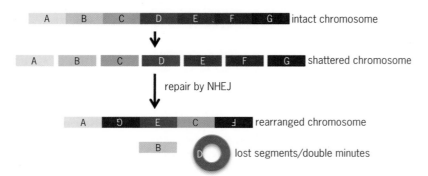

Fig. 2. Repair of shattered chromosomes by nonhomologous end joining (NHEJ). The resulting rearranged chromosome can suffer deletions and inversions.

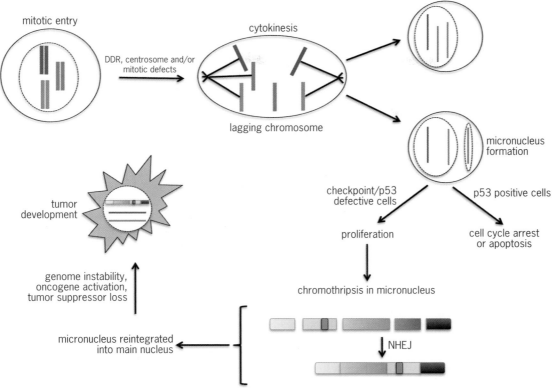

Fig. 3. A hypothetical model for the involvement of chromothripsis in tumor development. In this model, note that chromothripsis only occurs once the cell has already acquired other cancer-initiating mutations. Cytokinesis is the division of the cytoplasm following nuclear division. DDR = DNA damage response.

reported in p53-deficient tumor samples, and a link between chromothripsis and defects in DNA repair has also been suggested. This would imply that chromothripsis only occurs after other cancer-initiating mutations have taken place (**Fig. 3**).

Chromothripsis generation has the potential to substantially increase the landscape of chromosomal aberrations in a cancer cell in a very short period of time, either by being a tumor-initiating event or by being a consequence of genome instability, thus enhancing its tumorigenic potential. The most obvious chromosomal aberration that chromothripsis can cause is the deletion of a chromosome fragment, which is an event that can result in the loss of tumor suppressor genes that normally restrict tumor progression. Oncogene amplification has also been described in chromothriptic samples through the generation of double-minute chromosomes, which are small circular fragments of extrachromosomal DNA that are maintained in the cell because they confer some selective advantage. In addition, chromothripsis has the potential to generate oncogenic fusions: An otherwise inactive oncogene could be put under the control of a highly active promoter located in a different chromosomal region. Not surprisingly, the appearance of chromothriptic signatures has been correlated with a poor clinical outcome. Future efforts in identifying chromothripsis through genomic analyses of biopsy materials could have prognostic value and might also facilitate patient stratification when multiple therapeutic avenues exist.

For background information *see* APOPTOSIS; CANCER (MEDICINE); CELL CYCLE; CELL DIVISION; CHROMOSOME; CHROMOSOME ABERRATION; DEOXYRIBONUCLEIC ACID (DNA); DNA REPAIR; GENE; GENETICS; GENOMICS; ONCOGENES; ONCOLOGY; MITOSIS; MUTATION; PROTEIN; TUMOR SUPPRESSOR GENES in the McGraw-Hill Encyclopedia of Science & Technology. Josep Vicent Forment

Bibliography. A. Ciccia and S. J. Elledge, The DNA-damage response: Making it safe to play with knives, *Mol. Cell*, 40:179–204, 2010, DOI:10.1016/j.molcel.2010.09.019; K. Crasta et al., DNA breaks and chromosome pulverization from errors in mitosis, *Nature*, 482:53–58, 2012, DOI:10.1038/nature10802; J. V. Forment, A. Kaidi, and S. P. Jackson, Chromothripsis and cancer: Causes and consequences of chromosome shattering, *Nat. Rev. Cancer*, 12:663–670, 2012, DOI:10.1038/nrc3352; N. J. Ganem and D. Pellman, Linking abnormal mitosis to the acquisition of DNA damage, *J. Cell Biol.*, 199:871–881, 2012, DOI:10.1083/jcb.201210040; T. Rausch et al., Genome sequencing of pediatric medulloblastoma links catastrophic DNA rearrangements with TP53 mutations, *Cell*, 148:59–71, 2012, DOI:10.1016/j.cell.2011.12.013; P. J. Stephens et al., Massive genomic rearrangement acquired in a single catastrophic event during cancer development, *Cell*, 144:27–40, 2011, DOI:10.1016/j.cell.2010.11.055.

Circuit cavity electromechanics in the strong-coupling regime

Mechanical systems (such as levers, clockwork mechanisms, and pendulums) are the stuff of classical physics. In recent times, their attractiveness has been eclipsed by the advent of sophisticated, fast, and accurate electromagnetic circuits. But very recently, the mechanical sphere has reemerged into the limelight, mainly as a result of the advent of scanned probe microscopies. Scanning techniques have benefited from electromagnetic readout, either optically or using a microwave resonator. If the coupling between electromechanical and electromagnetic systems is made sufficiently strong, this allows the manipulation and detection of mechanical motion at the quantum level in a device that is enormous compared with the atomic scale at which we are accustomed to observing quantum behavior. Strong coupling has recently been achieved between two quite different types of resonator.

Resonators, physical systems that have a well-defined response at one or many specific frequencies, are the stuff of modern physics, and their use stretches back over centuries. Organ pipes, microwave cookers, nuclear magnetic resonance, quartz balances, and a great many other examples can be given. The key aspects that are usually demanded of a resonator are stability (the center response frequency does not shift much with changes in the environment) and accuracy (defined as the "sharpness" of the frequency response). The latter is often expressed by the quality factor or Q of the resonance, which is defined as the inverse of the fractional linewidth.

Generally, for applications purposes, isolated resonators have been preferred, as isolation leads to greater stability from environmental changes. However, more recently, researchers have begun to investigate the application potential of coupled resonators, that is, two or more resonant systems that interact with one another by some means, thereby altering their individual properties. The resonators may be similar (for example, in the case that all are electromagnetic resonators with similar resonant frequencies, as used, for example, in microwave filters for mobile telecommunications) or different (for example, in the case mainly under discussion in this article, an electromagnetic resonator coupled with a mechanical resonator). The coupling itself introduces more complex properties and, in the case of strong coupling, counterintuitive behavior. Recent experiments have achieved this strong-coupling regime for the first time, thereby throwing light on quantum-mechanical behavior in mechanical systems that consist of many trillions of atoms, far from the single-atom or single-molecule regime where we have come to expect this bizarre behavior. It already appears that quantum behavior governs the physics of a mechanical drumhead resonator that is almost large enough to be visible to the unaided eye. Erwin Schrödinger's thought experiment about

a cat being in a superposition of states was formulated to indicate that quantum mechanics does not apply to macroscopic objects such as cats. Where does the break between quantum and classical occur, then? Mechanical resonators that are almost visible to the unaided eye clearly lie on the quantum side of the frontier. *See* QUANTUM UNCERTAINTY IN MACROSCOPIC MEASUREMENTS.

Coupling strength defined. Controlled coupling between resonators (especially microwave thin-film resonators as used in mobile phones) is well understood. However, when it comes to coupling between different types of resonator, the topic has been less fully explored until recently. It is true that some 20 or 30 years ago, there was considerable research into coupling together small mechanical resonators (usually with resonant frequencies in the kilohertz range) with massive mechanically resonant bars. The latter were antennas for gravitational waves, and the small mechanical resonator was designed to efficiently absorb any resonant motion of the 1-metric-ton-scale antenna. Then the transferred energy, in the form of vibrations of the small resonant system, could be read out by some electromagnetic method. However, the coupling was always in the weak limit (as defined below).

Recent excitement has focused on direct coupling between a millimeter-scale microwave electromagnetic resonator and an adjacent micrometer-sized mechanical resonator. This coupling can be thought of as an interaction between photons of the electromagnetic resonator and phonons (quanta of vibration) in the mechanical resonator. Mechanical resonators can take any one of a number of forms, such as single- or double-clamped cantilevers (as small as single carbon nanotubes) and electrically conducting membrane resonators (especially interesting are those made of graphene). Equally, electromagnetic resonators can be made from a cavity or a coaxial resonator, a thin-film coplanar waveguide, or even lumped circuit L-C resonators. Each of the many possible pairs of types has been combined, although so far few combinations have approached the strong-coupling limit. The simplest way to envisage the origin of the coupling between the two systems is to imagine that a small distortion of the mechanical system in one direction (say along the x axis) will cause a frequency shift in the electromagnetic resonator's eigenfrequency ω_c. A useful parameter is the quantity G, which specifies how much the frequency shifts with a change in position of the mechanical component, as in Eq. (1).

$$G = d\omega_c/dx \qquad (1)$$

If the mechanical component is a conductor, then the gap between the two systems acts as a capacitor, the value of which depends on the spacing. This capacitor forms part of the electromagnetic system, and any change in its value will shift its resonant frequency. Thus, motion of the mechanical resonator affects the frequency of the microwave resonator.

However, one must also consider the effect of the radiation pressure from the cavity photons, which influences the stiffness (and therefore the resonant frequency) of the mechanical resonator.

Imagine a single photon being reflected from the part of the electromagnetic cavity that is also part of the mechanical resonator. A force will be applied, giving the movable mechanical component a displacement dx while the electromagnetic resonator suffers a frequency shift $d\omega_c$ (as a result of energy transfer to the mechanical system). The force exerted does work on the membrane equal to $F_{sp}.dx$, and the loss of energy is $\hbar d\omega_c$ ($\hbar$ is Planck's constant divided by 2π), so Eq. (2) is satisfied.

$$F_{sp} = \frac{\hbar d\omega_c}{dx} \qquad (2)$$

The coupling strength (or, equivalently, coupling rate) g is defined by Eq. (3). Here, x_{zp} is the zero-

$$g = Gx_{zp} = G\left(\frac{\hbar}{2m\Omega}\right)^{1/2} \qquad (3)$$

point motion of the mechanical resonator of effective mass m and mechanical resonant frequency Ω. This minimum motion is a consequence of the Heisenberg uncertainty principle when applied to a harmonic oscillator. To have any hope of approaching the strong-coupling regime, the displacement of the mechanical resonator caused by a single cavity photon should be as large as possible [that is, G in Eq. (1) should be maximized]. This is also the condition for ensuring that the cavity is a sensitive means for monitoring movement of the mechanical resonator. Thus, the displacement x_{sp} due to a single photon should be much greater than the zero-point motion x_{zp}. To maximize the parameter g, the mechanical resonator should have a soft spring and a low mass, and a small resonant frequency is also useful. The effective coupling strength g can also then be increased by an amount proportional to the square root of the number of photons in the electromagnetic resonator.

Conditions for observing quantum effects. But merely maximizing the coupling strength g is not sufficient to observe the counterintuitive results of the quantum regime that recent experiments have attained. For that, it is also necessary that the energy exchange between electromagnetic and mechanical systems takes place faster than energy is dissipated from either system. Explicitly, we can write this condition as requiring that $\Gamma_{th} \sim n_m \Gamma_m \ll g$ and $\kappa \ll g$, where Γ_{th} is the thermal decoherence rate, Γ_m and κ are the intrinsic dissipation rates of the mechanical oscillator and the cavity, respectively, and n_m is the equilibrium occupancy number of thermal phonons at the operating temperature.

This condition proved difficult to achieve until the use of superconducting microwave resonators, which enable extremely high quality factors Q. Achieving the values needed with the mechanical

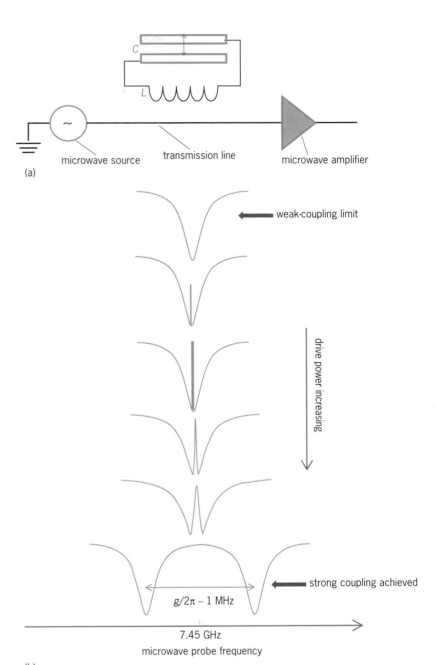

(a)

(b)

Fig. 1. Experiment to demonstrate the strong-coupling regime. (a) Schematic of the experiment. The microwave resonator consists of a superconducting thin-film inductor **L** coupled to an air-gap capacitor **C** (shown in green) made of superconducting aluminum foil. Its upper electrode is free to vibrate. A pure microwave source feeds a superconducting transmission line that is inductively coupled to the **LC** circuit (by proximity), and the transmitted power is fed to an ultra-low-noise cryogenic microwave amplifier. **(b)** Plot of the microwave transmission through the cavity, measured by a microwave probe signal whose frequency is swept through the cavity resonance while a microwave drive signal is applied at a frequency Ω below the unperturbed microwave cavity frequency (where Ω is the mechanical resonant frequency). As the drive power is increased, a narrow peak appears in the middle of the cavity response, with linewidth given by the unperturbed damping of the mechanical resonator. Further increases in drive power cause this peak to increase and broaden. Finally, when the strong-coupling regime has been achieved, the cavity response splits into two resolved resonances that are electromechanical coupled resonances, neither purely electromagnetic nor purely mechanical in nature. This is the strong-coupling limit.

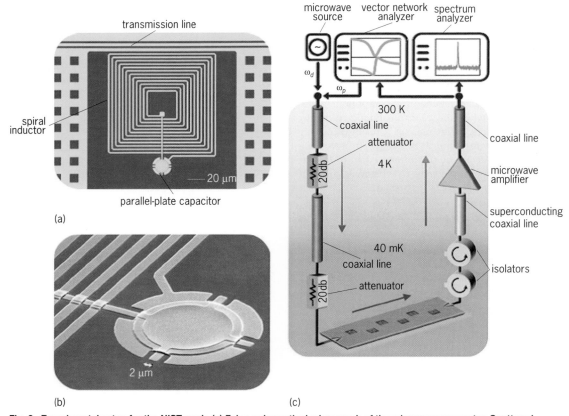

transmission line

spiral inductor

20 μm

parallel-plate capacitor

(a)

2 μm

(b)

microwave source

vector network analyzer

spectrum analyzer

ω_d

ω_p

300 K

coaxial line

attenuator

4 K

20db

coaxial line

40 mK

coaxial line

20db

attenuator

coaxial line

microwave amplifier

superconducting coaxial line

isolators

(c)

Fig. 2. Experimental setup for the NIST work. (a) False-color optical micrograph of the microwave resonator. Sputtered aluminum (gray) is patterned on a sapphire substrate (blue). (b) Scanning electron micrograph showing the upper plate of the capacitor, which is suspended approximately 50 nm above the lower plate and is free to vibrate. (c) Details of the coupled measuring circuit. Cryogenic attenuators and isolators ensure that thermal noise is reduced below the vacuum noise at microwave frequencies. The measured signal encoding the mechanical motion as modulated sidebands is decoded with either a vector network analyzer or a spectrum analyzer. Ω_d and Ω_p are the frequencies of the microwave drive and probe signals, respectively. (Courtesy of National Institute of Standards and Technology; adapted from J. D. Teufel et al., Sideband cooling of micromechanical motion to the quantum ground state, Nature, 475:359–363, 2011, DOI:10.1038/nature10261)

component is more straightforward. If both the strong-coupling condition and the low-dissipation conditions are satisfied, then the coupled system has to be treated as a single entity in terms of calculating resonant frequency response and time evolution of the system, given its initial conditions. Then, under suitable photon pumping conditions, the observed frequencies of the coupled system split into resonances that cannot be assigned to either system separately but are properties of the combined system.

Parametric driving processes, in which the excitation is applied at a frequency that is a multiple of a resonant frequency (and at a carefully controlled phase), or at a difference frequency within the coupled system, provide a means of enhancing the effective coupling strength but also of separating the drive frequency from the detection frequency, leading to improved dynamic range and signal-to-noise ratio.

Cooling a mechanical resonator to the ground state. The first successful attempt to achieve the ground state of a mesoscopic mechanical resonator by "brute-force" cooling was reported in 2010. It is necessary in this case to reduce the temperature

T to such a level that $T < h\Omega/k_B$, where h is Planck's constant and k_B is Boltzmann's constant. The highest-frequency mechanical resonators run at only a few gigahertz, requiring temperatures of a few tens of millikelvins, close to the current limits for cooling complete solids. The recent strong-coupling work, while still operating at similar temperatures, has used a different approach to cool a much lower-frequency (10 MHz) mechanical system to its ground state (on average, less than a single phonon). The method is known as sideband cooling and is similar to a method used to cool single atoms or ions using a system of lasers. It is also analogous to Raman spectroscopy, in which photons at a frequency below resonance can absorb the energy of a phonon before reradiating at the electromagnetic resonance. In this way, phonon energy is extracted from the mechanical system, corresponding to cooling. In order for the system to have a chance of sideband cooling to the quantum-mechanical ground state, another necessary condition, known as the resolved sideband condition, is that the electromagnetic resonator linewidth must be much less than the frequency of the mechanical resonator.

Strong-coupling experimental results. A breakthrough result, reported by a group at the National Institute of Standards and Technology (NIST) in Boulder, Colorado, in 2011, integrates the mechanical resonator (in this case a drumhead-shaped aluminum membrane some 15 μm in diameter) as an integral part of the microwave LC resonator (**Figs. 1** and **2**). A movement of only 1 nm by the membrane produces a frequency shift of 10 MHz in the LC-circuit eigenfrequency. Both components are cooled to around 20 mK, well below the superconducting transition temperature of the inductor and capacitor. The superconducting LC resonator has a Q value of 4.5×10^4 at a resonant frequency of 7.5 GHz. This translates into a decay rate of 170 kHz, considerably slower than the coupling strength of approximately 1 MHz. Likewise, the Q of the mechanical resonance is 3.6×10^5 at a resonant frequency of approximately 10 MHz, so the linewidth (and hence the decay rate), $\Gamma_m/2\pi$, equals approximately 30 Hz.

In a second breakthrough in the same year, the NIST group used sideband cooling to lower the phonon occupancy of the mechanical resonator to an average value close to zero.

Although the strong-coupling condition may be useful in the future for purely classical systems, the important outcome of this approach in the short term is to demonstrate a variety of quantum-mechanical behaviors on mesoscopic-scale mechanical systems.

The experimental results summarized here have all been achieved with microwave resonators. As an aside, it may seem counterintuitive to talk about the influence of a single microwave photon on a mechanical resonator, but this is essential if the quantum-mechanical nature of the electromechanical interaction is to be observed and understood. In any case, the exceptionally high Q values of superconducting microwave resonators coupled with millikelvin operating temperatures allow a single microwave photon to be detected.

Future outlook. As well as opening the way for more demonstrations of purely quantum-mechanical effects in mechanical systems, such as Rabi oscillations, squeezed states, and controlled superposition of states, experimenters have already embarked on more ambitious plans relating to quantum information processing with mechanical systems. By coupling another type of mesoscopic superconducting quantum interference device (SQUID) to the mechanical and electromagnetic system, it should be possible to make use of the very long decoherence times of the mechanical system to store and exchange qubit states. In this way, a mechanical quantum computer may be realized in the future, a return to the mechanical approach that heralded the dawn of the first classical computer age with Babbage's Difference Engine.

For background information *see* CAPACITANCE; CAVITY RESONATOR; GRAVITATIONAL RADIATION; LASER COOLING; MECHANICAL VIBRATION; NONRELATIVISTIC QUANTUM THEORY; PHONON; PHOTON; Q (ELECTRICITY); QUANTUM COMPUTATION; QUANTUM MECHANICS; RAMAN EFFECT; RESONANCE (ACOUSTICS AND MECHANICS); RESONANCE (ALTERNATING-CURRENT CIRCUITS); RESONANCE (QUANTUM MECHANICS); SQUEEZED QUANTUM STATES; SQUID; SUPERPOSITION PRINCIPLE; UNCERTAINTY PRINCIPLE in the McGraw-Hill Encyclopedia of Science & Technology.   Ling Hao; John Gallop

Bibliography. M. Blencowe, Quantum electromechanical systems, *Phys. Rep.*, 395:159–222, 2004, DOI:10.1016/j.physrep.2003.12.005; A. D. O'Connell et al., Quantum ground state and single-phonon control of a mechanical resonator, *Nature*, 464:697–703, 2010, DOI:10.1038/nature08967; M. Poot and H. S. J. van der Zant, Mechanical systems in the quantum regime, *Phys. Rep.*, 511:273–335, 2012, DOI:10.1016/j.physrep.2011.12.004; J. D. Teufel et al., Circuit cavity electromechanics in the strong-coupling regime, *Nature*, 471:204–208, 2011, DOI:10.1038/nature09898; J. D. Teufel et al., Sideband cooling of micromechanical motion to the quantum ground state, *Nature*, 475:359–363, 2011, DOI:10.1038/nature10261.

Color electronic paper

Electronic displays, such as transmissive (backlit) liquid-crystal displays (LCDs), have achieved image quality and panel sizes that were unimaginable as little as one decade ago. However, LCDs are still unable to outperform conventional ink on paper in several ways: you can't read your color LCD in bright sunlight; you can't take a large-size display and neatly roll or fold it up for storage in your pocket; and if you leave the image on your display, your smartphone battery will die long before you get home to charge it. If these issues could be resolved with a new display technology, then you would have an experience comparable to that of reading from paper. Pursuit of such a display is happening right now in the development of color electronic paper, or ePaper. This article reviews the rapid progress in the pursuit of color ePaper, which is now closing in on the attributes required for mass consumer acceptance.

ePaper overview. Like conventional printed paper, the tiny pixels in an ePaper display simply reflect light from the environment (sunlight, a lamp, or some other source), and therefore consume far less power than an LCD display, which requires an internal light source behind the display. There are dozens of technologies that are currently being developed, but to date the commercially dominant technology has been E Ink. E Ink is used in the traditional gray/black Amazon Kindle e-reader products. It is basically a thin film containing microspheres that are filled with electrically charged black and white particles. The white and black particles are oppositely charged (positive versus negative), so when a positive or negative voltage is applied to electrodes beneath the film, the electric field attracts the

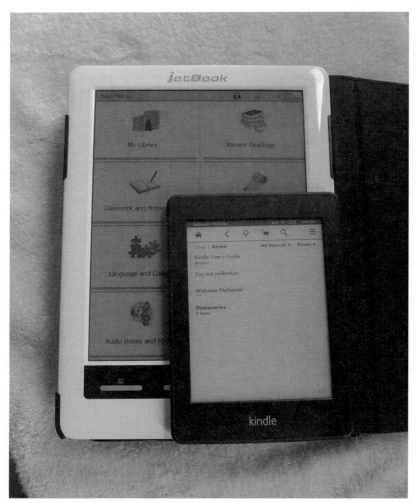

Fig. 1. A color E Ink product placed behind a monochrome E Ink product. (*Image courtesy of The Digital Reader*)

such as newspapers or magazines, then a color system like that used for print is a logical place to start. Printers use layers of cyan, magenta, and yellow inks to subtractively create reflective color; for example, a mixture of yellow and magenta will create red, and a mixture of all three colors creates black. Recently, Naijoh Yoshihisa and colleagues at Ricoh unveiled the first three-layer—cyan, magenta, and yellow—electrochromic display (**Fig. 2*b***). Electrochromism is not new; it goes back decades. Ricoh's innovation enables three layers of electrochromic material to be controlled by a single layer of electronics behind the display. In electrochromism, electrical charge is collected or depleted for special compounds, such as viologen, changing their oxidation state and switching them between a colorless and a colored state (Fig. 2*a*). Ricoh first clears the charges from all three layers (cyan, magenta, and yellow) to turn the display white. To create an image, a porous electrode next to each colored layer is used to move the desired amount of charge (and coloration) to each layer. First, the topmost layer (color) is charged using the topmost electrode. The amount of charge is controlled by the electronics at the bottom of the display. This charge flows through the two lower layers and porous electrodes without coloring them. Second, the middle layer is charged and colored without changing the color in the top layer or the bottom layer. Lastly, the bottom layer is charged and colored. The three layers then subtractively filter light, creating a compelling color image. This approach can allow high resolution and color gamut that is better than that seen on newsprint. The main downside is that electrochromism is a slow effect (the charging process requires several seconds to produce a full image). Therefore, progress has been made in creating color, but functionality like video is not currently possible, nor is it expected.

Hewlett-Packard electrokinetic display. In another recent discovery, Hewlett-Packard (HP) has created a new faster and brighter display through an electrokinetic approach that uses voltage to move charged colored particles through a fluid. As shown in **Fig. 3**, the electrokinetic display uses voltage and small micropits to compact colored particles inside pixels. The colored particles can be compacted so much that if you place a white reflector (like paper) behind the pixels, they will reflect about 60% of the light on the display. A color display is created by stacking cyan, magenta, and yellow pixel layers in a way similar to that used in the electrochromic display (Fig. 2*b*). Unlike in electrochromic displays, however, each layer in an electrokinetic display must have its own set of electronics. Each set of electronics requires a thin glass or plastic substrate on which the electronics (thin-film transistors) are fabricated. This poses a challenge, as each of the substrates creates a space (tens to hundreds of μm) between the overlapping cyan, magenta, and yellow pixels. If you look straight at the display, this is not a problem. But if you look at the display from an angle, the reflected light you are viewing does not pass through

oppositely charged particles, allowing the others to move to the top of the microspheres, where they can be seen by the viewer. A limitation of E Ink is that it switches too slowly to permit video or rapid point-and-click web browsing. Also, the image is too dim to create vibrant color images (**Fig. 1**). The brightness limitation of E Ink stems from the short dynamic range of the displays. Even when all the white particles are at the tops of the microspheres, the newer displays reflect just over 40% of the ambient light (the original E Ink reflected only about 35%). Compare this to white paper, which reflects between 80 and 90% of the ambient light.

To create color with E Ink, three color filter arrays (red, green, and blue) are added in front of the display, with each transmitting one-third of the visible spectrum. Therefore, a gray screen that starts at only 40% reflection becomes much darker when you filter out much of the limited light that is being reflected from it. Thus, the problem of how to create color ePaper is a daunting one. Three of the most promising current approaches will be discussed.

Ricoh electrochromic display. If the goal is to create color ePaper that is equivalent to printed color,

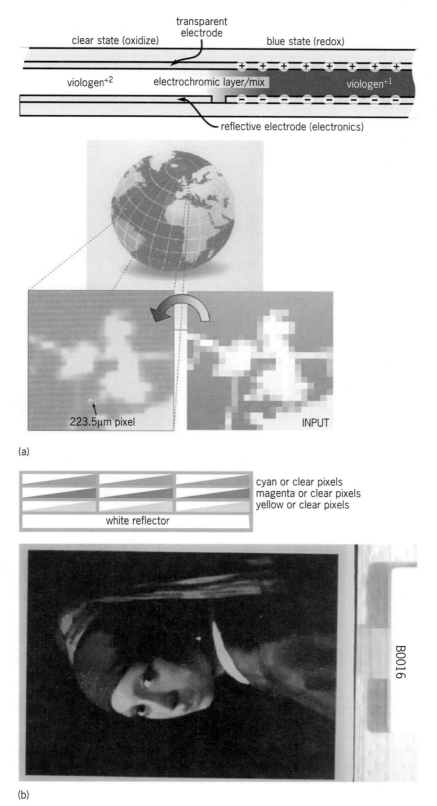

(a)

(b)

Fig. 2. Ricoh's three-layer electrochromic e-Paper display, which uses cyan-magenta-yellow subtractive color filtering. (*a*) Single-color pixel and display. (*b*) Full-color prototype. (*Photos courtesy of Ricoh Corp.*)

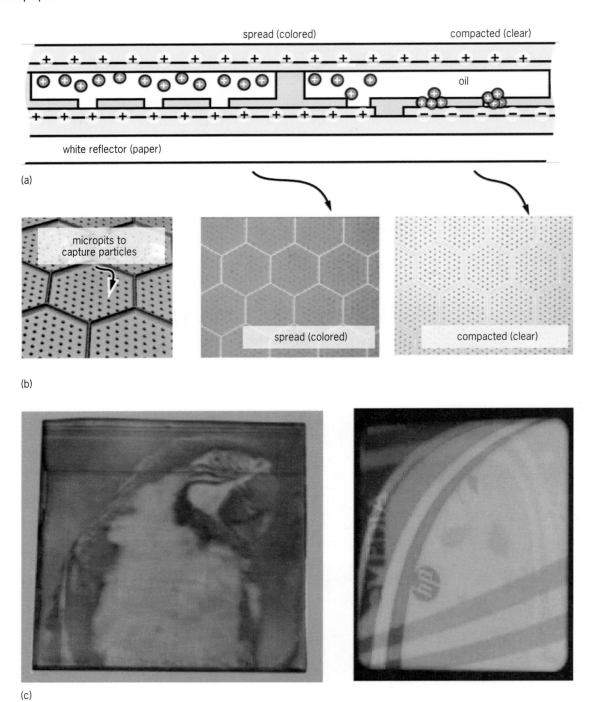

Fig. 3. HP's electrokinetic display technology, which, like the technology shown in Fig. 2*b*, also uses three-layer subtractive color filtering. (*a*) Single-color pixel. (*b*) Single-color operation. (*c*) Full-color prototype. (*Photos courtesy of HP*)

the overlapping pixels; instead, it passes through adjacent pixels, resulting in a washed-out image. Therefore, electrokinetic displays are currently limited to lower-resolution displays, such as billboards or grocery store signage. Color performance is quite good (as good as or better than that of newsprint), and switching speeds (hundreds of ms) are much faster than those of electrochromic displays, providing a user experience similar to E Ink in the Amazon Kindle products.

Gamma Dynamics electrofluidic display. In 2009, the University of Cincinnati reported a new elec-

trofluidic technology that, unlike E Ink or electrokinetic technology, uses voltage to move fluid with colored particles inside of it, instead of moving the colored particles through the fluid (as is done in electrophoretic and electrokinetic technology). This eliminates the fluid drag force on every particle and results in switching speeds that are about 100 times faster over similar distances for the particles. In 2011, this technique was improved and now involves moving a colored ink fluid through a highly reflective white film with ink holes (**Fig. 4***a*). To move the ink, opposite voltages are applied to the

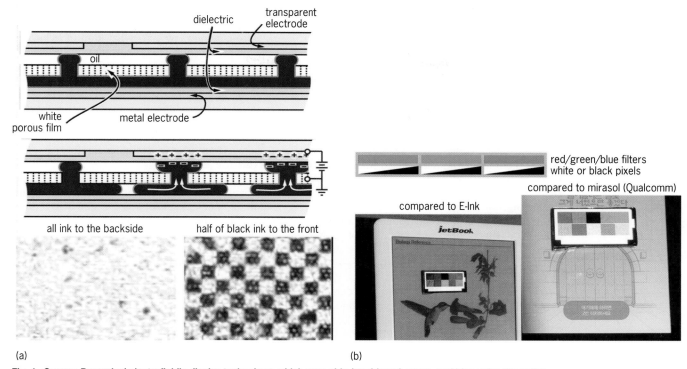

Fig. 4. Gamma Dynamics' electrofluidic display technology, which uses side-by-side red, green, and blue color filters like E-Ink. (*a*) Single black/white/gray pixel. (*b*) First-generation color demonstration. (*Photos courtesy of Gamma Dynamics Corp.*)

ink and to an electrode toward which the ink needs to move (opposite charges attract). If the black ink covers the film, it turns the pixel black; if the black ink is behind the film, then the pixel just shows the white color of the film. The film is also microporous, because as the ink moves through an ink hole, a second clear oil film needs to move through the micropores to the opposite side of the film. Switching speeds are fast (tens of ms, at least). If black ink and a white film are being used, this excludes the possibility of using the multilayered color approaches shown in Figs. 2 and 3. However, the white film is highly reflective, and it refocuses ambient light coming toward the viewer of the display from multiple angles. As a result, the white film can appear 200% reflective compared to white paper. This allows a conventional red, green, and blue color filter to be applied (similar to that used by E Ink), but with the capability of providing bright and saturated color. As shown in Fig. 4c, the color is newsprint quality or better, and far brighter than E Ink or Qualcomm's mirasol® technology. Because a single layer of pixels is used, higher resolutions are possible, like those found in e-readers and tablets. Furthermore, pixel switching speeds are fast enough to enable basic video. Electrofluidic technology is at a very early stage, and although it has many of the fundamental traits needed for the ultimate color ePaper, additional development is needed.

Outlook. It is clear that progress is being made toward creating a power-saving and read-in-sunlight display technology that also satisfies consumer demands for color and video capability. Overall, ePaper is best suited to achieve the long-term goal of foldable or rollable displays. The need for ePaper technologies remains, because LCD and emerging organic light-emitting device (OLED) technology cannot be used in many applications. Therefore, continued research in ePaper technology and improved commercial products as well are expected.

For background information *see* ELECTRIC FIELD; ELECTROCHROMIC DEVICES; ELECTROKINETIC PHENOMENA; ELECTRONIC DISPLAY; ELECTROPHORESIS; FLAT-PANEL DISPLAY DEVICE; OXIDATION-REDUCTION in the McGraw-Hill Encyclopedia of Science & Technology.   Jason Heikenfeld

Bibliography. B. Comiskey et al., An electrophoretic ink for all-printed reflective electronic displays, *Nature*, 394:253–255, 1998, DOI:10.1038/28349; M. Hagedon et al., Bright e-Paper by transport of ink through a white electrofluidic imaging film, *Nat. Comm.*, 3:1173, 2012, DOI:10.1038/ncomms2175; J. Heikenfeld et al., A critical review of the present and future prospects for electronic paper, *J. Soc. Inform. Display*, 19(2):129–156, 2011, DOI:10.1889/JSID19.2.129; T. Koch et al., Late-news paper: Roll-to-roll manufacturing of electronic skins, in *SID Int. Symp. Dig. Tech. Papers*, 40:738–741, 2009, DOI:10.1889/1.3256892; E. Kreit et al., Biological versus electronic adaptive coloration: How can one inform the other? *J. R. Soc. Interface*, 10(78): 20120601, 2013, DOI:10.1098/rsif.2012.0601; Y. Naijoh et al., Multilayered electrochromic display, in *Proc. 17th Int. Display Workshops*, Fukuoka, Japan, 2010.

Complex dynamics

Complex dynamics is a field of mathematics in which one studies dynamical systems on mathematical spaces, where these spaces are defined over the complex numbers $\mathbb{C}$. More generally, a dynamical system is a pair of objects (X, f), where X is a space (for example, X might be the real line $\mathbb{R}$ or the complex plane $\mathbb{C}$), and f is a transformation of the space X to itself. That is, f is a map (written $f : X \to X$) which takes a point $x \in X$ as input, and returns the point $f(x) \in X$ as output [the mathematical symbols "$x \in X$" mean that the point x is an element of the set X, and similarly for "$f(x) \in X$"]. In this setting, one can iterate the map f on the space X and study the behavior of subsequent iterates. In this article, we will consider a specific type of complex dynamical system: the space X will be the complex plane $\mathbb{C}$, and the transformation $f : \mathbb{C} \to \mathbb{C}$ will be a complex polynomial; that is, $f(z) = a_d z^d + a_{d-1} z^{d-1} + \cdots + a_1 z + a_0$, where the coefficients a_i are all complex numbers, $a_d \neq 0$, and z is a complex variable.

We will first discuss some fundamental notions from the field of complex dynamics, focusing mostly on quadratic polynomials. We will then discuss a major open problem in the subject that was recently solved.

Polynomials. Given an integer $d \geq 2$, consider the polynomial $f(z) = z^d$. The first iterate of f is just the polynomial itself. The second iterate of f (denoted as f^2) is the map composed with itself twice:

$$f^2(z) = f(f(z)) = (z^d)^d = z^{d^2}$$

The third iterate of the map f is the map composed with itself three times:

$$f^3(z) = f(f(f(z))) = ((z^d)^d)^d = z^{d^3}$$

Continuing in this way, we note that, for any integer $n > 0$, the nth iterate of the map f is $f^n(z) = z^{d^n}$. From the original map $f : \mathbb{C} \to \mathbb{C}$, we obtain infinitely many new maps, just by iterating:

$$f : \mathbb{C} \to \mathbb{C}, \quad f^2 : \mathbb{C} \to \mathbb{C},$$
$$f^3 : \mathbb{C} \to \mathbb{C}, \quad f^4 : \mathbb{C} \to \mathbb{C}, \ldots$$

Given a point $z_0 \in \mathbb{C}$, we define the orbit of z_0 to be the following sequence of complex numbers:

$$z_1 = f(z_0), \quad z_2 = f(z_1), \quad z_3 = f(z_2), \ldots$$

More succinctly, we begin with $z_0 \in \mathbb{C}$, and for $n > 0$, set $z_n = f(z_{n-1})$. A natural question to ask is: How does the orbit of z_0 change as z_0 varies?

For instance, in the case of $f(z) = z^d$, we note that if $|z_0| < 1$, then the sequence $n \to f^n(z_0)$ will converge to 0 as n tends to infinity. Conversely, if $|z_0| > 1$, then $f^n(z_0)$ will grow without bound; that is, the sequence $n \to f^n(z_0)$ will "escape to infinity" as n tends to infinity. And lastly, if $|z_0| = 1$, that is, if z_0 belongs to the unit circle, then the sequence $n \to f^n(z_0)$ also belongs to the unit circle; it may converge, or it may not.

More generally, we ask: what kind of behaviors emerge as z_0 changes? Is the dynamical system stable; that is, do the orbits for all possible starting points $z_0 \in \mathbb{C}$ behave in the same way [as in the example $f(z) = z^d$, for the cases $|z_0| < 1$ or $|z_0| > 1$]? Or is there an unstable (otherwise known as chaotic) part of $\mathbb{C}$, which is comprised of points where small perturbations of z_0 drastically affect the behavior of the associated orbit [as in the example $f(z) = z^d$, for the case $|z_0| = 1$]?

We will now introduce a natural subset of $\mathbb{C}$ that is associated to iterating a polynomial f, but we require a definition first. A subset $S \subseteq \mathbb{C}$ is bounded if there is a real number $R > 0$ so that the set S is contained in the disk (centered at the origin) of radius R. The filled Julia set of f is the set of all $z_0 \in \mathbb{C}$ so that the orbit of z_0 is bounded; equivalently, the filled Julia set K_f consists of all points $z_0 \in \mathbb{C}$ so that the orbit of z_0 does not escape to infinity. The filled Julia set for the map $f(z) = z^d$ is the closed unit disk in the complex plane, $K_f = \{z \in \mathbb{C} : |z| \leq 1\}$. **Figure 1** has a gallery of filled Julia sets associated to different quadratic polynomials.

The boundary of the filled Julia set also plays an important role. The boundary of a nonempty set $S \subseteq \mathbb{C}$ is a subset of $\mathbb{C}$ defined in the following way: A point $x \in \mathbb{C}$ belongs to the boundary of S if every disk centered at x contains points that are inside of S and contains points that are outside of S. For example, the boundary of the unit disk $\{z \in \mathbb{C} : |z| < 1\}$ is the unit circle $\{z \in \mathbb{C} : |z| = 1\}$. The Julia set of the polynomial f, denoted J_f, is the boundary of the filled Julia set K_f. For the example $f(z) = z^d$, the Julia set is the unit circle $J_f = \{z \in \mathbb{C} : |z| = 1\}$. The Julia set is precisely the set of points $z_0 \in \mathbb{C}$ where the dynamical system $f : \mathbb{C} \to \mathbb{C}$ is unstable. As mentioned above, if $|z_0| = 1$ (that is, if z_0 is in the Julia set), the orbits of points close to z_0 behave in very different ways.

A subset $S \subseteq \mathbb{C}$ has interior if it contains a small disk. The filled Julia sets in Fig. 1a and d have interior; however, the filled Julia sets in Fig. 1b and c do not have any interior. This is why the filled Julia sets in these pictures look so thin; the set K_f is colored in black, but the black is not readily visible since the sets have no interior. In Fig. 1, it is possible to see the kinds of intricate structure that Julia sets can exhibit; these sets are quite often fractal.

In each of the pictures in Fig. 1, the points $z_0 \in \mathbb{C}$ for which the associated orbit escapes to infinity are colored in gray. We may shade these gray points according to how fast the orbit escapes to infinity. For instance, if z_0 and w_0 are two points which are not in K_f, then the orbit of z_0 and the orbit of w_0 will escape to infinity. If these orbits escape to infinity at the same rate, then we color the points z_0 and w_0 with the same shade of gray.

Quadratic polynomials. Even just for quadratic polynomials, the shapes of the filled Julia sets K_f (and therefore of the Julia sets J_f) vary greatly

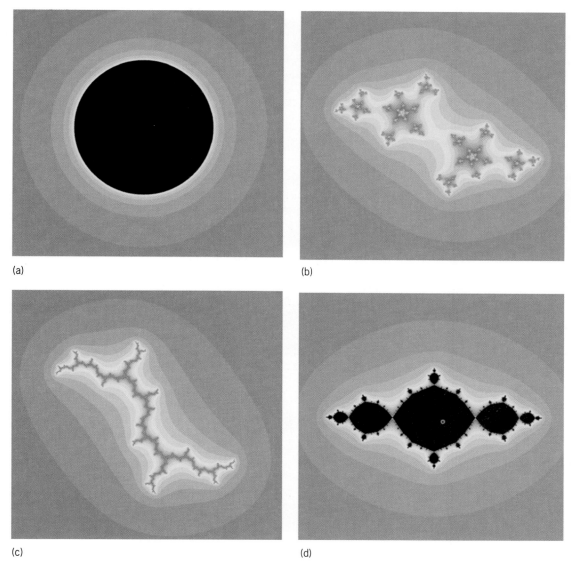

(a)   (b)

(c)   (d)

Fig. 1. The filled Julia set K_f is drawn in black for four specific polynomials: (a) $f(z) = z^2$; (b) $f(z) = z^2 - 0.67 + 0.67i$; (c) $f(z) = z^2 + i$; and (d) $f(z) = z^2 - 1$. The Julia set J_f is the boundary of K_f. In gray, we see the set of points $z_0 \in \mathbb{C}$ whose orbit escapes to infinity. The sets K_f drawn in Fig. 1b and c are very thin; in these cases, $K_f = J_f$.

depending on the quadratic polynomial f. Consider the family of quadratic polynomials $f(z) = z^2 + c$, where c is a complex parameter. For each $c \in \mathbb{C}$ we obtain a different polynomial f. Using the c-parameter plane, we can record information about the polynomial $f(z) = z^2 + c$; in particular, we are interested in the geometry of the set K_f. For instance, there are quadratic polynomials for which the filled Julia set is connected (roughly, this means that the set is in one piece), and there are quadratic polynomials for which the filled Julia set is disconnected (Fig. 1). We use this as a criterion to color the c-parameter plane in **Fig. 2**: color the parameter c_0 black if the filled Julia set of $f(z) = z^2 + c_0$ is connected, otherwise color c_0 gray.

The parameter space in Fig. 2 should be thought of as a space that is organized according to the different dynamical behaviors that emerge for the polynomial

$f(z) = z^2 + c$ as c varies. The set in black is the Mandelbrot set, $\mathcal{M}$, given by the equation below.

$$\mathcal{M} = \{c \in \mathbb{C} :$$

the filled Julia set of $f(z) = z^2 + c$ is connected$\}$

The set $\mathcal{M}$ records which quadratic polynomials have connected filled Julia sets; one beautiful mathematical result is that $\mathcal{M}$ itself is also connected; this is a theorem of Adrien Douady and John H. Hubbard from 1982. The Mandelbrot set is the most famous fractal, and it is universal in complex dynamics: It arises in other parameter spaces, not just in the parameter space associated to quadratic polynomials.

For the quadratic polynomial $f(z) = z^2 + c$, the point $z_0 = 0$ plays a special role; it is the unique critical point of f; that is, it is the point where the derivative $f'(z) = 2z$ vanishes. In each of the

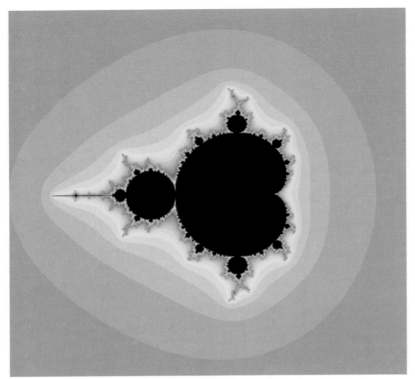

Fig. 2. This is the *c*-parameter plane for the family of quadratic polynomials *f(z)* = *z*² + *c*. In black is the Mandelbrot set $\mathcal{M}$.

pictures in Fig. 1, the critical point is in the center; note that the critical point is a "center of symmetry" in these pictures. It is a general principle in complex dynamics that the orbits of the critical points of the polynomial $f : \mathbb{C} \to \mathbb{C}$ provide information about the dynamics of f. One instance of this is the following theorem, which was proven by Pierre Fatou and Gaston Julia:

Theorem: Let $f(z) = z^2 + c$. The filled Julia set K_f is connected if and only if the critical point $z_0 = 0$ belongs to K_f.

A consequence of the theorem is that, for the polynomial $f(z) = z^2 + c_0$, c_0 is in the Mandelbrot set $\mathcal{M}$ if and only if the critical point 0 is in K_f, that is, if and only if the orbit of 0 under the polynomial $f(z) = z^2 + c_0$ is bounded. Therefore, if c_0 is not in the Mandelbrot set, then the orbit of the critical point 0 escapes to infinity. Because c_0 is not in $\mathcal{M}$, we will color it gray; we can shade it according to how fast the orbit of 0 (under the polynomial $f(z) = z^2 + c_0$) escapes to infinity. This is why there are many shades of gray in Fig. 2.

History. The field of complex dynamics was largely developed by Fatou and Julia in the early twentieth century (they worked independently). They never saw pictures of these striking fractal images; nevertheless, they established the foundations of the subject. However, after Fatou and Julia, complex dynamics was rather dormant from the late 1920s until the 1980s, when the field reawakened with the advent of computers. Mathematicians now had the ability to draw these sets and study the intricate geometry of these fractal objects. The subject further developed

with the groundbreaking work of Douady, Hubbard, Mikhail Lyubich, Curtis T. McMullen, John W. Milnor, Mitsuhiro Shishikura, Dennis Sullivan, William Thurston, and Jean-Christophe Yoccoz, to name a few of the pioneers. Complex dynamics has since developed into a rich area of mathematical research.

Julia sets with positive area. Fatou asked if there are polynomials $f : \mathbb{C} \to \mathbb{C}$ for which the Julia set J_f has positive area. This question remained unsolved for about 80 years. In 2005, it was ultimately resolved by Xavier Buff and Arnaud Chéritat. They successfully executed an approach designed by Douady to prove that there are quadratic polynomials f such that J_f has positive area. Any subset of the complex plane that has interior necessarily has positive area; however, it is possible to have a subset of the plane that does not have interior and yet can still have positive area. A line drawn in the plane will have area 0. However, if a curve in the plane undulates enough and accumulates on itself with complicated enough geometry, it is possible for the curve to have positive area even though the curve itself is "thin" (like a piece of string lying on the floor); this is precisely how one constructs space-filling curves. In Fig. 1, the Julia set associated with each of the four polynomials has area 0.

To mention some of the details of the revolutionary work of Buff and Chéritat, it is useful to change variables and rewrite our quadratic polynomials as $q(z) = \lambda z + z^2$, where $\lambda \in \mathbb{C}$ is a complex parameter. In this new form, we note that $q(0) = 0$, or that $z_0 = 0$ is a fixed point of the polynomial q. The number λ is called the multiplier of the fixed point at 0. If $|\lambda| < 1$, then 0 is an attracting fixed point, and points that are close to 0 will be mapped even closer by q. If $|\lambda| > 1$, then 0 is a repelling fixed point, and points that are close to 0 will be mapped further away by q. Lastly, if $|\lambda| = 1$, then 0 is an indifferent fixed point, and many different things can happen in this case.

If $|\lambda| = 1$, then we may write $\lambda = e^{2\pi i \theta}$ where θ satisfies $0 \le \theta < 1$. The number θ is called the rotation number of the fixed point. If θ is a rational number, then the fixed point $z_0 = 0$ is called parabolic; otherwise, the fixed point is called irrationally indifferent. There are two (mutually exclusive) ways in which the fixed point z_0 can be irrationally indifferent. Either there is a disk containing z_0 on which the polynomial q acts as a rotation (in which case the disk is called a Siegel disk), or there is not. In the first case, we say that z_0 is linearizable; otherwise, we say that z_0 is a Cremer point. Practically nothing is known about the dynamics of the polynomial q near a Cremer point; however, if z_0 is a Cremer point, then it is known that K_q has no interior. If K_q has no interior, it follows from the definition that $K_q = J_q$. If z_0 is a parabolic point, or if it is linearizable, then K_q does have interior (**Fig. 3**).

Douady conjectured that there is an angle θ satisfying $0 \le \theta < 1$ such that the polynomial $q(z) = e^{2\pi i \theta} z + z^2$ has a Cremer point at $z_0 = 0$,

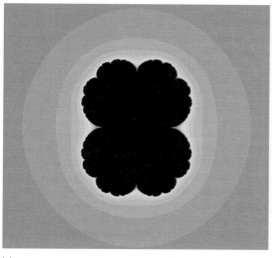

(a)   (b)

Fig. 3. The filled Julia sets (*a*) of a quadratic polynomial with a parabolic fixed point and (*b*) of a quadratic polynomial with a Siegel disk.

and the Julia set J_q has positive area. His strategy for establishing this result is as follows. The plan is to construct a sequence of numbers θ_n, each satisfying $0 \leq \theta_n < 1$, converging to θ, such that:

1. Each of the associated polynomials

$$q_n(z) = e^{2\pi i \theta_n} z + z^2$$

either has a Siegel disk at $z_0 = 0$, or a parabolic point at $z_0 = 0$.

2. The polynomial

$$q(z) = e^{2\pi i \theta} z + z^2$$

has a Cremer point at $z_0 = 0$.

3. The area of the interior of the filled Julia set K_{q_n} is bounded from below.

The idea is to obtain the sequence of polynomials q_n so that the filled Julia sets K_{q_n} have interior. Then, when θ_n converges to θ, the strategy is to control the amount of area that is lost, and since the polynomial q has a Cremer point at $z_0 = 0$, the filled Julia set K_q will have no interior. If the filled Julia set has no interior, then $K_q = J_q$, and if we have not lost too much area as θ_n converges to θ, the Julia set J_q must therefore have positive area. In 2001, Chéritat completed part of this program, and then in 2005, he and Buff finished it, resulting in the following theorem, finally putting to rest a question from about 80 years before.

Theorem 2. There exist quadratic polynomials $q : \mathbb{C} \to \mathbb{C}$ for which the Julia set J_q has positive area.

For background information *see* CHAOS; COMPLEX NUMBERS AND COMPLEX VARIABLES; FRACTALS; MEASURE THEORY; SET THEORY; TOPOLOGY in the McGraw-Hill Encyclopedia of Science & Technology.

Sarah Koch

Bibliography. X. Buff and A. Chéritat, Quadratic Julia sets with positive area, *Ann. Math.*, 176:673–746, 2012, DOI:10.4007/annals.2012.176.2.1; A. Chéritat, *Recherche d'Ensembles de Julia de Mesure de Lebesgue Positive*, Thesis, Orsay, France, 2001; A. Chéritat, The hunt for Julia sets with positive measure, in D. Schleicher (ed.), *Complex Dynamics, Families and Friends*, pp. 539–599, A K Peters, Wellesley, MA, 2009; A. Douady and J. H. Hubbard, *Études Dynamique des Polynômes Complexes*, Parts 1 and 2, Université de Paris-Sud, Département de Mathématique, Orsay, France, 1984–1985, reprint, Société Mathématique de France, Paris, 2007; J. Milnor, *Dynamics in One Complex Variable*, 3d ed., Annals of Mathematics Studies, Princeton University Press, Princeton, NJ, 2006.

Cortical gray matter changes in childhood-onset schizophrenia

Childhood and adolescence are turbulent periods of profound change, with a complex interplay among biological, psychological, emotional, and social factors as young people navigate their way to adulthood, assume adult roles and responsibilities, and develop relationships. Adolescence is also a risk period for the emergence of serious mental health disorders. A recent review of 21 studies surveying approximately 40,000 children and adolescents showed that 1 in every 4 youths will experience (in his or her lifetime) and meet the criteria of a mental disorder classified in the *Diagnostic and Statistical Manual of Mental Disorders* (DSM), which permeates to significant distress and impairment in psychosocial outcome.

Schizophrenia is the most severe, persistent, and disabling of the major mental illnesses, afflicting approximately 1% of the population worldwide. The disorder usually presents in late adolescence or early adulthood, with earlier age of onset in males compared with females. Schizophrenia is characterized by positive symptoms, which are reflective of an excess or distortion of normal functions, in particular delusions (false or irrational beliefs) and hallucinations (false perceptions), combined with negative symptoms, which are defined by the absence of normal behaviors, such as lack of drive or motivation (avolition), poverty of speech (alogia), reduction in emotional reactivity (blunted or flat affect), or the inability to experience pleasure (anhedonia). The early stages of the illness are characterized by repeated exacerbation of positive symptoms. Cognitive deficits are a prominent feature of the illness, affecting a diverse range of domains, and are strongly associated with impairments in behavioral functioning, problem-solving ability, and outcome of psychiatric rehabilitation. Although a high proportion of patients respond to initial treatment with antipsychotic medication, approximately 80% of patients relapse within 5 years of the first-episode schizophrenia.

There is a growing body of evidence suggesting that the pathophysiology of schizophrenia can be traced during the early stages of development. Recent imaging methodologies document significant brain maturation in normal individuals during adolescence and early adulthood. However, according to the neurodevelopmental theory of schizophrenia, early brain insults (damage, trauma, or injuries) cause dysfunction of the maturing brain, leading to the clinical expression of the disorder, and both environmental and genetic antecedents play a role in the phenotypic expression and pathophysiology of the disorder.

Childhood-onset schizophrenia (COS), with the onset of psychotic symptoms occurring before age 13, is a rare (1 in 30,000–50,000) and severe phenotypic variant of adult-onset schizophrenia. Most of the evidence for longitudinal changes in children and adolescents having a diagnosis of schizophrenia comes from an ongoing COS study at the National Institute of Mental Health (NIMH; based in Bethesda, Maryland), in which a large number of healthy subjects, COS probands (subjects), and their relatives have been prospectively scanned for the past 20 years. Current evidence suggests neurobiological continuity between COS and adult-onset illness, with diagnostic stability over time. Other features of COS include delays in developmental milestones (for example, speech and language, and motor coordination), more severe symptoms (as measured using clinical scales), resistance to antipsychotic treatment, and poor prognostic outcome compared with adult-onset schizophrenia.

Cortical development in typically developing children. The cortical tissue in the brain is composed of gray matter (GM; the somatodendritic tissue of neurons) and white matter (WM; the axonal compartment of myelinated connecting fibers). Structural magnetic resonance imaging (MRI) scanning has been used to estimate and model growth trajectories for different brain structures over time. Earlier volumetric studies have shown that cortical GM volume follows an inverted "U-shaped" trajectory that peaks in different regions during adolescence and early adulthood, suggesting heterogeneity in GM development across the major lobes; in particular, frontal and parietal lobe GM volumes peak at around 11 years of age, whereas temporal lobe GM continues to increase until the age of 14 years. On the other hand, WM volumes continue to increase linearly into adulthood, with peak levels occurring in the mid-forties. The developmental sequences of primary motor and sensory cortices mature at earlier ages, whereas brain regions associated with higher-order fronto-temporal and parietal associative cortices appear to mature at a later age. Subsequent studies have further shown that there is subregional heterogeneity of maturation events even within specific brain regions. For example, within the prefrontal cortex, the orbitofrontal cortex matures first, by the age of 3 years. These studies show that structural brain development works in parallel with important functional milestones in the brain, representing a complex interaction between development progression and environmental factors. This is also evident from a recent longitudinal NIMH pediatric study, which revealed that children having higher intelligence showed a plastic cortex with an initial acceleration and a longer phase of cortical thickness increase followed by a vigorous phase of cortical thinning. Thus, the "trajectory of change" in the thickness of the cerebral cortex appeared to be related to the level of intelligence.

Cortical GM development in patients with childhood-onset schizophrenia. Understanding GM maturation in healthy development has helped shed light on abnormal GM developmental patterns in COS. Neuroimaging and postmortem studies on subjects with adult-onset schizophrenia have shown smaller brain size, reduction in GM volume (particularly in the prefrontal and superior temporal cortices), and increased ventricular volume. Similarly, imaging studies on patients with COS have reported smaller brain size, larger lateral ventricles, and reduced prefrontal lobe volume compared to healthy subjects. During the adolescent period, patients with COS show progressive ventricular enlargement and a progressive loss of cortical GM that follows a parietal-frontal and parietal-temporal pattern, and the deficits are circumscribed to prefrontal and temporal cortices by late adolescence, merging into the typical adult pattern of prefrontal and temporal cortical GM loss in schizophrenia. The exaggeration of the normal developmental pattern of GM loss in COS during adolescent years suggests disruption of normal inhibitory controls in GM maturations, supporting the excessive synaptic pruning hypothesis in schizophrenia. As observed with GM, the WM growth also appears significantly delayed in COS during adolescence, suggesting a global brain development deficit in this severely ill population.

Neuroimaging advances in schizophrenia. Several lines of evidence indicate that schizophrenia is a disorder of functional and structural connectivity. Measurements of cortical thickness have provided a blueprint of the organizational properties of the human brain. Advances in psychiatric imaging methodology and analysis in resting-state or task-driven functional imaging and magnetoencephalography (a noninvasive technique for investigating human brain activity) can explore brain oscillations and neural networks that are abnormal in schizophrenia. Similarly, diffusion tensor imaging (a magnetic resonance method that measures the diffusion properties of water molecules) shows structural WM abnormalities in two regions reported to be significantly reduced in schizophrenia—namely, the left frontal lobe, which is traversed by WM tracts connecting the frontal lobe, thalamus, and cingulate gyrus; and the temporal lobe, which is traversed by WM tracts interconnecting the frontal lobe, insula, hippocampus-amygdala, temporal lobe, and occipital lobe. Overall, studies are beginning to provide unique insights into the abnormal neurocircuitries relevant to schizophrenia during the developmental age window. In addition, recent neuroimaging methodologies have begun combining genetic and imaging databases to study the association between a number of risk alleles (small-to-moderate effect size) and morphological and functional brain abnormalities. For example, a recent study of COS patients and their siblings showed that individuals with increased valine dosing of the *COMT* Val[158]Met genotype (where Val is the amino acid valine, and Met is the amino acid methionine) showed heightened loss of cortical GM in the prefrontal cortex in COS probands and healthy nonpsychotic siblings; however, the *COMT* genotype alone showed no diagnostic association with both groups. Interestingly, the Met/Met genotype appeared to normalize the GM loss in siblings during late adolescence, whereas normalization occurred at a later age in COS probands, indicating an age-dependent genetic influence on development.

In conclusion, COS studies, particularly with longitudinally acquired data, provide a unique opportunity for studying the pathophysiology of schizophrenia from a neurodevelopmental perspective. Neuroimaging advances together with the advent of high-density genetic microarray data will enhance the power of studying the underlying mechanisms of abnormal brain development in schizophrenia.

For background information *see* BRAIN; CENTRAL NERVOUS SYSTEM; DEVELOPMENTAL PSYCHOLOGY; MEDICAL IMAGING; MENTAL DISORDERS; NERVOUS SYSTEM (VERTEBRATE); NERVOUS SYSTEM DISORDERS; NEUROBIOLOGY; PSYCHOLOGY; SCHIZOPHRENIA in the McGraw-Hill Encyclopedia of Science & Technology.   Nora S. Vyas; Nitin Gogtay

Bibliography. J. N. Giedd and J. L. Rapoport, Structural MRI of pediatric brain development: What have we learned and where are we going?, *Neuron*, 67(5):728–734, 2010, DOI:10.1016/j.neuron.2010.08.040; N. Gogtay et al., Age of onset of schizophrenia: Perspectives from structural neuroimaging studies, *Schizophr. Bull.*, 37(3):504–513, 2011, DOI:10.1093/schbul/sbr030; J. L. Rapoport, J. N. Giedd, and N. Gogtay, Neurodevelopmental model of schizophrenia: Update 2012, *Mol. Psychiat.*, 17(12):1228–1238, 2012, DOI:10.1038/mp.2012.23; A. Raznahan et al., Catechol-*o*-methyltransferase (COMT) Val[158]Met polymorphism and adolescent cortical development in patients with childhood-onset schizophrenia, their nonpsychotic siblings, and healthy controls, *NeuroImage*, 57:1517–1523, 2011, DOI:10.1016/j.neuroimage.2011.05.032; P. Shaw et al., Intellectual ability and cortical development in children and adolescents, *Nature*, 440:676–679, 2006, DOI:10.1038/nature04513.

"Cruise ship" virus: new vaccine

Cruise ships have been in the news during the last several years because of a variety of mishaps, including mechanical failures causing nightmarish cruise experiences and ships running aground leading to passenger deaths. Another cruise ship hazard has been publicized as well: outbreaks of diarrhea and vomiting caused by norovirus, which is known as the "cruise ship" virus.

Background. Noroviruses are the most common cause of viral gastroenteritis in humans. Outbreaks of norovirus-caused disease on cruise ships have been annually documented by the U.S. Centers for Disease Control and Prevention since 1994 (see the **table** for a list of the cruise ship outbreaks in 2012). Cruise ships first became notorious for their outbreaks of this illness in 2002, when one of the Disney cruise line ships, the *Disney Magic*, had an outbreak that gained widespread attention in the press.

Noroviruses were originally named the "Norwalk virus" after an outbreak that occurred at an elementary school in Norwalk, Ohio, in 1968. These viruses belong to the *Caliciviridae* family, which includes single-stranded RNA viruses that lack an envelope and are referred to as "naked" (see **illustration**). These viruses are difficult to study because they do not have a suitable animal model and cannot be grown using tissue culture techniques. Noroviruses are classified into one of five different genetic groups or genogroups. Human outbreaks are usually caused by members of genogroups GI and GII.

Noroviruses are transmitted directly from person to person, and they also can be transmitted indirectly through food and water that have been contaminated by an infected individual. In addition, the viruses can be passed by contaminated inanimate surfaces, including ship railings and tables. The virus has been shown to survive several hours on these surfaces, enhancing its ability to spread within a confined population, such as is found on a cruise ship. Vomiting causes aerosolization of the virus, which can lead to infection through the respiratory tract. Flushing a toilet when diarrhea or vomit is present can also aerosolize the virus, potentially infecting other individuals. As the infectious dose is quite low (only 20 viral particles are required to cause

Cruise ship outbreaks in 2012

Cruise line	Cruise ship	Sailing dates in 2012	Causative agent
Cunard	*Queen Mary 2*	12/22–12/31	Norovirus
Princess	*Emerald Princess*	12/17–12/27	Norovirus
Prestige	*Oceania Riviera*	11/15–11/29	Norovirus
Holland America	*Amsterdam*	11/11–12/05	Norovirus
Princess	*Ruby Princess*	10/09–10/28	Norovirus and enterotoxigenic *Escherichia coli* (ETEC)
Princess	*Dawn Princess*	08/21–09/13	Norovirus
Royal Caribbean	*Rhapsody of the Seas*	08/24–08/31	Norovirus
Carnival	*Carnival Glory*	08/06–08/11	Norovirus
Princess	*Sun Princess*	07/08–07/21	Norovirus
Princess	*Ruby Princess*	02/26–03/04	Norovirus
Princess	*Crown Princess*	02/04–02/09	Norovirus
Celebrity	*Celebrity Silhouette*	01/29–02/10	Norovirus
Celebrity	*Celebrity Constellation*	01/28–02/11	Norovirus
Princess	*Crown Princess*	01/28–02/04	Norovirus
P & O	*Aurora*	01/04–01/26	Norovirus
Royal Caribbean	*Voyager of the Seas*	01/28–02/04	Norovirus

Source: Centers for Disease Control and Prevention, Atlanta, GA.

infection), aerosolization is a significant means by which the virus is passed from victim to victim.

After a person becomes infected with the virus, it travels through the gastrointestinal tract to the small intestine, where it begins to multiply. Symptoms of infection begin 24–48 hours after infection, and they include nausea, severe vomiting, watery diarrhea, and abdominal pain. Victims tend to feel weak and lethargic, and they may suffer from muscle aches (myalgia), headache, cough, and fever. In most patients, the disease is self-limiting and subsides in a few days. After recovery, patients can continue to shed the virus in their stools for 30 days or longer, allowing the continued spread of the virus. Severe disease is rare and is usually seen in the elderly, in the very young, and in patients who are immunocompromised, including transplant patients or people living with human immunodeficiency

virus (HIV) or acquired immunodeficiency syndrome (AIDS). Death in these groups is usually the result of severe dehydration, which should be closely monitored.

Development of a new vaccine. The U.S. Centers for Disease Control and Prevention estimates that 21 million people in the United States are infected with norovirus annually. Approximately 70,000 hospitalizations per year have resulted from these infections, including nearly 800 deaths. Based on these numbers, the need for an effective vaccine becomes obvious.

Leading the way in the search for a vaccine is Ligocyte Pharmaceuticals (based in Bozeman, Montana), which has developed two different vaccine formulations to prevent norovirus infections. The vaccines from Ligocyte Pharmaceuticals are based on proprietary viruslike particles (developed by the company's researchers) that are mixed with an adjuvant (a substance that enhances the strength of the immune response to the vaccine). These particles mimic the surface of the virus, triggering the immune system to produce antibodies that will bind to the norovirus during a natural infection. The vaccine formulation was first administered intranasally in the form of a dry powder. Ninety volunteers were given the vaccine, which was designed to induce an immune response in the gastrointestinal epithelium (the primary site of viral invasion). After the volunteers were given the vaccine, they were monitored for norovirus illnesses. About one-third of those given the vaccine acquired a norovirus infection; compared with a similar-sized placebo group, this was a reduction of about 33% because two-thirds of the placebo group developed a norovirus illness. Although this is a significant reduction, the company was interested in reducing the number of illnesses still further. Therefore, a second formulation was tested, which is a liquid vaccine designed for intramuscular (IM) injection.

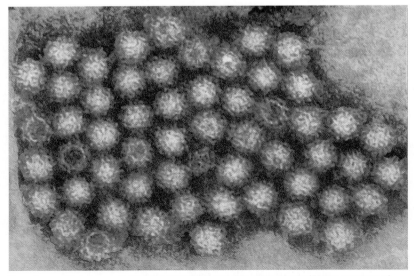

Norovirus particles revealed in a transmission electron micrograph. (*Photo courtesy of Charles D. Humphrey, Centers for Disease Control and Prevention, Atlanta, GA*)

Early trials of the IM vaccine demonstrated a significant antibody response by volunteers. The vaccine was injected twice in the arm with a 4-week gap between the initial vaccination and the booster shot. Volunteers who received the placebo did not produce antibodies specific to the virus, showing that the vaccine is specific to the targeted pathogen. Interestingly, there was no significant increase after the administration of the booster vaccine. This would seem to indicate that the initial dose may be the only one required to induce immunity. The IM vaccine also differs from the nasal powder in that it protects against two genetically different strains of the norovirus, whereas the nasal vaccine is only designed to protect against one. Therefore, the IM vaccine induces a broader response than the nasal powder and gives more immunity to the recipient.

The genetic diversity of noroviruses must be taken into account when developing a vaccine. As stated previously, there are five different genogroups; within these genogroups, there are a number of genetically different strains or genotypes. This means that the protection offered by a particular vaccine is limited to the genotype of virus that it is designed against. The strain of norovirus that is responsible for a particular outbreak may differ from that causing another outbreak, so a vaccine to combat one strain will not protect individuals from getting sick from a different strain. The dominant strain within a given population may change from year to year, thus requiring that vaccine developers monitor the strains present and predict which strain is most likely to cause disease over the course of a year. This type of surveillance and prediction has been in use for many years with the influenza vaccine, which is changed based on the strain of flu virus most likely to cause significant illness during the next flu season. Similarly, scientists could monitor for and predict future outbreaks of norovirus. As the vaccine is probably of limited duration (natural immunity occurring post-infection only lasts about 14 weeks), annual vaccinations will more than likely be required to give any type of regular protection.

Conclusions. Cruise ship outbreaks of norovirus illnesses receive a great deal of attention from the media and the public whenever they occur. However, the reality is that this virus is very prevalent in the population and that the number of cases documented annually in the United States calls for the development of an effective vaccine. Preliminary vaccine studies appear promising, but further testing and development may require several years before an effective vaccine can be used to protect the community. In the meantime, the best way for an individual to protect against infection is to use good hygiene practices. An individual should wash his or her hands thoroughly with soap and warm water after using the bathroom or changing a diaper, and definitely before eating or handling food. In addition, foods that are eaten raw (vegetables and fruit) should be washed thoroughly. If a person is sick with a stomach illness, he or she should not prepare food for others. If that person lives with others in a house, all surfaces that he or she touches should be washed and disinfected thoroughly. Clothes and linens used by the sick person should be handled using gloves, and they should be washed to prevent further spread of the illness. Until a vaccine becomes available for prevention of disease, these measures are the most effective means by which norovirus illnesses can be avoided.

For background information *see* ANTIBODY; DIARRHEA; EPIDEMIC; EPIDEMIC VIRAL GASTROENTERITIS; IMMUNITY; IMMUNOLOGY; INFECTIOUS DISEASE; PUBLIC HEALTH; VACCINATION; VIRUS; VIRUS CLASSIFICATION; WATER-BORNE DISEASE in the McGraw-Hill Encyclopedia of Science & Technology.

Marcia M. Pierce

Bibliography. M. K. Cowan, *Microbiology: A Systems Approach*, 3d ed., McGraw-Hill, New York, 2012; L. C. Lindesmith, E. F. Donaldson, and R. S. Baric, Norovirus GII.4 strain antigenic variation, *J. Virol.*, 85:231–242, 2011, DOI:10.1128/JVI.01364-10; A. D. LoBue et al., Alphavirus-adjuvanted norovirus-like particle vaccines: Heterologous, humoral, and mucosal immune responses protect against murine norovirus challenge, *J. Virol.*, 83:3212–3227, 2009, DOI:10.1128/JVI.01650-08; P. R. Murray, K. S. Rosenthal, and M. A. Pfaller, *Medical Microbiology*, 7th ed., Mosby, St. Louis, 2013; E. Nester, D. Anderson, and C. E. Roberts, Jr., *Microbiology: A Human Perspective*, 7th ed., McGraw-Hill, New York, 2012; M. Tan et al., Norovirus P particle, a novel platform for vaccine development and antibody production, *J. Virol.*, 85:753–764, 2011, DOI:10.1128/JVI.01835-10.

Data-mining and informatics approaches for environmental contaminants

New and emerging environmental contaminants are chemicals that have not been previously detected or that are being detected at levels significantly different from those expected in both biological and ecological arenas (that is, human, wildlife, and environment). Many chemicals can originate from a variety of sources, including consumer, agriculture, and industry as well as natural and/or anthropogenic disaster scenarios. For example, endocrine-disrupting chemicals (EDCs), pharmaceuticals, and personal care products (such as therapeutic, nontherapeutic, and veterinary drugs, as well as cosmetics and fragrances) are known to be present in many of the world's water bodies and thought to originate from a variety of sources, including improper disposal into municipal sewage, agribusiness, and veterinary practices. The detection and quantification of these chemicals from a toxicology and exposure perspective is paramount to understanding their effects on both the ecosystem and human health. EDCs act on the endocrine system and are known to alter sexual development and fertility in many vertebrate species. It is suspected that they may play a role in species population decline as well as public health issues.

Discriminating between potential contaminants and noncontaminants (for example, EDCs versus non-EDCs) can be an exhaustive and costly endeavor. In some cases, these methods rely on a specialized detection apparatus, discrete samples, and complicated sampling techniques as well as bioethical issues in testing methods that may require the sacrifice of animals. Currently, high-throughput screening (HTS) efforts (such as toxicity in vitro assays) are helping to reduce some of the challenges and hurdles to testing these chemicals. However, the analysis and interpretation of results require powerful data analytics to summarize and make sense of the data, due to the voluminous amount generated. Informatics-based approaches like cheminformatics hold the best possibility of deciphering the barrage of data within a statistical and chemical context.

Data mining and informatics. Informatics is a broad field of study encompassing computer science and information technology from the retrieval and storage of data to the mining of patterns that exist within the stored data streams. Data mining itself is one step along a process commonly known as data or knowledge discovery (KD). Data curation and storage are critical steps in this process, but analysis and interpretation help researchers to elucidate and summarize patterns and relationships within the data itself through sophisticated algorithmic and visualization-type techniques. Some examples of these data mining techniques include the location of predetermined groups (such as decision-tree analysis techniques), organization of data due to logical relationships (such as hierarchical and cluster analysis), identification of associations/dependencies (for example, associative rule mining), and prediction of patterns based on historical data (for example, predictive analytics). Many of these techniques are routinely applied in the retail, finance, and marketing sectors (for example, predicting consumer buying habits and trends in the market). Informatics-based approaches in the life sciences are largely dominated by cheminformatics and bioinformatics, which also employ the same techniques to understand the relationships (associations and patterns) related to chemical structures and properties and biological functions, respectively. Historically, this has been done with an eye toward discovery of new chemicals. This discovery aspect has apparent implications in both pharmaceutical and material sciences, but the same tools and techniques are beginning to be used in a variety of research areas (such as geographical information systems, environment- and genome-wide association studies). A visual representation using IBM's Many Eyes (http://www-958.ibm.com) service using 374 abstracts found in *PubMed* highlights the relationships of concepts found in the current literature (**Fig. 1**).

Chemical space and cheminformatics. Application of data-mining techniques in the arena of knowledge discovery for new and emerging chemicals encompasses a wide variety of chemicals from exposure biomarkers and pesticides to drugs and EDCs. Since "chemical space" is defined by the set of all

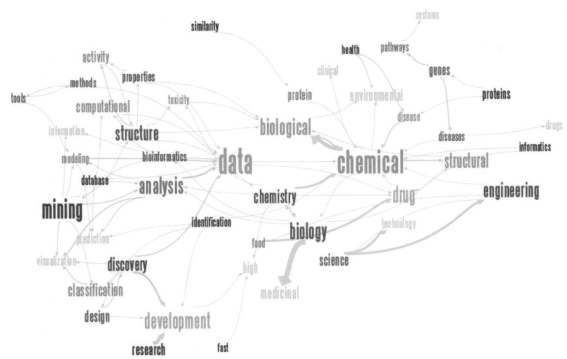

Fig. 1. IBM Many Eyes Phrase Net visualization, showing 48 of 1739 terms, of 374 abstracts queried from *PubMed* with the search query {"data mining"[All Fields] AND "chemical*"[All Fields] AND hasabstract[text]} illustrating the relationship of key concepts within data mining.

energetically stable stoichiometric combinations of atoms, nuclei, and electrons, it is not difficult to imagine that the possible combinations are astronomical, easily surpassing the current list of emerging contaminants. The number of small organic chemicals, alone, has been estimated to be on the order of 10^{60}. To sample and characterize this space, it would require multiple lifetimes at the current level of technology. Optimistically, this would be on the order of 10^{52} years, assuming most HTS efforts can process about 100,000 chemicals per day. A far more efficient approach would be to apply cheminformatics-based data-mining techniques to the subset of already known chemicals and arrive at a qualitative and potentially quantitative predictive framework (that is, through clustering, classification, association, and predictive analytics). This approach would provide the context for characterizing existing chemicals as well as new and emerging chemicals through a combination of molecular descriptor generation, molecular fingerprinting, and predictive analytics.

The description of chemical space is largely dictated by structure-based information. For example, one could define chemical space in terms of the subset of chemical properties (that is, molecular descriptors) that might be of interest to a particular biological activity or outcome. Molecular descriptors have a long history within cheminformatics and can be categorized as either mathematical constructs or empirical-based measurements that allow one to enumerate or quantify information about a chemical, spanning the range from simple quantification of a chemical's relative partition into oil and water (log $P_{o/w}$) to more complex quantum-mechanical-based descriptors that rely on the electron density of a molecule.

Molecular fingerprints, much like their name implies, are encoded structure-based information (such as molecular descriptors and fragments) that are ideally unique to a particular chemical. As variable or fixed-sized representations, they can encode structural keys related to both two- and three-dimensional (2D and 3D) molecular information. The power of molecular fingerprints is that they can be rapidly evaluated and compared to existing fingerprints in a database, thereby making similarity/dissimilarity searches trivial via standard similarity measures (such as Tanimoto Index). Chemical similarity is largely based on the principle that similar compounds have similar properties and, by association, chemicals can be grouped on the basis of some derived similarity in their selected molecular fingerprints (for example, P-glycoprotein inhibitors versus non-inhibitors). Calculated distance matrices in a database of chemicals can also aid in identifying observed structure in the data (that is, clustering of like properties and/or biological activity).

One of the classic predictive analytic methods of cheminformatics is quantitative structure-activity relationships, which seek to find statistical correlations between a finite set of structure-based features (for example, molecular descriptors) and their observed outcome (for example, molecular and/or biological activity). Due to the feature selection problem (that is, which descriptors to choose in the model) a variety of algorithms have evolved to use data-mining techniques, such as neural networks, support-vector machines, and ensemble average and kernel-based methods. Applicability domain issues (that is, the relevancy and applicability of a predictive model to a wide range of chemicals) are always prevalent in such models, as they rely heavily on the available data to "train" their predictive associations. In such cases, local models that are defined by their nearest-neighbors association may provide more predictive power than global models by interpolating within the data rather than extrapolating outside the data. However, these models may suffer from sparse data or small training sets, making it difficult to accurately quantify the applicability domain.

Visualization of multiple molecules of interest within a set of prescribed descriptor dimensions can convey rapid information on chemical similarity or dissimilarity as well as general clustering of chemicals. Reduced dimensionality visualization approaches, such as three-dimensional principal component analysis (3D-PCA) plots, can provide rapid visual insights. In this case, the similarity or dissimilarity of chemicals is based on the relative mapped positions of one molecular entity's structure-based properties with relation to another neighboring entity in a reduced Euclidean space composed of multiple molecular descriptors. To illustrate, **Fig. 2** shows a chemographic representation based on CHEMGPS-NP (http://chemgps.bmc.uu.se) of several open-access chemical databases that illustrate the representation of multidimensional data in identifying overlaps of datasets based on similar principal components.

Exposure science and pharmacokinetics. Detection of a chemical merely suggests its presence in the environment. However, a chemical's presence alone does not dictate the effect on ecosystem and human health because of many determining factors. Analogously, exposure to a chemical does not necessarily mean that an adverse effect (such as toxicity or disease) will arise. A complex and complicated relationship exists among many determining factors, including the physicochemical properties, the concentration in the environment, the subsequent fate and transport within both biology and the environment, and the discrete exposure related behaviors (that is, time-activity patterns) of the biological receptor (such as nontarget wildlife species and susceptible individuals/populations). Understanding these factors is a primary concern of exposure science which seeks to understand the continuum of processes from a chemical source to a tissue dose within an organism. The range of predicted physicochemical properties for new and emerging contaminants, however, may influence these key factors, thus making efforts at determining chemical similarity and their associated properties with predictive

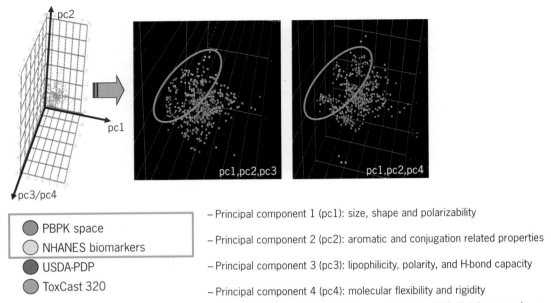

- Principal component 1 (pc1): size, shape and polarizability

- Principal component 2 (pc2): aromatic and conjugation related properties

- Principal component 3 (pc3): lipophilicity, polarity, and H-bond capacity

- Principal component 4 (pc4): molecular flexibility and rigidity

Fig. 2. CHEMGPS-NP representation showing the overlap of chemicals within three publicly available databases and literature PBPK chemical-specific PBPK models through 2010 PBPK model chemicals queried from literature up to 2010 NHANES IV (http://www.cdc.gov/nchs/nhanes.htm) chemicals; USDA-PDP (http://www.ams.usda.gov/AMSv1.0/pdp) chemicals; ToxCast™ (http://www.epa.gov/ncct/toxcast/) Phase 1 chemicals. The first four dimensions of the principal component analysis are plotted.

analytics a critical step in characterizing these chemicals.

Environmental fate and transport as well as its biological analogue, pharmacokinetics/pharmacodynamics, is described by the chemical's interaction within the system. In the pharmaceutical sciences, simple pharmacokinetic-based absorption-distribution-metabolism-elimination (ADME) rules of thumb are commonly used as a selective criteria in screening for drug candidates quickly and efficiently. The most famous of these is Lipinski's Rule of Five (RO5) and subsequent variations, which seek to identify "druglikeness" in candidate compounds (that is, orally active drugs for humans) based on its permeability/absorption into the body. As with many generalizations, it is far from perfect with many limitations due to its inability to cover all of drug space (that is, domain of applicability issues based on four simple molecular descriptors). But as a screening tool, it was transformative in the science, successfully showing that drug permeability could be screened based on simple molecular descriptors, thus reducing the pool of candidate drugs cheaply and efficiently.

From a human exposure perspective, ADME concepts can be used to characterize exposure potentials of chemicals based on a rate-limiting-step assumption of how chemicals enter and exit the body. If we assume that ADME, a step along the source-to-outcome continuum, describes the biological process whereby a chemical trespasses the body's barrier (absorption), is metabolized, distributed, and exits the body (elimination), then a simplified binary (fast/slow) diagram can illustrate the effect on exposure-dose relationships to categorize 16 unique

scenarios (2^4 possible combinations) or dose categorizations (**Fig. 3**). In these scenarios, two dominant exposure-dose themes are observed: (1) absorption limited (AL) via slow absorption and (2) elimination limited (EL) via fast absorption into the body. In this thought experiment, one could flag potential chemicals of concern based on their ability to enter quickly and exit slowly. For example, dose categories 13, 14, 15, and 16 would have the highest concerns given that elimination is slow and absorption is fast. Conversely, dose categories 1, 2, 3, and 4 would have the lowest concerns based on slow absorption and fast elimination. Assuming simple metabolic clearance (that is, no metabolic activation of toxicity pathways), inclusion of metabolism would delineate each category further by a faster/slower metabolism, which would result in quicker/slower clearance of a chemical thus reducing/increasing its dose at a target tissue. Since all steps in the ADME process can be influenced by its physicochemical properties, generic pharmacokinetic modeling should be used when possible to give context to the relative mappings of potential ADME behaviors alongside their predicted molecular descriptors.

Conclusions. Cheminformatics techniques are typically much less intensive to apply, but provide key insights into the nature of chemicals, especially in the context of knowledge discovery. For many contaminants, there is insufficient data available to parameterize models and perform the necessary risk-assessment studies. Data mining and informatics-based approaches allow us to induce predictive models as well as understand potential chemical similarities/dissimilarities of new and emerging contaminants to the environment and to public health.

Exposure makes the dose...

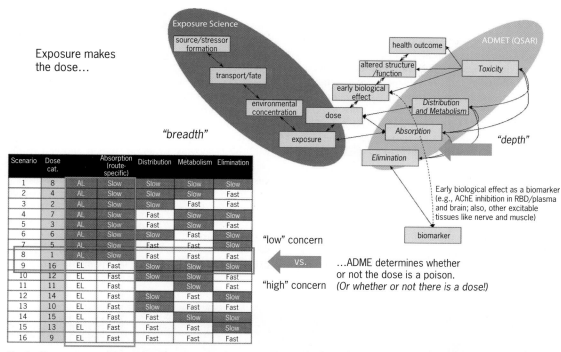

Scenario	Dose cat.	Absorption (route-specific)	Distribution	Metabolism	Elimination
1	8	AL Slow	Slow	Slow	Slow
2	4	AL Slow	Slow	Slow	Fast
3	2	AL Slow	Slow	Fast	Fast
4	7	AL Slow	Fast	Slow	Slow
5	3	AL Slow	Fast	Slow	Fast
6	6	AL Slow	Slow	Fast	Slow
7	5	AL Slow	Fast	Fast	Slow
8	1	AL Slow	Fast	Fast	Fast
9	16	EL Fast	Slow	Slow	Slow
10	12	EL Fast	Slow	Slow	Fast
11	11	EL Fast		Slow	Fast
12	14	EL Fast	Slow	Fast	Slow
13	10	EL Fast	Slow	Fast	Fast
14	15	EL Fast	Fast	Slow	Slow
15	13	EL Fast	Fast	Fast	Slow
16	9	EL Fast	Fast	Fast	Fast

"low" concern

"high" concern

vs.

...ADME determines whether or not the dose is a poison. *(Or whether or not there is a dose!)*

Early biological effect as a biomarker (e.g., AChE inhibition in RBD/plasma and brain; also, other excitable tissues like nerve and muscle)

Fig. 3. Sixteen dose categories (dose cat.) based on a hypothetical binary (fast/slow) stepwise pharmacokinetic scenario considering ADME only along the source-to-outcome continuum. A "low" and "high" concern dose scenario is highlighted within the red box in the table represented by dose cat. 1 and 16, respectively. The orange box highlights absorption limited (AL) and elimination limited (EL) scenarios.

However, care should also be taken when considering the exposure-dose relationships, especially with respect to pharmacokinetic-based ADME concepts. As more information via HTS studies becomes available, the associative power of these predictive models should become richer and more detailed, improving on the current state of the science. Ultimately, the ability to rapidly characterize the presence of new and emerging chemicals as well as their effects on individuals, populations, and ecosystems will have beneficial implications for both exposure risk assessment and risk mitigation.

[*Disclaimer:* The United States Environmental Protection Agency through its Office of Research and Development funded and managed the research described here. It has been subjected to Agency review and approved for publication. Mention of trade names or commercial products does not constitute endorsement or recommendation for use.]

For background information *see* ALGORITHM; CHEMOMETRICS; COMPUTATIONAL CHEMISTRY; DATA MINING; DATA REDUCTION; DATABASE MANAGEMENT SYSTEM; ENVIRONMENTAL ENGINEERING; ENVIRONMENTAL TOXICOLOGY; HAZARDOUS WASTE; MOLECULAR SIMULATION; MUTAGENS AND CARCINOGENS; NEURAL NETWORK; PHARMACOLOGY; RISK ASSESSMENT AND MANAGEMENT; TOXICOLOGY; TROPHIC ECOLOGY in the McGraw-Hill Encyclopedia of Science & Technology.

Daniel T. Chang; Michael-Rock Goldsmith; Christopher M. Grulke; Peter P. Egeghy; Yumei Tan; Jade Mitchell-Blackwood

Bibliography. D. T. Chang et al., In silico strategies for modeling stereoselective metabolism of pyrethroids, in J. B. Knaak, C. Timchalk, and R. Tornero-Velez (eds.), *Parameters for Pesticide QSAR and PBPK/PD models for Human Risk Assessment*, 254–269, American Chemical Society, 1099, Washington, DC, 2012; C. G. Daughton, Pharmaceuticals in the environment: Sources and their management, in M. Petrovic and D. Barcelo (eds.), *Analysis, Fate and Removal of Pharmaceuticals in the Water Cycle*, Elsevier Science, vol. 50, pp. 1–58, 2007; C. M. Dobson, Chemical Space and Biology, *Nature*, 432:824–828, 2004, DOI:10.1038/nature03192; P. P. Egeghy et al., The exposure data landscape for manufactured chemicals, *Sci. Total Environ.*, 414:159–166, 2012, DOI:10.1016/j.scitotenv.2011.10.046; M. R. Goldsmith et al., Informing mechanistic toxicology with computational molecular models, in B. Reisfeld and A. N. Mayeno, *What is computational toxicology, Meth. Mol. Biol.*, 929:139–165, 2012, DOI:10.1007/978-1-62703-050-2_1; M. F. Rahman, et al., Endocrine disrupting compounds (EDCs) and pharmaceuticals and personal care products (PPCPs) in the aquatic environment: implications for the drinking water industry and global environmental health, *J. Water Health*, 7(2):224–243, 2009, DOI:10.2166/wh.2009.021; Y. Tan et al., Reconstructing human exposures using biomarkers and other "clues," *J. Toxicol. Environ. Health B Crit Rev*, 15(1):22–38, 2012, DOI:10.1080/10937404.2012.632360.

Dawn's asteroid exploration

The objective of the Dawn mission is to study the origin of the solar system by taking a journey in space to map objects that have recorded the events of the earliest days of the solar system. The targets chosen were the second most massive asteroid in the main belt, 4 Vesta, which was first observed on March 29, 1807, by H. Olbers, and the most massive asteroid and dwarf planet, 1 Ceres, which was discovered on January 1, 1801, by G. Piazzi. These bodies are believed to be intact survivors of the tumultuous history of collisions experienced in the asteroid belt and the inner solar system as the giant planets formed and migrated. These two bodies are quite different. Vesta has a basaltic crust and an iron core somewhat like those of our Moon. Ceres is believed to contain a great deal of water in the form of hydrated minerals and possibly liquid water and ice. Vesta has revealed itself to terrestrial scientists through the howardite, eucrite, and diogenite (HED) meteorites that have fallen on Earth, but the meteorite record has revealed nothing about Ceres. *See* EVOLUTION OF ASTEROID 4 VESTA.

The Dawn mission was enabled by NASA's technological and programmatic innovation in the 1990s. The new technology was the development for flight of an ion-propulsion system using xenon ions accelerated to high speed. The programmatic innovation was the Discovery program, which allowed teams of scientists under the leadership of principal investigators to apply to NASA for the funds necessary to undertake state-of-the-art planetary missions. When this opportunity was announced in 1992, a team was formed with the support of the NASA Lewis Research Center (now the NASA Glenn Research Center). This team developed and proposed precursor concepts of the Dawn mission in 1994,

Fig. 1. Artistic rendering of the *Dawn* spacecraft in orbit about Vesta.

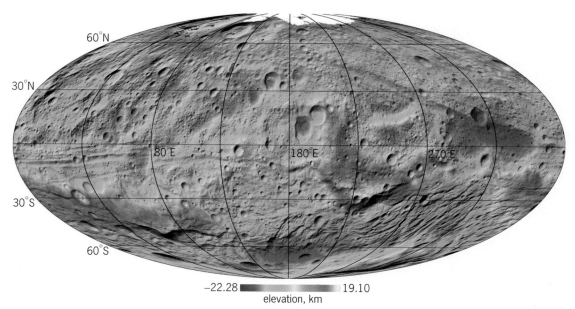

Fig. 2. Vesta topography obtained from images in the HAMO-1 and HAMO-2 orbits, shown as color-contoured Mollweide projection. Topography in kilometers (scale bar at bottom) is calculated relative to a reference ellipsoid of 285 × 285 × 229 km (177 × 177 × 142 mi). (*Courtesy of F. Preusker, German Aerospace Center*)

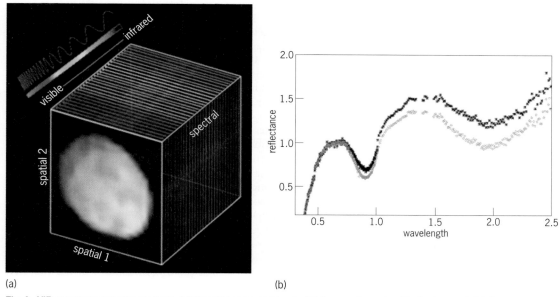

(a)   (b)

Fig. 3. VIR spectrometer observations. (*a*) Spectral cube obtained with the spectrometer. The instrument obtains a full-wavelength spectrum along a pixel-line array and builds up cubes by successive acquisitions as the spacecraft moves or by using its scan mirror. (*b*) Two examples of reflectance spectra in the visible and near-infrared range.

1996, and 1998. Finally, after the Deep Space 1 ion-propulsion demonstration mission was successfully executed under the NASA New Millennium Program, the Dawn mission was selected in 2001 for flight to Vesta and Ceres.

Spacecraft. The spacecraft (**Fig. 1**) was a joint undertaking of Orbital Sciences Corporation (Orbital) and the California Institute of Technology's Jet Propulsion Laboratory (JPL). Orbital developed the spacecraft bus, including the communication, atti-tude control, and power systems, while JPL provided deep space communication transponders and the ion-propulsion system. The Ion Propulsion System (IPS) comprises a high-power distribution system, three gimbaled ion thrusters, and a tank capable of carrying 425 kg (937 lb) of xenon for the long voyage. The thrusters operate one at a time and generate a thrust of 90 mN (0.020 lbf) by accelerating xenon ions with an electrostatic field to speeds of 40 km·s⁻¹ (25 mi·s⁻¹). Over the life of the mission,

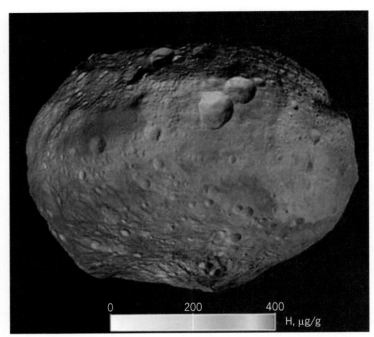

Fig. 4. Distribution of hydrogen (H) on the Vestan surface, seen by the gamma-ray and neutron spectrometer. (*Courtesy of T. Prettyman, Planetary Science Institute*)

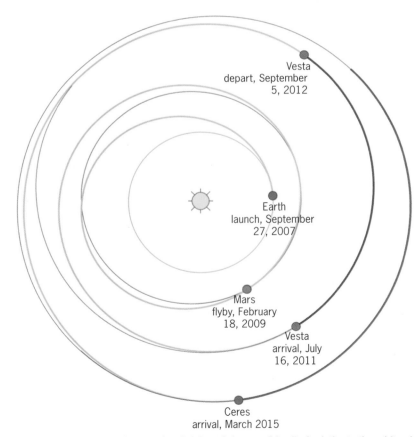

Fig. 5. Interplanetary trajectory showing *Dawn's* journey (blue line) relative to the orbits of Earth, Mars, Vesta, and Ceres, whose orbits are color-coded to match their symbols. The main mission events, including launch, the Mars flyby, the Vesta encounter, and arrival at Ceres, are indicated. The spacecraft will remain in orbit around Ceres at the end of the mission.

these engines are able to accelerate the spacecraft to more than 11 km·s⁻¹ (7 mi·s⁻¹), the same as the initial Boeing Delta-II heavy launch vehicle did in assisting *Dawn* to escape Earth's gravitational field. The spacecraft received a gravity assist from a Mars flyby that changed the inclination of its orbital plane. The IPS pushes the spacecraft out through the Sun's gravitational field to where it eventually matches orbits with first Vesta and next Ceres.

Vesta orbits the Sun in an elliptical orbit that ranges from 2.15 to 2.57 astronomical units (au). It rotates with a period of 5.34 h and has an obliquity of 27.46°. This results in a significant variation in solar illumination on the surface of Vesta in the course of a Vestan year. Vesta's orbit is inclined to the ecliptic by 7.1°, and the spacecraft's trajectory must achieve the same inclination. Ceres orbits from 2.55 to 2.99 au in an orbit inclined by 10.6° to the ecliptic. Its small obliquity results in fairly constant illumination conditions during the cerean year.

The instruments and the communication antenna are in fixed positions on the spacecraft, so that the spacecraft must optimize its pointing for communication, observations, and thrusting independently. It was built to reorient itself with either reaction wheels or hydrazine. The spacecraft was designed to store the data obtained while pointing at its targets and later turn to point its high-gain antenna and transmit the data to Earth.

Instruments. The *Dawn* spacecraft carries three scientific instruments. One of these is a framing camera provided by the Max Planck Institute for Solar System Research (Katlenburg-Lindau, Germany) in cooperation with the Institute for Planetary Research of the German Aerospace Center (Berlin, Germany). This instrument includes seven color filters tuned to help define geologic units on Vesta via color imagery. Images taken at various viewing angles allow stereographic reconstruction of the surface topography (**Fig. 2**). The second instrument is the Visible and Infrared (VIR) mapping spectrometer, spanning a wavelength range from 0.25 to 5 µm, provided by the Italian National Institute for Astrophysics (Rome, Italy), which identifies surface minerals through absorption features in the reflected light spectrum (**Fig. 3**). The third instrument is a gamma-ray and neutron spectrometer built by the Los Alamos National Laboratory. This instrument identifies the elemental composition of the surface and can infer the presence of water in the top meter of the surface through the identification of the hydrogen content (**Fig. 4**). Radiometric measurements of the precise distance between the spacecraft and the Earth allow the gravity field of the bodies to be determined accurately.

Cruise operations. The trajectory flown to date and the plans in mid-2013 are shown in **Fig. 5**. The spacecraft was launched from the Cape Canaveral Air Force Station on September 27, 2007, and flew by Mars on February 18, 2009, gaining a gravitational assist that included an inclination change. The spacecraft reached Vesta and entered orbit on July 16, 2011. It escaped Vesta's gravity field on September 5, 2012, when the incoming sunlight was grazing Vesta's north pole, then set sail on a course to Ceres to arrive in early 2015. A solar-electrically powered, ion-propelled spacecraft is a highly coupled system, so if, for example, the spacecraft cools more than expected, the additional heating required for it will allow less power to be provided to the thrusters and can affect the arrival date at the target. As a result, arrival dates always remain uncertain, unless they are arbitrarily fixed beyond the uncertainty of the estimate.

The solar arrays provided 10.3 kW at 1 au just after launch and will provide 1.3 kW at 3 au near the end of the mission. The arrays are articulated around their long axes so that they can be pointed toward the Sun to maximize power. The spacecraft can downlink data at rates from 10 bits per second to 124 kilobits per second.

Orbital operations. On approach and departure, when the spacecraft was on the lit side of Vesta and the camera and the VIR spectrometer could see all or most of the lit surface, it obtained "rotational characterizations" in which it took successive images as Vesta rotated under it. Also, smaller numbers of frames were obtained for navigational purposes. The major science gathering took place at three altitude ranges in circular polar orbits called Survey, the High Altitude Mapping Orbit (HAMO), and the Low Altitude Mapping Orbit (LAMO) [**Fig. 6**]. Two sets of observations were taken at the HAMO altitude (HAMO-1 and HAMO-2), once when the spacecraft was spiraling closer to Vesta, and later as the spacecraft was leaving Vesta, to look at areas of the surface that had been newly illuminated because the Sun had moved north. While some observations were obtained by all three instruments and the radio system for gravity in each of these three orbits, the Survey orbit was designed to optimize the VIR mapping spectrometer data. The HAMO orbit was designed to obtain global coverage with the framing camera and collect the stereo measurements needed to obtain the topography of Vesta. The LAMO orbit was designed to optimize the return from the gamma-ray and neutron detector and the gravity investigation. The VIR, framing camera, and gamma-ray and neutron data were all optimized with the instruments pointing toward the surface. The highest-quality gravity data were obtained by pointing the high-gain communication antenna toward the Earth, although data that were obtained continuously using the low-gain antennas were also of good quality.

Measurements. When a space mission is designed, a set of scientific objectives is formulated, and from those objectives, a set of "level 1" measurement objectives is derived. The mission then calculates what requirements (level 2, level 3, and so forth) are necessary to ensure that the measurements needed to meet the scientific objectives are made. The Dawn mission was quite successful at Vesta, obtaining far

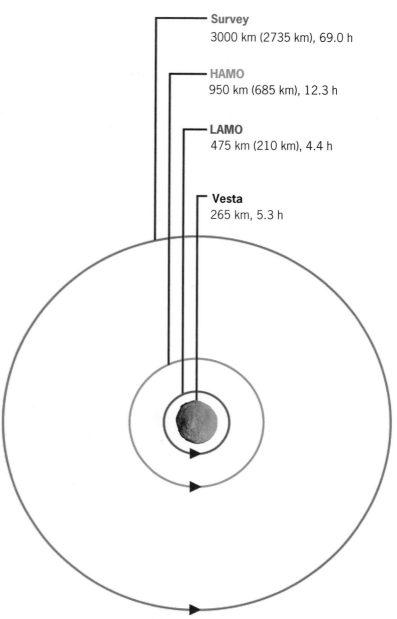

Fig. 6. Circular polar orbits used for mapping Vesta. Orbit radii are given, along with altitudes (in parentheses) and periods of revolution. The radius and rotation period of Vesta are also given. 1 km = 0.62 mi. (*Courtesy of C. T. Russell et al., Dawn completes its mission at 4 Vesta, Meteoritics Planet. Sci., 2013, in press, DOI:10.1111/maps.12091*)

more data than were required. Part of the reason for this success was the additional time that *Dawn* was able to stay at Vesta by arriving early and leaving late. This was enabled by the spacecraft systems working more efficiently than had been assumed in mission planning calculations. In total, more than 30,000 images were obtained with the framing camera, more than 18 million spectra with the VIR spectrometer, and more than 1680 h of pointed observations with the gamma-ray and neutron spectrometer. **Figure 7** shows the coverage of the surface of Vesta obtained from the VIR mapping spectrometer in the HAMO-2 orbit.

Fig. 7. Coverage of one hemisphere of the Vestan surface by the VIR mapping spectrometer in the HAMO-2 orbit.

For background information *see* ASTEROID; ASTRONOMICAL SPECTROSCOPY; CERES; COSMOCHEMISTRY; ION PROPULSION; METEORITE; PLANET; SOLAR SYSTEM; SPACE COMMUNICATIONS; SPACE PROBE; SPACECRAFT PROPULSION in the McGraw-Hill Encyclopedia of Science Technology.

Carol Anne Raymond; Christopher T. Russell
Bibliography. M. C. DeSanctis et al., The VIR spectrometer, *Space Sci. Rev.*, 163:329–369, 2011, DOI:10.1007/s11214-010-9668-5; T. H. Prettyman et al., Dawn's gamma ray and neutron detector, *Space Sci. Rev.*, 163:371–459, 2011, DOI:10.1007/s11214-011-9862-0; M. D. Rayman et al., Coupling of system resource margins through the use of electric propulsion: Implications in preparing for the Dawn mission to Ceres and Vesta, *Acta Astronautica*, 60:930–938, 2007, DOI:10.1016/j.actaastro.2006.11.012; C. T. Russell and C. A. Raymond, The Dawn Mission to Vesta and Ceres, *Space Sci. Rev.*, 163:3–23, 2011, DOI:10.1007/s11214-011-9836-2; H. Sierks et al., The Dawn framing camera, *Space Sci. Rev.*, 163:263–327, 2011, DOI:10.1007/s11214-011-9745-4; V. C. Thomas et al., The Dawn spacecraft, *Space Sci. Rev.*, 163:175–249, 2011, DOI:10.1007/s11214-011-9852-2.

Drop-in alternative jet fuel

The commercial aviation enterprise, propelled by a combination of concerns over the long-term use of petroleum-based jet fuel, and consistent with the 2008 Aviation Industry Commitment to Action on Climate Change and subsequent commitments, continues to pursue the development and commercialization of drop-in alternative jet fuel produced from sources of hydrocarbons other than petroleum. The concerns include supply and price stability, supply security, and environmental impact, all of which might be addressed by the wide-scale introduction of alternative jet fuel production. However, the environmental concern, primarily decoupling the growth of greenhouse gas emissions from the expected growth of the industry, has focused the industry's efforts on the commercialization of low-net-carbon fuels. These fuels, derived primarily from biologically created or waste-stream hydrocarbons (feedstocks), are often referred to as renewable jet fuel. Further, because these various concerns are also shared by the military and business aviation sectors, the turbine-powered aviation enterprise is now well aligned in its worldwide pursuit of drop-in renewable jet fuel development and commercialization.

Jet fuel background. Jet fuel is comprised primarily of relatively high-flash-point distillates of the kerosene type. A wide range of hydrocarbon molecules of various chain lengths and types are present in the fuel, from C_8 to C_{16} chains, and include normal, branched (iso-), and cyclic paraffins, as well as aromatics (**Fig. 1**).

The industry's governing jet fuel specifications [for example, ASTM D1655 (*Standard Specification for Aviation Turbine Fuels*) and MIL-STD 91-91] mandate both physical and performance (or fit-for-use) attributes that must be exhibited by the fuel, as opposed to mandating a specific composition. The **table** gives some examples of such specifications of physical attributes.

Mandating attributes rather than specific compositions allows for flexibility on the part of producers with regard to the type of petroleum used to feed a refinery, as well as the methodologies used in refining (preventing barriers to entry for new producers or production techniques). Jet fuel also typically contains several additives (for example, antioxidants, metal deactivator, electrical conductivity additive, leak detection additive, biocides, and icing inhibitor) to enhance aviation usability and safety. This blend of constituents delivers the levels of performance and safety demanded by the aviation enterprise.

Several specifications exist for specialized variants of jet fuel for use in specific sectors or regions, defining unique criteria such as enhanced freeze point and flash point, levels of static inhibitor, and whether the fuel can have a wider cut of distillates. The fuels are typically referenced by their own familiar names (for example, Jet A, Jet A-1, Jet B, JP-n, and TS-n), but they all originate from kerosene distillates produced from the refining of petroleum, and are governed by

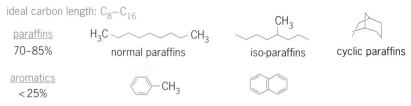

Fig. 1. Representative kerosene molecules: examples and typical fractions.

performance-based specifications approved by the industry. The work on developing renewable jet fuel can apply to any of the jet fuel types.

The aviation enterprise has optimized the performance of aircraft and engines around the use of jet fuel over the last 60 or more years. Jet fuel delivers both the energy density (mass and volumetric) necessary for efficient aircraft design as well as numerous other physical attributes that enable the safety and operability of aircraft.

Concept of drop-in replacements. As a result of these considerations, when the industry began to consider the production of fuels derived from hydrocarbon sources other than petroleum—that is, synthetic fuels—several issues had to be addressed. The entire industry recognized that it was not feasible to introduce a new distinct type of fuel that differed in the overall characteristics of existing jet fuel. Such an approach would lead to prohibitive expenditures being required in equipment (for example, fleet retrofit or replacement) and infrastructure (pipelines, storage, and hydrant systems). This quickly led to the concept of requiring any such fuel to be a "drop-in" fuel. That is, these synthetic fuels had to exhibit physical and performance attributes "essentially identical" to those of jet fuel. As such, they cannot contain alcohols, oxygen, or water—criteria that eliminate the possibility of using

Some physical requirements of aviation turbine fuels

Quality/property	Limitation	Jet A or Jet A-1	ASTM test method
COMPOSITION			
Acidity, total mg KOH/g	Max	0.10	
Aromatics, vol %	Max	26.5	
VOLATILITY			
Distillation temperature, °C			
10% recovered, temperature (T10)	Max	205	
Final boiling point, temperature	Max	300	
Flash point, °C	Min	38	
Density at 15°C, kg/m³		775–840	
FLUIDITY			
Freezing point, °C	Max	−40 Jet A	
	Max	−47 Jet A-1	
Viscosity, −20°C, mm²/s	Max	8.0	
COMBUSTION			
Net heat of combustion, MJ/kg	Min	42.8	
THERMAL STABILITY			
JFTOT* (2.5 h at control temperature)			
Temperature, °C	Min	260	
CONTAMINANTS			
Existent gum, mg/100 mL	Max	7	

*JFTOT = jet fuel thermal oxidation tester.

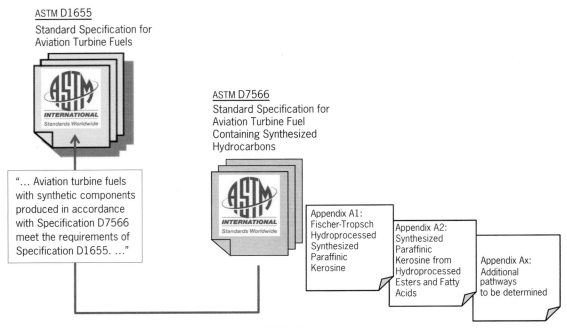

ASTM D1655
Standard Specification for
Aviation Turbine Fuels

ASTM D7566
Standard Specification for
Aviation Turbine Fuel
Containing Synthesized
Hydrocarbons

"… Aviation turbine fuels
with synthetic components
produced in accordance
with Specification D7566
meet the requirements of
Specification D1655. …"

Appendix A1:
Fischer-Tropsch
Hydroprocessed
Synthesized
Paraffinic
Kerosine

Appendix A2:
Synthesized
Paraffinic
Kerosine from
Hydroprocessed
Esters and Fatty
Acids

Appendix Ax:
Additional
pathways
to be determined

Fig. 2. Representative relationship of ASTM D1655 and ASTM D7566.

first-generation biofuels, as are used in other transportation modes. Further, the fuels must be fully miscible or fungible with current delivery and storage systems, and exhibit no settling or dissociative properties. In addition, new safeguards must be established to ensure that contamination by certain chemicals (that do not exist in petroleum and its supply chain but that could exist in nonpetroleum feedstocks) could not occur. Even given these criteria, technologists have shown that such fuels can be viably synthesized from feedstocks other than fossil sources.

The certification community subsequently developed two new specifications to govern the properties of proposed synthetic fuels:

1. ASTM D4054: *Standard Practice for Qualification and Approval of New Aviation Turbine Fuels and Fuel Additives*

2. ASTM D7566: *Standard Specification for Aviation Turbine Fuel Containing Synthesized Hydrocarbons*

In addition, language was added to ASTM D1655 that would allow the introduction of acceptable synthetic fuels, with additional safeguards and testing requirements, without impacting current producers of petroleum-based D1655 fuels (**Fig. 2**).

ASTM D7566 is formatted to enable the addition of successive synthetic production pathways, with any commensurate specification criteria, as appendices to the specification. At its creation, D7566 included Appendix A1, which enables the inclusion of blends of synthesized paraffinic kerosene from Fischer-Tropsch hydroprocessing of syngas (FT-SPK). This appendix allows FT-SPK to be produced from a broad range of feedstocks including coal, natural gas, biomass (and combinations thereof), as well as syngas streams originating from other industrial processes. In July 2011, D7566 saw the addition of Appendix A2, which enables the inclusion of blends of synthesized paraffinic kerosene from hydroprocessed esters and fatty acids (HEFA-SPK). This appendix allows HEFA-SPK to be produced from triglycerides or lipids that are produced by a broad range of plants, and as exist in animal fats. Since both of these fuel types lack the full range of molecules seen in petroleum-derived kerosene, they are at present limited to 50% maximum blend levels with D1655 fuels. In the case of HEFA-SPK, these fuels have been shown in some cases to deliver net greenhouse gas reduction in excess of 80% on a life-cycle basis, as compared to petroleum fuels, by virtue of the recycling of atmospheric CO_2 that occurs with the growth of the plant. Hence these bio-based fuels, and others like them that are being developed, hold the promise of enabling the net carbon reductions of interest to the aviation enterprise.

Achieving new specification approval. ASTM D4054, and documentation by the Commercial Aviation Alternative Fuels Initiative (CAAFI) entitled *Path to Alternative Jet Fuel Readiness* and *Fuel Readiness Level*, describe the process via which new production pathways can be added to ASTM D7566 as approved synthetic fuel types. The approval process is not trivial, and it can be lengthy, depending on several factors associated with the proposed technology and feedstocks. The steps are very briefly summarized as follows:

1. The prospective producer has modest fuel quantities tested to ensure that physical properties can be achieved, and that fit-for-use properties are likely to be achieved.

2. Testing of both neat and blended fuels are independently repeated and confirmed, and additional chemical characterization tests are completed.

3. The prospective producer engages with ASTM International Committee D.02, Petroleum and Lubricants, Subcommittee J, to initiate an evaluation process.

4. ASTM forms a formal task force which will have primary responsibility for overseeing and guiding the evaluation process.

5. Data are acquired through fuel, engine, component, and rig testing sufficient to address technical concerns of the user community; results are compiled into the "Research Report."

6. Initial balloting occurs at the subcommittee level when the Research Report and proposed specification are deemed ready for consideration by the task force. ASTM allows a period for comments and review. Comments are addressed to assuage concerns expressed (with additional data generation or research if required). These may be discussed and voted on at the semiannual ASTM meeting.

7. Final balloting at the committee level occurs when all subcommittee-level comments have been addressed. Ballots are considered passed with a unanimous affirmative vote, or when negative votes are withdrawn or overruled (as nonpersuasive) by the committee or subcommittee members. Upon passage of the ballot, ASTM adds the new fuel to the D7566 standard as a new appendix.

New synthetic production pathways. What the aviation enterprise and potential renewable jet fuel suppliers have "rediscovered" over the past decade is that hydrocarbons required for suitable jet fuel can be produced synthetically from a wide range of feedstocks or waste streams containing natural hydrocarbons (oils, sugars and starches, cellulose, hemicellulose, and lignin). Further, such production can occur using a broad range of natural and industrial processes, governed by standard biological and thermochemical practices, to "repurpose" hydrocarbons from an initial natural form to ones suitable for jet fuel. Numerous companies and entrepreneurs have announced interest in, or intentions of, producing renewable jet fuel blending components for the industry, and are engaged with CAAFI work teams to advance their interests. The following new pathways are currently undergoing evaluation by ASTM International for future incorporation into D7566:

1. Fischer-Tropsch synthetic kerosene with aromatics (FT-SKA) is a proposed modification of the FT-SPK process that produces a more balanced jet fuel blending component that contains aromatics in addition to the paraffins. This could potentially lead to increasing the blending limitation for FT-SKA versus FT-SPK.

2. Hydroprocessed depolymerized cellulosic jet (HDCJ) is produced from cellulosic feedstock such as forestry waste using a catalytically enhanced pyrolysis process. Unlike HEFA-SPK and FT-SPK, the HDCJ blending component may contain high levels of aromatics and is denser than conventional jet fuel. Consequently, it must also be blended to meet maximum density and aromatic requirements.

3. Alcohol-to-jet (ATJ) production pathways are also under evaluation. These pathways rely on the dehydration of alcohol to olefins, followed by oligomerization and fractionation to produce jet fuel blending components. Evaluations are underway for ATJ production both with and without aromatic content.

4. Direct sugar to hydrocarbon (DSHC) is a pathway that utilizes modified yeast to directly produce a long-chain hydrocarbon (rather than ethanol as in a standard distillation process) from a sugar feedstock.

5. Catalytic hydrothermolysis (CH) is a second pathway under evaluation that uses plant oils and animal fats as a feedstock. CH uses water as a catalyst to convert these bio-oils to hydrocarbon chain lengths in the kerosene range.

Other processes being proposed and evaluated include APR-SKA (using aqueous phase reforming), and "green crude" coprocessing in petroleum refineries of oils produced via pyrolysis or similar deconstruction processes.

CAAFI anticipates that approvals of the above pathways should start occurring in 2014 and continue at a regular pace for the next several years. At that point, fuels will technically be able to be produced by a very broad range of processes, from a very broad range of feedstocks. This should enable the local production of sustainable (environmental, social, and economical) renewable jet fuel consistent with local needs (predicated on local socioeconomic, geopolitical, and techno-agronomic conditions, coupled with strategic investments on the part of local entities).

Looking forward. At present, only modest quantities of approved renewable jet fuel are in production. This is the result of several factors, including immaturity of the feedstock supply chains, risk, lack of facilities or investment, and policies and other elements that skew markets and production toward other products. The next major milestone this nascent industry has adopted is to reach commercial-scale production targets of sustainable renewable jet fuel at reasonable cost, and enable the aviation enterprise to more readily achieve environmental goals. The U.S. Federal Aviation Administration (FAA) has an aspirational goal of 10^9 gallons (3.8×10^9 L) of renewable jet fuel usage per year by 2018. The U.S. Navy and U.S. Air Force have a combined similar target of about 10^9 gal of renewable jet fuel per year by the end of this decade.

In order to reach these ambitious goals, the entire aviation supply chain, including airlines, airports, manufacturers, fuel producers, and government agencies, are working through user and advocacy groups [including CAAFI, Sustainable Aviation Fuel Users Group (SAFUG), Brazilian Alliance for Aviation Biofuels (ABRABA), Aviation Initiative for Renewable Energy in Germany e.V. (AIREG), and Australian Initiative for Sustainable Aviation Fuels (AISAF)], working-group projects and initiatives [including Sustainable Aviation Fuel Northwest (SAFNW), Midwest Aviation Sustainable Biofuels Initiative (MASBI), Sustainable Aviation Biofuels for Brazil (SABB), Farm-to-Fly, and F2F2 (a continuation and expansion of Farm-to-Fly announced in April

2013)], and their own internal programs, in a concentrated effort, to identify the major challenges and execute strategies to facilitate commercial-scale deployment of alternative fuel production.

For background information *see* AIRCRAFT FUEL; AROMATIC HYDROCARBON; BIOMASS; CELLULOSE; COAL GASIFICATION; FISCHER-TROPSCH PROCESS; HEMICELLULOSE; KEROSINE; LIGNIN; PYROLYSIS; RENEWABLE RESOURCES; SYNTHETIC FUEL in the McGraw-Hill Encyclopedia of Science & Technology.

Steven Csonka

Bibliography. ASTM International, *Standard Practice for Qualification and Approval of New Aviation Turbine Fuels and Fuel Additives*, ASTM D4054-09, 2009; ASTM International, *Standard Specification for Aviation Turbine Fuel Containing Synthesized Hydrocarbons*, ASTM D7566, biannually; ASTM International, *Standard Specification for Aviation Turbine Fuels*, ASTM, D1655, annually.

Earliest evidence of bilaterians

Life has existed on Earth for almost 4 billion years, but most major groups of animals only appear in the fossil record approximately 542 million years ago (MYA) in a relatively short period of time known as the Cambrian explosion of life. During much of the Precambrian, living organisms were small, unicellular, and comparably simple. In this context, the Ediacaran Period (630–542 MYA) is arguably one of the most critical periods in evolutionary history. Complex animals with bilateral symmetry (that is, with a front end and a back end, as well as an up side and a down side) probably emerged in the Ediacaran, but the timing of their appearance and diversification is still a matter of debate. A major factor that negatively affects our understanding of Ediacaran life is that the first animals lacked skeletons or any external hard parts; thus, they had a very low preservation potential. As such, fossilized tracks and trails (known as ichnofossils or trace fossils) provide important evidence of the first bilaterians.

Molecular clock analyses, which predict the divergence times of taxa by comparing molecular data and fossil constraints, give dates ranging from 900–1100 MYA to 580 MYA for the emergence of stem-group bilaterians, but no definite bilaterian fossils had previously been found within this broad time interval. Putative microscopic bilaterian fossils from the Doushantuo Formation in China are probably about 580 million years old in age, but their attribution to bilaterians is controversial. Similarly, possible burrows estimated as 2.1 billion years old have been described, but the only universally accepted evidence for bilaterians comes from shallow-marine trace fossils in Russia that are slightly older than 555 million years old. However, a new discovery in Uruguay provides indisputable evidence for bilaterian burrows from shallow-water sediments that are at least 30 million years older than any previously reported trace fossils. Importantly, this new evidence has indicated that the animals likely evolved even earlier in Earth's history.

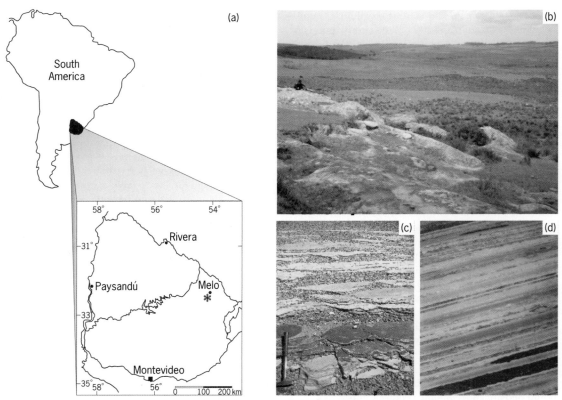

Fig. 1. (*a*) Map showing the location of the Tacuarí trace fossils. The asterisk indicates the fossil locality. (*b*) General view of the area. (*c*) Outcrop of the Tacuarí Formation showing the fine-grained strata where the trace fossils typically occur. (*d*) Close-up view of the strata shown in panel *c*. Note the thin laminated gray siltstones alternating with reddish sandy layers.

Geological setting and age. The oldest bilaterian trace fossils come from the Tacuarí Formation in east-central Uruguay (**Fig. 1**). The Tacuarí Formation comprises sedimentary rocks that were deposited by glaciers in a marine setting. The rocks were deposited as horizontal layers on the sea bottom. Sediment (for example, clays, sand grains, and gravel) was transported to the place of deposition by water and ice. Over long periods of time, these layers stacked into a thick sedimentary pile. Later, these layers were uplifted, deformed, and exposed as sedimentary strata at the surface as a result of plate tectonic movements (**Fig. 2**).

During sedimentation, tiny wormlike animals [maximum length: 1.5 cm (0.6 in.)] crawled over the soft sediment at the bottom of this ancient sea and left behind sinuous trails. These trails became buried and were fossilized as trace fossils. The trace fossils occur along bedding planes and were probably made by animals foraging in the wet sediment to obtain food (that is, organic matter). The bulk of the organic matter in the sea bottom was likely concentrated within microbial mats (multilayered structures of microorganisms) and also derived from the photosynthesis of phytoplankton organisms in the overlying, photic surface layers of the ocean. The preservation of the trace fossils was favored because of the depositional environment. The traces were preserved in muddy layers during periods of clay–silt sedimentation, which is typically associated with

calm conditions. Under these conditions, the morphologic details of traces were preserved in very fine detail when they became covered with sediment.

The age of the Tacuarí Formation is well constrained by zircon uranium–lead (U–Pb) ages from granitic dykes [discordant sheetlike bodies of magma (molten rock) cutting vertically, or almost vertically, through and across strata] that were injected into the rocks after the sediment was deposited (**Fig. 3**). Granites are common, coarse-grained igneous rocks formed by the slow cooling of magma located beneath the Earth's surface. Granites contain minerals such as quartz, feldspar, mica, amphibole, and tiny crystals of zircon. Zircon is a mineral that has zirconium (Zr), silicon (Si), and oxygen (O) in its crystalline structure. Trace amounts of uranium (U) and thorium (Th) are also trapped in the crystal before the magma solidifies. However, the uranium undergoes radioactive decay through a series of steps to become a stable form of lead (Pb). Being trapped in the crystal, Pb atoms build up in concentration with time. This makes the zircon especially valuable for dating rocks by simply calculating the amount of atomic decay of the radiogenic elements in the sample—that is, the U–Pb ratio. By dating the cross-cutting granite with the zircons that it contained, a minimum age of 585 ($\pm$3) million years old has been established for the traces. Similarly, by dating detrital (worn away) zircons located in the sedimentary rocks hosting the trace fossils, and which come from

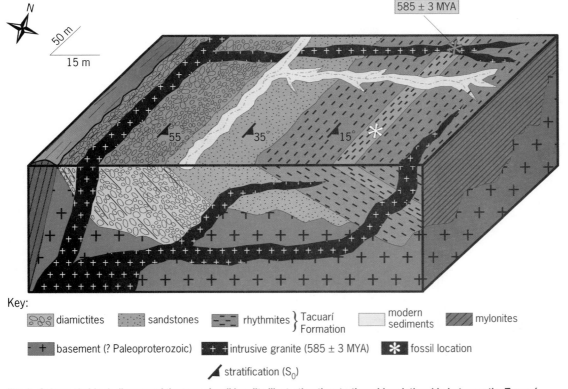

Fig. 2. Schematic block diagram of the trace fossil locality illustrating the stratigraphic relationship between the Tacuarí strata and the intrusive granite. The Tacuarí strata were initially deposited horizontally on the seafloor (on top of the red granite), and then were subsequently deformed (tilted and folded) and uplifted. Later, granite (black color in the figure) forced its way (intruded) into the whole sedimentary pile, which caused local metamorphic changes as a result of the emplacement temperature.

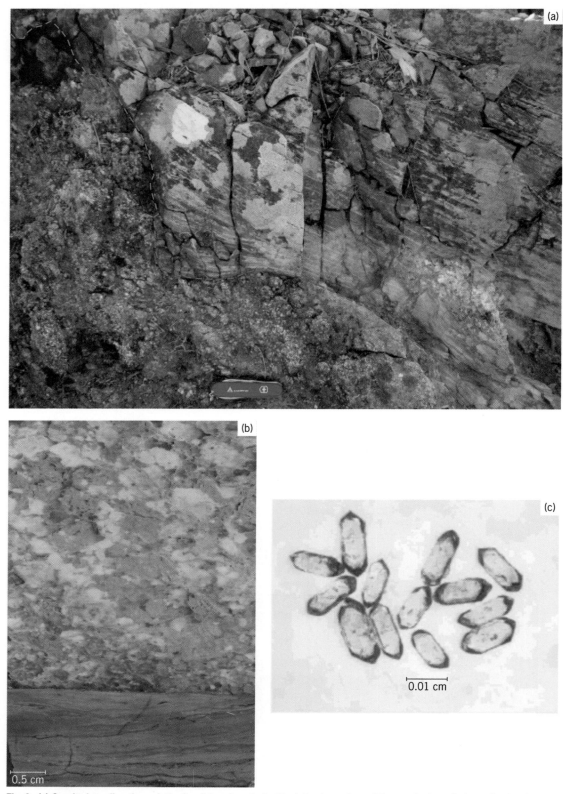

Fig. 3. (*a*) Granite intruding through the fossil-bearing strata. The intrusive nature of the granite is well shown by the sharp and discordant (perpendicular) contact between the granite and the sedimentary layers. (*b*) Close-up view from the granite and sedimentary strata contact. Note the "chilled" margin at the edge of the granite, in contact with the preexisting (country) rock; this occurs because of a faster cooling relative to the interior of the granite body (pink crystals: feldspar; light-gray crystals: quartz). (*c*) Zircon crystals from the intrusive granite (*photo courtesy of Larry M. Heaman*). These zircons were dated by several modern analytical techniques (see text for explanation).

the erosion of (older) source rocks, it was possible to place constraints on the maximum depositional age of these rocks at 600 ± 9 million years old.

Description and interpretation of the burrows. Trace fossils from the Tacuarí Formation are preserved on bedding planes in two ways (**Fig. 4**). The first type of preservation is as curving paired grooves (called a bilateral furrow), locally containing backfill, which is sediment that the animal pushed behind itself. When present, the backfill comprises very small, ovate sediment piles, and the long axes of these are oriented transverse to the burrow length. The second style of preservation is as irregular to massively filled burrows that generally exhibit minor positive relief from the lamination surfaces. Both types of burrows are narrow [2-3 mm (0.08-0.12 in.)] and unbranched, and some of the collected specimens pass laterally from one form to the other along the length of the burrow. The trace fossils commonly have raised lateral ridges adjacent to the burrow margins. The view from above the bedding plane reveals that the burrows curve back and forth, and that there are also abrupt changes in the curve radius, accompanied by slight lateral jumps. Three of the specimens show the burrow abruptly leaving the plane of preservation and reappearing 4-10 mm (0.16-0.4 in.) away.

The animals are not present with their traces; thus, it is difficult to determine what type of animal made these trace fossils. However, certain physical characteristics reveal many aspects of the animal's behavior and morphology. For instance, well-preserved bilateral furrows represent the bottom of the burrow. Irregularly and massively filled trace fossils suggest that the burrow was emplaced (positioned) within sediment, remained partially open as a tunnel, and then collapsed. Because of the shallow occurrence of these trace fossils within the sediment, it is likely that the animal grazed on organic material [possibly relict (remnant) biomat material] situated between sedimentary laminae (thin layers). Regularly curving trails additionally suggest that the trace makers were engaged in rudimentary searching for patchy food resources using a search pattern that improved the likelihood of finding food. As such, these trails represent early grazing traces. The presence of raised lateral ridges and the preservation of a beaded backfill show that the animal moved by expanding and extending its body and pushing against the sediment. The spacing of the backfilled beads reveals ponderous forward movement of less than 0.5 mm (0.02 in.) per wavelike muscular contraction. Serial indentations along the burrow margin have a similar spacing. The indents further show that the trace maker had some sort of prehensile "feet" and could extend those parts into the sediment to assist its motility. Abrupt changes in the meander radius with abrupt lateral jogs further suggest that the animal, although possibly elongate, did not exceed 1 cm (0.4 in.) in length. The bilateral furrow is indicative of the bilateral symmetry of the trace maker. When coupled

Fig. 4. Images of the Tacuarí trace fossils: Simple, sinusoidal (sine curve–shaped), and unbranched feeding trails preserved and oriented parallel to the silty–sandy layers (*a–d*).

with the mode of locomotion, this strongly points to an early bilaterian trace maker.

The combination of features seen in the Uruguay trace fossils are consistent only with those produced by bilaterian eumetazoans (the multicellular animals, except for the sponges, comprising the major portion of the animal kingdom). Crucially, these burrows extend the fossil record of bilaterian eumetazoans between 30 and 50 million years backward to approximately 585–600 MYA, which is a time coincident with the youngest ages for the appearance of bilaterians predicted by the molecular clock analyses.

For background information *see* ANIMAL EVOLUTION; ANIMAL KINGDOM; ANIMAL SYMMETRY; BILATERIA; CAMBRIAN; DEPOSITIONAL SYSTEMS AND ENVIRONMENTS; EDIACARAN BIOTA; FOSSIL; MARINE SEDIMENTS; PALEONTOLOGY; ROCK AGE DETERMINATION; SEDIMENTOLOGY; TRACE FOSSILS in the McGraw-Hill Encyclopedia of Science & Technology.

Ernesto Pecoits; Kurt O. Konhauser;
Natalie R. Aubet; Murray K. Gingras

Bibliography. M. Fedonkin et al., *The Rise of Animals: Evolution and Diversification of the Kingdom Animalia*, The Johns Hopkins University Press, Baltimore, MD, 2007; E. Pecoits et al., Bilaterian burrows and grazing behavior at >585 million years ago, *Science*, 336:1693–1696, 2012, DOI:10.1126/science.1216295.

Ecodriving

Ecodriving is a collection of driving behaviors and maintenance practices that can improve the fuel efficiency of driving. As a practice, ecodriving has gained attention among automakers, policy makers, and researchers because it costs little or nothing to implement and it can be applied to almost any passenger or freight vehicle immediately. Common ecodriving practices, such as accelerating slowly, braking gradually, and keeping tires properly inflated have been known for decades. Ecodriving offers numerous benefits, including fuel cost savings, fuel consumption and greenhouse-gas (GHG) reductions, greater safety and comfort, and less noise pollution. However, only recently, with concerns about increases in gasoline prices, foreign oil dependence, and climate change have these practices been viewed in a collective fashion to improve fuel economy. Studies in Europe, Japan, and the United States over the past 15 years report fuel-economy savings averaging 10–15%, depending on the ecodriving information conveyed and the study length. A core challenge of ecodriving is conveying the necessary information to the driver such that the practices are implemented appropriately and consistently.

There are two methods of conveying ecodriving information to drivers: (1) static ecodriving feedback and (2) dynamic ecodriving feedback. A static ecodriving intervention is simply the provision of information, such as a website, brochure, or classroom training program. With such interventions, drivers are taught about ecodriving beforehand, and they are not given any new information during or after their trips.

Technological advances have given rise to dynamic ecodriving feedback, which provides information directly to the driver during vehicle operation. Dynamic feedback requires an in-vehicle device that communicates regularly to the driver, usually as a visual interface embedded in or placed on the dashboard. In its most basic form, the interface reports the instantaneous fuel economy to the driver in numerical or graphical form, which allows the driver to gradually learn which behaviors result in better fuel economy. Advanced interfaces are under development that provide more directed feedback, such as accelerator-peddle pushback and instructions on how to drive to improve fuel efficiency in real time. Several automakers have developed original equipment manufacturer (OEM) dynamic ecodriving feedback systems. Initially, they were marketed in Europe and Japan. Recently, fuel-economy feedback information has become more widely available in vehicles sold throughout North America. Aftermarket devices are generally built to attach to a diagnostic port on the vehicle. They read real-time information reported to that port and process it into ecodriving feedback information for the driver. In the United States, the standard port to which such devices are attached is the on-board diagnostics (OBD-II) port, but other countries can have different standard ports. Both OEM and aftermarket systems use in-vehicle sensors to monitor accelerator use, engine and transmission efficiency, and speed to provide real-time information to drivers on average fuel economy and allow the driver to adjust driving behavior based on this feedback. Some of these systems go beyond individual monitoring and rank individual performance with those of others on the same system in social media forums, providing an incentive to compete with other motorists to engage in fuel-saving driving behavior. It is up to the driver to use this information to drive more efficiently or not. Drivers responding to the feedback can then teach themselves more efficient driving behaviors.

Overall, static ecodriving feedback, in the form of a website or brochure, is very low cost and simply informs individuals about how to drive more fuel efficiently. It is also effective at describing maintenance practices, which can maintain or improve fuel economy. Dynamic ecodriving feedback is more costly because it requires new technology that can process real-time driving situations and give the driver meaningful instruction. This more advanced feedback is given precisely when the driver needs it and is continuous over time.

Passenger-vehicle ecodriving strategies. Static ecodriving education programs convey to drivers a series of simple rules to maximize the fuel economy of existing cars while minimizing carbon emissions. The basic principles of ecodriving include anticipating changes in traffic, maintaining the vehicle properly, and minimizing brake use. The following are key driving and maintenance practices that educational programs promote:

1. Driving at the speed limit

2. Accelerating smoothly and coasting to stops and parking spots

3. Idling for no more than 30 s

4. Using the air conditioner rather than opening windows at speeds over 40 mi/h

5. Keeping tires inflated to the manufacturer's specifications

6. Using the lowest weight oil to improve kinematic viscosity

7. Changing air filters as recommended by the manufacturer

8. Avoiding unnecessary weight

9. Reducing aerodynamic drag by removing bike racks and roof racks.

Freight-vehicle ecodriving strategies. While many ecodriving strategies for passenger vehicles can be similarly applied to freight vehicles, certain practices are emphasized for truck drivers and fleet managers. A 2012 University of California, Berkeley, study conducted by the authors in conjunction with the California Air Resources Board helped to develop driving, maintenance, and additional practices for truck drivers and fleet managers for reducing fuel consumption. The following are some key practices.

Speed management. Reducing speed by just 5–10 mi/h (8–16 km/h) can improve truck fuel economy by 12% or more. Truckers are advised to maintain a steady highway speed, reducing the need for frequent acceleration and braking, thereby reducing fuel consumption. Fleet managers can govern top speeds through the engine control module (ECM). Many fleets choose to limit their drivers to a top speed of 60–65 mph (97–105 km/h).

Progressive shifting. Progressive shifting burns less fuel and prevents unnecessary wear on the engine. There are two ways to practice progressive shifting: (1) manually monitoring the tachometer by shifting gears at the minimum revolutions per minute (RPM) required to pick up the next gear or (2) activating the progressive shifting setting in the truck's computer, if available, to indicate when to shift gears.

Tires. Low tire pressure forces the engine to work harder, increasing fuel consumption and shortening the life of the tires. Tires that are properly inflated can reduce fuel consumption by 3–4%. Drivers should check the tires at least once per week using a tire pressure gauge. The proper tire inflation pressure is available on the vehicle's door-post sticker and in the owner's manual. Fleet managers can consider installing automatic tire inflation (ATI) systems, which monitor and adjust air pressure in tires automatically. They can also consider purchasing low-rolling resistance (LRR) tires, which can save 1.5–3% on fuel consumption. Fleets can further improve their tractor tire efficiency by converting to wide-base tires. Replacing the eight rear-axle tractor tires with four wide-base tires further improves tire-rolling efficiency and reduces the tractor weight by 400 lb (180 kg). Similar savings can also be achieved on trailer tires.

Aerodynamics. Aerodynamic technologies and retrofits can dramatically improve truck fuel efficiency. For flatbed trucks, objects should be packed tightly to avoid having large gaps, which can catch the wind. Any irregularly shaped objects should be covered with a tarp to minimize drag. Drivers and managers can consider installing aerodynamic fittings, such as rear fairings, front gap fairings, and side skirts. These fittings modify the air flows around the truck in a way that reduces drag. A combination of these can reduce fuel use by 10%. When purchasing a new tractor, fleets can consider U.S. Environmental Protection Agency (EPA) SmartWay certified models. All major truck manufacturers produce a SmartWay tractor model, which provides significantly improved fuel efficiency, in contrast to other models.

Idling control. Unnecessary idling leads to higher fuel and maintenance costs, serious health issues, and increased GHG emissions. One hour of idling burns about 1 gal (3.8 L) of diesel fuel and wears down the engine about the same as 7 mi (11 km) of driving. Reducing unnecessary idling can lead to significant cost savings. Drivers should turn off the engine when the vehicle is not in motion and follow the manufacturer's minimum recommendations for warm-up and cool-down times. During extended stays in the cab, drivers can use more efficient heating and air conditioning units available at certain truck stops.

Ecodriving programs and policies. Many countries have launched national ecodriving campaigns to educate and train individuals to drive more efficiently as a means of reducing GHG emissions and meeting emission-reduction targets. The methods used for education vary among countries. Generally, all programs include training, outreach, and educational components. Many also employ competitions and incentives to encourage the use of ecodriving techniques. The majority of the existing programs are located in Europe, with fewer programs in Asia and North America.

In the United States, the Alliance of Automobile Manufacturers launched EcoDrivingUSA™, a nationwide effort to increase fuel savings while reducing fuel consumption and emissions. The campaign began in 2008 with the support of the governors of California and Colorado, and it later expanded to include 16 more states and territories. However, due to budget constraints, the EcoDrivingUSA website and program was discontinued in Spring 2012. Several state departments of transportation have begun ecodriving campaigns. The North Carolina Department of Transportation began Drive Green, Save Green in April 2010, with a website of tips and instructional videos. The I-95 Corridor Coalition began its campaign in May 2011, modeled after Drive Green, Save Green. Moreover, U.S. cities have taken on the role of promoting fuel efficiency, including Denver's Driving Change program and New York City's anti-idling campaign Green NYC—Turn It Off.

Canada also has a comprehensive national eco-driving initiative, called ecoENERGY. The program is composed of two components: ecoENERGY for Personal Vehicles and ecoENERGY for Fleets. ecoENERGY for Personal Vehicles provides a variety of teaching tools, including online resources, publications, and driver tips, as part of the driver education program. ecoENERGY for Fleets primarily focuses on ecodriving for trucks and buses.

Outlook. Ecodriving continues to be a cost-effective method for curbing fuel consumption and GHG emissions, as research and programs continue to proliferate. Public education and outreach campaigns have been integral to ecodriving efforts in Europe for over a decade. At present, drivers, fleet operators, and policy makers have a growing body of knowledge and emerging technologies to assist in providing educational programs, driver training, and dynamic feedback devices for passenger and freight vehicles.

The future of ecodriving is dynamic interventions, which provide real-time, in-vehicle feedback that coaches individuals continuously while driving. Technologies that provide drivers with visual, audio, and tactile information or instruction will offer more comprehensive feedback. In the longer term, ecodriving will be coupled with connected vehicle technology, which will maximize the collective fuel efficiency of all vehicles on the road. Connected vehicles use a number of wireless technologies to communicate with other vehicles, the infrastructure, and the Internet or cloud. They include autonomous (driverless) and non-autonomous vehicle technologies that can improve fuel efficiency, safety, and mobility by providing real-time connectivity across the transportation system. The future of ecodriving will also enable more consistent and reliable measurement of fuel savings and emission reductions, which can ultimately be integrated into vehicle and climate policy.

For background information *see* AERODYNAMICS; AUTOMOBILE; BUS; CLIMATE MODIFICATION; CLOUD COMPUTING; TRANSPORTATION ENGINEERING; TRUCK in the McGraw-Hill Encyclopedia of Science & Technology.

Susan Shaheen; Elliot Martin; Nelson Chan
Bibliography. E. W. Martin et al., Dynamic ecodriving in Northern California: A study of survey and vehicle operations data from an ecodriving feedback device, *Proceedings from the Transportation Research Board 92nd Annual Meeting: TRB 92nd Annual Meeting Compendium of Papers*, Washington, DC, 2013; E. W. Martin, N. D. Chan, and S. A. Shaheen, How public education on ecodriving can reduce both fuel use and greenhouse gas emissions, *Trans. Res. Rec.*, 2287:163–173, 2012, DOI:10.3141/2287-20; S. A. Shaheen, E. W. Martin, and R. S. Finson, *Ecodriving and carbon footprinting: Understanding how public education can reduce greenhouse gas emissions and fuel use*, MTI Rep. 11-11, Mineta Transportation Institute, San Jose, CA, 2012.

Ecohydrology

Ecosystems are complex structures whose form and function depend on many interrelated links between climate, vegetation, soil, and water. Ecohydrology seeks to understand these linkages by determining how hydrological processes influence the distribution, structure, and function of plant communities, and how feedbacks from plant communities, in turn, affect hydrological processes. Implicit in ecohydrology is the recognition that vegetation, water, soil, and nutrients are intimately coupled, and this is true in both natural and human-dominated systems. While ecohydrology is centered at the interface of ecology and hydrology, in practice, it is much broader, and incorporates biogeochemistry and soil-related processes. Ecohydrology thus facilitates the study of environmental systems in an integrated and holistic way, which is necessary to (1) predict how systems will respond to changes in climate and land use, and how feedbacks will in turn modify climate, and (2) determine how to best manage water-dependent ecosystems for the provision of freshwater resources and associated ecosystem services. The relatively recent focus on ecohydrology is founded on longer-term research trends in hydrology, ecology, biogeochemistry, and geomorphology, which have looked at interactions between vegetation and the water cycle as primary controls on ecosystems structure. An ecohydrological approach, however, enables exploration of reciprocal interactions, which would otherwise not be possible.

Ecohydrology: the water balance, vegetation, and soil. Peter Eagleson, one of the pioneers of ecohydrology, investigated the interaction of hydrology, vegetation, and soil properties in water-limited systems. His central focus was on soil moisture, which is one of the key components of the water balance, and plants, which are a critical component of terrestrial ecosystems. Soil moisture remains at the heart of ecohydrology, but there has been increased recognition of the significance of other parts of the water balance in influencing the structure and function of ecosystems. The water balance is a key determinant of the composition, distribution, and productivity of vegetation, and in turn, the composition and distribution of plant communities regulate the partitioning of water among the different components of the water balance. The water balance can be described as the difference between water inputs (precipitation, infiltration, and seepage) and water outputs (evapotranspiration, runoff, and drainage). A simplified representation of the water balance relates the major hydrologic fluxes as shown in the equation,

$$P = Q + ET + \Delta S$$

where P is precipitation, Q is runoff, ET is evapotranspiration, and ΔS is change in storage of water. Vegetation alters the partitioning of water between different parts of the water balance in multiple ways. The spatial distribution and cover of plants and the shape and size of their crown and root systems determine the extraction of moisture and nutrients from the soil. Vertical exchanges of momentum, mass, and energy between the canopy and the atmosphere determine the partitioning of water losses between evaporation and transpiration. The size and shape of the canopy, along with root characteristics, also affect surface topography through sheltering the soil surface from the erosive force of raindrops and by binding soil together, thus increasing its resistance to erosion. It is therefore common for raised microtopography in the vicinity of vegetation, which in turn, governs surface runoff pathways and the characteristics of water redistribution and water losses from the system as runoff. The partitioning of water into different components of the water budget varies greatly across different climatic regimes. In arid climates, for example, approximately 95% of precipitation is lost to evapotranspiration (ET), while in more temperate climates, such as the Pacific Northwest, only 10% of precipitation is lost to ET (**Fig. 1**).

Soil is critical in determining the partitioning of water among the different components of the water balance and is fundamental to ecohydrology in general as it is the medium through which many ecohydrological feedbacks are manifest. Soil characteristics are remarkably heterogeneous in many systems because of spatial variability in geomorphology, soil-forming processes, and vegetation-soil feedbacks. As a result, soil-moisture content often exhibits great spatial variability in many systems, especially those that are water limited. Hydrologically, soil-moisture content controls infiltration rates, deep percolation, and runoff generation. Ecologically, soil-moisture content controls transpiration rates, carbon assimilation, and biomass production. Biogeochemically, soil-moisture content controls rates of decomposition, microbial activity, and mineralization. Soil-moisture dynamics may differ markedly from precipitation patterns, depending on soil characteristics and plant uptake of water. A further control on soil-moisture dynamics and spatial patterns of soil moisture is runoff, the redistribution of runoff across the landscape, and subsequent infiltration (termed runon). Not only does runoff (and runon) alter the spatial and temporal patterns of soil moisture, it also mobilizes and transports sediment and nutrients, which are then redeposited in lower energy locations within the landscape, thus altering surface microtopography, nutrient availability, and soil-moisture content.

Ecohydrological feedbacks and nonlinear responses. The two parent disciplines of ecohydrology, hydrology and ecology, have evolved over time using different methodological approaches. While hydrological studies have tended to favor the collection of long-term data sets and modeling studies, ecological studies have favored manipulative experimentation and hypotheses testing. These diverse approaches have remained relatively uncoupled in ecohydrological studies. Ecohydrological interactions and feedbacks occur across a range of scales, at the scale of individual plants, to the scale of communities and catchments, and beyond. Ecohydrological feedbacks are important in many, if not all, ecosystems. As population growth places even more pressure on water

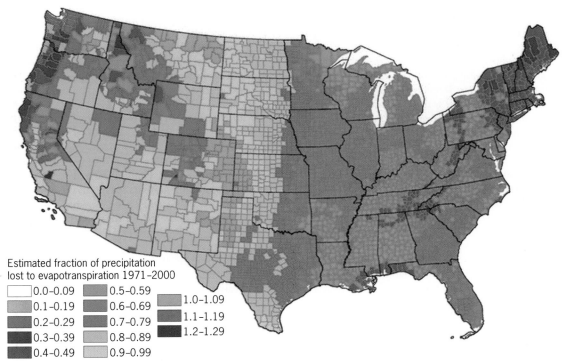

Fig. 1. Fraction of precipitation lost to evapotranspiration across the United States. (*Source: W. E. Sanford and D. L. Selnick, Estimation of evapotranspiration across the conterminous United States using a regression with climate and land-cover data, J. Am. Water Resour. Assoc., 49:217–230, 2013, DOI: 10.1111/jawr.12010*)

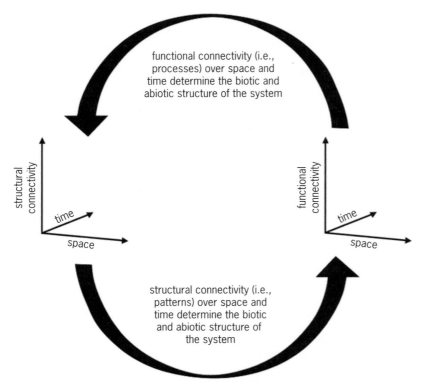

functional connectivity (i.e., processes) over space and time determine the biotic and abiotic structure of the system

structural connectivity (i.e., patterns) over space and time determine the biotic and abiotic structure of the system

Fig. 2. Feedbacks between the functional connectivity and structural connectivity of ecosystems determine the state of the system. Arrows show how ecohydrological structure (broken down into its biotic and abiotic components) affects ecohydrological function. These feedbacks between ecosystem structure and ecosystem function govern ecosystem dynamics and the provision of water resources and ecosystem services. (*Source: L. Turnbull, J. Wainwright, and R. E. Brazier, 2008*)

recognizes that understanding a system at one level of organization necessitates knowledge of the levels above and below and how the processes occurring at these different levels of organization are connected. Connectivity is thus an integral part of hierarchy theory. The concept of ecohydrological connectivity is one approach that is useful in understanding how processes (hydrological and ecological) and feedbacks are connected across both space and time (**Fig. 2**). Breaking down ecohydrology into its biotic and abiotic components, the evolution of a system can be considered in terms of how its structure affects its functional connectivity, or processes, and how these in turn affect its structural connectivity over space and time.

Application of ecohydrology to improve and manage ecosystems. Human modifications to natural ecosystems have substantially modified the hydrological cycle, for example, by deforestation, urbanization, and irrigation, and have altered the potential of ecosystems to provide plant-based resources, such as forageable grasses and crops. While many alterations are anticipated and intentional, such as urbanization and agricultural conversion, others are not. These unintentional changes often arise because of unanticipated nonlinearities in system response and have negative implications for water resources and the provision of essential ecosystem services. However, the mechanisms by which these changes occur and the dynamics by which they occur are often not well understood. There is increasing recognition that disturbances to one or more components of an ecosystem may alter critical feedbacks between biotic and abiotic processes.

Much of the ecohydrological research to date has been centered on water-limited systems, where ecohydrological interactions and feedbacks play a critical role in shaping the structure, function, and long-term evolution of these systems. In these systems, and indeed in all ecosystems characterized by reciprocal feedbacks between hydrology and biota, ecohydrology, as an integrative science, is necessary for their effective management. Thus, the utility of ecohydrology is in developing a mechanistic understanding of the system's structure and function to feed into development of potential management approaches that would be challenging to develop using nonintegrative, disciplinary approaches alone. Ecohydrological approaches, which by necessity are heavily centered on the role of feedbacks, can therefore lead to improved forecasts of environmental change, including identifying the potential for catastrophic behavior, and can also aid in identifying appropriate management strategies for resource preservation.

One of the classic case studies in ecohydrology is the role of ecohydrological feedbacks in propagating rangeland degradation in drylands (**Fig. 3**). Important drivers of initial vegetation losses are anthropogenic disturbances such as overgrazing and climatic disturbances such as drought. In a positive feedback loop, a reduction in vegetation cover results in an increase in runoff and erosion, causing

resources and the provision of ecosystem services, it is increasingly necessary to understand the ecohydrological mechanisms and consequences of ecosystem change. This understanding is necessary to devise appropriate strategies to mitigate undesirable changes that may arise. Ecohydrological feedbacks can be positive (self-reinforcing or amplifying) or negative (self-dampening or stabilizing). Because of these ecohydrological feedbacks, ecosystems often respond in a nonlinear way to perturbations, such as climatic forcing or anthropogenic disturbances. Predicting how a system will respond to perturbations in respect of the potential nonlinearities in system response necessitates understanding of how feedbacks render a system more susceptible to external perturbations (often via positive feedbacks) or increase the resilience of the system (often via negative feedbacks).

Thus, a critical component of ecohydrology, and one of its major challenges, is reconciling spatial complexity and cross-scale interactions. Hierarchy theory, which balances the search for mechanisms with an assessment of their significance at various spatial and temporal scales, is becoming increasingly used in ecohydrological studies to reconcile the different methodological approaches of hydrology and ecology, and to overcome some of the challenges imposed by cross-scale interactions. In a similar vein, recognizing that ecosystem dynamics cannot be understood fully without consideration of ecohydrological feedbacks, hierarchy theory

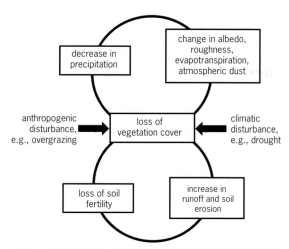

Fig. 3. Anthropogenic or climatic disturbances to rangelands in drylands cause a loss of vegetation cover that triggers positive ecohydrological feedbacks. The top feedback loop is concerned primarily with vertical fluxes between vegetation and the atmosphere, and the bottom feedback loop is concerned primarily with lateral fluxes that lead to progressive resource loss.

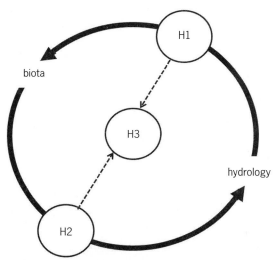

Fig. 4. H1: Hydrology can be used to regulate biota. H2: Biota can be used to regulate hydrological processes. H3: H1 and H2 can be integrated and used with technological innovation to improve and manage water-dependent ecosystems.

a loss of soil fertility, which leads to a further reduction in vegetation cover. A second positive feedback loop exists between vegetation and the atmosphere, whereby an initial reduction in vegetation cover causes a change in surface albedo and decreases evapotranspiration, which leads to a decrease in precipitation that reduces the amount of water available to support vegetation growth.

The concepts of ecohydrology may be applied to augment a system's resilience to anthropogenic changes (**Fig. 4**) by managing or preventing undesirable ecohydrological feedbacks or in conjunction with phytotechnology (using vegetation and its natural services for environmental quality improvements) to modify the type and strength of ecohydrological feedbacks to increase a system's resistance, for example, by using vegetation to reduce erosion.

Thus, the study of ecohydrology helps us to understand the critical links and feedbacks between hydrology and ecology and shows how these links may be used and manipulated to facilitate effective environmental management and environmental sustainability, which is becoming increasingly important as human activities continue to alter natural ecosystems at unprecedented rates. Ecohydrology provides an overarching paradigm for water management that is based on a holistic vision of the role of water in the environment and the influence of the ecosystem on hydrological processes. Ecohydrology alone does not facilitate the management of water resources, but it does provide the necessary scientific knowledge that can inform appropriate management strategies for effective water-resource management. The continued advances that are being made in understanding ecohydrological feedbacks over the range of spatial and temporal scales over which they operate and across a range of natural and human-disturbed environments improve our ability to increase the resilience of systems to natural and anthropogenic perturbations and improve our ability to develop adaptation strategies to mitigate adverse environmental consequences and manage water resources.

For background information *see* ALBEDO; BIOGEOCHEMISTRY; CLIMATOLOGY; DROUGHT; ECOLOGY; ECOSYSTEM; FRESHWATER ECOSYSTEM; GEOMORPHOLOGY; HYDROLOGY; SOIL; SOIL ECOLOGY; WATER CONSERVATION; WATER RESOURCES in the McGraw-Hill Encyclopedia of Science & Technology.

Laura Turnbull

Bibliography. P. S. Eagleson, *Ecohydrology: Darwinian Expression of Vegetation Form and Function*, Cambridge University Press, Cambridge, UK, 2002; B. D. Newman et al., Ecohydrology of water-limited environments: A scientific vision, *Water Resour. Res.*, 42(6):W06302, 2006, DOI:10.1029/2005WR004141; A. Porporato and I. Rodriguez-Iturbe, Ecohydrology—A challenging multidisciplinary research perspective, *Hydrolog. Sci. J.*, 47(5):811–821, 2002, DOI:10.1080/02626660209492985; B. P. Wilcox, Transformative ecosystem change and ecohydrology: Ushering in a new era for watershed management, *Ecohydrol.*, 3:126–130, 2010, DOI:10.1002/eco.104; M. Zalweski, Ecohydrology—The scientific background to use ecosystem properties as management tools toward sustainability of water resources, *Ecol. Eng.*, 16(1):1–8, 2000, DOI:10.1016/S0925-8574(00)00071-9.

Effects of invasive Burmese pythons in Everglades National Park

Although usually not as obvious as pollution, deforestation, or urban sprawl, the introduction of invasive alien species represents one of the foremost threats to global biodiversity. Billions of dollars are spent annually to prevent, manage, and mitigate the damage done by various invaders, including

Fig. 1. The Burmese python (*Python molurus bivittatus*) has been introduced from its native range in southern Asia to South Florida.

nition of their establishment in the early 2000s, these snakes have exploded across the Everglades and have recently been linked to severe declines of several once-common mammal species, raising concerns that they are causing fundamental damage to one of North America's most treasured ecosystems.

Burmese python invaders. The Burmese python (*Python molurus bivittatus*) [**Fig. 1**], which is one of the largest snakes in the world and a longtime mainstay of the exotic reptile trade, has been introduced to Florida from its native range in southern Asia. Giant snakes have been reported in the Everglades for decades. However, beginning in the 1990s, confirmed python observations from the mangrove forests of the southern portions of Everglades National Park (ENP) began to accumulate. These snakes were initially assumed to be released pets, but reproduction was confirmed in 2002. Furthermore, since that time, python populations have increased rapidly in both numbers and geographic range (**Fig. 2**). As of 2013, more than 2000 pythons have been removed, and the population has spread geographically to an area covering at least 8000 km² (3089 mi²) and encompassing all of ENP and Big Cypress National Preserve (located north of ENP). Burmese pythons captured in Florida have ranged up to 5.3 m (17.4 ft) in length and have

weeds, disease vectors, and feral pets. Invasive species come in many shapes and sizes, and they may alter native ecosystems in a multitude of ways. Few, though, have captured the attention of biologists, the media, and the public like the pythons that have recently invaded South Florida. Since the recog-

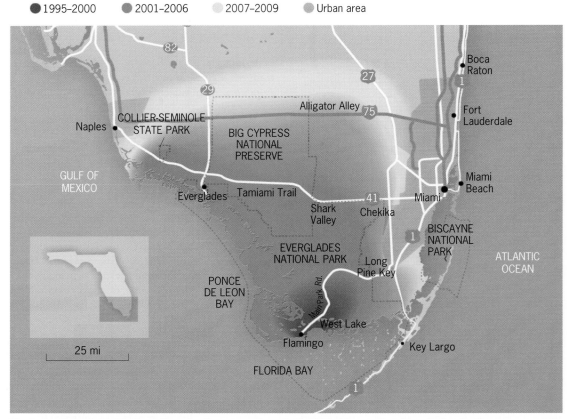

Fig. 2. Approximate distribution of invasive Burmese pythons in South Florida over time. The effects of pythons on mammals were assessed in the core of the python's range (along the Main Park Road in Everglades National Park), at recently invaded peripheral locations (Big Cypress National Preserve, Collier-Seminole State Park, Chekika, and Key Largo), and in extralimital locations (not shown) where pythons have not yet been documented. (*Map reprinted with permission from M. E. Dorcas and J. D. Willson, Invasive Pythons in the United States: Ecology of an Introduced Predator, University of Georgia Press, Athens, 2011*)

contained as many as 87 eggs. Although the exact circumstances that led to the introduction and establishment of pythons in Florida will probably never be known, the spatial distribution of captures and population growth models suggest that the invasive population probably stems from the introduction of a small number of pythons into the southern portions of ENP prior to the 1990s. This population probably remained undetected for a substantial period of time before snakes were encountered on a regular basis and establishment was confirmed.

Effects on native wildlife. Although these snakes could potentially pose a threat to humans, the primary concern related to the python invasion has been the effects that they could have on native wildlife. Thus, a major initial goal of the python research in the Everglades has been to document their diet. By examining the stomach contents of pythons collected from the Everglades, biologists from the National Park Service, the Smithsonian Institution, and the University of Florida have documented more than 40 prey species. As in their native range, Burmese pythons in Florida are generalist predators that feed predominantly on mammals and birds. The most common prey have been small to midsized mammals, such as rodents, rabbits, raccoons, and opossums. However, larger prey have also been found, including bobcats, otters, and white-tailed deer; in one case in 2011, an intact 36-kg (79-lb) doe was recovered from a 4.7-m-long (15.4-ft-long), 63-kg (139-lb) female python. Pythons also frequently consume marsh and wading birds, including rails, herons, egrets, and limpkins, and occasionally American alligators. Perhaps most alarmingly, pythons have been recorded as preying upon at least two federally listed species, the wood stork and the Key Largo woodrat.

In light of the wide array of native wildlife being consumed by pythons and the rapidly expanding python population, studies were aimed at evaluating whether python predation was affecting the populations of midsized mammals in the Everglades. Mammal encounter rates during systematic nocturnal road surveys along the same stretch of road in ENP before (1996–1997) and after (2003–2011) pythons became common in the area were compared. The investigations also evaluated mammal encounter rates in recent (2009–2011) road surveys that spanned the geographical spread of pythons in South Florida. Specifically, encounter rates in the core of the python's introduced range in ENP were compared to those in four peripheral locations that have been more recently invaded and two extralimital locations with similar habitats outside of the python's current range (Fig. 2). The results of these surveys were dramatic: Mammals had declined precipitously since pythons became common in ENP, and sighting rates of mammals were higher in peripheral locations and much higher in extralimital locations than in ENP (**Fig. 3**). The most severely affected mammal species were raccoons, which had declined by 99.3% in ENP since pythons became common; opossums, which had declined by 98.9%;

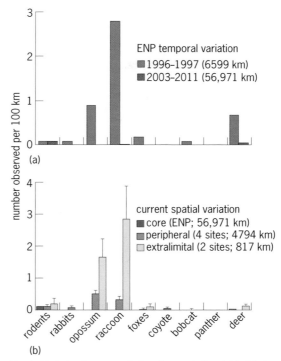

Fig. 3. Variation in mammal abundances in South Florida in relation to the Burmese python invasion. (*a*) Temporal variation in mammal encounter rates in Everglades National Park (ENP), as reflected in distance-corrected road survey counts before (1996–1997) and after (2003–2011) pythons became common in the region. (*b*) Current spatial variation in mammal encounter rates in core (ENP), peripheral, and extralimital regions of the python's range in Florida. Pythons have been recorded in the core region for more than a decade and only more recently in peripheral locations. (*Figure adapted from M. E. Dorcas et al., Severe mammal declines coincide with proliferation of invasive Burmese pythons in Everglades National Park, Proc. Natl. Acad. Sci. USA, 109:2418–2422, 2012, DOI:10.1073/pnas.1115226109*)

and rabbits, which were not documented at all in recent surveys in ENP. The fact that these declines correspond both spatially and temporally with the proliferation of pythons in the region and include a diverse assemblage of mammal species having differing ecologies strongly suggests that pythons are responsible.

Further consequences of the python invasion. The apparent severe impact of pythons on mammals in the Everglades is troubling for several reasons. First, midsized mammals, such as rabbits and raccoons, are typically common and important components of Florida ecosystems. Loss of these species may reduce prey for carnivores, including the Florida panther and the eastern diamondback rattlesnake, or may affect ecosystem processes such as vegetation dynamics and seed dispersal. Such indirect effects are probably complex and difficult to detect, and they may even be positive for some species. For example, reduced raccoon populations may increase the nesting success of turtles and birds. In addition, the severe declines in common mammal species that were the focus of the ENP study raise concerns for species that are more secretive or difficult to investigate, but are also potential prey for pythons. A decline in bobcat and fox observations has been documented in areas invaded by pythons, but these trends are difficult to interpret because of lower overall sample sizes. Wading birds such as herons and egrets are also common prey of pythons and may also be suffering from python predation. Loss of these beautiful and charismatic species not only would affect the Everglades ecosystem, but could result in a loss of tourism, which is a vital source of income for the region. Finally, although the factors that may limit the spread of pythons are poorly understood, several climate matching studies have suggested that pythons may be able to invade areas well beyond the Everglades. Different approaches have yielded conflicting results on the topic of python range expansion, but some suggest that much of the southern United States exhibits temperature and precipitation levels that are within the range of those in the areas inhabited by pythons in Asia. Only time will reveal the true degree to which pythons are able to expand beyond South Florida and the long-term effects of python predation in invaded ecosystems.

Prior to the establishment of pythons in Florida, the best-known case of a snake invasion was the introduction of brown tree snakes (*Boiga irregularis*) to the island of Guam in the South Pacific. Following their accidental introduction in the 1950s, brown tree snakes proliferated, eventually extirpated 10 of the island's 12 native forest birds, and contributed to declines or extirpations of several species of native bats and lizards. Removal of native vertebrates has resulted in reduced seed dispersal and germination for native plants and has altered invertebrate dynamics on the island. Considered together, the cases of the brown tree snake and the Burmese python raise concerns that snakes may be an emerging and highly destructive guild of invaders.

Snakes differ from comparable mammalian and avian predators in a variety of ways that may influence predator–prey dynamics. Many snakes occur in high densities, and, as ectotherms (animals that obtain most of their heat from the environment), they lead a low-energy lifestyle that allows them to survive long periods without prey. However, when there is an abundance of prey, snakes can rapidly and efficiently convert prey into growth and reproduction. For example, a female python can reproduce annually and can lay clutches of up to 100 eggs when it is well fed, but can survive for more than 1 year without feeding when prey are scarce. These life history characteristics may make invasive snakes particularly likely to reduce or extirpate native prey; however, with only two large-scale invasions to examine, general conclusions are difficult to draw. Recent years have seen a steep increase in the number of successful snake invasions. In addition to Burmese pythons, two other large constrictors, the African rock python (*Python sebae*) and the boa constrictor (*Boa constrictor*), are established in small areas of southern Florida. Boa constrictors have also invaded the islands of Cozumel (Mexico), Aruba, and Puerto Rico. Additionally, an established population of albino California kingsnakes (*Lampropeltis*

getula) has recently been discovered on the Canary Islands off of West Africa, and at least three species of water snakes (*Nerodia* species) native to eastern North America have been introduced in California. These recent invasions are troubling, but will provide unique opportunities to evaluate how snakes interact with prey populations and to assess the risks posed by snakes as invasive species.

For background information *see* BIODIVERSITY; BIOGEOGRAPHY; ECOLOGICAL COMMUNITIES; ECOLOGICAL COMPETITION; ECOSYSTEM; INVASION ECOLOGY; POPULATION ECOLOGY; POPULATION VIABILITY; PREDATOR-PREY INTERACTIONS; REPTILIA; SQUAMATA in the McGraw-Hill Encyclopedia of Science & Technology.

John D. Willson; Michael E. Dorcas

Bibliography. M. E. Dorcas and J. D. Willson, *Invasive Pythons in the United States: Ecology of an Introduced Predator*, University of Georgia Press, Athens, 2011; M. E. Dorcas et al., Severe mammal declines coincide with proliferation of invasive Burmese pythons in Everglades National Park, *Proc. Natl. Acad. Sci. USA*, 109:2418–2422, 2012, DOI:10.1073/pnas.1115226109; R. N. Reed et al., Ecological correlates of invasion impact for Burmese pythons in Florida, *Integr. Zool.*, 7:254–270, 2012, DOI:10.1111/j.1749-4877.2012.00304.x; G. H. Rodda, C. S. Jarnevich, and R. N. Reed, What parts of the U.S. mainland are climatically suitable for invasive alien pythons spreading from Everglades National Park?, *Biol. Invasions*, 11:241–252, 2009, DOI:http://dx.doi.org/10.1007/s10530-008-9228-z; R. W. Snow et al., Introduced populations of *Boa constrictor* (Boidae) and *Python molurus bivittatus* (Pythonidae) in southern Florida, pp. 416–438, in R. W. Henderson and R. Powell, eds., *Biology of the Boas and Pythons*, Eagle Mountain Publishing, Eagle Mountain, Utah, 2007; J. D. Willson, M. E. Dorcas, and R. W. Snow, Identifying plausible scenarios for the establishment of invasive Burmese pythons (*Python molurus*) in southern Florida, *Biol. Invasions*, 13:1493–1504, 2011, DOI:10.1007/s10530-010-9908-3.

ENCODE project

Many human diseases are caused by changes in the abundance or activity of proteins, and proteins are encoded by segments of DNA called genes. Therefore, a logical assumption is that identifying all the human genes could help in understanding human disease. The Human Genome Project was launched in 1990 with this specific goal in mind. This led to a push for sequencing the entire genome, which began in 1996, with a draft version of the human genome being published in 2001. One of the first big surprises that came from this era of human genomics had to do with the number of genes that was found. Based on the fact that genomic sequencing of a worm (which has only 959 cells and 1×10^8 nucleotides of DNA) had identified approximately

20,000 genes, it was assumed that humans would have approximately 150,000 genes (after all, a human is much more complicated than a worm). However, after the human genome was sequenced and "read" by computational programs that compared the results to known proteins and RNAs (the intermediary nucleic acids from which proteins are encoded), the results suggested that humans might have at most 30,000 genes; refinement of the analyses has since reduced this number to 20,000. In other words, a human has the same number of genes as a worm. In fact, only 5% of the 3×10^9 nucleotides in the human genome is covered by exons (DNA segments that encode proteins). This realization led to an intriguing question: If 95% of the genome is not involved in coding for proteins, then what does it do? A large international consortium called ENCODE (Encyclopedia of DNA Elements), funded by the National Human Genome Research Institute, began to address this question in 2004, and a pilot project was undertaken to study 1% of the human genome. However, ENCODE quickly advanced to studying the entire genome by 2007 because of technological improvements. The assays chosen by the ENCODE consortium focused on identifying regions of the genome that are "in use"—for example, regions that are transcribed into RNA or regions that control whether a gene is turned on or off. Since 2007, 442 scientists from 32 different institutes have studied 147 cell types and collected more than 1640 data sets; these efforts from the ENCODE consortium have shed light on several important questions in human biology.

What has been learned from ENCODE? Genome-scale experiments are expensive and time-consuming. Therefore, it is critical to approach such experiments in a well-controlled and efficient manner. One important aspect of the ENCODE project has been the development of new technologies and quality-control standards for these technologies. The ENCODE consortium published a description of current standards in 2012, and it is expected that updates will be published as new technologies and analytical programs are developed. Another important goal of the ENCODE project is to enable the community to access and use the data. Accordingly, all data are publicly available as soon as they are collected, and the ENCODE consortium has published a user's guide to illustrate how to access, download, and apply ENCODE data to studying the human genome. Another outcome from the ENCODE project was the realization that the data could not be understood by analysis of each assay in isolation. Rather, realization of the full impact of the information contained within the large-scale genomic data sets required the development of new integrative analytical methodologies. This becomes even more important when ENCODE data are compared to data from other large consortia (for example, the NIH Roadmap Epigenome Mapping Project and the 1000 Genomes project). A few insights from the ENCODE project are described below.

About 60% of the genome is transcribed into some form of RNA. Although protein-coding exons represent only 5% of the genome, the RNA transcripts that contain these exons can be very long as a result of the presence of introns (segments of DNA between the coding portions). It was discovered by ENCODE that most genes have a first exon that is quite far from the remaining exons; this can lead to a very long noncoding section at the beginning of the RNA. In addition, ENCODE studies showed that most genes have more than one promoter (the regulatory region that is responsible for initiating transcription of the gene). Because of the existence of alternative promoters and alternative usage of downstream exons, it is estimated that the human genome encodes approximately 80,000 different proteins (**Fig. 1**). Thus, although the human genome may be limited to 20,000 genes, there is a much greater diversity in the human set of proteins. ENCODE studies also revealed that there are thousands of cases in which DNA makes RNA, but RNA does not make protein (in contrast to the central dogma of molecular biology, which is that DNA makes RNA, and RNA makes protein). These RNAs that do not make proteins are called noncoding RNAs. Although their existence was known, their prevalence was unclear. The ENCODE studies identified more than 18,000 noncoding RNAs. This surprising finding revealed that the human noncoding RNA portfolio is just as diverse as the coding RNA portfolio.

About 95% of the genome lies within 8 kilobases of a protein–DNA interaction. Transcription of both coding and noncoding RNAs is controlled by DNA-binding transcription factors and their associated protein partners that bind to short regulatory regions close to the beginning of a gene (proximal elements or promoters) or far from a gene (distal elements or enhancers). Identifying a short regulatory region of approximately 200 base pairs (bp) in the human genome is like finding a needle in a haystack of 3 billion straws. However, the assays used by ENCODE provide a logical approach to identify and characterize regulatory elements. First, the regions of open chromatin (the DNA–protein complex) should be identified for the particular cell type under investigation. Most of the human genomic DNA is tightly wound around protein structures called nucleosomes, which are composed of proteins called histones. However, there are regions of the genome that are nucleosome-free, and these regions are the landing platforms for transcription

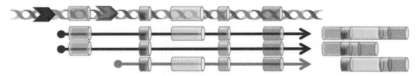

Fig. 1. More than one protein can be produced from a gene. RNAs can be produced from different promoters (blue and pink chevrons on the DNA helix), with longer transcripts incorporating additional coding exons (colored barrels). Different proteins also can be produced from a single transcript as a result of the alternative usage of internal exons. Three different proteins that could be produced from a single gene are shown in this example.

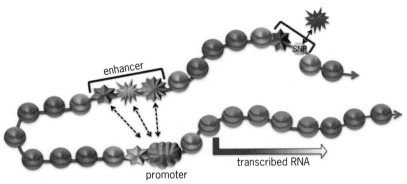

Fig. 2. The majority of the human genome is involved in a biochemical event. Studies from the ENCODE project indicate that approximately 80% of the human genome is "in use"; approximately 60% of the genome is transcribed into coding or noncoding RNAs, and approximately 20% is covered by transcription factors (star shapes) binding to DNase hypersensitivity sites (DHSs) at enhancers (brackets) or promoters (which are also bound by the general transcriptional machinery; orange shape). Dashed arrows indicate protein–protein interactions that mediate the looping of an enhancer to a promoter. The double arrowhead indicates that a single nucleotide polymorphism (SNP) can affect the binding of a transcription factor to an enhancer. The borders of the DHSs are marked by specifically modified nucleosomes. Round balls represent nucleosomes: blue balls represent nucleosomes having active modifications; pink balls represent nucleosomes within transcribed regions; and green balls represent other nucleosomes.

factors (**Fig. 2**). These regions are called DNase hypersensitivity sites (DHSs) because they can be digested easily with the enzyme DNase (this ability to be digested easily is the result of the lack of nucleosomes). ENCODE studies estimate that there are approximately 200,000 DHSs per cell type, with perhaps 3–5 million total DHSs in the genome (DHSs can be cell type–specific, and thus many of the sites are in different locations in different cells). Employing the sequencing technique of ChIP-seq, which uses antibodies to collect regions of the genome bound by transcription factors, ENCODE found that 98.5% of the binding sites for the transcription factors studied to date are within a DHS. Taken together, these results suggest that transcription factors densely decorate the entire genome.

The genome has a highly complex interactive structure. Because transcription units are very long and can be oriented in either direction in the genome, it is perhaps not surprising that coding regions of different genes can be interlaced; however, our understanding of the extent of this interlacing was greatly increased by the thorough annotation of human RNAs by ENCODE. In addition, studies from ENCODE showed that regulatory regions can be very far from the genes that they regulate. Distal regulatory regions called enhancers work by bending the DNA and forming a loop with a promoter (the regulatory region near the start of a gene). Although enhancer-mediated loops had been studied on a limited scale, the results from ENCODE greatly increased our knowledge of these structures, suggesting that, on average, each promoter is regulated by approximately four enhancers and each enhancer regulates approximately three different promoters.

Insights into human health. In addition to the annotation of regulatory elements by ENCODE, other groups have been studying human populations to determine the risks for human diseases. These studies are called GWAS (genome-wide association studies)

because they ask which regions of the genome are associated with an increased risk of a certain disease. This approach takes advantage of the fact that all humans are not identical. There are differences between ethnic populations and between individuals within a population. These differences are called single nucleotide polymorphisms (SNPs). In the 1000 Genomes project, 38 million SNPs have been identified in 1092 individuals from 14 populations, with an average of 3.6 million SNPs per person. Using these SNPs, investigators have linked different regions of the human genome to increased rates of certain diseases. However, these studies have encountered several problems. First, the regions associated with increased risk for a disease are very large, and there are a great number of SNPs contained within these regions. In addition, most of the SNPs are not within a protein-coding region and thus it is hard to understand how the nucleotide difference might cause an increased risk of disease. Fortunately, by combining GWAS and ENCODE data, it is possible to more clearly understand the underlying basis for a link between an SNP and a disease. The ENCODE project found that 34% of the GWAS SNPs are within a DHS, suggesting that they influence the activity of a regulatory region. In fact, although only 10% of human transcription factors have been studied to date, 12% of the GWAS SNPs actually overlap a binding site mapped by ENCODE. Such findings suggest that disease-linked SNPs may affect the binding of a transcription factor, which leads to altered gene expression and thereby increases the risk of a disease. However, many questions remain (for example, which gene is the target of the regulatory region?). DNA looping assays, genomic engineering to delete the regulatory region followed by analysis of global gene expression changes, and expression quantitative trait loci (eQTL) studies, which compare gene expression to SNP frequency across a population, can help further our understanding of population-based differences in the risk for human diseases.

Further exploration. So far, the ENCODE project has provided the scientific community with new experimental methods and standards, new data analysis programs, vast amounts of data deposited in public repositories, the knowledge of the structure and regulation of the human genome, insights into the functional effects of human variation, and (perhaps most importantly) the realization that the genomic frontier has not yet been fully explored. For example, although it is now known that approximately 80% of the genome is involved in a biochemical event, the identities of the proteins that bind to all of the DHSs in a given cell type are not known. In addition, experiments need to be expanded to include more cell types and more developmental and environmental conditions to link these studies more closely to human health. These experiments are ongoing and should provide important new insights into human biology in the coming years.

For background information *see* CHROMOSOME; DEOXYRIBONUCLEIC ACID (DNA); EXON; GENE;

GENETIC MAPPING; GENETICS; GENOMICS; HUMAN GENOME; INTRON; NUCLEOSOME; NUCLEOTIDE; POLY-MORPHISM (GENETICS); PROTEIN; RIBONUCLEIC ACID (RNA); TRANSCRIPTION in the McGraw-Hill Encyclopedia of Science & Technology.   Peggy J. Farnham

Bibliography. G. R. Abecasis et al., An integrated map of genetic variation from 1,092 human genomes, *Nature*, 491(7422):56–65, 2012, DOI:10.1038/nature11632;   S.   Djebali et al., Landscape of transcription in human cells, *Nature*,   489(7414):101–108,   2012,   DOI:10.1038/nature11233;   ENCODE   Project   Consortium, A user's guide to the encyclopedia of DNA elements (ENCODE), *PLoS Biol.*, 9(4):e1001046, 2011, DOI:10.1371/journal.pbio.1001046;   ENCODE   Project Consortium, An integrated encyclopedia of DNA elements in the human genome, *Nature*, 489(7414):57–74, 2012, DOI:10.1038/nature11247; P. J. Farnham, Thematic minireview series on results from the ENCODE project: Integrative global analyses of regulatory regions in the human genome, *J. Biol. Chem.*, 287(37):30885–30887, 2012, DOI:10.1074/jbc.R112.365940; R. C. Hardison, Genome-wide epigenetic data facilitate understanding of disease susceptibility association studies, *J. Biol. Chem.*, 287(37):30932–30940,   2012,   DOI:10.1074/jbc. R112.352427; S. G. Landt et al., ChIP-seq guidelines and practices of the ENCODE and modENCODE consortia, *Genome Res.*, 22(9):1813–1831, 2012, DOI:10.1101/gr.136184.111; A.   Sanyal   et   al., The long-range interaction landscape of gene promoters, *Nature*, 489(7414):109–113, 2012, DOI:10.1038/nature11279; L. D. Ward and M. Kellis, Interpreting noncoding genetic variation in complex traits and human disease, *Nat. Biotechnol.*, 30(11):1095–1106, 2012, DOI:10.1038/nbt. 2422.

Enhancers in development and evolution

Enhancers are noncoding sequences of deoxyribonucleic acid (DNA) that provide the information needed for gene regulation.

Challenges of development. Development of a multicellular organism is the process by which a fertilized egg, a single cell (which itself is a product of developmental processes producing eggs and sperm), divides to produce all of the specialized cells, tissues, and organs comprising a functional individual. It is often said that the "master plan" for directing this process is encoded in the genetic material that each cell inherits, but this statement is only partially true. It is indeed a plan in the sense that the information necessary for making an individual {the formulas for the building blocks of cells [proteins and ribonucleic acid (RNA)]} is encoded in the genetic material. However, the genetic material is much more dynamic than just a plan because it participates in its own readout through the activities of *cis*-regulatory sequences (the term *cis* is used to denote cases in which a regulating sequence is present on the same DNA molecule as the gene that it regulates). These *cis*-regulatory sequences are regions of DNA that dictate where, when, and how much to make of a gene product. This article describes how these regulatory sequences, called enhancers, work and their role in development.

Each mature cell (for example, a neuron residing in the forebrain or an insulin-secreting beta-cell residing in the pancreas) expresses a different (and unique) constellation of proteins and RNAs, comprising a subset of all the biological molecules encoded in the genetic material. How does each cell come to express its unique constellation of proteins and not any others? Moreover, what instructs some genes to be "turned on" and others to remain silent in a cell-type-specific temporal sequence through development? Enhancers are transcriptional regulators that fulfill these critical roles by integrating information to achieve the spatial and temporal control of gene expression in each cell.

What are enhancers? The genetic material—DNA—is a long linear array of nucleotides (the structural units of nucleic acids) packaged into tightly wound structures called chromosomes. Each chromosome contains instructions for the sequences of proteins and noncoding RNAs. For both items, short contiguous sequences along the chromosome, ranging from tens of bases to tens of thousands of bases, are transcribed from DNA into RNA. The DNA sequence contains specific sequences that inform the transcriptional machinery as to where to initiate the transcription of DNA to RNA and where it should terminate downstream in the sequence. Additional sequences located immediately upstream from the transcription initiation signal—the basal promoter—provide sequence-specific landing sites for the assembly of this molecular machinery. What then determines whether a gene is actively transcribed in a particular cell type? One component of this gene regulation involves changes in the structure of the chromosome itself; that is, regions of DNA along the chromosome containing a set of genes can be "opened" or "closed" to make those genes accessible (or not) for transcription.

Precise gene regulation is achieved through the activity of enhancers. These noncoding sequences (typically several hundred base pairs in length) contain clusters of short motifs (commonly 6–12 bases in length), with each having a binding affinity for a specific member of a class of DNA-binding proteins called transcription factors (TFs). TFs and their associated cofactors interact with the transcription machinery on the basal promoter to either activate (launch) or repress (hold back) the transcription machinery at a single nearby gene on the same DNA molecule (that is, they act only in "*cis*"). The term enhancer was coined by virtue of the method by which these sequences could be identified: An enhancer is the smallest piece of noncoding DNA that, when experimentally spliced in vitro to a proper promoter and an easily detected reporter gene [typically the bacterial gene encoding beta-galactosidase or a fluorescent protein such as green fluorescent protein (GFP)] and then placed back in the cell, drives the transcription of the reporter in a manner that recapitulates the expression of the native gene.

Enhancers constitute a remarkable molecular machine, and they act as a switch to turn on or keep off gene expression in a cell. A simple enhancer can contain as few as one binding site for a single activating TF, but more likely there are several binding sites. When the activating TF is present in the cell and is above a critical threshold concentration, it will be bound to its target sites and will turn on transcription of the regulated gene. Below the critical concentration, transcription of the gene will be kept off. Several features of enhancer biology are illustrated in even the simplest molecular switch. First, a certain minimum number of TF molecules must be bound to the enhancer for it to activate (turn on) gene expression. The switch is flipped "on" or "off" entirely depending on the concentration of the TF in the cell.

Second, because the property of a switch is determined by the configuration of the bound TF, the affinity of a sequence for its TF is important. In general, each TF recognizes not just a single DNA sequence, but a family of similar sequences (hence a "motif"), exhibiting a range of TF binding affinities. It is generally assumed that each base position in a motif acts independently to determine the overall TF binding affinity, and thus can be characterized by its position-weight matrix (PWM), that is, a $4 \times N$ matrix of base frequencies (where N is the length of the motif). Typical enhancers have multiple nonidentical binding sites for a TF whose binding affinities can be finely tuned by evolution. One peculiar consequence of a TF having affinity for many different short DNA sequences is that binding sites will occur not only within the segments of DNA recognized in a functional assay of the enhancer, but also at many additional sites in the DNA adjacent to these segments. There is an active debate as to whether these additional sites are "functional" and indeed whether enhancers are even discrete entities.

TFs have two opposing functionalities: They act either as activators of gene expression, as in the aforementioned example, or as repressors of gene expression to keep the genes turned off. These functionalities are solely dictated by the TF in most cases; however, they are context-dependent in other cases and depend on the binding of surrounding factors. Typical enhancers have binding sites for each of approximately six TFs, and both categories (activators and repressors) are represented. There are a variety of interactions between activators and repressors. The most important mechanisms are reasonably well understood, including direct competition between two different TFs for a particular binding site, cooperative binding of TFs, short-range repression (a repressor TF within 150 base pairs of an activator TF will generally block its activating potential), and long-range repression. The configurations of bound TFs on an enhancer, determined by the TF concentrations in a cell, are integrated via these mechanisms to determine the functional state of the enhancer. The nature of these interactions is governed by the physical configuration of the bound TFs, including their numbers and specific spacing along the DNA, and both of these are evolved properties. The architecture of an enhancer draws on the biophysical properties of the protein–protein interactions so as to make the enhancer act as a robust switch. A practical consequence is that an enhancer can very nearly have a binary property, meaning that a cell will tend to be either "on" or "off" over nearly the entire range of each TF concentration.

How are enhancers identified? In 1988, the first eukaryotic enhancer sequence was discovered in a monkey virus called SV40. In this case, noncoding sequences that could turn on (enhance) the expression of a reporter gene were identified. Any assay involved in this type of research needs to be carried out in the appropriate cell (and not a test tube) because this is where the necessary TFs and cofactors are present at appropriate concentrations. The gold standard for identifying an enhancer remains this empirical assay. In many cases, eukaryotic enhancers are organized along a single stretch of DNA. However, this does not have to be the case because many enhancers are also "dispersed," with the functional pieces being able to interact in the three-dimensional structure of the looped DNA. More recently, with the characterization of the TF sequence specificity, represented by a PWM, it is now possible to carry out searches computationally to identify stretches of noncoding DNA predicted to have tight clusters of the predicted TF binding sites. These computationally identified regions have a high likelihood of being functional enhancers. Functional enhancers evolve at rates substantially slower than functionally "unconstrained" DNA, and therefore they are predicted to have a phylogenetic (evolutionary developmental history) "shadow" of constraint, which can be revealed in an interspecific comparative analysis of noncoding sequences.

Where do enhancers reside? A rational designer might want to place the cis-regulatory sequences immediately in front of the basal promoter of the gene that is being regulated. However, the reality is much richer and is indeed one of the key reasons why multicellular organisms can even exist. Most genes are regulated by more than one enhancer, and in some cases by a dozen or more. A key feature of enhancers is that they act independently of each other. This independence is achieved by their physical separation along the noncoding DNA, and by other proteins bound to the noncoding DNA that "insulate" the activity of one enhancer from the activity of another enhancer. In the absence of insulators or spacing, enhancers will interfere with each other to generate inappropriate gene expression. Importantly, enhancers function equally well (at least in principle) in an orientation-independent manner (they can be flipped around on the DNA relative to the direction of the gene that they target), and enhancers can work equally well either in front (upstream) or in back (downstream) of a gene. In addition, because eukaryotic genes are broken into pieces (called exons) by the presence of noncoding

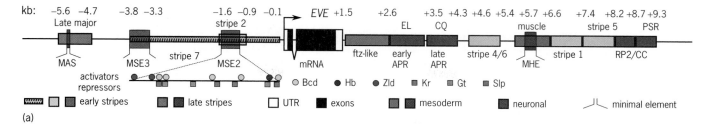

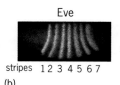

Eve

stripes 1 2 3 4 5 6 7

(b)

Schematic view of the *even-skipped* (*eve*) gene of the fruit fly, *Drosophila melanogaster*. (*a*) The transcript and all known functional regulatory regions are shown. The entire locus extends over approximately 15,000 base pairs (note the scale). Enhancers and minimal elements are color-coded by tissue and the timing of *eve* expression. The "stripe" enhancers, MSE3, 7, 2, 4/6, 1, and 5, control the expression of *eve* in an early stage of embryonic development, called the blastula. (*b*) Antibody staining and imaging with confocal microscopy of the Eve protein in early *D. melanogaster* blastoderm embryos. The numbered transverse stripes of *eve* expression in panel *b* correspond to the regulatory activities of the corresponding enhancers. A detailed diagram of the experimentally validated transcription factor (TF) binding sites in the MSE2 (the 489-base-pair minimal stripe 2 element) is shown in panel *a*; activators (Bcd: Bicoid; Hb: Hunchback; Zld: Zelda) are indicated by circles, and repressors (Gt: Giant; Kr: Kruppel; Slp: Sloppy-paired) are indicated by squares. Other terms: MSE3 (minimal stripe 3 element); MAS (minimal autoregulatory sequence); UTR (untranslated region); APR (anal plate ring); and MHE (muscle and heart enhancer); EL, CQ, RP2, and CC correspond to neuronal lineages derived from ganglion mother cells; and PSR (pairing-sensitive repression) is involved in the maintenance of *eve* expression in neurons.

sequences (called introns), enhancers can reside there as well. Enhancers have been found as far as 100,000 base pairs from the promoter with which they interact.

What roles do enhancers have in regulating development? The independent activity of enhancers is critical for the regulation of development. Most developmentally regulated genes, especially ones that themselves participate in development or cell fate specification, are expressed in more than one cell type or in a spatially regulated pattern, and at multiple time points in development. Enhancer independence allows a gene to achieve complex spatial and temporal regulation. One set of enhancers might trigger a gene's expression in embryonic tissue, another set might trigger expression in distinct tissues in the developing juvenile, and yet a third set might trigger expression in certain adult tissues. Importantly, all cells that lack the specific set and the appropriate concentrations of TFs for the enhancers of a gene will not express the gene. Such is the mechanism by which the regulated expression of genes ensures proper development and cell fate specification.

Enhancers in evolution. One fascinating feature of enhancer sequences is that they have the capability to evolve rapidly even as natural selection maintains functional constancy. A dramatic example of this involves the *even-skipped* stripe 2 enhancer (S2E), which is a sequence that drives the expression of a transverse stripe, approximately four cells in width, in the early blastula embryo of insects. This enhancer has been extremely well characterized in the fruit fly, *Drosophila melanogaster* (see **illustration**), and it also has been identified in the sepsid fly. The enhancer sequences from these two species, which diverged approximately 100 million years ago, are homologous (they share a common ancestor), but

they are unalignable at the DNA sequence level. Moreover, the predicted locations of the TF binding sites are distinctly different. Yet, when the sepsid S2E is placed in *Drosophila*, it makes an embryonic stripe in nearly the same location as observed with the native S2E. This shows that many different configurations of binding sites with identical regulatory potential are possible. One interesting corollary of this structural flexibility in enhancer architecture is that the enhancer sequences often tend to be polymorphic (existing in different forms) in natural populations, and this mutational variability can fuel rapid regulatory evolution. A popular, although controversial, view among evolutionists is that regulatory evolution (not protein evolution) is the primary source of adaptive change.

For background information *see* CHROMOSOME; DEOXYRIBONUCLEIC ACID (DNA); DEVELOPMENTAL BIOLOGY; DEVELOPMENTAL GENETICS; GENE; GENE SILENCING; GENETIC MAPPING; GENETICS; GENOMICS; TRANSCRIPTION in the McGraw-Hill Encyclopedia of Science & Technology.

Martin Kreitman; Carlos A. Martinez

Bibliography. S. B. Carroll, Evo-devo and an expanding evolutionary synthesis: A genetic theory of morphological evolution, *Cell*, 134:25–36, 2008, DOI:10.1016/j.cell.2008.06.030; E. H. Davidson, *The Regulatory Genome: Gene Regulatory Networks in Development and Evolution*, Academic Press, Burlington, MA, 2006; E. E. Hare et al., Sepsid *even-skipped* enhancers are functionally conserved in *Drosophila* despite lack of sequence conservation, *PLoS Genet.*, 4:e1000106, 2008, DOI:10.1371/journal.pgen.1000106; B. Ondek, L. Gloss, and W. Herr, The SV40 enhancer contains two distinct levels of organization, *Nature*, 333:40–45, 1988, DOI:10.1038/333040a0.

Evolution of asteroid 4 Vesta

There are two ways to study how our solar system formed. One way is to observe distant, apparently similar solar systems that appear to be younger than our own and then develop a statistical picture of the formation and aging process. A second way is to study materials and objects that have survived since the earliest days of our solar system and then attempt to decode this record. Our observation of younger distant systems indicates that solar systems like ours arise in cold nebulae of gas and dust in which a

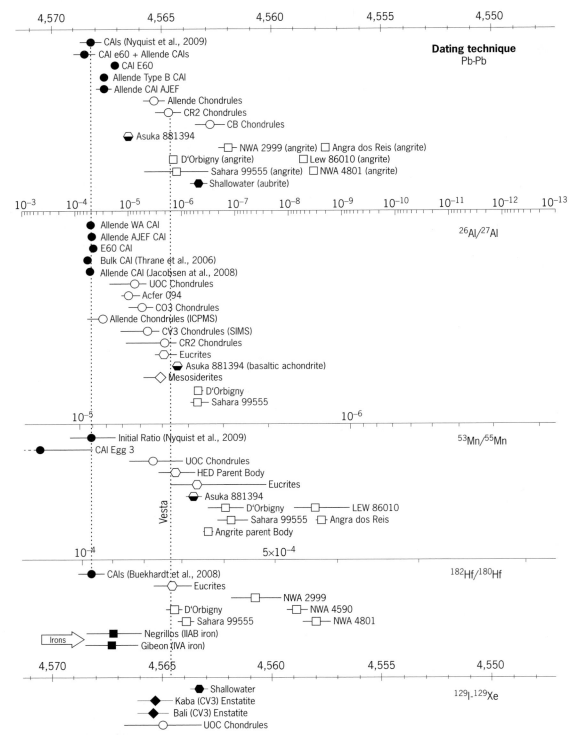

Fig. 1. Five dating techniques for meteorites using different elements that constrain the dates of events in the early solar system and the meteorites that have been studied using those techniques showing the dates obtained. (*From H. Y. McSween and G. R. Huss, Cosmochemistry, Cambridge University Press, 2010*)

large body of condensation forms as a result of a gravitational instability. This central rotating body is surrounded by a thin disk of gas and dust in which further condensation occurs.

A statistical picture such as this, however, is in many ways unsatisfactory because we wish to know our own particular history, which may be different from the norm. It is believed that early in the formation of our solar system a nearby supernova seeded the nebula with short-lived radioactive nuclei, in particular, ^{26}Al, which has a half-life of 7×10^5 yr. Any bodies condensing at this time would trap the ^{26}Al and its heat and then melt. The asteroid Vesta is believed to be one of the bodies that formed by accretion of primitive chondritic material (including live ^{26}Al) and melted, allowing iron to sink to its center and be surrounded by a silicate mantle. The silicate mantle solidified, was bombarded, and released chunks of rock that made their way to Earth via gravitationally induced scattering. Many pieces of early solar-system materials that reached Earth have been analyzed by geochemists using sensitive devices. These analyses have been used to develop a paradigm of the solar system's early history. It was the objective of the Dawn mission to test this paradigm by spending almost 14 months in orbit around Vesta from July 2011 to September 2012. *See* DAWN'S ASTEROID EXPLORATION.

Meteorite record. The study of meteorites and their geochemical properties has been an extremely productive means of elucidating what occurred in the early solar nebula and how silicate bodies formed, including the asteroids and terrestrial planets. Many dating techniques have been used, each of which is complementary to the others; combined, they provide a comprehensive and consistent history of the early solar system. **Figure 1** shows a summary of these measurements prepared by H. Y. McSween and G. R. Huss. Meteorites contain calcium-aluminum–rich inclusions (CAIs), the earliest-forming grains in our solar system that were incorporated into the chondritic material that later formed planetary bodies. These inclusions provide the evidence that a supernova seeded the solar system with short-lived ^{26}Al. If this very primitive ^{26}Al-rich material had accumulated in a small asteroid-sized body, the trapped heat would have melted the growing body. If the silicate melted, then the heavy materials (such as iron) could sink to the center of the body because of the asteroid's gravitational field. As illustrated in Fig. 1, the CAIs first appeared 4.568 billion years ago (BYA) and iron meteorites soon followed. The crust of Vesta, using the howardite-eucrite-diogenite (HED) meteorite clan as a proxy for the Vestan surface, appears to have been solid only 3 million years after the appearance of the CAIs. Asteroids associated with other meteorite families appear to have formed later, again as illustrated in Fig. 1.

The first member of the asteroid belt, 1 Ceres, was discovered in 1801; discoveries soon became almost routine, with 4 Vesta being discovered in

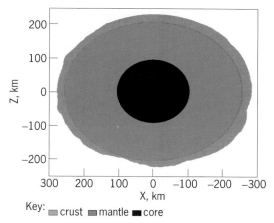

Fig. 2. Sketch of the interior of Vesta consistent with the shape, volume mass, and gravity measurements.

1807. Asteroids were subject to increasingly sophisticated investigation, but it was not until 1970 that T. B. McCord and coworkers realized that the infrared reflectance spectrum of Vesta showed that its surface was covered with a basaltic flow. Later it was shown that the HED meteorites had a similar spectrum and that Vesta might be the parent body of the HED meteorites. Where the finer-grained eucrites represent the upper crust, the coarser-grained (more slowly cooled) diogenites represent the lower crust and upper mantle, and the howardites are a brecciated mixture of eucrite and diogenite that resulted from impact shattering. When the opportunity arose for a principal investigator–led mission of the class capable of exploring Vesta from orbit, the Dawn mission was proposed; in 2001, it was accepted by NASA for flight. Based on the paradigm of the evolution of the solar system as deduced from the meteoritic record and on the hypothesis that Vesta was the HED parent body, the Dawn mission was prepared and launched in September 2007, just over 200 years after Vesta was first observed.

Confirmation of Vesta as the HED parent body. When Dawn slipped into orbit around Vesta in July 2011, some of the first measurements it made were of the gravity field and of the mass, shape, and volume of Vesta. These measurements constrain the interior structure of Vesta. **Figure 2** shows a sketch of the interior of Vesta that is consistent with the Dawn gravity data. There is a basaltic crust of eucrite on top of diogenite, a mantle of possibly olivine, and an iron core with a radius of about 110 km. The surface of Vesta is covered with eucrite (predominant in the north) and diogenite (predominant in the south). **Figure 3** shows the location of the two diagnostic absorption bands in the near-infrared (Band I and Band II, from the presence of two forms of the mineral pyroxene) plotted versus each other for the Vesta observations, compared to the oval regions defined for reflectance spectra of each of the three classes of meteorites (howardite, eucrite, and diogenite). The surface of Vesta is a regolith composed of a mixture of the original crustal materials, which were most probably originally layered. The surface

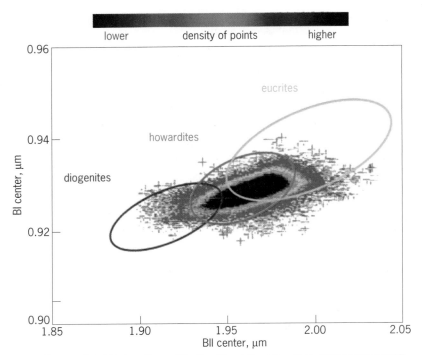

Fig. 3. Cluster plot of the locations of the Band I and Band II centers observed by the VIR mapping spectrometer compared with the location of those ratios in HED meteorites. *(After M. C. DeSanctis et al., Detection of widespread hydrated materials on Vesta by the VIR imaging spectrometer on board the Dawn mission, Astrophys. J., 758(2):L36, 2012b, DOI:10.1088/2041-8205/758/2/L36)*

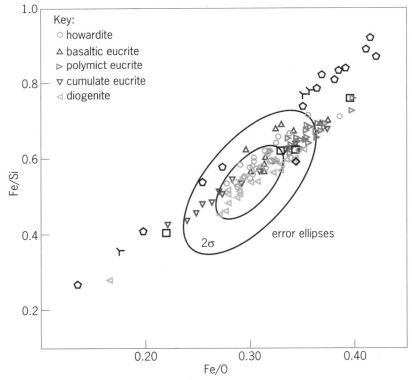

Fig. 4. Plot of the ratios of Fe/Si concentration versus Fe/O concentration for HED meteorites compared with the global ratio obtained at Vesta. *(After T. H. Prettyman et al., Elemental mapping by Dawn reveals exogenic H in Vesta's regolith, Science, 338(6104):242–246, 2012, DOI:10.1126/science.1225354)*

was expected to vary from eucritic to diogenetic in composition, as observed spectrally by the VIR (visible-infrared) instrument, with the majority of the surface indicating a mixture of both (howardite). This is precisely what was found, as shown in Fig. 3.

The measurement of elemental abundances made with the gamma-ray and neutron spectrometer supports this conclusion. **Figure 4** shows the ratios of iron to silicate versus the ratio of iron to oxygen measured at Vesta, compared with those same ratios in meteorites of different types. The best agreement is with the HEDs.

Since the geochemical and geophysical properties of Vesta are as expected from the HED meteorites, the Dawn science team has concluded that Vesta is indeed the parent body of the HED meteorites and that the history deduced from these meteorites is correct. At the same time, there are aspects of this history that are difficult to learn from the geochemistry, and the Dawn observations add important details to this story.

Bombardment of the Vestan surface. The asteroid belt is thought to have been a rather benign environment for planetary formation before the outer gas giants began to form. However, once Jupiter became a large point mass circling the solar system at a rate different from those at which the asteroids orbited, the asteroids were subjected to large perturbations in their motions by the gravitational pull of Jupiter, which forced them into collisions. This period is called the Jupiter Early Bombardment and was severe enough to be expected to remove a significant depth from Vesta's crust. Because it appears that the outer layer is at least partially still in place on Vesta, the timing and the location of Jupiter's formation may be constrained by Vesta's survival and the current state of the crust.

Later in Vesta's history, the giant planets moved into mutual resonances and migrated. This too resulted in a strong perturbation of asteroidal orbits, and Vesta was pummeled again, but probably not as hard. However, the Moon, which was finally in place orbiting the Earth during this Late Heavy Bombardment (LHB), suffered heavily because of the greater speeds of objects closer to the Sun and the resulting greater energy of any impacts. If we examine the Vestan cratering record, such as that shown in **Fig. 5**, we find that the number of craters versus their sizes for certain regions appears to approach cratering saturation about the time of the Late Heavy Bombardment, indicating that the entire surface of Vesta was bombarded. It is possible to relate ages derived from $^{40}Ar–^{39}Ar$ dating of lunar rocks with the LHB lunar cataclysm, so both Vesta and the Moon probably suffered from the same event. However, at Vesta the bombardment was gentler because of the lower speed of collisions at Vesta's orbit.

Vesta did continue to be bombarded, but either luck or the presence of its significant iron core protected it from complete destruction. **Figure 6** shows the topography of the southern hemisphere, which contains two large impact basins. It was known from

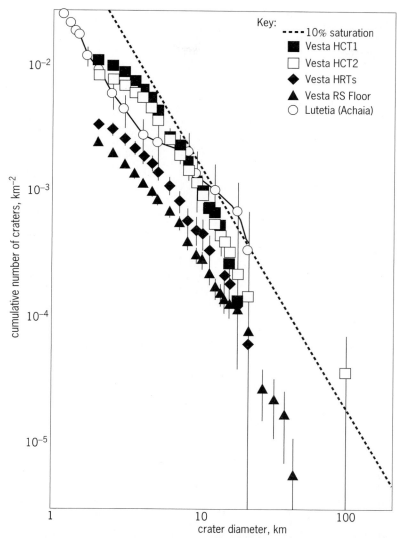

Fig. 5. The size–frequency distribution of craters on several different portions of the Vestan surface. HCT = Heavily Cratered Terrain (northern hemisphere); HRT = High Relief Terrain (equatorial); RS = Rheasilvia (southern hemisphere basin). (*Marchi et al., 2012*)

previous *Hubble Space Telescope* observations that Vesta has a large impact basin centered about its south pole, but the Dawn mission discovered that there were two basins and established their relative ages. The older and smaller Veneneia Basin dates from the period of the Late Heavy Bombardment or possibly as recent as 2 BYA, while the larger basin, Rheasilvia, was created only 1–2 BYA. The amount of material liberated during this collision was sufficient to populate the asteroid belt with a new set of kilometer-sized objects called the Vestoids, which have spectral reflectance similar to that of Vesta. Again the Dawn observations have provided a new layer of detail that brings greater understanding and confidence in the solar system paradigm.

Delivery of materials to Vesta. Vesta's surface is generally bright, but it is pockmarked with dark material. The bright materials are the pyroxene-rich diogenite and eucrite, but the dark material has no clear

spectral features that can be used for identification. The dark material appears to be carbonaceous material, examples of which can be found as dark clasts in HED meteorites. Although these dark deposits probably contain hydrous minerals, it is difficult to understand how they could have produced liquid, which seems necessary to produce the pits seen in the floors of several craters. It is possible that Vesta had subsurface ice that melted upon impact by a sufficiently large object.

The diversity of its surface materials makes Vesta a unique asteroid and a very colorful one. Although delivery of materials from elsewhere in the asteroid belt may be a possible source of this diversity, it is also possible that the interior of Vesta is not uniform and that a variety of different source regions were present on Vesta. Thus the story of Vesta's surface is not complete and much more work has yet to be done on the accumulated database.

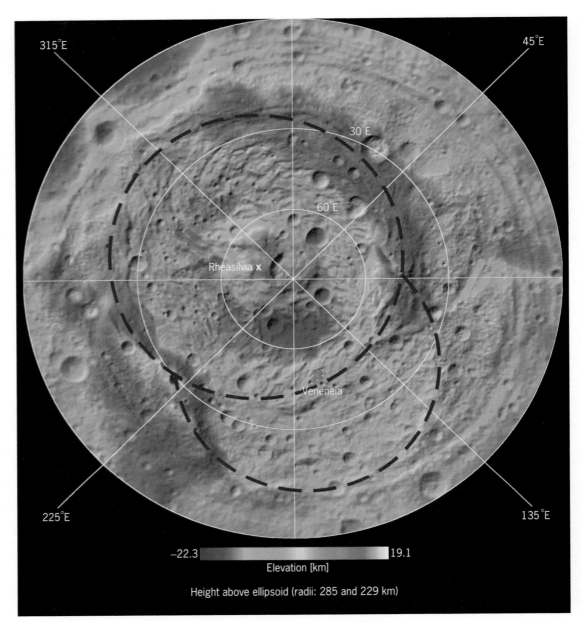

Fig. 6. Topography of the southern hemisphere showing the two giant impact basins.

For background information *see* ASTEROID; BASALT; COSMOCHEMISTRY; GEOCHEMISTRY; METEORITE; NEBULA; PYROXENE; REGOLITH; SOLAR SYSTEM; SPACE PROBE; SUPERNOVA in the McGraw-Hill Encyclopedia of Science & Technology.

Christopher T. Russell; Carol Anne Raymond

Bibliography. R. P. Binzel and S. Xu, Chips off of Asteroid 4 Vesta: Evidence for the parent body of basaltic achondrite meteorites, *Science*, 260(5105):186–191, 1993, DOI:10.1126/science.260.5105.186; R. P. Binzel et al., Geologic mapping of Vesta from 1994 Hubble Space Telescope images, *Icarus*, 128:95–103, 1997, DOI:10.1006/icar.1997.5734; G. J. Consolmagno and M. J. Drake, Composition and evolution of the eucrite parent body: Evidence from rare earth elements, *Geochim. Cosmochim. Acta*, 41(9):1271–1282, 1977, DOI:10.1016/0016-7037(77)90072-2; A. Coradini et al., Vesta and Ceres: Crossing the history of the solar system, *Space Sci. Rev.*, 163(1–4), 25, 2011, DOI:10.1007/s11214-011-9792-x; B. W. Denevi et al., Pitted terrain on Vesta and implications for the presence of volatiles, *Science*, 338(6104):246–249, 2012, DOI:10.1126/science.1225374; M. C. DeSanctis et al., Spectroscopic characterization of mineralogy and its diversity across Vesta, *Science*, 336(6082):697–700, 2012a, DOI:10.1126/science.1219270; M. C. DeSanctis et al., Detection of widespread hydrated materials on Vesta by the VIR imaging spectrometer on board the Dawn mission, *Astrophys. J.*, 758(2):L36, 2012b, DOI:10.1088/2041-8205/758/2/L36; R. Gomes et al., Origin of the cataclysmic Late Heavy Bombardment period of the terrestrial planets, *Nature*, 435:466–469, 2005, DOI:10.1038/nature03676; R. Jaumann et al., Vesta's shape and morphology, *Science*, 336(6082):687–690, 2012, DOI:10.1126/science. 1219122; S. Marchi et al., The violent collisional history of Asteroid 4 Vesta, *Science*, 336(6082):690–694, 2012, DOI:10.1126/science. 1218757; H. Y. McSween and G. R. Huss, *Cosmochemistry*, Cambridge University Press, 2010; T. B. McCord, J. B. Adams, and T. V. Johnson, Asteroid Vesta: Spectral reflectivity and compositional implications, *Science*, 168(3938):1445–1447, 1970, DOI:10.1126/science.168.3938.1445; T. H. Prettyman et al., Elemental mapping by Dawn reveals exogenic H in Vesta's regolith, *Science*, 338(6104):242–246, 2012, DOI:10.1126/science. 1225354; V. A. Reddy et al., Color and albedo heterogeneity of Vesta from Dawn, *Science*, 336(6082):700–704, 2012a, DOI:10.1126/science. 1219088; V. Reddy et al., Delivery of dark material to Vesta via carbonaceous chondritic impacts, *Icarus*, 221(2):471–1190, 2012b, DOI:10.1016/j.icarus. 2012.08.011; C. T. Russell et al., Dawn at Vesta: Testing the protoplanetary paradigm, *Science*, 336:684, 2012, DOI:10.1126/science.1219381; P. Schenk et al., The geologically recent giant impact basins at Vesta's south pole, *Science*, 336(6082):694–697, 2012, DOI:10.1126/science.1223272; J. E. C. Scully et al., Potential transient liquid water flow features in fresh craters on Vesta, Geological Society of America, *Abstr. Programs*, 44(7):278, 2012; T. J. Stubbs and Y. Wang, Illumination conditions at the Asteroid 4 Vesta: Implications for the presence of water ice, *Icarus*, 217(1):272–276, 2012, DOI:10.1016/ j.icarus.2011.11.007; P. C. Thomas et al., Impact excavation on Asteroid 4 Vesta: Hubble Space Telescope results, *Science*, 277(5331):1492–1495, 1997, DOI:10.1126/science.277.5331.1492; D. Turrini, G. Magni, and A. Coradini, Probing the history of solar system through the cratering records on Vesta and Ceres, *Mon. Not. R. Astron. Soc.*, 413:2439–2466, 2011, DOI:10.1111/j.1365-2966.2011.18316.x.

Feed-in tariff

The feed-in tariff (FIT) is an incentive scheme that is designed to encourage the development of renewable energy sources. Several sources of energy, such as fossil fuels, renewable energy sources, and nuclear fuels, are used to generate electricity. Electric power systems are developed and operated on landscapes that dictate the type of transmission system and the available sources of energy. They cost billions of dollars, taking decades to build, with typical asset lives spanning from a quarter to half a century.

The decision to use one or more energy sources is based on the intersection of multiple factors, which include policies, economics, and availability. Economic factors often take precedence in the absence of others. Historically, coal-based power plants were operated worldwide with a disregard for environmental pollution. However, energy policy makers worldwide have begun seeking alternatives to establish energy self-reliance and to reduce pollution. These policies, in addition to economic factors, have caused a change in the way energy is sourced and delivered.

Typically, it takes around half a century for a new energy source to mature in its technology and delivery methods. Creating and operating a supply chain of energy requires phenomenal drive and economic incentives. For example, the nuclear industry, which began in the 1950s, has relied significantly on subsidies to reach its current level of maturity. In 2011, 12.3% of the world's electricity production was provided by nuclear power stations. **Figure 1** shows the growth of the nuclear industry in France, the United States, and Japan over 50 years.

Today, the renewable energy supply is still in the early phase of its development life cycle. Renewable energy sources are mandated by a policy that seeks a pollution-free energy supply. Despite being abundant and free, renewable energy is not the most economically attractive source of energy. There are costs associated with equipment, installation, and maintenance, among other factors. Furthermore, there is a significant requirement for additional transmission and distribution capacity to integrate renewable energy sources. Although highly reliable equipment is used to provide renewable energy, the energy supply is intermittent. This intermittency creates additional operating costs, all of which must be borne by customers. As a result, it will require years of incentives to see the growth and maturity of renewable energy sources.

Operation and implementation. The feed-in tariff has been implemented in several ways and in several jurisdictions. The main schemes provide either constant rates or incentives for renewable energy sources. In the fixed-tariff scheme, renewable energy generators are paid a fixed rate in dollars per kilowatt hour that equals the cost and a nominal profit. In Canada, the province of Ontario has implemented an FIT system to incentivize growth of renewable energy sources (see **table**). These rates are much higher than those paid by customers today, who pay in the range of 5–10 cents per kilowatt hour for the existing generation mix.

The fixed-tariff system is particularly troublesome when a power system has an oversupply of generation, that is, the minimum generation is more than the system load. In this situation, customers are paid to consume more, that is, they pay negative prices. Even in those oversupply situations, renewable energy sources continue to supply energy and get paid at FIT rates, causing a significant financial burden to customers.

Other jurisdictions have focused on alternative incentive schemes. For example, New York State has implemented the New York Sun Competitive Photovoltaic (PV) Program. In this case, the New York State Energy Research and Development Authority

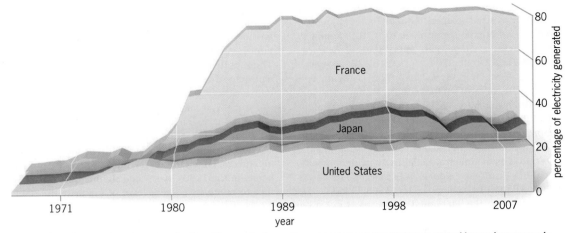

Fig. 1. Growth of nuclear energy production. The graph shows the percentage of electricity generated by nuclear power in France, Japan, and the United States. (*V. Smil, A skeptic looks at alternative energy, IEEE Spectrum, 49(7):46–52, July 2012; courtesy of Bryan Christie Design*)

(NYSERDA) seeks proposals for the installation of customer-sited photovoltaic projects of more than 50 MW capacity. Projects demonstrating viability are competitively selected based on their incentive bid in dollars per kilowatt hour. Each project has a site incentive given by the equation below.

(site incentive) = (incentive bid)
× (site estimated annual energy production)
× (3 years)

NYSERDA makes two up-front payments of 15% of the project site incentive when the project is completed and when the project is connected, respectively, and it makes performance payments each year for three consecutive years. For each year of the three-year performance period, the performance payment equals 70% of the applicant's incentive bid multiplied by the site's actual annual energy production in kilowatt hours. Thereafter, these

resources bid into the New York Independent System Operator (NYISO)-operated electricity market. When scheduled, they are paid at competitive market rates that are in addition to applicant incentives.

When the demand and price of energy is high, renewable energy sources become profitable. The drawback is that when the market price of energy is low, or negative, renewable energy generation leads to a financial loss for these sources. Renewable energy is intermittent and uncertain; as a result, this NYISO scheme ensures that renewable projects are economically viable for renewable generators and protects customers from their financial burden.

Figure 2 demonstrates how the above-mentioned policies have caused a shift in the wind-energy sector in the United States.

Drivers. The main driver for FIT is the policy aim of sourcing carbon-free energy. This policy is created to reduce pollution and fight climate change. Some jurisdictions have a significant source of renewable

Feed-in tariff prices for renewable energy projects in Ontario					
Fuel	Project size, kW	FIT price, ¢/kWh	Fuel	Project size, kW	FIT price, ¢/kWh
Solar, rooftop	≤10	54.9	Water	≤10,000	13.1
	>10	54.8		>10,000	12.2
	≤100* (250)			≤50,000	
	>100 (250)	53.9	Biomass	≤10,000	13.8
	≤500*				
	>500	48.7		>10,000	13.0
Solar, ground mount	≤10	44.5	Biogas on farm	≤100	19.5
	>10	38.8		>100	18.5
	≤ 500*			≤250	
	>500	35.0	Biogas	≤500	16.0
	≤5,000*				
	>5,000	34.7		>500	14.7
				≤10,000	
Wind	All sizes	11.5		>10,000	10.4
			Landfill gas	≤10,000	11.1
				>10,000	10.3

*New project size.
SOURCE: *Ontario Feed-in Tariff Program, Two-Year Review,* March 2012 (http://www.energy.gov.on.ca/en/fit-and-microfit-program/2-year-fit-review/appendix-4/)

generation. For example, in Canada, the province of Quebec generates more than 90% of its energy from hydroelectricity, which is a renewable source of energy. Hence, incentives in Quebec are low to transition into wind or solar energy. At the other extreme, the Danish system largely uses coal and is highly motivated to transition to renewable energy sources such as wind and solar energy.

Relation to carbon taxes. FIT is a policy used to encourage renewable energy supply, thus reducing carbon-intensive energy production. Renewable energy sources are one of the tools available to achieve the end result of sourcing carbon-free energy.

There are also other methods to achieve the same goal of sourcing carbon-free energy, for example, imposing carbon taxes or imposing limits on carbon emissions. A carbon tax is levied on processes such as electricity generation, with an aim of reducing carbon emissions and mitigating their associated harmful environmental impacts. Carbon taxes increase the cost of the energy being taxed, resulting in reduced energy consumption of that particular source of energy. When carbon emission limits are imposed, industries are mandated (and not incented) to reduce their emissions. Typically, they invest in various mechanisms such as sequestering or carbon capture to achieve emission reductions. In all cases, the cost of these additional investments would be passed directly and indirectly to customers. Further, these would result in the development of a carbon cap and trade system.

Impact on electricity market prices. In essence, all additional costs of sourcing and managing energy from renewables will be either passed to customers or subsidized by tax payers. In the first case, it is a direct translation of costs. In the latter case, it is an indirect transfer of costs to a larger base. Direct contracting of the renewable energy supply through the FIT mechanism also reduces opportunities for other generators to competitively sell energy into the market, depressing the market price. Further, with additional renewables in the system, the operator would have to procure a higher amount of reserves, ramping capacity, and so forth, creating additional market opportunities.

Implementation challenges. Integration of renewable energy sources poses several technical challenges. First, power systems must always balance demand and supply of energy in real time. Uncertainty in the energy supply from renewable energy sources poses a challenge for power system operators to maintain this demand-supply balance. Power system operators are now trying to procure additional capacities, such as advanced forecasting of wind and solar energy, additional generation reserves (spinning reserves), and additional operational flexibility (ramping capacity), to combat the uncertainty and intermittency of renewable energy sources.

Additional challenges arise from the characteristics of the electric distribution system. For example, distribution system lines in Ontario are very long, resulting in technical challenges to operation with

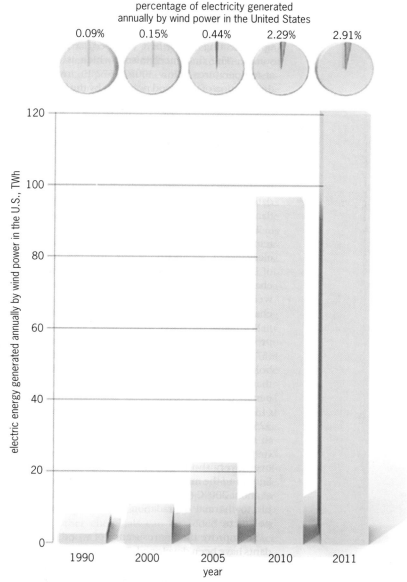

Fig. 2. Growth of wind electricity in the United States. The bar graph shows the electric energy generated annually in the United States, in terawatt-hours (1 TWh = 10^12 Wh), in the years shown. The pie charts show the percentages of the total electric energy generated annually in the United States that were generated by wind power in these years. (*V. Smil, A skeptic looks at alternative energy, IEEE Spectrum, 49(7):46–52, July 2012; courtesy of Bryan Christie Design*)

intermittent renewable energy sources. These challenges are being addressed through research and development initiatives.

For background information *see* AIR POLLUTION; CLIMATE MODIFICATION; ELECTRIC POWER GENERATION; ELECTRIC POWER SYSTEMS; ENERGY SOURCES; ENERGY STORAGE; GLOBAL CLIMATE CHANGE; NUCLEAR POWER; SOLAR ENERGY; WATER POWER; WIND POWER in the McGraw-Hill Encyclopedia of Science & Technology.

Bala Venkatesh; Rachel Lan Chung Yang
Bibliography. V. Smil, A skeptic looks at alternative energy, *IEEE Spectrum*, 49(7):46–52, July 2012, DOI:10.1109/MSPEC.2012.6221082.

Chemicals containing phosphorus are one of the oldest classes of fire retardants. Monoammonium and diammonium phosphates are used with nitrogen compounds because the synergistic effect allows less chemical to be used. Organophosphorus and polyphosphate compounds are also used as fire retardants. Ammonium polyphosphate at loading levels of 96 kg/m^3 (6 lb/ft^3) gives a flame-spread index of 15. This treatment generates a low smoke yield, but it is corrosive to aluminum and mild steel. Other formulations containing phosphorus are mixtures of (1) guanyl urea phosphate (GUP) and boric acid (BA) and (2) phosphoric acid, boric acid, and ammonia. The most effective chemical is phosphoric acid, with a weight loss of 61% as compared to 93% for untreated wood.

Borax and boric acid are the most often used fire retardants. Borates have low melting points and form glassy films upon exposure to high temperatures. Borax inhibits surface flame spread, but also promotes smoldering and glowing. Boric acid reduces smoldering and glowing combustion, but has little effect on flame spread. Because of this, borax and boric acid are typically used together. The alkaline borates also result in less strength loss in the treated wood and are less corrosive and hydroscopic. In addition, boron compounds are combined with other chemicals, such as phosphorus and amine compounds, to increase their effectiveness.

The most widely studied leach-resistant fire retardant system is based on amino-resins. Basically, the resin system consists of a combination of a nitrogen source (that is, urea, melamine, guanidine, or dicyandiamide) with formaldehyde to produce a methylolated (hydroxymethylated) amine. The product is then reacted with a phosphorus compound such as phosphoric acid. Other formulations can include mixtures of (1) dicyandiamide, melamine, formaldehyde, and phosphoric acid or (2) dicyandiamide, urea, formaldehyde, phosphoric acid, formic acid, and sodium hydroxide. Leach resistance is attributed to polymerization of the components within the wood. Another formulation uses a urea and melamine amino-resin. The stability of these resins is controlled by the rate of methylolation of the urea, melamine, and dicyandiamide.

For background information *see* BUILDINGS; CHARCOAL; COMBUSTION; FIRE; FIRE TECHNOLOGY; FLAMEPROOFING; POLYMER; THERMAL ANALYSIS; WOOD ANATOMY; WOOD ENGINEERING DESIGN; WOOD PROPERTIES in the McGraw-Hill Encyclopedia of Science & Technology.   Roger M. Rowell

Bibliography. S. L. LeVan, Chemistry of fire retardancy, pp. 531–574, in R. M. Rowell (ed.), *Chemistry of Solid Wood*, American Chemical Society, Washington, DC, 1984; R. M. Rowell (ed.), *Handbook of Wood Chemistry and Composites*, CRC Press, New York, 2012; F. Shafizadeh, The chemistry of pyrolysis and combustion, pp. 489–530, in R. M. Rowell (ed.), *Chemistry of Solid Wood*, American Chemical Society, Washington, DC, 1984.

Forensic isotope analysis

Are two cocaine "bricks" seized as part of two independent police operations part of the same drug-running operation or are they part of two different drug-dealing organizations operating in the same city? Are the hundreds of ecstasy tablets seized during the search of a suspected drug dealer's house linked to the handful of ecstasy tablets found on the suspect or are they, as per the suspect's defense, completely unrelated, having been stashed unbeknownst to him by a friend crashing at his home for a night? Was an unidentified homicide victim a local resident or had this person only recently moved to this location? When is one batch of methamphetamine not the same as another batch of methamphetamine? All these questions have two things in common. First, these are all questions typically asked in the context of a legal case, be it criminal or civil law. Second, these questions can all be answered by stable isotope forensics, which is the forensic application of stable isotope analytical techniques.

Stable isotopes. Almost all of the 92 naturally occurring chemical elements occur in more than one isotopic form. The vast majority of these isotopes are stable isotopes, which, unlike radioisotopes (radioactive isotopes), do not decay. The natural chemical elements are listed in the periodic table of chemical elements in order of increasing atomic number Z, which is defined by the number of protons in the nucleus of an atom. Isotopic atoms of the same chemical element share the same atomic number but differ in their atomic weight since they contain a different number of neutrons in their nuclei. A well-known example of a chemical element that exists in multiple isotopic forms is carbon (C), which in its major abundant isotopic form is made up of 6 protons and 6 neutrons, thus having an atomic weight of 12 atomic mass units. The chemical notation for this isotope is ^{12}C. However, carbon can also occur in two other isotopic forms: ^{13}C with one extra neutron, a stable isotope, and ^{14}C with two extra neutrons, a radioisotope whose existence is probably more widely known because of its use as a dating tool in archaeology (for example, carbon-14 dating).

Stable isotope analysis. In contrast to the global isotope abundance figures quoted for a given light element (see **table**), the abundance of a given light element in a chemical compound is subject to minute yet accurately measurable variation around its globally fixed natural abundance value. For example, the range of natural abundance variation for ^{13}C is of the order of 0.11 atom %, with the majority of organic compounds falling into a range from 1.1099 to 1.0539 at%, that is, a range of 0.056 at% in ^{13}C. These minute changes in isotope abundance at natural abundance levels cannot be reliably detected, let alone measured and quantified by analytical instruments such as the scanning mass spectrometers (MS) routinely used in a forensic chemistry

Stable isotopes of selected light elements and their global natural abundance to two significant decimals			
Chemical element	Major abundant isotope	First minor abundant isotope	Isotope ratio of first minor/major for scale calibration material
Hydrogen	^{1}H 99.985 at%	^{2}H 0.015 at%	0.00015576 VSMOW*
Carbon	^{12}C 98.89 at%	^{13}C 1.11 at%	0.0112372 VPDB†
Nitrogen	^{14}N 99.63 at%	^{15}N 0.37 at%	0.0036765 Air

*Vienna Standard Mean Ocean Water.
†Vienna Pee Dee Belemnite.

laboratory. This is due to a relative standard deviation (RSD) of typically 10% associated with ion-current measurement by scanning MS equipped with a single electron multiplier detector.

To overcome the limitations imposed by the scanning single-detector MS, isotope abundance is measured by magnetic-sector MS instruments with dedicated channels per isotope (multi-collector MS), expressing natural abundances of stable isotopes in a given material as the ratio of the heavier isotope over the lighter isotope of a given element (for example, ^{2}H/^{1}H or ^{13}C/^{12}C). Measured isotope ratios of a given sample are expressed relative to a contemporaneously measured isotope ratio of a standard of known isotopic composition and the results are expressed in the "delta notation" (δ). The δ-value of the heavier isotope **h** of a chemical element **E** for a given sample reported versus a given standard is defined by the equation below, where R_{sample} is the isotope

$$\delta^h E_{\text{sample/standard}} = \delta^h E_{\text{standard}} = (R_{\text{sample}}/R_{\text{standard}}) - 1$$

ratio of the heavier isotope over the lighter isotope (for example, ^{2}H/^{1}H) for the sample and R_{standard} is the isotope ratio for the international measurement standard, which in the case of ^{2}H is Vienna Standard Mean Ocean Water (VSMOW).

By virtue of its definition, the δ value of a scale defining international reference standard is 0. A positive δ value therefore means the sample has a higher abundance of the heavier isotope than the standard that defines the scale for a particular isotope, while a negative δ value means the sample has a lower abundance of the heavier isotope than the international reference standard. Since δ values derived from the above equation are numerically very small, they are either expressed as ‰ value, that is, as a multiple of 10^{-3} (for example, $\delta^2 H_{\text{VSMOW}} = -0.0095 = -9.5 \times 10^{-3} = -9.5‰$) or they are reported as a 1000-fold of a δ value but in this case as a dimensionless number (for example, $10^3 \delta^2 H_{\text{VSMOW}} = -9.5$).

Chemically indistinguishable yet not the same. If all chromatographic and spectroscopic data of two compounds correspond, it may be concluded that they are chemically indistinguishable. On this basis, sugar (or sucrose) obtained from sugarbeets and sugarcane are chemically the same but isotopically

different. The chemical formula for sucrose extracted from either plant is identical, namely $C_{12}H_{22}O_{11}$. However, compared to beet sugar, cane sugar is isotopically enriched in ^{13}C. While beet sugar typically exhibits $\delta^{13}C_{\text{VPDB}}$ values of around $-26‰$, $\delta^{13}C_{\text{VPDB}}$ values for cane sugar are typically found to be around $-11‰$ (**Fig. 1**).

With increasing frequency this same distinction between being chemically identical but not necessarily being the same is brought forward as a defense when the assertion is made that drug samples found in the possession of a suspect and drug samples found at the suspect's home may be chemically indistinguishable but they are otherwise completely unrelated (not the same). The "same" is understood as the sharing of a link, such as a common sample history or sample provenance. Multivariate stable isotope abundance analysis holds the potential to resolve this argument by providing an additional set of independent variables (for example, variables that are independent of other spectroscopic

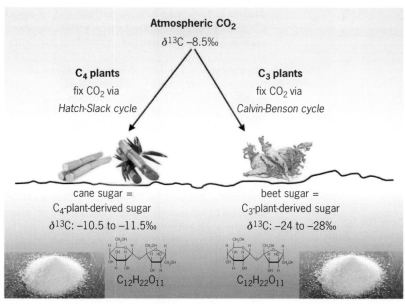

Fig. 1. Sugarcane and sugarbeets both produce sucrose, but due to the different routes of carbon dioxide (CO_2) fixation (Hatch-Slack cycle or C_4 pathway versus Calvin-Benson cycle or C_3 pathway) the associated different rates of mass discrimination toward ^{13}C lead to isotopically different sucrose being produced by either plant.

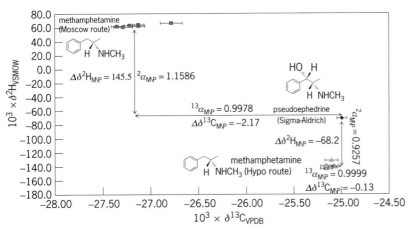

Fig. 2. Starting from the same precursor material (pseudoephedrine), different isotopic fraction factors α associated with different synthetic routes yield isotopically different products even though they are chemically identical, namely methamphetamine.

characteristics) that reflect how a compound was made and where.

In the same way differences in reaction kinetics (different rates of enzyme activity) or biochemical pathways result in differences in the stable isotopic composition of natural chemical compounds, such as sugar from different plant sources, differences in synthetic routes, or synthesis conditions yield isotopically different yet chemically identical synthetic compounds, including illegal drugs made in a clandestine laboratory. For example, the isotopic signature of methamphetamine made via the Moscow route is significantly different from the isotopic signature of methamphetamine made via the hypophosphorous route (**Fig. 2**).

Human provenancing. Probably one of the most impressive and, from a humanitarian point of view, the most important application of forensic isotope analysis is its ability to provide information about a person's geographic life history or life trajectory without requiring a person-specific database. International investigative authorities, such as Interpol, advocate that it is vital to identify a deceased person to allow the remains to be returned to the family for proper recognition and religious observance. Grieving and acceptance of death facilitate ultimate recovery and are an established and fundamental core facet of the reconciliation process with the death of a loved one. It is equally important for judicial matters related to the estate of the deceased that resolution is achieved at an early date.

Should a deceased be the victim of a violent crime, this adds to the need of positive identification, since a victim's identity will in most cases lead to the killer's identity. Murder investigations are particularly hampered in their efforts to establish a person's identity when a victim's body is badly deteriorated due to natural causes, such as decomposition or animal activity, or in cases where, for a variety of motives, post-mortem mutilation of the victim's body has taken place. In such cases, mutilation typically involves destruction of facial features, through destruction of dentition or through decapitation, and can extend to the removal of both hands and the lower legs. In the absence of any other distinguishing feature, such as jewelry, clothing, or body art, identification of mutilated murder victims becomes nearly impossible by traditional identification techniques unless the victim has a particular background, such as their fingerprints or DNA profile being on record in a national database. In the vast majority of such investigations, this is not the case.

Case examples. The two case examples discussed below illustrate the investigative power of forensic isotope analysis.

The case of the Scissor Sisters, Dublin, Ireland. One of the more high-profile cases our research group was involved with was the case of a dismembered body found by schoolboys in the Royal Canal near Ballybough, Dublin, Republic of Ireland, in 2005. The high level of attention and coverage the Irish media dedicated to this case was at first a reflection of the rather unusual and gruesome case circumstance, and later a reflection of the fact that the perpetrators of this crime were two sisters aged 23 and 31, who were dubbed by the media initially as "The Butcher Sisters" and later "The Scissor Sisters."

No match in the missing persons' files could be found and enquiries in the local community furnished no leads. After all attempts to identify the victim by traditional techniques did not reveal anything, the Garda Síochána (national police service of Ireland) detectives contacted the author asking if forensic isotope analyses could aid their investigation. Stable isotope signatures obtained from pubic hair, a toenail, and a slice of femoral bone taken midshaft revealed a man who had neither changed diet nor place of residence during the last 6 months of his life but who had not lived all of his life in Dublin or an area consistent with the stable isotope markers present in his tissues either (**Fig. 3**). Based on the remodeling rate for a midshaft femoral bone in males and a simple two-pool mixing model, we calculated the victim had immigrated to the Republic of Ireland 6.3 ± 3 years prior to death. Based on the ^{18}O signature in the oldest bone samples, we concluded that prior to immigration the victim had resided in a hot climate and near an equatorial region, specifically the countries comprising the Horn of Africa, such as Kenya or Somalia (Fig. 3).

These results and conclusions were reported to the investigating officer, who at the same time had developed several hypotheses, or leads, yet none of them strong enough to justify more resources being committed for a follow-up. In particular, one potential line of investigation required obtaining legal and financial authorization for cross-DNA matching procedures with DNA samples from presumed next-of-kin. According to the investigating officer, the results of the forensic stable isotope analysis provided him with the justification needed to pursue the DNA testing of both a child (believed to have been fathered by the victim) and the mother of this child. The DNA cross-match showed the victim to be the father of

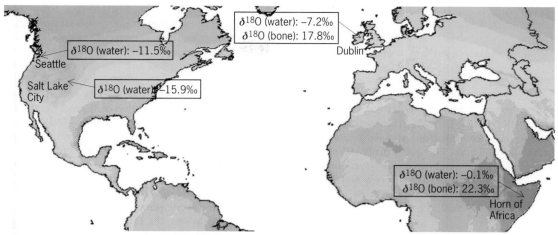

Fig. 3. Partial isoscape for ^{18}O abundance in water showing $\delta^{18}O_{VSMOW}$ values for local water in Dublin, the Horn of Africa, Salt Lake City, and Seattle. In relation to the case example "Scissor Sisters" $\delta^{18}O_{VSMOW}$ values for human bone phosphate (PO$_4$$^{3-}$) corresponding to Dublin and the Horn of Africa are also shown. The partial isoscape is based on a global ^{18}O isoscape available from Waterisotopes.org (http://www.waterisotopes.org).

that child, which in turn helped the police establish the victim's true identity. The deceased, Farah Swaleh Noor, was a 39-year-old man of African descent, originally from Kenya who had immigrated to Ireland in 1998; that is, 7 years prior to death, a figure that compared very favorably with our assessment of the victim having entered the country 6.3 ± 3 years prior to death. Once Mr. Noor's identity had been established, his two killers were quickly identified, ultimately leading to the convictions of two sisters, dubbed by the media "The Scissor Sisters," for murder and manslaughter on October 28, 2006 and their eventual sentencing to life and 15 years' imprisonment, respectively, on December 4, 2006.

Saltair Sally, Great Salt Lake, Utah. This case dates back to October 2000 when a pair of duck hunters walking along the south shore of the Great Salt Lake in Utah, just 30 m (100 ft) from Interstate 80, found buried in a shallow grave a plastic bag containing a white sock, an oversized t-shirt, a woven blue choker necklace, 12 bones, and a human skull. Police gathered what clues they could from the remains of "Saltair Sally," named after a resort near the place where her remains were found. The body was badly decomposed and dental records did not yield any results. A widely circulated composite sketch and description of her personal effects yielded no valuable information. In the absence of any means of identification, the case soon went cold.

Reviewing the case in 2007, the state medical examiner released a sample of Saltair Sally's long, blonde hair to be tested by stable isotope analysis, a new forensic technique that had been introduced in the intervening years. The hair sample was submitted to IsoForensics, a company founded by James Ehleringer of the University of Utah, and was duly prepared and analyzed by Lesley Chesson for ^{2}H and ^{18}O abundance and any changes thereof along the length of hair, that is, during Saltair Sally's last 2 years of life. If Saltair Sally had been living in Salt Lake City

during the last couple of months prior to her death, the hair closest to her scalp would reflect the isotopic signature of Salt Lake City's local water supply, which is depleted in ^{2}H. On the other hand, if she had most recently lived in Miami, for example, her hair's isotopic composition would be more enriched in ^{2}H, giving investigators a valuable clue about her recent geographic life history.

Stable isotope analysis revealed a changing ^{2}H/^{18}O signature within the 2 years leading up to Saltair Sally's death suggesting frequent changes in geographic location. The isotope signatures indicated she had moved at least three or four times, and it seemed there was a kind of cyclic pattern to her movements. She had moved from a region consistent with Salt Lake City and the Intermountain Western United States to a location in the Northwest with a water isotopic signature consistent with Seattle (Fig. 3). This pattern was repeated a couple of times in the years leading up to her death.

Armed with this new information, detectives refocused their investigation on the regions Chesson and her colleagues had suggested. Yet it was not until August 2012 that they caught a break in the case. Salt Lake Unified Police announced on August 7, 2012 that, with the help of stable isotope analysis, they had identified Saltair Sally. Her name was Nikole Bakoles. The cyclic pattern of travel between Salt Lake City and Seattle recorded in Saltair Sally's hair matched information provided in Bakoles' missing persons' report, which had been filed in 2003. A DNA test confirmed the match. Bakoles, who was aged 20 at the time of her death, was last seen in March 2000 when she was living in a hotel in a southern suburb of Salt Lake City with her boyfriend and young child. In the preceding years, she had traveled to Seattle occasionally to visit family members, a habit which was clearly recorded in the isotopic composition of her hair. Without that information, it is very likely Saltair Sally would never have been identified.

For background information *see* ATOMIC NUM-BER; CRIMINALISTICS; ISOTOPE; MASS SPECTROME-TRY; MASS SPECTROSCOPE; PERIODIC TABLE in the McGraw-Hill Encyclopedia of Science & Technology.
Wolfram Meier-Augenstein

Bibliography. B. Fry, *Stable Isotope Ecology*, Springer, New York, 2006; W. Meier-Augenstein, *Stable Isotope Forensics*, Wiley-Blackwell, Chichester, UK, 2010; T. J. T. Thomson and S. M. Black (eds.), *Forensic Human Identification*, CRC Press, Boca Raton, FL, 2007; J. B. West et al. (eds.), *Isoscapes: Understanding Movement, Pattern, and Process on Earth through Isotope Mapping*, Springer Science + Business Media, Dordrecht, the Netherlands, 2009.

Forensic photography

In general terms, forensic photography can be described as any type of photography and imaging that pertains to the law. This means photographs taken by police and forensic investigators for the purpose of expressing evidence and concepts in court or used during the forensic analysis of physical evidence. However, the expression forensic photography has several different meanings, depending on the discipline for which it is used. Forensic photography may include the following practices:

1. Crime scene photography
2. Scientific photography
3. Optical enhancement of evidence
4. Detection of latent (invisible) evidence
5. Interpretation of photographs as forensic evidence
6. Detection of photographic fakery

7. Production of visual media for court presentation (photographs, posters and charts, and so on).

This article will examine several different forms of forensic photography and describe the fundamental framework around forensic photography practices and their principles. The majority of images used in this article are those of shoemark evidence, used to highlight the level of variation of approaches within forensic photography as a discipline.

Crime scene photography. Crime scene photography is the recording of scenes at which a criminal incident has occurred. This type of forensic photography has two distinctively different approaches, depending on the outcome required. The first function of crime scene photography is to record items of evidence in situ, the location relating to the evidence, and the condition of the scene. This approach requires developing a visual narrative that can illustrate to the court the important crime scene circumstances relevant to the case. Visual narratives use a collection of images to illustrate a concept or account. The second function of crime scene photography is to preserve evidence that will require further laboratory analysis made directly from these photographs recorded at the scene. Physical evidence such as impression evidence of fingermarks and shoe marks undergo further forensic analysis in the laboratory and require the images to be taken using a forensic photography criterion to maintain the evidence integrity and in particular their dimensional integrity (**Figs. 1–3**).

An examination methodology for impression evidence and other pattern-based evidence applies a side-by-side comparison between the impression image found and recorded at the scene and a known or exemplar sample made in the forensic laboratory. This examination process involves the analysis of certain distinctive features inherent in both impressions to determine the source of the impression left at the scene. For example, a bloody shoemark left at the scene is compared with an exemplar impression made from a shoe seized by police from a possible suspect. This forensic examination determines whether the suspect's shoe is the source of the impression left at the scene or whether it may be eliminated as not having made the mark. Criminal offenders may be identified by impression evidence; alternatively, this evidence can quickly eliminate suspects from the investigation, which has important protective social benefits to potential suspects and offers resourcing benefits to investigating agencies.

Forensic photographs taken at a crime scene for this type of analysis must be recorded with minimal corruption of the dimensional integrity of the impression so that when a side-by-side comparison is conducted, both unknown and known impressions display similar and accurate dimensional qualities. The examination method also requires the known and unknown source images to be of the same magnification, which is usually 1:1 for shoemark examinations and 5:1 for fingerprints, further promoting the like-for-like qualities associated with this

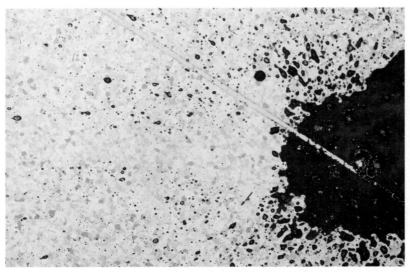

Fig. 1. Crime scene photograph of a bloodstain pattern. The bloodstains illustrated in this image were formed by blood dripping from a table and into a pool of blood on the floor. The photograph also reveals a void in the shape of a claw hammer, which indicates it may have been removed from the scene sometime after the incident. This is a complex condition of the scene, and the photograph provides the court with a method of explanation so that lay jurors can understand. (*Photo courtesy of Glenn Porter*)

(a)   (b)   (c)

Fig. 2. Note that the two additions to the image include a Bureau linear scale designed for shoemark evidence and the blue golf ball marker. The Bureau scale is used to establish scale, while the golf ball marker is used to indicate the lighting direction (note the shadow direction). These three images illustrate the differences in evidence representation when different lighting is used. (*a*) This image uses shadowless or directional lighting (positioned as close as possible to the lens axis), while (*b*) and (*c*) are side lighted from different directions. The interesting point to note is how impression evidence can appear to be either a depression or a relief impression by the application of different lighting. (*Photos courtesy of Glenn Porter*)

form of forensic comparison. The following forensic photography criteria are required to maintain dimensional integrity and accuracy of the evidential material recorded at the scene and are at the core of producing reliable forensic photographs:

1. Use a lens that is free from curvilinear distortion (macro lens).

2. Frame the image with the film plane from the camera parallel to the subject plane, to avoid rectilinear distortion (lens axis perpendicular to subject plane).

3. Correctly apply a linear scale to provide a representation of scale.

4. Apply suitable lighting methods for the type of evidence required (for example, side lighting for shoemark evidence).

5. Ensure that the photograph is highly resolved to ensure the recording of fine detail.

6. Digital editing (for example cropping, aspect ratio, resizing, and screen resolution settings) must also maintain the dimensional integrity of the subject.

Scientific photography. Forensic photography is considered to be predominately within the domain of scientific photography, in that it uses various scientific photography methods and instruments to record and analyze evidence. Forensic photography may include the recording of very small items (photomicroscopy and photomicrography), certain spectral ranges (ultraviolet or infrared radiation and monochromatic lighting), and specialized lighting techniques. Techniques also include the concepts of the scientific method in terms of documentation of the process, repeatability, and supporting concepts of evidence integrity and continuity. Special

scientific instrumentation may be used in addition to general-purpose camera and lighting equipment.

Enhancement methods. The enhancement of evidence is a critical function of forensic photography. Methods of enhancement may include chemical treatment, optical enhancement, or digital modification using imaging software. Enhancement may also use a combination of methods to achieve best results.

Optical enhancement as a tool in forensic photography relies on modification of the evidence

Fig. 3. A shoemark in dust is photographed at a scene using an electrostatic lifting device. This method transfers a dusty shoemark from a surface onto a Mylar film base. The Mylar film is highly reflective and offers several challenges when applying forensic photography principles to record this form of physical evidence. Specialized lighting methods were used to record this image. (*Photo courtesy of Glenn Porter*)

Fig. 4. A Polilight monochromatic light source being used by a forensic practitioner to examine a fingermark on a plastic drink bottle. (*Photo courtesy of Glenn Porter*)

units have LED (light-emitting diode) sources to produce a monochrome output at a specific wavelength.

Using monochromatic light sources rather than polychromatic light (all color or white light) allows for greater control over the specimen's reaction to the light source. Four different results are generally achievable by illuminating a specimen with monochromatic light: (1) the specimen may absorb the light and become darker (absorption); (2) the specimen may reflect the light and become lighter (reflection); (3) the specimen may transmit the light and become translucent (transmission); or (4) the light may excite the specimen to become fluorescent (photoluminescence). The purpose of optical enhancement with monochromatic light sources is to increase the visibility of the evidence, either by increasing contrast differences between the evidence and the background or by providing visualization through the specimen.

An example of how monochromatic lighting can improve evidence visibility is seen in **Fig. 5**. As previously explained, shoemark evidence is usually photographed at the crime scene and further analyzed by a comparison with an exemplar impression from a known source. These comparisons rely on very fine detail of corresponding marks caused by the shoe sole undergoing at least some damage during normal wear and recording this artifact in the impression deposition. These corresponding features are usually quite small and require a high degree of recording detail. With shoemark impressions in blood, the impression itself has a degree of resolution, which is the ability for the mark to record the critical detail required for the examination. Shoe soles that are heavily loaded with blood will make a heavy

according to photographic or optical principles. A basic technique of optical enhancement in forensic photography is the application of a monochromatic light source that provides control over how the specimen (evidence) appears. Monochromatic lighting is a single-color light source, and instruments such as the Polilight™ are designed especially for optical enhancement of forensic evidence. **Figure 4** shows a Polilight being used to examine a fingermark on a plastic bottle by a forensic examiner. Monochromatic light sources are essential specialized equipment for contemporary forensic photography practices. Portable units are also available and designed for hand-held use at crime scenes. These

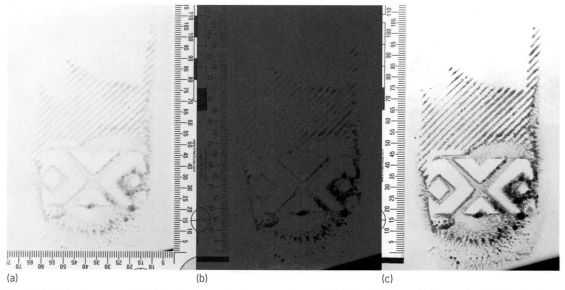

(a)   (b)   (c)

Fig. 5. Optical enhancement of a bloody shoemark using monochromatic lighting at 415 nm. (*a*) Image of a faint bloodstain shoemark without enhancement. (*b*) Image captured using a digital SLR camera and a Polilight set at 415 nm. (*c*) This image is part *b* with the color desaturated to produce a black-and-white image, eliminating the strong blue cast. (*Photos courtesy of Glenn Porter*)

and highly distinctive impression on a hard surface; however, these types of impressions usually lack the fine detail necessary for comparison and detection of distinctive identifying features. More suitable bloody shoemark impressions are usually impressions that have a lighter deposition so the fine detail or resolution of the impression retains the critical features required for the forensic comparison. This means that the best impressions are usually not the most obvious or clearly seen ones, but lighter impressions with finer detail. These latter impressions, however, although they contain better evidence (potentially more detail), usually do not produce an adequate level of contrast on light-colored surfaces. Optical enhancement of faint bloodstains involves manipulating the absorption properties of blood. Using a 415-nm monochromatic light source, the faint blood stain darkens, and the increased contrast results in better visibility without compromising important details. **Figure 6** is a chart illustrating the spectral distribution of a Polilight set on 415 nm. This wavelength is selected for bloodstain evidence because it is the peak absorption of the hemoglobin found in blood.

Modification of the recording spectrum is also conducted on radiation in the ultraviolet and infrared regions. Ultraviolet and infrared radiation photography uses spectra outside the human visual range and can therefore record evidence that cannot be seen with the naked eye. This type of imaging, sometimes referred to as invisible radiation photography, can provide contrast for visualization different from that of standard white light; infrared radiation, for example, can transmit through material to record items beneath the surface, such as bloodstains under paint. **Figure 7b** is an infrared photograph showing gunshot residue (GSR) on dark clothing, and compared to the standard white-light sample (Fig. 7a) provides greater visibility of the gunshot particles.

Enhancement of evidence may also be performed using digital imaging software such as Adobe Photoshop. **Figure 8** is a digital enhancement method for removing the busy patterned background of vinyl flooring material to improve the visual aspects of a shoemark impression. This method involves subtracting the background using the "Layers" function in Photoshop. The process for this method involves first taking a photograph of the shoemark using standard forensic photography criteria (Fig. 8a). Figure 8b was taken keeping the camera in the exact same alignment as the first (using a tripod); however, in this photograph the impression has been cleaned off. This photograph is essentially the same as the first but without the shoemark impression. The next steps are conducted in the forensic photography laboratory. They involve first inverting the image (producing a negative image) without the impression (Fig. 8c) and using layers to overlay this negative image (using about 50% opacity) over the original with the impression. The alignment of the positive and negative images allows them to cancel each other and eliminate the busy background,

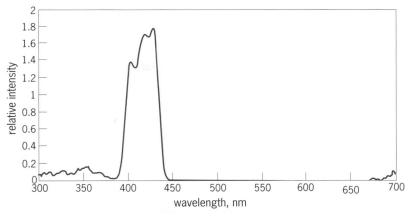

Fig. 6. Spectral distribution of a Polilight monochromatic lighting source set at 415 nm for the enhancement of faint bloodstain using absorption principles.

creating a mid-tone background that is easier to examine (Fig. 8d). The shoe-mark impression is not affected by the overlay because it is not recorded in the second image, only the background is modified.

Contemporary society is now dominated by visual forms of communication, and images are used seamlessly across many modern technologies. The volume of images taken today significantly exceeds the total number of images taken in previous years since the establishment of photography over 150 years ago. Cameras are ubiquitous within the modern community and are now installed in computers, tablet devices, and mobile phones. The application of surveillance cameras installed in public and private spaces, in combination with the fact most people carry a digital camera (mobile phone) on their person, increases the presence of cameras within the community and the overall surveillance on people who commit crimes. Criminal activity is now recorded from a range of sources, and the interpretation of this visual evidence has become a recent function for forensic photographers to report.

Images are also used as a form of demonstrating evidence that items existed or certain events actually took place, and the print and television media have exploited this thinking for many years. Images are used today as a form of witnessing and evidence and used within the legal environment as proof. Although the deliberate falsification of photographs is not a new concept, the increased accessibility of digital technology has led to situations where images have been falsified to commit fraud. These methods were previously only available to organizations with a high degree of technological skill. However, anyone with a computer and imaging-editing software can now falsify images for illegal intent. The detection of photographic fakes has become a function of forensic photography investigation and the methods used for this purpose are currently being developed. The current tools for image manipulation are relatively simple. Producing a falsified image that cannot be detected takes great skill by the operator and is usually beyond most novices. Forensic

(a)

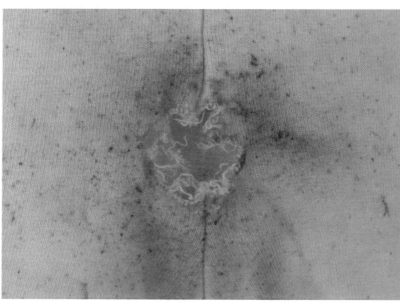

(b)

Fig. 7. Standard (*a*) white-light photograph of gunshot residue on dark clothing. (*b*) Infrared radiation photograph of the same specimen. (*Photos courtesy of Glenn Porter*)

methods of detection include the analysis of pictorial elements within the image (detecting inconsistencies in lighting, color, noise, perspective, size, and distortion) and forensic computing software to detect alterations in the digital image. This form of analysis by forensic photographers is increasing due to technology developments, as is the demand for photointerpretation examinations.

Forensic photography offers a range of practices from simple crime scene recording, evidence enhancement and analysis, the application of scientific instrumentation, the interpretation of surveillance recordings, and the examination of images to test their authenticity. Forensic photography remains a growing area as technology develops and society becomes more visually informed. This discipline is an essential area for sophisticated law enforcement agencies and remains an area of further research and development in the near future.

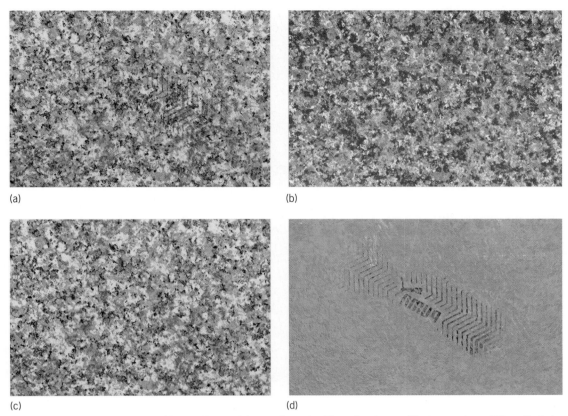

(a)

(b)

(c)

(d)

Fig. 8. Subtracting the background from a shoemark impression using Photoshop layers. (*Photos courtesy of Glenn Porter*)

For background information *see* CRIMINALISTICS; FORENSIC EVIDENCE; PHOTOGRAPHY; IMAGE PROCESSING in the McGraw-Hill Encyclopedia of Science & Technology.   Glenn Porter

Bibliography. G. Edmond et al., Law's looking glass: Expert identification evidence derived from photographic and video images, *Curr. Issues Crim. Justice*, 20(3):337–377, 2009; A. Farrar, G. Porter, and A. Renshaw, Detection of latent bloodstains beneath painted surfaces using reflected infrared photography, *J. Forensic Sci.*, 57(5):1190–1198, 2012, DOI:10.1111/j.1556-4029.2012.02231.x; G. Porter, A new theoretical framework regarding the application and reliability of photographic evidence, *Int. J. Evidence Proof*, 15(1):26–61, 2011, DOI:10.1350/ijep.2011.15.1.367; G. Porter, Visual culture in forensic science, *Austr. J. Forensic Sci.*, 39(2):81–91, 2007, DOI:10.1080/00450610701650054; G. Porter, Zak coronial inquest and the interpretation of photographic evidence, *Curr. Issues Crim. Justice*, 24(1):39–49, 2012.

Freeform optical surfaces

Freeform optical surfaces are generally defined as optical surfaces that are not rotationally symmetric. These surfaces have played important roles in nonimaging applications, such as illumination optics, for many years, but their use in imaging applications was considered to be rare until recently. Since the emergence of slow-servo diamond-turning fabrication technology around 2002, freeform optical surfaces have been gaining increasingly significant roles in imaging applications. The increased degrees of freedom of a freeform surface offer the opportunity to develop imaging systems with potentially smaller wavefront errors, fewer optical elements, smaller system packages, and lower weights as compared to rotationally symmetric surfaces.

Classes of optical surfaces. Optical surfaces are the interfaces between different optical media at which light is refracted or reflected, and are the basic building blocks for constructing optical elements such as lenses and mirrors. **Figure 1** illustrates the two-dimensional cross sections with the yOz plane of representatives of three different classes of optical surfaces: spherical surfaces, aspherical surfaces, and freeform surfaces. The optical axis of each surface is parallel with the z axis and the vertex O of each surface coincides with the origin of the yOz coordinate frame. The symbol R denotes the local radius of curvature of a surface, and this quantity is constant for a spherical surface, varies symmetrically about the y coordinate for an aspherical surface, and varies asymmetrically for a freeform surface.

Spherical surfaces and conics of revolution are the first class of surface shapes found in the vast majority of optical systems. This class of surface shapes includes the simple spheres, ellipsoid, paraboloid,

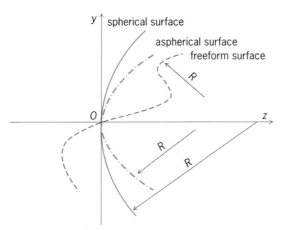

Fig. 1. Representatives of different types of optical surfaces.

and hyperboloid, which can be formed by rotating a circle, ellipse, parabola, and hyperbola, respectively, around an axis of symmetry. They inherently are rotationally symmetric and are easy to fabricate and test. For more than 125 years, the optics industry, including the manufacturing phases of design, fabrication, test, and assembly, has been developed primarily upon spherical and conic surfaces. The surface sag $z(r)$ of a spherical or conic surface, which is the z component of the displacement of the surface from the vertex at distance $r = \sqrt{x^2 + y^2}$ from the optical axis, is mathematically described by Eq. (1), where

$$z(r) = \frac{cr^2}{1 + \sqrt{1 - (1+k)c^2r^2}} \tag{1}$$

c is the curvature at the surface vertex and k is the conic constant. The conic constant is a quantity measuring the deviation of a conic section from being a circle.

Rotationally symmetric aspheres are the second class of common optical surfaces. Because of the lack of advanced fabrication and testing methods, this class of optical surfaces did not occur frequently in optical systems until around 2000. An aspheric surface can be described mathematically in many ways. As early as 1902, Ernst Abbe introduced a mathematical description of a rotationally symmetric asphere with a power series polynomial. Today, one of the most commonly adopted methods is to describe an aspheric surface in two parts, a conic section departure from a sphere as the first part, and aspheric deviations according to higher polynomial terms as the second part. The surface sag $z(r)$ of an aspheric surface is mathematically described by Eq. (2), where

$$z(r) = \frac{cr^2}{1 + \sqrt{1 - (1+k)c^2r^2}} + A_4r^4 + A_6r^6 + A_8r^8 + \dots \tag{2}$$

A_4, A_6, A_8 are the fourth-, sixth-, and eighth-order aspheric terms. Another newly adopted method is called the Q-type polynomial form, which characterizes an aspheric surface by its sag departure from

a base conic or alternatively by a root-mean-square slope departure from a best-fit sphere. The key benefits of adopting the Q-type polynomial form include data efficiency, effective estimation of surface manufacturability, and testability.

Freeform optical surfaces, which are the third class of surface shapes, are generally defined as optical surfaces that are not rotationally symmetric. This newly emerging class of optical surfaces demands both theoretical and technical advancements in several key areas, including methods of mathematical surface description, aberration theory, optical design, fabrication, and metrology. It is undergoing intensive research and development in the optics industry. The rest of this article will focus on freeform optical surfaces for imaging applications.

Representations of freeform optical surfaces. Developing efficient mathematical methods of describing freeform optical surfaces is critical for optical design, fabrication, and testing. Owing to the increased degrees of freedom, various forms of polynomials have been adopted in optical design to describe freeform optical surfaces. Some of these polynomial forms were adopted or evolved from those developed for rotationally symmetric optical surfaces to represent simple forms of freeform optical surfaces, while more sophisticated polynomial formulas are emerging to meet the needs of designing, fabricating, and testing more complex freeform surfaces.

An off-axis conic surface is perhaps the simplest type of freeform optical surface. It is a conventional conic surface or rotationally symmetric asphere with its center of symmetry decentered from the optical axis. The mathematical description of an off-axis conic surface can adopt the methods for a rotationally symmetric aspheric surface along with the necessary tilt and decenter information.

An anamorphic asphere is the second method of representing simple freeform optical surfaces. It is an aspheric surface with bilateral symmetry in both x and y directions without rotational symmetry. An anamorphic asphere surface is defined by four parts: two independent x- and y-radii of curvature, x- and y-conic constants, symmetric aspheric deviations from the conic surface according to higher polynomial terms, and asymmetric aspheric deformations from the conic surface according to higher polynomial terms. The surface sag $z(r)$ of an anamorphic asphere surface is mathematically described by Eq. (3), where c_x and c_y are the x- and y-curvatures

$$z(r) = \frac{c_xx^2 + c_yy^2}{1 + \sqrt{1 - (1+k_x)c_x^2x^2 - (1+k_y)c_y^2y^2}} + \sum_{n=2}^{10} A_{2n}[(1 - B_{2n})x^2 + (1 + B_{2n})y^2]^n \tag{3}$$

at the vertex, k_x and k_y are the x- and y-conic constants, the A coefficients are the symmetric terms, and the B coefficients are the asymmetric terms. If the curvatures are equal, the conic constants are equal, and the B coefficients are all zeros, the equation reduces to that of a standard rotationally symmetric polynomial asphere.

An xy-polynomial surface is the third method of representing freeform optical surfaces. It is an extension of the polynomial representation of an aspheric surface by expanding the power series into the form of $x^m y^n$. Although this method of surface representation is sufficiently general to represent a large variety of surface shapes that are not rotationally symmetric, its key limitation is the fact that the polynomial terms are nonorthogonal bases such that the individual coefficients for the different polynomial terms are not independently associated with the frequency content of the Fourier transform of a freeform surface. Consequently, individual polynomial coefficients can be neither added nor deleted readily, nor facilitate estimates of surface manufacturability.

A Zernike polynomial surface is the fourth and a more effective approach to the mathematical description of freeform optical surfaces. It mathematically describes a freeform optical surface with a circular aperture as a summation of a conic base and the deviation from a conic surface in terms of a summation of orthogonal polynomials, where the choice of the orthogonal polynomials currently can have several different forms. This surface descriptor has dominated the optical testing industry since the 1970s, and it is gaining popularity in describing freeform surfaces in optical design.

A significant advantage of using polynomials with orthogonal bases as freeform surface descriptors lies in their independence and numerical robustness among basis elements. A limitation of some of the existing orthogonal bases is that these bases are often defined over specific aperture shapes that constrain the aperture shapes of the freeform elements.

Optical design. Like designing optical systems with rotationally symmetric surfaces, incorporating freeform optical surfaces into an optical system is not only a practice of optical engineering, but also a practice of art in the sense that the prior experiences and intuition of optical designers play a large role in the process of optimizing a system. Commercial optical design software, such as CODE V by Synopsys Inc. and Zemax by Radiant Zemax LLC, provides support for designing optical systems with freeform optical surfaces to some extent. For example, the most recent version of CODE V (V10.5), available in early 2013, supports the modeling of freeform surfaces, from the simple off-axis conic and anamorphic asphere representations, and representation with xy polynomials, to a variety of forms of Zernike representations.

Unlike the simple spheres and conic surfaces, freeform optical surfaces provide far more degrees of freedom for shape control and optimization. This characteristic has a great impact on the practice of optical system design and optimization. For example, one important departure from designing rotationally symmetric systems is the sampling of the imaging fields. Sampling a few points along a single direction of an imaging field is typically sufficient for simulating and optimizing the optical performance of a rotationally symmetric system. A system incorporating one or more freeform optical surfaces requires a far larger number of sampling points, typically in an array format across both the x and y directions of the imaging fields, because of the potentially rapid change of local surface shapes. During the design and optimization process, determining the appropriate and adequate constraints for optimization is a far more complex process than dealing with simple spheres or conics. Inadequate constraints in an optimization process can lead to results that are either not machinable or irrecoverable. Evaluating and balancing system performance across the imaging field is another major challenge in the design process because of the larger number of field samples and the complex surface shapes. The aberration theory for freeform optical systems is still evolving.

Surface fabrication. The fabrication of freeform optical surfaces for imaging applications is enabled by the recent advancement of the slow-servo diamond-turning technique, also known as 5-axis or c-axis diamond turning, as well as computer-controlled small-lap polishing. Diamond turning is a multistage process of mechanical machining of precision elements using computer numerical control (CNC) lathes or derivative machine tools equipped with natural or synthetic diamond-tipped tool bits. It is capable of achieving subnanometer-level surface finishes and submicrometer-form accuracies, and thus is widely used to fabricate high-quality optical elements. The Moore Nanotech 350FG Ultra-Precision Freeform Generator is one of the leading diamond-turning machines capable of fabricating high-precision freeform optics.

The process chain required for fabricating a freeform surface based on 5-axis diamond-turning techniques consists of several potentially iterative steps. The process begins with importing the surface geometry that has been designed and created into the computer-aided-machine (CAM) system to evaluate the surface accuracy and machinability in a specific material. Occasionally, the initial surface geometry may require additional refinement to address specific problems identified during the evaluation step. Based on the results of the evaluations, the proper machining method, tool, and process are determined. Materials play a large role in determining the machining method. For example, natural or synthetic diamond tools are appropriate for machining nonferrous metals, plastics, crystals, and silicon, while glass or tungsten carbide molds can be machined only with grinding technology. Diamond tools are available in fast-tool servo, slow-slide servo, raster machining, and micro milling, while grinding is available only in slow-slide servo and raster machining. With a selected machine method, further analysis is performed with regard to the design of a tool path and to determine the minimum allowed tool radius, the required sweep of the tool, and the minimum required tool clearance.

Applications. Freeform optical surfaces have a much longer history of applications to nonimaging illumination optics, and interest in these applications continues to grow rapidly. With the increasingly intensive development of optical design, fabrication, and testing capabilities, freeform optical surfaces are beginning to appear in many types of imaging applications, from head-mounted displays and head-up displays, to compact cameras. **Figure 2** demonstrates the use of freeform optics in the design

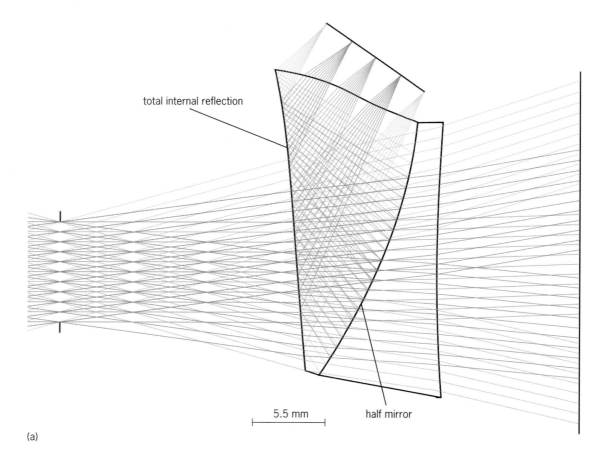

(a)

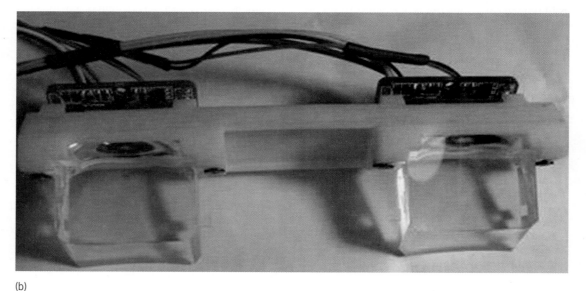

(b)

Fig. 2. Head-mounted display system employing freeform optical surfaces. (*a*) Diagram of the design, showing ray paths (*after D. Cheng et al., Design of an optical see-through head-mounted display with a low f-number and large field of view using a free-form prism, Appl. Optics, 48:2655–2668, 2009, DOI:10.1364/AO.48.002655*). (*b*) Optics prototype (*photo courtesy of Dewen Cheng*).

of a high-performance compact eyepiece for a head-mounted display system. Traditionally, such eyepieces require a number of lenses made of rotationally symmetric optical surfaces. The use of freeform optical surfaces creates the opportunity to reduce the optics into a monolithic element consisting of multiple freeform surfaces, which enables not only a much smaller package size but also dramatically less weight than rotationally symmetric optics.

For background information *see* ABERRATION (OPTICS); COMPUTER-AIDED DESIGN AND MANUFACTURING; COMPUTER NUMERICAL CONTROL; GEOMETRICAL OPTICS; LENS (OPTICS); MIRROR OPTICS; OPTICAL SURFACES; SURFACE (GEOMETRY) in the McGraw-Hill Encyclopedia of Science & Technology.   Hong Hua

Bibliography. D. Cheng et al., Design of an optical see-through head-mounted display with a low f-number and large field of view using a free-form prism, *Appl. Optics*, 48(14):2655–2668, 2009, DOI: 10.1364/AO.48.002655; G. W. Forbes, Shape specification for axially symmetric optical surfaces, *Opt. Express*, 15:5218–5226, 2007, DOI:10.1364/OE.15.005218; J. R. Rogers, A comparison of anamorphic, keystone, and Zernike surface types for aberration correction, paper 76520B-8 (8 pp.), in J. Bentley, A. Gupta, and R. N. Youngworth (eds.), *International Optical Design Conference 2010*, Proc. SPIE 7652, SPIE, Bellingham, WA, 2010, DOI:10.1117/12.871025; K. P. Thompson, Multinodal fifth-order optical aberrations of optical systems without rotational symmetry: Spherical aberration, *J. Opt. Soc. Am. A.*, 26:1090–1100, 2009, DOI:10.1364/JOSAA.26.001090; Y. Tohme, Trends in ultra-precision machining of freeform optical surfaces, in *Optical Fabrication and Testing*, Rochester, NY, October 21–24, 2008, Optical Society of America, Washington, DC, 2008; F. Zernike, Diffraction theory of knife-edge test and its improved form, the phase contrast method, *Mon. Not. Roy. Astron. Soc.*, 94:377–384, 1934.

Fungal meningitis outbreak

Although normally a rare infection, fungal meningitis received a great amount of attention in the United States in 2012. Meningitis is a swelling of the protective membranes (meninges, derived from the Greek *meninx*) covering the brain and spinal cord. According to health officials, tainted injections of a pain-relieving steroid [injectable preservative-free methylprednisolone acetate (MPA)] custom-produced by a Massachusetts-based company (the New England Compounding Center) triggered an outbreak of the disease in 15 states during a 4-month time period in 2012. These injections were used to treat severe back pain. The first outbreak was reported in Tennessee and then spread to 14 other states (Florida, Idaho, Indiana, Maryland, Michigan, Minnesota, New Hampshire, New Jersey, New York, North Carolina, Ohio, Pennsylvania, Texas, and Virginia). This outbreak was linked to the contami-

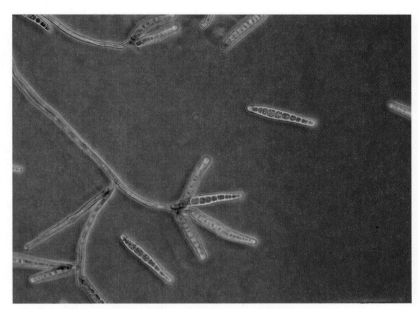

Exserohilum rostratum, which was the agent responsible for the fungal meningitis outbreak in 2012. (*Photo courtesy of the Centers for Disease Control and Prevention, Atlanta, GA*)

nated shots and led to almost 300 cases, including 23 deaths.

The pharmacy company. The New England Compounding Center is a compounding pharmacy, which is a legitimate and often very useful operation that mixes special-order drugs at the request of physicians. This type of practice is growing in the United States and elsewhere as drug shortages and the awareness of allergies and adverse reactions to pharmaceutical ingredients increase. Typically, a physician will write a prescription for a compound drug that is free of preservatives or allergens (for example, lactose) or will request drugs in formulations that are not available from a local commercial pharmacy.

Causative agent. The responsible fungus was *Exserohilum rostratum*, which is very common in the environment (see **illustration**). It is found in soil and on plants, especially grasses, and thrives in warm and humid climates. Infection by *Exserohilum* is very rare in humans and is not contagious (not transmitted from person to person). However, *Exserohilum* has been known to cause several different types of infections, including infection of the skin or cornea (the clear, front part of the eye) following trauma to the skin or eye, respectively. *Exserohilum* also can cause more invasive forms of infection in the sinuses, lungs, lining of the heart, and bones, and these infections are thought to be more prevalent in individuals with weak immune systems. The fungus spreads through the bloodstream from somewhere else in the body (such as the injection sites for back pain) and into the central nervous system.

Diagnosis, disease, and treatment. If fungal meningitis is suspected, samples of cerebrospinal fluid and blood are collected and sent to a laboratory

The most commonly compounded drugs	
Drug category	Examples
Hormones	Estrogen and progesterone pills can be reformulated as creams or pellets, or made without peanut oil, which can cause allergic reactions in some women.
Thyroid medications	Compounded thyroid hormone (thyroxine) can be made in very specific doses (based on the patient's needs) and free of cellulose fillers, which can affect absorption of the thyroxine.
Pain medications	Sterile spinal injections to treat severe back pain have been in very short supply in the United States. This has driven many hospitals, clinics, and physicians to stock compounded drugs.
Allergy-free drugs	Some drugs contain allergens such as lactose, and compounded drugs can be made without this allergen.
Preservative-free and better-tasting drugs	Compounded drugs can be made that eliminate the adverse reactions to the various additives used in many drugs. They also can be made to have improved taste (especially for children).

where specific tests are performed. Fungal meningitis, which is not contagious, is a tenacious disease that can be treated only with powerful antifungal medications, usually given through an intravenous line in the hospital. The length of treatment depends on the status of the patient's immune system. Longer treatments are required for patients with immune systems that do not function well (for example, patients with AIDS, diabetes, or cancer). The antifungal drugs have to be given intravenously and are very difficult to use. They are very toxic, and the dose has to be sufficient to have therapeutic effects while minimizing the risk of damage to the liver and kidneys. Signs and symptoms of fungal meningitis may include fever, headache, stiff neck, nausea, vomiting, photophobia (sensitivity to light), and altered mental states.

Scenario. In these cases of fungal meningitis, patients obtained the prescription at their local commercial pharmacy and were probably aware that they were getting a compounded drug. However, occasionally in the clinical setting, shelves will be stocked with a compounded variety because of shortages of the usual ordinary drug formulation. Compounded drugs are also often cheaper, making them even more attractive. In these instances, both the patient and physician may not have been aware that a compounded drug was being used. This happened with the injectable methylprednisolone that was linked to the fungal meningitis outbreak in the United States in 2012.

Current regulation. One of the reasons for this outbreak is that compounded drugs, unlike most other drugs, are not regulated by the U.S. Food and Drug Administration for safety and quality. Instead, they are overseen with little regulation by state pharmacy boards. In 2013, the U.S. Congress is currently exploring tighter regulations—too late for the 2012 fungal meningitis victims, but not too late to prevent future outbreaks, especially considering the large number of the most commonly compounded drugs (see **table**).

Prevention. No specific activities are known to cause fungal meningitis. Individuals should avoid soils and other environments that are likely to contain fungi. People with weak immune systems (for example, HIV-positive individuals) should avoid bird droppings and avoid digging and dusty activities, particularly if they live in a geographic region where fungi exist.

For background information *see* COMPOUND (CHEMISTRY); FUNGAL ECOLOGY; FUNGAL INFECTIONS; FUNGI; MEDICAL MYCOLOGY; MENINGES; MENINGITIS; MYCOLOGY; PHARMACY; PHARMACEUTICAL CHEMISTRY in the McGraw-Hill Encyclopedia of Science & Technology.   John P. Harley

Bibliography. M. A. Kainer et al., Fungal infections associated with contaminated methylprednisolone in Tennessee, *New Engl. J. Med.*, 367:2194–2203, 2012, DOI:10.1056/NEJMoa1212972; A. C. Pettit et al., The index case for the fungal meningitis outbreak in the United States, *New Engl. J. Med.*, 367:2119–2125, 2012, DOI:10.1056/NEJMoa1212292; R. M. Smith et al., Fungal infections from contaminated methylprednisolone—preliminary report, *New Engl. J. Med.*, 2012, DOI:10.1056/NEJMoa1213978; B. Todd, Fungal meningitis outbreak, *Am. J. Nurs.*, 113(2):52–57, 2013, DOI:10.1097/01.NAJ.0000426691.81083.93.

Future of fungal genomics for energy and the environment

Fungi are very important with regard to the economy and ecology. They decompose dead organic matter and recycle nutrients in various ecosystems, including soil. Some fungi, such as mushrooms and yeasts, are used for food and medicine. Others can cause human and plant diseases. More than a million species in the kingdom Fungi cover more than a billion years of evolutionary history. The evolutionary innovations encoded in their genomes can be deciphered using genomics.

The first eukaryotic genome to be sequenced was that of the fungus *Saccharomyces cerevisiae*, which dramatically changed the biological sciences and led to the development of a whole spectrum of new tools and discoveries in genetics and molecular biology. Following this initial genome sequencing, several dozen fungal genomes have been sequenced by the Fungal Genome Initiative, led by the Broad Institute in Cambridge, Massachusetts; these fungi have been predominantly those of medical importance. Fungi are also important for plant health. Some, such as mycorrhizal fungi (that is, fungi that form symbiotic relationships in and on the roots of host plants), help plants to extract nutrients from the soil; others, such as rusts and rots, can kill plants. Most fungi contribute significantly to carbon cycling.

To address questions related to energy and the environment, the U.S. Department of Energy (DOE) Joint Genome Institute (JGI) has been developing genomic resources and tools to explore fungal diversity at large. To facilitate fungal genomics efforts, JGI has partnered with the scientific community around the world and started several large-scale genomics initiatives. The first of them, the Genomic Encyclopedia of Fungi for Energy and Environment, is focused on the analysis of groups of fungi that are important for growing biomass and converting it into biofuels. The second initiative, the 1000 Fungal Genomes Project, aims to explore fungal diversity across the Fungal Tree of Life [the classification of Fungi based on phylogenetic (evolutionary) relationships] and to provide references for studying fungal communities in soil and other ecosystems. The third initiative will provide functional information for the sequenced genes and genomes using the functional genomics of individual fungi and fungal communities.

Using these initiatives, JGI solicits genomics proposals for sequencing and analyzing large amounts of genomic data from researchers around the world to solve various energy and environmental problems. To enable these analyses, JGI has also developed a Web-based fungal genomics resource, MycoCosm, which provides tools to analyze more than 200 fungal genomes and promotes user participation in data submission, annotation, and analysis (see **illustration**).

Genomic Encyclopedia of Fungi for Energy and Environment. The Genomic Encyclopedia of Fungi for Energy and Environment initiative aims to analyze groups of diverse fungi that share the same traits, lifestyle, secretions, and other features for energy- and environment-related science and applications. The two initial focus areas involve fungi that (1) can positively or negatively affect plant health and bioenergy crops and (2) encode genes, pathways, and other parts that are important for developing efficient biorefineries for biofuel production.

Plant health maintenance is critical for sustainable growth of biofuel feedstocks, and fungi [mutualists, parasites, and other microbial components of the rhizosphere (the soil region subject to the influence of plant roots and characterized by a zone of increased microbiological activity)] can dramatically affect this. Mycorrhizal fungi, for example, enter into symbiotic relationships with plants and effectively extend the host root system toward regions of decaying organic matter to provide nutrients such as nitrogen and phosphorus. Comparison of the first two sequenced genomes of mycorrhizal fungi, the poplar symbiont *Laccaria bicolor* and the black truffle *Tuber melanosporum*, has revealed dramatic differences in their gene sets and their interactions with host plants, justifying a more comprehensive study of 25 mycorrhizal fungi. While sequencing of these

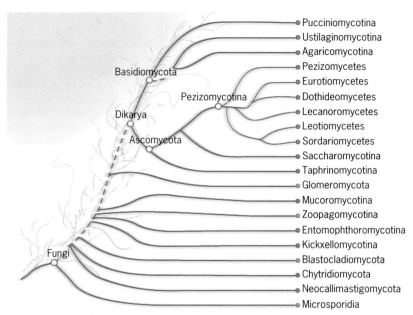

The JGI fungal genomics portal, MycoCosm (http://genome.jgi.doe.gov/programs/fungi/index.jsf).

genomes is in progress, a dozen new plant pathogens from the fungal class of Dothideomycetes have been sequenced and analyzed in the largest comparative study of its kind to date. This study revealed genomic differences and aligned some of them with different strategies of pathogenicity, including the expansion of genes involved in secondary metabolism and plant cell wall degradation in fungi-killing plants (necrotrophs) in comparison to those parasitizing from inside plants (biotrophs). When this is followed by in-depth analyses and functional genomics studies, it should lead toward the development of new methods of controlling the growth of pathogenic fungi and protecting plants from catastrophic events (such as the 1970 epidemic of corn leaf blight, which wiped out the entire corn crops of several states in the United States).

Biorefinery methods convert the biopolymers composing the plant cell wall (lignocellulose) into simple sugars (glucose and xylose) and then into biofuels using fungal strains optimized for large-scale industrial processes. Knowing the enzymes and processes employed by diverse fungi in lignocellulose degradation and sugar fermentation, and also understanding the molecular biology of the strains adopted by industry, are essential for developing robust platforms for biomass-to-biofuel production on an industrial scale. Comparison of the genomes of the white rot fungus *Phanerochaete chrysosporium* and the brown rot fungus *Postia placenta* revealed very different mechanisms of lignocellulose degradation for each of them. This led to the sequencing of 30 more wood-decay fungi from the class Agaricomycetes to build the most comprehensive catalog of lignocellulolytic enzymes and reconstruct white and brown rot evolution. Sugars produced by these processes include xylose, which is processed poorly by industrial strains of *S. cerevisiae*, but efficiently by other yeasts (for example, *Pichia stipitis*). Comparative genomics of several xylose-fermenting yeasts suggested missing genes, which have been added to *S. cerevisiae* to enable more complete sugar processing during biomass decomposition. Another way to improve industrial enzyme-producing or sugar-fermenting strains of fungi is to replace them with thermophilic fungi (that is, fungi that thrive at high temperatures). Two of these, *Thielavia terrestris* and *Myceliophthora thermophila*, have displayed good biomass decomposition potential at high temperatures and have been sequenced to produce complete chromosomes, which can be used as detailed maps for further genome engineering and strain improvement. The research community will continue to add new chapters of the Encyclopedia to explore a number of different areas—for example, the roles of fungi in ecology, the secrets of endophytes (fungi that live within, but are not necessarily parasitic on, plants) and extremophiles (organisms that live and thrive in environments with extreme conditions), and the potential of fungi for bioremediation (the use of a biological process to clean up a polluted environmental area).

1000 Fungal Genomes. Despite the growing number of fungal genome sequencing projects, sequenced fungi represent only a tiny fraction of the natural fungal diversity created by more than a million different species. The majority of the fungal species in soil or other environments are not characterized and do not have any genome information. They may be a potentially rich source of valuable metabolic pathways and enzyme activities, and there is thus a need for a systematic survey of phylogenetically diverse genome sequences. To address this need, an international research team, in collaboration with JGI, has embarked on a 5-year project (the 1000 Fungal Genomes Project) to sequence 1000 fungal genomes from across the Fungal Tree of Life. The goal is to fill in gaps in the Fungal Tree of Life by sequencing at least two reference genomes from each of the more than 500 recognized families of Fungi. With several culture collections participating and with growing interest from the entire mycological community, this project aims to provide genomic references to inform research on plant–microbe interactions and environmental metagenomics (the analysis of many genomes simultaneously). The MycoCosm portal provides integrated information for ongoing genome sequencing projects, the list of known families of Fungi, and tools for nominating new species and assigning them to families with no sequenced genomes. Any researcher can nominate fungal species in these families and can send DNA samples to JGI for sequencing and annotation.

Functional genomics of fungal systems. Whereas traditional genomics focuses on genome sequencing and computational analysis of predicted genes, functional genomics should provide experimental data on the function of these genes. There have been revolutionary changes in sequencing technologies, but not as much in the biochemical characterization of genes and proteins, creating a growing gap between the available sets of sequences and functions. However, initiatives such as the Human ENCODE project (which seeks to build a comprehensive parts list of the functional elements in the human genome) give promise of developing high-throughput techniques that could be applicable to fungi and other organisms. These may include new experimental techniques for examining and delineating a number of genomic features [including, for example, interactions of chromatin (the wrapping of the genome into a complex between DNA and proteins); DNA accessibility and structure; modifications of histones (a large class of proteins associated with nucleic acid molecules); transcription factor binding sites; DNA methylation; promoters; and transcriptional silencers].

Sequence-based high-throughput approaches such as transcriptomics (the study of the entire complement of RNA that has been transcribed from DNA in a cell or, more likely, a population of cells) and proteomics (the study of the total protein complement of a cell, a tissue, or an entire organism) have been successfully utilized for many fungi. Large collections of deletion mutants for the model yeast *S. cerevisiae* and the filamentous fungus *Neurospora crassa* help in better portraying the role of individual genes (by using resequencing and transcriptomics), and there is a need for further collections to be developed for a significantly larger number of fungi. Transcriptome analysis of systems consisting of an interacting host and fungal pathogens or symbionts can shed light on changes in both and can help provide information on their interactions. Large-scale transcriptomics studies of several pathogen–host and mycorrhizal fungi–host systems are also currently in progress at JGI, along with the *N. crassa* ENCODE project. Moreover, initial efforts on metatranscriptomics of complex fungal communities (such as soil) could ultimately lead to understanding the interactions in these communities and modeling their responses to environmental changes.

Conclusions. Fungi encode processes that are important for the economy and ecology in their genomes. Dramatic changes in genome sequencing in the last few years have opened the doors to massive genome explorations. To integrate the large amounts of genomics data and to better coordinate the efforts of a large research community, new tools have been developed and several genomic initiatives have been launched at JGI to study large groups of fungi relevant to bioenergy, explore the phylogenetic diversity of fungi at the scale of 1000 genomes, and develop fungal genomics of model systems and microbial communities.

For background information *see* BIOMASS; FUNGAL BIOTECHNOLOGY; FUNGAL ECOLOGY; FUNGAL GENETICS; FUNGAL GENOMICS; FUNGAL PHYLOGENETIC

CLASSIFICATION; FUNGI; LIGNIN-DEGRADING FUNGI; MUSHROOM; MYCOLOGY; MYCORRHIZAE; RECOMBINANT FUNGAL BIOTECHNOLOGY; YEAST in the McGraw-Hill Encyclopedia of Science & Technology.
Igor V. Grigoriev

Bibliography. R. M. Berka et al., Comparative genomic analysis of the thermophilic biomass-degrading fungi *Myceliophthora thermophila* and *Thielavia terrestris*, *Nat. Biotechnol.*, 29(10):922–927, 2011, DOI:10.1038/nbt.1976; D. Floudas et al., The Paleozoic origin of enzymatic lignin decomposition reconstructed from 31 fungal genomes, *Science*, 336(6089):1715–1719, 2012, DOI:10.1126/science.1221748; I. V. Grigoriev et al., Fueling the future with fungal genomics, *Mycology*, 2(3):192–209, 2011, DOI:10.1080/21501203.2011.584577; R. A. Ohm et al., Diverse lifestyles and strategies of plant pathogenesis encoded in the genomes of eighteen Dothideomycetes fungi, *PLoS Pathogens*, 8(12):e1003037, 2012, DOI:10.1371/journal.ppat.1003037; D. J. Wohlbach et al., Comparative genomics of xylose-fermenting fungi for enhanced biofuel production, *Proc. Natl. Acad. Sci. USA*, 108(32):13212–13217, 2011, DOI:10.1073/pnas.1103039108.

Gamma-ray spectroscopy of neutron-rich fission fragments

In a nuclear fission reaction, a large number of fission fragments are produced in various discrete quantum excited states. The characterization of these excited states along different isotopic chains with increasing mass numbers, for various elements, is necessary for understanding, microscopically, the evolution of the individual and collective motion of the nucleons (the intrinsic structure) in a complex nuclear many-body system as a function of its temperature (excitation energy), rotation (spin), and neutron-proton asymmetry (isospin). However, such a characterization for each set of isotopes is experimentally very challenging. The traditional approach uses correlations among the coincident characteristic gamma rays emitted by a given fission fragment, or correlations with the gamma rays emitted by its complementary partner (or partners), to identify the excited states of interest. In the experiments that will be discussed in this article, the sensitivity of the method of using prompt gamma rays for the spectroscopy of fission fragments is extended toward more neutron-rich exotic nuclei (nuclei with ratios of neutron number N to atomic number Z much larger than those found in nature), lying farther away from the valley of stability. This is done by measuring gamma rays in coincidence with the detection in a large-acceptance spectrometer of fission fragments that are isotopically identified by their atomic (Z) and mass (A) numbers.

Probing nuclei in energy-spin-isospin space. Key questions in nuclear physics address both the understanding of how regular and simple patterns emerge in the intrinsic structure of nuclei and distinguishing the degrees of freedom, which govern the dynamics of their collisions. Observables are understood in terms of the fundamental interaction between the individual constituents (nucleons). The relevant theoretical models are best tested while following the evolution of the intrinsic properties along isotopic chains of elements toward the extremes of excitation energy, spin, and isospin. Near these extremes, surprising phenomena have been observed, such as neutron "halos and skins," the appearance of new nuclear "magic numbers" (shell gaps) or their disappearance (relative to those historically known close to the valley of stability), nuclear shape coexistence, and new forms of radioactivity.

Nuclear reactions between the isotopes available in nature combined with the measurement of the promptly emitted gamma rays are primary tools that are used to explore the intrinsic features of excited nuclei. Fusion-evaporation reactions offer the possibility of accessing nuclear states at very large spin (approximately $60\hbar$, where $\hbar$ is Planck's constant divided by 2π) and high excitation energy (approximately 100 MeV), but primarily in neutron-deficient nuclei. Multinucleon transfer reactions populate moderately neutron-rich nuclei (having a few additional neutrons as compared to stable nuclei) at relatively high spin (approximately $20\hbar$) and excitation energy. In recent years, low-intensity secondary beams of exotic nuclei produced in high-energy nuclear reactions (approximately 50 MeV/nucleon or higher) have been used to probe low-spin states (equal to or less than $10\hbar$) in nuclei far from stability using direct nuclear reactions. Fission of heavy neutron-rich nuclei, either produced in spontaneous fission or in reactions with intense stable beams, is one of the most efficient ways to populate exotic neutron-rich nuclei far away from the valley of stability and also at relatively high spins, up to approximately $20\hbar$.

The process of nuclear fission produces a mass distribution (over 400 nuclei) spanning a wide range of elements and isotopes. These nuclei, formed within a similar range of excitation energy and spin, de-excite toward their ground states by the emission of characteristic gamma rays. These fingerprints of a variety of nuclear configurations and shapes provide insights into both single-particle and collective motion of nuclei at a relatively large isospin. The yields of neutron-rich exotic nuclei are as low as 1 in 10^5 fissions, while the number of gamma rays emitted per fission event is greater than 10. Therefore, observing and identifying gamma rays from a nucleus of interest produced sparingly becomes equivalent to looking for a needle in a haystack, and requires an increase in both sensitivity and selectivity. This increase can be achieved by using an efficient and selective fragment separator and a highly efficient gamma-ray detection system, coupled with reactions involving inverse kinematics (heavy-ion beams interacting with light target atoms) and intense beams.

Method. Fragments from fusion and transfer-induced fission were produced in interactions of a uranium-238 (^{238}U) beam, at an energy of 1.29 GeV and intensity of approximately 10^9 particles per second, with a 10-μm-thick beryllium-9 (^{9}Be) target. These measurements, made at Grand Accélérateur National d'Ions Lourds (GANIL), with a very large angular acceptance (approximately 0.1 steradian) and high-resolution magnetic spectrometer (VAMOS++), in coincidence with an efficient gamma-ray detector (EXOGAM), additionally exploited the experimental advantages offered by reactions in inverse kinematics. Because of the inverse kinematics, the resulting fragments are strongly forward-focused within a cone of approximately 25° and have large velocities. These characteristics favor both efficient collection and the isotopic identification of either one of the fission fragments in VAMOS++ (placed at 20° with respect to the beam axis). **Figure 1** illustrates the various aspects of the measurement. VAMOS++ covered 14° of the polar and 60° of the azimuthal angles, respectively. Its very large acceptance is attained primarily on account of the two large-aperture magnetic quadrupoles, which focus the incoming ions on to the detection system located approximately 7.5 m (25 ft) downstream from the target. Additionally, ions are dispersed by

the magnetic dipole as per their magnetic rigidity, $B\rho$. This can be expressed by the equation below,

$$B\rho \approx \frac{A}{q} * V$$

where B and ρ are the magnetic field and the radius of curvature of the ion trajectory, and A, q, and V are the mass number, atomic charge, and velocity of the ion, respectively. The action of a magnetic dipole is illustrated in Fig. 1d, where ions with various values of $B\rho$ (indicated by the color scale) are dispersed to different positions at the detection system; a range of up to 40% in $B\rho$ of the ions is covered within a single measurement. Typical ion trajectories in VAMOS++ with a given magnetic rigidity but with different scattering angles are shown in Fig. 1d. The detection system located at the focal plane (Fig. 1f) of VAMOS++ has a large active area of 100×15 cm (40×6 in.). It is composed of: a multiwire parallel-plate avalanche counter (MWPPAC) to obtain the time of flight, two drift chambers for determination of the position in two dimensions, three segmented ionization chambers for the energy loss, and silicon detectors arranged in a wall structure for the residual energy of the ions. The measurements of time of flight (with respect to a start detector located near the target) and positions of incoming

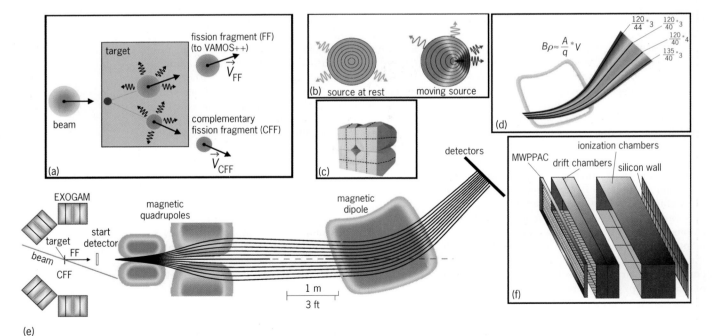

Fig. 1. Experiment for measurements on fission fragments. (*a*) The fission reaction in inverse kinematics and the resulting forward-focused fission fragment (FF) and complementary fission fragment (CFF), which promptly emit gamma rays. Only one of the fragments (FF) is detected in the VAMOS++ spectrometer. (*b*) Doppler effect on gamma-ray energies emitted from a moving source, detected in the laboratory system. The energy of the measured gamma ray, emitted in motion, varies as a function of the laboratory angle between the velocity of the emitter and the direction of the gamma ray. Here, blue and red indicate measured gamma rays with higher and lower energies, respectively. (*c*) Segmented clover high-purity germanium (HPGe) detector. The electrical segmentation of each detector is also illustrated. (*d*) Magnetic rigidity: The dispersion by a magnetic dipole of ions having different magnetic rigidities B_ρ (indicated on the color scale) is illustrated. Examples of different combinations of A, q, and V are shown. (*e*) Experimental setup, showing the EXOGAM gamma-ray array around the target. VAMOS++ is placed at 20° relative to the axis of the beam. The trajectories of ions with a given magnetic rigidity but different scattering angles are also shown. (*f*) Detection system: The ensemble of particle detectors used to identify the fission fragments. MWPPAC = multiwire parallel-plate avalanche counter.

ions, along with the known ion-optical properties of VAMOS++, led to the determination of $B\rho$, the velocity vector of the fission fragment, $\vec{V}_{FF}$, and A/q on an event-by-event basis. The Z identification of the fission fragment was obtained from the correlation of the energy loss and the total energy (E_{TOT}, the sum of the energy loss and the residual energy), as shown in **Fig. 2a**. The q and A values of the fission fragment were derived from the combination of the measured values of A/q, E_{TOT}, and $\vec{V}_{FF}$, and are

shown in Fig. 2b. Thus, a complete identification of the fission fragment was obtained. The prompt gamma rays emitted from the excited fission fragment and the complementary fission fragment were detected in coincidence in the EXOGAM gamma array (Fig. 1e). It consisted of 11 Compton-suppressed segmented clover high-purity germanium (HPGe) detectors, located around the target at a distance of 15 cm (6 in.). A clover detector is a closely packed arrangement of four HPGe detectors resembling a

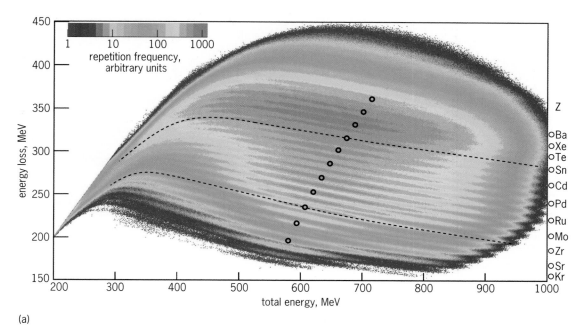

(a)

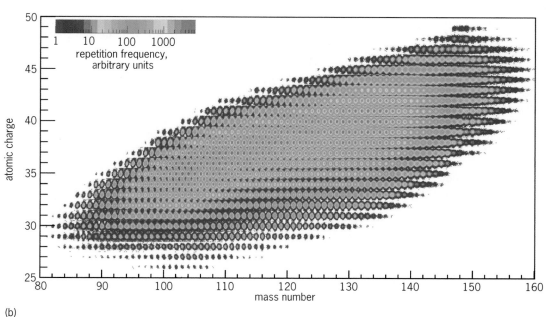

(b)

Fig. 2. Identification spectra. (*a*) The relationship between the energy loss and the total energy of fission fragments, measured in the detection system of VAMOS++, resulting in a correlated band for each element. (The color scale represents the repetition frequency for a given event.) The locus of the centroids of such correlated bands for zirconium (Zr, $Z = 40$) and tin (Sn, $Z = 50$) are shown by broken lines to guide the eye. A few of the different bands for even atomic numbers are also marked and labeled. The detector resolution decreases for higher values of Z, limiting the elemental identification. (*b*) Correlation between atomic charge and mass number for the detected fission fragments. (The color scale represents the repetition frequency for a given event.)

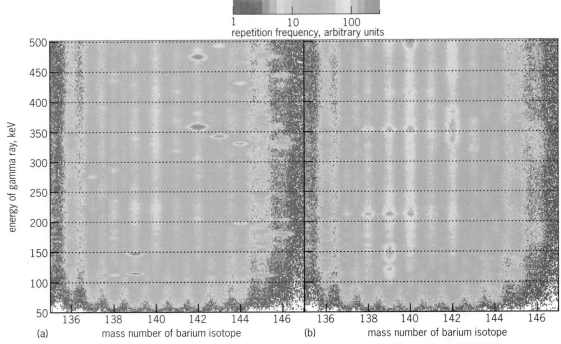

(a) mass number of barium isotope   (b) mass number of barium isotope

Fig. 3. Gamma-ray energy spectra as functions of the mass number of barium (Ba, $Z = 56$) detected in VAMOS++ using two different Doppler corrections on the same data set. (The color scale represents the repetition frequency for a given event.) (*a*) Data that are Doppler corrected using the velocity $\vec{V}_{FF}$ of a fragment detected in VAMOS++. The characteristic gamma rays (the more intense regions for a given mass number *A*) correspond to the isotopes of Ba. (*b*) Data that are Doppler corrected using the velocity $\vec{V}_{CFF}$ of a complementary fragment not detected in VAMOS++. The characteristic gamma rays can be seen to be different from those in part (*a*), and correspond to the complementary fragment, primarily isotopes of zirconium (Zr), depending on the Doppler correction made.

cloverleaf (Fig. 1*c*). The electrical segmentation of each of the HPGe detectors provides a finer localization of the gamma-ray interaction. Since the gamma rays are emitted by nuclei in motion and undergo the Doppler effect (Fig. 1*b*), they were transformed to the rest frame (of the emitter) by combining the direction of the gamma ray (using the segmentation of EXOGAM) and the velocity $\vec{V}_{FF}$ measured in VAMOS++. Additionally, using two-body kinematics, the velocity $\vec{V}_{CFF}$ of the complementary fission fragment, undetected in VAMOS++, was inferred, and the corresponding gamma-ray spectrum could also be obtained.

Over 400 different isotopes in the range $Z = 32$–63 have been detected and identified in coincidence with gamma rays. **Figure 3***a* shows the gamma-ray energy spectrum, Doppler corrected using $\vec{V}_{FF}$, as a function of the mass numbers (*A*) of barium ($Z = 56$) isotopes detected in VAMOS++. The present method thus allows us to obtain directly for a given *Z* the energies of the gamma rays as a function of *A* corresponding to the decay of their various excited states. Such a figure thus allows a direct visualization of the evolution of the gamma-ray spectrum for each nucleus (*Z*, *A*), and thus an idea of the changing nuclear structure along a given isotopic chain. In Fig. 3*b* the same set of events, but with the gamma-ray energy spectrum obtained using $\vec{V}_{CFF}$, reveals among other things the characteristic gamma rays of isotopes of zirconium ($Z = 40$),

which is the complementary element of barium arising from a fusion-fission reaction.

Figure 4 shows the most neutron-rich isotope for a given element that could be characterized in the present work as compared to the those obtained using the high-fold gamma-coincidence method, highlighting the large increase in sensitivity for this region of *Z*. [In the high-fold gamma-coincidence

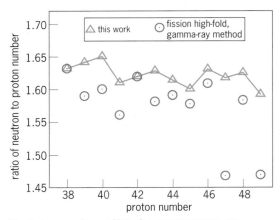

Fig. 4. Increase in sensitivity for prompt gamma-ray spectroscopy of fission fragments. The ratio of neutron to proton number as a function of atomic number (*Z*), a measure of neutron richness, for the most neutron-rich nuclei characterized in this work are compared with those studied using the conventional high-fold gamma-ray method.

method, gamma rays are recorded only when a large number of detectors (fold) fire in coincidence. The fold is related to the multiplicity of gamma rays in an event and thus to the angular momentum populated in the fragment.] The advantage of the present method, in addition to the very high sensitivity and selectivity, is that both the prompt gamma rays in single mode as well as higher-fold gamma-ray cascades in coincidence with isotopically identified nuclei can be measured. In particular, the characterization of nuclei for which A or Z or both are odd numbers, having a relatively larger number of closely spaced gamma rays, is also easier. Such a combination of experimental facilities, used in the present work, also opens new avenues to understand the dynamics of the fission process, which is still an open problem. The advances in the isotopic identification of the fission fragments aided by ongoing developments of high-efficiency next-generation gamma-ray tracking detectors (such as AGATA and GRETA) will further enrich the scope of future research and uncover yet undiscovered aspects of nuclear structure at fairly high spin in extremely neutron-rich nuclei.

For background information *see* DOPPLER EFFECT; EXOTIC NUCLEI; GAMMA-RAY DETECTORS; GAMMA RAYS; I-SPIN; IONIZATION CHAMBER; ISOTOPE; MASS SPECTROSCOPE; NUCLEAR FISSION; NUCLEAR REACTION; NUCLEAR SHAPE COEXISTENCE; NUCLEAR SHELL MODEL AND MAGIC NUMBERS; RADIOACTIVITY; SPIN (QUANTUM MECHANICS); TIME-OF-FLIGHT SPECTROMETERS in the McGraw-Hill Encyclopedia of Science & Technology.   Navin Alahari; Maurycy Rejmund

Bibliography. D. C. Carey, *Optics of Charged Particle Beams*, Harwood Academic Publishers, Chur, Switzerland, 1987; R. F. Casten, *Nuclear Structure from a Simple Perspective*, 2d ed., Oxford University Press, Oxford, UK, 2000; G. Gilmore, *Practical Gamma-Ray Spectrometry*, 2d ed., Wiley, Chichester, UK, 2008; J. Kantele, *Handbook of Nuclear Spectrometry*, Academic Press, London, 1995; C. Wagemans, ed., *The Nuclear Fission Process*, CRC Press, Boca Raton, FL, 1991.

Green cloud architecture

Recently, cloud computing has become very popular and has emerged as a widely accepted computing and service paradigm. Although cloud computing has been widely adopted, the research on cloud computing is still at an early stage. An Internet data center (IDC) is a common system for hosting cloud computing. However, the power consumption of these data centers is having a huge impact on the environment. A number of state-of-the-art research techniques have been proposed for improving data-center energy efficiency. The aim is to reduce energy consumption and at the same time provide the desired quality of service (QoS). Green cloud architecture (GCA) is an IDC architecture that aims to reduce data-center power consumption. The advantage of this architecture is that it guarantees real-time

performance, while saving in the total energy consumption of the IDC. The GCA also helps consolidate the workload and achieves significant energy savings for the cloud-computing environment. This architecture was created to address the issues in the cloud-computing environment, such as improving resource use and reducing power consumption. One of the challenges of this architecture is how to make scheduling decisions for performance-sensitive applications, such as online gaming servers.

Need for the green cloud architecture. According to the Climate Group and the Global e-Sustainability Initiative (GeSI), personal computer ownership will quadruple to 4 billion devices from 2007 to 2020. It is estimated that laptops will overtake desktops by then. Carbon dioxide (CO_2) emissions will increase significantly over the same time period and laptops will be the main source of global information technology and communication sector emissions. In addition, mobile-phone ownership will almost double to nearly 5 billion by 2020, which also will result in CO_2 emission growth. The **table** shows the CO_2 emissions for 2007 and predicted CO_2 emissions for different sectors for 2020. Environmental impact and power consumption are becoming crucial metrics for the sectors, as indicated in the table.

In a cloud data center, devices that are not directly providing the services are contributing primarily to power consumption; for example, cooling and electrical devices. Cloud providers can significantly improve the power usage efficiency (PUE) of their data centers by using the most energy-efficient technologies. State-of-the-art green data-center designs for large cloud services can achieve 40% more power efficiency than traditional data centers. Green cloud-computing solutions not only aim at saving energy but also at reducing operational costs and the carbon footprint on the environment.

Different green cloud architectures. A number of different GCAs have been defined for green cloud computing with the common goal of reducing energy consumption. This type of architecture helps in modeling subclouds, where each cloud encapsulates a specific business need that meets the requirements of the end users and businesses. One of these architectures is shown in **Fig. 1**. In this architecture, user requests are submitted through a middleware known as the Green Broker. This middleware selects

Global carbon footprint for information and communication technologies (ICT)*		
	Emissions, MtCO$_2$e	
ITC sector	2007	2020
PCs and peripherals	407	643
Telecommunications	307	349
Data centers	116	259

From SMART 2020: Enabling the low carbon economy in the information age. (http://www.smart2020.org/publications/)
MtCO$_2$e = metric tons (tonne) carbon dioxide equivalent.
*ICT accounted for 2% of all global emissions in 2007

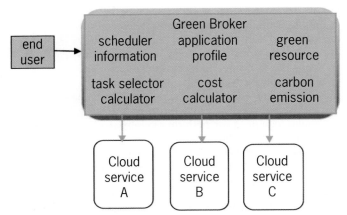

Fig. 1. Green cloud architecture. (*From V. Srimathi et al., Green cloud environmental infrastructure, Int. J. Eng. Comp. Sci., 1(3):168–177, 2012*)

the "greenest" cloud provider to complete the user's request, which is of three types: software, platform, or infrastructure. These services are stored in a public directory known as the carbon emission directory. This directory also maintains the data related to energy efficiency that includes PUE, cooling efficiency of the data center, the network cost, and the carbon emission rate of electricity used. The middleware uses the current status of energy parameters and selects the set of services for end users that will provide the most efficient PUE.

Figure 2 shows an integrated green cloud architecture (IGCA), which provides a client-oriented

green cloud middleware, allowing the manager to define the job of each department and specify the related QoS level and the service level agreements (SLA) involved. This architecture consists of the client, a client-oriented green cloud middleware, and the Green Broker. The client provides the description of the job, such as the associated budget, QoS, and SLA to the middleware. The IGCA then provides three options for carbon emission for user request completion: on the client's personal computer (local), on a server in a private cloud, and on a server in a public cloud. Thus, it provides the flexibility for the manager to choose an option based on factors such as SLA, budget, and security-level requirements.

Advantages of green cloud architecture. GCA can help in managing technology resources, improving productivity, decreasing costs, and at the same time make a positive impact on the environment. Different architectures have their own advantages, but all of them are geared toward reducing power consumption while keeping the services and QoS available to the consumer.

Technology performance. GCA provides the adaptability, scalability, reliability, and security features that are the basic needs of any business today. Most importantly, there is assurance of security and an environment of reliability for mission-critical data.

Business productivity. In terms of business-related advantages, GCA provides availability of the latest technology and solutions that are accessible from any location, thus increasing employee productivity. The major advantage for the consumer is QoS; that is,

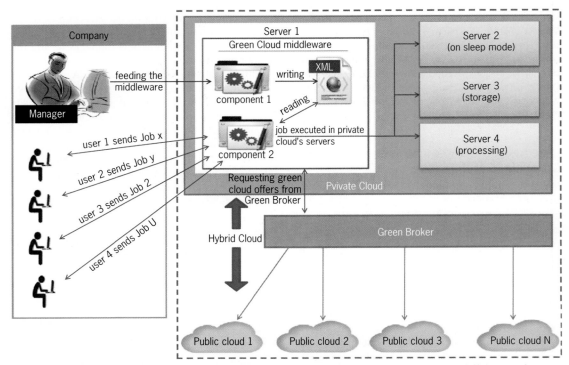

Fig. 2. Integrated green cloud architecture. (Copyright © 2012 IEEE. *Reprinted with permission from M. Hulkury and M. Doomun, Integrated Green Cloud Computing Architecture, International Conference on Advanced Computer Science Applications and Technologies [ACSAT], Kuala Lumpur, Malaysia, November 26–28, 2012, pp. 269–274, Conference Publishing Services [CPS], 2012*)

consumers are likely to receive a service that is always available.

Cost management. GCA not only aims at saving energy but also at saving operational costs. This is achieved by minimized expenditures on servers, other equipment, maintenance costs, support costs, and electric bills.

Environmental impact. The main advantage of GCA is the impact on the environment by decreasing its carbon footprint. This can be achieved by efficiently managing the energy infrastructure and using a flexible green cloud architecture.

Energy consumption and efficiency have become some of the most indispensable issues. GCA helps in achieving efficient energy management and reducing the carbon footprint for a positive impact on the environment. The flexibility of the GCA will not only provide a QoS to the consumer but, at the same time, will be cost-efficient and environment friendly.

For background information *see* CLOUD COMPUTING; COMPUTER SECURITY; DISTRIBUTED SYSTEMS (COMPUTERS); GLOBAL CLIMATE CHANGE; INDUSTRIAL ECOLOGY; INTERNET in the McGraw-Hill Encyclopedia of Science & Technology.

Ramon A. Mata-Toledo; Pranshu Gupta

Bibliography. M. Ali, Green cloud on the horizon, *Cloud Computing*, 5931:451–459, 2009, DOI:10.1007/978-3-642-10665-1_41; Y. B. Choi, Y.-S. Choi, and Y. B. Song, From green computing to green communications: A new application of Green-Tech, in *Proceedings of the 39th Annual Meeting of the Southeast Decision Sciences Institute (SEDSI 2009)*, Charleston, South Carolina, February 18–20, 2009, http://www.sedsi.org/2012_Conference/pdf/2012sedsiproceedingscombined.pdf; S. Garg et al., Green cloud framework for improving carbon efficiency of clouds, *Euro-Par 2011 Parallel Processing*, 6852:491–502, 2011, DOI:10.1007/978-3-642-23400-2_45; S. Garg and R. Buyya, Green cloud computing and environmental sustainability, in S. Murugesan and G. Gangadharan (eds.), *Harnessing Green IT: Principles and Practices*, pp. 315–340, Wiley, Chichester, West Sussex, UK, 2012; M. Hulkury and M. Doomun, Integrated green cloud computing architecture, pp. 269–274, in *Proceedings of the International Conference on Advanced Computer Science Applications and Technologies (ACSAT)*, Kuala Lumpur, Malaysia, November 26–28, 2012, Conference Publishing Services (CPS), 2012; D. Jadhwani et al., Study of efficient utilization of power using green computing, *Proc. Int. J. Adv. Comp. Res.*, 2(6):108–113, 2012; L. Liu et al., Green-Cloud: A new architecture for Green Data Center, in *Proceedings of the 6th International Conference Industry Session on Autonomic Computing and Communications Industry Session*, ICAC '09 6th International Conference on Autonomic Computing, Barcelona, Spain, June 15–19, 2009, Association for Computing Machinery (ACM), New York, 2009; R. Mata-Toledo and P. Gupta, Green data center: How green can we perform?, *J. Technol. Res.*, 2(1):1–8, 2011; S. J. Prakash, K. Subramanyam, and U. D. S. V. Prasad, Towards energy efficiency of green computing based on virtualization, *Int. J. Emerg. Trends Eng. Develop.*, 2(7):415–423, 2012; V. Srimathi, D. Hemalatha, and R. Balachander, Green cloud environmental infrastructure, *Int. J. Eng. Comp. Sci.*, 1(3):168–177, 2012.

Hantavirus outbreak

Hantavirus pulmonary syndrome (HPS) is a very rare and highly lethal respiratory illness. It was first reported in the United States during the spring of 1993. The most recent outbreak occurred among people visiting California's Yosemite National Park in June 2012. There were 10 confirmed cases, and the National Park Service initiated a public health campaign to heighten public awareness, detection, and prevention of the disease.

Background. In mid-May 1993, a Native American marathon runner in rural New Mexico came down with severe flu-like symptoms. He had a headache, fever, severe body aches, and cough, and he became extremely short of breath, prompting him to seek medical attention twice. His chest x-ray was normal, suggesting that he did not have pneumonia. His doctor prescribed antibiotics and sent the patient home, but his condition worsened. He collapsed and died of respiratory failure at an Indian Health Service (IHS) emergency room.

Two days before the patient became ill, his fiancée died from the same mysterious respiratory illness. Both victims died from fluid buildup in their lungs. Normally, with each breath, the air sacs or alveoli of the lungs take in oxygen and release carbon dioxide. In this situation, however, the lung alveoli were filled with fluid instead of air; this prevented oxygen from being absorbed into the bloodstream, causing shortness of breath and eventually death. Personnel at the IHS were baffled by these two cases and called in the New Mexico Office of Medical Investigations. It was soon determined that five more similar deaths had occurred. All of the individuals were previously healthy. The Special Pathogens Branch of the Centers for Disease Control and Prevention (CDC) was notified and began an investigation, partnered with the IHS, the Navajo Nation, the University of New Mexico, and the state health departments of Arizona, New Mexico, Colorado, and Utah.

By mid-June 1993, the investigation teams identified 24 similar cases. The majority of patients were previously healthy adults between 20 and 40 years of age; among these, half died. The mysterious virulent disease was reported in a region of Arizona, Utah, Colorado, and New Mexico referred to as the Four Corners region of the United States (**Fig. 1**). Experts worked intensely to narrow down a list of possibilities, including bubonic plague, influenza, other emerging viral diseases, and exposure to herbicides. Virologists at the CDC finally identified the culprit as an Old World hantavirus (a member of the Bunyaviridae family of RNA viruses). The term Old World

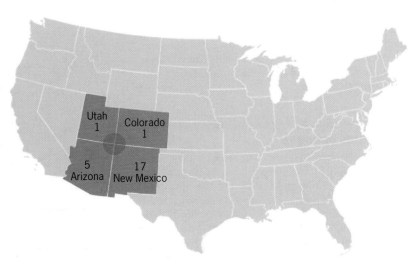

Fig. 1. Locations of the 24 confirmed cases of hantavirus pulmonary syndrome (HPS) during the 1993 Four Corners outbreak in the United States. (*Figure adapted from http://summitcountyvoice.com/2010/12/29/clearing-the-air-in-the-four-corners-region*)

been associated with severe respiratory illness. Why then did this unique hantavirus make an appearance? It was known that chronically infected, but apparently healthy, wild rodents harbor hantaviruses in their droppings, urine, and saliva. The hantaviruses could be aerosolized when humans came into contact with contaminated items such as blankets or food-storage areas. The hantavirus enters the human respiratory tract through the inhalation of contaminated air particles. Therefore, investigators trapped rodents in barns, woodpiles, and people's homes. The new hantavirus was isolated from the deer mouse (*Peromyscus maniculatus*). It was likely that the hantavirus was present in rodent populations for a long time in the Four Corners region, but an unusually mild winter and increases in spring rainfall led to an abundance of pinyon nuts on which the deer mice feed. The end result was an increased deer mice population in the summer and greater opportunities for people to come in contact with the infected rodents.

Infected individuals during the 1993 Four Corners region outbreak experienced a rapid course of illness that was approximately 50% fatal. This new or emerging disease in the United States was named hantavirus pulmonary syndrome (HPS). Researchers determined that the hantavirus was not transmitted from person to person. The new virus was originally named the Four Corners disease virus and then Muerto Canyon virus; later, the name was changed to Sin Nombre virus ("no name virus").

refers to those parts of the world known before the voyages of Christopher Columbus; it includes Europe, Asia, and Africa and their surrounding islands. This Old World virus had entered the New World and is now referred to as a New World hantavirus in scientific and medical reports.

Hantaviruses had not been previously associated with human disease in North America. Moreover, hantaviruses found elsewhere in the world had not

Fig. 2. Locations and names of the unique rodent reservoir of New World hantaviruses. Common animal names are given in green text. Pathogenic hantaviruses are given in red text (a skull and crossbones symbol is also shown). (*Adapted from Fig. 1 of A. McNeil, S. T. Nichol, and C. F. Spiropoulou, Hantavirus pulmonary syndrome, Virus Res., 162:138–147, 2011*)

More New World hantaviruses. Until the 1993 description of HPS in the Four Corners outbreak, most (Old World) hantavirus outbreaks were reported in the military field. During the Korean War (1951–1953), U.S. Army physicians had been confronted with what is now referred to as hemorrhagic fever with renal syndrome (HFRS). Soldiers in the field were found to suffer from sudden fever, hemorrhages, multiorgan failure, and shock. However, it was not until 1978 that the first hantavirus known to cause Korean hemorrhagic fever (KHF) was identified. The hantavirus was isolated from the lungs of striped field mice trapped in fields and in dwellings near farms in Korea. This first identified hantavirus was called Hantaan, after the river that runs near the famous 38th parallel between North Korea and South Korea, where most of the battles were fought and most KHF cases were recorded.

After the 1993 Four Corners region outbreak, numerous studies revealed at least 20 different New World hantaviruses, with each one being associated with a unique rodent host that is persistently infected, although without causing disease (**Fig. 2**). Moreover, not all of them cause disease in humans. For example, antibodies against the Prospect Hill hantavirus have been found in mammals trapped in Minnesota and Maryland, but have not been associated with any human disease. However, other hantaviruses cause HPS or HFRS in humans. For example, the Andes virus (the cause of an HPS outbreak in southwestern Argentina in 1995) has been associated with the most HPS cases to date; in addition,

the Andes virus is the only hantavirus to have been associated with human-to-human transmission.

HPS cases have varied widely across North America and South America. In the United States, as of mid-December 2012, there were 616 confirmed cases in 34 states since 1993 (**Fig. 3**). Of these, 27 cases had an unknown location of exposure. The incubation period of HPS ranges from 1 to 6 weeks. Mortality rates of confirmed cases range from 23 to 56% in the United States. New Mexico has the highest number of cases (90).

Diagnosis and treatment. HPS and influenza share similar symptoms, making early diagnosis difficult. A history of potential rural rodent exposure would strongly suggest HPS, prompting testing. Blood tests can reveal antibodies against hantaviruses. There is no vaccine to prevent or cure New World hantavirus infections, and there is no specific treatment. Treatment for HPS is supportive care. Intubation or mechanical ventilation may be necessary to assist respiration and to prevent the lungs from filling up with fluid. In extreme cases, a method called extracorporeal membrane oxygenation is used to pump blood through a machine that removes carbon dioxide and adds oxygen to make sure the patient has a sufficient supply of oxygenated blood. Ribavirin (an antiviral) was used to treat HPS during the 1993 outbreak in an open clinical trial, but it did not improve patient outcome, presumably because patients were treated too late during the course of the disease. The prognosis of patients improves with early diagnosis, immediate hospitalization, and facilitated breathing

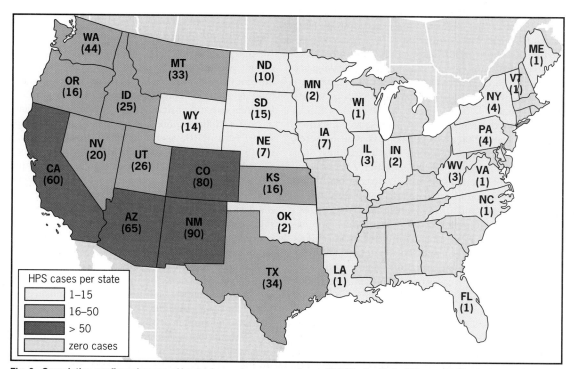

Fig. 3. Cumulative confirmed cases of hantavirus pulmonary syndrome (HPS) in the United States (1993–2012) by locations of exposure. There were 616 total cases in 34 states. Of these, 27 cases had an unknown state of exposure. (*Figure adapted from http://www.cdc.gov/hantavirus/surveillance/state-of-exposure.html*)

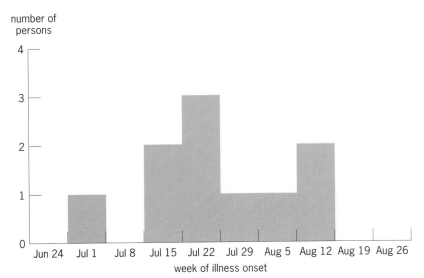

number of
persons

week of illness onset

Fig. 4. Timeline of the 2012 hantavirus outbreak in Yosemite National Park, California, in which park visitors were exposed to infected deer mice. (*Source: http://www.cdc.gov/ hantavirus/outbreaks/yosemite/epi.html*)

support. Ribavirin has been shown to be effective at reducing hantavirus replication in hamster animal model studies of lethal HPS caused by Andes hantavirus.

Yosemite National Park outbreak. In mid-August 2012, two residents of California were confirmed to be suffering from HPS after an overnight stay in Yosemite National Park. In early September 2012, the World Health Organization (WHO) issued a global warning to travelers from 39 other countries who may have come into contact with contaminated rodent droppings or saliva while staying at the signature tent cabins in Curry Village in Yosemite National Park. Deer mice infestations were discovered in the insulation of the tent cabins, and all 91 of these cabins were closed indefinitely in late August 2012. Trapping and control of deer mice and educational interventions for staff and visitors were implemented.

Based on the number of cabin reservations, the CDC speculated that up to 10,000 park visitors were at risk for exposure to cabin dust containing Sin Nombre hantaviruses. By mid-October 2012, there were 10 confirmed cases of hantavirus infection in visitors to Yosemite National Park: 8 in California, 1 in Pennsylvania, and 1 in West Virginia. Three cases were fatal. The timeline of the full outbreak is presented in **Fig.** 4. This cluster of cases in Yosemite National Park was unusual. Fortunately, Sin Nombre hantavirus is not contagious. Before this outbreak, there were 58 cases of HPS in California since 1994; of these cases, two were people who visited Yosemite National Park before 2012.

Outlook. HPS is a very rare and highly lethal respiratory disease first recognized in the United States in 1993. Hantaviruses are transmitted to humans via aerosols of infectious excreta from chronically infected, but apparently healthy small mammals, mainly wild rodents. Vaccination programs are be-

ing implemented to prevent Old World hantavirus infections in some East Asian countries. American and European vaccines may be expected in the not too distant future, but they will likely have limited use (for example, these vaccines may be used only by the military and other professionals at high risk, such as foresters and mammalogists).

For background information *see* ANIMAL VIRUS; DISEASE; EPIDEMIC; IMMUNOLOGY; INFECTIOUS DISEASE; PUBLIC HEALTH; VACCINATION; VIRULENCE; VIRUS; VIRUS CLASSIFICATION in the McGraw-Hill Encyclopedia of Science & Technology.   Teri Shors

Bibliography. California Department of Public Health et al., Hantavirus pulmonary syndrome in visitors to a national park—Yosemite Valley, California, 2012, *Morb. Mortal. Wkly. Rep.*, 61(46):952, 2012; F. Koster et al., Outbreak of acute illness—Southwestern United States, 1993, *Morb. Mortal. Wkly. Rep.*, 42(22):421–424, 1993; H. W. Lee, P. W. Lee, and K. M. Johnson, Isolation of the etiologic agent of Korean hemorrhagic fever, *J. Infect. Dis.*, 137(3):298–308, 1978, DOI:10.1093/infdis/137.3.298; A. McNeil, S. T. Nichol, and C. F. Spiropoulou, Hantavirus pulmonary syndrome, *Virus Res.*, 162:138–147, 2011, DOI:10.1016/j.virusres.2011.09.017; S. T. Nichol et al., Genetic identification of a hantavirus associated with an outbreak of acute respiratory illness, *Science*, 262:914–917, 1993, DOI:10.1126/science.8235615; D. Safronetz et al., *In vitro* and *in vivo* activity of ribavirin against Andes virus infection, *PLoS ONE*, 6(8):e23560, 2011, DOI:10.1371/journal.pone.0023560.

Heads-up displays

Heads-up displays (HUDs) are graphic displays that do not require users to divert their eyes from their current fields of view. They were first developed for military aviation. Today, the scope of their application has expanded dramatically, notably to civilian aircraft and automobiles, as well as to personal devices. Early HUDs were stationary devices permanently mounted in a cockpit; many still are. However, for some applications mobility is essential, and helmet-mounted displays, a subset of HUDs, were developed. As technology improved, virtual retinal displays were developed. These small devices write high-resolution images directly onto the viewer's retina and significantly extend the potential applications for HUDs.

The term augmented reality, first coined in 1990, is used today to describe the augmentation of real-world views with computer-generated sensory input. The term subsumes heads-up displays in that HUDs are examples of augmented reality. However, not all examples of augmented reality are HUDs. For instance, augmented reality includes overlaying data on indirect views of the real world, such as smartphone images, while HUDs are restricted to adding information to direct views of the real world.

Fig. 1. Rockwell Collins 3500 HUD marketed for small to mid-sized commercial aircraft. (*Rockwell Collins*)

History of HUDs. The precursors for HUDs were pre-World War II optical-sighting technologies for military aircraft, first used in Germany in 1918. The reflector gunsight allowed the user to see an illuminated projection of a gun's aiming point superimposed on the field of view.

Just before World War II, the gyro gunsight was developed to enhance existing reflector gunsights by superimposing airspeed and other data to improve the accuracy of aircraft guns. During the 1940s, the enhanced sights improved rapidly, offering ever more information. The British AI Mk VIII air-interception radar was an early example of information being projected onto the aircraft windscreen, allowing pilots to perform an intercept without diverting their eyes.

In the 1950s, the reflector gunsight image was projected onto a cathode-ray tube (CRT) controlled by computers in the aircraft and enhanced with basic flight information. This began the era of the modern HUD.

During the 1950s and 1960s, HUD displays became commonplace in military aircraft. In the 1970s, commercial aircraft began incorporating HUDs in the cockpit, and today they are common in most commercial and corporate aircraft (**Fig. 1**).

Many applications have been developed specifically for avionics and military use. For military use, various data concerning weapons targeting have been added to HUD displays. In the 1980s, HUDs were also developed for vertical-takeoff-and-landing aircraft, as well as for short-takeoff-and-landing aircraft. These applications are particularly helpful when landing on and taking off from aircraft carriers.

Enhanced vision systems (EVS) are used for HUDs in low-light conditions caused by either darkness or weather. In these systems, an image of the outside scene, captured from a nose-mounted infrared camera, is overlaid on the HUD display to provide a clearer vision of the outside than the pilot actually has (**Fig. 2**).

Camera positions vary for EVS systems to be as close as possible to the pilot's eye position. The registration of the EVS image on the real-world view is a critical concern for these systems.

In more extreme conditions, HUDs have been designed to project synthetic vision systems (SVS), in which a synthetic view of the outside is projected together with the data from the HUD (**Fig. 3**). The synthetic image is constructed from terrain databases and instrument readings, such as altitude. As seen in Fig. 3, a host of critical information is projected by the HUD, including airspeed, altitude, flight path, stabilizer settings, and pitch of the aircraft.

Synthetic vision systems do not conform to the definition of heads-up displays because they are not overlaying information on a real-world view. The same is true, but to a lesser extent, for enhanced-vision systems. However, each is a valuable navigational aid when conditions demand.

Components of HUDs. Heads-up displays typically consist of a data projector driven by a computer. Many types of projectors have been used, including cathode-ray tubes, liquid-crystal displays, and plasma displays.

The projector is coupled to an optical collimator that enables the image to be projected some distance without parallax. The collimator limits the angle of view for the HUD by providing a cylinder of collimated light. The display is visible only if the user's point of view is from somewhere within that cylinder. Typically, this area is large enough for a reasonable amount of head movement on the part of the viewer.

The collimator focuses the image at infinity, which enables viewers to read the displayed information without having to refocus their eyes from the scene they are observing.

The image is commonly redirected by a combiner, a specialized beam splitter that reflects only the wavelengths of light used to form the image, allowing all other wavelengths to pass through.

The use of different displays marks the succeeding generations of HUDs. The first generation uses CRTs. The second generation uses liquid-crystal displays illuminated by light-emitting diodes. The third generation of HUDs uses optical waveguides to produce images directly in the combiner without need for a traditional projection system. The fourth generation uses a scanning laser beam to write images directly on the display medium.

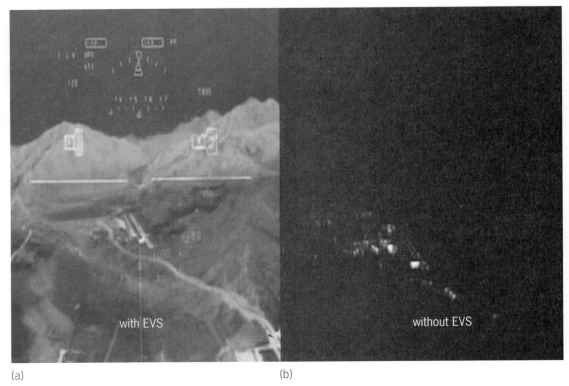

(a)   (b)

Fig. 2. Gulfstream Enhanced Vision System™ (EVS): (*a*) infrared image versus (*b*) visual image. (*Copyright © Gulfstream Aerospace Corporation*)

The HUDs of the refractive design have the advantage that viewers can move their heads and still see the information being displayed. With reflective HUDs, viewers need to remain relatively stationary to view the display. With reflective HUDs, however, there is no need for a collimating lens, and the display is brighter, although the engineering of the curved combining glass adds complexity to the design.

HUDs can be fixed in their mounting, such as in a cockpit or automobile dashboard, or they can be mobile, such as in a helmet-mounted display. Modern fighter jets, such as the F-16, use both fixed HUDs and helmet-mounted displays simultaneously. Some modern jets rely solely on helmet-mounted displays and forego fixed-mounted HUDs.

Effectiveness of HUDs. In examining the use of HUDs in avionics, A. Ingman concluded, "HUD aids the instrument scanning process in phases of flight with high workload, such as takeoff, approach and landing resulting in increased situational awareness, flight precision and flight safety."

It has been found that, depending on several factors, it can take up to 2 seconds for a pilot to stop looking at the scene ahead, change focus to an instrument panel, assimilate information, and refocus on the scene ahead.

Typically, HUDs used in avionics replicate information from flight instruments, such as altitude, speed, heading, and aircraft attitude. They also project a flight path symbol showing where the aircraft is going in relation to the real-world view. Without HUDs, pilots have to infer the actual flight path from interpretation of the instrument readings, making it more difficult to correct for aircraft drift in cross winds (a critical factor for landing on aircraft carriers). Comparisons between the use

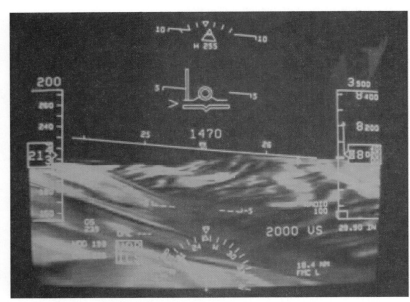

Fig. 3. Synthetic vision system (SVS) HUD. (*NASA*)

of HUDs and conventional flight methods have found that using HUDs improves track, speed, and altitude maintenance.

O. Goteman, K. Smith, and S. Dekker found that the use of HUDs improved the touchdown performance of pilots in terms of lateral accuracy in both normal and limited-visibility situations. No evidence was found that the additional information presented to pilots by HUDs interfered with their decision making during the critical landing process.

HUDs in automobiles. In the late 1960s, the use of HUDs was tested in cars by the Bureau of Public Roads of the U.S. Department of Transportation. The application tested was for directional instructions with possible implications for hazard warnings on motorways.

In 1988, three years after acquiring Hughes Aircraft Co., General Motors began incorporating HUDs in automobiles, selling 54 HUD-equipped Oldsmobile Cutlass Supreme Indy 500 pace car replicas. The HUD unit was on top of the dashboard and projected images in the center of the driver's view that appeared to be located near the front bumper of the car. This image placement was used to reduce driver "blind times," the time it takes to refocus the eyes from near to far fields. Vehicle speed, turn signals, and low-fuel warnings were projected. Drivers could adjust the brightness and vertical position of the display.

In 1988, Nissan sold the first production cars to incorporate HUDs. The Nissan 240SX models incorporated them from 1989 to 1994. The vehicle speed only was projected in the bottom left of the driver's visual field, appearing to be about 1 m from the eye. The Nissan HUD was located beneath the dashboard, projecting through a small hole onto the windshield combiner. BMW was the first European car maker to offer HUDs, in 2003.

Cost was an obstacle to automotive HUD development. Aircraft cockpit HUDs cost as much as $100,000 each, with complex lens systems and image generation and projection equipment. Automobiles required greatly simplified and less expensive versions of this technology for it to be viable.

In January 2013, *The Wall Street Journal* reported that automakers are implementing HUDs as a result of improving technology and the increasing role of automotive Internet connections. Automotive HUDs today offer brighter, larger, and sharper images as a result of improved light-emitting diode (LED) lighting and better mirrors. **Figure 4** shows the HUD image from a 2013 BMW. In the future, laser steering technology is expected to improve the display quality even further.

Instrument makers predict that information may someday be displayed on the entire windshield, with different content for passengers and drivers. Already, HUDs can project almost any kind of information onto windshields, including smartphone messages and videos. Car makers must choose judiciously which information enhances driving safety

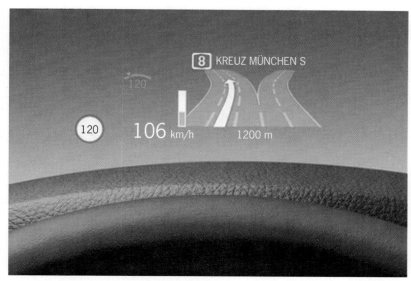

Fig. 4. HUD image from 2013 BMW. (*BMW AG*)

and which information becomes a distraction for drivers. The 2013 Lexus GS offers one of the most comprehensive HUDs, including speed and engine RPMs, as well as navigation instructions, radio stations, and lane-change and collision warnings.

Today, the use of HUDs is still limited to luxury cars because the average cost is about $1000. In 2012, worldwide sales of automobile HUDs exceeded 800,000 units. This figure is expected to rise rapidly in coming years. There are still several important automakers, such as Mercedes-Benz, on the sidelines waiting for the right time to implement HUDs. However, with Audi, BMW, and Lexus all offering HUDs, Mercedes-Benz is expected to offer this option in the near future.

Special-purpose HUDs have been developed for police vehicles to display computer output to drivers. Also, there are automotive aftermarket companies selling a range of HUDs that can be retrofitted to any car. One example is the Springteq GPS navigation display developed in 2010, which was the first product to integrate GPS satellite navigation in an all-in-one HUD display. The projector for this display is mounted temporarily on the car's dashboard when it is needed.

The future of HUDs on automobiles may not be limited to the windshield. In 2009, Light Blue Optics showed a prototype HUD for an automobile side-view mirror (**Fig. 5**) at the Society for Information Display's *Vehicles and Photons 2009* symposium.

The prototype in Fig. 5 has the advantage of being substantially more compact than other HUDs, allowing it to be housed in the side-view mirror. The holographic projector uses liquid-crystal-on-silicon panels to modulate the light in forming the image.

Helmet-mounted HUDs. There are applications where it is necessary or desirable to have heads-up displays mounted on the viewer, such as on a helmet or goggles. This subset of heads-up displays

Fig. 5. Prototype side-view mirror HUD. (*Light Blue Optics*)

is referred to as helmet-mounted displays (HMDs), or, in weapons applications, helmet-mounted sights. These afford the viewer greater freedom of movement while maintaining the overlay of critical information on the user's field of view.

Helmet-mounted displays for military avionics were developed in the 1960s and implemented during the 1970s. Early helmet-mounted display systems projected defocused images onto small screens such as the inner surface of glasses close to the user's

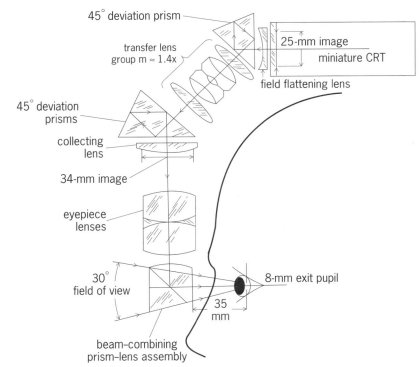

Fig. 6. Diagram of 1969 head-mounted heads-up display. (*Reprinted from M.H. Freeman, Head-up displays: Part 2, Optics Technology, 1(4):175–182, 1969, DOI:10.1016/S0374-3926(69)80001-3; copyright © 1969, with permission from Elsevier*)

eyes. The image would appear focused only if the viewer's eyes were focused at a particular depth. The early head-mounted apparatuses were cumbersome. **Figure 6** shows a 1969 diagram of a head-mounted display.

The limited brightness of these displays restricted their use to indoor applications. Over time, miniaturization, improved optical systems, and brighter projectors made helmet-mounted HUDs more comfortable and more effective. Also, as the Internet grew and wireless and GPS technologies became ubiquitous, the capabilities of HMDs increased dramatically. **Figure 7** shows a 2008 HMD optimized for helicopter pilots.

The 2008 Elbit Systems Jedeyes HMD provided the widest field of view yet achieved with a heads-up display. The ultrawide visor incorporates two 2250 × 1200-pixel displays that offer sharp, high-resolution, 3D imagery. The Jedeyes HMD processes input from unmanned aerial vehicles, digital maps, and various on-board and off-board sensors.

As with stationary HUDs, HMDs were adopted for civilian uses as the technology improved and became more affordable. Today, helmet-mounted displays are available for motorcycle helmets, scuba diving masks, swimming goggles, and ski goggles. For example, the Recon Mod HUDs in ski goggles provides information about speed, altitude, vertical drop, distance, navigation, jump analytics, buddy tracking, call display, SMS texts, and music-player control. Similar to the automotive industry, HUD designers for sports goggles must be judicious in presenting crucial information without allowing the displays to become distracting for users.

Virtual retinal displays. Personal HUD systems have evolved with the development of displays that project information directly on the viewer's retina. Some of these systems use low-powered lasers to write the images directly onto the retina. An alternative method is to use a micro display, such as an organic light-emitting diode (OLED) display, that is projected onto the retina through a lens system.

Virtual retinal displays (VRDs) do not produce a real image for the user to view. Instead, they create a virtual image on the retina that appears to be at a distance from the viewer.

For laser-writing systems, three lasers are required for a color image. They must each be modulated to match the intensity of color required in any section of the image. The lasers are then scanned to place the image on the retina. The scanning mode can be either vector or raster, with raster scanning having the advantage that it can be driven by standard video sources. A block diagram of VRD components is shown in **Fig. 8**.

When projecting the scanned image onto the viewer's retina, the goal is for the exit pupil from the VRD to be coplanar with the entrance pupil of the eye. The lens and cornea of the eye focus the beam on the retina, placing it in relation to the angle at which the beam enters the eye. The angle is varying during the raster image construction, and the persistence of vision of the eye allows the viewer to see the whole pattern as a stable image.

The retinal scanning technique grew from the invention of the flying-spot ophthalmoscope in 1980. The first virtual retinal display was invented by Kazuo Yoshinaka of Nippon Electric Company in 1986. Later work at the University of Washington in the Human Interface Technology Lab resulted in a similar system in 1991. Further research at the University of Washington, funded partly by Microvision, Inc., led to a series of prototypes with higher resolution, full-color images, smaller optics, and improved eye-tracking techniques.

In using VRDs to augment reality, eye tracking is necessary to maintain alignment between virtual images and real objects. The eye-tracking system signals the computer graphics generator with the instantaneous position and orientation of the eye so that the system can generate graphics, allowing the virtual elements to appear stable relative to viewed objects. A variety of eye-tracking methods have been used with VRDs, with the shared-aperture method having been shown to be effective for cockpit applications. The consumer-oriented VRDs that are coming on the market do not incorporate eye tracking because of the added complexity and cost. Instead, the display images are in the peripheral vision of the user, who glances at them as needed.

Virtual retinal displays have significant advantages over other display technologies. They are small, lightweight, and energy efficient. They have large fields of view, high image resolution, large color gamuts (range of colors), high contrast, and high brightness. Plus, they offer the potential for true 3D displays. Advances in related fields, such as nanotechnology, laser diodes, and holographic optical elements, are being incorporated into successive generations of VRD designs.

Virtual retinal displays in the form of glasses are beginning to emerge on the market. In 2013, Recon Instruments began releasing general-purpose VRD glasses aimed at a spectrum of sporting activities, but also marketed for working professionals, including law-enforcement officers, doctors, electrical technicians, and others (**Fig. 9**).

The Recon Jet is a rugged pair of multipurpose sports glasses that is versatile enough to fulfill the needs of many types of users. The screen is mounted in the lower right corner of the field of vision, allowing users to devote most of their concentration to the task at hand. It has a dual-core processor, dedicated graphics, 2 gigabytes of storage, Wi-Fi, Bluetooth, GPS, and a comprehensive suite of sensors, including altimeter, gyroscope, magnetometer, thermometer, and accelerometer. It also has a built-in 8-megapixel camera capable of 1080 HD video at 30 frames per second. Speakers and microphone are also built in.

The onboard sensors, camera, connectivity, and audio enable the glasses to present an array of data to the wearer. However, the versatility of the device for different occupations is enabled by applications

Fig. 7. Elbit Systems JEDEYE™ helicopter helmet-mounted display. (*Copyright © Elbit Systems Ltd.*)

that customize the display information for specific tasks with information from databases or input from off-board sensors.

In 2013, Google announced the open beta test of Google Glass (**Fig. 10**), a lightweight personal VRD heads-up display that is expected to push the boundaries of augmented reality. Google Glass augments the scene before the viewer. Through voice activation, the viewer can photograph and videorecord that augmented scene and send the resulting files. Google Glass interfaces with the Internet through

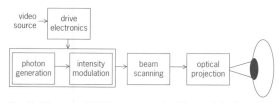

Fig. 8. Diagram of VRD components. [*Human Interface Technology Lab (HITLab)*]

Fig. 9. Recon Jet heads-up display sunglasses. (*Recon Instruments*)

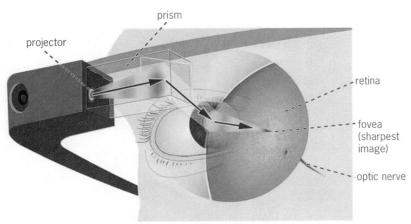

Fig. 10. Diagram of Google Glass imaging method. (*Image courtesy of Martin Missfeldt under a Creative-Commons-License CC-BY, http://www.brille-kaufen.org/en/googleglass/*)

Wi-Fi or Bluetooth via the wireless service on the user's cellphone or tablet computer.

Google has released the Application Programming Interface (API) to encourage third-party developers to create apps that will extend the capabilities of the device. Other manufacturers of HMDs had previously done the same, but none has had the reach of Google.

Outlook. Heads-up displays have evolved dramatically since their invention more than a half-century ago. The growth has been both within the avionics industry and branching out to an ever-increasing number of new applications. Technological developments have enabled systems that are smaller, lighter, more efficient, more capable, more portable, and of higher optical quality than was imagined at their inception. The specialized avionic, military, medical, and industrial HUDs continually incorporate technological advances to become ever more capable, convenient, accurate, and useful.

The era of the Internet, mobile communications, and the information age in general has steadily increased the data sources accessible for the augmented reality provided by heads-up displays. The advent of HUDs using virtual retinal displays promises to make the technology ubiquitous, and the development of applications by the public at large will expand the functionality of these devices just as it has for cell phones and tablet computers.

For background information *see* AIRCRAFT INSTRUMENTATION; CATHODE-RAY TUBE; COMPUTER GRAPHICS; ELECTRONIC DISPLAY; EYE (VERTEBRATE); HOLOGRAPHY; LIGHT-EMITTING DIODE; LIQUID CRYSTAL DISPLAY; LIQUID CRYSTALS; VISION in the McGraw-Hill Encyclopedia of Science & Technology.

Anthony Stanton

Bibliography. Chester Dawson, Car makers take a serious look at heads-up displays, *The Wall Street Journal*, January 26, 2013; M. H. Freeman, Head-up displays—A review, *Opt. Technol.*, pp. 63–70, August 1969; M. H. Freeman, Head-up displays—Part 2, *Opt. Technol.*, pp. 175–182, August 1969; O. Goteman, K. Smith, and S. Deffer, HUD with a velocity (flight-path) vector reduces lateral error during landing in restricted visibility, *Int. J. Aviation Psychol.*, 17(1), pp. 91–108, 2007, DOI:10.1080/10508410709336939; D. Graham-Rowe, Heads-up displays go holographic, *MIT Technol. Rev.*, October 2009; A. Ingman, *The Heads-Up Display Concept, a Summary with Special Attention to the Civil Aviation Industry*, School of Aviation, Lund University, Lund, Sweden, March 2005; J. K. Lauber et al., *An Operational Evaluation of Head-up Displays for Civil Transport Aircraft*, NASA Tech. Pap. 1815, NASA Ames Research Center, Moffett Field, CA, 1982; L. H. McCarty, Automotive heads-up display projects information inexpensively, *Design News*, pp. 112–113, March 13, 1989; K. McWalter, Heads-up displays come to autos, *Design News*, pp. 120–122, October 3, 1988; L. H. Sverdrup and Mikhail Belenkii, *Dynamic Foveal Vision Display*, U.S. Patent Application 20120105310, filed November 3, 2010; M. Tidwell et al., The virtual retinal display—A retinal scanning imaging system, *Proc. Virtual Reality World, 1995*, pp. 325–333, 1995; R. H. Webb, G. W. Hughes, and O. Pomerantzeff, Flying spot TV ophthalmoscope, *Appl. Opt.*, 19(17):2991–2997, 1980; Harry Woodman, *Early Aircraft Armament: The Aeroplane and the Gun up to 1918*, p. 239, Smithsonian Institution Press, Washington, DC, 1989.

Health benefits of edible and medicinal mushrooms

Edible and medicinal mushrooms (MMs) have an established history of use in traditional Eastern Asian therapies. Many species of mushrooms have been used in traditional medicine for thousands of years. The use of mushrooms in traditional medicine has been well documented throughout Asia, Europe, and Africa (including Algeria, Egypt, and Yoruba populations in Nigeria and Benin). There is also a long history of the traditional use of mushrooms as curatives in Mesoamerica (especially for species of the genus *Psilocybe*). A very special role was assigned to fly agaric (*Amanita muscaria*) in Siberian and Tibetan shamanism, Buddhism, and Celtic myths. Many important MM species are rarely eaten as food because they are woody and have a bitter taste.

Active substances and characteristics. MMs have valuable health benefits. Mushrooms contain several biologically active substances in their fruit bodies, cultured mycelia, cultured broths, and spores. These include high-molecular-weight polysaccharides (mainly β-D-glucans), heteroglucans, chitinous substances, peptidoglucans, proteoglucans (β-D-glucans linked to proteins), lectins, RNA components, dietary fibers, secondary metabolites (organic substances such as lactones, terpenoids, steroids, statins, phenols, alkaloids, and antibiotics), and metal-chelating agents.

Many, if not all, mushrooms contain biologically active polysaccharides in their fruit bodies, cultured mycelia, and cultured broths. The data on mushroom polysaccharides have been summarized for approximately 700 species. Particularly, and most importantly for modern medicine, polysaccharides with antitumor and immunostimulating properties have been identified. Several of the mushroom polysaccharide compounds have undergone phase I, II, and III clinical trials and are used extensively and successfully as drugs to treat various cancers and other diseases in Asia.

A total of 126 medicinal functions are thought to be produced by MMs and fungi, including antitumor, immunomodulating, antioxidant, radical scavenging, cardiovascular, antihypercholesterolemia, antiviral, antibacterial, antiparasitic, antifungal, detoxification, hepatoprotective, and antidiabetic effects. The best known medicinal mushrooms are *Ganoderma lucidum* (lingzhi or reishi), *Lentinus edodes* (shiitake) [see **illustration**], *Grifola frondosa* (maitake), *Cordyceps* species (caterpillar mushrooms), *Trametes versicolor* (turkey tail), *Flammulina velutipes* (winter mushroom), *Agaricus brasiliensis* (royal sun mushroom), *Pleurotus* species (oyster mushrooms), *Hericium erinaceus* (lion's mane), *Hypsizygus marmoreus* (beech mushroom), *Tremella mesenterica* (yellow brain mushroom), *Tremella fuciformis* (silver ear mushroom), *Phellinus linteus* (black hoof mushroom), *Schizophyllum commune* (split gill mushroom), and *Inonotus obliquus* (chaga).

Mushrooms are rich in proteins, chitin (dietary fibers), vitamins, and minerals. They are also low in total fat, but with a high proportion of unsaturated fatty acids, and have no cholesterols. As for the characteristics of taste, mushrooms serve as a delicious foodstuff and also as a source of food-flavoring substances (because of their unique flavors). In addition to the volatile 8-carbon compounds, the typical mushroom flavor consists of water-soluble taste components such as soluble sugars, polyols, organic acids, free amino acids, and nucleotides.

Lentinus edodes (shiitake), which is a notable medicinal mushroom. (*Photo courtesy of Keith Weller, Agricultural Research Service, USDA*)

Beneficial nutritional effects. Regarding the beneficial nutritional effects of mushrooms, the following facts should be noted:

1. Mushrooms have a low energy level, which is beneficial for weight reduction.

2. Mushrooms have significant levels of purine, which is beneficial for the diets of persons suffering from metabolic diseases.

3. Mushroom carbohydrates are composed chiefly of dietary fibers (such as β-glucan, heteroglycan, and chitin), mannitol, and trehalose, which are beneficial for diabetics.

4. Mushrooms have a very low sodium concentration, which is beneficial for the diets of persons suffering from high blood pressure.

5. Mushrooms have a high content of several key vitamins, providing an important orthomolecular aspect. This means that a significant part of the daily requirement of different essential vitamins can be covered by the consumption of mushrooms.

6. Mushrooms have high contents of potassium and phosphorus, providing another important orthomolecular aspect.

7. Finally, mushrooms have a high content of selenium, which is regarded as an excellent antioxidant.

Most mushroom-derived preparations and substances are not used as pharmaceuticals ("real" medicines) or botanical drugs, but rather they constitute a novel class of products having a variety of names: medicinal mushroom dietary supplements (MMDSs), mycopharmaceuticals, tonics, functional foods, nutraceuticals/nutriceuticals, phytochemicals, biochemopreventives, and designer foods. MMDSs have been used for centuries throughout Asia (especially China, Japan, Korea, and Russia), but only recently has the extent of their benefits been recognized by Western countries. Western medicine has made little use of MM products partly because of their complex constituents, unknown mechanisms, and the lack of acceptable pharmacological purity.

MM products and their effects. Several types of MM products are available on the market today:

1. Artificially cultivated fruit body powders, hot water or alcohol extracts of these fruit bodies, or the same extract concentrates and their mixtures.

2. Dried and pulverized preparations of the combined substrates, mycelia, and mushroom primordia after the inoculation of an edible semisolid medium (usually grains).

3. Biomass or extracts from mycelia harvested from submerged liquid cultures grown in a fermentation tank.

4. Naturally grown, dried, mushroom fruit bodies in the form of capsules or tablets.

5. Spores and their extracts.

MMs belong to a class of immunomodulators known as biological response modifiers (BRMs), adaptogens, or immunoceuticals, which are capable of stimulating various immune functions. The regular intake of MMDSs may enhance the immune response of the human body, thereby increasing its resistance to disease and, in some cases, causing regression of the disease state. MMDSs enhance the cellular immune function and stimulate immunity in the body, generally to help maintain the correct balance between cellular and humoral immunity. MM polysaccharides and other compounds prevent oncogenesis, show direct antitumor activity against various synergetic tumors, and prevent tumor metastasis. Their activity is especially beneficial when used in conjunction with chemotherapy.

In particular, BRMs have been used as antitumor MMDSs and immunotherapeutic drugs. BRMs modify the host's biological response by stimulating the immune system, which may result in various therapeutic effects. The criteria for BRMs are as follows: (1) they should cause no harm and place no additional stress on the body; (2) they should help the body adapt to various environmental and psychological stresses; and (3) they must have a nonspecific action on the body, supporting all the major systems including the nervous, hormonal, and immune systems as well as regulating functions. The application of BRM immunotherapy has become an additional kind of cancer treatment, which can be used together with surgery, chemotherapy, and radiotherapy. In Japan, 25% of all anticancer drugs (including Krestin, Lentinan, and Sonifilan) are substances prepared from different species of MMs.

Overall, the best implementation of MMDSs is for the prevention or stabilization of immune disorders and other dysfunctions of the immune system, including autoimmune disorders (especially in immunodeficient and immunodepressed patients, and patients undergoing chemotherapy or radiotherapy), different types of cancers, chronic bloodborne viral hepatitis infections, different types of anemia, hypercholesterolemia and hyperlipidemia, HIV/AIDS, the herpes simplex virus (HSV), chronic fatigue syndrome, Epstein-Barr virus, chronic gastritis and gastric ulcers caused by *Helicobacter pylori*, and dementia (especially for patients exhibiting Alzheimer's disease).

Conclusions. Mushroom-derived products are not a substitute for modern medicine. However, it should be recognized that, generally, mushroom-derived products are a special category of substances that can serve a patient better under certain circumstances (for example, they can enhance a patient's well-being). Furthermore, in some situations, they can serve to supplement other treatments (for example, they can complement modern medicine). As mentioned previously, mushrooms are used as health foods, MMDSs, and medicines (drugs and botanical drugs). Approximately 400 clinical studies on MMDSs have been undertaken since the 1970s, and more than 10,000 scientific papers dedicated to studying different aspects of MM use have been published in scientific journals.

The medical establishments of Western and Eastern medicine have adopted different regulatory systems for herbal and mushroom preparations. Most Western countries follow the rules of the World Health Organization (WHO) and the Dietary Supplement Health and Education Act (DSHEA), in which plant or MM extracts are defined as DSs, and clinical studies are not required before DSs are introduced to the market. China and several other Asian countries define many of the same herbs and some MMs as drugs, and therefore clinical studies are needed. The target for the future should be to integrate those regulations, standards, and practices from Western and Eastern medicine that have been proven the most valuable in the quest for health benefits in the twenty-first century.

For background information *see* CANCER (MEDICINE); ETHNOMYCOLOGY; FUNGAL BIOTECHNOLOGY; FUNGAL ECOLOGY; FUNGI; MUSHROOM; MUSHROOM PHARMACY; MYCOLOGY; NUTRITION in the McGraw-Hill Encyclopedia of Science & Technology.   Solomon P. Wasser

Bibliography. S. T. Chang and S. P. Wasser, The role of culinary-medicinal mushrooms on human welfare with a pyramid model for human health, *Int. J. Med. Mushrooms*, 14(2):95–134, 2012, DOI:10.1615/IntJMedMushr.v14.i2.10; M. Powell, *Medicinal Mushrooms: A Clinical Guide*, Mycology Press, Somerset, UK, 2010; R. Rogers, *The Fungal Pharmacy*, North Atlantic Books, Berkeley, CA, 2011; P. Roupas et al., The role of edible mushrooms in health: Evaluation of the evidence, *J. Funct. Foods*, 4:687–709, 2012, DOI:10.1016/j.jff.2012.05.003; S. P. Wasser, Medicinal mushroom science: History, current status, future trends, and unsolved problems, *Int. J. Med. Mushrooms*, 12(1):1–16, 2010, DOI:10.1615/IntJMedMushr.v12.i1.10; S. P. Wasser, Medicinal mushrooms as a source of antitumor and immunomodulating polysaccharides, *Appl. Microbiol. Biotechnol.*, 60:258–274, 2002, DOI:10.1007/s00253-002-1076-7.

Heart regeneration

Heart disease is responsible for one in every four deaths in the United States. Approximately 600,000 deaths per year are attributed to heart disease, making it the leading cause of death in both men and women. Heart tissues obtain their oxygenated blood supply through a series of spider leg–like blood vessels called coronary arteries. The primary cause of heart attacks is a block (myocardial infarction) in this coronary network, thus precluding downstream cardiac cells from receiving oxygen and nutrients. Subsequent cardiomyocyte (heart muscle cell) death is a precursor to the replacement of functional cardiac muscle with scar tissue. Scarring leads to further pathology and loss of cardiac output.

The field of regenerative medicine aims to repair or replace diseased tissues by tapping into a cell's potential to become a variety of different cell types. There are at least two avenues of research contributing to these efforts. One combines the knowledge of stem cells outside of the organism with our understanding of the in vivo genetic switches that guide these cells toward specific fates. The other involves the elucidation of tissue regeneration in select model organisms that exhibit this amazing capability naturally. A convergence of both approaches makes a future of "cells made to order" more likely.

Cardiac stem cells. Perhaps there is no subfield of biology bursting with more therapeutic promise than stem cells. Stem cells are unspecialized cells that divide to produce two cells (daughter cells) with different purposes. Whereas one daughter cell remains a stem cell, the other daughter becomes a progenitor cell with restricted potential before fully differentiating into its specialized cell type.

Numerous studies have shed light on genetic markers that highlight the development of the embryonic heart. It is not surprising that these same markers are often used to identify embryonic-like stem cells in the adult heart. A small population (1%) of cells within the adult mouse heart expresses *kit* and/or *sca1* genes; when the cells are followed inside or outside the animal, they have the ability to differentiate into cardiomyocytes. These observations suggest that therapeutic stimulation of these adult stem cells could drive cardiac repair. More important, this avenue would circumvent the immune rejection that is expected from using exogenous embryonic stem cell transplantation.

Differentiation of embryonic cells to specific cell fates is associated with epigenetic changes within the genome (the term epigenetics describes the study of heritable changes in gene expression that are not the result of changes in DNA sequences). Early animal cloning studies unveiled the ability of the egg cytoplasm to erase these epigenetic markers and to "reprogram" the nucleus to a more embryonic-like state. Since then, investigators have narrowed down the reprogramming factors to two or three genes (for example, *Nanog* and *Oct4*). These induced pluripotent stem cells (iPS cells) can then be directed to a cardiac fate in a culture dish using several different culture conditions. The difficulty, at least for some culture methods, is determining the proper conditions to drive a more efficient transition to a cardiac state. Treatments with fibroblast growth factor (FGF), bone morphogenetic protein (BMP), and Wnt growth factor families, often concurrently, have shown the greatest inductive efficiency. Not surprisingly, these factors mirror the cardiogenic milieu in the early embryo.

Turn toward the zebrafish model system. Recent evidence suggests that cells within the adult mammalian heart maintain their ability to be renewed throughout an individual's life. This was surprising because cardiac cells were considered to be postmitotic (mature cells that are no longer capable of undergoing mitosis) and difficult to coax back into the cell-division cycle. This is even more puzzling because the adult mammalian heart fails to mount a successful regenerative event following acute injury. To uncover the reasons for this, investigations have been conducted using model organisms that regenerate their cardiac tissues naturally. For example,

newt cardiomyocytes are known to be nonproliferative unless they are provided with an injury stimulus. Logically, if an investigator finds a gene expression profile specific to a regenerative organism, it might be possible to therapeutically "tweak" this program to induce cardiac tissue repair in humans.

The zebrafish has become the ideal system in which to carry out these types of studies. In 2002, investigators surgically removed a portion of the ventricular muscle and then watched this part regenerate back in less than 2 months. Another, less-invasive injury model, wherein diphtheria toxin was delivered to the heart using an inducible transgene (genetic material from one organism that has been experimentally transferred to another), unveiled a similar regenerative response. The noncontractile scar tissue that builds up in mammals is not present in these fish. Knockdown techniques (manipulations to decrease gene expression) of zebrafish pathways involved in heart regeneration often lead to increased scar tissue, suggesting that there is an inverse relationship between the ability to regenerate and the level of cardiac scarring. Instead, zebrafish cardiomyocytes proliferate in order to repair the cardiac muscle wall.

Although the prevailing view is that newly regenerated cardiac tissue is derived primarily from preexisting cardiomyocytes, the transition between "old" and "new" was not worked out until recently. A series of fluorescence-encoding transgenes used in developmental timing assays showed that injury stimulates at least a partial dedifferentiation of cardiomyocytes near the injury site. This partial loss of contractile gene expression is consistent with analyses showing an activation of cardiogenic genes. This change in the differentiated state is likely to facilitate cardiomyocyte proliferation.

A recent study unveiled an important role for the endocardium, which is a thin layer of endothelial cells lying underneath cardiac muscles. Surgical resection (removal) of the ventricular apex (tip) induces the expression of two genes, *retinaldehyde dehydrogenase 2* (*raldh2*) and *heart of glass*, within the atrial endocardium, on the side of the heart opposite the injury. A few hours later, expression becomes uniform within the entire endocardium before becoming restricted to the injury site. In addition, several intriguing details have been observed: (1) Injury stimulates expression as early as 1 hour, suggesting that these genes may act as part of an initiator of the regenerative cascade. (2) The response to injury is organ-wide and is similar to what is observed during mammalian liver regeneration. This might reflect a requirement by distant cells to sense injury. (3) The *raldh2* gene encodes the rate-limiting enzyme for retinoic acid (RA) synthesis, thus implicating the RA pathway in zebrafish heart regeneration. (4) Expression within the endocardium unlocks one key relationship between the underlying endocardium and proliferative cardiomyocytes.

Overexpression of two transgenes designed to knock down RA signaling during zebrafish heart regeneration shows that normal RA signaling is required for maintaining cardiomyocyte proliferation near the injury site. As a result, scar tissue builds up in these hearts. Coronary artery ligation injuries in the nonregenerative mouse heart fail to induce a similar upregulation (increase of gene expression) of RA genes within the endocardium. It is tempting to speculate that insufficient RA is one reason for the inability to regenerate adult mouse cardiac tissue.

Neonatal mouse heart. These results could help explain one newly discovered phenomenon. It turns out that the neonatal mouse heart has the ability to be regenerated, but this ability is lost 1 week after the mouse's birth. Because of the small size of a newborn mouse heart and its coronary vasculature, scientists used a surgical resection injury to stimulate organ-wide cardiomyocyte proliferation. It is not clear why such a sharp regenerative/nonregenerative transition point exists in the early mouse heart, but comparisons between the "before" and "after" states could bring a wealth of knowledge. For example, the embryonic mouse heart is more similar to the adult zebrafish heart because both of them are highly trabeculated (noncompacted or "spongy"), with many individual fingerlike projections of cardiac muscle bathed in a significant amount of endocardium. The adult mouse heart is not as "spongy" and instead has a single thick muscle wall with a single inner endocardial layer. Because the endocardium acts as an important signaling source for proliferative cardiomyocytes after injury, the fact that the adult zebrafish and embryonic/neonatal mouse hearts have more of it is a very important detail that should not be ignored.

In an attempt to unveil the entire bank of genetic changes that characterize this postnatal transition, investigators enlisted microarray technology. Microarrays allow for an unbiased assessment of tens of thousands of gene expression differences between two or more cell populations. By comparing mouse hearts at 1 and 10 days after birth, it was discovered that a small noncoding RNA (microRNA or miRNA), called miR-195, is rapidly upregulated in the 10-day hearts. Because miRNAs are known to target multiple gene transcripts and prevent their translation to proteins, the increased levels of miR-195 automatically thrust its target genes into the spotlight. Indeed, miR-195 was shown to regulate cell cycle gene expression and limit cardiomyocyte proliferation directly.

Conclusions. It is an exciting time for regenerative medicine. Decades of work have brought a deep understanding of the genetics of cell fate decisions. Elucidation of genetic markers has allowed investigators to identify, extract, culture, transplant, and determine the differentiated state of cardiac stem cells. Recent observations indicate that adult mammalian hearts have passed through a transition where they no longer support the full regeneration of injured cardiomyocytes. This puts researchers in a position to compare the cellular and genetic changes that occur at this postnatal transition point. More tractable model organisms, such as the zebrafish, which exhibit robust capacities to regenerate cardiac tissue, have been instrumental in unveiling explanations for why higher organisms lose this regenerative ability. These interweaving approaches provide hope that it might be possible to routinely repair cardiac tissue and enhance the quality of life.

For background information *see* CARDIOVASCULAR SYSTEM; CELL CYCLE; CELL DIFFERENTIATION; CELL DIVISION; CELL FATE DETERMINATION; DEVELOPMENTAL BIOLOGY; HEART (VERTEBRATE); HEART DISORDERS; MICRORNA; MORPHOGENESIS; MUSCLE; MUSCLE DEVELOPMENT AND REGENERATION; PATTERN FORMATION (BIOLOGY); REGENERATIVE BIOLOGY; STEM CELLS; TRANSPLANTATION BIOLOGY in the McGraw-Hill Encyclopedia of Science & Technology.

Robert J. Major

Bibliography. O. Bergemann et al., Evidence for cardiomyocyte renewal in humans, *Science*, 324:98–102, 2009, DOI:10.1126/science.1164680; J. Kajstura et al., Cardiomyogenesis in the adult human heart, *Circ. Res.*, 107:305–315, 2010, DOI:10.1161/CIRCRESAHA.110.223024; K. Kikuchi and K. D. Poss, Cardiac regenerative capacity and mechanisms, *Annu. Rev. Cell Dev. Biol.*, 28:719–741, 2012, DOI:10.1146/annurev-cellbio-101011-155739; K. Kikuchi et al., Retinoic acid production by endocardium and epicardium is an injury response essential for zebrafish heart regeneration, *Dev. Cell*, 20:387–404, 2011, DOI:10.1016/j.devcel.2011.01.010; F. Mouquet et al., Restoration of cardiac progenitor cells after myocardial infarction by self-proliferation and selective homing of bone marrow–derived stem cells, *Circ. Res.*, 97:1090–1092, 2005, DOI:10.1161/01.RES.0000194330.66545.f5; E. R. Porrello et al., MiR-15 family regulates postnatal mitotic arrest of cardiomyocytes, *Circ. Res.*, 109:670–679, 2011, DOI:10.1161/CIRCRESAHA.111.248880; E. R. Porrello et al., Transient regenerative potential of the neonatal mouse heart, *Science*, 331:1078–1080, 2011, DOI:10.1126/science.1200708; V. F. M. Segers and R. T. Lee, Stem-cell therapy for cardiac disease, *Nature*, 451:937–942, 2008, DOI:10.1038/nature06800.

Hellbender salamanders

Hellbenders are North America's largest and most spectacular salamanders (**Fig. 1**), reaching lengths of 75 cm (30 in.) and weights of 3 kg (6.6 lb) or more. Several folktales have arisen to explain the name "hellbender," but the earliest references attribute the name to the slow, twisting movement of these creatures when moving under water, analogous to the fanciful suffering of tortured souls in hell.

Description. Hellbenders are one of only three living species of the salamander family Cryptobranchidae [order Urodela (Caudata), class Amphibia], which is one of the oldest living families of salamanders. Members of the Cryptobranchidae family have changed very little through their evolutionary

Fig. 1. **Hellbender in a Tennessee Valley river.** (*Photo courtesy of Michael Freake*)

history, with fossil species extending as far back as the Oligocene (23 million years ago) and being remarkably similar to living species. Hellbenders are sometimes confused with mudpuppies *Necturus maculosu*s, which may be found in the same habitat. However, hellbenders can be recognized by a large laterally flattened tail, five toes on the hind feet, and a distinctively wide, dorsoventrally flattened head and body. In addition, there are extensive folds and wrinkles of skin along the sides of the body. These folds are richly supplied with blood vessels and are used for gaseous exchange. The color of hellbenders varies from green to reddish brown, and most individuals have irregular dark spots and blotches on their back. Hellbenders have an entirely aquatic life cycle. Typically, they are found in swift, cool, clear, and well-oxygenated rivers with abundant large flat rocks that provide cover and nesting sites. However, hellbenders are tolerant of fairly high temperatures, and some populations in the Ohio Valley inhabit relatively warm, low-flow streams with significant sediment loads. There are even records of hellbenders from still-water sections of rivers created by dams; however, it is not clear if they represent viable reproducing populations or merely accidental vagrants. Their secretive lifestyle means that they are rarely encountered by most people visiting their habitat, although they are often caught by anglers using bait. The presence of a viable population of hellbenders in a stream is a very strong indicator of water quality, and there is a growing public appreciation for the species as a result of the educational efforts of zoos, wildlife agencies, and researchers.

Species. Currently, two subspecies of hellbenders are recognized—the eastern hellbender *Cryptobranchus alleganiensis alleganiensis*, and the Ozark hellbender *Cryptobranchus alleganiensis bishopi*—which are distinguished by differences in spot and blotch patterns on the dorsum and throat. Ozark hellbenders are restricted to watersheds in the Ozark highlands of southern Missouri and northeastern Arkansas that drain into the Mississippi River. Eastern hellbenders occupy a much larger area, ranging from central Missouri, through the Ohio/Susquehanna system as far north as New York, and down through the New River and Tennessee

River systems as far south as northern Georgia (**Fig. 2**).

Life cycle. The life cycle of hellbenders starts with the external fertilization of large egg masses (200–400 eggs) that are laid under large nesting rocks in the fall. These fertilized eggs are then guarded by the male until spring. At this point, approximately 5-cm (2-in.) gilled larvae emerge. This stage lasts 1–1.5 years. By the time that the hellbenders reach 12–13 cm (4.8–5.2 in.) in length, the external gills are lost, and the folds and wrinkles on the body become obvious. Sexual maturity develops between 3 and 6 years of age, and hellbenders have lived more than 30 years in captivity. Meanwhile, growth studies on tagged hellbenders suggest that they may live to at least 50 years of age in the wild. Most studies have shown that mature hellbenders move very little, even from year to year, and they are solitary during the nonbreeding season, aggressively defending shelter rocks from other hellbenders. It is common to find substantial injuries from these encounters, including loss of digits and even limbs. In most populations, hellbenders remain under their cover rocks during the day, with activity typically occurring at night. Hellbenders primarily ambush crayfish and small fish passing near their cover rocks, using powerful suction feeding. Some populations may have a significant ecological effect in limiting crayfish abundance.

Decline of hellbenders. Historically, it appears that hellbenders were widespread and abundant across much of their range. However, most populations have seen dramatic declines in recent decades. The reductions are so severe that, in 2011, the United States Fish and Wildlife Service listed the Ozark hellbender as an endangered species under the Endangered Species Act (ESA). The eastern hellbender is currently a candidate species for listing under the

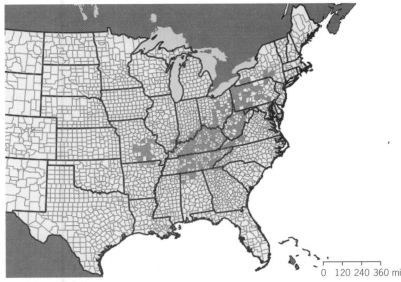

Fig. 2. **Historic range of hellbenders.** [*Image courtesy of USGS National Amphibian Atlas, Hellbender (Cryptobranchus alleganiensis), Version no. 2.2, USGS Patuxent Wildlife Research Center, Laurel, MD, 2012*]

ESA. Of the 17 states with hellbender populations, most classify the species as endangered, rare, or a species of concern. Numerous factors have contributed to the decline of hellbenders, including loss of habitat to dam construction, increased stream sediment deposition from land-use changes (especially loss of forest cover in headwaters), acid mine drainage, persecution from fishers who wrongly assume that hellbenders are poisonous or predators of game fish, collection for the pet trade, and disease. Investigators have described a massive decline in well-studied hellbender populations over a 20-year period, as well as a 70–80% decrease in abundance, a shift in age structure to primarily old individuals with very few juveniles, and a decline in body condition in some populations. Numerous reports of hellbenders having infections from the fungus *Batrachochytrium dendrobatidis* are of great concern, especially because this fungus is believed to have played a significant role in the catastrophic reductions of amphibians around the world and has been identified in both wild and zoo populations of hellbenders. The fungus is capable of causing disease (chytridiomycosis) in hellbenders. It is associated with severe tissue abnormalities and poor wound healing in some populations, but appears to have little effect in other populations, suggesting that other factors causing immune suppression may be required to trigger disease. Meanwhile, ongoing research is investigating the role of other disease agents, including *Ranavirus* and biofilm-forming opportunistic fungi and bacteria. Many healthy populations of hellbenders are found in areas where the headwaters are located within protected public lands, which maintain extensive forest cover. Continued development of rural areas for housing, timber harvesting, and industry pose a great threat to the remaining hellbender populations. Thus, efforts should be made to preserve the vegetation and forests along streams, especially as stream temperatures are likely to rise in the future because of projected changes in climate.

Conservation and management. Given the lack of successful reproduction and recruitment in declining populations, intensive efforts are being made to propagate hellbenders in captivity. In 2011, the St. Louis Zoo announced the first natural mating of captive hellbenders, resulting in surviving larval hellbenders. In 2012, the Nashville Zoo successfully used hormone-induced ovulation and artificial fertilization of eggs to produce viable young. Other zoos have raised hellbenders from wild-collected fertile egg masses, and researchers are monitoring the progress of these hellbenders as they are released back into the wild to increase population densities.

Successful conservation and management of hellbender populations also require a good understanding of the genetic relationships of hellbenders. Recent investigations using mitochondrial and microsatellite DNA markers have shown that hellbender populations in their natural range appear to have fairly low genetic variation. However, at least eight major genetic groups, which are quite different from each other, have been identified. This genetic information will be important in guiding future captive breeding and release programs to preserve genetic variation and local adaptations. Another recent development using genetic tools is the ability to test river waters for the presence of hellbender DNA (environmental DNA or eDNA). Typically, field surveys for hellbenders are conducted using snorkeling gear and lifting tools to find hellbenders under rocks. This has a number of drawbacks, being extremely time consuming and labor intensive. In addition, field surveys are often ineffective in deeper, murkier rivers, failing to find any hellbenders if the population densities are low. Wildlife managers need reliable and up-to-date data on the presence or absence of hellbenders, and eDNA offers a rapid and reliable method of identifying whether hellbenders are present.

For background information *see* AMPHIBIA; CONSERVATION OF RESOURCES; ECOLOGICAL COMMUNITIES; ENDANGERED SPECIES; FUNGAL ECOLOGY; LISSAMPHIBIA; POPULATION ECOLOGY; POPULATION VIABILITY; URODELA in the McGraw-Hill Encyclopedia of Science & Technology.   Michael Freake

Bibliography. J. T. Briggler, K. A. Larson, and K. J. Irwin, Presence of the amphibian chytrid fungus (*Batrachochytrium dendrobatidis*) on hellbenders (*Cryptobranchus alleganiensis*) in the Ozark Highlands, *Herpetol. Rev.*, 39:443–444, 2008; P. Daszak et al., Emerging infectious diseases and amphibian population declines, *Emerg. Infect. Dis.*, 5:735–748, 1999, DOI:10.3201/eid0506.990601; M. A. Nickerson and C. E. Mays, The hellbenders: North American "giant salamanders," *Milw. Public Mus. Publ. Biol. Geol.*, 1:1–106, 1973; J. W. Petranka, *Salamanders of the United States and Canada*, Smithsonian Institution Press, Washington, DC, 1998; S. J. Sabatino and E. J. Routman, Phylogeography and conservation genetics of the hellbender salamander (*Cryptobranchus alleganiensis*), *Conserv. Genet.*, 10(5):1235–1246, 2009, DOI:10.1007/s10592-008-9655-5; M. Tionne, J. R. Johnson, and E. J. Routman, Microsatellite analysis supports mitochondrial phylogeography of the hellbender (*Cryptobranchus alleganiensis*), *Genetica*, 139:209–219, 2011, DOI:10.1007/s10709-010-9538-9; B. A. Wheeler et al., Population declines of a long-lived salamander: A 20+-year study of hellbenders, *Cryptobranchus alleganiensis*, *Biol. Conserv.*, 109:151–156, 2003, DOI:10.1016/S0006-3207(02)00136-2.

Homo floresiensis: further insights

A tiny skeleton was revealed to an unsuspecting world in October 2004. The bones of this skeleton belonged to a new kind of human that was nicknamed "the hobbit" because it was so small. The bones were discovered during an archeological excavation in Liang Bua cave on the island of Flores in

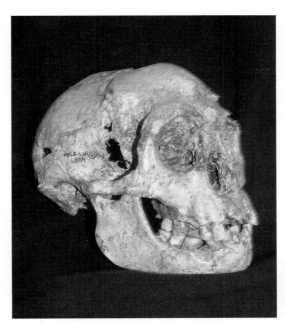

Fig. 1. *Homo floresiensis* (LB1) skull and jaw. Note the retreating forehead and low, small cranium; the mound of bone over the eye orbit; the forward-sloping face; and the lack of a protruding chin. (*Photo courtesy of Debbie Argue*)

Indonesia. The excavation team of Indonesian and Australian researchers was led by Michael Morwood and Tony Djubiantono under the auspices of the Indonesian National Research Centre for Archaeology. The excavation aimed to find insights into the origins of the first Australians. No one could have imagined that the finds would throw the scientific world into a frenzy of excitement and controversy.

Archeological evidence. The most spectacular find was located at a depth of 6 m (19.7 ft). It was an 18,000-year-old skeleton of an individual just over 1 m (3.28 ft) in height. The skeleton was first named LB1 (**Fig. 1**), in reference to the cave (Liang Bua) in which it was found. The remains included the skull, leg bones, parts of the pelvis, hands, feet, and some other fragments. Based on the evidence of the pelvis, LB1 was probably female. Although it is not known how she died, the archeological evidence indicates that she had not been deliberately buried; rather, after death, she had sunk into mud in a shallow pool of water, where the body was slowly covered by silt.

There were many other human bones from a number of individuals found throughout the 13 m (42.7 ft) of excavation. These remains were in stratigraphic levels that have been dated to 10,200–100,000 years before the present. They were all from individuals who were only 1 m (3.28 ft) in height. They walked upright, with relatively short legs, which resulted in their arms extending much lower than those of modern humans, and they had long feet. Their wrists and shoulder joints were quite unlike those of *Homo sapiens*: the wrists were more like those of African apes, and the shoulders faced forward somewhat and could not rotate like

those of modern humans; in fact, the shoulders were quite similar to those of an early member of our genus, *H. ergaster*, who lived 1.5 million years ago in Africa. They lacked a protruding chin and had a short forehead that sloped backward (**Fig. 1**). A mound of bone framed the upper and side regions of the orbits. The size of the brain was small, even for such a short being, but it had a relatively large frontal lobe. In *H. sapiens*, this part of the brain is associated with capabilities for planning, for learning from mistakes, and for passing on knowledge from generation to generation.

Homo floresiensis. When the bones of the diminutive human LB1 were first discovered, there was uncertainty with regard to what species they belonged to; thus, they were initially studied in relation

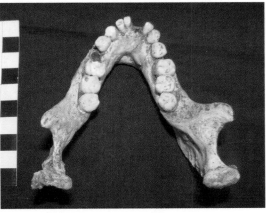

(a)

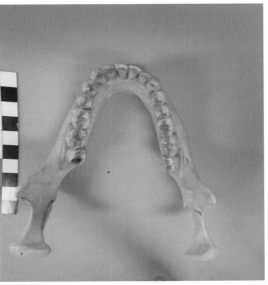

(b)

Fig. 2. Comparison of mandibles. (*a*) View of a *Homo floresiensis* mandible. Note the internal buttressing at the inside front of the jaw. In addition, this individual had a full complement of adult teeth. (*b*) View of a *Homo sapiens* mandible. Note the lack of buttressing inside the front of the jaw. Size differences between the two species can be seen by reference to the scales in the images. (*Photo courtesy of Debbie Argue*)

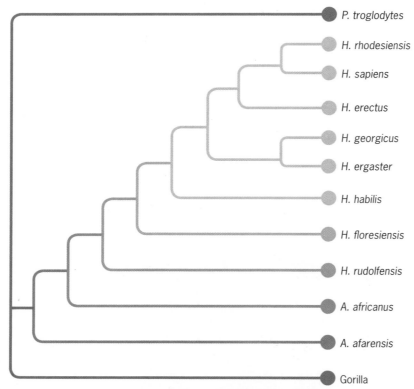

Fig. 3. Phylogenetic tree showing the most likely placement for *Homo floresiensis*. (*Illustration courtesy of L. Abbott, Biotext Pty Ltd, Canberra, Australia*)

to those of *H. erectus, H. ergaster, H. georgicus, H. sapiens,* and *Australopithecus africanus.* Further investigations showed that LB1 comprised a mix of archaic and modern characteristics. Because LB1 was unlike any other species of human, it was declared to be a new species of *Homo* and given the name *H. floresiensis.* In addition, two competing hypotheses were presented—specifically, (1) *H. floresiensis* is an early hominin similar to the earliest member of our genus, *Homo,* but until now known only from East Africa, which somehow got to Flores Island, Indonesia, and survived there until recently; and (2) *H. floresiensis* is a dwarfed descendant of *H. erectus,* the only known non-sapiens hominin to once have existed in Southeast Asia. In this latter case, *H. floresiensis* is said to be the result of a biological response to specific ecological conditions faced by species genetically isolated on islands.

Evolutionary implications. *Homo floresiensis* challenged the existing paradigms of human evolution. It had been thought that *H. erectus* was the earliest hominin to live in the archipelago that is now Indonesia and had been present there approximately 1 million years ago. It seemed now that an archaic species, either a very early archaic species of *Homo* or a dwarfed *H. erectus,* lived on Flores during the period that modern humans were present on nearby New Guinea and Australia, although, as yet, it is not known whether the two species were ever present on the same island or landmass at the same time.

The claim that another hominin, let alone one of such primitive form, lived in the Indonesian region at the same time as modern humans presents an enormous challenge to the predominant ideas about human evolution. Contemporary understandings of human evolution are based on a conceptual framework of a "branching tree," containing species of *Australopithecus* (who lived between about 4 million years ago and a little less than 2 million years ago), *H. habilis* (who lived about 2 million years ago), and subsequently, on different branches, a range of hominin species, including *H. ergaster, H. erectus, H. heidelbergensis, H. neanderthalensis,* and (finally) *H. sapiens.* There are debates about the relationships among all these species, as well as arguments about possible temporal overlaps in the existence of *H. erectus* and *H. sapiens* and of *H. neanderthalensis* and *H. sapiens.* However, until the discovery of *H. floresiensis,* it was thought that our species, *H. sapiens,* had been the sole remaining species of *Homo* for more than 30,000 years.

Pathological condition or a new species? It is hardly surprising that serious disputes erupted immediately after the announcement of the discovery of *H. floresiensis.* The challenges to the status of the new form, as a new species of *Homo,* centered on its very small stature and its tiny brain. It was suggested that LB1 was a modern human who suffered from a pathological condition. Different investigators suggested different pathologies, including microcephaly, Laron syndrome, and hypothyroid cretinism. The first condition, microcephaly, is characterized, primarily, by a marked reduction of brain growth, although microcephalic people may exhibit other abnormalities, such as short stature, joint defects, and cognitive impairment. Laron syndrome is a rare condition expressed in consanguineous families (that is, individuals that have a common recent ancestor) that produces short stature, underdeveloped musculature, shallow orbits, and small hands and feet. The third condition, hypothyroid cretinism, is caused by an iodine deficiency that results in thyroid malfunction in some individuals in a population and, like the other pathologies, leads to very short stature and some abnormalities in the limbs.

However, there are several reasons why these interpretations may be rejected. First, they prioritize the limited features of just one specimen, that is, the small stature and brain size of LB1, but the excavation at Liang Bua produced skeletal remains of other similar individuals. Bearing in mind that all the possible pathologies mentioned are rare conditions, it is unlikely that all individuals in an excavation would show the same abnormalities. Furthermore, the absence of human remains of modern form is itself evidence that pathology is an unlikely explanation.

Second, the skeletal remains from Liang Bua span a period of about 90,000 years. The pathology-based hypotheses fail to explain how rare conditions such as microcephaly or Laron syndrome, or even cretinism, could have been sustained in a single population for such a long time. Rather, the available evidence suggests a flourishing population of *H. floresiensis*.

Other facts also show that *H. floresiensis* is not a pathology-afflicted modern human. The archaic head shape, facial features, mandibular structure, shoulder and wrist structures, and the long arms and feet on a very short body are not accounted for in these interpretations. The arm-to-leg ratio, the form of the palate, and the existence of mounds of bone above the orbits are just a few of the characteristics that reveal that the remains found at Liang Bua are not those of *H. sapiens*. In addition, *H. floresiensis* has a particular buttressing structure on the inside of the front of the jaw that is never found in modern humans (**Fig. 2**). The buttressing in modern humans is on the front of the jaw, in the form of a chin.

Conclusions. Thus, *H. floresiensis* is seemingly an archaic member of our genus, with good cognitive skills, who lived until recently. Where did it fit, then, on our family tree? Recent studies compared the characteristics of *H. floresiensis* with those of other *Homo* species, including *H. sapiens* and *H. erectus*, and some *Australopithecus* species. The results showed that *H. floresiensis* was nowhere near *H. erectus* on the family tree, and the hypothesis that these two species were closely related could not be supported; hence, it is highly unlikely that *H. floresiensis* is a dwarfed form of *H. erectus*. Instead, *H. floresiensis* is located very close to the earliest member of our genus, *H. habilis*. It might even have shared a common ancestor with that species, branching from our family tree at an early stage in the evolution of the genus, *Homo*, possibly around 1.4–2 million years ago (**Fig. 3**). However, remarkably, *H. floresiensis* lived as recently as 10,200 years ago, which is a period that is 1–2 million years after the disappearance of similar hominins from Africa. Therefore, the evidence indicates that *H. floresiensis* likely represents a remnant population of very early hominins on this remote Indonesian island, and this conclusion has far-reaching implications with regard to human evolution—which is quite a feat for such a little individual.

For background information *see* ANTHROPOLOGY; ARCHEOLOGICAL CHRONOLOGY; ARCHEOLOGY; BIOGEOGRAPHY; EARLY MODERN HUMANS; FOSSIL; FOSSIL HUMANS; ISLAND BIOGEOGRAPHY; PALEOGEOGRAPHY; PHYLOGENY; PHYSICAL ANTHROPOLOGY in the McGraw-Hill Encyclopedia of Science & Technology.

Debbie Argue

Bibliography. L. Aiello, Five years of *Homo floresiensis*, *Am. J. Phys. Anthropol.*, 142:167–179, 2010, DOI:10.1002/ajpa.21255; D. Argue et al., *Homo floresiensis*: A cladistic analysis, *J. Hum. Evol.*, 57:623–639, 2009, DOI:10.1016/j.jhevol.2009.05.002; D. Falk, *The Fossil Chronicles: How Two Controversial Discoveries Changed Our View of Human Evolution*, University of California Press, Berkeley, 2012; M. Morwood and P. van Oosterzee, *A New Human*, HarperCollins, New York, 2007; M. Morwood and P. van Oosterzee, *The Discovery of the Hobbit*, Random House, Sydney, 2007.

Human microbiome and disease

On the basis of cell numbers, people can be considered to be more microbial than human. Humans are colonized by trillions of microbes. For example, every surface of our bodies that is exposed to the outside world, including the eyes, mouth, sinuses, lungs, and gut, is a unique niche for the habitat of specialized microbial passengers that live their lives in mutualistic symbioses with us, who are their hosts (they need us, and we need them). If the total biomass of our microbial cargo (microbiota) could be weighed, it is estimated that it would equate to approximately 3 lb (1.36 kg). Yet, the role of the microbiota in maintaining health and promoting disease has only been suitably appreciated within the last few decades. Why is this? Part of the reason is that many of the microbes within our microbiota are difficult to culture using traditional microbiology techniques. For example, the microbes of the distal gut region are mostly fastidious, anaerobic species with very strict metabolic requirements that are not met by the use of standard culture media. In addition, our microbiota is a collection of complex microbial ecosystems. Thus, to understand microbial behavior, each ecosystem is best studied as a whole; this is in contrast to traditional microbiology, which is largely a reductionist practice involving the study of individual species in the absence of others. The recent surge of activity in human microbiota research is chiefly a result of emerging technologies that have allowed the handling of large and multifaceted data sets, providing both a window to view microbial ecosystem composition and a lens through which to view microbe–microbe and host–microbe interactions.

Human microbiota composition. The Human Microbiome Project (HMP), an effort led by the National Institutes of Health (NIH) in the United States, has been instrumental in pioneering a first detailed look at the composition of the normal human microbiome (the genetic material contained within the microbiota). This effort has been aided by similar projects in other countries, including the MetaHIT project (a European Union–led effort that has focused on the gut microbiome). One of the more remarkable findings of the HMP effort, which sampled a population of 242 healthy adults, was the wide microbial diversity detected (more than 5000 different microbial taxonomic profiles were found in total). The greatest diversity of bacterial species was discovered in the large intestine, and the least diversity was found on the skin. The vast majority of the human microbiota belongs to just three bacterial phyla, that is, Actinobacteria, Bacteroidetes, and Firmicutes, with minor components belonging to seven further phyla, including Proteobacteria and Fusobacteria.

The microbial profiles of individual hosts have been found to be unique, rather like fingerprints. Despite this, the functionality of the ecosystems from the same body site of different individuals seems to be conserved, suggesting that microbial ecosystems with similar functions can be constructed in many ways. The evidence for this conserved functionality has been indicated by the discovery of several distinct gut ecosystem types (enterotypes) among different species.

Although only a small number of longitudinal studies have been undertaken, it is apparent that the microbiota of a given individual is remarkably stable through time. This is particularly true for the gut microbiota, which seems to be established early in life (shaped by the microbiota in the birth canal and in breast milk, and later by the introduction of a solid diet) and persists henceforth through life. Because of this early establishment, there is the growing realization that any interference in this important colonization process (for example, delivery through an elective Caesarean section, or bottle-feeding) may be detrimental to an infant's future health.

Human microbiota function. Most early surveys of the human microbiota were simply catalogues of the taxa present, which provides valuable information but alone cannot describe function. The introduction of modern methodologies (for example, whole-genome shotgun sequencing methods) has allowed the genetic potential of microbes to be evaluated in the context of their ecosystems. Already, it has been shown that microbial ecosystems (particularly those of the gut, which have been the most studied so far) demonstrate a great deal of cooperation. For example, multiple bacterial species can be seen to contribute to complex trophic webs consisting of various biochemical pathways. In the gut, the outputs of these pathways are generally beneficial to the host, including short-chain fatty acids (which can be used as energy sources, growth stimulators,

and immune system modulators) and vitamins (for example, the vitamin B complex and vitamin K).

As well as providing metabolic outputs, it is thought that the presence of a healthy ecosystem on a given body surface is in itself a barrier to infection with pathogenic species. This process, termed competitive exclusion, contributes to disease resistance and may be effected both by the sheer physical presence of the microbiota and by the microbial cross-talk that may influence the virulence (gene expression) of the pathogens.

One of the more remarkable attributes of the microbiota is its ability to stimulate and "educate" the host immune system. Specific microbial species seem to stimulate the innate and adaptive immune systems in different ways, leading to a delicate balance between pro- and anti-inflammatory effects driven by subsets of immune cells (for example, T cells). The net, homeostatic effect of this complex interaction may be disrupted if the microbiota is altered.

Conceptualizing microbiome-related disease. In general, diseases caused by microbes are thought to be the effects of individual pathogens; this is because medical microbiology has largely focused on the pathogenic traits of individual species during acute infections. Although this is valuable work and has yielded many therapeutic advances, it is also becoming clear that many chronic diseases are associated with an aberrant microbiota signature (see **table**). For many of these diseases, it is not yet clear whether altered microbial profiles (dysbioses) are a cause or an effect of the disease. To understand this, detailed longitudinal studies that follow individuals at risk of developing certain chronic diseases will be required. Several of these studies are currently in

Summary of observations of microbiota dysbiosis in selected disease states

Microbiota site studied	Disease or syndrome	Summary of observations
Gut	Inflammatory bowel disease (ulcerative colitis and Crohn's disease)	Decrease in diversity; reduced levels of some beneficial bacterial species, including *Faecalibacterium prausnitzii* and *Akkermansia muciniphila*
	Irritable bowel syndrome	Increase in *E. coli*, *Dorea*, and *Ruminococcus* spp.; decrease in *Bifidobacterium* spp.
	Clostridium difficile infection	Decrease in diversity; increase in *Clostridium difficile* and Proteobacteria
	Obesity	Increased ratio of Firmicutes to Bacteroidetes; increased prevalence of methanogenic Archaea
	Type 1 diabetes	Decreased ratio of Firmicutes to Bacteroidetes; decrease in *Lactobacillus*, *Bifidobacterium*, and *Prevotella* spp.
	Celiac disease	Increased Proteobacteria in duodenum
	Colorectal cancer	Increased abundance of *Fusobacterium nucleatum*
	Infantile eczema	Increased abundance of *Clostridium* clusters IV and XIVa; tendency toward a more diverse, adultlike microbiota; reduced Bacteroidetes spp.
Vagina	Bacterial vaginosis	Reduced *Lactobacillus* spp.
Skin	Psoriasis	Reduced abundance of *Staphylococcus* and *Propionibacterium* spp.
Lung	Asthma	Increased diversity; increased presence of Proteobacteria
	Cystic fibrosis	Reduced diversity; increased *Streptococcus* spp.
	Chronic obstructive pulmonary disease (COPD)	Microbiome is seeded from the oral cavity; oral pathogens predominate in COPD lung samples
Nasopharynx	Acute otitis media	Reduced diversity; replacement of commensal bacterial species with pathogens
Mouth	Periodontitis	Increased microbial diversity and biomass; reduced Actinobacteria; increased *Porphyromonas gingivalis*

progress. For example, the Genetics, Environmental, Microbial (GEM) Project, which is a Canadian effort that follows the healthy siblings of patients with inflammatory bowel disease (IBD) through time, is collecting biological specimens for retrospective analyses in the event that these individuals go on to develop the disease.

If a healthy microbial community is perturbed, the outcome of that perturbation generally is a result of the functional redundancy built into the ecosystem, which in turn is related to the level of biological diversity in the system. Thus, in comparison to simple ecosystems, diverse microbial consortia are able to more readily withstand the stresses applied to them. This disturbance resistance is also associated with the inherent ecological balance (equilibrium) that establishes itself within a given ecosystem. This is best conceptualized using a cup-and-ball diagram; here, a stable ecosystem sits within a deep recess, which requires a large amount of applied stress to dislodge it, whereas a dysbiotic ecosystem is placed in a more shallow depression from which it is much more easily displaced (see **illustration**). A displaced ecosystem will eventually settle into a new equilibrium that may be less balanced and thus more susceptible to future perturbations. In this way, damage to an ecosystem may accrete (accumulate) over time

if no recovery is made. In extreme cases, this could lead to ecosystem collapse, whereby the function is lost.

The hygiene hypothesis suggests that ecosystem damage may be the result of an increased trend toward an oversanitized environment, which prevents the development of a healthy, diverse microbial ecosystem, particularly in childhood, and which is biasing individuals toward a tendency for microbiota collapse and associated health consequences. More recently, the missing microbiota hypothesis has been proposed, whereby changing health and lifestyle practices are interfering with the normal process of microbial transmission from parent to child, leading to microbial extinction events that can accumulate over generations. Both hypotheses fit well with the increasing trends of certain chronic diseases seen since the wide introduction of broad-spectrum antibiotics in the 1960s.

Microbiota therapeutics. Along with the work being done to understand the role of microbiota perturbations in chronic diseases, it is becoming clear that novel therapeutic interventions that aim to correct dysbiotic ecosystems may represent powerful new tools in the fight against certain diseases. The best example of this therapeutic approach is the use of fecal bacteriotherapy (stool transplant) for the

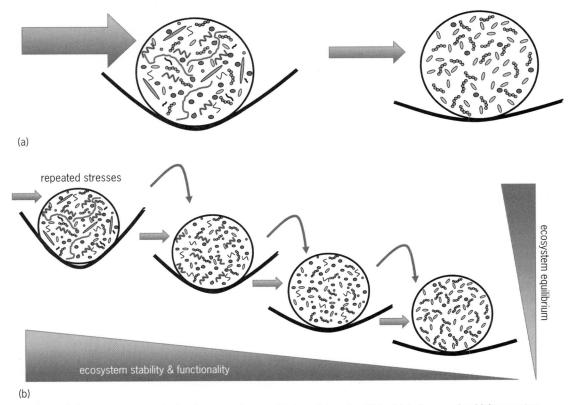

(a)

(b)

Cup-and-ball diagrams to conceptualize the ecosystem equilibrium of the microbiota. (*a*) A diverse microbial ecosystem requires a large amount of applied force (blue arrow; for example, an antibiotic disturbance) to push it out of its stable equilibrium (deep recess); in comparison, a less diverse ecosystem, shown on the right of the panel, requires comparatively less force to be displaced from its state of equilibrium (shallow recess). Note that a less diverse ecosystem does not necessarily have fewer numbers of microbial cells because the remaining species adapt to fill the niche. (*b*) Repeated stresses (blue arrows) can remove diversity from an ecosystem, pushing it into less-stable equilibrium states within which the ecosystem function and stability may be diminished.

treatment of recurrent *Clostridium difficile* infection (CDI). CDI, which leads to a severe diarrheal disease that is often nosocomial (acquired in a hospital), is the result of a colonic microbial ecosystem collapse caused by the use of antibiotics. Under these circumstances, *C. difficile* takes advantage of the vacated niche in the gut, proliferates in the absence of competitive exclusion, and secretes toxins that lead to diarrheal symptoms. Any antibiotic treatment aimed at destroying *C. difficile* may prove futile because the host's protective microflora may have been damaged beyond repair; in this case, the pathogen can easily proliferate again once the antibiotics are stopped. To address this issue, the transplantation of gut microbiota sourced from a healthy donor directly into a patient's gut has been shown to be upwards of 80% efficient in curing CDI, presumably by reinstating a healthy microbial ecosystem (along with its inherent protective attributes). Although fecal bacteriotherapy is a crude example of a therapeutic ecosystem correction, its effectiveness heralds a new era whereby microbial ecosystems, or their bioactive products, may be used to correct disease. In the case of CDI, steps toward this, using defined microbial ecosystems (simplified mixtures of gut-derived bacterial species), have already been successfully taken. The concept should be equally applicable to any disease with microbiota dysbiosis as a root cause.

Conclusions. In summary, there is an increasing trend toward viewing the human microbiota as a microbial organ, recognizing its chief functions, and understanding how damage to this critical ecosystem may affect human health.

For background information *see* BACTERIA; BACTERIOLOGY; DIGESTIVE SYSTEM; DISEASE; GASTROINTESTINAL TRACT DISORDERS; INFECTION; INFLAMMATORY BOWEL DISEASE; MEDICAL BACTERIOLOGY; MICROBIAL ECOLOGY; MICROBIOTA (HUMAN); PATHOGEN; PUBLIC HEALTH; VIRULENCE in the McGraw-Hill Encyclopedia of Science & Technology.

Emma Allen-Vercoe

Bibliography. W. M. DeVos and E. A. J. DeVos, Role of the intestinal microbiome in health and disease: From correlation to causation, *Nutr. Rev.*, 70(suppl. 1):S45–S56, 2012, DOI:10.1111/j.1753-4887.2012.00505.x; E. A. Grice and J. A. Segre, The human microbiome: Our second genome, *Annu. Rev. Genom. Hum. Genet.*, 13:151–170, 2012, DOI: 10.1146/annurev-genom-090711-163814; T. Looft and H. K. Allen, Collateral effects of antibiotics on mammalian gut microbiomes, *Gut Microbes*, 3:463–467, 2012, DOI:10.4161/gmic.21288; V. Robles Alonso and F. Guarner, Linking the gut microbiota to human health, *Br. J. Nutr.*, 109(suppl. 2):S21–S26, 2013, DOI:10.1017/S0007114512005235; The Human Microbiome Project Consortium, Structure, function and diversity of the healthy human microbiome, *Nature*, 486:207–214, 2012, DOI:10.1038/nature11234; M. Wilson, *Bacteriology of Humans: An Ecological Perspective*, Blackwell Publishing, Oxford, UK, 2008.

Hypersonic spectroscopy for materials characterization

Hypersonic spectroscopy is the measurement of the relative interaction of different very high frequencies of sound with a solid elastic sample. The description "hypersonic" indicates that the frequencies are greater than 1 gigahertz (GHz, 10^9 or one thousand million oscillations per second). The elastic properties of materials, quantitatively describing the deformation of the material caused by applied forces, are measured by this technique, and the high frequencies, corresponding to a short wavelength for the sound, make the technique ideal for investigating materials with very small features of the order of micrometers (1 μm = 10^{-6} m, one millionth of a meter). The internal movements of the material caused by the wave can be in the direction of energy propagation of the wave (a longitudinal wave, such as sound) or perpendicular to it (a transverse wave), so that the waves, as they go through the material, are more correctly described as elastic waves rather than sound waves.

Experimental techniques. There are three standard approaches for hypersonic spectroscopy (**Fig. 1**). The first consists of generating the elastic wave using a transducer that is driven with a high-frequency electrical signal and then launching the wave through the sample to a receiving transducer. The receiver converts the transmitted waves back into an electrical signal that can be analyzed in detail using an electronic analyzer. Thus, the system essentially is a loudspeaker-and-microphone pair that can operate at hypersonic frequencies.

The second approach, called picosecond ultrasonics, uses the technique of pump-probe laser spectroscopy, and is analogous to striking a bell or a fine china plate and then listening to the subsequent ringing of the material. In this case, a very short pulse of light strikes the sample, causing a shock wave through the material that sets the sample vibrating. A delayed laser pulse, the probe beam, then measures an optical property of the sample at a later and variable time so that the hypersonic vibrations of the sample can be measured.

The third method, Brillouin scattering of light, is the measurement of the inelastic scattering of laser light from the material. Inelastic here refers to a change in the energy of the scattered light because it has interacted with a single quantum of the allowed vibrations of the material. Measuring the very small changes in the energy of the light gives the energy and amplitudes of the allowed hypersonic vibrations of the material.

The descriptions of these three techniques already indicate that there is an intrinsic link between the vibrations of a sample of material and how elastic waves move through that material. We can understand this by considering organ pipes and guitar strings. The note, that is, the frequency, of an organ pipe is determined by the time it takes sound to travel up and down the length of the organ pipe.

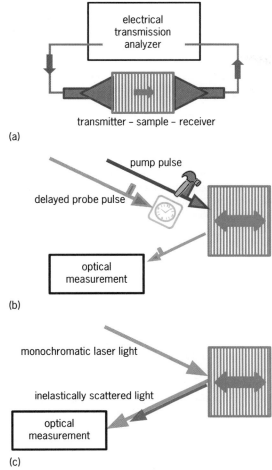

(a)

(b)

(c)

Fig. 1. Techniques for hypersonic spectroscopy.
(*a*) Transmission through sample using transducers.
(*b*) Picosecond ultrasonic measurement by pump-probe spectroscopy. Sample is vibrating after shock wave from pump pulse. (*c*) Brillouin scattering of light. The small (red) component has lost energy because of vibrations of the material. Most of the incident light is reflected with no change of energy.

Thus, a range of pipe lengths is required to give the required range of notes for an organ; the sound wave trapped in the pipe gives a set vibration frequency for the air in the pipe. For a guitar string, the open string fundamental note is tuned by changing the tension on the full fixed length of the string, which changes the velocity of the wave along the wire. This wave velocity then resonates in varying lengths as the string is stopped against the frets when the guitar is played. So, to generalize this idea, sound waves confined in a length of material produce the typical vibrations of material of that size and shape, and the frequency of vibration itself depends on the velocity of sound in the material. Furthermore, the velocity of sound in a material depends on the elastic properties of a material.

Better is smaller, faster, and greener. The inexorable progress of technology with constantly added functionality, for example, to phones and tablets, is inherently linked to the production of new devices or the miniaturization and improvement of existing tech-

nologies. Hypersonic spectroscopy measures the elastic properties of materials, and as devices are miniaturized, the typical vibration frequencies increase to hypersonic values. The important wavelengths of sound waves interacting with a structure are those that have a length comparable to or less than the size of features of the structure. This will be true for any natural feature of the structure being measured, but interesting properties are increasingly being engineered into materials as they are constructed either from shapes of one material or patterns built into composite materials. Hypersonic spectroscopy gives the ability to measure the key response frequencies and key lengths in these artificial engineered materials.

Tuning silicon with nanoholes. Porous silicon is produced by taking a single crystalline wafer, as would normally be used in the production of integrated circuits, and etching it by passing a current through it while it is in contact with an acidic etchant. Under the right conditions, the silicon is "porosified," with pores being produced that tunnel from the surface down into the silicon wafer. The pores progress into the sample at a controllable rate and with a controllable fraction of silicon removed. The final porous silicon has a porosity, normally stated as a percentage, that is the volume fraction of the material that is now air rather than silicon. This means that the material properties of the porous silicon can be tuned to a desired value. A sample of porous silicon that is 0% porous is silicon, a sample that is 100% porous is air, and a sample that is 50% porous is a 50/50 mix of silicon and air that will have material properties somewhere between those of silicon and air. Porous silicon samples can have porosities of up to 95%.

Moreover, the pores produced typically have diameters measured in nanometers. Mesoporous silicon, the type used for hypersonic devices, has pores that are approximately 10–30 nm in diameter, and through control of the etching process, the porous silicon can be produced in layers that change porosity over chosen lengths between 300 and 10,000 nm. This makes the interaction of both sound and light waves with the material particularly interesting.

A wave with a wavelength much greater than the pore size will experience the blended-material property of silicon and air. If the wavelength is roughly the length of the designed layer structure, it will experience reflections, vibrations, and critical frequencies related to that structure. Only a wave with much shorter wavelength will sample the effect of the pores that are giving the blended tunability of the averaged material properties. The doors of microwave ovens demonstrate this idea. Oven microwaves have a frequency of 2.45 GHz, which corresponds to a wavelength of 122 mm (4.80 in.). Inside the glass, the oven doors have a metal sheet with an array of small holes (pores), approximately 1 mm (0.04 in.) in diameter. The microwaves are much longer in wavelength than the size of the holes, and therefore interact with the averaged property of the

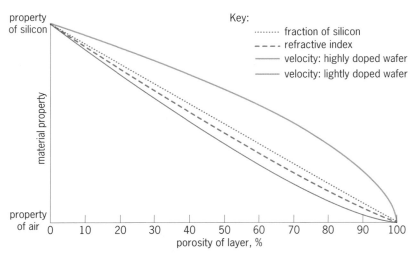

Fig. 2. The dependence of the material property of a porous silicon layer on porosity, showing the change from the properties of silicon to those of air. The dotted line (blue) shows the decrease in the silicon content. The broken line (red) shows the change in refractive index. The upper solid line (green) is the velocity dependence observed for a layer etched from a highly doped silicon wafer. The lower solid line (purple) is the velocity dependence from a lightly doped silicon wafer. Doping relates to the deliberate introduction of selected impurities in the original crystalline silicon.

metal-and-air, thus acting as if sealed in a solid metal box.

The different ways that sound and light average out the effect of the pores in porous silicon can be compared graphically (**Fig. 2**). The refractive index of porous silicon is the key optical parameter to describe how light interacts with the material and the response is roughly proportional to the silicon content with the same dependence of refractive index on porosity found for all mesoporous silicon samples. The velocity of hypersound in the mate-

rial depends on the elastic properties and varies for different classes of mesoporous samples. It is affected by how the silicon is interconnected around the pores, and this is determined by the exact conditions used to produce the pores; this is a complication that, when mastered, gives greater options for the control of the elastic properties of the material.

Multilayered mirrors. Controlling the etching of porous silicon to give a pattern by repeating two layers, A and B [ABAB... ABAB], has the effect of partially reflecting the waves many times at the interfaces between the different layers (**Fig. 3**). This gives a strong net response at a critical wavelength dependent on the overall thickness of one pair of layers, AB. The response is a mirror effect with very strong reflectivity over a range of wavelengths, called a band gap for the wavelength band that cannot propagate through the mirror. This response for optical waves, called a photonic band gap, has been used for 20 years for optical devices in porous silicon, and recent results have demonstrated the effect for hypersonic waves, giving a mirror with an acoustic or phononic band gap. The term "phononic" is often used because it neatly parallels "photonic" and also relates to the idea of the phonon, the quantum particle of vibration.

Similar band-gap results are also seen if the sharp interfaces at the boundaries between the A and B layers are removed and a smooth sinusoidal profile is used for the effective material constants. These structures are called rugate filters; the corrugations of the material properties cause critical wavelengths of interaction for waves passing through the material.

The properties of porous silicon multilayers mean that they can simultaneously provide a photonic band gap for light at technologically useful wavelengths while also presenting an acoustic band gap for hypersonic waves. Future advances may enable these features to be combined to give a hypersonic acoustooptic device, where sound controls light signals for telecommunications or computing applications.

For background information *see* ACOUSTOOPTICS; ELASTICITY; INTERFERENCE FILTERS; LASER SPECTROSCOPY; LATTICE VIBRATIONS; MUSICAL INSTRUMENTS; NANOSTRUCTURE; PHONON; PHOTONIC CRYSTAL DEVICES; PHOTONICS; REFLECTION OF ELECTROMAGNETIC RADIATION; REFRACTION OF WAVES; SCATTERING OF ELECTROMAGNETIC RADIATION; SOUND; ULTRASONICS; VIBRATION; WAVE MOTION in the McGraw-Hill Encyclopedia of Science & Technology.   Paul A. Snow

Bibliography. P. A. Deymier, *Acoustic Metamaterials and Phononic Crystals*, Springer, Berlin, 2013; J. D. Joannopoulos et al., *Photonic Crystals: Molding the Flow of Light*, 2d ed., Princeton University Press, Princeton, NJ, 2008; M. J. Sailor, *Porous Silicon in Practice: Preparation, Characterization and Applications*, Wiley VCH, Weinheim, Germany, 2012; P. A. Snow, Phononic crystals in porous silicon, in L. T. Canham (ed.), *Porous Silicon: The Handbook*, Springer, London, 2014.

Fig. 3. Scanning electron microscope image of a layer structure etched in porous silicon. The bright layers are of low porosity (55%) and the dark layers of high porosity (75%). The white bar corresponds to a length of 2 μm. The structure is a mirror, at the appropriate wavelengths, for both light (a photonic crystal) and sound (a phononic crystal). The pores of approximately 30 nm are too small to be resolved in this image. The arrows indicate a subset of the partial reflections occurring at the interface between the layers.

Incentive-sensitization disease model of addiction

Drug addiction is a disorder in which compulsive patterns of drug-taking and drug-seeking behavior occur despite negative consequences. Dysfunctions in both cognitive and behavioral patterns are common in the disorder. The incentive-sensitization theory of addiction describes how drug-induced changes in the brain may contribute to the transition from casual drug use to addiction. According to this theory, repeated exposure to drugs of abuse promotes the progressive sensitization of neuronal activation within specific brain reward circuitry. For example, animal models of drug abuse suggest that hyperactivation (sensitization) of dopamine (DA) signaling [dopaminergic neurotransmission] within a brain region known as the nucleus accumbens (NAcc) may underlie the transition from experimental to excessive (sensitized) self-administration of a drug. Sensitized self-administration of a drug is thought to be attributable to compulsive drug "wanting" and craving, and it is dissociable from simple "liking" of a drug, which may decrease with repeated drug use.

Environmental stimuli and cues. Drugs of abuse cannot be administered in isolation from salient discrete and contextual stimuli. A discrete stimulus may be an instrument used in drug taking (for example, a syringe, a spoon, or a razor blade), whereas a drug-related context is often a location where drugs are administered (for example, a basement, a friend's house, or a park). If an individual always administers drugs in the presence of these cues, then these stimuli become associated with (or conditioned to) drug availability. Therefore, conditioned stimuli have the capacity to tightly control behavior. Even after long periods of withdrawal, they can induce craving and potential relapse into drug abuse. DA neurotransmission may also be tightly controlled by conditioned cues because animal and human studies often uncover sensitized DA release only while the subject is exposed to drug-related stimuli. However, although this is the case, sensitization of DA neurotransmission also occurs in experimental paradigms that prohibit or minimize the regulation by conditioned cues. For example, amphetamine-evoked sensitized DA release can be measured in vitro from brain slices taken from psychostimulant-exposed rats. Taken together, these findings suggest that the sensitization of brain reward systems is a nonassociative process because it does not require learning about the drug-related cues. In contrast, conditioning is an associative process because it requires learning of the predictive nature of the drug cues. Furthermore, the attribution of incentive salience to these conditioned stimuli enables these cues to motivate and direct drug-seeking behaviors, increasing the chances of reinforcement. The degree to which conditioned stimuli exert control over behaviors varies across a population. For example, although a conditioned cue that predicts reward becomes attractive and wanted in a subset of outbred rats termed "sign-trackers," "goal-tracker" rats exhibit conditioned responses toward the location where the reward is delivered. DA signaling appears to be essential to the attribution of incentive salience to reward-predictive cues in sign-tracker rats.

Self-administration studies. Self-administration studies are an important link between the animal model theory of sensitization and the human condition of addiction. Drug-naïve animals (that is, animals that have not previously been exposed to a drug) can be trained to press a lever for an available drug using low-effort fixed-ratio schedules with high drug doses. In contrast, rats that have previously been exposed to drugs will readily self-administer low drug doses and will increase their responding for a higher dose of the drug when tested under a progressive ratio (PR) schedule (in which the number of lever presses needed to obtain a drug infusion increases progressively). Importantly, microdialysis studies have determined that drug-exposed rats that are working harder to obtain a drug on the PR schedule show enhanced NAcc DA overflow compared to previously saline-exposed controls, indicating the role of sensitized DA release in promoting increased drug self-administration. These results suggest that drug-induced sensitization of neural systems can lead to the defining characteristics of addiction, namely, a craving for a drug and increased motivation to take that drug.

Brain and neuronal activity. The activity of DA neurons in the ventral tegmental area (VTA) and the release of DA in ventral forebrain terminal sites such as the NAcc mediate the reinforcing effects of addictive drugs (see **illustration**). Glutamate (glutamatergic) and DA transmissions within the VTA govern the induction of drug sensitization because this sensitization is antagonized by the local blockade of DA and glutamate receptors. These findings are supported by studies showing that single and repeated injections of systemic cocaine can facilitate long-term potentiation (LTP) and increase α-amino-3-hydroxy-5-methyl-4-isoxazole propionic acid (AMPA)/N-methyl-D-aspartate (NMDA) glutamate receptor ratios in the VTA. Glutamatergic activation can switch DA neurons from their baseline tonic excitation pattern to firing in phasic bursts, thereby enhancing the NAcc DA levels thought to be necessary for enhanced locomotor responding and self-administration of drugs. Importantly, the sensitized DA release is still observed in NAcc slice preparations in the absence of VTA DA cells of origin. These findings suggest that the aforementioned changes in VTA plasticity (the capacity to alter its structure and network) may induce long-lasting enhancements in the synthesis and trafficking of DA and other molecules to neuron terminals, thereby promoting sensitization of the DA release in the NAcc.

In contrast to these VTA neuroadaptations underlying the induction of sensitization, the neuroadaptations underlying the expression of sensitization occur in dopaminergic terminal fields such as the NAcc. One protein that is thought to contribute

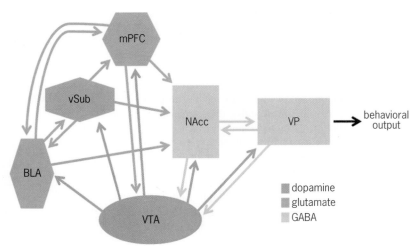

Simplified schemata of the mesocorticolimbic dopamine system. Dopaminergic projections from the ventral tegmental area (VTA) are sent to the basolateral amygdala (BLA), ventral subiculum (vSub), medial prefrontal cortex (mPFC), nucleus accumbens (NAcc), and ventral pallidum (VP). The mPFC sends glutamatergic projections to the VTA, BLA, and NAcc, whereas the BLA and vSub send glutamatergic projections to each other, as well as to the NAcc and mPFC. The NAcc and VP send inhibitory GABAergic (γ-aminobutyric acid) projections to each other, as well as to the VTA. Projections from the VP target premotor areas associated with the initiation of behaviors, such as motor activation.

to various molecular signaling cascades underlying the expression of both psychostimulant and opiate drug sensitization is calcium/calmodulin-dependent kinase II (CaMKII). Activation of CaMKII is required for the sensitized DA release from DA terminals in the NAcc. Furthermore, transiently increasing CaMKII levels in neurons of the NAcc enhances amphetamine-induced locomotion and self-administration, whereas decreasing active CaMKII levels abolishes the sensitized responding for drugs. Sensitized responding to psychostimulants resulting from CaMKII expression is thought to at least partially result from increased expression or activation of glutamatergic AMPA receptors. For example, AMPA receptor antagonists block the expression of sensitization, and microinjections of an AMPA receptor agonist into the NAcc produce enhanced responding in psychostimulant-exposed rats. In addition, CaMKII phosphorylates the transcription factor ΔFosB, a truncated form of the immediate early gene *FosB*, which has been shown to accumulate in NAcc neurons following repeated drug exposure. A complicated interaction between CaMKII and ΔFosB may contribute to the regulation of AMPA receptor function, dendritic spine plasticity, and drug sensitization. The levels of both CaMKII and ΔFosB are increased in the NAcc of postmortem brain tissues sampled from human cocaine addicts, demonstrating the potential importance of studying these molecules when searching for novel pharmacotherapies to treat and prevent drug addiction.

Different classes of addictive drugs have different effects on the various neuroadaptations. AMPA receptors are expressed on dendritic spines of medium spiny neurons in the NAcc that receive conver-

gent dopaminergic and glutamatergic inputs. These spines have been reported to undergo long-lasting changes following repeated drug exposure: psychostimulant drugs increase NAcc dendritic spine size and density, whereas opiate drugs produce the opposite effect. Because repeated intermittent exposure to either of these classes of drugs leads to sensitized behavioral and neurochemical responses, it is difficult to attribute changes in dendritic spine morphology to sensitization processes. Similarly, increased AMPA receptor expression on dendritic spines in the NAcc is seen in psychostimulant-exposed (but not opiate-exposed) rats. These and other findings suggest that the neuronal mechanisms underlying the development and expression of sensitization may not be completely shared across drug classes.

It is also possible that psychostimulant-induced changes in dendritic spine morphology and AMPA receptor expression are more closely related to associative conditioning than to nonassociative sensitization processes. For example, repeated exposure to amphetamine in the VTA leads to the sensitization of behavior and neurotransmission, but it does not affect the development of locomotor conditioning and actually decreases NAcc spine density. In addition, although several studies have implicated AMPA receptor expression in behavioral sensitization, mutant mice lacking these receptors display sensitization, but not associative contextual conditioning. Because the expression of AMPA receptors and changes in dendritic spine morphology have been linked to the formation of learned associations, these findings suggest that spine synaptic plasticity following repeated drug exposure may reflect conditioning and possibly the attribution of incentive salience to reward-predictive cues.

Conclusions. The results discussed suggest a dynamic and complex relationship between the development of nonassociative sensitization and the associative conditioning processes that are thought to underlie the transition from drug experimentation to drug dependence. Although the repeated exposure to drugs of abuse is thought to transform drug "wanting" to drug craving, the attribution of incentive salience to drug-associated cues may guide behavioral responses to increase the chances of reinforcement. Sensitization of behavioral responding to drugs may rely on enhanced neurotransmission in brain regions such as the NAcc, and exposure to drug-conditioned cues may influence this neurotransmission. Dopaminergic and glutamatergic overflow in the NAcc may influence synaptic signaling cascades within dendritic spines on medium spiny neurons, influencing the striatal output pathways necessary for the generation of appetitive behaviors. Whereas basic animal research has uncovered these neuroadaptations that result from repeated drug exposure and self-administration, studies of human drug addicts are beginning to confirm these neural plasticity findings, thereby supporting the incentive-sensitization theory of drug addiction.

For background information *see* ADDICTIVE DISOR-DERS; AMPHETAMINE; BRAIN; COCAINE; NEUROBIOL-OGY; OPIATES; PHARMACOLOGY; PSYCHOLOGY; PSY-CHOPHARMACOLOGY; PSYCHOSOMATIC DISORDERS; PSYCHOTHERAPY; PUBLIC HEALTH; SYNAPTIC TRANS-MISSION in the McGraw-Hill Encyclopedia of Science & Technology.   Bryan F. Singer; Terry E. Robinson

Bibliography. T. E. Robinson and K. C. Berridge, The neural basis of drug craving: An incentive-sensitization theory of addiction, *Brain Res. Rev.*, 18:247–291, 1993, DOI:10.1016/0165-0173(93)90013-P; T. E. Robinson and B. Kolb, Structural plasticity associated with exposure to drugs of abuse, *Neuropharmacology*, 47(suppl. 1):33–46, 2004; B. F. Singer et al., Amphetamine-induced changes in dendritic morphology in rat forebrain correspond to associative drug conditioning rather than nonassociative drug sensitization, *Biol. Psychiatry*, 65:835–840, 2009, DOI:10.1016/j.biopsych.2008.12.020; P. Vezina, Sensitization of midbrain dopamine neuron reactivity and the self-administration of psychomotor stimulant drugs, *Neurosci. Biobehav. Rev.*, 27:827–839, 2004, DOI:10.1016/j.neubiorev.2003.11.004; P. Vezina et al., Sensitization of midbrain dopamine neuron reactivity promotes the pursuit of amphetamine, *J. Neurosci.*, 22:4654–4662, 2002.

Infectious salmon anemia

Infectious salmon anemia (ISA) is a serious viral disease of marine-farmed Atlantic salmon (*Salmo salar*). It is caused by the ISA virus (ISAV), which belongs to the genus *Isavirus* in the family Orthomyx-oviridae; other members of this family include the influenza viruses. ISA is arguably the most economically important viral disease of marine-farmed Atlantic salmon when considering production losses, the loss of export markets, and the associated social impacts. The 2007–2011 ISA outbreak in the Atlantic salmon industry in Chile is a powerful example of the economic significance of ISA; projected losses for this period were estimated to be approximately US$1 billion (that is, 50% of the economic value of the Chilean salmon industry), and full recovery of the industry is not expected before 2013. Therefore, eradication of the disease and control of the viral infection have been priorities for the Atlantic salmon industry, regardless of where the disease has occurred. In addition, because the farmed fish are reared in the same marine water column with wild fish, the mere presence of ISAV invariably elicits strong opposition to aquaculture from environmental groups.

Virus spread regionally and internationally. ISAV is stable in seawater. Its transmission between aquaculture farms can be linked to many fish-farming practices, including the movement of boats carrying live fish, the sharing of personnel and equipment (for example, nets and barges), the movement of infected fish, and the movement of the virus

through the water column resulting from the proximity to fish slaughterhouse processing plants or other fish farms. It also can be transmitted in ballast water. Sea lice (*Lepeophtheirus salmonis*) may serve as mechanical vectors. Migratory wild salmonids

(a)

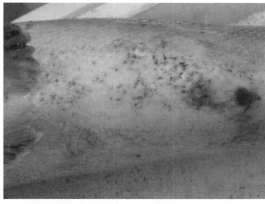

(b)

(c)

Gross lesions in affected Atlantic salmon with ISA.
(*a*) Atlantic salmon with exophthalmia (marked eyeball protrusion) and pale gills. (*b*) Atlantic salmon with petechial hemorrhages (that is, hemorrhages marked by small red or purple spots) on the abdomen. (*c*) Atlantic salmon with a very dark liver and hemorrhages on the visceral adipose tissue. [*Adapted from M. G. Godoy et al., First detection, isolation and molecular characterization of infectious salmon anaemia virus associated with clinical disease in farmed Atlantic salmon (Salmo salar) in Chile, BMC Vet. Res., 4:28, 2008*]

(Atlantic salmon, rainbow trout, brown trout, and sea trout) may be subclinically infected and may serve as carriers, particularly in cases where the virus has spread over long distances (similar to the spreading of avian influenza viruses by migratory wild birds). The shipment of infected and contaminated fish eggs is thought to have been responsible for the introduction of ISAV to Chile.

Clinical manifestation. Clinical signs of ISA include anorexia (loss of appetite), lethargy, and anemia (a condition marked by significant decreases in hemoglobin concentration and in the number of circulating red blood cells). Mortality in a fish cage on a fish farm rises slowly and can vary from 0 to 90%. The virus may be present in a fish cage for up to 6 months before significant mortality is noted. Stressful events, such as handling of fish (for example, during sorting, treatment, splitting, and moving of cages), may initiate disease outbreaks on infected farms. The dead fish have pale gills resulting from anemia, blood-tinged fluid in peritoneal and pericardial cavities, and pinpoint hemorrhages of the internal organs and the membrane lining the abdominal cavity (see **illustration**).

Historical perspective. ISA was first recognized as a new disease entity in Atlantic salmon in 1984 on the southwestern coast of Norway. The situation developed into an epidemic, which peaked in 1990, forcing the Norwegian authorities to impose a series of biosecurity measures that significantly reduced disease outbreaks, but did not eliminate them. The World Organization for Animal Health [Office International des Epizooties (OIE)] recognized the disease in 1990 and named it ISA. The disease was first reported outside of Norway in 1996 in New Brunswick, Canada. Subsequently, ISA was detected in Scotland in 1998, the Faroe Islands (Denmark) in 1999, Maine (USA) in 2000, and Chile in 2007. ISAV is now endemic in fish populations in Norway, New Brunswick, Scotland, the Faroe Islands, Maine, and Chile, and virulent strains of the virus have been replaced by low-pathogenic variant ISAVs called HPR0 viruses, but the dynamics of this evolution are not clearly known. Only Norway and Canada reported ISA outbreaks in 2012. The 2012 outbreaks in Canada occurred in Nova Scotia and Newfoundland.

Pathogenesis. No natural outbreaks of ISA have been reported in fish other than farmed Atlantic salmon; however, the virus can be detected by genomic sequencing methodologies [such as polymerase chain reaction (PCR) procedures, which copy and amplify the sequence of a defined region of a DNA molecule] in feral fish (see **table**). Experimental infection of several Pacific salmon species (various species of *Oncorhynchus*), Arctic char (*Salvelinus alpinus*), and herring (*Clupea harengus*) with ISAV resulted only in subclinical infection. The only other fish species conclusively shown to develop clinical disease and die because of ISAV infection is rainbow trout (*Oncorhynchus mykiss*), and this occurred following experimental infections with highly pathogenic ISAV isolates or using genetically susceptible juvenile rainbow trout. The virus specifically targets red blood cells and endothelial cells (the virus attaches to the *N*-acetyl-4-*O*-acetylated sialic acid receptor), and thus virus replications occur in several organs, particularly the heart, liver, kidney, and spleen, causing a generalized infection of the vascular system. The most extensive and prolonged virus replication is in heart tissue.

Prevention and control. ISA is an OIE-listed disease. It is therefore a reportable disease and is subjected to OIE trade standards. Discovery of a reportable disease often leads to expensive eradication or control efforts, and suspect populations may be quarantined until a definitive diagnosis can be made. Good management and increased biosecurity by fish farm managers in combination with early detection of infection through enhanced surveillance and use of rapid and sensitive diagnostic methods are important keys to prevention of the spread of ISAV. Vaccination is used in North America (New Brunswick and Maine) and in the Faroe Islands; since 2010, it also has been used in most parts of Norway and in Chile. Up to six different vaccines, most of them consisting of inactivated whole ISAV emulsified with adjuvant

---

Timeline (chronological history) of the detection of ISAV in wild fish

Year of sample and test used*	Country (location)	Wild fish species with ISAV
1998–1999, virus isolation and RT-PCR	UK (Scotland)	Sea trout, Brown trout, Atlantic salmon
2000, RT-PCR	Canada (New Brunswick)	Salmonids
RT-PCR	UK (Scotland)	Atlantic salmon
2000, RT-PCR	UK (Scotland)	Sea trout, Brown trout, Atlantic salmon
2001, RT-PCR	West Greenland	Atlantic salmon
2001, RT-PCR	USA (Maine)	Atlantic salmon
2000–2002, virus isolation and RT-PCR	USA (Maine)	Pollock,[†] Atlantic cod[‡]
1998, 2001–2003, RT-PCR	Norway (western Norway)	Salmonids (wild trout, Atlantic salmon)
1995–2002, Antibody ELISA	USA (Maine and Massachusetts)	Atlantic salmon
2010, RT-PCR	Denmark	Atlantic salmon[§]
2010, RT-PCR	Chile (an estuary in southern Chile)	Free-living *Salmo salar* (escapees)

*RT-PCR: reverse-transcriptase polymerase chain reaction; ELISA: enzyme-linked immunosorbent assay.
[†] Pollock taken from inside a marine cage containing ISA-diseased salmon was weakly RT-PCR-positive for ISAV.
[‡] Atlantic cod taken from a marine cage in a well boat holding clinically ISA-diseased salmon was CPE-positive (that is, it showed a positive cytopathic effect, or the observable disruption of a cell culture monolayer by the virus).
[§] Danish salmon produced for restocking purposes.

(a material that enhances the action of a drug or antigen) and administered by intraperitoneal injection, are available commercially. An oral vaccine is also available for the Chilean market. However, the efficacy of these vaccines in the presence of the widespread HPR0 infections is not known.

For background information *see* ANEMIA; ANIMAL VIRUS; AQUACULTURE; FISHERIES ECOLOGY; MARINE CONSERVATION; MARINE FISHERIES; SALMONIFORMES; VIRUS; VIRUS CLASSIFICATION in the McGraw-Hill Encyclopedia of Science & Technology.

Frederick S. B. Kibenge

Bibliography. L. Cottet et al., Infectious salmon anemia virus—genetics and pathogenesis, *Virus Res.*, 155:10–19, 2011, DOI:10.1016/j.virusres.2010. 10.021; M. G. Godoy et al., First detection, isolation and molecular characterization of infectious salmon anaemia virus associated with clinical disease in farmed Atlantic salmon (*Salmo salar*) in Chile, *BMC Vet. Res.*, 4:28, 2008, DOI:10.1186/1746-6148-4-28; F. S. B. Kibenge et al., Countermeasures against viral diseases of farmed fish, *Antiviral Res.*, 95:257–281, 2012, DOI:10.1016/j.antiviral.2012.06.003; F. S. B. Kibenge et al., Infectious salmon anaemia virus: Causative agent, pathogenesis and immunity, *Anim. Health Res. Rev.*, 5:65–78, 2004, DOI:10.1079/ AHR200461.

Integrated process for traffic project evaluation and decision making

Although individual techniques are available, a method that integrates operations, safety, economics, stakeholder perceptions, and uncertainty into a decision-making tool for traffic projects is lacking. The typical stakeholders of traffic projects include motorists, pedestrians, bicyclists, adjacent businesses and residents, and responsible agencies. A three-level project decision-making process that encompasses planning and screening in Level 1, feasibility and performance analysis in Level 2, and evaluation and decision making in Level 3 has been developed to replace the traditional piecemeal approach.

This integrated method is solidly based on three nationally accepted U.S. manuals. Traffic operations are addressed using the *Highway Capacity Manual* (HCM), safety conditions are evaluated using the *Highway Safety Manual* (HSM), and cost-benefit analysis (cost-effectiveness) is based on the *User Benefit Analysis for Highways Manual* (AASHTO Red Book). These are integrated into a planning level and screening analysis. Feasibility and performance analysis follows to examine site-specific constraints and produce performance measures. A multiple-attribute evaluation under uncertainty and fuzziness (MAFU) introduces fuzziness in stakeholder preference and uncertainty in performance measurement. MAFU is designed to determine the alternative that can best achieve a compromise among all competing objectives and conflicting interests. A brief case study demonstrates the application of the integrated

method and compare its reliability to that of the traditional method.

Traffic projects. Traffic projects involve the improvement of vehicular and pedestrian operations, the improvement of safety, and in some cases both. Traffic improvements must be done in a cost-effective manner to maximize the benefits from increasingly leaner budgets.

Typically the traffic office of a highway or transportation agency initiates a traffic analysis and collects safety input from another office. Often its planning office integrates all inputs, receives cost information from the design and construction offices, and provides an evaluation of options. In some cases, traffic operations projects do not include any explicit safety analysis. This fragmented and sequential process is far inferior to a comprehensive and simultaneous procedure.

In addition, trade-off analysis is involved given the potentially conflicting interests or priorities of the various stakeholders. For example, motorists prefer more traffic lanes and longer greens (traffic signals), users of nonmotorized vehicles prefer dedicated lanes and long greens, and pedestrians prefer short crossings (that is, fewer and narrower lanes) and frequent walk times (that is, shorter greens for traffic). In addition, some traffic projects affect access to adjacent parcels of land and in some cases affect the value of adjacent properties; therefore, the perspectives of landowners, shopkeepers, and neighborhood residents may need to be incorporated into the decision-making process. The typical failure to incorporate such perspectives in engineering and decision making exacerbates the NIMBY ("not in my backyard") reaction to projects.

Integrated decision-making process. A comprehensive method for considering multiple project objectives, stakeholder preferences, and performance attributes is inherently complicated. Currently there are no methods that integrate operations, safety, economic performance, stakeholder perceptions, and uncertainty into a multiattribute decision-making tool. A research team from the University of Hawaii at Manoa combined the three nationally accepted manuals, HCM, HSM, and AASHTO Red Book, with risk analysis (we used R Project for Statistical Computing) to develop the integrated decision-making process for the traffic projects, as shown in **Fig. 1**. The process consists of three levels: planning and screening, feasibility and performance, and evaluation and decision making.

Level 1: Planning and screening. Level 1 is designed to assess whether proposed traffic projects have a strong potential for providing net benefits in both traffic operations and safety. The output of this level indicates whether the significant additional effort needed for detailed feasibility investigations and performance analysis is justified. This level is also important for developing a prioritized list of traffic improvement projects for a set of candidate locations. For example, in a large city, several congested intersections might need investigation for improvement

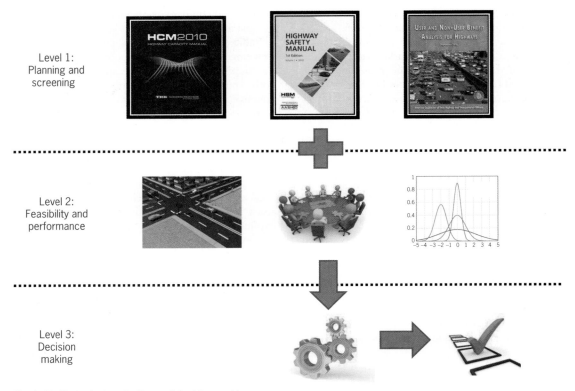

Fig. 1. Traffic project evaluation and decision-making process.

projects. This planning process assists in selecting the most suitable types of projects (mitigation action) and the most promising locations for Level 2 analysis.

Traffic operations analysis is based on HCM and yields in-vehicle delay and level of service (LOS) for the traffic facility. The number of annual traffic collisions by vehicle class and accident severity is estimated with the HSM. The cost-benefit analysis involving the direct costs for project design, planning, construction, and maintenance and the direct benefits from travel time savings and safety risk mitigation is based on guidelines in the AASHTO Red Book. Fuel consumption and emissions savings from congestion mitigation projects are not assessed, so the overall benefits tend to be underestimated and are thus conservative. Consumption and emission estimates require sophisticated simulation models, which are applied in Level 2. Level 1 is designed to provide the justification to proceed with the detailed analysis in Level 2.

Level 2: Feasibility and performance. The five common factors in a feasibility study are technological feasibility, economic feasibility, legal feasibility, operational feasibility, and construction/scheduling feasibility. Level 2 assesses the feasibility of traffic projects by considering site-specific constraints and construction impacts.

The feasibility analysis examines whether the selected alternative can be implemented given time, financial, legal, environmental, and social constraints. For example, if a traffic project includes

a turn-removal option, the availability of rerouting roads and the potential legal restrictions on removing the accessibility of some important buildings (such as a fire station or a hospital) should be carefully taken into account. The dimensions and optimum size of large traffic projects (such as a tunnel or interchange) may be restricted by the project budget and available right-of-way. Other challenges, such as construction impacts, sight-line blockage, and the difficulty of underground utility relocation, may also limit the potential application of a traffic project at a specific location.

Each project that is found to be feasible is then subjected to detailed performance analysis. Unlike the basic traffic analysis in Level 1, the traffic project is treated as it functions in the real-world road network. Performance analysis reveals the traffic, environmental, and other regional impacts on the adjacent road network and surrounding communities. This is accomplished by explicitly modeling the location of each vehicle, bus, and pedestrian using advanced traffic microsimulation tools such as Aimsun, PTV Vissim, or TransModeler, along with EPA's Motor Vehicle Emission Simulator (MOVES). Traffic operation, safety, noise, and energy indices are quantified at this level. These outputs enable the quantification of the performance indicators and their associated uncertainties for subsequent decision making in Level 3.

Level 3: Decision making. The delivery of a traffic project typically occurs several years after the planning and performance analysis. Therefore,

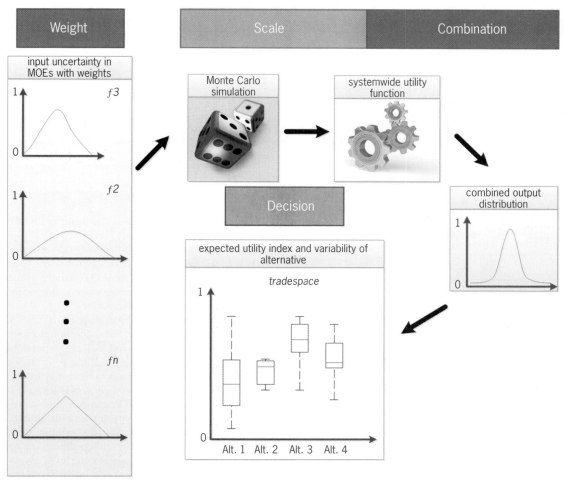

Fig. 2. Project decision-making process. MOEs are the measures of effectiveness, and *f1*, *f2*, and *fn* are examples of distributions that MOEs may follow.

performance outputs are based on predicted future traffic and environmental conditions. In infrastructure projects, the future is synonymous with uncertainty and risk. Level 3 integrates quantitative uncertainty and risk analysis into the decision-making process. In addition, Level 3 analysis determines which project alternative can best achieve a compromise among all competing project objectives and conflicting stakeholder interests. Its fuzzy analytic hierarchy process (FAHP) captures the vagueness in stakeholder preferences. Its multiple-attributes utility theory (MAUT) generates and combines dimensionless performance indicators. Its probabilistic Monte Carlo simulation (MCS) models output uncertainties and trade-off analysis.

The decision-making process shown in **Fig. 2** has four stages: weight, scale, combination, and decision. In the weight stage, performance attributes of a traffic project, including operation, safety, accessibility, and environmental factors, are given weights using FAHP. Scaling is one of the key stages in this process. In this stage, single-attribute utility functions are established for each attribute to provide a dimensionless measurement. Risk parameters are assigned to each function to describe the risk toler-

ance of the decision maker. In addition, a quantification of uncertainty in performance measurement is made at this stage. The combination stage includes the development of a systemwide multiattribute utility function that combines the single-attribute utility functions in order to determine the utility value of each alternative. In the decision stage, the expected utility index and variance are calculated using the systemwide multiattribute utility function. Because of the uncertainty in performance measurement, MCS is used to develop a "tradespace" to visually assist in trade-off analysis among alternatives. The decision is made by simultaneously comparing a statistical summary of the utility values of each alternative, including expected values, confidence interval, and variance. This process is demonstrated in the following case study.

Case study. This case study demonstrates outputs using both the traditional project evaluation process and the three-level integrated process. A proposed congested intersection improvement project includes three alternatives: do nothing (DN), left-turn prohibition (LTP), and a low-clearance underpass (LCUP). Safety, operation, environment, and energy are the chosen dimensions for this evaluation.

Results for three alternatives with traditional and integrated process

Analysis scenario	Weights of performance attributes					Do nothing		LTP[1]		LCUP[2]	
	Safety	Operation	Environment	Energy	Sum	Expected utility	Std. dev.[3]	Expected utility	Std. dev.	Expected utility	Std. dev.
Traditional process only	N/A	N/A	N/A	N/A	N/A	0.050	0.029	0.199	0.017	0.345	0.044
Three-level integrated process	0.50	0.40	0.05	0.05	1.00	0.005	0.003	0.025	0.004	0.053	0.007

[1] LTP = left-turn prohibition
[2] LCUP = low-clearance underpass
[3] Std. dev. = standard deviation

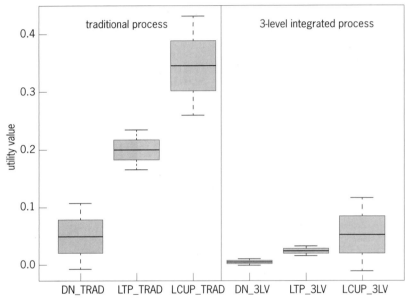

Fig. 3. Tradespace of case study for project decision making with traditional (**TRAD**) and three-level integrated (**3LV**) processes. DN = do nothing. LTP = left-turn prohibition. LCUP = low-clearance underpass. N_Sim = 10,000.

As shown in the **table** and **Fig. 3**, the maximum variance of the expected utility is produced by using the traditional analysis, in which the uncertainty in stakeholder perceptions and traffic performance are not quantified. The variance of the expected utility value is substantially reduced by the three-level integrated process, where the trade-offs among stakeholder preferences on performance attributes are analyzed and the uncertainty in performance analysis is considered. Therefore, the integrated project evaluation and decision-making process produces more reliable outputs and reduces the uncertainty for each alternative. Since Monte Carlo simulation is involved in this part, the number of simulations (N_Sim) is large, as Fig. 3 indicates, but they are executed quickly on a modern PC.

Outlook. A framework was developed to integrate operations, safety, economic, stakeholder objectives, and uncertainty analysis into a multiattribute decision-making framework for traffic projects. With adjustments, this process can become a generic tool applicable to large-scale transportation infra-structure projects, especially if the projects involve (1) considerable uncertainty regarding the estimation of performance indicators, (2) multiple stakeholders with conflicting interests in their expectations of the project, and (3) changes in the underlying assumptions that produce a significant variation in the ranking of alternatives.

Although the full three-level process is recommended for project evaluation and decision making, each level can lead to decision making, depending on the characteristics and scope of the project. For example, the planning-level assessment may be sufficient to determine whether a project is suitable if the project budget, land-use limitations, and potential adverse impacts are not major concerns. If there is limited uncertainty regarding the estimation of performance indicators and conflicts among stakeholders are minimal, then a planning-level assessment combining feasibility and performance analysis (that is, Levels 1 and 2) would probably suffice. However, only Level 3 analysis involves multiple stakeholders and uncertainty evaluation, so that it yields much less uncertain outcomes than basic analysis (Level 1).

For background information *see* FUZZY SETS AND SYSTEMS; HIGHWAY ENGINEERING; MONTE CARLO METHOD; TRAFFIC-CONTROL SYSTEMS; TRANSPORTATION ENGINEERING in the McGraw-Hill Encyclopedia of Science & Technology.

Panos D. Prevedouros; Xin Alyx Yu

Bibliography. American Association of State Highway and Transportation Officials, *Highway Safety Manual*, AASHTO, Washington, DC, 2001; American Association of State Highway and Transportation Officials, *A Manual of User Benefit Analysis for Highways*, 3d ed., AASHTO, Washington, DC, 2010; Federal Highway Administration, *The Transportation Planning Process: Key Issues, A Briefing Book for Transportation Decisionmakers, Officials, and Staff*, FHWA-HEP-07-039, FHWA, Washington, DC, 2007; D. Ruppert, *Statistics and Data Analysis for Financial Engineering*, Springer, New York, 2010; K. C. Sinha and S. Labi, *Transportation Decision Making: Principles of Project Evaluation and Programming*, Wiley, Hoboken, NJ, 2007; Transportation Research Board, *Highway Capacity Manual*, 5th ed., TRB, Washington, DC, 2011;

X. A. Yu and P. D. Prevedouros, Left turn prohibition and partial grade separation for signalized intersections: Planning level assessment, *J. Transp. Eng.*, 139(4):399–406, 2013 doi:10.1061/(ASCE)TE.1943-5436.0000511.

Intensity frontier of particle and nuclear physics

The main goal of fundamental particle physics is to identify the basic building blocks of nature, understand their properties, and decipher how these building blocks, generically referred to as particles, interact with one another. The ultimate goal is to reveal the most basic laws of physics, which, in principle, would allow us to get as close as possible to understanding how, in principle, everything works. We are, of course, very far away from getting anywhere close to this goal, which may or may not be achievable. However, over the last century or two, this pursuit has led to many paradigm-shifting surprises, a deeper understanding of nature, and fantastic achievements, from the discovery of atoms, electrons, nuclei, and quarks, to the development of quantum mechanics, personal computers, and nuclear power plants, to revealing the secrets of how stars burn and how the universe looked almost 14 billion years ago.

Frontiers. Research in fundamental physics is pursued in a variety of ways, from the collision of protons at ultrahigh energies to satellite observations of the universe when it was less than 400,000 years old, to precision measurements of the flux of neutrinos produced in the Earth's atmosphere in gigantic multikiloton detectors located deep underground. Recently, it has become convenient to categorize these different avenues in terms of three distinct frontiers of fundamental physics that are being explored by experimental and theoretical nuclear and particle physicists. The boundary between the frontiers is fuzzy, and their goals and capabilities are often complementary. A healthy research program in all three frontiers is required in order to properly advance our understanding of fundamental physics.

Energy frontier. The energy frontier consists of efforts to directly study the behavior of matter at the smallest achievable distance scales (or, according to Heisenberg's uncertainty principle, the highest momentum and energy scales). It is the realm of high-energy particle accelerators like the Tevatron at the Fermi National Accelerator Laboratory (Fermilab), which stopped collecting data in 2011, and the Large Hadron Collider (LHC), which is currently operational at the European Organization for Nuclear Research (CERN), the highest-energy particle accelerator ever built. Energy-frontier experiments have the ability to directly produce new, unknown, sometimes very heavy particles and directly study their interactions and measure their properties. Recent achievements include the discovery of the top quark at the Tevatron in 1995 and the discovery of a new particle, consistent with the long-sought Higgs boson, at the LHC, announced on July 4, 2012.

Cosmic frontier. The cosmic frontier consists of research efforts through which one attempts to learn more about fundamental particle physics by looking up to the cosmos and measuring the properties of astrophysical sources, like supernovae and active galactic nuclei, or measuring the global properties of the universe itself, like the distribution of clusters of galaxies or the different properties of the cosmic microwave background. The best (and only confirmed) evidence for the existence of dark matter, for example, comes from the exploration of the cosmic frontier.

Intensity frontier. The intensity frontier consists of research efforts aimed at studying, as precisely as possible, the properties and interactions of the known basic ingredients of matter (the current fundamental particles) or combinations of these ingredients, such as protons and neutrons, nuclei, or atoms. Achievements of intensity-frontier research include the discovery that matter and antimatter can be fundamentally distinguished from each other—a phenomenon called CP-invariance violation—and, at the very end of the twentieth century, the observation that neutrinos can change species as they travel, which ultimately led to the discovery of nonzero neutrino masses.

Many intensity-frontier efforts make use of particle accelerators. Unlike in energy-frontier research, here the goal is not to achieve the highest possible energies. Instead, it is often the intensity or the quality of the particle beam that determines the reach of an accelerator-based intensity-frontier experiment. Intense proton beams are required in order to pursue precision measurements of the properties of neutrinos and muons and to search for physics processes that are either exceedingly rare or simply forbidden by our current understanding of the laws of physics.

There are several ongoing and near-future proposals to take advantage of Fermilab's existing accelerator complex and many of its potential future upgrades, and to develop a comprehensive intensity-frontier research program for the current decade and beyond. Concrete proposals include, among several other ideas, the search for CP-invariance violation in the neutrino sector and searches for absurdly rare physics processes involving muons. These examples are fleshed out in a little more detail later in this article. There is considerable intensity-frontier activity at several other nuclear and particle physics facilities as well, including CERN and the Japanese Proton Accelerator Research Complex (J-PARC).

Neutrinos. Neutrinos are fundamental matter particles, like the electron and the quarks that make up the proton and the neutron. Unlike all other matter particles, neutrinos do not participate in processes mediated by electromagnetic interactions, which govern almost all familiar physics processes, or by strong interactions, which are responsible for binding quarks into neutrons and protons and binding those into atomic nuclei. Neutrinos are known to interact only via the so-called weak interactions, which mediate certain nuclear decay processes (such as nuclear beta decay), and gravity. As far as all accessible particle physics processes are concerned, gravitational interactions are exceedingly feeble and can always be safely neglected, which means that neutrinos can be "seen" only through the eyes of the weak interactions. The weak interactions, for the energies of interest, are indeed quite weak, rendering the neutrinos virtually interaction-free. For this reason, neutrinos are by far the most elusive and hence least well understood of all the matter particles.

There are three known species, or flavors, of neutrinos. They are distinguished by the way they undergo charged-current weak interactions: One neutrino flavor (ν_e) interacts only with electrons (e), another flavor (ν_μ) interacts only with muons, while a third flavor (ν_τ) interacts only with taus. Muons (μ) and taus (τ) are heavy cousins of the electrons. All three are electrically charged matter particles that do not interact via the strong interactions. Muons are much heavier (around 200 times) than electrons, while taus are heavier still (around 17 times heavier than muons).

Oscillations. Until more or less the turn of the century, it was widely believed that neutrinos were exactly massless, as predicted by the so-called standard model of particle physics. Experiments capable of studying the flavor evolution of neutrinos over large distances revealed otherwise through the observation of a phenomenon called neutrino oscillations. In a nutshell, the following was observed: Muon neutrinos—that is, neutrinos created in physics processes involving muons—can be detected, with some nonzero probability, as tau neutrinos (that is, neutrinos detected via physics processes involving taus) as long as the distance between the detector and the production of the neutrino beam is large enough. The probability depends sinusoidally on the distance and the (inverse of the) neutrino energy; hence, these types of phenomena are referred to as neutrino flavor oscillations. Experiments have also observed, sometimes indirectly, the oscillation of electron neutrinos into muon neutrinos and into tau neutrinos.

Probing the difference between matter and antimatter. Several well-defined fundamental physics questions can be addressed only with next-generation "precision" neutrino oscillation experiments. Among them is the quest for CP-invariance violation among neutrinos, a physics phenomenon that has never been observed and is expected to play a central role when it comes to understanding how the universe turned out to be mostly, but not completely, empty.

Interactions that violate the discrete symmetry CP (combined charge conjugation and parity) in effect can distinguish particles from antiparticles and are required if we are ever to understand why the universe is mostly devoid of matter (there are more than a billion photons for every proton and electron in the universe) and why there is no primordial antimatter, as far as we can measure. Of the known interactions,

only the weak one violates CP invariance, a phenomenon that has been observed in the quark sector. The amount of CP violation observed in the quark sector, however, is too small and seems not to play a role in understanding why the universe has a little bit of matter but no antimatter. CP-invariance violation in the neutrino sector not only may be much more significant but also may be the answer we have been looking for.

In neutrino oscillations, CP-invariance violation manifests itself in a very simple way: the probability that, say, a muon neutrino will oscillate into an electron neutrino is equal to that of a muon antineutrino oscillating into an electron antineutrino only if CP invariance is exact. If the probabilities are different, CP invariance is violated. The size of the difference is proportional to the degree to which CP invariance is violated. In order to perform such a measurement, one needs (1) a very intense, very well understood beam of muon neutrinos, and (2) a very large detector, located far away from the neutrino source, that is capable of observing electron neutrinos efficiently and precisely. For the neutrinos with energies in the range of those available at Fermilab, the required source-detector distance is several hundred kilometers. In practice, the effect one is looking for is a several percent difference between neutrino and antineutrino oscillation probabilities, while the probabilities themselves are at the level of several percent (**Fig. 1**). With current neutrino beams and detector technologies, we could perform such a measurement only if we were to build detectors with a mass of around several tens of thousands of tons, and only after waiting a very long time, say, a couple of decades. (One should remember that neutrino interactions are very weak.) New, much more intense beams are being planned and new detector technology is being developed in order to circumvent these technical difficulties. The current generation of neutrino oscillation experiments, including the NuMI

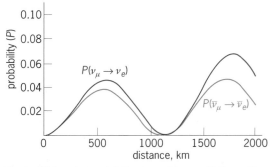

Fig. 1. CP-invariance violation in neutrino oscillations. The graph plots the probability (*P*) for a muon neutrino (ν_μ) and a muon antineutrino ($\bar{\nu}_\mu$) to be detected as, respectively, an electron neutrino (ν_e) and an electron antineutrino ($\bar{\nu}_e$) as a function of the source-detector distance, in kilometers. The curves are computed given everything we know about neutrino oscillations, except for the assumption that the amount of CP-invariance violation, something that we do not know, is quite large. If CP-invariance violation is absent or very small, the two curves are expected to be indistinguishable. 1 km = 0.6 mi.

Off-Axis ν_e Appearance (NOνA) experiment at Fermilab and the Tokai to Kamioka (T2K) experiment in J-PARC, will serve as excellent stepping-stones—while expanding our understanding of neutrinos and their interactions along the way—for designing bigger, more powerful, better (and cheaper) neutrino experiments. Among the proposed next-generation experiments are the Long Baseline Neutrino Experiment (LBNE) at Fermilab and the Hyper-Kamiokande experiment in Japan. There are several other innovative ideas that are being pursued by the American and the world neutrino community.

Rare muon processes. Neutrino oscillations reveal that a neutrino's flavor is not a conserved quantum number. What was produced as an electron neutrino can change into a muon neutrino as long as one is willing to wait long enough. The concept of flavor, however, extends to charged leptons as well, and we expect new phenomena involving electrons, muons, and taus.

An example of such a phenomenon is the decay of a muon into an electron and a photon. There is no known interaction that mediates this decay, but the existence of neutrino oscillations guarantees that it must happen (**Fig. 2**). Since we do not know neutrino properties and interactions in detail, however, we do not know the probability with which a muon will decay in this way. The most pessimistic guess is really tiny but not zero. We can safely state that at least one in about 10^{54} muons (an astronomically large number) will decay in this way. Current searches for this most rare decay process—which

has never been observed—tell us that at most one in around 10^{13} (ten trillion) muons decays in this way. We are still a long way from being sensitive to the one-in-10^{54} level.

Not only will the pursuit of these very rare processes reveal new neutrino properties, but they are also very sensitive to the existence of new particles and new interactions that can convert muons into electrons, even if these particles are very heavy or if the new interactions are very feeble. Indeed, it is estimated that searches for rare muon processes are sensitive to particles with masses as large as 10,000 TeV/c^2 (around 10,000,000 times as heavy as a proton). In a way, these rare particle searches are sensitive to new hypothetical fundamental particles so heavy that not even our most powerful particle accelerators can produce them (by a factor of more than 1000).

Today and in the near future, the ultimate way to look for muons turning into electrons is not, it turns out, to search for muon-to-electron-plus-photon decays. The most sensitive searches involve a process referred to as muon-to-electron conversion in nuclei, which works as follows. A muon is shot into a piece of matter. It gets captured by a nucleus and forms what is called a muonic atom, which is like a regular atom except that one of the electrons has been replaced by a muon. In the absence of neutrino masses or new forces, the fate of a muonic atom is one of two: Either the muon decays into an electron and two neutrinos (this is how muons normally decay) or the muon "collides" with the nucleus and converts into a muon neutrino (and the nucleus changes into a different nucleus, but we are not interested in that). Both processes are mediated by the weak interactions, and it turns out that the latter is more likely than the former. The violation of lepton flavor allows one to consider a third possibility: The muon and the nucleus can "collide," yielding an electron and another nucleus—muon-to-electron conversion in nuclei.

The Mu2e proposal at Fermilab aims at extending the sensitivity to muon-to-electron conversion by four orders of magnitude—a factor of 10,000. A similar proposal called COMET is actively being pursued at J-PARC. This challenging experiment requires the production of a very intense muon beam that one shoots at a target. One does not care about having a very high energy beam (after all, all the muons will eventually stop and get captured by nuclei), but one does care about the "purity" of the beam. One of the key challenges is to make sure that the muon beam contains only muons. (For example, the presence of even a minute number of pions, which are not too different from muons, would destroy the experimental sensitivity.) More intense proton beams, of the type being considered for next-generation neutrino experiments, would also significantly enhance our ability to search for these rare muon processes. Preliminary studies indicate that another factor-of-100 improvement in sensitivity is within reach, and more progress can be envisioned with new

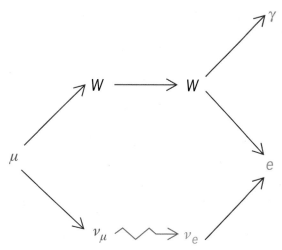

Fig. 2. Diagram of a muon-to-electron-plus-photon decay that results from neutrino oscillations. According to quantum mechanics, there is a nonzero probability that a muon (μ) will manifest itself as a W boson and a muon neutrino (ν_μ). Since the W boson is much heavier than the muon, this happens for only a tiny fraction of a second, after which, most of the time, the W boson and the neutrino "recombine" into a muon. A very tiny fraction of the time, the W boson will emit a photon (γ), while the muon neutrino will oscillate into an electron neutrino (ν_e). When this happens, the W boson and the electron neutrino "recombine" instead into an electron (e). The end result is the extremely rare muon decay into a photon and an electron.

technological developments in beam and detector designs.

Other accelerator-based intensity-frontier research. At an accelerator complex like Fermilab, several other intensity-frontier activities, both within the broad areas of neutrino and muon physics and beyond, can be envisioned. In the realm of neutrinos, there are several activities related to the pursuit of new neutrino states, referred to as sterile neutrinos; precision measurements of neutrino scattering on nucleons and nuclei; and the development of new types of neutrino beams. In the realm of muons, there are precision measurements of the muon magnetic dipole moment and the pursuit of potentially new strategies for searching for other very rare and yet-to-be-observed muon processes, including muon decays into two electrons and one positron.

Understanding quark properties and interactions is also within the purview of accelerator-based intensity-frontier research. There are proposals to explore rare flavor-changing decays of strange mesons (like the charged and neutral kaons), and a new electron-positron collider facility dedicated to studying the properties of mesons containing bottom quarks is under consideration at KEK, Japan. There are also proposals to look for the never-observed phenomenon of neutron-antineutron oscillations and to search for very light, very weakly coupled new particles at different types of beam-dump experiments.

For most of the accelerator-based activities just described, the main ingredient is a very intense, versatile proton beam. Intense means "as many protons per unit time as possible," and versatile means, among other qualifiers, "available in an array of energies" and "with a malleable time structure." Such an investment is expected to buy a rich, diverse fundamental physics research program that is capable of shining light on the least understood of the fundamental matter particles, the neutrinos, and capable of revealing, through the search for very rare or completely forbidden processes, the existence of new particles, interactions, and phenomena that cannot be exposed in any other way. Over the past many decades, intensity-frontier research has played a key role in advancing our understanding of nuclear and particle physics. Along with research in the other frontiers of fundamental physics, it is expected to continue to surprise us and move us closer to understanding the most fundamental ingredients of nature.

For background information *see* ANTIMATTER; COSMIC BACKGROUND RADIATION; COSMOLOGY; DARK MATTER; ELEMENTARY PARTICLE; FUNDAMENTAL INTERACTIONS; GALAXY, EXTERNAL; HIGGS BOSON; INTERMEDIATE VECTOR BOSON; LEPTON; NEUTRINO; PARTICLE ACCELERATOR; QUARKS; STANDARD MODEL; SYMMETRY LAWS (PHYSICS); TIME-REVERSAL INVARIANCE; UNCERTAINTY PRINCIPLE; UNIVERSE; WEAK NUCLEAR INTERACTIONS in the McGraw-Hill Encyclopedia of Science & Technology.

André de Gouvêa

Bibliography. S. Bilenky, *Introduction to the Physics of Massive and Mixed Neutrinos*, Lecture Notes in Physics, Springer, Berlin, Heidelberg, 2010; A. Franklin, *Are There Really Neutrinos?: An Evidential History*, Perseus Publishing, Cambridge, MA, 2001; A. de Gouvêa and N. Saoulidou, Fermilab's intensity frontier, *Annu. Rev. Nucl. Part. Sci.*, 60:513–538, 2010, DOI:10.1146/annurev-nucl-100809-131949; W. J. Marciano, T. Mori, and J. M. Roney, Charged lepton flavor violation experiments, *Annu. Rev. Nucl. Part. Sci.*, 58:315–341, 2008, DOI:10.1146/annurev.nucl.58.110707.171126.

Kangaroo genome

The tammar wallaby (*Macropus eugenii*) [**Fig. 1**] is a small member of the kangaroo family that has become an important emerging model system for understanding many aspects of mammalian biology. Its utility in scientific research is the reason why this specific marsupial species was chosen for detailed genome sequencing. Marsupials are true mammals, possessing fur and producing milk to nourish their young. However, they differ from the other groups

(a)

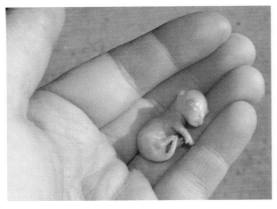

(b)

Fig. 1. Tammar wallaby (*Macropus eugenii*). (*a*) An adult, female tammar wallaby weighs approximately 6 kg (13 lb) and stands 45 cm (18 in.) in height. (*b*) A tammar wallaby pouch young at approximately 20 days after birth. At this stage, the hind limb is still smaller than the forelimb.

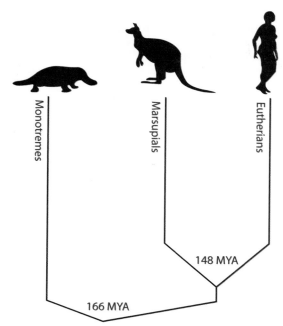

Fig. 2. Evolutionary tree of the extant mammalian lineages. MYA, million years ago.

of mammals [monotremes, such as the platypus; and eutherians, which include all mammals except monotremes and marsupials (for example, humans, elephants, whales, and bats)] because of their unique mode of reproduction. Marsupials give birth to very small and underdeveloped young, similar to the early fetal stages in eutherians. These young then complete the majority of their growth and development attached to a teat in the adult female's pouch. It is this alternative mode of reproduction that has made them extremely useful for the study of mammalian development. Specifically, because the young are in a pouch, they are easy to observe and experimentally manipulate throughout development. Marsupials also occupy a unique evolutionary niche because they have been evolving independently from eutherian mammals for approximately 160 million years (**Fig. 2**). This evolutionary distance enables the marsupial genome to be an exceptionally powerful tool for understanding the human genome and the critical components that define a mammal.

Sequencing the kangaroo genome. The kangaroo genome contains approximately 2.9 billion base pairs (just slightly smaller than the human genome). It contains about 18,250 genes, similar to the number in humans. However, a significant proportion of the kangaroo's genes are unique or highly diverged from their human counterparts. Interestingly, many of these novel genes could be classified as associated with reproduction, immune function, and lactation, which are all unique aspects of the biology of marsupials.

Smell genes. The olfactory receptor (OR) genes, which are responsible for the ability to detect odors, comprise one of the largest gene families in the mammalian genome. Humans have approximately 600 OR genes, and about half of these genes are no longer functional. Dogs have approximately 800 OR genes, with around 200 being no longer functional. The marsupial genome has one of the largest collections of mammalian ORs, with more than 1500 OR genes, representing almost 10% of all their genes. Part of the reason for the tammar wallaby's exceptional sense of smell may be to help the newborn young locate the pouch. Newborn young are blind (Fig. 1*b*), and they lack complete development of many of their organ systems when they have to make the journey from the mother's urogenital sinus to the pouch. The young crawl up their mother's abdomen and then locate the pouch opening based on smell. Once inside the pouch, this smell can guide them to a teat to begin feeding. Perhaps the expanded family of OR genes in the marsupial genome helps guide the newborn on their perilous journey to the pouch.

Immune genes. The major histocompatibility complex (MHC) is an essential part of the human body's natural defense mechanisms and is responsible for presenting foreign molecules to the immune cells. There are many MHC genes in the human genome, forming a large cluster on chromosome 6. It was thought that the grouping of these MHC genes together was essential for their function. However, in the kangaroo, the MHC genes are found spread throughout the genome across almost all the chromosomes. Even more of a surprise was that one whole class of MHC genes found in all eutherian mammals was missing from the tammar wallaby genome. Despite this apparent reduction in immune genes, kangaroos are surprisingly resilient to infection. When the young are born, they have not yet developed their own immune system. This poses quite a problem for the young as they transition into the warm, moist, and often quite dirty environment of the pouch, which is a perfect breeding ground for bacteria and fungi. The young are protected from infections by a family of antimicrobial peptides delivered in the mother's milk and made by the young themselves. These peptides are effective against many problematic drug-resistant human pathogens and may prove to be useful in biomedicine.

Body plan genes. The vertebrate body plan is highly variable, even among mammals. Eutherian mammal body plans include forms adapted for flight and for terrestrial and aquatic environments. A large part of the early development of the mammalian embryo into these different forms is controlled by a set of highly conserved master regulatory genes called the HOX genes. HOX genes control the placement and patterning of the limbs, which are especially unique in the kangaroo. The early developing kangaroo has a greatly accelerated development of the forelimbs, enabling the young to crawl into the pouch at a very early developmental time point. In fact, at birth, the hind limb is barely developed and is referred to as a "paddle," resembling a flat disk without any digits. As the young develop in the pouch, the growth and differentiation of the hind limb take place at a greatly accelerated rate; then, once the young are ready to exit the pouch, they have greatly elongated footplates and hind limbs evolved for hopping. Interestingly, the hind limb is also missing a toe and has two fused digits.

Overall, examining the expression of the HOX genes in the marsupial limb is providing important insights into the role of these genes in limb patterning and the control of digit formation in the hands and feet. Investigations of the tammar wallaby's HOX cluster have uncovered many unique features, which are now being examined in great detail in a range of mammals.

Reproduction genes. One of the many unique features of the kangaroo genome is the content of its sex chromosomes. Marsupials, like humans, have an X/Y sex chromosome system, where XY individuals are male and XX individuals are female. The X chromosomes of marsupials and humans share a large region of identity, but humans have several other large chunks of their genome added onto the X chromosome. The X chromosome is a unique place for a gene to be located in the genome because there is only a single copy in males. Interestingly, the X chromosome has a disproportionately large number of genes associated with testis and brain development on it. In humans, these X-linked testis and brain genes are located within both the conserved region and the added region of the X chromosome. However, in marsupials, the content of this added region is located on the autosomes (nonsex chromosomes) and not on the sex chromosomes. Examining the function of these marsupial autosomal genes destined to join the human X chromosome showed that they already had a function in testis and brain development before being added to the X chromosome. This suggests that the X chromosome has selectively recruited useful testis and brain genes from the genome throughout its evolution.

Another interesting feature of marsupials is that the young are born in a sexually indifferent state, that is, before their gonads have made a decision to become male or female. Sex is determined by a gene on the Y chromosome called SRY. In males, the presence of the Y and SRY triggers a testis to form; on the other hand, in females, an ovary is formed in the absence of Y and SRY. Thus, sex in marsupials, and indeed in all mammals, is under the control of a genetic switch. Interestingly, sex can be reversed early in development in marsupials by exposure to hormones. Estrogen has the ability to change XY gonads, which are destined to become testes, into ovaries. In humans, exposure of a developing male fetus to estrogenic chemicals can also cause defects in testis formation. Hence, the tammar wallaby is being used as a model system to understand the effect that estrogen can have on sexual development in mammals.

Lactation genes. Marsupials have a very long and sophisticated lactation period in which the developing young undergo the majority of their growth and development. As the young develop, their nutritional demands change, and the composition of the milk produced by the mother undergoes alterations. Initially, the milk is very high in carbohydrates, but low in fat; then, as development proceeds, the milk switches completely to become very high in fat and very low in carbohydrates. This molecular control over the milk's nutrient content is of major interest to the dairy industry.

Overall, many highly conserved genes controlling lactation have been identified in the tammar genome. Interestingly, but perhaps not surprisingly, a large number of the novel genes identified have also fallen into the category of lactation. Thus, it seems that kangaroos have developed a number of new genes and control mechanisms to control milk production and nutrient content.

Conclusions. The kangaroo genome sits in a unique evolutionary place because marsupials are the closest living mammalian relatives to eutherians, including humans (Fig. 2). Analysis of the marsupial genome has provided many insights into the human genome. In particular, the marsupial genome has shed light on the functioning of the immune system, the development of the mammalian body plan, the controls over sexual development, and the forces that shape the human genome as it evolves. Marsupials also have many unique aspects to their genome that may be of use to the dairy industry and the biomedical field (for example, marsupial peptides could be a source of unique and effective antimicrobials).

For background information *see* ANIMAL EVOLUTION; CHROMOSOME; DEVELOPMENTAL BIOLOGY; DEVELOPMENTAL GENETICS; ESTROGEN; EUTHERIA; GENE; GENETIC MAPPING; GENOMICS; HOMEOTIC (HOX) GENES; KANGAROO; LACTATION; MARSUPIALIA; OLFACTION; PHYLOGENY in the McGraw-Hill Encyclopedia of Science & Technology.   Andrew J. Pask

Bibliography. K. Y. Chew, HOXA13 and HOXD13 expression during development of the syndactylous digits in the marsupial *Macropus eugenii*, *BMC Dev. Biol.*, 12:2, 2012, DOI:10.1186/1471-213X-12-2; A. J. Pask et al., Oestrogen blocks the nuclear entry of SOX9 in the developing gonad of a marsupial mammal, *BMC Biol.*, 8:113, 2010, DOI:10.1186/1741-7007-8-113; M. B. Renfree et al., Genome sequence of an Australian kangaroo, *Macropus eugenii*, provides insight into the evolution of mammalian reproduction and development, *Genome Biol.*, 12:R81, 2011, DOI:10.1186/gb-2011-12-8-r81; J. Wang et al., Ancient antimicrobial peptides kill antibiotic-resistant pathogens: Australian mammals provide new options: *PLoS One*, 6(8):e24030, 2011, DOI:10.1371/journal.pone.0024030.

Ketamine and depression

The world of medicine has long known ketamine hydrochloride to be a dissociative anesthetic agent, typically used intravenously for pediatric surgical procedures. Ketamine's principal action in the brain is on *N*-methyl-D-aspartate (NMDA) receptors, where

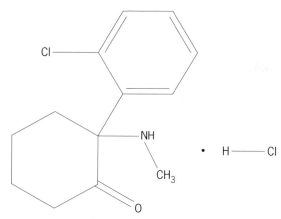

Fig. 1. The chemical structure of ketamine hydrochloride [(±)-2-(o-chlorophenyl)-2-(methylamino)cyclohexanone hydrochloride].

it blocks the action of the brain's principal excitatory neurotransmitter, glutamate.

As a derivative of phencyclidine (PCP), ketamine (**Fig. 1**) shares some notoriety as a commonly abused club drug, going under the street names K and Special K. It is a schedule III controlled substance in the United States. At lower, so-called subanesthetic doses (at which consciousness is largely preserved), ketamine produces dissociative (out-of-body) and hallucinogenic effects. These effects led to its early study in psychiatric research, as a pharmacological model of psychosis.

Depression, antidepressants, and treatment resistance. Major depressive disorder is defined as a depressed mood or a loss of pleasure in daily activities consistently for at least a 2-week period. There is a decline in social, occupational, or educational functioning. Depression remains one of the most significant causes of disability and lost productivity worldwide.

Medications, neuromodulatory treatments, psychotherapy, and social interventions potentially play an important role in the treatment of depression. Nevertheless, it is estimated that more than one-third of patients treated for depression will not adequately improve. Treatment-resistant depression (TRD) is generally diagnosed when a patient has not derived significant clinical benefit from two or more adequate trials of conventional antidepressant medications.

When selecting any psychiatric medication, patients and their prescribers must weigh the potential benefits versus risks. The great suffering of people with TRD can justify the use of more efficacious treatments that carry greater risk. Lesser-used antidepressants and combinations of medications may be employed. Electroconvulsive therapy (ECT) is currently the most effective, validated treatment for TRD.

A paradigm shift. Since the 1950s, when the serendipitous finding of the antidepressant effects of antituberculous drugs prompted a focus on the monoamine neurotransmitters, serotonin and norepinephrine, the formulary (list of prescribed drugs) for depression has steadily grown. However, until recently, novel antidepressant agents continued to focus on monoamine neurotransmitter systems without a significantly increased efficacy (albeit there was improved tolerability). Ketamine has now significantly broken that mold, leading to new frontiers in both the pathophysiology and treatment of depression.

Ketamine has distinguished itself from conventional antidepressants through its rapid effect (4 h versus 2 weeks), its efficacy (2 out of 3 patients respond versus 1 out of 2), and its hypothetical mechanism of action (glutamatergic systems versus monoaminergic systems). Unfortunately, the benefits are transient, tending to last less than a week. There is also the potential for its abuse and for a range of adverse effects. Therefore, clinical trials of ketamine have tended to study subjects with TRD; who have a favorable risk-to-benefit ratio.

Clinical trials. Inspired by growing laboratory evidence for the role of NMDA receptor antagonists in depression, the first placebo-controlled trial of ketamine for major depression was conducted at Yale University School of Medicine (New Haven, CT) in 2000. For a while, subsequent published evidence for ketamine's antidepressant effect in humans primarily consisted of case reports or non-placebo-controlled (open-label) studies, which were potentially subject to bias. It is only in the past few years that research groups [including those from the National Institute of Mental Health and the Icahn School of Medicine at Mount Sinai (formerly the Mount Sinai School of Medicine)] have added a handful of placebo-controlled trials, which more strongly support the clinical effects of ketamine. These trials have focused on a single, intravenous infusion (lasting 40 minutes) of racemic ketamine hydrochloride (at a dose of 0.5 mg/kg body weight). Clinical targets have mainly been subjects suffering from TRD (including those unresponsive to ECT), bipolar depression (major depression in the context of bipolar disorder), and suicidal ideation.

There has been a range of clinical evidence in humans to date, with the majority of patients being studied since 2011. A dozen case studies, totaling 16 patients, have reported a rapid antidepressant response with regimens ranging from one to six ketamine infusions. The durations of response range from 1 day to several weeks. Open-label studies more systematically illustrate the effects of ketamine, but they lack a placebo/control comparison. A dozen such studies, involving 120, mostly unmedicated, treatment-resistant depressed patients, most clearly support a rapid, transient response in approximately 40–60% of the patients, which occurred at 4 hours after a single 0.5 mg/kg intravenous infusion. Two further open-label studies have tested repeated dose regimens in a total of 34 subjects, showing a response rate of 50–71% and an extended median duration of effect of 18 days (after the last infusion). Controlled trials in this field have also been supportive of an effect, commonly comparing the response of ketamine and a nonpsychoactive, saline placebo within each subject. Six trials of this nature

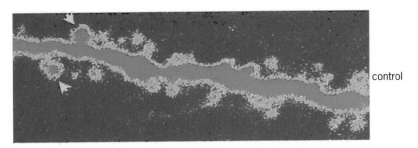

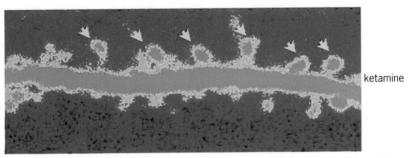

Fig. 2. Two-photon microscopic images of rodent neurons after treatment with ketamine (*bottom panel*), showing increased synaptic spine density (*yellow arrows*), as compared to controls (*top panel*). (*Figure courtesy of R. S. Duman*)

have been published, involving 81 depressed patients (including those with bipolar depression), and they have shown a peak response rate of 40–79% within 72 hours of a single intravenous administration. Finding a rigorous control condition is a challenge with ketamine, which has both an immediate intoxicating effect and a downstream antidepressant effect. Results of ongoing trials using a psychoactive control, midazolam, should be informative.

Attempts to extend the fleeting benefits of single-dose ketamine with an oral NMDA receptor antagonist, riluzole, proved ineffective. However, there is hope of sustaining ketamine's effect through repeated intravenous dosing regimens, which would be similar to the way that ECT is administered (three treatments per week with tapering frequency). Alternative routes of administration, particularly intramuscular, may also be of interest.

Another conceptually appealing application has been the use of ketamine as the anesthetic agent

for ECT treatments. This, in fact, has been long practiced when struggling to induce therapeutic seizures in a patient. Ketamine will not increase the seizure threshold as much as conventional anesthetics. Sadly, the evidence for a cumulative benefit of ECT and ketamine is not compelling. The mechanism of interaction of these two treatments remains unclear, and it is likely that ketamine's antidepressant effect is particular to the lower, subanesthetic dose range.

Although a compelling novel mechanism for treating depression with ketamine is elucidated, practicality and safety may constrain the clinical utility of ketamine to a jump start for other biological, psychological, and social interventions.

Mechanism of action. Recent investigations into the potential mechanism of action of ketamine have brought about a breakthrough, extending our understanding of the pathophysiology of depression as a whole. It has long been thought that chronic stress, associated with depression, may damage neurons (especially in the hippocampus and the rest of the limbic system), reducing the number of connections (synapses) between them. Laboratory studies in rodent models of depression show that a single ketamine dose induces a rapid behavioral response (equivalent to an antidepressant response), which is correlated with a rapid increase in the protein building blocks, number, and function of the synaptic connections in the prefrontal cortex (a brain region associated with mood and higher cognitive function) [**Fig. 2**].

By consolidating these various findings, investigators have proposed a model in which ketamine transiently reverses the synaptic deficits in the prefrontal cortex (**Fig. 3**). Brain-derived neurotrophic factor (BDNF) is a protein secreted to promote the normal growth of neurons and the formation of synapses (synaptogenesis). It is an important player for maintaining the balance of neurochemical factors necessary for synaptic function and regular mood (synaptic homeostasis). A component of this healthy equilibrium is the cycling of glutamate A1 (GluA1) receptors to and from the synapse, making the receptors functionally available. The depression

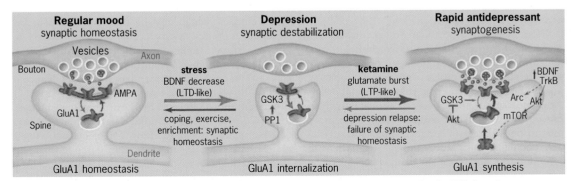

Fig. 3. The synaptogenic basis of depression and the action of ketamine. See text for more details. LTD, long-term depression. LTP, long-term potentiation. (*Figure courtesy of R. S. Duman and G. K. Aghajanian, Synaptic dysfunction in depression: Potential therapeutic targets, Science, 338(6103):68–72, 2012, DOI:10.1126/science.1222939*)

state is characterized by a disruption of the equilibrium (synaptic destabilization). GluA1 receptors are internalized and become unavailable at the synapse. Furthermore, BDNF levels were shown to be reduced in stress and depression, causing synapse loss and neuronal atrophy.

Ketamine's primary action is the blockade of NMDA receptors on inhibitory (GABAergic) interneurons, unleashing a burst of glutamate into the synapse. The glutamate acts on AMPA receptors (glutamate receptors that also bind the glutamate agonist AMPA) to signal a complex interplay of neurochemical factors (including BDNF, mTOR, TrKB, and Akt) [Fig. 3]. The end result is the restoration of GluA1 cycling and functional synaptic connections (synaptogenesis). Additionally, ketamine (through the inhibition of postsynaptic NMDA receptors) may deactivate an enzyme called eukaryotic elongation factor 2 kinase, disinhibiting the rapid production of synaptic proteins such as BDNF. BDNF levels are increased by a range of proven antidepressant treatments, including ketamine.

Vitally, this model accounts for the relative rapidity of ketamine's effects. Ketamine's eventual disinhibition of BDNF release (along with other essential components for functional synapses) utilizes an ever-ready, efficient physiological mechanism for generating synaptic connections. This stands in contrast to conventional antidepressants, which are thought to rely on more extensive changes in the neuronal architecture.

A word of caution. Reports of ketamine's potential clinical benefits must be interpreted with the utmost caution. Any therapeutic use of ketamine for depression is experimental, requires hospital monitoring, and has not received the general approval from the U.S. Food and Drug Administration. Furthermore, the unsupervised, nonprescription use of this drug is extremely dangerous and can be fatal. Acute adverse effects include increased heart rate and blood pressure, dangerous behavioral changes, and disturbing perceptual changes. Chronic side effects include ulcerative cystitis, cognitive and memory impairments, liver damage, structural brain damage, and drug abuse or dependence.

Future outlook. The past few years have brought a wave of laboratory studies and clinical trials that augment our theoretical and practical knowledge of ketamine and major depression. Work exploring ketamine's potential role in the reversal of depression-related synaptic loss shows great promise; however, both the pathophysiology of major depression and the mechanism of ketamine's action remain unconfirmed. In addition, there are a number of outstanding clinical questions: What is the optimal dose and route of administration? How is it possible to sustain the response? What are the long-term side effects of this treatment?

More than 50 clinical trials pertaining to ketamine and depression have been registered to date in the United States. Novel agents with similar glutamatergic properties are also being developed and stud-

ied with the hope of comparable benefits and attenuated side-effect profiles. Whether ketamine itself becomes established in general psychiatric practice remains to be seen. Its reported effects, thus far, have nevertheless garnered considerable attention and are catalyzing a paradigm shift in our understanding of, and approach to, major depression.

For background information *see* AFFECTIVE DISORDERS; BRAIN; MENTAL DISORDERS; NERVOUS SYSTEM (VERTEBRATE); NEUROBIOLOGY; NEURON; PHARMACOLOGY; PHARMACY; PSYCHOLOGY; PSYCHOPHARMACOLOGY; PSYCHOSOMATIC DISORDERS; PSYCHOTHERAPY; STRESS (PSYCHOLOGY); SYNAPTIC TRANSMISSION in the McGraw-Hill Encyclopedia of Science & Technology.   John Daniel Cahill

Bibliography. M. aan het Rot et al., Ketamine for depression: Where do we go from here?, *Biol. Psychiatry*, 72(7):537–547, 2012, DOI:10.1016/j.biopsych.2012.05.003; A. E. Autry et al., NMDA receptor blockade at rest triggers rapid behavioural antidepressant responses, *Nature*, 475(7354):91–95, 2011, DOI:10.1038/nature10130; R. M. Berman et al., Antidepressant effects of ketamine in depressed patients, *Biol. Psychiatry*, 47(4):351–354, 2000, DOI:10.1016/S0006-3223(99)00230-9; R. S. Duman and G. K. Aghajanian, Synaptic dysfunction in depression: Potential therapeutic targets, *Science*, 338(6103):68–72, 2012, DOI:10.1126/science.1222939; R. S. Duman et al., Signaling pathways underlying the rapid antidepressant actions of ketamine, *Neuropharmacology*, 62(1):35–41, 2012, DOI:10.1016/j.neuropharm.2011.08.044; E. T. Kavalali and L. M. Monteggia, Synaptic mechanisms underlying rapid antidepressant action of ketamine, *Am. J. Psychiatry*, 169(11):1150–1156, 2012, DOI:10.1176/appi.ajp.2012.12040531; J. W. Murrough et al., Rapid and longer-term antidepressant effects of repeated ketamine infusions in treatment-resistant major depression, *Biol. Psychiatry*, 2012, DOI:10.1016/j.biopsych.2012.06.022.

Laser Microjet technology

The water-jet-guided laser processing technology, Laser Microjet®, combines the advantages of laser material processing with water-jet technology. The capability of water jets to guide light was used already in musical fountains in the Renaissance. The light was coordinated with music to perform shows and surprise spectators. In 1993, at the Swiss Federal Institute of Lausanne this principle was applied to material treatment, yielding a radical new process for industrial applications.

In **Fig. 1** a schematic principle of the Laser Microjet is shown. A water jet emerges from a nozzle in a water chamber. Water in the chamber is under a pressure of 2–70 MPa (20–700 bar). The resulting water jet has a diameter between 25 and 100 μm, being approximately 83% of the nozzle diameter. In the top of the water chamber, which has a height of 300–500 μm, is a quartz window that is transparent

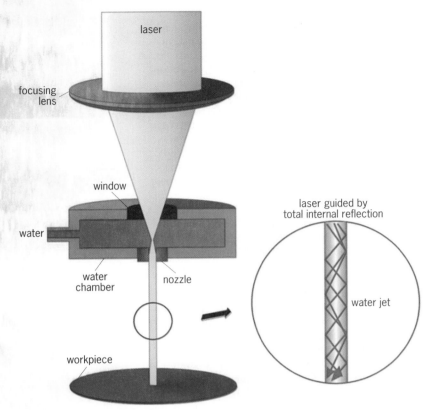

Fig. 1. Laser Microjet technology.

to laser light. The laser beam is thus focused inside the nozzle and transmitted by total reflection inside the water jet. Thus the water jet acts as a fluid optical waveguide of variable length that remains stable while processing the material. The material is only ablated by the laser, the force exerted by the water jet being small. The force on the workpiece is less than 80 mN at 10 MPa (100 bar) water pressure and 0.1 mm jet diameter; it therefore allows processing of very fine workpieces.

The Laser Microjet technology offers various interesting advantages in comparison with dry lasers. The water jet ensures the consistency of the spot diameter and enables a working distance equal to the coherence length of the water jet, which can be longer than 10 cm (it is typically 1000 times the nozzle diameter; see **Fig. 2**). Laser Microjet can be used effectively with complex profiles and contours where normal access would be impeded or impossible.

The water jet has other beneficial effects for precision cutting; for example, water cooling reduces the heat-affected zone and burrs on the back side of the sample. The water jet also removes the molten material, reducing contamination in the sample by leaving the sample clear of debris. All advantages are shown in more detail in **Fig. 3**. Therefore, more parallel cuts are achieved, the aspect ratio of the cut is increased, and chipping and microcracks are reduced.

These advantages result in more parallel cuts, increasing the aspect ratio of the cut and reducing chipping and microcracks. The lasers used in the Laser Microjet are typically solid state Nd:YAG and its frequency-doubled and frequency-tripled versions, with output powers from 50–400 W. Fiber lasers are also used. By using the much more affordable and reliable nanosecond lasers, results comparable to picosecond lasers can be obtained.

The Laser Microjet technique is used in industries that require precision micromachining for their products, such as the semiconductor market, the automotive industry (fuel-injection nozzles, catalytic converters, spark plugs), the watch industry (watch hands, precision metal parts), and recently the diamond industry.

Watch industry. The hands on today's watch mechanisms, both the pure mechanical and the battery-powered quartz-driven varieties, are precision mechanical parts that place demanding requirements on the manufacturers, especially for items destined for the luxury markets.

Modern watch hands are produced in a great variety of styles, qualities, and colors. High-grade parts are made of solid gold or tempered steel and have a polished pipe or head. Otherwise brass is generally used, and protected and decorated with either a thin galvanized layer of gold or rhodium or with some kind of lacquer. There are many different types and shapes of hands, each adapted to the use as well as to the aesthetics of the watch.

The base materials used for the watch industry are usually brass or steel. The thickness of the materials varies typically from 150–200 μm.

Manufacturing parts such as watch hands places very high demands on the producer. The delicate parts are made from material that is extremely susceptible to thermal effects possibly causing warping and mechanical deformation due to thinness. Postmanufacturing requirements for the removal of contaminants, deposition, or burrs should be avoided or minimized to avoid unnecessary loss in parts yield due to the added handling processes.

Cutting such fine mechanical parts with conventional dry nanosecond lasers would cause burrs due to heating effects and also deposition of ablated materials. The alternative method of stamping the parts from the sheet metal is inflexible (because stamp dies are required for each new or modified design) and leaves burrs, which require additional processing steps before the parts can be used.

As a "cold" and "wet" laser, the Laser Microjet is ideally suited for high-precision cutting of watch-hand materials. The Laser Microjet is a highly stable and reliable technology that can precisely cut complex-shaped metal pieces from brass or steel that have clean, sharp burr-free edges and a very low contamination level. Moreover, its high speed enables optimal production rates (5–10 mm/s for 200-μm-thick sheets) and leaves no mechanical or thermal deformation. Some examples are shown in **Fig. 4**. This eliminates the need for postprocessing,

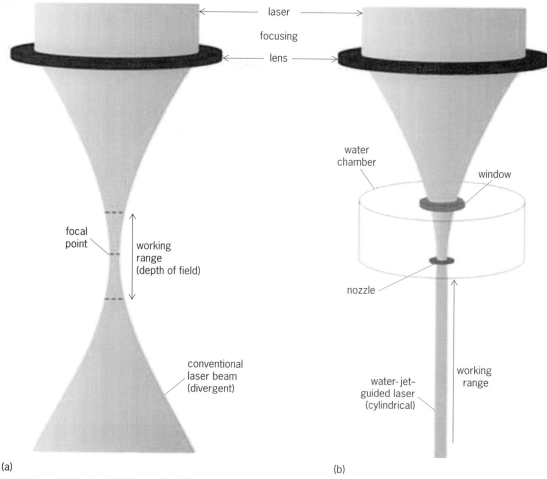

laser

focusing

lens

focal point

working range (depth of field)

conventional laser beam (divergent)

water chamber

window

nozzle

water-jet–guided laser (cylindrical)

working range

(a)

(b)

Fig. 2. Laser technology. (*a*) **Conventional laser.** (*b*) **Laser Microjet.**

as is required with traditional processes such as stamping.

The Laser Microjet can also process narrower kerf (cut) widths, resulting in increased parts count from the sheet material. Water-jet-guided laser technology is ideally suited for flexible and versatile production, such as for luxury products where small- to medium-sized series are required, without compromising quality. It is also a perfect marketing and prototyping tool, as customers can submit several designs, and have the cut pieces in hand for evaluation just minutes later.

Because of the significant advantages over other manufacturing methods, in particular the negligible thermal and mechanical stress as well as the burr- and contaminant-free parts produced, the Laser Microjet process is proving to be the ideal method for cutting watch-hand material today.

Diamond cutting. Diamond is the preferred precious stone for use in jewelry because of its hardness and its high dispersion of light. Finished diamonds are graded and certified as per the four Cs, which are carat, cut, color, and clarity.

The carat is the standard unit of measure in the diamond industry and one carat (= 200 mg) has 100

points. As the size of a diamond goes up, the price goes up exponentially. Prices can range from $2000 to $60,000 per carat. The two preferred cuts are round (Brilliant) and square (Princess). Other cuts are trapezoid (Baguette), octagon (Emerald), heart, pointed oval (Marquise), oval, pearl-shape, and rectangular.

The color of a diamond is graded from D to Z. Examples are: D, E, F (colorless, most valued) or S, T, U, V (light yellow).

The clarity of a diamond is graded from F (flawless, perfect), IF (internal flawless), VVSI (very, very small inclusions, 2 grades), VSI (very small inclusions, 2 grades), to SI (small inclusions, 3 grades) and I (imperfect, 3 grades).

The process of shaping a rough diamond into a polished gemstone is both an art and a science. The choice of cut is often decided by the original shape of the rough stone, location of the inclusions and flaws to be eliminated, the preservation of the weight, popularity of certain shapes among consumers, and many other considerations.

Even with modern techniques, the cutting and polishing of a raw diamond crystal into a finished stone always results in a dramatic loss of weight; rarely less

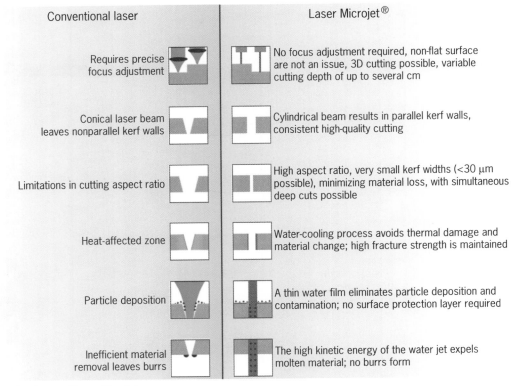

Fig. 3. Advantages of Laser Microjet.

Conventional laser		Laser Microjet®
Requires precise focus adjustment		No focus adjustment required, non-flat surface are not an issue, 3D cutting possible, variable cutting depth of up to several cm
Conical laser beam leaves nonparallel kerf walls		Cylindrical beam results in parallel kerf walls, consistent high-quality cutting
Limitations in cutting aspect ratio		High aspect ratio, very small kerf widths (<30 μm possible), minimizing material loss, with simultaneous deep cuts possible
Heat-affected zone		Water-cooling process avoids thermal damage and material change; high fracture strength is maintained
Particle deposition		A thin water film eliminates particle deposition and contamination; no surface protection layer required
Inefficient material removal leaves burrs		The high kinetic energy of the water jet expels molten material; no burrs form

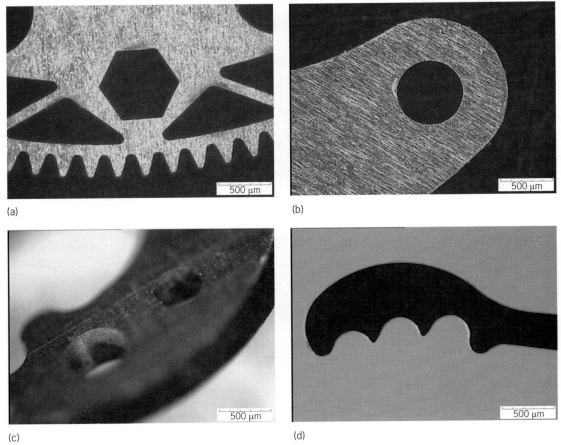

(a)

(b)

(c)

(d)

Fig. 4. Manufactured watch parts. (*a*) Brass. (*b*) Durnico steel. (*c*) Copper beryllium (CuBe). (*d*) Durnico steel.

than 50%. Within the Laser Microjet technology the weight loss during decreased width can be reduced efficiently. In **Fig. 5** a scheme for a diamond cut with the conventional laser and cut in the Laser Microjet is shown. With the conventional laser a weight loss of 2–4% occurs due to the V-shaped kerf width and postprocessing steps. The latter is not required for the Laser Microjet technology. The weight loss for this technology is between 0.5 and 1.5%. For both cutting technologies the weight loss depends on the size of the stone, the sawing depths, and the position of the kerf.

To optimize their yield from raw diamonds, manufacturers have invested heavily in equipment to plan how a diamond should be cut. Sophisticated diamond-planning systems, equipped with laser and video camera systems, enable the raw stone to be viewed three-dimensionally so that flaws such as inclusions can be detected and marked. Thereafter, the software proposes various cutting options and recommends an option with the highest yield in terms of market value. After the selection of a cutting option, a laser-marking machine marks a brown line along which the diamond must be cut.

After cutting, the diamond is shaped and polished with multiple facets in order to exhibit its brilliance. There are a number of factors to quantitatively judge the quality of cut: proportion, polish, symmetry, and the relative angles of various facets. A diamond with facets cut only a few degrees out of alignment can result in a poorly performing stone in terms of brilliance.

The advantages of this cutting process are clean, smooth, and parallel sliced surfaces, reduced weight loss, lower risk of breakage in so-called "stress" diamonds, and an increased cutting depth as compared to conventional lasers.

Currently, diamonds are cut using conventional infrared and green lasers, identified as "dry" lasers. The conical laser beams in these dry lasers have several limitations: they require a precise focal length, leave non-parallel walls, and have a small cutting aspect ratio. Furthermore, the increased heat leaves particles and reduces the luster in the cut surfaces. The greatest danger, however, is the risk of breakage in stress diamonds. In the case of low-quality diamonds, such breakage losses could average 1.7% over a period of a year.

The raw diamond stone sufficiently absorbs the 532-nm green wavelength of the Microjet laser. The diamond can be cut without any breakage and uneven surfaces. Non-parallel cutting surfaces are completely avoided. In addition, the cutting aspect ratio is such that large diamonds can be cut in a single operation instead of cutting from two sides, as is the case for conventional lasers.

Because of the huge improvement in the quality and productivity compared to conventional laser cutting, the Laser Microjet process is being considered as the preferred choice for cutting of diamonds.

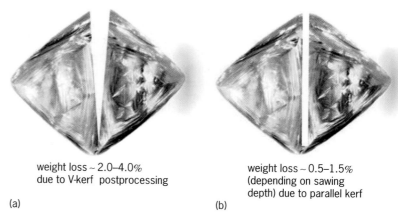

weight loss ~ 2.0–4.0% due to V-kerf postprocessing

weight loss ~ 0.5–1.5% (depending on sawing depth) due to parallel kerf

(a)   (b)

Fig. 5. Cut diamond. (a) Conventional laser. (b) Laser Microjet.

For background information *see* DIAMOND; GEM; LASER; WATCH in the McGraw-Hill Encyclopedia of Science & Technology.

Pablo Moreno; Bernold Richerzhagen

Bibliography. B. Richerzhagen, Industrial applications of the water jet guided laser, *Ind Laser User*, 28:28–30, 2002; B. Richerzhagen et al., Water jet guided laser cutting: A powerful hybrid technology for fine cutting and grooving, in *Advanced Laser Applications Conference & Exposition: ALAC 2004*, Ann Arbor, MI, September 20–22, 2004; J. A. Porter, Y. A. Louhisalmi, and J. A. Karjalainen, Cutting thin sheet metal with a water jet guided laser using various cutting distances, feed speeds and angles of incidence, *Int J Adv Manuf Tech*, 33:961–967, 2007, DOI:10.1007/s00170-006-0521-7.

LED roadway lighting: the Los Angeles conversion project

LED (light-emitting diode) roadway lighting has many advantages over traditional forms, including greater energy efficiency, increased visibility, better lighting uniformity, and longer life. The roadside lighting conversion project now in progress in Los Angeles is the largest of its type in the world.

Background. The City of Los Angeles owns the second-largest municipal street lighting system in the United States with over 210,000 streetlights, including more than 400 distinct fixtures styles. Before the LED conversion, each year these streetlights consumed approximately 197,000,000 kWh of electricity. The system is operated and maintained by the Bureau of Street Lighting.

The Los Angeles Bureau of Street Lighting pays a variable rate per fixture to the Los Angeles Department of Water and Power, the municipal utility company. Rates for streetlight fixtures are calculated by the Department of Water and Power based on the real kWh use of the fixtures. Annually, the Bureau of Street Lighting's electricity bill totals approximately $15 million, or nearly 29% of the Bureau's $52 million operating budget. Funding for the bureau is provided primarily by the Street Lighting Maintenance Assessment Fund (SLMAF), a yearly assessment paid by city residents for the operation and maintenance of the Los Angeles street lighting system; the SLMAF generates $42 million per year for the Bureau of Street Lighting.

Project description. On February 16, 2009, former President Bill Clinton and Los Angeles Mayor Antonio Villaraigosa announced a major public works project to retrofit 140,000 modern "cobrahead" fixtures with energy-efficient LED fixtures. The Los Angeles LED Conversion Project, launched in the 4th quarter of 2009, was the result of a collaborative effort between the Los Angeles Bureau of Street Lighting, the Los Angeles Mayor's Office, the Los Angeles Department of Water and Power, and the Clinton Climate Initiative. The $57 million retrofit, scheduled to be completed within 4 years of its launch date.

The LED Conversion Project has been divided into four discrete yearlong phases. For the first three phases of the project, through June 2012, the deployment and installation of the LED fixtures was entirely focused on local/residential streets. With roadways ranging from 30–40 ft (9–12 m) in width, the required illumination levels range from 0.4 to 0.9 foot-candles (fc). To achieve the lower level requirements, fixtures with 20 LEDs (37 W) were used. For wider streets and higher pedestrian activity, fixtures with 40 LEDs (95 W) were installed. All LED fixtures have variable drivers with the ability to increase or decrease the drive current, which in turns affects the lumen output of the fixture. Through actual field measurements of illuminance, the LED retrofits were able to achieve foot-candle levels comparable to old technology (100-W high-pressure sodium lights, HPS) and in some cases surpass previous lighting levels. By June 2012, 84,410 LED fixtures were installed on residential streets.

Beginning in July 2012, the deployment and installation shifted to major and collector streets throughout the city. The existing streetlights on major streets range from 200-W HPS to 400-W HPS. For this type of roadway configuration, which can have widths of up to 100 ft (30 m), the required illumination levels range from 0.9 to 1.7 fc, and up to 3.4 fc for some intersections. Depending on the type of system (that is, staggered, opposite, and so on) and existing mounting height, replacement LED fixtures contained from 60 (136 W) to 160 (275 W) LEDs. The achieved lighting levels were comparable to existing levels based on the Illuminating Engineering Society of North America (IESNA) RP8 specification, which recommends lighting levels and uniformity ratios appropriate to roadway classification and pedestrian use.

As LED technology changes every 6 months, one challenge for the bureau has been to adopt design standards for new LED street lighting projects. As the technology evolves and products become more efficient, the bureau works closely with LED manufacturers to specify and develop the LED fixtures that will provide the illumination requirements while increasing efficacy (lumens per watt) and reducing overall production costs.

Energy and cost. The Bureau of Street Lighting is in charge of maintenance and operation of the entire street lighting system in the City of Los Angeles. The energy provided by the Department of Water and Power comes from a variety of sources including 26% from natural-gas generation stations, 52% from coal-burning power plants, 11% from nuclear power plants, and 11% from hydropower and other sources.

For the LED Conversion Project, the energy and cost savings have been quantified in the **table** and are represented by the inauguration dates for each phase.

The Bureau of Street Lighting worked in partnership with the Clinton Climate Initiative to successfully create economic and financial analyses for the LED Conversion Project, taking into account the total light fixtures to be replaced, cost per fixture for new equipment, cost of operation and maintenance per fixture, and estimated life expectancy of the fixtures. In addition, LED fixtures are manufactured without hazardous materials, which are harmful to the environment. Through extensive product testing and evaluation it was concluded that LED lighting could provide energy savings of more than 50%. Based on manufacturing tests, the life expectancy of LED fixtures totals more than 70,000 h, equivalent

---

LED Conversion Project energy and cost savings

Phase I
September 2009–June 2010

Total Units Installed	19,953
Energy Cost Savings[†]	$655,071
Energy Use Savings[*]	7.41 GWh
CO_2 Emissions Savings[*]	4,384 MT

Phase II
July 2010–June 2011

Total Units Installed	30,108
Energy Cost Savings[†]	$1.189M
Energy Use Savings[*]	13.45 GWh
CO_2 Emissions Savings[*]	7,951 MT

Phase III
July 2011–June 2012

Total Units Installed	36,991
Energy Cost Savings[†]	$1.712M
Energy Use Savings[*]	19.37 GWh
CO_2 Emissions Savings[*]	11,465 MT

Phase IV
July 2012–Present

Total Units Installed	47,031
Energy Cost Savings[†]	$3.18M
Energy Use Savings[*]	35.38 GWh
CO_2 Emissions Savings[*]	20,919 MT

[†] Energy Cost Savings reflected in US dollars.
[*] Energy use and CO_2 emissions savings compared to traditional (HPS) installations.
  1 GWh = 1 million kWh; 1 MT = 1000 kg

Conventional street lighting | LED street lighting

(a)

(b)

(c)

Conventional versus LED street lighting in Los Angeles, California. (*a*) 6th Street Bridge. (*b*) Hoover Street. (*c*) Ocean Front Walk, Venice.

to 12–15 years, although the manufacturers do not warranty the fixture to last that long. The Bureau of Street Lighting in Los Angeles specifies a warranty that provides for the full replacement of the luminaire due to any failure for 6 years. The warranty provides for the repair or replacement of defective electrical parts (including light source and power supplies/drivers) for a minimum of eight years from the date of purchase. Reduction of lighting output by more than 10% of the LED package within 6 years constitutes luminaire failure. The approved compa-

nies currently being used by the bureau for LED replacement include Beta LED, Cree, Leotek Electronics, and Hadco.

The bureau also partnered with the Department of Water and Power to secure a 7-year, $40 million loan at 5.25% interest that is being repaid through energy and maintenance savings over the loan term. Additionally, the bureau is contributing $3.5 million directly from the Street Lighting Maintenance Assessment Fund. Furthermore, the Department of Water and Power is providing a rebate based on the kWh reduced by the project totaling $16.3 million.

Impact and project evaluation. As of July 1, 2013 the bureau had installed 140,000 LED fixtures. The total nominal wattage from all LED fixtures is approximately 11,000 kW and the City of Los Angeles will save an estimated $10 million a year in energy and maintenance. In addition, the 64% energy savings reduces CO_2 emissions by approximately 46,000 metric tons. For the environment, this reduction translates to 9500 cars off the road and enough energy to provide electricity for 6800 homes.

Aside from the environmental impact, light pollution will be decreased greatly as the LED fixtures are able to direct the light efficiently onto the roadways and sidewalks. The Bureau of Street Lighting has received favorable feedback from city residents on the initial phases of the project. Residents have reported improved visibility from the broad spectrum LED light source. In addition, the Los Angeles Police Department has stated that safety has improved across neighborhoods in the city, and the increased lighting has assisted helicopter operators during nighttime operations (see **illustration**).

The economic impact of the project can be readily measured as the overall energy consumption decreases as the LED installations increase. Currently, the Bureau of Street Lighting is saving over $6.7 million in energy costs. Furthermore, the reduction in maintenance and relamping costs adds to the monetary savings. The LED Conversion Project has created an unforeseen opportunity where the Bureau has been able to auction removed street lighting units (as opposed to simply recycling them). The energy savings, combined with the continued fall in the price of LED fixtures in the U.S. market means that upon completion, the project payback will be notably less than the 7 years originally anticipated.

Even though the LED Conversion Project focused on cobrahead streetlight replacement, it is only the beginning of a broader plan to convert every streetlight to energy saving technologies, such as LEDs. The bureau is formulating a plan to replace other styles of lighting fixtures over the next 5 to 10 years. As technology advances, more opportunities will become available and suitable for ornamental and historic lighting.

Given the size and magnitude of the project, both economic and environmental, the bureau sees this project as an opportunity to share the results and benefits with constituents in the City of Los Angeles. The bureau has also partnered with the Mayor's and Council offices to bring this information to schools and to children throughout the city to show how a simple idea can produce results that affect everyone, including future generations.

For background information *see* GLOBAL CLIMATE CHANGE; LIGHT-EMITTING DIODE; LIGHT PANEL; LUMINOUS EFFICACY; SODIUM-VAPOR LAMP; TRANSPORTATION ENGINEERING in the McGraw-Hill Encyclopedia of Science & Technology.   Ed Ebrahimian

Lymphangiogenesis

Lymphangiogenesis is the formation of new lymphatic vessels that are part of the lymphatic system carrying the fluid called lymph. Lymphatic vessels regulate tissue homeostasis, immune cell trafficking, and the absorption of dietary fats. Lymphangiogenesis occurs primarily during embryonic development. In adults, this biological process is closely associated with several pathologies, including lymphedema (a type of tissue swelling), cancer, chronic inflammation, autoimmunity, and transplant rejection. The recent explosion of interest in lymphangiogenesis is the result of its involvement in transplant rejection and tumor metastasis, as well as the identification of specific lymphatic markers that have paved the way for new research. Nowadays, lymphangiogenesis is clearly viewed as a therapeutic target. This paper will provide an overview of the lymphatic functions, the factors governing lymphangiogenesis processes, and the therapies being developed to target pathological lymphangiogenesis.

Lymphatic system. The lymphatic system, described by Gasparo Aselli in 1627 as "milky veins," is a one-way vascular network that works in parallel with the blood circulation. It drains most of the body's organs, with the exceptions of bone marrow, the retina, the central nervous system, and some avascular tissues (the cornea, cartilage, hair, nails, and the epidermis). In tissues, small arteries release large amounts of liquid and macromolecules (plasma) because of the blood pressure. This fluid, which spreads (extravasates) into the interstices of all body tissues (that is, the interstitial space), is then absorbed back by highly permeable lymphatic capillaries, which are blind-end vessels formed by a single layer of lymphatic endothelial cells (LECs) [**Fig. 1**]. Therefore, lymphatic capillaries constitute the absorptive part of the lymphatic vascular tree. Once inside the lymphatic vessels, the absorbed interstitial fluid, cells, and macromolecules are collectively called lymph. The lymph moves from the lymphatic capillaries into collecting lymphatics covered by smooth muscle cells and finally returns back to the blood circulation via the subclavian veins (a pair of large veins that return blood from the arms and upper extremities to the heart) [Fig. 1]. The lymph is filtered by lymph nodes (organs that are localized all along the lymphatic vessels) and returns into the blood circulation via the thoracic duct and the right lymphatic duct, draining into the left and right subclavian veins, respectively. In healthy adults, 1–2 L of interstitial fluid are drained every day into the venous circulation. In addition to draining fluid, the lymphatic system plays an important role in immune defenses by transporting extravasated leukocytes, antigens, and activated antigen-presenting cells to the lymph nodes, where an immune response is triggered. The lymphatic system also contributes to the absorption and transport of intestinal fatty acids and fats.

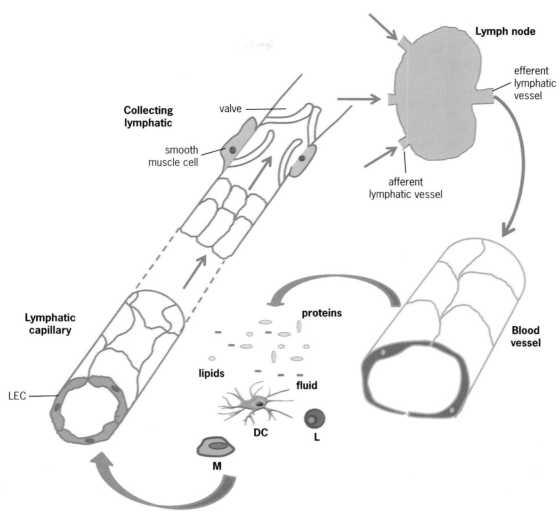

Fig. 1. Schematic overview of the function of the lymphatic vasculature. Fluid containing proteins, lipids, and other solutes leaks out from blood vessels, percolates through the interstitial tissue, and then is absorbed back by highly permeable lymphatic capillaries, which are blind-end vessels formed by a single layer of lymphatic endothelial cells (LECs). In addition to draining fluid, the lymphatic system plays an important role in immune defenses by transporting immune cells such as lymphocytes (L), macrophages (M), and dendritic cells (DC). Once inside the lymphatic vessels, the absorbed interstitial fluid, cells, and macromolecules are collectively called lymph. The lymph moves from the lymphatic capillaries to collecting lymphatics covered by contractile smooth muscle cells that allow fluid propulsion. The collecting lymphatics also contain valves to prevent backflow. The lymph then enters the lymph nodes by afferent lymphatic vessels, which are present throughout all parts of the periphery of the lymph nodes. Once filtered by the lymph nodes, the lymph exits by efferent lymphatic vessels and returns to the blood circulation.

Because of its numerous roles, several pathologies are associated with the lymphatic system (**Fig. 2**). Dysfunction in the lymphatic system because of abnormal vessel development (often associated with genetic disorders), obstruction of the lymphatic vessels, or lymph node removal following surgery causes the localized accumulation of fluid and proteins in the interstitium (interstitial tissue), which is characteristic of lymphedema. Unfortunately, lymphedemas are usually progressive and lifelong pathological disorders, and curative treatments are not available yet. According to the mechanism of pathogenesis, lymphedemas are classified into primary (congenital) or secondary (acquired) lymphedemas. Lymphangiogenesis also plays a key role in several disorders. Because of its activation in an inflammatory environment and its crucial role in the induction of immune responses, lymphangiogenesis is a key mediator of graft rejection. Indeed, lymphatic vessels transport antigen-presenting cells from the graft to the regional lymph nodes, where they initiate a T cell (immune cell) response. Once activated, T cells leave the lymph nodes and infiltrate the graft via blood vessels, where they mediate the transplant rejection. Lymphangiogenesis occurs also during tumor development, allowing tumor cells to enter the lymphatic system, metastasize to lymph nodes, migrate into the bloodstream, and disseminate through other organs. For these reasons, lymph node metastasis leads to poor patient survival.

Development of lymphatic vessels. Lymphangiogenesis is primarily an embryonic event. During embryogenesis, the lymphatic vessels develop after the establishment of the blood circulation, at around

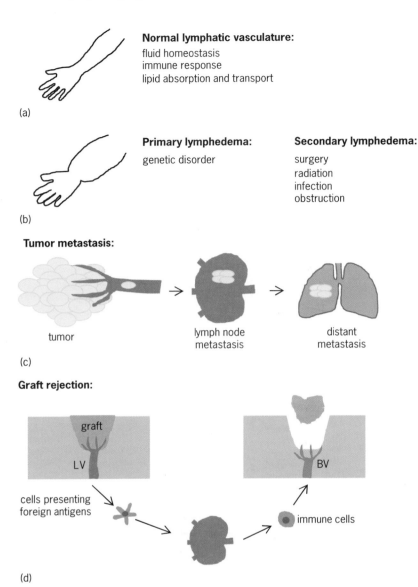

Normal lymphatic vasculature:

fluid homeostasis
immune response
lipid absorption and transport

(a)

Primary lymphedema:

genetic disorder

Secondary lymphedema:

surgery
radiation
infection
obstruction

(b)

Tumor metastasis:

tumor → lymph node metastasis → distant metastasis

(c)

Graft rejection:

graft

LV

cells presenting foreign antigens

BV

immune cells

(d)

Fig. 2. Common pathologies associated with the lymphatic system. (*a*) The main function of lymphatic vessels is to regulate fluid homeostasis. It is also implicated in immune defenses by transporting leukocytes, antigens, and activated antigen-presenting cells to the lymph nodes. In addition to these functions, the lymphatic system contributes to the absorption and transport of intestinal fatty acids and fats. (*b*) Malformation of or damage to the lymphatic vasculature leads to a type of tissue swelling called lymphedema. Lymphedema can occur on its own (primary or hereditary lymphedema), or it can be induced (secondary lymphedema) by surgery, radiation, injury, or pathological conditions (infection). Secondary lymphedema is the most common form. (*c*) The lymphatic vasculature is one of the key mediators of tumor metastasis. Indeed, lymphatic vessels act as a conduit for tumor cells, allowing them to migrate toward regional lymph nodes and farther to the bloodstream and other organs, leading to distant metastasis. (*d*) Because of its implication in the immune defenses, the lymphatic system also plays a role in graft rejection. Shortly after transplantation, antigen-presenting cells migrate out of the graft through lymphatic vessels (LV) and infiltrate the recipient's draining lymph nodes, where they present the donor antigens and activate T cells (immune cells). Activated T cells leave the lymph nodes and infiltrate the graft via blood vessels (BV), where they mediate the graft rejection.

in a subpopulation of blood endothelial cells in the cardinal vein is necessary for LEC progenitors to bud off from the vein. The prox-1 expression by LECs is also mandatory for the maintenance of LEC identity. The expression of prox-1 in LEC precursors induces the expression of the vascular endothelial growth factor receptor 3 (VEGFR-3) at the LEC cell surface, allowing LEC sprouting and migration from the cardinal vein along a vascular endothelial growth factor C (VEGF-C) gradient. The LEC migration leads to the formation of primitive jugular lymph sacs. Further lymph sacs are formed near major veins, and a lymphatic plexus (network) develops from these lymph sacs. The lymph nodes will develop in those regions occupied by the lymph sacs. The primary lymphatic network is further remodeled into a mature lymphatic system composed of capillaries and collecting vessels.

Adult lymphangiogenesis is closely associated with tissue inflammation and occurs in wound healing, chronic inflammation, autoimmunity, allograft rejection, and tumor metastasis. In adults, newly formed lymphatic vessels arise mainly from the preexisting lymphatic vasculature. However, several studies have shown that, during pathological conditions, bone marrow–derived cells can transdifferentiate into LECs that are incorporated into the existing lymphatic vasculature. The lymphangiogenesis processes in adults are similar to those observed in embryos (that is, sprouting from a preexisting lymphatic vessel, proliferation, and migration). In a similar manner to developmental lymphangiogenesis, prox-1 is necessary to induce LEC sprouting from the preexisting lymphatic vessels in inflammation-induced lymphangiogenesis. The overexpression of prox-1 induced by small cell-signaling proteins (inflammatory cytokines) induces the upregulation of VEGFR-3, allowing the LECs to migrate. Therefore, prox-1 expression precedes VEGFR-3 upregulation by 2–3 days, and elevation of both proteins is mandatory to induce lymphangiogenesis.

Factors governing lymphangiogenesis. Lymphangiogenesis is orchestrated by a tightly controlled balance between factors that stimulate or inhibit LEC activities; these factors are named prolymphangiogenic and antilymphangiogenic factors, respectively. The most potent prolymphangiogenic factors belong to a family of growth factors (the VEGFs) controlling the functions and survival of vascular cells. Members of the VEGF family include VEGF-A, VEGF-B, VEGF-C, VEGF-D, and placental growth factor (PlGF), but only VEGF-A, VEGF-C, and VEGF-D are involved in lymphangiogenesis. Several other growth factors have also been identified as inducers of lymphangiogenesis, including fibroblast growth factor-2 (FGF-2) and angiopoietin-1 and angiopoietin-2 (see **table**). Prolymphangiogenic growth factors are produced by different cell types to induce the growth of new lymphatic capillaries. Prolymphangiogenic factors also can be produced by tumor cells themselves. In addition, macrophages (white blood cells present at inflammatory sites or in tumors) are

embryonic week 6–7 in humans and at embryonic day 10 in mice. The venous origin of the lymphatic system, proposed by Florence Rena Sabin in the early part of the twentieth century, has been confirmed in mice. The anterior cardinal vein has been identified as the first source of LEC precursors (**Fig. 3**). The expression of the prospero homeobox 1 (prox-1) gene

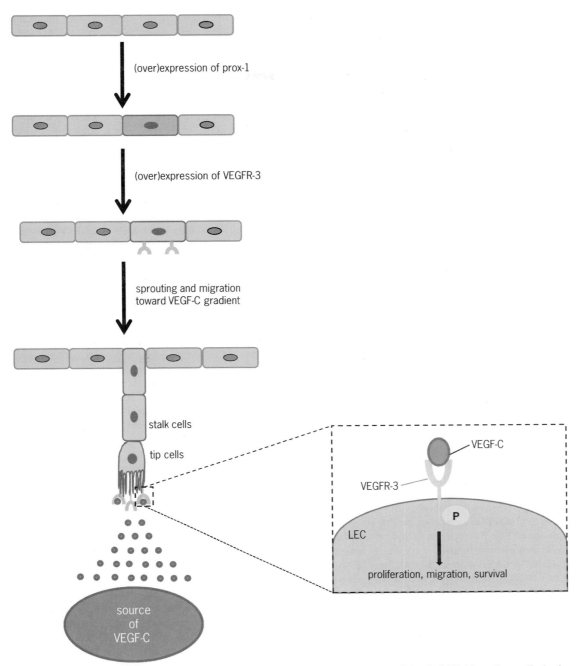

Fig. 3. Different steps of the lymphangiogenic process. Sprouting of lymphatic endothelial cells (LECs) from the cardinal vein (in embryos) or from a preexisting lymphatic vessel (in adults) requires that a subset of cells express (in embryos) or overexpress (in adults) prox-1. The prox-1 positively regulates VEGFR-3 expression at the cell surface, allowing LECs to sprout and migrate toward a VEGF-C gradient. The tip cell, characterized by cellular extensions (filopodia), senses the microenvironment and guides the neolymphatic vessel toward the source of the VEGF-C. Stalk cells behind the tip cell have a high proliferative rate, allowing vessel elongation. The binding of VEGF-C to VEGFR-3 leads to VEGFR-3 phosphorylation (P) and activation (rectangle on the right). Once activated, the VEGFR-3 induces a cascade of intracellular signals, leading to cell migration, proliferation, and survival.

viewed as important sources of lymphangiogenic factors. All members of the VEGF family stimulate cellular responses by binding to receptors (VEGFRs) expressed at the cell surface. Among the three VEGFRs, only VEGFR-2 and VEGFR-3 are expressed by LECs in adults. VEGFR-2 is activated primarily by VEGF-A, but cleaved forms of VEGF-C and VEGF-D may also activate this receptor. VEGFR-3 is activated by VEGF-C and VEGF-D (see table). These receptors are anchored to the LEC cell surface via a transmembrane domain, and binding of prolymphangiogenic factors to their receptors induces their activation through the addition of a phosphate group (phosphorylation) to the intracellular part (Fig. 3). Receptor activation induces a cascade of intracellular signals leading to cell migration, proliferation, and

---

Main prolymphangiogenic growth factors and their receptors

Prolymphangiogenic receptors	Prolymphangiogenic factors
VEGFR-2	VEGF-A Proteolytically processed VEGF-C Proteolytically processed VEGF-D
VEGFR-3	VEGF-C, VEGF-D
FGFR-1	FGF-2
FGFR-3	FGF-2
Tie-2	Ang-1, Ang-2
Insulin-like growth factor receptor	Insulin-like growth factor-1, -2
PDGFR	PDGF-BB

Abbreviations: Ang, angiopoietin; FGF, fibroblast growth factor; FGFR, fibroblast growth factor receptor; PDGF-BB, platelet-derived growth factor BB; PDGFR, platelet-derived growth factor receptor; VEGF, vascular endothelial growth factor; VEGFR, vascular endothelial growth factor receptor.

---

survival. Among the receptors of the prolymphangiogenic factors, VEGFR-3 is the most studied, and it is prominently expressed by specialized LECs called tip cells (Fig. 3). Tip cells are present at the leading edge of lymphatic sprouts and are characterized by small membranous extensions (filopodia) that sense the microenvironment. By expressing VEGFR-3, tip cells are guided toward the source of the VEGF-C and VEGF-D. Stalk cells, which follow the tip cells, have a high proliferative capacity and contribute to the vessel elongation. This differentiation of LECs into stalk cells or tip cells explains the directional migration against a gradient of a lymphangiogenic factor.

During lymphangiogenesis, the migrating LECs have to progress in a complex meshwork of proteins (an interstitial matrix) composed of fibrillar collagens and glycoproteins (for example, fibronectin). Because a dense matrix inhibits the LEC invasion, LECs need to degrade the matrix in order to create the space through which the cells can move. Matrix degradation can be achieved by proteases (protein-digesting enzymes) such as matrix metalloproteinases (MMPs). MMPs are zinc-dependent endopeptidases that degrade various extracellular matrix components. There are 24 human MMPs classified according to their structure and substrate specificity. Interstitial collagen is cleaved by several collagenases (MMP-1, MMP-2, MMP-8, MMP-13, and MMP-14). Up to now, only MMP-2 has been described to play a role in lymphangiogenesis by degrading collagen and allowing cell migration. Mice lacking MMP-2 do not show any physiological abnormalities, but they show defects in the lymphangiogenesis induced by inflammation. By degrading the extracellular matrix, proteases also generate fragments that can play a role in lymphangiogenesis. The best example is endostatin or neostatin-7 (fragments of collagen XVIII), which inhibits lymphangiogenesis. Once the matrix is degraded, LECs can move by adhering to the remodeled matrix. The main receptors involved in the LEC migration are integrins, which are cell surface adhesion receptors that establish a link between the cytoskeleton and the matrix component. Cells can move because of a cyclic process that involves cell adhesion at the leading edge of the cells, which provides traction; cell contraction at the cell body; and detachment at the trailing edge, which allows forward movement. Integrins mediate both the adhesion at the leading edge and the de-adhesion at the trailing edge, and both are essential for efficient cell migration. The main integrins involved in lymphangiogenesis are $\alpha 9\beta 1$, $\alpha 4\beta 1$, and $\alpha 5\beta 1$. Mice lacking the integrin $\alpha 9\beta 1$ die shortly after birth because of a lymphatic defect. Moreover, integrins not only play a role in cellular adhesion and migration, but they contribute to the stimulation of VEGFR-3 by VEGF-C. Indeed, integrins $\alpha 9\beta 1$ and $\alpha 5\beta 1$ are also found to interact with VEGFR-3 and play a role in the directional migration toward VEGF-C.

Targeting lymphangiogenesis. Several studies are aimed at identifying therapeutic targets that inhibit lymphangiogenesis to prevent tumor spread or graft rejection. Most preclinical studies have focused on the VEGF-C/VEGFR-3 pathway in order to impair receptor activation and then reduce LEC sprouting and migration toward tumor cells or a transplant. A common strategy is to prevent the binding of VEGF-A, VEGF-C, or VEGF-D to their respective receptors. Neutralizing antibodies against VEGF or VEGFR have been tested. Neutralizing antibodies are antibodies directed against a specific antigen, thus blocking its activity. Neutralizing antibodies trap a specific target (VEGF or VEGFR) and prevent the VEGF binding to their receptors. Because the VEGFRs are anchored to the surface of LECs, another approach is to block the VEGFR activation by using a soluble form of VEGFR (sVEGFR) that clears the VEGF from the extracellular milieu. Interestingly, soluble forms of the VEGFRs are naturally found in the human body. For example, sVEGFR-3 is expressed by epithelial cells in the cornea (a transparent tissue located at the most anterior part of the eye) to maintain lymphatic avascularity. Indeed, the cornea is devoid of blood and lymphatic vessels to ensure an optimal vision. However, after an injury or a corneal transplantation, sVEGFR-3 levels decrease, whereas the expression of VEGFR-3 levels increases, stimulating lymphangiogenesis. Another strategy that interferes with lymphangiogenesis is to inhibit the phosphorylation of VEGFRs by using chemical inhibitors. It is important to note that these inhibitors are broad-spectrum inhibitors that target multiple growth factor receptors. An additional strategy is to selectively downregulate the expression of the VEGF or VEGFR by using a small interference RNA (siRNA) approach. In this case, the siRNA inhibits gene expression by causing the degradation of a specific messenger RNA (mRNA) whose sequence is complementary to the siRNA. All strategies targeting the VEGF/VEGFR pathway decrease tumor or inflammatory lymphangiogenesis, but do not completely inhibit it. This indicates that additional pathways should be targeted for more efficient antilymphangiogenic therapies. Unwanted side effects also have to be considered because lymphangiogenesis is induced after wounding, and the inhibition of lymphangiogenesis may interfere with tissue regeneration.

Furthermore, some preclinical studies have aimed at promoting lymphangiogenesis in order to cure lymphedema. Lymphedema is most commonly caused by the removal or damage of lymph nodes, and it is one of the most common side effects of breast cancer treatments. There is no cure available to treat lymphedema. However, the overexpression of VEGF-C or VEGF-D in preclinical animal models of lymphedema leads to the formation of new lymphatic capillaries and reduced edema. These results look encouraging, and the process could decrease the discomfort resulting from lymph node resection. To date, lymph node transplantations have been performed following breast cancer surgery, but the transplanted lymph nodes are incorporated into the existing lymphatic vasculature at low frequency. In a mouse model, the overexpression of VEGF-C in lymph nodes improves the success rate of the lymph node transplantation. However, it is important to remember that VEGF-C promotes the lymphatic metastasis of tumor cells, and an overexpression of VEGF-C can lead to an increase of metastasis if some tumor cells are still present.

Despite recent advances in the understanding of lymphangiogenic processes, few factors (except those involved in the VEGF-C/VEGF-D/VEGFR-3 signaling system) have been identified. Identification of new factors involved in the growth and development of the lymphatic vasculature is mandatory to delineate more approaches for the molecular manipulation of lymphatic vessels. Regarding lymphatic vessels as a therapeutic target, important questions remain to be answered, especially in terms of treatment efficacy and patient safety.

For background information *see* CANCER (MEDICINE); CLINICAL IMMUNOLOGY; DISEASE; EDEMA; GROWTH FACTOR; IMMUNOLOGY; INFLAMMATION; LYMPHATIC SYSTEM; NEUTRALIZING ANTIBODY; TRANSPLANTATION BIOLOGY; VASCULAR DISORDERS in the McGraw-Hill Encyclopedia of Science & Technology.   Jenny Paupert; Agnès Noël

Bibliography. Y. Cao, Why and how do tumors stimulate lymphangiogenesis?, *Lymphat. Res. Biol.*, 6(3/4):145–148, 2008, DOI:10.1089/lrb.2008.1007; M. Lähteenvuo et al., Growth factor therapy and autologous lymph node transfer in lymphedema, *Circulation*, 123(6):613–620, 2011, DOI:10.1161/CIRCULATIONAHA.110.965384; A. W. Lund and M. A. Swartz, Role of lymphatic vessels in tumor immunity: Passive conduits or active participants?, *J. Mammary Gland Biol. Neoplasia*, 15(3):341–352, 2010, DOI:10.1007/s10911-010-9193-x; C. Norrmén et al., Biological basis of therapeutic lymphangiogenesis, *Circulation*, 123(12):1335–1351, 2011, DOI:10.1161/CIRCULATIONAHA.107.704098; J. Paupert, N. E. Sounni, and A. Noël, Lymphangiogenesis in post-natal tissue remodeling: Lymphatic endothelial cell connection with its environment, *Mol. Aspects Med.*, 32(2):146–158, 2011, DOI:10.1016/j.mam.2011.04.002.

Manipulation of heat flow

Artificial materials engineered to exhibit properties that do not typically exist in nature are often called metamaterials, and these unique materials have attracted a significant amount of scientific interest in recent years. Just as conventional materials owe their properties to the average response from an ensemble of atoms and molecules, in "artificial" materials, each structural unit plays the role of an atom. The material properties are controlled not only by what elements are used and their individual properties, but also by the way they are arranged collectively in lattice-like geometrical patterns with prescribed spatial variations. This immense flexibility is one of the main reasons why material engineering has become such an explosive catalyst in so many scientific disciplines. For example, metamaterials applied to the manipulation of electromagnetic waves have demonstrated some counterintuitive concepts such as a negative index of refraction, which allows light to bend at the interface of materials in a direction opposite to what you would observe from any ordinary materials. The concept of artificial material engineering has extended beyond conventional material science and it has now started to be applied to the manipulation of heat flow.

Heat conduction. Heat current is everywhere. Heat flows wherever there is a temperature difference, and as we are very much aware from our daily lives, it flows from hot to cold. Heat conduction is a diffusive energy flow and is not a wave phenomenon governed by the so-called wave equation. In that sense, heat conduction differs significantly from energy propagation in the form of waves exemplified by light and sound. However, some clear analogies and common properties exist among these disparate physical phenomena. One such example is that it is possible to manipulate their flow path with anisotropic material properties. An anisotropic property here refers to a physical property that has a different value when measured in a different direction. To control heat flux in unconventional manners, for example, one needs to prescribe various structural elements that play the role of atoms and design overall structures that exhibit different thermal conductivities at the same point in space if measured in different directions. Thermal conductivity has to be not only spatially varying, but also direction dependent. Mathematically that means that the conductivity of the material needs to be a tensor, not a scalar.

Heat flux manipulation. Anisotropic materials do exist in nature. For example, quartz and graphite can exhibit direction-dependent thermal conductivities due to their inherent internal structures. It would be ideal to be able to build up materials with such anisotropy from the ground up, tailored to our specific needs to force the heat flux to follow the paths of our interest. That is easier said than done. Even with the recent technological advances in nanofabrication and characterization, we still lack the ability to build materials one atom at a time and scale things up to a macroscopic size. One therefore needs a different approach: a practical one that approximates the same end result. One such approach is to construct a layered composite. If one looks at a set of stairs from very far away, it appears to be a smooth continuous slope. By stacking discrete layers of materials characterized by constant but individually different thermal conductivities, we can mimic materials with a smooth gradient in their conductivity profiles. What is important here, again, is the arrangement. For example, if one constructs a material by alternating elements characterized by high and low thermal conductivities, just as in the case with electric current in resistor networks, heat would prefer to flow in the parallel direction rather than in the series direction. That is a bit oversimplified, as more complicated heat-flow patterns can appear depending on the exact geometry of the material placement and the configurations of externally applied heat flux. However, the principle is clear. By using only isotropic materials that exist in nature, one can design and construct anisotropic materials with uniquely engineered thermal conduction properties.

Recipe. There is a wide parameter space that one can explore for determining the exact spatial distribution of thermal conductivities. It turns out that it is so wide that, given a particular heat flux manipulation of interest, the process of figuring out the exact elements required along with the specific patterns and configurations to place those elements in can be quite daunting. To make that process more efficient, a recipe called coordinate transformation can be used. The conduction equation is mathematically form invariant when one moves from one coordinate system to another. One can then view the bending of heat current as a mere coordinate transformation, or more precisely a distortion of space from such transformation. Once the adequate coordinate transformation that achieves the required heat flux distortion is found, formulations in linear algebra allow the same transformation to be used to transform the thermal conductivities to the values necessary for such distortion. Since the mathematical transformation that achieves a particular operation is generally not unique, it makes the most sense to choose the one that gives the conductivity profiles that can easily be assembled; for example, a layered configuration. The parameter space that needs to be explored becomes a bit narrower, and this provides researchers with an appropriate starting point for designing and assembling composites. The coordinate transformation approach was initially discussed in the context of electrical impedance tomography where, given current-voltage measurements on a sample, its electrical conductivity profile can

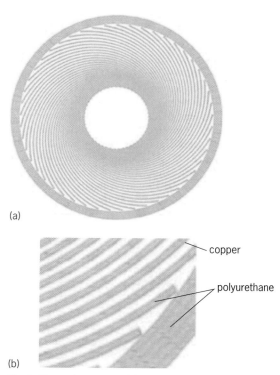

(a)

copper

polyurethane

(b)

Fig. 1. Thermal metamaterial configuration. (*a*) A hollow cylindrical material consisting of layers of polyurethane and copper arranged in a spiral pattern. (*b*) Close-up view.

not be uniquely determined. The same principle was developed further and applied to more recent metamaterial work such as cloaking a spatial region from electromagnetic waves.

Local heat current inversion. An interesting example of heat flux manipulation using thermal metamaterial is the local inversion of heat current. A hollow cylindrical material with artificial thermal properties is embedded in a block of ordinary material (**Fig. 1**). In this case the engineered material consists of approximately 100 layers of polyurethane and copper in a spiral configuration designed with the aid of coordinate transformation discussed above. A heat source and a sink are applied at the two ends of the block to externally force the heat to flow from left to right. Simulations reveal the designed functionality of this material (**Fig. 2**). The temperature profile rotates within the composite to invert the temperature gradient in the inner region. The heat flux lines become distorted within the artificial material in such a way that it forces heat to flow from right to left in the inner region to be able to get out to the heat sink. Such local inversion of heat flux has been experimentally observed (**Fig. 3**). Even with the direction of heat flow strictly imposed from outside, it is possible to design material properties such that heat current becomes manipulated passively and it flows backwards in a targeted region.

Outlook. Heat current manipulation using thermal metamaterials is a step toward a more robust control of heat flux. Thermodynamics is a well-established discipline in science and the concept of heat has

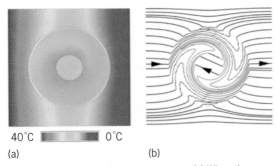

40°C ▬▬ 0°C

(a)   (b)

Fig. 2. Simulations of thermal responses. (*a*) When the metamaterial is embedded in a host medium (agar-water block) and subjected to an external thermal gradient, the temperature profile rotates to invert the gradient in the inner region, while making minimum perturbation to the outside. (*b*) Heat-flux lines are distorted and forced to flow from right to left in the inner region, while they continue to flow from left to right in the exterior region.

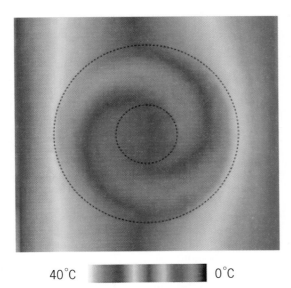

40°C ▬▬▬▬ 0°C

Fig. 3. Experimentally observed temperature profile showing the inversion of the thermal gradient in the inner region with respect to the outside. Dotted lines outline the inner and outer diameters of the metamaterial.

been known for a long time. That often makes us forget how difficult it really is to manipulate heat current. Compared to the field of electrical conduction, which is armed with nonlinear solid-state devices, the field of thermal conduction is still in its infancy. Given that temperature differences exist everywhere and the resultant heat flow is often just wasted, it is worthwhile to consider various possible means to manipulate, control, and more speculatively process heat current. With engineered thermal functionalities available, one property that seems within reach is the ability to switch on and off those functionalities. For example, with materials that exhibit temperature-dependent thermal conductivities, particular functionalities can be turned on and off with a temperature change in the environment. Such nonlinear thermal materials may pave the way for more sophisticated thermal management. Simultaneous manipulations of thermal and electrical

conductivities could potentially lead to new types of thermoelectric materials. It is not clear at the moment how small one can make these thermal metamaterials, and that is a topic that will require further investigation along with the thermal responses in the transient regime. What is exciting is that, with further advancement in material growth, synthesis, and fabrication, more complicated structures should become feasible to assemble. Not restricted by the layered structures, truly graded materials tailored with multi-functionalities could be experimentally investigated and applied to various scientific fronts in the future.

For background information *see* COMPOSITE MATERIALS; CONDUCTION (HEAT); COPPER; HEAT; HEAT TRANSFER; MATERIALS SCIENCE AND ENGINEERING; POLYURETHANE RESINS; THERMAL CONDUCTION IN SOLIDS in the McGraw-Hill Encyclopedia of Science & Technology.   Yuki Sato

Bibliography. A. Greenleaf, M. Lassas, and G. Uhlmann, Anisotropic conductivities that cannot be detected by EIT, *Physiol. Meas.*, 24:413, 2003, DOI:10.1088/0967-3334/24/2/353; A. Greenleaf, M. Lassas, and G. Uhlmann, On nonuniqueness for Calderon's inverse problem, *Math. Res. Lett.*, 10:685–693, 2003; S. Guenneau, C. Amra, and D. Veynante, Transformation thermodynamics: Cloaking and concentrating heat flux, *Optic. Express*, 20:8207–8218, 2012, DOI:10.1364/OE.20.008207; U. Leonhardt, Optical conformal mapping, *Science*, 312:1777–1780, 2006, DOI:10.1126/science.1126493; S. Narayana and Y. Sato, Heat flux manipulation with engineered thermal materials, *Phys. Rev. Lett.*, 108:214303, 2012, DOI:10.1103/PhysRevLett.108.214303; J. B. Pendry, D. Schurig, and D. R. Smith, Controlling electromagnetic fields, *Science*, 312:1780–1782, 2006, DOI:10.1126/science.1125907.

Mars Science Laboratory

The *Mars Science Laboratory* is an advanced, instrumented roving vehicle designed to assess whether its landing site on Mars contains evidence of past or present habitable environments. Named *Curiosity*, the rover landed inside Gale crater on August 6, 2012, with the intention of exploring a tall central mound of layered sediments within the crater.

Spacecraft characteristics. NASA's *Mars Science Laboratory* represents the most advanced spacecraft ever sent to the surface of another planet (**Fig. 1**). The space agency sponsored an essay contest in 2009 to choose the rover's name. The winning entry, *Curiosity*, was submitted by Clara Ma, who at the time was a sixth-grade student.

Curiosity utilizes a six-wheeled design, as have previous Martian rovers, which provides the ability to traverse uneven terrain and some degree of redundancy should any of the individual wheels fail. Roughly the size of a Mini Cooper automobile, the rover has an overall length of 9.8 ft (3.0 m), a width

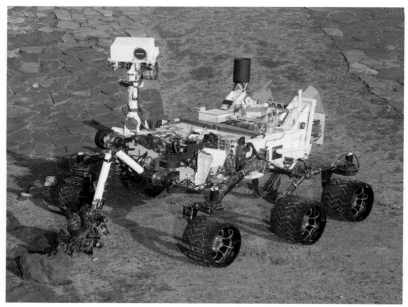

(a)

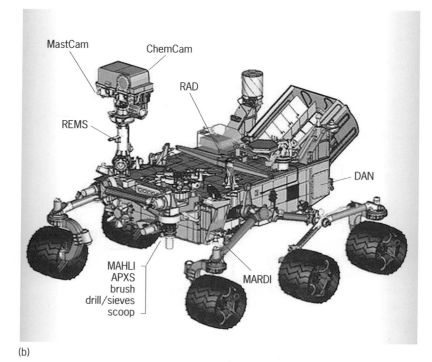

(b)

Fig. 1. Engineering model of NASA's *Mars Science Laboratory*. (a) Photograph. (b) Schematic diagram, showing locations of instruments. CheMin and SAM are inside the rover. (*NASA/JPL*)

(1.6 cm) across and up to 2 in. (5 cm) deep. The resulting rock dust is then scooped up and repeatedly sifted to screen out particles larger than 0.04 in. (1 mm) or 0.006 in. [150 micrometers (μm)]. Then the powder is deposited in inlets for one of three analytical instruments housed within the main spacecraft body.

Designed by NASA to survive for at least an entire Martian year, 687 Earth days, the rover is powered by 10.6 lb (4.8 kg) of plutonium dioxide. Heat from the radioactive decay of the plutonium is used to generate electricity for the electronic systems and instruments on board and also to warm the spacecraft's interior during frigid Martian nights, during which temperatures can drop to $-130°$F ($-90°$C). Earlier rover designs relied on solar-cell arrays for electricity.

Curiosity carries 10 scientific instruments with a total mass of 165 lb (75 kg), roughly half the total mass of NASA's previous Martian rovers, *Spirit* and *Opportunity*. These instruments (see **table**) provide an unprecedented ability to study the surface of Mars, at scales that range from panoramas of the landing-site terrain to microscopic close-ups, to the atomic abundances and crystal structure of minerals found within individual rocks.

Curiosity is essentially a roving geological laboratory. Three instruments in particular—the Alpha Particle X-ray Spectrometer (APXS), Chemistry and Camera (ChemCam), and Chemistry and Mineralogy (CheMin)—operate in concert to reveal not only the elemental composition of Martian surface rocks but also the specific minerals they contain.

A fourth experiment, Sample Analysis at Mars (SAM), focuses on chemical compounds relevant to life. Actually a suite of three analytical tools that fit into a box about the size of a microwave oven, SAM examines gases in the thin Martian atmosphere and those created by heating powdered rock samples to very high temperatures. The first of these tools, a mass spectrometer, identifies gases by the molecular weight and electrical charge of their ions. The second, a tunable laser spectrometer, records the absorption of specific wavelengths of light to reveal the relative abundances of water vapor, carbon dioxide, and methane. It can also detect specific isotopes of various atoms. The third, a gas chromatograph, separates a mixture of gases into its different components and is especially sensitive to organic compounds, which tend to have higher molecular weights.

During the rover's construction, technical difficulties and significant budget overruns led to some loss of instrumental capability (for example, zoom lenses for MastCam, the rover's primary cameras) and also forced a launch delay from 2009 to 2011.

Gale crater and Aeolis Mons. The Martian surface is crisscrossed by networks of channels that bear a very strong resemblance to dry river beds on Earth. These range in size from less than 300 ft (100 m) wide to broad flood channels nearly 40 mi (60 km) wide.

of 9.1 ft (2.8 m), and a mass of 1982 lb (899 kg). Rising vertically from the box-shaped main body is an instrumented mast whose top is 7 ft (2.1 m) above the ground.

Attached to the vehicle's front is a multijointed arm that can extend to a length of 6.2 ft (1.9 m). At its end is a complex turret with two instruments and three sampling mechanisms. In normal operation, a drill grinds into a rock to create a small hole 0.63 in.

Instruments carried by *Mars Science Laboratory*

Name	Abbreviation	Purpose
Alpha Particle X-ray Spectrometer	APXS	Placed by arm against rocks and soils to identify elemental abundances
Chemistry and Camera	ChemCam	Near-infrared laser vaporizes pinhead-size samples up to 23 ft (7 m) away. Optics direct light from the white-hot vapor to three spectrometers
Chemistry and Mineralogy	CheMin	Powdered samples are exposed to a beam of x-rays, which scatter within crystals in characteristic ways to reveal mineral compositions
Dynamic Albedo of Neutrons	DAN	Detects hydrogen (in water) at depths of up to 20 in. (50 cm)
Mars Descent Imager	MARDI	Examines ground underneath rover; also used during descent to surface
Mars Hand Lens Imager	MAHLI	Color camera on arm; resolves detail down to 0.00055 in. (14 μm) across
Mast Camera	MastCam	Color cameras at top of mast with lens focal lengths of 34 and 100 mm
Radiation Assessment Detector	RAD	Measures high-energy particles emitted by Sun and cosmic sources
Rover Environmental Monitoring Station	REMS	Measures meteorological conditions and intensity of ultraviolet sunlight
Sample Analysis at Mars	SAM	Heats rock powders to 1800°F (1000°C); determines elemental and isotopic abundances in heated samples and in atmospheric gas

Fig. 2. Gale crater on Mars. The landing target (ellipse at upper left) for NASA's Mars Science Laboratory mission is about 12 mi (20 km) long. Near the crater's center is Aeolis Mons (Mount Sharp), a massif of layered sediments that is 3 mi (5 km) tall. (*NASA/JPL/ ESA/DLR/FU Berlin/MSSS*)

Today Mars is too cold and its atmosphere too thin for liquid water to remain stable on its surface. However, geologists believe that in the distant past the Martian climate was more clement, with a denser, warmer atmosphere. These conditions allowed water to flow freely over its surface and perhaps were conducive to life.

Curiosity's primary scientific objective is to seek evidence of past or present environments suitable for microbial life. With this in mind, mission managers chose the interior of Gale crater as the landing site. Named for Walter Frederick Gale (1865–1945), the crater is 96 mi (154 km) across (**Fig. 2**). Small channels, likely cut by flowing water long ago, run down the inner rim and onto the crater's interior. At the center of Gale is a layered massif that rises 3 mi (5 km) above the flat crater floor. Although officially named Aeolis Mons, this feature is widely known as Mount Sharp in honor of pioneering planetary geologist Robert P. Sharp (1911–2004).

Images and spectra taken by orbiting spacecraft show that Aeolis Mons consists of stratified layers much like those in Arizona's Grand Canyon. Clay minerals near its base begin just 1000 ft (300 m) above the crater floor, sulfate-rich deposits dominate its middle layers, and the summit is capped by still-younger material that might be a sediment-filled system of fractures. This sedimentary sequence, em-placed over the past 3.8 billion years, no doubt holds crucial details about ancient Martian environments and the role of water in shaping them. *Curiosity* should have direct access to these various layers thanks to a canyon incised into the mountain's northern flank.

Mission overview. *Curiosity* was launched on November 26, 2011, and arrived at Mars after an interplanetary journey of 352 million mi (567 million km) over 8½ months. During its descent and deceleration through the Martian atmosphere, the spacecraft was enclosed in a protective aeroshell. Small thrusters continually adjusted the aeroshell's orientation to provide optimum lift, which helped guide the craft to its landing zone with unprecedented accuracy. A parachute deployed at an altitude of about 7 mi (11 km), and during the final approach to the surface the rover was suspended from a rocket-powered descent stage. The interval from entering the uppermost atmosphere to landing lasted about 7 min, and touchdown occurred on August 6, 2012, at 5:17:57 Universal Time.

NASA officials decided to name the touchdown site Bradbury Landing to honor noted science-fiction writer Ray Bradbury (1920–2012), who died two months before *Curiosity* reached its destination. The rover landed about 5 mi (8 km) from the lowermost slopes of Aeolis Mons (**Fig. 3**), but the mission's

Fig. 3. *Curiosity* took this self-portrait, comprising 55 separate images, in October 2012 using a camera at the end of its robotic arm. In the distance at the upper right is a portion of Aeolis Mons (Mount Sharp), about 5 mi (8 km) from the landing site. (*NASA/JPL/MSSS*)

scientists and engineers did not command the rover to head directly there. Instead, *Curiosity* spent most of its first year on Mars exploring Bradbury Landing and a nearby convergence of three distinct terrain types known collectively as Glenelg. Along the route to Glenelg the rover passed outcrops of loosely cemented gravel and silt very similar in appearance to what is commonly found in dry streambeds on Earth.

An exposure of layered mudstone served as the target for *Curiosity*'s first drilling test, which occurred in February 2013. After sifting the resulting rock powder to remove small pebbles, a small sample was heated and analyzed by the SAM instrument, which detected the presence of water, carbon dioxide, oxygen, sulfur dioxide, and hydrogen sulfide. This suite of compounds suggests that the rock contains abundant smectite, a group of claylike minerals that forms in the presence of water. Calcium sulfates in the sample indicate the water probably had a relatively neutral pH and was not strongly salty. Taken together, the results suggest that this portion of the crater floor, a shallow depression dubbed Yellowknife Bay by the mission team, is covered with sediments deposited long ago in a lake.

Curiosity spent several months in this location, in part because an electronic glitch halted science activities for about a month and in part because communications were suspended for a few weeks when Mars passed very near the Sun as seen from Earth. After normal operations resumed, a second drilling test occurred in May 2013. The rover was to begin its trek toward Aeolis Mons a few months later, arriving at the base of the towering mound and beginning its slow ascent in mid-2014.

For background information *see* MARS; SPACE PROBE in the McGraw-Hill Encyclopedia of Science & Technology.   J. Kelly Beatty

Bibliography. J. Bell, *Postcards from Mars: The First Photographer on the Red Planet*, Penguin Group, New York, 2006; E. Lakdawalla, Touchdown on the red planet, *Sky Telesc.*, 124(5):20–27, November 2012; National Aeronautics and Space Administration, *Mars Science Laboratory Landing* (press kit), July 2012; W. Sheehan, *The Planet Mars: A History of Observation and Discovery*, University of Arizona Press, Tucson, 1996.

Masdar, sustainable desert city

As we progress scientifically and technologically worldwide in response to global warming, accelerating sea-level rise, and climate change, there has been an intensified effort to move effectively toward the use of natural renewable energy resources not only in transportation, but also in industry and building construction. Masdar City, under construction outside the city of Abu Dhabi in the United Arab Emirates (UAE), is the world's first planned self-energizing, sustainable desert city.

In Arabic, *masdar* as a verb means "to source," and as a derivative noun means "a sourcing." The sole sourcing in the case of Masdar City (literally Source City) applies to the use of renewable energy resources primarily for electric power generation. This is in lieu of fossil fuel combustion, with its inherent intensive and extensive carbon dioxide (CO_2) emissions.

In a novel, exemplary leadership fashion, Masdar intends to plant the seeds for progressive developmental practices based on traditional forms, with a special focus on innovative, sustainable environmental systems planning and architectural design, as we move away from energy-wasteful robust centralized electric power generation, transmission, and distribution technologies and toward localized self-generating net-zero or even net-plus electric power energy-conservation systems based on renewable energy resources.

Masdar City is the world's very first car- and truck-free, wasteless, carbon-neutral (from lack of fossil fuel combustion) self-generating (via sole dependency on several renewable energy sources), electrically powered progressive modern sustainable desert city. It is the 2006 conceptual brainchild of H.H. General Sheikh Mohammed bin Zayed Al Nahyan, crown prince of Abu Dhabi and deputy supreme commander of the UAE Armed Forces, who in 2007 retained the architectural firm Foster + Partners as city planners. Masdar City is 6.4 km^2 (2.5 mi^2) in area and is intended to eventually include business enterprises, while providing goods and services for a population of 40,000 residents and 50,000 commuters.

Ultimately, based on the success of the current 10-MW photovoltaic (PV) solar farm (which generates more electric power than is currently being consumed) and rooftop PV solar panels, Masdar City plans additional solar collector arrays and wind farms outside the existing city boundaries.

Desert environment. The Arabian Peninsula, primarily occupied by Saudi Arabia, is about 95% desert, with some of the world's highest sand dunes located in the UAE. In 2010, Saudi Arabian desert temperatures were recorded as the Earth's hottest at 55°C (131°F). Abu Dhabi's daytime and nighttime temperatures can differ by as much as 33°C (60°F) in the winter months and as much as 45°C (81°F) during the summer, when the surface of the desert sands can reach 82°C (180°F). Average monthly temperatures from January to August can vary from 22°C (72°F) to 39°C (102°F); however, extreme temperatures can reach 50°C (122°F). With cloudless blue skies prevailing, the average rainfall is minimal: only 3 cm (1.2 in.) during the months of December, January, and February, for a total of 9 cm (3.6 in.) annually. In addition, the hottest months (June through September) bring sporadic life-threatening sandstorms, which can reduce visibility to just a few meters. Ground-level wind speeds can approach 97 km/h (60 mi/h), blowing fine, powdery sand deposits onto roadways, plazas, flat rooftops, and photovoltaic panels as well as onto automobiles and trucks. The UAE normally experiences 8–10 severe sandstorms each year; however, possibly because of global warming, in 2006 Abu Dhabi experienced 128 wind events lasting from a few hours to an entire day.

In several developed neighboring countries in the region and in the urban areas of the Arabian Peninsula, including the city of Abu Dhabi, it has been traditional to incorporate wood and finished masonry wind scoops, wind catchers, wind towers, or wind ventilation chimneys, known as *barjeel* or *malqaf* in Arabic, to provide natural air conditioning and ventilation as well as natural lighting to the interior spaces of dwellings and other architectural structures. Normally, these traditional *barjeel* are designed to advantageously collect the cold, dense nighttime air currents from all compass directions. These air currents naturally spiral downward, descending in a vortex fashion to central courtyard colonnades, and then naturally migrate to the surrounding rooms as a result of convective air pressure differentials, causing the heavier cooler air to sink and the lighter warm air to rise and escape.

The courtyards are often planted with native fruit and shade trees and are connected to enclosed domestic vestibule entryways and to completely shaded pedestrian alleyways and narrow, winding streets that originally served carts and also served as an ingenious human and animal waste collection and disposal system with minimal use of water transport.

Planning and design. Foster + Partners laid out the basic right-angled urban matrix grid for Masdar City in 2007. After its 2008 groundbreaking, it was to be rapidly completed by 2016. However, that date has been extended to 2025 because of the far-reaching financial impacts of the ongoing economic recession, which was also a serious consideration in the decision to reduce the overall budget. The Foster grid layout is interrupted by intermittent greenways and a planned high-speed curvilinear rail line as well as interspersed recreational park areas. The plan's on-site fringe areas also contain provisions for extensive innovative solar power and wind power generation facilities as well as geothermal renewable energy systems, traditional updraft wind (ventilation chimney) towers, a desalination plant, and self-sustaining agricultural farms.

Like the sustainable multistory desert city of Shibam in Yemen, which was originally constructed of adobe mud in its current strictly regulated basic forms (achieving heights of 11 stories) in the sixteenth century on ancient ruins built on a major rock outcropping during the third century, Masdar City has been planned and designed as an elevated walled city and is also edged with an external tree belt to guard against desert winds and sandstorms.

Masdar City incorporates the 10 ecologically based environmental systems planning and design principles of the One Planet Living® model promulgated by BioRegional: (1) zero carbon, (2) zero waste, (3) sustainable transport, (4) local and sustainable (construction and building products) materials, (5) local and sustainable (organic) food, (6) sustainable (and recycled) water, (7) natural habitats and wildlife (biodiversity preservation and conservation), (8) culture and heritage, (9) equity and fair trade (negotiable conflict resolution), and (10) health (harmonious ecosystem) and happiness (joy of accomplishment). Many of these Masdar City planning and design principles relate to more than one of the three basic spheres of social, economic, and environmental sustainability.

Foster + Partners created the relatively low- and midrise Masdar City based on the 10 principles just listed as basically a Cartesian grid matrix, strongly taking into consideration daily and seasonal sun orientation angles within the proposed modern walled city, creatively segmented by sparse diagonal on- and off-site linkages. They also designed the six-story Masdar Institute of Science and Technology (MIST) on a raised platform 7.3 m (24 ft) above the surrounding sandy terrain.

Masdar Institute of Science and Technology (MIST). Following the award of the Masdar City conceptual city planning commission to Foster + Partners in 2007, Phase 1A of the MIST master development plan as designed by Foster + Partners was completed in January 2010 through the use of three daily work shifts based on construction documents prepared by international planners, architects, and engineers RW Armstrong. As a result, MIST's classrooms, laboratories, library, and apartments, along with ancillary facilities, were initially operational in September 2010 (**Fig. 1**). Two months after the first six buildings were constructed, Phase 1B of the MIST master plan was initiated, with construction completion and occupancy planned for September 2012.

MIST is a graduate-level university campus devoted to entrepreneurial research and the focused study of sustainability in a relatively harsh, hostile, forbidding desert environment. Foster + Partners' basic design principles for the new city plan have been incorporated into its first Masdar architectural design project; that is, high-density compactness in a mixed-use development that contains laboratory, library, and recreational space, along with student housing, accessible public transport, and pedestrian-oriented narrow streets and courtyards that provide shade and emphasize walkability, relaxation, and social interchange. The six-story reinforced concrete frame selected for the structural system allows for a raised concrete slab almost 8 m (25 ft) above the desert sands. There is also some accommodation for a small fleet of remotely controlled driverless electric personal rapid transit (PRT) podlike cars below the raised slab, as no highway-type vehicles are permitted within the science and technology complex. As with Masdar City, the basic geometry of the plan and its sections is orthogonal, based on the Cartesian coordinate system of perpendicular x, y, and z axes, with the exception of the

Fig. 1. Desert view of the first buildings of the Masdar Institute of Science and Technology. (*Nigel Young/Foster + Partners*)

contemporaneously styled traditional grilled verandas of formed concrete (normally these would be of light wood cantilevered construction known as *mashrabiya*, *shanasheel*, or *rushan*), which serve as breezier, cooler sitting or sleeping areas in the hot daytime desert environment. At MIST, these indoor-outdoor non-air-conditioned spaces are curvilinear and add some flair to the multiple stories. Another exception to the orthogonal plan is the superimposed diagonal grid, which capitalizes on the Sun's orientation with the renewable solar rooftop overhanging perimeter PV panels.

In addition to graduate student apartments and scientific and technological research and development laboratories, the architectural spaces in Phases 1A and 1B call for a library research and study center and a large multiuse hall, while Phase 2 includes a conference hall and Phase 3 a mosque.

Comparative thermal-imaging-camera analyses by Foster + Partners in 2011 proved the firm's design theories with respect to the primary architectural and environmental systems planning and design, energy conservation, and gross CO_2 plus greenhouse gas (GHG) emission-reduction and emission-negation aspects of the MIST project. The thermal imaging vividly showed the strikingly high contrast with streets in Abu Dhabi, with MIST's predominantly pedestrian plaza surfaces and arcade spaces being much cooler, at a reported differential of 11.1°C (20°F) at midday in October. Therefore, the ventilated spaces at the conscientiously planned and designed podium level, which is almost 8 m (25 ft) above the shifting desert sands, convey the intrinsic value of thoughtful city planning and architectural and engineering design in reducing both energy consumption and CO_2 emissions; this is superbly manifested in the computational fluid dynamics (CFD) thermal [infrared thermometry (IRT)] imaging data that have been published. Much of this planning and design success is attributable to the use of traditional tall, narrow pedestrian pathways and the PV cantilevered overhead panels to shade plazas from the sun, and especially to the triangularly extruded enhanced structural steel-framed wind tower designed by Foster + Partners (**Fig. 2**). The wind tower is 45.8 m (150 ft) tall—about 15 or 16 stories. This innovative design is based on the traditional Arabian desert cooling and ventilating *barjeel*, except that these architects, engineers, and planners have added (1) sensor-controlled horizontal louvers, (2) horizontal micro-mist jets, (3) a weather monitoring station, and (4) a vertical tubular downdraft (inner sock) to achieve significant pedestrian-level success.

Of specific concern, however, in the thermal imaging analysis are the orange (hot) and yellow (hotter) readings on architectural reflective and absorbent surfaces at the end of the MIST courtyard and above the notated second story at the right, and the light yellow (very hot) and white (hottest) heat radiation recorded on the underside of the diagonally oriented rooftop PV solar panels. This may require some reflective thermal insulation below the elevated (by the equivalent of about one story) solar roof panels or some non-fossil-fuel-burning micro wind turbines to better ventilate this open reflective rooftop story, including atticlike areas where

Fig. 2. Passive wind tower at the Masdar Institute, designed to provide a cooling breeze on the plaza. (*Nigel Young/Foster + Partners*)

the solar panels are vertically splayed at an angle so that they also serve as natural illuminating skylights. However, of utmost importance would be further comparative analysis of not only exterior spaces but also interior occupied spaces through thermal imaging camera documentation. The lack of more lush and functional xeriscape landscaping is disturbing, as this would not only dissipate heat radiation by serving as natural fans and shading elements in outdoor pedestrian circulating and socializing spaces, but also serve in the natural symbiotic photosynthesis exchange of oxygen (O_2) and CO_2 among trees, plants, and humans, because this is of paramount importance in energy conservation (including that of human beings) and the reduction of CO_2 and other GHG emissions that green plants can often capture.

One of the distinctive features of the Foster + Partners' planning and architectural design studies, which also applied to MIST, is that they took a more comprehensive inclusive (versus exclusive) systems approach. Therefore, instead of attempting to oversimplify complex sets of interrelated and interdependent architectural and architectural engineering planning and design problems within a very challenging environment and changing economic and social conditions, they very successfully managed to expand horizons, enabling the entire team of players to achieve an integrated system of multiple subsystems and sub-subsystems. Furthermore, such forward-thinking architecture exemplifies a functional and aesthetic sensitivity to local and regional culture in ways that demonstrate Foster + Partners'

keen understanding of the underlying design and construction principles that their predecessors employed with their available technologies. Foster + Partners wisely adapted these valuable historical principles for use with more advanced engineering and construction technologies.

Masdar Headquarters and Masdar City center. Designated by the owner, Mubadala Development Company (an investment entity owned by the Abu Dhabi government), as the "centerpiece" of Masdar City, the Masdar Headquarters will also serve as the secretariat of the International Renewable Energy Agency (IRENA). Because of the need for cost reductions during the current economic downturn, although there have been two award-winning designs produced for the city center, superstructure construction has not commenced beyond expensive reinforced concrete foundations.

AS + GG design. The very first piece of innovative architecture for the Masdar City center, Masdar Headquarters, was designed by architects Adrian Smith and Gordon Gill of AS + GG Architecture of Chicago for Abu Dhabi Future Energy Company, as the very first self-energizing positive-energy building in the Middle East.

Masdar Headquarters, approaching a minimal high-rise height of 10 commercial stories, was designed as a mixed-use facility with direct access to an underground rapid transit station and an underground personal transit system, including underground pedestrian access to elevators, escalators, and emergency exit stairways (required by the life safety code). The architectural design includes ground-level retail shops, commercial office space, and upper-level residential apartment units, a prayer assembly space, landscaped areas, and upper- and lower-level public gardens (**Fig. 3**).

To meet Masdar City's energy-saving and emission-reductions targets, AS + GG designed both active and passive integrated renewable energy systems after thorough CFD analyses with simulated wind ventilation tests. These tests led to innovative design concepts not only in architectural forms and spaces, but also in functionality beyond the typical visual, acoustical, thermal comfort, and solar daylighting relationships between the interior and exterior spaces. Due consideration was given to aiding the flow of cooling and dehumidifying air by using an inventive hyperbolic paraboloid-shaped series of daytime updraft/nighttime downdraft wind cones, which are triangulated latticed curvilinear spaceframe conical structures, ultimately creating an immense seven-acre sun-shading spaceframe roof plane with maximum photovoltaic solar-energy-harvesting capabilities. The circular open-well daylighting canopies are aligned with traditional courtyard oases that were systemically integrated in the environmental systems planning and architectural design process (**Fig. 4**).

AS + GG Architecture's progressive curvilinear design for the Masdar Headquarters wind cones is based on the centuries-old traditional regional

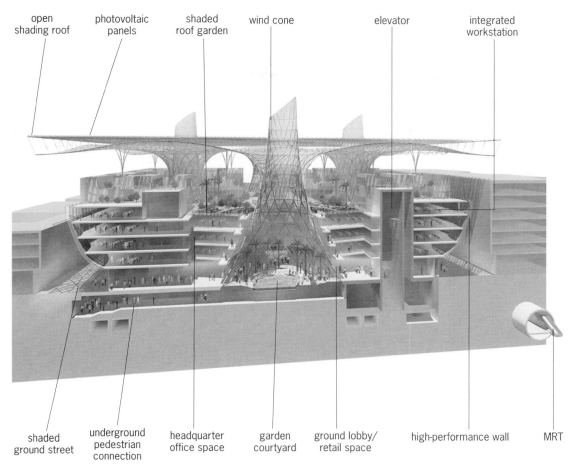

open
shading roof

photovoltaic
panels

shaded
roof garden

wind cone

elevator

integrated
workstation

shaded
ground street

underground
pedestrian
connection

headquarter
office space

garden
courtyard

ground lobby/
retail space

high-performance wall

MRT

**Fig. 3. Cross-sectional drawing of the AS + GG design for Masdar Headquarters. MRT = Masdar Rapid Transit.
(*Copyright © Adrian Smith + Gordon Gill Architecture*)**

rectilinear baffled or louvered and seasonally modulated wind towers. The integration of the wind cones with the natural daylighting light wells in the solar-powered roof canopy creates shaded interior spaces as well as magnificent multilevel courtyards, which many consider "oases," with operable wind-cone triangular ventilating windows. Supplemental energy for air conditioning of other deep interior spaces is provided by the rooftop seven-acre combined solar farm and wind farm, with energy-supplying wind turbines at about 45.7 m (150 ft) above ground level, where the wind speeds and wind power are greatest, and also by the use of subterranean geothermal natural renewable energy sources.

The AS + GG Masdar Headquarters was projected to produce 3% more energy than it consumed, making it a carbon-negative facility. The breakdown of energy savings resulted in 52% being attributed to passive design strategies, 20% coming from active systems efficiencies, and 31% being derived from renewable sources of on-site electrical generation, for a total of 103%, resulting in the projected 3% excess.

That this is possible in the extremely hot desert climate of the Arabian Peninsula is truly remarkable. Climatic conditions in the temperate zones, where the United States and Europe are located,

are completely different, and therefore active rather than passive design systems dominate in those areas to such an extent that mechanical, electrical, and plumbing (MEP) engineering design fees and associated construction costs have soared; more than half of the architectural and engineering design fees are going to MEP consultants, and the architects and structural engineers are being shortchanged in areas of design coordination. For Masdar Headquarters, AS + GG and its engineering consultants commendably used the design fees that in the temperate zones would have been spent on MEP design fees (including significant equipment layouts in addition to design specifications and a review of shop drawings) to come up with very inventive passive cooling systems using true renewable natural energy sources rather than inefficient, wasteful fossil-fuel-generated electricity.

In late November 2008, midway into the project design development and the preparation of construction documents, Mubadala reconvened the competition design jury, as the UAE was experiencing financial difficulties in the bond market owing to the real estate glut in Dubai. As a result of the need for cost reductions, the AS + GG design would not be built.

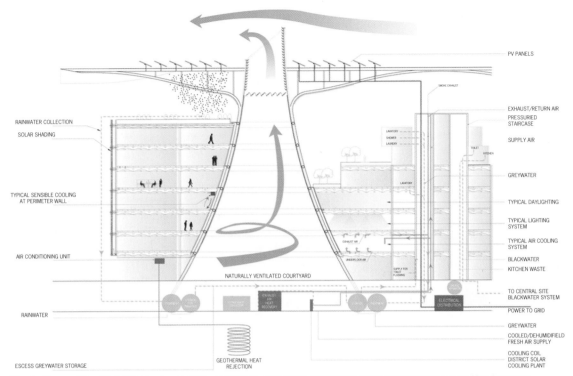

Fig. 4. Some of the AS + GG energy, cooling, ventilation, and other environmental strategies for Masdar Headquarters. (*Copyright © Adrian Smith + Gordon Gill Architecture*)

LAVA design. On September 1, 2009, Masdar City declared LAVA (Laboratory for Visionary Architecture) and its team of planning and design professionals (sans contractors) as the final-stage design competition winners. Although its published submissions are respectful of the AS + GG design proposals for Masdar Headquarters, in a sense LAVA upstaged AS + GG aesthetically as well as functionally, with core planning and design concepts that are more conducive to balanced social, environmental, and economic interactions. To date, superstructure construction has not yet commenced beyond caissons.

One of the very strong planning and design concepts offered by LAVA in its competition submission is the central open plaza gathering place within the city center, with very ingeniously designed kinetic solar-shading open-close sunflower umbrellas (**Fig. 5**).

The city center includes a five-story avant-garde hotel, a convention center, and an indoor-outdoor entertainment complex and dining court, along with small boutique retail and convenience shops and a long-stay hotel.

Current construction. Construction of a scaled-back Masdar Headquarters began at the end of 2012, and it is expected to be completed in 2014. In addition, Siemens' Middle East regional headquarters is expected to be occupied in 2013. Both buildings feature the latest technology in the areas of energy production and savings, water conservation, and green building practices.

Masdar Headquarters. The new phased Masdar Headquarters by design concept architects Woods Bagot and contractor Brookfield Multiplex of Australia has been substantially reduced in size (by 67%) to essentially a highly simplified, sustainable compact office building complex with some living accommodations, a seven-story skylighted open lobby formed by three surrounding building blocks, and vertical transportation connectors, in keeping with Masdar City's mandated cost-reduction measures during the global economic downturn (**Fig. 6**). The new complex will also house IRENA. Construction is proceeding on the new facility, using some of the existing reinforced concrete caissons and grade beam foundations that were to be used in the AS + GG design.

Siemens headquarters. Siemens' regional headquarters, in the center of Masdar City, features a "sawtooth fenestration" glazing system on two of its solar-shading façades, very similar to the one incorporated by AS + GG Architecture in its initial award-winning Masdar Headquarters proposal, and a PV overhanging roof panel system similar to the one used in MIST (**Fig. 7**). In certain installations worldwide, these "sawtooth" baffled vertical solar-shading devices have been dynamically used for almost half a century as kinetic open-close opaque louvers to reduce air-conditioning loads before the recent applications of PV panels and thin-film solar technologies. The Siemens building is expected to operate at a 45% reduction in energy consumption and a 50% reduction in water consumption, compared with international standards. Siemens has long been working globally for clean renewable energy, sustainability, and "smart" cities. In 2007, 50% (3.3 billion) of the world's population and 80% (248 million) of the U.S. population resided in cities, and this is projected to reach at least 70% (5.7 billion people) worldwide by 2050 or sooner, including 90% (360 million) of the U.S. population. Currently, cities create 70% of GHG globally and use 67% of the energy produced and 60% of the total water used by humans.

Directive foresights. As a consequence of Abu Dhabi's investment in Masdar City, many constructive actions are being implemented worldwide in developed and developing nations. Furthermore, in conjunction with the implementation of master development plans for Masdar City, Abu Dhabi has asserted the need for a regionally adaptable, environmentally conscious rating system of its own creation known as the Pearl Rating System (PRS), launched in 2012 by Abu Dhabi's Urban Planning Council (UPC) as part of its Estidama (Sustainability) Initiative, patterned after the Cascadia Green Building Council's Living Building Challenge Program [which exceeds the U.S. Green Building Council's (GBC) highest "Platinum" award standard, having a maximum grant of five pearls].

Foster + Partners and AS + GG Architecture were directed to follow the Pearl Rating System, which ensured that these firms and their engineering would exceed the standards of both the U.S. Leadership in Energy and Environmental Design (LEED) and the UK Building Research Establishment Environmental Assessment Method (BREEAM) in their systemic planning and design work for Masdar.

PRS understandably assigns a higher weighted importance to the water component, given the arid desert environment with only insignificant amounts of annual rainfall, leading to a need for energy-intensive coastal water desalinization. It also assigns a higher comparative percentage to indoor environmental quality and building materials, but in all other areas (including site selection, natural systems, energy, and innovation), PRS provides reduced weighted percentages. However, the UPC claims that, compared to the voluntary BREEAM and LEED programs, mandatory PRS is more progressive and comprehensive, as it is an advanced part of a more holistic integrated hierarchical system relating to the Estidama integrative design process (IDP) and the Plan Abu Dhabi 2030. In compliance with established development codes and imminent incorporation within building codes, before the environmental systems planning and design processes are permitted to be initiated, thorough contextual analyses are required, including energy modeling and strategically projected efficiencies, water conservation, and the potential for habitat biodiversity with a much reduced human waste loading and resulting carbon footprint.

As a further outcome of Masdar City's success to date, net-zero city planning proposals are in the policy-development stage or being planned in several locales on other continents, including Lancaster,

(a)

(b)

Fig. 5. Rendering of LAVA's design for the Masdar city center, showing the solar-powered sunflower umbrellas (a) opened and (b) closed. *[Visuals by LAVA (Laboratory for Visionary Architecture)]*

California; Las Vegas, Nevada; Chongming and Dongtan, China; Amsterdam under Amsterdam, Netherlands, and other less formulated proposals. The questions remaining become (1) will there be adequate prolonged investment funding, as Masdar's completion timetable has been extended to 2025, and (2) will the time be available before Earth reaches the fast-approaching tipping point of unstoppable global warming? The National Oceanic and Atmospheric Administration (NOAA) recently reported that in May 2013, the daily mean CO_2 concentration reached 400 ppm at its CO_2 and GHG monitoring station atop Mauna Loa, Hawaii.

In his 2012 annual report issued during the first quarter of 2013, Masdar CEO Dr. Sultan Ahmed Al Jaber stressed the primary importance of continuing to achieve diversified renewable energy Estidama

Fig. 6. Rendering of the Woods Bagot design for Masdar Headquarters. (*Woods Bagot*)

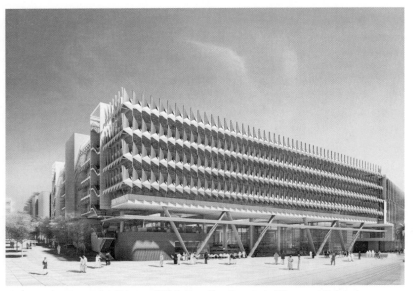

Fig. 7. Rendering of the Siemens Middle East Headquarters. (*Sheppard Robson*)

goals rather than dwelling on relatively minor setbacks in budgetary funding and construction start dates.

For background information *see* ARCHITECTURAL ENGINEERING; BUILDINGS; DESERT; GLOBAL CLIMATE CHANGE; GREENHOUSE EFFECT; SOLAR ENERGY; STRUCTURAL ANALYSIS; STRUCTURE (ENGINEERING); WIND POWER in the McGraw-Hill Encyclopedia of Science & Technology.   Andrew Charles Yanoviak

Bibliography. C. Alexander, *A Pattern Language: Towns, Buildings, Construction*, Oxford University Press, Oxford, UK, 1977; E. Bacon, *Design of Cities*, Penguin Group, New York, 1967; Le Corbusier, *The Radiant City: Elements of a Doctrine of Urbanism to Be Used as the Basis of Our Machine-Age Civilization*, Orion Press, New York, 1967; N. R. Foster, *Architecture and Identity: Responses to Cultural and Technological Change*, Taylor & Francis, London, 2000; R. B. Fuller, *Utopia or Oblivion: The Prospects for Humanity*, Bantam Books, New York, 1972; G. Gill and A. Smith, *Towards Zero Carbon:*

The Chicago Central Area Decarbonization Plan, Images Publishing Group, Sydney, Australia, 2011; K. Lynch, *The Image of the City*, Harvard University Press, Cambridge, MA, 1960; I. L. McHarg, *Design with Nature*, Wiley, New York, 1968; S. Moholy-Nagy, *Matrix of Man: An Illustrated History of Urban Environment*, Pall Mall, London, 1968; V. Olgyay, *Design with Climate: Bioclimatic Approach to Architectural Regionalism*, Princeton University Press, Princeton, NJ, 1963; M. Quantrill, *The Norman Foster Studio: Consistency Through Diversity*, Taylor & Francis, London, 2000; A. Smith, *Architecture of Adrian Smith, SOM: Toward a Sustainable Future*, Images Publishing Group, Sydney, Australia, 2007; A. C. Yanoviak, Structural design of the highrise towers, in *2010 McGraw-Hill Yearbook of Science and Technology*, McGraw-Hill, New York, 2010; A. C. Yanoviak, Self-energizing high-rise towers, *2013 McGraw-Hill Yearbook of Science and Technology*, McGraw-Hill, New York, 2013.

Measurement of aircraft fuel efficiency

Air travel has become an integral part of modern society, connecting the world with predictable, rapid, and safe transport. Because fuel consumption is a significant portion of aviation operating costs, the aviation industry has been continually striving to improve aircraft fuel efficiency. With the rising global concern regarding environmental impacts, aviation fuel efficiency has received increased attention from national and international governing organizations, which have initiated significant efforts to improve fuel efficiency. Under the Fixed Wing and Environmentally Responsible Aviation programs, NASA has been identifying and evaluating technologies and future aircraft and engine architectures to reduce fuel consumption by about 50% compared to the current state of the art. To achieve the goal of 1.5% annual energy efficiency improvement across the U.S. National Airspace System (NAS) by 2020, the U.S. Federal Aviation Administration (FAA) has invested significant resources in the Continuous Lower Emission, Energy, and Noise (CLEEN) and Next Generation Air Transportation System (NextGen) programs. Furthermore, the International Civil Aviation Organization (ICAO) is seeking global policy measures to promote further improvement in aircraft fuel efficiency by developing an aircraft carbon dioxide (CO_2) emissions standard. (Because aircraft CO_2 emissions are directly proportional to fuel consumption for a given fuel type, the ICAO's CO_2 standard is based on aircraft fuel efficiency performance.)

The success of any policy or technology development program that promotes aviation efficiency improvements relies on the ability to measure fuel efficiency adequately. Whether it is for the purpose of negotiating an aircraft purchase contract, monitoring efficiency improvement of the NAS, optimizing airline network structure and fleet deployment strategy, or developing advanced technologies, it is imperative for every program to have a metric with which the fuel efficiency of different aircraft or air transportation systems can be objectively and consistently measured and compared. Critical decisions associated with policy making, future aircraft technology development, and aircraft acquisition and deployment strategies are often based on the comparison of different alternative options using these metrics. This article reviews diverse fuel efficiency metrics that have been used in the aviation sector by various stakeholders such as governments, airlines, manufacturers, environmental groups, and international organizations. Then this article discusses the proper use of metrics depending on their use and the context for quantifying aircraft fuel efficiency.

Fuel efficiency metrics in air transportation. The modern aviation industry is bursting with impressive claims about recent fuel efficiency gains, but not all these claims are easily understood or verified. When it is said that modern aircraft fuel efficiency has improved by 70% from the early turbojet aircraft in the 1950s, what exactly does that mean and how is it calculated? When an airframe manufacturer announces its new aircraft model claiming 15% fuel efficiency improvement from its previous model or 5% better fuel economy than its competitor, what does that mean and how is it calculated? How does the International Air Transport Association (IATA), an international industry trade group of airlines, set its target of fuel efficiency improvement by 1.5% a year annually until 2020, and how can we tell whether the goal is reached?

One popular philosophy in defining efficiency across the sectors is to measure a ratio of energy input to useful work output. This approach is also analogous to the concept of cost versus benefit. Fuel burn, which is measured by weight (in kilograms or pounds), volume (in liters or gallons), grams of CO_2 emission, or energy content (in joules or BTUs), can be considered the "cost" of air travel. The benefit, which is useful work output or productivity, is often defined as a product of a load parameter that represents aircraft capacity (such as seats, passenger counts, or payload weight) and a travel distance parameter. One such metric, BTUs per passenger-mile, compares aviation cost and benefit relative to other modes of transportation (**Fig. 1**). This basic structure of fuel or energy consumption normalized by passenger-mile is often observed in fuel efficiency metrics used in the transportation sector, and is useful in comparing efficiencies of different modes of transportation, giving comparable metric values between air, cars, rail, and buses.

Several fuel efficiency measures commonly used in civil air transportation are provided in **Table 1**. Most metrics in the table include some form of fuel (W_F), load (L), and flight distance (D) parameters as part of the metrics. In aviation, the amount of traffic is commonly measured by revenue-passenger-kilometers (RPK) for passenger aircraft and revenue-ton-kilometers (RTK) for cargo aircraft. Common measures of air transportation capacity are

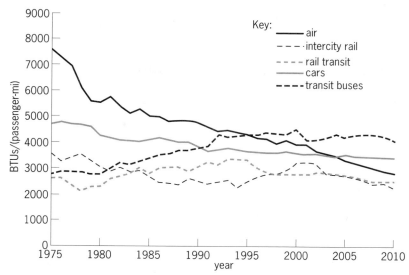

Fig. 1. Energy use (measured in BTUs) per passenger-mile by mode of transportation. (*Adapted from United States Government Accountability Office, Aviation and Climate Change, Report to Congressional Committees, 2009; data source: U.S. Department of Energy*)

available-seat-kilometers (ASK) for passenger aircraft and available-ton-kilometers (ATK) for cargo aircraft. The first four metrics in Table 1 normalize fuel consumption by one of these productivity or work output measures that combine the load and distance terms by multiplying them ($L \times D$).

The last two metrics take the form of fuel/distance without incorporating a load term. This "liters-per-kilometer" type of fuel efficiency metric has been widely used across different transportation modes to simply measure the amount of fuel required to travel a certain distance. Such metrics are also used in the form of kilometers-per-liter, gallons-per-mile, or miles-per-gallon to represent either fuel/distance or distance/fuel. In this article, all the metrics are presented in a form where a reduction is understood as improvement, for example, fuel/distance. The "1/specific air range" metric measures incremental fuel burned for an aircraft to travel a unit air distance; this is noted as $-dW_F/dR$, where W_F and R denote fuel mass and air distance, respectively. This metric is the inverse of specific air range (SAR), a common measure of aircraft cruise efficiency. These metrics do not account for disparity in size or loading capacity of the transportation unit, so they can be applied only to aircraft in a similar class (that is, aircraft binned by their size). When aircraft in different classes are compared, the use of these metrics alone would not be sufficient. In such a case, addition of one or more new parameters, often called correlating parameters, to an independent axis (for example, on the x axis) can complement the metric (for example, on the y axis).

Proper use of aviation fuel efficiency metrics. Although the metrics listed in Table 1 look similar to each other, taking a general form of fuel normalized by distance (W_F/D) or fuel normalized by load and distance [$W_F/(L \times D)$], they actually measure vastly

TABLE 1. Fuel efficiency metrics commonly used in civil aviation

Metrics	Units	Description	Recommended uses and caveats
Fuel/revenue-passenger-kilometers (fuel/RPK)	kg/(passenger-km) MJ/(passenger-km) g CO_2/(passenger-km)	Measure system-wide efficiency of passenger aircraft fleet, accounting for how aircraft are operated.	Useful for evaluation of historical fleet operational efficiency trends. Not appropriate for evaluation of individual aircraft fuel efficiency technology level.
Fuel/revenue-ton-kilometers (fuel/RTK)	kg/(ton-km) MJ/(kg·km) g CO_2/(kg·km)	Measure system-wide efficiency of cargo or passenger aircraft fleet, accounting for how aircraft are operated.	Useful for evaluation of historical fleet operational efficiency trends. Not appropriate for evaluation of individual aircraft fuel efficiency technology level.
Fuel/available-seat-kilometers (fuel/ASK)	kg/(seat-km) MJ/(seat-km) g CO_2/(seat-km)	Fuel burned normalized by passenger transport capacity.	Useful for airline economics analysis. Highly sensitive to seat counts.
Fuel/available-ton-kilometers (fuel/ATK)	kg/(ton-km) MJ/(kg·km) g CO_2/(kg·km)	Fuel burned normalized by cargo transport capacity.	Useful for airline economics analysis. Highly sensitive to maximum payload capacity.
Fuel/distance	kg/km MJ/km g CO_2/km	Popular measure of any transportation mode including aviation.	Useful for measuring combined effect of aircraft fuel efficiency technology level and the choice of the mission distance.
1/specific air range (1/SAR)	kg/km MJ/km g CO_2/km	Aircraft cruise efficiency measure; instantaneous fuel/distance.	Most suitable for measuring aircraft fuel efficiency technology level as selected by ICAO CAEP* for the Aircraft CO_2 Certification Standard.

*Committee on Aviation Environmental Protection.

different aspects of aircraft or aviation system fuel efficiency. No single fuel efficiency metric is perfectly applicable to all problems. Therefore, it is important to understand the different characteristics of the metrics that have been presented in order to choose the most suitable metric for a specific application.

Fleet-level fuel efficiency versus aircraft-level fuel efficiency. Ensuring the proper use of metrics for quantifying aviation fuel efficiency begins with determining the scope of the context being considered. Typical problems examine fuel efficiency either for an individual aircraft or for many aircraft combined into an aggregate fleet-wide system. The most commonly used metrics to evaluate fleet-wide efficiency are the fuel/RPK and fuel/RTK metrics. In particular, the fuel/RTK metric has received more attention recently because it is better suited for capturing aggregate commercial aviation traffic including cargo traffic and passenger traffic with belly freight. These metrics measure aggregated fuel performance, calculated as the expression below, where N is the total

$$\frac{\sum_{i=1}^{N} W_{Fi}}{\sum_{i=1}^{N} L_i \times D_i}$$

number of system operations fulfilled by all aircraft types in the network for a given time frame, such as a month, a quarter, or a year. When calculated for a sufficiently large number of operations, these metrics can successfully provide useful insight on air transportation system efficiency among different regions of the world; different types of airlines, such as low-cost carriers versus legacy carriers; and different airline network structures, such as hub-and-spoke versus point-to-point. These metrics are intended to measure efficiency of an air transportation system as a whole, including aircraft fuel efficiency, weather impacts, traffic congestion, and route efficiencies. One should note the sensitivity of this measure to the load factor—the ratio of revenue passenger and cargo payload to the maximum payload capacity of an aircraft—which can become a dominant factor in the fuel/RTK metric. Because these highly aggregated fuel/RTK metrics do not distinguish among contributions from individual aircraft, weather, traffic demand, or network structure, it is generally inappropriate to decompose such metrics into component impacts. Although aggregate metrics are very useful for monitoring system performance, other metrics are better suited for tracking individual contributing factors. As an example, the increase in energy/RPK of transit buses over the past three decades (Fig. 1) may not indicate a degradation of vehicle fuel efficiency technology but rather may indicate a decline of passenger counts.

As-operated versus as-designed metrics. Second, it is important to understand differences between metrics that are intended to measure aircraft efficiency as they are "operated" as opposed to as they are "designed." Even when N is equal to 1 in the RTK metric, it is essentially

$$\left(\frac{W_F}{L \times D}\right)_{operated}$$

and it should be differentiated from

$$\left(\frac{W_F}{L \times D}\right)_{designed}$$

Characteristics of these two metric types are compared in **Table 2** along several dimensions. RTK or RPK metrics can be especially useful for monitoring

TABLE 2. Comparison between operational usage versus designed capability fuel efficiency measures

$$\left(\frac{W_F}{L \times D}\right)_{\text{operated}} \quad \text{versus} \quad \left(\frac{W_F}{L \times D}\right)_{\text{designed}}$$

W_F	Fuel burned in real operations as reported by the airlines. Includes weather effects, off-nominal performance, and off-optimal flight trajectory due to traffic.	Estimated fuel burn from performance models or mission planning software. Typically uses consistent assumptions for nominal performance and flight trajectory.
L	Revenue passengers or revenue payload.	Seats or cargo capacity.
D	Radar track distance.	Great circle distance or air distance.

system performance over time, but they are recognized to include factors that are strictly beyond the control of the aircraft designer or operator, such as weather and traffic congestion. As opposed to the RTK and RPK metrics, the fuel/ASK or fuel/ATK metrics are based on aircraft capacity and designed performance independent of their operational usages. Thanks to the ability to compare fuel efficiency at a consistent set of conditions, independent of operational constraints, these metrics have been used in numerous studies that evaluate different aircraft design alternatives or technology alternatives. Such metrics have also been used to evaluate fuel economy of different aircraft in similar classes for airline fleet acquisition, lease, or fleet allocation purposes.

Impact of technology versus mission specifications. The third important aspect for determining proper metrics for measuring aviation fuel efficiency is to consider what improvements or changes in aircraft attributes should be credited toward an improvement in a metric. More specifically, one may want to apply different weighting on technological improvement or changes in mission capabilities. Aircraft fuel burn is largely determined both by parameters related to technology characteristics and by the parameters that define what mission the aircraft performs (**Fig. 2**). Depending on how a metric is constructed, particularly what is used for the load term (L), its sensitivity to those parameters can change significantly.

For instance, payload-based metrics such as fuel/ASK and fuel/ATK metrics are highly sensitive to differences in mission capabilities such as number of seats, maximum payload capacity, and mission range parameters. The only pure comparison of technology occurs when comparing aircraft of equal mission capabilities, but then fuel burn is an equally effective metric [that is, $D_1 = D_2$ and $L_1 = L_2$, so that

$$\left(\frac{W_F}{L \times D}\right)_1 \quad \text{versus} \quad \left(\frac{W_F}{L \times D}\right)_2$$

reduces to W_{F1} versus W_{F2}]. Therefore, these metrics are less effective when one wants to measure fuel-efficiency technology levels across aircraft with differing capabilities. The Boeing 737 aircraft family, which evolved in three technological generations corresponding to the originals, the classics, and the new generations, serves as a distinct example that can illustrate the inability of those payload-based metrics to distinguish technology levels. Some variants of the originals introduced to the market in the

1960s show much better scores for the fuel/ATK and the fuel/ASK metrics than some of the new-generation models of the late 1990s technology. Another example is the comparison of a passenger aircraft and its freight variant. When a passenger aircraft is converted to a freighter aircraft, maximum payload weights are often increased by more than 50% without incorporating new technology (for example, a 95% increase in maximum payload capacity from a Boeing 777-200LR to a 777-200F). The ATK-based metrics give a much better score to those aircraft variants with higher maximum payload capacity. Therefore, these metrics are not suitable for measuring technological differences among aircraft of different mission capabilities or for monitoring the technological progression of a fleet over time.

There may be a circumstance where a change in mission capabilities must be credited as well as technological improvement. Nevertheless, one should note an important characteristic of those payload-based metrics, which is their disproportional sensitivities with respect to disparate payload and flight distance. ATK and ASK metrics credit an increase in payload and range at an equal weighting. For example, 10 tons of payload transported over 1000 km is equal to 1000 tons of payload transported over 10 km in terms of ATK. On the other hand, increasing range capability is generally more demanding than increasing payload capability in terms of requiring additional fuel. As a result, these metrics tend to favor shorter-range and larger-payload-capacity aircraft. The appropriate weighting between payload and range may differ for the context, but it is extremely challenging (or may not be possible) to find a weighting that is equitable for a wide range of civil transport types.

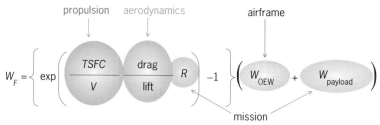

Fig. 2. Aircraft cruise fuel burn by rearranging the Breguet range equation. Aircraft fuel burn is determined by the mission-related parameters (W_{payload} and R) and the aircraft design- and technology-related parameters (W_{OEW}, TSFC/V, and lift/drag). TSFC is thrust-specific fuel consumption (that is, the ratio of the weight of fuel consumed per unit time to thrust), V is air speed, R is air range flown, lift/drag is lift-to-drag ratio, W_{OEW} is operating empty weight, and W_{payload} is payload weight.

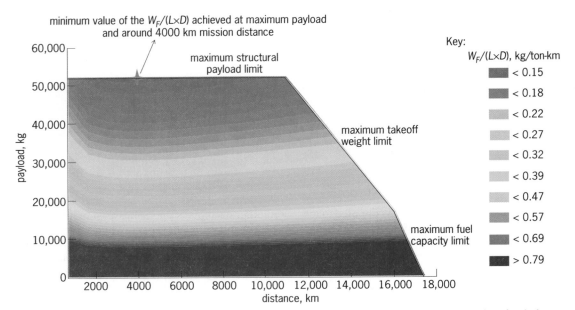

Fig. 3. Variation of $W_F/(L \times D)$ metric for a large twin-aisle aircraft within its maximum payload-range envelope (analysis using Environmental Design Space, an FAA aircraft environmental impact modeling tool suite). For a large twin-aisle aircraft model similar to the Boeing 777-200ER with GE90 engines, the fuel/ATK metric value varies from about 0.14 kg/(ton-km) to infinity depending on which evaluation point is measured. The minimum metric value is for a mission of about 4000 km with full cabin passengers and belly freight. This diagram illustrates the sensitivity of the metric to the choice of a mission used to evaluate this metric. The metric is particularly sensitive to payload, and the more the payload weight the lower the metric value. The metric sensitivity to mission distance cannot be ignored either. For a fixed payload weight, the metric (effectively fuel/distance, because the payload term is a constant) shows nonlinear trends with respect to flight distance. The metric value decreases as the mission distance increases, reaching a minimum value at about 4000 km and then increasing again. This trend is due to the fact that the fuel/distance ratio decreases initially as fuel burned for taxi, takeoff, approach, and landing is not credited covering a certain distance, and that fixed cost is amortized as the flight distance increases. For flight distances longer than 4000 km, the fuel/distance ratio increases again because the cost of carrying fuel to fly long range outweighs the amortization effect. 1 km = 0.62 mi, 1 kg = 2.20 lb.

For the purpose of differentiating aircraft technology levels for aircraft in diverse mission capabilities, the fuel/distance and 1/SAR metrics can be considered as better candidates. In order to account for differences in aircraft size or capacity, these metrics should be associated with those characteristics as correlating parameters. The fuel/distance metric is not completely independent of mission capabilities. The metric is still sensitive to the choice of mission distance, due to the nonlinear relationship between fuel burn and mission length, even though fuel burn is normalized by mission distance (**Fig. 3**). Compared to the metrics discussed above, the 1/SAR metric is least sensitive to aircraft mission capabilities and is independent of their utilizations, most accurately capturing fuel efficiency technology of diverse aircraft classes and types when used with a proper correlating parameter. In fact, the ICAO's Committee on Aviation Environmental Protection (CAEP) Working Group 3, consisting of subject-matter experts, has developed a metric that is based on 1/SAR as a basis for the ICAO Aircraft CO_2 Certification Standard.

Metric identification and application process. Identification of appropriate metrics for quantifying aviation fuel efficiency is a challenging task, and therefore a technically thorough process must be established for successful metric identification and application. A successful process should clearly iden-

tify the use and context of fuel efficiency metrics; establish criteria to evaluate the metrics objectively; populate metric candidates based on flight physics, literature review, and expert opinions; prepare quality technical data to test metric candidates against the criteria; and select a metric (or metrics) that best meets the purpose. For the successful measure of aircraft fuel efficiency, one must understand the interaction of aircraft design, mission, and technology and their relative contributions to the metric. For the purpose of differentiating aircraft fuel efficiency technology levels, a metric that does not confound the effect of mission and technological improvement should be used.

For background information *see* AIRCRAFT ENGINE PERFORMANCE; AIRCRAFT FUEL; AIRCRAFT PROPULSION; SPECIFIC FUEL CONSUMPTION in the McGraw-Hill Encyclopedia of Science & Technology.

Dongwook Lim; Taewoo Nam;
Michelle Kirby; Graham Burdette

Bibliography. P. Belobaba, A. Odoni, and C. Barnhart (eds.), *The Global Airline Industry*, Wiley, Chichester, UK, 2009; J. Hileman et al., Payload fuel energy efficiency as a metric for aviation environmental performance, in *Proceedings of the 26th International Congress of the Aeronautical Sciences*, Anchorage, AK, September 14–19, 2008; International Civil Aviation Organization, Aircraft CO_2 emissions standard metric system, ICAO Fact

Sheet, Montreal, Canada, July 11, 2012; M. Kirby and D. Mavris, The environmental design space, in *Proceedings of the 26th International Congress of the Aeronautical Sciences*, Anchorage, AK, September 14–19, 2008; J. J. Lee, Can we accelerate the improvement of energy efficiency in aircraft systems?, *Energy Conversion Manage.*, 51:189–196, 2010, DOI:10.1016/j.enconman.2009.09.011; D. Lim et al., An investigation of the potential implications of a CO_2 emission metric on future aircraft designs, in *Proceedings of the 27th International Congress of the Aeronautical Sciences*, Nice, France, September 19–24, 2010; United States Government Accountability Office, *Aviation and Climate Change*, Report to Congressional Committees, 2009.

Metabolic engineering of biochemical pathways

The goal of metabolic engineering is to enable the host organism to be more productive in forming a desired metabolite compound. This objective is accomplished through employing a designed genetic modification strategy to enhance the performance of the host organism. As people seek efficient and environmentally benign routes for the production of useful products, the ability to manipulate organisms and take advantage of the reactions that they can catalyze provides an avenue for future gains toward these beneficial goals. Thus, this new way of engineering cells aids in the formation of novel and lower-cost products for industry, food, and medicine.

Removal of competing pathways. Metabolic pathways for the production of a particular compound connect with other pathways that form other compounds through the use of a common intermediate. Because the objective is to have a high level of production of the desired product of the pathway, removing the other pathways that use intermediates can provide more for the subsequent conversion to the desired product (**Fig. 1**). This is especially important if an intermediate is the precursor of a variety of compounds: for example, pyruvate serves as the precursor of many compounds; and if the other major uses of pyruvate are prevented through deletion of the genes encoding those enzymes of alternative pathways that could use pyruvate, then more pyruvate is available for formation of the desired product.

Not only must the metabolic pathways that use the carbon intermediates be considered in this situation, but a metabolic engineer must also consider the use of cofactors (specific substances required for the activity of an enzyme, such as a coenzyme or metal ion) and reducing equivalents that go into making the product. If these are not fully available for the reactions of the desired pathway, this can limit the productivity of the process. As an example, the reaction that forms ethanol from acetyl-coenzyme A (acetyl-CoA) and the reaction that converts pyruvate to lactate both compete for a cofactor, specifically the reduced coenzyme form of nicotinamide adenine dinucleotide, NADH. Eliminating

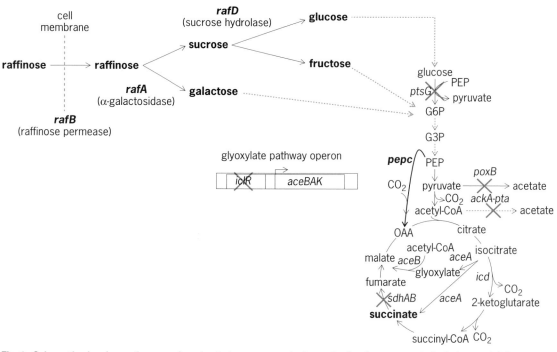

Fig. 1. Schematic showing pathway engineering to increase succinate production from soy carbohydrates containing raffinose, galactose, sucrose, and glucose. A red "×" indicates competing metabolic pathways that were inactivated (acetate and fumarate) and the negative regulator (*iclR*) that was inactivated to derepress the expression of the glyoxylate pathway (*aceBAK* genes).

the ethanol-forming reaction leaves more NADH available for the conversion of pyruvate to lactate.

Overexpression of pathway genes. In the natural state, an organism has control and regulatory mechanisms to avoid making too much of a compound, so cell resources can be balanced and preserved for the best distribution for cell growth. These regulatory processes limit the ability to engineer the cell for high production of a specific compound. Regulatory mechanisms that are common include feedback inhibition at the enzyme level and regulation of gene expression of the pathway enzymes by a repression-type mechanism. In the feedback-inhibition mechanism, a key enzyme, usually early in the metabolic pathway, is sensitive to the product compound of the pathway such that the enzyme has reduced activity when the level of the product compound of the pathway is high in the cell. One way of overcoming this limitation to production is to isolate a feedback-resistant mutant of the enzyme. These mutants can be isolated and often have an alteration in the enzyme, so the enzyme does not respond to or bind the inhibitory compound. Such mutations can be included in the cell genome and would be important in any plan to overexpress the genes encoding the enzymes of the pathway.

The other major way to achieve high productivity is to increase the levels of the pathway enzymes in the cell. This is done by one of several genetic strategies. One strategy is to clone the DNA segment encoding the pathway enzymes onto a multicopy plasmid (a circular extrachromosomal genetic element; **Fig. 2**) that will be introduced into the cell and thus raise the level of enzymes because those genes are now present in increased copy number (note that many widely used plasmids have copy numbers of 10–50 or more per cell). The number of copies of the pathway genes can also be amplified in the chromosome of the host, and methods are available for tandem amplification or sequential introduction of additional copies at multiple independent locations within the chromosome.

Another widely used strategy is to enhance formation of the pathway enzymes by placing the coding regions of the genes under strong regulatory signals that either (1) improve the transcription of the gene (promoter) so that more copies of the messenger RNA encoding the pathway enzymes are made or (2) alter the translation start region (ribosome binding site) so that the messenger RNA is translated more efficiently. In this regard, the use of known highly efficient RNA polymerase binding sites (promoters) and stable highly efficient translation signals can be used, or the naturally occurring signals can be mutated to give signals that are more active. A number of vectors have been made that have highly efficient transcription and translation signals, and the gene of interest can be placed into these constructs for expression. In many cases, this strategy works well. However, there are several other problems that can limit expression of functional proteins, including the tendency of some proteins to be digested by cell proteases or to aggregate within the cell; in these cases, special hosts can be used that afford improved functionality through a protease-minus phenotype or an increased chaperone content.

Beyond the overexpression of the enzymes acting directly on the pathway carbon skeleton, the cofactors (for example, NADH or coenzyme A) involved in the pathway can also be enhanced by increasing the level of expression of those genes involved in the biosynthesis of the appropriate form of the cofactor. In addition, another metabolic factor that can affect overall yield and growth is an imbalance of intermediates along the pathway. Sometimes certain intermediate metabolites can become toxic and inhibit cell processes; therefore, a correct balance of the upstream and downstream enzymes needs to be present to avoid excessive buildup of any toxic intermediate.

Computational analysis of complex metabolic networks. Recently, databases of enzymes and reactions have become available (for example, KEGG and BRENDA) that provide a great deal of information on the properties of individual enzymes and the pathways that involve different compounds. The information from these data sources can allow the most suitable enzyme to be used for a particular step in the proposed pathway (regardless of whether it is from the original host or not). The compilation of cellular reactions has enabled the construction of genome scale models encompassing the suite of thousands of reactions in simple cells. Computational models of cell growth and theoretical performance can provide information on the effects of eliminating specific pathways or enzymes on the metabolite pattern, and such models are useful in metabolic engineering. These large databases and the huge amount of new information from genomic sequencing provide the basis for finding new enzymes and pathways for use by metabolic engineers. However, although these databases provide possible enzymes to test,

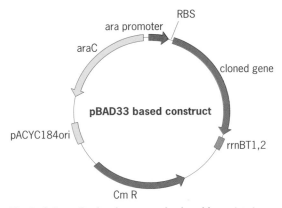

Fig. 2. Schematic showing a generic plasmid construct carrying a cloned gene expressing the desired enzyme (cloned gene) under the control of the L-arabinose promoter system and the araC regulatory protein. Terms: RBS, ribosomal binding site; rrnBT1,2, transcription termination site; Cm R, chloramphenicol resistance; pACYC184ori, origin of replication of the plasmid.

the properties of the enzymes (for example, the rate catalyzed by the enzyme; the conditions of temperature, pH, and substrate concentration for an optimal enzyme reaction; and the stability of the enzyme) are not known in many cases. Thus, it is useful to synthesize a number of genes that are able to encode and express a desired enzyme activity. The advances in DNA synthesis have allowed this screening approach to be taken in industrially important processes where new enzymes are needed.

Conclusions. Numerous advances have provided the basis for the creation of cells that can perform new functions and generate established products more efficiently. These include technological advances that have allowed the genome sequencing of many organisms, the ease of DNA synthesis allowing construction of genes encoding enzymes of choice, the synthesis of multiple genes involved in a whole biosynthetic pathway, the development of genetic tools for modification of many species, the analysis and application of global cellular information from systems biology "-omics" (for example, genomic, transcriptomic, proteomic, and metabolomic analyses), and computational advances. As these technologies are applied through metabolic engineering, a greater impact of these engineered organisms and their products on the marketplace is anticipated.

For background information *see* BIOCHEMICAL ENGINEERING; BIOCHEMISTRY; BIOTECHNOLOGY; CELL (BIOLOGY); ENZYME; FERMENTATION; GENE; GENE AMPLIFICATION; GENETIC ENGINEERING; METABOLISM; MICROBIOLOGY; MOLECULAR ENGINEERING; MUTATION; PLASMID in the McGraw-Hill Encyclopedia of Science & Technology.   Ka-Yiu San; George N. Bennett

Bibliography. M. Papagianni, Recent advances in engineering the central carbon metabolism of industrially important bacteria, *Microb. Cell Fact.*, 11:50, 2012, DOI:10.1186/1475-2859-11-50; J. H. Shin et al., Production of bulk chemicals via novel metabolic pathways in microorganisms, *Biotechnol. Adv.*, 2012, DOI:10.1016/j.biotechadv.2012.12.008; C. D. Smolke (ed.), *The Metabolic Pathway Engineering Handbook*, vol. 1: *Fundamentals*, vol. 2: *Tools and Applications*, CRC Press, Boca Raton, FL, 2012; G. Stephanopoulos, A. A. Aristidou, and J. Nielsen, *Metabolic Engineering: Principles and Methodologies*, Elsevier Science/Academic Press, San Diego, 1998; C. Thakker, K-Y. San, and G. N. Bennett, Production of succinic acid by engineered *E. coli* strains using soybean carbohydrates as feedstock under aerobic fermentation conditions, *Bioresour. Technol.*, 130C:398–405, 2012, DOI:10.1016/j.biortech.2012.10.154.

Metal-organic frameworks

Metal-organic frameworks (MOFs) are hybrid materials composed of organic bridging ligands that connect metal ions or small metal clusters to form one-, two-, or three-dimensional crystalline networks. Their propensity to exhibit extremely high surface areas (beyond 6000 m^2/g) and impressive porosities (up to 90% free volume) has attracted significant interest from scientists and engineers in designing porous MOFs for gas storage and separations. The facile tunability of MOF materials also allows for their engineering to suit many other applications such as catalysis, drug delivery, and molecular sensing.

The interest in MOFs is due in large part to three fundamental characteristics that render a level of control seldom found in other materials: crystallinity, reticular synthesis, and ease of imparting functionality. Crystallinity refers to the highly ordered, periodic structure formed by connecting metal ions or small metal clusters with organic bridging ligands. X-ray crystallographic studies allow precise determination of the MOF structure, facilitating investigation of structure–property relationships to an extent that is not possible for other materials.

Reticular synthesis pertains to the rational design and construction of the framework by using known molecular building units, insofar as this can be done. The proposed concepts of MOF design are based on the invariance of connectivity between the building blocks (that is, the metal connecting points and bridging ligands). Exploratory syntheses remain commonplace in MOF chemistry, and the relationships within crystallization remain complex and unresolved.

Crystal engineering of MOFs can be accomplished via judicious choice of the metal and bridging ligand, as the shape of the ligand and metal connecting point determine the connectivity of the final material. For example, terephthalic acid (commonly referred to as H_2BDC) has two sites located para to one another, creating a linear bridging ligand, while isophthalic acid has two sites located meta to each other, creating a bent bridging ligand. When combined with Cu(II), using H_2BDC as a ligand creates a two-dimensional (2D) MOF, while using isophthalic acid results in discrete metal-organic polyhedra. Varying the number of coordinating moieties changes connectivity, as can be seen with the tritopic ligand benzene-1,3,5,-tricarboxylic acid (H_2BTC) forming the structure HKUST-1 (see **Fig. 1**) when combined with a Cu(II) salt. Combining solutions of different ligands can also be used to change the topology of the framework, providing limitless possibilities for the design of new MOF structures.

Varying the metal or metal-cluster connecting point, also known as the secondary building unit (SBU), will change the MOF structure as well. Certain metals are known to form well-characterized geometric shapes, allowing for an additional level of design. For example, Cu(II) regularly forms a copper paddlewheel when two Cu atoms are bridged by four different carboxylate groups, with a generic formula of $Cu_2(O_2CR)_4$. Zn(II) often forms a tetrahedron when four Zn atoms are bound with a central μ_4-oxygen (an oxygen atom bound equally to four different atoms) and six bridging carboxylate groups orient in an octahedral fashion around the Zn_4O^{6+}

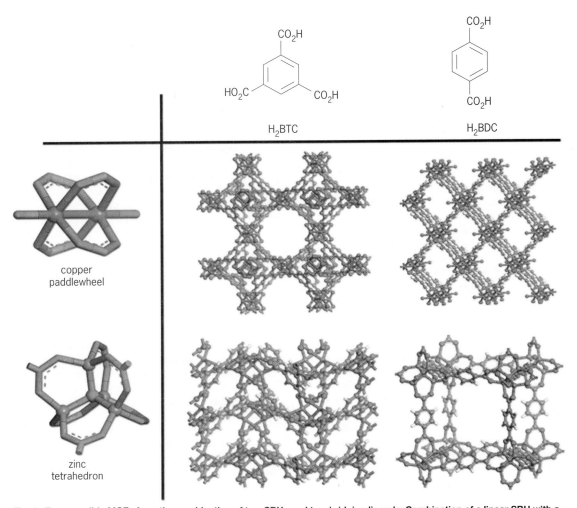

Fig. 1. Four possible MOFs from the combination of two SBUs and two bridging ligands. Combination of a linear SBU with a linear bridging ligand yields a 2D lamellar structure (upper right). In contrast, a tritopic ligand with a linear SBU (upper left) or a linear ligand with tetrahedral SBU (bottom right) yield the 3D structures HKUST-1 and MOF-5, respectively. Copper, zinc, carbon, oxygen, and hydrogen are green, blue, gray, red, and white, respectively.

cluster. Zr(IV) forms a highly stable and extensively studied $Zr_6O_4(OH)_4(O_2CR)_{12}$ SBU, in which the organic bridging ligands are oriented away from the central Zr cluster with one carboxylate spanning each edge of the octahedral structure. The location of the metal coordinating groups on the ligand and the geometry of the SBU often provide insight into the expected structure of the resulting MOF. For instance, the combination of a planar SBU (for example, the copper paddlewheel) with a linear organic bridging ligand (for example, terephthalic acid) will result in a 2D MOF composed of planar sheets. In contrast, combining the Zn tetrahedron with H_2BDC yields the cubic three-dimensional (3D) structure known as MOF-5. Figure 1 displays four possible MOFs formed using combinations of H_2BDC or H_2BTC with copper paddlewheel or zinc tetrahedron SBUs.

The archetypical isoreticular series of MOFs was synthesized using the $Zn_4(\mu_4\text{-}O)(O_2CR)_6$ SBU and linear dicarboxylate ligands of various lengths. As shown by O. M. Yaghi and colleagues, simple

extension of H_2BDC through the addition of phenyl rings to [1,1'-biphenyl]-4,4'-dicarboxylic acid (H_2BPDC) or [1,1':4',1''-terphenyl]-4,4''-dicarboxylic acid (H_2TPDC) results in the formation of an isoreticular series of MOFs (IRMOFs) with different pore dimensions. **Figure 2** displays two isoreticular series of MOFs formed from linear bridging ligands with different SBUs. Although these simple examples may make engineering of MOFs appear straightforward, they are intended only to illustrate a concept. Reticular design is not trivial. Metals do not always form the anticipated SBU, ligands do not always coordinate to the SBUs in the manner desired, and different metal salts and solvents can drastically affect the final MOF topology. Research in this discipline remains active.

Another noteworthy characteristic intrinsic to MOFs is the ease of imparting functionality by taking advantage of the relatively mild conditions of MOF synthesis. Bridging ligands can be prepared to include a secondary functional group, which can either be modified after assembly of

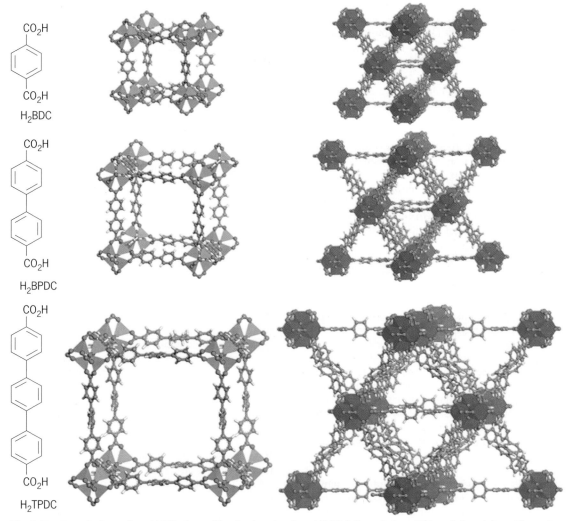

CO₂H

CO₂H

H₂BDC

CO₂H

CO₂H

H₂BPDC

CO₂H

CO₂H

H₂TPDC

Fig. 2. Two isoreticular series of MOFs formed by simple extension of H₂BDC through the addition of phenyl rings. The series on the left is from O. M. Yaghi and coworkers and uses the zinc tetrahedron SBU. The series on the right is from K. P. Lillerud and colleagues and contains a zirconium oxide SBU. Zinc, zirconium, carbon, oxygen, and hydrogen are blue, dark gray, gray, red, and white, respectively.

the MOF in a process known as postsynthetic functionalization, or used as originally synthesized. For example, W. Lin and coworkers prepared an isoreticular series of MOFs with orthogonal hydroxyl functions on 1,1′-Bi-2-naphthol (BINOL)–derived bridging ligands. Postsynthetic functionalization with Ti(OⁱPr)₄ yielded a catalytic site, and the resulting Ti-BINOLate MOFs were used to catalyze the addition of diethylzinc to aldehydes. J. T. Hupp and colleagues demonstrated the second functionalization technique by constructing a MOF from N,N′-bis(salicylidene)ethylenediamine [salen] ligands metallated with Mn, which were then used as prepared to catalyze the epoxidation of 2,2-dimethyl-2*H*-chromene.

An alternative technique for functionalizing MOFs relies on the swapping of ligands or metals from the final crystalline framework in a process called postsynthetic exchange. Several publications by S. M. Cohen and coworkers demonstrate that by immers-ing MOFs in solutions containing a similar metal or ligand, even highly stable and robust frameworks undergo ligand and metal exchange while retaining the original crystallinity. This technique provides a unique means to functionalize an otherwise inert MOF by exchanging a functionalized linker for an unfunctionalized linker. Similarly, exchanging metals allows for the preparation of MOFs with topologies that are otherwise inaccessible by direct synthetic techniques. This was recently demonstrated by M. R. Hill and coworkers, who exchanged Ti in a MOF possessing a topology that had only been synthesized using Zr-based SBUs. The resulting reduction in mass was leveraged to drastically increase the mass-weighted uptake of carbon dioxide.

Synthesis. MOFs are prepared by self-assembly, often under hydro- or solvothermal conditions. Final structures are dictated by many parameters, including pH, concentration, and temperature. Temperature in particular plays an important role, as the dielectric properties of solvents change as a function of temperature, leading to weakened interactions of solvent molecules and increased dissociation. As a result, with all other parameters constant, different MOFs can be synthesized solely by changing the temperature.

Solvent also plays a large role, as the organic bridging ligand is typically soluble, and use of different solvents can result in the formation of different frameworks. Dimethylformamide (DMF) is used frequently in MOF synthesis because of its impressive solubilizing properties for a wide range of organic groups and metal salts. DMF decomposes at elevated temperatures, hydrolyzing into formic acid and dimethylamine. As solution pH gradually increases, coordinating moieties on organic ligands are deprotonated to favor metal binding and subsequent nucleation of crystalline MOFs. Bulky solvents can also be used as templates to suppress framework catenation, a phenomenon in which two (or more) identical frameworks intergrow at the expense of pore volume.

Applications. Considering the vast and diverse means by which MOFs can be designed, characterized, and tuned, it is no surprise their potential uses are equally numerous and varied. MOFs have been investigated for applications such as drug delivery, ion exchange, molecular shuttling, scaffolds for nanoparticles, nonlinear optics, sensors, and sorbents. Although discussion of all MOF applications is beyond the scope of this article, the use of MOFs in gas separations and storage as well as application in catalysis will be discussed.

Gas storage and separations. Selective, efficient, and reversible storage of gasses is a scientific challenge of substantial proportion for which MOFs have shown great promise. Materials for hydrogen, methane, or carbon dioxide (CO_2) adsorption and storage is of utmost importance for averting the pending energy crisis and mitigating global climate change. However, different physical properties for each gas prompt the need for unique sorbent materials. Hydrogen has weak interactions and a low enthalpy of adsorption, requiring cryogenic temperatures for reasonable loading. In contrast, CO_2 sequestration suffers from the energy needed to liberate bound CO_2 to regenerate the capture material. Furthermore, mixed gases and the presence of other contaminants demand sorbent selectivity and stability under a wide range of conditions.

Porous materials separate gases via several mechanisms: size or shape exclusion, in which certain components are blocked from entering the pores of an adsorbent; thermodynamic equilibrium, in which adsorbate surface or adsorbate packing induce preference for one type of adsorbent over another; kinetic effects, in which certain components are able to enter the pores more rapidly and thus become adsorbed faster; and quantum sieving effects, in which micropores separate light molecules according to their different diffusion rates. MOFs are ideal platforms for gas storage and separation because their

high surface areas and fundamental characteristics allow for systematic tuning to optimize each of these separation mechanisms. Crystallinity facilitates rapid transportation of gas molecules through the pores and channels, permitting access to all gas-binding sites, while high surface areas allow for greater physisorption of gases on the surface of the bridging ligands. Reticular synthesis allows the design of materials possessing optimal pore size for gas adsorption and the incorporation of air- and moisture-stable SBUs. Additional gas-binding sites can be obtained for some SBUs by removing the coordinating solvent molecules using heating or vacuum. Finally, ligands in the MOF can be tuned to include gas-binding functional groups or to modify the electronic properties of the framework to enhance gas adsorption.

Certain MOFs have a framework supported in large part by coordination bonds and other weak interactions such as hydrogen bonding or van der Waals interaction. These materials, known as dynamic MOFs, have the ability to distort in response to external stimuli such as pressure, temperature, or the adsorption of certain guest molecules. This structural modulation with preservation of crystallinity and morphology is a phenomenon known as "breathing," and can prompt either the inclusion or evacuation of guest molecules. G. Férey and coworkers investigated a MOF formed from Al and H_2BDC that showed drastic shrinkage of cell volume by approximately 40%, while subsequent studies on an analogous Cr MOF revealed breathing effects to be related to the enthalpy of adsorption of the gas molecule. With gas separation influenced by factors such as pore aperture and rate of diffusion, this unique subgroup of the MOF family has tremendous potential for pressure- or temperature-dependent shape-selective separations, which is far beyond the capabilities of traditional sorbents.

Catalysis. The ability to incorporate diverse functional groups into porous MOFs makes them excellent candidates as solid catalysts. Unlike traditional heterogeneous catalysts, in which active sites can only be located on the outermost surface of the material, the well-defined pores and channels of MOFs allow rapid transport of substrates into the MOF and endow size- and shape-selective properties. Additionally, the crystalline nature of the framework allows precise knowledge of the active catalytic site, uniform catalyst loading, and investigation of the structure–activity relationships while eliminating intermolecular catalyst-deactivation pathways.

As discussed earlier, catalysts can be included via postsynthetic modification of an orthogonal functional group, or precatalysts can be synthesized directly into the bridging ligand prior to MOF assembly. Alternatively, opportunistic catalysts take advantage of the metal present in the SBUs, with accessible coordination sites employed as catalysts after activation by removal of the coordinated solvent. These different techniques of imparting catalytic activities are displayed in **Fig. 3**. The mild conditions for MOF synthesis facilitate incorporation of delicate

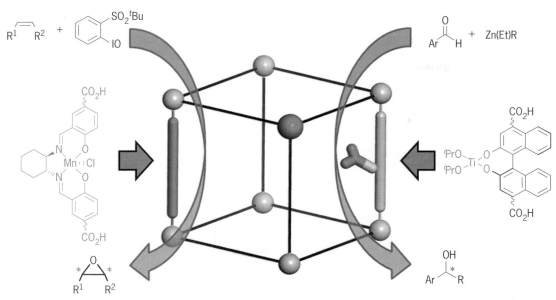

Fig. 3. Methods for functionalizing a MOF for catalysis. The red sphere represents opportunistic catalytic sites available by activating the MOF SBU. The red column on the left represents the use of bridging ligands synthesized to include a precatalyst, such as the Mn-salen–derived ligand, which can be used for asymmetric epoxidation. On the right, an orthogonal functional group on a BINOL-based ligand is postsynthetically modified by reacting with Ti(^{i}PrO)$_4$ and used for diethylzinc additions to aldehydes.

functional groups, such as precatalysts or enantiopure chiral ligands, making MOFs particularly exciting for asymmetric catalysis.

Asymmetric catalysis imparts chirality to a substrate molecule, yielding the stereoisomer products in unequal amounts. These reactions commonly use chiral coordination complexes as homogeneous catalysts, in which bulky ligands create a chiral environment around the active catalytic site. It was speculated that chiral MOFs would provide an ideal platform for this type of reaction, as the ligands could be functionalized to include a catalyst and the framework could create a chiral environment in the MOF channels. While initial efforts using MOFs for asymmetric catalysis showed promising results, only recently was this relationship between pore size and enantioselectivity demonstrated decisively. Preparing an isoreticular series of homochiral MOFs with Cu(II)- and BINOL-derived ligands elongated at the 4, 4', 6, and 6' positions, W. Lin and coworkers investigated the Ti(^{i}PrO)$_4$-catalyzed addition of diethylzinc to aldehydes of varying bulk. Although surface reactivity ensured complete conversion for most reactions, enantioselectivity was observed only in substrates that were small enough to diffuse through the channels of the MOFs. The enantioselectivity could be modulated by using isoreticular MOFs with shorter ligands, as smaller pore apertures decrease the rate of diffusion.

Outlook. MOFs are a novel class of materials with well-ordered structures and properties that can be systematically tuned by a variety of techniques. Their high porosity, large surface areas, modifiable nature, and synthetic scalability make them interesting platforms for diverse applications. With their utility already demonstrated in catalysis, gas separations, and storage, MOFs have shown great promise in enabling novel technological breakthroughs in the twenty-first century.

For background information *see* ASYMMETRIC SYNTHESIS; CATALYSIS; COORDINATION CHEMISTRY; CRYSTAL STRUCTURE; LIGAND; SUPRAMOLECULAR CHEMISTRY; X-RAY CRYSTALLOGRAPHY in the McGraw-Hill Encyclopedia of Science & Technology.

Carter W. Abney; Wenbin Lin

Bibliography. J. H. Cavka et al., Zirconium inorganic building brick forming metal organic frameworks with exceptional stability, *J. Am. Chem. Soc.*, 130:13850–13851, 2008, DOI:10.1021/ja8057953; S.-H Cho et al., A metal-organic framework material that functions as an enantioselective catalyst for olefin epoxidation, *Chem. Commun.*, 24:2563–2565, 2006, DOI:10.1039/B600408C; M. Eddaoudi et al., Systematic design of pore size and functionality in isoreticular MOFs and their application in methane storage, *Science*, 295:469–472, 2002, DOI:10.1126/science.1067208; D. Farrusseng (ed.), *Metal-Organic Frameworks: Applications from Catalysis to Gas Storage*, Wiley, 2011; L. Ma, J. Falkowski, C. Abney, and W. Lin, A series of isoreticular chiral metal-organic frameworks as a tunable platform for asymmetric catalysis, *Nat. Chem.*, 2:838–846, 2010, DOI:10.1038/nchem.738; M. Kim et al., Postsynthetic ligand exchange as a route to functionalization of 'inert' metal-organic frameworks, *Chem. Sci.*, 3:126–130, 2012, DOI:10.1039/C1SC00394A; C. H. Lau, R. Babarao, and M. R. Hill, A route to drastic increase of CO$_2$ uptake in Zr metal organic framework UiO-66, *Chem Commun.*, 35:3634–3636, 2013, DOI:10.1039/C3CC40470F;

L. R. MacGillivray (ed.), *Metal-Organic Frame-works: Design and Application*, Wiley, 2010; M. Schröder (ed.), *Functional Metal-Organic Frame-works: Gas Storage, Separation, and Catalysis*, Springer, 2010; C. Serre et al., Very large breathing effect in the first nanoporous chromium (iii)-based solids: MIL-53 or $Cr^{III}(OH)\cdot\{O_2C\text{-}C_6H_4\text{-}CO_2\}\cdot HO_2C\text{-}C_6H_4\text{-}CO_2H\}_x\cdot H_2O_y$, *J. Am. Chem. Soc.*, 124:13519–13526, 2002, DOI: 10.1021/ja0276974; Special issue featuring metal-organic frameworks, *Chem. Rev.*, 112:673–1268, 2012; Special issue featuring metal-organic frameworks, *Chem. Soc. Rev.*, 38:1201–1508, 2009.

MicroRNA biogenesis pathway

The discovery of microRNAs (miRNAs) is one of the major scientific breakthroughs in recent years, revolutionizing our understanding about gene regulation. In general, miRNAs are short, single-stranded RNAs [approximately 22 nucleotides (nt) in length], and they are expressed by all multicellular eukaryotes. Although miRNAs do not encode any proteins directly, they can regulate the expression of about 60% of all protein-coding genes in humans. The high sequence conservation of many miRNAs among distantly related organisms suggests strong evolutionary pressures and participation in essential processes. In fact, miRNAs have been shown to participate in the regulation of almost every cellular process investigated to date.

Lin-4 was the first miRNA to be determined. It was found in the roundworm, *Caenorhabditis elegans*, in the early 1990s. However, miRNAs were not recognized as a distinct class of gene regulators having conserved functions until the early 2000s, when the second miRNA, let-7, was identified. Since then, miRNA research has revealed more and more important functions for these small RNAs. At present, there are 25,141 miRNAs identified in 193 species, and there are more than 2000 miRNAs existing in humans. This article provides an overview about the biosynthesis and biological functions of miRNAs.

Mechanism of miRNA formation. With regard to the encoding of genomic miRNAs, genes are transcribed by either RNA polymerase II or RNA polymerase III to generate long primary transcripts (pri-miRNAs) [see **illustration**]. The typical structure of a pri-miRNA includes a double-stranded (ds) stem of approximately 33 base pairs, a terminal loop, and two flanking, unstructured, single-stranded RNA regions. This structure is critical for a microprocessor to cleave pri-miRNAs and release a hairpin intermediate (pre-miRNA). The key components of the microprocessor are a ribonuclease (RNase) III enzyme called Drosha and a dsRNA-binding protein termed DGCR8 [also called Pasha (partner of Drosha)]. DGCR8 can recognize and bind the single-stranded RNA and dsRNA junction on the pri-miRNA and can bring Drosha to its substrate. Drosha cleaves

the stem part of a pri-miRNA at approximately 11 nucleotides away from the single-stranded segments, thereby liberating the pre-miRNA, which has a 5′ monophosphate and a 3′ 2-nt hydroxyl overhang (see illustration). In addition to the microprocessor, several other proteins, including the heterogeneous nuclear ribonucleoprotein A1 (hnRNP A1) and RNA helicases p68 and p72, have been found to function as accessory proteins for conversion of a subset of pri-miRNAs to pre-miRNAs.

Analysis of mouse cells lacking Drosha or DGCR8 has demonstrated that the biogenesis of most cellular miRNAs is dependent on these two proteins. However, a few miRNAs are still produced even when Drosha is absent, indicating that there are Drosha-independent miRNA biogenesis pathways existing in the cells. In addition to the canonical miRNA biogenesis pathway, several studies have shown that certain introns released during the RNA splicing process can also form the hairpin structure with a 5′ monophosphate and a 3′ 2-nt hydroxyl overhang, which mimics the pre-miRNA and enters the miRNA processing pathway without Drosha-mediated cleavage (see illustration). These pre-miRNAs are named mirtrons (pre-miRNA/introns) and have been identified in *Drosophila*, *C. elegans*, and mammals.

After processing by Drosha/DGCR8, pre-miRNAs are exported to the cytoplasm by Ran [a small protein that binds with guanosine-5′-triphosphate (GTP) and is essential for the translocation of RNA through the nuclear pore] and exportin-5 (a member of the Ran-dependent nuclear transport receptor family). In the cytoplasm, Ran-GTP is hydrolyzed by Ran GTPase-activating protein (Ran-GAP) to Ran–guanosine diphosphate (Ran-GDP), and the pre-miRNA is released from exportin-5. The pre-miRNAs are cleaved into short-lived miRNA duplexes by an enzyme protein called Dicer. The loading of the miRNA into its effector complex, called the RNA-induced silencing complex (RISC), is asymmetric, which is determined by the relative thermodynamic characteristics of the 5′ termini of the miRNA duplex. The strand with the less-stable 5′ end is favored or exclusively loaded into the RISC and becomes the mature miRNA (see illustration).

Function of miRNAs. After loading, miRNA guides the RISC and binds to the 3′ untranslated region (3′UTR) of target messenger RNAs (mRNAs). The RISC contains argonaute proteins (the catalytically active RNases), which can inhibit protein synthesis by either repressing translation or promoting degradation of target mRNAs. Efficient binding requires continuous base pairing of miRNA nucleotides 2 to 8 to the target sequence. This region on the miRNA is also called the seed region, which determines the target specificity of the miRNA. However, functional miRNA sites containing mismatches or even bulged nucleotides in the seed region have also been identified, as exemplified by the *Lin-41* mRNA targeted by *let-7* miRNA in *C. elegans*. Complementarity of the miRNA 3′ half is quite relaxed, although it stabilizes the interaction, particularly when the seed matching

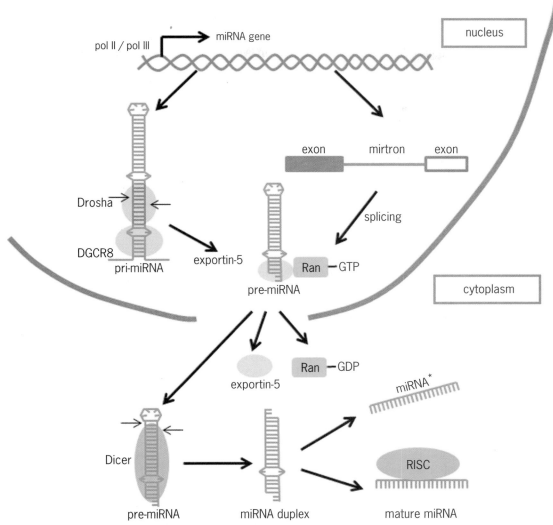

The miRNA biogenesis pathway. The miRNA genes are transcribed by either RNA polymerase II (pol II) or RNA polymerase III (pol III) to generate long primary transcripts (pri-miRNAs). The typical structure of a pri-miRNA includes a double-stranded (ds) stem of approximately 33 base pairs, a terminal loop, and two flanking, unstructured, single-stranded RNA regions. This structure is critical for a microprocessor to cleave pri-miRNAs and release a hairpin intermediate (pre-miRNA). The key components of the microprocessor are a ribonuclease enzyme called Drosha and a dsRNA-binding protein termed DGCR8. Drosha cleaves the stem part of a pri-miRNA, thereby liberating the pre-miRNA. In addition, certain introns released during the RNA splicing process can also form the hairpin structure, which mimics the pre-miRNA and enters the miRNA processing pathway without Drosha-mediated cleavage. These pre-miRNAs are named mirtrons. After processing by Drosha/DGCR8, pre-miRNAs are exported to the cytoplasm by Ran [a small protein that binds with guanosine-5′-triphosphate (GTP)] and exportin-5. In the cytoplasm, Ran-GTP is hydrolyzed to Ran–guanosine diphosphate (Ran-GDP), and the pre-miRNA is released from exportin-5. The pre-miRNAs are cleaved into short-lived miRNA duplexes by an enzyme protein called Dicer. The loading of the miRNA into its effector complex, called the RNA-induced silencing complex (RISC), is asymmetric, which is determined by the relative thermodynamic characteristics of the 5′ termini of the miRNA duplex. The strand with the less-stable 5′ end is favored or exclusively loaded into the RISC and becomes the mature miRNA. The other strand of the miRNA (designated miRNA*) is typically degraded.

is suboptimal. In addition, an adenine (A) residue at position 1 of the miRNA and an adenine (A) or uracil (U) residue at position 9 improve the activity of the miRNA, although they do not need to base-pair with any mRNA nucleotides. In the 3′UTR of the target mRNA, there are usually multiple binding sites, for either the same or different miRNAs, which are required for effective repression. When these sites are close to each other, they tend to act cooperatively.

The emergence of miRNAs does not make it easier to understand gene regulation, but it is possible to get closer to the real picture by integrating them into the existing gene regulatory networks. Each miRNA regulates more than one gene, whereas each gene is regulated by multiple miRNAs. Many miRNA targets are transcription factors, which can further regulate the downstream gene expression. On the other hand, as observed in other genes, miRNA expression is also regulated by transcription factors. It is clear that the potential regulatory effect of miRNAs is enormous. However, for most miRNAs, only their sequence and basic expression data are known, and the functional data are available for a tiny fraction of the miRNAs discovered at present.

Disease and miRNAs. As a class of important gene regulators, miRNAs have been demonstrated to play critical roles in many physiological processes, including differentiation and maintenance of cell identity in the hematopoietic system, establishment of muscle phenotypes, morphogenesis of epithelial tissues, organogenesis, and metabolic processes. Accordingly, deregulated miRNA expression has been found in many human diseases, offering the possibility of using miRNAs as diagnostic and prognostic markers. In particular, cancer researchers have shown that miRNA expression signatures provide a more accurate method for cancer subtype classification than mRNA expression profiling. Some miRNA expression profiles also have predictive prognostic power; for example, in chronic lymphocytic leukemia, a specific miRNA expression signature composed of 13 miRNAs has been reported to establish prognosis. In addition, overexpression of miR-210 in breast cancer is associated with an increased risk of recurrence and a reduced chance of relapse-free survival.

Surprisingly, miRNAs have been found recently to exist in a stable form in body fluids, including serum, urine, saliva, tears, breast milk, and seminal fluid. These extracellular miRNAs are packaged in exosomes (small secreted membrane vesicles of endocytic origin) or RNA-binding proteins, which protect them from being degraded by the large amounts of RNase found in body fluids. Although a few studies have implicated the roles of extracellular miRNAs in intercellular communication, their biological function is largely unknown. However, these extracellular miRNAs hold a larger promise to become clinical biomarkers because their expression patterns are associated with various pathophysiological conditions, and body fluid samples are easy to obtain by noninvasive methods in clinical settings.

As mentioned previously, miRNAs play important roles in human diseases, including cancer, heart diseases, infectious diseases, and inflammatory diseases. Because of their differential expression patterns, it has been suggested that miRNAs could be potential targets for medical therapy. It has been shown in vitro and in animal models that the introduction of miRNA mimics or miRNA inhibitors into diseased cells or tissues can induce favorable therapeutic responses. Because a unique miRNA can affect cellular processes by regulating the expression of multiple proteins, miRNA-based therapies may be more effective than drugs that target single proteins. At present, many targeted miRNA therapies for various diseases are being studied. So far, the only miRNA-based therapy tested in human beings is the miR-122 inhibitor (also known as miravirsen or SPC3649), which is used to treat hepatitis C virus (HCV) infection. The miRNA known as miR-122 is liver-specific and is essential for HCV replication. Researchers have designed locked nucleic acid (LNA) oligonucleotides complementary to miR-122,

which can specifically and stably inhibit the activity of miR-122. Intravenous delivery of this miR-122 inhibitor has been tested in HCV chronically infected chimpanzees and healthy human volunteers. The results have indicated that the miR-122 inhibitor can efficiently reduce the HCV viral load in serum and liver, and there are no dose-limiting toxicities. Presently, it is being tested in a phase-2 clinical trial to treat HCV chronically infected patients. Preliminary results are very promising, and this miR-122 inhibitor may become the first miRNA-based therapy used in clinics.

Conclusions. Although miRNAs are simple in structure, these gene regulators are extremely important to cells. Their biosynthesis is a multistep process and is subjected to sophisticated controls at different levels. Based on sequence complementarities, a mature miRNA can recognize target mRNAs, bring the effector enzyme complex (RISC) to these target mRNAs, and regulate protein synthesis. Moreover, because of the connection between miRNAs and many human diseases, these miRNAs have the potential to become promising targets for diagnosis and treatment.

For background information *see* ENZYME; GENE; GENETICS; MICRORNA; MOLECULAR BIOLOGY; NUCLEOTIDE; PROTEIN; RIBONUCLEIC ACID (RNA); TRANSCRIPTION in the McGraw-Hill Encyclopedia of Science & Technology.   Ning Xu Landén

Bibliography. D. P. Bartel, MicroRNAs: Target recognition and regulatory functions, *Cell*, 136:215–233, 2009, DOI:10.1016/j.cell.2009.01.002; Y. W. Kong et al., MicroRNAs in cancer management, *Lancet Oncol.*, 13:e249–e258, 2012, DOI:10.1016/S1470-2045(12)70073-6; J. Winter et al., Many roads to maturity: MicroRNA biogenesis pathways and their regulation, *Nature Cell Biol.*, 11:228–234, 2009, DOI:10.1038/ncb0309-228; J.-S. Yang and E. C. Lai, Alternative miRNA biogenesis pathways and the interpretation of core miRNA pathway mutants, *Mol. Cell*, 43(6):892–903, 2011, DOI:10.1016/j.molcel.2011.07.024.

Mining Internet search and social media for epidemiology

Many pervasive and multifactorial disorders of modern noncommunicable and noninfectious diseases, such as obesity, asthma, migraine, and autism, need to be better understood, defined, and explored. Recently, medical and public health researchers have begun to take advantage of the huge increase in the amount of information available via the Internet and the concomitant advance in data science technology to explore potential disease-related factors and the temporal and spatial relationships among them at a variety of population levels.

An individual's disease or health status can be thought of as a complex balance of a variety of biological, environmental, and lifestyle factors (**Fig. 1**). Quantifying these factors for large numbers of individuals can elucidate meaningful trends and aid in

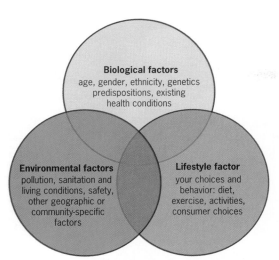

Fig. 1. Overlapping domains give rise to an individual's health status, which is a complex function of biological, environmental, and lifestyle factors. Being able to capture electronically information of this type that has been voluntarily journaled or streamed by individuals has tremendous value in public health modeling and methods.

hypothesis generation. Historically, our knowledge of lifestyle and environmental factors and their interactions has been limited. To overcome this obstacle, epidemiology researchers are now using new methods to collect disease-factor information from publically available big data web-based or social-media-based streams. The data streams of social media contain gigantic volumes of mentions relating to symptoms, treatments, activities, events, consumer products use, and other related human behaviors. Surveillance of social media through search-term analysis can identify meaningful geographic and temporal patterns in these mentions, and that information can be compared with other available public data, such as census, public health, housing, weather, and environmental data, to better understand, quantify, and visualize the causes and origins of diseases.

Search volume analysis. Search volume analysis involves a quantitative investigation of the aggregate search-term volume from a variety of search engines such as Google or Yahoo, using publically available tools such as Google Trends™. These approaches provide temporal and spatial information about what people are searching for, and hypothetically, what they are doing, eating, or buying. This approach can be fine-tuned to validate the assumption that there is a correlation between human activities or behaviors and information-seeking patterns by comparing them to global, national, or local epidemiological statistics. It provides a rational starting point for identifying the optimal seasons and locations in which to administer informative surveys. The search volume approach does not assist in directly identifying demographic information, but it can be combined with census data to glean or infer the demographics of populations in different places.

The key step in search volume analysis is the development of appropriate search terms for a

given research question (for example, a set of disease symptoms). Text analysis (for example, the generation of wordclouds that represent the frequency with which words are used in social media), set-generation methods (such as Google Sets™), and crowdsourcing approaches [such as Mechanical Turk (https://www.mturk.com)] can be useful in developing meaningful sets of search terms.

Google Trends analyses have recently been used to examine the temporal properties of Lyme disease outbreaks. Another simple example of a disease-related search volume analysis is shown in **Fig. 2**. We performed a Google Trends analysis of the term "migraine" in 40 different languages. The global, geographically specific relative search volume results were compared against migraine prevalence for 14 different global regions as reported by the World Health Organization (WHO). Despite the simplicity of the search term, a significant correlation could be seen. This example could be refined to target specific countries or symptoms, or to correlate these results to other global data (such as weather).

We have also recently applied search volume analysis to elucidate trends in consumer product

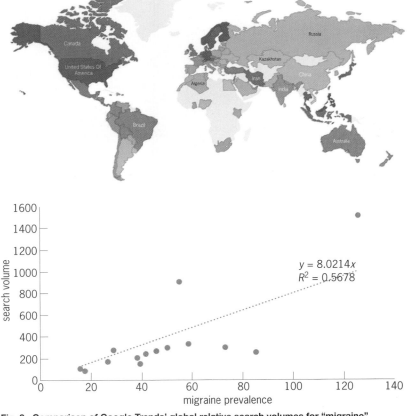

Fig. 2. Comparison of Google Trends' global relative search volumes for "migraine" compared to the World Health Organization (WHO) migraine prevalence data. The map of the world is colored according to the frequency (normalized search term volume) of the term "migraine," in 40 different languages (darker is higher search term volume). The source of the data is from "migraine" and "migraines" in multiple languages: http://goo.gl.mesbb (this is the shortened URL). The graphic was rendered in many-eyes.org. The plot was made in Excel (underneath the map) against regional WHO migraine prevalence data.

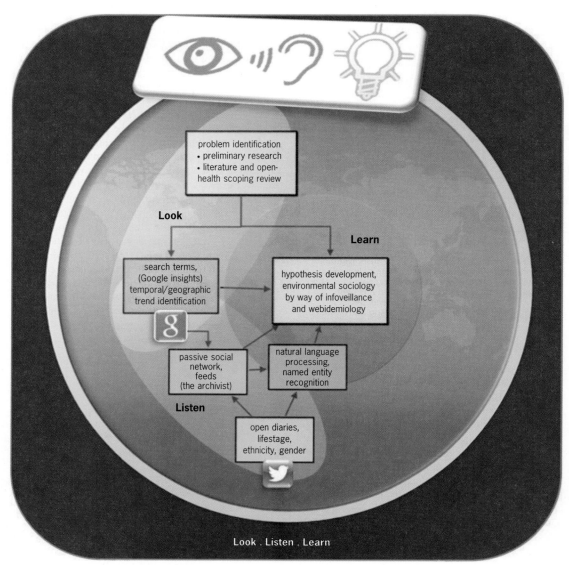

Fig. 3. The look, listen, and learn paradigm.

use, which could be useful in the risk assessment of chemicals. Preliminary studies determined that there is a high degree of correlation between the Google Trend search volumes associated with a set of terms describing different types of cleaning products or personal care products and the numbers of those products actually found in homes in prior field studies. This finding will allow us to extrapolate our methods to predict product use for product categories for which we have little or no data.

Mining of social media (microblogging) streams. Another approach to exploring symptoms and related factors is to deal directly with massive amounts of microblogging data such as from Twitter or Tumblr. These microblogging environments can provide information similar to that of the search volume approach. The effort requires the development of natural language processing (NLP) methods, such as a named-entity recognition (NER) term tokenizer that identifies the key taxonomy for a given domain

of interest. Appropriate taxonomies are required to more accurately identify and capture the representation of terms related to a specific symptom, disease, human activity, or behavior. An advantage of these methods over search volume analysis is that they can provide immediate correlations between symptoms and activities by tracking the use of the search terms by individuals. Geographic information can be collected as well, because users can set their microblog entries (such as the tweets posted in Twitter) to be geocoded. In addition, it is easier to extract demographic information for individuals from these data through user-provided profiles or from information within the microblog streams themselves.

One useful method we are developing is the mapping of microblog entries to the generalized activity and location codes described in the U.S. Environmental Protection Agency's (EPA) Consolidated Human Activity Database (CHAD), which the agency uses in assessments of exposure to air and chemical

TABLE 1. Some useful data streams by type, source, and accompanying open-access resource URL, with most of these containing geographically specific information

Data type	Source	URL
Asthma statistics	The global burden of asthma: executive summary of the Global Initiative for Asthma Program (GINA) Dissemination Committee Report	http://onlinelibrary.wiley.com/doi/10.1111/j.1398-9995.2004.00526.x/full
Pollen data	American Academy of Allergy, Asthma & Immunology	http://www.aaaai.org/global/nab-pollen-counts.aspx
Air quality	Air Now	www.airnow.gov
U.S. Census	U.S. Census Bureau	http://www.census.gov/main/www/access.html
National Air Toxics Assessments	U.S. Environmental Protection Agency (EPA)	http://www.epa.gov/nata/
American Housing Survey (housing information)	U.S. Census Bureau	http://www.census.gov/housing/ahs/
Diet and SES (Food Environment Atlas)	U.S. Department of Agriculture Economic Research Service	http://www.ers.usda.gov/data-products/food-environment-atlas/go-to-the-atlas.aspx#.UZ4keKLqnxA
Weather forecast	National Weather Service (National Oceanic and Atmospheric Administration)	http://www.weather.gov/forecastmaps
List of World Health Organization (WHO) regions and subregions	WHO	http://www.who.int/entity/healthinfo/statistics/gbdestimatesregionallist.xls
Migraine statistics	WHO	http://www.who.int/healthinfo/statistics/bod_migraine.pdf
Fine particulate matter ($PM_{2.5}$) map of Earth (served as comparison)	National Aeronautics and Space Administration (NASA)	http://www.nasa.gov/topics/earth/features/health-sapping.html
Weather/activity relationship (served as comparison)	NASA	http://icp.giss.nasa.gov/education/urbanmaap/projects/projects_asthma5.html
Human activities (Consolidated Human Activity Database)	U.S. EPA	http://www.epa.gov/heasd/chad.html
Human activities (American Time Use Survey)	U.S. Department of Labor, Bureau of Labor Statistics	http://www.bls.gov/tus/

pollutants. It has previously been shown that NLP can be used to translate spoken word diaries directly into CHAD codes, and we are extending this to text-based diaries. This advance will allow us to map microblog entries directly to activities and locations relevant to pollutant exposures, and then to correlate them with disease symptoms or other relevant factors. To this end we have also begun taxonomy development related to CHAD activities in a simple nine-person "how would you tweet that?" experiment.

There have been numerous attempts to mix both search volume-derived data and microblogging data into the mainstream of predicting, extrapolating, and anticipating human behavior as it relates to disease and epidemic outbreaks, such as Google Flu Trends (http://www.google.org/flutrends/us/#US) or Health Map (http://healthmap.org/en/). Those projects have found this method to be quite useful, which is why using this method to alleviate the big-data problem of elucidating the etiology of diseases seems plausible.

The look, listen, and learn paradigm. We have found a "Look, Listen, and Learn" paradigm that formalizes and combines the aforementioned methods (illustrated in **Fig. 3**) to be extremely useful in framing our approach to new questions. We can start from a global perspective, using aggregated data that contain temporal and spatial information related to specific keyword search terms, and then work our way down to the levels of populations, communities, and individuals, where we can collect detailed information from social-media data streams. This paradigm can be summarized as follows.

Look: problem identification and key-factor term development. The step starts by defining public-health problem targets (such as asthma, migraine, obesity, or psoriasis). An analysis of the medical literature (through pubmed.org) identifies keywords for search formulation (and also for inventory information that could potentially to be used later to validate the methods). In addition, open-health websites (such as curetogether.com) can be explored for potential symptom- or treatment-related search terms. Text analyses or visualizations (such as wordclouds) can be useful in extracting important terms from large volumes of abstracts or other text.

Listen: aggregate search-term volume analysis at different spatial, geographic, and temporal scales. This step involves using search-term volume analysis (by Google Trends, for example) at global (multilingual), population (monolingual), and community levels to elucidate potential temporal and geographical trends and identify target locations or populations of interest.

Learn: target populations and times of interest for detailed social media analysis leading to hypothesis generation. This step includes fine-tuning the analysis of any key identified locations and seasons through the NLP mining of geocoded social streams (microblogs), which have been appropriately anonymized. In this way, more detailed information can be explored, identifying hourly as opposed to seasonal patterns or demographic details gleaned from social media profiles, or other activities or factors.

Many of the factors explored in those three steps can be mapped against other available data to elucidate data gaps, visualize variations in disease prevalence over time or seasons, and explore correlations among potential factors. A selection of freely available spatial and temporal data and some useful tools are provided in **Tables 1** and **2**.

This paradigm can be used for scoping analysis

TABLE 2. Useful tools for performing passive web-based analysis of disease factors

Tool	Definition of tool	How tool was used	URL	Reference for definition
Cure Together	Free public site that allows people around the world to share quantitative information about their medical conditions, including symptoms and treatments that worked best for them	Used to identify self-described symptoms and treatments	http://curetogether.com/	http://curetogether.com/blog/about/
Google Maps	Map service viewed in web browser that provides geocodes	Used to retrieve geocodes	https://maps.google.com/	http://support.google.com/maps/bin/answer.py?&hl=entopic=1687350&safe=on&answer=144352
Google Scholar	Freely accessible web search engine that provides a simple way to broadly search for scholarly literature across many disciplines and sources	Used to search for literature, in order to get an idea of factor and information landscape of disease in question	http://scholar.google.com	http://www.google.com/intl/en/scholar/about.html
Google Sets	A tool within Google Drive that identifies keywords that are semantically related	Used to generate symptoms that correspond with illness or disease	https://drive.google.com	http://www.ncbi.nlm.nih.gov/pmc/articles/PMC3635219/
Google Trends	Public web facility by Google that shows how often a particular search term is entered relative to the total search volume across various regions of the world, and in various languages	Used to identify trends geographically, using the keywords from Many Eyes, Google Scholar, and PubMed	http://www.google.com/trends/	http://en.wikipedia.org/wiki/Google_Trends
Many Eyes	Free site from IBM that provides data visualization tools. Site allows users to upload datasets and produce graphic representations.	Used to visualize relationships in abstracts and help formulate query or keywords	http://www.many-eyes.com	http://www.many-eyes.com (Google search)
Nice Translator	Site that provides an improved interface for translating text on the Web	Used to translate terms (symptoms) and identify other languages within a text	http://www.nicetranslator.com/	http://nicetranslator.com/blog/about
Patients Like Me	A health data-sharing platform	Used to identify self-described symptoms and treatments	http://www.patientslikeme.com/	http://www.patientslikeme.com/about
PubMed	Provides free access to the MEDLINE database, of indexed citations and abstracts to medical, nursing, dental, veterinary, health care, and preclinical science journal articles	Used to search for literature, in order to get an idea of factor and information landscape of disease in question	http://www.ncbi.nlm.nih.gov/pubmed	http://www.nlm.nih.gov/services/pubmed.html
Tweet Archivist	Twitter analytics tool used to search, archive, analyze, visualize, save, and export tweets based on a search term or hashtag	Used to capture geocoded tweets	http://www.tweetarchivist.com/	http://www.tweetarchivist.com/ (Google search)

and hypothesis generation. Advantages and disadvantages of this approach are discussed in **Table 3**. Although these methods will never take the place of more traditional methods in epidemiology, they have the potential to inform the design of future focused studies that optimize the selection of geographic and seasonal sampling patterns, relevant cohorts, and studied factors.

TABLE 3. Benefits and disadvantages of passive web-based methods for exploring disease factors (the look, listen, and learn paradigm)

Benefits [Pros (+)]	Disadvantages [Cons (−)]
Extremely useful and relevant tool for **"real-time" screening** of a wide-cast set of variables and undiscovered factors with minimum burden	**Not structured** epidemiological queries
Passive interrogation methods reduce Hawthorne effect and study participant biases common to traditional active survey methods	**"Web-savvy" demographics may vary** from actual population demographics (age, gender, ethnicity, and socioeconomic status)
Can be modified on the fly by language (that is, use nicetranslator.com), terms, rapidly regenerated, and is essentially **"free"** in terms of cost	Social media monitoring by some (for example, government) may **appear "big brother"**...what are the ethical implications?
This form of information modeling can give rise to **understanding either data gaps, population variability, or technology penetration.**	**Technology penetrance** in certain populations may be an issue (some counties, states, and countries have fewer technology resources for a variety of reasons, including socioeconomic factors, government censorship, and so forth)

[*Disclaimer:* The United States Environmental Protection Agency through its Office of Research and Development funded and managed the research described here. It has been subjected to Agency review and approved for publication. Mention of trade names or commercial products does not constitute endorsement or recommendation for use.]

For background information *see* ENVIRONMENTAL ENGINEERING; EPIDEMIOLOGY; GEOGRAPHIC INFORMATION SYSTEMS; INTERNET; NATURAL LANGUAGE PROCESSING; PUBLIC HEALTH; RISK ASSESSMENT AND MANAGEMENT in the McGraw-Hill Encyclopedia of Science & Technology.

Kristin Isaacs; Christopher M. Grulke; Raina D. Brooks; Madeline Reich; Ryan Edwards; Michael-Rock Goldsmith

Bibliography. H. A. Carneiro and E. Mylonakis, Google trends: a web-based tool for real-time surveillance of disease outbreaks, *Clin. Infect. Dis.*, 49(10):1557-1564, 2009, DOI:10.1086/630200; G. Eysenbach, Infodemiology and infoveillance: Framework for an emerging set of public health informatics methods to analyze search, communication and publication behavior on the Internet, *J. Med. Internet Res.*, 11(1):e11, 2009, DOI:10.2196/jmir.1157; C. Guinn and D. J. Reeves, Using a spoken diary and heart rate monitor in modeling human exposure to airborne pollutants for EPA's Consolidated Human Activity Database, in G. A. Uzochukwu et al. (eds.), *Proceedings of the 2007 National Conference on Environmental Science and Technology*, pp. 197-203, Springer Science, New York, 2009; M. J. Paul and M. Dredze, You are what you tweet: Analyzing Twitter for public health, http://www.cs.jhu.edu/~mdredze/publications/twitter_health_icwsm_11.pdf, Association for the Advancement of Artificial Intelligence, 2011; A. Seifter, A. Schwarzwalder, K. Geis, and J. Aucott, The utility of "Google Trends" for epidemiological research: Lyme disease as an example, *Geospat. Health.* 4(2):135-137, 2010.

Mitochondrial pyruvate carrier

The metabolite pyruvate occupies a pivotal position at the junction of a number of different metabolic pathways, including cytoplasmic glycolysis, mitochondrial carbohydrate oxidation, glucose production, fatty acid biosynthesis, and amino acid metabolism. As a result of this prominent placement in the metabolic network, the fate of pyruvate has large consequences on the behavior of cells and organisms. A great deal of the metabolic regulation that is prominently implicated in the determination of metabolic status acts directly or indirectly to control the quality and quantity of pyruvate consumption. The most obvious difference in the fate of the pyruvate within the cell is whether or not it is taken into the mitochondria [specialized compartments (organelles) that provide ATP for most eukaryotic cells]. Because the cytoplasmic and mitochondrial enzymes that metabolize pyruvate are spatially separated, the metabolic pathways and opportunities that involve pyruvate can differ, depending on whether the pyruvate is located in the cytoplasm or it enters the mitochondria. Because of this critical role in metabolic regulation, the process of mitochondrial pyruvate transport has been the subject of extensive study over the past several decades. These historical studies have provided great insight into the existence, function, kinetics, and substrate specificity of the mitochondrial pyruvate carrier (MPC), whose molecular identity remained a mystery prior to 2012.

MPC research. Prior to the mid-1970s, there was substantial uncertainty about the existence of a specific transporter that would enable the entry of pyruvate into mitochondria. Being a weak acid, pyruvate can traverse membranes in the absence of a carrier. However, in 1974, investigators determined that modified hydroxycinnamates are specific inhibitors of mitochondrial pyruvate transport activity. This discovery essentially proved the existence of a specific transporter and led to a great deal of study into the activity of this carrier. The kinetics, substrate specificity, and even some molecular information emerged over the ensuing decade. Although invaluable, none of these lines of investigation culminated in the discovery of the proteins that make up the MPC or the genes that encode them.

In 2012, two research groups described the molecular identification of a two-protein complex that is either the MPC or an obligate component of it. The entrée for these groups into this fruitful endeavor came with the identification of proteins in mitochondrial extracts for which no function had previously been described in the literature. The phylogenetic structure of the protein superfamily that contains these two proteins is an important part of the biochemical story. The MPC superfamily comprises two subfamilies (MPC1 and MPC2), which are related to one another, but are clearly distinct. It appears that every eukaryotic species has at least one member of each of these two subfamilies. Humans express one functional protein in each of the subfamilies, previously named BRP44L and BRP44 and now named MPC1 and MPC2.

Because of the high degree of conservation and the power of the model system, these investigators began to study the role of the MPC family using the yeast *Saccharomyces cerevisiae*. Yeast has one *MPC1* gene, but two MPC2 subfamily genes, *MPC2* and *MPC3*, which appear to be largely redundant, depending on the environment. It was found that the loss of *MPC1* or the loss of *MPC2* and *MPC3* conferred a defect in mitochondrial pyruvate metabolism that was manifested both in defects of carbohydrate metabolism and of branched-chain amino acid and lipoic acid biosynthesis. Through a series of steady-state metabolomics measurements, it was concluded that the loss of *MPC1* (or *MPC2*) impaired the conversion of cytosolic pyruvate into mitochondrial acetyl–coenzyme A (acetyl-CoA, which is a substrate for mitochondrial ATP production). In this case, mutants accumulated excess pyruvate and other glycolytic intermediates, and they had decreased accumulation of acetyl-CoA.

The function of the MPC genes appeared to be conserved across species as both *Drosophila melanogaster MPC1* and human *MPC1* fully rescued the metabolic and growth defects of yeast mutants lacking *MPC1*. This was confirmed using analysis of fly mutants lacking the single *MPC1* ortholog (a gene whose encoded proteins fulfill similar roles in different species). These mutants exhibited a profound defect when fed a carbohydrate diet, losing motility within hours and dying within a few days. Detailed and careful metabolomics studies again pinpointed a metabolic blockade between cytosolic glycolysis, and its product pyruvate, and the mitochondrial tricarboxylic acid (TCA) cycle (also known as the Krebs or citric acid cycle), involving acetyl-CoA.

Further studies determined the precise metabolic step that was impaired in the MPC mutants. The two possibilities were a loss of the activity of the pyruvate dehydrogenase complex, which converts mitochondrial pyruvate to acetyl-CoA, and a loss of mitochondrial pyruvate uptake (import). It was found that the activity of the pyruvate dehydrogenase was only marginally lower in MPC mutants, at least in a medium containing adequate amino acids. Parenthetically, it is interesting that there was a statistically significant decrease in the ex vivo activity of pyruvate dehydrogenase, implying some sort of intimate relationship between the MPC and the pyruvate dehydrogenase complex. Nonetheless, the defect that seems to be much more relevant was detected as a failure of pyruvate uptake into mitochondria that were purified from an *mpc1* mutant strain. A role for the MPC proteins in mitochondrial pyruvate uptake was further demonstrated by the discovery of a mutant of *MPC1* that conferred resistance to UK-5099 (an inhibitor of mitochondrial pyruvate transport).

Human MPC abnormalities. It was also shown that small interfering RNA (siRNA)–mediated knockdown of either *MPC1* or *MPC2* in mammalian cells also led to a decrease in both basal and maximal pyruvate oxidation. This led to the exciting hypothesis that mutations in either human *MPC1* or *MPC2* might cause a subset of metabolic defects that appear to be mutations in the pyruvate dehydrogenase complex, but have normal activity of that complex. To this point, there are patients with these characteristics that have no known genetic basis for their disease presentation. One example of such a patient was described in 2003. By analyzing the fibroblasts derived from this patient, it was decided that the defect was likely to involve mitochondrial pyruvate uptake. Eventually, the aberration was mapped genetically to an interval on chromosome 6 that included human *MPC1* (which was an unstudied gene in 2003). Two additional patients were also identified, with a similar (albeit less severe) disorder. With the identification of the *MPC1* and *MPC2*

genes, it was possible to sequence them and determine if one of them was mutated in these patients. *MPC2* was found to be wild type, but *MPC1* contained mutations in all three patients. The two mutations found were both nonsynonymous and changed residues that were absolutely conserved across the *MPC1* orthologs (note that a nucleotide change is termed nonsynonymous if it changes the amino acid sequence of a protein). When those mutant forms of human *MPC1* were introduced into yeast, they were found to be partially or completely inactive, in a manner that correlated with the disease severity in the patients.

Impact and implications for the future. All of these data convincingly establish that MPC1 and MPC2 are required for mitochondrial pyruvate transport in three different eukaryotic species. It is another matter to say that they are the mitochondrial pyruvate carrier, that is, these two proteins are sufficient for mitochondrial pyruvate uptake. However, recent data have largely answered that question: The expression of mouse *MPC1* and *MPC2*, but not either one on its own, conferred enhanced pyruvate uptake on the bacterium *Lactococcus lactis*. This pyruvate transport also exhibited characteristics of the native MPC, specifically dependence on a proton gradient and sensitivity to an inhibitor of mitochondrial pyruvate transport (UK-5099).

These data demonstrate that the molecular identity of the mitochondrial pyruvate carrier has been discovered at last. Why did it take so long to discover? It seems that the major reason was the complete novelty of the structure encoded by *MPC1* and *MPC2*. MPC1 and MPC2 physically interact, and both of them are absolutely required for pyruvate transport. In addition, the MPC complex is rather large [approximately 150 kilodaltons (kDa)] and seems to contain many molecules of MPC2. Not only is this type of organization unlike any other known transporters, but the primary sequences of MPC1 and MPC2 do not exhibit homology to any known transporters. These issues that created great challenges in the past now create incredible opportunities to understand the structural basis of this heretofore mysterious transporter complex. Moreover, along with this novel structure, there are new potential modes of regulation yet to be discovered. Does the cell control the transport activity of the MPC as a means to determine the fate of pyruvate? If the answer is yes, then understanding that regulation and the pathways that control it will provide a new window into the principles of cellular metabolic control.

The impact of the MPC on human disease also remains to be determined. A number of diseases are characterized by impaired pyruvate oxidation, including most cancers and heart disease, in addition to inborn errors of metabolism. Does the loss of MPC expression or activity underlie some of the pathology associated with these devastating diseases? With the discovery of the genes and proteins that encode the MPC, this field of disease genetics is now ready for harvest.

For background information *see* BIOCHEMISTRY; CELL (BIOLOGY); CELL METABOLISM; CELL ORGANIZATION; CITRIC ACID CYCLE; ENERGY METABOLISM; METABOLISM; MITOCHONDRIA in the McGraw-Hill Encyclopedia of Science & Technology.   Jared Rutter

Bibliography. D. K. Bricker et al., A mitochondrial pyruvate carrier required for pyruvate uptake in yeast, *Drosophila*, and humans, *Science*, 337:96–100, 2012, DOI:10.1126/science.1218099; M. Brivet et al., Impaired mitochondrial pyruvate importation in a patient and a fetus at risk, *Mol. Genet. Metab.*, 78:186–192, 2003, DOI:10.1016/S1096-7192(03)00016-7; A. P. Halestrap, The mitochondrial pyruvate carrier: Has it been unearthed at last?, *Cell Metab.*, 16(2):141–143, 2012, DOI:10.1016/j.cmet.2012.07.013; S. Herzig et al., Identification and functional expression of the mitochondrial pyruvate carrier, *Science*, 337:93–96, 2012, DOI:10.1126/science.1218530.

Mobile modeling in the molecular sciences

The art of modeling in the molecular sciences is highly dependent on the available computational technology, underlying data, and ability to collaborate. With the ever-increasing market share of mobile devices, tablets will likely overtake laptops as the computer of choice in the coming years. As the world population shifts to mobile architectures for their primary computing devices, modeling tools need to evolve to provide the required functionality in the portable and interactive tactile environment afforded by these devices. Mobile modeling in the context of molecular sciences is focused on using smartphone or tablet devices to perform a variety of modeling tasks, including but not limited to molecular modeling, geometry optimization, chemical-structure-based calculations, structure-activity relationship (SAR) generation, and database lookups.

The primary benefit of mobile technologies in molecular sciences is the simplistic and intuitive nature of the touchscreen interface that yields a faster learning curve and wider accessibility to nonspecialists. Software is distributed through app stores, which facilitates installation, provides continuous updating, and eliminates the need for centralized information technology (IT) support. The small and portable nature of the devices allows science to be done immediately on idea formation rather than delaying until in an office setting. This makes it ideal for the new generation of telecommuters who can maximize research time and minimize downtime by modeling whenever the opportunity arrives.

Mobile devices also introduce some challenges. The simple touchscreen interface limits the complexity of interactions. For example, a molecular visualization interface (such as Sybyl®, Maestro, or MOE) accessed through a Windows desktop commonly has specific functions based on which mouse button a user presses, such as for atom selection, rotation, and menu call-up. Switching to an interface

that has only one type of click and drag action and yet provides equivalent functionality can be difficult. The precision of a finger on a screen is very low compared to that of a mouse or trackpad, and the screen is partially obscured with each operation. In addition, the smaller screen size of portable devices not only makes viewing complex macromolecules difficult, it also limits the real estate available for adding buttons to increase interface functionality.

The benefits and detriments of mobile devices for complicated scientific applications will likely have little effect on the penetration of such devices within the scientific community. As mobile becomes mainstream for the less complicated functions commonly completed via a desktop computer, scientific software developers must actively work to provide equivalent functionality for mobile environments. Efforts by a small community of focused scientists already provide access to key data resources, chemical structure building and viewing applications, and molecular-modeling software, yielding expanded molecular-science toolkits for experts and novices alike.

Mobile database access. Because of the abundance of data on molecular entities, many investigations of chemicals start with simply ascertaining available knowledge. To that end, numerous apps provide focused sets of information [such as Green Solvents (http://pubs.acs.org/doi/abs/10.1021/sc3000509) and TB Mobile (http://www.ncbi.nlm.nih.gov/pubmed/23497706). These relatively simplistic apps provide users with ways to explore collated sets of chemical information that are self-contained within the app.

Apps that act as a portal to large online databases allow for much broader use. Such apps provide a significant advantage over the corresponding website by solving the problem of allowing users to draw chemical structures for use as queries, as well as leveraging the improved performance and functionality of a native app for browsing the results. Apps, such as ChemSpider Mobile, SPRESImobile, and Mobile Reagents, are tied to a specific service. Apps, such as the Mobile Molecular DataSheet (MMDS) and MolPrime$^+$, provide searching as a secondary feature and facilitate access to *PubChem* (http://pubchem.ncbi.nlm.nih.gov/), ChEBI (http://www.ebi.ac.uk/chebi/), and ChemSpider (http://www.chemspider.com), in addition to their primary structure-data management capabilities. Such apps provide users with access to millions of chemical structures online with precomputed properties, associated experimental data, and links to additional data across the Internet. In the case of the ChemSpider Mobile app, more than 28 million chemicals can be accessed online with linked information, including patents, publications, chemical vendors, and a myriad of other related data types. The open availability of the ChemSpider web services allows for the pairing of diverse interfaces, including the mobile-app client, making use of the server-based searching and data storage (**Figs. 1** and **2**).

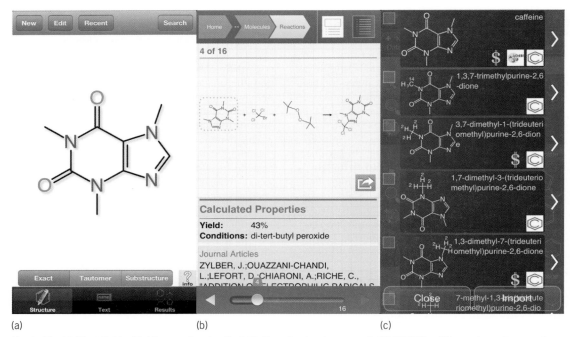

(a)   (b)   (c)

Fig. 1. The (*a*) ChemSpider Mobile app showing the initiation of a structure search. (*b*) SPRESImobile app browsing reaction hit results. (*c*) Mobile Molecular DataSheet (MMDS) app browsing results of a similarity search across multiple databases.

Molecular visualization. Apps are available for sketching and visualization of two-dimensional (2D) structures, three-dimensional (3D) structural models, molecular properties, and collective trends such as structure-activity analysis. Many of the apps currently available primarily are visualization tools, but increasingly they are able to link up with web services to generate models from user-provided data.

Mobile molecular collaboration platform. Mobile apps have access to strong collaboration features,

owing to their origins as portable communications devices. Because apps are typically quite modular relative to desktop software, a workflow often operates by passing documents between different apps, and between heterogeneous platforms by sending and receiving e-mail attachments, downloading data from the Internet, and interacting with online storage services such as Dropbox.

It is also possible to connect with services, such as Twitter, for chemical data, images, and commentary.

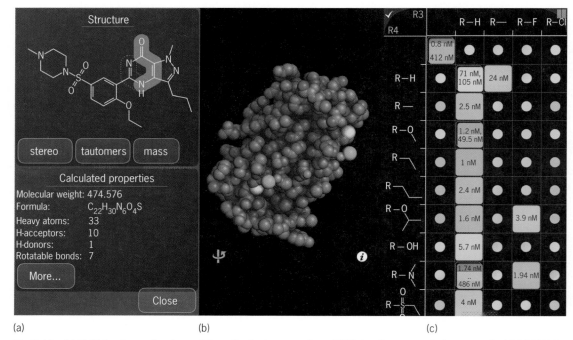

(a)   (b)   (c)

Fig. 2. The (*a*) MolPrime+ app showing an interactive tautomer explorer. (*b*) Molecules app rendering a protein. (*c*) SAR Table app showing actual and predicted activity for *R*-group correlation.

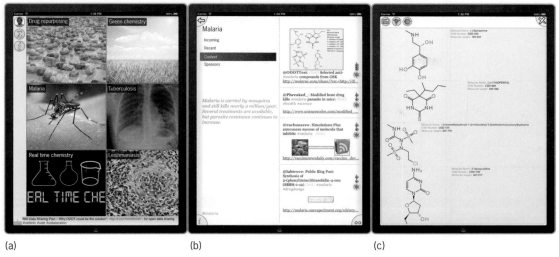

Fig. 3. Topic display for (*a*) the Open Drug Discovery Teams app. (*b*) Recent documents for the malaria topic. (*c*) In-app preview of a datasheet containing structures of malaria inhibitors.

Using specific hash tags corresponding to topics of interest is a way to publish data to projects in an app, such as Open Drug Discovery Teams (http://www.ncbi.nlm.nih.gov/pubmed/23198003), which has an app-based interface for presenting scientific data on rare and neglected diseases as well as other research topics of interest; it is also chemistry aware, as shown in **Fig. 3**. Many of these apps can be used in an integrated workflow as data is passed from one app to another (https://www.jstage.jst.go.jp/article/cbij/13/0/13_1/_article).

Mobile systems modeling. The interactions between chemicals and their environments have long been the domain of dynamics simulation software (such as MATLAB®). Because pharmacokinetic and pharmacodynamic models are typically crafted in the form of ordinary differential equations (ODEs), any ODE solver can theoretically be used to run such models. Coding an ODE solver is not complicated and several have been made available on both the Google Play store and iTunes App Store. As computational power in mobile devices increases, it may well be that developing more complex models that use these software tools is the next frontier for the mobile molecular sciences. Math Minion (http://www.redtree.com/mm) is a particularly well-developed example of the mobile capabilities for generating and running a mobile physiologically based pharmacokinetic (PBPK) model.

Math Minion provides users with a graphical interface for formulating models. The interface allows the definition of all relevant variables in a dynamic simulation and the necessary ODEs to be simulated. In addition, Math Minion will automatically analyze the units defined for all parameters, make conversions, and note inconsistencies. Math Minion has been used to implement a functional model of styrene pharmacokinetics (**Fig. 4**).

With such modeling function freely available, models for use in preclinical and clinical environments are sure to follow. Such models could direct scientists in pharmaceutical development on the proper dosing for animal studies, inform doctors on how to optimize radio-contrasting agents in radiology or anesthetics prior to surgery, and protect field risk assessors (for example, abandoned or active hazardous waste sites; environmental risk assessment; waste management) by allowing them to quickly determine if an environmental exposure is likely to cause high internal doses. A framework such as Math Minion can enable the development of dynamic system models that detail the influence of a chemical on its environment over time and feed into a plethora of other realms of the molecular sciences.

Server-side and cloud applications. In addition to the numerous client-side mobile applications that can be used in molecular sciences, many server-side web-enabled applications can be used to round out missing functionalities. Although these fall between mobile and traditional formats (often allowing access via both mediums), they are accessible via mobile devices using focused app interfaces or through web browsers. Key abilities that may not be otherwise accessible on mobile platforms because of computational or storage limitations can still be accessed on mobile devices as long as the necessary infrastructure is available elsewhere. Many tools (including some of those mentioned above such as ChemSpider Mobile) rely on the connected nature of mobile devices to provide users with the functionality they need on the devices they desire.

While many of these tools have interfaces specially formatted for mobile devices that provide a seamless integrated feel (for example, apps that link to data sources or mobile formatted websites), there are many tools that were originally designed for traditional computing environments that can outperform the current mobile tools. For example, to examine the interactions between a set of compounds and a protein of interest, several servers (for example, Dock Blaster http://blaster.docking.org, SwissDock http://www.swissdock.ch/, Docking

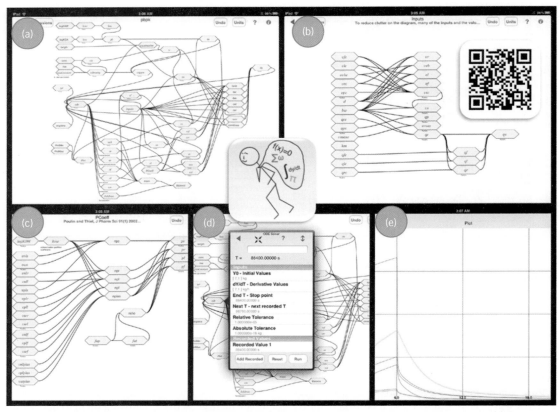

Fig. 4. A five-compartment physiologically based pharmacokinetic (PBPK) model of styrene inhalation in a rat. (*a*) The complete visual representation of expression, variables, solvers, and plots through a "mind-map" interface. (*b*) An expanded section containing various physiological input parameters. (*c*) Chemical-specific tissue partitioning parameters derived by the Poulin and Thiel (2002) approach. The LogP can be calculated using other apps such as the ChemSpider mobile app. (*d*) The ordinary differential equation (ODE) solver performing relevant integrations for chemical disposition across each compartment. (*e*) The final tissue concentration plots. The entire model can run on an iPod touch, iPhone, iPad, or iPad mini and on the Mac OSX environments. The model runs about an order of magnitude faster on the Mac, but still only takes a few seconds to run on the iOS devices and can be downloaded (http://goo.gl/VMfPs).

Server at http://www.dockingserver.com/web/) provide mobile modelers with access to protein-ligand docking capabilities. Web-based toolkits for application or generation of statistical quantitative structure-activity relationship (QSAR) models also are available (for example, Chembench http://chembench.mml.unc.edu/ and OCHEM http://ochem.eu). Because many of these web-based tools are designed for desktop environments and require formatted file inputs, file manipulation applications and/or nonnative web browsers with file-system access functions are required.

Outlook. Although many tools exist for scientific mobile apps, few are tailored exclusively to the mobile modeler in comparison to the offerings in a desktop environment, leaving much room for further development. While it has been documented that rather complex molecular-science investigations can be completed by combining several apps, integrated research environments still remain elusive in the mobile environment. However, the recent inclusion of Windows 8 in new mobile devices blurs the distinctions between traditional computing and mobile computing. The expansion of molecular-science software available to scientists working exclusively on mobile devices will continue to accelerate.

[*Disclaimer:* The United States Environmental Protection Agency through its Office of Research and Development funded and managed the research described here. It has been subjected to Agency review and approved for publication. Mention of trade names or commercial products does not constitute endorsement or recommendation for use.]

For background information *see* CLOUD COMPUTING; DATABASE MANAGEMENT SYSTEM; ENVIRONMENTAL ENGINEERING; ENVIRONMENTAL TOXICOLOGY; HAZARDOUS WASTE; HAZARDOUS WASTE ENGINEERING; MOLECULAR SIMULATION; TOXICOLOGY in the McGraw-Hill Encyclopedia of Science & Technology.

Christopher M. Grulke; Alex M. Clark;
Antony J. Williams; Sean Ekins;
Craig Morris; Michael-Rock Goldsmith

Bibliography. A. M. Clark, S. Ekins, and A. J. Williams, Redefining cheminformatics with intuitive collaborative mobile apps, *Mol. Inform.*, 31(8):569–584, 2012, DOI:10.1002/minf.201200010; A. Clark, A. J. Williams, and S. Ekins, Cheminformatics workflows using mobile apps, *Chem-Bio Inform. J.*, 13:1–18, 2013, DOI:10.1273/cbij.13.1; S. Ekins, A. M. Clark, and A. J. Williams, Incorporating green chemistry concepts into mobile chemistry applications and their potential uses,

ACS Sustainable Chem. Eng., 1(1):8–13, 2013, DOI:10.1021/sc3000509; S. Ekins, A. M. Clark, and A. J. Williams, Open drug discovery teams: A chemistry mobile app for collaboration, *Mol. Inform.* 31(8):585–597, 2012, DOI:10.1002/minf.201200034; P. Poulin and F-P. Thiel, Prediction of pharmacokinetics prior to in vivo studies. 1. Mechanism-based prediction of volume of distribution, *J. Pharm. Sci.*, 91(1), 2002, DOI:10.1002/jps.10005; J. C. Ramsey and M. E. Andersen, A physiologically based description of the inhalation pharmacokinetics of styrene in rats and humans, *Toxicol. Appl. Pharmacol.*, 73:159, 1984, DOI:10.1016/0041-008X(84)90064-4; A. J. Williams and H. Pence, Smart phones, a powerful tool in the chemistry classroom, *J. Chem. Educ.*, 88(6):683–686, 2011, DOI:10.1021/ed200029p; A. J. Williams, S. Ekins, R. Apodaca, A. Clark, and J. Jack, Mobilizing chemistry in the world of drug discovery, *Drug Discov. Today*, 16(21-22):928–939, 2011, DOI:10.1016/j.drudis.2011.09.002. http://www.scimobileapps.com/index.php?title=Main_Page.

Modern methods of flow visualization

Our everyday life is surrounded by flows, either natural or engineered. Examples of the former category include the flow of air breathed in and out of our lungs, and examples of the latter include the flows of fuel and air injected into the combustion chambers of vehicles. However, the fundamental physics of flows remains poorly understood in the so-called turbulent regime, the regime that attracts practically all the interest from researchers and engineers. As experience teaches us, a good first step toward solving a problem is usually to "see" the problem. Flow visualization is the art and science of making flow patterns visible so that researchers can "see the flow," providing a starting point for further study and understanding.

Visualization techniques. Most of us developed our first impressions and intuitions of flows via visualization techniques provided by nature without actually realizing it. For instance, even though air is invisible (or transparent) to our eyes, we developed an intuitive feeling of air flows by making everyday observations, ranging from the buffeting leaves in the wind to the smoke rising from a cigarette. These two examples illustrate two categories of flow visualization techniques. In the first example, the leaves act as probes to help visualize the wind flow. In the second example, the smoke particles, tiny black particles generated by the burning of the cigarette (**Fig. 1***a*), visualize the air flow around the cigarette by both tracking the flow and scattering light so that we can see them.

These seemingly simple and completely natural examples actually illuminate the underlying principles of flow visualization techniques actively used in the most advanced flow studies. In the terminology of flow visualization, techniques that involve stick-

ing probes (the buffeting leaves) into the flow are categorized as intrusive techniques, and those that do not are categorized as nonintrusive techniques. Researchers have invented, and are still inventing, a variety of flow probes to visualize different aspects of flows. And engineers still use smoke guns to visualize the flow around a vehicle to understand the aerodynamics of its body and to make it more "streamlined," so that drag can be reduced and mileage improved.

The disadvantage of intrusive techniques, as the name suggests, is that the probe itself disturbs the flow to be visualized. Consider the buffeting leaves

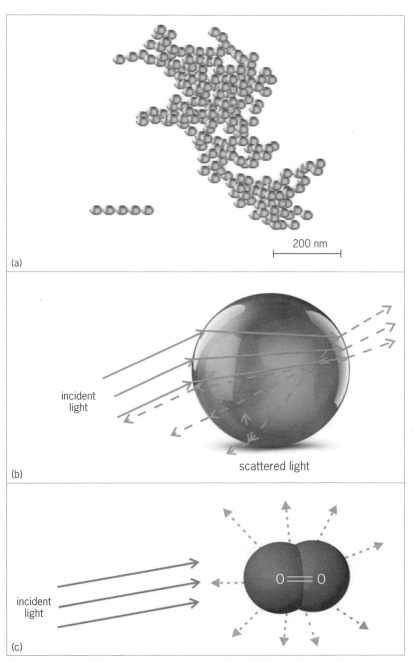

Fig. 1. Light scattering by small particles and molecules. (*a*) A smoke particle. (*b*) Scattering by a spherical particle. (*c*) Scattering by a molecule.

again: What we see from the motions of the leaves is actually a convoluted result produced by the interactions between the wind flow and the leaves. As beautiful as such motions are, researchers often want to see *just* the wind flow, that is, its pattern without interference from the leaves. Such research needs motivate the search for nonintrusive techniques, which aim at visualizing the target flow pattern without the use of probes.

The cigarette example mentioned above illustrates the key concept of nonintrusive techniques. These techniques require a tracer that can both track the flow and be detected optically. The smoke particles happen to meet both requirements in the cigarette example (and also in smoke gun applications). These particles are small in size: typically smaller than a few micrometers (in comparison, the diameter of a human hair ranges from 20 to 200 μm). Consequently, these particles are light in weight and can float in air and track the motions of the target air flow faithfully. Furthermore, the optical refractive index of these particles is significantly different from that of air, so they scatter light and we can see them. Should the smoke particles have the same refractive index as air, they would just be invisible and transparent to our eyes, like air. Hence, in some sense,

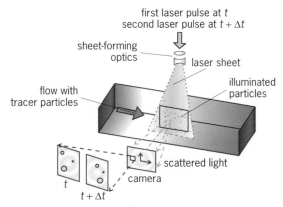

first laser pulse at t
second laser pulse at $t + \Delta t$

sheet-forming optics

laser sheet

flow with tracer particles

illuminated particles

scattered light

camera

t $t + \Delta t$

Fig. 2. Schematic of a velocity measurement using particle imaging velocimetry (PIV).

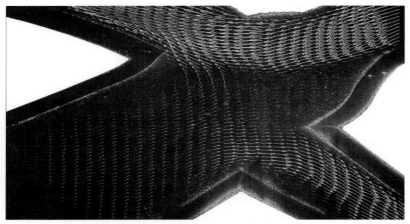

Fig. 3. Example of a velocity measurement in an artificial heart valve.

nonintrusive techniques use the tracer particle and light (usually generated by a laser in research) as the flow probe, in contrast to the physical probes used in intrusive techniques.

It is not always easy (it is actually very challenging in many applications) to find a flow tracer that can meet both of these requirements. For example, many practical flows have high temperatures, or they are corrosive (for example, combustion flows in energy-generating devices), and finding a tracer that can survive in the flow itself is challenging.

Light scattering. The remainder of this article focuses on nonintrusive techniques. As already mentioned, optical detection of the flow tracer is necessary in these techniques, and such detection is often accomplished by light scattered by the tracer. Therefore, the scattering of light will now be discussed.

The smoke particle introduced in the earlier discussion is actually quite complex (Fig. 1*a*). These particles are the result of the aggregation of many smaller particles (so-called primary particles) in complicated ways. Because of their complicated structure and geometry, the explanation of how these particles scatter light is quite involved. A simpler explanation of light scattering uses an ideal spherical particle (Fig. 1*b*). Some flow tracers (for example, glass beads used as flow tracers to visualize water flows) do have an approximately spherical shape. Whenever there is a mismatch in refractive index between the particles (for example, smoke particles or glass beads) and their surrounding media (for example, air or water), the particles will scatter light (a collection of photons). Light will reflect and refract at the interface of the particles and their surrounding media according to the basic laws of optics (Fig. 1*b*). Such reflection and refraction redistributes the photons in the incident light (that is, the light used to illuminate the particles) in various directions. We will be able to see the particle if some of the scattered photons reach our eye or camera.

Molecules can also scatter photons. (Figure 1*c* illustrates the scattering of light by an oxygen molecule.) Although the mechanism of scattering by molecules is different from that by particles, the end result of relevance to optical detection is that this scattering also redistributes the photons in the incident light in various directions (Fig. 1*c*). So molecules also can be used as flow tracers.

Particle image velocimetry (PIV). Now, we are ready to examine PIV, a representative flow visualization technique, in depth. The PIV technique visualizes (or measures) the flow velocity in a plane (**Fig. 2**). The technique involves seeding small particles (ranging from glass beads and oil droplets to metal powders) in the target flow. A laser is used to illuminate the particles, serving as the incident light (Fig. 1). The laser output is focused into a sheet (typically with a thickness less than 1 mm) to visualize a two-dimensional planar region in the flow. The laser generates two pulses (that is, two bursts of light), each with a duration of the order of nanoseconds. These two light pulses are generated consecutively at times

t and $t + \Delta t$, with Δt being the delay of the second pulse relative to the first. In practice, Δt can range from milliseconds to microseconds depending on the application (1 ms = 1000 μs and 1 μs = 1000 ns). As a result, the particles in the flow are illuminated twice; and each time, an image of the particles is recorded by a camera using the light scattered by the particles. Because these two images are taken at two different times (t and $t + \Delta t$) and the particles are displaced by the flow during Δt, the positions of the particles will be different on these two images. The PIV technique determines such displacements of the particles by comparing the two images recorded. Once the displacement is obtained, velocity can be calculated by simply dividing the displacement by Δt.

In summary, the PIV technique, as its name suggests, visualizes the flow velocity by imaging seeded particles. Such visualization was accomplished without sticking any physical probes into the flow to be visualized.

The PIV technique has found application in a wide range of engineering and scientific disciplines. Two examples from the author's research group will be given to illustrate the range of applications. The first example is a velocity measurement in an artificial heart valve using PIV (**Fig. 3**). In this measurement, the arrows show the local direction of the flow and the colors show the local magnitude of the flow (red corresponding to the highest flow velocity and blue to the lowest flow velocity). As a second example, PIV is used to study high-speed flows encountered in air-propulsion engines. The design and optimization of these engines, which may have the potential to save billions of dollars of fuel costs in both civilian and military aircraft, involve some of the most intricate and challenging flow patterns at combustion temperature and high speeds, well beyond 100 m/s (224 mi/h). Such visualization techniques provide powerful insights into flow patterns, which are difficult to obtain otherwise, for researchers to understand fundamental flow physics and for engineers to design better devices.

For background information *see* AIRCRAFT PROPULSION; FLUID MECHANICS; LASER; MOLECULE; PHOTON; REFLECTION OF ELECTROMAGNETIC RADIATION; REFRACTION OF WAVES; SCATTERING OF ELECTROMAGNETIC RADIATION; SCHLIEREN PHOTOGRAPHY; SHADOWGRAPH OF FLUID FLOW; TURBULENT FLOW; VELOCIMETER; WIND TUNNEL in the McGraw-Hill Encyclopedia of Science & Technology.   Lin Ma

Bibliography. F. Mayinger and O. Feldmann, *Optical Measurements: Techniques and Applications*, Springer-Verlag, New York, 2001; M. Raffel et al., *Particle Image Velocimetry: A Practical Guide*, Springer-Verlag, New York, 2007; M. Samimy et al., *A Gallery of Fluid Motion*, Cambridge University Press, Cambridge, UK, 2004; H. C. van de Hulst, *Light Scattering by Small Particles*, Dover Publications, New York, 1981; M. Van Dyke, *An Album of Fluid Motion*, Parabolic Press, Stanford, CA, 1982.

Molecular gadolinium complexes for magnetic resonance imaging

The ability to peer noninvasively into the human body has made magnetic resonance imaging (MRI) an indispensable diagnostic technique in modern medicine. Ever since Paul Lauterbur first applied the known principles of nuclear magnetic resonance (NMR) to imaging nearly 40 years ago, the rapid development of improved instrumentation and new applications has pushed MRI to the forefront of those imaging modalities available to the clinician. The setup of a typical MRI scanner used today is comparable to that of a standard NMR spectrometer used routinely for structural characterization of a sample prepared in a relatively small tube. MRI, however, employs the water proton signal in a much larger human "sample" and relies on the abundant water distribution throughout tissue and magnetic field gradients in different directions to generate the image. Although detailed soft-tissue images can be obtained with MRI thanks to the inherent nuclear spin of the water proton, administering a paramagnetic contrast agent before the scan can further enhance the image in certain instances. Small-molecule coordination complexes of gadolinium(III) are most often used for this purpose, and the effect of such agents can be quite dramatic (**Fig. 1**).

Water proton relaxation. In a typical NMR or MRI experiment, when a sample is placed in the external magnetic field (B_0), a small excess of water-proton magnetic spins align with B_0 along the longitudinal axis (z axis, **Fig. 2**). These spins combine to produce a net magnetization vector that precesses around B_0 before a 90° pulse of radio-frequency radiation is used to move the vector from the original longitudinal z axis to the x–y transverse plane. Energy is then lost by the spins to their surroundings, as the net magnetization vector is restored to its original position along the z axis in a process called spin–lattice or longitudinal (T_1) relaxation (Fig. 2). Observable magnetization can also be lost from the x–y plane due to mutual swapping of energy between the individual spins that comprise the net magnetization vector in a process known as spin–spin or transverse (T_2) relaxation. Critical to the success of MRI is the fact that the T_1 and T_2 relaxation times of water protons are different in different types of tissue (healthy versus diseased tissue, for example). This phenomenon leads to variations in the signal intensity that ultimately produce the observed contrast in a magnetic resonance image. Tissues with water protons that undergo fast longitudinal (T_1) relaxation generally yield greater image intensity (that is, they appear brighter in the resulting image) than those with longer values, because the magnetization vector along the z axis is greater in the tissue with the fastest relaxation. Conversely, fast transverse (T_2) relaxation results in lower signal intensity, because faster disappearance of the magnetization vector in the transverse plane results in less magnetization available for detection.

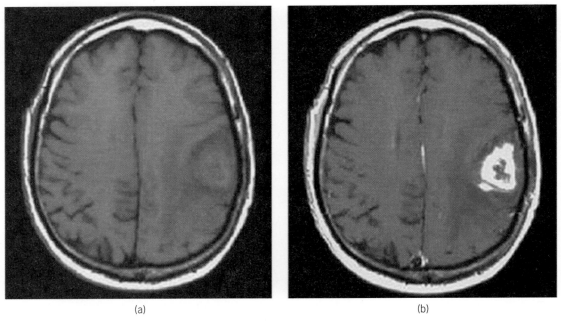

Fig. 1. MRI scan of a human brain (*a*) without and (*b*) with the administration of MultiHance, a Gd(III)-based contrast agent, revealing details of tumor tissue. *(Images courtesy of Bracco Imaging S.p.A., Colleretto Giacosa, Ivrea, Italy)*

Achieving sufficient magnetic field homogeneity throughout a typically small NMR sample for chemical structure elucidation is straightforward, but accomplishing such for MRI work is much more challenging because of the larger sample size of the human body. Consequently, only small volume elements, called voxels (generally $<10^{-5}$ mm^3), can be observed at any particular time to ensure that B_0 satisfies the resonance conditions for the in vivo water protons present in the entire volume probed. Spatial information of protons with differing resonance frequencies is encoded by introduction of a linear magnetic field gradient in addition to the existing static field. Following a 90° pulse, the decay signal is Fourier-transformed to generate a one-dimensional (1D) projection of signal amplitude along a certain direction throughout the patient. Computer algorithms are then used to build up these projections into two-dimensional (2D) and three-dimensional (3D) images of water distribution in tissue and produce the final MR image.

Gadolinium-based MRI contrast agents. Although the natural magnetic properties of the water proton make contrast possible, introduction of a paramagnetic substance can increase proton relaxation rates, leading to further signal enhancement. Such param-agnetic compounds are called contrast agents, and they function by increasing the relaxation rates of water protons in the immediate surroundings of the tissue in which they localize. Gadolinium(III) was used in the first approved contrast agent in 1988 and has become the most widely used metal for the production of paramagnetic contrast agents today. This lanthanide ion's seven unpaired electrons combined with a relatively long electronic relaxation time make it an ideal candidate for a proton relaxation agent. Although Gd-based agents increase both the longitudinal and transverse relaxation rates, the change in tissue is significantly greater with respect to the longitudinal rate ($1/T_1$). Consequently, such agents are best visualized in the clinical setting using T_1-weighted scans.

Commercial contrast agents utilize the octadentate polyaminocarboxylate DTPA (diethylene-triaminepentaacetic acid) or DOTA (1,4,7,10-tetraazacyclododecane-1,4,7,10-tetraacetic acid) ligands, which present combinations of nitrogen and oxygen donor atoms for the Gd(III) ion (**Fig. 3**). Following intravascular injection, these nonspecific extracellular agents quickly distribute between plasma and interstitial spaces; they are eliminated via the renal route within several hours. Other

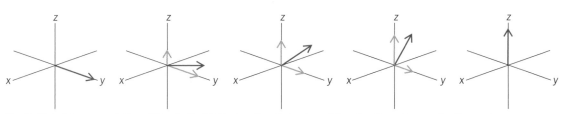

Fig. 2. Pictorial representation of longitudinal (T_1) relaxation. Following a 90° pulse, the net magnetization vector recovers along the z axis as energy is lost to the surroundings in the form of heat.

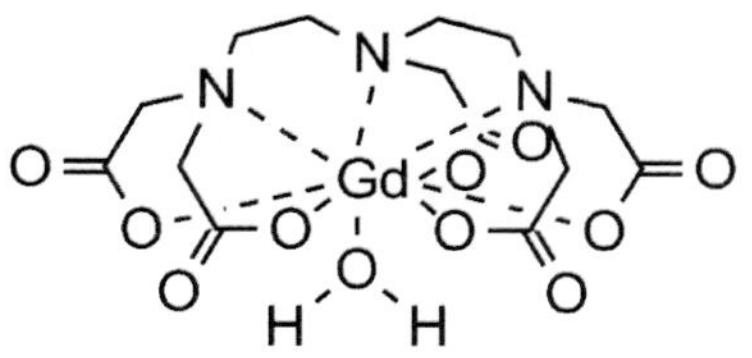

$[Gd(DTPA)(H_2O)]^{2-}$
(Magnevist)

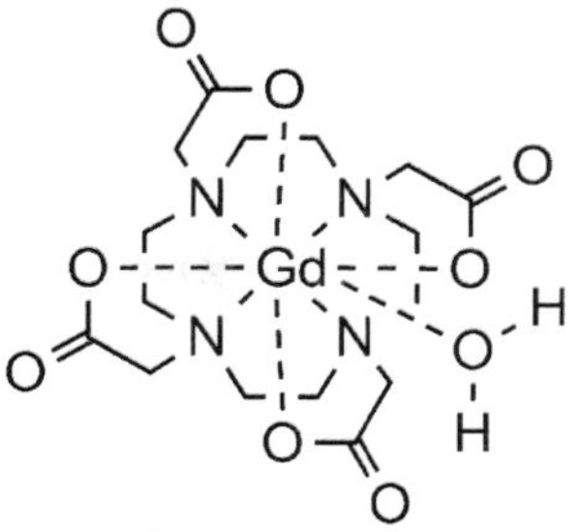

$[Gd(DOTA)(H_2O)]^{-}$
(Dotarem)

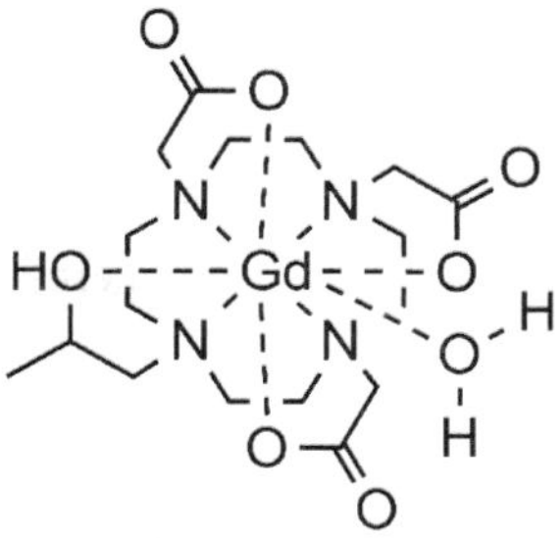

$[Gd(HP\text{-}DO3A)(H_2O)]$
(Prohance)

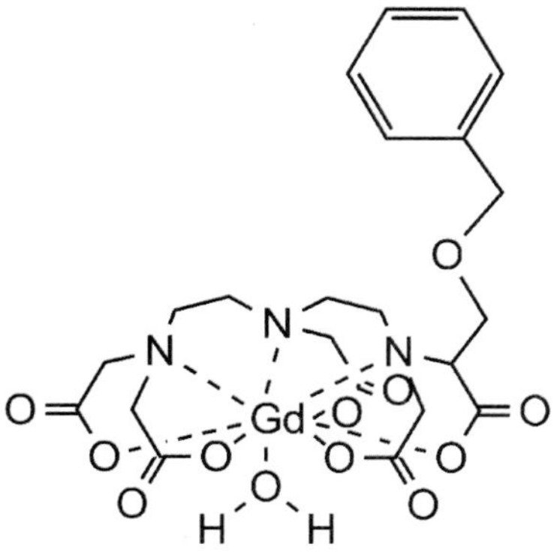

$[Gd(BOPTA)(H_2O)]^{2-}$
(MultiHance)

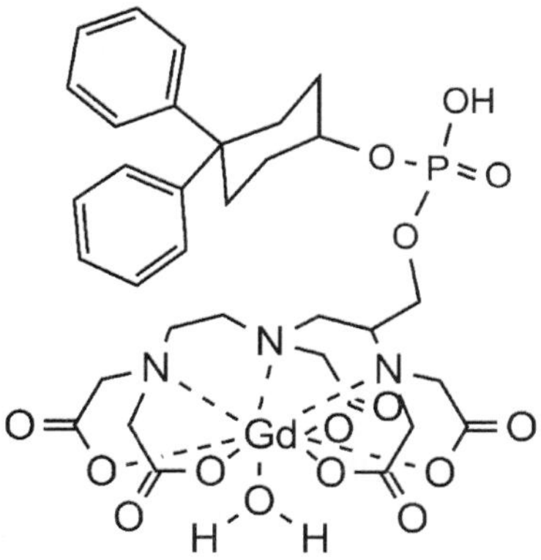

[MS-325]
(Vasovist)

Fig. 3. Aminocarboxylate-based MRI contrast agents.

derivatives of DTPA, known by their commercial names MultiHance and Vasovist (MS-325), are designed specifically as targeted agents. MultiHance is known to target the hepatobiliary system and acts as a liver-imaging agent, whereas Vasovist noncovalently binds with the blood protein human serum albumin (HSA). Upon binding HSA, water-proton relaxation rates increase and the longer in vivo retention times enable magnetic resonance angiography applications.

Relaxivity and Solomon-Bloembergen-Morgan theory. Gd-based contrast agents are typically assessed on the basis of their relaxivity value, or how much the relaxation rates of water protons are increased in the presence of a known concentration of agent. The observed relaxation rate of water stems from both a diamagnetic and a paramagnetic contribution. The paramagnetic component is linearly related to the concentration of paramagnetic contrast agent in solution. Relaxivity is thus defined as the increase in relaxation rate per concentration of the agent present, or the slope of a plot of $(1/T_i)_{\text{obs}}$ versus concentration, as shown in the equation below.

$$(1/T_i)_{\text{obs}} = (1/T_i)_{\text{diamagnetic}} + r_i[\text{Gd}] \qquad i = 1, 2$$

Current agent development focuses primarily on attaining higher inner-sphere, longitudinal relaxivity, r_{1p}, from protons of water molecules bound directly to the Gd(III) ion within the complex. The well-documented Solomon-Bloembergen-Morgan (SBM) equations of paramagnetic relaxation theory describe the relationship among several parameters related to complex design and the consequent relaxivity value. These parameters include q, the number of inner-sphere, metal-bound water molecules (or the hydration number); τ_M, the mean water residence time of the bound water (inverse of the water exchange rate); τ_R, the complex rotational correlation time; and T_{1e}, the electronic longitudinal relaxation time of the metal ion (**Fig. 4**). Electronic relaxation is often difficult to tune for a given Gd(III) complex, but the remaining parameters can be rationally influenced through ligand design and, in the case of τ_R, conjugation to macromolecular structures to further augment relaxivity. Current commercial agents possess relaxivities that are small relative to what is theoretically possible, with r_{1p} values of only 4-5 mM^{-1} s^{-1}. SBM theory reveals the need to maximize the hydration number q ($q = 1$ for all commercial agents) and optimize τ_M (τ_M ranges from 150 to 1000 ns in commercial agents) and the rotational correlation time τ_R to obtain high relaxivity. Achieving an optimal combination of these parameters is necessary for enhanced agents, but it must also come without sacrificing chelate stability to avoid

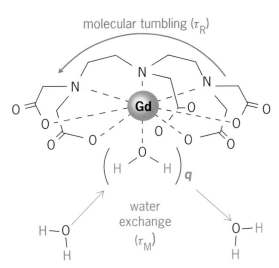

Fig. 4. Schematic of selected key factors that affect proton relaxivity, r_{1p}.

potential toxicity problems that may arise in vivo due to free Gd(III).

Recent strategies in design of contrast agents. In recent years, synthetic chemists have pursued numerous derivatives of the classic DTPA/DOTA ligand scaffolds as well as new ligand designs in an attempt to generate stable, high-relaxivity agents. Much of this effort has involved either the study of the underlying coordination chemistry at the Gd(III) center to affect q and water exchange, or conjugation to larger structures to slow molecular tumbling (reorientation). With regard to enhanced water coordination and exchange, complexes with higher hydration numbers relative to commercial agents have been attained via structural modifications to the DTPA or DOTA platform. In such cases, $q = 2$ complexes are obtained by removing one of the coordinating carboxylate units within the octadentate ligand motif to generate a heptadentate ligand, allowing room for an additional bound water molecule. Relaxivity is particularly sensitive to increasing q, as doubling the hydration number typically leads to an approximate doubling in the complex relaxivity value, all other parameters held constant. In studies reported by A. Merbach and coworkers, increasing the steric bulk at the metal center for other octadentate DTPA- or DOTA-based complexes can also lead to faster water exchange rates, favoring higher relaxivities.

Although much research has been directed toward the modification of known DTPA or DOTA derivatives, efforts involving other ligand systems have also shown promise. For example, S. Aime and coworkers have reported the heptadentate AAZTA ligand, which is relatively straightforward to synthesize and binds Gd(III) to yield a q of 2 (**Fig. 5**). Further, the two water molecules remain bound in the presence of biologically relevant anions that might otherwise have displaced the waters, leading to decreased relaxivity in vivo. In work published in 2012, M. Botta and coworkers described the Gd(III) complex of another heptadentate ligand, OBETA [ethylene glycol-bis(2-aminoethyl ether)-N,N,N′,N′-tetraacetic acid], which adds an ether oxygen donor to an aminocarboxylate design (Fig. 5). Despite the presence of only seven ligand donor atoms, chelate stability remains quite high, which, when combined with an increased q and relaxivity of 7.2 mM^{-1} s^{-1}, reveals the promise of such an agent.

As mentioned above, it is important to monitor the effect of new binding motifs (or structural modifications to existing DTPA/DOTA ligands) on chelate stability, particularly when moving to lower-denticity ligands, as this can lead to weaker ligand–metal binding and potential in vivo toxicity. Work by K. N. Raymond and coworkers has demonstrated the possibility of achieving high hydration numbers ($q = 2$ or 3), fast water exchange, and high chelate stability using the hexadentate hydroxypyridinone (HOPO) ligand scaffold (Fig. 5). These efforts have led to relaxivities as high as 13 mM^{-1} s^{-1}, approximately three times the values seen for commercial agents. Recent work has also included tethering Gd-HOPO complexes to larger dendrimeric and virus capsid structures to slow molecular rotation in solution (τ_R) and attain even higher relaxivities.

Conjugation to macromolecules and further application. Following optimization of the coordination-chemistry properties to enhance relaxivity of small-molecule Gd(III) chelates, association with macromolecular structures can both increase relaxivity further and enable a wider range of clinical applications. Since the pioneering work of R. B. Lauffer and coworkers with MS-325, a number of new complexes have been reported that take advantage of the relaxivity gains observed upon conjugation to larger molecules through either noncovalent binding or via covalent linkages. As noted in the case of MS-325 and the Gd-HOPO family of complexes, slowing molecular rotation in solution favors high relaxivity, and several other successful attempts have included the attachment of dendrimers or other polymeric structures to the classic DTPA/DOTA compounds. Upon conjugation, the small-molecule chelate takes on a molecular tumbling time that is consistent with that of the macromolecule, leading to higher relaxivities and other useful imaging properties.

Among some of the promising Gd-based macromolecular agents currently under development are systems composed of chelates attached to biocompatible nanoparticles or liposomes. In addition to

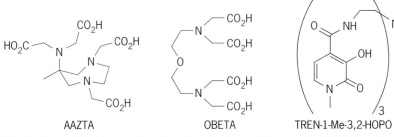

AAZTA   OBETA   TREN-1-Me-3,2-HOPO

Fig. 5. Chemical structures of ligands for the development of new potential Gd-based MRI contrast agents.

slower rotation, these nano-sized frameworks can function as targeted agents with improved biocompatibility. For example, one liposomal system reported by R. V. Bellamkonda and coworkers possesses increased blood circulation times and shows enhanced brain-tumor imaging in a rat glioma model. Finally, other routes toward slower rotation and higher relaxivity have been further coupled with efforts to generate bioresponsive agents. In recent work reported by T. J. Meade and coworkers, a DOTA-based Gd(III) complex was developed to link covalently to the versatile HaloTag reporter protein. Upon binding, a sixfold relaxivity increase is noted for the bound versus free complex, and the conjugation to HaloTag should enable enhanced imaging of cellular processes. As such systems employing new molecular architectures with enhanced relaxivity and biocompatibility emerge, the breadth of application of Gd-based MRI probes will continue to grow.

For background information *see* CHELATION; COORDINATION CHEMISTRY; COORDINATION COMPLEXES; DENDRITIC MACROMOLECULE; DIAMAGNETISM; GADOLINIUM; LIGAND; LIPOSOMES; MAGNETIC RELAXATION; MAGNETIC RESONANCE; MEDICAL IMAGING; NUCLEAR MAGNETIC RESONANCE (NMR); PARAMAGNETISM in the McGraw-Hill Encyclopedia of Science & Technology.

Eric J. Werner; Tavya G. R. Benjamin

Bibliography. Z. Baranyai et al., Lower ligand denticity leading to improved thermodynamic and kinetic stability of the Gd^{3+} complex: The strange case of OBETA, *Chem. Eur. J.*, 18:7680–7685, 2012, DOI:10.1002/chem.201200265; P. Caravan, Strategies for increasing the sensitivity of gadolinium based MRI contrast agents, *Chem. Soc. Rev.*, 35:512–523, 2006, DOI:10.1039/b510982p; E. Karathanasis et al., MRI mediated, non-invasive tracking of intratumoral distribution of nanocarriers in rat glioma, *Nanotechnology*, 19:315101, 2008, DOI:10.1088/0957-4484/19/31/315101; A. E. Merbach and E Tóth (eds.), *The Chemistry of Contrast Agents in Medical Magnetic Resonance Imaging*, Wiley, 2001; E. Terreno et al., Challenges for molecular magnetic resonance imaging, *Chem. Rev.*, 110:3019–3042, 2010, DOI:10.1021/cr100025t.

Natural killer T cells

Natural killer T cells constitute a unique and distinct subset of immune cells (T cells) that are known to influence and regulate immune and inflammatory responses. These cells possess a very limited T-cell antigen receptor diversity and often express cell surface proteins more typically expressed by natural killer cells.

Background. In carrying out adaptive (acquired) immunity, populations of T and B lymphocytes (white blood cells) respond to a myriad of foreign molecules, called antigens. Despite this, each lymphocyte and its daughter cells have specificity for

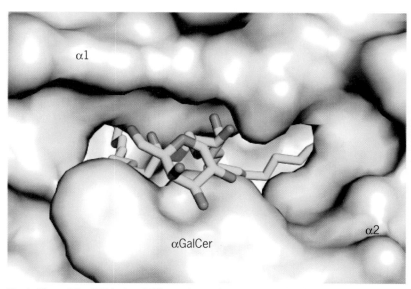

Fig. 1. View of the CD1d–glycolipid complex surface contacted by the iNKT cell TCR (T-cell antigen receptor). The view is looking down from the TCR perspective. The backbone structure of the glycolipid αGalCer (carbons in yellow; oxygens in red) is shown as bound in a space-filling representation of CD1d (gray shading). The antigen is bound within a cleft formed by two antiparallel α-helical CD1d domains labeled α1 and α2. The hexagonal galactose sugar portion of the glycolipid is protruding at the CD1d surface, where it can be contacted by the TCR, whereas most of the fatty acid chains are buried within the CD1d and thus are not visible.

one type of antigen. The clonal specificity of lymphocytes is imparted by their antigen receptors, which are cell surface proteins composed of two polypeptides. The expression of each chain of the antigen receptor is dependent upon the random rearrangement of two or three segments of DNA, encoding regions termed V (variable) and J (joining); in some cases, there is also a D (diversity) segment. The multiple V, D, and J segments can join in a combinatorial fashion, and rearrangement is frequently coupled with the variable removal and/or addition of a few nucleotides at the junctions of the joined segments. Therefore, not only does DNA rearrangement commit the lymphocyte to expression of a single type of antigen receptor, but it also is a powerful mechanism for the creation of enormous antigen receptor diversity. Upon an infection or other immune challenge, those T and B cells with receptors that are reactive to the foreign antigen are activated, and they proliferate and ultimately produce "memory" T and B cells, which are more rapidly activated if there is a subsequent challenge with the same antigen. This is the essence of the clonal selection theory, which is a cornerstone of modern immunology. The generation of a protective immune memory is the goal of vaccination.

Despite the great antigen receptor diversity, it has become apparent that there are populations of cells with unusual phenotype and behavior within the T lymphocyte pool that have a very limited T-cell antigen receptor (TCR) diversity and that exhibit the rapid responses characteristic of memory T cells, even without a previous known antigen challenge. In addition, these T cells often express cell surface proteins more typically expressed by natural killer

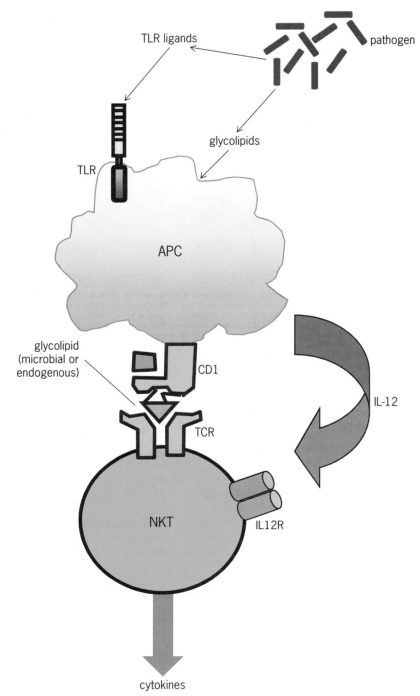

Fig. 2. Mechanisms driving the activation of iNKT cells during infection. Glycolipids produced by pathogens inside or outside the antigen-presenting cell (APC) can be assembled by the APC into complexes with CD1d that are recognized by the iNKT cell TCR (T-cell antigen receptor). This leads to iNKT cell cytokine production. Pathogens also can provide ligands for Toll-like receptors (TLRs) expressed by APCs, which drive the production of cytokines (such as IL-12) that in turn activate iNKT cells. Furthermore, infection may promote the production of endogenous glycolipids that can bind CD1d and that are recognized by the iNKT cell TCR, typically in conjunction with IL-12. Note that these mechanisms are not mutually exclusive.

thus led to the general moniker "NKT" cells. This article will discuss the properties of a major population of these NKT cells that have limited TCR diversity.

Characterization. The most extensively characterized NKT cell population, and the most abundant in mice, lacks diversity in one of its antigen receptor chains, specifically the α chain. It comprises an identical or invariant Vα14 rearrangement to Jα18 in mice, and similar V and J elements are used in human NKT cells. These cells are frequently called type I NKT cells or invariant NKT cells (iNKT cells) in order to distinguish them from NKT cells having more diverse TCRs. Most T lymphocytes recognize peptide fragments bound to or presented by proteins on other cells encoded within the major histocompatibility complex (MHC). (Note that the MHC is a family of genes that encode cell surface glycoproteins that regulate interactions among cells of the immune system.) In contrast, iNKT cells recognize glycolipids (compounds having solubility properties of a lipid and containing one or more molecules of a covalently attached sugar) that are presented by CD1d, which is a protein related to the MHC antigen-presenting molecules.

The first identified antigen that activates iNKT cells was obtained from a marine sponge. It was discovered because it had strong activity in an experimental screen for natural substances that prevented tumor metastases in the liver of mice. The structure of this compound was determined to be a glycolipid known as α-galactosylceramide (αGalCer). αGalCer was later shown to prevent tumors by activating iNKT cells, and it is a highly potent antigen for them. Furthermore, iNKT cells can be identified by staining with fluorescently labeled artificially formed tetramers (molecules consisting of four structural subunits) of CD1d loaded with αGalCer. Structural analyses revealed that CD1d has two hydrophobic pockets in which the lipid chains of the bound glycolipids, such as αGalCer, are buried. The glycolipid sugar moiety of the glycolipid is exposed at the CD1d surface, where it is available to make contact with the TCR α-chain (**Fig. 1**). Consistent with this, the invariant TCR α-chain (in contrast with the TCR β-chain) drives most of the binding interaction to the glycolipid plus CD1d.

The differentiation of iNKT cells, like that for other T lymphocytes, takes place within the thymus. However, it diverges from the differentiation of other thymic T cells at the immature, CD4/CD8 double-positive (DP) stage. It has been shown that the interaction of NKT cell progenitors with other thymus cells that express CD1d delivers essential TCR-mediated signals that are important for directing iNKT cell development. Nascent type iNKT cells undergo a developmental process distinct from other T cells, which involves multiple rounds of proliferation and the expression of cell surface proteins otherwise found on memory T cells and/or NK cells. As mature cells, iNKT cells are relatively infrequent in lymph nodes, but they are well represented in a number of sites, including blood, spleen, bone

(NK) cells. NK cells are an innate population of lymphocytes that respond to and kill infected cells, although they lack the gene rearrangements that produce highly diverse antigen receptors. Coexpression by some lymphocytes of TCRs and NK receptors has

marrow, and adipose tissues; in mice, they are very abundant in the liver. In humans, iNKT cells tend to be less frequent than in mice, although the frequency can vary greatly in the blood (note that the reason or reasons for this frequency variation in the blood are presently unknown).

Immunological role. The role of iNKT cells in the immune system has been probed extensively, especially in experiments using mice that cannot generate these lymphocytes because of targeted mutations. For example, iNKT-deficient mice have been shown to have a number of defects in their response to bacterial pathogens. Subsequent research has led to the identification of bacterial glycolipids derived from a number of bacteria that can stimulate iNKT cells in a CD1d-dependent manner; the sources include gram-positive and gram-negative strains, commensals, and pathogens. The bacterial glycolipid antigens generally have two hydrophobic carbon chains and a sugar with a particular stereochemistry of the bond to the lipid (an α-linkage) that is not found in mammals. These data suggest that the recognition of bacterially derived glycolipids could be a driving force in the conservation of iNKT cells.

Interestingly, iNKT cells have also been implicated in the response to pathogens that apparently do not express antigens for their TCR, including the herpes family of viruses. The iNKT cell activation in the absence of exogenous TCR antigens has been shown to be dependent on the stimulation of antigen-presenting cells (APCs) by bacterially or virally derived ligands for the Toll-like family of receptors (TLRs); these TLR-activated cells then produce cytokines (intercellular signals), such as interleukin-12 (IL-12), which in turn stimulate iNKT cells (**Fig. 2**). In other cases, stimulation of APCs during infections has been shown to increase the production of self-glycolipid antigens that, in conjunction with IL-12, stimulate iNKT cells. The ability of iNKT cells to be activated either by cytokines or by self-antigens plus cytokines suggests that they could have a broad role in regulating many types of immune responses (in addition to those prompted by bacterial infections). In fact, studies in mice indicate that these cells play an important role in a wide variety of autoimmune diseases, sterile inflammatory reactions (such as the ischemia reperfusion injury that occurs after the temporary loss of blood flow), and the response to cancers. In some cases, there are correlative data suggesting that iNKT cells could play similar roles in humans. However, it is important to note that iNKT cells play a beneficial role in some disease models, such as models of type 1 diabetes, whereas they are promoters of disease in other models.

One of the hallmarks of the iNKT cell response to αGalCer is the production of a diverse group of cytokines. This diverse cytokine response is a potential problem when considering their mechanism of action, or possible use in immune therapies, because one type of cytokine, for example, IL-4, which is typical of the so-called type 2 response, may counteract the activity of another cytokine, such as interferon γ (IFNγ), which is the major cytokine of type 1 responses. However, the prevalence in different contexts of one type of cytokine versus another might account for the diverse and sometimes opposing effects attributed to these cells. Because IFNγ is thought to be the cytokine primarily responsible for the anticancer activity of αGalCer, there is now considerable interest in the synthesis of αGalCer variants with an enhanced ability to induce this cytokine.

In addition, recent work has revealed the existence of functional subsets of iNKT cells; the selective activation of a subset also could partially explain the diverse effects of iNKT cell activation in different studies. For example, the treatment of mice with αGalCer has been shown to induce the differentiation of iNKT cells to become similar to those T lymphocytes specialized for promoting B cell responses. Moreover, a separate subset of iNKT cells has been defined that is specialized to produce the cytokine IL-17, which is important for fighting certain infections.

Clinical potential and outlook. Is the stimulation or inhibition of iNKT cell activity likely to find use in the clinic? The fact that αGalCer, the prototypical iNKT cell antigen, was discovered through an experimental screen for agents with anticancer activity has alerted researchers to the potential of glycolipid antigens for tumor immunotherapy. Clinical trials of αGalCer-mediated iNKT cell activation are being carried out for head and neck cancers and lung cancers. One caveat, however, is the aforementioned lower frequency of these cells in the blood in most humans, although these cells may be more frequent in other sites, such as adipose tissues. It should be noted that there is at least one additional population of cells with a limited TCR α repertoire, collectively known as mucosal-associated invariant T (MAIT) cells. Although they are not CD1d-reactive, MAIT cells have some similarities with iNKT cells, and they are more frequent in humans than in mice. Thus, the principles learned from modulating iNKT cell activity in mice may be extendable to studies on MAIT cells in humans.

For background information see ANTIGEN; BLOOD; CANCER (MEDICINE); CELL (BIOLOGY); CELLULAR IMMUNOLOGY; CYTOKINE; GLYCOLIPID; IMMUNITY; IMMUNOLOGIC CYTOTOXICITY; IMMUNOLOGY; IMMUNOTHERAPY; INFECTION; PROTEIN in the McGraw-Hill Encyclopedia of Science & Technology.

Isaac Engel; Mitchell Kronenberg

Bibliography. P. J. Brennan, M. Brigl, and M. B. Brenner, Invariant natural killer T cells: An innate activation scheme linked to diverse effector functions, *Nat. Rev. Immunol.*, 13:101–117, 2013, DOI:10.1038/nri3369; E. Girardi and D. M. Zajonc, Molecular basis of lipid antigen presentation by CD1d and recognition by natural killer T cells, *Immunol. Rev.*, 250:167–179, 2012, DOI:10.1111/j.1600-065X.2012.01166.x; L. Wu and L. Van Kaer, Natural killer T cells in health and disease, *Front. Biosci.*, S3:236–251, 2011, DOI:10.2741/148.

Natural quasicrystals

The regularly repeating atomic arrangement in crystals is called periodic. The hexagons in a honeycomb lattice (**Fig. 1***a*) or the square tiles in bathroom tiling are examples of periodic tessellations. According to the laws of mathematics discovered in the nineteenth century, periodicity can only occur for certain rotational symmetries, such that one-, two-, three-, four-, and sixfold symmetry are allowed, but crystals or periodic tilings with five-, seven-, eight-, or higher-fold symmetry axes are strictly forbidden. About thirty years ago, however, a new kind of material that violates these rules was hypothesized and dubbed quasicrystals (short for quasiperiodic crystals), and, independently, a synthetic example was discovered in the laboratory. Since then, over a hundred different quasicrystals have been made in the laboratory using highly controlled synthetic methods.

Quasicrystals have an atomic arrangement that is quasiperiodic (two or more types of atomic clusters each repeat at regular intervals like in a crystal); however, the ratio of intervals is irrational (not expressible as a fraction) so that the combined arrangement of atoms never exactly repeats. Because they are quasiperiodic, they can violate the mathematical theorems and have any of the rotational symmetries forbidden to crystals, including fivefold symmetry in the plane and icosahedral symmetry (the symmetry of a soccer ball) in three dimensions. An example is the fivefold symmetric Penrose tiling composed of two tile shapes that repeat with frequencies whose ratio is the famous irrational number known as the "golden ratio" (Fig. 1*b*).

The search in nature. Are quasicrystals energetically stable and robust like crystals? Or are they metastable oddities? If some are truly stable materials, then it is conceivable that they formed under natural conditions, just like crystalline minerals. Thus, the question arises, is it possible that quasicrystals formed through natural geologic processes long before they were discovered in the laboratory? In 2009, a new kind of mineral was discovered in the collection of the Museo di Storia Naturale of the Università degli Studi di Firenze, Italy. The mineral, the first naturally forming quasicrystal, has chemical composition $Al_{63}Cu_{24}Fe_{13}$ (where the numbers indicate percentages) and has the symmetry of an icosahedron. Because an icosahedron includes six independent fivefold symmetry axes, it is a superforbidden symmetry for crystals (**Fig. 2**). In 2010, the new mineral was officially accepted by the Commission on New Minerals, Nomenclature and Classification of the International Mineralogical Association as the first natural quasicrystal and named icosahedrite for the symmetry of its atomic structure.

The search for natural quasicrystals began in 1984 as an informal hunt by P. J. Steinhardt through major museum collections soon after quasicrystals were found in the laboratory; but these modest efforts yielded no results. Then, in 1998, a systematic search was initiated using a scheme for identifying quasicrystals based on x-ray powder diffraction data. X-ray powder diffraction patterns are obtained by scattering x-rays from a mixture of many grains oriented at random angles. Although the random angles make it difficult to determine the symmetry of a sample, the advantage of using powder diffraction data for the search was that there exists a collection of over 80,000 patterns in the International Center for Diffraction Data Powder Diffraction File (ICDD-PDF) that includes nearly 9000 mineral patterns in addition to a majority of diffraction patterns of synthetic phases. The key to the search strategy was to identify quantitative figures-of-merit that could be applied to powder patterns and could separate known quasicrystals and promising quasicrystal candidates from the vast majority of powder patterns in the ICDD-PDF. Using these figures-of-merit, the search ranked all the patterns in the catalog and identified six minerals among the 100 most promising candidates. Each of the minerals was acquired and studied by transmission electron microscopy (TEM) and x-ray diffraction from a single grain to check for forbidden symmetry, but, in the end, no new quasicrystals, synthetic or natural, were discovered in the original study. The paper included at the end an offer to share the names of additional candidates on the list with any collaborators willing to test minerals from their collection. Six years later, the call was answered by L. Bindi who began by testing samples on the list that were also in the collections of the Museo di Storia Naturale of the Università degli Studi di Firenze (Italy). A year later, when no successes were found among candidates on the list, the decision was made to test minerals that were not listed in the ICDD-PDF catalog altogether but whose compositions were similar to known quasicrystals synthesized in the laboratory. The search soon focused on a sample labeled

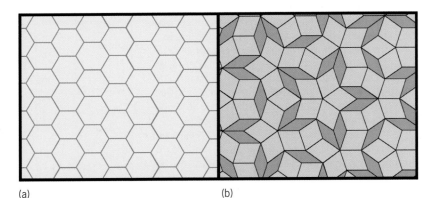

(a)   (b)

Fig. 1. Crystals are composed of atoms or atom clusters that repeat at equal intervals, such as (*a*) the hexagons in a honeycomb lattice. Crystals can have six-, four-, three-, two-, and onefold symmetry, but fivefold, sevenfold, and higher-fold symmetries are mathematically forbidden. Quasicrystals can be decomposed into two (or more) atom clusters that repeat at different frequencies whose ratio cannot be expressed as a ratio of integers. An analogy is (*b*) the Penrose tiling, a tessellation composed of two types of tiles arranged with fivefold symmetry. As the tiling is extended, the ratio of fat and skinny tiles is equal to the ratio of successive Fibonacci numbers that approaches the famous irrational number, the golden ratio: $\tau = (1 + \sqrt{5})/2 = 1.618....$

Fig. 2. The symmetry of a solid is determined by bombarding it with electrons along different directions and examining the scattering pattern. If the atoms are disordered, the pattern consists of diffuse rings, but if the atoms are highly ordered, as in crystals or quasicrystals, the pattern is an array of spots. The spot pattern has a symmetry that reflects the symmetry of the atomic arrangement along the electron-beam direction. The patterns obtained for icosahedrite, the first natural quasicrystal, show that it has icosahedral symmetry, the symmetry of a soccer ball. By aiming the beam at the solid along symmetry axes analogous to the indicated axes of a soccer ball, patterns with (*a*) five-, (*b*) three-, and (*c*) twofold symmetry are observed, just what is expected if examining an icosahedral quasicrystal down the corresponding axes.

"khatyrkite" (catalog number 46407/G; **Fig. 3**), acquired by the Florence museum in 1990 and catalogued as coming from the Khatyrka region of the Koryak Mountains in the Chukotka Autonomous Okrug (district) on the northeastern part of the Kam-

chatka peninsula. (Khatyrkite is a crystalline alloy of copper and aluminum and icosahedrite was found in very small and rare grains in close association with it together with other well-known rock-forming minerals.) At first, there was no direct evidence that the

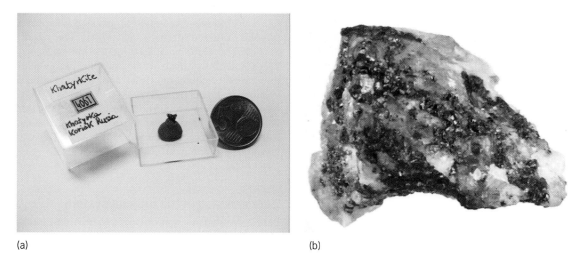

(a)   (b)

Fig. 3. Pictures of the original rock sample containing the first natural quasicrystal. (*a*) The original box with the rock sample attached to plastiline and marked as coming from the Khatyrka River in far eastern Russia. (*b*) High-resolution image of the sample (approximately 3 mm in size) showing that it is a "rock," an aggregate of several minerals. The dark regions are the metal alloys, including icosahedrite.

Florence sample actually came from that location. However, through a remarkable investigation worthy of a detective novel, the history of the sample was traced back to its original unearthing in a blue-green clay bed along the Listvenitovyi stream, off the Iomrautvaam tributary of the Khatyrka River.

What about the origin? A puzzling aspect for geologists was the presence of metallic aluminum in the quasicrystal grains as well as some of the other mineral phases found in the rock. Aluminum normally oxidizes unless placed in a highly reducing environment, as is done in the laboratory or in industry. Hence, serious consideration had to be given to the possibility that the sample was slag or an accidental byproduct of some anthropogenic process. Over the next two years, more data was collected that provided overwhelming evidence that the rock was formed by some natural process. Among the data was the discovery of a grain of icosahedrite trapped within stishovite (a form of silicon dioxide that only forms at very high pressures of 100,000 atm or more), which indicated that the quasicrystal had to have formed at pressures that only occur under exotic conditions, either very deep under the surface of the Earth, near the boundary between core and mantle, or in space, through the collisions of meteors and asteroids. To distinguish the two possibilities, the team collaborated with scientists at Princeton, the Smithsonian Institution in Washington, DC, and Caltech in a series of ion-probe experiments that measure the ratio of oxygen isotopes. The results were unmistakable: The oxygen isotopes matched precisely the known abundances in a form of meteorite known as carbonaceous chondrite, among the oldest meteorites to have formed in our solar system.

Establishing that the material is indeed natural and meteoritic was based on the analyses of the Florence sample only. The only hope for pushing the exploration further was to find new samples. But the only real chance of finding more samples with the same remarkable properties would have been to return to the place where the original samples were found: the Listvenitovyi stream in the Koryak Mountains in far eastern Russia. Despite the difficulties and the unlikely possibility of finding more samples, a geological expedition to Chukotka in far eastern Russia was undertaken in 2011. The extraordinary journey to one of the most remote places on the planet resulted in the unexpected discovery of new samples that have firmly established that the quasicrystal and the rock containing it are definitely part of a carbonaceous chondritic meteorite (officially named Khatyrka, after a river in Chukotka), with calcium aluminum inclusions that date back 4.5 billion years ago (BYA) to the formation of the solar system.

Implications. What does it mean to have found the first mineral with forbidden symmetry in nature? In geology, the discovery of a natural quasicrystal has opened a new chapter in the study of mineralogy, forever altering the conventional classification of mineral forms. In condensed matter physics, the discovery has pushed back the age of the oldest quasicrystals by orders of magnitude and has had an impact on our view of how difficult it is for quasicrystals to form. To have found a natural quasicrystal has also been a way of studying quasicrystal stability over annealing times and conditions not accessible in the laboratory and demonstrates that these materials are not inherently delicate, metastable oddities that may only be synthesized for ideal compositions and under highly controlled laboratory conditions. Identifying materials that form quasicrystals has always relied significantly on trial-and-error and serendipity, and searching through nature could prove to be an effective complement to laboratory methods. Finally, the discovery has suggested new geologic or extraterrestrial processes of formation. What remains is to determine exactly how the collisions of asteroids produced quasicrystals and never-before-seen combinations of aluminum and copper metallic alloys. The research team will be performing a series of follow-up experiments to determine more precisely the conditions under which the novel minerals formed and the implications for the evolution of the early solar system.

For background information *see* COSMOCHEMISTRY; CRYSTAL STRUCTURE; CRYSTALLOGRAPHY; ELECTRON MICROSCOPE; METEORITE; MINERALOGY; QUASICRYSTAL; SOLAR SYSTEM; X-RAY CRYSTALLOGRAPHY; X-RAY DIFFRACTION in the McGraw-Hill Encyclopedia of Science & Technology.

Luca Bindi; Paul J. Steinhardt

Bibliography. L. Bindi et al., Natural quasicrystals, *Science*, 324:1306–1309, 2009, DOI:10.1126/science.1170827; L. Bindi et al., Icosahedrite, $Al_{63}Cu_{24}Fe_{13}$, the first natural quasicrystal, *Am. Mineral.*, 96:928–931, 2011, DOI:10.2138/am.2011.3758; L. Bindi et al., Evidence for the extraterrestrial origin of a natural quasicrystal, *Proc. Natl. Acad. Sci. USA*, 109:1396–1401, 2012, DOI:10.1073/pnas.1111115109; D. Levine and P. J. Steinhardt, Quasicrystals: A new class of ordered structures, *Phys. Rev. Lett.*, 53:2477–2480, 1984, DOI:10.1103/PhysRevLett.53.2477; P. J. Lu et al., Identifying and indexing icosahedral quasicrystals from powder diffraction patterns, *Phys. Rev. Lett.*, 87:275507, 2001, DOI:10.1103/PhysRevLett.87.275507; D. Shechtman et al., Metallic phase with long-range orientational order and no translational symmetry, *Phys. Rev. Lett.*, 53:1951–1954, 1984, DOI:10.1103/PhysRevLett.53.1951; P. J. Steinhardt and L. Bindi, In search of natural quasicrystals, *Rep. Progr. Phys.*, 75:092601-092611, 2012, DOI:10.1088/0034-4885/75/9/092601.

Neuroscience in the judicial system

Rapid advances in neuroscience have broad implications for our understanding of human behavior. The extent of the legal system's interest in this information as well as the range of concerns related to the use of neuroscience in court are reflected in publications so numerous that an exhaustive review here is impractical. As a result, this article is limited to discussions about the use of scientific evidence in court, limitations on such use of neuroscience, select examples of such use, and concerns as to whether the field is prepared to manage the demands for this knowledge.

Law and scientific evidence. The legal system relies upon an adversarial process to resolve disputes. Through the introduction of evidence and argument, the opposing parties attempt to persuade the trier of fact to decide in their favor. In civil litigation, such as personal injury cases, the plaintiff must prove by a preponderance of the evidence that the defendant behaved improperly and caused an injury for which the plaintiff should be compensated by the defendant. In criminal cases, the prosecution must prove beyond a reasonable doubt that a criminal act occurred (the *actus reus*) and that the defendant had criminal intent (*mens rea*).

The defendant's state of mind is critical in both types of cases. Whether or not the defendant intentionally or negligently caused the injury in a civil case affects the nature of the liability and the size of the damage award if the plaintiff prevails. Defenses in criminal cases include lack of criminal intent, justification, or excuse: The defendant committed the crime, but should not be held responsible. The insanity defense is the most familiar excuse defense: At the time of the offense, the defendant suffered from a mental disease or defect of sufficient severity that he or she should not be held responsible for the criminal act in question. The criteria for the insanity defense vary among jurisdictions, but elements can include inability to appreciate the wrongfulness or nature of the act, or inability to conform one's behavior to the requirements of the law. The insanity defense is rarely raised and even more rarely successful. The chances of success are greatest where the illness or defect is severe and can be documented through observable behavior or an abnormality supported by physical evidence.

Neuroscientific evidence is potentially of great value in both civil and criminal litigation. Proposed and attempted uses have included determining the presence and nature of a mental disease or defect, detecting deception on the part of witnesses or the parties, and documenting the presence of injuries (such as chronic pain) or specific mental conditions (such as posttraumatic stress disorder).

Efforts to introduce neuroscientific research into the courts have met with mixed success because of the rules of evidence that govern the use of expert testimony. In federal courts in the United States, the admissibility of scientific evidence is governed by Rule 702 of the Federal Rules of Evidence. Rule 702 allows for the introduction of scientific evidence through the testimony of expert witnesses where the judge is convinced that the expert's testimony meets certain criteria of scientific soundness (see **table**). Even when expert scientific testimony meets these standards, it may be excluded pursuant to Federal Rule 403, where "its probative value is substan-

---

Rule 702: Testimony by expert witnesses

A witness who is qualified as an expert by knowledge, skill, experience, training, or education may testify in the form of an opinion or otherwise if:
(a) the expert's scientific, technical, or other specialized knowledge will help the trier of fact to understand the evidence or to determine a fact in issue;
(b) the testimony is based on sufficient facts or data;
(c) the testimony is the product of reliable principles and methods; and
(d) the expert has reliably applied the principles and methods to the facts of the case.

---

tially outweighed by the danger of unfair prejudice, confusion of the issues, or misleading the jury, or by considerations of undue delay, waste of time, or needless presentation of cumulative evidence." Individual states have similar rules of evidence.

Concerns about the use of neuroscience in court. The exciting developments in neuroscience have sparked the imagination of researchers, clinicians, and those eager to apply those developments in real-world settings, including the judicial system. This proposed use of neuroscience in court has generated a number of concerns, including some that relate to the following issues.

1. Research studies have commonly portrayed certain areas of the brain as being specifically responsible for certain emotions and functions. However, this model is being displaced by the understanding that the brain operates via interconnected networks that share multiple functions.

2. Biomarkers attributed to specific disorders, behaviors, or emotions are derived from data that are averaged from large groups of subjects and therefore have limited applicability to identifying disorders in individual subjects. Attempts to address this by using computational techniques to assign individuals to diagnostic categories achieve accuracies of no greater than 80%, with no demonstrated superiority over traditional diagnostic approaches.

3. The attribution of biomarkers to specific diagnoses assumes that the diagnoses and their criteria are valid and stable. Diagnostic criteria are periodically modified, and diagnoses are added or eliminated in the *Diagnostic and Statistical Manual of Mental Disorders*. As a result, biomarkers for a specific diagnosis are of questionable validity if that diagnosis is determined to no longer exist or if its criteria are changed. Additionally, a 2013 study demonstrates that the same genetic variations are associated with five major psychiatric disorders, raising further questions about the specificity of diagnostic categories.

4. The majority of studies use healthy controls and sick subjects, and studies of criminal behavior tend to utilize violent, incarcerated offenders, thus failing to include data from those criminal offenders who escape prosecution and incarceration and from white-collar criminals.

5. Experimental studies of brain function intended to emulate acts of aggression, experiencing pain, and deception utilize stimuli that have minimal emotional impact or personal significance to the subjects. This limits the application of these studies in the courtroom, where false-positive and false-negative findings will have significant consequences for individuals and society.

6. Research studies at best demonstrate a correlative relationship between brain activity and specific behaviors and diagnoses, but do not establish causality. The inability of neuroimaging studies to distinguish between correlation and causation was part of the Supreme Court's rationale in overturning (in 2011) a California statute that barred the sale of violent video games to minors. California had offered neuroimaging evidence of the effect of violent video games on the brains of adolescents. Justice Stephen Breyer, in his dissent, wrote that "[c]utting-edge neuroscience has shown that 'virtual violence in video game playing results in those neural patterns that are considered characteristic for aggressive cognition and behavior'." In his majority opinion, however, Justice Antonin Scalia suggested that the evidence would not pass the Federal Rules of Evidence tests for admissibility.

7. In addition to being developed in laboratory settings, as opposed to real-world situations, deception detection techniques utilizing functional neuroimaging and brain electrical activity are susceptible to covert countermeasures that significantly reduce their accuracy. In 2012, the United States 6th Circuit Court of Appeals upheld a trial judge's refusal to admit functional magnetic resonance imaging (fMRI) lie detection evidence under Rule 702. The defendant had offered fMRI lie detection evidence to prove that he was generally truthful in denying that he had committed health care fraud. The court held that the trial judge had not erred in refusing to admit the evidence under Rule 702, noting that the technology "had not been fully examined in real-world settings" and that the testing was not consistent with tests administered in research studies.

The concerns about the use of neuroscientific evidence in court also extend to Rule 403, that is, that the probative value is outweighed by the risk of prejudice, confusion of the issues, or misleading the jury. Neuroscience evidence has been shown to significantly affect the decisions of lay decision makers, even in cases where that evidence is largely irrelevant or based on faulty science. Mock jurors were less likely to recommend the death penalty for defendants deemed to be at risk of future dangerousness when neuropsychological and neuroimaging evidence was presented, and the introduction of evidence of a biomechanism explaining psychopathic behavior to judges sentencing mock defendants in hypothetical cases appears to lead them to issue shorter sentences.

In spite of these concerns, neuroscientific evidence can add value in specific cases, for example, informing the decision maker of mitigating factors in a criminal case, providing clarity in clinical situations, or corroborating other evidence of mental or physical disease or defect. For example, in 2012, a federal trial court judge in Iowa granted a defendant's petition for relief from her convictions on five counts of murder and her four death sentences and one life sentence. The judge found that the defendant's initial trial counsel had provided ineffective assistance at the guilt and mitigation phases when it chose not to introduce expert testimony suggesting that the defendant suffered from possibly inherited brain impairments, did nothing toward using that information at the mitigation stage, and did not follow up on a defense psychologist's recommendation for neuropsychological testing and neuroimaging. The judge specifically pointed out that additional mitigating evidence was available from several experts who had found that the defendant had numerous cognitive deficits.

Judges and juries are not always swayed by neuroscientific evidence. In 2008, a jury in Louisiana was unconvinced by expert testimony, including neuroimaging results, indicating that a defendant suffered from fetal alcohol syndrome and other cognitive problems such that she should be spared the death penalty for her first-degree murder conviction. The Supreme Court of Louisiana rejected the defendant's arguments that the brain imaging evidence in and of itself demonstrated that she was not competent to stand trial and that she was mentally retarded (intellectually disabled), and thus not subject to the death penalty. The Supreme Court noted that a sanity board had found her competent after evaluation by two psychiatrists, and that the issue of mental retardation (intellectual disability) had properly been left to the jury.

Ready or not? The U.S. legal system as a whole has taken a cautious approach to neuroscientific evidence, applying the standard rules of evidence to determine whether information from a given study or technique should be admissible in a given matter. To date, the judicial system appears to have successfully taken an approach that subjects neuroscientific testimony to the same standards of scrutiny that apply to other expert testimony. Exceptions to this have and will occur, however, with neuroscientific evidence excluded or admitted when, upon further reflection, it should not be.

A key element in determining the proper use of this information will be neuroscientists themselves. It remains an open question whether neuroscientists are prepared to withstand the numerous pressures and temptations posed by requests to move their research findings from the laboratory to the real world. The request to describe one's work in a public forum and have it used to make important societal decisions is difficult to resist. The same is true of the financial incentives that come with being an expert witness or establishing a commercial venture that offers neuroscientific techniques for applications in nonexperimental settings such as corporate or national security. The temptation to overstate the certainty and applicability of research findings in such circumstances is strong, and any failure to prevent this raises the risk of significant societal harm through distortion of the judicial system and damage to the credibility of the science.

For background information *see* BRAIN; COGNITION; CRIMINALISTICS; EMOTION; FORENSIC EVIDENCE; MEDICAL IMAGING; MOTIVATION; NEUROBIOLOGY; PSYCHOLOGY; SOCIOBIOLOGY in the McGraw-Hill Encyclopedia of Science & Technology.

Ronald Schouten; José A. Hidalgo

Bibliography. D. J. Church, Neuroscience in the courtroom: An international concern, *Wm. Mary Law Rev.*, 53(5):1825–1854, 2012; K. D. Davis, E. Racine, and B. Collett, Neuroethical issues related to the use of brain imaging: Can we and should we use brain imaging as a biomarker to diagnose chronic pain?, *Pain*, 153(8):1555–1559, 2012, DOI:10.1016/j.pain.2012.02.037; J. M. Eggen and E. J. Laury, Toward a neuroscience model of tort law: How functional neuroimaging will transform tort doctrine, *Colum. Sci. Technol. Law Rev.*, 13:235–306, 2012; H. T. Greely and A. D. Wagner, Reference guide on neuroscience, pp. 747–812, in *Reference Manual on Scientific Evidence*, 3d ed., National Academies Press, Washington, DC, 2011; S. Henry and D. Plemmons, Neuroscience, neuropolitics and neuroethics: The complex case of crime, deception and fMRI, *Sci. Eng. Ethics*, 18:573–591, 2012, DOI:10.1007/s11948-012-9393-4; K. A. Lindquist and L. F. Barrett, A functional architecture of the human brain: Emerging insights from the science of emotion, *Trends Cognit. Sci.*, 16(11):533–540, 2012, DOI:10.1016/j.tics.2012.09.005; D. S. Weisberg et al., The seductive allure of neuroscience explanations, *J. Cognit. Neurosci.*, 20(3):470–477, 2008, DOI:10.1162/jocn.2008.20040.

New generation of concretes

Concrete is an artificial building material that looks like stone. The origin of the word concrete came from the Latin *concretus*, which means to hold together or formable rock. Although it looks like a homogeneous material, concrete is actually a composite material composed of coarse stones (the coarse aggregate) and sand (the fine aggregate) embedded in a binder (the cement paste, asphalt, or other binders) that fills the interparticle spaces among the sand and stone particles and binds them together.

Ordinary portland cement concrete. Depending on the type of binder being used, concrete can be classified as hydraulic cement concrete, nonhydraulic cement concrete, asphalt concrete, or polymer concrete. Both hydraulic and nonhydraulic cement need water to mix and react, while only hydraulic cement can gain strength in water because of the insolubility of the hydration products. The ancient Egyptians built the pyramids by gluing stone blocks using a mixture of water and burned gypsum, a type of nonhydraulic cement. Ordinary portland cement (OPC) belongs to the family of hydraulic cement. The common term cement paste refers to a mixture of OPC and water. Cement paste becomes mortar when sand is added, and mortar becomes concrete after coarse stones are included.

A typical OPC consists of about 65% calcium oxide (CaO), 23% silica (SiO_2), 4% alumina (Al_2O_3), and a small percentage of other inorganic compounds. The major reactive compounds in OPC are alite (tricalcium silicate), belite (dicalcium silicate), tricalcium aluminate, and tetracalciumaluminoferrite. A small amount of gypsum is commonly added to control the hydration speed of OPC. Soon after it was patented in 1824 by British inventor Joseph Aspdin, portland cement quickly took over the market for cement in building materials. Today, OPC is the most widely used manufactured material in the world. But as we are becoming more aware of protecting the Earth, a new era of alternative concretes is on its way to make our buildings and infrastructures greener and more sustainable.

The need for alternatives to ordinary portland cement. Ordinary portland cement is manufactured in a highly energy-intensive process in which raw materials need to be heated above 1300°C to melt in a kiln (oven). A rough estimate is that 100–200 kWh is required to make one ton of OPC. In addition to high energy consumption, OPC is the third largest source of CO_2 emission and contributes to 5% of the total CO_2 emission in the world. For every ton of OPC manufactured, one ton of CO_2 is liberated to the atmosphere through the decomposition of raw materials and the burning of the fossil fuels. Therefore, the construction-materials industry is under increasing pressure to reduce the energy used in production of OPC and greenhouse-gas emissions.

Geopolymer. Geopolymer, a new type of ceramic-like material, is drawing the attention of material scientists and civil engineers from academia, industry, and government. The concept of geopolymer dates back to the 1930s when V. D. Glukhovsky first developed alkali-activated slag (a waste material from metal production) cement in the Ukraine and used it in a number of structures, some of which are still standing up today. The name geopolymer was first introduced by Joseph Davidovits, a French chemist, in the 1980s.

Compared to OPC, geopolymer is more environmentally friendly because its production requires less energy and generates lower CO_2 emissions for a number of reasons. First, geopolymer can be made at room temperature and does not need any curing at elevated temperature. Because industrial byproducts are used as raw materials, geopolymer essentially consumes zero energy. Second, little or only a very small amount of CO_2 is generated in the manufacturing process of geopolymer, meaning it can fully or partially solve the problem of high CO_2 emissions of OPC. Third, industrial solid wastes, especially fly ash, can be incorporated as a raw material for geopolymer. Fly ash is a byproduct of the

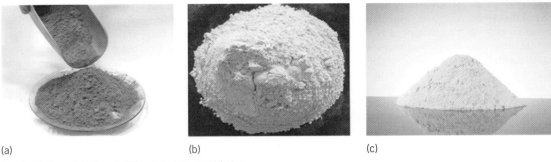

(a)   (b)   (c)

Fig. 1. Photos of (*a*) fly ash, (*b*) metakaolin, and (*c*) slag.

coal combustion process and usually needs to be disposed of in landfills or ash ponds. However, there have been tremendous concerns about its environmental effects because of toxic constituents, such as arsenic and mercury, which could be leached from the fly ash into underground aquifers and contaminate drinking water. The U.S. Environmental Protection Agency (EPA) is currently evaluating a proposal to regulate fly ash as a hazardous waste. If fly ash can be converted to geopolymer, however, the toxic constituents will be encapsulated inside the concrete.

In addition to the above-mentioned advantages, geopolymer also exhibits superior mechanical properties, has a very short set time (time to gain enough strength), and is very durable. Mortar and concrete made with geopolymer can easily have a compressive strength of 83 MPa (12,000 psi), which is twice the normal compressive strength of OPC. While OPC usually has a set time of 2–4 h, geopolymer can set as quickly as two minutes, giving it a huge advantage for use as a repair material. In addition, the full strength of geopolymer can be reached in several days or even several hours, compared to 28 days as is the case for OPC. Concrete made with OPC is known to have a number of potential durability problems, such as acid attack, alkali–silica reaction (damage to the concrete caused by expansive aggre-

gates), and cracking due to freezing and thawing. Geopolymer inherently has a denser structure and is thus far less susceptible to harsh environmental conditions.

Geopolymer is normally made by either a one-part or two-part method. The one-part method is very much like making OPC mortar, whereby a pre-blended mixture of aluminosilicate or calcium aluminosilicate and activation chemicals is mixed with water and cured. In the two-part method, the chemicals are dissolved in the water first to form an activation solution and then an aluminosilicate powder or a calcium-aluminosilicate powder is mixed with the activation solution. The aluminosilicate or calcium-aluminosilicate powder usually contains one or more of the following ingredients: fly ash, slag, metakaolin (burned kaolin clay), and micro kaolin clay (**Fig. 1**). The activation chemicals include alkali-metal hydroxides, alkaline-earth metal hydroxides, alkali-metal silicates, and alkali-metal aluminates. Sometimes a retarder is also used, such as borax or sodium phosphate. A common mix design can use class F (low calcium content) fly ash and water glass (sodium silicate, Na_2SiO_3, made by dissolving silica in a sodium hydroxide, NaOH, solution). The resultant geopolymer has a dense, ceramic-like and three-dimensional microstructure that is significantly different from that of OPC (**Fig. 2**).

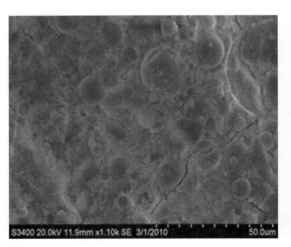

(a)   (b)

Fig. 2. Scanning electron microscope photos of (*a*) ordinary portland cement (OPC) and (*b*) geopolymer pastes.

Because of its distinct properties, geopolymer has potential applications ranging from replacing OPC in concrete, to making building products, to even some high-tech applications. In Australia, geopolymer has been used to make concrete pavements and bridge decks. In the United States, companies are making geopolymer bricks, pavers, and tiles. Besides applications in the construction industry, fire-resistant geopolymer coatings for airplanes and electronic circuits have been proposed.

Alternatives to OPC. Calcium aluminate cements (CACs) are a specialty class of cements containing primarily monocalcium aluminate (CA or $CaO \cdot Al_2O_3$) and sometimes C12A7 ($12CaO \cdot 7Al_2O_3$) or CA2 ($CaO \cdot 2Al_2O_3$). CAC concrete has several distinct advantages over traditional OPC concrete, including rapid strength gain upon setting and enhanced resistance to abrasion, sulfate attack (concrete cracking due to sulfate), and alkali–silica reaction. Furthermore, production of CAC results in lower CO_2 emissions than OPC production. However, widespread use of CAC is limited by a process called "conversion," which occurs in hydrated CAC over time, whereby metastable hydrates convert to stable hydrates, leading to an increase in porosity and subsequent decrease in strength.

Calcium sulfoaluminate (CSA) cements contain ye'elimite (C_4A_3S or $4CaO3Al_2O_3SO_3$) as a major constituent. Because of their ability to bind heavy metals, CSA cements are of interest in applications for hazardous-waste encapsulation. CSA cements currently are receiving more general attention because their production generates low CO_2 emissions.

Supersulfated cements are binders free of OPC, and generally composed of slag, calcium sulfate ($CaSO_4$), and an alkaline activator. The main constituents of supersulfated cements are 70–90% slag, 10–20% calcium sulfate, and generally low quantities of an alkaline activator, mainly portland cement or clinker. Besides portland cement or portland cement clinker, other activators, including calcium hydroxide [$Ca(OH)_2$], potassium hydroxide (KOH), and sodium carbonate (Na_2CO_3), are reported. The slow hardening of supersulfated cements during the first few days makes it necessary to apply moisture to building materials during curing. Supersulfated cements exhibit a lower capillary porosity and good durability to chemical and physical attacks.

Cost effectiveness. In the United States, the price of portland cement has increased more than 20% since 2012, and this trend in the price may become even worse in the foreseeable future. Likewise, from 2007 to 2011, the Chinese national cement price increased 39%. International cement prices also increased significantly because of increases in fuel prices. A new EPA regulation, which will go into effect in 2013, will set much stricter emission limits for the U.S. cement industry. This new regulation will cost billions of dollars in plant upgrades, which could lead to job outsourcing, higher prices, and ultimately plant closures, according to the Portland Cement Association. In light of this cement price hike, finding an alternative binder to reduce cement use and promote sustainable construction is required as quickly as possible.

The cost of geopolymer depends on the cost of the raw materials, such as fly ash, metakaolin, NaOH, and water glass. Generally the cost of geopolymer is comparable to portland cement at about $80–110/ton for portland cement and $50–100/ton for geopolymer. Some additional costs may result from the quality control required for geopolymer products, such as concrete, tiles, and bricks.

For background information *see* ALKALI METALS; ALKALINE-EARTH METALS; CEMENT; COMPOSITE MATERIAL; CONCRETE; MORTAR in the McGraw-Hill Encyclopedia of Science & Technology.　　Lin Shen; Li Ai

Bibliography. M. Juenger et al., Advances in alternative cementitious binders, *Cement Concr. Res.*, 41:1232–1243, 2011, DOI:10.1016/j.cemconres.2010.11.012; Z. Li, *Advanced Concrete Technology*, John Wiley & Sons, Hoboken, NJ, 2011; A. M. Neville, *Properties of Concrete*, 4th ed., Longman Group, London, 1995; A. Palomo, M. W. Grutzeck, and M. T. Blanco, Alkali-activated fly ashes: A cement for the future, *Cement Concr. Res.*, 29(8):1323–1329, 1999, DOI:10.1016/S0008-8846(98)00243-9.

New planktonic symbiosis found in the ocean

Symbiosis is the long-term biological interaction of two species. The three major types of symbiosis are mutualism, where both partners benefit from the relationship; commensalism, where one partner benefits and the other is neither harmed nor benefited; and parasitism, where one partner benefits at the expense of the other. A well-known mutualistic symbiosis in the ocean is that of reef-building corals and zooxanthellae (algal dinoflagellates that reside in the coral polyp). The coral receives carbohydrates and oxygen from the dinoflagellate partner as a result of photosynthesis. In return, metabolic waste products from the coral are used by the algal symbiont. This type of symbiosis has been directly observed both in the laboratory and in the field.

Although less known, the planktonic symbiosis among diatoms (algae of the class Bacillariophyceae) of the genus *Rhizosolenia* and filamentous cyanobacteria (blue-green algae) of the genus *Richelia* has been studied extensively. *Richelia*, along with a free-living cyanobacterium, has traditionally been credited with the bulk of nitrogen fixation in the ocean. Recently, however, a mutualistic symbiosis between a member of the unicellular nitrogen-fixing cyanobacterium Group A (UCYN-A) and a single-celled eukaryotic alga was discovered. This was the first report of a partnership between a unicellular cyanobacterium and a prymnesiophyte (an alga of the class Prymnesiophyceae). Although the name *Candidatus Atelocyanobacterium thalassa* has been proposed for this cyanobacterium, it is referred to as UCYN-A throughout the literature. UCYN-A provides fixed nitrogen to its algal host while receiving fixed carbon in exchange. UCYN-A has proven difficult to cultivate, and it is difficult to visualize under the microscope because of its small size (less than 1 μm in diameter). As a result, much of what is known about UCYN-A and its symbiotic relationship is based on flow cytometry coupled with metagenomic studies and isotopic analyses. UCYN-A is particularly significant in that it has a reduced genome, lacking the genes that are associated traditionally with the major metabolic pathways of cyanobacteria. The genome is also structurally similar to that of chloroplasts (plant cell plastids). This suggests the possibility that UCYN-A is on an evolutionary path analogous to that of the ancestor of chloroplasts.

Relationship between UCYN-A and its algal host. UCYN-A is a widespread and uncultivated diazotroph (an organism capable of fixing nitrogen). The relationship of UCYN-A with its algal partner is mutualistic. The absence of major metabolic pathway genes is unprecedented, further suggesting that UCYN-A is an obligate (dependent) symbiont. Quantitative isotopic analysis and tracer experiments with ^{13}C and ^{15}N have confirmed active atmospheric nitrogen fixation in UCYN-A and demonstrated the transfer of nitrogen and carbon between the partners. This was facilitated by nanoscale secondary ion mass spectrometry (nanoSIMS).

The symbiotic relationship can also be characterized by the location of the symbiont. It is unclear whether UCYN-A is an endosymbiont (a symbiont organism that lives within the body of the host) or whether it resides on the surface of the host as an epiphyte. However, an extracellular association is suggested by halogenated in situ hybridization SIMS imaging and by the ease with which the association is disrupted during sample handling and processing. Based on DNA sequence analysis, the algal partner of UCYN-A is most closely related to *Braarudosphaera bigelowii*, which has calcareous plates that may easily be dislodged. It is possible that the UCYN-A may be attached to these plates or may be found under these plates. Then, during the experimental procedures, the plates may be dislodged or dissolved.

UCYN-A genome. UCYN-A was initially discovered in 1998 using amplification and sequencing of the *nif*H gene, which codes for one of two highly conserved proteins that make up the enzyme nitrogenase (which is required for nitrogen fixation). Based on this analysis, UCYN-A appears to be most closely related to a unicellular cyanobacterium of the genus *Cyanothece*. In 2008, investigators established the absence of photosystem II (PSII) in UCYN-A, suggesting a novel metabolism, as it was the first reported cyanobacterium that is unable to undergo oxygenic photosynthesis. This prompted the whole genome sequencing of the cyanobacterium. Using metabolic reconstructions inferred from the assembled genome of UCYN-A, several metabolic pathways (in addition to PSII) were found to be incomplete or missing altogether, including the carbon fixation pathway and the biosynthetic pathways of several amino acids and purines. An incomplete tricarboxylic acid (TCA) cycle (which is required for aerobic respiration in cells) has been observed in many cyanobacteria, and various enzymes involved in the TCA cycle are absent (for example, alpha-ketoglutarate dehydrogenase and NADH oxidase). Moreover, a complete absence of the TCA cycle has been cited in *Mycoplasma* and *Nanoarchaeum*. With regard to UCYN-A, just a single enzyme related to the TCA cycle is present. In addition, the accessory pigment phycoerythrin is absent. In fact, this was the missing component from the genome that initially hinted at a possible symbiotic relationship for UCYN-A because it implied that UCYN-A would need to obtain nutrients (specifically carbon) from another source.

When compared with those of closely related species, the genome of UCYN-A is relatively small (1.44 megabases). *Crocosphaera watsonii*, a phylogenetically related species, has a genome that is nearly four times the size of that of UCYN-A. The genome consists of a single circular chromosome including approximately 1200 genes. Interestingly, it contains inverted repeats of ribosomal RNA operons (distinct genes that are expressed and regulated as a unit), making it structurally similar to those of many chloroplasts. Additionally, UCYN-A appears to be highly conserved throughout its global distribution.

Nitrogen fixation. Nitrogen is important to biological organisms as a major component of amino acids (the building blocks of proteins). Nitrogen fixation is the process by which atmospheric nitrogen (N_2) is reduced to ammonia (NH_3), which is a form that organisms are able to use. This process requires the enzyme nitrogenase, which is sensitive to oxygen and is deactivated in its presence. The lack of PSII, the oxygen-evolving component of photosynthesis, makes it possible for UCYN-A to fix nitrogen during the day. This is important in the oligotrophic (nutrient-deprived) environment of the open ocean because nitrogen can be a limiting nutrient. It also has important implications for the global nitrogen budget. Prior to the discovery of a diverse diazotrophic microbial population in the oligotrophic oceans, it was thought that the bulk of nitrogen fixation in the oceans could be attributed to two genera (*Trichodesmium* and *Richelia*). However, the nitrogen budget did not seem to balance out. The contribution of nitrogen from UCYN-A and other newly discovered diazotrophs may provide the missing nitrogen inputs required to balance the global nitrogen budget.

Implications for endosymbiosis. The endosymbiotic theory asserts that mitochondria and chloroplasts originated as free-living bacteria that were engulfed by larger prokaryotes. Over time, these bacteria lost the genes that were necessary for a free-living lifestyle, making them completely dependent on the host cell. Mitochondria are thought to have originated from proteobacteria, and chloroplasts are thought to have originated from cyanobacteria. Each has its own genome, which is believed to be a relic of the respective bacterial ancestors. The size of the genome is reduced relative to that of bacterial cells. UCYN-A has an unprecedented reduction in genome size and appears to specialize in nitrogen fixation, analogous to the specialization of chloroplasts with regard to photosynthesis. There are currently no known nitrogen-fixing plastids or eukaryotes. Perhaps the symbiotic relationship between UCYN-A and a prymnesiophyte is providing a snapshot in time of an evolutionary pathway that will lead to a new eukaryotic cell type containing a nitrogen-fixing plastid.

Conclusions. The symbiotic relationship between UCYN-A and a prymnesiophyte similar to *Braarudosphaera bigelowii* is a novel and exciting discovery. It is suggestive of a possible evolutionary pathway leading to a nitrogen-fixing plastid within a eukaryotic cell. It will be important to definitively determine whether UCYN-A is an endosymbiont or an epiphyte. This will be difficult to achieve because of the small size of the cyanobacterium and the potentially fragile calcareous plates of its algal host. New and gentler methods for sample processing and handling will be necessary. Efforts toward the successful cultivation of UCYN-A should continue. An increased understanding of symbiont host interactions and the nutritional requirements of UCYN-A based on genomic information can be used to bolster this effort. Continued metagenomic and metatranscriptomic analyses of seawater samples using genes such as *nif*H will be critical in determining whether there are yet undiscovered nitrogen-fixing organisms in the open ocean that may be contributing to the global nitrogen budget. Additionally, these types of analyses may reveal other unicellular cyanobacteria in symbiotic association with prymnesiophytes, with genomes that are more streamlined than that of UCYN-A.

For background information *see* ALGAE; CELL PLASTIDS; CYANOBACTERIA; MARINE ECOLOGY; MARINE MICROBIOLOGY; MICROBIAL ECOLOGY; MUTUALISM; NITROGEN FIXATION; OCEANOGRAPHY; PHOTOSYNTHESIS; PHYTOPLANKTON; PLANT–ANIMAL INTERACTIONS; PRYMNESIOPHYCEAE in the McGraw-Hill Encyclopedia of Science & Technology.

Patricia A. Waikel

Bibliography. J. A. Fuhrman and D. G. Capone, Nifty nanoplankton, *Nature*, 412:593–594, 2001, DOI:10.1038/35088159; A. W. Thompson et al., Unicellular cyanobacterium symbiotic with a single-celled eukaryotic alga, *Science*, 337:1546–1550, 2012, DOI:10.1126/science.1222700; H. J. Tripp et al., Metabolic streamlining in an open-ocean nitrogen-fixing cyanobacterium, *Nature*, 464:90–94, 2010, DOI:10.1038/nature08786; J. P. Zehr, Interactions with partners are key for oceanic nitrogen-fixing cyanobacteria, *Microbe*, 8(3):117–122, 2013.

New spider: Trogloraptor marchingtoni

Trogloraptor marchingtoni is a newly discovered and unique spider species. It inhabits caves in the Pacific Northwest of the United States and has important implications for cave conservation and the evolution of spiders.

Earth is home to millions of species of animals and plants, and humans have probably discovered less than half of these species. This certainly applies to spiders because more than 100 previously unknown species of spiders are discovered each year. Most of these new species fit comfortably into some well-known category, such as one of the more than 110 described spider families. These families comprise groups of closely related species that are clearly distinct from members of other families. For example, North American spiders are well known, with most families and most genera being identified in the literature. However, a large, bizarre, cave spider, first collected in 2010, defied all efforts at identification. This discovery of *Trogloraptor marchingtoni*, a new species of spider from caves in the Pacific Northwest of the United States, represents a very rare event. *Trogloraptor marchingtoni* is a new species that is so evolutionarily distinct from all other spiders that a new family needed to be proposed to contain it. Worldwide, the last time that a new family needed to be proposed to accommodate a newly discovered spider was in 2000 for the South African spider species placed in the genus *Chumma* (spiny-backed spiders, family Chummidae), and the last time that such a discovery was made in North America was in the 1890s, with the discovery of the first known coneweb spiders (family Diguetidae) and desert sand spiders (family Homalonychidae). The discovery of *Trogloraptor* is a reminder that remarkable organisms await discovery even in supposedly well-known corners of the world. *Trogloraptor* highlights the conservation importance of caves and the biogeographic interest of the Pacific Northwest, and compels researchers to rethink the evolution of a major spider group, the superfamily Dysderoidea (goblin spiders and their kin).

Discovery of Trogloraptor. A team of citizen scientists from the Western Cave Conservancy (Santa Cruz, CA) and arachnologists from the California Academy of Sciences (San Francisco, CA) found a new group of spiders living in caves in southwest Oregon. Charles Griswold, Tracy Audisio, and Joel Ledford, all from the California Academy of Sciences, collected, analyzed, and described this new family. The genus name, *Trogloraptor*, means cave robber or cave grabber, in reference to their life in caves and presumed manner of catching prey with their extraordinary claws. The species name, *marchingtoni*, honors Neil Marchington, a cave biologist with the Western Cave Conservatory, who helped discover the new species. The new family name, Trogloraptoridae, is based on the sole included genus.

Biology of Trogloraptor. This spider has been collected in the dark zone of limestone caves in the

Fig. 1. Female *Trogloraptor marchingtoni* spider climbing on a cave ceiling in Oregon. (*Photo courtesy of Joel Ledford*)

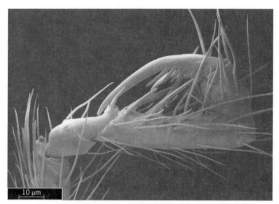

Fig. 2. Scanning electron micrograph of a front side view of the claws of the third leg of a female *Trogloraptor marchingtoni* spider. (*Photo courtesy of Charles E. Griswold and Tracy Audisio*)

Klamath-Siskiyou region of southwest Oregon. It was found hanging beneath a few strands of silk that were attached to the cave roof (**Fig. 1**). In general, the spiders are approximately 4 cm (1.6 in.) in width when their legs are extended. Their extraordinary, raptorial claws (**Fig. 2**) suggest that they are fierce, specialized predators, but their prey and attack behavior remain unknown. Nothing has been observed of their mating behavior either. Like most spiders, *Trogloraptor* spiders have three claws at the end of each leg, but their claws are much longer than those of most species. Uniquely, the tarsus (the last leg segment, or foot, of a spider) in *Trogloraptor* is flexible and set with a row of vicious spikes, against which the claws fold much like a switchblade knife. In general form (although different in the details), the claws of *Trogloraptor* resemble those of the *Doryonychus* spiders (family Tetragnathidae) from Hawaii and the long-claw spiders (family Gradungulidae) of Australia and New Zealand. These latter two groups of spiders have been observed to snap at and impale prey on their claws, and *Trogloraptor* may catch prey in similar ways.

Evolutionary affinities of Trogloraptor. The anatomy of *Trogloraptor* has forced arachnologists to revise their understanding of spider evolution. Uniquely among animals, male spiders have their first pair of leglike appendages, called pedipalps, modified to deliver sperm to the female spiders. *Trogloraptor* spiders belong among those spiders with simple male genitalia (this group is called the Haplogynae) and, similar to other members of the Haplogynae, the males have simple, bulb-shaped pedipalps (**Fig. 3**). Like most Haplogynae spiders, *Trogloraptor* spiders have only six eyes (most spiders have eight); uniquely, the middle eyes are widely separated (Fig. 3). Other anatomical details clearly distinguish them from most spiders in this group. Most families among the Haplogynae have the chelicerae (the spider's "jaws") fused at the base, but these are freely moveable in *Trogloraptor*. Strong evidence suggests that *Trogloraptor* spiders are close relatives of goblin spiders (Oonopidae and related families), which also have freely moveable chelicerae. The spinnerets (silk-spinning organs) of *Trogloraptor* have a peculiar morphology: The base of the anterior pair is crossed by a diagonal band of soft tissue. This peculiarity also occurs in goblin spiders and their kin (superfamily Dysderoidea, including the families Dysderidae, Oonopidae, Orsolobidae, and Segestriidae) and represents a synapomorphy (a shared evolutionarily derived feature) that unites these spiders as an evolutionary lineage. Unpublished molecular data from various genes [including the mitochondrial cytochrome c oxidase I (CO1), nuclear histone 3 (H3), and ribosomal 16S, 18S, and 28S rRNA genes] also suggest that the *Trogloraptor* spiders belong among the goblin spiders and their kin.

Furthermore, *Trogloraptor* spiders possess a mosaic of ancient features and evolutionary novelties, leading to a reconsideration of evolution among the Haplogynae spiders. Most spiders breathe through

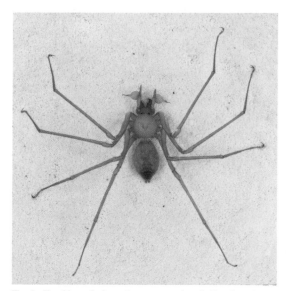

Fig. 3. Top (dorsal) view of a preserved male *Trogloraptor marchingtoni* spider. (*Photo courtesy of Vic Smith and Tracy Audisio*)

"book lungs" (many-layered leaflike blood- and air-filled spaces within the abdomen) and through tracheae (pipes that deliver gases directly to the tissues). Goblin spiders have their tracheae made of bundles of numerous tubes, whereas most Haplogynae spiders have tracheae that are highly reduced. In contrast, *Trogloraptor* spiders have simple, long, thin tracheae, constituting a primitive morphology found widely among spiders. The occurrence of this simple breathing apparatus in *Trogloraptor* suggests parallel evolutionary modifications of the tracheae in Haplogynae spiders: toward complex, elaborate bundles in goblin spiders and their kin, and toward reduction in all the others. Whereas the selective forces behind these developments remain unknown, this new knowledge of *Trogloraptor* suggests a primitive pattern from which this evolution occurred.

Trogloraptor biogeography and conservation. Western North America, especially the Klamath-Siskiyou region of northern California and southern Oregon, is rich in biodiversity, particularly with respect to its endemic plants and invertebrates. This area is particularly notable for relicts, that is, primitive relatives of otherwise widespread lineages. The coast redwood, *Sequoia sempervirens*, is a notable example. The coastal tailed frog (*Ascaphus truei*, Ascaphidae) and mountain beaver (*Aplodontia rufa*, Aplodontiidae) are considered the world's most primitive living frog and rodent species, respectively. Primitive arachnids (spiders, harvestmen, ticks, and scorpions) and myriapods (centipedes and millipedes) also occur in the Pacific Northwest. For example, the millipede family Microlympiidae is known from a minute species living in the Olympic Mountains of Washington, and several families of the branch-footed harvestman (Opiliones, Travunioidea) are found here. The California turret spider and the folding door trapdoor spiders (family Antrodiaetidae) retain vestiges of abdominal segmentation, similar to scorpions and whip spiders and reminiscent of fossil spiders known from the Paleozoic Era. Northern California also harbors the eight-eyed caponiid spider *Calponia* (bright lungless spiders) in the family Caponiidae: Most members of this family have their eyes reduced to two in number, and thus *Calponia* represents a primitive form. Finally, *Archoleptoneta*, also from California, differs from all other members of the spider family Leptonetidae (midget cave spiders) because it retains a primitive mechanism for producing sticky silk that comprises a fuzzy mass of electrostatically charged fibers. The turret spiders and folding door tarantulas, the eight-eyed *Calponia*, and the *Archoleptoneta* all comprise relatively ancient spider lineages characterized by the retention of ancestral character states. If the Trogloraptoridae (cave robber) spiders are the most primitive living members of the Dysderoidea, then this group is another case of a notable relict from western North America.

Other *Trogloraptor* individuals have been collected in old-growth redwood forests in northern California. These specimens were not found in caves, but deep beneath boulders and logs in ancient forests. Only juvenile specimens are known, and they lack the mature genital organs necessary for the description of a new species. Unpublished molecular analyses, using the previously mentioned genes, demonstrate that these specimens belong to a species distinct from *Trogloraptor marchingtoni*.

Conclusions. In summary, the remarkable *Trogloraptor* species long went undiscovered in what was thought to be a well-studied part of the world. The survival of these unique, relictual spiders in caves and ancient old-growth forests underscores the importance of preserving these habitats. It should not be surprising to find additional *Trogloraptor* species in caves and ancient forests in the Pacific Northwest. If such a large and bizarre spider could have gone undetected for so long, who knows what else may lurk undiscovered in this remarkable part of the world.

For background information *see* ARACHNIDA; ARANEAE; BIODIVERSITY; CAVE; CLASSIFICATION, BIOLOGICAL; PHYLOGENY; PREDATOR-PREY INTERACTIONS; SPECIATION; SPECIES CONCEPT; SPIDER SILK in the McGraw-Hill Encyclopedia of Science & Technology.   Charles E. Griswold

Bibliography. R. Foelix, *Biology of Spiders*, 3d ed., Oxford University Press, Oxford/New York, 2011; C. E. Griswold, T. Audisio, and J. Ledford, An extraordinary new family of spiders from caves in the Pacific Northwest (Araneae, Trogloraptoridae, new family), *ZooKeys*, 215:77–102, 2012, DOI:10.3897/zookeys.215.3547; C. E. Griswold et al., Atlas of phylogenetic data for entelegyne spiders (Araneae: Araneomorphae: Entelegynae) with comments on their phylogeny, *Proc. Calif. Acad. Sci.*, 56(suppl. II): 1–324, 2005; R. Jocqué and A. Dippenaar-Schoeman, *Spider Families of the World*, Royal Museum for Central Africa, Tervuren, Belgium, 2006; J. Ledford and C. E. Griswold, A study of the subfamily Archoleptonetinae (Araneae, Leptonetidae) with a review of the morphology and relationships for the Leptonetidae, *Zootaxa*, 2391:1–32, 2010; H. Levi and L. Levi, *Spiders and Their Kin: A Golden Guide*, St. Martin's Press, New York, 1996; J. Miller et al., Phylogeny of entelegyne spiders: Affinities of the family Penestomidae (NEW RANK), generic phylogeny of Eresidae, and asymmetric rates of change in spinning organ evolution (Araneae, Araneoidea, Entelegynae), *Mol. Phylogenet. Evol.*, 55:786–804, 2010, DOI:10.1016/j.ympev.2010.02.021; N. I. Platnick et al., Spinneret evidence and the higher classification of the haplogyne spiders (Araneae, Araneomorphae), *Am. Mus. Novit.*, 3016:1–3, 1991; M. J. Ramírez, Respiratory system morphology and the phylogeny of haplogyne spiders (Araneae, Araneomorphae), *J. Arachnol.*, 28:149–157, 2000, DOI:10.1636/0161-8202 (2000)028[0149:RSMATP]2.0.CO;2; D. Ubick et al., eds., *The Spider Genera of North America: An Identification Manual*, American Arachnological Society, Stockton, CA, 2005.

Olduvai Gorge

Olduvai Gorge (or Oldupai Gorge) is an important paleoanthropological site located in northern Tanzania. It is a site of significant hominin remains and has provided notable evidence for the understanding of early human evolution.

Description and discovery. Olduvai Gorge (**Fig. 1**) is situated on the southeastern edge of the Serengeti plain in northern Tanzania. It comprises a main gorge, spanning 46 km (28.6 mi) from its inception at the Lake Ndutu-Masek system to its end in the Olbalbal depression to the east, and a secondary or side gorge, spanning approximately 16 km (10 mi) from the foot-slope (lower slope) of the Lemagrut volcano to the junction with the main gorge. The gorge has a depth of approximately 100 m (328 ft) and is a record of the last 2 million years. This comprehensive record of human evolution is preserved in the form of thousands of fossils of the animals and hominins that roamed a diverse succession of paleolandscapes (**Fig. 2**). This record is supplemented by paleobotanical evidence [plant pollen, phytoliths (fossilized plant silica bodies), and macroremains] and by the geochemical indicators of vegetation preserved in different sedimentary facies [observable attributes (such as overall appearance or composition) of one part of a rock or stratigraphic unit as contrasted with other parts of the same rock or unit].

The uplift of the volcanic highlands to the east and south of the Serengeti plain formed the Olduvai basin approximately 2 million years ago (MYA). A fluctuating lake surrounded by a diversity of habitats sheltered mammal life, which were abundant during most of the geological sequence. The fossiliferous (fossil-containing) deposits are underlaid by a metamorphic rock basement, which outcrops today in the form of inselbergs (isolated mountains). Researchers have defined a sequential series of geological beds; from most ancient to most recent, these are Bed I (2–1.8 MYA), Bed II (1.8–1.3 MYA), Bed III (1.3–1.1 MYA), Bed IV (1.1–0.9 MYA), Masek (0.8–0.6 MYA), Ndutu (0.5–0.01 MYA), and Naisiusiu (0.05–0.01 MYA).

Olduvai Gorge was discovered by Wilhelm Kattwinkel in 1911 and initially explored by Hans Reck in 1913. In 1926, Louis Leakey and Hans Reck carried out a preliminary joint exploration. Then, starting in 1931, Louis Leakey led several expeditions in the company of his wife, Mary Leakey. The exploratory expeditions undertaken by Louis and Mary Leakey from 1931 to 1947 had the following goals: establishing a sequence of the evolutionary stages of culture across all beds; surveying the gorge to identify as many sites as possible for future excavations; and obtaining a picture of the geology of the gorge and its relevance to the climatic history of East Africa. The next stage of research at Olduvai, initiated in the early 1950s by Louis and Mary Leakey, focused on finding and excavating the "living floors" (the levels within an archeological site upon which a group of people lived and worked) to reconstruct

Fig. 1. A general view of Olduvai Gorge. (*Photo courtesy of Manuel Domínguez-Rodrigo*)

the behavior of "early man." Subsequently, extensive open-air excavations were carried out at some sites (specifically, BK and SHK) in Bed II. In the meantime, surveys continued in Bed I, with hominin fossils being discovered at the sites MK and FLK. The cranium of *Zinjanthropus boisei* (Zinj; later renamed *Paranthropus boisei*) was the most spectacular discovery found at FLK.

The discovery of Zinj switched the focus of attention from the Bed II "living floors" to the Bed I "living floors," and it provided the impetus for significant funding for further research. This marked a crucial moment in East African paleoanthropology. For paleontology, it led to the discovery of some of the most important hominin fossils in decades, including the first remains of *Homo habilis*. For archeology, it enabled the prolonged excavation of several sites during the 1960s and the horizontal exposure of some of the most impressive "living floors." Still today, some of these sites (for example, FLK Zinj) remain the most extensive open-air excavations of early Pleistocene archeology in Africa.

The abundant, well-preserved fossils and artifacts from these Olduvai Bed I sites have constituted the basis for the core of opinions about early human behavior since the 1960s. Early taphonomic (fossil preservation) work on these assemblages, along with the evidence of butchery, appeared to corroborate the basically anthropogenic (influenced by humans) nature of the "living floors," but this perspective actually catalyzed more extensive debate rather than bringing consensus or closure to it.

After Mary Leakey retired in 1986, work at the gorge was continued by Fidelis Masao and Robert Blumenschine. The Olduvai Paleoanthropological and Paleoecological Project (TOPPP) was initiated in 2006. This project was aimed at integrating archeology and paleoecology and is still active. Among its discoveries, the following should be stressed for their importance to human evolution studies: Several archeological sites constitute palimpsests (superimposed unrelated layers or collections of artifacts) formed with minimal hominin input in the accumulation of fauna, whereas those sites that are anthropogenic (for example, FLK Zinj in Bed I or BK in Bed II) show clear taphonomic evidence that hominins were systematically having primary access to carcasses ranging in size from gazelles to zebras. Also, after 1.5 MYA, hominins were frequently exploiting large mammals heavier than 1 ton of weight. This supports the hypothesis that early humans were hunters and that meat was an integral part of their diet. Additionally, most sites occurred in the vicinity of freshwater springs, showing that hominins, as well as other animals, were drawn to these permanent sources of water across time.

Importance of FLK Zinj. Mary and Louis Leakey discovered *Zinjanthropus boisei* (Zinj) at the site known as FLK in 1959. At that time, it was the oldest significantly intact hominin fossil from Olduvai Gorge. From the 1960–1961 excavation of level 22, that is, the FLK Zinj layer, approximately 2500 early stone tool (Oldowan) artifacts and 3500 fossil

Fig. 2. Example of faunal remains exploited by *Homo erectus* at the BK site. (*Photo courtesy of Manuel Domínguez-Rodrigo*)

bone specimens were reported, including remains of *Homo habilis* and *Zinjanthropus* (= *Paranthropus*) *boisei*. The site is recognized as one of the prime examples of a localized, dense concentration of Oldowan tools and fossilized bones. The significance of the site for understanding the origins of sophisticated hominin behavior, such as foraging strategies, is documented by abundant butchered bones and evidence of repeated transport of portions of at least 48 large mammal carcasses (mostly bovids) to this location on the paleolandscape.

The reasons why this unique archeological site occurred at this specific location in the Olduvai basin have remained a mystery. FLK Zinj was considered to have occupied an undetermined spot in a barren lacustrine (lake) floodplain based on the original interpretation of its geological context as a "near-lake" location. However, recent discoveries have shown that this spot was near a freshwater source available to hominins that was less than 200 m (656 ft) away from the high-density patch of stone tools and butchered bones observed at the site. At the Zinj site itself, abundant phytoliths from woody dicotyledons and palms were found, attesting to the presence of trees or shrubs. Hence, the paleoenvironmental context at FLK Zinj appears to offer a spring-fed watering hole and an adjacent woodland that would have provided a relatively safe location (away from carnivores) for hominins to butcher animals. The spring would have provided an attraction because of the abundance of fauna, and the woodland would have served as a temporary respite of safety for the multipurpose activities of hominins producing tools and consuming animals.

Thus, the site seems to have been a sort of primitive version of a home base that these early hominins used repeatedly over time and in which some basic features of human behavior, such as intentional food-sharing, seem to have taken place. This interpretation has been made by several researchers based on the taphonomically documented data that every depositional event involved the transport of fleshed carcasses or carcass parts belonging in several instances to animals weighing more than 100 kg (220 lb). This food surplus was much more than needed by individual hominins. Because it was introduced repeatedly into the same spot, it probably had a socio-adaptive function, such as food-sharing, which is similar to that seen in modern hunter-gatherers.

Early humans at FLK Zinj: hunters or scavengers? Traditional interpretations of hominin strategies of carcass acquisition revolve around the debate over whether early hominins hunted or scavenged. A popular version of the scavenging scenario is the carnivore-hominin-carnivore hypothesis, which argues that hominins acquired animal resources primarily through the opportunistic scavenging of animal carcasses that had been abandoned and defleshed (had their flesh removed) by predatory felids (wild cats). Its main empirical support comes from the analysis of tooth mark frequency and distribution at the FLK Zinj site. It was claimed that certain bones exhibited a high frequency of tooth marks, which was only explainable if felids had preceded hominins in carcass defleshing. Recent reevaluations of the assemblage show that previous estimates of tooth marks on the FLK Zinj assemblage were artificially high because natural biochemical marks were mistaken for tooth marks. The revised estimates are similar to those obtained in experiments in which hyenas intervene in bone modification only after thorough butchery by humans. Furthermore, the analyses of percussion marks (that is, marks or pits made by blows from a stone), notches, and breakage patterns provide data that are best interpreted as the results of hominin activity (hammerstone percussion and marrow extraction).

Cut marks occur on more than 250 fossil bones from the FLK Zinj site, and they cluster on meaty bones and on sections of these bones where no scraps of flesh would have survived the carnivores' initial consumption of their prey. They have been documented on all the anatomical sections of the animals: inside their rib cages [indicating evisceration (disemboweling)], on the ends of some limb bones (indicating dismembering), and on the shafts of limb bones (showing filleting). Cut marks at the FLK Zinj site occur in similar frequencies to those experimentally replicated when butchering fully fleshed carcasses.

These multiple lines of evidence indicate that hominins had early access to fleshed carcasses that were transported, processed, and accumulated at the FLK Zinj site. Hominins did not acquire these animals by being passive scavengers. Therefore, meat consumption was one of the key elements in the progression of human evolution.

Hominin discoveries. So far, more than 80 hominin remains have been discovered at Olduvai Gorge. The main ones are:

OH 5: Also popularized as *Zinjanthropus*, it is one of the most complete crania of *Paranthropus boisei* to date.

OH 7, OH 8, OH 13, OH 16, and OH 24: Important specimens of *Homo habilis*, the earliest maker of stone tools.

OH 9: One of the oldest remains of *Homo erectus* (*ergaster*) in East Africa.

OH 62: A partial skeleton of a purported *Homo habilis* female, which is extremely gracile (slender and small-bodied) and primitive.

OH 65: One of the best-preserved maxillary (upper jaw) bones of *Homo habilis* to date.

There also have been a number of important recent discoveries, including the following:

OH 80: A partial skeleton of *Paranthropus boisei* found at BK (upper Bed II), showing that arboreality (tree climbing) was still an important part of the locomotor repertoire of hominins at 1.3 MYA.

OH 81: A parietal (skull) fragment of a 1.5 million-year-old child found at SHK (Bed II), bearing pathology (porotic hyperostosis, or bone porosity on the surface of the skull) suggestive of nutritional deficiency (anemia), which indirectly indicates a physiology adapted to a high-quality diet in which meat was important.

Olduvai Gorge is one of the best fossiliferous locations in Africa to study the evolution of the genus *Homo*, namely from *Homo habilis* to *Homo erectus*, both anatomically and behaviorally. This is aided by the study of the evolution and progression of early stone tool (Oldowan) sites into more advanced stone tool (Acheulean) sites. Most of the behavioral models that have been proposed since the 1960s have been based on the evidence from the Olduvai sites or have been tested against the gorge's archeological record. Therefore, the gorge and its sites occupy a privileged place in the study of human evolution.

For background information *see* ANTHROPOLOGY; ARCHEOLOGICAL CHRONOLOGY; ARCHEOLOGY; EARLY MODERN HUMANS; FOSSIL; FOSSIL HUMANS; PALEOECOLOGY; PALEOGEOGRAPHY; PALEOLITHIC; PHYLOGENY; PHYSICAL ANTHROPOLOGY; PREHISTORIC TECHNOLOGY; TAPHONOMY in the McGraw-Hill Encyclopedia of Science & Technology.

Manuel Domínguez-Rodrigo

Bibliography. M. Domínguez-Rodrigo, R. Barba, and C. P. Egeland, *Deconstructing Olduvai*, Springer, New York, 2007; M. Domínguez-Rodrigo et al., Paleoecology and human behavior during Bed I at Olduvai Gorge (Tanzania), *Quaternary Res.* (special issue), 74(3):301–424, 2010, DOI:10.1016/j.yqres.2010.07.016; R. Hay, *The Geology of Olduvai Gorge*, California University Press, Los Angeles, 1976; M. D. Leakey, *Olduvai Gorge*, vol. III, Cambridge University Press, Cambridge, UK, 1971; R. Blumenschine et al. (eds.), Five Decades after *Zinjanthropus* and *Homo habilis*: Landscape Paleoanthropology of Plio-Pleistocene Olduvai Gorge, Tanzania, *J. Hum. Evol.* (special issue), 63(2):247–438, 2012, DOI:10.1016/j.jhevol.2012.05.005.

Oral immunotherapy

Oral immunotherapy (OIT), also known as oral desensitization, is a method of inducing the body's immune system to tolerate a food that causes an allergic overreaction. OIT involves the regular administration (challenge) of small amounts of an allergen (food) by mouth. It is an active treatment of antibody [immunoglobulin E (IgE)]–mediated food allergies, including cow's milk allergy (CMA), hen's egg allergy (HEA), and peanut allergy. The aim of OIT is the achievement of desensitization or tolerance. The desensitization state can be achieved by the majority of the individuals treated with specific immunotherapies. A longer duration of desensitization may result in permanent tolerance. Currently, many questions remain unanswered, involving allergen dosage and formulation, the induction of full tolerance, the transition of OIT to clinical practice, and the risk-to-benefit assessment. Still, the specific active treatment of food allergy is poised for clinically important advances, and the immunomodulatory treatment of allergic diseases has probably found a new tool in OIT.

Background. Over the past few decades, the prevalence of allergic diseases has increased substantially, especially in developed countries. Although the prevalence of asthma and eczema has stabilized, the prevalence of food allergy and anaphylaxis (a generalized or localized tissue reaction occurring within minutes of an antigen–antibody reaction) continues to rise.

A meta-analysis of more than 50 articles from different countries examined the prevalence of food allergies using various criteria. The self-reported prevalence of allergy was found to be 1.2–17% for milk, 0.2–7% for eggs, 0–2% for fish, 0–10% for shellfish, and 3–35% for other foods. Experiments involving food challenges provided lower estimates: 0–3% for milk, 0–1.7% for eggs, 0.2–1.6% for peanuts, and 1–10.8% for other foods. Some food allergies, such as those to cow's milk, hen's eggs, wheat, and soy, resolve over time in the majority of allergic children, whereas other food allergies, such as those to peanuts, tree nuts, and fish, tend to persist throughout life.

There is currently no effective treatment for food allergies. Management is only supportive, comprising avoidance of the concerned food, early recognition of the allergic reaction symptoms, and initiation of an appropriate emergency treatment. To some extent, the avoidance of food allergens is difficult to achieve, particularly with commercially prepared foods. Furthermore, 40–100% of the deaths from food anaphylaxis involve the ingestion of foods that have been catered or prepared away from the home.

Therefore, a safe and affordable therapeutic approach is necessary, and it should be offered at least to patients who are at risk of severe adverse reactions. In this sense, allergen-specific immunotherapy (SIT) or allergen desensitization by injection is capable of modifying the IgE-mediated immune response and of achieving long-term protection. For this rea-

son, the immunotherapy approach was regarded as an attractive strategy to treat food allergies since the 1980s, but the first attempts involving peanut extracts led to an unacceptable rate of severe adverse events. Thus, the oral administration of foods to achieve tolerance or desensitization was proposed, and this appears particularly suitable for allergies to cow's milk, hen's eggs, and peanuts. Several clinical studies have been done, and some trials are currently in progress to better define the indications, contraindications, and practical aspects of OIT.

Immunotherapy for CMA. There has been a good amount of research concerning OIT for CMA (**Table 1**). In an OIT protocol for the treatment of a variety of food allergies, desensitization was induced in 75% of the participants. The most common food allergy was milk, followed by eggs and fish. In another study, individuals receiving OIT experienced a significant decrease in food-specific IgE levels in comparison with age-matched food allergic controls. Using a 6-month OIT protocol, 15 of 21 children were fully desensitized and 3 children were partially desensitized.

In addition, tolerance inductions by OIT and an allergen elimination diet were analyzed in 47 children who were allergic to cow's milk or hen's eggs. The patients were randomly assigned to OIT or an elimination diet as a control group. Clinical reevaluations of the relevant food allergy were performed by food challenge after a median of 21 months. A similar percentage (35%) in both the treatment and control groups displayed tolerance by being able to eliminate therapy, although a number of "partial responders" to OIT were seen, which increased the rate in the treatment group to 64%. Therefore, the patients who reached total tolerance were able to resume the intake of "previous culprit foods" without the risk of any further appearance of the allergic symptoms. Similar results have been reported in other trials, including a number of double-blind, placebo-controlled (DBPC) trials, with the vast majority of children achieving full tolerance.

Another research group studied 60 children (5 years of age or older) with histories of severe allergic reactions to milk ingestion. Approximately 80% of the participants had high milk-specific IgE levels. Half of the patients received immunotherapy for one year, and the other half were observed with conventional elimination management. OIT was carried out for 10 days in the hospital and continued until a dose of 20 mL of pure cow's milk was reached. Of those treated with OIT, 36% were able to tolerate a single feeding of 150 mL, 54% could ingest 5–50 mL, and 10% (three children) interrupted the study because of serious adverse effects. Conversely, most children in the observation group saw no changes in their milk-reaction thresholds, and none could tolerate 5 mL. Again, similar results of high desensitization were observed in other trials.

Immunotherapy for HEA. Patients allergic to hen's eggs have been studied in a number of OIT clinical trials (**Table 2**). In one study, seven children with mild symptoms [urticaria (hives)] were treated with

TABLE 1. Clinical trials of oral desensitization for cow's milk allergy

Research author	Design	Number of patients	Age range, years	Female patients	Duration of induction	Initial dose	Tolerance	OIT discontinued because of side effects
Staden et al., 2007	Randomized, open controlled study	25	1–13	16/25 (64%)	67 days	0.02 mg of cow's milk (CM) protein	Full tolerance: 9/25 (36%); tolerant with regular intake: 3/25 (12%); partial tolerance: 4/25	9 (36%)
Skripak et al., 2008	Randomized, DBPC study	13 OIT; 7 avoidance	6–17	5 (38%) OIT; 3 (43%) avoidance	8 weeks	0.4 mg of CM protein	Full tolerance: 12/30 (37%); partial tolerance: 16/30 (53%)	1/20 (5%)
Zapatero et al., 2008	Prospective study	18	>4 (mean age, 5.05)	3 (17%)	2 days	0.05 mL of CM	Full tolerance: 15/18 (83%); partial tolerance: 1/18 (5.5%)	1/18 (11%); 1/18 (11%): failed
Longo et al., 2008	Randomized, open controlled study	30 OIT; 30 avoidance	5–17	9 (30%) OIT; 12 (40%) avoidance	10 days (hospital) + 3 months (home)	1 drop of CM in 10 mL of water	Full tolerance: 11/30 (37%); partial tolerance: 16/30 (53%)	3/30 (10%)
Pajno et al., 2010	Randomized, single-blind, soy milk–controlled trial	15 OIT; 15 avoidance	4–10	7 (46.7%) OIT; 6 (40%) avoidance	18 weeks	1 drop of CM diluted 1:25	Full tolerance: 10/15 (77%); partial tolerance: 1/15 (6.6%)	2/15 (13%); 2/15 (13%): failed
Martorell et al., 2011	Randomized, open controlled study	30 OIT; 30 avoidance	2 (24–36 months)	11 (36.7%) OIT; 15 (50%) avoidance	2 days	1 mL of CM diluted 1:100	Full tolerance: 27/30 (90%); partial tolerance: 1/30 (3%)	1/30 (3%): no tolerance; 1/30 (3%): abandoned study
Salmivesi et al., 2012	Randomized, DBPC study	16 OIT; 8 avoidance	6–14	Not detailed	24 weeks	0.06 mg of CM protein	16 OIT (89%) and 8 in the placebo group (80%) successfully completed the OIT protocol	0%

Abbreviations: DBPC, double-blind, placebo-controlled; OIT, oral immunotherapy.

Sources of research: U. Staden et al., Specific oral tolerance induction in food allergy in children: Efficacy and clinical patterns reaction, *Allergy*, 62:1261–1269, 2007, DOI:10.1111/j.1398-9995.2007.01501.x; J. M. Skripak et al., A randomized, double blind, placebo-controlled study of milk oral immunotherapy for cow's milk allergy, *J. Allergy Clin. Immunol.*, 122:1154–1160, 2008, DOI:10.1016/j.jaci.2008.09.030; L. Zapatero et al., Oral desensitization in children with cow's milk allergy, *J. Investig. Allergol. Clin. Immunol.*, 18:389–396, 2008; G. Longo et al., Specific oral tolerance induction in children with very severe cow's milk–induced reactions, *J. Allergy Clin. Immunol.*, 121:343–347, 2008, DOI:10.1016/j.jaci.2007.10.029; G. B. Pajno et al., Oral immunotherapy for cow's milk allergy with a weekly up-dosing regimen: A randomized single-blind controlled study, *Ann. Allergy Asthma Immunol.*, 105:376–381, 2010, DOI:10.1016/j.anai.2010.03.015; A. Martorell et al., Oral desensitization as a useful treatment in 2-year-old children with cow's milk allergy, *Clin. Exp. Allergy*, 41:1297–1304, 2011, DOI:10.1111/j.1365-2222.2011.03749.x; S. Salmivesi et al., Milk oral immunotherapy is effective in school-aged children, *Acta Paediatr.*, 102:172–176, 2012, DOI:10.1111/j.1651-2227.2012.02815.x.

OIT, and six of them tolerated significantly more egg proteins than at the study onset. In another study, children (5–11 years of age) suffering from HEA received OIT (40 children) or placebo (15 children) in a randomized DBPC trial. After 10 months of therapy, none of the children who received placebo and 55% of those who received OIT passed the oral food challenge and were considered to be desensitized; after 22 months, 75% of the children in the OIT group were desensitized.

In addition, in a randomized, controlled open study with 20 children allergic to hen's eggs, 8 out of 10 children (80%) in the active OIT group achieved a daily intake of 25 mL over a 6-month period. One child could tolerate up to 2 mL/day, whereas another child failed the desensitization. In contrast, only two children in the control group (20%) could tolerate eggs after 6 months. Other studies have achieved similar successful results.

Immunotherapy for peanut allergy. Because severe adverse reactions can occur following the accidental ingestion of peanuts, OIT has become a major focus of treatment (**Table 3**). In one open study, a case series of four boys (aged 9–13 years) with challenge-confirmed peanut allergies underwent peanut OIT (the gradual escalation of ingested peanut proteins). After 6 weeks, all patients tolerated at least 2.4 g (10 peanuts), with a median 50-fold increase in the dose threshold for reactivity following a repeat oral food challenge.

Further trials (including DBPC trials) have been carried out with more patients, and similar results of tolerance have been observed. For example, one OIT study enrolled 39 children (median age, 57.5 months; 64% male) who experienced adverse symptoms to peanuts. Twenty-nine subjects completed the peanut challenge over the course of 36 months. Among them, 27 children were able to tolerate 3.9 g of peanuts. In fact, peanut-specific IgE antibody concentrations decreased significantly by 12–18 months. Moreover, in another study of 23 children (aged 3–14 years) with severe challenge-confirmed IgE-mediated peanut allergies (including asthma and other allergic reactions after accidental peanut ingestion), 14 of the children (61%) reached the protective peanut dose of 500 mg after a median of 7 months.

In addition, in a further DBPC study, 40 subjects (12–37 years of age; median, 15 years) were randomized to peanut or placebo sublingual immunotherapy

TABLE 2. Clinical trials of oral desensitization for hen's egg allergy

Research author	Design	Number of patients	Age range, years	Female patients	Duration of induction	Initial dose	Tolerance	OIT discontinued because of side effects
Buchanan et al., 2007	Open study	7	1–16	Not detailed	1 day (rush phase); 2 weeks (buildup phase)	0.1 mg of powdered egg white	Full tolerance: 2/7 (28.5%); partial tolerance: 2/7 (28.5%)	3/7 (43%)
Itoh et al., 2010	Open study	6	7–12	2 (33%)	Variable (9–18 days)	One-tenth of the threshold dose for each patient	Full tolerance: 6/6 (100%)	None (0%)
Vickery et al., 2010	Open study	8	1–16	3 (37.5%)	1 day (rush phase), followed by buildup phase	0.1 mg of powdered egg white	Full tolerance: 4/8 (50%); partial tolerance: 3/8 (37.5%)	None (0%)
García Rodriguez et al., 2011	Prospective open study	23	5–17	6 (26%)	5 days	0.001 mL of egg white	Full tolerance: 20/23 (86.9%); partial tolerance: 2/23 (8.6%)	1/23 (4.3%)
Burks et al., 2012	Randomized, DBPC study	40 OIT; 15 placebo	5–11	Not detailed	22 months	Not detailed	Full tolerance: 11/40 (27.5%)	5/40 (12.5%)
Meglio et al., 2012	Randomized, controlled open study	10 OIT; 10 placebo	>4 (median age, 8.7)	5 OIT; 3 placebo	181 days	0.27 mg of hen's egg (HE) proteins (1 drop of raw HE diluted 1:100)	Full tolerance: 8/10 (80%); partial tolerance: 1/10 (10%)	1/10 (10%)
Dello Iacono et al., 2013	Randomized, controlled open study	10 OIT; 10 placebo	5–11	10 OIT (50%)	176 days	1 drop of a blended emulsion of 45 mL of raw HE and 150 mL of amino acid–based infant formula (corresponding to 0.015 mL of HE emulsion)	Partial tolerance: 9/10 OIT (90%); no tolerance: 1/10 (10%)	None (0%)

Abbreviations: DBPC, double-blind, placebo-controlled; OIT, oral immunotherapy.

Sources of research: A. D. Buchanan et al., Egg oral immunotherapy in nonanaphylactic children with egg allergy, *J. Allergy Clin. Immunol.*, 119:199–205, 2007, DOI:10.1016/j.jaci.2006.09.016; N. Itoh et al., Rush specific oral tolerance induction in school-age children with severe egg allergy: 1 year follow-up, *Allergol. Int.*, 59:43–51, 2010, DOI:10.2332/allergolint.09-OA-0107; B. P. Vickery et al., Individualized IgE-based dosing of egg oral immunotherapy and the development of tolerance, *Ann. Allergy Asthma Immunol.*, 105:444–450, 2010, DOI:10.1016/j.anai.2010.09.030; R. García Rodriguez et al., Oral rush desensitization to egg: Efficacy and safety, *Clin. Exp. Allergy*, 41:1289–1296, 2011, DOI:10.1111/j.1365-2222.2011.03722.x; W. A. Burks et al., Oral immunotherapy for treatment of egg allergy in children, *N. Engl. J. Med.*, 367:233–243, 2012, DOI:10.1056/NEJMoa1200435; P. Meglio et al., Oral food desensitization in children with IgE-mediated hen's egg allergy: A new protocol with raw hen's egg, *Pediatr. Allergy Immunol.*, 24:75–83, 2013, DOI:10.1111/j.1399-3038.2012.01341.x; I. Dello Iacono et al., Specific oral tolerance induction with raw hen's egg in children with very severe egg allergy: A randomized controlled trial, *Pediatr. Allergy Immunol.*, 24:66–74, 2013, DOI:10.1111/j.1399-3038.2012.01349.x.

(SLIT). The results of the trial showed a modest level of desensitization in a majority of test subjects compared with placebo controls.

Safety of OIT. In all immunotherapy trials, safety is of paramount importance. The appearance of adverse reactions during OIT is reported frequently. In some studies, 100% of CMA patients have experienced adverse reactions during the desensitization period; however, OIT had to be discontinued in less than 20% of the subjects.

For HEA patients, the rate of appearance of unwanted effects is quite high (reaching 78%); however, only 9% of the children have withdrawn from these studies. A large peanut OIT study revealed that the frequency and severity of adverse reactions were greatest on the initial rush induction days and least during the home-dosing phases. Approximately 93% of the subjects experienced some symptoms [mostly upper respiratory tract (79%) and abdominal (68%) symptoms] during the initial rush induction, and four patients (12%) withdrew because of persistent adverse reactions. During the subsequent buildup phase, adverse reactions occurred after 46% of the buildup doses, with 29% of the patients experiencing upper respiratory tract symptoms and 24% experiencing skin symptoms. Severe systemic side effects have been reported independently of the schedule, and mild reactions such as abdominal pain, itchy throat, gritty eyes, watery eyes, transient erythema, and sneezing usually do not require the cessation of the desensitization process.

However, when rhinitis, dyspnea (shortness of breath), asthma, generalized urticaria, and hypotension occur as a single symptom or in combination, OIT should be postponed or stopped. Adverse reaction events are largely unpredictable, and they can occur during home dosing. In addition, systemic reactions have occurred with previously tolerated doses during exercise, viral illness, or bouts of suboptimal controlled asthma. Of note, these reactions are usually well controlled by antihistamines, steroids, or epinephrine.

TABLE 3. Clinical trials of oral desensitization for peanut allergy

Research author	Design	Number of patients	Age range, years	Female patients	Duration of induction	Initial dose	Tolerance	OIT discontinued because of side effects
Clark et al., 2009	Open study	4	9–13	0	6 weeks	5 mg	4/4 (100%) tolerated 2.38 g protein (equivalent to 10 peanuts)	none
Jones et al., 2009	Open study	39	1–16	25 (64%)	1 day	0.1 mg peanut protein	Full tolerance: 27/29 (93%); partial tolerance: 3/29 (7%)	4/39 (10%); 6/39 (15%)
Blumchen et al., 2010	Randomized, open controlled study	23	3–14	Not detailed	7 days	0.03 g	Full tolerance: 14/23 (61%); partial tolerance: 1/23 (4%)	1/23 (4%)
Varshney et al., 2011	Randomized, DBPC study	19 OIT; 9 placebo	1–16	10/19 OIT (53%); 0/9 placebo (0%)	1 day	0.1 mg peanut protein	Full tolerance: 16/19 (84%)	3/19 (16%)
Fleischer et al., 2013	Randomized, DBPC, multicenter trial; SLIT	40	12–37 (median, 15)	13 (32%)	44 weeks	0.000165 mg	14/20 (70%) tolerated doses of varying amounts	4/40 (10%)

Abbreviations: DBPC, double-blind, placebo-controlled; OIT, oral immunotherapy.
Sources of research: A. T. Clark et al., Successful oral tolerance induction in severe peanut allergy, *Allergy*, 64:1218–1220, 2009, DOI:10.1111/j.1398-9995.2009.01982.x; S. M. Jones et al., Clinical efficacy and immune regulation with peanut oral immunotherapy, *J. Allergy Clin. Immunol.*, 124:292–300, 2009, DOI:10.1016/j.jaci.2009.05.022; K. Blumchen et al., Oral peanut immunotherapy in children with peanut anaphylaxis, *J. Allergy Clin. Immunol.*, 126:83–91, 2010, DOI:10.1016/j.jaci.2010.04.030; P. Varshney et al., A randomized controlled study of peanut oral immunotherapy: Clinical desensitization and modulation of the allergic response, *J. Allergy Clin. Immunol.*, 127:654–660, 2011, DOI:10.1016/j.jaci.2010.12.1111; D. M. Fleischer et al., Sublingual immunotherapy for peanut allergy: A randomized, double-blind, placebo-controlled multicenter trial, *J. Allergy Clin. Immunol.*, 131:119–127, 2013, DOI:10.1016/j.jaci.2012.11.011.

Future developments. Before further advances in understanding the efficacy and mechanism of action of OIT can be made, there are still some needs that must be met.

Allergen dosage and formulation. There is a noticeable difference among the published controlled trials with regard to the amount of allergen administered. It is also likely that OIT performed with native foods is more effective than other routes such as SLIT; however, it may be accompanied by more side effects. Moreover, the quality of the allergen vaccines is critical for treatment. In general, standardized vaccines of known potency and shelf life should be used. Currently, the vaccines containing food proteins and prepared by companies or hospital dispensaries are not available as standardized products. Both the bacteriological load and biological activity of these products are undetermined. Hence, the use of fresh material for OIT is advisable for achieving the goal of both desensitization and tolerance.

Tolerance. The goal of OIT is permanent oral tolerance, which is established when the food can be ingested without the appearance of allergic symptoms despite periods of withdrawal. In contrast, desensitization is marked by the requirement that the patients regularly ingest the food allergen (or allergens). Therefore, when ingestion is interrupted or discontinued, the protective effect of OIT may be lost or significantly decreased.

Currently, it is unclear whether oral desensitization is the first step toward permanent oral tolerance. As with other kinds of immunotherapy (for example, immunotherapy involving inhalant allergens), the duration of desensitization could be pivotal for achieving tolerance. Although clinical desensitization and immune modulation have been demonstrated with OIT, the strength of the current evidence from clinical trials is insufficient concerning the induction of tolerance.

OIT in clinical practice. OIT is time consuming and subject to side effects. In contrast, many children with CMA or HEA develop tolerance spontaneously, and they can be managed properly with a simple avoidance regimen. Therefore, more clear indications concerning eligible patients and the predictive factors for OIT are urgently needed.

Conversely, individuals with permanent IgE-mediated food allergies deserve better treatment methods than a strict allergen avoidance. Recent review articles, meta-analyses, and reports have been published. So far, the clinical trials have resulted in quite positive effects. Thus, the time is ripe for the clinical practice of OIT in selected medical centers and under strict medical supervision.

For background information *see* ALLERGY; ANAPHYLAXIS; ANTIBODY; ANTIGEN; ANTIGEN-ANTIBODY REACTION; ASTHMA; CELLULAR IMMUNOLOGY; CLINICAL IMMUNOLOGY; EGG (FOWL); FOOD ALLERGY; IMMUNOGLOBULIN; IMMUNOLOGY; MILK; PEANUT in the McGraw-Hill Encyclopedia of Science & Technology.

Giovanni B. Pajno; Lucia Caminiti; Stefania Arasi

Bibliography. K. Anagnostou et al., Efficacy and safety of high-dose peanut oral immunotherapy with factors predicting outcome, *Clin. Exp. Allergy*, 41:1273–1281, 2011, DOI:10.1111/j.1365-2222.2011.03699.x; J. L. Brozek et al., Oral immunotherapy for Ig-E mediated cow's milk allergy: A systematic review and meta-analysis, *Clin. Exp. Allergy*, 42:363–374, 2012, DOI:10.1111/j.1365-2222.2011.03948.x; H. R. Fisher, G. Du Toit, and

G. Lack, Specific oral tolerance induction in food allergic children: Is oral desensitization more effective than allergen avoidance?: A meta-analysis of published RCTs, *Arch. Dis. Child.*, 96:259–264, 2011, DOI:10.1136/adc.2009.172460; R. S. Gupta et al., The prevalence, severity and distribution of childhood food allergy in the United States, *Pediatrics*, 128:9–17, 2011, DOI:10.1542/peds.2011-0204; I. H. Ismail and M. L. Tang, Oral immunotherapy for the treatment of food allergy, *Isr. Med. Assoc. J.*, 14:63–69, 2012; C. A. Keet et al., The safety and efficacy of sublingual and oral immunotherapy for milk allergy, *J. Allergy Clin. Immunol.*, 129:448–455, 2012, DOI:10.1016/j.jaci.2011.10.023; A. Nowak-Wgrzyn and H. A. Sampson, Future therapies for food allergies, *J. Allergy Clin. Immunol.*, 127:558–573, 2011, DOI:10.1016/j.jaci.2010.12.1098; U. Nurmatov et al., Allergen-specific oral immunotherapy for peanut allergy, *Cochrane Database Syst. Rev.*, 9:CD009014, 2012, DOI:10.1002/14651858.CD009014.pub2; G. B. Pajno, Oral desensitization for milk allergy in children: State of the art, *Curr. Opin. Allergy Clin. Immunol.*, 11:560–564, 2011, DOI:10.1097/ACI.0b013e32834cd298; G. Passalacqua, M. Landi, and G. B. Pajno, Oral immunotherapy for cow's milk allergy, *Curr. Opin. Allergy Clin. Immunol.*, 12:271–277, 2012, DOI:10.1097/ACI.0b013e3283535b93; R. J. Rona et al., The prevalence of food allergy: A meta-analysis, *J. Allergy Clin. Immunol.*, 120:638–646, 2007, DOI:10.1016/j.jaci.2007.05.026; S. H. Sicherer, Epidemiology of food allergy, *J. Allergy Clin. Immunol.*, 127:594–602, 2011, DOI:10.1016/j.jaci.2010.11.044; R. A. Wood et al., The natural history of milk allergy in an observational cohort, *J. Allergy Clin. Immunol.*, 131:805–812, 2013, DOI:10.1016/j.jaci.2012.10.060; J. P. Yeung et al., Oral immunotherapy for milk allergy, *Cochrane Database Syst. Rev.*, 11:CD009542, 2012, DOI:10.1002/14651858.CD009542.pub2.

Origin of grasslands

Grasslands are the foundation of agriculture, providing the grains and proteins for a hungry world. Forty million years ago (MYA), there were no well-drained grasslands. However, today grasslands occupy approximately 40% of the land area of our planet. Grasslands have been considered to be adapted to areas of diminished precipitation on the downwind side of topographic obstacles that are created by mountain uplift and the tectonic reorganization of ocean currents. Now, there is an alternative hypothesis: Grasslands were a biological force for global change through the coevolution of grasses and animals that eat mainly grasses (grazers), creating cooler and drier conditions because of the light color of the grasses, limited evaporation of water from plants into the atmosphere, and deep organic soils. Organisms in coevolutionary trajectories adapt to each other rather than to their environments, so they can be forces for global change. For example, humans are a force for global warming and, by ploughing and harvesting, they have undone the cooling effects of grasslands. However, carbon farming techniques can offset human-induced global warming.

Soils. Soils play a critical role in the carbon cycle by fueling photosynthesis and by storing organic carbon. Plant-reduced organic compounds and the export of bicarbonate and nutrient cations in solution are forces for global cooling because soils, lakes, and oceans keep carbon away from the atmospheric greenhouse gases, including carbon dioxide and methane. The evolution and global expansion of grasslands and their newly evolved, carbon-rich soils (Mollisols) may have induced global cooling and ushered in the Pleistocene glaciation. In these soils, highly unstable clays are stabilized within clods that are the size of corn kernels by coatings of organic matter from the guts of earthworms and the exudates of fibrous roots. Grassland soils have unusually high organic carbon contents and fertilities for well-drained soils.

Coevolution. Coevolution is the coordinated evolution of two different kinds of organisms that are mutually interdependent, such as grasses and grazers. For example, the high-crowned and continuously growing teeth of hoofed animals have adapted to the abrasive grasses of the open dusty plains, whereas slender limbs with hard hooves have evolved as a means of running escape from predators on grassy plains. In turn, grasses evolved underground horizontal stems (rhizomes), underground sod, telescoped internodes, intercalary meristems, and abundant opal phytoliths (microscopic opaline silica bodies of plants) to withstand more effectively the onslaught of hard hooves and molars.

The fossil record of grasses extends back 80 million years. However, during the Cretaceous time of dinosaurs and into the early Tertiary time of primitive mammals, grasses were restricted to marshes and streamsides. The evidence from fossilized soils and phytoliths indicates that dryland grasses were common approximately 40 MYA, but modern sod-forming grasses evolved about 19 MYA. This matches the schedule of tooth complexity of fossil mammals, suggesting that animals were eating a mixture of grass and other leaves by the Eocene epoch and grazing by the Miocene epoch. It also matches the mammalian reorganization in outer limb length and the reduction of digits in going from paws to hooves by 19 MYA. In addition, this is the same geological age of the earliest fossilized herds of mammalian skeletons and the frontal brain lobe (prorean gyrus) associated with pack-hunting behavior in fossil dog brains. Lastly, the earliest fossil dung cakes, rather than dung pellets common in older rocks, are found to date back to 19 MYA. The features were all important selection pressures in the evolution of sod grasslands and their distinctively organic soils.

Paleosol and paleoclimate data. Small ellipsoidal clods of soil (crumb peds) and fine root traces have allowed the identification of Mollisols and sod grasslands from fossil soils (paleosols) [**Fig. 1**], but other

Fig. 1. Grassland Mollisols (*a*, *b*) and dry woodland Aridisols (*c*, *d*) of the semiarid woodlands that they replaced:
(*a*) Onuria paleosol, middle Miocene (14 MYA), Fort Ternan mammal quarry, Kenya; (*b*) modern Mollisol and wooded
grassland near Lake Nakuru, Kenya; (*c*) Tut paleosol, early Miocene (20 MYA), near Songhor, Kenya; (*d*) modern
Aridisol and dry woodland (mallee) near Damara Station and Mungo Lake, New South Wales, Australia. The lengths of
the hammer handles in panels *a* and *c* are 25 cm (10 in.). Soil horizon labels describe surface horizons (A) and
subsurface horizons enriched in carbonate (Bk) and clay (Bt).

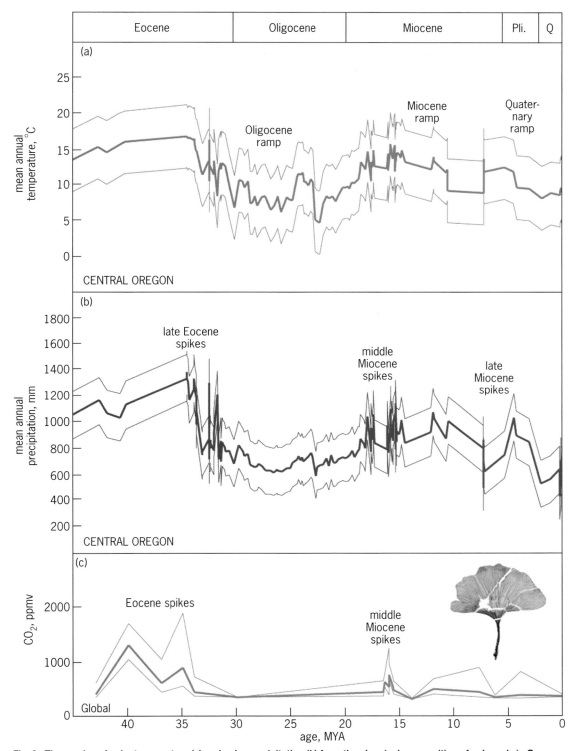

Fig. 2. Time series of paleotemperature (*a*) and paleoprecipitation (*b*) from the chemical composition of paleosols in Oregon, and atmospheric carbon dioxide (CO_2) levels (*c*) from the fossil *Ginkgo* stomatal index, which suggest a CO_2-greenhouse control of paleoclimate over the past 45 million years. Pli. = Pliocene; Q = Quaternary.

features of these ancient soils are evidence of the paleoclimates during grassland origins: For example, the drier the climate, the shallower the depth of soil carbonates. Thus, the depths for modern soils of known precipitation levels can be used to calculate the precipitation for paleosols (in this calculation, burial compaction needs to be taken into account and compensated). From these kinds of paleosol data, bunch grasslands appeared during warm–wet climate spikes about 35 MYA, and sod grasslands appeared about 19 MYA. By 8 MYA, tall grassland ecosystems with deep calcareous soils expanded into the humid regions of North America, Africa, and Asia. This tall grassland expansion coincided with a shift in the carbon isotopic composition of soil nodules and mammal teeth and bones, indicating the evolution of the carbon-conservative C_4 photosynthetic pathway in many grasses. Therefore, grasslands were a biological force that displaced earlier kinds of arid shrublands and woodlands, and then they expanded their geographic and climatic range during warm–wet greenhouse periods. Grasslands did not merely fill in arid regions.

Climate change can be inferred from a variety of sources. For example, paleoclimatic proxies of fossil soils have been used to determine climate change: Spikes of high temperature (**Fig. 2***a*) and precipitation (Fig. 2*b*) dating to 35 MYA are followed by a cooling and drying period (ramp) about 34–19 MYA, and there are additional transient spikes dating to 19–16 MYA and 8–7 MYA. Another paleoclimatic proxy for atmospheric carbon dioxide is the stomatal index of *Ginkgo* fossils (Fig. 2*c*).

Explanations for cooling. Mountain uplift, particularly of the Himalayas, has been invoked as a cause of paleoclimatic cooling over the past 30 million years. This idea was based on the ratios of strontium isotopes in marine carbonates, which were mistakenly considered evidence of enhanced silicate weathering. In the Himalayas, strontium isotope variations reflect carbonate weathering, which has little impact on atmospheric carbon dioxide. Paleosol proxies for carbon-dioxide-linked silicate weathering show that chemical weathering declined with mountain uplift.

Paleoclimatic cooling over the past 30 million years has also been explained by the completion of the Antarctic Circumpolar Current, which occurred as Australia and South America drifted away from Antarctica with seafloor spreading. This had the effect of thermally isolating Antarctica from warm currents. The cold, nutrient-rich Antarctic waters thus became biologically productive, burying carbon in marine clays. The growth of ice in Antarctica also raised the planetary albedo (the reflecting properties of a surface) and locked away much atmospheric water vapor. Computer modeling indicates that the increase of albedo in Antarctica could not explain the observed global cooling unless the levels of carbon dioxide in the atmosphere also declined.

A final explanation for the long ramps of paleoclimatic cooling over the past 30 million years is grassland coevolution. Grass–grazer coevolution created the sods and soils of grasslands, cooling the atmosphere by means of increased soil carbon storage and solar reflection, along with reduced evapotranspiration. Grassland soils have as much as 10 wt% organic carbon to depths of more than 1 m (3.28 ft), whereas comparable amounts of soil carbon under nearby dry woodlands seldom are deeper than 10 cm (4 in.). Fire is less harmful to grasses with their underground rhizomes, than for woody plants, and this allows grasslands to spread at the expense of woodlands, while leaving a residue of grass char (charcoal). Grasslands are also light colored (albedo: 17–19%), especially when covered by snow (albedo: >50%), whereas woodlands are dark (albedo: 9–14%) and seldom completely covered with snow. Grassland expansion also has increased the planetary losses of solar energy by reflection. Sod grasslands have moist soil but dry air. In contrast, woodlands and forests transpire as much water as they can before reaching their permanent wilting point. Theoretically, water would be a greater problem for global warming than carbon dioxide, except that water is easily rained out, which is not an option for carbon dioxide. The retention of grassland soil water vapor thus desiccated the atmosphere over geological time.

Implications for the future. If the spread of organic-rich grasslands and their fertile soils was an engine for global cooling over the past 30 million years, could this engine be used to combat the present-day global warming? Techniques for carbon sequestration of grassland soils include planned grazing, that is, increasing the stocking density to match the effects of herds maintained by pack-hunting predators in African grasslands. Small pens defined by electric or other fences limit cattle to as much feed as needed for a single day or week; this is followed by rotation to the next pen as the previous pen recovers. Weeds and grasses are eaten and covered in manure. Only the most vigorous and palatable grasses regrow, obviating the need for chemical weed control. Other carbon-building techniques involve the successive use of pasture by several different animals to mimic the grazing succession of African savannas. Another technique is pasture cropping, in which seed is drilled through the grass-covered soil that has been reduced to stubble and fertilized by grazing. Building soil carbon also builds soil fertility, structure, and moisture, offsetting atmospheric carbon dioxide.

For background information *see* CARBON; FOSSIL; GRASSLAND ECOSYSTEM; PALEOBOTANY; PALEOCLIMATOLOGY; PALEOSOL; PLANT EVOLUTION; PLANT GEOGRAPHY; SOIL; SOIL CHEMISTRY; SOIL ECOLOGY in the McGraw-Hill Encyclopedia of Science & Technology.   Gregory J. Retallack

Bibliography. E. K. Berner and R. A. Berner, *Global Environment: Water, Air, and Geochemical Cycles*, Prentice-Hall, Upper Saddle River, NJ, 1996; M. Kiely, *Carbon Farming Handbook*, Carbon Farmers of Australia, Goolma, New South Wales, Australia, 2010; G. J. Retallack, Global cooling by grasslands in the geological past and near future, *Annu. Rev. Earth Planet. Sci.*, 42:1–18, 2013; G. J. Retallack, Mallee model for Mesozoic and early Cenozoic mammalian communities, *Palaeogeogr. Palaeoclimatol. Palaeoecol.*, 342/343:111–129, 2012, DOI:10.1016/ j.palaeo.2012.05.009; G. J. Retallack, *Soils of the Past*, Blackwell, Oxford, UK, 2001; C. A. E. Strömberg, Evolution of grasses and grassland ecosystems, *Annu. Rev. Earth Planet. Sci.*, 39:517– 544, 2011, DOI:10.1146/annurev-earth-040809- 152402.

Origins of symbolic behavior

A central focus of the discussions surrounding the behavioral origins of *Homo sapiens* in Africa and Eurasia has been when and where our ancestors first behaved in ways similar to ourselves. A term commonly used in the literature to describe this process is modern human behavior. It can be defined as behavior that is mediated by socially constructed patterns of symbolic thinking, actions, and communication that allow for material and information exchange and cultural continuity between and across generations and contemporaneous communities. The capacity for symbolic thought is not the key defining factor for modern human behavior; rather, it is the use of symbolism to organize behavior. In other words, early humans were first behaviorally modern when symbols became an intrinsic part of their daily lives.

What is symbolic material culture? A symbol can be explained as a sign that has no natural or resembling connection with its referent; it only has a conventional one. Symbols cannot exist in isolation, but generally form a part of systems in which they are interlinked. Examples of symbol use by early *H. sapiens* include the use of syntactic (complex) language and the production of material culture that carried symbolic meaning. The latter is frequently referred to as symbolic material culture, and examples include the first jewelry and abstract engravings. A symbolically mediated culture is one in which individuals understand that artifacts are imbued with meaning and that these meanings are construed and depend on collectively shared beliefs. This criterion is crucial. It explains how human norms and conventions differ from the ritualized behaviors found in nonhuman primates. In simple terms, this means that people were able to use the artifacts that they made to organize (mediate) their social world in much the same way as we do today. Within each group of people, artifacts may have possessed meanings that were understood only within that group; for example, the design of a bead necklace may have carried a specific meaning that was not understood by people who were not a part of that group. This is not dissimilar to how material culture now identifies people who belong to a specific group; for example, wearing a cross identifies a person as a Christian.

Models for the origins of symbolic behavior. There are complex theoretical arguments relating to the origins and applications of symbols by early humans, in particular relating to changes in brain organization and cognitive functions that may best explain this phenomenon. It is argued that early behavioral innovations—for example, the use of symbols and syntactical (complex) language—must be related to a previous expansion of the higher association areas of the temporal and parietal cortices underlying a higher theory of mind, perspective taking, and attentional flexibility. In this essay, the focus is on presenting the archeological evidence associated with *H. sapiens* in Africa and Eurasia. It is in the former continent that the origins of symbolic behavior lie.

Three current archeological models that have been applied to the origins of symbolically mediated behavior and cognitive modernity are (1) a late and rapid appearance at approximately 50–40 KYA (thousand years ago) associated with the European Upper Paleolithic and the Later Stone Age of sub-Saharan Africa, (2) an earlier and more gradual evolution rooted in the African Middle Stone Age (approximately 300–40 KYA), and (3) a discontinuous evolution rooted in both the African Middle Stone Age and the Mousterian (Middle Paleolithic) of Eurasia.

Until relatively recently, model 1 held sway as archeologists, linguists, and anthropologists supposed that the first manufacture of symbolic material culture, and its assumed involvement in the past organization of social behavior, was likely to have been a recent event, not older than 40 KYA, and that it occurred in Europe. The association was made with *H. sapiens* and not Neandertals, even though they coexisted in Europe prior to 30 KYA. There was good reason to believe this model. The cave paintings from Western Europe (for example, the Lascaux caves in France) were thought to date to at least 30 KYA, as were small, carved statuettes from Germany and France. The Neandertal Mousterian culture did not, apparently, contain symbols such as these. The Upper Paleolithic was also unparalleled elsewhere in the world, and the evidence for symbolic material culture in Africa and Eurasia was sparse and not highly regarded. Material culture that could equate with that from the European Upper Paleolithic was recorded in Africa, but only after about 40 KYA and in the period known as the Later Stone Age. There are some isolated examples in Asia.

In the twenty-first century, a number of discoveries at African archeological sites provided evidence for changes in technology, social organization, and economy during the Middle Stone Age, specifically a period before 50 KYA. These discoveries support model 2. The basis of model 2, that is, a gradual emergence in Africa model, is that the appearance of modern cognitive behaviors in Eurasia, associated with *H. sapiens*, is the end result of an out-of-Africa dispersal of an already symbolic species at about 60 KYA or earlier.

Model 3 evolved because it seemed that, prior to 50 KYA in Africa, the use of symbolically mediated culture was discontinuous. This conclusion may have resulted from the fact that only a small number of archeological sites from this period have been excavated. In Europe, new archeological evidence suggested that Neandertals, independent of *H. sapiens*, may have produced symbolic material culture prior to 40 KYA.

Archeological evidence for symbolic behavior. The earliest archeological evidence for symbolic behavior comes from the Middle Stone Age (approximately 250–50 KYA) in Africa. During this period, and especially after approximately 100 KYA, groups of early

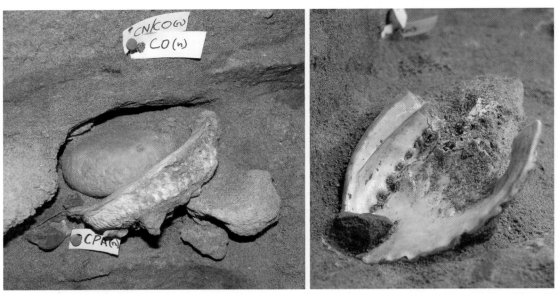

Fig. 1. Ochre-processing toolkits, dated to 100 KYA, from Blombos Cave, South Africa. (*Photos courtesy of C. Henshilwood and G. Moéll Pedersen*)

H. sapiens began to invest significant time and energy in the nonidiosyncratic alteration of the appearance of their material culture. Probably for the first time in prehistory, our ancestors began to live in societies in which people cared about how others saw the world and about transforming their environment in a way that met the expectations of others. In other words, they lived in a world of shared meanings.

Several behavioral innovations appear significantly earlier than 100 KYA in Africa. At Twin Rivers in Zambia and at Kapthurin in Kenya, there is convincing proof of the symbolic use of pigments at about 200 KYA associated with early *H. sapiens*. The use of ochre is also attested at Pinnacle Point Cave in South Africa by approximately 164 KYA. If pigment use is an archeological indication of symbolic behavior, as has been suggested by many investigators, then the origin of these abilities has to be considered more ancient than commonly accepted.

Symbolically related innovations appear in Africa at 100–60 KYA. These include the following:

1. The first known production of a multicomponent pigmented compound (paint) at 100 KYA and the earliest use of a container (in this case, an abalone shell) also at 100 KYA. The contents of the shells from Blombos Cave in South Africa indicate a planned sequence of actions in order to produce and store the ochre-rich compound. The ability to source, combine, and store substances that enhance technology or social practices represents a benchmark in the evolution of complex human cognition (**Fig. 1**).

2. Ochre pieces and bone fragments engraved with abstract patterns dated to approximately 75 KYA (**Fig. 2**). The engraved ochres, associated with the remains of *H. sapiens*, constitute some of the most ancient persuasive evidence for symbolic behavior.

3. Convincing evidence for the use of personal ornaments, consisting of perforated marine shells, is found at sites in South Africa, North Africa, and the Near East dated to 100–70 KYA (**Fig. 3**).

4. The deliberate heating of stone raw materials to enhance knapping (aesthetic shaping) at 75 KYA, and the first known application at 75 KYA of pressure flaking on the pretreated stone materials.

5. The recovery of hundreds of pieces of ostrich eggshell deliberately incised with distinct parallel or cross-hatched geometric motifs dated at approximately 60 KYA.

Discussion. Despite significant advances in recent years, it must also be emphasized that well-dated archeological sites between approximately 300 and 100 KYA are rare, so the evolution of *H. sapiens* and the earliest emergence of symbolic behavior during this key period are still poorly understood. There might have been a sudden surge in human innovation at approximately 100 KYA, but the possibility of a much longer and gradual evolution of modern symbolic behavior following a mosaic pattern is clearly probable.

Another possibility is that, despite the appearance of anatomically modern humans at approximately 200 KYA, neural reorganization within the human brain was not a punctuated event, but happened gradually between 200 and 100 KYA. Depending on selective criteria that may have favored or disfavored novelty and change, periods of rapid innovation or stasis might have followed. Until a clearer picture of human evolution between 300 and 100 KYA has emerged, it is hard to produce a detailed argument about the earliest links between neural and behavioral evolution in early *H. sapiens*; however, it seems

Fig. 2. Ochre pieces engraved with abstract designs from the 75-KYA levels at Blombos Cave, South Africa. (*Photos courtesy of C. Henshilwood and F. d'Errico*)

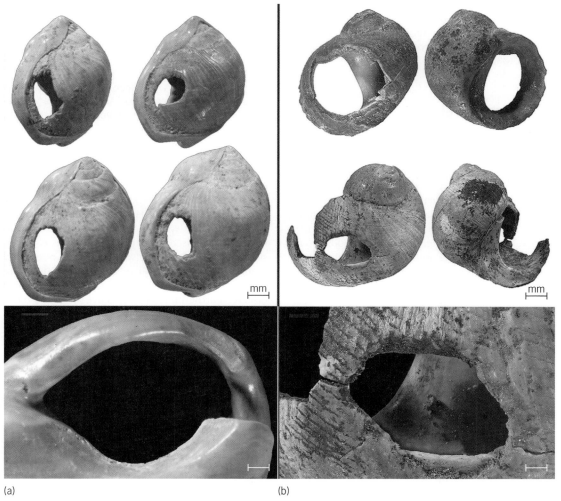

(a)   (b)

Fig. 3. Perforated marine shells. (*a*) *Nassarius kraussianus* shell beads from the 72-KYA levels at Blombos Cave, South Africa; (*b*) *Afrolittorina africana* shell beads from the approximately 72-KYA levels at Sibudu Cave, KwaZulu Natal, South Africa. (*Images courtesy of F. d'Errico and C. Henshilwood*)

plausible that the building blocks for social systems mediated by symbolic behavior were laid during this time.

For background information *see* ANTHROPOLOGY; ARCHEOLOGICAL CHEMISTRY; ARCHEOLOGICAL CHRONOLOGY; ARCHEOLOGY; COGNITION; EARLY MODERN HUMANS; FOSSIL HUMANS; NEANDERTALS; PALEOLITHIC; PHYSICAL ANTHROPOLOGY; PREHISTORIC TECHNOLOGY in the McGraw-Hill Encyclopedia of Science & Technology.

Christopher Henshilwood

Bibliography. I. Davidson, The archeology of cognitive evolution, *WIREs Cognit. Sci.*, 1(2):214–229, 2010; F. d'Errico et al., The search for the origin of symbolism, music and language: A multidisciplinary endeavour, *J. World Prehist.*, 17(1):1–70, 2003, DOI:10.1023/A:10239980201043; C. S. Henshilwood and F. d'Errico, *Homo Symbolicus: The Dawn of Language, Imagination and Spirituality*, John Benjamins, Amsterdam, 2011; C. Henshilwood and B. Dubreuil, The Still Bay and Howiesons Poort, 77–59 ka: Symbolic material culture and the evolution of the mind during the African Middle Stone Age, *Curr. Anthropol.*, 52:361–400, 2011, DOI:10.1086/660022; C. S. Henshilwood and C. W. Marean, The origin of modern human behaviour: Critique of the models and their test implications, *Curr. Anthropol.*, 44(5):627–651, 2003, DOI:10.1086/377665.

Fig. 1. Internal, vascular discoloration caused by Panama disease (TR4) on a Cavendish banana cultivar on Hainan Island, China. (*Photo courtesy of Randy C. Ploetz*)

Panama disease of bananas

Panama disease, also known as fusarium wilt of bananas (*Musa* species), is one of the most destructive fungal diseases of plants. It is caused by a soilborne fungus, *Fusarium oxysporum* f. sp. *cubense* (Foc), and has affected bananas across the globe.

Bananas and plantains. Bananas and plantains (which are a type of banana) are produced in more than 120 countries. They rank among the world's most valuable primary agricultural commodities. In total, bananas are the fourth most valuable food after rice, wheat, and milk. In 2009, the combined global production of bananas and plantains was about 132 million metric tons (145.5 million tons) and valued at US $35 billion. Approximately 85% of the total output is consumed on farms or sold in local or regional markets. They are often staple foods and an important dietary source of carbohydrates; for example, the per capita consumption of these fruits in Uganda exceeds 293 kg (645 lb) per year. Locally consumed fruits are produced by hundreds of distinct cultivated varieties (cultivars) of the *Musa* species. In contrast, the cultivars used in export commerce are virtually all from the Cavendish subgroup.

Panama disease. Fusarium wilt is a most notable disease of bananas. It is known commonly as Panama disease because it was in that country that some of the first damage was noted in 1890. Foc infects the roots and xylem (the water-conducting portion of the vascular system) of susceptible cultivars. As the infected xylem is damaged, it develops a brownish red discoloration (**Fig. 1**); the oldest leaves and then progressively the younger leaves wilt, yellow, and die (**Fig. 2**); and the entire plant ultimately collapses (**Fig. 3**).

Over the course of the first half of the twentieth century, Panama disease was responsible for massive losses for the export plantations in tropical America and Western Africa. Several factors were instrumental in these epidemics. 'Gros Michel,' the banana that was used for export at the time, is highly susceptible to Panama disease, and the plantation monoculture (cultivation of a single crop) of this cultivar facilitated the epidemic development of the disease. Furthermore, the practice of using traditional seed pieces (that is, "suckers") to establish plantings, which were often infected with Foc, hastened its spread. Once the soils were contaminated with Foc, they could not be successfully replanted with 'Gros Michel'. By the mid-1900s, uncontaminated soils were so uncommon that 'Gros Michel' was abandoned. The export trade then converted to cultivating members of the Cavendish subgroup.

The Cavendish cultivars are the world's most productive, naturally occurring bananas. They are the most prevalent bananas worldwide, with combined local and export totals of 26 and 13%, respectively, of all production. Although their fruits are more fragile than those of Gros Michel, the Cavendish cultivars are essentially immune to race 1 of Foc, which devastated Gros Michel. By the 1960s, the export

Fig. 2. External symptoms of Panama disease caused by TR4 on a Cavendish banana cultivar on Hainan Island, China. (*Photo courtesy of Randy C. Ploetz*)

production of bananas was based almost entirely on the Cavendish cultivars.

Tropical race 4. For decades, Cavendish plantations thrived in soils that were heavily infested with the race 1 pathogen. For the most part, Panama disease was a minor concern in global production. This changed abruptly at the end of the twentieth century. In the 1990s, there was an increased demand for bananas in the global market. To accommodate this, Cavendish monocultures were planted in Indonesia and Malaysia. Surprisingly, these plantations soon succumbed to another pathotype of Foc, specifically tropical race 4 (TR4) [Figs. 1 and 2]. Ironically, both Cavendish and TR4 originated in Southeast Asia; however, because monocultures of Cavendish had not been grown in that location, TR4 was not known. Typically, production in the region relies on small-scale heterogeneous plantings of several types of bananas and other crops; and large, uniform plantings of bananas are not used. Once monocultures were attempted, though, the widespread presence of TR4 was revealed, and vast and unexpected damage developed.

TR4 is now recognized in Australia, China, Indonesia (including Java, Sulawesi, and Sumatra), Malaysia, and the Philippines. It is the most serious threat that global banana production has faced. TR4 affects a far greater range of banana cultivars than race 1, and diverse plantains, cooking bananas, and dessert bananas are susceptible (in aggregate, the susceptible cultivars are responsible for more than 80% of the current output). The great fear is that the export and subsistence production in Africa,

the Americas, and the Indian subcontinent would be devastated if TR4 spreads to those areas.

Disease management. Panama disease management is constrained by a limited number of options. Unfortunately, no efficacious biological, chemical, cultural, or physical treatments exist to protect susceptible cultivars. Biocontrol measures have been effective for short periods in mainly greenhouse experiments. Limited or questionable efficacy has been associated with fungicide injections and soil fumigation treatments. Likewise, soil amendments (materials added to a soil), heat treatment, flooding, and other means have led to limited success at best. The only approaches that are truly effective are exclusion of the pathogen from areas in which susceptible cultivars are produced, and the use of resistant cultivars in contaminated soils.

Mitigating the TR4 threat depends in large part on effective quarantine measures in the producing nations. Keeping the pathogen out of uncontaminated areas would be far more effective than attempting to eliminate or restrict the movement of the pathogen once it had moved to a new area. The latter goals are especially difficult with a soilborne pathogen that induces symptoms at 2–9 months after infection. Moreover, the early detection of TR4 infection is extremely difficult because of the cryptic (unrecognized) infection by Foc, the slow development of Panama disease epidemics, and the fact that all pathotypes of Foc cause the same external and internal symptoms. Although a specific molecular protocol has been developed to identify TR4, it could

Fig. 3. External symptoms of Panama disease caused by race 1 on Manzano, a highly susceptible dessert banana, in South Florida. (*Photo courtesy of Randy C. Ploetz*)

Fig. 4. Internal symptoms of Panama disease on a partially resistant FHIA hybrid in South Africa. This FHIA hybrid was created by Fundación Hondureña de Investigación Agrícola (the Honduras Foundation for Agricultural Research). (*Photo courtesy of Randy C. Ploetz*)

still contaminate new locations before any clear indications of its presence were evident.

Breeding programs. Few bananas resist TR4. Virtually all of the world's important bananas are susceptible, including the Cavendish subgroup, the plantains, a wide range of cooking bananas, and many different dessert bananas. Although some primitive (progenitor) diploid (having two complete chromosome pairs) bananas are resistant, as are a few hybrids that have been produced by breeding programs, these bananas possess substandard agronomic, postharvest, or organoleptic (sensory) characteristics.

The first banana breeding center was started in 1922, but the improvement programs have made limited progress in developing disease-resistant cultivars (**Fig. 4**). Banana breeding is confronted with significant hurdles: Important cultivars are essentially sterile and are virtually useless as male or female parents; resistant, fertile parents typically possess poor agronomic and fruit characteristics; and other technical issues impede the production of acceptable, disease-resistant hybrids. Given these obstacles, several nonconventional strategies have been tried, albeit with minor success. For example, somatic cell culture (somaclonal) variants that have been developed in Taiwan have filled a niche in that location and have been used on a small scale in TR4-affected

areas in Asia; however, they possess relatively low tolerance to TR4 and must be replanted after one or two cropping cycles.

Recently, transgenic bananas (that is, bananas that possess transferred genes) have been developed for different breeding targets. Genetic modification holds great promise for the production of disease-resistant bananas because the desirable traits of superior but sterile bananas, such as the Cavendish cultivars, might be modified for one characteristic, for example, disease resistance. Although progress has been impeded by the technical difficulties associated with banana transformation, the ineffectiveness of the transgenes that have been used so far, and the complexity of plant diseases that are caused by fungi, novel approaches to these problems may be ultimately successful.

Conclusions. In summary, TR4 has the potential to cripple the global production of bananas. Although it is restricted to Southeast Asia, TR4 could devastate the export and subsistence production of this crop if it becomes more widely distributed. Awareness of the problem, ongoing vigilance in quarantine efforts, and new programs to develop resistant cultivars and effective management strategies are needed.

For background information *see* AGRICULTURAL SCIENCE (PLANT); BANANA; BREEDING (PLANT); FRUIT; FRUIT, TREE; FUNGAL INFECTIONS; FUNGI; GENETICALLY ENGINEERED PLANTS; HORTICULTURAL CROPS; PLANT PATHOLOGY in the McGraw-Hill Encyclopedia of Science & Technology.   Randy C. Ploetz

Bibliography. M. A. Dita et al., A molecular diagnostic for tropical race 4 of the banana Fusarium wilt pathogen, *Plant Pathol.*, 59:348–357, 2010, DOI:10.1111/j.1365-3059.2009.02221.x; S.-C. Hwang and W.-H. Ko, Cavendish banana cultivars resistant to Fusarium wilt acquired through somaclonal variation in Taiwan, *Plant Dis.*, 88:580–588, 2004, DOI:10.1094/PDIS.2004.88.6.580; R. C. Ploetz, Fusarium wilt of banana is caused by several pathogens referred to as *Fusarium oxysporum* f. sp. *cubense*, *Phytopathology*, 96:653–656, 2006, DOI:10.1094/PHYTO-96-0653; R. C. Ploetz, Panama disease: An old nemesis rears its ugly head—Part 1. The beginnings of the banana export trades, *Plant Health Progr.*, December 2005, DOI:10.1094/PHP-2005-1221-01-RV; R. C. Ploetz, Panama disease: An old nemesis rears its ugly head—Part 2. The Cavendish era and beyond, *Plant Health Progr.*, March 2006, DOI:10.1094/PHP-2006-0308-01-RV; R. C. Ploetz and A. C. L. Churchill, Fusarium wilt: The banana disease that refuses to go away, *ISHS Acta Horticult.*, 897:519–526, 2011.

Partially cable-supported girder bridge

Generally, we can group all existing bridges in the world into four basic types: girder bridges, cable-stayed bridges, suspension bridges, and arch bridges (**Fig. 1**).

Fig. 1. Four bridge types. (*a*) Girder bridge. (*b*) Suspension bridge. (*c*) Cable-stayed bridge. (*d*) Arch bridge.

In the case of a girder bridge, the girder is self-supporting. In all the other types of bridges, the girder is supported by cables or spandrels. The girder in these bridges is usually very weak and relies entirely on the cables to carry all loads, which include the self-weight of the girder and all superimposed loads. In a cable-stayed bridge or a suspension bridge, the cables transfer the loads to the towers, which then carry the loads to the foundation. In an arch bridge, the loads from the cables, or spandrels, transfer the loads to the arch ribs, which carry the load to the foundation. In a way, we can label these three types of bridges as cable-supported bridges, where the cables, together with the towers or the arch ribs, are the primary carrying members, while the girder is a secondary member. Because the girder is only a secondary member that is supported by cables, the stiffness of the girder is not important. As a matter of fact, in the design of most arch bridges, cable-stayed bridges, and suspension bridges, the girder is usually made so slender that its flexural capacity can be neglected. For example, the precast concrete girder of the 340-m-span Skytrain Bridge in Vancouver, Canada is only 1.10 m deep, with a span-to-girder depth ratio of 309.

However, in a short- or medium-span bridge, the girder itself does possess a certain amount of capacity. What if we reverse the roles of the two structural elements, having the girder as the primary member and the cable support as the secondary member? This way, we will be able to fully utilize the capacity of the girder and the cable system. This is the concept of the partially cable-supported girder bridge. When we utilize the girder capacity to the fullest extent, the supporting cables and towers or arch ribs can be minimized to save cost.

Various forms. A partially cable-supported girder bridge can have different forms. Besides stay cables,

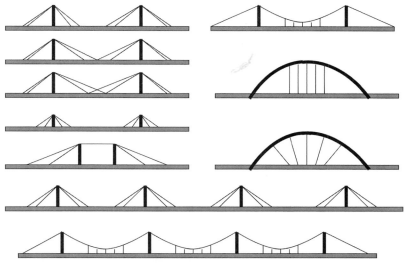

Fig. 2. Possible partial cable support systems.

the partial support can come from a suspension system or an arch system. **Figure 2** shows examples of several possible schemes of partial cable support. A partially cable-supported girder can have numerous variations of forms. If the cables are designed to carry a portion of the load for the entire length of the bridge, a partially cable-supported girder bridge will look exactly like a regular cable-supported bridge, except the towers may appear more slender. If the cables are designed to apply to only a portion of the bridge, the appearance of the bridge will be different. This difference, in many instances, may be just what is preferred in the design for aesthetic or other reasons. In many instances, the tower height of a cable-supported bridge may be restricted, such as by the flight path of a nearby airport. This can be the reason for using a partially cable-supported system.

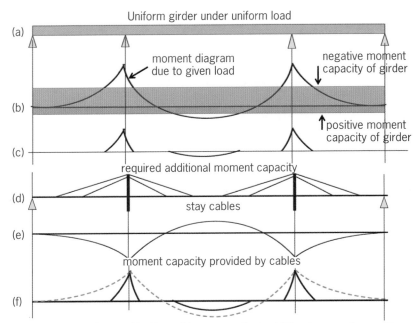

(a) Uniform girder under uniform load

(b) moment diagram due to given load / negative moment capacity of girder / positive moment capacity of girder

(c) required additional moment capacity

(d) stay cables

(e) moment capacity provided by cables

(f) Moment capacity provided by cables vs. required additional moment capacity

Fig. 3. The concept of a partially cable-stayed girder bridge. (*a*) A simplified three-span girder. (*b*) Moment diagram reflecting given loads and moment capacities of the girder structure. (*c*) Moment not covered by the girder capacity = difference. (*d*) Assumed cable-stay system. (*e*) Moment diagram reflecting moment capacities of the cable forces. (*f*) Moment due to cable forces must exceed the difference not covered by the girder capacity.

Design concept. Figure 3 describes the design procedure for a partially cable-stayed girder bridge. Figure 3*a* illustrates a three-span girder under a uniform load. Figure 3*b* represents the bending-moment capacity of the girder under the given load with the positive and negative bending-moment capacities of the girder. Portions of the girder do not have sufficient capacity to resist the bending moment caused by the load on the girder and the difference is plotted on Fig. 3*c*. To make the structure work, a cable-stay system (Fig. 3*d*) that will produce a bending-moment capacity (Fig. 3*e*) to make up the difference can be added.

There are many combinations of cable forces that can produce bending moments that will satisfy or exceed the demand requirements not provided by the girder's moment capacity (Fig. 3*f*). We can take this advantage to assign cable forces in such a way as to simplify fabrication and/or construction. To simplify construction of the girder, for example, we can select a set of cable forces that will have the same vertical component. This will allow us to have one design for all the cable anchorage points. Alternatively, we can assign the same force to all the cables to simplify cable manufacturing.

A partially cable-stayed girder bridge is an economical solution because it fully utilizes the capacity of both the girder and the stay-cable system.

Extradosed bridge. The extradosed bridge is a special type of partially cable-supported girder bridge. It does not, however, have all the freedoms found in the design of a partially cable-supported girder bridge.

The original idea of an extradosed bridge was to raise the prestressing tendons near the pier to gain a larger eccentricity in order to increase the efficiency of the tendons. Eventually these external tendons were made into actual cables with similar corrosion protection requirements, but these cables are still designed as prestressing tendons that allow a higher stress than typical stay cables. The basis for this is the fact that these cables are loaded mainly by permanent loads. The live-load stress variation in these cables is usually small due to two requirements by definition: a stiff girder and very flatly inclined cable geometry. These cables are not effective under live load and consequently are not sensitive to fatigue because the inclination of the cables is very flat. On the other hand, because of these requirements, an extradosed bridge can only be considered a special case in the use of a partially cable-supported girder. Following are two examples of partially cable-supported girder bridges that have been opened to traffic.

Jiayue Bridge. One example of a partially cable-supported girder bridge is the Jiayue Bridge (**Fig. 4**) over the Jialing River in the City of Chongqing, China. The bridge deck is about 70 m above water level in a beautiful and delicate landscape setting.

Navigation dictates that the main span must be at least 230 m at this location. A prestressed concrete girder would be too bulky for such a setting. A conventional cable-stayed bridge with tall towers over the already very deep gorge is also aesthetically not acceptable. We decided to cut the height of the tower to an acceptable level and to increase the capacity of the girder to carry a larger portion of the loads. This resulted in a partially cable-stayed bridge. It is not a real extradosed bridge, even though it looks like one, because the towers are taller and therefore the cables are more efficient than the cables in a conventional extradosed bridge. In this case, the cables are designed to fulfill the same requirements as a regular cable-stayed bridge.

For this bridge, the girder carries about 55% of the total load, while the cable system carries the remaining 45% of the load.

Fig. 4. The Jiayue Bridge.

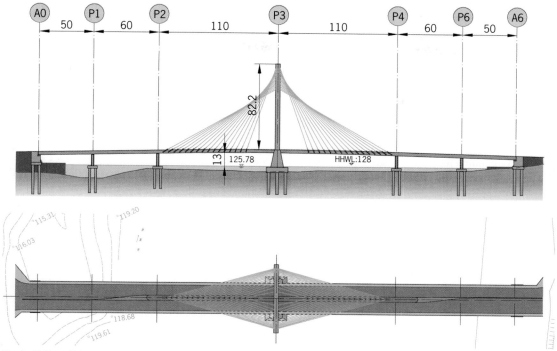

Fig. 5. Taijiang Bridge elevation. A = abutment. P = pier. Distances in m.

Taijiang Bridge. The Taijiang Bridge in Sanming, China is one of the first bridges designed as a partially cable-supported girder bridge. The bridge connects to urban roads on both banks of the river, thus determining the bridge elevation, which in turn fixed the allowable girder depth to a maximum of 3.0 m. The main spans are 110 m. The depth-to-span ratio is 1:36.7, which is beyond the reach of a regular girder bridge. The city desired to have a "signature" bridge. In a design competition, the city selected the bridge scheme of the cable-stayed bridge with an arch type tower (**Fig. 5**). The original design utilized a steel girder to reduce weight, but the available budget would not permit the use of a steel girder. In China, a steel girder usually costs about twice as much as a concrete girder. But a concrete girder is much heavier. If the bridge were designed as a conventional cable-stayed bridge, the heavier concrete would have required a much stronger tower and larger cables, which would have been just as expensive as a full steel girder. To make this bridge scheme possible the partially cable-supported girder bridge concept was applied.

As mentioned above, we first designed the girder to take as much load as possible. Obviously the girder by itself was not able to support all the loads on the bridge. By comparing the capacity of the girder with the maximum required capacity, it was possible to determine how much the cables and tower had to carry. This is simply the difference between the requirement in the maximum/minimum moment diagram and the bending capacity of the girder. The next step was to assign the forces in the cables to

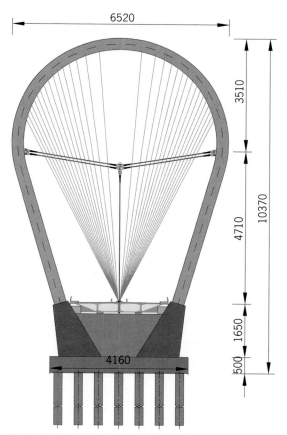

Fig. 6. Taijiang Bridge tower. Distances in cm.

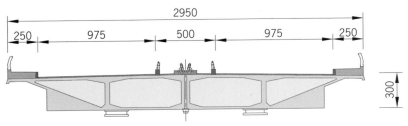

Fig. 7. Taijiang Bridge girder cross section at the tower. Distances in cm.

create a bending-moment diagram that could cover this requirement, as shown in Fig. 3d–f. With a girder depth-to-span ratio of 36.7, the girder by itself could carry about 50% of the loads on the bridge. The cables therefore were only required to carry about 50% of the load. This savings was very significant.

Another advantage in this design concept is that the assignment of cable forces is rather simple. As long as the cable forces, as a group, can create a

bending moment that can cover the requirement, it will be satisfactory. In the Taijiang Bridge, the tower is curved (**Fig. 6**), which was more advantageous to reduce the force in the top cables. This could be done by increasing the force in the middle cables. The middle cables were actually the most effective cables for creating a higher bending moment in the girder.

Because the bridge is symmetrical in both transverse and longitudinal directions, we could adjust the forces in the cables to eliminate all out-of-plane forces in the arch rib. Because all the cables were anchored at the longitudinal axis, or center line, of the bridge deck, the arch did not experience any transverse load, no matter what load was acting on the bridge deck. Certainly, there will be eccentric loading on the deck, but the eccentricity will be taken up by the torsional moment of the deck (**Fig. 7**).

Outlook. In a country like China with a large population and a relatively mountainous landscape, many smaller cities are built between two mountain ranges with a river in the middle, and small- to medium-span bridges are needed to connect the two halves of the city. Useable land is scarce in these cities, so the geometry of the bridge is often severely restricted, as in the case of the Taijiang Bridge (**Fig. 8**). The partially cable-supported girder bridge will always be a good bridge concept to apply to achieve both aesthetics and economy.

For background information *see* ARCH; BRIDGE; CONSTRUCTION ENGINEERING; FOUNDATION; LOADS; TRANSVERSE; PRECAST CONCRETE in the McGraw-Hill Encyclopedia of Science & Technology.

Man-Chung Tang

Bibliography. M. C. Tang, First person: Rethinking bridge design: A new configuration, *Civ. Eng.*, 77(7):38–45, July 2007.

Fig. 8. The Taijiang Bridge.

Particle movement subject to a fluctuating fluid force

The movement of particles from an erodible surface by a flowing fluid is a fundamental physical phenomenon that occurs in many industrial processes and is applicable to biological flows and a wide range of natural phenomena. The erosion and transport of sediment caused by the flow-boundary interaction is a central problem in Earth surface dynamics, where the global amount of sediment eroded annually over the continental surface of the Earth is estimated to be between 80 and 100 billion metric tons. Approximately 20 billion metric tons make it all the way to the ocean, with the rest deposited in reservoirs, lakes, rivers and their floodplains, and wetlands. Additionally, the smaller grains are carriers of various chemicals and pollutants. Human activities, such as deforestation and the increase of impervious surfaces, as well as climate change, tend to exacerbate erosional problems through the redistribution of rainfall in terms of surface and subsurface runoff and enhancement in the frequency of extreme meteorological events. In October 2012, Hurricane Sandy provided a vivid and very painful demonstration of the power that such extreme events possess and the massive and catastrophic erosion damage that they can cause. The effects of the rearrangement of the eroded material over the surface of the Earth is not at all well understood, nor is the mechanism that initiates the process—the dislodgement of a sediment grain from an erodible boundary. Fundamentally, the physical mechanism for particle motion must be related to an unbalanced force on the particle and the application of Newton's laws of motion.

Steady and unsteady forces. We are most familiar with direct contact, mechanical forces, such as between a golf club and the ball on the tee. Such mechanical contact forces are generally easier to characterize than the hydrodynamic forces that arise due to fluid motion, for example, fluid drag. An example of the latter is the aerodynamic force exerted on the flying golf ball, or the aerodynamic drag on an automobile driving down the highway or on an airplane. Both mechanical and flow-induced forces may be steady or unsteady. Traditionally, fluid forces

have been classified as unsteady if the associated flow is unsteady as well. If the golf ball is blown off of the tee by a wind gust, that is an unsteady force, induced by an unsteady wind velocity. Similar flows that induce unsteady forces may also be oscillatory, such as the flow of blood through our arteries and veins. Unsteady forces are particularly important as they relate to fatigue in mechanical parts, and, in the case of unsteady fluid forces, wave-induced vibration of structures such as oil platforms, sea walls, and submerged pipelines and cables, or turbulence-induced vibration or motion of submerged bodies, among many other phenomena.

However, turbulent flows, which are by far the most commonly encountered flows in natural systems and industrial processes, even when steady in the time-average sense, possess an inherently irregular and highly fluctuating nature. To illustrate, the drag force time history experienced by a small (12.7-mm- or 0.5-in.-diameter) exposed sphere positioned on a bed of like spheres at the bottom of a laboratory water channel is shown in **Fig. 1**. In a

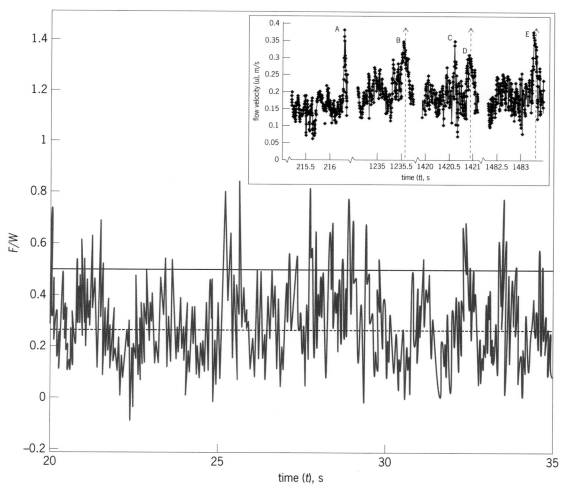

Fig. 1. The drag force on a sphere resting on a bed of identical spheres is plotted as a function of time *t*. The drag force *F* has been nondimensionalized by dividing it by the particle weight *W*. The time-averaged drag force is represented by the broken line, while the corresponding critical force required to dislodge the particle is shown by the solid line. The inset is a composite of several flow velocity time series measured one diameter upstream of the sphere, representing several extreme velocity events. (*Inset from P. Diplas et al., The role of impulse on the initiation of particle movement under turbulent flow conditions, Science, 322:717–720, 2008, DOI:10.1126/science.1158954*)

more general sense, this behavior is representative of the same phenomenon typically encountered in a natural stream or river. For the conditions in this experiment the force varies rapidly, randomly, and over a wide range. This variation occurs because the flow is turbulent. For reference in this figure, the mean drag force is indicated with a broken horizontal line. Because the flow conditions are steady (that is, the flow rate, water depth, and so forth, do not vary) the drag force is constant and steady "in-the-mean."

Entrainment paradox. If this spherical sediment grain were free to move, according to Newton's laws, grain motion would be initiated when the instantaneous applied force exceeds the force resisting motion. For this particular spherical particle, the force of resistance, the so-called critical or threshold force, F_{cr}, is indicated in Fig. 1 by the solid horizontal line. It is observed that the mean drag is less than F_{cr}, but that the fluctuating drag force frequently exceeds the critical value. If only the mean drag force is considered, it would appear that no sediment entrainment should occur. To overcome the limitations of the time-averaged approach and explain the frequent movement of multiple particles that have been reported from numerous field and laboratory observations under flow conditions similar to those shown in Fig. 1, it has been advocated by Hans Albert Einstein (in 1950) and many other researchers that the grain really responds to the instantaneous force. For those instances when the instantaneous drag exceeds the critical force one would expect that the grain can be eroded from the sediment bed. This is the current state-of-the-art in our understanding of the physical mechanism responsible for the entrainment of individual particles from a sediment bed. Paradoxically, recent experiments have demonstrated that the particle is not necessarily eroded even if the fluctuating force exceeds the critical. In the inset of Fig. 1, a representative flow velocity time history measured upstream of the sediment particle is shown. The velocity of the fluid upstream of a sediment particle is well correlated with the drag force applied to the grain—high flow-velocity fluctuations are associated with high force fluctuations. The inset shows several very strong, high-flow-velocity events, all of which correspond to high-drag-force events (all above the critical level). But, not all of these events resulted in full sediment particle entrainment. It is therefore concluded that an object subject to rapidly fluctuating forces is not necessarily entrained even when the applied hydrodynamic force exceeds the critical value. This finding is termed the particle entrainment paradox.

Resolution of the paradox: impulse. Newton's second law of motion is stated mathematically in the equation below. Here, F is the net applied force and

$$F = \frac{d(mV)}{dt}$$

mV is the momentum of the body of mass m and velocity V. If the force is a pulse having magnitude $F(t) > F_{cr}$, lasting for a set interval of time T, this equation can be solved to show that the final momentum of the body (assuming the body is initially at rest) is equal to the product of the force magnitude averaged over T and its duration, that is, $F_{av} \cdot T$. This product is termed the impulse, I. It is therefore evident that under unsteady forcing conditions, force magnitude and duration are equally important in determining the momentum delivered to the mobile grain. The impulse concept provides the resolution to the sediment entrainment paradox. For a mobile grain to be completely dislodged from its resting pocket on the sediment bed, it must acquire a minimum momentum, or equivalently, the flow should impart an impulse exceeding a critical value, to carry it at least to the next adjacent pocket. Therefore, the grain dislodgement criterion is not based on a critical force concept but rather on critical impulse, determined for each pocket geometry and grain size characteristics. When we deal with steady-state forces, then the criterion devolves into a critical force. That the temporal duration of the applied force is relevant to grain entrainment is demonstrated qualitatively in the inset of Fig. 1. Of the several high-velocity events displayed, only events B, D, and E resulted in grain entrainment. Events A and C are equally strong in magnitude but their duration is too short to fully entrain the grain. It is consistently found that flow events must have both sufficient force magnitude (above the critical) and duration to entrain the grain. The role of temporal duration and the existence of a critical impulse is demonstrated quantitatively in **Fig. 2**, where the results of a series of carefully designed experiments are exhibited.

Electromagnet experiments. In these experiments, spherical grains were used to create an idealized

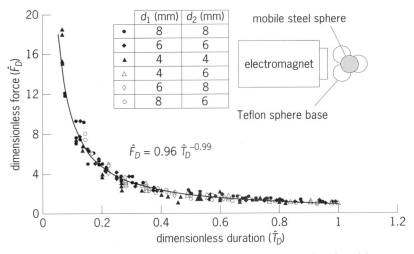

Fig. 2. The dimensionless force on a magnetic sphere is plotted as a function of the dimensionless duration that is required to just cause full-grain dislodgment. The magnetic sphere is resting on a base of Teflon™ spheres. The inset is a sketch (top view) of the geometric arrangement of the electromagnet that induces the force and the mobile, magnetic grain. In the inset table, d_1 is the mobile grain diameter and d_2 is the base diameter. The equation represents the best-fit line to the data and confirms within experimental error that to dislodge the sphere the force and duration are inversely related, consistent with the impulse concept for the initiation-of-entrainment criterion.

model of a sediment bed with a single exposed steel sphere resting upon a bed of Teflon™ spheres. The inset in Fig. 2 shows a top view of the arrangement. An electromagnet (on the left) under computer control was used to induce a wide range of different combinations of lateral force magnitudes and durations to dislodge the steel sphere via rolling. In addition, several different combinations of mobile grain size (diameter) to bed grain size were tested. The table inset in Fig. 2 displays the various combinations (d_1 is the diameter of the steel sphere and d_2 is the diameter of the Teflon spheres). Those combinations of force and duration that just result in complete dislodgment (no more and no less) are plotted. The result is consistent (within experimental error) with a critical value of the impulse, $I_{critical}$, where $I_{critical}/T$ is a hyperbola on the (F, T) plane. The values of the force and duration in Fig. 2 are dimensionless values, using relevant physical characteristics of the mobile grain.

Further considerations and implications. Additional experiments performed in a laboratory flume, using a laser Doppler velocimeter to obtain the velocity record at a point located one diameter upstream and along the centerline of a boundary-fixed grain, allowed for the calculation of the time history of the impulse and its statistical distribution. An example is shown in **Fig. 3**. The resulting distribution is skewed with a long right tail. In the same figure, a separate hypothetical distribution associated with the critical impulse necessary to dislodge a wide range of particle sizes and relevant pocket arrangements is provided. The overlap region identifies the grain sizes susceptible to particle dislodgement by the particular flow considered here. This schematic alludes to the statistical and intermittent nature of particle dislodgement for near-threshold-flow conditions. Furthermore, it provides additional credence to the

idea originally proposed by Einstein that, strictly speaking, there is no such thing as a critical flow in a stream or other environment, even under steady turbulent flow. Because of the highly fluctuating nature of both force magnitude and the corresponding duration, it is highly unlikely that a given flow will generate impulsive events all of which exceed a specific critical value necessary for grain dislodgement. Instead, it is more appropriate to refer to the probability of particle dislodgement under given turbulent flow conditions. Finally, the long tail of the impulse distribution demonstrates the ability of the flow to occasionally entrain much coarser particles than would otherwise be expected or predicted. This explains the movement of boulders in streams under flow conditions below those traditionally perceived as necessary for their entrainment. These extreme events of very high impulse content, usually removed from the data record as outliers, are characteristic of long-tailed distributions and play an important role in natural processes.

For background information *see* DYNAMICS; EROSION; FLUID MECHANICS; FORCE; IMPULSE (MECHANICS); LINEAR MOMENTUM; NEWTON'S LAWS OF MOTION; SEDIMENTOLOGY; TURBULENT FLOW; VELOCIMETER in the McGraw-Hill Encyclopedia of Science & Technology.

Panayiotis Diplas; Clinton L. Dancey

Bibliography. A. O. Celik et al., Impulse and particle dislodgement under turbulent flow conditions, *Phys. Fluid.*, 22:046601, 2010 (13 pp.), DOI:10.1063/1.3385433; P. Diplas et al., The role of impulse on the initiation of particle movement under turbulent flow conditions, *Science*, 322:717–720, 2008, DOI: 10.1126/science.1158954; H. A. Einstein, The bed load function for sediment transportation in open channel flows, *US Dept. Agr. Tech. Bull.*, 1026:1–71, 1950; J. P. M. Syvitski et al., Impact of humans on the flux of terrestrial sediment to the global coastal ocean, *Science*, 308:376–380, 2005, DOI:10.1126/science.1109454.

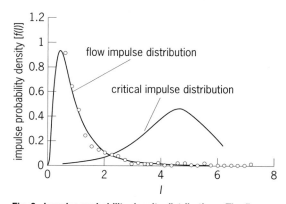

Fig. 3. Impulse probability density distributions. The flow impulse distribution is the measured distribution in turbulent open channel flow for conditions near the threshold of motion. The second curve is a hypothetical representation of the minimum (critical) impulse required to dislodge grains from the sediment bed. The overlap region of these distributions represents those sediment grains that will be entrained. The impulse parameter, *I*, plotted here has been nondimensionalized. (*From A. O. Celik et al., Impulse and particle dislodgement under turbulent flow conditions, Phys. Fluid., 22:046601, 2010, DOI:10.1063/1.3385433*)

Pepducins

Pepducins are membrane-tethered intracellular peptides that are chemically synthesized to target receptors. More specifically, these chemical reagents are cell-penetrating lipidated peptides that are designed to alter the signaling involved with G-protein-coupled receptors (GPCRs), as well as their intracellular signaling, which is typically done via G-proteins [a large family of proteins that bind GTP (guanosine 5′-triphosphate) in intracellular signaling pathways]. Pepducins penetrate the cell by means of a lipid group that is attached to the peptide; this lipid (for example, the fatty acid palmitate) appears to tether the peptide to the membrane. The peptides typically mimic the sequence of a portion of the membrane-adjacent cytoplasmic section of a GPCR. A GPCR has seven transmembrane regions, three cytoplasmic loops, and a cytoplasmic tail. In many GPCRs,

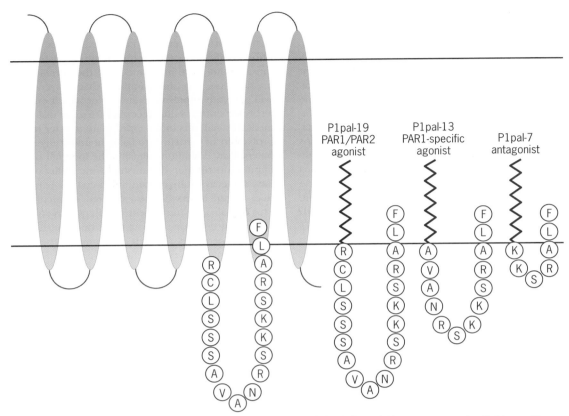

A schematic seven-transmembrane G-protein-coupled receptor (GPCR) is indicated. The sequence region that is used for pepducin design is shown in the third intracellular loop. Three derived pepducins, each with a different activity, are shown on the right.

this tail is palmitoylated (modified by the addition of palmitate), creating another point of membrane tethering, which is analogous to adding a fourth loop to the protein. The diverse range of GPCRs signals through a smaller set of G-proteins. There are four main classes of G-proteins based on the type of alpha subunit that they contain (i, q, s, and $12/13$), and each activates distinct signaling pathways within the cells. Consistent with their less specialized roles in transmitting the signal, G-proteins have a more widespread tissue distribution than many GPCRs. Accordingly, it is attractive to target GPCRs to maximize the specificity of the responses to the particular extracellular signals that they mediate.

Mechanisms of pepducins. It is believed that the pepducin peptides will typically dangle from the membrane, with the lipid tail being embedded in the membrane (see **illustration**). The peptide moiety is then free to participate in protein interactions. It can do this in one of two ways. First, it can compete with the receptor for the binding of signaling partners, such as G-proteins. However, the evidence is generally more consistent with a second mechanism of action. Specifically, the peptide moiety can interact directly with components of the receptor itself, which is accomplished essentially by competing with other segments of the receptor to alter intrareceptor protein loop/tail interactions. Such a mechanism of action may be facilitated

because many GPCRs participate in homodimer (a protein made of paired identical polypeptides) and heterodimer (a protein made of paired polypeptides that differ in their amino acid sequences) interactions, with the swapping of components playing a potential role.

Pepducins may enter the cell by a variety of potential mechanisms. In the simplest mechanism, the pepducin, which is initially embedded in the extracellular side of the cell membrane, "flips" into the inner leaflet. Although the theory of pepducin action is well advanced, the practical evidence is lagging because the physical localization and membrane positioning of the pepducins and the structural characterization of the membrane-adjacent complexes in live cells have not been completely determined. Nevertheless, the available evidence surrounding the actions of certain pepducins at relatively low concentrations is suggestive of receptor-specific (rather than nonspecific) mechanisms of action. It is possible that the targeting of pepducins to the membrane via the lipid anchor contributes to their ability to act at low concentrations because the pepducins are limited to one orientation (tethered to the membrane) and are limited to the chemical target search space of a two-dimensional surface, rather than seeking targets in a three-dimensional cytoplasmic space. Avoiding the off-target effects of peptidic reagents is an important feature of the design of pepducins, and this targeting of the pepducins by the lipid attachment may enhance their effectiveness. A second feature of lipidation is that the tethering of the peptide can aid in the formation of specific structures, in particular favoring alpha-helix formation, which would be poorly supported by the short non-lipidated peptide in solution. Thus, peptides modeled on the membrane-adjacent regions of receptors are more likely to adopt configurations that resemble those adopted in vivo as a result of the membrane tethering.

Design of pepducins. Pepducins that possess agonist and antagonist activities have been developed from all three cytoplasmic loops of the GPCRs. This is suggestive of a general "disruptive" model of pepducin action, shifting the delicately balanced decision making of the receptors in determining whether to adopt an activated or an inactivated conformation. Pepducins have also been designed that mimic the N-terminus of G-proteins, presumably altering receptor function by interfering with natural G-protein binding. At present, there are no clear models that will predict in advance whether a peptide will agonize or antagonize a particular receptor. The synthesis of a pepducin can start off with a screening program to identify a series of peptides from a receptor, and this is allied with an assay that is sensitive to the function of that receptor. Deletion and replacement of selected residues can help in optimizing the pepducin's function. In practice, the design of pepducins owes something to chance: The peptides are created, and the resulting bioactivity is hard to predict. By creating a variety of overlapping peptides and then exploring the effects of mutating key residues or altering their lengths, scientists have been able to generate a library of compounds with diverse agonist and antagonist effects and specificities for different sets of related GPCR proteins. Choosing a peptide that acts at low concentrations provides a useful tool for exploring the molecular biology of the receptor's action. This can be brought further into in vivo models and even clinical trials.

Actions of pepducins. The success of pepducins is well illustrated by the protease-activated receptor family (PAR1 to PAR4). P1pal-19 is a 19-mer pepducin (that is, a 19-subunit oligomer) that mimics the third intracellular loop of PAR1, which causes calcium mobilization and platelet activation (see illustration). It is an agonist of the PAR1 receptor and its homologue PAR2. A truncated 13-mer version of this pepducin is an agonist of PAR1, but not PAR2, showing that the specificity of the receptors can be modulated by varying the pepducin design. Antagonists were also generated from this same region by truncating all but the last seven residues of the pepducin (P1pal-7). P1pal-19 has a number of features that may stabilize its interaction with the plasma membrane, including the membrane-embedded palmitate; a hydrophobic C-terminus that mimics the transmembrane residues and permits potential additional tethering within the membrane; penetration of the membrane; and pos-

itively charged residues at both membrane boundaries, which may be stabilized by interactions with negatively charged lipids in the cytoplasmic membrane inner leaflet. Other pepducins do not have all these features, which may alter their cellular distribution. For example, Pal-CLTYAWHTSFKAL mimics the first half of the second cytoplasmic loop of a developmentally important GPCR named Smoothened and may not associate with the membrane at its C-terminus; it is seen to move to the intracellular membranes after the initial cell membrane localization. Thus, the manner of tethering is likely to alter not only the conformation of the pepducin, but also its distribution and concentration in the appropriate cellular compartment. Such shifts in cellular localization may have implications for pepducin action over time that need to be carefully considered, particularly because pepducins may continue to exert some cellular signaling effects long after they are cleared from the plasma.

Perhaps one of the most promising features of pepducins that target GPCRs involves their mechanism of action. In most cases, these compounds apparently bind to the receptor itself, rather than to G-proteins or other signal mediators. This is advantageous because G-proteins mediate many signaling pathways and are less specific targets than the receptors. Nevertheless, some caution is still required: whereas studies of closely related receptors indicate a strong specificity for certain pepducins, this does not preclude the possibility that these reagents may interact with other more distantly related GPCRs; hence, experimental designs need to allow for this possibility.

Applications of pepducins. The clinical applications of pepducins are as vast as the activities of GPCRs, with potential roles in stem cell activation, angiogenesis modulation, and treatments for cardiovascular disease and cancer. The injection of pepducins into tissues can lead to a local distribution, which is advantageous for many clinical applications. Intravenous injections can lead to a more general distribution. To date, however, pepducins that are capable of crossing the blood–brain barrier have not been designed. There is good evidence for the action of certain pepducins in vivo, indicating their promise as therapeutic agents. So far, studies of pepducins have been carried out over relatively short time periods, and their long-term stability, receptor desensitization, and off-target effects remain to be charted. Beyond GPCRs, lipidated receptor–related peptides show considerable promise, but the understanding of the probable mechanisms of action of these peptides lags behind that of pepducins that target GPCRs. However, it does indicate the important potential of widespread screening of many receptors for protein-sequence-derived reagents that act intracellularly on receptor function. The success of pepducins also opens up the broader possibilities of developing nonpeptidic lipidated compounds that act via similar membrane-tethered mechanisms. Such compounds may have enhanced druglike properties and specificities. As a first step in this direction, alternative (retro-inverso) versions of the Smoothened pepducins have been created, in which the sequence is replaced with a reversed sequence (and reversed palmitate) using D-amino acids. These not only have slightly altered activities, but they should be much more resistant to proteolysis (protein fragmentation by the addition of water to the peptide bonds) in any in vivo setting.

For background information *see* BIOCHEMISTRY; BIOMEDICAL CHEMICAL ENGINEERING; CELL (BIOLOGY); CELL BIOLOGY; CELL MEMBRANES; LIPID; PEPTIDE; PROTEIN; PROTEIN ENGINEERING; SIGNAL TRANSDUCTION in the McGraw-Hill Encyclopedia of Science & Technology.

Denis C. Shields; Kevin T. O'Brien

Bibliography. L. Covic et al., Pepducin-based intervention of thrombin-receptor signaling and systemic platelet activation, *Nat. Med.*, 8:1161–1165, 2002, DOI:10.1038/nm760; R. J. Edwards et al., Bioinformatic discovery of novel bioactive peptides, *Nat. Chem. Biol.*, 3:108–112, 2007, DOI:10.1038/nchembio854; J. M. Janz et al., Direct interaction between an allosteric agonist pepducin and the chemokine receptor CXCR4, *J. Am. Chem. Soc.*, 133:15878–15881, 2011, DOI:10.1021/ja206661w; L. Johannessen et al., Peptide structure stabilization by membrane anchoring and its general applicability to the development of potent cell-permeable inhibitors, *ChemBioChem*, 12:914–921, 2011, DOI:10.1002/cbic.201000563; K. O'Callaghan, A. Kuliopulos, and L. Covic, Turning receptors on and off with intracellular pepducins: New insights into G-protein-coupled receptor drug development, *J. Biol. Chem.*, 287:12787–12796, 2012, DOI:10.1074/jbc.R112.355461.

Perilipins: primary regulators of cellular lipid storage

Perilipins (derived from the Greek words for "surrounding lipid") are primary regulators of cellular lipid storage and the major surface coat proteins of cytoplasmic lipid droplets (CLDs). CLDs are unique cellular compartments for the storage of free fatty acids (FFAs) and sterols as triacylglycerides (TAGs) and cholesterol esters (CEs), which are the precursors for energy metabolism, membrane synthesis, signaling moieties, and steroid hormones. TAG/CE storage also serves to buffer the damaging effects of excess FFAs or cholesterol on membranes that can change the organelle surface fluidity and charge, which affects functions such as transport, receptor signaling, and the release of lipid metabolites and reactive oxygen species (ROS) that can induce insulin resistance, inflammatory responses, and apoptosis (programmed cell death). The balance between TAG storage and FFA utilization is critical. The pathophysiological consequences of defective lipid storage are illustrated by obesity and lipodystrophies, where the inability to store excess dietary lipids in the CLDs

of specialized white adipose cells causes increased lipid deposits (ectopic fat) in nonadipose tissues, including skeletal and heart muscles, the liver, and the pancreas. Ectopic fat is associated with lipotoxicity, insulin resistance, dyslipidemia, type 2 diabetes, and cardiovascular disease. Hence, the packaging and location of CLDs in adipose and nonadipose tissues are critical for lipid homeostasis, energetics, and insulin sensitivity.

Perilipins: CLD proteome signatures. CLDs have a neutral lipid core surrounded by a phospholipid/sterol monolayer that provides a water/lipid interface to dock regulatory proteins. The perilipins (Plins) are generally the most abundant coat proteins of isolated CLDs (see **illustration**). The Plins comprise a multiprotein family (defined by their primary sequence homology through their N-termini) and are conserved in species as diverse as *Dictyostelium* (a soil-living ameba) and mammals. There are five Plin genes (*Plins 1–5*) in mammals, with additional protein forms (for example, Plin1a and Plin1c) derived from tissue-specific messenger RNA (mRNA) splice variants.

Each Plin protein has a unique tissue distribution, although individual cells often express more than a single Plin type. Plin1a is expressed in white adipose tissue (WAT) and brown adipose tissue (BAT), whereas Plin1c is found in steroidogenic tissues. Plin2 and Plin3 are more widely distributed, with Plin2 being highly expressed in the liver. Plin4 is observed in adipocytes, the heart, and skeletal muscles, and Plin5 is restricted to oxidative tissues, primarily the heart, BAT, and skeletal muscles. The Plins also display differential targeting to neutral lipid

adipocyte

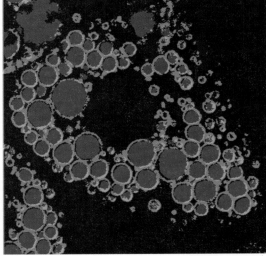

Plin1   neutral lipids

Perilipins localize to the surface of cytoplasmic lipid droplets (CLDs). Plin1 is the founding member of the perilipin family of lipid droplet–targeting proteins. Differentiated adipocytes accumulate large cytoplasmic lipid droplets, which are stained for neutral lipids (*red*) and immunostained with Plin1 antibody (*green*).

cargos. Plins 1a, 1b, and 5 preferentially associate with TAG-containing CLDs, whereas Plins 1c and 4 preferentially localize to CE-containing CLDs. Plins 1d, 2, and 3 show no preference. It is not fully understood how the Plins target CLDs and interact with their surfaces. Two motifs, a domain called PAT (which stands for Perilipin, ADRP, and TIP47) and an 11-residue-long (11-mer) repeat, within the conserved N-terminal region, contribute to the CLD targeting, but these regions are insufficient to define the specificity of Plin interactions with the CLD surfaces.

The tissue-specific expression and subcellular compartmentalization differences suggest that the Plin family members mediate separate and perhaps unique functions. Recent progress toward understanding Plin function has focused on the relationship of Plin-deficient mouse models and lipid homeostasis.

Plin1 in adipocytes: "professional" storage cells. Plin1 is the most extensively studied family member and is most highly expressed in WAT and BAT, that is, cells specialized for regulated whole body energy storage and maintenance. Results from $plin1^{-/-}$ ($plin1$-deficient) mice and cultured cells underscore an important role for Plin1a to coordinate TAG storage and hydrolysis.

Plin1a is a strategic scaffold at the CLD surface for the assembly/disassembly of multiprotein lipolytic complexes upon Plin1a phosphorylation (addition of a phosphate group)/dephosphorylation (removal of a phosphate group). In insulin-stimulated basal cells, Plin1a is unphosphorylated, and the adipocyte CLD hydrolytic enzymes [adipose triglyceride lipase (ATGL) and hormone sensitive lipase (HSL)] are cytosolic; the ATGL coactivator CGI-58 (comparative gene identification-58) preferentially binds to unphosphorylated Plin1a at the surface of the CLD, apart from ATGL. Thus, under basal conditions, lipases are sequestered from CLDs and lipolysis is suppressed.

Upon β-adrenergic stimulation, adenylyl cyclase is activated and cyclic adenosine monophosphate (cAMP) accumulates. Both Plin1a and HSL are phosphorylated by protein kinase A (PKA), resulting in lipase reorganization, with phosphorylated HSL (pHSL) binding phosphorylated Plin1a (pPlin1a) at the CLD surface, dissociation of CGI-58 from pPlin1, and interaction of CGI-58 and ATGL at the CLD surface, collectively activating adipocyte lipolysis. Plin1a interacts with an isoform of optic atrophy 1 (OPA$_1$), which is a PKA-anchor protein (AKAP) that tethers PKA type 1 and type 2 subunits at the CLD surface to facilitate Plin1a phosphorylation.

WAT from $plin1^{-/-}$ mice shows both the loss of basal lipolytic suppression and impaired β-adrenergic activation. Under basal conditions, lipases are not fully sequestered from the CLD surfaces; under stimulated conditions, lipases are not fully recruited to the CLD and activated. In response to high basal activation, WAT is reduced approximately 70% in $plin1^{-/-}$ mice, promoting ectopic

lipid accumulation and hepatic insulin resistance. Naturally occurring genetic errors in human $Plin1$ further support Plin1a as an essential lipase scaffold and regulator.

Plin1 interacts with other proteins at the CLD surface to facilitate FFA flux through CLDs to protect adipocytes from FFA toxicity and promote whole-body lipid storage to adipocytes, suppressing ectopic lipid accumulation. The significance of Plin1 is highlighted by the serious metabolic consequences that occur in $plin1$-deficient mice and humans.

Plin2: a coat protein adapted for multicell storage. Plin2 protects cultured fibroblast CLDs against intracellular neutral lipases. Although Plin2 is the major perilipin in $plin1^{-/-}$ WAT CLDs, Plin2 does not compensate for the Plin1 regulatory role in WAT lipolysis. Several $plin2$-depletion mouse models have been developed that exhibit similar overall phenotypes.

In comparison to $plin2^{+/+}$ controls, $plin2$-deficient mice exhibit a decreased hepatic CLD content in response to starvation or a high-fat diet challenge, and they also have a reduced weight gain on an extended high-fat diet. The $plin2$-deficient mice are partially protected against CLD accumulation in the subcutaneous WAT. The subcutaneous WAT depot has increased expression of uncoupling protein 1 (UCP1), which is a protein that separates oxidative metabolism from adenosine triphosphate (ATP) synthesis, with released energy dissipated as heat. Accordingly, the subcutaneous WAT may contain thermogenically active "beige" adipose cells. Many of these phenotypes are similarly observed in $plin2$ ASO (antisense oligonucleotide)–treated adult mice.

The leptin-deficient obese mouse model shows defects in systemic glucose and lipid homeostasis and extensive hepatic steatosis (fatty liver). Mice with the combined absence of both leptin and Plin2 show improvement in all assayed parameters and protection against leptin-deficient obesity. Overall, these $Plin2$ mouse models indicate an in vivo role for Plin2 in hepatic lipid sequestration, confirming Plin2 as a negative regulator of lipolysis. The absence of Plin2 is compensated by an increase in Plin3 and Plin5 levels and may augment lipolytic products that activate peroxisome proliferator-activated receptor α (PPARα) and promote FFA utilization, thus limiting lipotoxicity.

Plin5 in "oxidative" cells. Plin5 is expressed in oxidative cells and induced when energy is required from mitochondrial β-oxidation of FFAs during fasting or exercise. Cell culture studies indicate that Plin5 regulates CLD accumulation and lipolysis. Plin5, like Plin1, is a scaffolding protein for key lipolytic proteins. Plin5 will interact with CGI-58 and HSL, but also with ATGL. ATGL and CGI-58 may compete for the same Plin5 binding site, suggesting a molecular mechanism for lipolytic regulation distinct from Plin1, although involving the similar lipolytic protein set.

Plin5 uniquely tethers mitochondria and CLDs, perhaps to maximally couple lipolysis and energy production and to buffer excess FFAs for prevention of mitochondrial membrane damage. Plin5 may offer a protective feedback mechanism at the CLD surface to regulate ATGL-mediated CLD hydrolysis and the TAG/FFA cycle.

The function of Plin5 in the heart has been studied in different mouse models. For example, *plin5*$^{-/-}$ mice lack ectopic cardiac CLD accumulation upon starvation and a high-fat diet, and they show age-related cardiac dysfunction that can be suppressed by antioxidants. The CLDs present are also dissociated from the mitochondria. Cardiac-specific overexpression of Plin5 drives cardiac steatosis (fatty heart), without impairing cardiac function, and this is possibly the result of persistent CLD–mitochondrial coupling and the coactivation of antioxidative pathways. These relationships and the function of Plin5 in other oxidative tissues, including BAT, remain to be fully investigated in the context of systemic lipid and glucose homeostasis, obesity, and exercise or cold.

Plin3 and Plin4: works in progress. Plin4 is the largest and most unconventional perilipin, with the 11-mer repeat region expanded to approximately 900 amino acids. Plin4 was first identified in adipocytes, but its expression is also observed in heart and skeletal muscles. Disruption of *Plin4* in mouse models did not cause perturbations in adipocyte differentiation or metabolism, but it did decrease cardiac CLDs, resulting in reduced levels of Plin5. Cardiac mitochondrial function was unaffected upon fasting or genetic- or dietary-induced obesity. Because *Plin4* and *Plin5* are closely linked in the genome, the *Plin4* deletion may impair sites required for *Plin5* expression. Future studies will clarify the relationships between these genes/proteins.

Plin3 is the least protective to lipolytic action on CLDs. Although Plin3 is widely distributed, it is the most abundant Plin of the small intestine, which is a primary site for dietary lipid absorption. Plin3 may facilitate CLD hydrolysis for repackaging of lipids for the export of chylomicrons (extremely small lipid droplets). Plin3 is highly induced by a bolus of dietary fat, but not by chronic dietary fat, which promotes Plin2 expression. Here, an increased Plin2 presence may suppress lipid absorption and toxicity. A *Plin3* mouse model is not yet available for the study of energy homeostasis.

Conclusions. The perilipins sequester lipids by protecting CLDs from lipase action. Their relative protective nature and expression are adapted to the balance of lipid storage and utilization in specific cells. Plin1 in adipocytes allows prime energy storage and efficient energy export. Plin2 is adapted to medium-level storage facilities, whereas storage via Plin3 may be more transient. Plin5 regulates the subpopulation of CLDs associated with mitochondria. The function of Plin4 remains an enigma. Significant analyses have defined the molecular aspects of the action of Plin1. The mechanistic functions of the other Plins are less clear, but they remain prime tools to understand both the function of nonadipose CLDs in metabolic diseases and their effects on overall body energy homeostasis.

For background information *see* ADIPOSE TISSUE; DIABETES; ENERGY METABOLISM; GENE; HOMEOSTASIS; INSULIN; LIPID; LIPID METABOLISM; MITOCHONDRIA; OBESITY; PROTEIN; TRIGLYCERIDE (TRIACYLGLYCEROL) in the McGraw-Hill Encyclopedia of Science & Technology.

Alan R. Kimmel; Carole Sztalryd

Bibliography. P. E. Bickel, J. T. Tansey, and M. A. Welte, PAT proteins, an ancient family of lipid droplet proteins that regulate cellular lipid stores, *Biochim. Biophys. Acta*, 1791:419–440, 2009, DOI:10.1016/j.bbalip.2009.04.002; A. S. Greenberg et al., The role of lipid droplets in metabolic disease in rodents and humans, *J. Clin. Invest.*, 121:2102–2110, 2011, DOI:10.1172/JCI46069; A. R. Kimmel et al., Adoption of PERILIPIN as a unifying nomenclature for the mammalian PAT-family of intracellular lipid storage droplet proteins, *J. Lipid Res.*, 51:468–471, 2010, DOI:10.1194/jlr.R000034; T. C. Walther and R. V. Farese, Jr., Lipid droplets and cellular lipid metabolism, *Annu. Rev. Biochem.*, 81:687–714, 2012, DOI:10.1146/annurev-biochem-061009-102430; H. Wang and C. Sztalryd, Oxidative tissue: Perilipin 5 links storage with the furnace, *Trends Endocrinol. Metab.*, 22:197–203, 2011, DOI:10.1016/j.tem.2011.03.008; R. Zechner et al., FAT SIGNALS—lipases and lipolysis in lipid metabolism and signaling, *Cell Metab.*, 15:279–291, 2012, DOI:10.1016/j.cmet.2011.12.018.

Personal chemical exposure informatics

Chemical exposure science is the study of human contact with chemicals (from manufacturing facilities, everyday products, and waste) in the environments. It advances knowledge of the mechanisms and dynamics of events that cause or prevent adverse health outcomes. Personal chemical exposure (PCE) is a subtopic within exposure science that focuses on the individual (**Fig. 1***a*). This primarily considers who you are (the receptor), what you are doing (activity), and what you interact with or use in what you are doing (products, articles, feeding, exercising, hygiene, and so on).

A receptor's chemical exposure can also be obtained mathematically (deterministically or probabilistically, or both) by knowing one's location and the time spent in that location. This contextually limits the choices of what you are doing to a tractable probability. Chemical exposure, in general, is a function not only of the chemical, but also of the individual receptor's biology, environment, and the lifestyle factors that make up an individual's personal experience (Fig. 1*b*). By combining individual habits with chemical residue or composition knowledge, a full picture of that individual's personal chemical exposure can be obtained.

When coupled with a chemical-specific hazard characterized by known dose-response relationships

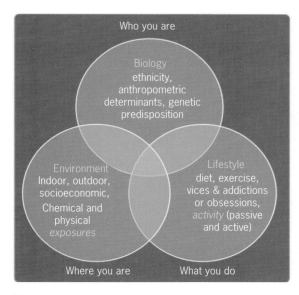

(a)

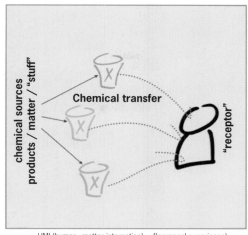

HMI (human - matter interaction) = f(personal experience)
PCE (personal chemical exposure) = f(chemical residue, and HMI)

(b)

Fig. 1. The three information domains that directly affect personal chemical exposure related to (*a*) who, what, and where of an individual. (*b*) Nearfield chemical exposure from one's local environment results as chemical transfer between various sources of chemicals (red, green, and blue cups of idealized chemicals X), and is a function of how receptors (humans) interact with products, materials, or articles (matter) and the chemical residue constituents of those products.

(such as toxicological characterization, adverse outcome pathways (AOPs), and exposure thresholds), PCE holds the potential to estimate personalized (or individual) risk by bringing exposure into the "risk mix." In **Fig. 2**, a visual overview of the published literature related to personal chemical exposure reveals information about chemical exposure sources, exposure routes, and scientific methods and data that characterize personal exposure more generally.

Personal chemical exposure informatics (PCEI) is the sum or combination of all informatics resources required to make personal chemical exposure extrapolations (via modeling and simulation approaches) at the crossroads of a biological receptor with the chemical constituents it interacts with (interactome) and how those exposures relate to health in a lifetime (exposome). Moreover, the more generalized analogs, personal informatics systems, we know that people want to get information about themselves to reflect on, and that systems that support this activity need to be effective and simple to use. The nature of the data PCEI tools need to handle is diverse and ranges from chemical, biological, social, and geographical data types, including but not limited to:

1. Air quality (indoor/outdoor)

2. Pollution [for instance, listed on TSRI (toxic substances release inventory)]

3. Location (GPS data)

4. Time activity journals (that is, American Time Use Survey/Comprehensive Human Activity Database)

5. Product use in those activities (exposure factors such as the *Exposure Factors Handbook*)

6. Material composition (articles and consumables; that is, National Library of Medicine's Household Product Database)

7. Water quality [(for instance, the Environmental Working Group's National Drinking Water Database (http://www.ewg.org/tap-water/)]

8. Anthropometric determinants

   a. Species, life stage, gender, ethnicity or strain, underlying physiological/genomic data

   b. Dietary, metabolic output/physical activity, and so on

   c. Chemical and species-specific ADME (pharmacokinetics or Absorption, Distribution, Metabolism, and Elimination).

In addition, PCEI needs collection and correlation of proxies that allow one to deduce or infer these variables. The complexity of PCEI needs an information model that contains all the required data sources and proxies necessary to model personal chemical exposure. This information model and required data streams to extrapolate personal chemical exposure (PCE) are shown in **Fig. 3**. Specifically, the aim of PCEI is to better understand the exposure sources present in microenvironments. Some of these efforts have been explored through a proof-of-concept study for the first step of Systems Reality Modeling (http://www.epa.gov/heasd/research/srm.html). Despite its preeminence in the source-exposure dose-effect continuum, chemical source information is generally not well integrated in exposure and risk assessment. In exposure studies, source information is often collected in an ad hoc fashion either by the investigators attempting to inventory products in homes or offices or by the study of participants attempting

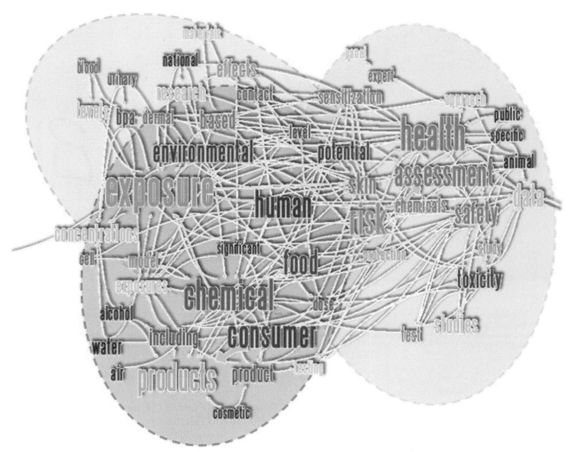

Fig. 2. A text-mining visualization of personal chemical exposure according to the *PubMed* literature search for ("everyday exposure" OR "consumer exposure" OR (("consumer product" OR "consumer products") AND exposure)) AND chemical) with advanced filters: "Humans" provides 224 research articles (on May 23, 2013). The resulting text abstracts were imported into Many-eyes.com and visualized using a phrase net analysis. Key themes are circled in colored ovals related to (red) sources of everyday exposures, (yellow) exposure routes for these everyday exposures, and (blue) key areas of research involved in safety assessment. The shortened URL for the underlying data is http://goo.gl/qSjWe.

to interpret chemical information from consumer product labels. An approach that will significantly increase the collection efficiency, amount, and quality of source data one can collect in a short period of time is outlined in Figs. 3, 4 and 5. This approach holds the potential to reduce the uncertainty and errors in real-time data acquisition and interpretation.

Integrating personal time-activity use into PCEI: from information model to workflow. Although it is vital for exposure modeling to gather current time-location activity profiles of the U.S. population to better understand relevant routes of exposure, these profiles are difficult to obtain. The state-of-the-science in gathering these data is time-consuming, expensive, and subject to a number of limitations. It places a great burden on participants to provide data, leading to noncompliance with study protocols, biases in activity reporting, and even participant dropout. Thus, to increase data collection efficiency and simultaneously reduce participants' burden of filling out conventional time-activity diaries, an innovative approach that monitors individuals anonymously in real time without solicitation is much needed.

Sociological researchers have been surprised by the growing subset of the population who volunteer their time-activity information to the public via social media (such as in tweets, status updates, and check-ins). This is ideal for making the development of a tool for converting such free-form texts into a structured set of knowledge, with the proviso that the sole reliance on information from social media may lead to limited scope and possible bias. Thus, developing an activity-tracking app for smartphones to reduce the burden on participants in traditional observational studies is vital for PCEI. Such apps would have a great potential to collect real-time activity data with high spatial and temporal resolution when installed on a smartphone with other monitoring apps, such as GPS for tracking location, accelerometer for tracking movement, calorie-tracker for recording food consumption, and time-logger for recording time-activity information. While social media and other available data streams (for example, geospatial location) can potentially provide a wealth of untapped information to mine human activity data, the challenge of separating the noise from relevant data will also need to be dealt

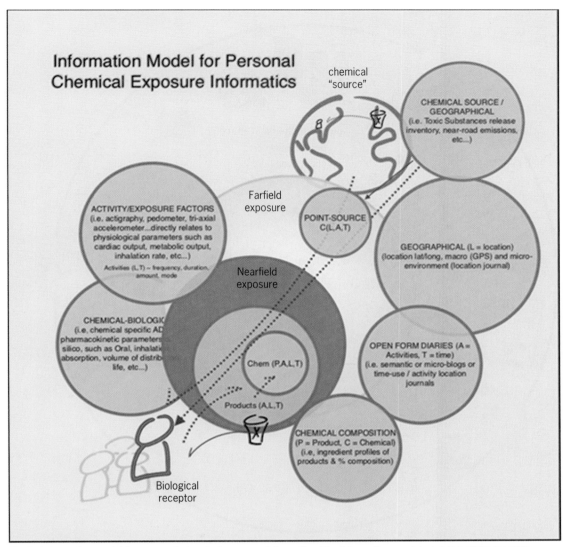

Fig. 3. Information model for personal chemical exposure informatics. The information model contains all the requisite information for calculating chemical transfer from a chemical source to a biological receptor (an individual). C = Chemical, P = Product, A = Activity, T = Time, L = Location. Depending on the individual biological receptors and the activities and locations of those individuals, they will have a unique set of activities, with a corresponding set of products with known chemical formulations and specific chemical exposures. The exposure profile of an individual is unique, and at the aggregate level there may be some community/population-based similarities, or even occupational-related chemical exposures that can be deduced using such an approach.

with. However, at a minimum, developing a preliminary tweet/microblog codification algorithm, which can be further optimized by including knowledge of location/activity co-occurrence, is also needed for PCEI. Such passive interrogation methods show a great deal of promise for increasing the quality and quantity of data to inform the exposure, epidemiology, and behavioral sciences, but with minimum participant burden.

With an eye toward mobile computing as the desired computational environment to deploy personal chemical exposure informatics, we have designed a workflow that captures the interactions of individuals with their local environment (Fig. 4 from *a* to *b*) and provides individuals with the ability to explore their personal chemical exposures.

Integrating the disparate information piece into a PCEI product for smartphone apps. Ideally, integrating the disparate data streams (Fig. 3, geographical chemical release information, geographical position data, exposure factors, activity logs, chemical composition, and uptake/intake) into a "mashup" that uses and combines this data will allow for a real-time exposure assessment based on a particular real-time scenario. Within the local environment, personal chemical space (bar-coded products associated with an inventory that links concentrations and use) could be linked with location and activity information to determine exposure, based on contact with the chemical substances within the products. Exposure for particular products could then be assessed by mined text mapped to archived

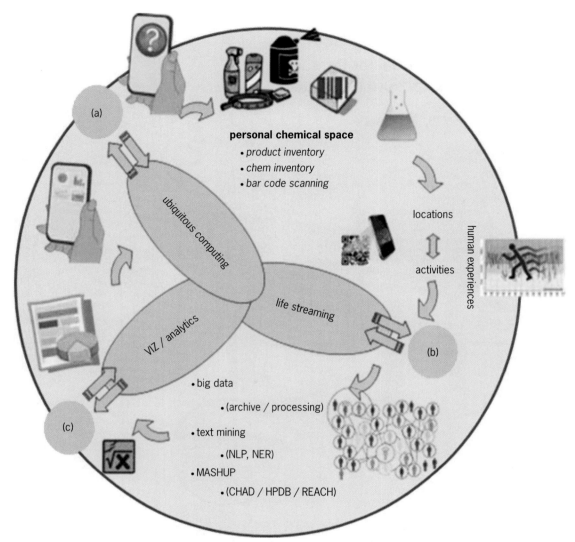

personal chemical space
- *product inventory*
- *chem inventory*
- *bar code scanning*

Fig. 4. Integrating personal time-activity use into PCEI: From information model to workflow. To inform on human-matter interaction and personal chemical exposure, we propose the use of a PCEI workflow, including (*a*) ubiquitous computing, (*b*) life-streaming and appropriate data-mining, and (*c*) visual analytics and modeling/mashups to make use of big data and to inform the individual of personal chemical exposures from everyday household products. NLP = Natural Language Processing, NER = Named Entity Recognition, CHAD is the Comprehensive Human Activity Database (http://www.epa.gov/heasd/chad.html), HPDB is the Household Product Database, and REACH is the European CHemical REgulation program: Registration, Evaluation, Authorisation, and Restriction of Chemical substances.

big data (the collection, storage, and management of huge amounts of data) containing activities, frequencies, and durations mapped to typical product use information from CHAD (Consolidated Human Activity Database), the HPDB (Household Products Database), SPIN (Substances in Preparations In the Nordic countries), and REACH (Registration, Evaluation, Authorisation, and Restriction of Chemical substances). A computational evaluation of exposure will be determined for each given product. These analytics could be relayed back to the user for each product scanned in their personal space. This combination of visualization and aggregation would generate a user-friendly presentation of the exposure assessment, thereby increasing the functionality of the data streams for the user. Users could then have an accurate representation of the sum-

mative chemical exposure potential of their local environment.

Using the information models, PCEI workflow, and user interface (UI) one can conceivably develop a research tool (either smartphone app or desktop/web application) that allows for simulation of exposures within local environments (Fig. 5). A user could specify day-to-day activities in a series of scenarios and obtain a virtual exposure assessment drawing on information from the mashed-up data streams. These simulations would allow for the exploration of potential exposures on virtual subjects in a myriad of microenvironments without the limitations of obtaining new location, activity, and chemical-specific data.

Modeling and simulation using data derived from PCEI increases the predictive capacity of individuals,

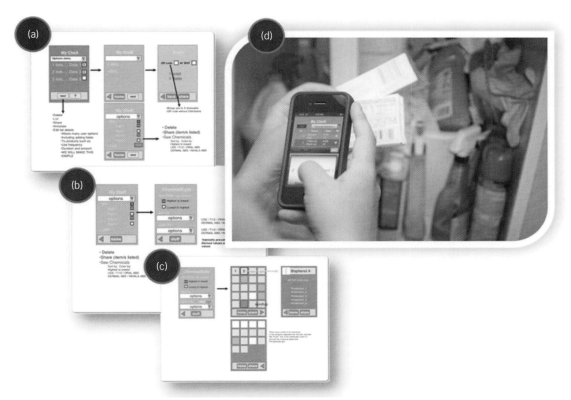

Fig. 5. The designed mock-up of a smartphone user interface (UI) to (*a*) enter a chemical inventory, with options to select and share subset product lists and (*b*) create sublists and identify how to visualize the chemical exposure by a variety of sorting and coloring schemes such as half-life or absorption, with (*c*) a sharable tactile link table color-coded according to a desired scheme that links each chemical to toxicity resources such as ACToR (http://actor.epa.gov). (*d*) A prototype in the proper contextual setting—at home.

researchers, industries, and regulators because it can be used to extrapolate exposure information for new chemicals. The simulation models can include visualization with mathematical models that describe the exposure processes from source to receptor to calculate the impact of product use on chemical exposure, which can be linked to health effects and subsequently to decisions to mitigate potentially harmful exposures or to promote more sustainable health decisions.

[*Disclaimer:* The United States Environmental Protection Agency through its Office of Research and Development funded and managed the research described here. It has been subjected to Agency review and approved for publication. Mention of trade names or commercial products does not constitute endorsement or recommendation for use.]

For background information *see* DATABASE MANAGEMENT SYSTEM; ENVIRONMENTAL ENGINEERING; ENVIRONMENTAL TOXICOLOGY; MODEL THEORY; RISK ASSESSMENT AND MANAGEMENT; SIMULATION; TOXICOLOGY in the McGraw-Hill Encyclopedia of Science & Technology.

Michael-Rock Goldsmith; Christopher M. Grulke; Daniel T. Chang; Yuemei Tan; Raina D. Brooks; Curtis C. Dary; Daniel A. Vallero

Bibliography. Summary Report for Personal Chemical Exposure Informatics: Visualization and Exploratory Research in Simulations and Systems (PerCEIVERS), Rep. no. EPA/600/R13/041, June 26–27, 2012 (http://www.epa.gov/heasd/documents/chemical_info.pdf); I. Li, A. Dey et al., A stage-based model of personal informatics systems, in *proc., CHI* 2002, ACM Press, 2010.

Persuasive technology

Increased interactivity and engagement of users through modern information and communication technologies have opened up many opportunities for influencing the behaviors of information-system users. For example, the fostering of healthier lifestyles through Web access has become one of the most prominent areas for future health-care improvement, and other application areas include directing users toward promoting greener energy behaviors and using stronger passwords in their Web accounts. Psychological theories, including the elaboration likelihood model, can be used to explain some of these behavioral changes. The elaboration likelihood model suggests that there are two routes for persuading people: Approaching through the central route underscores reason and argument, whereas approaching through the peripheral route builds upon emotions, social cues, and often several arguments. Other theories of persuasion suggest that there are six generic persuasive strategies to influence people's behaviors: social proof, scarcity, reciprocity, liking, commitment and consistency, and authority.

Development of persuasive technology. Theoretical frameworks and conceptual models that pay closer attention to mapping the lessons learned from psychological studies with the characteristics of modern information and communication technologies are needed. From this viewpoint, the design and development of systems that maintain powers to influence their users are the essential features. In the late 1990s, the psychologist B. J. Fogg (at Stanford University) suggested persuasive technology as a field to study any interactive information technologies intentionally designed for changing users' attitudes or behaviors. Since then, persuasive technology has received growing interest among both researchers and practitioners. Based on these investigations, persuasive systems have been defined as computerized software or information systems designed to reinforce, change, or shape attitudes or behaviors (or both) without using coercion or deception.

Many forms of attempted influence do exist, including deception and coercion as well as monetary inducements. These means may be effective for producing behavioral changes, but the voluntary nature of persuasive systems by definition excludes deception and coercion. An ideal system literally persuades its users to adopt the target behavior. These persuasive systems may use either computer-mediated or computer–human persuasion. Computer-mediated persuasion means that people are persuading others through computers, for example, instant messages or social networking systems. Some patterns of interaction, which are similar to social communication, may be used in computer–human persuasion, even if the Web cannot communicate in the same way that humans do. However, in the case of persuasive systems, there always are stakeholders who have the intention of influencing someone's attitudes or behaviors because computers do not have intentions of their own.

Persuasive systems design model. Fogg's seminal work on persuasive technology, which stated that information technology may play the role of a tool, a medium, or a social actor for its users, was the first conceptualization suggested for helping software designers. The persuasive systems design (PSD) model is a more recent and state-of-the-art approach for designing and evaluating persuasive systems. The PSD model defines seven postulates or core issues that are common for all persuasive systems. According to this model, information technology, at least philosophically, is never neutral; rather, it always influences its user (or users) in one way or another. Moreover, the ability to build persuasive systems requires insight from both software design and psychology. Some of the lessons learned from psychology are that people like their views about the world to be organized and consistent, persuasion is often incremental, and the direct and indirect routes are key persuasion strategies. Software design requirements

are equally important. For example, persuasive systems should be both useful and easy to use, which is much easier said than done, and persuasion through these systems should always be transparent and must always be unobtrusive to a user's primary tasks.

After obtaining a deeper understanding of these persuasion postulates, the next step, according to the PSD model, is a careful analysis of the contexts for persuasion (the intent, event, and strategy for persuasion) to discern opportune and inopportune moments for delivering the message (or messages). This step is where a number of issues must be resolved. These include the intended outcome, change, and message; the route that will be used to deliver the message; the user models and use situations; and many technological issues. Analyzing the context for persuasion is needed for all application domains, ranging from evaluating software specifications in the early stages of systems development to studying full-fledged commercial applications.

The PSD model also defines four categories of software features for persuasive systems, namely primary task support, computer–human dialogue support, perceived system credibility, and social influence. Thus, different types of persuasive software features, which have psychological grounding, can be implemented, supporting the user's primary activities, representing information fluently in the computer–human dialogue, conveying the credibility of information being presented, and leveraging social influence. For example, provision of positive feedback and virtual trophies after attaining a goal leverages the computer–human dialogue support features of praise and virtual rewards. Leveraging social influence through software features that support social learning, comparison, and facilitation, as well as normative influence, recognition, competition, and cooperation, can provide highly persuasive user experiences. However, the model does not put forward a claim that all imaginable software features should be implemented into a persuasive system or that more is always better.

Behavior change support systems. Of course, nudging people to do small things is much easier than helping them to carry out a longer process of change through full-fledged persuasive systems, which are known as behavior change support systems (BCSSs). In addition to being a special case of a persuasive system, a BCSS also has characteristics of its own. A BCSS places more emphasis on the actual outcome than a persuasive system, which emphasizes more the persuader's intent than measuring the actual outcome in most cases (this applies even if its developers were interested in the outcomes as well). Another special characteristic of BCSSs is that a much stronger emphasis on a positive user experience and a high level of engagement (also known as stickiness) is required to motivate users to interact with them regularly over an extended period of time. What distinguishes research into persuasive and behavior change support systems from research into other information systems is that they are inherently transformative, deliberately attempting to cause a cognitive and/or an emotional change in the mental state of a user to transform the user's current state into another planned state and to cause a corresponding change in the user's behaviors.

In implementing persuasive systems, many different kinds of issues need to be addressed. Some of these are technical, but many stem from users and they may also relate to organizations, cultures, or society. These issues may also regard an end user's personal goals or social environments. Furthermore, the development of persuasive systems cannot be narrowed down to being a mere user interface issue. A variety of topics beyond human–computer interaction, including approaches, methodologies, processes, and tools to develop persuasive systems and ways for studying their organizational, social, and end-user effects, must be analyzed. In addition, BCSSs must be made available for their users without breaks, and they have to address a variety of cultural issues. Finally, information technologies vary in terms of their limitations and opportunities.

Other aspects. In terms of academic research, affective computing, which more directly focuses on the emotions that systems evoke, may be recognized as a sister field or subfield of persuasive technology. Thus far, most persuasive technology research has placed its emphasis on experimental studies and design research, with less emphasis on real-life studies, qualitative approaches, or theoretical developments, which eventually will be needed to advance persuasive technology as a scientific field. In addition, there has been surprisingly little research into the ethical considerations relating to persuasive technology, perhaps because of the strong emphasis on experimental and design research. Ethical considerations (for example, the ethics involved in cases in which computer-mediated persuasion potentially takes place without the user being aware of it, or motives and designer bias behind a service that is not being clearly explicated) almost automatically arise on par with developing persuasive technology solutions. However, research awareness and action on these and other ethical considerations seem to be on the increase.

Outlook. Overall, the general audience should become more aware of the various ways in which people can be influenced through information technology designs, whereas application domain experts and Web developers should obtain deeper understanding of persuasive systems and their development. This is especially important because the contemporary and future Web will keep opening up a myriad of opportunities for building software that aims at persuading people.

For background information *see* BRAIN; CLIENT-SERVER SYSTEM; HUMAN-FACTORS ENGINEERING; HUMAN-MACHINE SYSTEMS; INFORMATION PROCESSING (PSYCHOLOGY); INFORMATION TECHNOLOGY; INTERNET; MOTIVATION; PSYCHOLOGY; SOFTWARE; WORLD WIDE WEB in the McGraw-Hill Encyclopedia of Science & Technology. Harri Oinas-Kukkonen

Bibliography. R. B. Cialdini, *Influence: Science and Practice*, 4th ed., Allyn & Bacon, Boston, 2001; B. J. Fogg, *Persuasive Technology: Using Computers to Change What We Think and Do*, Morgan Kaufmann, San Francisco, 2003; H. Oinas-Kukkonen, A foundation for the study of behavior change support systems, *Personal Ubiquitous Comput.*, July:1–13, 2012, DOI:10.1007/s00779-012-0591-5; H. Oinas-Kukkonen and M. Harjumaa, Persuasive systems design: Key issues, process model, and system features, *Commun. Assoc. Inf. Syst.*, 24:485–500, 2009; R. E. Petty and J. T. Cacioppo, *Attitudes and Persuasion: Classic and Contemporary Approaches*, William C. Brown, Dubuque, IA, 1981.

Planck mission

The Planck mission is a satellite mission to explore the cosmic microwave background radiation (CMB). The discovery of this radiation in 1964 opened up a new era in observational cosmology. It was soon confirmed that CMB photons almost exactly reproduce the blackbody spectrum corresponding to a temperature of 2.7 K, confirming their cosmological origin as remnants of the very early big bang phase of the evolution of the universe, when it was very dense and very hot. Early in 1992, the *Cosmic Background Explorer* (*COBE*) satellite, designed by NASA, detected for the first time small temperature anisotropies at a level of $\Delta T/T \sim 10^{-5}$. These small variations carry important information about the distribution of matter and radiation when the photons decoupled from hot matter some 380,000 years after the big bang. Late in June 2001, NASA launched another specially designed satellite, the *Wilkinson Microwave Anisotropy Probe* (*WMAP*), and placed it at the second Lagrange (L2) point of the Sun-Earth system to measure the temperature anisotropy of the CMB with much increased accuracy. The *WMAP* satellite was equipped with several bolometers operating at five different frequencies spanning the range from 23 to 94 GHz, and a special optical system for differential measurements of the sky temperature. The *WMAP* satellite produced a detailed map of temperature anisotropies that enabled the determination with high precision of several parameters that specify the basic properties of the universe, and independently confirmed the existence of dark matter and dark energy.

Launch, orbit, and spin. The Planck mission, originally called COBRAS/SAMBA, is a third-generation satellite mission to explore the CMB, following *COBE* and *WMAP*. It was approved by the European Space Agency (ESA) in 1996, and the *Planck* satellite was launched on May 14, 2009, on an Ariane 5 rocket from the Guiana Space Center, at Kourou, French Guiana. The *Planck* satellite was launched together with the *Herschel* telescope. The two satellites separated about 30 min after launch. Early in July 2009, *Planck* reached its operational Lissajous orbit with an average amplitude of 400,000 km (250,000 mi) around the second Lagrange point (L2) of the Sun-Earth system, 1.5×10^6 km (0.9×10^6 mi) away from the Earth. The *Planck* spacecraft spins at 1 revolution per minute and normally operates with its spin axis pointing directly away from the Sun. The line of sight of the telescope is positioned at an angle of 85° to the spin axis, and the instruments scan a circular sector of the celestial sphere with a radius of 85° once per spacecraft revolution. As *Planck* orbits L2, it makes one revolution around the Sun per year.

Spacecraft design. The main objective of the Planck mission is to measure the very small temperature anisotropies of the CMB. To reach the required level of angular resolution and sensitivity, the *Planck* satellite has been specially designed. The optical design of *Planck* is of the Gregorian type, with a 1.5-m (59-in) primary and smaller secondary mirrors. They collect the ambient microwave radiation and direct it to the focal plane of the instrument (**Fig. 1**).

Detectors. The received microwave signal is, however, contaminated by foreground emissions of gas and dust in the Milky Way and all other galaxies and clusters of galaxies. To identify and properly subtract foreground radiation, *Planck* is equipped with two sets of detectors that survey the sky in nine frequencies covering the frequency range from 30 to 857 GHz. The Low Frequency Instrument (LFI) is composed of 22 radiometers fed by corrugated horns and special transducers to separate the two orthogonal linear polarizations. They operate at three frequency bands centered at 30, 44, and 70 GHz. The High Frequency Instrument (HFI) is composed of 52 bolometers that operate at six frequency bands centered at 100, 143, 217, 353, 545, and 857 GHZ. Of these bolometers, 20 are sensitive to total power, and the remaining 32 are polarization-sensitive bolometers, arranged in orthogonally oriented pairs.

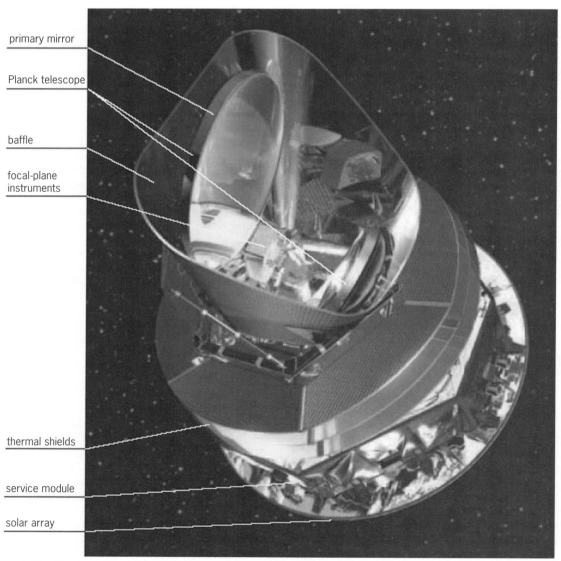

primary mirror

Planck telescope

baffle

focal-plane instruments

thermal shields

service module

solar array

Fig. 1. The *Planck* satellite and its main elements. (*Courtesy of ESA, AOES Medialab*)

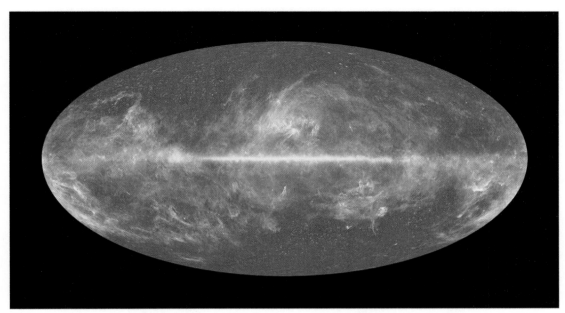

Fig. 2. The multifrequency all-sky image of the microwave sky prepared using data from *Planck*, covering the electromagnetic spectrum from 30 to 857 GHz. (*Copyright © ESA, HFI, and LFI consortia, July 2010*)

Cooling system. To measure the temperature variations of the CMB with a sensitivity of $\Delta T/T \sim 2 \times 10^{-6}$ and an angular resolution of 5 arcminutes, the LFI and HFI detectors need to be cooled to cryogenic temperatures; the LFI detectors require an operational temperature of 20 K, while the HFI detectors need to be cooled down to 0.1 K. These operational temperatures are achieved through a cooling chain that uses several temperature steps involving a combination of passive cooling and a sophisticated active cooling system. The key elements of the *Planck* spacecraft's passive cooling system are the three V-groove thermal shields and the telescope baffle. The active cooling is done in three steps: a closed-cycle hydrogen sorption cooler cools the HFI to 18 K, a Joule-Thomson closed-cycle system with helium-4 (^{4}He) as the working medium cools the HFI focal plane unit to about 4 K, and the final and coldest stage of the active cryogenic cooling chain is the dilution cooler that cools the HFI detectors to 0.1 K. The working principle of the 0.1-K cooler is based on unusual properties of the helium-3/helium-4 (^{3}He/^{4}He) mixture at a temperature below 1 K. The 0.1-K cooler is an open system—at the end of the cooling process, the gas mixture is vented into space.

Observations and results. After the testing and calibration of all the instruments on board and of the pointing system, *Planck* began continuously scanning the sky on August 13, 2009. On January 14, 2012, the HFI instrument stopped collecting data because the detector had run out of coolant, ending its ability to detect CMB photons. The LFI instruments were to operate until the end of *Planck*'s mission, which was set for late September 2013.

Map of the microwave sky. The Planck Consortium delivered the first map of the microwave sky soon after performing the first full scan of the sky (**Fig. 2**). The disk of our galaxy is the dominant object, immersed in giant streams of cold dust at only about 12 degrees above absolute zero and extending far above and below the Milky Way. The streams have a filamentary structure breaking into dense clumps of matter that have not been seen before. *Planck* mapped the Orion and Perseus regions very precisely, revealing many glowing structures of dust and gas where new stars are forming.

First scientific results. In January 2011, the Planck Collaboration released the first scientific results of *Planck*'s mission. *Planck* has discovered a new class of galaxies that are very distant, very cold, shrouded in dust, and forming stars at rates that are 10–1000 times higher than in nearby galaxies. Early in the 1970s, R. Sunyaev and Ya. B. Zeldovich predicted that the CMB photons will be scattered by hot gas that exists in the central parts of clusters of galaxies, shifting their energy distribution. Searching for such distortions of the CMB spectrum, *Planck* discovered 189 clusters of galaxies, including 20 that had not been known before. The very sensitive LFI and HFI instruments detected and cataloged several thousand previously unknown compact cold objects. Data collected by *Planck* instruments helped to solve the puzzle of anomalous microwave emission that is emerging from dust-dominated regions of the Milky Way. It turned out that this radiation is produced by nanoscale dust particles that rotate up to 10^{10} times per second.

Diffuse emission and carbon-monoxide distribution. A year later, the Planck Consortium presented two maps revealing a mysterious diffuse emission from the central region of the Milky Way and the first all-sky distribution of carbon monoxide. The diffuse emission is synchrotron-like, but with a distinctly different

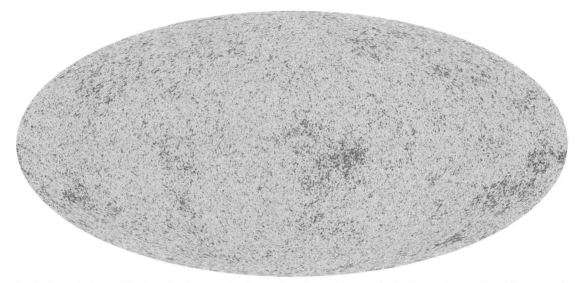

Fig. 3. The anisotropy of the cosmic microwave background as observed by *Planck*. The blue regions on this picture are slightly colder than the orange ones; their temperature difference is about 10 microkelvins (μK). This picture also shows the distribution of matter in the universe 380,000 years after the big bang. The blue regions are slightly denser than the orange ones; the relative difference is of the order of 10^{-5}. (*Copyright © ESA and Planck Collaboration*)

characteristic: its intensity does not decline fast enough with increasing frequency. The distribution of carbon monoxide is strongly linked with the distribution of molecular hydrogen, which is otherwise difficult to detect.

Cosmological data. On March 21, 2013, the Planck Consortium released the first set of cosmological data. The final map of the CMB anisotropies is shown in **Fig. 3**. From this map, it was possible to derive the basic parameters that characterize the universe. *Planck* confirmed with high precision that the universe is flat and that it is composed of standard (baryonic) matter, dark matter, and dark energy. In comparison with previous measurements, *Planck* is seeing more standard matter and more dark matter, but less dark energy (**Fig. 4**). Accord-

ing to *Planck*, the universe is expanding slightly more slowly, with a Hubble constant, $H_0 = 67.3 \pm 1.2$ km/s/Mpc, that is noticeably less than previous astronomical measurements, translating into a slightly older universe with an age of $\tau = 13.81 \pm 0.05$ billion years. The observed statistical characteristics of CMB anisotropies are fully consistent with predictions of a simple inflationary model that assumes the adiabatic and Gaussian character of primordial density fluctuations with a power-law spectrum with spectral index $n_s = 0.9616 \pm 0.0094$. This means that the amplitude of a density perturbation is proportional to the linear size of the perturbation to the power $-n_s$. The *Planck* satellite observed for the first time effects of gravitational lensing of the CMB photons on elements of the large-scale structure,

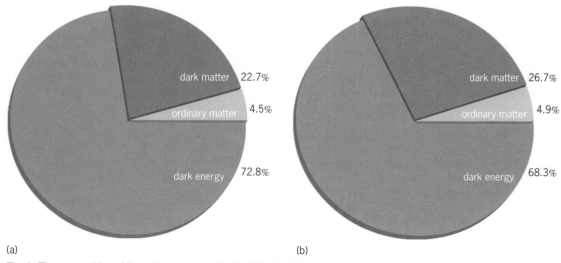

(a)   (b)

Fig. 4. The composition of the universe as revealed by *Planck*. (*a*) Before Planck. (*b*) After Planck. (*Copyright © ESA and Planck Collaboration*)

including the Sunyaev-Zeldovich clusters of galaxies. In addition to being consistent with the predictions of a simple inflationary model, the properties of the large-scale structure are consistent with the existence of only the three known types of neutrinos. *Planck* was able to detect polarization on small angular scales. The observed level of polarization is consistent with the predictions of a simple model of inflation. Quite surprisingly, the observed properties of CMB anisotropies derived from *Planck*'s data are fully consistent with a six-parameter lambda cold-dark matter (ΛCDM) cosmological model. The full set of cosmological data, including polarization, will be released by the Planck Consortium in 2014.

For background information, *see* BIG BANG THEORY; BOLOMETER; COSMIC BACKGROUND RADIATION; COSMOLOGY; CRYOGENICS; DARK ENERGY; DARK MATTER; GALAXY, EXTERNAL; GRAVITATIONAL LENS; HEAT RADIATION; HUBBLE CONSTANT; INFLATIONARY UNIVERSE COSMOLOGY; INTERSTELLAR MATTER; MILKY WAY GALAXY; NEUTRINO; SPACE PROBE; TELESCOPE; WILKINSON MICROWAVE ANISOTROPY PROBE in the McGraw-Hill Encyclopedia of Science & Technology.   Marek Demianski

Bibliography. J. Boslough and J. Mather, *The Very First Light: The True Inside Story of the Scientific Journey Back to the Dawn of the Universe*, rev. and updated, Basic Books, New York, 2008; A. Liddle, *An Introduction to Modern Cosmology*, Wiley, Chichester, UK, 2003; P. J. E. Peebles, L. A. Page, Jr., and R. B. Partridge, *Finding the Big Bang*, Cambridge University Press, Cambridge, UK, 2009; G. Smoot and K. Davidson, *Wrinkles in Time: Witness to the Birth of the Universe*, Harper Perennial, New York, 2007.

Plasmonics

Plasmonics, the study of optical resonance in metallic nanostructures, was unknowingly used hundreds of years ago by alchemists and glassmakers to make stained-glass windows and colorful goblets that incorporated various small metallic particles into the glass. The various colors exhibited in the glass matrix are the result of the nanometallic particles in the glass scattering different wavelengths of light. How the light is scattered depends on the size and shape of the particles because of the plasmonic resonance of a metal, which is generated by the collective movement of free electrons in response to incident light waves. One form of the excited plasmons, called the localized surface plasmon resonance, depends strongly on the nanoscale size, shape, and specific metal material. A consequence of this resonance is that the local electric field is enhanced by several orders of magnitude compared to the electric field associated with the incident optical field. Another form of the plasmonic resonance is generated at the surface of a metallic film: The excited collective oscillations of the free electrons follow the momentum of the incident wave traveling on the metallic surface, called the propagating surface plasmon resonance.

Plasmonics has great potential for applications in a variety of fields, including (1) healthcare, where the metallic nanoparticles can be used as a scattering label for cancer detection or for monitoring the protein-protein interaction on metallic films, and (2) nanophotonics and nano-optics, where plasmons can be used to confine light down to the nanometer scale to enhance its interaction cross section with adjacent quantum nanostructures, nanoparticles, and molecules. Two applications will be discussed to show the important role of plasmonics: the development of a nanosensor with the potential for single-molecule detection, and a nanolaser whose emitting wavelength is larger than the dimensions of the laser itself in all three dimensions, with the potential for superresolution imaging and displays.

Nanosensor. Identifying a single molecule, or, more precisely, a very low concentration of molecules, without labeling has been an ultimate goal in biological detection from pathogen monitoring to early cancer diagnosis. Labeling with fluorescent tags has traditionally been used to signal the presence of minute amounts of a specific protein effectively. Fluorescence occurs when light is absorbed from an external excitation source by a fluorescent tag called a fluorophore and subsequently emitted. The period of excitation and emission lasts until the excitation source (typically a laser) is turned off or the fluorophore is consumed. While a concentration of tens of picograms per milliliter ($1\ \text{pg/ml} = 10^{-12}\ \text{g/ml}$) of protein can be detected with the labeling technique, fluorescent tags present their own challenges, including potential interference with the biological events under investigation that may cause erroneous or false-positive signals, as well as photobleaching. Moreover, finding a biomolecule that can attach the fluorescent tag while keeping strong binding strength with the targeted protein is arduous. Meanwhile, the fluorescence from a single molecule remains undetectable. Amplification approaches like concentration enrichment and the polymerase chain reaction (PCR) have been explored to increase the fluorescent signals. In concentration enrichment, special approaches are used to accumulate the biomolecules in a certain area. In PCR, a single piece of deoxyribonucleic acid (DNA) can be amplified across several orders of magnitude, generating thousands to millions of copies of a particular DNA sequence to make the attached fluorescent tags detectable. However, the mechanical or chemical applications involved in these two approaches are often time-consuming and species-limited. Recent progress in plasmonics shows that highly sensitive, label-free techniques that detect biomolecules without exogenous fluorescent tags are feasible.

The unique capability of plasmonics for field localization and enhancement has made a profound contribution to Raman spectroscopy. A Raman spectrum is a measurement of the inelastic scattering

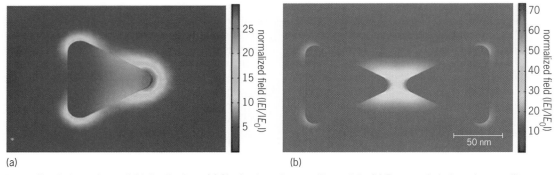

Fig. 1. Simulations of near-field distributions. (*a*) Single triangular metallic particle. (*b*) Two coupled triangular metallic particles, showing more than twice the maximal local field compared to the single particle. The color bars show the field normalized to the incidence, that is, the ratio of the near-field distribution |*E*| to the incident electric field |E_0|.

of monochromatic laser light interacting with a molecule (termed Raman scattering). The laser light interacts with the molecular vibrations and rotations, resulting in a shift of the energy of the scattered photons. This shift in energy gives information about the signatures of the molecule, and thus can be used for its label-free identification. The drawback is that the Raman scattering cross sections of molecules are very small (far smaller than fluorescence cross sections), making the Raman scattering approach impractical for low-concentration detection. However, it was found that the Raman signal increases significantly when the molecules are placed either on a roughened metallic film or on nanoparticles. The increase in the Raman signal on metallic surfaces occurs because of an enhancement and localization of the electric field provided by plasmonic resonances. When the incident light strikes the metallic surface, the surface plasmons are excited, resulting in an enhanced local electric field, which in turn boosts the interaction cross section and the Raman scattering signal of the interrogated molecules. Since the enhancement of the surface-enhanced Raman scattering (SERS) signal by the electromagnetic effect is approximately proportional to the fourth power of the localized electric field, various methods for maximizing the optical field localization on the nanometer scale to allow the detection of molecules at low concentration have been investigated.

Nanoparticles were first used as SERS substrates, but they were soon replaced by nanoparticle assemblies that offered a higher local field at the interstitial sites because of coupling between particles. However, the random locations of the hot spots made the substrate unsuitable for quantitative analysis of the species. Other approaches were also pursued: electron beam lithography and focused ion beams were employed to fabricate finely defined nanostructures, such as bowtie structures, that could achieve high local fields at their tips (**Fig. 1**). Subsequently, researchers studied the resonant coupling of nanocrescents or half-shell structures, and of the ring and disk structure (where coupled multiple dipoles are involved). It was shown in two-dimensional (2D) nanocrescents that decreasing the tip distance will

localize the field to a smaller volume and therefore increase the value of its complex amplitude.

There is also a new engineered 3D version of the nanocrescent, the "nanotorch" structure, which yields smaller tip-to-tip spacing (smaller rim diameter) with a higher local field. Furthermore, to avoid randomly oriented nanocrescent structures, a fabrication method was demonstrated in which the nanotorches are upright on their carrier substrate with controllable rim diameter and deterministic orientation (**Fig. 2**). The simulated local electric field distribution in Fig. 2 shows that the maximal field is located at the edges of the nanotorch. The coupling effectiveness in the nanotorch particles is shown in the Raman spectra in **Fig. 3**. When the 260-nm opening of the nanotorch shrinks to 140 nm, the measured Raman intensity increases by 6 times, with an average enhancement factor of 1.6×10^6 (compared to the bulk Raman signal without any metal structures). It is well known that the different Raman modes, that is, peaks, have different Raman cross sections and enhancement factors when the metal is used. In some cases, differences of up to two orders of magnitude could be seen. Figure 3*a* clearly shows that SERS enhancement factors are unequal for the different Raman modes.

The most important features of this method are the individual nanostructure detections with tens of nanometers of detection area and the high reproducibility among different nanotorch particles on the same chip (Fig. 3*b*). These features enable the spatial resolution of practical biodetection to shrink from the current state of the art of tens of micrometers to tens of nanometers, greatly affecting applications of single-molecule (that is, low-concentration) detection.

Nanolaser. Plasmonics also can be used to make ultracompact lasers toward the nanometer scale, that is, smaller than their emission wavelengths. The small size and extremely low power of these nanolasers could make them very useful components for future optical circuits packed onto tiny computer chips. Other applications for nanolasers could include tiny biochemical sensors or high-resolution imaging and displays. Recent efforts have been directed at reducing the size of lasers below

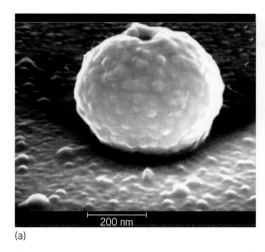

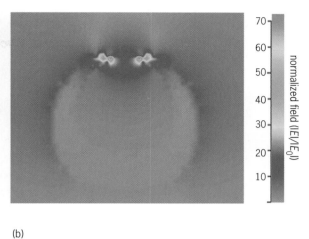

(a)

(b)

Fig. 2. Nanotorch. (*a*) Scanning electron micrograph (SEM). (*b*) 3D electric field distribution. The color bar shows the field normalized to the incidence, that is, the ratio of the near-field distribution |*E*| to the incident electric field |*E*₀|. (*From H. M. Chen et al., Controllable orientation of nanotorch structures leading to uniform surface enhanced Raman scattering detection, Nanoscale 4:7664–7669, 2012, DOI:10.1039/c2nr32305b)*

their emission wavelength in some or all dimensions using surface plasmons, nanowires, metallic cavities, and metallo-dielectric cavities. Most recently, by utilizing a plasmonic coaxial nanoresonator, the smallest telecommunication-frequency laser to date was demonstrated.

All lasers require a certain amount of "pump power" from an outside source to begin emitting a coherent beam of light or "lasing." A laser's threshold is the point where this coherent output is greater than any spontaneous emission produced. The smaller a laser is, the greater is the pump power needed to reach the point of lasing. To overcome this issue, a new design was established for nanolasers that uses quantum electrodynamics (QED) effects in coaxial nanocavities to alleviate the threshold constraint. Like a coaxial cable hooked up to a television receiver (only at a much smaller scale), the laser cavity consists of a metal rod enclosed by a ring of metal-coated quantum wells of semiconductor material. By designing a plasmonic coaxial resonator that supports the cutoff-free transverse electromagnetic mode, subwavelength-size nanocavities with modes far smaller than the operating wavelength are achieved. When fully exploited, this approach can completely eliminate the threshold constraint by reaching so-called thresholdless operation, which occurs when every photon emitted by the gain medium is funneled into the lasing mode. The most remarkable conclusion is that nanocoaxial resonators can support a single electromagnetic mode with arbitrarily small volume when the resonator size becomes deeply subwavelength. With such a single-mode nanoresonator, thresholdless narrowband emission with a broadband semiconductor gain medium was demonstrated, realizing the smallest telecommunication- frequency source to date.

Figure 4 shows a schematic diagram of the cavity design and a scanning electron microscope (SEM) image of a fabricated device. At the heart of the cavity lies a coaxial waveguide that supports

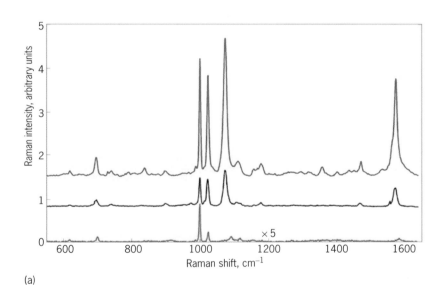

(a)

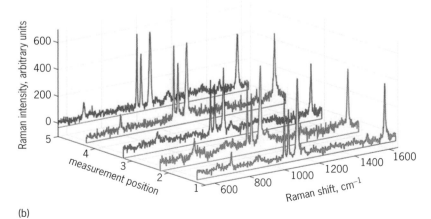

(b)

Fig. 3. Raman spectra of benzenethiol. (*a*) Spectra for a 140-nm opening nanotorch (top), for a 260-nm opening nanotorch (middle), and without metallic structures (bottom; the signal is amplified 5 times for visualization). (*b*) Uniformity plot of 5 nanotorches at different locations within the same chip. *(From H. M. Chen et al., Controllable orientation of nanotorch structures leading to uniform surface enhanced Raman scattering detection, Nanoscale 4:7664–7669, 2012, DOI:10.1039/c2nr32305b)*

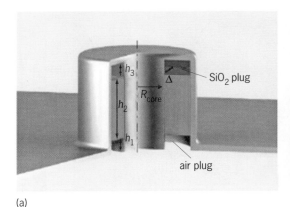

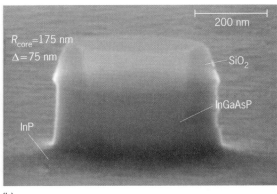

(a)

(b)

Fig. 4. Nanoscale coaxial laser cavity. (a) Schematic of a coaxial laser cavity that has an inner core radius of $R_{core} = 175$ nm; a gain-medium ring with a thickness of $\Delta = 75$ nm; a lower plug height of $h_1 = 20$ nm; a quantum-wells height of 200 nm covered by a 10-nm overlayer of indium phosphide (InP), resulting in a total gain-medium height of $h_2 = 210$ nm; and an upper plug height of $h_3 = 30$ nm. **(b)** Scanning electron microscope (SEM) image of the constituent rings. A side view of the rings comprising the coaxial structures is seen. The rings consist of silicon dioxide (SiO_2) on top and a quantum-well gain region underneath. (*From M. Khajavikhan et al., Thresholdless nanoscale coaxial lasers, Nature 482:204–207, 2012, DOI:10.1038/nature10840*)

plasmonic modes and is composed of a metallic rod enclosed by a metal-coated semiconductor ring. The thin layer of low-index silicon dioxide (SiO_2 plug) at the top of the device is to prevent the formation of undesirable surface plasmonic modes at the top interface between the metal and the gain medium. Desirable surface plasmonic modes, on the other hand, exist at the interface between the metal sidewalls and the semiconductor. To reduce the lasing threshold, the coaxial structures are designed

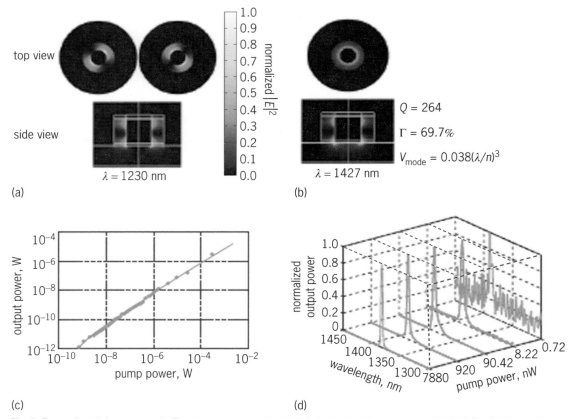

(a)

(b)

(c)

(d)

Fig. 5. Properties of the structure in Fig. 4 at a temperature of 4.5 K: simulation of electromagnetic field distribution and thresholdless lasing behavior. (a) Field distribution at a wavelength of 1230 nm and **(b)** a wavelength of 1427 nm. **Q** stands for quality factor; Γ factor gives the extent of energy confinement to the semiconductor region; V_{mode} is the effective modal volume (λ = wavelength, n = refractive index). The electric field intensities are normalized to their maximums. **(c)** Light-light curve. **(d)** Spectral evolution; the output powers are normalized to their maximums. (*From M. Khajavikhan et al., Thresholdless nanoscale coaxial lasers, Nature, 482:204–207, 2012, DOI:10.1038/nature10840*)

to maximize the benefits from the modification of the spontaneous emission resulting from the cavity QED effects. Because of their small size, the number of resonant modes of nanocoaxial cavities is sparse, which is a key requirement for obtaining high spontaneous emission coupling into the lasing mode of the resonator. The resonant modes can be further modified by tailoring the geometry, that is, the radius of the core, the width of the ring, and the heights of the gain medium and the low-index dielectric plugs. The number of modes supported by the resonator that can participate in the lasing process is ultimately limited to those that occur at frequencies within the semiconductor gain bandwidth. **Figure 5** shows the electromagnetic field distribution of the cavity modes and the thresholdless lasing behavior at a temperature of 4.5 K.

The implication of this work is threefold. First, nanoscale coaxial lasers have a great potential for future nanophotonic circuits on a chip. Second, the thresholdless operation and scalability provide the first systematic approach toward the realization of QED effects, that is, the realization of the interaction between light and matter in subwavelength resonant structures, specifically the realization of quantum metamaterials, in which the dielectric constant of a medium is tailored by using periodic artificial electromagnetic materials to enhance the light-matter interaction. Finally, this new family of resonators paves the way for in-depth study of the unexplored physics of the gain-resonator–plasmonic-field interaction.

The recent progress in the field of plasmonics presented here shows its most promising applications. There are other potential applications of plasmonics, including nanolithography, super-lens imaging, negative-index materials, and cloaking. Recent work on plasmonics has brought to light new aspects of various applications whose concepts are derived from the ancient use of metals. The combination of metals and dielectric materials on the nanometer scale leads to many novel properties that do not exist in nature. In the near future, we will witness the impact of these techniques on applications such as healthcare, communications and computing, super-resolution imaging, displays, and other technologies.

For background information *see* BIOSENSOR; COAXIAL CABLE; FLUORESCENCE; LASER; NANOPARTICLES; NANOSTRUCTURE; NEGATIVE REFRACTION; PLASMON; POLYMERASE CHAIN REACTION (PCR); QUANTUM ELECTRODYNAMICS; RAMAN EFFECT; WAVEGUIDE in the McGraw-Hill Encyclopedia of Science & Technology.

Lin Pang; Yeshaiahu S. Fainman

Bibliography. M. P. Nezhad et al., Room-temperature subwavelength metallo-dielectric lasers, *Nat. Photon.*, 4:395–399, 2010, DOI:10.1038/nphoton.2010.88; L. Pang et al., Spectral sensitivity of two-dimensional nanohole array surface plasmon polariton resonance sensor, *Appl. Phys. Lett.*, 91:123112 (3 pp.), 2007, DOI:10.1063/1.2789181; H. Raether, *Surface Plasmons on Smooth and Rough Surfaces and on Gratings*, Springer, Berlin, 1988; K. A. Tetz et al., Excitation and direct imaging of surface plasmon polariton modes in a two-dimensional grating, *Appl. Phys. Lett.*, 86:111110 (3 pp.), 2005, DOI:10.1063/1.1883334.

Postharvest treatments of fruit

Successful fruit storage is based on the application of suitable technologies that reduce metabolic rates (thereby avoiding changes in color, composition, texture, flavor, and nutritional status), reduce water loss (which otherwise would result in loss of marketable weight, shriveling, softening, and loss of crispness and nutrition), minimize bruising (friction damage and other mechanical injuries), and prevent the development of physiological and pathological disorders. There have been two recent advances that improve fruit quality maintenance after harvest. The first advance is the further development of dynamic controlled atmosphere (DCA) storage methodologies, based on the measurement of the physiological and metabolic responses of fruit to low oxygen. The second advance is the discovery and commercialization of the inhibitor of ethylene action, namely 1-methylcyclopropene (1-MCP). Understanding these technologies requires comprehension of the biology of the ripening and senescence of fruit while it is in storage.

Fruit can be classified as climacteric or nonclimacteric, with many popular fruits belonging to each category (**Table 1**). The ripening of climacteric fruit is associated with an increase in respiration coinciding with major events such as color change, softening, and the production of aroma volatiles. The respiratory climacteric stage is mediated by the onset of production of the plant hormone ethylene, which is necessary for normal ripening processes to occur. Increased ethylene production is not required for the ripening of nonclimacteric fruit. Both climacteric and nonclimacteric fruit can be affected by exposure to exogenous (outside) sources of ethylene (ethylene-producing fruits and vegetables, damaged commodities, and contamination).

TABLE 1. Examples of fruits (including vegetable fruits) classified according to respiratory behavior during ripening

Climacteric	Nonclimacteric
Apple	Blackberry
Apricot	Cherry
Blueberry	Cranberry
Muskmelon	Cucumber
Nectarine	Eggplant
Peach	Grape
Pear	Pea
Plum	Pepper
Tomato	Raspberry
	Strawberry
	Summer squash
	Watermelon

TABLE 2. Summary of recommended controlled atmosphere (CA) storage conditions for selected fruit types

Fruit type	Temperature range, °C	CA	
		O₂, %	CO₂, %
Apple	0–5	1–2	0–3
Apricot	0–5	2–3	2–3
Avocado	5–13	2–5	3–10
Banana	12–16	2–5	2–5
Blackberry	0–5	5–10	15–20
Blueberry	0–5	2–5	12–20
Cherimoya and atemoya	8–15	3–5	5–10
Cherry, sweet	0–5	3–10	10–15
Cranberry	2–5	1–2	0–5
Durian	12–20	3–5	5–15
Fig	0–5	5–10	15–20
Grape	0–5	2–5 or 5–10	1–3 or 10–15
Grapefruit	10–15	3–10	5–10
Kiwifruit	0–5	1–2	3–5
Lemon	10–15	5–10	0–10
Lime	10–15	5–10	0–10
Lychee (litchi)	5–12	3–5	3–5
Mango	10–15	3–7	5–8
Nectarine	0–5	1–2 or 4–6	3–5 or 15–17
Nuts and dried fruits	0–10	0–1	0–100
Olive	5–10	2–3	0–1
Orange	5–10	5–10	0–5
Papaya	10–15	2–5	5–8
Peach, clingstone	0–5	1–2	3–5
Peach, freestone	0–5	1–2 or 4–6	3–5 or 15–17
Pear, Asian	0–5	2–4	0–3
Pear, European	0–5	1–3	0–3
Persimmon	0–5	3–5	5–8
Pineapple	8–13	2–5	5–10
Plum	0–5	1–2	0–5
Pomegranate	5–10	3–5	5–10
Rambutan	8–15	3–5	7–12
Raspberry	0–5	5–10	15–20
Strawberry	0–5	5–10	15–20
Sweetsop (custard apple)	12–20	3–5	5–10

Exposure of unripe climacteric fruit to ethylene can cause earlier-than-desirable ripening, although ethylene treatment is used routinely to initiate the ripening of some fruits before their distribution to retail markets (for example, bananas and tomatoes). Exposure of nonclimacteric fruits increases their respiration rates, resulting in more rapid depletion of energy reserves and increased water loss.

Controlled atmosphere storage. Controlled atmosphere (CA) storage involves decreasing oxygen concentrations and increasing carbon dioxide concentrations in storage. This decreases the respiration rate of the fruit and inhibits ethylene production and action.

Each fruit type has a safe concentration range of oxygen and carbon dioxide (based on the tolerance of each fruit for these gases) [**Table 2**], and these concentrations may be affected by growing region and cultivar. The benefits of CA storage include slower ripening and senescence (the processes that lead to ripening), alleviation of certain physiological disorders (for example, chilling injury of avocado and superficial scald of apples), and direct or indirect effects of postharvest pathogens on development. Fruit can be damaged if concentrations of oxygen are too low or if concentrations of carbon dioxide are too high. CA-related injuries include irregular ripening, failure to ripen, initia-

tion and aggravation of certain physiological disorders, development of off-flavors and off-odors, and increased susceptibility to decay as a result of injury.

Apples are the major fruit type using CA storage. Other fruits that use CA storage include pears, kiwifruit, peaches, persimmons, and pomegranates. CA storage has limited use because it requires significant capital investment. For other products, structures must be airtight and refrigerated, with precise temperature control and equipment to modify the room atmosphere. The volume of these storage rooms is also large to maximize the value of the equipment. Therefore, the return on investment is usually limited to long-lived commodities that are stored for months (not days or weeks). Tent CA storage systems with lower-cost oxygen and carbon dioxide control monitors are now available, and they have been used for local-market strawberries.

The economic importance and long-term storage potential of apples have driven the development of new CA technologies. In standard CA storage, the concentrations of oxygen and carbon dioxide are maintained in the 2–3% range. However, this has increasingly been replaced by ultralow oxygen (ULO) storage. Some cultivars in certain growing regions can be routinely stored in low oxygen concentrations of 1–1.5% provided that high-quality storage

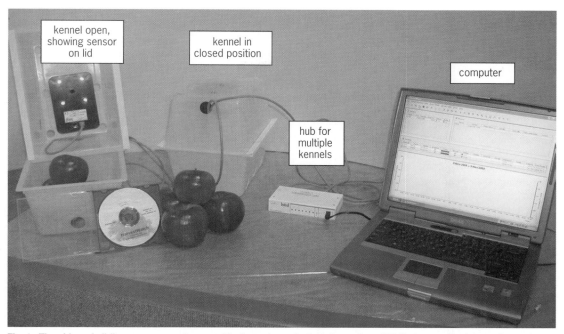

Fig. 1. The chlorophyll fluorescence system used in dynamic controlled atmosphere (DCA) storage. Each kennel contains approximately six fruits and is placed inside the DCA storeroom. The number of kennels in each DCA store is operator-determined. (*Photo courtesy of and reproduced with permission from Agriculture and Agri-Food Canada, copyright © Her Majesty the Queen in Right of Canada*)

rooms and computerized monitoring and maintenance of gas levels are available.

Recently, DCA storage, in which storage oxygen is lowered to concentrations that are close to the anaerobic compensation point where fermentation occurs, has been developed. The metabolism of the fruit in response to low oxygen concentrations is monitored, and the concentrations are changed as necessary to avoid fermentation. Therefore, instead of maintaining safe, static, but above-optimal oxygen concentrations around the fruit, it is possible to adjust the oxygen concentration continuously.

The first DCA system to be patented and developed on a commercial scale is HarvestWatch™. This system uses DCA–chlorophyll fluorescence (DCA-CF) to sense fluorescence changes in real time to assess whether the fruit is under stress from low oxygen (or high carbon dioxide). Containers of fruit are fitted with a sensor and a fluorescence interactive response monitor (FIRM) that can detect changes in fluorescence signals (**Fig. 1**). The storage operator makes appropriate changes to the oxygen concentration based on the fluorescence signals.

Figure 2 illustrates the change in the fluorescence signal (Fα) over time as the oxygen concentration around a fruit is lowered. The signal increases when the concentration reaches a critical point. The oxygen concentration is then increased to safe levels, and the fluorescence signal decreases.

The dynamic control system (DCS) is based on fruit ethanol accumulation and on respiratory changes (for example, the respiratory quotient, which represents the ratio of oxygen uptake to carbon dioxide production by the fruit). Airtight rooms

are required, along with the appropriate CA technology and expertise. It is also assumed that the fruits are of high quality and that the monitored fruits are representative of the entire storage room.

1-Methylcyclopropene. 1-Methylcyclopropene (1-MCP) belongs to a class of compounds known as cyclopropenes. In the 1990s, the discovery of

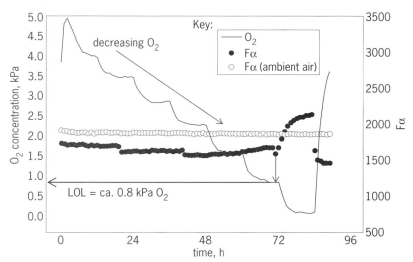

Fig. 2. An example of the chlorophyll fluorescence (CF)–based dynamic controlled atmosphere (DCA) storage technique. The fruit-derived CF signal (Fα) is used to identify the low oxygen limit (LOL) of the fruit (apples) in a kennel. The O_2 concentration is gradually decreased over time until the Fα sharply increases at approximately 72 h, indicating the LOL of the fruit. By extrapolation down to the O_2 trace and then to the left-hand y-axis, the LOL for this kennel is approximately 0.8 kPa O_2. With the addition of 0.2 as a safety margin, the recommended DCA setting would be 1.0 kPa O_2. (*Figure courtesy of and reproduced with permission from Agriculture and Agri-Food Canada, copyright © Her Majesty the Queen in Right of Canada*)

cyclopropenes as inhibitors of ethylene perception represented a major breakthrough for controlling ethylene responses in horticultural products. Ethylene inhibition makes it possible to control ripening and senescence, especially in climacteric fruit.

1-MCP was first commercialized by Floralife, Inc. It is unstable in the liquid phase, but it can be stabilized when complexed with α-cyclodextrin. This process made it possible to release 1-MCP from the complex in order to expose it to produce. Floralife, Inc., obtained regulatory approval from the U.S. Environmental Protection Agency (EPA) in 1999 for use on floriculture and ornamental products. The 1-MCP formulation was marketed under the name EthylBloc®. The rights to 1-MCP were subsequently acquired by AgroFresh (formerly a subsidiary of Rohm and Haas and now part of Dow AgroSciences). EPA approval for the use of 1-MCP on edible food products was obtained in 2002. By 2011, regulatory approval had been obtained in more than 40 countries. 1-MCP is registered for use on apples, apricots, Asian pears, avocados, bananas, cherimoyas, cucumbers, dates, guavas, kiwifruit, limes, mangos, melons, nectarines, papayas, peaches, pears, peppers, persimmons, pineapples, plantains, plums, plumcots, squashes, and tomatoes.

1-MCP has been rapidly approved because it is gaseous and easily applied, it leaves no residues in the treated produce, and it is active at very low concentrations. Fruit must be treated in a tightly enclosed area, such as a storage room, greenhouse, trailer, or shipping container.

Many ripening and senescence processes are affected by 1-MCP. Some of the processes that are affected include pigment properties, softening and cell wall metabolism, flavor and aroma properties, and nutritional properties. Both nonclimacteric and climacteric products are affected, but the degree to which they are affected may vary.

Several generalizations can be made about the responses of fruit to 1-MCP:

1. Genotype, cultivar, and maturity effects can be highly variable.

2. Climacteric fruits are affected by 1-MCP treatment, but the capacity to interrupt ripening after it has been initiated varies by fruit and the attributes studied.

3. Nonclimacteric fruits also respond to 1-MCP, providing insights into ethylene-dependent and ethylene-independent events during ripening.

4. Treated fruits are firmer, slower to soften, and slower to change peel color, and they develop proper aroma and flavor. Importantly, when 1-MCP concentrations and exposure periods are appropriate, the final quality of the ripened fruit is similar to that of the untreated product.

5. The effect of 1-MCP on physiological disorders is dependent on the role of ethylene. 1-MCP decreases senescent-related and ethylene-induced disorders (senescent breakdown of apples and water soaking of watermelons). It can increase the susceptibility of apples to CA storage–related disorders (carbon dioxide injury). Some chilling-related disorders (woolliness and internal breakdown of peaches and nectarines, and chilling injury of citrus and bananas) can be increased by inhibition of ethylene production. Other chilling-related disorders are decreased by inhibition of ethylene production (superficial scald of apples and pears, and internal flesh browning of avocados and pineapples).

6. Disease incidence can be increased, decreased, or unaffected by 1-MCP, depending on the product. Results are not always consistent because of the complex interactions of the host, pathogen, and environment.

Outlook. The apple industry has benefited from the use of 1-MCP, and it is used around the world to maintain fruit quality from harvest to the consumer. This success is largely associated with a fruit for which maintenance of at-harvest quality and only minimal softening are desirable. Challenges exist for the use of 1-MCP in fruits that ripen to a melting texture or have major color changes. A failure to ripen normally has been shown in avocados, bananas, pears, and tomatoes when the fruits were treated at an early ripening stage or when the applied 1-MCP concentration was too high. Fruit must ripen uniformly to develop the quality characteristics (texture, flavor, aroma, and color) that the consumer expects. Despite these challenges, the SmartFresh™ commercial formulation of 1-MCP has been used successfully to treat avocados, bananas, melons, pears, persimmons, and tomatoes as a result of a careful attenuation of 1-MCP concentrations and a proper evaluation of ripening stage at harvest.

For background information *see* AGRICULTURAL SCIENCE (PLANT); APPLE; ETHYLENE; ETHYLENE (PLANT PHYSIOLOGY); FOOD MANUFACTURING; FRUIT; FRUIT, TREE; PLANT GROWTH; PLANT HORMONES; PLANT METABOLISM; PLANT PHYSIOLOGY; PLANT RESPIRATION in the McGraw-Hill Encyclopedia of Science & Technology.   Christopher B. Watkins

Bibliography. K. C. Gross, C. Y. Wang, and M. Saltveit, *The Commercial Storage of Fruits, Vegetables, and Florist and Nursery Crops*, Agriculture Handbook 66, U.S. Department of Agriculture, Beltsville, MD, 2004; D. J. Huber, Suppression of ethylene responses through application of 1-methylcyclopropene: A powerful tool for elucidating ripening and senescence mechanisms in climacteric and nonclimacteric fruits and vegetables, *HortScience*, 43:106–111, 2008; R. K. Prange et al., History, current situation and future prospects for dynamic controlled atmosphere (DCA) storage of fruits and vegetables, using chlorophyll fluorescence, *Acta Horticulturae*, in press (http://harvestwatch.net/history.html), 2013; C. B. Watkins, Overview of 1-MCP trials and uses for edible horticultural crops, *HortScience*, 43:86–94, 2008; C. B. Watkins, Postharvest ripening regulation and innovation in storage technology, *ISHS Acta Horticulturae*, 796:51–58, 2008.

Powder mixing

Powder mixing is one of the most important processes in many industries, including pharmaceuticals, food, catalysts, cement, chemicals, cosmetics, energetics, and plastics, to name a few. Surprisingly, powder mixing remains a poorly understood process, and up until very recently, most industries neglected its importance and complexity. In manufacturing processes, this neglect often leads to process and product failures. The goal of a mixing process is to yield a sufficiently homogenous mixture with desired material properties. However, "sufficient" and "desired" depend on the specific industry, the final product, and its applications.

The complexity of the powder mixing process is a result of several factors. First, powders have complex rheological characteristics. Powders can have multiple rheological phases within the same process, and rheological behavior may vary depending on the processing history and environmental

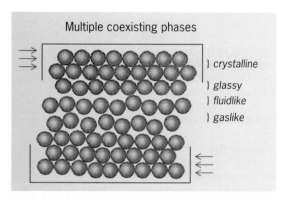

Fig. 1. Coexisting phases in powder flow behavior and mixing. Crystalline (solid), glassy/fluidlike (liquid), and gaslike. [Image from F. J. Muzzio et al., Solids mixing, chap. 15, in E. L. Paul, V. A. Atiemo-Obeng, and S. M. Kresta (eds.), Handbook of Industrial Mixing—Science and Practice, John Wiley & Sons Inc., 2003]

conditions. In fact, powders can behave as solids, liquids, and gases all in one process, depending on the applied stress and the interactions among particles (**Fig. 1**). In many industries, the high blend-uniformity standards required in final products and the desired quality and performance make powder mixing a challenging process.

Most research in powder mixing in the past 20 years has been driven by the pharmaceutical industry and its regulatory agencies. More than 80% of all pharmaceutical products are powder-based. Most pharmaceutical powders are hard-to-mix materials that require careful dosing and control to ensure that a product contains the right amount of drug and that upon administration the drug is delivered at the correct rate and to the right location in the human body. Nevertheless, most advances in understanding pharmaceutical powder mixing apply readily to other powder-based industrial processes.

Mixing mechanisms. Recent powder mixing research has focused on characterizing the mixing and de-mixing mechanisms found in common mixers used in a wide range of industries. Three mechanisms have been proposed for powder mixing: convection, dispersion, and shear. Convective mixing (macro-mixing) occurs when groups of particles are transported from one location to another by the main flow. Diffusive mixing (micro-mixing) refers to the dispersive comingling of particles due to velocity fluctuations. Shear mixing, which is also a micro-mixing effect, is caused by slipping planes within the powder bed, driven by the same external forces that drive convective and dispersive mixing. In most applications, these mechanisms act concurrently and interact in complex ways, and their relative importance is scale-dependent. Thus, the interactions of different mixing mechanisms, along with the complex rheological properties of powders, make powder mixing a difficult process to predict and control.

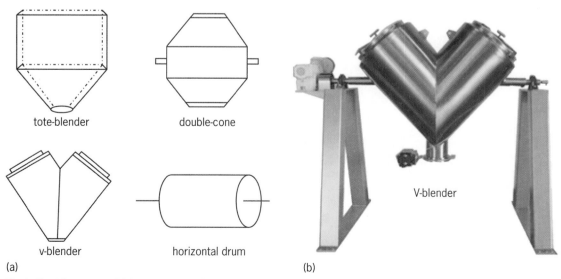

tote-blender

double-cone

v-blender

horizontal drum

V-blender

(a) (b)

Fig. 2. Tumbling mixers. (a) Schematics and (b) actual V-blender setup.

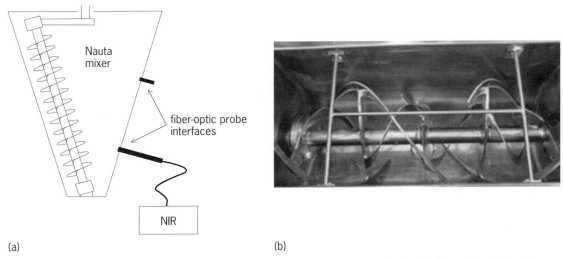

(a)   (b)

Fig. 3. Convective mixers. (a) Schematic of the Nauta mixer with in-line near-infrared (NIR) probe (*image from O. Berntsson et al., Quantitative in-line monitoring of powder blending by near infrared reflection spectroscopy, Powder Technol., 123:185–193, 2002*). (b) Ribbon blender (*image from F. J. Muzzio et al., Evaluating the performance of a ribbon blender, Powder Technol., 186:247–254, 2008*).

Mixing mechanisms have been studied experimentally and numerically for several mixer geometries. Depending on the external force that drives the flow (such as gravity or shear), one mechanism will predominate, but the others will also occur. For illustration purposes, let us consider the most common mixers used in batch mixing applications by the pharmaceutical industry. The most common powder mixers are tumblers (for example, V-blenders, Y-blenders, and double-cones; **Fig. 2**) and convective mixers (for example, ribbon and paddle mixers; **Fig. 3**). Tumbling mixers have fast convection, while dispersion is much slower. To induce greater dispersion in tumbling mixers, asymmetric vessels, internal baffles, and/or rotating impellers are used. Convective mixers (agitated mixers) have faster dispersion due to the use of impellers (mechanical means), but can lead to both high-shear zones and stagnant unmixed areas, which affect the final quality of the mixture. Shearing occurs in all types of mixers, especially in high-shear mixers because of the rapid impeller velocities used.

Batch versus continuous mixing. Broadly speaking, two powder mixing methods are used in many industries: batch and continuous. In batch mixing, a specific total amount of ingredients are mixed in an individual vessel. The ingredients are loaded and agitated for a certain amount of time until a homogeneous mixture is obtained. Afterward, the blend is discharged out of the vessel for the next unit operation (such as granulation, tableting, or packaging). In continuous mixing, the ingredients are fed in a fixed proportion using controlled feeding mechanisms and flow continuously through a device where they are agitated as they flow along. The time the powder spends inside the mixer is variable and is characterized by the residence-time distribution. The average time particles spend in the mixer is given by the ratio of the bulk amount of powder in the mixer, known as the holdup, and the overall feed rate. This quantity is known as the mean residence time. At the outlet, the powder flows continuously into the next unit operation (**Fig. 4**). Understanding feeding mechanisms and their variability is critical to continuous powder mixing.

Most powder mixing processes in the pharmaceutical industry are batch processes. Despite much research and predictive modeling, control and scale-up of batch mixing is still far from being fully implemented, particularly for convective mixers. Continuous mixing has begun to gain popularity because of its several advantages over batch processes, including the opportunity to implement meaningful on-line analytical methods and modeling techniques for

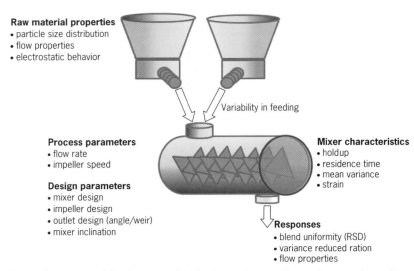

Fig. 4. Continuous mixing: loss-in-weight feeders and convective continuous mixer suite with important process parameters and characterization techniques.

process monitoring and control, leading to finished products with improved quality. Improved continuous mixers, feeding systems, and on-line analytical techniques can greatly improve continuous mixing and processing overall. With continuous mixing, the same equipment used for process development can be used in manufacturing. Therefore, product scale-up can be eliminated or reduced, accelerating the introduction of new products to the market. Additional advantages include significant reductions in the equipment footprint and the ability to integrate continuous mixing with other continuous processes such as roller compaction, extrusion, tableting, or packaging. This can yield greater production efficiency. Overall, these advantages can significantly reduce time and costs during the development and manufacturing of powders.

Material properties of powders. Several powder characterization techniques have been used to understand the material properties of powders and powder mixtures and to predict and control the performance of batch and continuous mixing processes as well as consecutive processing. Common material properties used to characterize blends include particle-size distribution, particle shape (**Fig. 5**), electrostatic behavior, and the hydrophobicity caused by lubricant shearing and smearing dur-

ing mixing, roller compaction, capsule filling, and compression.

Material properties related to powder cohesion include the bulk and tapped density, the angle of repose, the angle of internal friction, compressibility, dilation, flow indices, and flow functions. Importantly, although a mixture might be prepared from the same materials, lot-to-lot differences in raw materials, equipment differences (such as mixer size, mixer type, and total strain), and changes in environmental conditions can affect a blend's final properties.

Powder cohesion has been correlated to the mixing performance of several mixers. In tumbling mixers, for example, large differences are obtained among free-flowing materials and cohesive materials. Free-flowing materials tend to segregate in tumbling mixers (**Fig. 6**), while cohesive materials in low concentration tend to agglomerate (**Fig. 7**). In such cases, a convective mixer might be a better choice for mixing these materials.

Rheological properties of powder mixtures have also been studied and correlated to the performance of consecutive processes such as tableting and capsule filling. In these cases, the variability of tablet or capsule weights is greater for more cohesive powder mixtures. Blend hydrophobicity has been

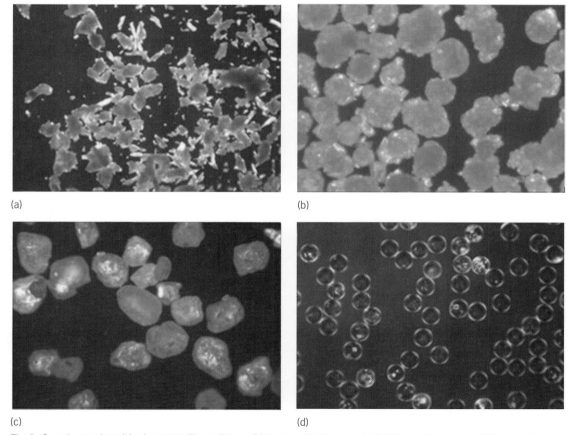

(a) (b) (c) (d)

Fig. 5. Sample powders: (*a*) microcrystalline cellulose; (*b*) lactose; (*c*) white sand; (*d*) 150-μm glass beads. Differences in particle shapes and sizes are commonly encountered in all powdered-based industries.

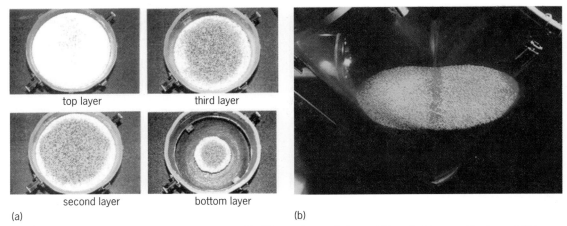

Fig. 6. Blend segregation. Segregation of particles with different sizes and shapes (*a*) in a double-cone blender and (*b*) in a V-blender.

back-correlated to the amount of shear rate and total strain experienced, and forward-correlated to longer disintegration and dissolution times in pharmaceutical tablets.

On-line monitoring. In recent years, companies have made increasing use of on-line blend testing methods, mainly near-infrared (NIR) spectrometers with fiber-optic sensors (Fig. 3). Such approaches are highly desirable because they allow real-time

monitoring of blending performance, thus enabling real-time control of the process. In batch mixing, on-line monitoring techniques monitor the process and determine when a homogeneous mixture has been achieved. In continuous mixing, the powder mixture is monitored at the outlet of the mixer (**Fig. 8**). If fluctuations in concentration and/or blend homogeneity are detected, appropriate actions can be taken to correct the problem. To be able to do this in

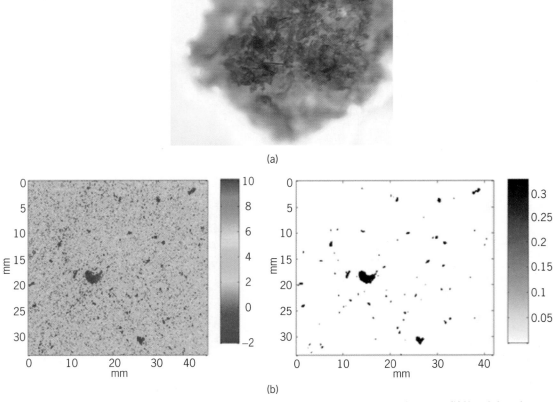

Fig. 7. Drug agglomeration. (*a*) Scanning electron microscope image of acetaminophen agglomerate. (*b*) Near-infrared chemical image of a mixture with acetaminophen. Blue spots on the left show the highest intensity where acetaminophen agglomerates are detected. The dark spots on the right confirm that these are acetaminophen agglomerates.

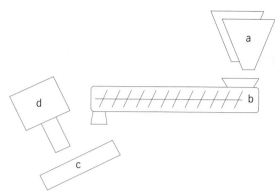

Fig. 8. Continuous mixer with in-line near-infrared (NIR) spectrometer. (*a*) Two powder feeders. (*b*) Continuous blender. (*c*) Metal chute. (*d*) Wireless NIR spectrometer (*image from A. U. Varanase et al., Real-time monitoring of drug concentration in a continuous powder mixing process using NIR spectroscopy, Chem. Eng. Sci., 65:5728–5733, 2010*).

an automated fashion, closed-loop control methodologies must be in place.

Failure modes. Powder mixing processes also have well-defined failure modes. From a product quality perspective, a manufacturing process fails when it generates a product with unacceptably high product performance variability. The definition of appropriate product performance criteria and acceptable variability obviously varies among industries and from product to product, and achieving a meaningful definition is often the first serious challenge in developing a systematic approach for optimizing a blending process. Blending processes fail partly because we understand powders much less than other materials, and partly because blending processes are difficult to characterize. The following is a summary of the different failure modes encountered in powder mixing.

Insufficient mixing time. In a number of cases, the mixing process is stopped before it reaches completion; that is, the blend would have been more homogeneous if the mixing process had been allowed to continue. In spite of efforts to validate blending times, this situation is actually quite common, and is due to two little known facts. First, performance of most blending processes is quite sensitive to the manner in which ingredients are loaded into the blender. In most blenders, mixing across planes of symmetry occurs only by dispersion (a very slow process), and if the blender is loaded asymmetrically, mixing can take much longer than if the blender is loaded symmetrically. Second, mixing performance is also very sensitive to blender fill level. If the volumetric fill level exceeds 70–80% of the total blender volume, mixing becomes very slow. Because of variations in the density of raw materials, fluctuations in blend density can cause differences in fill level that can slow a blending process significantly. Similar problems might be encountered with continuous mixers. The mean residence time might not be sufficient to filter the feeding fluctuations and mix the ingredi-

ents homogeneously. If the holdup (the amount of powder in the continuous mixer at steady-state flow) is low, the ingredients might not experience enough shearing to become homogeneously mixed.

Segregation. When powder flows, free-flowing particles with sizes larger than about 200 μm tend to move individually (in contrast to smaller cohesive particles, which tend to move in associated loose clumps). Moreover, free-flowing particles that have large differences in size tend to follow different paths, often ending in different places (Fig. 6). Thus, in free-flowing blends in which there are large differences in the particle sizes of ingredients (for example, 50% differences in the mass median diameter, d_{50}), ingredients can segregate spontaneously during flow. Such segregation can and does occur in blenders, but it typically becomes much more intense when a blend is discharged from a blender into a receiving container (such as a bin, drum, feed pipe, or large hopper). When such a blend is subsequently compressed into tablets or filled into capsules, large differences in blend composition can often be detected. Continuous mixing and processing can significantly reduce segregation, because only a small amount of powder is flowing at any given time and the powder flows directly to the next continuous processing stage.

Agglomeration. In dry blends that contain a small amount of a critical ingredient (typically less than about 3% by weight), when such ingredients are often present in small particle size (less than 30 μm), agglomeration of the ingredient can occur, often leading to intermittent "superpotency" of the ingredient in both powder samples and in the finished product (Fig. 7). This phenomenon can occur for a number of reasons:

1. The ingredient is highly cohesive, as is the case for micronized materials or for materials that are intensely electrostatic.

2. The material is intensely hydrophilic and is taking moisture from other ingredients or from the environment.

3. The material has high affinity for another minor ingredient with a low melting point (a classic example is a solid lubricant, such as magnesium stearate, used in pharmaceuticals) and is granulating in situ due to the mechanical shear imparted by the blending process.

4. The ingredient was not properly delumped prior to loading it into the blender.

5. The ingredient has a strong tendency to stick to metal and becomes agglomerated as it sticks to blender surfaces for long times.

Sampling issues. The most common tools used to assess powder blend uniformity are thief samplers (**Fig. 9**). These devices have been shown to exhibit many problems, including undersampling and oversampling of certain ingredients, segregation of the blend during sampling, sticking of ingredients to thief surfaces, and inconsistency in sampling location due to inappropriate flow of the blend into thief cavities. These issues, and the fact that usually only

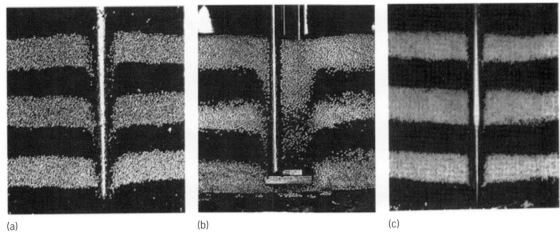

(a) (b) (c)

Fig. 9. Thief sampling probes and common issues in sampling. (*a*) Side-sampling thief probe. (*b*) End-sampling thief probe. (*c*) End-sampling thief probe.

a small number of samples (about 10) are collected, can lead to nonrepresentative results, causing rejection of good blends and acceptance of poor blends.

Sensing issues. On-line sensing methods are widely used, with NIR spectroscopy being the most common. Although such methods are very useful for monitoring processes, several potential problems need to be avoided. Sensors can become coated by powder, introducing measurement error. Calibration models need to be periodically maintained to account for ingredient variability. In some cases, multiple sensors may be needed to ensure that the blender is monitored adequately. In continuous mixing, because the powder is continuously moving (flowing), changes in powder velocity and density need to be included in the model.

Outlook. In recent years, our understanding of powder mixing has grown substantially. Nevertheless, much research is still required. As technology is developed to characterize granular materials, powder mixing can be studied in more detail. A higher level of understanding, the development of predictive models, and the use of in-process monitoring are leading to more controllable and more efficient mixing processes. Although most powders are mixed in batch mode, continuous mixing is gaining in popularity, leading to rapid development of new powder mixing technologies for the first time in several decades.

For background information *see* BULK-HANDLING MACHINES; CHEMICAL ENGINEERING; FLOW OF GRANULAR SOLIDS; INFRARED SPECTROSCOPY; MIXING; PARTICULATES; RHEOLOGY; UNIT OPERATIONS in the McGraw-Hill Encyclopedia of Science & Technology.

Juan G. Osorio; Fernando J. Muzzio

Bibliography. J. Bridgwater, Fundamental powder mixing mechanisms, *Powder Technol.*, 15:215–236, 1976, DOI:10.1016/0032-5910(76)80051-4; R. Hogg, Mixing and segregation in powders: Evaluation, mechanisms and processes, *KONA Powder Particle J.*, 27:3–17, 2009; F. J. Muzzio et al., Solids mixing, in E. L. Paul, V. A. Atiemo-Obeng, and S. M. Kresta (eds.), *Handbook of Industrial Mixing—Science and Practice*, Wiley, New York, pp. 887–985, 2003; L. Pernenkil and C. L. Cooney, A review on the continuous blending of powders, *Chem. Eng. Sci.*, 61:720–742, 2006, DOI:10.1016/j.ces.2005.06.0162006.

Priapulida (penis worms): implications of embryonic development

Priapulida is a phylum of marine worms, often termed penis worms. Priapulids are important animals because of the insights provided by the evolutionary implications of their embryonic development.

Background. Most animals (for example, worms, flies, and mammals) have a bilaterally symmetrical body, with an anterior head and a posterior end, and a dorsal side and a ventral side. Bilaterally symmetrical animals are divided into two main groups, the Deuterostomia and the Protostomia, traditionally based on the fate of the blastopore (an early opening of the embryo associated with the formation of the gut). In the Deuterostomia (literally, second mouth), the blastopore gives rise to the anus of the animal. In the Protostomia (literally, first mouth), the blastopore usually becomes the adult mouth, but in some cases it becomes either the anus or both the mouth and the anus simultaneously. This variability observed within the Protostomia complicates our understanding of the exact fate of the blastopore in the ancestor to all bilaterally symmetrical animals. However, the recent discovery that the blastopore develops into an adult anus in a key group of marine worms, the Priapulida, belonging to the Protostomia, offers illuminating insights into this basic evolutionary question.

Priapulida. Priapulida is a small group (approximately 20 described species) of marine worms that live in the sand or mud bottoms of shallow and deep waters. They vary in size from large species such

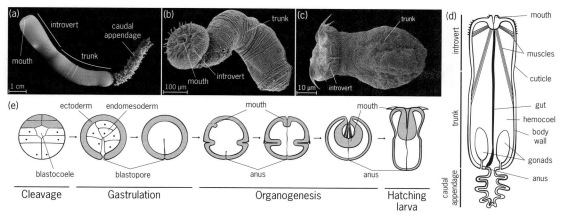

Fig. 1. Morphology and embryonic development of the Priapulida. (*a*, *b*) Adults of *Priapulus caudatus* (*image courtesy of B. C. Vellutini*) and *Meiopriapulus fijiensis* (*image courtesy of M. Sørensen*), respectively. (*c*) A hatching larva of *Priapulus caudatus* (*image courtesy of B. C. Vellutini*). (*d*) A schematic representation of the basic body plan of an adult priapulid. (*e*) A schematic representation of the priapulid embryonic development.

as *Priapulus caudatus* [mature adults are usually 6–8 cm (2.4–3.2 in.) in length] to small priapulids such as *Meiopriapulus fijiensis* [mature adults are 2–3 mm (0.8–1.2 in.) in length] that live between sand grains (**Fig. 1***a*, *b*). Most of the large priapulids inhabit cold waters, often in the Arctic and Antarctic regions, whereas the smallest species seem to exhibit a wider distribution, including tropical waters. The largest priapulid species consume other worms, such as annelids, whereas the small-sized priapulids eat bacteria or other small organisms that live in sediment particles.

Priapulids have a bilaterally symmetrical, cylindrical body divided into a trunk and an anterior introvert, and some species bear one or two caudal appendages of unknown function (respiration and chemoreception have been proposed as possible functions) [Fig. 1*a–c*]. The introvert can retract into the trunk; successive eversions and retractions of this region enable the priapulids to burrow and move within the mud or sand. The body is covered by a chitinous cuticle, is annulated in the trunk, and presents multiple and diverse microscopic scales and spines (scalids) that are used for sensory reception, locomotion, and feeding. As is observed in insects and roundworms, priapulids molt (shed) their cuticle regularly throughout their life as they mature and increase in size. The mouth is located in an anterior terminal position, and the anus is at the posterior end of the trunk, near the base of the caudal appendage (or appendages), if present (Fig. 1*d*). Internally, the priapulid body is a cavity filled with a lymphatic tissue (hemocoel) that acts both as a hydrostatic skeleton (a skeleton composed of fluid that is kept under pressure) and as a system to transport oxygen and nutrients to the rest of the body (Fig. 1*d*). The body wall is composed of an epidermis and the muscular layers. Priapulids usually have separate sexes, and the gonads develop inside the internal cavity, associated with the excretory system, in the posterior region of the trunk (Fig. 1*d*).

The fossil record indicates that priapulids were abundant and important members of the marine fauna in the Cambrian period, which is when most of the present-day animal groups appeared. The fossil record also indicates that living priapulids have changed little from their ancestors, both at the morphological level and at the ecological level. Molecular data further support the idea that priapulids should be considered as evolutionarily conservative animals because their genomic information changes more slowly than the rates observed for other commonly studied animals. In the current animal tree of life (phylogenetic tree), priapulids are close relatives of more diverse and specialized groups, such as arthropods (including spiders, insects, and crustaceans) and nematodes (roundworms). This feature, together with their conserved morphology and molecular repertoire, makes the Priapulida a key group for understanding animal evolution, and in particular bilaterian evolution.

Embryonic development. Despite their relevance for evolutionary studies, the embryonic development of priapulids is poorly known. Although the first report on *P. caudatus* was made in 1949, a more detailed and complete description of the embryonic development of this species was obtained only recently, when new culture methodologies and modern staining techniques were developed. As in all large priapulid species, fertilization is external. In *P. caudatus*, the zygote divides completely to give rise to a number of cells (blastomeres) that are radially arranged and define a small cavity (blastocoele) in the inner part of the embryo (Fig. 1*e*). This early process of cell division, called cleavage, is similar to that observed in other related animals, such as crustaceans, roundworms, and horsehair worms.

Gastrulation is the process in which some blastomeres move inside the embryo to form a more complex, multilayered embryo (Fig. 1*e*). The cells that remain in the surface of the embryo form the ectoderm, which will develop into the epidermis and nervous system. The cells in the interior of the embryo are called the endomesoderm and will later form the digestive system, muscles, excretory system, and gonads. Endomesodermal cells often ingress into the embryo at a discrete point called the blastopore, which usually adopts the form of a hole. In *P. caudatus*, gastrulation occurs at the future posterior pole of the embryo and involves the formation of a blastopore that closes by the end of the process (Fig. 1*e*).

After gastrulation, the different cell types, tissues, and organs of the embryo are formed. During this process, which is called organogenesis, the mouth develops in the ventral side of the embryo as an invagination of ectodermal cells and progressively moves toward a terminal anterior position (Fig. 1*e*). Simultaneously, the region where the blastopore opened develops into the anus. The division of the body into an anterior introvert and a more posterior trunk is established at this point. Late organogenesis is not clearly characterized, but it seems to involve at least the development of the different muscle layers and the maturation of sensory structures (such as the scalids). At the end of the embryogenesis, the introvert region retracts inside the trunk, and eventually the embryo hatches through the eversion of the introvert, which pushes and breaks the eggshell. The hatching larva already shows the basic body organization of an adult priapulid (Fig. 1*c*). Through a series of molts, the hatching larva acquires the definitive cuticular pattern of scalids and matures into an adult priapulid.

Division of the Bilateria into the Protostomia and the Deuterostomia. The division of bilaterally symmetrical animals (Bilateria) into the Protostomia (for ex-ample, flies, flatworms, and snails) and the Deuterostomia (for example, mammals, fish, and sea stars) has major implications for our understanding of animal evolution (**Fig. 2**). In the Deuterostomia (second mouth), the blastopore always becomes the anus, and the mouth forms anew from the surface anterior ectoderm (Fig. 2). The Protostomia (first mouth) was originally defined as the group of animals in which the blastopore gives rise to the mouth. This name has prevailed, despite the fact that there is real variability in the fate of the blastopore within this group and even among related species. The blastopore can become either the mouth or the anus, and therefore defining the ancestral fate of the blastopore in the Protostomia is complex (Fig. 2). Nevertheless, some theories about the origin of the Bilateria propose that the blastopore originally developed into both the mouth and the anus, thereby attempting to explain the variability in the types of gastrulation.

The blastopore becomes the anus in *P. caudatus*; thus, priapulids show deuterostomic development (Fig. 1*e*). The presence of deuterostomic development in this ancestral group of animals that is included within the Protostomia suggests that the deuterostomic development observed in other closely related protostomes, such as some arthropods and related nematodes, is an ancestral characteristic rather than a derived characteristic (Fig. 2). This has two direct consequences for our understanding of animal evolution. First, the split of bilaterally symmetrical animals into the Deuterostomia and the Protostomia cannot be solely based on the differences in the ancestral fate of the blastopore of each group. Indeed, there is currently no morphological

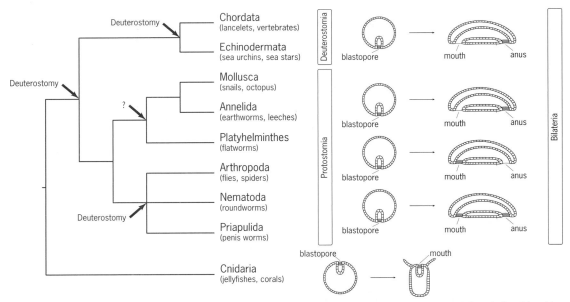

Fig. 2. The division of bilaterally symmetrical animals into the Deuterostomia and the Protostomia, and the relationship with the fate of the blastopore in each group. In the Deuterostomia, the blastopore always becomes the anus, and the mouth forms anew from the surface anterior ectoderm. In the Protostomia, there is real variability in the fate of the blastopore, and the blastopore can become the mouth, the anus, or the precursor of both. The fate of the blastopore (that is, where it ends up later in morphogenesis) is shown in *green*.

or embryological characteristic that can be used to define the Deuterostomia and the Protostomia, although both groups are consistently classified and well supported by modern molecular systematic methods. Second, the presence of deuterostomic development across different groups of bilaterally symmetrical animals (that is, in the Deuterostomia and in the major groups within the Protostomia) suggests that this was the ancestral mode of development for the Bilateria (Fig. 2). This implies that the mouth and the blastopore developed independently in the last common ancestor to all bilaterians, contrary to what is observed in extant jellyfishes (Cnidaria) [Fig. 2]. These findings play against the most accepted evolutionary theories, highlighting the importance of extending developmental studies to a broader range of animals in the pursuit of a better understanding of animal evolution.

For background information *see* ANIMAL EVOLUTION; ANIMAL KINGDOM; DEUTEROSTOMIA; DEVELOPMENTAL BIOLOGY; ECDYSOZOA; GASTRULATION; INVERTEBRATE EMBRYOLOGY; INVERTEBRATE PHYLOGENY; PRIAPULIDA in the McGraw-Hill Encyclopedia of Science & Technology.

José M. Martín-Durán; Andreas Hejnol

Bibliography. F. Maderspacher, Breakthroughs and blind ends, *Curr. Biol.*, 19:R272–R274, 2009, DOI:10.1016/j.cub.2009.03.043; J. M. Martín-Durán et al., Deuterostomic development in the protostome *Priapulus caudatus, Curr. Biol.*, 22:2161–2166, 2012, DOI:10.1016/j.cub.2012.09.037; M. Q. Martindale, Evolution of development: The details are in the entrails, *Curr. Biol.*, 23:R25–R28, 2013, DOI:10.1016/j.cub.2012.11.023; C. Nielsen, *Animal Evolution: Interrelationships of the Living Phyla*, 3d ed., Oxford University Press, Oxford, UK, 2012; E. E. Ruppert, R. S. Fox, and R. D. Barnes, *Invertebrate Zoology: A Functional Evolutionary Approach*, 7th ed., Brooks/Cole Thomson, Belmont, CA, 2004; M. J. Telford and D. T. J. Littlewood, *Animal Evolution: Genomes, Fossils, and Trees*, Oxford University Press, Oxford, UK, 2009; S. A. Wennberg, R. Janssen, and G. E. Budd, Early embryonic development of the priapulid worm *Priapulus caudatus, Evol. Dev.*, 10:326–338, 2008, DOI:10.1111/j.1525-142X.2008.00241.x.

Primate visual signals

Primates are unusual mammals. Unlike the majority of mammals, which rely on a strong sense of smell for navigating the world, primates are characterized by a shift away from an ancestral reliance on olfaction toward an increasing use of the visual sense. Primates possess more forward-facing eyes that allow a greater resolution of depth distances (stereoscopy) and an increased number of color receptor types in the retina, allowing for a greater discrimination of different wavelengths of light. This increased reliance on vision may have originally been associated with improved foraging on colorful fruits, but it has led primates to communicate with each other using a wide range of visual signals (see **illustration**).

Color visual signals. The catarrhine primates, that is, the Old World monkeys and apes (including humans), have evolved trichromacy (red–green–blue color vision: the presence of three different types of color receptors) through the duplication of a coding gene. This excellent color vision has led to a prevalence of color visual signals all over the bodies of Old World monkeys, including mandrills, drills, geladas, baboons, macaques, guenons, and mangabeys. Species in these groups are not only the most colorful monkeys, but they are also the most colorful of all mammals. Recent studies of these color signals have utilized digital photography to collect images of wild primates while controlling for differences in ambient light and camera settings using color standards. The signals captured in these images are then analyzed for differences in color (chromatic variation), luminance (achromatic variation: lightness and darkness), and other aspects of signal form (for example, shape and pattern). By combining measures of such signals with hormonal and genetic information measured from fecal or urine samples, and detailed behavioral observations, a raft of recent field studies have aimed to investigate the proximate mechanisms and ultimate function of primate visual signals. These studies include investigations of the bright red sexual swellings of female baboons and chimpanzees, which increase in size near the time of ovulation and signal female fertility; the chest patch of the male gelada, which is redder among harem-holding males than roving bachelor males, thereby signaling harem-holding status; and the striking red and blue muzzle of the male mandrill, where the contrast between the two colors signals dominance rank and appears to represent a close-to-optimal chromatic contrast for maximum detectability. Work on the comparative neuroscience of primate vision has revealed the peak spectral sensitivities of the different photoreceptors possessed by different species (that is, the wavelengths of light to which they are most sensitive). This enables the signals expressed by primates to be analyzed and interpreted within mathematical models of visual space, which are specific to each species and incorporate information on the spectral sensitivities and relative abundance of each receptor type within the eye.

Other types of visual signals exhibited by primates, such as gestures and facial expressions, are more ephemeral than color patches and swellings, lasting for just a few seconds. Many primates use gestures during communication, and these may act as signals (where evolutionary selection has acted on their communicative function) or cues (where no such selection has acted, but where they can nonetheless be used by receivers to infer information about the signaling individual). Recent studies have shown that they are used flexibly according to the audience, and can be modified, for example, in the presence of infants. Another type of short-term

Examples of primate visual signal diversity. Top row: Bald uakari (*Cacajao calvus*); ring-tailed lemur (*Lemur catta*); emperor tamarin (*Saguinus imperator*); mantled guereza (*Colobus guereza*). Middle row: Mandrill (*Mandrillus sphinx*); De Brazza's monkey (*Cercopithecus neglectus*); Diana monkey (*Cercopithecus diana*). Bottom row: Common squirrel monkey (*Saimiri sciureus*); common guenon (*Cercopithecus pogonias*); gelada (*Theropithecus gelada*); collared mangabey (*Cercocebus torquatus*). (*Images reproduced from W. A. Allen and J. P. Higham, Analyzing visual signals as visual scenes, Am. J. Primatol., 75:664–682, 2013, DOI:10.1002/ajp.22129*)

flexible signal given by primates is facial expression. Charles Darwin was highly interested in the facial expressions of primates, and the facial expression repertoires of species such as chimpanzees are now well documented. Such facial expressions can play critical roles in mediating transient social interactions. For example, when a subordinate rhesus macaque is approached by a dominant individual, a bare-teethed fear-grin is given as a signal of submission. Many primate vocalizations are accompanied by facial expressions in an obligate fashion, and this extends to humans, where it is impossible to form the words by which we communicate without concomitant movement of the lips. An increasing focus in primate communication research is the natural links between the signals expressed and detected in different sensory modalities. Studies have shown behavioral advantages to exhibiting such multimodal stimuli; they are easier to detect for receivers.

Polymorphic color vision. One of the most interesting features of primate perception is that some lemurs and almost all New World monkeys have polymorphic color vision (the presence of multiple different color vision phenotypes within the same population of one species). These species have evolved allelic variations in their opsin genes such that each X chromosome possesses a SW (short-wave) receptor and a type of MW (medium-wave) or LW (long-wave) receptor (but not both, unlike the X chromosomes of catarrhine primates). This means that all males, and homozygous females, exhibit some form of dichromacy. However, heterozygous females are functionally trichromatic. This adds a new layer of complexity to the system. Imagine a scene of ripe red fruits against a backdrop of green leaves, where some group females are trichromatic and see the red fruits clearly, whereas other group females and all group males are dichromatic and see only green. Molecular studies have suggested that the presence of different color vision phenotypes in populations is the result of balancing selection (rather than being a transitional state), with different phenotypes being better suited to solving different tasks. For example, insects that are camouflaged against predation by trichromatic primates may be more easily seen by dichromatic primates.

The latest research on these systems is combining the genotyping of individuals in primate groups from fecal samples, while undertaking detailed observations of their feeding behavior, to improve our understanding of the advantages and disadvantages of different visual system types. The invasive work on captive primates that was previously necessary to evaluate the spectral sensitivities of primate photoreceptors has been replaced with new noninvasive techniques. Fecal samples can be collected and genotyped, and the genes coding for the photoreceptors can be expressed in vitro. The sensitivity of the photoreceptor cells to different wavelengths of light can then be assessed directly. The combination of genotyping and the assessment of wavelength sensitivities, the measurement of behaviors, and the measurement and analysis of fruits, leaves, and other important aspects of the environment in species-specific visual spaces create a powerful set of methods for evaluating the balancing selective forces maintaining polymorphic vision. Although the significance of such variability in vision for understanding feeding behavior continues to be investigated, there is as yet little work on what such variability means for the detection of camouflaged predators, such as snakes and jaguars, or the evaluation of the visual signals of potential mates.

Multimodal signals. Increasingly, visual signals are being seen in the context of other signals given in other modalities, as the whole signaling system may be evolving together. For example, it may be that the large sexual swellings exhibited by female baboons represent a visual signal attracting many males; however, the most accurate information on female fertility may be accessible only through olfactory cues available to just one of those males, the one who is able to use his social dominance to consort with the female and control access to her. As such, the role of the visual signal in communicating fertility may be only one element in a multimodal system, in which all elements must be understood before the role of any one signal can be fully elucidated.

Future research. Some of the most interesting new research directions in primate visual signaling include the extension of communication from its dyadic nature (with one individual signaling to a second individual) into more realistic communication networks that include other bystanders. Eavesdroppers, whether they are conspecific (same-species) group members or predators, exert strong selective pressures on signals. For example, rhesus macaque mothers are much more likely to allow a crying infant to have access to the nipple during weaning when dominant unrelated individuals are close by because these individuals may physically punish the mother or the infant for the highly aversive crying. Finally, another type of effect that is increasingly being studied relates to the familiarity between the individuals giving signals and those perceiving them. Imagine a situation in which someone you know well gives a particular facial expression. You may well recognize what your friend is feeling and thinking, but other individuals present who do not know your friend may misunderstand what that facial expression means. This is a familiarity effect between signalers and receivers, and studies of primates have started to show that such effects may be present in non-humans too. Phenomena such as these are likely to complicate primate visual communication even further.

For background information *see* ANIMAL COMMUNICATION; BEHAVIORAL ECOLOGY; COLOR; COLOR VISION; EYE (VERTEBRATE); PERCEPTION; PHOTORECEPTION; PRIMATES; SOCIAL MAMMALS; SOCIOBIOLOGY; STEREOSCOPY; VISION in the McGraw-Hill Encyclopedia of Science & Technology.   James P. Higham

Bibliography. B. J. Bradley and N. I. Mundy, The primate palette: The evolution of primate coloration, *Evol. Anthropol.*, 17:97–111, 2008, DOI:10.1002/evan.20164; F. B. M. de Waal, Darwin's legacy and the study of primate visual communication, *Ann. N.Y. Acad. Sci.*, 1000:7–31, 2003, DOI:10.1196/annals.1280.003; J. P. Higham et al., Familiarity affects assessment of facial signals of female fertility by free-ranging male rhesus macaques, *Proc. Royal Soc. B.*, 278:3452–3458, 2011, DOI:10.1098/rspb.2011.0052; T. Hiwatashi et al., An explicit signature of balancing selection for color vision variation in New World monkeys, *Mol. Biol. Evol.*, 27:453–464, 2010, DOI:10.1093/molbev/msp262; D. Osorio and M. Vorobyev, A review of the evolution of animal colour vision and visual communication signals, *Vis. Res.*, 48:2042–2051, 2008, DOI:10.1016/j.visres.2008.06.018; S. Semple and J. P. Higham, Primate signals: Current issues and perspectives, *Am. J. Primatol.*, 75:613–620, 2013, DOI:10.1002/ajp.22139; M. Stevens, *Sensory Ecology, Behaviour and Evolution*, Cambridge University Press, Cambridge, UK, 2013.

Prosocial behavior

Prosocial behavior is any behavior intended to promote (or prevent declines in) another person's welfare. It comes in many varieties, from the rare case of saving the life of a stranger to more mundane behaviors like giving a parent a hug, holding a door open for someone, or listening to a friend's problems. It also includes giving goods, services, information, advice, or money to other people. However, prosocial behavior also includes actions with less tangible benefits, such as expressing affection, recognizing others' accomplishments, and celebrating the source of another's positive emotions with that person. Even intentionally refraining from doing something one would ordinarily do, so somebody else benefits, is a form of prosocial behavior. Refraining from eating the last piece of pie so that another person can enjoy it is a prosocial act. Behavior can also be prosocial even if it does not succeed in benefiting someone. Hunting for a friend's lost wallet, even if it is never found, and striving to comfort someone who is beyond consolation count as prosocial actions. On the flipside, behavior that benefits another person is not prosocial if it was not intended to support that person's welfare. Dropping a $20 bill that another person finds and keeps is not prosocial if one did not intend to drop it for that person's benefit.

Categorizing prosocial behavior. How can the various types of prosocial behavior be classified or categorized? There is no one correct typology. Rather, different typologies are useful for different research purposes. Someone interested in evolutionary fitness (an organism's ability to survive and reproduce) might classify behaviors as prosocial according to whether they advance fitness. For example, behaviors that benefit the actor but hurt the recipient can be categorized as selfish and not prosocial; those that benefit both organisms can be categorized as cooperative; and those that benefit the recipient while costing the actor can be categorized as altruistic. The question from an evolutionary perspective then becomes the following: Why does each kind of helping behavior exist? Psychologists, however, most often focus on the proximate explanations of prosocial behavior, such as people's motivations, and they group them together in terms of the nature of those proximal motivations. For instance, psychologists might classify acts according to whether those acts arise from a sense of duty versus interpersonal attraction, whether they arise from empathy for another versus a desire to relieve one's own distress, and whether or not the acts are costly to perform. These are not mutually exclusive categories; rather, they represent a variety of approaches that are useful for guiding research designed to answer different questions.

Observations and analyses. In studying prosocial behavior, most attention has been devoted to establishing its antecedents. Many situational factors have been identified. For instance, if the signals indicating that somebody needs assistance are ambiguous, people are less likely to help. One well-known series of studies has shown that the number of people present when situations suggest that help is needed influences whether or not people intervene: the greater the number of people present, the less likely any one of them will help.

From a human economics (homo economicus) view of behavior, it is in people's rational self-interest to maximize their rewards and minimize their costs. Some researchers have thus argued that people engage in a behavior that promotes the welfare of others because it has been positively reinforced over the course of their life spans or when it will benefit them personally. They should be less likely to help when doing so is costly. One reason that prosocial behavior is rewarded may be that people collectively have settled upon norms of fairness, reciprocity, and justice, and people reward one another when such norms are followed. People can also preserve their reputations by acting in a prosocial manner. In one study, people paid about three times as much for a beverage by dropping money into an "honor box" when they were exposed to cues of being watched; that is, people paid more when a poster depicting

a pair of eyes was displayed above the honor box compared to when they were exposed to a poster depicting nature scenes.

Yet another well-established proximal predictor of prosocial behavior is mood. Happy people consistently offer more help than people experiencing no particular emotion; people feeling guilt and gratitude act more prosocially than others; and sadness increases helping when helping others would boost one's mood. One of the most well-documented forces motivating prosocial behavior is the empathy felt upon exposure to another person's distress. Empathy is especially likely to occur when the target person is similar to the potential helper and may result in truly altruistic behavior. In fact, there is a long-standing debate in the literature over whether exposure to another person's unfortunate circumstances results in helping through motivating people to help another for egoistic reasons (to reduce their own personal distress; the negative state relief model) or whether empathic feelings inspire helping behavior that is done for the ultimate purpose of reducing the other person's negative state (the empathy–altruism hypothesis). Evidence exists for both positions.

Psychologists have also searched for individual differences related to behaving prosocially. Gender and chronic differences in empathy have received a particularly large amount of attention. It is safe to say that a chronic tendency to feel empathic toward others is a clear precursor to greater levels of prosociality. With regard to gender, numerous studies have suggested that men and women do not differ greatly in their overall tendencies to act prosocially; however, the nature of the help offered is different. Women's prosocial behavior is more geared toward forming and maintaining close relationships, whereas men's prosocial behavior seems to have more individualistic motives.

Aside from studying motivations, researchers have also focused on the consequences of prosocial behavior for the person doing it. A number of studies have demonstrated that giving money to others and engaging in acts of kindness makes people happier. This may be true primarily when recipients are people with whom one wishes to build or maintain close relationships. In such cases, the act of helping serves to build desired relationships, which may be why it feels good. When one does not desire a close relationship with a recipient, helping can actually make one feel worse.

Relational context. Obviously, and by definition, prosocial behavior is interpersonal. It also is a truism that any interaction between two or more people takes place within the context of some kind of relationship. This is the case even if that interaction is between people who have never met before; this is simply one type of relationship (that is, one between strangers). The relationship between people is therefore critical for predicting when prosocial behavior will occur as well as what its outcomes will be. As predicted by kin selection theory, people who are more closely related are more likely to engage in prosocial behavior with one another than people who are less closely or not at all related.

However, beyond the category of kinship, the relational context should be considered more broadly. For instance, people have communal relationships, typically with romantic partners, friends, and family, in which they give benefits in response to the partner's needs and desires without expecting anything in repayment. Other relationships, such as those with strangers and acquaintances, operate on a tit-for-tat basis in most situations (except for emergencies and when the cost of doing so is extremely minimal). Unsurprisingly, most help is given in communal relationships. Importantly, these communal relationships also vary in strength, with people feeling more responsibility for some people's needs than for others (for example, more responsibility for a child than for a casual friend). The type of relationship, the relationship stage, and the priority of that relationship within one's larger social network are a few of the factors that can powerfully influence whether prosocial behaviors will take place.

Prosocial behavior in human infants and nonhuman primates. Recent research has gone beyond adult humans to demonstrate a basic motivation to act prosocially in both human infants and nonhuman primates. Capuchins reliably give food to conspecifics (individuals of a single species) in role-playing (dictator game) scenarios, and chimpanzees appear to have a basic motivation to act altruistically, suggesting that the phylogenetic (evolutionary developmental) roots of human altruism in the domain of instrumental helping may be ancient. However, despite a tendency to cooperate readily with kin and reciprocating partners, chimpanzees (unlike humans) often fail to take advantage of opportunities to deliver benefits to familiar individuals at no cost to themselves. Furthermore, prelinguistic children as young as 14–18 months of age spontaneously help adults achieve their goals by engaging in unrewarded instrumental helping behavior (for example, helping an adult pick up dropped clothespins), although the infant's relationship with the adult can influence whether this help occurs.

Outlook. Prosocial behavior is a topic that has captured the interest of many clinical, developmental, health, personality, and social psychologists. It also has interested researchers in other fields, including sociology, anthropology, and ecology. Although it is difficult to do justice to the rich and extensive literature on this topic, future investigations will surely build upon the scaffolding provided in this paper.

For background information *see* BEHAVIOR GENETICS; BRAIN; COGNITION; MOTIVATION; NEUROBIOLOGY; PERSONALITY THEORY; PSYCHOLOGY; SOCIAL MAMMALS; SOCIOBIOLOGY in the McGraw-Hill Encyclopedia of Science & Technology.

Erica J. Boothby; Margaret S. Clark

Bibliography. C. D. Batson, *Altruism in Humans*, Oxford University Press, New York, 2011; M. S. Clark et al., Putting pro-social behavior in relational context, in D. A. Schroeder and W. Graziano (eds.), *Handbook of Prosocial Behavior*, Oxford University Press, Oxford, UK, 2013; J. Dovidio et al., *The Social Psychology of Prosocial Behavior*, Lawrence Erlbaum, Mahwah, NJ, 2006; A. H. Eagly, The his and hers of prosocial behavior: An examination of the social psychology of gender, *Am. Psychol.*, 64:644–658, 2009, DOI:10.1037/0003-066X.64.8.644.

Quantum cascade lasers

A quantum cascade laser is an infrared semiconductor laser in which electrons travel through a series of quantum wells and emit infrared light at wavelengths that depend on the precise dimensions of the wells. Since the invention of the laser in 1960, researchers have been pushing to expand the functionality of lasers into all ranges of the electromagnetic spectrum. Of particular interest are small, compact, and versatile devices that can be used in multiple portable applications. The semiconductor laser diode perfectly fits this description and has enabled applications from laser pointers to optical telecommunications in the visible and near-infrared range. Yet, the mid- to far-infrared range has been harder to conquer. This is mainly due to scarcity of semiconductor materials with suitable optical (band gap) and structural properties. The solution to the band-gap limit was provided in the early 1990s by a team at Bell Laboratories. Using traditional compound semiconductors as building blocks and exploiting the consequences of quantum mechanics, they succeeded in demonstrating a new type of infrared semiconductor laser, the quantum cascade laser (QCL).

Electrons in a box. The infrared lasers invented at Bell Labs rely on the quantum mechanical solution to the problem of a particle in a box. In contrast to classical mechanics, quantum mechanics predicts that a particle in a box can occupy only a state with a discrete energy belonging to a set of exactly defined values. Each of these energies depends on the size and shape of the box. Moreover, the transition energy between two allowed states increases with decreasing box size and, therefore, can be tailored to needs simply by engineering the geometry of the box. The Bell Labs team's radical idea was to manipulate these states to generate laser light. In QCLs, the particles are electrons in the conduction band of semiconductors, and the box is an active region comprised of two or more quantum wells. Each quantum well is a sandwich of a lower-band-gap semiconductor layer surrounded by two layers of a different, higher-band-gap semiconductor. The wavelength of emitted light is not determined by the band gap of any of the materials, but rather by the exact dimensions of the quantum wells. Only two different semiconductors are needed to build the quantum wells, and there are endless possibilities to combine the

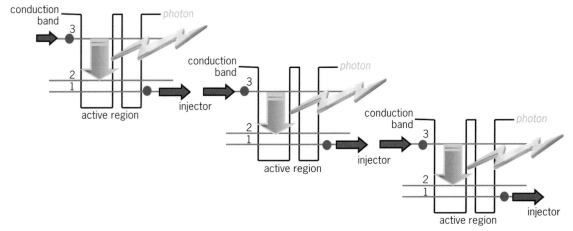

Fig. 1. Schematic diagram of the electron path in the light-emitting section of a quantum cascade laser. The electrons fall down a staircase of quantum levels similar to a waterfall and get a chance to emit a photon in each active region. A single device may contain 30–100 active region/injector sections.

two types of layers into devices that operate in a broad, previously inaccessible infrared range.

Cascade effect. The quantum cascade lasers were named after the innovative device layout utilized to inject electrons into and extract them from an active region. After emitting light in one active region, the electrons are recycled and reinjected into another downstream active region. The charge ends up cascading down a staircase of quantized energy levels similar to a waterfall. The steps of the staircase are discrete energy levels of a complex sequence of precisely designed quantum wells.

Figure 1 shows schematically the path electrical charge takes in QCLs. The electrons are guided to and accumulated into the high energy level 3 of one active region. They emit light through a transition from level 3 to level 2 in the active region. To clear

the path for more electrons to emit light, or, in technical terms, to maintain population inversion, the staircase is carefully engineered so that electrons quickly exit the lower laser level 2 through tunneling and heat (longitudinal-optical phonon) emission. Then they are reinjected into the next downstream active region by a section called the injector. The injector is also a sequence of quantum wells designed to ensure optimal charge transport. Since each device typically contains 30–100 active-region/injector sections, the electrons get a chance to emit more than one photon at one pass through the structure. This cascading scheme is the main reason for the successful operation of a QCL and for the high optical power achievable with these devices.

Fabrication techniques. A QCL typically has hundreds of nanometer-size semiconductor layers that need to be assembled with exquisite accuracy. Molecular-beam epitaxy was first used to grow QCL structures and is still the technique of choice for the most demanding structures. Molecular-beam epitaxy uses an ultrahigh-vacuum environment to deposit semiconductors one atomic layer at a time. **Figure 2** shows a modern molecular-beam epitaxy system currently being used to grow QCL materials. More recently, metal-organic chemical vapor deposition has also been demonstrated to grow high-performance laser material. Both techniques allow the rigorous control of the layer thicknesses and reproducibility over the extended period of time necessary to grow full QCL structures.

The present is bright. In the two decades since its invention, QCL technology has evolved tremendously. Using a single material combination (InGaAs/InAlAs), devices were demonstrated in the entire mid-infrared range. A major breakthrough was the demonstration of a QCL in the terahertz (far-infrared) range. High-power (multiwatt) continuous-wave emission at room temperature has been achieved in the mid-infrared range. It is noteworthy that QCLs are relatively inefficient when compared to laser diodes, but the record wall-plug-efficiency—

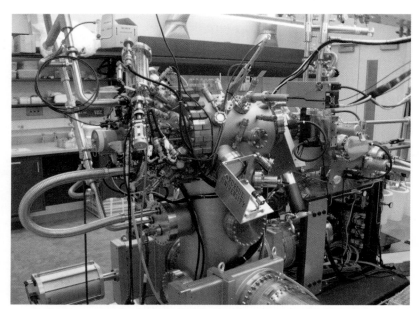

Fig. 2. Modern molecular-beam epitaxy system used to grow ultrahigh-purity arsenide materials. Molecular beam epitaxy was originally used to demonstrate a QCL.

the ratio of optical power emitted to total consumed power—has been rapidly increasing, recently exceeding 50% at low temperature. The lasers can operate at single and multiple wavelengths, in single or multiple modes. Even single devices can be tuned over a broader spectral range than diode lasers. This property makes them particularly suitable for applications. Most importantly, QCLs have moved beyond the realm of research laboratories and into commercial production. Several companies are now providing high-performance lasers, and their cost has come down dramatically over the past few years as they penetrate new product markets.

Sensing opportunities. The QCL spectral range makes them ideally suited for chemical and biological sensing applications. Most of the chemical compounds of interest for environmental, health or defense applications have strong absorption lines in the mid-infrared. For this reason, the mid-infrared is also known as the molecular fingerprint region. Matching

the laser wavelength with one of these absorption lines allows for extremely sensitive spectroscopic detection of these chemicals at levels as low as parts per billion. The first proof-of-principle demonstrations used single lasers and targeted small molecules such as NO, NH_3, CH_4, CO, and so forth for environmental monitoring purposes. More recently, the sensors have evolved into systems employing several lasers for enhanced spectral coverage. If the laser frequency does not overlap with any water or carbon dioxide bands, the QCL infrared beams undergo minimal attenuation and can propagate long distances through the atmosphere. For this reason, they can be used for either standoff or remote chemical detection. **Figure 3** shows the experimental setup that was used to examine the chemical composition of smoke affecting the health of the residents of a small fishing village in Ghana. QCL-based sensing research has been performed for air and food quality testing, medical diagnosis, and detection of

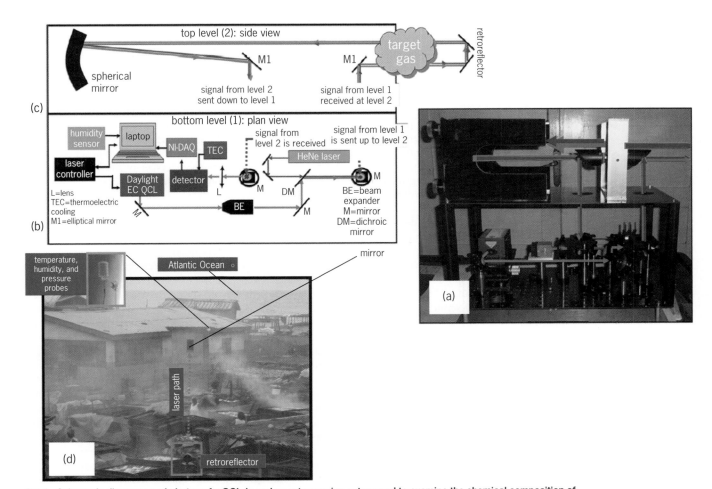

Fig. 3. Schematic diagrams and photos of a QCL-based remote-sensing setup used to examine the chemical composition of smoke in a fishing village in Ghana. The actual sensor (shown in part *a* and detailed in part *b*) was located on level 1 of the building in the center of part *d*. The sensor used an external-cavity QCL provided by Daylight Solutions, Inc., San Diego (Daylight EC QCL). The QCL infrared beam (red line) was combined with an alignment visible beam (purple line) from a HeNe laser on level 1 and routed to level 2 of the building. The laser beams were directed out the window, across a fish market to a retroreflector and then returned to the sensor on level 1 for measurement. The outside laser beam path on level 2 is shown schematically in part *c* and indicated in part *d*. The laser detection was done with an infrared detector and a National Instruments data acquisition system (NI-DAQ). (*Courtesy of Ekua N. Bentil and Charles L. Amuah, Princeton University*)

explosives. Commercial systems using QCL technology have been deployed to test automotive exhaust, to inspect production lines for aerosol leaks, and to check for weapons in airports. Possibly the most fascinating applications involve noninvasive medical diagnosis of cancer and liver disease with breath analysis.

Prospects. Current research in QCL technology is aggressively pursuing device performance optimization to increase power output and efficiency, as well as broadband tunability. Further QCL advances may eventually revolutionize the way we perform infrared spectroscopy. Ideally, a single tunable laser that can scan over the entire infrared range would make possible a spectrometer on a chip. Such a device would be smaller, faster, and more accurate than Fourier-transform infrared spectrometers, the devices in wide use today, and may ultimately replace them. In addition to a multitude of practical applications, the novel laser spectrometers would enable new types of chemical physics investigations of large molecules with complex spectra, molecular dynamics experiments, and studies of condensed phases. Because of the high power and narrow linewidth, the lasers will be ideally suited not only to probe but also to drive chemical reactions by selectively depositing energy into molecular states for infrared photochemistry studies, multiple resonance experiments, and so forth.

Aside from chemical physics applications, there are other applications of QCLs that are still in their infancy. Proof-of-concept experiments of QCLs in light detection and ranging (LIDAR) have already been demonstrated, but these applications are expected to really take off in the near future. QCLs are also potentially interesting for free-space optical communications.

In parallel with traditional device development efforts, researchers worldwide pursue novel directions for light generation based on the ideas of the quantum cascades. Because of the fundamental properties of the commonly used QCL materials, there are still some slices of the infrared that are not easily accessible with semiconductor lasers and for which new concepts need to be explored. Ongoing research aims to exploit new classes of materials (nitrides, antimonides) and nonlinear light generation for near- and far-infrared light emission. Integration of QCL active material with novel optics such as photonic crystals, microcavities, optical circuits, and metamaterials is also being pursued to improve sensor technologies. Based on their outstanding track record, the QCLs are likely to open many more exciting research opportunities and may even find their way into consumer products in the not too distant future.

For background information *see* CRYSTAL GROWTH; INFRARED SPECTROSCOPY; LASER; LIDAR; PHOTONIC CRYSTAL DEVICES; QUANTIZED ELECTRONIC STRUCTURE (QUEST); SEMICONDUCTOR HETEROSTRUCTURES in the McGraw-Hill Encyclopedia of Science & Technology.   Oana Malis

Bibliography. F. Capasso, High-performance mid-infrared quantum cascade lasers, *Opt. Eng.*, 49: 111102, 2010, DOI:10.1117/1.3505844; F. Capasso et al., Quantum cascade lasers, *Phys. Today*, 55(5): 34–40, 2002, DOI:10.10.1063/11485582; R. Kohler et al., Terahertz semiconductor-heterostructure laser, *Nature*, 417:156–159, 2002, DOI:10.1038/417156a; A. Kosterev et al., Application of quantum cascade lasers to trace gas analysis, *Appl. Phys. B*, 90: 165–176, 2008, DOI:10.1007/s00340-007-2846-9.

Quantum uncertainty in macroscopic measurements

The effects of quantum mechanics should be present in objects of all size scales. However, we rarely encounter quantum superposition (such as an object existing in two places at once) or quantum uncertainty (an intrinsic spread in the location of an object like that represented by the orbitals of electrons in an atom) in objects on the scale of our everyday experience. These more exotic quantum properties are absent in systems that are strongly coupled to their environments. Quantum superpositions exist only as long as they remain unobserved. If enough information to determine the position of an object is available in the surrounding environment, then quantum superpositions collapse. Similarly, quantum position uncertainty, while always present, is easily obscured by motion induced from thermal vibrations or collisions with air molecules amongst other sources. However, recent experiments with specially designed objects, many of which are macroscopic, or visible to the unaided eye, are able to explore quantum effects on larger size scales.

Heisenberg microscope. In the 1920s, shortly after the development of quantum theory, Werner Heisenberg came up with a famous example illustrating a quantum consequence of measurement. He envisioned a position measurement stripped down to its simplest form. We observe a single free electron through a microscope by the scattering of a photon, a single particle of light (**Fig. 1**). The position resolution, Δx, is proportional to the photon wavelength. If the photon is scattered in one direction, the electron must recoil in the opposite direction, conserving the total momentum of the system. This disturbance to the electron's motion is an example of measurement backaction. The momentum of a slowly moving electron is given by its mass times its velocity, while the photon momentum increases for shorter wavelengths and is proportional to Planck's constant, $\hbar$, a number that governs the size of quantum effects. Since the photon could have passed through any point on the lens to arrive at the detector, its exact trajectory, and hence momentum, is uncertain. Correspondingly, the direction of the final momentum of the electron is also uncertain by an amount Δp. Heisenberg estimated the product of the position measurement uncertainty and added momentum uncertainty to be $\Delta x \Delta p \approx \hbar$.

A more general result is summarized by the Heisenberg measurement-disturbance uncertainty limit $\Delta x \Delta p \geq \hbar/2$, which holds for most common position measurement schemes. Put simply, a better position measurement requires a larger disturbance to the system being measured. For instance, using more photons to make a better measurement will result in an increased recoil momentum of the electron. Typically, this limit is only important in the microscopic world. Measuring the position of a grain of sand to better than the size of a single atom requires a disturbance to its velocity of only a miniscule 10^{-14} m/s.

Optomechanical systems. In the last decade, experimenters have developed a variety of mechanical elements that interact strongly with laser light, allowing for precise position measurement. The elements are also highly mechanically isolated from their environment, allowing quantum effects to become visible over other noise (**Fig. 2**). Designs include trapping light in an optical cavity so that light makes multiple reflections off of the mechanical element. Mechanical isolation is achieved by careful choice of materials and geometry, allowing for millions of oscillations before mechanical energy escapes from the system or is lost to internal friction. Experiments are usually performed inside vacuum chambers, which limit interactions with air molecules, and in refrigerators at very low temperatures, less than a few kelvin, which limit thermally induced vibrations.

The device shown in Fig. 2(*d*) is a membrane optomechanical cavity. Two mirrors trap a standing wave of light produced by the interference between left- and right-going reflections. This standing wave creates a natural ruler with an increment of $\lambda/2$, where λ is the micrometer-scale optical wavelength. A thin, partially reflective, highly tensioned, glass membrane is placed between the mirrors. The membrane is a square 0.5 mm on a side (easily visible to the unaided eye), but is much less than λ thick. If the membrane moves along the standing wave to a position of different intensity, the interference of the reflected light inside the cavity changes in a way that varies the laser transmission. The membrane vibrates at a particular resonance frequency, flexing like the head of a drum. These vibrations are sensed as a modulation on the light exiting the cavity, constituting a measurement of the membrane's position.

Continuous position measurement. The measurement imprecision and backaction in a membrane optomechanical cavity stem from the particle nature of the laser beam used to make the measurement. The light inside the cavity consists of around 100 million individual photons at any given time. Each photon either reflects off or transmits through the partially reflective membrane at random. The photons buffet the membrane like the constant pitter-patter of many individual drops of rain striking a rooftop. The random momentum kicks from the reflected photons cause the membrane to vibrate, creating an extra position uncertainty. These random recoils are termed radiation pressure shot noise, and cause the measure-

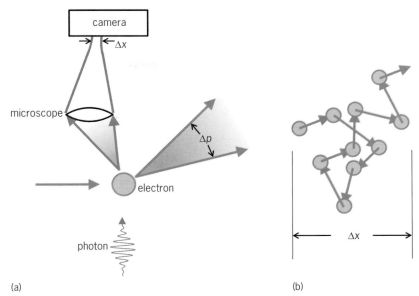

Fig. 1. Heisenberg microscope. (a) Measuring the position of an electron leaves its final momentum uncertain. (b) Repeated position measurements yield different results. The path of the electron diffuses through space, changing direction at each measurement and leading to increased position uncertainty in the long run.

ment backaction. The measured signal is the average number of photons detected at the cavity output in a short time interval. The exact number of photons that arrive in one measurement interval will vary as the square root of the average photon number due to the independent random nature of the individual photons. The effect is called photon shot noise, causing an inherent measurement imprecision in the system.

The results of such a position measurement are displayed in **Fig. 3**. As the measurement laser power is increased, the signal level goes up in proportion, while the imprecision from the shot noise rises only with the square root of the laser power. This results in an increasing signal-to-noise ratio. However, with increased laser power, the extra disturbance due to random photon momentum kicks results in an increased backaction. The sum of these two effects is plotted as the purple curve in Fig. 3. Each point on the purple curve reaches the lower bound of the Heisenberg uncertainty limit. The point where the sum of the imprecision and backaction is minimized is called the standard quantum limit. At this laser power, the system can be used to most sensitively measure outside forces on the mechanical element. In the actual experiment, the membrane's thermal motion prevents reaching the full sensitivity of the standard quantum limit. However, at large enough laser power, the measurement backaction from radiation pressure shot noise becomes larger than the thermal motion for this macroscopic object.

Many other measurement techniques, not involving laser light, can also achieve high sensitivity. Researchers have also used electromagnetic fields in the microwave domain and superconducting

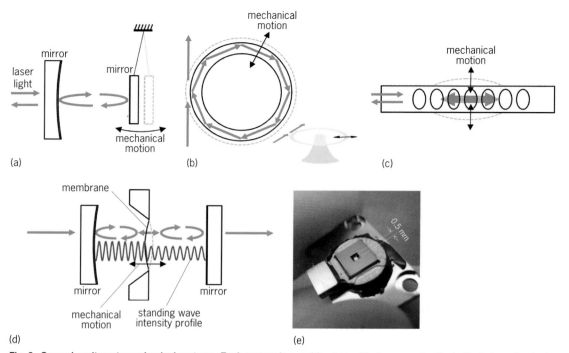

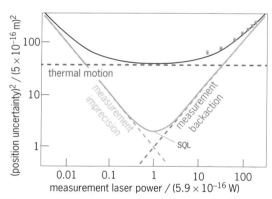

Fig. 2. Several cavity optomechanical systems. Each system is capable of sensitively measuring the indicated mechanical motion with laser light (red). (*a*) A mirror is suspended as a pendulum. Mirrors can be anywhere from micrometers to centimeters in size. (*b*) Light can circulate around the edge of a thin glass disk. The optical pressure is in the radial direction. Typical disks are tens to hundreds of micrometers in diameter. (*c*) Light is confined in the center of a long, thin beam by scattering off of a series of wavelength-scale holes. The optical force dilates the width of the beam. The beam is less than 1 μm in width. (*d*) The drum mode of a membrane placed in an optical cavity. The membrane is millimeter-scale in two dimensions, but is less than 100 nm thick. Also shown in blue is the laser standing-wave intensity profile. (*e*) Image of membrane described in (*d*).

Fig. 3. Quantum limits of continuous position measurement for a membrane optomechanical cavity. The dashed lines represent different sources of position uncertainty: measurement imprecision due to photon shot noise (green), measurement backaction due to radiation pressure shot noise (blue), and thermal motion (brown). The sum of the measurement imprecision and backaction yields the purple curve. Along this curve the measurement reaches the Heisenberg uncertainty limit. The standard quantum limit (SQL) is labeled at the point of least total uncertainty. The experimentally measured data (orange circles) has an additional contribution from thermal motion, but approaches the purple curve at high measurement strength. The data have been corrected for the optical cooling effect of the measurement laser. In this experiment the mechanical motion is read out with a separate laser of much weaker power than the measurement laser to separate the effects of measurement imprecision and backaction.

mechanical elements. Other experiments employ single-electron transistors or other solid-state devices to make sensitive position measurements. The electrical currents used are made up of many individual electrons, leading to an electron shot noise limit to the measurement imprecision, akin to the optical case, and to measurement backaction as the electrostatic force from the individual electrons randomly kick the mechanical element. *See* CIRCUIT CAVITY ELECTROMECHANICS IN THE STRONG-COUPLING REGIME.

Another type of measurement consists of coupling a piezoelectric mechanical element to a nonlinear microwave circuit known as a superconducting quantum bit, or qubit. The effective particles, or quantized states, of the qubit are not single photons or electrons, but consist of macroscopic states of currents flowing through the system. The coupling is so strong that the backaction from a single measurement can involve removing nearly all of the mechanical energy from the system. The low temperature achieved in this system and strong coupling lead to a behavior quite different from the random kicks described above. When the measurement interaction is turned on, the energy of the system oscillates periodically back and forth between the qubit and mechanical element, a hallmark of quantum coherence.

Gravitational wave detectors. One important application of quantum-limited position measurement is the detection of gravitational waves. When distant, massive objects such as neutron stars or black holes rapidly accelerate or orbit one another, a gravitational wave is radiated out from the system. This wave potentially can be detected on Earth, resulting in a new type of astronomy capable of observing the universe in a way unlike current telescopes observing the electromagnetic spectrum. The challenge lies in the detection of the weak signals from gravitational waves. Two unbound objects on Earth are expected to change their separation by only 1 part in 10^{-21} of the distance between them in response to the largest expected gravitational waves. To increase the signal size, gravitational-wave observatories such as LIGO use test masses separated by several kilometers. The distance between the masses is measured with a laser interferometer. The test masses are made extremely large, on the order of tens of kilograms, to limit the effects of other sources of motion including radiation pressure shot noise from the measurement laser. However, the next generation of gravitational-wave observatories is expected to be limited by the quantum effects of position measurement.

Many clever ideas that have been developed evade the measurement backaction. In a simple example, a pendulum-suspended test mass is observed for only a short time at the bottom of each swing. Any disturbance from the measurement process will change the amplitude of pendulum motion, thus not violating the Heisenberg uncertainty limit, but will not change the point in the period of the swing when the test mass reaches the bottom. A gravitational wave, however, can still disturb the pendulum's swing in a detectable way.

Conclusions. In the spirit of Heisenberg's conceptual experiment, many recent actual experiments are exploring the nature of quantum measurement on objects of a macroscopic scale. In each experiment a real force can be identified that enforces the Heisenberg uncertainty limit. This force is associated with the quantized or particlelike nature of the measurement field. As researchers make progress in understanding and controlling macroscopic systems, quantum mechanics may become more familiar to our daily lives.

For background information *see* ELECTRICAL NOISE; GRAVITATIONAL RADIATION; LIGO (LASER INTERFEROMETER GRAVITATIONAL-WAVE OBSERVATORY); PHOTON; QUANTUM MECHANICS; QUANTUM THEORY OF MEASUREMENT; RADIATION PRESSURE; SIGNAL-TO-NOISE RATIO; SUPERPOSITION PRINCIPLE; UNCERTAINTY PRINCIPLE in the McGraw-Hill Encyclopedia of Science & Technology.

Thomas P. Purdy

Bibliography. M. Aspelmeyer, P. Meystre, and K. Schwab, Quantum optomechanics, *Phys. Today*, 67(7):29–35, July 2012, DOI:10.1063/PT.3.1640; B. C. Barish and R. Weiss, LIGO and the detection of gravitational waves, *Phys. Today*, 52(10):44–51, 1999, DOI:10.1063/1.882861; T. P. Purdy, R. W. Peterson, and C. A. Regal, Observation of radiation pressure shot noise on a macroscopic object, *Science*, 339:801–804, 2013, DOI:10.1126/science.1231282; V. Vedral, Living in a quantum world, *Sci. Amer.*, 304(6):38–43, June 2011, DOI:10.1038/scientificamerican0611-38.

Regulation of cotton lint growth

Cotton is one of the world's economically important crop plants and is the most prevalent natural source for the textile industry. Approximately 33 million hectares (81.5 million acres), or 5% of the world's arable land, is used for cotton planting, producing an annual global textile mills market value of $630.6 billion in 2011. Cotton lint, which is the industrial name for cotton fiber, is a single-celled trichome (plant appendage) produced from the ovule epidermis. Apart from its economic value, cotton is also an excellent model system for studying cell elongation, cell wall biosynthesis, and polyploidization (chromosomal multiplication). Recent progress with regard to ethylene, very long chain fatty acids (VLCFAs), reactive oxygen species (ROS), and calcium signaling has contributed toward deciphering the molecular mechanisms that regulate lint cell expansion. This information has enabled the proposal of a linear cell-growth mode that may be common to cotton lint and similar cell types.

Cotton lint production and development. Cotton, in the *Gossypium* genus, constitutes 5 tetraploid ($2n = 4x = 52$) and 45 diploid ($2n = 2x = 26$) species, which are believed to have originated from a common ancestor approximately 5–10 million years ago. The tetraploid *Gossypium hirsutum* (upland cotton) accounts for more than 90% of the world's cotton lint production, and a further 5–8% is produced from the tetraploid *Gossypium barbadense* (Creole or extra-long staple cotton). Cotton lint development consists of four overlapping stages: lint initiation [from –3 to 1 days post-anthesis (after flowering), DPA], elongation (5–20 DPA), secondary cell wall synthesis and deposition (15–45 DPA), and maturation/dehydration (40–60 DPA). Only about 30% of ovule epidermal cells will differentiate to mature cotton lint (with a final length of approximately 3 cm and a width of 15–20 μm), whereas others may develop into short fibers called fuzz (with a length of 5–6 mm). Vigorous cell expansion (peak growth rates of more than 2 mm/day) coupled with specific upregulation of metabolite syntheses are observed in upland cotton during the most active elongation period. Cellulose synthesis dominates the period of secondary cell wall biosynthesis. The quality and productivity of cotton lint depend mainly on the first three stages, which respectively determine the number of lint cells present on each ovule, the final lint length, and the strength of each lint cell.

Ethylene positively regulates cotton lint growth. Genetic investigations showed that several metabolic pathways, including ethylene biosynthesis and fatty acid biosynthesis/elongation, were significantly upregulated during lint cell elongation. The last two key steps in ethylene biosynthesis are the conversion of S-adenosyl-L-methionine to 1-aminocyclopropane-1-carboxylic-acid (ACC) and further oxidative cleavage of ACC to ethylene, which are catalyzed by ACC synthase (ACS) and ACC oxidase (ACO), respectively. Three of the four ACO genes (ACO1, ACO2, and ACO3) are expressed at high levels during the period of fiber elongation. Further analyses showed that the expression levels of ACO1, ACO2, and ACO3 were higher in individual lint cells than in ovules with fibers removed. ACO1 and ACO3 were highly expressed in elongating lint cells, with low levels found in roots, stems, and leaves, whereas ACO2 was only detected in lint cells. In an ovule culture system, wild-type ovules released more than 60 nmol ethylene/day/gram fresh weight (gfw), whereas ovules from a fuzzless-lintless (fl) mutant released less than 3 nmol ethylene/day/gfw. When ethylene was applied in the culture media, lint lengths increased in a dose-dependent manner compared to wild-type ovules. Treatment with $0.1~\mu$M ethylene increased lint length by more than fourfold (5.15 ± 0.62 mm versus 1.2 ± 0.1 mm without ethylene). No lint growth was observed when $1~\mu$M L-(2-aminoethoxyvinyl)-glycine (AVG), an ethylene biosynthesis inhibitor, was added to the culture media. This inhibitory effect was nullified by simultaneous ethylene application, suggesting that the AVG effect was related specifically to ethylene biosynthesis. These data suggest that ethylene plays a specific and important role in promoting lint cell growth.

VLCFAs act upstream of ethylene. VLCFAs act as precursors of sphingolipids, seed triacylglycerols, suberin, and cuticular waxes. They are essential for membrane biosynthesis in all organisms and may serve directly as signaling molecules. Rapidly elongating fiber cells contain three to five times the level of VLCFAs than those of mutant ovules or wild-type ovules with fiber cells removed. Addition of saturated VLCFAs with 20 to 30 carbon atoms (C20 to C30), especially C24:0 VLCFAs (that is, VLCFAs with 24 carbon atoms and 0 double bonds), to cultured wild-type cotton ovules significantly promoted lint cell elongation. Application of $2~\mu$M acetochlor (2-chloro-N-[ethoxymethyl]-N-[2-ethyl-6-methyl-phenyl]-acetamide, ACE), an inhibitor of VLCFA biosynthesis, to the culture media completely blocked lint growth. The ACE inhibition was overcome by exogenously applied C24:0 VLCFAs, suggesting that VLCFAs are necessary and sufficient for this process. Addition of ethylene nullified the growth inhibition by ACE, whereas C24:0 VLCFAs were ineffective in reversing the AVG effect. Furthermore, exogenous C24:0 VLCFAs induced a rapid and significant increase of all ACO transcripts, with a concomitant elevation of ethylene production. Application of C24:0 VLCFAs in growth media resulted in significant root hair elongation of wild-type Arabidopsis plants and complemented the cut1 dwarf mutant phenotype (CUT1 encodes

an enzyme that catalyzes the first step in VLCFA biosynthesis). Promotion of Arabidopsis root hair and stem elongation was accompanied by upregulation of specific ACO transcripts. Thus, VLCFAs or VLCFA derivatives may exert their functions by upregulating ethylene biosynthesis, and hence VLCFAs may act upstream of ethylene.

Ethylene positively regulates pectin biosynthesis. Comparative proteomic studies using 10-DPA wild-type and fl mutant cotton ovules have revealed a large number of proteins required for lint growth. Seven protein spots related to pectin cell wall polysaccharide biosynthesis were accumulated in wild-type samples. All these proteins accumulated significantly in response to either ethylene or C24:0 VLCFA treatments, suggesting that ethylene or VLCFAs directly targeted cell wall polymer production. Primary lint cell walls contained substantially higher amounts of pectin, whereas more hemicellulose was found in ovule samples of both genotypes. Significant lint growth was observed when cell wall pectin precursors were added to the ovule culture medium. The short root hairs of Arabidopsis uer1-1 and gae6-1 mutants were complemented either by genetic transformation of the respective cotton complementary DNA (cDNA) or by adding specific pectin precursors to the growth medium. When the pectin precursors produced by the cell wall polysaccharide biosynthesis pathways were used in the chemical complementation assay, cut1 and ein2-5 Arabidopsis seedlings that showed defects in C24:0 biosynthesis and ethylene signaling, respectively, produced root hair lengths similar to those of the wild-type. These results indicate that ethylene and C24:0 VLCFAs promote cotton lint and Arabidopsis root hair growth by activating the pectin biosynthesis network.

Calcium activates ethylene biosynthesis. Calcium signaling plays crucial roles in a wide range of growth and developmental processes. A significant Ca^{2+} ion influx at the growing tip of wild-type cotton lint initials (young cells), but not in fl mutant ovules, has been observed using a scanning ion-selective electrode technique. The Ca^{2+} influx was highest at the tip and then gradually decreased toward the basal part of the developing lint cell. The Ca^{2+} influx reached a peak mean value in +1-DPA lint apices, which was approximately four times higher than for −1-DPA ovules. Only a constant and very low Ca^{2+} influx was detected in mutant ovules at any growth stage (**Fig. 1**). Transcripts of GhPOX1, which encodes a class III plant peroxidase involved in oxidoreduction of H_2O_2, predominantly accumulated in rapidly elongating lint cells. Addition of the NADPH oxidase inhibitor DPI or the peroxidase inhibitor SHAM to the ovule culture medium inhibited both ROS production and lint elongation. Systematic studies found that total Ca^{2+}-dependent protein kinase (CPK) activities increased consistently in wild-type ovules, but not in fl mutant ovules, soon after lint initiation. Applying chemicals such as

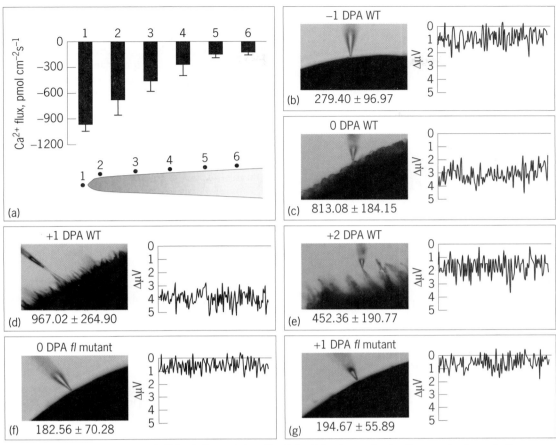

Fig. 1. Observation of significant Ca²⁺ ion influx early in cotton lint cell development using the scanning ion-selective electrode technique. (*a*) Ca²⁺ influx profile along a young, rapidly growing wild-type lint cell. Ca²⁺ fluxes [measured as microvolts and converted into ion fluxes (pmol cm⁻¹ s⁻¹)] were recorded for 3 min at each position. (*b–e*) Net Ca²⁺ influxes recorded from wild-type (WT) cotton ovules at −1, 0, +1, and +2 days post-anthesis (DPA). (*f, g*) Net Ca²⁺ influxes recorded from fuzzless-lintless (*fl*) mutant ovules at 0 and +1 DPA. Each panel shows a bright-field image indicating the exact position of the Ca²⁺-specific microelectrode (*left*) and one representative electrograph (*right*). All data are reported as mean ± SD with $n = 10$ throughout the figure.

trifluoperazine (TFP) and *N*-(6-aminohexyl)-5-chloro-1-naphthalenesulfonamide, which inhibit CPK activity, into ovule culture medium completely blocked lint growth. Significant inhibition of lint growth occurred when ovules were cultured in the presence of TFP or in the absence of exogenous Ca²⁺ ions, suggesting that Ca²⁺ influx to lint tips is required for cell growth. Cotton ACS2, a major enzyme responsible for the second to last step in ethylene biosynthesis, was specifically phosphorylated by CPK1. This modification resulted in significantly higher ACS activity and elevated ethylene evolution, suggesting a possible posttranscriptional regulatory mechanism that connects Ca²⁺, CPK, ethylene production, and cotton lint growth.

A linear cell-growth mode for cotton lint and similar cell types. Typically, unidirectional and rapidly growing cells such as pollen tubes, root hairs, leaf trichomes, and fungal hyphae follow a tip-growth mode. The establishment of tip growth requires a tip–high calcium gradient and an elevated ROS concentration. Microtubules and actin filaments are arranged as long bundles along the length of the tip-

growth cell (**Fig. 2***a*). They form a meshwork in the subapical zone, but not in the apical dome, to facilitate vesicle transport and docking to the apex. Although cotton lint cells were previously suggested to expand via a diffuse-growth mode, fundamentally decisive experimental data are not yet available. In diffuse growth (Fig. 2*b*), the cortical microtubules and newly deposited cellulose microfibrils are transversely oriented with respect to the growth axis. It has been suggested by the robust Ca²⁺ gradient and high ROS production in elongating cotton lint that a linear cell-growth mode (Fig. 2*c*) accounts for the existence of similar pathways between tip-growth and diffuse-growth cells. This new growth mode is further supported by the finding that a large number of genes important for vesicle coating and trafficking (such as syntaxin, clathrin, and vesicle transport SNARE) are preferentially expressed during lint cell elongation. The linear cell-growth mode may be common among different cell types that respond positively to ethylene signaling.

Conclusions. The plant hormone ethylene upregulates cotton lint growth. The ethylene effect is

tip growth

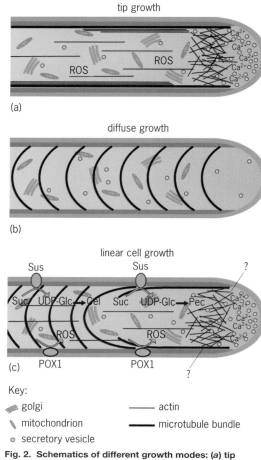

(a)

diffuse growth

(b)

linear cell growth

(c)

Key:

- golgi — actin
- mitochondrion — microtubule bundle
- secretory vesicle

Fig. 2. Schematics of different growth modes: (a) tip growth; (b) diffuse growth; (c) linear cell growth. Terms: Sus, sucrose synthase; Suc, sucrose; UDP-Glc, uridine diphosphate–glucose (involved in pectin cell wall polysaccharide biosynthesis); Cel, cellulose; ROS, reactive oxygen species; Pec, pectin; ?, lacks experimental data.

brought about by activating biosynthesis of primary cell wall components, especially pectin, and also by promoting significant cellular ROS production. A highly localized Ca^{2+} gradient at the growing lint tips precedes endogenous ethylene evolution. Many genes involved in vesicle coating and transport are preferentially expressed in the cytoplasm of rapidly elongating lint cells. VLCFAs, especially C24:0 VLCFAs, induce a rapid and significant increase of all ACO transcripts that are required for ethylene production. Further elucidation of this newly proposed linear cell-growth mode using other similar cell types will strengthen our understanding of cell growth and plant development.

For background information *see* AGRICULTURAL SCIENCE (PLANT); BIOLOGICAL OXIDATION; CALCIUM; COTTON; ETHYLENE; ETHYLENE (PLANT PHYSIOLOGY); NATURAL FIBER; PECTIN; PLANT CELL; PLANT GROWTH; SIGNAL TRANSDUCTION in the McGraw-Hill Encyclopedia of Science & Technology.   Yu-Xian Zhu

Bibliography. W. Q. Mei et al., Cotton GhPOX1 encoding plant class III peroxidase may be responsible for the high level of reactive oxygen species production that is related to cotton fiber elongation, *J. Genet. Genomics*, 36:141–150, 2009, DOI:10.1016/S1673-8527(08)60101-0; C. Y. Pang et al., Comparative proteomics indicate that biosynthesis of pectic precursors is important for cotton fiber and *Arabidopsis* root hair elongation, *Mol. Cell. Proteomics*, 9:2019–2033, 2010, DOI:10.1074/mcp.M110.000349; Y. M. Qin and Y. X. Zhu, How cotton fibers elongate: A tale of linear cell-growth mode, *Curr. Opin. Plant Biol.*, 14:106–111, 2011, DOI:10.1016/j.pbi.2010.09.010; Y. M. Qin et al., Saturated very-long-chain fatty acids promote cotton fiber and *Arabidopsis* cell elongation by activating ethylene biosynthesis, *Plant Cell*, 19:3692–3704, 2007, DOI:10.1105/tpc.107.054437; Y. H. Shi et al., Transcriptome profiling, molecular biological and physiological studies reveal a major role for ethylene in cotton fiber cell elongation, *Plant Cell*, 18:651–664, 2006, DOI:10.1105/tpc.105.040303.

Renal denervation as therapy for hypertension

Hypertension is a growing public health problem and remains a leading cause of cardiovascular diseases. The sympathetic nervous system (SNS), which is part of the autonomic nervous system, has long been recognized as playing an important role in the pathogenesis of hypertension. Invasive and nonspecific surgical sympathectomy (disruption of the sympathetic nerves) was performed successfully several decades ago to improve the survival of patients with severe hypertension and related complications. However, surgical sympathectomy had high rates of complications and severe side effects [including postural hypotension (a drop in blood pressure due to a change in body position), impotence, and incontinence], and it was largely abandoned after the advent of modern pharmacological therapy for hypertension. Despite the availability of several classes of effective antihypertensive medications, resistant hypertension remains common and accounts for approximately 10–12% of all drug-treated hypertension. Minimally invasive and targeted renal denervation (disruption of the renal sympathetic nerves) is now possible with a catheter-based approach, and clinical trials have shown impressive blood pressure (BP) reductions and favorable side-effect profiles in the treatment of drug-resistant hypertension.

Renal sympathetic hyperactivity and hypertension. The SNS is part of the autonomic nervous system that helps maintain the BP and heart rate. Sympathetic hyperactivity has been implicated in the pathogenesis of hypertension, and the sympathetic activity increases in parallel to the severity of the hypertension. The innervation (nerve stimulation) of the kidneys is done mostly by the SNS, and the activation of the renal SNS is often greater than that of the other organs involved in hypertension. The **illustration** is a schematic depiction of the physiological effects of activating the renal SNS. The efferent (outflow)

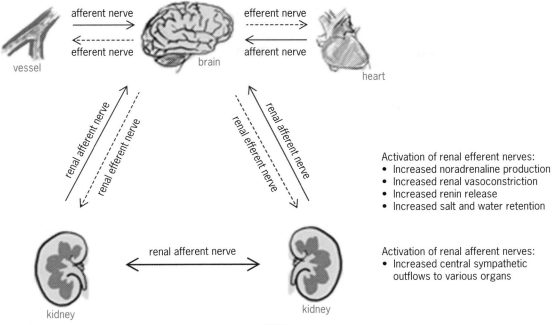

Effects of activating the renal sympathetic nervous system (SNS).

renal sympathetic nerves carry the central sympathetic outflow to the kidneys, and the activity of the efferent renal SNS is regulated by several factors, including the central sympathetic outflow, vagal tone (activity of the parasympathetic nervous system), and cross-talk between the kidneys. The activation of the efferent renal sympathetic nerves results in the increased production and release of renal noradrenaline (a vasoactive hormone), greater constriction of the renal vasculature, increased activity of renin (an important enzyme released by the kidneys), and enhanced sodium and water retention, which all lead to increased BP.

The afferent (inflow) renal sympathetic nerves are the sensory nerves that regulate the central sympathetic outflow by sending sensory information from the chemoreceptors and mechanoreceptors located in the kidneys to the central nervous system. The activation of the afferent renal sympathetic nerves as the result of renal injuries, including ischemia (lack of adequate blood perfusion) and hypoxia (lack of adequate oxygen supply), stimulates sympathetic centers in the brain and increases the central sympathetic outflow to the kidneys and the other vital cardiovascular organs, including the heart and blood vessels, which also result in higher BP.

The renal SNS plays an important role in BP control by regulating volume and sodium homeostasis and the release of renin and noradrenaline. Adequate renal function, however, does not seem to depend on the integrity of the renal SNS. As seen in transplanted kidneys, adequate renal function is maintained despite complete destruction of the renal SNS. Given the unique anatomy of the renal SNS, where nerve fibers enter the kidneys along the wall

of the main renal artery, targeted renal denervation is possible using an ablation (disruption) device placed directly in the renal artery by a catheter-based approach.

Description and results. The first minimally invasive renal denervation device used in humans was carried out by placing a percutaneous ("through the skin") femoral catheter in the main renal artery and delivering radio-frequency energy to ablate (disrupt) the renal nerves lying within the outer layer of the artery wall at several discrete sites along the main renal artery. The denervation procedure is minimally invasive and has a short procedure and recovery time. The results from the initial trials on renal denervation have shown impressive BP reduction and minimal systemic side effects. The **table** summarizes the results of the major trials on catheter-based renal denervation.

In the first proof-of-concept study, 45 patients with resistant hypertension and preserved renal function had impressive BP reductions after bilateral renal denervation. The effectiveness of the renal denervation was confirmed by a reduction in the renal and overall sympathetic activities, resulting in lowered renal and overall noradrenaline levels and renin activity, improved cardiac baroreflex sensitivity (which helps to maintain the baroreceptor reflex mechanism that regulates BP), and decreased muscular sympathetic nerve firings toward the normal level. The initial proof-of-concept study was later expanded to enroll 153 subjects with resistant hypertension and preserved renal function. This study, called Symplicity HTN-1, resulted in similarly impressive and durable BP reductions up to 36 months post-procedure. The safety of the renal denervation

Results of major trials on catheter-based renal denervation

Trial	Design	Size, n	Age, years	Baseline BP, mmHg	Average number of BP medications, n	Baseline GFR, mL/min/ 1.73 m²	Mean BP reduction, mmHg						
							1 month	3 months	6 months	12 months	18 months	24 months	36 months
Symplicity HTN-1	Uncontrolled	153	57	176/98	5.1	83	19/9	21/10	22/10	27/14	26/14	29/14	31/16
Symplicity HTN-2	Randomized controlled	106	58	178/97	5.2	77	20/7	24/8	32/12	28/10	32/12	29/10	
Symplicity HTN-3	Randomized controlled	530											

Terms: BP = blood pressure; GFR = glomerular filtration rate (the rate at which blood plasma is filtered).

procedure was equally impressive, with a very low rate of procedure- and device-related complications (including only 3 cases of groin pseudoaneurysms and 1 case of renal artery dissection occurring before the radio-frequency ablation) and the absence of renovascular injury or renal function deterioration up to 2 years post-procedure.

A randomized controlled trial, called Symplicity HTN-2, was conducted to further examine the efficacy of the renal sympathetic denervation. It enrolled 106 patients with resistant hypertension and preserved renal function and assigned them randomly to either a renal denervation group or a control group. The denervation group had impressive BP reductions post-procedure, whereas the control group had no significant change in BP despite their similar baseline characteristics. At the end of the 6-month follow-up, individuals in the control group were crossed over to receive renal denervation. The data, which are now up to 2 years post-procedure, confirm durable BP reductions in both the initial denervation group and the cross-over group. Again, no serious procedure- or device-related complications or significant changes in renal function were noted.

So far, the available results are all based on trials conducted outside of the United States, including Australia, New Zealand, and Europe. Therefore, an ongoing randomized, single-blinded controlled trial, called Symplicity HTN-3, is being carried out at multiple centers in the United States to gain the regulatory approval of this procedure in the United States. The Symplicity HTN-3 trial is expected to enroll 530 patients with resistant hypertension and preserved renal function and to provide the strongest evidence on the catheter-based renal denervation procedure. It will be the largest trial on renal denervation and will compare the catheter-based renal denervation to a catheter-based sham procedure. In anticipation of the potential benefits of renal denervation, patients who are enrolled in the sham procedure group will be offered catheter-based renal denervation upon completion of 6 months of follow-up.

The effects of renal denervation on renal hemodynamics and function, and on the vasculature, were examined in more detail in a group of 88 patients with resistant hypertension and preserved renal function. Besides the similarly impressive reductions in BP and a significant decrease in the renal resistive index (an assessment for renal arterial disease), there were no detectable changes in renal function or signs of renal injury, and no renal artery stenoses (constrictions), dissections, or aneurysms during the 6 months of follow-up.

More recently, a pilot study of 15 patients with resistant hypertension and moderate-to-severe impairment of renal function showed similarly impressive and durable BP reductions up to 1 year after renal denervation. In addition, nighttime (ambulatory) BP levels decreased significantly, restoring a more physiologic nocturnal dipping pattern. Again, there were no significant changes noted in renal function up to 12 months post-denervation. In a feasibility study, 9 out of 12 patients with resistant hypertension and end-stage renal disease were able to undergo the renal denervation procedure and had similarly impressive and durable BP reductions up to 12 months post-procedure. The lowering of the renal and overall sympathetic activity was confirmed by a decrease in renal noradrenaline production and muscle sympathetic nerve firings. These pilot studies of patients with impaired renal function and end-stage renal disease support the potential utility of renal denervation in treating patients who comprise a significant portion of the resistant hypertension population.

Furthermore, the results from several studies suggest that renal denervation has an impact that goes beyond its effect to control BP. For example, it can improve cardiac function, including left ventricular hypertrophy (cardiac muscle thickening) and diastolic function, and other conditions associated with sympathetic hyperactivity, including sleep apnea and glucose intolerance.

Taking into account the available data on the catheter-based renal denervation procedure, a position statement in 2012 by the European Society of Hypertension endorsed the use of renal denervation. However, the statement also recommended that it should only be used in true drug-resistant hypertension and be performed in very experienced medical centers. The optimism of renal denervation will remain guarded at the present time because of the complicated mechanism of hypertension and the lack of long-term results with regard to outcome.

Conclusions. Drug-resistant hypertension remains common. The catheter-based renal denervation procedure has shown impressive BP reductions and a favorable safety profile with no significant procedure- or device-related complications. Despite the promising results so far, ongoing follow-up is necessary to confirm the long-term efficacy and safety of renal denervation. While awaiting answers from the ongoing studies on renal denervation, the field of catheter-based renal denervation is expanding rapidly with the emergence of new ablation devices using different configurations and methods. With the reduction of both the renal and overall sympathetic activities, it is possible that the benefits of renal denervation can extend beyond BP control to other cardiovascular conditions affected by overall sympathetic hyperactivity.

For background information *see* AUTONOMIC NERVOUS SYSTEM; BIOMEDICAL ENGINEERING; CARDIOVASCULAR SYSTEM; HEART DISORDERS; HYPERTENSION; KIDNEY; KIDNEY DISORDERS; NERVE; NERVOUS SYSTEM (VERTEBRATE); SYMPATHETIC NERVOUS SYSTEM in the McGraw-Hill Encyclopedia of Science & Technology.   Yonghong Huan; Debbie L. Cohen

Bibliography. M. D. Esler et al., Renal sympathetic denervation for treatment of drug-resistant hypertension: One-year results from the Symplicity HTN-2 randomized, controlled trial, *Circulation*, 126(25):2976–2982, 2012, DOI:10.1161/CIRCULATIONAHA.112.130880; M. D. Esler et al., Renal sympathetic denervation in patients with treatment-resistant hypertension (The Symplicity HTN-2 Trial): A randomised controlled trial, *Lancet*, 376(9756):1903–1909, 2010, DOI:10.1016/S0140-6736(10)62039-9; S. Ewen et al., Percutaneous renal denervation: New treatment option for resistant hypertension and more?, *Heart*, 99:1129–1134, 2013, DOI:10.1136/heartjnl-2012-301725; H. Krum et al., Catheter-based renal sympathetic denervation for resistant hypertension: A multicentre safety and proof-of-principle cohort study, *Lancet*, 373(9671):1275–1281, 2009, DOI:10.1016/S0140-6736(09)60566-3; Symplicity HTN-1 Investigators, Catheter-based renal sympathetic denervation for resistant hypertension: Durability of blood pressure reduction out to 24 months, *Hypertension*, 57(5):911–917, 2011, DOI:10.1161/HYPERTENSIONAHA.110.163014.

Responses to acute sun exposure in large whales

Although there has been a net decrease of emissions of ozone-depleting substances (which are compounds that contribute to stratospheric ozone depletion, including chlorofluorocarbons and hydrofluorocarbons) in recent years, ozone loss occurs every year over the North Pole and South Pole, and large amounts of solar ultraviolet radiation (UV)

continue to reach our biosphere. These high levels of UV represent a significant threat to the Earth's ecosystems, and there is now evidence that, as happens in humans, some wild species are developing UV-induced skin cancer. So far, the majority of published studies on the effects of UV on wildlife have focused on amphibians, fishes, and invertebrates, largely ignoring the effects on large marine mammals, which are unable to avoid continuous exposure to UV because of their physiological and life-history constraints. Indeed, whales spend extended periods of time at the ocean's surface to breathe and socialize, and they lack the epidermal protection that would be conferred by fur, feathers, or scales. Interestingly, reports of skin lesions in whales have increased in the last decade. Whereas the causes of some lesions have been identified [for example, tattoo skin disease (lesions in the form of black punctiform stippled patterns), caused by poxvirus], the causes of many others (for example, blister-type lesions) remain unknown. It is possible that the large amounts of UV reaching the oceans play a role in the development of these whales' lesions. Knowing that the levels of UV are not expected to change for several decades and that UV has been recognized as one of the most injurious environmental factors for marine ecosystems, it is pressing to investigate the extent of the damage to whales caused by UV.

Sun exposure and lesions. If whales are affected by sun exposure and consequently develop sunburn lesions, some species or individuals might be more sensitive than others. For example, in humans, light-skinned individuals, whose skin presents low amounts of melanin (a pigment that plays an important role in photoprotection), have a higher risk of developing sunburn lesions compared to dark-skinned individuals. Long-lasting effects of repetitive sun exposure can lead to lethal skin cancer, and this risk is 10- to 100-fold higher in light-skinned individuals than in dark-skinned individuals. By extrapolating the photoprotective role of skin pigmentation that is known to occur in humans and laboratory animals, it is possible to hypothesize that whales with paler pigmentation are more sensitive to UV and thus will present higher levels of UV-induced skin lesions than whales with darker pigmentation. In addition, the amount of time that a whale spends daily at the sea surface would be associated with the duration of sun exposure, which might also determine the degree of sunburn, as is observed in laboratory animals exposed to UV for different lengths of time. To test these hypotheses, investigations were carried out that relied on both the distinct skin coloration of blue whales (*Balaenoptera musculus*), fin whales (*Balaenoptera physalus*), and sperm whales (*Physeter macrocephalus*) and their distinct sea-surface behavior (time spent at the sea surface) [**Fig. 1***a*].

Investigations and evidence. A total of 184 skin biopsies (106 from blue whales, 55 from fin whales, and 23 from sperm whales) were collected between 2007 and 2009 in the Gulf of California, Mexico. This

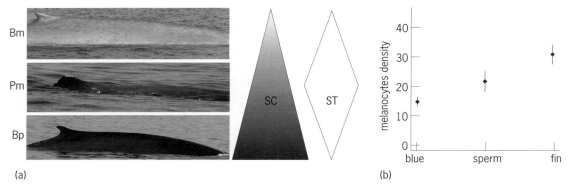

(a)   (b)

Fig. 1. Sun exposure and whales. (*a*) Differences in skin color (SC) and time spent at the surface (ST) among blue whales (*Balaenoptera musculus*, Bm), sperm whales (*Physeter macrocephalus*, Pm), and fin whales (*Balaenoptera physalus*, Bp). (*b*) Melanocyte counts in blue whales (*n* = 53), sperm whales (*n* = 17), and fin whales (*n* = 45). Bars: ±SE (standard error).

region is situated near tropical latitudes, where UV levels can reach cancer radiation doses and where, between January and June, the three aforementioned whale species are seasonally sympatric (occupying the same range). Thin formalin-fixed skin sections of the whales' epidermis were placed on microscope slides and stained with routine hematoxylin and eosin (histologic dyes) to detect and quantify UV-induced epidermal lesions. Specialized stains were used to identify UV-induced glycogen deposition and cells undergoing programmed cell death (apoptosis); these cells are called apoptotic cells or sunburn cells. Knowing that melanocyte cells (cells that produce the melanin pigment, found deep in the epidermis) play a central part in protecting the skin from UV by increasing epidermal melanin concentrations, the individual density of melanocytes using the whales' skin sections was evaluated. Epidermal levels of melanin were also estimated for each individual. Finally, high-quality photographs were used to count gross blisters on a normalized area of the backs of the three whale species.

Evidence of sun-induced lesions in whales included the presence of gross blisters and microscopic lesions characteristic of skin inflammation, such as the abnormal accumulation of fluid in epi-

dermal cells (intracellular edema), the infiltration of immune cells (leukocyte infiltration), and the formation of microvesicles. Occurrences of cytoplasmic vacuoles and epidermal glycogen deposition, generally observed after 24 hours of UV exposure in humans, were also observed in the whale skin sections. Knowing that apoptosis plays a key role in eliminating severely damaged cells that could lead to uncontrolled cell proliferation such as skin cancer, it was interesting to observe that levels of apoptosis in the whale epidermis were relatively high, suggesting that these animals are able to remove sun-damaged cells. Interestingly, melanin formed supranuclear caps over the sun-exposed side of the whale epidermal cells' nuclei. In humans, such melanin formation protects the nuclear DNA from UV insults. At the DNA level, whales present UV-induced lesions in their mitochondrial DNA. Taken together, these results prove that whales can and do experience UV-induced damage.

Variation among whale species. Sun-induced skin abnormalities varied among the whale species. As expected, fin whales, because of their darker pigmentation, had the lowest levels of blisters and microscopic lesions (**Fig. 2**). Furthermore, the most pigmented whales, that is, those with the highest levels of melanocytes and melanin, had the lowest levels of lesions, including cytoplasmic vacuolation and intracellular edema. A similar relationship was observed when looking at UV-induced mitochondrial DNA lesions. These results suggest that increased pigmentation protects the skin from cellular and molecular damage, similar to what occurs in humans. In addition, a direct relationship between pigmentation and apoptotic cells was observed, suggesting that darker whales are better able to remove potentially precancerous UV-damaged cells via melanin-mediated apoptosis, as described in humans. Together, the findings suggest that whale skin pigmentation plays an important photoprotective role. Work is currently in progress to study the capacity of whales to modulate their level of pigmentation as a response to fluctuating levels of UV. Similar abilities have been described so far for only a few wild species, such as fish and zooplankton.

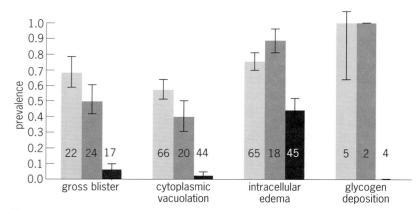

Fig. 2. Prevalence of gross blisters and microscopic epidermal abnormalities in blue whales (light gray bars), sperm whales (dark gray bars), and fin whales (black bars). Sample sizes are indicated in the figure. Bars: ±SE (standard error).

Arguably, the dark pigmentation of fin whales might not be the only reason for their comparatively lower prevalence of lesions compared to blue whales. Another, nonexclusive explanation might include the different migratory patterns of the two species. Indeed, whereas blue whales migrate annually from higher latitudes with relatively lower levels of UV to lower latitudes with relatively higher levels of UV, fin whales are resident in the Gulf of California, where UV levels are high for most of the year. Thus, blue whales receive acute doses of UV upon their arrival in the Gulf of California, whereas fin whales do not. Interestingly, blue whales sampled at the beginning of the season showed a higher prevalence of UV-induced microscopic damage than those sampled at the end of the season, strengthening the hypothesis that blue whales receive high doses of UV upon their arrival, followed by some acclimatization, as is known to happen in humans. In addition to skin color and migratory behavior, the duration of UV exposure might play a role in the occurrence of sunburn in whales. Indeed, although sperm whales are resident in the Gulf of California and have significantly higher densities of melanocytes compared to blue whales (Fig. 1*b*), the two species showed comparable levels of sun-induced skin lesions (Fig. 2). The extended duration, up to 6 h at a time, that sperm whales can remain at the surface while resting might explain such high levels of lesions in this species compared to the similarly dark fin whales, which generally spend less than 10 min at a time at the sea surface.

Other factors. Finally, it was interesting to observe that blue whales sampled in 2009 showed a markedly higher prevalence of gross blisters compared to samples obtained in the previous years. A similar trend was observed for cytoplasmic vacuolation. These patterns raise the possibility that the year 2009 might have been particularly intense in terms of UV exposure. As levels of UV are directly related to ozone-layer thickness under clear sky conditions, it is tempting to speculate that the high prevalence of lesions observed in 2009 resulted from severe ozone-layer thinning. However, no evidence of a reduction in the ozone layer from 2007 to 2009 was found. A more parsimonious explanation might be that the observed trend reflects month-to-month variations in ozone levels and thus UV exposure. In addition, as there was no evidence that the population is aging, the results are unlikely to reflect an age-related decrease in repair mechanisms.

Outlook. In conclusion, a previously ignored environmental stressor, specifically the high UV levels that continue to reach our biosphere, can affect whales, particularly those with lightly pigmented skin and those that spend sustained periods of time at the sea surface. This new field of research may be useful for whale management plans and conservation efforts. More important, because of their long life expectancy and their extended distribution, whales could reflect UV variation across large spatial and temporal scales and thus could be considered as UV barometers of the ocean.

For background information *see* APOPTOSIS; BURN; CANCER (MEDICINE); CELL (BIOLOGY); CETACEA; INFLAMMATION; OZONE; PIGMENTATION; SKIN; SKIN DISORDERS; STRATOSPHERIC OZONE; ULTRAVIOLET RADIATION; ULTRAVIOLET RADIATION (BIOLOGY) in the McGraw-Hill Encyclopedia of Science & Technology.

Laura M. Martinez-Levasseur; Diane Gendron; Robert J. Knell; Edel A. O'Toole; Manuraj Singh; Amy Bowman; Mark Birch-Machin; Karina Acevedo-Whitehouse

Bibliography. A. Bowman et al., Mitochondrial DNA, a reliable biomarker for measuring the effect of cumulative ultraviolet irradiation exposure in whales (cetaceans), in *Annual Meeting of the British Society for Investigative Dermatology*, Wiley-Blackwell, Exeter, UK, 2012; M. Llabrés et al., Impact of elevated UVB radiation on marine biota: A meta-analysis, *Global Ecol. Biogeogr.*, 22(1):131–144, 2013, DOI:10.1111/j.1466-8238.2012.00784.x; L. M. Martinez, Effects of solar radiation on cetaceans, PhD dissertation, Queen Mary University of London, 2011; L. M. Martinez-Levasseur et al., Acute sun damage and photoprotective responses in whales, *Proc. R. Soc. Lond. B Biol. Sci.*, 278:1581–1586, 2011, DOI:10.1098/rspb.2010.1903; R. L. McKenzie et al., Ozone depletion and climate change: Impacts on UV radiation, *Photochem. Photobiol. Sci.*, 10:182–198, 2011, DOI:10.1039/C0PP90034F; Y. Yamaguchi, J. Beer, and V. Hearing, Melanin mediated apoptosis of epidermal cells damaged by ultraviolet radiation: Factors influencing the incidence of skin cancer, *Arch. Dermatol. Res.*, 300:43–50, 2008, DOI:10.1007/s00403-007-0807-0.

Restoration of the American chestnut tree

The American chestnut (*Castanea dentata*) [**Fig. 1**] was once known as the "king of the forest" and was the single most prevalent hardwood tree in the eastern half of the United States. In those forests, nearly one out of every four canopy trees was an American chestnut. Some of these trees were giants, reaching heights in excess of 30 m (98 ft) and having diameters (at breast height) in excess of 3 m (9.8 ft). They often were free of branches for the first 15 m (49 ft). The natural range of the American chestnut extended from Maine down to the northern parts of Georgia, Alabama, and Mississippi, and west to the greater Ohio River Valley and the western end of Lake Erie.

During the first half of the twentieth century, an Asian fungus (*Cryphonectria parasitica*), inciting a disease known as chestnut blight (**Fig. 2**), was accidently imported into the United States. Chestnut blight was first observed on American chestnut trees in New York City's Bronx Zoo in 1904. The fungus spread quickly and more than four billion trees were destroyed across nearly 200 million acres

Fig. 1. American chestnut trees (*Castanea dentata*) in North Carolina (circa 1910). These magnificent examples of the American chestnut were photographed in the early twentieth century near the present-day location of the Great Smoky Mountains National Park. (*Photo courtesy of the Forest History Society*)

was a staple in many American households prior to the chestnut blight. Families depended on the nut as a major food source and as a cash crop. Millions of bushels of the sweet-tasting nuts were hauled to cities such as New York and Philadelphia and sold during the Christmas holidays. Many railroad cars were filled to the brim each year for shipment to urban areas. Farm families in the Appalachian Mountains fattened their hogs and other livestock on the nuts, and children would fill their pockets with chestnuts to snack on at school.

The most important hard mast (hard shelled seeds) for wildlife almost assuredly was produced by the American chestnut. Hard mast commonly available to wildlife includes acorns, hickory nuts, beechnuts, and walnuts. Mast provides wildlife with critical nutrients during the fall and winter months when other foods are scarce in the forest. The chestnut's plentiful, reliable nut crop likely provided more nourishment than any other hard mast. Many species likely benefited from chestnuts, including whitetailed deer, bears, raccoons, wild boars, squirrels, mice, wood rats, wild turkeys, grouse, crows, and blue jays.

Restoring the American chestnut. The American Chestnut Foundation (TACF) was established in 1983 with one clear mission: to restore the American chestnut to the eastern woodlands of the United States to benefit the environment, wildlife, and society.

Backcross breeding program. Since 1983, TACF has been working to restore the American chestnut tree by breeding blight-resistant trees using a backcross tree breeding method developed by the plant geneticist Charles Burnham. The goal of the backcross breeding program is to develop a population of trees with the growth characteristics of the American chestnut while maintaining genes from the Chinese parent that confer resistance to chestnut blight. Burnham's plan predicted that chestnuts should have adequate American type plus blight resistance by the third generation of the third backcross (B_3F_3) [**Fig. 3**].

The backcross breeding program intends to continue breeding beyond the B_3F_3 level, but trees at the B_3F_3 level of breeding are considered to be suitable for the start of a long-term process of testing and reintroduction. As more advanced lines of potentially blight-resistant trees are developed, TACF will switch over to using these trees for testing and reforestation efforts.

Overall, the breeding program selects for trees that exhibit both American chestnut growth characteristics and enough blight resistance to allow the tree to reproduce sexually; this is a basic requirement for the breeding program's success. To maximize the genetic diversity among the chestnut trees, a network of state chapters throughout the historic range of the American chestnut has been established. These chapters breed American chestnuts indigenous to their states. The reasons for

(81 million hectares) of forestland. Most of the trees succumbed to the blight. Chestnuts that did not initially die were often cut down to preserve the timber for future use.

In a short span of 50 years, the American chestnut was gone from the landscape of America as a forest canopy tree. As such, chestnut blight is recognized as one of the worst ecological disasters of the twentieth century. Although American chestnut trees are still common in American forests today, they exist as small saplings growing from seeds or the root system of parent trees originally infected by the blight during the early twentieth century; the saplings are continually knocked back by repeated attacks of chestnut blight and rarely reach the canopy.

Historically, the American chestnut was an important tree for both wildlife and society. The chestnut

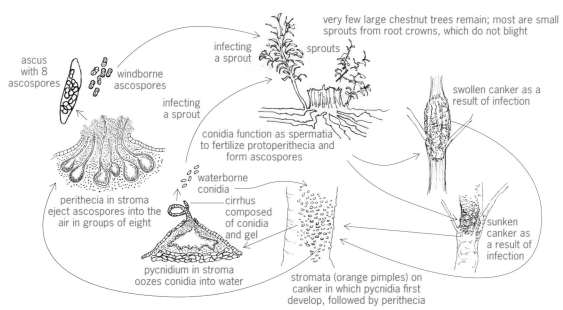

Fig. 2. Diagram of the disease cycle of chestnut blight, incited by *Cryphonectria parasitica*. One of the reasons that *Cryphonectria parasitica* is so lethal to American chestnuts is that it has two different ways of reproducing and multiple ways of being transported. Ascospores (sexually produced fungal spores) are windborne, and conidia (asexually produced spores) are waterborne. In addition, conidia can be transported from tree to tree by adhering to birds, mammals, or insects, and they can even pass through the digestive system of mites. (*Illustration courtesy of The American Chestnut Foundation*)

using indigenous chestnut trees within the breeding program are to develop blight-resistant trees that are adapted to the environment peculiar to the state and to increase the overall genetic diversity of trees in the program. The state chapter system has developed more than 450 breeding orchards, representing more than 70,000 chestnut trees. Therefore, the breeding program incorporates genetic characteristics from local chestnut trees through state chapter breeding programs as well as blight resistance from multiple types of Asian chestnuts.

During the spring of 2009, TACF partnered with the United States Department of Agriculture (USDA) Forest Service, the USDA Forest Service Southern Research Station, and the University of Tennessee to initiate testing of the first lines of potentially blight-resistant chestnuts (B_3F_3). Additional plantings have been installed, and growth characteristics and blight resistance are being continually monitored in these trees (**Fig. 4**).

In addition to the plantings initiated with the USDA Forest Service, TACF has established other B_3F_3 plantings on both private and public lands to secure data on resistance and growth of the B_3F_3 trees. Presently, it is still too early in the testing process to make any meaningful evaluation of the B_3F_3 trees, beyond that they have enhanced blight resistance compared to the American chestnut. However, as mentioned previously, the B_3F_3 tree is not necessarily the end of the breeding efforts. On the contrary, the B_3F_3 represents the beginning of a continual process of additional breeding and testing, both in structured field trials and in actual reintroduction efforts.

Ink disease. The backcross breeding program extends beyond breeding blight-resistant chestnut trees. It is also engaged in a breeding program designed to develop trees resistant to ink disease. Ink disease is incited by the organism *Phytophthora cinnamomi*, as well as other species of *Phytophthora*. Many chestnut plantings have failed as a result of ink disease, mainly in the southeastern United States where this organism is common. Although chemical treatment for *Phytophthora* is effective in orchard situations, this is not a practical approach for reintroducing the American chestnut to the wild. Current efforts (in particular, at Chestnut Return Farm in Seneca, South Carolina) are now focused on selecting for chestnuts that have resistance to both blight and ink disease.

Biotechnology. The use of biotechnological methodologies is another pathway that is being used to develop blight-resistant trees. In partnership with the State University of New York–College of Environmental Science and Forestry (SUNY–ESF), Pennsylvania State University, the University of Georgia, North Carolina State University, Clemson University, and the USDA Forest Service, TACF collaborators are experimenting with transgenic (gene transfer) approaches to confer blight-resistance. Genetic markers are also being identified and mapped that will help to accelerate and improve traditional breeding programs. During the spring of 2011, TACF's New York State chapter and SUNY–ESF planted their first transgenic chestnuts for testing and evaluation.

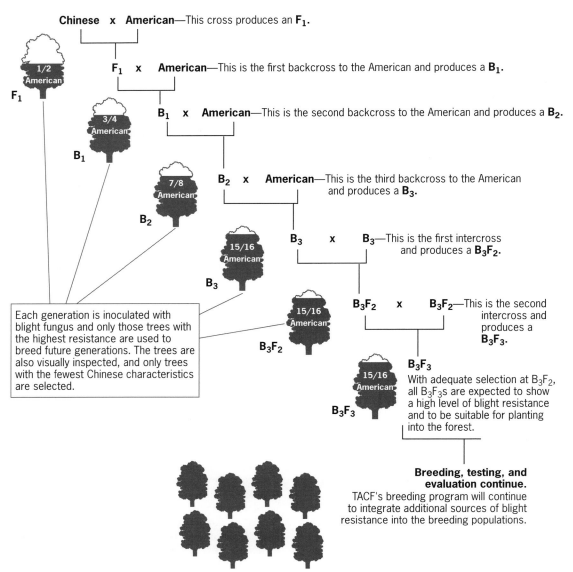

Each generation is inoculated with blight fungus and only those trees with the highest resistance are used to breed future generations. The trees are also visually inspected, and only trees with the fewest Chinese characteristics are selected.

Chinese x American—This cross produces an **F₁**.

F₁ x American—This is the first backcross to the American and produces a **B₁**.

B₁ x American—This is the second backcross to the American and produces a **B₂**.

B₂ x American—This is the third backcross to the American and produces a **B₃**.

B₃ x B₃—This is the first intercross and produces a **B₃F₂**.

B₃F₂ x B₃F₂—This is the second intercross and produces a **B₃F₃**.

B₃F₃ With adequate selection at B₃F₂, all B₃F₃s are expected to show a high level of blight resistance and to be suitable for planting into the forest.

Breeding, testing, and evaluation continue. TACF's breeding program will continue to integrate additional sources of blight resistance into the breeding populations.

Fig. 3. **The American Chestnut Foundation's unique backcross breeding program requires a minimum of six generations of breeding to produce a blight-resistant chestnut tree that is 15/16ths American and 1/16th Chinese. The backcross breeding program begins by crossing an American chestnut and a Chinese chestnut. This is followed by three successive generations of crossing back to American chestnut trees to restore American characteristics. In between each breeding step, the trees are inoculated with blight fungus (*Cryphonectria parasitica*), and only those trees showing strong blight resistance and American characteristics are chosen to breed additional generations. For the final two generations, trees with proven blight resistance are intercrossed with each other to eliminate genes for susceptibility to blight introduced from the American parents. (*Illustration courtesy of The American Chestnut Foundation*)**

In 2012, the New York State chapter/SUNY–ESF partnership developed several transgenic recombination events based on the oxalate oxidase (*OXO*) gene (which enhances plant disease resistance activity) combined with a vascular promoter gene that expresses levels of blight resistance equal to the level exhibited by the Chinese chestnut. In addition, researchers are working on further transgenic events based on the same *OXO* gene combined with a different promoter gene that is showing 30 to 200 times the expression of the *OXO* gene in lab assays compared to using the vascular promoter.

Outlook. The loss of the American chestnut resulted in a tremendous blow to the eastern forests of the United States. This loss affected society, wildlife, and the productivity of the forests. The American Chestnut Foundation's mission is to restore the American chestnut to the eastern woodlands to benefit the environment, wildlife, and society. To achieve this monumental task, a structured, yet diverse program has been developed that will span many generations. This program is now at a juncture where trees are being planted in real forest environments and where they are being closely evaluated. Breeding will continue for many more decades, but efforts will expand in scope to include ecological and silvicultural aspects of the restoration program.

Fig. 4. Young chestnut seedlings growing at Meadowview Research Farms in Virginia. These young seedlings are part of the research and breeding program conducted by The American Chestnut Foundation. In 2009, potentially blight-resistant chestnuts were planted in real forest environments. (*Photo courtesy of The American Chestnut Foundation*)

For background information *see* CHESTNUT; FOREST AND FORESTRY; FOREST MANAGEMENT; NUT CROP CULTURE; POPULATION ECOLOGY; POPULATION VIABILITY; REFORESTATION; SILVICULTURE; TREE; TREE DISEASES in the McGraw-Hill Encyclopedia of Science & Technology.

Bryan Burhans; Frederick V. Hebard

Bibliography. A. Barakat et al., Chestnut resistance to the blight disease: Insights from transcriptome analysis, *BMC Plant Biol.*, 12:38, 2012, DOI:10.1186/1471-2229-12-38; S. Barilovits, First year results on the use of phosphate compounds for managing *Phytophthora* root rot in American chestnut seedlings, *TACF J.*, XXIII(1):22–32, 2009; C. R. Burnham, P. A. Rutter, and D. W. French, Breeding blight-resistant chestnuts, *Plant Breed. Rev.*, 4:347–397, 1986; S. Jeffers, J. James, and P. Sisco, Screening for resistance to *Phytophthora cinnamomi* in hybrid seedlings of American chestnut, pp. 188–194, in *Phytophthoras in Forests and Natural Ecosystems*, USDA Forest Service, Pacific Southwest Research Station, Albany, CA, 2009.

RGB workflow

Preparing a colored photograph for commercial printing requires converting it into color separations corresponding to the percentages of cyan, magenta, yellow, and black (CMYK) ink needed in each part of the image. To optimize printed quality, the CMYK separations then have to be adjusted by a process known as "color correction," which traditionally involved altering the CMYK values on the printing plates or the files from which they were made. Recent technology advancements have enabled a more powerful color correction workflow in which images are edited in units of RGB light instead of CMYK inks. The RGB workflow has revolutionized printing, with numerous benefits for printers and print buyers alike.

To appreciate the significance and benefits of the RGB workflow, a basic understanding of the principles of color photography and color printing is required. In showing that the two disciplines evolved together and that printing is simply an extension of photography, this article will show why RGB color correction has largely replaced CMYK methods.

Principles of color photography. The origins of color photography can be traced to two important discoveries. The first, by Sir Isaac Newton in 1672, was that white light is composed of many different colors, or wavelengths, in what is now called the visible spectrum (**Fig. 1***a*). The second, by James Clerk Maxwell in the 1850s, was that by varying the intensities of just three—red, green, and blue—lights, virtually any color in the spectrum, including white, could be created (Fig. 1*b*).

Maxwell's discovery revealed that the human visual system is not sensitive to individual wavelengths, but is sensitive to just three general sensations of red, green, and blue (RGB). This was the clue that unlocked the secret to natural-color photography.

The earliest surviving color photograph is Maxwell's Tartan Ribbon, made in 1861 by taking three black-and-white color-separated negatives through red, green, and blue filters (**Fig. 2**). At the time, photographic plates were insensitive to red light, so the experiment was only partially successful (as shown by the drab coloring), but the concept was correct. Today's digital cameras use the same principle, capturing the scene on a single black-and-white "chip" whose millions of pixels are covered with a pattern of microscopic red, green, and blue filters.

To view his photographs in color, Maxwell projected three black-and-white positive copies of the

(a)

(b)

Fig. 1. The principles on which color photography is based. (*a*) Newton's discovery that white light consists of a large number of individual colors. (*b*) Maxwell's discovery that with only three beams of red, green, and blue light, virtually any color can be produced. (*Copyright © HutchColor, LLC*)

Fig. 2. Tartan Ribbon. The earliest surviving color photograph, from 1861.

camera negatives onto a white screen through the same RGB filters, but this was an awkward and impermanent approach.

Louis Ducos du Hauron solved the impermanence problem by converting the RGB separation negatives into positives, dyeing each with its opposite color, then transferring the dye images in register onto a white base. The red positive was dyed cyan (the product of blue and green light), the green positive was dyed magenta (the product of red and blue light), and the blue positive was dyed yellow (the product of red and green light). This was the birth of modern color printing.

Although they were more convenient to view, du Hauron's prints were less colorful than Maxwell's projected images largely because of impurities in the available dyes.

Principles of color printing. Modern color printing uses the same principles pioneered by Maxwell and du Hauron, whereby a physical photograph (slide or print) is color-separated by scanning or rephotographing it through red, green, and blue filters. (Digital camera files avoid this step.) The RGB values are then converted to cyan, magenta, and yellow (CMY) ink percentages, with black (K) added to enhance contrast (**Fig. 3**).

Although they are better than du Hauron's dyes, today's inks are still far from ideal. For example, a perfect cyan ink should reflect all blue and green light and absorb all red light, but in practice some red light is reflected and some blue and green light is absorbed, effectively contaminating cyan with unwanted magenta and yellow ink. Similarly, a perfect magenta ink should reflect all red and blue light and absorb all green, but in practice a large amount of blue light is absorbed, effectively contaminating magenta ink with a large percentage of yellow.

Color correction. Ink impurities can be reduced or color corrected by adjusting the relative strength of the color separations prior to printing (**Fig. 4**). For example, if the yellow separation is lightened in proportion to the magenta separation in areas where both inks print, the yellow contaminant that is already present in magenta ink can be effectively subtracted. And if the magenta and yellow separations are lightened in proportion to cyan, the yellow and magenta contaminants in cyan ink can be effectively subtracted.

The tools with which ink impurities are color corrected have multiple uses, including:
- Compensating for ink impurities
- Adjusting for variations in the printing process
- Correcting for errors or limitations in the original photograph
- Applying creative effects, such as making a blue sky "bluer" or roses "redder."

Traditionally, it was the CMYK color-separation values that were color corrected, partly because that was the medium available, but also because printing was poorly standardized and unpredictable. Ink colors and the way they reacted on press varied

Fig. 3. Principles of color photography. (*a*) A scene is photographed through (*b*) red, green, and blue filters, making (*c*) three color-separation images, from which (*d*) cyan, magenta, and yellow positive dye images are made; when registered together on a white substrate, these produce (*e*) a full-color print. (*Copyright © HutchColor, LLC*)

dramatically from press to press, so a different set of CMYK separations (and color corrections) was needed for each press run.

Advances in color printing. In the last decade, printing quality and predictability have dramatically increased thanks to standardized ink colors, improved press specifications such as G7® and GRACoL®, and automated CMYK conversions via International Color Consortium (ICC) color management

(described later). The need to custom-compensate for ink impurities or press variations has been virtually eliminated, yet prepress color correction remains a vital tool to:

- Correct for under- or over-exposure
- Remove color casts (for example, a blue tint produced by overcast sky)
- Improve the color accuracy of a product or subject

(a)

(b)

Fig. 4. A CMYK file printed (*a*) without and (*b*) with color correction to compensate for ink impurities. Colors in image a appear dirty and desaturated as a result of unwanted ink contamination. (*Copyright © HutchColor, LLC*)

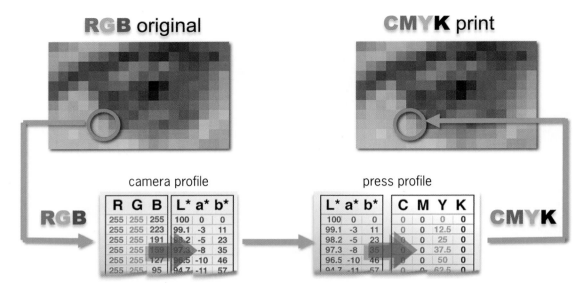

Fig. 5. Conversion of an RGB camera file into CMYK via two device profiles. (*Copyright* © *HutchColor, LLC*)

- Make editorial changes to meet the client's creative intent.

Because the main reasons for color correction are now photographic, and because the fundamental units of color photography are RGB, the most logical units in which to make color corrections are now RGB and not CMYK.

The impact of digital photography. Until the late 1990s, photographic slides or prints were color-separated on drum scanners whose built-in color computers translated RGB optical values directly into CMYK percentages. When digital files began arriving, there was no way to feed them into the scanner computer, so a new way was needed to convert RGB into CMYK.

The perfect solution arrived in the form of ICC color management and software like Adobe Photoshop®, which allowed quick, intuitive color corrections while viewing an RGB camera file on a computer screen. By making the corrections before converting to CMYK, creative personnel (such as photographers or artists) with little or no CMYK knowledge could now make their own editorial color corrections.

The impact of ICC color management. Crucial to this new RGB workflow was the ability to convert to CMYK after all editorial color corrections were complete. This was enabled by ICC color management, introduced in 1994.

ICC color management facilitates fast, automated translation of colored image data between two or more devices (for example, a camera and a printing press) by linking their device profiles. An ICC profile acts as a translation dictionary, or look-up table, between a device's native image values (RGB for scanners, cameras, or monitors; CMYK for desktop printers or printing presses) and a profile connection space (PCS). The PCS is usually CIELAB (also known as L* a* b*, pronounced "L-star," "a-star," "b-star"), which is one of several ISO-standard CIE (Commis-

sion Internationale d'Eclairage) color spaces based on human color vision research.

When a camera profile is assigned to an RGB image in software like Photoshop, each pixel is translated from RGB into L*a*b* values that represent the color seen by the eye. To convert the image into CMYK, the L*a*b* values are looked up in an appropriate output profile to find the CMYK values necessary to print that color (**Fig. 5**).

A clever pair of ICC rules ensures that no matter how much an RGB image is color-corrected, the resulting pixel values will always translate into rational L*a*b* units, for which optimum CMYK values will always be found in any CMYK profile:

First, in every RGB profile, every RGB value from 0, 0, 0 (infinite black) to 255, 255, 255 (pure white) is included with its equivalent L*a*b* value. Second, in every press profile, regardless of the range of colors the press can print, every possible L*a*b* value must be accepted and translated, if not into that exact color, then into the nearest color available on that printing system.

ICC conversions have relegated the skill-intensive process of correcting for ink limitations to a simple look-up table at the end of the workflow, freeing the creative and prepress workflows to focus on optimizing each RGB image visually, without necessarily knowing how it will be printed. More important, the image can be output on any number of different printing processes, without having to repeat the editorial adjustments.

Soft-proofing (display simulation). Another critical requirement of the RGB workflow is that the monitor on which visual corrections are made must have its own custom ICC profile; if it does not, it will not show the true colors of the original RGB image or the final print. Just having a custom ICC display profile is not enough for critical work, however, because RGB images often contain colors that are outside the printable gamut, so the color on the screen will often

Fig. 6. Ideal soft-proofing environment with an adjustable-brightness D50 viewing booth alongside the display. (*Copyright* © *HutchColor, LLC*)

be more brilliant or more saturated than the press can print. This is solved by soft-proofing.

Soft-proofing converts a proxy of the RGB image into CMYK, then converts the CMYK values into monitor RGB using ICC profiles. Colors outside the printable gamut are therefore displayed as they will really print, avoiding disappointment on press.

On a professional soft-proofing workstation, a viewing booth equipped with ISO-standard D50 lighting is located next to the monitor and adjusted to the same brightness level (**Fig. 6**). When the monitor is calibrated to match the color of the booth light, a critical visual comparison can be made between the soft proof and a physical print. Without such a system, variations in room lighting make it impossible to compare the soft proof reliably with a physical print.

RGB workflow overview. A successful RGB workflow for editorial image corrections typically requires:

- A desktop computer (Mac or PC)
- Adobe Photoshop
- A high-quality monitor
- A custom ICC monitor-profiling utility
- A CMYK profile of the printing process (for soft-proofing or CMYK conversion).

The typical steps in an RGB prepress workflow are:

- Open the RGB image in image editing software
- Make color corrections or editorial adjustments as needed
- Switch to soft-proofing mode to check how the colors will look on press
- Save a copy of the RGB image in case future adjustments are needed

- Assemble the image into a printable document in Adobe InDesign® or equivalent software
- Save the finished document as a PDF file, or whatever format is required
- Convert to CMYK just prior to printing (ideally done by the printer).

Workflow comparison: RGB versus CMYK. Compared to working in CMYK, an RGB workflow offers numerous quality, simplicity, versatility, and cost benefits. A major economic benefit is that RGB color corrections or creative edits have to be done only once, regardless of how many ways the RGB file will be printed (**Fig. 7***a*). Once optimized, an RGB image can be reproduced accurately on any number of output devices simply by converting it to the appropriate CMYK profiles. A CMYK workflow is potentially more expensive because color and creative edits must be repeated for each output process (Fig. 7*b*).

Speed, ease, and safety. RGB color correction is faster, easier, and safer than correcting in CMYK because there are no arcane CMYK rules. For example, the total of all four CMYK ink percentages allowed in the blackest image areas varies according to the printing process and is typically well below the theoretical 400% maximum. Too much ink can lead to poor drying, smudging, or bleed-through to the other side of the page. Simply lightening or darkening a CMYK image can push the CMYK total out of bounds, forcing a skilled CMYK color corrector to constantly check that the correct total is preserved.

By contrast, the ideal maximum black in an RGB image is always 0, 0, 0 RGB, which the output profile will always convert to the optimum CMYK values. Other critical CMYK parameters, such as ink correction, gray balance, and tonal reproduction, are also

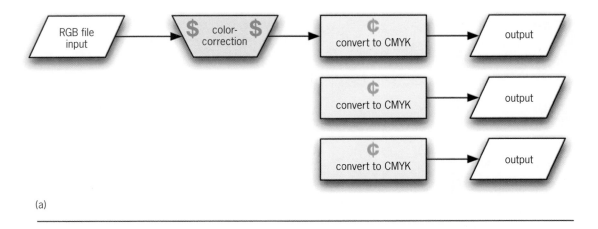

(a)

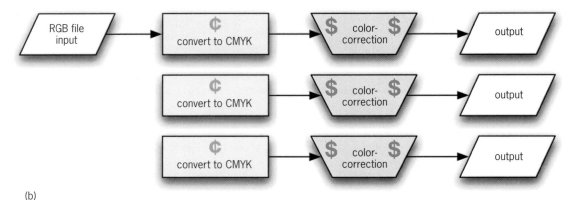

(b)

Fig. 7. RGB versus CMYK workflow. (*a*) An RGB workflow is more cost-effective because the skill-intensive color correction process has to be done only once, followed by any number of inexpensive CMYK conversions. (*b*) Costs are generally greater in a CMYK workflow because color correction and creative edits must be repeated for each output process. (*Copyright* © *HutchColor, LLC*)

built into the CMYK profile, so it is impossible for even the most extreme RGB corrections to produce incorrect CMYK percentages if the correct CMYK profile is applied at the end of the workflow.

Photorealism and range of correction. Perhaps the most compelling benefit of an RGB workflow is the range and photorealism of possible corrections. By manipulating the camera file's RGB values, a photograph can be virtually "retaken" to correct for photographic problems.

Subliminal RGB data resident in the original camera file can be amplified in a way similar to the action of light on film or on the sensor chip. Like the latent image in an undeveloped film, this residual detail, normally hidden from view, can be effectively "redeveloped" to compensate for inaccurate camera exposure.

If the RGB file is first converted to CMYK, such corrections are no longer possible because the subliminal RGB data are lost in the CMYK conversion. This is clearly illustrated when an underexposed image has to be lightened, as shown in **Fig. 8**.

In defense of CMYK. In spite of the obvious advantages of RGB, a few apparently logical arguments can be made in defense of CMYK, with the most common being, "We print with CMYK inks, so they must be the best color correction units." This was true when the primary reason for color correction was ink or press issues, but those have been solved by standardized printing and ICC profiles. Today's corrections almost exclusively address photographic or creative issues, which are more logically (and effectively) manipulated in RGB.

Another seemingly logical argument is, "Four variables give more control than three." This is true if the goal is to control a four-color printing process. But to control a tricolor photographic process, the reverse is actually true because the black separation, being derived from the original RGB values, adds no new pictorial information. In fact, the act of creating the black separation actually destroys subliminal color data, with the result that they can no longer be used to make photorealistic exposure or color corrections.

The cases where CMYK is preferable are the creation of colored text or artificial blocks of color. For example, if a designer wants a pure yellow object, the best approach is to define it as 0% cyan, 0% magenta, 100% yellow, and 0% black. If the same yellow block is specified in RGB, after conversion to CMYK

Fig. 8. Photographic image correction. (*a*) Original underexposed image. (*b*) Corrected in RGB. (c) Corrected in CMYK. Notice the smoother, more photorealistic reproduction of dark colors in the RGB-corrected image. (*Copyright* © *HutchColor, LLC*)

it may contain an unwanted pattern of fine magenta or cyan halftone dots (the small dots you can see on any printed page), depending on the particular RGB and CMYK profiles. Of course, the actual color of the final object will now depend on the yellow ink and may be slightly different from what the artist intended.

Summary. In the past, images intended for printing were color corrected by manipulating the CMYK printing-ink values. Thanks to recent technological advances, the preferred workflow today is RGB-based.

Time Inc. was the first major publisher to adopt RGB workflows in the late 1990s. By the mid-2000s, most other publishers, advertising agencies, printers, and brands had followed for economic and quality reasons.

For background information *see* COLOR; COLOR VISION; INK; LIGHT; PHOTOGRAPHY; PRINTING in the McGraw-Hill Encyclopedia of Science & Technology.
Don Hutcheson

Self-healing polymers

Polymer materials are found in a variety of applications for everyday life and are most often used to reduce costs and improve material properties. These materials are versatile, lightweight, and can be molded at will. With advancements in polymer chemistry, the functionality of polymer materials has greatly increased, particularly from the viewpoint of mechanical, electronic, and optical properties. However, the goal of generating self-healing polymers, which possess the ability to heal autonomously in response to damage, has remained unachieved until recently. Self-healing polymers could contribute to the extension of polymer lifetime and reduction of waste, and bring us closer to realizing an environmentally sustainable society. In addition, self-healing polymers can be expected to contribute to the development of reliable restorative materials that

may benefit fields such as space development and artificial organs.

After some preliminary but fragmentary work on self-healing polymers in the twentieth century, the idea of self-healing polymers was spotlighted as accessible by pioneering work at the beginning of this century. This work employed the microencapsulation of a "healing agent" (in this case, a bifunctional monomer) that would be released after a crack in the polymer breached the microcapsules, and subsequently the agent polymerized after contact with an initiator or catalyst embedded within the polymer matrix. Since this seminal work, plenty of self-healing materials have been reported and some are now available commercially. More strategies toward the development of self-healing polymers have been proposed (**Fig. 1**). Both physical and chemical strategies have been explored, with the latter further classified into three separate branches, making use of healing agents, noncovalent interactions, and reversible covalent bonds.

Physical strategy. Physical strategies for obtaining self-healing polymers are particularly effective in the field of polymer coatings. Polymer coatings are usually applied to improve the surface properties of a substrate, such as adhesion, wettability, corrosion

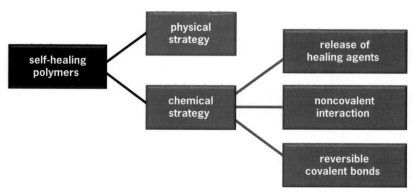

Fig. 1. Classification of self-healing polymers.

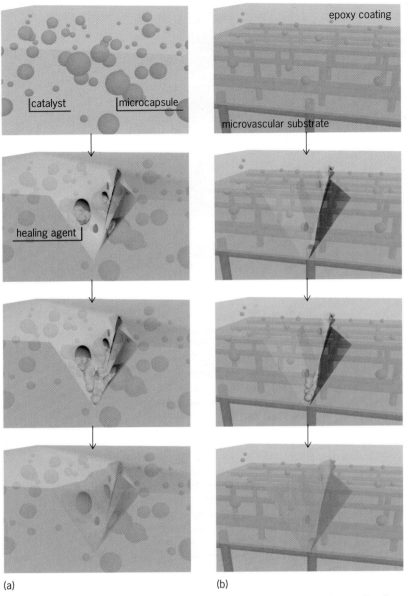

(a)   (b)

Fig. 2. Schematic representation of self-healing materials based on the release of healing agents. (*a*) Microencapsulation system. (*b*) Artificial microvascular system.

cially available as automobile coatings, laptop housings, protective films for mobile device screens, and so on. However, once the polymer coating is cracked severely enough to reach the substrate, the film no longer exhibits self-healing behavior. Physically self-healing polymers that are cut this severely cannot typically be repaired by bringing the cut surfaces into contact with each other.

Release of healing agents. Various synthetic and self-healing materials have been inspired by biological self-healing processes. In one of the most influential ideas in the field of self-healing polymers (**Fig. 2***a*), microcapsules containing fluid healing agents are embedded in a polymer matrix. A bifunctional liquid monomer, dicyclopentadiene, is incorporated into the microcapsules to serve as the healing agent, and a Grubbs (ruthenium-based) catalyst is dispersed into the epoxy matrix to trigger polymerization. When a crack in the bulk polymer breaks open the microcapsules, liquid monomer flows into the crack by capillary action. The catalyst can subsequently react with the monomer to yield a cross-linked polymer by ring-opening metathesis polymerization. As a result, the crack can be successfully sealed and the mechanical properties can be recovered to some extent. This pioneering work motivated many researchers to develop similar self-healing systems using microcapsules containing monomers or catalysts.

Artificial microvascular systems, which enable multiple healing cycles, have also been successfully incorporated into polymer materials. This bio-inspired design incorporates a three-dimensional microvascular network embedded in the substrate that delivers a healing agent to cracks in the polymer coating (Fig. 2*b*). In this system, crack damage to the epoxy coating can be healed repeatedly by continuous delivery of healing agents. This sophisticated self-healing system mimics that of human skin, in which a minor cut triggers blood flow from capillary networks in the underlying dermal layer of skin. Such microvascular network systems can deliver not only healing agents, but also molecular signals, coolants, or other chemical species that provide additional functionality such as self-diagnosis or self-cooling.

Noncovalent interaction. Noncovalent interactions, such as ionic interactions and hydrogen bonding, are reversible and thus good candidates for the construction of self-healing polymers. When noncovalent interactions are introduced to cross-linking points in polymers, cross-links gain the ability to reversibly dissociate and associate under certain conditions. Because noncovalent interactions are weaker than covalent bonds present throughout the polymer skeleton, the cross-linking points are preferentially dissociated by external mechanical stress. The dissociated parts exist in an unstable state and tend to associate autonomously or through external stimulation such as heating. Poly(ethylene-*co*-methacrylic acid) [EMAA] copolymers and ionomers (for example, the sodium ionomer Na-EMAA) are

resistance, wear resistance, and scratch resistance. Polymer coatings were traditionally validated based on their lifetime, and classical coatings concentrated on increasing stiffness to protect the substrate from mechanical shock. Self-healing polymer coatings are based on a completely different concept, which considers not only the lifetime of the coating but also the stability of its appearance. Well-designed soft films can temporarily absorb impact energy as viscoelastic strain, which results in dent formation. The viscoelastic strain can be recovered gradually, and the dent simultaneously disappears. Although this mechanism includes no chemical reaction in the self-healing process, the appearance of the polymer coating can be completely recovered. Some physically self-healing polymer coatings are currently commer-

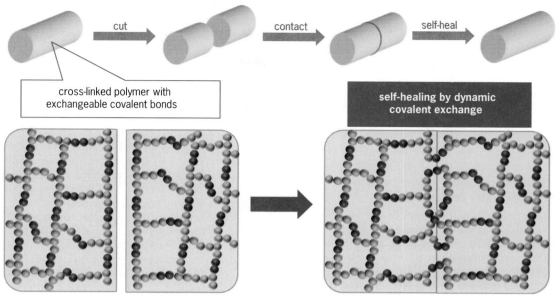

Fig. 3. Schematic representation of self-healing by exchangeable dynamic covalent bonds.

representative examples. These are thermoplastic polymers with physical cross-links composed of carboxylates and metal ions, which exhibit self-healing ability. Self-healing organic/inorganic hybrid hydrogels physically cross-linked with ionic interactions have also been reported.

Pure hydrogen-bonding networks are also useful for designing self-healing materials. One representative example is the cut-healing of thermoreversible rubber materials. The preparation of these rubber materials is simple: A mixture of fatty diacid and triacid is condensed with diethylene triamine and reacted with urea, giving a mixture of oligomers equipped with complementary hydrogen-bonding groups. When this rubber material is cut into two pieces and the pieces are contacted for some time at room temperature, they self-heal autonomously and recover their mechanical properties. In addition, hydrogen-bonding thermoplastic elastomers showing high modulus (stiffness), toughness, and spontaneous healing capability have been successfully developed using a sophisticated multiphase synthesis. Smart, self-healing systems employing host-guest interactions have also been constructed. The macrocyclic oligosaccharides, cyclodextrins, as host molecules, generate cross-linked polymer hydrogels with cyclodextrin pendant groups and corresponding guest moieties. This material showed self-healing behavior through molecular recognition. Various types of self-healing materials based on noncovalent interaction, including coordination bonding, have also been reported.

Reversible covalent bonds. An approach based on reversible (dynamic) covalent bond formation can potentially provide higher mechanical strength for self-healing materials, compared to noncovalent systems. Classical systems based on Diels-Alder/retro Diels-Alder cycloaddition reactions, thiol-disulfide redox reactions, and reversible reactions of imine moieties have been investigated. More recently, the concept of dynamic covalent chemistry was introduced for the molecular design of self-healing polymer materials (**Fig. 3**). Exchange reactions based on disulfide, trithiocarbonates, and thiuram disulfide have all been used for the design of self-healing materials. Furthermore, some of these materials with autonomously exchangeable dynamic covalent bonds do not require external stimulation to heal, which means they may have a potential for application under extreme conditions and in places that cannot be easily accessed.

Finally, a simple self-healing polymer system has recently been discovered using siloxane equilibration. A cross-linked polymer network containing active silanolate ($\equiv$Si–O$^-$) end groups can be prepared by tetramethylammonium silanolate-initiated ring-opening copolymerization of octamethylcyclotetrasiloxane and a cross-linker. The resulting silicone rubber, with a living and reactive network, is stable under water, oxygen, and carbon dioxide. After the silicone rubber is cut in half and rejoined, the pieces can completely heal by thermally activated equilibration of reversible covalent bonds among different network isomers and cyclic oligomers. Although this classical system requires heating to heal, it is undoubtedly one of the most simple and robust self-healing polymer systems.

For background information *see* CHEMICAL BONDING; COORDINATION CHEMISTRY; DIELS-ALDER REACTION; EPOXIDE; HYDROGEN BOND; INTERMOLECULAR FORCES; POLYMER; POLYMER COMPOSITES; RING-OPENING POLYMERIZATION; SUPRAMOLECULAR CHEMISTRY in the McGraw-Hill Encyclopedia of Science & Technology.   Hideyuki Otsuka

Bibliography. X. Chen et al., A thermally remendable cross-linked polymeric material, *Science*, 295:1698–1702, 2002, DOI:10.1126/science.1065879; P. Cordier et al., Self-healing and thermoreversible rubber from supramolecular assembly, *Nature*, 451:977–980, 2008, DOI:10.1038/nature06669; S. K. Ghosh (ed.), *Self-Healing Materials*, Wiley-VCH, 2009; S. R. White et al., Autonomic healing of polymer composites, *Nature*, 409:794–797, 2001, DOI:10.1038/35057232; S. van der Zwaag (ed.), *Self-Healing Materials*, Springer, 2007.

Sewage water reclamation

"Reduce, reuse, and recycle" is one of the catchphrases used by the environmentally conscious community, and most people are enthusiastic about recycling in order to minimize the effects of humans and their activities on the environment. In 2012, however, a ski resort in northern Arizona won the right to use sewage effluent to produce artificial snow after a decade of combined opposition efforts by environmental groups and Native American tribes. Why were these groups so set against this use of water? What led to their protests against this ruling? This article will explore both the positive and negative impacts of reclaimed water use.

Background. Reclaimed water is defined as the end product of wastewater reclamation that meets water quality requirements for biodegradable materials, suspended matter, and pathogens. This water is used in both agricultural and industrial applications in many states and cities across the United States and in many locales around the world.

Historically, the development of cities leads to an increased need to dispose of sewage (wastewater) and stormwater. The invention of indoor plumbing in the 1800s required additional sewage disposal because the waste is mixed with water to flush it away from the home. This contaminated water is carried into the sewage treatment system, where it is allowed to separate into solids (known as sludge) and liquids. The system is aerated to decrease the amount of odor that is produced, and the water is then put through a series of refining treatments to further purify it from its contaminants (see **illustration**). The end result is water that is nearly indistinguishable from typical surface waters or groundwaters. Although not considered potable (drinkable), this water is considered safe for many potential uses, including irrigation of agricultural crops and other industrial applications.

Safe or not safe: current uses of reclaimed sewage water. Using reclaimed water to save and conserve potable water for drinking has essentially been pioneered by the state of California. Los Angeles County in California has been using reclaimed sewage water for landscape irrigation since 1929. The Irvine Ranch Water District (IRWD), also in California, has a recycled water system serving more than 400 miles (644 km) of the state. Various studies of reclaimed water indicate that it is highly comparable to groundwater and surface water in its components, although there is a higher level of chlorine by-products in the reclaimed water because of the disinfection step required during the treatment.

On the world stage, Israel is known as the leader in the proportion of water that it recycles, with 80% of its sewage water reclaimed and used in irrigation in agricultural or public landscaping. Spain is another country that relies heavily on reclaimed water, and Florida and California are the leading areas for water reclamation in the United States. A U.S. National Research Council report in 2012 recommended the expansion of the use of treated wastewater for beneficial purposes, including irrigation, industrial applications, and the augmentation of drinking water supplies. Currently, states do not share a common set of regulations for the reuse of treated water. Hence, the committee involved in making this report recommended the establishment of federal regulations in the hopes of providing a minimum standard of protection for the public. Potable water frequently contains a small percentage of treated wastewater that has been released upstream of the municipality using it as a water source. Therefore, the potential risks of a conventional drinking water source that contains a small percentage of treated wastewater are equal to or exceed the risks involved in drinking reclaimed water, based on the measurement of 24 chemical and 4

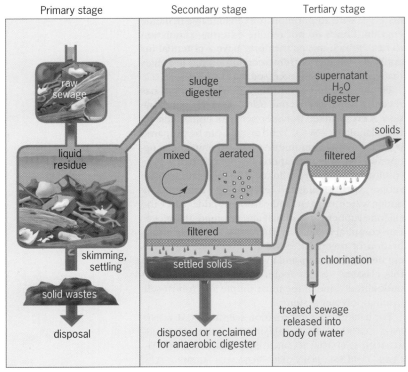

Primary stage   Secondary stage   Tertiary stage

Stages of sewage water treatment. (*Courtesy of M. K. Cowan, Microbiology: A Systems Approach, 3d ed., McGraw-Hill, New York, 2012*)

microbial contaminants. The committee suggested that the reliability of each treatment system would have to be examined in order to quantify the uncertainty in the risk assessment for both nonpotable and potable reclaimed water uses.

Political ramifications of the federal ruling. The ski resort in question, Arizona Snowbowl (near Flagstaff, Arizona), will be the first in the world to use 100% sewage effluent in producing artificial snow. When stated in this way, it is not surprising that the reaction of the public would be unfavorable. The U.S. Forest Service, which owns the land where the resort is located, says that the water meets the highest possible standards for nonpotable water. The reality is that snowmaking has become essential to these resorts because of climate change. Insufficient snow is being produced naturally, and a ski resort must open by Thanksgiving, or by Christmas at the latest, to remain profitable. To produce this snow, water must be brought to the resort. However, the use of potable water in the western United States is a source of contention between different states. Moreover, the number of people living in these states has increased exponentially in the last 50 years; in turn, this has decreased the available potable water that can be obtained directly from natural aquifers.

Two major groups protested the plan to use reclaimed water for snowmaking: Native Americans and environmental groups. The Native American protesters, consisting of 13 different tribes, consider the mountain area sacred and are absolutely against the use of the sewage effluent water, which they view as a desecration. Members of the tribe have held protests and hunger strikes, with many of their members being arrested for their acts of protest. However, despite their efforts, the federal appeals court has ruled in favor of the ski resort.

Most of the objections by environmental groups to the use of the reclaimed water for snowmaking were based on the chemicals that were found in the water during an independent study. This study found that the water contained a number of substances that cause disruption of the endocrine system in humans. These include hormones, pharmaceutical drugs, antidepressants, steroids, and, most significantly, antibiotics. Federal guidelines do not require that the Forest Service examine the potential effects of these substances, thereby making it possible for the city of Flagstaff to consider the water safe for snowmaking.

To add to this concern over endocrine-disrupting substances, an additional study has shown that there is a risk of antibiotic resistance developing in the bacteria found in the treated water. Genes confer specific mechanisms of antibiotic resistance to bacteria; moreover, these genes can be passed among different species of bacteria found within the same environment. The presence of antibiotics in recycled water can lead to increases in the presence of these genes because the bacteria undergo evolution-ary pressure to survive. Such antibiotics are present in the water that has been designated as safe for the production of artificial snow at Snowbowl.

In another study done on the Flagstaff recycled water, it was found that the concentration of antibiotic resistance genes (ARGs) increased dramatically at the point of use (for example, at sprinkler heads in irrigated landscapes). The presence of these genes in the reclaimed water is significant; further studies may indicate the presence of antibiotic-resistant bacteria because the genes must be carried by the bacteria in order to be replicated. Considering that the end use of the water is to produce snow used for skiing, the potential presence of these antibiotic-resistant bacteria becomes more alarming. These bacteria, when introduced to the body via a cut or scrape of the skin, would pose a difficult challenge for therapy if infection were to occur.

Current water quality standards require the presence of no more than 23 coliforms (colon and fecal bacilli) per 100 mL of recycled water. This standard only examines for the presence of indicator organisms; it is not actually testing for the presence of waterborne pathogens. No standards are mandated for the presence or absence of ARGs in reclaimed water. This may be a required next step in testing recycled water for safety.

Conclusions. Reclaimed water will be of increasing importance as climate changes continue to occur. However, as recycled water is currently regulated by state governments rather than the federal government, the current lack of mandates on substances found in these waters leaves cities and other institutions in the United States without guidance on how to manage their water resources. In the meantime, the use of reclaimed water by the Snowbowl resort and other similar businesses will continue to be disputed by environmental groups and the Native Americans who are most invested in the affected lands.

For background information *see* ANTIBIOTIC; BACTERIA; ENVIRONMENTAL ENGINEERING; FILTRATION; GENE; INDUSTRIAL WASTEWATER TREATMENT; RECYCLING TECHNOLOGY; SEWAGE; SEWAGE COLLECTION SYSTEMS; SEWAGE SOLIDS; SEWAGE TREATMENT; WASTEWATER REUSE; WATER SUPPLY ENGINEERING; WATER TREATMENT in the McGraw-Hill Encyclopedia of Science & Technology.   Marcia M. Pierce

Bibliography. M. K. Cowan, *Microbiology: A Systems Approach*, 3d ed., McGraw-Hill, New York, 2012; T. Helgeson, *A Reconnaissance-Level Quantitative Comparison of Reclaimed Water, Surface Water, and Groundwater*, WateReuse Research Foundation, Alexandria, VA, 2009; P. R. Murray, K. S. Rosenthal, and M. A. Pfaller, *Medical Microbiology*, 7th ed., Mosby, St. Louis, 2013; National Research Council, *Use of Reclaimed Water and Sludge in Food Crop Production*, National Academy Press, Washington, DC, 1996; E. Nester, D. Anderson, and C. E. Roberts, Jr., *Microbiology: A Human Perspective*, 7th ed., McGraw-Hill, New York, 2012.

Sloan Digital Sky Survey: new instruments and projects

The Sloan Digital Sky Survey (SDSS) is an astronomical imaging and redshift survey, begun officially in 2000, designed to map a large volume of the universe and of our own Milky Way Galaxy. Discoveries in this survey have contributed to the understanding of the solar system, the Milky Way, the evolution of galaxies, and the early universe. The SDSS has exploited the efficiency of charge-coupled devices (CCDs) to efficiently make wide-field images of one-third of the sky, and the flexibility of fiber optics to obtain more than 2.6 million spectra, making all of the data publicly available.

It has progressed through three distinct phases (SDSS-I, SDSS-II, and SDSS-III). By 2008, SDSS-I and SDSS-II had completed two major surveys: the Legacy survey of galaxies and quasars that was the original motivation for the facility, and a search for nearby supernovae by repeatedly imaging a single area of sky. SDSS-III began in 2008 and continues through 2014. It completed the SDSS's imaging survey of the sky, made several hardware upgrades, and began four major new projects. There are plans for a fourth phase to extend operations until 2020.

Completion of the imaging survey. The Sloan Foundation Telescope, installed at the Apache Point Observatory (APO) in New Mexico, has a 2.5-m (98-in.) primary mirror, a modest size by modern standards. However, its optical design (called Ritchey-Chrétien) delivers an undistorted image over a large angular patch of sky (3°, or six times the diameter of the full moon). From 1998 through 2009, the SDSS used an imaging camera to take images of 14,500 square degrees of night sky in five wavelength bands called u, g, r, i, and z (with wavelength centers from 350 to 900 nm), thus measuring the colors of the 470 million stars and galaxies it detected. **Figure 1** shows the distribution of galaxies it observed. The imaging camera was retired at the end of 2009, and all of its data was publicly released in 2011.

SDSS as a spectroscopic facility. The Sloan Foundation Telescope is now operated in a fully spectroscopic mode, using an optical spectrograph and a near-infrared (1.6-μm) spectrograph. Optical fibers situated in the telescope focal plane direct the light of stars, galaxies, and quasars to these spectrographs, allowing the flexible observation of many objects simultaneously. Since 2008, SDSS has conducted four major surveys in this mode: Sloan Extension for Galactic Understanding and Exploration (SEGUE), Baryon Oscillation Spectroscopic Survey (BOSS), Multi-Object APO Radial Velocity Exoplanet Large-Area Survey (MARVELS), and APO Galactic Evolution Experiment (APOGEE).

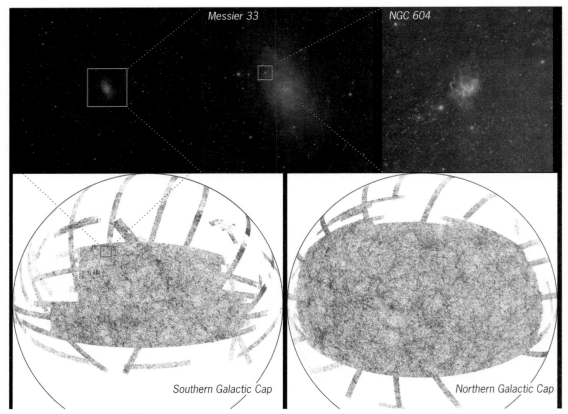

Fig. 1. SDSS image of the night sky. Bottom panels show the light from galaxies detected in the imaging survey on two halves of the sky. (The Galactic Caps are the halves of the sky on each side of the plane of the Milky Way. One is most easily viewed from our Southern Hemisphere, and one from the North.) The top panels show a sequence of zooms onto a bright, nearby galaxy called Messier 33, and then onto an H II region inside it named NGC 604. (*Courtesy of the Sloan Digital Sky Survey III*)

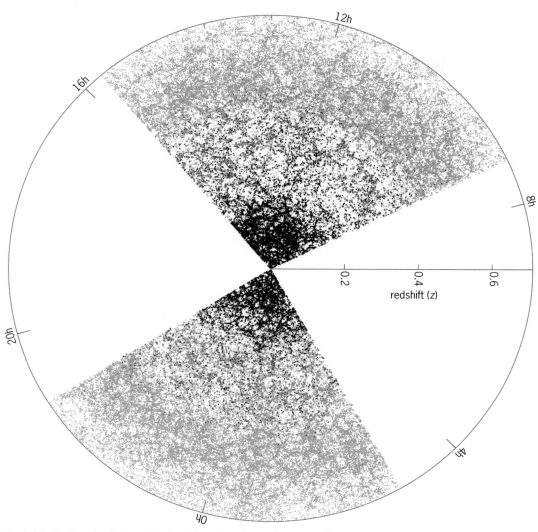

Fig. 2. Distribution of galaxies within 2° of the celestial equator from the SDSS. In this polar plot, the radius indicates the distance from the Milky Way Galaxy, and the angle is the right ascension. The universe is shown out to 6 billion years into the past. The black points show galaxies measured by SDSS-I and SDSS-II in the Legacy survey. The red points show galaxies measured by SDSS-III in the BOSS survey. The BOSS survey of quasars probes yet further distances, not shown on this plot. Blank areas have not been surveyed by the SDSS. (*Courtesy of the Sloan Digital Sky Survey III*)

SEGUE. In 2009, SDSS-III completed the SEGUE survey of Milky Way stars, which obtained more than 300,000 optical spectra (in the range between 380 and 900 nm). For each star, the spectrum reveals its temperature, its radius, and the abundances of its elements, as well as how fast it is moving from its Doppler shift. Studying this many individual stars reveals the history of the growth of the Milky Way Galaxy. The elements heavier than helium—such as carbon, nitrogen, oxygen, iron, and others, all referred to in the nomenclature of astronomy as "metals"—were created primarily in stellar processes. Thus, the very earliest stars to form, a handful of which have now been found by SEGUE, have tiny abundances of those metals. Each generation of stars enriches the gas in metals according to patterns that depend on how the star-formation rate is changing and how the winds of stars and supernovae interact with the surrounding gas. Astronomers are

using the observed patterns in SEGUE's observation to reconstruct the history of the Milky Way Galaxy. Meanwhile, the motions of the stars are related to the mass of the Milky Way Galaxy, and thus the measured Doppler shifts allow SEGUE to measure the dark-matter content of the Galaxy, which in terms of mass is its primary constituent.

BOSS. After the end of SEGUE in 2009, SDSS-III upgraded the optical spectrograph to include more fibers, increasing the number from 640 to 1000, and increasing its efficiency. This new spectrograph is used in BOSS, which between 2009 and 2014 is mapping the more distant universe, beyond the region covered by the Legacy survey. BOSS targets distant galaxies and quasars, and measures their speed of recession. Through the well-known Hubble law, these speeds are proportional to galaxy distances by a factor known as the Hubble constant, which is effectively a measure of how fast the universe is

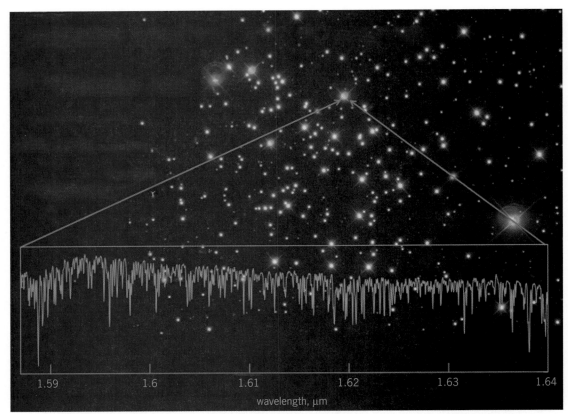

Fig. 3. One of 100,000 APOGEE spectra, for a star in the stellar cluster Messier 67, which is filled with stars approximately the age of the Sun. The features in the spectrum are caused by atoms and molecules in the atmosphere of the star, and measuring them allows us to determine the abundances of various elements. [*Courtesy of Peter Frinchaboy (Texas Christian University), Robert Lupton (Princeton University), and the Sloan Digital Sky Survey III*]

expanding. The spectroscopic measurements can then be used to make a three-dimensional map of the universe (**Fig. 2**).

BOSS's primary goal is to measure how the universe expanded over time. It does so by measuring the angular scale of the baryon acoustic oscillation (BAO). The BAO is a statistical feature of the way matter clusters in the universe, whose physical scale is very well known (around 450 million light-years). With three-dimensional maps based on galaxy redshift, we can convert the observed scale of the feature in the redshift map into an actual distance, and thus determine the Hubble constant. BOSS is measuring very distant galaxies and quasars whose light has taken billions of years to reach Earth, and therefore BOSS can use this technique to measure the expansion rate of the universe over the past history of the universe. In this manner, BOSS has already made the most accurate measurements of the expansion history at 6 billion and 11 billion years in the past.

These measurements provide precise constraints on the contents of the universe. In particular, they measure the total amount of dark matter (both inside and outside galaxies) as well as the amount and nature of dark energy, a mysterious component that appears to be causing the universe to accelerate.

MARVELS. The MARVELS program aimed to monitor the radial velocities of thousands of bright stars with the goal of discovering substellar companions and exoplanets. From 2008 through 2012, it used the "bright time" when the Moon was near full to observe the radial velocities of bright stars, searching for the telltale wobbles that would be caused by an orbiting planet. Using a specially designed interferometric spectrograph, it represented the first attempt to perform precise radial velocity observations of many objects simultaneously. It found several dozen substellar companion candidates.

APOGEE. The latest instrument to be installed on the Sloan Foundation Telescope is the APOGEE spectrograph, which observes high-resolution spectra in the near-infrared (around 1.6 μm). Its goals are similar to SEGUE: to unravel the history of the Milky Way Galaxy by observing the motions and elemental abundances of its stars. However, the new infrared spectrograph has substantial advantages. With its high resolution, it can more accurately measure a larger number of elements and more accurately determine stellar velocities. Furthermore, the central parts of our Galaxy and much of its disk are obscured by intervening dust; the effects of this obscuration are much less in the near-infrared, allowing APOGEE to observe effectively far more of the extent of the Galaxy.

APOGEE was commissioned in 2010 and will operate at least through 2014, using the telescope time when the Moon is near full. In its first year of operation alone, it took around 100,000 high signal-to-noise spectra, many times more of their kind than all previous projects combined (**Fig. 3**). It has discovered new structures as well as very poorly metal-enriched stars in the center of the Milky Way Galaxy, provided new determinations of the motions of stars within the Galaxy, and even found a number of substellar companions, including planets.

Projects and instruments after 2014. Planning for the fourth phase of SDSS, to commence in 2014 with three projects, is now underway. First, the BOSS program will be expanded by mapping the expansion of the universe between 6 and 11 billion years ago. Second, new instrumentation will be built to observe around 10,000 distant galaxies in fine detail; instead of a single spectrum of the center of each galaxy, up to several hundred spectra will be observed across the extent of each one. Third, the APOGEE program will continue to map the stars in our galaxy. These projects all will continue to use the Sloan Foundation Telescope, which will remain in 2014 the most efficient and powerful wide-field spectroscopic facility in the world.

For background information *see* ASTRONOMICAL IMAGING; ASTRONOMICAL SPECTROSCOPY; CHARGE-COUPLED DEVICES; COSMOLOGY; DARK ENERGY; DARK MATTER; DOPPLER EFFECT; EXTRASOLAR PLANETS; GALAXY, EXTERNAL; HUBBLE CONSTANT; INFRARED ASTRONOMY; MILKY WAY GALAXY; OPTICAL FIBERS; SLOAN DIGITAL SKY SURVEY; SPECTROGRAPH; STAR; STELLAR POPULATION; TELESCOPE; UNIVERSE in the McGraw-Hill Encyclopedia of Science & Technology.   Michael Blanton

Bibliography. B. Bok and P. F. Bok, *The Milky Way*, 5th ed., Harvard University Press, Cambridge, MA, 1981; W. L. Freedman (ed.), *Measuring and Modeling the Universe*, Carnegie Observatories Astrophysics Series, vol. 2, Cambridge University Press, Cambridge, UK, 2004; F. Levin, *Calibrating the Cosmos: How Cosmology Explains Our Big Bang Universe*, Springer, New York, Astronomers' Universe Series, 2006; L. S. Sparke and J. S. Gallagher, III, *Galaxies in the Universe: An Introduction*, 2d ed., Cambridge University Press, Cambridge, UK, 2007.

Small modular reactors

The commercial use of nuclear power began in 1957 with the 60-MWe (megawatts of electric power) Shippingport reactor. Less than 15 years later, most new commercial plants built in the United States had capacities nearly 20 times larger, a trend that continues today worldwide. Currently, the only new plant designs available on the world market are in the 1100–1600-MWe range, including several designs from France, Japan, the Republic of Korea, Russia, and the United States. During the past few years, a number of reactor designers have turned to develop a new generation of commercial nuclear power plants with much smaller capacities. Commonly designated as small modular reactors (SMRs), they are generally characterized by having an electrical output of less than 300 MWe, are substantially

fabricated in a factory and transported to a site for installation into a fixed building structure, and operated in combination with one or more identical reactor modules.

Currently, there are nearly 30 SMR designs being commercially developed worldwide, motivated by three key drivers: enhanced safety, reduced cost, and increased flexibility. Improved safety is accomplished by lower fuel inventory, greater use of passive safety features, and the elimination of design features that are vulnerable to potential accidents. The smaller physical size contributes to added flexibilities in fabrication, construction, and siting. Finally, lower total capital cost and shorter construction time contribute to reduced investment risk and cash outlay profiles.

Technologies. Reactor technology is typically categorized by the type of coolant used to remove heat from the reactor core, and includes: water (H_2O or D_2O), gas (helium or carbon dioxide), and liquid metal (sodium, lead, or lead-bismuth). Of the 435 commercial nuclear plants operating worldwide, 416 are water-cooled, 17 are gas-cooled, and 2 are sodium-cooled. Small modular reactors employ the same fundamental technologies but differ from large plants in the physical scale of the components. Although some SMRs are downsized replicas of large plant designs, most SMRs use different engineering principles to eliminate many components. An example of this simplification is the integral primary system design approach in which all or nearly all of the primary system components are contained in a single pressure vessel. **Figure 1** shows a simplified comparison of a loop-type pressurized-water reactor (PWR) design typical of most large operating reactors and an integral primary system design, sometimes referred to as an iPWR. An integral configuration greatly simplifies the design in two ways: (1) it eliminates the external piping and vessels, and (2) it eliminates the need for active backup safety systems required to mitigate the extreme consequences resulting from a major break in any of the external pipes or vessels.

Design options. The International Atomic Energy Agency (IAEA) recently reviewed more than 60 SMR designs under development in 13 countries worldwide. These designs, roughly half of which are being developed by commercial reactor vendors, include all reactor technology categories, that is, water-, gas-, metal-, and salt-cooled systems. In the United States, eight SMR designs have been substantially developed by commercial vendors: four light-water reactors, three gas-cooled reactors, and one sodium-cooled reactor.

Introduced in 2007, the 45-MWe NuScale Power reactor design is the smallest and most modular of the water-cooled SMRs currently being commercialized in the United States. The primary deployment model for NuScale is to construct multimodule plants comprised of up to 12 units. An individual module, which includes the primary reactor vessel housed in a compact steel containment vessel and coupled to a small turbine-generator power

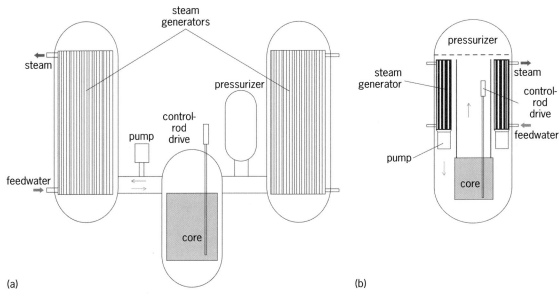

Fig. 1. Comparison of (*a*) traditional loop design with (*b*) integral design.

conversion unit, is intended to be completely factory fabricated. **Figure 2** shows a model of the reactor module and a cutaway view of a 12-module plant. The compact iPWR relies on natural circulation of the primary coolant and uses redundant helical-coil steam generators within the reactor vessel. Modules are refueled independently while the remaining modules continue to generate electricity.

In 2009, Generation mPower announced the 180-MWe mPower reactor design, which also uses

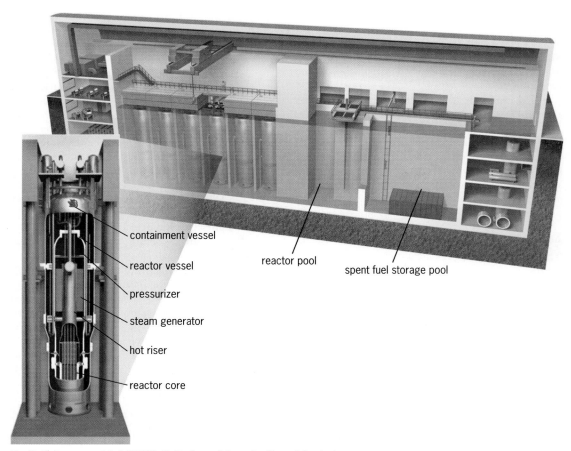

Fig. 2. Cutaway model of 45 MWe NuScale module and a 12-module plant.

an integral primary system configuration and is designed to be deployed in a two-module plant with independent steel containment domes and power conversion systems. The mPower module contains similar fuel and fuel assembly design as existing PWR plants and employs forced circulation of the primary coolant using pumps mounted external to the reactor vessel (**Fig. 3**). The compact reactor vessel allows for truck or rail shipment of the factory-fabricated module to the plant site.

Two additional water-cooled SMRs were introduced in the United States subsequent to NuScale

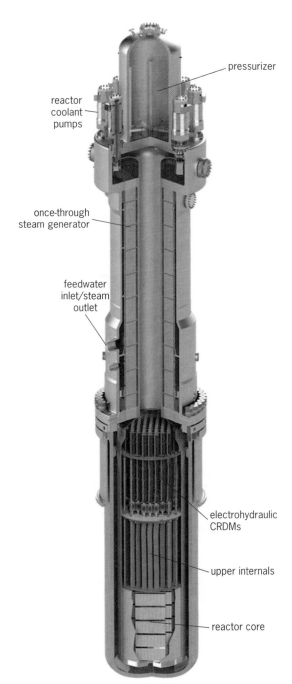

pressurizer

reactor coolant pumps

once-through steam generator

feedwater inlet/steam outlet

electrohydraulic CRDMs

upper internals

reactor core

Fig. 3. Cutaway model of a 180 MWe mPower module. CRDM = control-rod drive mechanism.

and mPower: the Westinghouse W-SMR design (225 MWe) and the Holtec SMR-160 design (160 MWe). While the forced-circulation W-SMR design uses an iPWR configuration, the natural-circulation SMR-160 more closely models a one-loop PWR configuration. All four water-cooled SMR designs use the same low-enriched uranium dioxide fuel that is used in existing commercial nuclear plants.

Three reactor vendors have been working in parallel to develop a high-temperature helium-cooled demonstration SMR. A Westinghouse-led design is based on the Pebble Bed Modular Reactor (PBMR) design that was previously developed by PBMR Ltd. in South Africa. A General Atomics design is the direct-cycle modular high-temperature reactor (MHR), which is based substantially on a plant design being developed jointly with Russia for the disposition of surplus plutonium stockpiles. The third design is Areva's New Technology Advanced Reactor for Energy Supply (ANTARES) design, which uses a prismatic block arrangement for the moderator similar to the MHR but uses an indirect gas and steam cycle power conversion system. In the case of the PBMR, tiny robust graphite-coated fuel particles are distributed within 6-cm-diameter (2-in.) graphite balls, similar in size to a billiard ball, and randomly placed in a large graphite hopper. The MHR and ANTARES prismatic designs use the same coated fuel particles, but the fuel is formed into long rodlets and placed in large hexagonal blocks that are tightly stacked to form the reactor core. All three designs have a nominal power capacity of 280 MWe.

Rounding out the eight commercial U.S. SMR designs is General Electric's Power Reactor Innovative and Safe Module (PRISM) sodium-cooled reactor. The PRISM design was one of the first advanced reactor designs to employ significant use of passive safety features and was designed as a power module to be used in multiples to form a large-electrical-capacity power plant. The current PRISM design has a power of 300 MWe and is intended to be colocated with an electro-refining fuel recycle facility to provide a closed fuel cycle with dramatically enhanced fuel utilization.

Motivations. The current rush to design, license, and deploy new SMRs is motivated by their promise of enhanced safety, affordability, and flexibility. The potential for smaller reactors to enhance plant safety beyond existing large plants comes from: (1) the potential to eliminate design vulnerabilities, (2) the opportunity to passively remove residual decay heat, and (3) the reduced inventory of radionuclides that potentially can be released in an accident. As an example, the iPWR configuration described earlier eliminates the potential for a high-consequence large-break loss-of-coolant accident. Some SMR designs also use gravity-driven natural circulation of the coolant during normal operation, thus eliminating the possibility of a pump failure event and reducing or eliminating the need for emergency power during a station blackout event. Removal of the residual decay heat in a reactor core is made easier since the smaller reactor core produces less heat than a large core. Similarly, the inventory of radionuclides produced by the fission process in the fuel is less for small cores since the total quantity of radionuclides is roughly proportional to the power level. Some SMR units have power levels less than 5% of a large reactor and therefore will have less than 1/20th of the radionuclide inventory for potential release during a severe accident.

The affordability of SMRs comes from having a lower sticker price. Values of $6–10 billion have been cited for recent purchases of large nuclear plants. This substantial cost, and the financing challenge it creates, present an insurmountable barrier for all but the largest utilities. Small modular reactors offer the potential for improved affordability because of: (1) a lower total plant cost, and (2) the ability to add new generating capacity incrementally. Estimates of initial plant cost are in the range of $1–3 billion for SMR plants with total outputs of 200–500 MWe. Also, cash flow or capital-at-risk is much different for a multiunit SMR plant than for a single-unit large plant. The owner has the flexibility to stagger the construction or installation of the modular units, allowing the first unit to generate revenue earlier. The lower financing cost resulting from the reduced debt profile and the ability of the owners to better match their demand profile further reduces the total life-cycle cost of the plant.

Regarding operational flexibility, SMRs allow the owner to build new capacity at a rate that more closely matches demand growth. Additionally, the smaller generating capacity provides for better grid stability, especially in small-grid regions. Finally, several plant features allow greater flexibility in plant siting, such as the smaller plant "footprint" of most modern SMRs (40 acres or 16 hectares, compared to 400–500 acres or 160–200 hectares for a traditional large plant) and reduced water usage because of the smaller amount of rejected heat.

Challenges for deployment. Despite the several benefits of smaller-sized reactors, many technical and institutional challenges must be addressed and overcome. From a technical perspective, design innovations, such as integral primary systems and passive safety systems, will require comprehensive testing and demonstration through separate effects tests, scaled simulators, or perhaps even a prototype. Examples of some nontraditional components include helical-coil steam generators, internal control-rod drive mechanisms, and internal coolant pumps. In the case of the non-light-water-reactor designs, significant material and fuel qualification efforts may be needed in addition to new component and systems testing. Material and fuel qualification will be especially important for SMR designs that are intended to have very long fuel-cycle lengths—some designs claim cycle lengths as much as 10–15 times longer than current light-water-reactor fuels.

A number of institutional challenges also exist for the deployment of new SMR designs. The most significant challenge will be the regulatory approval of the new designs. The U.S. Nuclear Regulatory Commission (NRC) is already working to adapt the existing licensing framework to SMRs; however, there are many explicit and implicit biases in the process in favor of large light-water-reactor plants. The NRC is currently working to expand the framework to be both size and technology neutral.

International interests. Surging interest in SMRs is a global phenomenon in terms of both customer interest and new SMR designs. From a customer perspective, many emerging countries are experiencing rapid growth in electricity demand (8–10% per year), yet are severely constrained in the size of power plants that they can afford and operate on their regional grids. Collectively, these countries represent more than half of the anticipated global energy demand growth in the next few decades, and thus a significant customer base for new SMR designs.

In terms of new international SMR designs, the Republic of Korea achieved design approval from their regulator for the 100-MWe SMART (System-integrated Modular Advanced Reactor) SMR design, which is intended for export as a cogeneration facility for generating electricity and desalinating water. In Russia, construction is nearly complete for the first 35-MWe KLT-40S SMR that is being built in pairs on barges to service remote communities along the Russian northern coast. Other SMR designs are in various stages of commercial development in Argentina, China, France, and Japan.

For background information see NUCLEAR FUELS; NUCLEAR POWER; NUCLEAR REACTOR in the McGraw-Hill Encyclopedia of Science & Technology.

Daniel T. Ingersoll

Bibliography. M. D. Carelli, B. Petrovic, and C. W. Mycoff, Smaller sized reactors can be economically attractive, Pap. 7569, in *Proceedings of the International Conference on Advanced Power Plants (ICAPP 2007)*, Nice, France, May 13–18, 2007; D. T. Ingersoll, Deliberately small reactors and the second nuclear era, *Progr. Nucl. Energ.*, 51:589–603, 2009, DOI:10.1016/j.pnucene.2009.01.003; International Atomic Energy Agency (IAEA), *Status of Innovative Small and Medium Sized Reactor Designs: Reactors with Conventional Refueling Schemes*, IAEA-TECDOC-1485, 2006; International Atomic Energy Agency (IAEA), *Status of Innovative Small and Medium Sized Reactor Designs: Reactors without Onsite Refueling*, IAEA-TECDOC-1536, 2007.

Smart net-zero energy buildings

Buildings account for about one-third of the total final energy consumption and roughly 40% of primary energy in most developed countries, while 30–40% of greenhouse-gas (GHG) emissions are usually attributed to buildings. Buildings are connected with infrastructure such as roads, electricity grids, district heating and cooling grids, waste collection systems, water supply networks, and communication systems.

The design of buildings, their shapes, and their density affect our quality of life in a profound way. The flow of energy from the Sun and electricity grids maintains our civilization and everyday life. The design of our built environment, our lifestyles, and our work habits directly determine the required energy consumption to maintain an acceptable indoor environment, but also significantly influence transportation energy consumption.

Buildings typically account for more than half of total electricity consumption. They are largely responsible for the peaks in electricity demand associated with space heating, cooling, lighting, and appliances. These peaks, if not reduced and shifted in time, will impose additional requirements to build new power plants. Without a major transformation in the way we design, build, and operate buildings, we cannot expect to meet our goals for reductions in GHG emissions and for clean air quality. Mechanisms that allow a building to act as a net energy generating and storage system can provide the basis for this transformation.

Smart buildings. Modern buildings provide services to their occupants, such as lighting, heating, cooling, indoor environment control, elevators, security, and monitoring functions. There are many possible definitions for smart buildings, and they are often associated with the existence of comprehensive automation (management) systems (building automation systems; BAS). However, the existence of BAS does not necessarily make buildings smart. It is the control strategies, information flow, actions, and techniques employed by the BAS that optimize building operation and make it "smart." The term smart building, as used in this article, denotes two major expected characteristics of such buildings:

1. A building that optimally controls its indoor environment (heat, daylight and artificial light, sound, and air quality) and is responsive to occupant needs so as to provide good indoor comfort for work, leisure activities, and rest.

2. A building that optimizes its operation to substantially reduce energy consumption costs, while optimally interacting with community, city, and country energy grids, both electrical and thermal (for example, district heating and cooling).

Smart buildings interacting in an optimal way with smart electricity grids can shift and reduce peak demand for electricity by optimizing production, storage, and utilization of energy. Smart buildings can become net energy producers over a year through efficient integration of energy efficiency measures such as use of LED (light-emitting diode) lighting, optimal insulation levels, and advanced windows with renewable energy systems such as building-integrated photovoltaic systems (BIPVs). However, the routine design of such buildings poses major challenges and requires significant innovations in how we design, construct, and operate them.

Evolution from traditional buildings to smart net-zero energy buildings. Buildings have evolved over time as largely passive systems, that is, passive filters between the outdoor and indoor environments. They used to be massive structures made of stone and bricks. In the twentieth century, buildings evolved into structures with increasingly high levels of environmental control, in part through the addition of insulation such as fiberglass and polystyrene. The adoption of double-glazed windows with an insulating airspace led to the adoption of larger fenestrations (openings such as windows, doors, and so on) in both homes and workspaces. Large fenestrations connect us in a more direct manner with our outdoor environment through views, but they lead to increased heating and cooling energy consumption when they are excessive. The need for daylight and views is associated with human evolution on Earth under the Sun's rays, with a peak wavelength that is near the color green.

Thus, fenestration and daylight increasingly drive building design. The invention of electric lighting and its adoption in the early twentieth century contributed to an opposite trend of reduction in window areas and reliance on artificial light, particularly from 1950 to 1970. This trend has been reversed in the last 20–30 years, with increasingly large window areas, as insulating windows with special coatings to reduce heat transfer and optimize transmission of solar radiation have become widespread. In addition, the benefits of daylight for health and enhanced productivity are increasingly recognized.

In the past 20 years, the potential of solar radiation incident on building surfaces to satisfy all our energy needs has contributed to the widespread acceptance of net-zero energy buildings as a technically feasible long-term goal (for most regions). A net-zero energy building (NZEB) is defined as one that, in an average year, produces as much energy (electrical plus thermal) from renewable energy sources as it consumes. When the energy production is on-site, the NZEB definition is most strict. A number of NZEB definitions have been developed by the International Energy Agency.

The visible part of solar radiation (nearly half of total solar radiation) is useful as daylight. Almost all solar radiation can be converted to useful heat for space heating or other purposes, such as heating water, drying clothes, or solar cooling using passive and active solar systems. Photovoltaic (PV) technology, which converts solar radiation to electricity, has recently experienced significant advances and dramatic reductions in cost (often at least 90% cost reduction per watt generating capacity in the last 10 years).

Most inhabited areas receive significant amounts of sunshine that enable the design of technically feasible NZEBs with current solar and energy-efficiency technologies. For example, in Canada between latitudes 40–53° N, where most of the population lives, a suitably oriented facade or roof on a typical building receives up to about 6.4 kWh/m^2 per day, and the

Challenges toward smart NZEBs		
Building systems	Current buildings	Future smart net-zero energy buildings
Building fabric/envelope	Passive, not designed as an energy system	Optimized for passive design and integration of active solar systems
Heating, ventilation, and air-conditioning (HVAC)	Large oversized systems	Small HVAC systems optimally controlled; integrated with solar, combined heat and power; communities have seasonal storage and district energy
Solar systems/renewables, generation	No systematic integration—an afterthought	Fully integrated: daylighting, solar thermal, photovoltaics, hybrid solar, geothermal systems, biofuels, linked with smart microgrids
Building automation systems	Not used effectively	Predictive building control to optimize comfort and energy performance; online demand prediction/peak demand shifting and reduction

incident solar energy usually far exceeds the building's total energy consumption. PV panels integrated on the roof and facade can typically convert 6–20% of the Sun's energy into electricity, and 50–70% of the remainder can be extracted as heat from the PV panels, while 10–30% can be used for daylighting in semitransparent systems. Combined solar-energy use efficiencies of the order of 80% can be achieved if proper integration strategies are implemented, and up to half of solar radiation can be used as daylight, useful heat, or electricity.

The energy generation function in NZEBs using solar energy as daylight, useful heat, and electricity requires a transformation of the way buildings are designed and operated to be cost-effective and affordable. The key challenges to overcome toward smart NZEBs are summarized in the **table** for each of the four major building subsystems, where the current buildings are contrasted with the expected characteristics of smart NZEBs.

Smart net-zero energy building concepts. The convergence of the need for innovation and the requirement for drastic reductions in energy use and GHG emissions provides a unique opportunity to transform the way we conceive buildings and their energy systems. Energy efficiency measures need to be simultaneously considered with solar system integration and on-site generation of useful heat and electricity using a whole-building approach.

Building energy design is currently going through a period of major changes driven largely by three key factors and related technological developments:

1. The adoption in most developed countries and by influential engineering societies such as the American Society of Heating, Refrigerating, and Air-Conditioning Engineers (ASHRAE) of net-zero energy as a long-term goal for new buildings.

2. The need to reduce the peak electricity demand from buildings through optimal operation, thus reducing the need to build new central power plants that often use fossil fuels.

3. The need to efficiently integrate new advanced energy technologies into buildings, such as controlled shading and daylighting devices, solar systems, and different types of thermal storage.

A key requirement of high-performance building design is the need for rigorous design and operation of a building as an integrated energy system that must have a good indoor environment suited to its functions. In addition to the extensive array of HVAC (heating, ventilation, and air-conditioning), lighting, and automation technologies developed over the last 100 years, there are many new building envelope technologies such as vacuum insulation panels, advanced fenestration systems (for example, electrochromic coatings for so-called smart windows), solar thermal technologies for heating and cooling, solar-electric or hybrid systems, and combined heat and power (CHP) technologies. A high-performance building may be designed with optimal combinations of traditional and advanced technologies depending on its function and on the climate.

Solar gain and daylight control through smart-window systems, in which the transmission of solar radiation can be actively controlled, remains a challenge in building design and operation because of the simultaneous effects on instantaneous and delayed heating and cooling loads, and on thermal and visual comfort. Solar gains may be controlled through a combination of passive and active measures, with the passive measures employed during design and active measures, such as positioning of motorized venetian blinds, employed during operation. Since solar gains have delayed effects because of building thermal mass, there is significant benefit in predictive control and optimal operation of passive and active storage that utilizes real-time weather prediction.

New building technologies, such as phase change materials (PCM), active façades with advanced daylighting devices, and building-integrated solar systems, open up new challenges and possibilities to improve comfort and to reduce energy use and peak loads, which need to be taken into account in developing optimal control strategies. The energy requirements and control needs of commercial and residential buildings are usually quite different. For example, in commercial buildings, cooling and lighting play major roles, while in houses, especially in cold-climate regions, space heating and domestic hot water heating dominate energy consumption.

Plug-loads from appliances and office equipment represent a large portion of building energy consumption, and their share is increasing as HVAC

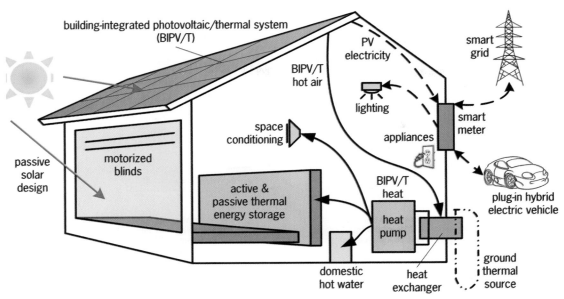

Fig. 1. Schematic illustrating the concept of a smart NZEB that combines passive and active solar technologies as well as interaction with a plug-in hybrid electric vehicle (PHEV).

and lighting systems become more energy efficient. Demand-response strategies, such as scheduling of appliances, are becoming more popular as a way to significantly reduce the impact of plug loads on peak electric demand.

The design of a smart NZEB requires the following three key concepts:

1. An integrated approach to energy efficiency and passive design (**Fig. 1**).

2. An integrated approach to building design and operation. Optimized net-zero energy buildings need to be designed based on anticipated operation so as to have a largely predictable and manageable impact on the grid. Smart buildings optimally linked with smart grids will enable a reduction in the need to build new power plants.

3. The concept of solar optimization requires optimal design of building form and orientation so as to provide the maximum capture of solar energy from near-south facing facades and roofs for conversion to solar electricity, useful heat, and daylight.

These three concepts are particularly important in the design of new communities where there exist many alternative optimal solutions. **Figure 2** shows the impact of roof orientation for three houses in a curved street on electricity production (positive) from a roof BIPV system on a clear day in February in Montreal and a typical electricity demand curve (load, negative). As shown in the load curve, two peaks are often observed, one in the morning and one in the evening, with both associated with the appliance and hot water usage, lighting, and possibly peaks in space heating and cooling. A NZEB will have equal areas under the demand and generation profiles averaged over a typical year.

Integration of photovoltaic solar technologies into the building envelope. Full integration requires an innovative approach to building design in which building

envelope components perform several controlled functions, such as generating solar heat and electricity in building-integrated photovoltaic/thermal (BIPV/T) systems or transmitting daylight and producing electricity in semitransparent photovoltaic (STPV) systems. Integration improves the cost effectiveness by having the PV panels provide additional functions. The following are some recognized methods of beneficial integration.

Integrating the PV panels into the building envelope (BIPV). This strategy could involve, for example, replacing roof shingles or wall cladding with PV panels. It has significant advantages over the more usual add-on strategy. Not only does it eliminate an extra component (for example, shingles), but it also eliminates

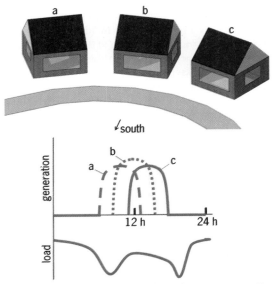

Fig. 2. Impact of roof BIPV orientation on generation profile (load also shown).

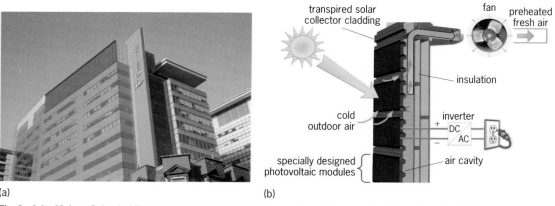

Fig. 3. John Molson School of Business (JMSB) building BIPV/T system. (*a*) Top right section of facade. (*b*) Schematic illustrating the system concept. 70% of the transpired collector cladding area is covered by specially designed PV modules; the system generates up to about 25 kW electricity and 75 kW of thermal energy used to directly heat ventilation air.

penetrations of a pre-existing envelope that are required in order to attach the panel to the building.

Integrating heat collection functions into the PV panel (STPV). As previously noted, PV panels typically convert about 6–20% of the incident solar energy to electrical energy, and the remaining solar energy (normally lost as heat to the outdoor environment) is available to be captured as useful heat. In this strategy, a coolant fluid, such as water or air, is circulated next to the panel, extracting useful heat. The coolant also serves to lower the temperature of the panel, which is beneficial because the panel efficiency increases with lower panel temperature. This strategy can be adopted in either an open-loop or a closed-loop configuration. In one open-loop configuration, outdoor air is passed under PV panels and the recovered heat can be used for space heating, preheating of ventilation air, or heating domestic hot water, either by direct means or through a heat pump.

Integrating light transmission functions into the PV panel (BIPV/L). This strategy uses special PV panels (semitransparent PV windows) that transmit sunlight. As was the case for the previous strategy, this strategy draws on the fact that only a fraction of the incident solar energy goes into electricity, and much of the remainder can be used for other purposes, in this case, for useful light, thereby saving on the energy that electrical lights would otherwise draw.

The John Molson School of Business (JMSB) building at Concordia University in Montreal demonstrates a new open-loop, air-based BIPV/T system that achieved peak combined efficiencies of about 55% (13% electrical and 42% thermal). Reduction of cost is a complex issue for building-integrated solar systems, particularly BIPV/T systems, since part of their cost needs to be attributed to an increase in building value (**Fig. 3**).

Design of appropriate incentive measures and policies may help accelerate deployment of building-integrated solar systems and contribute to long-term reduction in costs by helping this new industry grow. For example, the introduction of a renewable energy feed-in tariff (FIT) program in Ontario

marked a turning point for photovoltaics in Canada. In 2010, Ontario installed approximately 150 MW of solar PV systems, up from less than 2 MW in 2008. The price of photovoltaic panels has dropped rapidly with an average price of just under $1 per watt peak capacity (electricity generated at full sun), making them suitable energy producing cladding materials on most building surfaces facing between East, South, and West. For example, a 50-square-meter (538-square-foot) roof surface can accommodate a 7-kW PV system, with panels costing about $6000–7000 and total system cost of about $20,000, including inverter, wiring, and installation. Such a system can produce between 7000–10,000 kilowatt-hours annually in most locations, readily accommodating the electricity needs of an energy-efficient 150-m^2 (1600-ft^2) house (family of four), such as the EcoTerra near-net-zero energy demonstration house near Montreal, resulting in near-net-zero energy consumption. Integration of such a system with heat pumps can help convert excess electricity (that the grid might not be able to absorb) into stored heat or cooling for later usage, helping solve a potential grid bottleneck problem. *See* FEED-IN TARIFF.

For background information *see* BUILDINGS; CO-GENERATION SYSTEMS; ELECTRIC POWER GENERATION; ELECTRIC POWER SYSTEMS; ENERGY CONVERSION; ENERGY STORAGE; GLOBAL CLIMATE CHANGE; SOLAR ENERGY in the McGraw-Hill Yearbook of Science & Technology.   Andreas K. Athienitis

Bibliography. ASHRAE, *ASHRAE Vision 2020—Producing Net Zero Energy Buildings*, Atlanta, GA, 2007; A. K. Athienitis et al., A prototype photovoltaic/thermal system integrated with transpired collector, *Solar Energy*, 85(1):139–153, 2011; A. K. Athienitis S. A. Kalogirou, and L. Candanedo, Modeling and simulation of passive and active solar thermal systems, in A. Sayigh, (ed.), *Comprehensive Renewable Energy*, vol. 3, pp. 357–417, Elsevier, Oxford, UK, 2012; A. K. Athienitis and M. Santamouris, *Thermal Analysis and Design of Passive Solar Buildings*, James & James, London, 2002; A. K. Athienitis, M. Stylianou, and J. Shou, A methodology for building thermal dynamics studies and control applications, *ASHRAE Trans.*, 96(pt 2):839–848 1990; Y. Chen, A. K. Athienitis, and K. Galal, Modeling, design and thermal performance of a BIPV/T system thermally coupled with a ventilated concrete slab in a low energy solar house, Part 1: BIPV/T system and house energy concept, *Solar Energy*, 84(11):1892–1907, 2010; International Solar Energy Society (ISES), *Solar Energy: State of the Art*, James & James, London, 2001; K. Voss and E. Musall (eds.), *Net Zero Energy Buildings, 2011*, Detail Green Books, Munich, Germany, 2011.

Solar Dynamics Observatory

The Solar Dynamics Observatory (SDO) is part of NASA's fleet of heliophysics spacecraft and is the first mission in NASA's Living With a Star (LWS) program. The LWS program is NASA's contribution to the National Space Weather Program. The LWS mission's primary goal is to understand how the Sun changes and the effects of solar variability on life and society. Such understanding is necessary because we live on the Earth, which is embedded in the extended variable atmosphere of the Sun. LWS is a combination of science missions, engineering missions, and science investigations to both improve our understanding of the sources of space weather and be better able to develop space hardware that can survive space weather events.

Development history. The LWS concept was developed in the late 1990s and early 2000s. The SDO was quickly recognized as the logical first mission because the Sun is the source of the variability that the following missions will study. The SDO Science Definition Team was formed in 2000, and a science definition report was published in 2001. SDO development began in early 2002, with plans for a 2006 launch. The SDO definition study recommended seven instrument concepts to meet the mission's science objectives. Three instrument suites, which collectively provide four of the seven capabilities, were approved in 2003. SDO was ready for launch at the end of 2008. When the *Atlas-V 401* launch vehicle was ready, SDO was launched on February 11, 2010, from Cape Canaveral, Florida. The three instruments are the Extreme Ultraviolet Variability Experiment (EVE), developed by the University of Colorado Laboratory for Atmospheric and Space Physics (LASP); the Atmospheric Imaging Assembly (AIA), developed by the Lockheed-Martin Solar and Astrophysics Laboratory (LMSAL, part of the Lockheed-Martin Advanced Technology Center in Palo Alto, California); and the Helioseismic and Magnetic Imager (HMI), developed by the Stanford University Hansen Experimental Physics Laboratory (HEPL). The SDO itself was developed and is operated by the NASA Goddard Space Flight Center (GSFC) in Greenbelt, Maryland.

Goals. The science goals for the SDO mission are summarized in the SDO Definition Study Report as:

1. What mechanisms drive the quasiperiodic 11-year cycle of solar activity?

2. How is active-region magnetic flux synthesized, concentrated, and dispersed across the solar surface?

3. How does magnetic reconnection on small scales reorganize the large-scale field topology and current systems? How significant is it in heating the corona and accelerating the solar wind?

4. Where do the observed variations in the Sun's total and spectral irradiance arise, and how do they relate to the magnetic activity cycles?

5. What magnetic field configurations lead to the coronal mass ejections (CMEs), filament eruptions, and flares that produce energetic particles and radiation?

6. Can the structure and dynamics of the solar wind near Earth be determined from the magnetic field configuration and atmospheric structure near the solar surface?

7. When will activity occur, and is it possible to make accurate and reliable forecasts of space weather and climate?

Spacecraft. The SDO is a three-axis stabilized spacecraft powered by solar panels with telemetry from steered antennas (**Fig. 1**). The 3100-kg (6834-lb) launch weight of the SDO spacecraft includes 1450 kg (3197 lb) of fuel and the 290-kg (639-lb) set of instruments. The spacecraft is 4.5 m (14.8 ft) tall and 6.5 m (21.3 ft) wide with the solar panels extended. After release from the *Atlas* launch vehicle, it raised itself to a near-circular orbit at 42,164 km (26,200 mi), inclined at 28.5°. The orbit is such that SDO is above a longitude of −102°, which provides good access for the 18-m (59-ft) Ka-band dishes installed at White Sands Air Force Base in New Mexico.

The spacecraft's structure and its electronics and control system were designed and fabricated at GSFC. The instruments are mounted around the sunward end of the spacecraft, with solar panels and antennas mounted on the sides. Both the instrument electronics and the spacecraft electronics are near the back, with the fuel tanks filling most of the interior. The instruments are all upgraded versions of existing instrument designs with changes to allow the higher resolution and higher cadence needed to meet the demanding SDO mission goals.

The science data are sent to the instrument Science Operation Centers (SOCs) directly from White Sands. The science data telemetry coverage is continuous at 130 Mbit/s and amounts to 1.4 TB (1.4×10^{12} bytes) per day. The data are online and available at the respective centers within about 2 min of observation time. SDO has sufficient fuel to keep its orbit steady and the spacecraft pointed at the Sun for many more decades. The EVE SOC at LASP manages instrument operations and receives the data. HMI and AIA are managed by a joint SOC (JSOC), with instrument operations being managed at LMSAL and data received at HEPL. SDO itself and

Fig. 1. Complete SDO spacecraft waiting for launch. (*NASA; SDO*)

the ground data system are operated by NASA at GSFC.

EVE instruments. The EVE measures the solar extreme ultraviolet (EUV) irradiance in the 0.1–105-nm range. These wavelengths of solar output provide most of the energy creating the Earth's ionosphere that affects communications and the energy that heats the thermosphere, causing drag on low-orbit satellites. The measurements are made with a combination of instruments to get both a detailed high-resolution spectrum at a 10-s cadence and the emission in several narrow bands at a very high cadence, 0.25 s. The required high accuracy is obtained with a combination of special onboard

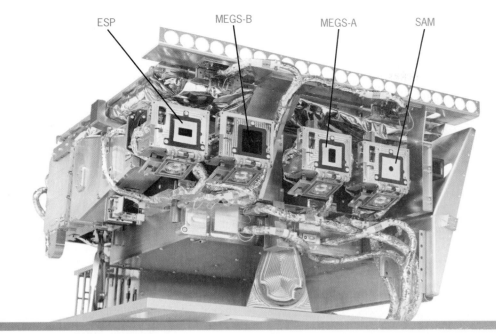

Fig. 2. The EVE optical package. (*SDO; EVE*)

calibration channels and a multiyear sequence of calibration rocket flights. The separate instruments in the EVE suite are the two Multiple EUV Grating Spectrographs (MEGS-A and MEGS-B), a pinhole camera to verify pointing (Solar Aspect Monitor or SAM), and the EUV SpectroPhotometer (ESP) for the fast narrow spectral bands (**Fig. 2**). EVE generates about 7 Mbit/s of telemetry data.

AIA telescopes. The AIA makes images of the Sun's coronal brightness in seven spectral lines in the extreme ultraviolet (EUV) at a 12-s cadence and in two bands in the ultraviolet (UV) at a 24-s cadence, and one broadband visible image each hour. The EUV bands are each chosen to include emissions from one or a few spectral lines emitted from plasma at very high temperatures (millions of degrees). The plasma is constrained to move along magnetic field lines in the corona and maps out the magnetic structures that are the direct sources of space weather events. These images show the detailed and dynamic corona in beautiful detail. The AIA consists of four similar telescopes, each designed to observe in two wavelength bands (**Fig. 3**). Each EUV telescope has half of each mirror coated with multilayers designed to reflect only a very narrow wavelength band. Seven of the eight half-mirrors are tuned for EUV bands. The final half-mirror reflects UV and visible radiation. Light from this half-mirror passes through a rotating filter wheel that selects one of two UV bands or broadband visible light. Thus, there are 10 types of images that can be made with the AIA. Each telescope has a 16-megapixel fast-readout charge-coupled device (CCD) camera with 0.6 arc second per pixel (1.2-arc second resolution). The instrument is operated to produce two images from each telescope

each 12 s. This is fast enough to capture the dynamic corona in action.

The AIA instrument is an enhanced version of two earlier instruments. The first of these is the Extreme Ultraviolet Imaging Telescope (EIT), one of a dozen instruments on the Solar and Heliospheric Observatory (SOHO). SOHO, a joint mission of the European Space Agency (ESA) and NASA, was launched in December 1995, and its mission has been extended at least through 2014. EIT, with tens of images per day, each covering about 1.5 solar diameters of the low corona, demonstrated early in the SOHO program that the corona was much more dynamic and contained much finer structure than had been appreciated before. This led almost immediately to the Transition Region and Coronal Explorer (TRACE) Small Explorer mission (launched in 1998). TRACE made higher-resolution, higher-cadence observations, similar to EIT, but provided only a small field of view for each image. EIT and TRACE in combination showed that, alone, moderate-cadence images taken in different spectral lines in sequence could not sort out spatial versus temporal changes in coronal structure. This shortcoming was a strong motivation for a "full-disk, high-cadence, multiple-simultaneous-lines" version of EIT, which was the concept that is now realized in the AIA. **Figure 4** shows a sample AIA image of the low corona.

HMI instrument. The HMI instrument consists of a visible-light 495-cm (195-in.) focal-length telescope with a 14-cm (5.5-in.) aperture, a polarization analyzer, a narrowband tunable filter, and two 16-megapixel CCD cameras (**Fig. 5**). HMI makes a sequence of images in six wavelengths across one spectral absorption line of iron, FeI at 617.3 nm.

Fig. 3. AIA telescope assembly. (*SDO; AIA*)

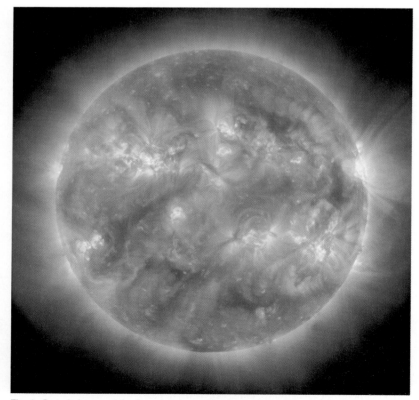

Fig. 4. Sample image of the Sun showing a mix of 1- and 10-million-kelvin plasma measured in the extreme ultraviolet with the SDO/AIA 19.3-nm filter. This image was obtained at about 0 h Universal Time (UT) on April 10, 2013. (*SDO; AIA*)

This line is sensitive to magnetic fields, so by observing in multiple polarizations with samples across the line, HMI can determine both the motion of the photosphere and the magnetic field in the photosphere. The HMI image scale is 0.5 arc second per pixel (1-arc second resolution), and it makes 12 images per camera each 45 s. The data are combined to produce Dopplergrams (maps of solar surface motion) and line-of-sight magnetograms (maps of the magnetic field) at a 45-s cadence, and all components of the magnetic field are averaged into 12-min samples.

The HMI instrument is an enhanced version of the Michelson Doppler Imager (MDI) instrument on SOHO. MDI was designed to generate full-disk Dopplergrams and magnetograms. MDI's full-disk Dopplergrams each minute for 60 days each year helped to usher in the new techniques of local-area helioseismology. MDI data also showed that a continuous stream of multiple magnetograms per day could enable a new understanding of magnetic fields in the corona—important for an understanding of space weather. These two findings together were the motivation for a higher-resolution, full-disk, continuously observing instrument to replace MDI, a concept that was realized in the HMI. **Figure 6** shows a sample visible-light HMI image, and **Fig. 7** shows a sample HMI magnetogram.

Related missions. The combination of HMI, AIA, and EVE meets most of the science data requirements for better understanding of the sources of space weather and possibly learning how to make both short- and long-term predictions of future space

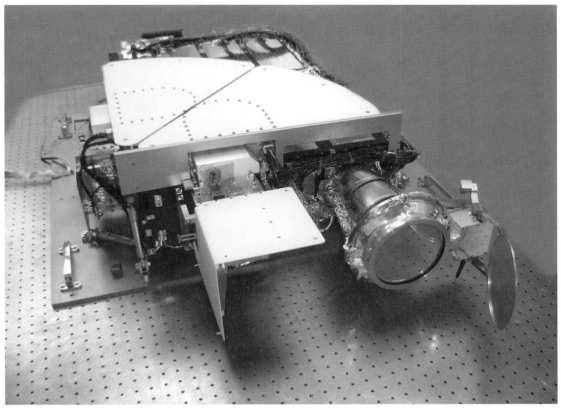

Fig. 5. HMI optics unit. (*HMI; SDO*)

weather. Some necessary capability was not included on SDO. One such key instrument is a wide-field coronagraph to allow measurements of CMEs as they head toward Earth. SOHO has such an instrument, the Large Angle and Spectrometric Coronagraph (LASCO). SOHO operations are being continued so that LASCO data can be available to be combined with SDO observations for both space weather status and solar science investigations. Another mission component is detailed EUV spectral information at high spatial resolution and cadence. The Interface Region Imaging Spectrograph (IRIS) mission, launched on June 27, 2013, will fill this gap in data. The third instrument concept omitted from SDO is a photometric mapper, which is, in part, met by the French Picard mission. The combination of SDO and these other missions meets the data goals outlined in the SDO definition study.

A number of other missions provide important complementary data. The Solar Terrestrial Relations Observatory (STEREO) pair of spacecraft provides the needed data for a full heliospheric view of the Sun and dynamic coronal events. The Hinode mission provides very-high-resolution, small-field-of-view data for selected regions, enabling the acquisition of significant knowledge about the physical processes in the solar atmosphere. The Reuven Ramaty High Energy Solar Spectroscopic Imager (RHESSI) mission, providing imaging at very high energy in flaring regions, adds significantly important

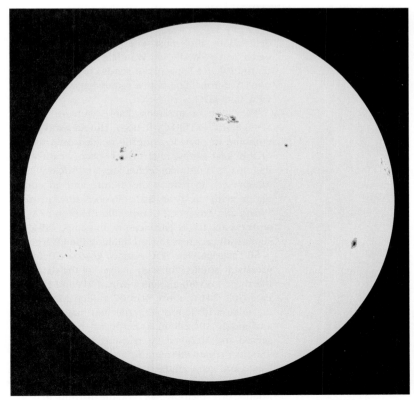

Fig. 6. Sample image of the Sun seen in visible light as measured by the HMI instrument on April 10, 2013, at 0 h UT. Solar limb darkening has been removed to show more detail near the limb. The color is artificial. The filter used passes 617.3-nm light. (*SDO/HMI*)

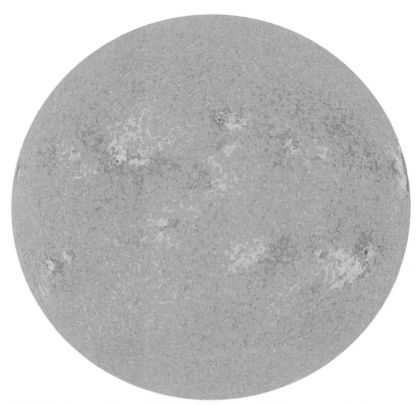

Fig. 7. Sample magnetic map of the Sun obtained by the HMI instrument on April 10, 2013, at 0 h UT. Yellow and orange colors show the magnetic field pointing into the Sun, while green and blue sections show the field pointing out of the Sun. Gray areas have a weak field averaged over a pixel. The locations of the sunspots seen in Fig. 6 have very strong fields. These fields extend into the corona and are the source of the structures seen in Fig. 4. (*SDO/HMI*)

seums, websites, educational material, and social media.

For background information *see* ASTRONOMICAL IMAGING; CHARGE-COUPLED DEVICES; CORONAGRAPH; DOPPLER EFFECT; HELIOSEISMOLOGY; IONOSPHERE; SATELLITE (SPACECRAFT); SOLAR CORONA; SOLAR MAGNETIC FIELD; SOLAR WIND; SPECTROGRAPH; SUN; TELESCOPE; THERMOSPHERE; ULTRAVIOLET ASTRONOMY in the McGraw-Hill Encyclopedia of Science & Technology.   Philip H. Scherrer

Bibliography. E. Drobnes et al., The *Solar Dynamics Observatory* (SDO) Education and Outreach (E/PO) Program: Changing perceptions one program at a time, *Sol. Phys.*, 275:391–406, 2012, DOI:10.1007/s11207-011-9917-0; J. R. Lemen et al., The *Atmospheric Imaging Assembly* (AIA) on the *Solar Dynamics Observatory* (SDO), *Sol. Phys.*, 275:17–40, 2012, DOI:10.1007/s11207-011-9776-8; W. D. Pesnell, B. J. Thompson, and P. C. Chamberlin, The *Solar Dynamics Observatory* (SDO), *Sol. Phys.*, 275:3–15, 2012, DOI:10.1007/s11207-011-9841-3; P. H. Scherrer et al., The *Helioseismic and Magnetic Imager* (HMI) Investigation for the *Solar Dynamics Observatory* (SDO), *Sol. Phys.*, 275:207–227, 2012, DOI:10.1007/s11207-011-9834-2; T. N. Woods et al., *Extreme Ultraviolet Variability Experiment* (EVE) on the *Solar Dynamics Observatory* (SDO): Overview of science objectives, instrument design, data products, and model developments, *Sol. Phys.*, 275:115–143, 2012, DOI:10.1007/s11207-009-9487-6.

data about the most energetic emissions from flares. ESA's SWAP (Sun Watcher with Active Pixel) on the *PROBA2* spacecraft sends coronal images in one UV coronal line with a somewhat wider field of view than SDO.

The suite of missions that is now in place—SDO, SOHO, STEREO, RHESSI, Hinode, and IRIS—combine to provide critically needed observations of the solar output that drives space weather and its impacts on human technology and society. Each mission fills in part of the picture and, in combination with the near-Earth missions now in place [Wind and Advanced Composition Explorer (ACE)] and new and future Earth-centric missions, will allow significant progress toward fulfilling the LWS goals.

SDO science. The SDO science goals are being aggressively studied through analysis of the data from the three instrument suites: AIA, EVE, and HMI. To date (July 2013), more than 67 million AIA images, 2.2 million HMI Dopplergrams and magnetograms, and nearly 10 million EVE spectra have been observed and archived. As of June 2013, more than 450 peer-reviewed scientific articles have been published and many studies are continuing.

Education and public outreach. In addition to the science investigation, SDO and the instrument teams support education and public outreach activities by participation in public science events, science mu-

Solar sailing

Solar sailing is a form of space travel that uses pressure provided by sunlight for propulsion. Traveling through the heavens on starlight may sound like science fiction, but that is what solar sailors aim to accomplish. James Clerk Maxwell's equations describe the momentum and pressure that light imparts on objects in its path. While these equations are perhaps intimidating, the concept is simple enough; sunlight will create a pressure on a surface that it strikes. This simple idea underpins the concept of solar sailing. Solar pressure is not all that dissimilar from the pressure one feels when standing in a breeze. However, the solar pressure felt on Earth is roughly 1,000,000 times weaker than the wind pressure from a gentle breeze (15 km/h or 9 mi/h). In fact, it is not until several hundred kilometers of altitude that solar pressure finally surpasses the drag from residual atmosphere.

Solar-sail designs. A solar sail is a spacecraft that harnesses the pressure provided by sunlight. As solar pressure is so very small, the design of a solar sail must maximize the amount of sail area while minimizing the mass of the craft. In its simplest form, a solar-sail spacecraft consists of a large area of reflective material, held in the "wind" of sunlight, joined to the spacecraft bus. The designs and shapes of solar sails vary significantly. A very simple design consists of four structural members, joined in the center of the craft, supporting four triangular pieces of sail material. A small sail employing this construction was built and successfully flown by NASA in 2010 (**Fig. 1**).

A more complex design uses centripetal motion to deploy and support itself. The Japan Aerospace Exploration Agency (JAXA) launched, deployed, and sailed a craft of this construction in 2010. This craft, named *IKAROS*, is the first solar sail to be operated beyond the influence of the Earth's atmosphere and as such should be considered the first demonstration of solar sailing.

A third solar-sail design uses an elegant deployable-beam system to periodically attach the sail material along the length of the boom. NASA's Space Technology Mission Directorate (STMD) is supporting the fabrication of a sail of this design in preparation for a planned 2014 flight. This mission, named Sunjammer, will further advance the potential of propellant-less solar sails (**Fig. 2**).

Sunjammer mission. The Sunjammer mission is being led by the private company L'Garde Inc. of Tustin, California. Sunjammer is named after a short story written by Sir Arthur C. Clarke. In the story, the protagonist builds and flies an enormous solar sail in a solar-sail yacht race. This story is thought to be the first to use the term "solar sail."

Objectives. The Sunjammer mission is being designed with the following objectives as guidance:

1. *Sunjammer* will demonstrate segmented deployment of a solar sail with an area of 1200 m^2 (12,900 ft^2).

2. *Sunjammer* will have small solar sails called beam-tip vanes at the corners of the larger sail, which can be pointed with control motors. Using these control surfaces, *Sunjammer* will demonstrate three capabilities of the spacecraft: the ability to actively control the angle of the sail about the Sun-sail line (attitude control), the natural tendency of the sail to passively return to its "trim" orientation about the other two axes when disturbed (passive stability), and the ability to retrim to a new passively stable orientation about those two axes by changing vane angles.

3. *Sunjammer* will execute a navigation sequence with mission-capable accuracy.

4. *Sunjammer* will fly to and maintain position at the Lagrangian stability point L1, located on the Earth-Sun line, about 1.5×10^6 km (0.9×10^6 mi) toward the Sun from Earth; or at pole sitter positions, which are unique orbital trajectory positions located above and below the Earth-Sun line. (The angle between a line from *Sunjammer* to the center of the Earth and the Earth-Sun line could reach approximately 20°.)

Upon completion of this Technology Demonstration Mission (TDM) flight, mission planners will have a flight-proven scalable solar-sail design. This relatively inexpensive mission will greatly advance the solar-sail technology in which NASA has already invested. Indeed, it will provide NASA and the

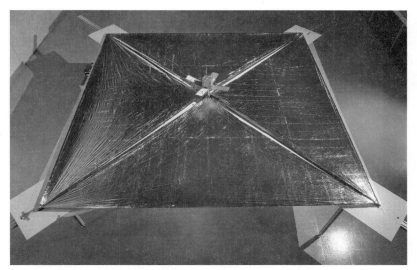

Fig. 1. Nanosail-*D*, demonstrating a simple solar-sail design. (*Courtesy of NASA*)

Fig. 2. Rendering of *Sunjammer* solar sail

Fig. 3. NASA in-space propulsion sail deployment in 2005.

United States with a solar-sailing technology and capability that is second to none.

Spacecraft design. The *Sunjammer* design relies on inflatable, rigidizable technology in the sail structure. The sail structure consists of four conically stowed, inflatably deployed, cold-rigidized booms. These four booms are connected at the center of the sail area to the sailcraft bus. This design was matured through the execution of several programs including the NASA In-Space Propulsion (ISP) efforts, which culminated in several deployments (**Fig. 3**). The sail area is built from 5-micrometer (μm) Kapton. During previous efforts, Kapton of this gauge was unavailable. However, the promise of projects like this has incited investment in research to develop Kapton of sufficiently low thickness as to be credible for use in large solar-sail projects. As previously mentioned, *Sunjammer* will use gimbaled control vanes at each corner of the sail area to control altitude. The vanes will rely on the same technology as the sail area. The use of vanes makes the *Sunjammer* design truly propellantless. This will be an important feature for future mission planners who envision ultralong solar-sail flights.

The *Sunjammer* spacecraft is split into two distinct portions: the sailcraft and the carrier. The sailcraft is the portion of the spacecraft that will perform the solar-sail demonstration after being boosted to Earth-escape orbit. The carrier is the portion of the spacecraft that is expendable after deployment of

the sailcraft. **Figure 4** shows the assembled spacecraft and the separated sailcraft and carrier.

The mission is built around the desire to fly a sail beyond the bounds of an Earth orbit. Also, the mission is targeted to be inexpensive. These two constraints drive much of the design of the entire spacecraft and, more directly, the design of the carrier. First, in order to achieve the low-cost constraint, this mission is planned as a secondary payload. As a secondary payload, the mission is forced to conform to several regulations and requirements. Specifically, *Sunjammer* is being designed to meet Evolved Expandable Launch Vehicle (EELV) Secondary Payload Adapter (ESPA) standards. This conformance, among other things, puts volume and mass constraints on the spacecraft. Second, in order to obtain Earth escape from a commercially available launch, the spacecraft has its own propulsion system.

Demonstration flight details. Less than 2 days after launch, the solar sail will be deployed to full size and separated from the carrier. Within 6 days of launch, the sail will be calibrated and trimmed. For the next 30 days, the sail will navigate to demonstrate and fulfill navigation requirements discussed earlier. Thirty-six days after launch, the sail should have met all of the program-level requirements (PLRs) governing the program, which NASA has defined as the minimum things the project needs to accomplish. At this point, L'Garde desires to continue the mission to fly the sail near L1 and finally to a sub-L1

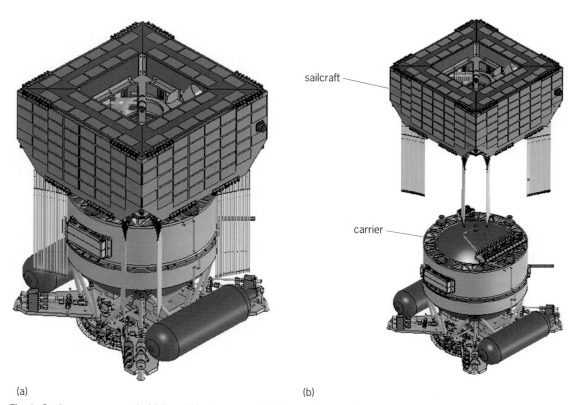

(a)   (b)

Fig. 4. *Sunjammer* spacecraft. (*a*) Assembled spacecraft. (*b*) Separated sailcraft and carrier.

location. Along the way, the onboard magnetometer and plasma detector will be measuring particles from the Sun and comparing the results with those from the National Oceanic and Atmospheric Administration's (NOAA's) *Advanced Composition Explorer* (*ACE*) satellite. These important instruments are being provided by the UK Space Agency and will be instrumental in demonstrating the usefulness of solar sails in this particular application. L'Garde intends to operate the spacecraft for 1 year, after which the ultimate goal is to hand over operation of the spacecraft to an interested party. The spacecraft can then be used directly by another organization to demonstrate its capabilities.

The *Sunjammer*, with its planned 2014 launch, should fully demonstrate the propellantless propulsion potential of solar sails and pave the way for mission designers to build operations around sail technology. The technologies required for future larger-sail missions will be demonstrated in this single mission. The STMD is providing the necessary leadership and support to demonstrate this important technology.

For background information *see* ELECTROMAGNETIC RADIATION; MAXWELL'S EQUATIONS; POYNTING'S VECTOR; RADIATION PRESSURE; SOLAR ENERGY; SPACE PROBE; SPACE TECHNOLOGY in the McGraw-Hill Encyclopedia of Science & Technology.

Nathan Barnes

Bibliography. G. Greschik and M. M. Mikulas, Design study of a square solar sail architecture, *J. Spacecraft Rockets*, 39:653–662, 2002; C. R. McInnes, *Solar Sailing: Technology, Dynamics and Mission Applications*, Springer, London, 1999, reprint, Springer, Berlin, 2004.

Space flight, 2012

The year 2012 was a year of transition for space travel and exploration. NASA's space shuttles were all moved to museums around the country. The largest planetary rover, *Curiosity*, was landed by NASA on Mars. The private company SpaceX conducted the first-ever commercial supply mission to the *International Space Station* (*ISS*). China launched its first female astronaut and North Korea its first successful satellite.

Human space flight. NASA transferred the space shuttle *Discovery* to the Smithsonian's National Air and Space Museum during a ceremony on April 19 at the Stephen F. Udvar-Hazy Center in Chantilly, Virginia (**Fig. 1**).

On April 27, three members of the Expedition 30 crew undocked from the *ISS* and returned safely to Earth after a $5^1/_2$-month mission. Commander Dan Burbank of NASA and Russian Flight Engineers Anatoly Ivanishin and Anton Shkaplerov landed in their *Soyuz TMA-22* spacecraft in Kazakhstan after undocking from the space station's Poisk module.

NASA Flight Engineer Joseph Acaba, Russian Soyuz Commander Gennady Padalka, and Russian Flight Engineer Sergei Revin blasted off for the *ISS* on May 15 from the Baikonur Cosmodrome in Kazakhstan. After docking with the *ISS*, they joined Expedition 31 Commander Oleg Kononenko of the Russian Federal Space Agency and Flight Engineers Don Pettit of NASA and André Kuipers of the European Space Agency (ESA) on May 17.

On May 22, a demonstration mission for NASA's Commercial Orbital Transportation Services (COTS) program launched from Cape Canaveral Air Force Station in Florida aboard SpaceX's Falcon 9 rocket and its Dragon cargo vehicle. The mission carried supplies and experiments to the *ISS* and brought back experiment results and used equipment on May 31, splashing down a few hundred miles west of Baja California, Mexico. It was the first mission by a commercial company to resupply the *ISS*.

On June 16, China launched *Shenzhou 9*, a spacecraft carrying three taikonauts (Chinese astronauts), including the first female one, Liu Yang, to the Tiangong 1 space station. Also onboard was Jing Haipeng, the first taikonaut to fly twice into space. They undocked and landed back on Earth on June 29 in Mongolia.

On July 1, three members of the Expedition 31 crew undocked from the *ISS* and returned safely to Earth, landing their *Soyuz TMA-03M* spacecraft in Kazakhstan. Commander Kononenko and flight engineers Pettit and Kuipers had spent $6^1/_2$ months (193 days) in space, 191 of them aboard the station. While in space the crew worked on more than 200 experiments on biology, combustion, and robotics, involving scientists from around the world.

NASA Flight Engineer Sunita Williams, Russian Soyuz Commander Yuri Malenchenko, and Japan Aerospace Exploration Agency Flight Engineer Akihiko Hoshide took off from the Baikonur Cosmodrome in Kazakhstan on July 15. On July 17, they joined Expedition 32 Commander Padalka and Flight Engineers Acaba and Revin.

July 23 saw the passing of a U.S. space flight legend, Sally Ride. She was the first American woman to fly in space. Ride also was the youngest astronaut to fly into space, being 32 at the time of her first mission. Her death was due to pancreatic cancer.

In August NASA awarded contracts to Boeing, Sierra Nevada, and SpaceX to develop capability to launch humans to the *ISS*.

On August 25, Neil Armstrong, who became the first human to walk on the Moon in 1969, died at age 82 of complications from coronary artery bypass surgery.

NASA's Kennedy Space Center in Florida welcomed the arrival of the agency's first space-bound *Orion* capsule in July. *Orion* will be one of the most advanced spacecraft ever designed for human space flight, capable of sustaining astronauts for long periods of time, providing safe reentry from deep space, and an emergency abort capability. The *Orion* at Kennedy will launch on Exploration Flight Test-1, which will be a crewless test mission, in 2014.

Fig. 1. Shuttle *Discovery* on its carrier aircraft flies over Washington, DC, on its way to its final exhibit place at the National Air and Space Museum.

ISS Expedition 32 Commander Padalka and Flight Engineers Acaba and Revin undocked from the station and returned to Earth safely on September 16, after more than 4 months in space.

Another SpaceX Falcon 9 rocket carrying a Dragon spacecraft lifted off from Cape Canaveral Air Force Station on October 7, beginning NASA's first contracted cargo delivery flight. NASA designated the flight to the *ISS* SpaceX CRS-1. Under NASA's Commercial Resupply Services contract, SpaceX will fly at least 12 cargo missions to the space station through 2016 for a cost of $1.6 billion. To dock, Dragon was grappled into place by the *ISS* robot arm on October 10. It returned to Earth with *ISS* experiment results on October 28.

NASA astronaut Kevin Ford and Russian cosmonauts Evgeny Tarelkin and Oleg Novitskiy launched aboard a Russian Soyuz rocket on their mission to the *ISS* on October 23. The three took off from the Baikonur Cosmodrome in Kazakhstan. They joined Expedition 33 Commander Williams and Flight Engineers Hoshide and Malenchenko, who had been living aboard the orbiting laboratory since July. On November 18, Williams, Hoshide, and Malenchenko of the Expedition 33 crew undocked from the station and returned safely to Earth.

The year in human space flight ended on December 19 with the launch of Tom Marshburn of NASA, Roman Romanenko of the Russian Federal Space Agency (Roscosmos), and Chris Hadfield of the Canadian Space Agency. They docked their *Soyuz TMA-07M* spacecraft with the *ISS* on December 21.

Robotic solar system exploration. In February, new images from NASA's *Lunar Reconnaissance Orbiter* (*LRO*) spacecraft showed that the Moon's crust is being stretched, creating small valleys in several areas on the lunar surface. Scientists believe this geologic activity occurred less than 50 million years ago, which is recent compared to the Moon's age of more than 4.5 billion years.

March saw NASA's twin *Gravity Recovery And Interior Laboratory* (*GRAIL*) spacecraft in orbit around the Moon officially begin their science collection phase. During this phase, scientists obtained a high-resolution map of the lunar gravitational field to learn about the Moon's internal structure and composition in unprecedented detail. These data provide a better understanding of how Earth and other rocky planets in the solar system formed and evolved. NASA intentionally crashed the two spacecraft into the surface of the Moon on December 17 when their mission was over (observations of their impact by the *LRO* provided more data about the Moon's composition). NASA named the lunar site where the two spacecraft hit the Moon in honor of the late astronaut Sally Ride.

The MARSIS radar instrument on board ESA's *Mars Express* orbiter discovered subsurface low-density

Fig. 2. One of the first images of the surface of Mars as seen from the navigation cameras on NASA's *Curiosity* rover. Gale Crater can be seen in the distance. Part of the rover is visible in the foreground. (*NASA*)

material around the Martian north polar cap. This finding helps to support theories that the northern lowlands of Mars were once covered by a large body of water. A great deal of evidence points to the fact that, although Mars is essentially a dry planet today, it was once much wetter.

NASA's *Dawn* space probe revealed unexpected details on the surface of the large asteroid Vesta. New images and data highlight the diversity of Vesta's surface and reveal unusual geologic features, some of which were never previously seen on asteroids. *Dawn* found that some areas on Vesta are nearly twice as bright as others, providing information about the asteroid's history. The dark materials seem to be related to impacts and their results. Carbon-rich asteroids could have hit Vesta at speeds slow enough to create some of the smaller deposits without blasting away the surface. If impacts occurred at higher speeds, volcanic basaltic crust would be melted, creating a darker surface. *Dawn* was launched in September 2007 and left Vesta in September 2012, headed for rendezvous with its second destination, Ceres, in early 2015. *See* DAWN'S ASTEROID EXPLORATIONS; EVOLUTION OF ASTEROID 4 VESTA.

Data from NASA's Cassini mission revealed that Saturn's moon Phoebe has more planetlike qualities than previously thought. This conclusion is based on data from multiple instruments collected during a *Cassini* close fly-by. *Cassini* showed Phoebe to have originated in the far-off Kuiper belt in the outer solar system and to be similar in composition and density to Pluto. It is now believed that Phoebe was captured by Saturn.

NASA's *LRO* spacecraft in June returned data that indicate that ice makes up as much as 22% of the surface material in Shackleton crater, located on the Moon's south pole. *LRO* found that the crater is brighter than other nearby craters, which is consistent with the presence of small amounts of ice. This information will help researchers understand crater formation and study other uncharted areas of the Moon.

On August 5, NASA's most advanced Mars rover, *Curiosity*, landed on the Red Planet. The rover, weighing about one ton, completed the most complex descent and landing ever done on Mars. The landing culminated a 36-week flight from Earth and began a 2-year science mission. *Curiosity* has begun its 2-year baseline of experiments to determine whether life ever existed on the Red Planet. The rover completed check out of its 10 science instruments, sent back detailed photos (**Fig. 2**) and weather observations, and has scooped up some soil to perform an analysis. *See* MARS SCIENCE LABORATORY.

A NASA spacecraft orbiting Mercury provided evidence for the hypothesis that the planet harbors abundant water ice and other frozen volatile materials within its permanently shadowed polar craters, much as Earth's Moon does. The data originate from NASA's *MESSENGER* spacecraft. Its onboard instruments have been studying Mercury up close since arriving in orbit in March 2011.

Other activities. After 16 years of service in space, NASA's *Rossi X-ray Timing Explorer* (*RXTE*) made its last observation on January 4. The satellite provided unprecedented views into the extreme environments around white dwarfs, neutron stars, and black holes. After performing engineering tests, controllers at NASA's Goddard Space Flight Center in Greenbelt, Maryland, successfully decommissioned the satellite on January 5.

Observations made in February by the NASA/ESA *Hubble Space Telescope* have identified a new type

Fig. 3. The Hubble Extreme Deep Field (XDF), containing some of the most distant objects ever identified. It shows about 5500 galaxies, many in their very early stage of formation. (*NASA*)

of planet with a water surface and water-laden atmosphere. It is larger than Earth and smaller than Uranus. The planet, named GJ1214b, orbits a red dwarf star 40 light-years from Earth.

On June 13 NASA's *Nuclear Spectroscopic Telescope Array* (*NuSTAR*) launched over the central Pacific Ocean on a Pegasus XL launch vehicle. It is providing unprecedented spatial and spectral coverage of the x-ray region. *NuSTAR* is using instruments to see the highest energy x-ray light from the universe.

Astronomers using NASA's *Spitzer Space Telescope* have detected what they believe is a planet two-thirds the size of Earth on July 18. The exoplanet candidate, called UCF-1.01, is 33 light-years from Earth. This object is the nearest known world to our solar system that is smaller than Earth. The planet is very near its star and is believed to have very high surface temperatures.

Launched on August 30, the NASA Radiation Belt Storm Probes (RBSP) mission uses the first dual spacecraft to investigate the radiation belts that surround Earth. These two belts, named for their discoverer, James Van Allen, circle the Earth and contain highly charged particles. The

spacecraft were renamed the Van Allen Probes in November.

In September, astronomers released a new, improved series of images to create a portrait of our deepest-ever view of the universe. It was called the eXtreme Deep Field, or XDF, and combines 10 years of NASA/ESA *Hubble Space Telescope* observations of a patch of sky within the original famous Hubble Ultra Deep Field observations. The XDF is a small fraction of the angular diameter of the full Moon and contains about 5500 galaxies (**Fig. 3**).

Late in the year, *Hubble* also found seven early galaxies from a distant population that formed more than 13 billion years ago. These observations have suggested a candidate for the record of the most distant galaxy found to date, which exhibits a large redshift of 11.9. They have also helped unlock the very earliest years of cosmic history. The galaxies are seen as they were when the universe was less than 4% of its current age.

Launch summary. In 2012 there were 78 launches, with 73 successful. During the year there were 20 commercial launches. American launch vehicles launched two commercial missions in 2012. Russia had 7 commercial launches. The Sea Launch

Space launches in 2012		
Country of launch	Attempts	Successful
Russia	24	22
China	19	19
United States	13	13
Europe	10	10
Russian-Ukrainian Zenit-3SL	3	3
Iran	3	1
India	2	2
Japan	2	2
North Korea	2	1
Total	78	73

consortium successfully launched three commercial missions. Europe had six commercial launches and China two. Five launches were failures; of these, two were Russian, two Iranian, and one North Korean.

Russia once again led in launches in 2012 with 24. Seven of these were commercial and of the other 17, eight were devoted to the *ISS*. Four crewless Progress modules were launched on Soyuz launch vehicles on *ISS* supply missions. Four were crewed Soyuz missions. A Russian launch failure was with the Proton M booster. A second Proton M launch was a partial failure when the rocket's upper stage failed to place a satellite in the intended orbit, but the satellite's onboard propulsion enabled it to reach the correct orbit.

Four Russian launches were for military purposes. Three were civilian missions, using the Soyuz twice and the Proton M once. Launch vehicles used by Russia were Proton M (10), Soyuz (9), Soyuz 2 (2), Rockot (1), Soyuz U (1), and Proton K (1).

For the United States the most launches were the three with the Atlas V-401. Two launches used the Falcon 9 Dragon, and one apiece used the Atlas V-501, Atlas V-531, Atlas V-551, Delta IV-Heavy, Delta IV-Medium+4,2, Delta IV-Medium+5,2, Delta IV-Medium+5,4, and Pegasus XL. All launches were successful.

China continues to rely on a variety of Long March launch vehicles. Five were Long March 3B; three each used the 3C and 2D; two each used the 2C, 4B and 4C; one each used the 2F and 3A. Two launches were commercial. There was one Chinese human space flight in 2012. Seven launches carried government civil missions (communications, meteorological, remote sensing, and scientific) and nine were military.

Seven European launches used the Ariane 5 variants, with one being an Autonomous Transfer Vehicle (ATV) robotic vehicle to carry supplies to the *ISS*. Two Soyuz 2 launches were considered European because they launched from the European French Guiana complex. The Vega rocket made its inaugural launch for Europe.

Japan placed their crewless *ISS* supply spacecraft HTV into orbit on their H-IIB vehicle. Also, an H-IIA vehicle launched Sun-synchronous orbit (SSO) payloads successfully.

India had two successful noncommercial launches of its PSLV launcher.

Iran attempted three Safir 2 rocket launches and two were failures. A remote-sensing satellite launch was successful in February.

Multinational Sea Launch launched the Zenit 3SL from the Pacific Ocean three times successfully in 2012.

The North Korean Unha 3 rocket launched twice. The first attempt in April was unsuccessful. The second, a launch in December, placed North Korea's first satellite into orbit.

For background information *see* ASTEROID; ASTROPHYSICS, HIGH-ENERGY; EXTRASOLAR PLANETS; GALAXY, EXTERNAL; HUBBLE SPACE TELESCOPE; KUIPER BELT; MARS; MERCURY (PLANET); MOON; SATELLITE (ASTRONOMY); SATURN; SCIENTIFIC AND APPLICATIONS SATELLITES; SPACE BIOLOGY; SPACE FLIGHT; SPACE PROBE; SPACE PROCESSING; SPACE SHUTTLE; SPACE STATION; SPACE TECHNOLOGY; SPITZER SPACE TELESCOPE; VAN ALLEN RADIATION; X-RAY ASTRONOMY; X-RAY TELESCOPE in the McGraw-Hill Encyclopedia of Science & Technology.

Donald Platt

Bibliography. *Aviation Week & Space Technology*, various 2012 issues; ESA Press Releases, 2012; NASA Public Affairs Office, News Releases, 2012; *The Annual Compendium of Commercial Space Transportation: 2012*, Federal Aviation Administration, February 2013.

Sports and brain injury

Sport-related concussion (SRC) has become the focus of increasing concern for clinicians, researchers, sporting organizations, and athletes because of its reported prevalence, its acute effects, and the fears about its potential long-term neurological consequences. Concussion is among the most frequent injuries experienced by athletes participating in contact and collision sports (for example, football, hockey, and wrestling), and it occurs at all levels of participation. From 1997 to 2007, visits to hospital emergency departments for 8- to 13-year-old children affected by concussion in organized team sports doubled, and those for 14- to 19-year-old teenagers more than tripled. The true incidence of SRC is thought to be higher than that reported in epidemiological studies because of a tendency by athletes to not recognize or report these injuries.

Over the past several years, a longitudinal model for understanding and studying the acute and potential long-term effects of concussion has emerged. During the acute phase, SRC is known to cause serious symptoms and functional impairments that gradually improve over time in the majority of cases. However, in very rare instances, catastrophic outcomes in the form of death or permanent disability have been associated with diffuse cerebral swelling or second-impact syndrome in the case of athletes who sustain multiple SRCs over a short time frame. In addition, a small percentage of athletes are reported to have prolonged recovery, persistent symptoms, or functional impairments after concussion, which is commonly referred to as postconcussion syndrome. More recently, there are growing concerns about the long-term neurologic consequences of repetitive concussion, including early onset of dementia or chronic traumatic encephalopathy (CTE).

Without question, enormous strides have been made in advancing the basic and clinical science of concussion over the past few decades, but many questions remain unanswered. These advances now provide evidence-based approaches to concussion diagnosis, assessment, management, and prevention. This paper presents a brief overview of the current evidence base and highlights critical directions for future research.

Acute recovery following sport-related concussion. The first area of investigation involves the acute recovery following SRC, including an examination of its clinical signs and symptoms as well as the neurophysiologic changes during the acute recovery period.

Clinical signs and symptoms. Concussion causes physical symptoms (for example, headache and dizziness), cognitive deficits (for example, deficits in memory, attention, and processing speed), and other functional impairments almost immediately after injury. In the vast majority of cases, a single concussion appears to be a relatively benign neurologic event, followed by a rapid and complete recovery within several days for most athletes, and within 1–2 weeks for an overwhelming majority of individuals. A small proportion of athletes appear to require more time to fully recover from concussions, although the reasons for their more prolonged recovery are unclear. Whereas limited research found a lengthier recovery time in younger athletes, other work with high school and college athletes has suggested that the primary risk factors for prolonged recovery (that is, recovery beyond the typical 7–10 days) were initial indicators of more severe injury (unconsciousness, posttraumatic amnesia, and acute symptom severity) rather than age or other individual factors.

Neurophysiologic changes during the acute recovery period. Animal brain injury models have detailed a complex cascade of ionic, metabolic, and physiological events following concussion that culminate in axonal injury and temporary neuronal dysfunction. Modern biomedical advances (for example, functional neuroimaging and electrophysiological testing) that enabled a powerful translation from earlier animal work to applied clinical research on the physiological effects of concussion in humans have documented metabolic and physiological changes in the brain after concussion that correlate with postconcussive symptoms and performance on neurocognitive testing during the acute postinjury phase. Abnormal patterns of brain blood flow on functional magnetic resonance imaging (fMRI) appear to correlate with clinical symptoms during the acute recovery period (7–10 days), and atypical activation patterns on fMRI are highly related to persistent symptomatology during the subacute period, which lasts months after SRC. Diffusion tensor imaging (DTI), which is a variant of MRI that models the brain's white matter integrity, appears to be particularly sensitive to the neurophysiological abnormalities (for example, axonal injury) that may persist beyond the typical window of clinical recovery after concussion. Questions remain about how long such effects persist and for whom. Another question for future work to address is whether there is an interaction between when athletes resume physical activity (that is, return to play) after SRC and the time course of their neurobiologic recovery.

Long-term risks associated with multiple concussions. There has been much concern about the long-term consequences of multiple concussions, especially with regard to persistent neurophysiologic changes and neurodegenerative disease.

Clinical signs and symptoms. Despite the typically transient effects of single concussions, there is growing concern that repeated SRCs could cause persistent symptoms, neurocognitive changes, or the development of degenerative brain disease years after athletic participation. For example, athletes having had multiple historical concussions report more postconcussive symptoms than those having had one concussion, although findings may be confounded by an erroneous recall of concussion histories or preexisting differences between these groups. In partial support of this possibility, professional football players followed prospectively (that is, as multiple concussions occurred) showed similar signs and symptoms after their first and second concussions, with the exception that they reported more somatic symptoms after their repeat injury. Future studies will be better able to tease apart individual risk factors for concussion incidence and recovery and the persistent effects of concussions.

A small body of work has begun to examine the potential for recurrent concussions to increase the risk for psychiatric disorders. However, an overlap between symptoms of concussion and those of depression complicates their differential diagnosis and this area of research. On the one hand, retired professional football players with a history of multiple mild head injuries have a threefold risk of lifetime depression. In contrast, given that professional football players have a below-average rate of suicide, this does not appear to translate to increased suicidality.

Cognitive changes as measured by traditional neuropsychological tests may also persist following exposure to repeated concussions. For example, executive functioning, memory, divided attention, and response inhibition have all been cited as being weaker in individuals who have had multiple concussions. However, numerous studies have found no reliable association between neuropsychological measures and concussion history. As both head and nonhead injuries are associated with lower intellectual ability and achievement in children, it is possible that cognitive deficits that have been attributed to concussions in some studies may be the result of personal factors generally common to sustaining injuries, leading to an overestimation of the extent to which cognitive differences between groups exist because of differences in concussion histories.

Persistent neurophysiologic changes following multiple concussions. Athletes reporting histories of multiple concussions have shown differences in brain event–related potential responses, with some evidence that electrophysiological changes following SRC can normalize given enough time to recover. Although there are not enough reports to draw strong conclusions, neuroimaging techniques such as fMRI are increasingly being used to evaluate the potential long-term effects of repeat concussions and hold promise for detecting subtle changes in neurobiology that could accumulate with recurrent mild head injuries.

Neurodegenerative disease. With the accumulation of high-profile cases of serious cognitive and psychiatric difficulties in professional athletes, there is increasing concern about the potential for recurrent concussions to increase the risk for developing neurodegenerative diseases (such as Alzheimer's disease and CTE). Older rugby players with a history of repeat concussions report more subjective memory complaints, and retired professional football players with a history of 3 or more (versus 0) concussions have a fivefold risk of being diagnosed with mild cognitive impairment (MCI). Although there were no differences in the rates of Alzheimer's disease in the sample of football players, the multiply concussed group tended to be diagnosed with Alzheimer's disease at an earlier age.

CTE is of particular concern given recently reported cases in retired football players and other nonboxing athletes. Clinically, CTE is thought to be similar to other progressive neurodegenerative diseases, with presenting symptoms including impaired cognition, mood, and behavior. However, CTE is pathologically and clinically distinct from other dementias. Gross pathological findings include neurofibrillary tangles and glial tau inclusions [abnormal deposits of a microtubule-associated protein (tau) in glial cells] that preferentially involve various regions of the brain (for example, the cortical sulci, medial temporal lobe, diencephalon, and brainstem). CTE research is in its infancy, and numerous issues require further investigation. Clinical criteria for the diagnosis of CTE, which currently relies on a postmortem examination, need to be established and tested. There is currently no imaging modality or biochemical marker that can accurately and reproducibly detect the presence of concussion or the development of CTE. Additionally, the incidence and prevalence of CTE have not been established because the autopsy-based case series model is limited by ascertainment bias. Finally, a causal relationship between repetitive head injury and clinical symptoms (for example, cognitive, behavioral, and emotional changes) is confounded by numerous factors, including the presence of comorbid medical and mental health conditions.

Conclusions and future directions. Great strides have been made in our knowledge base about the natural history of SRC. During the acute period following SRC, athletes commonly experience physical, cognitive, and emotional symptoms that resolve within several days for most players. However, emerging neuroimaging data suggest that pathophysiologic changes may persist beyond the point of clinical recovery. Furthermore, select athletes may be at risk for the development of persistent symptoms or neurologic changes (including early onset of dementia or CTE), particularly following exposure to repeated SRCs, although it is unclear who is at greatest risk and what factors predict outcome. Unfortunately, the data on SRC are often limited by small sample sizes, reliance on retrospective self-reports, and correlational research designs that lack adequate control for potential confounding factors. Future work that accumulates larger samples, follows athletes prospectively, and incorporates advanced neuroimaging and biomarker technologies will enhance our understanding of SRC and inform injury prevention and management strategies.

For background information *see* ALZHEIMER'S DISEASE; BRAIN; COGNITION; CONCUSSION; INTELLIGENCE; MEDICAL IMAGING; NERVOUS SYSTEM DISORDERS; NEUROBIOLOGY; SPORTS MEDICINE; TRAUMA in the McGraw-Hill Encyclopedia of Science & Technology.

Michael A. McCrea; Lindsay D. Nelson; Julie K. Janecek

Bibliography. H. G. Belanger and R. D. Vanderploeg, The neuropsychological impact of sports-related concussion: A meta-analysis, *J. Int. Neuropsychol. Soc.*, 11(4):345–357, 2005, DOI:http://dx.doi.org/10.1017/S1355617705050411; M. W. Collins et al., Sport-related concussion, pp. 498–516, in N. Zasler, D. Katz, and R. Zafonte, eds., *Brain Injury Medicine: Principles and Practice*, 2d ed., Demos Medical Publishing, New York, 2012; K. M. Guskiewicz et al., Cumulative effects associated with recurrent concussion in collegiate football players: The NCAA Concussion Study, *JAMA*, 290(19):2549–2555, 2003, DOI:10.1001/jama.290.19.2549; M. McCrea et al., An integrated review of recovery after mild traumatic brain injury (MTBI): Implications for clinical management, *The Clinical Neuropsychologist*, 23(8):1368–1390, 2009, DOI:10.1080/13854040903074652; P. McCrory et al., Consensus statement on concussion in sport: The 3rd International Conference on Concussion in Sport held in Zurich, November 2008, *Br. J. Sports Med.*, 43(suppl. 1):i76–i90, 2009, DOI:10.1136/bjsm.2009.058248; A. C. McKee et al., The spectrum of disease in chronic traumatic encephalopathy, *Brain*, 136(pt. 1):43–64, 2013, DOI:10.1093/brain/aws307.

Strength loss in decayed wood

Wood is a durable engineering material when used in an appropriate manner, but it is susceptible to biological decay when a log, sawn product, or final product is not stored, handled, or designed properly. Even before the biological decay of wood becomes visually apparent, the decay can cause the wood to become structurally unsound. The progression of decay to that critical state depends heavily on temperature and moisture conditions. As a preventative measure, wood preservatives are chemical treatments applied to wood to protect less-durable wood species from decay. To ensure that these treatments are effective in providing protection, the wood preservation industry typically uses a suite of standard test methods to evaluate the efficacy of wood preservatives to combat wood decay microorganisms. The two standardization agencies in the United States are the American Wood Protection Association (AWPA) and the American Society for Testing Materials (ASTM).

The initial evaluation for determining the feasibility and potential effectiveness of a preservative is based on laboratory tests of small wood blocks, both treated and untreated, which are challenged against wood-rotting fungi. The soil block test (AWPA E10 or ASTM D1413) requires 12–16 weeks of exposure (depending on the test block dimensions) to various decay fungi (for example, brown- or white-rot fungi), and more time is needed for preparing and conditioning the samples before and after the test. The weight loss of treated blocks over this exposure period provides a measure of the minimum amount of preservative necessary for preventing decay under optimum conditions, and it allows the determination of the amount of preservative needed for long-term field testing (aboveground or in-ground field tests). Field tests usually take a minimum of five years of exposure to fully evaluate the effectiveness of preservatives against outdoor hazards. Furthermore, it has been known for years that there can be a significant loss of strength in biologically degraded wood, especially wood under attack from brown-rot fungi, and this strength loss appears long before there is very much weight loss. Accelerated laboratory tests based on strength measurements of early decayed wood are being developed and standardized as early indicators of the performance of wood preservatives. Recently, a standard for predicting aboveground performance has been developed that is based on the compressive strength loss of wood sticks after four weeks in an accelerated fungal exposure (AWPA E22-12). A key for developing accelerated testing methods is to use accurate and quantitative measurements that are important indicators of performance in service conditions. Bending elasticity and compression tests have been used for small specimens, and dynamic modulus of elasticity (MOE) tests have been used for larger size specimens. This article explores the issue of weight loss versus strength loss as a result of decay in the evaluation of wood preservatives.

Decay fungi. Decay fungi are multicellular filamentous microorganisms that use the structural components of wood as food. **Figure 1** shows the decay cycle of wood. The fungal spores are spread by the wind, insects, or animals. They germinate on moist, susceptible wood, and the hyphae (mycelial filaments) spread throughout the wood. These hyphae

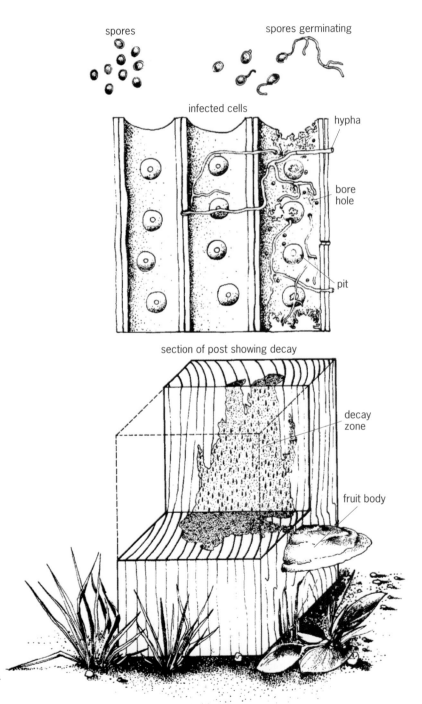

Fig. 1. The wood decay cycle. (*Figure adapted from Forest Products Laboratory, Wood Handbook: Wood as an Engineering Material, Gen. Tech. Rep. FPL-GTR-190, Forest Products Laboratory, U.S. Department of Agriculture Forest Service, Madison, WI, 2010*)

secrete enzymes that attack the wood cells, causing the wood to deteriorate. After serious decay, a new fruiting body may form.

In the early or incipient stage of wood decay, serious strength losses can occur before the decay is even detected. Strength properties related to sudden loads, such as toughness or impact bending, are most sensitive to decay. When affected by incipient decay, unseasoned wood may become discolored, but it is harder to detect on dry wood. The advanced stages of wood decay are easier to detect. Decayed wet wood will break across the grain, whereas sound wood will splinter.

Decay fungi need food (hemicelluloses, cellulose, and lignin), oxygen (air), the proper temperature [10–35°C (50–95°F); optimum: 24–32°C (75–90°F)], and moisture (above the fiber saturation point; approximately 30% moisture content) to grow. Free water must be present (from rain, condensation, or wet ground contact) for the fiber saturation point to be reached and decay to occur. Air-dried wood will usually have no more than 20% moisture content, so decay will not occur. However, there are a few water-conducting fungi that transport water to dry wood and cause a decay called dry rot. When free water is added to wood to attain 25–30% moisture content or higher, decay will occur. Yet, wood can be too wet for decay. If wood is soaked in water, there is not enough air for the fungi to develop.

Brown-rot fungi. Brown-rot fungi decompose the carbohydrates (that is, the cellulose and hemicelluloses) of the wood. The lignin is left intact, making the wood browner in color (hence, the name brown-rot). Brown-rot fungi mainly colonize softwoods, but they can be found on hardwoods as well. Because of the attack on the cellulose, the strength properties of the brown-rot decayed wood decrease quickly, even in the early stages. When extreme decay is attained, the wood becomes a very dark, charred color. After the cross-grain cracking, the wood shrinks, collapses, and finally crumbles. Brown-rot fungi first use a low-molecular-weight system to break down (depolymerize) the cellulose within the cell wall, and then they use specific enzymes (endocellulases) to further decompose the wood.

White-rot fungi. White-rot fungi decompose all of the structural components (that is, the cellulose, hemicelluloses, and lignin) of the wood. As the wood decays, it becomes bleached (in part from the lignin removal) or "white" with black zone lines. White-rot fungi occur mainly on hardwoods, but they can be found on softwoods as well. The degraded wood does not crack across the grain until it is severely degraded. It keeps its outward dimensions, but feels spongy. In general, the strength properties decrease gradually as the decay progresses; however, the toughness can decrease more rapidly. White-rot fungi have a complete cellulase enzyme complex and also the ability to degrade lignin.

Soft-rot fungi. Soft-rot fungi are related to molds. They usually occur in wood that is constantly wet, but they can also appear on surfaces that encounter wet–dry cycling. Typically, the decayed wood is shallow in depth and "soft" when wet, but the undecayed wood underneath is still firm. Upon drying, the decayed surface is fissured. The wood becomes darker (dull-brown to blue-gray) when decayed by soft-rot fungi. Soft-rot fungi have a system that first frees the lignin in the wood, allowing the cellulase decay enzymes access to the substrate.

Methods for evaluating wood decay in a testing environment. The evaluation of wood decay is complicated because different fungi can attack different wood species in diverse ways. The history of the exposure is also important. In the evaluation of the efficacy of wood preservatives, multiple methods are used to compare the deterioration of preservative-treated wood to untreated wood (as a negative control) and also to wood that has been treated with an established effective preservative (as a positive control). Depending on the test conducted, difficulties can be encountered, including the inability to control for wood moisture content variation during the test, depletion of the wood preservatives during the test (for example, by leaching), biomass weight gain from fungal colonization, and the lack of differentiation between localized and entire specimen decay.

Laboratory decay tests. Laboratory decay tests expose the treated wood to fungi that are known to aggressively degrade less-durable and untreated wood. These tests are based on weight loss or strength loss (or both) and help to determine the threshold treatment level that is needed to prevent the decay of wood that will be in contact with the soil. These tests are typically performed before field testing. Often, metal- or biocide-tolerant strains of wood decay fungi may be used in these tests. Laboratory decay tests are optimized to provide ideal conditions for fungal biodegradation.

Outdoor in-ground field tests. Outdoor in-ground field tests expose treated wood stakes and untreated controls to various natural organisms under severe conditions. Wood stakes are placed in the soil and rated visually over an extended period of time. Usually two different sites are chosen with different moisture and temperature climates, soil properties, and types of organisms present.

Outdoor aboveground field tests. Outdoor aboveground field tests expose treated wood and untreated controls to the weather (usually in an area with a warm, wet climate), and they are visually rated over an extended period of time. The exposures are usually not as severe as in-ground field stake tests. The wood samples are installed and designed to trap moisture and create ideal conditions for aboveground decay.

Strength tests. Strength tests are a way of comparing the mechanical properties of wood, including treated versus untreated wood exposed to similar conditions. Changes in the mechanical properties can be indications that the wood has been damaged by biological decay or even from the chemical treatment or process. AWPA Standard E22-12 is an accelerated laboratory method for testing the efficacy of preservatives against decay fungi using compressive strength, which may be used as an indicator of aboveground performance.

Bending, compression, hardness, and the torsional properties of wood at various stages of fungal decay have been measured. Static bending has been shown to be a viable method of measuring decay in the laboratory. Tests to determine the MOE with static bending require specialized equipment and controlled conditions, and these tests are usually done in a laboratory. A dynamic methodology called dynamic MOE (MOE$_{dyn}$) is another way to determine the MOE and is highly correlated with the static MOE. It was initially developed on the basis of an ultrasonic pulse excitation methodology; however, a more recent MOE$_{dyn}$ method has been developed using resonant vibration excitation technology. With this type of nondestructive measurement, there are fewer sample dimension and configuration restrictions, and on-site measurements can be performed with the equipment. Handheld spring-loaded plunger devices have also been used to correlate wood hardness with the extent of decay. A strong correlation exists at higher weight losses, but the measurements are affected by grain orientation and moisture content, making it difficult to detect the early stages of decay.

Other methods. Methods to detect the presence of fungal antigens have been developed (immunodiagnostics) and are very sensitive to detecting the incipient stages of decay, but they do not provide information on the progressive development of the decay. However, genetic profiles of microbial communities in wood decay environments are being developed. Establishing relationships between the progression of these measurements and strength properties could provide quicker methods for incipient and early wood decay evaluation.

Near-infrared (NIR) spectroscopy has been used to detect and quantify the chemical biodeterioration of wood. The coupling of NIR spectroscopy with multivariate regression or principal components analysis has allowed good correlations to be made between NIR measurements and both mass loss and compressive strength loss of brown-rotted wood. However, more research is needed to determine if this method is capable of detecting the early stages of decay and other types of fungi.

Effect of decay on the strength of wood. Decay initially affects toughness, or the ability of wood to withstand impacts. This is generally followed by reductions in strength values related to static bending. Eventually, all strength properties are seriously reduced. Strength losses during the early stages of decay can be considerable, depending to a great extent on the fungi involved and to a lesser extent on the type of wood undergoing the decay. In laboratory tests, the losses in toughness ranged from 6% to more than 50% by the time that a 1% weight loss had occurred in the wood as a result of fungal attack. Further, the weight loss of wood in the range of 5–10% equates to a reduction of the mechanical properties in the range of 20–80%. At weight losses

of 10% or less, the decay is detectable only microscopically. A wood that shows visible signs of decay most likely has greatly reduced strength values. There is no method known to estimate the amount of strength loss from just visually inspecting the decayed wood.

Of the three main components of wood, that is, cellulose, hemicelluloses, and lignin, the initial losses in strength from early brown-rot decay are the result of the attack on the hemicelluloses and then the cellulose. At low weight losses in the decayed wood, there can be significant reductions in the degree of polymerization of the holocellulose (the total polysaccharide fraction of the wood); for example, at only 10% weight loss of sweetgum decayed by a brown-rot fungus, the degree of polymerization of the holocellulose dropped from 1500 to 300. The wood's mechanical properties decrease when the side chains of the hemicelluloses (such as arabinose and galactose) are degraded enzymatically by chemical reactions, including hydrolysis, dehydration, and oxidation. The initial strength loss of 5–20% is related to the initial degradation of the hemicelluloses, followed by the degradation of the main-chain backbones of the hemicelluloses. After 40–60% strength reduction, the glucose and lignin are degraded. This helps explain the shortcomings of using mass loss to detect the early stages of decay.

Figure 2 shows the effect of decay by a brown-rot fungus (*Gloeophyllum trabeum*) on the weight loss and mechanical properties of wood. It shows that the loss in bending strength occurs before any measurable weight loss. At a 10% weight loss, there is an approximately 40% loss of strength (modulus of rupture, MOR) and a 70–80% loss in energy properties, such as the work to the maximum load (WML).

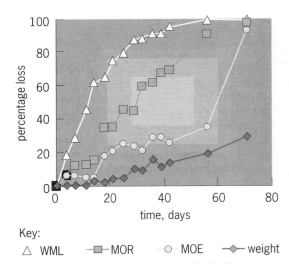

Key:
△ WML ▪ MOR ○ MOE ◆ weight

Fig. 2. The effect of wood decay caused by the brown-rot fungus *Gloeophyllum trabeum* on weight loss and mechanical properties. WML, work to the maximum load; MOR, modulus of rupture; MOE, modulus of elasticity. [*Figure adapted from S. F. Curling, C. A. Clausen, and J. E. Winandy, Relationships between mechanical properties, weight loss, and chemical composition of wood during incipient brown-rot decay, For. Prod. J., 52(7/8):34–39, 2002*]

Average strength loss in decayed wood

Time, weeks	Wood blocks			Wood stakes		
	Weight loss, %	MOE reduction, %	MCS reduction, %	Weight loss, %	MOE reduction, %	MOR reduction, %
1	0	3	6	0	5	2
2	3	13	21	0	8	2
3	9	22	37	1	7	8
4	18	34	53	3	9	19
5	26	53	71	7	12	22

Note: The brown-rot fungus *Postia placenta* was used in the tests. MOE, modulus of elasticity; MCS, maximum compressive strength; MOR, modulus of rupture. [*Table adapted from C. A. Clausen and S. N. Kartal, Accelerated detection of brown-rot decay: Comparison of soil block test, chemical analysis, mechanical properties and immunodetection, For. Prod. J., 53(11/12):90–94, 2003*]

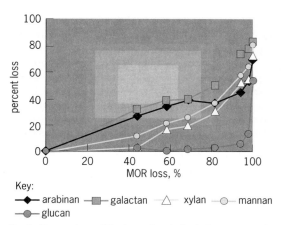

Key:

—◆— arabinan —■— galactan —△— xylan —○— mannan
—●— glucan

Fig. 3. Comparison of the loss of carbohydrate components with the loss in bending strength (modulus of rupture, MOR) caused by the brown-rot fungus *Gloeophyllum trabeum*. [*Figure adapted from S. F. Curling, C. A. Clausen, and J. E. Winandy, Relationships between mechanical properties, weight loss, and chemical composition of wood during incipient brown-rot decay, For. Prod. J., 52(7/8):34–39, 2002*]

Figure 3 shows a comparison of the loss of the carbohydrate components with the loss in bending strength (MOR) as the result of the decay caused by a brown-rot fungus (*Gloeophyllum trabeum*). The chemical composition is directly related to the strength loss (MOR).

The **table** shows the losses in MOE and maximum compressive strength (MCS) in wood exposed to a brown-rot fungus (*Postia placenta*) in the standard ASTM soil block and in-ground tests. The data show that there are critical losses in MOE and strength measurements in both types of tests, even when there are low levels of weight loss.

In service, the heterogeneous nature by which decay fungi consume and deconstruct wood makes the field evaluation of strength properties difficult. This known, rapid loss in strength properties, which can occur prior to visual detection or weight loss, combined with the fact that wood is susceptible to other hazards if it is not prepared, stored, or treated properly, means that wood suspected of deterioration should be inspected by a professional and repaired or replaced if necessary. Wood handled and treated in a proactive manner to prevent attack by decay and other hazards reduces the risk of strength losses and makes wood a cost-effective building material.

For background information *see* BIODEGRADATION; CELLULOSE; ENZYME; FUNGAL ECOLOGY; FUNGI; HEMICELLULOSE; LIGNIN; LIGNIN-DEGRADING FUNGI; STRENGTH OF MATERIALS; WOOD ANATOMY; WOOD DEGRADATION; WOOD ENGINEERING DESIGN; WOOD PRODUCTS; WOOD PROPERTIES in the McGraw-Hill Encyclopedia of Science & Technology.

Rebecca E. Ibach; Patricia K. Lebow

Bibliography. American Society of Testing and Materials, *2012 Annual Book of ASTM Standards*, Section 4: Construction, vol. 04.10: Wood, ASTM International, West Conshohocken, PA, 2012; American Wood Protection Association, *2012 AWPA Book of Standards*, AWPA, Birmingham, AL, 2012; R. A. Eaton and M. D. C. Hale, *Wood: Decay, Pests and Protection*, Chapman & Hall, New York, 1993; Forest Products Laboratory, *Wood Handbook: Wood as an Engineering Material*, Gen. Tech. Rep. FPL-GTR-190, Forest Products Laboratory, U.S. Department of Agriculture Forest Service, Madison, WI, 2010; T. P. Schultz et al., *Development of Commercial Wood Preservatives: Efficacy, Environmental, and Health Issues*, ACS Symposium Series 982, American Chemical Society, Washington, DC, 2008; R. A. Zabel and J. J. Morrell, *Wood Microbiology, Decay and Its Prevention*, Academic Press, San Diego, 1992.

Symmetry-adapted no-core shell model

The symmetry-adapted no-core shell model (SA-NCSM) is a nuclear-structure many-body theory that capitalizes on dominant symmetries discovered in atomic nuclei. It is designed, by utilizing cutting-edge computer resources, to provide nuclear system simulations from first principles (ab initio), which means the interaction between the constituent protons and neutrons of a nucleus is realistic—typically tied to underlying quark-gluon considerations—and hence powers the model with a predictive capability. The SA-NCSM builds upon a novel symmetry-adapted concept that winnows the configurations available to protons and neutrons to only the physically most relevant ones, thereby conquering a previously unknown realm. On the

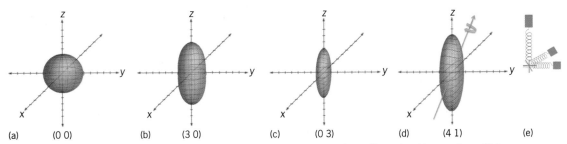

Fig. 1. Spheroids. (*a*)–(*d*) Labeling by two numbers, (λ μ). (*e*) Analogy to the three-dimensional harmonic oscillator.

one hand, particles can occupy configurations not accessible heretofore but key to important correlations, and on the other hand, new regions of heavier nuclear species are opened, for the first time, to ab initio investigations. These include some rare isotopes, which are inaccessible by current experiments and ab initio methods but are key in cosmic processes that are mainly nuclear-reaction driven, such as stellar evolution and explosions (including novae, supernovae, and x-ray bursts) as well as the formation of elements (nucleosynthesis).

Emergent simplicity in complex nuclei. Complex many-body dynamics often display striking simplicities. Consider a water droplet in space: It forms a sphere, the state of the lowest energy. Remarkably, this system, made up of a huge number of molecules, can be described by just one quantity, the radius of its spherical shape. Other deformation and rotation features of the droplet, such as waves along the surface, are possible, but these come at a cost of increasing the energy of the droplet. And even then, simple deviations from a spherical shape can be described by just two quantities. For example, the $\{a_z, a_x, a_y\}$ radii in each direction describe a variety of spheroids; for example, $\{3, 3, 3\}$ is a sphere, $\{5, 2, 2\}$ is a football-like shape, $\{4, 4, 1\}$ is a frisbee-like shape, and $\{6, 2, 1\}$ is a triaxial spheroid (**Fig. 1**). And since the sum of the three radial measures is fixed at 9 in these examples, only two numbers,

(λ μ), are necessary to describe departures from a sphere, namely, $\lambda = a_z - a_x$ and $\mu = a_x - a_y$, rendering, for these examples, the (λ μ) values (0 0), (3 0), (0 3), and (4 1) for spherical, prolate, oblate, and triaxial shapes, respectively.

Likewise, a nucleus—described by the momentum (p_i) and position (r_i) coordinates as well as the spin (s_i) of each particle—can be described by its "geometry" and associated rotations in addition to its spin degrees of freedom, as utilized in the SA-NCSM. The complementarity of the two pictures, dynamics versus geometry, means that the number of all possible configurations is the same in both cases, and hence, impossible to handle even on modern-day computers except for the lightest of nuclei. Notwithstanding, the SA-NCSM framework exposes an extraordinarily simple feature in nuclei that is masked in other ab initio approaches; in particular, the emergence, without a priori (prior) constraints, of simple orderly patterns that favor large spatial deformation and low intrinsic spins (**Fig. 2**). As a result, a general nuclear state is a superposition of only a relatively small number of various deformed configurations, a feature that can be employed to guide a truncation and augmentation of ultralarge model spaces, thereby making solutions feasible.

Nature's symmetry patterns. Simple patterns are associated with symmetries or conserved quantities, mathematically described by group theory. For example, rotations in the three-dimensional coordinate space are described by the SO(3) group generated by the angular momentum; it conserves, for example, the length of a vector. The three-dimensional spherical quantum harmonic oscillator with an oscillation frequency Ω—the harmonic-oscillator potential being a rough approximation to the one inside a nucleus—is described by the SU(3) group. In analogy to the spheroids in the coordinate space, but with the unit of length replaced by a harmonic-oscillator excitation quantum of energy $\hbar\Omega$ ($\hbar$ being Planck's constant divided by 2π), the numbers of quanta in the $x, y,$ and z directions define (λ μ) labels (Fig. 1). A link has been established between (λ μ) and the deformation of the nuclear surface in the limit of large deformation, so they too describe the nuclear geometry; for example, (λ 0) is associated with prolate deformation (Fig. 1*b*). The SU(3) transformations conserve the total number of harmonic-oscillator quanta (the harmonic-oscillator energy) and any

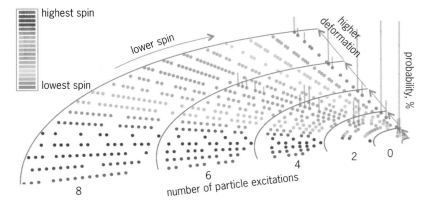

Fig. 2. Highly structured mix of dominant intrinsic spins and spatial deformation in ab initio low-energy solutions. The example shown is for the beryllium-8 (⁸Be) ground state, using a realistic interaction called N³LO. Dots represent all configurations of a given spin and deformation available to this state, while bars represent the few configurations that make up this state (with probabilities on a logarithmic scale).

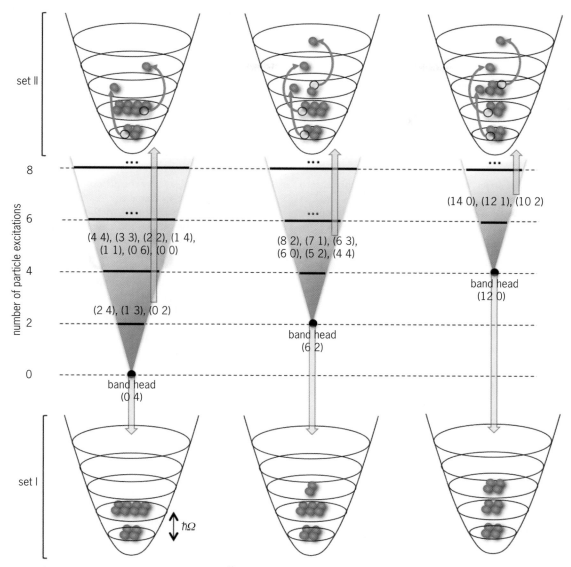

set II

8

6

(14 0), (12 1), (10 2)

number of particle excitations

(4 4), (3 3), (2 2), (1 4),
(1 1), (0 6), (0 0)

(8 2), (7 1), (6 3),
(6 0), (5 2), (4 4)

4

band head
(12 0)

2

(2 4), (1 3), (0 2)

band head
(6 2)

0

band head
(0 4)

set I

$\hbar\Omega$

Fig. 3. Selected symplectic slices for carbon-12 (^{12}C). Basis states of a slice are shown by pairs of numbers (λ μ) that label deformation. Basis states are built by consecutive excitations (in the *x*, *y*, and *z*-directions) of a particle two shells up (set II) over a band head (set I) of a given nucleon distribution over the harmonic-oscillator shells.

deformation (λ μ), while changing its orientation in space. Furthermore, deformation configurations of special interest are those needed to account for experimentally observed enhanced electric E0 and E2 transitions (carrying orbital angular momentum zero and two, respectively) between two nuclear states. These configurations are reached by transformations that change the total number of quanta by two and are generated by the mass quadrupole moment and the monopole operator. The overarching symmetry is described by the symplectic Sp(3,R) group. It divides the space of harmonic-oscillator shells, each of which has a fixed harmonic-oscillator energy, into "vertical slices" that are comprised of states of a definite deformation (**Fig. 3**). Namely, the slices are built over a band head (set I) by consecutive one-particle excitations two shells up (set II), together with a smaller correction of excitations of two particles a

shell up for eliminating the spurious center-of-mass motion (not shown in the figure). Operators of foremost physical significance, such as the many-particle kinetic energy, the harmonic-oscillator Hamiltonian, the mass quadrupole moment, the monopole operator, and the angular momentum operator, act within a single symplectic slice, thereby giving the Sp(3,R) symmetry a special role in physics.

Symmetry-adapted model. In the harmonic-oscillator-based shell model, each particle can occupy one of the single-particle states, as determined by the harmonic oscillator, and all possible configurations for all the particles within a nucleus define the model space (Fig. 3). This space is infinite, so typically, as dictated by physics, spaces are truncated based on the total harmonic-oscillator excitation quanta, $N_{\max}$, above the lowest harmonic-oscillator-energy configurations. For example, $N_{\max} = 2$ spaces include these lowest-energy many-particle configurations (no excitations) together with excitations of two particles a shell up or a particle two shells up, both increasing the harmonic-oscillator energy by $2\hbar\Omega$ (called $2\hbar\Omega$ excitations). The no-core shell model (NCSM) keeps all particles active (there are no particles "frozen" in a core), and it has already achieved a successful ab initio description of the structure of light nuclei, from the deuteron up through oxygen-16 (^{16}O). However, it is limited by the combinatorial growth in the size of the model spaces as N_{max} or the number of particles increase. The model space of the SA-NCSM is organized into linear combinations of the configurations used in the NCSM, with good SU(3) symmetry [definite $(\lambda\ \mu)$ quantum numbers], and with good total (of all the particles) orbital momentum **L** and total spin **S**, as well as total angular momentum, $\mathbf{J} = \mathbf{L} + \mathbf{S}$, and its projection, M_J. With this space

organization, the model is a multiple-shell generalization of J. P. Elliott's model, the first shell model that utilized SU(3) symmetry for particles in the last partly filled harmonic-oscillator shell (valence shell) to achieve a successful description of rotational features in light nuclei such as neon-20 (^{20}Ne) and magnesium-24 (^{24}Mg); and beyond, when the symplectic symmetry is further employed, it is a microscopic realization of the famous Bohr-Mottelson collective model.

The SA-NCSM approach, like the NCSM, calculates the eigenvalues and eigenvectors of the nuclear Hamiltonian using state-of-the-art computational resources. It is understood that the lowest eigenvalues and eigenvectors correspond to the experimental regime and that the quality of the results is related to the degree of convergence of the solutions, which, in turn, is linked to the size and appropriateness of the selected model space. The SA-NCSM novel feature is the model-space winnowing based on symmetry considerations.

Missing piece. The underlying concept of the SA-NCSM is illustrated in projecting ^{12}C and ^{16}O low-lying states obtained in large-scale ab initio NCSM calculations onto symplectic slices. Namely, a small fraction of the symmetry-adapted model space, typically several orders of magnitude less than that of the corresponding NSCM approach, suffices to represent a large fraction, typically about 90% or more, of the physics. For example, for ^{12}C, a level of more than 80% has been achieved by only three symplectic slices. This, in turn, has enabled a symmetry-adapted study that, while down-selecting to the most relevant symplectic slices and microscopic interaction terms, shows, for the first time, the significance of shell-model spaces expanded up through $N_{max} = 20$, much beyond current NCSM limits. It addresses a long-standing challenge, namely, understanding, from a no-core shell-model perspective, highly deformed spatial configurations and alpha-cluster substructures within low-lying 0^+ states in light nuclei, for example, the elusive Hoyle state (the second 0^+ state in ^{12}C, key to the stellar triple-alpha process).

Unprecedented reach of ab initio investigations. The SA-NCSM points to a path forward by exploiting exact and near symmetries of nuclei to resolve the scale explosion of the conventional NCSM model space, to account for higher-lying correlations that are essential to collective features such as enhanced transition rates, and to reach intermediate-mass nuclei. Ab initio calculations are now feasible for nuclei with particles filling the third ("sd") harmonic oscillator shell; the SA-NCSM results for silicon-24 (^{24}Si) in an $N_{max} = 6$ space are shown in **Fig. 4**. The model space size is only 3×10^6; for comparison, the $N_{max} = 6$ NCSM calculations require a currently inaccessible 8×10^9 space size. The results are strongly affected by the realistic interactions employed and whether forces among three particles are included or not. Nonetheless, the outcome reveals the efficacy of the SA-NCSM for providing solutions and

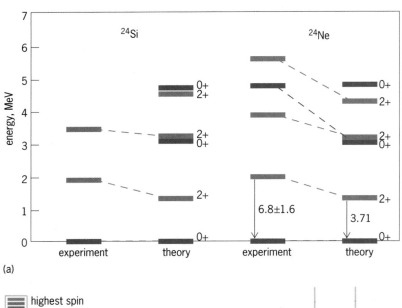

(a)

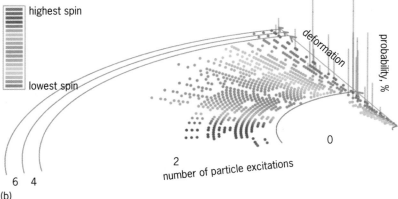

(b)

Fig. 4. Ab initio SA-NCSM calculations in an $N_{max} = 6$ selected model space for ^{24}Si (a) Energy levels for ^{24}Si shown together with its mirror nucleus ^{24}Ne, for which more experimental data is available. Arrows represent E2 transitions, given with their strength in Weisskopf units (1 unit = 4.1 e^2fm^4 for mass 24). (b) Selected model space used for calculations of the ^{24}Si ground state. Dots represent all configurations of a given spin and deformation available to this state, while bars represent the few configurations that make up this state (with probabilities on a logarithmic scale). The ultralarge model spaces for 4 and 6 numbers of particle excitations are winnowed to only a tiny fraction of configurations made available to this state based on low-spin and high-deformation considerations.

capturing the underlying physics, while ongoing efforts focus on improving accuracy by examinations of model spaces and interactions.

The results further anticipate the likely significance of SU(3) and symplectic symmetry for an extension of ab initio methods to even heavier nuclei, where the associated SU(3) shell model, called pseudo-SU(3) shell model, has been observed; that is, in a particular reference frame, the spin of a particle (pseudospin) interacts only weakly with its complementary orbital angular momentum, just as for spin and orbital angular momentum in light nuclei, and the associated pseudo-SU(3) shell model has been shown to play a key role in modeling the deformation of medium-mass nuclei and strongly deformed nuclei of the rare-earth and actinide regions.

For background information *see* ANGULAR MOMENTUM; GIANT NUCLEAR RESONANCES; GROUP THEORY; HARMONIC MOTION; HARMONIC OSCILLATOR; NUCLEAR SHELL MODEL AND MAGIC NUMBERS; NUCLEAR STRUCTURE; NUCLEOSYNTHESIS; STELLAR EVOLUTION; SURFACE (GEOMETRY); SYMMETRY LAWS (PHYSICS) in the McGraw-Hill Encyclopedia of Science & Technology.

Tomas Dytrych; Kristina D. Launey; Jerry P. Draayer

Bibliography. B. R. Barrett, P. Navratil, and J. P. Vary, Ab initio no core shell model, *Prog. Part. Nucl. Phys.*, 69:131–181, 2013, DOI:10.1016/j.ppnp.2012.10.003; A. Bohr and B. R. Mottelson, *Nuclear Structure*, Benjamin, New York, vol. 1, 1969, vol. 2, 1974; T. Dytrych et al., *Ab initio* symplectic no-core shell model, *J. Phys. G: Nucl. Part. Phys.*, 35:123101, 2008, DOI:10.1088/0954-3899/35/12/123101; J. P. Elliott, Collective motion in the nuclear shell model. I. Classification schemes for states of mixed configurations, *Proc. Roy. Soc.*, A245:128–145, 1958; B. R. Mottelson, Elementary modes of excitation in the nucleus, in S. Lundqvist (ed.), *Nobel Lectures, Physics 1971–1980*, pp. 236–254, World Scientific, Singapore, 1992; D. J. Rowe, Microscopic theory of the nuclear collective model, *Rep. Progr. Phys.*, 48:1419–1480, 1985, DOI:10.1088/0034-4885/48/10/003.

TAL effectors

Transcription activator–like (TAL) effectors are DNA-binding proteins found in plant pathogenic bacteria of the genus *Xanthomonas*. During infection, they are injected by the bacteria into the host plant's cells, where they enter the nucleus, bind to host DNA, and ramp up the expression of host genes that are important for the infection to progress or for symptoms to develop (or both). Different TAL effectors bind to different DNA sequences, and this sequence specificity directs them to their target genes. Identification of the targets of TAL effectors has led to important insights into plant diseases caused by *Xanthomonas* and how to control these diseases. TAL effectors were recently discovered to recognize their corresponding DNA sequences in a straightforward and predictable way based on the sequences of amino acids at certain positions in a structurally repetitive part of the proteins. This discovery has simplified the identification of TAL effector targets and has enabled customization of TAL effectors for a variety of applications that depend on targeting specific DNA sequences, including reprogramming gene expression and making changes to DNA in living cells.

Each TAL effector contains four functional parts: at one end, a secretion signal that directs translocation of the protein out of the bacterium and into the plant cell; at the other end, a nuclear localization signal that allows the protein to enter the host cell nucleus and a transcription activation domain that enables the TAL effector to increase expression of the host gene to which it binds; and in the middle, the structurally repetitive region that directs binding of the protein to its corresponding specific DNA sequence (**Fig. 1**). The repeated structure in this DNA recognition domain consists typically of a 34-amino-acid sequence that is nearly identical from repeat to repeat, except at positions 12 and 13. These two positions are called the repeat variable diresidue (RVD). When a TAL effector binds to DNA, each repeat interacts with a single base in the binding site. The identity of the base bound by each repeat is determined by the amino acids that make up the RVD of that repeat. Thus, the number of repeats and the string of RVDs that they present determine the number and sequence of bases in the DNA that are recognized by the protein. Because of this recognition code, if the sequence of RVDs in a TAL effector is known, its genomic target can be predicted. Also, repeats with different RVDs can be assembled to create custom TAL effectors that bind to novel DNA sequences.

TAL effectors in plant disease and disease resistance. Different species of *Xanthomonas* cause diseases in more than 350 plant species, including many economically important crops and ornamentals such as rice, wheat, cotton, citrus, pepper, walnut, strawberry, and geranium. TAL effectors play important roles in many of these diseases. TAL effector targets that enhance the ability of *Xanthomonas* to infect the host plant are called susceptibility genes. Identification of these susceptibility genes is an important step toward understanding the disease process, and it informs efforts to breed resistant crops. One possible strategy is to look for wild relatives of a crop that have susceptibility gene variants that lack the TAL effector binding site, and are therefore immune to activation, and breed those variants into the crop to reduce its susceptibility to disease.

Some TAL effectors increase expression of resistance genes, which activate plant immune responses to limit bacterial infection. Likely, such resistance genes have evolved as susceptibility gene mimics to counter attacks by pathogens that use TAL effectors. Identification of these genes and incorporation into commercial crop varieties through breeding programs has been an effective strategy to protect those crops from disease. However, it is

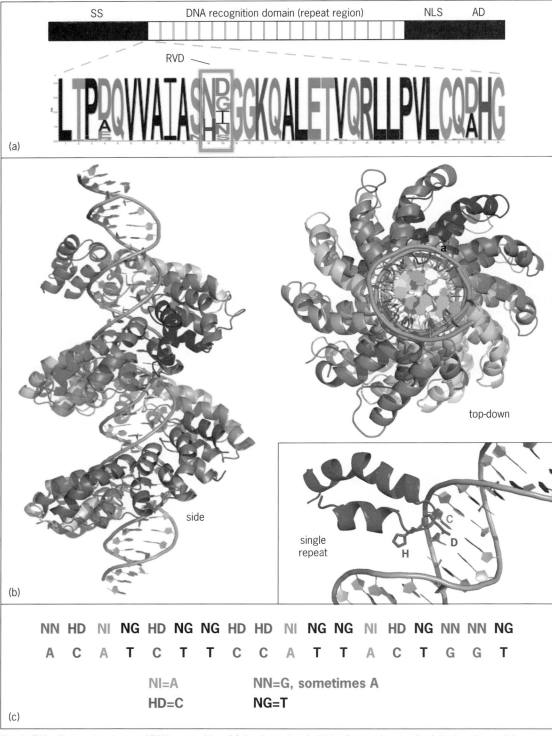

Fig. 1. TAL effector structure and DNA recognition. (*a*) A schematic of a TAL effector showing (*top*) the locations of the secretion signal (SS), the repeat-containing DNA recognition domain, the nuclear localization signal (NLS), and the activation domain (AD), and (*bottom*) a representation of the amino acid sequences of 2363 TAL effector repeats, using the single letter code for each amino acid. At each position, the frequency of a given amino acid is represented by the height of the letter (the taller the letter, the more common the amino acid). The repeat-variable diresidue (RVD) resides at positions 12 and 13 (boxed). Note the greater diversity of amino acids found at these positions. (*b*) A TAL effector DNA recognition domain bound to DNA. The DNA (gray) is encircled by the DNA recognition domain. Each TAL effector repeat is shown in a different color. The repeats interact with one base each, all on the same DNA strand. The inset shows a close-up of one repeat interacting with a single base. The repeat forms two helices and a loop. The loop contains the RVD: in this case, the amino acids histidine (H) and aspartic acid (D), which interact with a cytosine (C, red). For clarity, the side chains of only the RVD amino acids are shown. With some exceptions, different RVDs each specify the identity of a single base, so the string of RVDs present in the repeat region of a TAL effector defines the DNA sequence to which the protein binds. (*c*) A representative string of RVDs and the nucleotide sequence that it would specify. The four most common RVDs and their specificities are shown at the bottom.

possible for *Xanthomonas* to overcome resistance. For example, *Xanthomonas* strains may acquire mutations in a TAL effector that otherwise targets a resistance gene, or they may lose the TAL effector altogether so that the resistance gene is not activated. One way to prevent such mutations is to select resistance genes targeted by TAL effectors that cannot be readily mutated or lost because they are necessary for the bacteria to infect host plants. Another broader strategy is to engineer a resistance gene to include binding sites for many TAL effectors, making it difficult for the pathogen to acquire enough mutations to overcome the resistance without losing its inherent ability to infect. Multiple TAL effector binding sites can also be added to a resistance gene to make it effective against diverse strains of the pathogen or even different pathogens that use different TAL effectors. In addition, it is now possible to take advantage of TAL effectors themselves to generate disease-resistant plant varieties: As genome editing tools, these proteins can be used to modify resistance genes in a plant directly, or to remove from a plant genome the TAL effector binding sites in susceptibility genes that a pathogen relies on.

TAL effectors as biological tools. Custom TAL effectors have become increasingly important tools for genome editing because they can be easily targeted to bind DNA sequences of interest. The TAL effector DNA recognition domain has been fused to a DNA-cutting enzyme called *Fok*I to create TAL effector nucleases (TALENS). These proteins can be used to create precisely targeted double-strand breaks in DNA, either in a test tube or in living cells. Because two molecules of *Fok*I must come together to cut DNA, TALENs made using *Fok*I are designed in pairs to bind to the opposite strands of the DNA and bring the *Fok*I portions together across a short spacer, where the cut is made (**Fig. 2**). In eukaryotic cells, these breaks are repaired by one of two pathways. In nonhomologous end joining (NHEJ), the DNA on either side of the break is rejoined, often with inser-

tions or deletions of one to a few base pairs that can disrupt or knock out gene function. In homologous recombination (HR), the break is repaired by incorporating a piece of DNA with ends that are similar in sequence to the cut ends. By providing such a DNA patch along with the TALENS, researchers can use HR to swap in (substitute) virtually any sequence at the cut site, either to modify the existing sequence or to introduce new genetic material altogether. TALEN-mediated, site-specific DNA modifications resulting from NHEJ or HR have been demonstrated in a variety of organisms and cell types, including human cells. When these DNA modifications are created in germline cells (which include sperm and egg cells, and the cells that generate them), the modifications can be inherited by the organism's offspring. This allows researchers to generate lines or populations of organisms with the same genetic modifications. These lines are used for studying the effects of the genetic changes. In the case of crops or livestock, for example, germline cell modification can be used to develop new varieties with better quality or yield.

The potential of custom TALENs as gene therapy tools for human medicine has also generated considerable excitement. TALEN-mediated HR could be used to correct disease-causing genetic mutations, either by editing an existing gene or by inserting new genetic material to compensate for a nonfunctioning or mutated gene copy. TALENs could also be used to make cells resistant to certain types of infection. Clinical trials using a different type of targetable DNA-cutting enzyme, a zinc-finger nuclease, are currently under way to treat HIV by engineering T cells to no longer express the gene for a receptor protein that is necessary for the virus to infect. Such engineered T cells are then put back into the patient to reestablish a functional immune system. Custom TALENs have proven easier to target than zinc-finger nucleases, they cleave their intended targets with high efficiency, and they rarely cleave other sites in

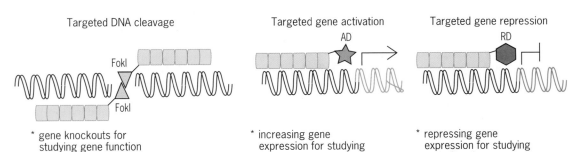

Targeted DNA cleavage

*Fok*I

*Fok*I

* gene knockouts for studying gene function
* insertion of new genes for improving crops and livestock
* therapies for genetic and retroviral diseases

Targeted gene activation

AD

* increasing gene expression for studying gene function
* synthetic biology

Targeted gene repression

RD

* repressing gene expression for studying gene function
* synthetic biology

Fig. 2. Major DNA targeting applications of TAL effectors. TAL effector DNA recognition domains can be fused to DNA-cleaving enzymes such as *Fok*I to create double-strand breaks at desired locations in a genome. Because two molecules of *Fok*I are required to cut the DNA, two TAL effector–*Fok*I fusions must be targeted to opposing sequences on either DNA strand. Making such breaks in the DNA allows researchers to disrupt genes, insert new DNA, or edit existing DNA sequences at those locations for basic research, biotechnology, or medical purposes. TAL effectors with their own activation domain (AD) or alternative activation domains can be similarly customized to drive expression of genes of interest in different organisms. Similarly, the AD can be replaced with a repressor domain (RD) to create targeted off-switches for genes.

the genome. Thus, TALENs could be used in a similar way to treat HIV and other diseases. Finally, it has been suggested that TALENs may be an effective therapy for other retroviral diseases, including herpes simplex virus and the chickenpox virus, by targeting the viral genome itself. Retroviruses insert copies of their genomes into the host genome. These latent genome copies make it virtually impossible to completely cure a cell of the virus. By targeting the latent viral genome copies for cleavage with TALENs, it may be possible to effectively eliminate all functional copies of the virus from the host.

In addition to their use in TALENs, custom TAL effector DNA recognition domains have been used to increase expression of specific genes in yeast, plants, and animal cells. In plants, the existing activation domain is typically used. In other organisms, different activation domains have been substituted that function better in those organisms. Custom TAL effectors have also been used for reducing or shutting down expression of target genes by replacing the activation domain with a repressor domain. The ability to tightly control the expression of specific genes using TAL effectors is useful for researchers who study gene function. It is also important for synthetic biology applications, where, for example, novel metabolic pathways are created from genetic building blocks whose expression must be carefully regulated.

Future research. Despite the established utility and future promise of TAL effectors and TALENs, several challenges remain. Engineering plant disease resistance based on TAL effectors requires identifying the important TAL effectors in a bacterial population. However, accurate sequencing and assembly of the repeat encoding portions of TAL effector genes and mutational analysis to determine the TAL effector contributions to virulence are still costly and time consuming. Fortunately, sequencing methods continue to improve and can be expected to speed up the process. The evolutionary origin of TAL effectors is still an open question to which few clues have emerged. Questions also remain about the best way to design custom TAL effectors and TALENs. Although TAL effector repeats can be assembled in any order to target a specific sequence, some TALENs appear to function more efficiently than others. This may be the result of differences in the inherent strength with which different RVDs bind their target nucleotides, with more efficient TALENs including more strong-binding RVDs. Differences in activity may also result from factors such as chromatin status (the degree of compactness of the target DNA in the cell) or the presence of alterations to the DNA (for example, cytosine methylation) that affect the ability of TAL effectors to recognize the intended sequence. Also, most RVDs do not bind exclusively to their preferred nucleotide, and TAL effectors can bind to targets with several mismatches. The design of TALENs with minimal binding to unintended sites is especially important because such off-target DNA cleavage could cause unforeseen consequences such as cell death or cancer. The discovery of new RVDs with higher specificities for a single nucleotide, combined with better understanding of the effects of mismatches, will be necessary to design custom TAL effectors and TALENs with the least possible chance of off-target activity. Finally, another important area for ongoing research is the exploration of uses for TAL effectors beyond gene regulation and targeted DNA cleavage.

For background information *see* AGRICULTURAL SCIENCE (PLANT); DEOXYRIBONUCLEIC ACID (DNA); GENE; GENETIC ENGINEERING; GENETICALLY ENGINEERED PLANTS; GENETICS; MUTATION; PATHOTOXIN; PLANT PATHOLOGY; PROTEIN; PROTEIN ENGINEERING; RECOMBINATION (GENETICS) in the McGraw-Hill Encyclopedia of Science & Technology.

Katherine E. Wilkins; Erin L. Doyle; Adam J. Bogdanove

Bibliography. J. Boch et al., Breaking the code of DNA binding specificity of TAL-type III effectors, *Science*, 326:1509–1512, 2009, DOI:10.1126/science.1178811; A. W. Hummel and A. J. Bogdanove, The roles of transcription activator–like (TAL) effectors in virulence and avirulence of *Xanthomonas*, pp. 107–122, in G. Sessa (ed.), *Molecular Plant Immunity*, Wiley-Blackwell, Oxford, UK, 2012; A. N.-S. Mak et al., TAL effectors: Function, structure, engineering and applications, *Curr. Opin. Struct. Biol.*, 23(1):93–99, 2012, DOI:10.1016/j.sbi.2012.11.001; A. N.-S. Mak et al., The crystal structure of TAL effector PthXo1 bound to its DNA target, *Science*, 335:716–719, 2012, DOI:10.1126/science.1216211; M. J. Moscou and A. J. Bogdanove, A simple cipher governs DNA recognition by TAL effectors, *Science*, 326:1501, 2009, DOI:10.1126/science.1178817.

The electrical nature of thunderstorms

Although lightning had long been a subject of myth and speculation, it was not until electricity was discovered that natural philosophy could start developing a scientific understanding of lightning and the electrical properties of thunderstorms. Beginning with experiments proposed by Benjamin Franklin in the eighteenth century, scientists soon learned that lightning is a giant spark, that thunderstorms contain charge, and that weak electric currents flow vertically through the atmosphere in fair weather. Little more was learned about lightning and atmospheric electricity for over a hundred years, while scientists were learning about electricity and magnetism.

Further progress had to await the development of new instruments early in the twentieth century, but even then, progress remained slow. By the 1950s, scientists had learned that (1) most thunderstorms have a large positive charge over a large negative charge, sometimes with a small positive charge below the negative charge; (2) most flashes that strike ground lower negative storm charge, but strikes to towers and tall buildings often lower positive charge; and (3) the diurnal (24-h) variation in some electrical properties of fair-weather regions of the lower atmosphere is synchronized worldwide, behavior attributed to the similar diurnal variation in the total number of thunderstorms throughout the world and caused, in turn, by the diurnal variation in the area of continents heated by the Sun.

Since 1975, advances in laboratory studies and new technologies for observing storms and lightning have led to increasingly rapid progress in our understanding of how thunderstorms become electrified and produce lightning. Furthermore, we have discovered electrical phenomena produced by thunderstorms that were barely suspected previously. Although questions certainly remain, this article reviews the considerable progress that has been made.

Processes electrifying storms. Several processes involving water particles can contribute to electrifying various regions of thunderstorms. However, a large body of evidence has convinced scientists that the process causing thunderstorms to become electrified and accounting for the majority of charge produced by updrafts is the charge exchanged during rebounding collisions between riming ice particles (called graupel, typically a few mm or less in diameter) and smaller ice particles. Riming means that a graupel particle is collecting liquid droplets and freezing them quickly enough to maintain each droplet's shape, so strong electrification requires ice particles in a mixture with liquid droplets. In storms, this mixed-phase region is between 0 and −40°C. Small droplets can remain liquid at temperatures less than 0°C, but all particles have frozen by the time the temperature has dropped to −40°C. Liquid droplets colder than 0°C are said to be supercooled.

Details of the microphysics governing this exchange are still uncertain, but laboratory studies and numerical storm simulations show that enough charge can be exchanged by the collisions to account for the principal charge regions of storms. The amount and direction of the charge exchange depend on several factors, including the environmental temperature, the size of the ice particles, the rate at which graupel collects liquid droplets, and the nature of substances dissolved in the water.

It appears that over most of the mixed-phase region of most storms, graupel particles gain negative charge and small ice particles gain positive charge. However, graupel tends to gain positive charge between roughly 0 and −10°C and at all temperatures in mixed-phase regions of updraft having unusually large concentrations of liquid droplets. After charge is exchanged during collisions, sedimentation causes graupel to fall below the small ice particles, so a region of the charge carried by small ice particles emerges above the region of collisions and a region of the charge carried by graupel emerges below the region of collisions. A subsequent section discusses how these tendencies affect the distribution of charge in storms.

Once a storm becomes electrified, the electric forces produced by the initial electrification can

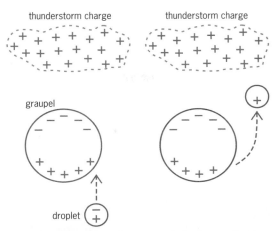

Fig. 1. Charge exchange between polarized graupel and droplets in an electrified storm.

create additional charge regions by other processes. The following are two examples.

1. Electric force polarizes both liquid and frozen water particles. "Polarize" means electric force induces positive charge on one side of a particle and negative charge on the opposite side. When polarized graupel particles collide and rebound from smaller polarized liquid particles, they exchange charge, as shown in **Fig. 1**. Then sedimentation of the graupel again causes two oppositely charged regions to emerge from a neutral region of collisions.

2. Electric force produces electric currents. Because it takes more electric force to produce a given current in cloudy air than in clear air, any force created around a cloud boundary produces a larger current in the clear air. The abrupt change in the current causes charge to build up along the cloud boundary, and the force from the charge on the boundary increases the current inside the cloud and decreases it outside. The process continues until the charge on the boundary itself produces just enough force to make the current the same on both sides of the boundary. The charge on the boundary is called a screening layer, because it reduces the magnitude of the force outside the cloud produced by charge inside the cloud.

Typical gross distribution of charge in thunderstorms. The principal charge regions in the updraft of typical thunderstorms can be explained by the behavior of the charge exchange between riming graupel and smaller ice particles during rebounding collisions. The net result of these processes is shown in **Fig. 2** for a typical thunderstorm. A large upper positive charge region is formed of cloud ice particles that have gained positive charge from their collisions with graupel at roughly −10 to −40°C in a storm updraft. The graupel from these collisions contributes to the large, midlevel negative charge region. As noted previously, rebounding collisions in an updraft at 0 to −10°C tend to put positive charge on graupel. When there are sufficient collisions in this temperature range, the graupel produces a small lower positive region, and the

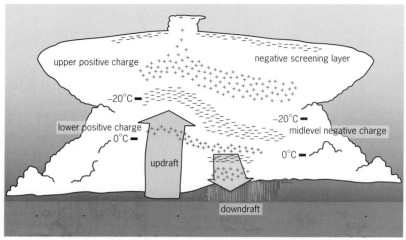

Fig. 2. Conceptual model of the charge distribution in a typical thunderstorm.

small ice particles contribute to the large midlevel negative region. A screening layer containing negative charge typically forms quickly on the upper cloud boundary in response to the upper positive charge.

Outside the updraft, the vertical distribution of charge becomes more complicated, as additional processes contribute charge. Rebounding collisions of polarized frozen particles colliding with polarized small liquid particles probably are responsible for at least some charge regions. Near and below the melting level, the process of melting may also contribute charge.

As the duration and size of storms increase, the distribution of charge becomes increasingly complex. Besides the effects of lightning on charge, which will be discussed later, long-lasting storms have a series of updraft pulses, each typically lasting a few tens of minutes. As an updraft pulse weakens and dissipates, the precipitation and charge it carries fall, with the larger precipitation particles tending to fall faster. Thus, the upper positive charge produced by

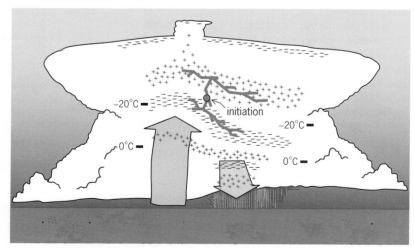

Fig. 3. Initiation and development of a typical in-cloud lightning flash.

an older pulse can be at the same altitude as the midlevel negative charge from a newer pulse.

Lightning. When the electric force produced by the charge regions of a storm becomes large enough, it produces lightning. Lightning initiation is thought to involve free electrons that are produced continually throughout the atmosphere by radiation such as cosmic rays. Very large electric forces can accelerate particularly energetic free electrons so much between collisions with neutral molecules that they strip additional electrons from the molecules with which they collide. If the electrical conditions are favorable, the number of electrons increases rapidly to create a self-propagating discharge that becomes lightning.

In storms, the electric force is largest between a region of positive charge and a region of negative charge, as one expects from physics, so that is where flashes tend to be initiated. Flashes then develop bidirectionally outward from the region of initiation, with one end developing toward and within a region of positive charge and the other end developing toward and within a region of negative charge, as shown in **Fig. 3**.

Because the lightning channel is an excellent electric conductor, the electric forces created by thunderstorm charge regions induce electric currents to flow freely over the surface of developing channels, so that positive charge collects on channels propagating through the negative charge region of a storm and negative charge collects on channels propagating through the positive charge region of a storm. When the flash dissipates, it leaves this charge behind on gaseous ions. The charge is then captured by precipitation and by small cloud particles having negligible fall speeds. The captured charge adds to the local storm charge and usually reduces the net magnitude of charge in a given region. Thus, once lightning begins, it starts producing regions of reduced charge within what had been a more uniform charge region.

The charge from lightning in some regions can be larger than the charge already on water particles, so the net charge is not just reduced, its polarity is reversed. Even if the lightning does not reverse the net storm charge anywhere along its channel, it can cause subsequent regions of charge to form by sedimentation, if most of the original charge is on larger, relatively sparse precipitation particles and most of the captured charge is on many small cloud particles.

Lightning can extend below, above, or to the side of thunderstorms. The most obvious of these to most people are cloud-to-ground flashes. Roughly 90% of cloud-to-ground flashes lower negative charge and most are initiated by the large electric force occurring between a midlevel negative charge and a smaller positive charge below it, as shown in **Fig. 4**. If the downward-directed end of a developing flash reaches the lower positive charge in a region with too little charge to completely capture further development, the developing lightning channel can continue propagating to ground. As a channel approaches ground, a spark typically is drawn upward to meet it. When the two connect, it creates basically a short circuit to the charge on the ground, producing an upward surge in current typically peaking at 10–20 kA and decreasing to half the peak value in 10–100 microseconds. It is this current surge that makes the channel very bright, and the surge travels back up the channel at 10–50% of the speed of light.

The maximum horizontal extent of lightning inside a storm approaches the horizontal extent of the storm itself. Flashes typically span 10–20 km horizontally and can extend more than 100 km. Since the top of the channel to ground is typically 3–8 km high, the horizontal channels inside a storm often are much longer than the channel to ground.

It had been thought that essentially all cloud-to-ground flashes that lowered positive charge to ground were triggered by tall buildings and other tall structures. With the advent in the 1980s of networks of stations that automatically determine the location and peak current of lightning strikes to ground, it was found that roughly 5–10% of naturally occurring cloud-to-ground flashes lower positive charge. However, such flashes were found to form a much larger fraction of cloud-to-ground flashes in dissipating storms, in many winter storms, in some severe storms, and in the region of widespread lighter precipitation (called the stratiform region) that can trail the deeper convection in large storm systems (called mesoscale convective systems). The basic charge distribution that initiates most flashes lowering positive charge to ground appears similar to the distribution that initiates most flashes lowering negative charge, except that the charge polarities are reversed, with the midlevel charge being positive and the small lower charge being negative.

The ways in which this polarity reversal arises probably are different for the different situations in which positive cloud-to-ground flashes occur. In dissipating storms, for example, the major charge regions have descended, and the precipitation carrying the lower positive charge and, perhaps even precipitation carrying some of the midlevel negative charge, has fallen to ground. The positive charge a flash lowers to ground then comes from what had been the upper positive charge region. Similarly, in mesoscale convective systems, particles tend to descend as they are carried from strong updrafts in the leading line of storms back into the stratiform region. The positive charge lowered to ground in the trailing stratiform region typically is the upper positive charge in the leading line of storms that has descended gradually to a level near 0°C behind the line and has been maintained at that level by processes that are not yet well understood. Winter storms are somewhat different in that no subsequent descent of charge is required. If the temperature of a cloud base is cold enough, the lower positive charge is negligible, and the upper positive charge is closer to ground and supplies the charge for cloud-to-ground flashes.

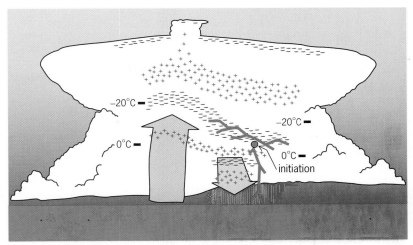

Fig. 4. Initiation and development of a typical cloud-to-ground lightning flash.

Research since 2000 has found that severe storms provide a much different scenario. Severe storms have extremely large flash rates, sometimes hundreds of flashes per minute, because the rate at which their exceptional updrafts carry liquid and frozen water through the mixed-phase region is much larger than in typical storms. Although this is a contributing factor in producing positive cloud-to-ground flashes, it is insufficient by itself, as most cloud-to-ground flashes in many severe storms lower negative charge to ground. While the cause is not well understood, all hypotheses that have been offered thus far include some mechanism that limits the amount of precipitation-size particles being lifted into the mixed-phase region. In that situation, fewer liquid droplets have been captured at warmer temperatures, and the resulting liquid water content of the mixed-phase region can remain large enough that graupel gains positive charge, regardless of temperature. Thus, the large upper charge region in the storm has negative charge and the large midlevel charge region has positive charge, a distribution inverted from the usual polarity. The lower negative charge region needed to initiate most positive cloud-to-ground flashes can be provided by older adjoining updraft pulses in which charge has fallen, such as the remnants of a normal-polarity updraft on the right side of the newer inverted-polarity region in **Fig. 5**.

Severe storms having inverted-polarity charge distributions in all or part of the storm have been observed in many locales. Some evidence suggests that inverted-polarity updrafts are more likely to produce large hailstones. In the United States, such storms are most prevalent in a swath stretching northeastward from western Kansas into the Dakotas and Minnesota. They are almost never observed in southeastern states.

Additional electrical properties of storms. Some storms and storm systems have other unique electrical characteristics. Strong isolated storms, for example, produce large anvil clouds that can contain

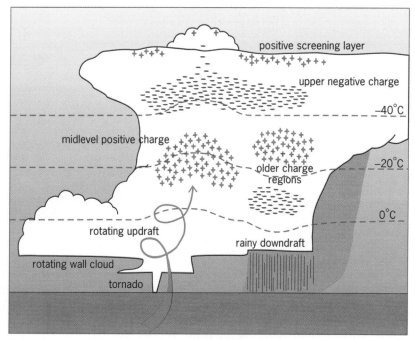

Fig. 5. Conceptual model of an updraft with an inverted-polarity charge distribution.

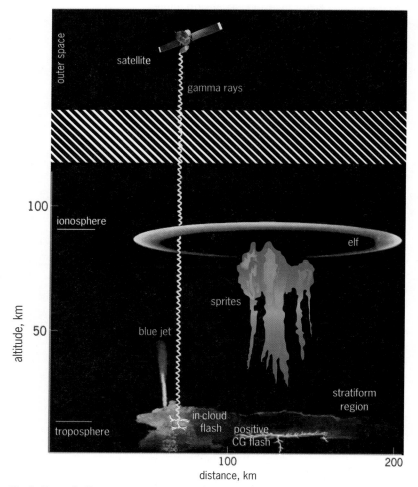

Fig. 6. Recently discovered electrical phenomena produced above storms by thunderstorms and mesoscale convective systems.

considerable charge. Anvils are produced as the mass in vertical updrafts approaches the top of a storm. Much of the mass then starts losing its buoyancy relative to the surrounding air and so starts being pushed horizontally away from the updraft into an anvil. This anvil material carries the same charge as resides in the upper region of storms, so lightning from the main body of the storm can propagate into an anvil. Although the charge is expected to decrease with distance, the decrease is slower than had been expected, and lightning sometimes propagates as much as 30 km into an anvil.

Anvil lightning can be enhanced further in supercell storms, which occur when a storm interacts with environmental winds to create a rotating updraft, such as the updrafts providing the parent rotation of violent tornadoes shown in Fig. 5. Supercell storms can maintain their characteristic structure for several hours, and their anvils can stretch more than 100 km from the parent storm. Recent research has found that in some supercell storms, lightning not only propagates into anvils, but electrical structures can evolve in ways that initiate lightning in anvils up to roughly 100 km from the main body of the storm. Sometimes this is caused by anvils of adjoining storms converging, sometimes enough convection can develop in an anvil itself to create a new region of electrification, and in some cases we cannot see an obvious cause.

A strong storm can also produce unusual electrical discharges in transient cloud turrets that extend above the rest of the storm. The height of most of the storm is determined by the equilibrium level at which the buoyancy of air lifted by the updraft falls to zero. However, the updraft core can have enough momentum to continue higher, to a level at which the deceleration by negative buoyancy stops the upward motion and causes the air eventually to descend back to the equilibrium level. In supercell storms, turrets can extend as much as 5–6 km above the rest of the storm. Observations by recently deployed lightning-mapping systems have found that very small discharges can occur continually in these overshooting turrets for anywhere from several minutes to more than an hour, the duration depending on the lifetime of the turret or of sequential turrets. A contributing factor in producing these discharges is the rapid decrease with altitude in the magnitude of the electric force needed to initiate discharges, so initiation requires much less energy in storm turrets. However, it is still unclear what storm processes produce these discharges. The only mechanism suggested thus far is that turbulent eddies in the screening layer, or updraft, bring small regions of opposite charge close enough together to create the force needed for initiation.

In 1989, low-light video cameras serendipitously were pointed above a large storm system and observed transient faint discharges that have been named sprites. Since then, scientists have learned much about sprites and have uncovered a host of other electrical phenomena above storms, as shown in **Fig. 6**. Sprites carry electric current up to the ionosphere, roughly 90 km above ground. They can have several forms and can occur singly or in clusters, but typically last only a few milliseconds. They almost always are triggered by flashes that lower large amounts of positive charge to ground from a long horizontal layer of charge (several tens of kilometers long) in the stratiform region of a large storm system. Some positive cloud-to-ground flashes also produce a quickly expanding ring of light (called an elf) at approximately the same altitude as the top of sprites.

Two other classes of phenomena above storms are less well understood. One is the various categories of blue jets, which are cone-shaped spurts of light that emerge from the top of some severe storms. They are classified by the distance they extend upward above a storm: blue starters extending roughly 20 km, blue jets extending 40–50 km, and giant blue jets extending 70 km to the lower ionosphere. Blue jets are not triggered by flashes detected within the storm, but the triggering phenomenon remains unknown at this writing.

Gamma-ray flashes are lightning flashes within a storm that emit energetic gamma-rays detected by satellites. Not every flash produces upward gamma rays, but the characteristics of flashes that produce this radiation have not yet been discovered.

For background information *see* ATMOSPHERIC ELECTRICITY; CLOUD; CLOUD PHYSICS; ELECTRIC CHARGE; ELECTROSTATICS; IONOSPHERE; LIGHTNING; MESOMETEOROLOGY; PRECIPITATION (METEOROLOGY); STORM ELECTRICITY; THUNDERSTORM; TORNADO in the McGraw-Hill Encyclopedia of Science & Technology.   Donald R. MacGorman

Bibliography. W. A. Lyons, R. A. Armstrong, E. A. Bering III, and E. Williams, The hundred year hunt for the sprite, *EOS, Trans. Am. Geophys. Union*, 81:373–380, DOI:10.1029/00EO00278; D. R. MacGorman and W. D. Rust, *The Electrical Nature of Storms*, Oxford University Press, New York, 1998; V. A. Rakov and M. A. Martin, *Lightning: Physics and Effects*, Cambridge University Press, 2003; M. A. Uman, *The Lightning Discharge*, Dover, New York, 2001.

Tongue Drive System

The Tongue Drive System is an assistive technology that allows individuals with severe disabilities, such as those with tetraplegia, to control their environment using free, voluntary tongue motion. The tongue does not receive nearly as much attention and appreciation as it deserves. While tirelessly playing its vital roles in communication, ingestion, and breathing, the tongue has many additional inherent capabilities that allow it to be an ideal control channel for individuals who cannot use their hands because of severe physical disabilities or double amputations. Even able-bodied individuals can benefit from the tongue's rich motor capabilities in environments where the extremities' motion is limited, such as those in spacesuits or heavy gear for underwater or high-temperature operations. The tongue may even be employed in demanding conditions that require multitasking, such as controlling sophisticated surgical robots, drones, machinery, gaming, and even driving, where engaging both hands may not be sufficient.

Motivation. Here are a few characteristics of the tongue that place it in this unique position:

1. The area of the motor cortex occupied by the tongue and mouth rivals that of the fingers and the hand. Therefore, the tongue is capable of sophisticated motor control and manipulation tasks with many degrees of freedom, which is evident from its role in speech and ingestion. In fact, one can intuitively touch every single tooth in one's mouth with the tip of the tongue very rapidly and accurately without thinking, concentration, or prior training.

2. The tongue musculature is controlled by a cranial nerve that directly connects it to the brain. Cranial nerves generally escape severe damage in spinal cord injuries and most neuromuscular diseases. Therefore, even individuals with the highest-level spinal cord injuries, that is, cervical level 2–4, who may not be able to breathe on their own, still maintain their tongue motion.

3. Tongue muscle fibers are similar to those of the heart in terms of being quite fatigue resistant, allowing us to frequently talk and eat throughout the day without feeling pain or fatigue in the tongue. Therefore, unlike many other devices, a tongue-operated assistive technology is expected to be accessible and usable throughout the day.

4. The nerves controlling the tongue muscles receive a wealth of vestibular input. Therefore, the position of the tongue is reflexively adjusted with changes in the body position, allowing tongue-based devices to be easily operated in any desired posture, such as sitting on a wheelchair or lying in bed. Other devices, such as eye trackers, may need quite a bit of adjustment following user displacements.

5. Unlike neuroprosthetic devices, which require high-risk and costly brain surgery for direct access to the brain signals, noninvasive access to the tongue is readily available without surgery.

6. The tongue's location inside the mouth affords users of intraoral assistive devices with considerable privacy. Like everyone else, individuals with disabilities do care about their appearance, and do not want to attract unwanted attention. Therefore, if the assistive technology can be located inside the mouth, without leaving any overt sign of disability, it would be more likely to be widely accepted by potential end users.

These benefits were the motivation behind the design and development of a new wireless, wearable, and unobtrusive assistive technology, the Tongue Drive System (TDS). The number of people with disabilities is increasing among all age groups. A study initiated by the Christopher and Dana Reeve Foundation showed that 1 in 50 people in the United States is living with paralysis, and 16% of these individuals (about 1 million) have stated that they are unable to move and cannot live without continuous help.

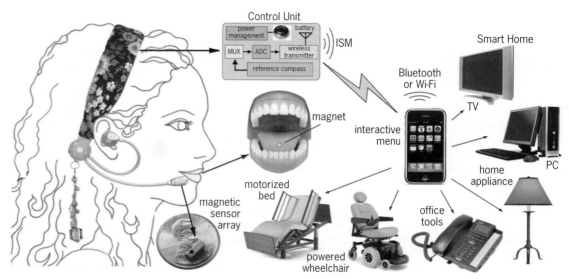

Fig. 1. External Tongue Drive System (eTDS) built in the form of a wireless headset. Magnetic sensors mounted near the cheeks record the changes in the magnetic field generated by a small magnet attached near the tip of the tongue, and wirelessly send it to a smartphone, which translates the tongue movements to a set of user-defined commands for a variety of target devices. ADC, analog-to-digital converter; ISM, Industrial, Scientific, and Medical band; MUX = multiplexer.

Moreover, the National Institutes of Health reports that 11,000 cases of severe spinal cord injuries from automotive accidents, acts of violence, and falls add every year to this population. Sadly, 55% of individuals with spinal cord injuries are between 16 and 30 years old, and they will need special care for the rest of their lives. This is why the spinal cord injury is considered one of the most expensive types of disability to families and the society as a whole.

Operation. A TDS can infer the users' intentions based on the voluntary positions, gestures, and movements of their tongues and translate them into certain user-defined commands that are simultaneously available to the TDS users in real time. These commands can be used to control the movements of

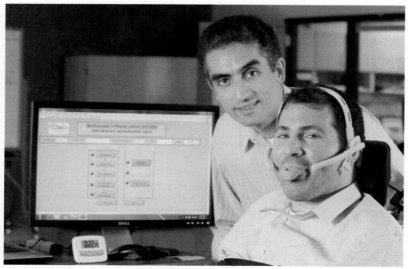

Fig. 2. An eTDS end user with spinal cord injury at level C4 showing off his magnetic tongue piercing.

a cursor on the PC screen, thereby substituting for a mouse or touchpad, or to substitute for the joystick function in a powered wheelchair. A TDS operates by detecting the position of the tongue. It does this by measuring the changes in the magnetic field that is generated by a small magnetic tracer that is attached to the tongue. An array of magnetic sensors inside or around the mouth continuously measures the magnetic field in a few strategic positions.

In the current version of the TDS (**Fig. 1**), changes in the magnetic field that result from tongue movements are wirelessly transmitted to a smartphone (iPhone), carried by the user, which runs a sensor signal processing (SSP) algorithm to infer seven tongue commands (extendable to 25, almost one command per tooth). These commands are either executed locally on the smartphone to make a phone call, for example, or sent to other target devices in the user's environment, such as a PC or a powered wheelchair, via Bluetooth, Wi-Fi, or a universal interface. The SSP algorithm is also responsible for attenuating sources of external interference such as the effects of Earth's magnetic field that result from head motion.

To test-drive the TDS, the magnetic tracer, which is a small permanent magnet the size of a lentil, can be temporarily attached near the tip of the tongue using dental adhesives. For long-term use of the system, the user should receive a magnetic tongue piercing (**Fig. 2**), which looks like an ordinary tongue barbell made of titanium or acrylic with the permanent magnetic tracer embedded in its upper ball. Another option, which will be explored in the near future, is to implant the magnetic tracer after it is coated with biocompatible polymers in the user's tongue using a hypodermic needle.

The first few generations of TDS prototypes have been built in the form of headsets (Figs. 1 and 2),

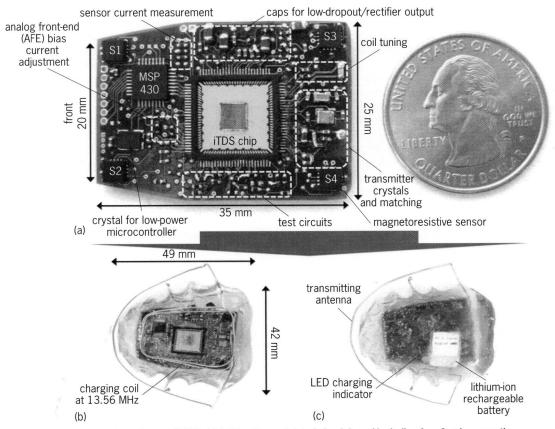

Fig. 3. Intraoral Tongue Drive System (iTDS). (*a*) A 35 × 25-mm printed circuit board including four 3-axis magnetic sensors on the four corners and an application-specific integrated circuit (ASIC). (*b*) Top view and (*c*) bottom view of charging coil and rechargeable battery sealed inside dental acrylic and molded based on the user's dental impression. The transmitting antenna is a metal spring wire that also helps the retainer stay in place.

which are not only convenient to use but also look like wireless headphones worn by many able-bodied individuals on a daily basis. In the external TDS (eTDS) headset, four 3-axis magnetic sensors are held bilaterally near the user's cheeks on a pair of adjustable poles and the wireless transceiver and battery are either embedded in the headband (Fig. 1) or hidden behind the ears (Fig. 2).

Trials. Several human subject trials have been conducted on able-bodied volunteers, as well as two rounds of clinical trials with participants who had tetraplegia as a result of high-level spinal cord injuries. In these studies, the performance of individuals who had no prior experience with the TDS was measured in accessing PCs and smartphones for point-and-click and on-screen maze navigation tasks, as well as in driving wheelchairs in an obstacle course over 6 consecutive weeks. These trials also compared their performance executing the same tasks using a mouse and a keypad for able-bodied participants, and a popular assistive technology known as sip-and-puff for tetraplegic participants. During these trials, all participants were able to learn how to use the TDS within the first session. As they gained more experience, they moved the computer cursor more quickly and accurately, and maneuvered through the obstacle course faster with very few col-

lisions. The results clearly demonstrated the usability and effectiveness of the TDS. Unlike brain-computer interfaces, most of which require concentration and lengthy training periods, the results showed a rapid learning process with this assistive technology, most of which occurred during the first session, that is, a steep performance improvement from the first to the second session.

Intraoral TDS. A new intraoral version of the TDS (iTDS) is currently under development, which entirely fits inside the mouth in the form of a dental appliance. It contains small magnetic field sensors that are mounted on its four corners near the roof of the mouth. The iTDS (**Fig. 3**) also includes a rechargeable lithium-ion battery and an induction coil to charge the battery when the retainer is placed in the charging cup of the universal interface. The transceiver circuitry fits in the space available on the retainer, covered with a water-resistant material that is vacuum-molded inside dental acrylic based on the user's dental impression.

Multimodal TDS. The multimodal TDS (mTDS), yet another version that is under development, combines the magnetic sensors with a microphone and 3-axis inertial sensors, all on the same wireless headset. The mTDS can provide an unprecedented level of access and control capability to those with high-level physical disabilities in terms of bandwidth, flexibility, and adaptability to effectively utilize any remaining abilities of the end users including but not limited to speech, free voluntary tongue motion, and head motion.

For background information *see* BIOMEDICAL ENGINEERING; MEDICAL CONTROL SYSTEMS; MOBILE COMMUNICATIONS; MOTOR SYSTEMS; PROSTHESIS; SPINAL CORD DISORDERS; TONGUE; WIRELESS FIDELITY (WI-FI) in the McGraw-Hill Encyclopedia of Science & Technology.   Maysam Ghovanloo

Bibliography. X. Huo and M. Ghovanloo, Evaluation of a wireless wearable tongue-computer interface by individuals with high-level spinal cord injuries, *J. Neural Eng.*, 7:026008, 2010, DOI:10.1088/1741-2560/7/2/026008; X. Huo and M. Ghovanloo, Tongue Drive: A wireless tongue-operated means for people with severe disabilities to communicate their intentions, *IEEE Comm. Mag.*, 50(10):128–135, October 2012, DOI:10.1109/MCOM.2012.6316786; E. R. Kandel et al., *Principles of Neural Science*, 5th ed. McGraw-Hill, New York, 2013; J. Kim et al., Evaluation of a smartphone platform as a wireless interface between Tongue Drive System and electric-powered wheelchairs, *IEEE Trans. Biomed. Eng.*, 59:1787–1796, 2012, DOI:10.1109/TBME.2012.2194713; National Institute of Neurological and Communicative Disorders and Stroke, Office of Scientific and Health Reports, *Spinal Cord Injury: Hope Through Research*, NIH pub. 81-160, U. S. Dept. of Health and Human Services, Public Health Service, National Institutes of Health, 1981, http://www.ninds.nih.gov/disorders/sci/detail_sci.htm; H. Park et al., A wireless magnetoresistive sensing system for an intraoral tongue-computer interface, *IEEE Trans. Biomed. Circ. Syst.*, 6:571–585, 2012, DOI:10.1109/TBCAS.2012.2227962.

Touch-screen display

A touch-screen display is an electronic display that allows a user to interact with a computer system by touching an area or areas on the display. Touch-screen displays have been in use for many years in ATMs, checkout registers, and other applications, but gained mass popularity only recently with the introduction of smartphones and tablets. Moreover, it seems that touch is becoming the standard way of interacting with screens, and it is expected to penetrate over to larger displays, such as notebook computers and other monitors.

Technologies for touch sensing. Four main approaches are used to implement touch-screen displays: capacitive, optical over the display, optical in the display, and resistive.

Capacitive touch sensing. This approach is by far the most popular for tablet and smartphone displays. Capacitance is an electrical quantity describing the ratio between the charge accumulated on an object and its electric potential (voltage). Thus, capacitive touch sensing is based on the idea that we impose

a known voltage on an object (called an electrode) and measure the amount of charge accumulated on it. A change in the amount of charge needed to hold a fixed potential will indicate a change in the capacitance of the electrode. Capacitance is impacted by neighboring objects, and specifically by their material composition and geometric configuration. A finger approaching the touch sensor will cause a change of capacitance, and thus be detected. The change detected will depend mainly on the proximity of the finger and on its size (**Fig. 1**). Different electrode configurations can be used to achieve tailored sensitivity or design constraints. Specifically, in most modern display touch systems, a variant based on mutual capacitance phenomena is used (**Fig. 2**). Mutual capacitance sensing is very similar to the measurement described before, only this time we measure the charge accumulated on one object, while changing the voltage on a different (nearby) object. Thus, two electrodes are involved here. Again, a finger approaching will change this mutual capacitance. The reason for using mutual capacitance is the ability to have a more localized measurement of capacitive change, and thus enable multiple finger interaction.

Optical over the display. Used mainly with larger displays, this method is based on sending rays of light parallel to the display, and by using detectors (cameras or simpler photodetectors) to determine which rays of light are "broken" by an object touching the screen (**Fig. 3**). By geometric computation, one can calculate the shape and location of the object touching the screen. No actual touch of the finger and the screen is needed. It is enough for the finger to cross this "sheet of light" near the surface. In addition, as long as the material touching the screen is opaque, and thus blocks the light, any object will do, and not only a finger.

Optical in the display. As in the optical-over-the-display method, rays of light are sent across the screen. However, this time these rays are trapped within the outside layer (usually glass) of the screen itself (**Fig. 4**). Based on the phenomenon of total internal reflection (TIR), the light is guided within the glass slab, from source point to receiving detector. This is similar to the guiding of light in a fiber-optic cable. When a finger touches this guiding glass, some of the light "escapes" out, in what is known as frustrated total internal reflection (FTIR). This reduction in the amount of light can be detected, and serves to identify the location of the touching object. In this case, unlike the previous one, the finger has to be physically in contact with the glass.

Resistive. Probably the first method to gain mass adoption was the resistive method, which was used extensively in ATMs, casino machines, gas stations, and so forth. The method is based on establishing a simple electrical connection between two surfaces as a result of pressure. Two conductive layers with a small air gap between them are placed over the display (**Fig. 5**). When the finger touches the top surface and presses on it, the top conductive layer

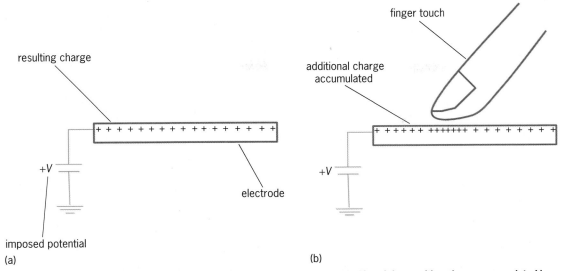

Fig. 1. Capacitive touch sensor. (*a*) **A single electrode is brought to a potential +*V*, and the resulting charge accumulated is recorded and determines the capacitance of the electrode.** (*b*) **The electrode is still held at potential +*V*, but because of the proximity of the finger, more charge is accumulated, thus increasing the capacitance measured.**

comes into electrical contact with the bottom layer. If the electrical resistance of the conductive layer is known, the location of the contact point can be calculated.

Capacitive in-cell touch sensing. One more method that has received much attention recently (because of its use in high-end smartphones) is the capacitive in-cell touch sensing approach. This method is identical to the capacitive touch sensing described previously in terms of its physical operation. However, the electrodes used for sensing the capacitance are embedded within the display itself, rather than being on top of the display. As previously mentioned, capacitive touch sensing can measure proximity of the finger, and thus the sensor does not have to be exactly on the most outside-facing surface. The advantages of using the in-cell approach are the saving in thickness of the device, and higher integration. The main problems are performance (the farther the electrode from the finger, the harder it is to sense) and manufacturing (high cost).

Comparison of methods, and challenges. With the penetration of touch sensing into many consumer devices, it becomes apparent that some of the methods are better fit for specific applications. A few common requirements will be noted, and it will be seen how the above four sensing methods comply.

Design for aesthetics is a driving force in many of the consumer electronics smartphones and tablets. These are expected to be thin and light, and with the display occupying the whole front area. In this category, the need of optical-over-the-display technology to have special accommodations for light emitters and detectors on top of the screen is a big drawback. All the other methods can be integrated with the display in a much thinner form.

Responsiveness, perhaps more vaguely termed the "feeling" of touch sensing, is an important factor

as well. In capacitive touch sensing, no pressure is required for the touch to register, and even a very light swipe of the finger will be recorded as touch. This is to be contrasted with resistive touch, where a deliberate force (albeit small) is needed to create a contact between the two layers. In the FTIR-based method (in the glass), the mechanism of coupling light into the finger depends on the wetness of the finger and the direct optical contact between the glass and finger. This results in slower responsiveness than afforded with capacitive sensing.

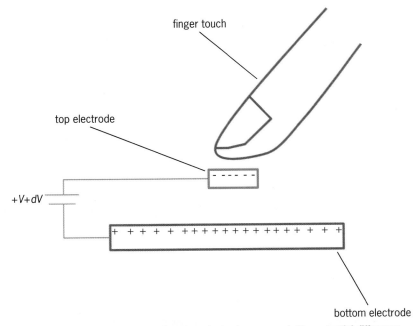

Fig. 2. In mutual capacitance sensing, two electrodes are used. The potential difference between them is changed by a small amount *dV*, and the resulting change of charge on one of them is examined. In the presence of a finger, this amount of charge differs, and indicates change in the mutual capacitance.

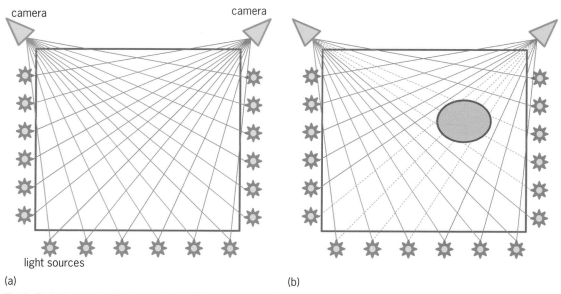

Fig. 3. Optical-over-the-display method. (*a*) Two cameras are inspecting the surface parallel to the display, while 18 light sources are distributed around the edges. Each camera in this specific scenario has a view of 12 of the light sources. (*b*) Once a finger approaches the screen, it breaks the line of sight from some of the light sources. By analyzing the known geometry and the broken rays, one can calculate the location (and size) of the obscuring object.

Cost is of course an important factor for deployment, and moreover, the scaling of the cost of the solution with the size of the screen. Resistive touch is considered the least expensive. The main difference between optical-based and capacitive methods is the scaling with size. Whereas capacitive cost scales as the area of the display, the cost of an optical-based solution scales as the perimeter. Thus, for larger screens, optical-based methods are less expensive. The breakeven point is considered currently to be around 33 cm (13 in.); above that size, optical sensing might be preferred.

Multitouch is yet another requirement that was brought to the forefront only in recent years. Whereas resistive touch sensing can detect only one point of contact, capacitive and optical can detect many. This consideration became paramount with the introduction of two-finger gestures like zoom and pinch.

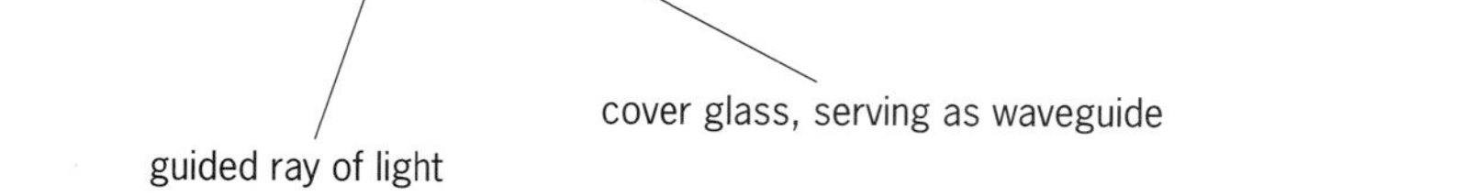

There are many more aspects to compare by (resolution, working with a stylus, true multitouch, and so forth), but presently there is no winning method for all applications. For example, the resistive method, which is not favorable in terms of the "feeling" of touch, inability to do multitouch, the need for calibration, and so forth, is still dominant in cash registers, ATMs, and other places where multitouch is not needed and low cost is of high significance.

Future directions. As hard as it is to predict the future, one can be fairly confident that touch interface will be an expected means of interaction with a computer. The mouse and keyboard might still be present, but not solely anymore.

A natural extension of the touch interface is the ability to interact using a stylus. This will transform the interaction into the realm of pencil-and-paper, where people can write on the screen and draw comfortably. There are still many challenges to get this means of interaction to work well (such as parallax, cost, and texture-feeling), but many attempts are being made along this path.

Another point of extension is the detection of pressure. Adding pressure to touch sensing enables the sensor to do a better job of identifying the intention of the user. For example, the user can be required not merely to put a finger over a button on the display, but to actually press it to activate it.

Another means of interaction, somewhat orthogonal to touch, is gesture sensing. This technology involves devices based on cameras, or 3D sensors, to detect hand waving and gesturing from afar.

Fig. 4. Optical-in-the-display method. Looking through a cross section of the cover glass on the display, we see one light source launching light into the glass, which serves as a waveguide. When the finger touches the glass, some of the light leaks outside, and thus the camera on the other side will note a reduction in light intensity. In practice, many light sources and many detectors are placed on the side of the cover glass, enabling the detection and localization of multiple fingers.

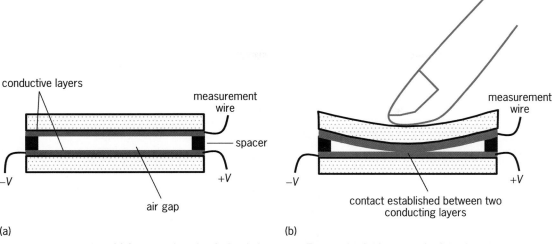

Fig. 5. Resistive method. (*a*) Cross section of typical resistive sensor. Two conductive layers are laminated on transparent material (glass, clear plastic, or a similar material), and are kept with a small space between them (usually about 40 μm). (*b*) Pressure by a finger touch causes the two layers to be in contact, and closes a "switch" to be measured.

Such devices became very popular in video-game interactions, and are finding some headway in general consumer devices. However, in most relevant cases, gesture is an augmenting technology, just like the stylus, and is not meant to replace touch interaction.

To conclude, it seems inevitable that the coming few years will witness a proliferation of touch displays to all computing devices, and even beyond that, to other surfaces with which humans interact, such as car dashboards, appliances, and maybe even tables and walls. This article has outlined some of the prominent technologies to enable this evolution.

For background information, *see* CAPACITANCE; COMPUTER PERIPHERAL DEVICES; ELECTRICAL RESISTANCE; ELECTRONIC DISPLAY; HUMAN-COMPUTER INTERACTION; MULTIMEDIA TECHNOLOGY; REFLECTION OF ELECTROMAGNETIC RADIATION in the McGraw-Hill Encyclopedia of Science & Technology.

Zachi Baharav

Bibliography. B. Mackey, 43.1: Invited paper: Trends and materials in touch sensing, *SID Symp. Digest Tech. Papers*, 42(1):617–620, 2011, DOI:10.1889/1.3621396; Special issue: The best times for touch, *Inform. Display*, vol. 26, no. 3, March 2010; G. Walker, A cornucopia of touch technology, *Inform. Display*, 22(12):14–20, 2006; O. Wassvik et al., 50.1: Invited paper: PSD (Planar Scatter Detection), a new method for optical touch screens, *SID Symp. Digest Tech. Papers*, 42(1):726–728, 2012, DOI:10.1889/1.3621428.

Transposable elements in plants

A genome (the genetic endowment of a species) is often thought to be composed of genes (the basic units of inheritance in the form of DNA sequences) whose function is to provide a selective advantage to an organism. However, these DNA sequences actu-

ally only represent a small portion of most eukaryotic genomes. Instead, in the case of plants, the dominant part of the average plant genome is made up of endogenous parasites known as transposable elements (TEs). TEs are stretches of DNA that are able to replicate themselves within a genome. The DNA of TEs does not have to provide a benefit for the organism in order to persist. It has only to outreplicate the rest of the genome. In plants, TEs have been wildly successful at doing this. Indeed, the average stretch of plant DNA is almost certainly a TE whose function is to make more of itself. Ongoing replication and subsequent deletion of these molecular parasites largely explain the enormous variation in DNA content that is observed in plants.

Kinds of transposable elements. Broadly speaking, TEs can be divided into those that transpose via an RNA intermediate and those that do not, with the former using a copy-and-paste mechanism for transposition and the latter employing a cut-and-paste mechanism (**Fig. 1**). Elements that use an RNA intermediate are called retrotransposons, or retrons. These elements use a reverse transcriptase (a type of polymerase) to convert RNA expressed by the TE into DNA, which is then reinserted into the genome at a new location. Cut-and-paste elements physically excise the TE DNA and move it to a new location. The gap at the site of excision is then repaired by host enzymes. Depending on the timing of excision and the repair pathways available, this can result in restoration of the element at the original position as well as an insertion at a new position. Note that transposition requires proteins encoded by the elements. Elements that encode these proteins are referred to as autonomous. Elements that can only transpose in the presence of autonomous elements are referred to as nonautonomous. A TE system is composed of all the elements that can transpose in response to a given autonomous element. Moreover, TEs are divided into larger families and superfamilies

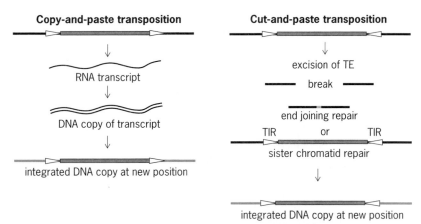

Fig. 1. Two common modes of TE transposition: (*left*) copy-and-paste transposition and (*right*) cut-and-paste transposition. In copy-and-paste transposition, an RNA copy of the element is reverse-transcribed into DNA and then reintegrated into a new position in the genome. In cut-and-paste transposition, the DNA of the element is physically cut from its original position and integrated into a new position. Repair of the donor position can result in a loss of the element at the original position or a restoration of the element when a sister chromatid (which retains the element) is used as a template to repair the break. TIR refers to the terminal inverted repeats that characterize the ends of many cut-and-paste TEs.

based on sequence similarity and similarities in the transposition mechanism.

Effects of the activity of transposable elements. Because TEs insert themselves into new positions in the genome, they can alter normal gene function. The simplest example of this is an insertion into the exon of a gene [an exon is the segment or segments of a gene coding its final messenger RNA (mRNA)], which prevents its translation into a protein. However, there are many other, more subtle effects as well, with some of them providing a selective benefit to the host. Indeed, there is ample evidence that TEs have been co-opted by their hosts in a variety of ways. This has been the case for several TE-induced mutations associated with domestication and crop

improvement, including those involved in the loss of red pigment in white grape varietals as well as "sticky" varieties of millet. Because TEs also carry sequences important for regulating expression, insertion of TEs can also alter patterns of gene expression, which is a process that has given rise to the loss of branching observed in modern corn and the deep red color of blood oranges. In some cases, genes encoded by TEs can themselves be co-opted; thus, rather than promoting transposition, they take on important functions for the host.

Despite the occasional advantages conferred by TE activity, most TE-induced mutations, like most mutations in general, are either neutral or deleterious, and very high levels of TE activity can cause stunted growth, infertility, and chromosomal rearrangement. To cope with the danger posed by TEs, plants, like all eukaryotes, have evolved an elaborate immune system whose function is to monitor and inactivate these molecular parasites. They do so by epigenetically silencing autonomous TEs so that they are unable to produce the proteins necessary for transposition.

Epigenetic silencing. Epigenetic changes are heritable changes in gene expression in the absence of changes in the DNA sequence. Transgenerational epigenetic changes are those that are propagated from one generation to the next. Although many host genes are targeted for epigenetic silencing, the vast majority of silenced genes in plant genomes are those encoded by TEs.

Epigenetic silencing involves modification of both DNA and histones (the proteins around which DNA is wound). These modifications result in a compact mix of DNA and proteins referred to as heterochromatin. In plants, the modification of DNA that is associated with heterochromatin involves the addition of a methyl group to cytosine bases. The addition of methyl groups to specific sites on one histone, histone H3, is also associated with the formation of heterochromatin and the prevention of productive transcription of TEs. New DNA and histone DNA methylation can be triggered by the presence of small RNAs (generally 20–26 nucleotides in length). In plants, small RNAs are produced from double-stranded RNAs via the activity of a class of enzymes called DICERs, which cleave double-stranded RNAs into shorter RNAs. These small RNAs are then incorporated into a complex that invariably includes an ARGONAUTE protein. Plants generally encode several different DICER and ARGONAUTE proteins, which vary with respect to their targets. Some small RNAs direct the cleavage of mRNAs. Others are associated with the inhibition of translation. Those that are specifically responsible for triggering DNA methylation and histone modification are generally 24–26 nucleotides in length. These small RNAs are also involved in maintaining DNA methylation once it has been established (**Fig. 2**). This is because methylated DNA is often transcribed by a plant-specific polymerase, PolIV. The transcript produced by PolIV is converted into double-stranded

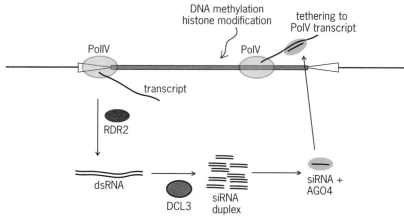

Fig. 2. Maintenance of DNA methylation at a silenced TE. The specialized polymerase, PolIV, produces a transcript from a methylated TE. This transcript is converted into double-stranded RNA (dsRNA) because of the activity of RNA-DEPENDENT RNA POLYMERASE2 (RDR2). The resulting dsRNA is then processed into shorter small RNAs (siRNAs) by DICER-LIKE3 (DCL3). One strand of these short RNA duplexes is then loaded onto a protein complex that includes ARGONAUTE4 (AGO4). This complex then guides the small RNA to a scaffold RNA produced by a second plant-specific RNA polymerase, PolV. Together, these components recruit DNA and histone methyltransferases, which reinforce heterochromatin formation at the TE.

RNA by an RNA-dependent polymerase, RDR2. The newly synthesized double-stranded RNA is cleaved by DICER-LIKE3, producing small RNAs that are incorporated into a RNA–protein complex that can reinforce DNA methylation and histone modification (Fig. 2). It is this feedback mechanism that helps to ensure stable transgenerational silencing.

Although this system of self-reinforcing silencing would seem to be sufficient to keep TEs inactive, plants have additional strategies for maintenance of silencing. The best evidence for this comes from pollen, which is the haploid male sex cell of plants. Pollen contains three nuclei. Two of these nuclei, the generative nuclei, are destined to separately fertilize the egg and the endosperm (a nutritive tissue in the seed that does not form part of the germline); this process is referred to as double fertilization. The third nucleus, the vegetative nucleus, is responsible for the physiological functions of pollen. As such, it does not participate in fertilization. It appears that plants exploit this fact in order to gain information concerning potentially damaging TEs. In the vegetative nucleus, DNA methylation is lost, resulting in increased expression and even new TE transpositions. Because the vegetative nucleus is not transmitted to the next generation, and each plant produces millions of pollen grains, the effect of this activity on the ability of plants to reproduce is minimal. However, this activation of TEs in the vegetative nucleus also results in the production of a novel class of small RNAs that can be transmitted to the genera-

tive nuclei, where TE silencing is then reinforced. Interestingly, a similar process appears to occur in the endosperm and in young seedling leaves. In each case, it would appear that plants permit expression of RNA from TEs in tissues that are adjacent to the germinal lineage in order to reinforce silencing in that lineage.

Triggering of silencing. Much of what is known about TE silencing involves the means by which TEs are held in a silenced state. However, there are instances in which TEs have yet to be recognized and silenced. The small RNAs associated with the maintenance of silencing do not appear to have an effect on these elements. Instead, an additional trigger is required. One well-documented trigger involves RNA transcripts derived from a rearranged autonomous element in which a portion of the element was duplicated and inverted (**Fig. 3**). Because two parts of this transcript are complementary to each other, the transcript forms a double-stranded hairpin, which is then processed into small RNAs that can trigger heritable silencing of active versions of the element. After silencing, the presence of the trigger is no longer necessary, and silencing can be stably maintained via the maintenance pathway. This process represents an elegant solution to the problem of active TEs. In order to survive, all TEs must replicate themselves. In doing so, they often produce rearranged or aberrant copies, including some that will inevitably produce transcripts that trigger silencing. Thus, the more successful a given TE is at increasing its copy

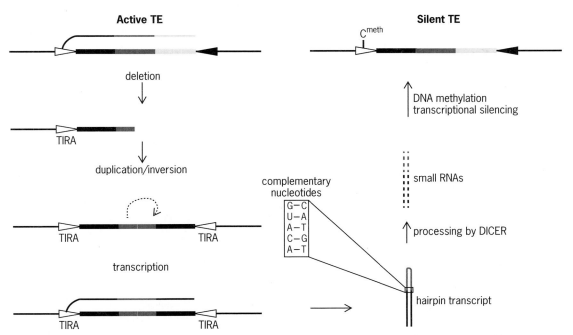

Fig. 3. A trigger for TE silencing. Silencing of TEs can be triggered by aberrant RNAs that are produced by rearranged autonomous elements. In this case, a TE has suffered a deletion of one half of the element, followed by a duplication and inversion of the remaining portion of the TE. Expression of this mirror-image version of the element results in a transcript that exhibits self-complementarity along its length. This complementarity of sequence leads to the formation of a double-stranded hairpin, which is processed by a DICER protein into siRNAs, which then initiate heterochromatin formation and transcriptional silencing of all copies of the original, unrearranged TE. TIRA refers to the terminal inverted repeats that characterize the ends of many cut-and-paste TEs.

number, the more likely it is that at least one copy of the element will produce an aberrant transcript that can serve as an "antigen" that will trigger silencing of the entire transposon system.

A great deal is known about the means by which TEs are held in check. However, it is also known that TEs can undergo rapid copy number expansion and can be responsive to a wide variety of environmental influences. This suggests that TEs are competent to regularly evade epigenetic silencing, just as many viruses are capable of evading our immune response to them. An interesting topic for future research will be the coevolution of host-encoded silencing systems and the strategies for escape from those systems employed by TEs.

For background information *see* DEOXYRIBONUCLEIC ACID (DNA); DNA METHYLATION; GENE; GENE SILENCING; GENOMICS; HISTONE; MUTATION; POLLEN; PROTEIN; REVERSE TRANSCRIPTASE; RIBONUCLEIC ACID (RNA); TRANSCRIPTION; TRANSPOSABLE ELEMENTS in the McGraw-Hill Encyclopedia of Science & Technology.   Damon Lisch

Bibliography. N. L. Craig et al. (eds.), *Mobile DNA II*, ASM Press, Washington, DC, 2002; M. Gigal and O. Mathieu, A "mille-feuille" of silencing: Epigenetic control of transposable elements, *Biochim. Biophys. Acta*, 1809(8):452–458, 2011, DOI:10.1016/j.bbagrm.2011.04.001; J. R. Haag and C. S. Pikaard, Multisubunit RNA polymerases IV and V: Purveyors of non-coding RNA for plant gene silencing, *Nat. Rev. Mol. Cell Biol.*, 12(8):483–492, 2011, DOI:10.1038/nrm3152; D. Lisch, Epigenetic regulation of transposons in plants, *Annu. Rev. Plant Biol.*, 60:43–66, 2009, DOI:10.1146/annurev.arplant.59.032607.092744; D. Lisch, How important are transposons for plant evolution?, *Nat. Rev. Genet.*, 14(1):49–61, 2013, DOI:10.1038/nrg3374; H. Saze et al., DNA methylation in plants: Relationship to small RNAs and histone modifications, and functions in transposon inactivation, *Plant Cell Physiol.*, 53(5):766–784, 2012, DOI:10.1093/pcp/pcs008.

Trusted systems

Webster's New World Dictionary defines trust, as a noun, as the "firm belief or confidence in the honesty, integrity, reliability, justice, etc. of another person or thing." The *Oxford English Dictionary* defines trust, in its adjectival form of trusted, as "committing someone or something to the safekeeping of."

The concept of trust implies a domain (or context) and an object that denotes a relationship of trust. The word trust is used with people, organizations, and objects. Usually the term is associated with a specific situation. For example, a person can be trusted to perform a task and not another. It is also possible to associate a degree of trust to the object itself or the action associated with a context that it executes. For example, in the U.S. credit system, the possibility of granting a loan is subject to an applicant having a good credit record; this record is institutionalized and it is available for inquiring. The assessment contained in this record may also change over time, indicating that trust is an element that can change over time.

The understanding of trusted technology and trusted computing concepts, tracking the evolution of products and their needs in the commercial sector, has evolved since the introduction of the technology and computing concepts in the early 1970s. Currently the trusted system concept, as it relates to the information world, refers to computer systems that are concerned with trust for modeling procedures, software quality assessment, decision making, security of communications systems, and, more recently, trust on websites for e-commerce, product downloads, and the like. The trust concept has to be modeled, specified, and adequately addressed. More advanced approaches of trust include calculus-based trust, knowledge-based trust, and institution-based trust. Recently, trust has been adapted to wireless communication networks which, if modeled adequately, can resolve many problems within this communication context.

In the field of computer science, researchers have been working to develop theories, technologies, and applications of trusted systems as evidenced in the different specialized conferences that address topics such as computing systems, trusted modules, platforms, networks, services, and applications from their fundamental features and functionalities to design principles, architecture, and implementation technologies. Trust as a concept has many very different applications, which causes divergence in trust-management terminology. An overview of the principal trust research areas includes:

1. Policy-based trust (network security credentials, trust negotiation, security policies and trust languages, distributed trust management, and effect of credential type)

2. Reputation-based trust (decentralization and referral trust, trust metrics in a web of trust, trust in peer-to-peer networks and grids, and application-specific reputation)

3. General models of trust (general characteristics of trust, computational and online trust models, game theory and agents, and software engineering)

4. Trust in information resources (trust concerns on the web, semantic web, trust using hyperlinks, filtering information based on trust, filtering the semantic web, subjectivity analysis, provenance information, content trust, site design, and human factors).

Some concepts associated with trust. As we can see, the set of topics associated with trust are wide-ranging and numerous. Here, we will consider some of the most relevant topics related to the concept of trust.

Trust relationship. Audun Jøsang defines trust as a directional relationship between two parties that can be called trustor and trustee. This relationship has a scope. By scope we mean that it applies to a specific purpose or domain of action. Trust influences the trustor's attitudes and actions, but can also have effects on the trustee and other elements in the environment. For example, a trustor could be a service provider practicing electronic commerce on the Internet, and a trustee could be either a business partner or an individual requiring access to the trustor's services, as represented by an identifiable agent in the network. There are trust pseudo-transitivity relationships; that is, the trustor A has a trust relationship with the trustee B and the trustee B becomes in the same way a trustor of another trustee C, then the trustor A may have a trust relationship with the trustee C by transitivity. This transitivity relationship may eventually end since C, in turn, can trust another entity D. However, trustor A may not necessarily trust entity D.

When searching about trusted systems in the literature, it is common to find the related concept of reputation. In fact, there is an important relationship as well as some differences between these two concepts.

Trust and reputation systems. Reputation is defined as beliefs or opinions that are generally held about someone or something. Reputation systems can help to evaluate the trust that allows individual decision making. These reputation systems increase an assessment system based on good or bad past experiences from a trustee. Current trust models have to make the relationship between trust and reputation clear; the relationship is dependent on context and time. A reputation system aggregates information about the past behavior of a group of entities in the form of the community's shared perception of them. This information may include information from book reviewers, perceived fairness to online companies, and perceived competence and reliability. Reputation systems have been found to benefit computer-aided human-to-human interaction by reducing the level of uncertainty about new acquaintances to a manageable level.

Audun Jøsang establishes the following differences between trust and reputation systems. Trust systems produce a score that reflects the relying party's subjective view of an entity's trustworthiness, whereas reputation systems produce an entity's (public) reputation score as seen by the whole community. Secondly, transitivity of trust paths and networks is an explicit component in trust systems, whereas reputation systems usually do not take transitivity into account, or only in an implicit way. In addition, trust systems take subjective expressions of (reliability) trust about other entities as input, whereas reputation systems take ratings about specific (and objective) events as input. Some other authors have tried to describe the principal components associated with the construction and development of trusted systems.

Trust-based system components. A. Srinivasan and coworkers have proposed four important components of reputation and trust-based systems: infor-

mation gathering, information sharing, information modeling, and decision making. Information gathering is the process by which a node collects information about the nodes it relates to. Information sharing is concerned with dissemination of first-hand information gathered by nodes. Information modeling is concerned with combining the first-hand and second-hand information meaningfully into a metric, its maintenance, and its updating. Decision making is concerned with the decisions made based on the information provided by the information-modeling component. The basic decision is a binary decision—who to trust and who not to.

Several approaches have been tried to formalize the concept of trust through expressions or mathematical concepts; all of them aim to represent a single value called a trusted value.

Trust modeling. The problem of somehow representing human thoughts and feelings in a computer system is quite evident in trust management. Trust modeling is concerned with the representational and computational aspects of trust values. Early trust values were modeled as scalar values of trust. Other models have included different measures such as subjective probability, possibilities, belief, and fuzzy values. More advanced models include trust values in a framework of modal logic. Trust values are expressed as numbers or labels, thus their domains can be binary, discrete, or continuous.

A critical aspect within the security component of a network is the concept associated with the trust-management model. As we know, a crucial element in the communication systems is the fidelity and backup of the information transmitted in a network. There have been different approaches to the security component. They range from the development of preventive measures to the implementation of corrective measures. A mechanism that has become very popular on the Internet is the use of a certificate of security. For example, banking systems use a certificate or electronic document to determine if the person who is conducting an electronic transaction is the right and authorized person to carry out such transaction. A protection protocol established to confirm the execution of the transaction may notify the user via some other media such as email or text messaging. If the notified person has not authorized an electronic transaction, the person can contact the bank to cancel the transaction.

Trust management model. The trust management problem is a distinct and important component of security in network services. Trust management is a unified approach to specifying and interpreting security policies, credentials, and relationships, which allows direct authorization of security-critical actions.

A trust-management system provides direct authorization of security-critical actions and decouples the problem of specifying policy and authorization from that of distributing credentials. In general, it combines the notion of specifying security policy with the mechanism for specifying security credentials. Nowadays, the trust-management model has an important challenge, it has to be more dynamic and adaptable; that is, the system must determine how much unknown individuals should be trusted, sometimes without knowing anything about them. The behavior of the trustee should be considered as well as the monitoring and re-evaluation of trust.

Trust-management research has its roots in authentication and authorization. In the context of authentication, trust is established by means such as digital certificates. The trust-management approach to distributed-system security was developed as an answer to the inadequacy of traditional authorization mechanisms. Trust-management engines avoid the need to resolve "identities" in an authorization decision. Instead, they express privileges and restrictions in a programming language. This allows for increased flexibility and expressivity as well as standardization of modern and scalable security mechanisms. At the authentication level, trust is monotonic (invariant) across time and attached to a certain identity or membership.

Real-life situations lead us to make decisions with some degree of uncertainty. In fact, we generally have to make decisions without complete knowledge of all the elements concerning a particular fact or situation. A classic example is a medical decision, where sometimes a procedure or treatment is done without knowing the exact cause or origin of a disease.

Decisions with some degree of uncertainty are generally made taking into account a cost/benefit analysis. For example, medicines are prescribed despite their having side effects, because in some cases the need for medicines outweighs the side effects they can cause.

Trust-based decisions. From a decision point of view, trust is the extent to which one party is willing to participate in a given action with a given partner, considering the risks and incentives involved. Consequently, a trust decision is binary and based on the balance between trust and risk, and it has some sort of effect on the trustee. The aspect of risk is dealt with explicitly based on the costs and benefits of the considered engagement. Trust is a very useful tool that has been used to facilitate decision making in diverse fields ranging from ancient fish markets to state-of-the-art e-commerce. For over three decades, formal studies have been done on how trust can affect decision-making abilities in uncertain conditions.

There are only a few computational trust models that explicitly take risk into account. Some ideas have been taken from economic models. The decision model has to include risk-trust analysis, probability of success, gain and risk attitude, and benefits and risk relationships.

In recent times, an area that has gained in relevance and importance is e-commerce. Contracting services on the Internet is increasingly common because of its accessibility and ease of use. In many cases, the experience of a friend or reviewer is very helpful in the use of a website as a place of inquiry, or

reference, or for commercial operations. For other websites, despite being reliable sites, there are valuation measures expressed by the experience of previous users about a product or service. This is the case, for example, for the websites of hotels or lodgings, where judgments about criteria such as cleanliness, noise level, attention, value, location, accessibility by common carriers, and other information set the rules that can lead a customer to decide on a product or service.

Trust and commerce. Trust is complex and multidimensional in nature, and a critical aspect of e-commerce. The concept has been widely recognized as an important factor affecting consumer behavior, especially in the e-commerce context where uncertainty abounds.

As e-commerce increases on the Internet it will be necessary to install a new system to help customers be trustful about sites or services. The Internet environment is uncertain and consumers' perceived uncertainty deters their adoption of online shopping. Trust contributes to e-commerce success by helping consumers overcome uncertainty and with making decisions.

Transaction-economics research demonstrates that uncertainty increases transaction cost and decreases acceptance of online shopping. Trust is necessary only when there is uncertainty.

Online purchase renders a customer vulnerable in many ways because of the lack of proven guarantees that an e-vendor will not behave opportunistically. The Internet is a complex social environment, which still lacks effective regulation. When a social environment cannot be regulated through rules and customs, people adopt trust as a central social complexity-reduction strategy. Therefore, online customers have to trust an e-vendor from which they purchase; otherwise, the social complexity will cause them to avoid purchasing.

As a consequence, the early optimism associated with the Internet has been replaced by cynicism and diminishing trust in the Internet as a reliable platform for building markets and communities.

For background information *see* COMPUTER PROGRAMMING; COMPUTER SECURITY; DECISION THEORY; INTERNET; RISK ASSESSMENT AND MANAGEMENT in the McGraw-Hill Encyclopedia of Science & Technology.   Ana Aguilera; Rodolfo Canelón

Bibliography. M. D. Abrams and M. V. Joyce, Trusted system concepts, *Comput. Secur.*, 14(1):45–56, 1995, DOI:10.1016/0167-4048(95)97025-6; D. Artz and Y. Gil, A survey of trust in computer science and the Semantic Web, *J. Web Semant. Sci. Serv. Agents World Wide Web*, 5(2):58–71, 2007, DOI:10.1016/j.websem.2007.03.002; M. Blaze et al., The role of trust management in distributed systems security, pp. 185–210, in J. Vitek and C. D. Jensen (eds.), *Secure Internet Programming: Security Issues for Mobile and Distributed Objects*, Springer-Verlag, Berlin, 1999; A. Jøsang, Trust and reputation systems, pp. 209–245, in A. Aldini and R. Gorrieri (eds.), *Foundations of Security*

Analysis and Design IV, Springer-Verlag, Berlin, 2007; S. Ries, J. Kangasharju, and M. Mühlhäuser, A classification of trust systems, pp. 894–903, in R. Meersman et al. (eds.), *On the Move to Meaningful Internet Systems 2006: OTM 2006 Workshops*, Springer-Verlag, Berlin, 2006; S. Ruohomaa and L. Kutvonen, Trust management survey, pp. 77–92, in P. Herrmann et al. (eds.), *iTrust*, Springer-Verlag, Berlin, 2005; A. Srinivasan et al., Reputation and trust-based system for ad-hoc and sensor networks, pp. 375–404, in A. Boukerche (ed.), *Algorithms and Protocols for Wireless Ad-Hoc and Sensor Networks*, Wiley, Hoboken, NJ, 2008.

Tunneling bacteria and tunneling of wood cell walls

Wood exposed to natural environments can deteriorate because of the interaction of a wide variety of biotic (living) and abiotic (nonliving) factors. Biotic factors are induced by the actions of living organisms. Abiotic factors include all physical and nonliving chemical factors (for example, soil, water, and atmosphere), which influence living organisms. Among biotic factors, fungi and bacteria are considered to be important for degradation of the wood polymers, that is, cellulose, hemicelluloses, and lignin. Whereas biological degradation of lignocellulosics is a significant contributor to the carbon cycle in natural ecosystems, deterioration of wood products is of concern with regard to economic reasons. Therefore, microbial degradation of wood and its protection against microbial decay have been intensively studied for decades.

Competition in nature with faster wood-degrading fungi, such as white and brown rot fungi, has led wood-degrading bacteria to evolve adaptations that are well suited to their population growth and for obtaining nutrients from wood. Wood-degrading bacteria are able to degrade intact wood. In contrast, purely cellulolytic bacteria cause little or no degradation of wood. Based primarily on micromorphological patterns of degradation, wood-degrading bacteria have been placed into two distinct groups: tunneling and erosion. This review relates to tunneling bacteria.

Bacterial morphology and size. Tunneling bacteria (TB) are short gram-negative, nonflagellated rods (**Fig. 1**), measuring 1.5–2.00 μm in length and 0.5 μm in diameter, with rounded ends; in contrast, erosion bacteria (EB) have flattened or slightly conical ends. However, variable forms of TB have also been observed during tunneling of cell walls, particularly in situations where TB abruptly change the direction of tunneling or have to negotiate pathways through cell wall regions that are difficult to degrade. A dumbbell shape is a common form during TB penetration across the middle lamella, and it is likely that bacteria degrade only a small portion of this highly lignified cell wall region in order to squeeze through when traversing the middle lamella. A pear shape is a form that is commonly associated with bacteria at the front of the tunnels and during the initial penetration of the cell wall by TB colonizing the cell lumen. Having penetrated the S_3 layer and on coming in contact with the richest food source, that is, the S_2 layer, TB revert back to their usual form. It is probable that the form changes may be related to conservation of energy and enzymes during cell wall penetration and degradation. Physical constraint of the substrate may also be a factor because slender, elongated forms of TB and slender tunnels have been observed during long-distance tunneling of the S_1 layer, which is a very thin cell wall layer with microfibrillar orientation essentially perpendicular to the S_2 layer. Thus, TB are considered to be pleomorphic (variable in size and shape). High-resolution images obtained using transmission electron microscopy (TEM) have provided evidence of membranous cell walls, typical for gram-negative-type bacteria.

Tunneling mode of attack. TB colonization of wood is likely to be facilitated by the adherence of TB to wood surfaces with the help of an extracellular slime that they abundantly produce. Judging from studies of microbial attachment to solid surfaces, compositionally the slime produced by TB may consist of mucopolysaccharides (polysaccharides containing an amino sugar and uronic acid). Subsequent to colonizing wood surfaces, TB preferentially penetrate into and colonize rays (vascular strips of short horizontal cells that extend in a radial direction), which being nutrient-rich serve as the initial source of food and thus are the main pathways of bacterial entry into wood. From rays, TB enter into the lumens of other wood elements [including tracheids

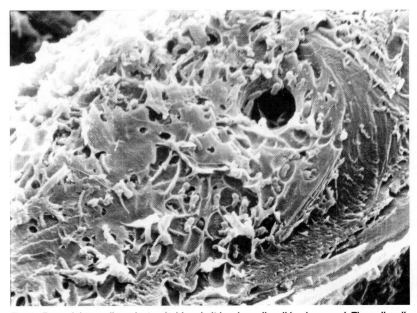

Fig. 1. Bacterial tunneling of a tracheid and pit border cell wall in pine wood. The cell wall contains holes and is also pitted. Pitting is caused by bacterial tunneling. In some pitted regions, tunnels are recognizable. Tunneling bacteria (rod-shaped) are widely present. (*Scanning electron micrograph courtesy of Thomas Nilsson*)

(elongate, spindle-shaped xylem cells) in softwoods, and vessels, fiber-tracheids, and fibers in hardwoods], mainly via pits but also through direct penetration of cell walls. The sequence of penetration into and attack of lignocellulosic secondary cell walls from the cell lumen has been examined in detail, and a combination of light and electron microscopy has provided much of the information known about wood degradation by TB. Bacterial attachment to the lumen face of the S_3 wall is a prerequisite to cell wall penetration, and TEM images have provided evidence of the involvement of the slime sheath in bacterial attachment: The slime forms a continuous layer covering the lumen face of the bacteria, thereby securing the bacteria. TEM images also reveal an intricate pattern of bacterial entry into the cell wall through the S_3 layer and subsequent tunneling of the S_2 layer, which being the thickest part of the cell wall appears to be a preferred source of nutrients for TB. The initial TB penetration through the S_3 layer appears to be a point penetration, with TB assuming a pear shape and with the pointed end of the bacterium serving as the advancing front. This may be a strategy for the TB to conserve energy by concentrating enzymes and radicals within a small cell volume to optimize degradation.

Once in contact with the S_2 wall, TB divide and degrade the adjacent wood cell wall with repeated divisions and tunneling (**Fig. 2**), initially producing a pattern of radiating branches from a central point, which appears as a rosette when viewed with a light microscope. The variable direction of tunneling, particularly within the S_2 layer, indicates that there is no influence of microfibrillar orientation on the course of cell wall tunneling. However, TEM images showing long-distance tunneling within the extremely thin S_1 wall along the length of microfibrils suggest that there may be a relationship in some situations.

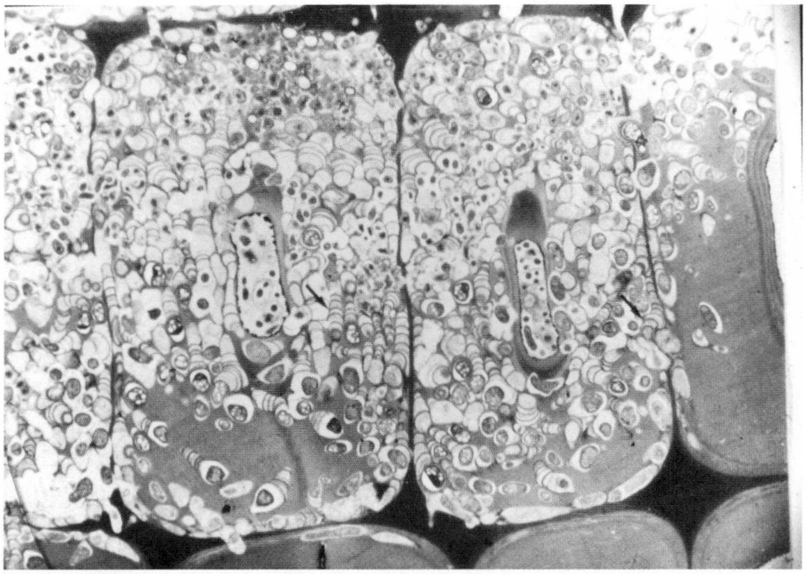

In TEM images (**Figs. 3** and **4**), individual tunnels are clearly resolved and are readily identifiable because of their unique and characteristic features. The tunnels have a banded appearance, typically containing periodic crescent-shaped bands (also referred to as cross-walls). The shape of the bands reveals the direction of tunneling, as the band concavity faces the bacterium within a tunnel. Scanning electron microscopy (SEM) images suggest that tunnels may in fact be slime tubes within which TB can glide. The bands within tunnels represent concentrated deposits of the slime in places where bacteria stop to recharge their battery of enzymes and other cell wall–degrading agents. Because the slime is needed for bacterial movement and thus has to be continuously produced, its accumulation in places (appearing as tunnel bands) suggests that TB do not move at the same speed, and stop or slow down in places during tunneling. Interband regions of tunnels may appear empty, suggestive of complete cell wall degradation. Generally, however, they contain a diffuse granular material, which may represent a mixture of slime and lignin degradation products, as the material positively stains with potassium permanganate (a reagent widely used to contrast lignin in wood ultrastructure work). The presence of tunnels densely filled with granular deposits in some substrates, such as dead stems of the fern *Pteridium*, points to substrate-related differences. *Pteridium* stems are highly lignified, and it is likely that, in lignin-rich substrates, TB cannot degrade lignin as rapidly or efficiently as in substrates that are less highly lignified, resulting in greater accumulations of lignin residues within tunnels. Lignin type may be another factor. The granular material in the tunnels present in degraded wood treated with copper-chrome-arsenate (CCA) preservative may also contain CCA components. TEM-EDX (energy dispersive X-ray analysis) studies have provided evidence of the presence of high concentrations of CCA components within the extracellular slime, which suggests that TB may have a capacity to remove CCA from adjacent cell wall regions, and sequestration and selective binding of CCA to the extracellular slime thus prevent CCA entry into bacterial cells.

What determines the direction of TB movement or tunneling is a mystery. A relationship with the orientation of cellulose microfibrils remains speculative, as TB tunnel in all directions regardless of microfibrillar orientation, with the exception of the S_1 layer, where tunneling has been observed to follow the long direction of microfibrils. Another intriguing feature of TB degradation of wood cell walls is that TB do not cross any other's path, although spatially they may come very close to one another during tunneling (as judged by TEM views showing separation of closely placed tunnels by an extremely thin wall segment in places). This leads to the important

Fig. 2. Bacterial tunneling of *Homalium foetidum* wood cell walls. Parts of the fiber cell walls are heavily degraded and are filled with tunnels and tunnel remains. Intact tunnels and tunneling bacteria (arrows) are present in partially degraded cell wall regions. Tunneling bacteria have penetrated all cell wall regions, including the middle lamella. (*Transmission electron micrograph courtesy of Adya P. Singh*)

question of how TB communicate with one another in a solid substrate, such as the wood cell wall, where porosity is limited to the pore size of approximately 2 nm.

Some bacteria tunnel in the S_2 layer only for a short distance and then form cavities, whereas others tunnel continuously for longer distances and produce branches at random. The resulting decay patterns become either quite compact or extended with a rhizoform (rootlike) branching. The variable attack modes suggest that tunneling can be caused by a number of probably closely related bacterial species. TB does not appear to cause any other forms of degradation besides tunneling. Cellulosic lignin-free substrates such as cotton and cellophane are also degraded by TB through tunneling. No signs of erosion of the substrates have been observed.

In the final stages of attack, a typical honeycomb structure remains. Such wood has lost almost all strength and has a butterlike consistency.

Wood substrates. TB attack most types of wood. The fact that they can tunnel through the lignin-rich middle lamella, including the highly lignified cell corners, suggests that TB can degrade lignin in addition to cellulose and hemicelluloses. Purely cellulolytic bacteria cannot degrade wood, unless it has been extensively fragmented or delignified. In contrast, TB can attack even highly lignified softwoods and hardwoods, including *Pinus sylvestris* and *Alstonia scholaris*. They also attack a large number of wood species reputed for their high natural durability, such as the highly durable wood of *Eusideroxylon zwageri*. Wood samples treated with various fungicides mixed with copper-containing chemicals and those treated with creosote are degraded by TB. Wood samples that have been chemically modified through acetylation (bonding of an acetyl group onto an organic molecule) and furfurylation (addition of furfuryl alcohol), making them completely resistant to attack by white, brown, and soft rot fungi, are still degraded by TB. Therefore, TB can be considered to be ultimate degraders because of their extraordinary capacity for degradation of toxic or chemically complex woody substrates. The biochemical agents used for degradation of attack are not known, but the ability of attacking widely different substrates strongly suggests involvement of free radicals in addition to a typical setup of enzymes.

The role of TB in nature is to degrade woody substrates recalcitrant to fungal degradation. TB may cause considerable damage to wood products, whether treated or not, if exposed in environments where they are highly active. The potential of TB for the removal of complex pollutants from our environments should be explored.

Why tunneling? Wood degradation by bacteria occurs at much slower rates compared to degradation by wood-degrading fungi, particularly white and brown rot fungi. Therefore, TB have evolved strategies that allow them to utilize wood as a source of nutrition without entering into direct competition with these fungi. These strategies include

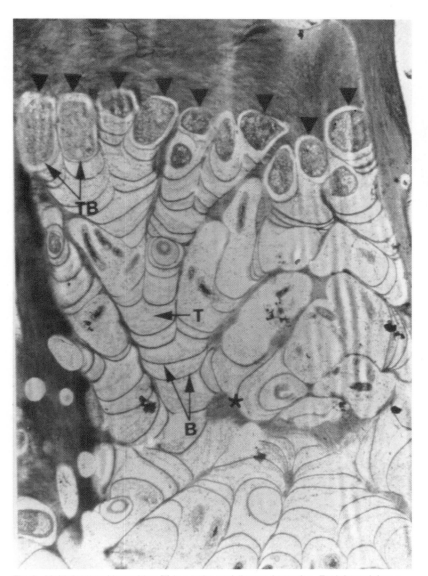

Fig. 3. Multiple tunnel branching (T) in a palm-and-fingers formation. Each branch has a single bacterium at the advancing front (arrowheads), suggestive of coordinated tunneling by tunneling bacteria (TB). Tunnels (T) contain characteristic crescent-shaped periodic bands (B). The asterisk marks a void in the heavily degraded cell wall region of the pine wood. (*Transmission electron micrograph courtesy of Adya P. Singh*)

utilization of the substrate without being exposed to the external environment and any organisms (for example, amebae and nematodes) that can predate on them in natural environments, as well as adaptations to degrade substrates that are difficult for white and brown rot fungi to degrade (for example, wood with high lignin and extractives content; or wood treated with toxic preservatives, such as CCA). Furthermore, these strategies probably minimize the loss of enzymes, particularly those that are not cell wall–bound and are produced extracellularly, and radicals through dilution or diffusion in moist or aquatic environments where the TB degradation of wood cell walls takes place. As observed in the TEM images, TB are separated from the wood cell wall matrix only by the extracellular slime covering, the slime tube, and thus are in close vicinity to

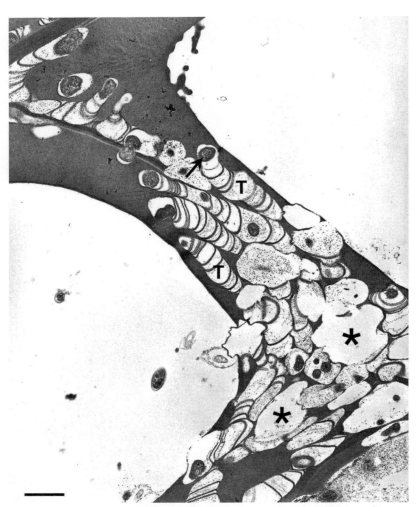

Fig. 4. Bacterial tunneling of *Alstonia scholaris* wood cell walls. Tunnels (T) contain crescent-shaped periodic bands and a bacterium at the advancing front (arrow). Tunneling bacteria are variously shaped and have penetrated all cell wall regions, including the middle lamella. Asterisks mark voids in the heavily degraded cell wall regions. (*Transmission electron micrograph courtesy of Adya P. Singh*)

TB attack has been found in many samples of driftwood collected from beaches in North America, Europe, Australia, and New Zealand. Wood samples exposed in seawater collected at various sites have been found to be often attacked by TB. Studies on wooden shipwrecks and exposure of wooden stakes into sediments at the bottom of a sea show that TB are quite oxygen demanding. This is in contrast to EB, which can be active at near-anaerobic conditions; this explains why EB are the most important degraders of wooden shipwrecks. Wood samples exposed in soils and collected from various land sites have been attacked by TB. Overall, TB occur most frequently in fertile soils and are extremely active in composts. However, TB are absent from poor acid soils.

Identity of TB. TEM images and gram-staining of wood sections with TB suggest that these bacteria are typically gram-negative. However, taxonomic identification has so far not been done because of the fact that it has not been possible to obtain pure cultures. By treating infected wood samples with antifungal antibiotics and letting TB tunnel into cellophane, followed by a subsequent washing with sterile water, mixed cultures have been obtained containing four or five different types of bacteria. Such cultures could be used to reproduce the typical tunneling observed in wood fibers. So far, however, all experiments with pure bacterial cultures have failed to result in tunneling. Molecular and immunological approaches for identification may provide more promising results. The unique feature of TB to be directly associated with an exact site of degradation should enable the use of fluorescently tagged antibodies (FISH techniques) to identify at least a specific group of bacteria.

[Acknowledgment: Adya Singh thanks the Korean Ministry of Education, Science and Technology and the Korean Federation of Science and Technology Societies for supporting this work.]

For background information *see* BACTERIA; BIODEGRADATION; CELL WALLS (PLANT); CELLULOSE; HEMICELLULOSE; LIGNIN; MICROBIAL ECOLOGY; WOOD ANATOMY; WOOD DEGRADATION; WOOD PROPERTIES in the McGraw-Hill Encyclopedia of Science & Technology.   Thomas Nilsson; Adya P. Singh

Bibliography. C. G. Björdal, Evaluation of microbial degradation of shipwrecks in the Baltic Sea, *Int. Biodeterior. Biodegrad.*, 70:126–140, 2012, DOI:10.1016/j.ibiod.2012.01.012; G. Daniel and T. Nilsson, Developments in the study of soft rot and bacterial decay, pp. 37–62, in A. Bruce and J. Palfreyman (eds.), *Forest Products Biotechnology*, Taylor and Francis, London, 1998; J. A. Drysdale, T. Nilsson, and M. E. Hedley, Decay of preservative-treated softwood posts used in horticulture in New Zealand: III. A survey to assess the types and importance of decay, *Mater. Org. (Berl.)*, 21:273–290, 1988; M.-L. Edlund and T. Nilsson, Performance of copper and non-copper based wood preservatives in terrestrial microcosms, *Holzforschung*, 53:369–375, 1999, DOI:10.1515/HF.1999.061; T. Nilsson and

the substrate. Degrading substances (enzymes and radicals) that are produced have only to cross the slime matrix to reach the substrate. Studies based on fungal systems have shown the slime sheath to be highly porous; therefore, assuming that a similar texture is present in the slime sheath produced by TB, a mechanism of degradation, which involves contact of enzymes and radicals with the lignocellulosic matrix following diffusion across the porous slime sheath, is proposed.

Ecology. TB often occur together with other types of wood-degrading microorganisms, including white and soft rot fungi and EB. No specific interactions have been reported. Wood samples exposed in soil and suffering from extensive TB attack are often gnawed at the surface by millipedes and springtails. The surface parts of samples exposed in marine environments with extensive TB and fungal attack are ingested by *Limnoria lignorum* (wood gribbles). Studies on soil, wood samples, and seawater have shown that TB possess a worldwide distribution.

D. Holt, Bacterial attack occurring in the S_2 layer of wood fibres, *Holzforschung*, 37:107–108, 1983, DOI:10.1515/hfsg.1983.37.2.107; T. Nilsson, A. P. Singh, and G. Daniel, Ultrastructure of the attack of *Eusideroxylon zwageri* wood by tunneling bacteria, *Holzforschung*, 46:361–367, 1992, DOI:10.1515/hfsg.1992.46.5.361; A. P. Singh, Certain aspects of bacterial degradation of *Pinus radiata* wood, *IAWA Bull.*, 10:405–415, 1989; A. P. Singh, T. Nilsson, and G. Daniel, Bacterial attack of *Pinus sylvestris* wood under near-anaerobic conditions, *J. Inst. Wood Sci.*, 11:237–249, 1990; A. P. Singh, T. Nilsson, and G. Daniel, Ultrastructure of the attack of two high lignin tropical hardwood species, *Alstonia scholaris* and *Homalium foetidum*, by tunneling bacteria, *J. Inst. Wood Sci.*, 11:26–42, 1987.

Vasa: the state of deterioration

The seventeenth-century Swedish Royal warship *Vasa* (**Fig. 1**) is the largest preserved maritime-archeological wooden object in the world. The ship is fascinating in many ways, being an artifact of marine and shipbuilding history. In particular, the chemistry taking place in the wood of the *Vasa* turns out to be spectacularly interesting. In the midst of being a piece of living history, a battle—one of a completely different kind than originally intended—is still raging within the ship. This chemical battle is tightly linked to the future of this Swedish national treasure.

Shipwreck and silent changes. When the warship *Vasa* made its dramatic short maiden voyage and sank in Stockholm harbor in 1628, several chemical processes started to take place (**Fig. 2**). The wood was slowly but steadily saturated with water, which in turn allowed the transport and exchange of other substances between the surrounding waters and the wooden structure. For example, the hull was held together by more than 5000 iron bolts, but nearly all of them had completely corroded away by the time that the ship was salvaged in 1961, more than three centuries after it capsized (Fig. 2). While submerged, the iron had oxidized to iron(II) ions, which had penetrated into the wood. Subsequent analyses have shown that the iron content varies throughout the ship between 0.1 and 2% by mass. The microbiological activity in the water and bottom sediment was also important. As Stockholm grew from a relatively small town to a large city, the aquatic environment of its harbor turned more and more anaerobic (lacking in oxygen). Untreated city sewage was dumped into the harbor, creating large amounts of hydrogen sulfide. This led to an influx of reduced sulfur in the surface of the wood, primarily thiol groups bound to the lignin, but also elemental sulfur and various types of iron sulfides. The time spent on the bottom thus gave rise to microbially affected surface wood with different forms of sulfur and inner parts impregnated by iron(II) ions.

Comprehensive conservation. After the salvage of the *Vasa*, a long and tedious preservation process started. The basic approach for preserving wet archeological wood is to ensure that the water-saturated material does not shrink or crack because this would do irreparable damage to the structure. To circumvent this problem, it is necessary to replace the water, thereby stabilizing the wood cells mechanically and preventing an internal collapse. In this case, polyethylene glycol (PEG) was used, which is a substance with excellent properties for the task: It is water soluble and chemically stable, and it has a low vapor pressure. In total, nearly 250 metric tons (275 short tons) of PEG was sprayed on and in the *Vasa* between 1961 and 1979 (Fig. 2). The ensuing drying process then took over until the beginning of the 1990s, when the ship was moved to its present location in the Vasa Museum (Fig. 1). Some shrinkage and subsidence were noted and expected, but overall the conservation process was deemed a success. Chemically speaking, it also meant that the

Fig. 1. The seventeenth-century warship *Vasa* on display at the Vasa Museum in Stockholm.

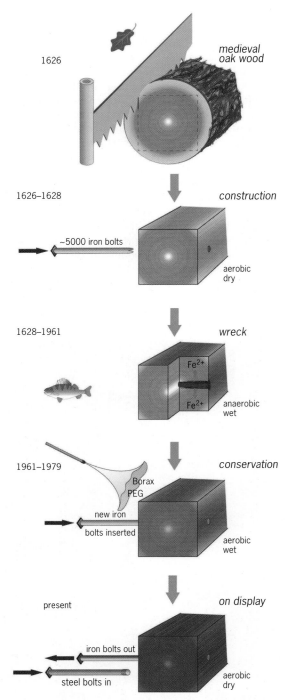

1626

medieval oak wood

1626–1628   *construction*

~5000 iron bolts

aerobic dry

1628–1961   *wreck*

Fe²⁺

Fe²⁺

anaerobic wet

1961–1979   *conservation*

Borax PEG

new iron bolts inserted

aerobic wet

present   *on display*

iron bolts out

steel bolts in

aerobic dry

Fig. 2. Overview of the environmental changes and different regimes that a piece of Vasa oak wood has been subjected to over the years.

already sulfur- and iron-rich wood was further impregnated with new compounds, PEG and antifungal boric acid, as well as being exposed to oxygen in the air (Fig. 2).

Dramatic discovery. The *Vasa* quickly turned into a popular tourist attraction. However, the rainy summer of the year 2000 exhibited periodically high air humidity, which varied quite a lot on daily, weekly, and monthly cycles. Around the same time, white

and yellow precipitations were discovered on many places of the hull, particularly in the inner parts of the ship. When the humidity increases, wood and PEG absorb water, allowing soluble compounds present inside the wood to go into solution. If the humidity later is lowered, the water and these compounds are transported to the surface, where they may precipitate and remain. The fluctuating humidity in the museum hall thus acted as a pump, transporting such compounds to the surface. The precipitations turned out to be acidic sulfur and iron compounds, and the hypothesis was that the sulfur in the wood had formed sulfuric acid. Dramatic news about the *Vasa* echoed in headlines and stories around the world, telling people to "go see her before she crumbles." These discoveries led the Vasa Museum curators to contact researchers who became involved in the project through Swedish national research funds.

Interesting interior. Further analyses, however, indicated additional problems that were not visible on the surface, but rather inside the wood. There is a well-established view of wood as consisting of thin fibers of cellulose, surrounded by hemicelluloses and lignin. The building blocks of cellulose are polymerized glucose units, whereas hemicelluloses contain other sugars, but with shorter average chain lengths. Lignin is a much more complicated network of branched organic molecules. The cellulose brings strength to the wood, the lignin provides flexibility, and the hemicelluloses act as a putty between them. Altogether, these components are integrated in the ultrastructure of the cell walls (**Fig. 3**), enabling wood to have the properties that it is known for. The exposed postsubmerged oak wood from the *Vasa*, however, did not only contain these three main components, but also large amounts of other compounds (the aforementioned iron and sulfur compounds). Through electron microscopy investigations, it has been possible to observe that the iron compounds are not separated from the woody components, but instead have attached and even integrated themselves with the cell walls (**Fig. 4**). Also, the compositions of the cellulose and hemicelluloses have changed, primarily deeper into the wood, through depolymerization, with reduced mean chain lengths. Not surprisingly, when compared to recent wood, the Vasa wood has a decreased mechanical tensile strength. Moreover, the wood was shown to be acidic where these changes had occurred. The low pH values could be an effect of sulfuric acid; however, somewhat surprisingly, the most acidic and degraded regions were found where the sulfur concentration was very low. X-ray absorption spectroscopy showed that the iron inside the wood existed as both iron(II) and iron(III) ions, with predominantly chloride and carboxylate ions as counterparts. Iron(II) ions are generally more soluble and hence more chemically active than the triply charged form, which often yields insoluble compounds (for example, rust). Iron(II) in the presence of elemental oxygen also allows for the possible formation of radicals that are highly reactive and can cause severe, irreparable damage to most biological molecules, including cellulose.

Model experiments have shown that such radical reactions indeed have taken place, where the concurrent formation of low molecular organic acids (primarily oxalic acid, but also substantial amounts of acetic, formic, and glycolic acids) can explain the low pH values detected in the wood. The radical chain reaction is fueled by additional amounts of oxygen unless it is stopped by antioxidants. Recent results show that PEG may provide such inhibitory effects, which would explain why the wood degradation is accentuated in PEG-free areas of the wood. Then again, the presence of oxalic acid, probably formed by oxidation of the wood components, may induce cellulose degradation in a second step (hydrolysis). Thus, the chemical reactions linked to the presence of iron compounds in an aerobic environment have led to reactions leading to acidification, depolymerization, and decreased mechanical stability. The acute danger of the initially noticed sulfuric acid is much smaller, in both effect and spread, whereas the degradation resulting from the presence of iron is much worse when considered from a long-term preservation point of view.

Pressure and precautions. Because the *Vasa* is bearing her own weight, estimated to be 1000 metric tons (1100 short tons), an extremely high constant pressure is put on parts of the hull, which makes it sensitive to changes in mechanical wood properties resulting from chemical deterioration. In the current research, the focus is on how fast the deterioration processes are proceeding today and may proceed in the future. Another factor of the enormous convoluted chemical puzzle that the *Vasa* has turned out to be concerns the role of water and oxygen levels in the degradation process. In 2004, a crucial measure was taken by the Vasa Museum for both the ship and other exhibited objects. The climate-control system was upgraded, and this has stabilized the temperature and relative humidity in the whole museum. This means that the chemical and mechanical changes in the wood resulting from the previous climate fluctuations have been stabilized. However, regular measurements of different parts of the hull show that the ship is under several forms of slow deformation, including hogging (in which the ship's hull curves up in the center), sagging, and subsidence, up to a few millimeters per year. Thus, there is a need for a completely new support structure that takes into account these types of deformation to preserve the ship for the future. The current research project for constructing a new supporting ship cradle, *Support Vasa*, will end in 2016, after which the construction can begin. The only limitations for this project are to make sure that no further damage is induced, chemically or mechanically, and to keep any aesthetic interference to a minimum. Furthermore, while developing a new hull-supporting structure, the bolts inserted in the 1960s are being replaced by acid-resistant stainless-steel rods (Fig. 2).

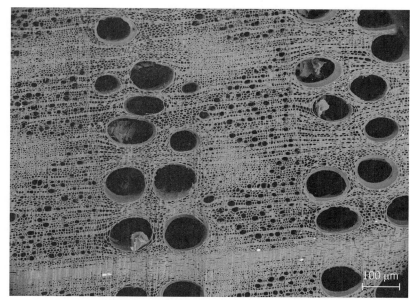

Fig. 3. Scanning electron microscopy image of a cross section of recent oak wood. The intricate morphology and cell wall structure provide high strength to the wood.

In the most pessimistic scenario, the progression will effectively break down the entire hull. However, there are positive indications that the rates of degradation were more intense during the preservation period when both water and oxygen were highly abundant. Thus, the present degradation rates should be significantly reduced in the controlled museum environment. Finally, once these processes are understood, a second salvage operation will lift the rescued wreck from the bottomless pit of eternal degradation.

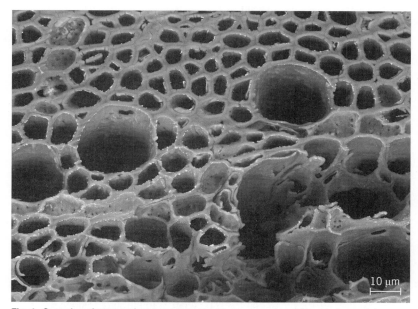

Fig. 4. Scanning electron microscopy image of a cross section of Vasa oak wood. Iron compounds have impregnated the wood and can be detected as particles or hot spots (*white*) integrated on and in the cell walls.

For background information *see* ARCHEOLOGY; ART CONSERVATION CHEMISTRY; CELL WALLS (PLANT); CELLULOSE; HEMICELLULOSE; LIGNIN; SHIPBUILDING; WOOD ANATOMY; WOOD DEGRADATION; WOOD ENGINEERING DESIGN; WOOD PROPERTIES in the McGraw-Hill Encyclopedia of Science & Technology.

Gunnar Almkvist; Daniel Lundberg

Bibliography. G. Almkvist and I. Persson, Distribution of iron and sulfur and their speciation in relation to degradation processes in wood from the Swedish warship *Vasa*, *New J. Chem.*, 35(7):1491–1502, 2011, DOI:10.1039/c1nj20056a; I. Bjurhager et al., State of degradation in archeological oak from the 17th century *Vasa* ship: Substantial strength loss correlates with reduction in (holo)cellulose molecular weight, *Biomacromolecules*, 13(8):2521–2527, 2012, DOI:10.1021/bm3007456; C. O. Cederlund, *Vasa I: The Archaeology of a Swedish Warship of 1628*, National Maritime Museums of Sweden, Oxbow Books, Oxford, UK, 2006; B. Håfors, The role of the *Wasa* in the development of the polyethylene glycol preservation method, pp. 195–216, in R. M. Rowell and R. J. Barbour (eds.), *Archaeological Wood: Properties, Chemistry, and Preservation*, American Chemical Society, Washington, DC, 1990; W. P. Henry, Non-enzymatic iron, manganese, and copper chemistry of potential importance in wood decay, pp. 175–195, in B. Goodell, D. D. Nicholas, and T. P. Schultz (eds.), *Wood Deterioration and Preservation: Advances in Our Changing World*, American Chemical Society, Washington, DC, 2003; E. Hocker, G. Almkvist, and M. Sahlstedt, The *Vasa* experience with polyethylene glycol: A conservator's perspective, *J. Cult. Herit.*, 13(3):S175–S182, 2012, DOI:10.1016/j.culher.2012.01.017; M. Sandström et al., Deterioration of the seventeenth-century warship *Vasa* by internal formation of sulphuric acid, *Nature*, 415(6874):893–897, 2002, DOI:10.1038/415893a.

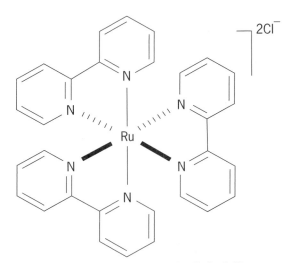

Fig. 1. Visible-light photoredox catalyst Ru(bpy)₃Cl₂.

Visible-light-assisted synthesis

A century ago, Giacomo Ciamician, a pioneer of modern photochemistry, envisioned a future where solar energy could be converted and stored through artificial photosynthetic processes, providing a clean alternative to fossil fuels. Subsequently, natural sunlight has been recognized as a free and sustained energy resource with its use holding the potential for tremendous environmental benefits. Numerous attempts have been made by the chemical community to design suitable photosynthetic systems that mimic natural photofunctional organisms. However, the inability of many organic molecules to absorb sunlight in the visible range of the spectrum has severely impeded the development of visible-light photochemistry.

Nature's efficient exploitation of solar energy conversion and electron transfer has offered inspiration for applying photosensitizers or photocatalysts in visible-light-assisted artificial photosynthesis. Among them, ruthenium(II) polypyridine complexes are commonly used because of their excellent photochemical and electrochemical properties, and have been extensively applied in established water splitting and photovoltaic and solar-cell systems. However, it is only recently that the application of visible-light photoredox catalysis in organic synthesis has drawn widespread attention with exciting reports from the D. W. C. MacMillan, T. P. Yoon, and C. R. J. Stephenson research groups. For recent reviews on photoredox catalysis, see J. M. R. Narayanam and C. R. J. Stephenson (2011) and F. Teplý (2011).

Traditionally, photochemical processes utilize ultraviolet (UV) light to generate radicals; however, such a high-energy light source can greatly reduce reaction selectivity and efficiency. Visible-light-assisted photoredox catalysis, conversely, has proved successful under milder conditions with high chemoselectivity observed in many cases. This review will discuss recent highlights in this fast growing area of research, and focus mainly on the use of the commercially available tris(2,2′-bipyridine)ruthenium dichloride complex (Ru(bpy)₃Cl₂) [**Fig. 1**].

General information of Ru(bpy)₃²⁺. Upon visible-light irradiation ($\lambda_{max} = 452$ nm), Ru(bpy)₃²⁺ will absorb a photon and generate an excited state [*Ru(bpy)₃²⁺, $\tau = 890$ ns in acetonitrile], which is sufficiently long to promote bimolecular energy- and electron-transfer reactions. Compared to its ground state, this excited state is more redox active, undergoing single-electron transfer (SET) via two distinct pathways. In the reductive quenching pathway, electron transfer from the reductive quenchers to the photocatalyst generates a strong reductant Ru(bpy)₃⁺ [−1.33 V vs. SCE (saturated calomel electrode)]; whereas, in the oxidative quenching pathway, electron transfer to the oxidative quenchers generates a strong oxidant Ru(bpy)₃³⁺ (+1.29 V vs. SCE). Therefore, depending on the chemical species present in the reaction, Ru(bpy)₃²⁺ can initiate both

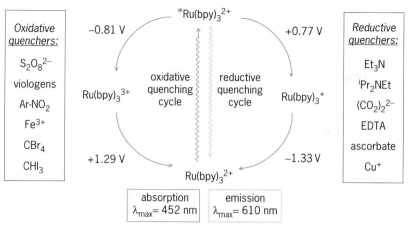

Fig. 2. Current view of photoredox catalyst Ru(bpy)$_3^{2+}$ (potentials are volts vs. SCE in CH$_3$CN).

photoreductive and oxidative transformations, respectively (**Fig. 2**).

Synthetic applications of Ru(bpy)$_3^{2+}$ employing the reductive quenching pathway. Photoreductive reactions include asymmetric α-alkylations, cycloadditions, dehalogenations, and trifluoromethylations.

α-Alkylation of aldehydes combining SOMO organocatalysis and photoredox catalysis. α-Alkylation of aldehydes with alkyl halides is a widely used strategy for C—C bond formation in organic synthesis. In 2008, MacMillan and coworkers successfully demonstrated that by

combining both photoredox catalysis and singly occupied molecular orbital (SOMO) organocatalysis, the enantioselectively catalytic α-alkylation of aldehydes in dimethylformamide (DMF) could be achieved (**Scheme 1**). Single-electron reduction of α-bromocarbonyl compound (**2**) occurs in the presence of the strong reductant Ru(bpy)$_3^+$, giving the electron-deficient alkyl radical (**5**). This reactive intermediate can then be trapped directly by the electron-rich enamine (**6**), generated from the condensation of aldehyde (**1**) with imidazolidinone

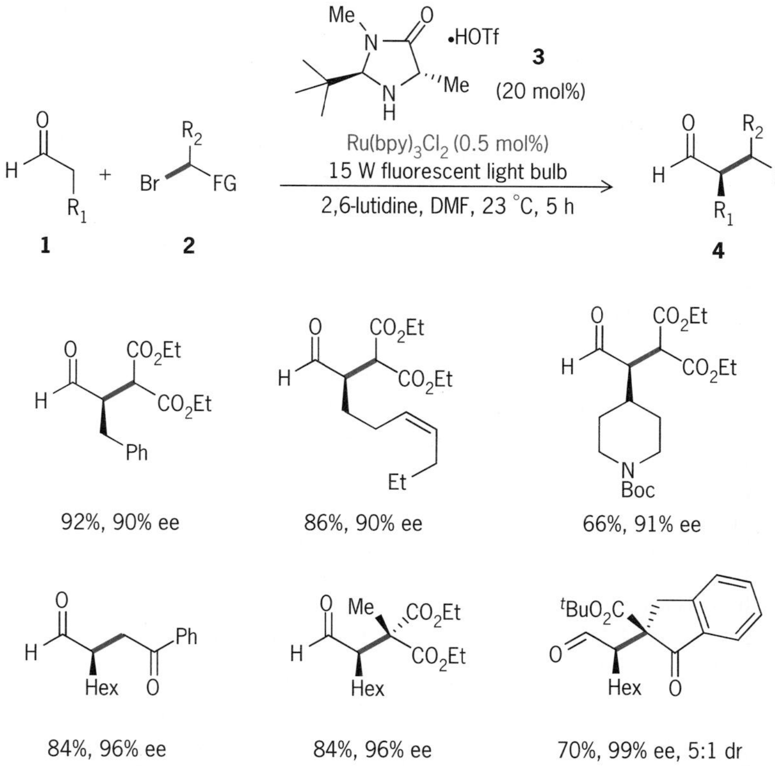

Scheme 1. Asymmetric α-alkylation of aldehydes by MacMillan. (See D. A. Nicewicz and D. W. C. MacMillan, Science, 322:77–80, 2008, DOI:10.1126/science.1161976)

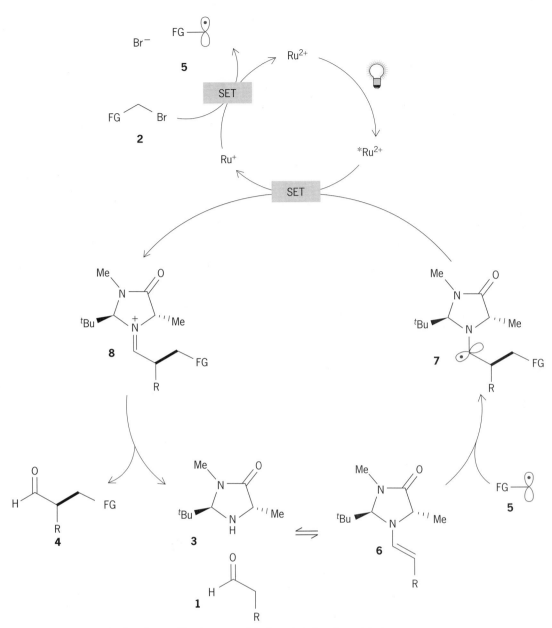

Fig. 3. Proposed mechanism for combined organocatalysis and photoredox catalysis.

catalyst (**3**). The resulting α-amino radical (**7**) is oxidized by *Ru(bpy)$_3$$^{2+}$ providing the corresponding iminium (**8**) and regenerating Ru(bpy)$_3$$^+$. The α-alkyl aldehyde product (**4**) is obtained from hydrolysis of iminium (**8**). This overall process operates with typically high levels of enantioselectivity for a range of aldehyde and bromide coupling partners (**Fig. 3**).

Visible-light-assisted [2+2] cycloaddition of enones. The same year, Yoon and coworkers reported a [2+2] cyclization of bis(enones) using visible-light photoredox catalysis (**Scheme 2**). A variety of symmetric and asymmetric enones and α,β-unsaturated carbonyl compounds are suitable substrates for this transformation, providing excellent yields and diastereomeric ratios (dr) of the cyclobutane products.

The method proceeds with high functional group tolerance and readily tolerates the formation of all-carbon quaternary stereocenters. Interestingly, complementary products could be readily accessed; the intramolecular reactions provide all *cis*-cyclobutane products, while intermolecular dimerizations of untethered enones provide all *trans*-cyclobutanes. The proposed mechanism for this transformation initiates with irradiation of Ru(bpy)$_3$$^{2+}$ to generate *Ru(bpy)$_3$$^{2+}$. Single-electron reduction by the reductive quencher *N,N*-diisopropylethylamine (^{i}Pr$_2$NEt) affords Ru(bpy)$_3$$^+$, which is capable of reducing the lithium-activated enone to give radical enolate (**11**). 1,4-Addition, followed by cycloaddition via radical addition to the enolate, provides the

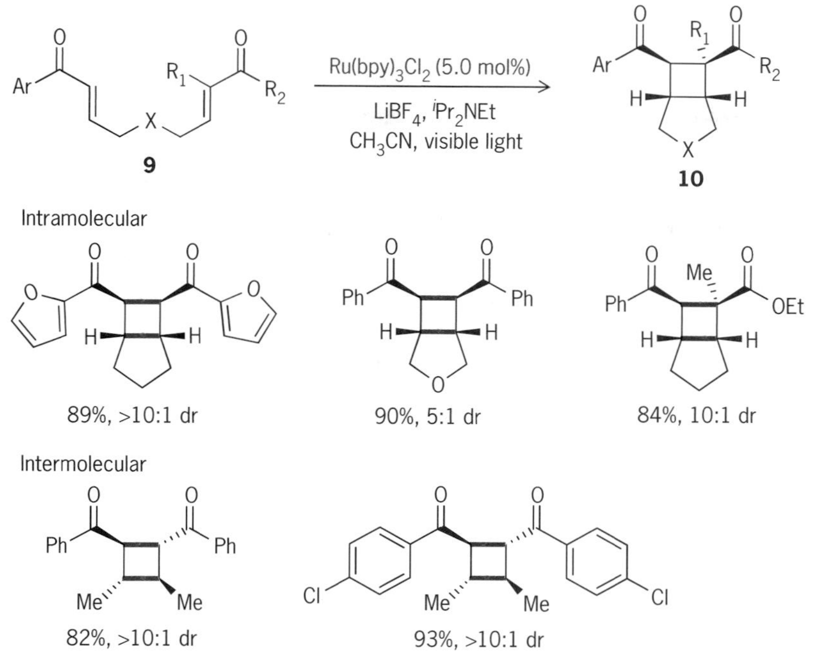

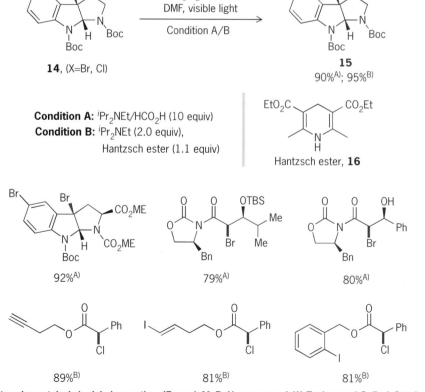

Scheme 2. Visible-light-assisted [2+2] cycloaddition by Yoon. (*From M. A. Ischay, M. E. Anzovino, J. Du, and T. P. Yoon, J. Am. Chem. Soc., 130:12886–12887, 2008, DOI:10.1021/ja805387f*)

Condition A: $^{i}Pr_2NEt/HCO_2H$ (10 equiv)
Condition B: $^{i}Pr_2NEt$ (2.0 equiv),
          Hantzsch ester (1.1 equiv)

Hantzsch ester, **16**

Scheme 3. Photoredox catalysis in dehalogenation. (*From J. M. R. Narayanam, J. W. Tucker, and C. R. J. Stephenson, Electron-transfer photoredox catalysis: Development of a tin-free reductive dehalogenation reaction, J. Am. Chem. Soc., 131:8756–8757, 2009, DOI:10.1021/ja9033582*)

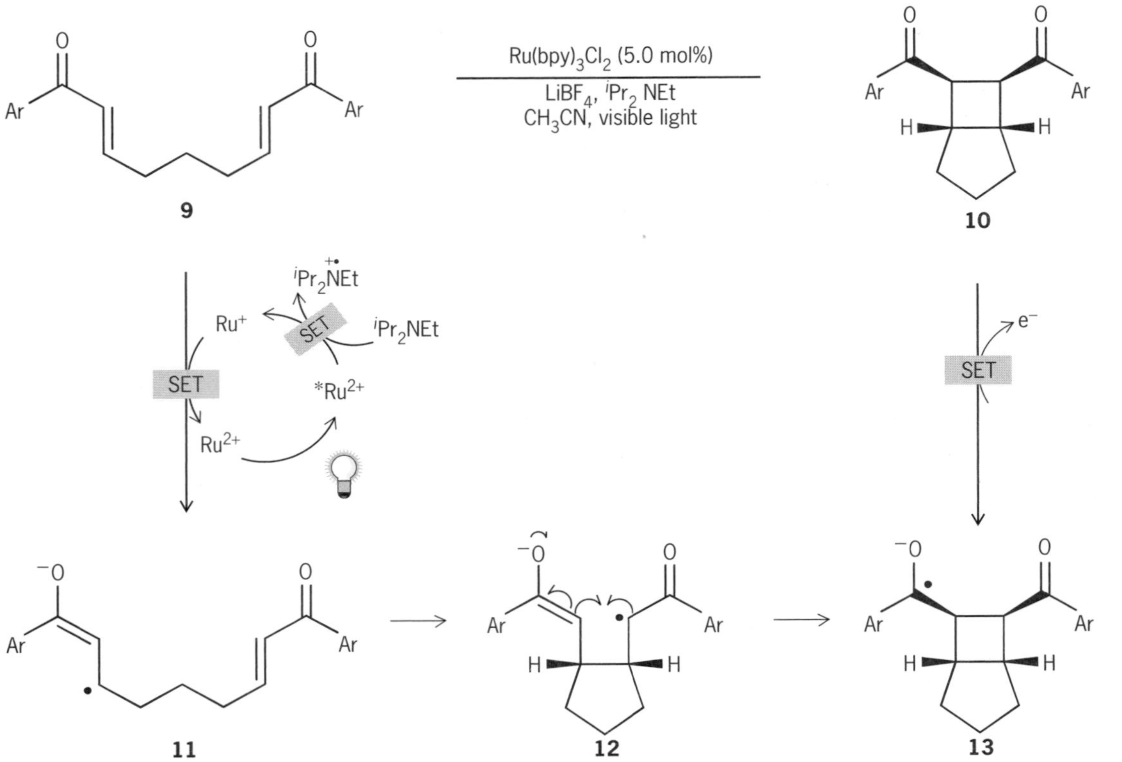

Fig. 4. Proposed mechanism for visible-light-assisted [2+2] cycloaddition.

ketyl radical (**13**). Oxidation, either by *Ru(bpy)$_3$²⁺ or the ⁱPr₂NEt radical cation, leads to the [2+2] cycloaddition product (**10**) [**Fig. 4**].

Reductive dehalogenation using photoredox catalysis. Stephenson and coworkers first reported a visible-light-assisted reductive dehalogenation. Using Ru(bpy)$_3$Cl$_2$, in combination with ⁱPr₂NEt as the reductive quencher, halogens α to an electron-withdrawing group (such as carbonyl or aryl group) are successfully reduced (**Scheme 3**).

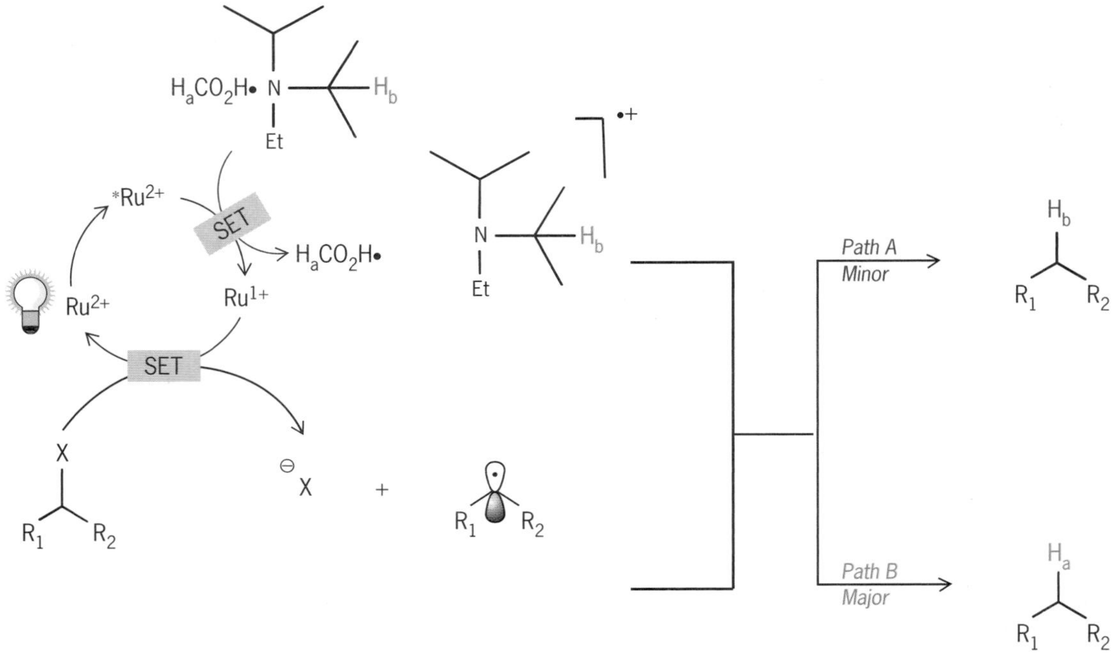

Fig. 5. Proposed mechanism for reductive dehalogenation.

The reaction circumvents the use of toxic tin reagents. The excellent chemoselectivity and high functional group tolerance results from the unique properties of Ru(bpy)$_3{}^{2+}$ and mild conditions required for the transformation, atypical of traditional methods. The authors provided two sets of reaction conditions for this transformation: **A.** Ru(bpy)$_3$Cl$_2$ (1.0 mol%), ^{i}Pr$_2$NEt (10 equiv) and formic acid (HCO$_2$H, 10 equiv); or **B.** Ru(bpy)$_3$Cl$_2$ (1.0 mol%), ^{i}Pr$_2$NEt (10 equiv) and Hantzsch ester (**16**, 1.1 equiv). Condition **B** proved particularly effective for the less activated halogen substituents. This reaction proceeds via the reductive quenching pathway with single-electron reduction by ^{i}Pr$_2$NEt to generate Ru(bpy)$_3{}^+$. This Ru(I) complex then reduces the carbon-halogen bond followed by either one of two distinct hydrogen atom abstraction pathways: (A) hydrogen abstraction from formic acid (H$_a$, minor); or (B) hydrogen abstraction from ^{i}Pr$_2$NEt (H$_b$, major) to furnish the reduced products (**Fig. 5**).

Trifluoromethylation combining photoredox catalysis and SOMO organocatalysis or transition-metal catalysis. In addition to the successful application of dual catalysis in the α-alkylation of aldehydes, MacMillan and coworkers extended this approach to the α-trifluoromethylation of aldehydes (**17**) with equally impressive enantioselectivity. In an analogous reaction mechanism to that reported for the α-alkylation, the key photocatalytic step involves the reduction of α-trifluoromethyl iodide [CF$_3$I, (**18**)] by Ir(ppy)$_2$(dtb-bpy)PF$_6$ to generate a CF$_3$ radical (**21**), which then participates in the organocatalytic pathway. This approach ultimately provides trifluoromethyl aldehydes (**20**) in good yields and with excellent enantioselectivity (**Scheme 4**).

79%, 99% ee

61%, 93% ee

68%, 99% ee
>20:1 dr

via:

21

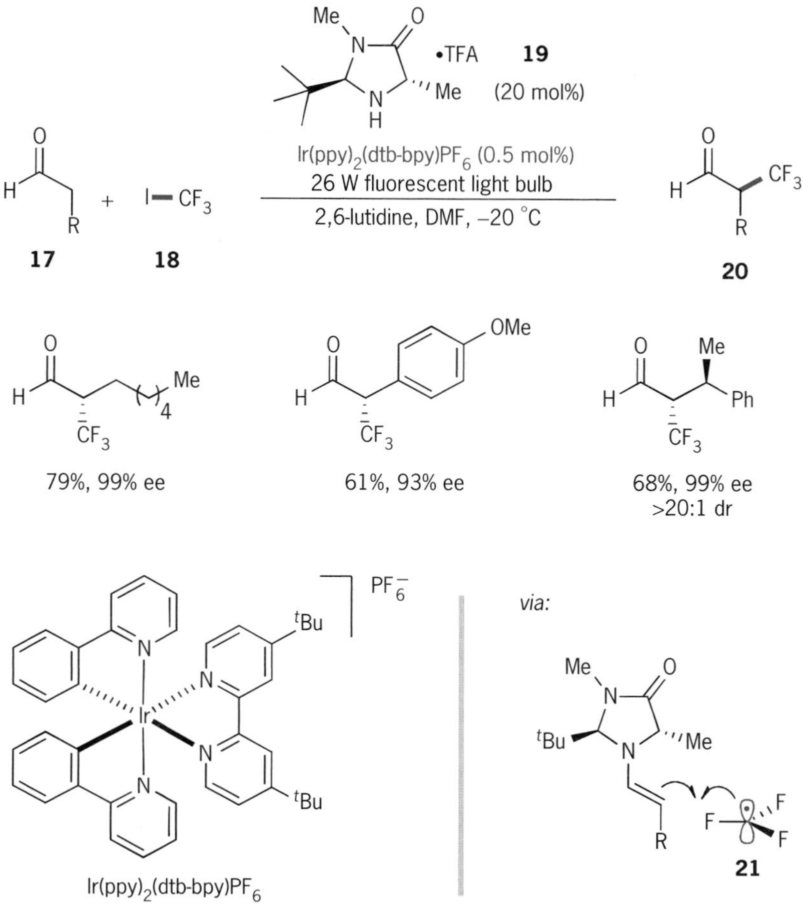

Scheme 4. α-**Trifluoromethylation of aldehydes. (*From D. A. Nagib, M. E. Scott, and D. W. C. MacMillan, Enantioselective α-trifluoromethylation of aldehydes via photoredox organocatalysis, J. Am. Chem. Soc., 131:10875–10877, 2009, DOI:10.1021/ja9053338*)**

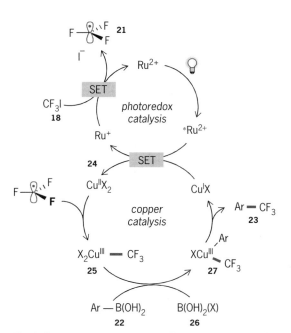

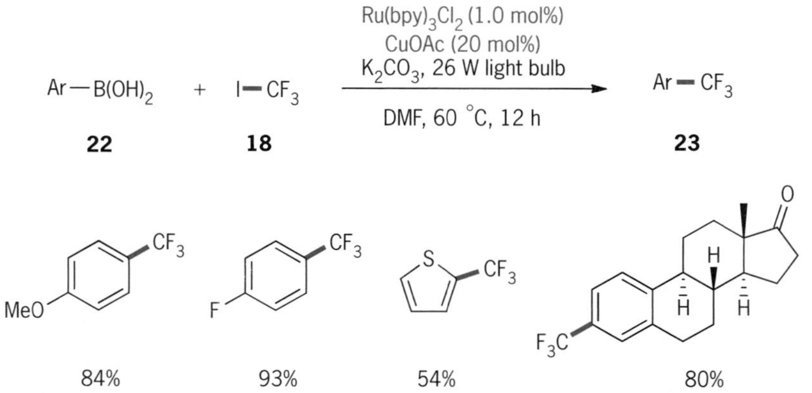

Fig. 6. Proposed mechanism for trifluoromethylation of boronic acids.

Ru(bpy)$_3$Cl$_2$ (1.0 mol%)
CuOAc (20 mol%)
K$_2$CO$_3$, 26 W light bulb

DMF, 60 °C, 12 h

84%

93%

54%

80%

Scheme 5. **Trifluoromethylation of boronic acids by Sanford. (*See Y. Ye and M. Sanford, J. Am. Chem. Soc., 134:9034–9037, 2012, DOI:10.1021/ja301553c*)**

In 2012, M. Sanford and coworkers reported a catalytic cross-coupling reaction of arylboronic acids (**22**) and CF$_3$I to form the C—CF$_3$ bond. The convergence of photoredox catalysis with transition-metal catalysis enabled the generation of an active "Cu-CF$_3$" complex that couples with arylboronic acids to form trifluoromethylated arenes and heteroarenes in good yields (**Scheme 5**). The proposed

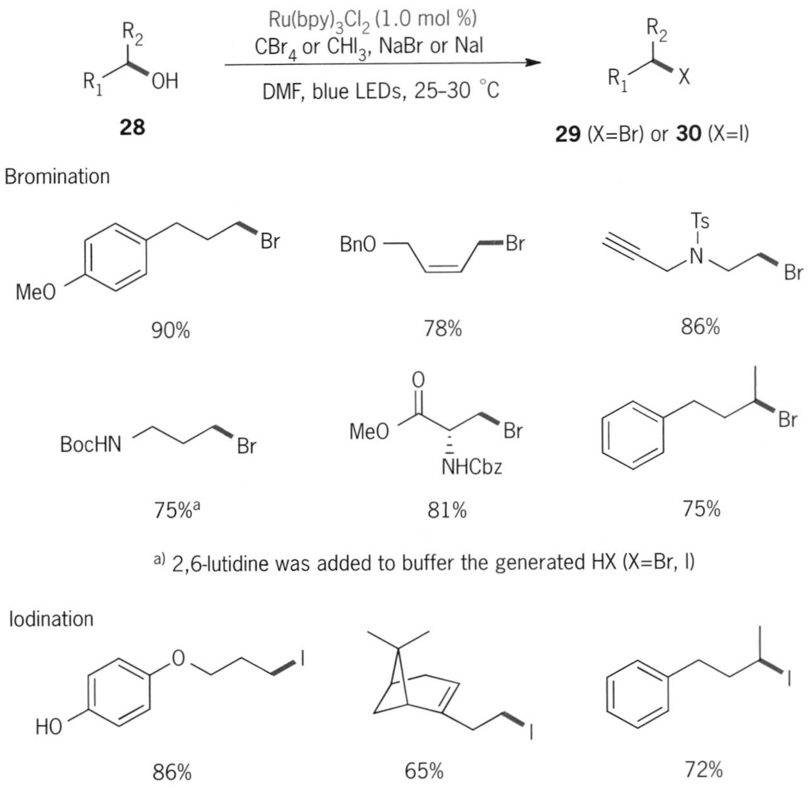

28 → 29 (X=Br) or 30 (X=I)

Ru(bpy)$_3$Cl$_2$ (1.0 mol %)
CBr$_4$ or CHI$_3$, NaBr or NaI
DMF, blue LEDs, 25–30 °C

Bromination

90%   78%   86%

75%[a]   81%   75%

[a] 2,6-lutidine was added to buffer the generated HX (X=Br, I)

Iodination

86%   65%   72%

Scheme 6. Photoredox catalysis in halogenation by Stephenson. (*See C. Dai, J. M. R. Narayanam, and C. R. J. Stephenson, Nat. Chem., 3:140–145, 2011, DOI:10.1038/nchem.949*)

36 + 37 → 40

Ru(bpy)$_3$Cl$_2$ (1.0 mol%)
NHC catalyst (5.0 mol%)
m-DNB, DCM, visible light

NHC catalyst, **38**   *m*-DNB, **39**

81%, 92% ee   75%, 92% ee   84%, 92% ee

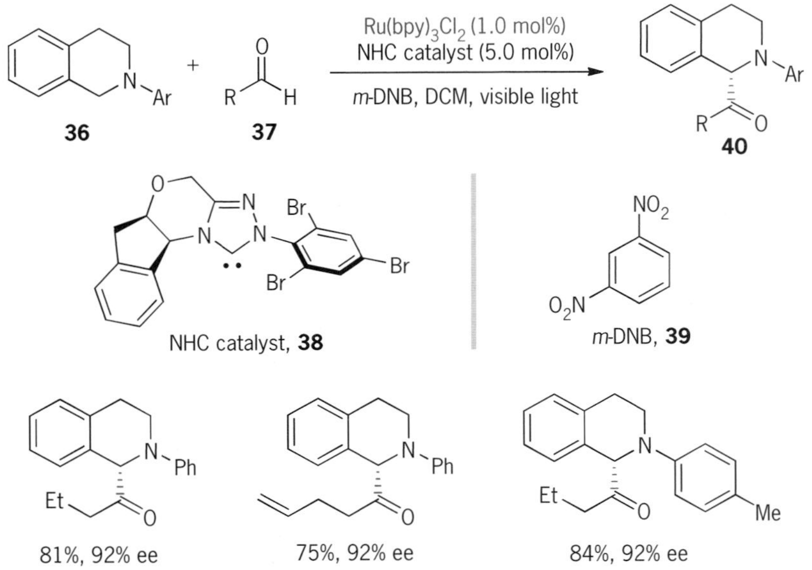

Scheme 7. α-Acylation of tertiary amines using dual catalysis by Rovis. (*See T. Rovis and D. A. DiRocco, J. Am. Chem. Soc., 134:8094–8097, 2012, DOI:10.1021/ja3030164*)

boronic acid (**22**) generates (**27**), which followed by reductive elimination provides trifluoromethylated product (**23**).

Because the CF$_3$ substituent is a common functional group found in various pharmaceutical agents, these methods provide a potential means of functionalizing molecules and drug candidates, even at a late stage.

Synthetic applications of Ru(bpy)$_3^{2+}$ employing the oxidative quenching pathway. These include carbon-carbon and carbon-halogen bond forming reactions.

Visible-light-assisted halogenation. Compared to the intensive research directed toward the reductive quenching pathway of Ru(bpy)$_3^{2+}$, the oxidative quenching pathway has found limited applications in organic synthesis, despite potential access to the strong oxidant Ru(bpy)$_3^{3+}$.

Recent research by Stephenson and coworkers has shown that reduction of polyhalomethane (CBr$_4$ or CHI$_3$) in DMF using Ru(bpy)$_3$Cl$_2$ can efficiently convert alcohols (**28**) into the corresponding bromides (**29**) or iodides (**30**) via the in situ generation of a Vilsmeier-Haack reagent (**Scheme 6**). Both CBr$_4$ and CHI$_3$ serve a dual role as the stoichiometric oxidative quenchers and the halogen sources. The reaction is typified by mild conditions, excellent yields, and broad functional group tolerance. Moreover, the absence of phosphine reagents aids product purification and increases atom economy, when compared to the classical Appel reaction.

As an example, the bromination reaction is postulated to proceed via a single-electron reduction of CBr$_4$ to generate the CBr$_3$ radical (**31**). Trapping of this electron-deficient radical by DMF generates a highly stabilized radical (**32**), which can be oxidized by Ru(bpy)$_3^{3+}$ to form an iminium intermediate (**33**) and regenerate Ru(bpy)$_3^{2+}$. Addition of the bromide ion to (**33**) produces the Vilsmeier-Haack reagent (**34**) in situ. Both (**33**) and (**34**) are able to react with alcohol (**28**) to give the reactive intermediate (**35**). Finally, (**35**) undergoes S$_N$2 displacement by bromide, to provide the bromide product (**29**) in typically excellent yield (**Fig. 7**).

α-Acylation of tertiary amines combining photoredox catalysis and NHC catalysis. The functionalization of tetrahydroisoquinolines via visible-light photoredox catalysis has received much attention. However, extension to an asymmetric C—C bond forming protocol remains a significant challenge. Recently, T. Rovis and coworkers demonstrated a highly asymmetric dual catalysis approach, combining photoredox catalysis and nucleophilic heterocyclic carbene (NHC) catalysis (**Scheme 7**). Chiral NHC catalyst (**38**) is used to generate chiral acyl anion species (**43**) from aldehyde (**37**), which serves as the competent nucleophile for the enantioselective addition to photoredox-generated iminium (**42**). Subsequent displacement of (**38**) from complex (**44**) affords product (**40**). In this report, *meta*-dinitrobenzene (**39**) is used as the sacrificial oxidative quencher of Ru(bpy)$_3$Cl$_2$. The configuration at the newly formed C—C center is controlled by the chiral

mechanism, shown in **Fig. 6**, begins with reduction of *Ru(bpy)$_3^{2+}$ by Cu(I) as the reductive quencher to give Ru(bpy)$_3^+$, which in turn reduces CF$_3$I. The resulting CF$_3$ radical (**21**) combines with the oxidized Cu^{II} species (**24**) to afford an active Cu^{III}-CF$_3$ complex (**25**). Transmetallation with

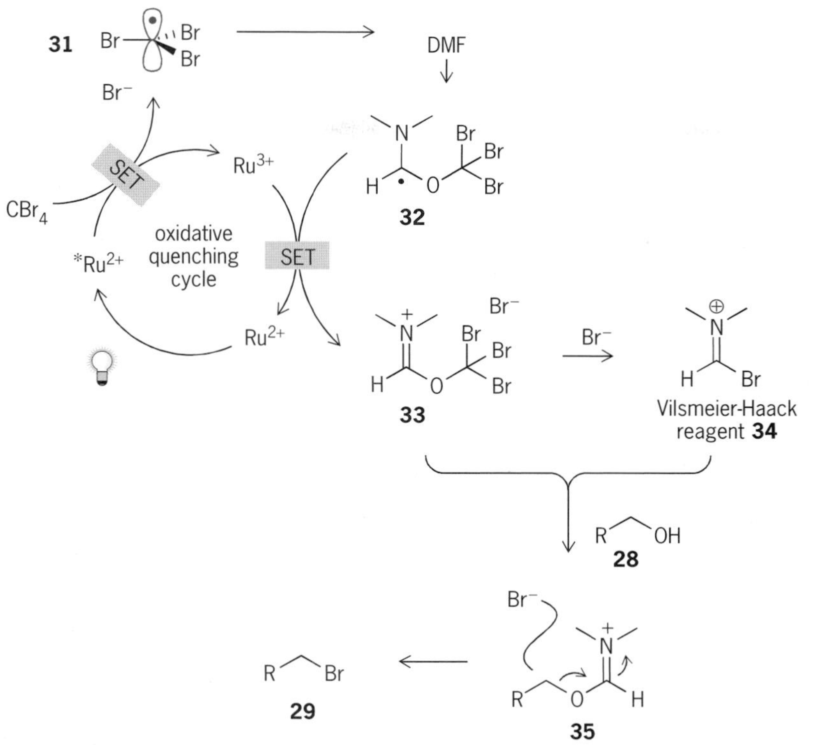

Fig. 7. Proposed mechanism for photocatalytic halogenation.

NHC catalyst. A range of aliphatic aldehydes bearing common functional groups reacted efficiently with N-aryltetrahydroisoquinolines (**36**) to provide α-acylamine products in good yields with high enantioselectivities (**Fig. 8**).

Outlook. The re-emergence of photoredox catalysis following the seminal publications of MacMillan, Yoon, and Stephenson has led to a wide variety of new synthetically efficient processes. In this review, we have discussed the applications in carbon-carbon and carbon-halogen bond formations, as well as the reduction of activated carbon-halogen bonds. Visible-light photoredox catalysis has also proved amenable to combination with other catalytic systems, such as SOMO, NHC, and transition metal catalysis. These transformations demonstrate the unique advantages of visible-light photocatalysis, typified by high chemoselectivity, mild reaction condition, and ease of operation. Although this review mainly focuses on the introduction of Ru(bpy)$_3$Cl$_2$, the tuning of photochemical properties of the catalysts can be readily achieved by variation of both the ligand and metal center. This key feature has driven the remarkable recent growth rate in this field and will no doubt continue to power further novel and exciting chemical discoveries.

For background information *see* ASYMMETRIC SYNTHESIS; CATALYSIS; ELECTROMAGNETIC RADIATION; ELECTRON-TRANSFER REACTION; INORGANIC PHOTOCHEMISTRY; ORGANIC PHOTOCHEMISTRY; ORGANIC SYNTHESIS; OXIDATION-REDUCTION;

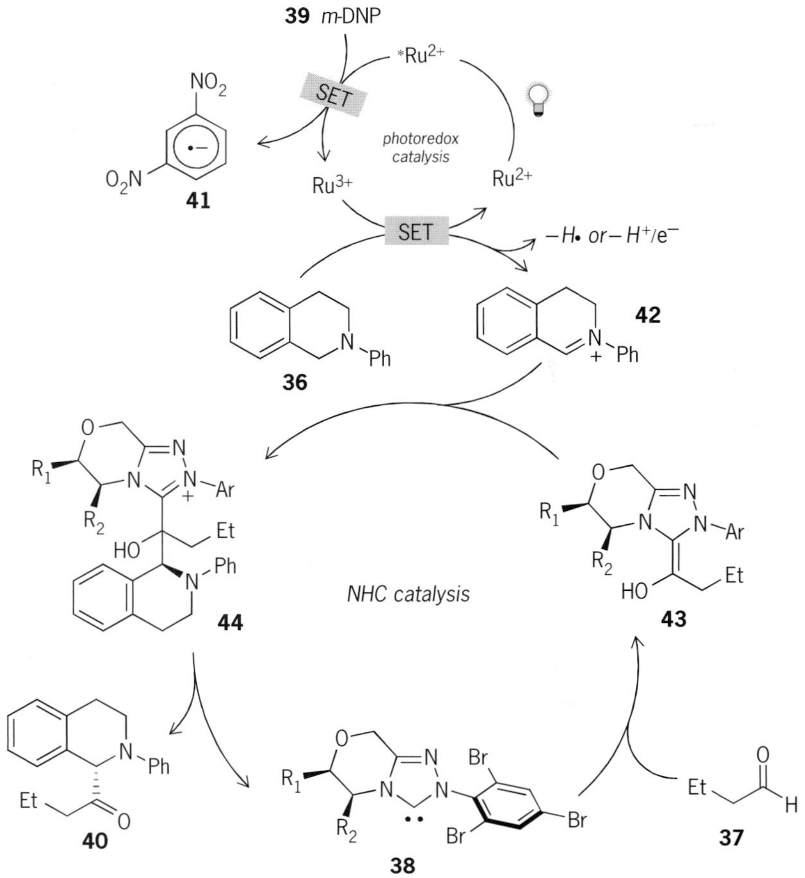

Fig. 8. Proposed mechanism for α-acylation of tertiary amines.

PHOTOCHEMISTRY in the McGraw-Hill Encyclopedia of Science & Technology.

Chunhui Dai; Corey R. J. Stephenson

Bibliography. C. Dai, J. M. R. Narayanam, and C. R. J. Stephenson, Visible-light-mediated conversion of alcohols to halides, *Nat. Chem.*, 3:140–145, 2011, DOI:10.1038/nchem.949; M. A. Ischay, M. E. Anzovino, J. Du, and T. P. Yoon, Efficient visible light photocatalysis of [2+2] enone cycloadditions, *J. Am. Chem. Soc.*, 130:12886–12887, 2008, DOI:10.1021/ja805387f; D. A. Nagib, M. E. Scott, D. W. C. MacMillan, Enantioselective α-trifluoromethylation of aldehydes via photoredox organocatalysis, *J. Am. Chem. Soc.*, 131:10875–10877, 2009, DOI:10.1021/ja9053338; J. M. R. Narayanam and C. R. J. Stephenson, Visible light photoredox catalysis: Applications in organic synthesis, *Chem. Soc. Rev.*, 40:102–113, 2011, DOI:10.1039/B913880N; J. M. R. Narayanam, J. W. Tucker, and C. R. J. Stephenson, Electron-transfer photoredox catalysis: Development of a tin-free reductive dehalogenation reaction, *J. Am. Chem. Soc.*, 131:8756–8757, 2009, DOI:10.1021/ja9033582; D. A. Nicewicz and D. W. C. MacMillan, Merging photoredox catalysis with organocatalysis: The direct asymmetric alkylation of aldehydes, *Science*, 322:77–80, 2008, DOI:10.1126/science.1161976; T. Rovis and D. A. DiRocco, Catalytic asymmetric α-acylation of tertiary amines mediated by a dual catalysis mode: *N*-heterocyclic carbene and photoredox catalysis, *J. Am. Chem. Soc.*, 134:8094–8097, 2012, DOI:10.1021/ja3030164; F. Teplý, Photoredox catalysis by [Ru(bpy)$_3$]$^{2+}$ to trigger transformations of organic molecules. Organic synthesis using visible-light photocatalysis and its 20th century roots, *Collect. Czech. Chem. Commun.*, 76:859–917, 2011, DOI:10.1135/cccc2011078; Y. Ye and M. Sanford, Merging visible-light photocatalysis and transition-metal catalysis in the copper-catalyzed trifluoromethylation of boronic acids with CF$_3$I, *J. Am. Chem. Soc.*, 134:9034–9037, 2012, DOI:10.1021/ja301553c.

Wake-wash prediction

Moving ships generate waves called wake wash, which may be harmful to the shoreline or to other users of the waterway. Estimating the impact of these waves and controlling their formation requires the ability to predict their characteristics. Ship wake-wash prediction is one component of minimizing a ship's environmental impact.

Ship-generated waves have an effect upon other users of the waterway, upon the soils and sediment of the shoreline, and upon the structures along the shore. These effects may include shoreline erosion, with potential environmental and legal consequences. A landmark case in the United States was the introduction of high-speed ferry service between the cities of Bremerton and Seattle, Washington, where unanticipated shoreline impact led to severe restrictions upon the service. Cases such as the Bremerton situation have given rise to an increased awareness of the issues associated with ship wake wash, and have led to improved techniques for wake-wash prediction.

Wake-wash characteristics. A ship moving through the water generates a series of waves. These waves are the result of the ship displacing the water out of the way for it to pass. The waves represent a pressure field in the water, generated by pressures upon the body surface of the ship. The energy represented in this pressure field is a large part of the resistance of the ship. The details of wave generation are complex, and have formed a field of study for over 300 years, from at least the time of Lord Kelvin.

Water waves are characterized by height (amplitude), wavelength or frequency, and wave direction. Ships actually produce some waves at all directions and frequencies, but there are two components of this spectrum that predominate. These are waves that generate a characteristic feather pattern, comprising a set of diverging waves in a chevron shape, and a set of transverse waves, which are more-or-less perpendicular to the ship's direction of travel.

The ship's waves are not single waves, but are actually a collection of many waves of different frequencies, and originate from different points along the ship's hull. In the far field, when the ship is far enough away that it may be represented by a single point in space, the wake-wash field may be adequately described by a directional wave spectrum.

Ship wave making is generally studied in an infinite ocean, but for certain applications it may be important to consider the water depth in which the ship is operating. This is because the characteristics of the ship-generated waves change substantially when the ship speed is large in relation to the depth (called supercritical operation). The details of this change vary from ship to ship, but the point is that the calculation of the ship wave characteristic must take into account the specific depth of the route.

Wake-wash propagation. As the waves move away from the ship, they undergo transformations and changes. In infinitely deep water, these transformations are a result of the fact that waves propagate at different speeds depending upon their frequency. Further, the water particles in an ocean wave exhibit orbital motion, which provides a dissipative mechanism that causes the energy in the wave to slowly decay.

In water of finite depth, there are also complex influences from the seabed upon the waves. The most common of these is an effect that causes all waves in shallow water to travel at the same speed, despite differences in their wavelength. This phenomenon causes waves to pile up on each other, and gives rise to the experience of breaking waves on a beach.

Wake-wash impacts. Wake-wash impacts may be of many different types. Further, different aspects of the wake-wash system give rise to different types of impact. And, of course, the nature of the shoreline, the use of the shoreline, and the shoreline structures all contribute to determining what type of impact may be considered harmful in a particular case. In consequence, it is not possible to definitively list all possible impact mechanisms or to propose a one-size-fits-all wake-wash criterion.

Marine animals and plants, such as fish, crabs, and eelgrasses, may be disturbed or even washed away by wake wash. The soils and sediments along the shore may be transported by wake wash. Soil transport may result in the destruction of marine habitat, either by undercutting existing habitat or by burying habitat under newly arriving sediments.

Soil transport may also result in undercutting of shoreline structures such as docks, piers, bulkheads, and seawalls. In other cases, the mere splashing of waves, such as a spray jet thrown upward from a seawall, may constitute damage to a flowerbed or a homeowner's lawn located at the top of that seawall.

The study of the damage mechanisms includes the application of geological sciences and even local law to determine what type of impact constitutes "damage." These topics are outside the scope of the present article, which is restricted to the prediction of the nature of the wake-wash system that arrives at the beach. What effect this wave system has upon the beach, and whether that effect is harmful, is the domain of other disciplines.

Types of prediction. The importance of the wave physics from the standpoint of wake-wash prediction is the fact that the waves that arrive at the shoreline do not have the same characteristics as the waves close to the ship. Thus, at least two types of prediction are needed: predicting the waves created by the ship, and predicting the waves experienced at the shore.

The most common technique is to predict the waves created at the ship, and then apply a second wave-propagation model to predict the transformation of these waves as they reach the shore. This procedure results in a general-purpose model of the wave associated with the ship, and a site-specific model of the wave transformation associated with any specific shoreline location. Finally, a coastal-engineering model uses the characteristics of the arriving waves to estimate the impact upon soils, sediments, structures, and beaches.

Prediction of ship-generated waves. There are basically two ways to predict the wave field that is generated by the ship: One may use measurements of physical assets, or one may use mathematical predictions. Each method has its own merits and demerits.

Prediction by physical models. The ship-generated waves may be predicted in several ways. The most accurate is of course not to predict the waves per se, but instead to measure them directly via full-scale tests of the ship itself. This method, however, requires the availability of the ship and is thus not useful during design or other early investigative phases.

The most accurate small-scale or predictive technique is to build a model of the ship and test it in a ship-model testing tank. The test is run at a range of speeds and loading conditions representative of all possible operations of the ship, and the ship-generated wake-wash wave train is measured. The wave characteristics can be scaled directly to full scale by well-understood principles. The drawback to the model testing method is its expense, associated with the construction of the physical model and the employment of an expensive testing facility.

Prediction by analog methods. During early investigative phases, when the ship design is not firmly decided, it is desirable to have a numerical predictive method, rather than the two physical predictive methods described above. Two such methods are predominant.

The first method is the use of computational fluid dynamics (CFD). CFD constructs a numerical analog of the ship—a digital ship in a digital sea. CFD methods on modern computers may be very fast and of high resolution, and are excellent practical tools.

The drawback to CFD is that the actual mathematics of fluid flow (the Navier-Stokes equations) cannot be solved. The CFD tool therefore uses some simplification or subset of these equations, thus creating an analog of the fluid flow, but not a fully accurate solution.

The simplest CFD tools (which, despite being called simple, are still very powerful and complex) use the principle of potential flow. Potential flow is generally accurate for representing flows that are incompressible, irrotational, and inviscid. These restrictions are a good model of ship waves in the far field, in deep water. In the ship's near field, however, viscosity plays a substantial role that potential flow will not capture. This viscosity can lead to froth, breaking waves on the bow or stern, and other phenomena that will not be represented accurately by CFD. At the shoreline, a potential-flow CFD model will again suffer because it is not able to represent correctly the viscosity experienced along the seabed.

In response to these shortcomings of potential flow models, some CFD tools use Reynolds-averaged Navier-Stokes (RANS) models. These models include the effect of viscosity in a broadly distributed manner. The RANS model will capture large-scale viscous effects such as the ship boundary layer, but does not always accurately predict small-scale effects such as a breaking bow or stern wave.

Unfortunately, there is no simple way of knowing whether a model that uses CFD is likely to be missing some part of the phenomenon, and thus of knowing whether the wake-wash prediction is likely to be wrong or not.

The second analog method is to rely on measurements of similar ships. Many ship designers, builders, and owners maintain libraries of measured wake-wash characteristics. Based on these characteristics, it may be possible to predict the wake-wash characteristics of a new, untested vessel by assuming various similarities with a parent ship. There is no accepted technique for this type of prediction by analogy, nor is there any accepted way of estimating the accuracy of the method a priori.

Prediction of the wake-wash propagation. The next step to predicting the total impact of the ship-generated waves upon the shoreline is to determine the changes, discussed above, that this wave field undergoes as it propagates from the ship to the shore.

The nature of the wave transformations may be predicted in a number of ways. It is possible to build a ship wave model big enough to go all the way to the shoreline, in which case the propagation effect is included. This technique is impractical in physical model testing, but may be practical in a CFD model.

Alternatively, a mathematical model of the propagation problem may be set up separate from the wave-generation model. This propagation model would then be supplied with the characteristics of the ship-generated waves, and would produce as output a set of characteristics of the modified waves as they arrive at the shoreline. In this case, the model will most likely be a stand-alone mathematical tool, and the wave characteristics will take the form of directional wave spectra, as both input and output.

Prediction of shoreline impact. Finally, the mathematical representation (spectrum) of the wave system that arrives at the beach will be passed to a set of geophysical and coastal process models to determine the nature and extent of sediment transport and related events. The prediction of these impacts is addressed in articles on civil engineering, coastal engineering, and sediment transport. *See* PARTICLE MOVEMENT SUBJECT TO A FLUCTUATING FLUID FORCE.

For background information *see* COASTAL ENGINEERING; COMPUTATIONAL FLUID DYNAMICS; FLUID MECHANICS; OCEAN WAVES; POTENTIAL FLOW; SEDIMENTOLOGY; SHIP POWERING, MANEUVERING, AND SEAKEEPING; SURFACE WAVES; TOWING TANK; VISCOSITY; WAKE FLOW; WAVE MOTION in the McGraw-Hill Encyclopedia of Science & Technology.

Chris B. McKesson

Bibliography. E. Friedrich, Ruling slows fast ferry, *The Kitsap Sun*, July 27, 1999; *Guidelines for Managing Wake Wash from High-Speed Vessels*, Report of Working Group 41 of the Maritime Navigation Commission, International Navigation Association, 2003; S. Stumbo et al., The prediction, measurement, and analysis of wake wash from marine vessels, *Mar. Tech. Soc. J.*, 36(4):248–260, 1999; *Wake Wash and Shore Protection*, Marine Vessel Environmental Protection Bulletin GM 3.2, *Society of Naval Architects and Marine Engineers Technical & Research Bulletin*, in press.

White space

White space, often called TV white space, is strictly a method to access radio spectrum owned by others. However, the term has become more widely used to describe applications that might be deployed in such a white-space spectrum. To understand white space, recall that all wireless communications needs some radio spectrum. For cellular communications, this is dedicated spectrum, often sold at auction. For applications such as Wi-Fi, this is unlicensed spectrum, set aside by the regulator to allow all to make use of it on an unprotected basis. As evidenced by the high prices paid at auction, spectrum is in scarce supply, and finding bands that can be repurposed for new uses is becoming ever harder. This scarcity stimulated a search to find ways to make more intensive use of the existing bands. Observations of licensed spectrum use showed that often there appeared to be only about 20% in use at any particular time and place, prompting the concept of shared use, whereby others could opportunistically access the unused parts of the spectrum as long as they did not cause interference to the license holders. An analogy would be someone using a house left vacant by the owners while they were away on vacation subject to it being left in an identical state such that the owners were unaware of any such usage. Research into such access methods, sometimes called cognitive access or dynamic spectrum access (DSA), has been underway since around 2000, with significant annual events such as the IEEE Communications Society Dynamic Spectrum Access Networks (DySPAN) conference.

Focus on TV bands. Shared access could occur in any frequency band, but proponents chose to focus on the band used for terrestrial television broadcasting. This tends to span the frequency band around 400–800 MHz, varying somewhat from country to country. This band is advantageous because the relatively low frequencies allow radio signals to propagate further, because it is harmonized around the world, and because television transmitters are static and well-characterized. To look at a plan of television coverage at a particular frequency, the plan is often drawn as an overlay on a map, with colors indicating the level of coverage. Those areas where there is no coverage are uncolored and hence, left white—giving the name "white spaces." Television transmitters typically do not use the same frequencies in neighboring areas to avoid interference. The net result of this practice is that, in any particular area, only about 25% of the frequencies may actually be in use, in principle leaving the remainder for white-space devices.

While television reception is the major use of this band, it is also used for "program making" services such as wireless microphones, and in some countries for a variety of other applications including radio astronomy and hospital wireless systems. In order for any shared use to be allowed, it must be possible to ensure that it does not interfere with any of these existing applications. This issue has proven complicated and contentious. Initial thinking focused on the white-space device sensing whether the spectrum was in use in an area by looking for existing transmissions, but experiment and theory showed that it was too difficult to make a device sufficiently sensitive to ensure that it received transmissions in all circumstances. So subsequent work has moved to a geolocation database approach whereby devices determine their location, for example, using GPS; they report this location to a database using preexisting communications channels (that is, not white space); and then the database determines which frequencies are available for use for the device. The database does this through having as input the known locations of licensed transmitters in the band, the anticipated locations of receivers, and a set of rules to derive availability for white-space usage. These rules include understanding how sensitive television receivers are to interference and predicting how far interfering signals might travel.

Balance between protection and innovation. Although the database approach and the concept sound simple, practical application is much more complex. Some television receivers are more sensitive to interference than others. Some viewers may have wrongly aligned antennas, poor mast-mounted amplifiers, or other issues. Some white-space devices might be higher above ground than anticipated, resulting in stronger interfering signals. None of these factors can be precisely modeled, and so approximations and judgements need to be made. The greater the protection afforded to existing license holders, the less white-space spectrum there is available for shared use because power levels from white-space devices would be reduced, sometimes to the point where applications would become unviable. Quite where this balance should lie has been the subject of much debate, study, and controversy. However, the geolocation database approach does allow for changes to rules as more experience is gained. If, for example, interference to license users were to prove greater than expected, the rules within the database could be modified to add additional margin. In principle, this could be done nearly instantaneously. This still leaves the question as to whether regulators should start conservatively and increase allowed power levels over time or start optimistically and reduce them if interference is experienced. Logic and experience suggest that latter, optimistic approach, but risk aversion and strong representation from existing license holders means that the former, conservative approach is more generally adopted. Regulations in the United States, enacted in 2012, were relatively optimistic, allowing radiated power levels up to 4 W from fixed devices. However, Ofcom in the United Kingdom, which was finalizing its regulations in mid-2013, appeared to be heading toward more conservative levels. Other countries continue to monitor developments.

Likely applications. Interest in white space has resulted predominantly from its possible use for innovative new applications. Its open, shared access, but somewhat uncertain availability, suggest that it is suitable for new ideas where unlicensed spectrum enables rapid trials and early deployments, but less suited for applications such as cellular, which tend to work with dedicated spectrum bands. Experience shows that predictions of applications are often proven incorrect but that such predictions are useful in charting future courses. During the process of enabling white-space access, three key applications areas have emerged: rural broadband, machine communications, and enhanced Wi-Fi.

Rural broadband. Rural broadband enables those living in remote areas to have faster Internet access. Providing broadband for all has long been a goal of many developed countries and has sometimes been given additional funding, such as stimulus funding in the United States. Solutions to rural broadband vary from laying fiber, through local radio distribution, to satellite systems. The use of television white space brings an additional option. Its advantages are that the radio signals propagate further than solutions using cellular or Wi-Fi bands, making the economics of remote provision more viable. It is also relatively easy to deploy in white space as both ends of the link are static and can be carefully provisioned to avoid interference with licensed users. The underlying wireless technologies tend to be repurposed from other applications with greater economies of scale and include the IEEE 802.22 standard, based on Worldwide Interoperability For Microwave Access (WiMax). Rural broadband use of white space is anticipated to grow, but by its very nature will remain a relatively low-volume application.

Machine communications. Machine communications, sometimes known as machine-to-machine (M2M) or the Internet of Things (IoT), is a rapidly emerging area. Clear benefits are foreseen from enabling billions of devices to communicate including smart energy meters; cars; city infrastructure such as garbage bins, parking spaces, and bridges; healthcare monitoring devices; and much more. Analysts predict that, by 2020, there could be 50 billion connected devices—an order of magnitude more than the number of mobile phones. Machines need to use wireless technologies that are extremely inexpensive, have a 10-year battery life, have a range of more than 8 km (5 mi) to enable ubiquitous coverage, and are optimized to short messages from large numbers of devices. Such wireless technologies did not previously exist, but the advent of white space has resulted in the development of a new standard called Weightless, which is optimized for machines and for the challenges of white-space operation. Weightless has been published as a finalized standard, and by 2013 early deployments were occurring in countries such as the United States and Singapore. If successful, this application will revolutionize our lives and generate extraordinary value from the shared use of white-space spectrum.

Enhanced Wi-Fi. Enhanced Wi-Fi uses the greater propagation at television-band frequencies to deliver a Wi-Fi system with a range of up to 1.6 km (1 mi), compared to today's range of around 100 m (300 ft). This enhanced range could be useful in achieving widespread coverage of cities and towns with Wi-Fi. However, the narrower bandwidths and possible interference suggest that data rates will be lower than those users currently enjoy from Wi-Fi systems. Work is near completion on a variant of the IEEE

802.11 Wi-Fi standard termed 802.11af. At present, it is unclear quite what such enhanced Wi-Fi might be used for, but there is substantial interest from some major software and computer companies.

Predicting future developments. During 2012, white space moved from a concept to a reality with the type approval of the first equipment in the United States and the near completion of key standards. The first volume deployments occurred during 2013, and in 2014 it should be clearer what the white space will be used for and whether it will become a key driver for innovation and valuable new services. If the concept of shared access proves successful, then it is likely to expand into other frequency bands, especially those used by government, and we may see the deployment of some services and applications, particularly in the machine communications space, that will have a major impact on our way of life.

For background information *see* MOBILE COMMUNICATIONS; RADIO SPECTRUM ALLOCATION; RADIO-WAVE PROPAGATION; TELEVISION; WIMAX BROADBAND WIRELESS COMMUNICATIONS; WIRELESS FIDELITY (WI-FI) in the McGraw-Hill Encyclopedia of Science & Technology.   William Webb

Bibliography. P. Marshall, *The Reallocation Imperative: A New Vision for Spectrum Policy*, Aspen Institute, Washington, DC, 2012; W. Webb, *Understanding Weightless*, Cambridge University Press, Cambridge, UK, 2012.

Nobel Prizes for 2013

The Nobel Prizes for 2013 included the following awards for scientific disciplines.

Chemistry. The chemistry prize was awarded jointly to Martin Karplus of Harvard University, Cambridge, Massachusetts, United States, Michael Levitt of Stanford University, Stanford, California, United States, and Arieh Warshel of the University of Southern California, Los Angeles, California, United States, for the development of multiscale, multiphysics models for complex chemical systems—that is, models that work for both large and small molecules and that incorporate both classical and quantum physics.

Today, for scientists who are studying the chemical processes or reactions of complex molecules such as drugs or biomolecules, the first step is to simulate the behavior of these systems on a computer. Thanks to developments in the computational application of theoretical chemistry and to computer power having doubled at least 20 times since 1970, scientists can frequently use simulations to gain a fairly accurate understanding of the questions they are trying to answer before starting any experimental work.

Historically, however, putting this approach into practice in chemistry was difficult. Prior to 1970, programs based on classical mechanics, which describe interactions among atoms, were able to model the atomic structures of large molecules but not their functions (for example, their chemical reactions). Meanwhile, programs based on quantum mechanics, which describe the electronic structure of atoms and molecules, were able to model changes in the structures of molecules during reactions, but only for very small and simple molecules because of the vast amount of computing power required.

Yet Karplus, Levitt, and Warshel found a way to simulate chemical reactions among more complex molecules by developing multiphysics models that calculated their properties in terms of classical and quantum mechanics simultaneously. From a modeling point of view, combining classical and quantum models is not simple because the disparate programs need to share or link information to make accurate descriptions. The main problem was that the quantum model was accurate but not efficient because of the infeasible amounts of computing power needed to describe all the atoms in the molecules of a chemical system.

The solution was to focus the quantum model on only the atoms of interest in a molecule or reaction and then to use the classical model for the remaining atoms. Karplus and Levitt first demonstrated this approach for small molecules in 1972. By 1976, Levitt and Warshel had developed a similar program that was able to describe how the enzyme lysozyme cleaves a glycoside chain in a peptide. By using hybrid models that incorporated approximate, computationally simpler methods, Levitt and Warshel were able to develop highly accurate simulations of enzymatic reactions. Even more significantly, they found that their program applied to all kinds of large molecules. Today such multiscale models are used routinely in chemical engineering, materials science, molecular biology, and pharmaceutical development, to name just a few applications.

For background information *see* BIOCHEMISTRY; COMPUTATIONAL CHEMISTRY; COMPUTER PROGRAMMING; ENZYME; MODEL THEORY; MOLECULAR SIMULATION; PHYSICAL CHEMISTRY; PROTEIN; QUANTUM CHEMISTRY; QUANTUM MECHANICS; SIMULATION in the McGraw-Hill Encyclopedia of Science & Technology.

Physics. The physics prize was awarded to François Englert, professor emeritus at Université Libre de Bruxelles in Brussels, Belgium, and Peter W. Higgs, professor emeritus at University of Edinburgh, United Kingdom, for the theory of how particles acquire mass. In 1964, the theory was proposed independently by Higgs and by Englert and Robert Brout (who died in 2011). Their ideas were confirmed by the detection of the fundamental particle predicted by the theory, called the Higgs particle or Higgs boson, which was announced on July 4, 2012.

Modern physics is based on relativity and quantum theory, which are united in relativistic quantum field theories, in which four-dimensional space-time is filled with invisible fields. All phenomena are seen as collections of vibrations in these quantum fields, and these vibrations pass through the field in small packages, called quanta, which appear to us as particles. There are matter fields with matter particles and force fields with force particles, the mediators of forces. In quantum electrodynamics (QED), the first quantum field theory, which was fully developed in the late 1940s, the force particle is the massless photon, the quantum of the electromagnetic field, and the matter particles are electrons and other charged particles.

Four fundamental forces are known in the universe: the electromagnetic interaction described by QED, the gravitational interaction, the weak nuclear interaction, and the strong nuclear interaction. With the remarkable success of QED, there were attempts to develop similar quantum field theories for the strong and weak nuclear interactions, with the more distant goal of developing theories that would unify electromagnetism and the two nuclear interactions, as J. C. Maxwell's theory had unified electricity and magnetism in the nineteenth century. To that end, theorists devised what are known as gauge theories, which embody crucial symmetry principles.

However, efforts to construct gauge theories of the strong and weak nuclear interactions soon encountered a fundamental roadblock. While the gravitational and electromagnetic interactions have virtually infinite range, the strong and weak nuclear interactions have very short ranges, on the order of 10^{-15} and 10^{-18} m, respectively. It follows, basically from the uncertainty principle, that whereas the long-range gravitational and electromagnetic interactions are mediated by massless particles, the short-range nuclear forces must be mediated by massive particles, with masses inversely proportional to the range of the force. Yet the mathematics of gauge theories simultaneously appears to require that the particles that mediate the force be massless.

These conflicting requirements seemed to pose a barrier to such theories explaining nuclear forces. Many physicists began to turn away from quantum field theories and sought alternative approaches to understanding the universe, particularly after the inauguration of higher-energy particle accelerators around 1959, which led to the discovery of a plethora of new particles seemingly beyond the power of a quantum field theory to explain.

Nevertheless, in the early 1960s, Murray Gell-Mann and others did classify the particles using the symmetry group SU(3), and then introduced the quark concept. The strongly interacting particles, such as the proton and neutron, were now understood to be composed of quarks, which were the truly fundamental entities. Thus, there were a limited number of fundamental particles in the world: the quarks (which now number 6), the leptons (which now number 6 as well), and the force carriers for the four fundamental interactions. However, there was still no dynamical theory for the quarks.

In 1961, Sheldon Glashow attempted to construct a unified gauge theory of the weak interaction and electromagnetism—what would come to be called the electroweak interaction. He explicitly introduced large masses for three of the four force carriers while leaving the fourth massless. However, the theory was not renormalizable, which meant that the mathematical series used to calculate values in the theory could not be rid of infinitely large quantities; in short, the theory was flawed but it pointed the way to subsequent efforts.

A number of attempts were made in the early 1960s to construct gauge-invariant theories with massive force particles by taking advantage of spontaneous symmetry breaking, a phenomenon in which the state of a system is less symmetrical than the fundamental equations governing the system. The hope was that spontaneous symmetry breaking would permit massive force carriers in a gauge-invariant theory by hiding the symmetries requiring them to be massless. However, a new barrier to this goal appeared to arise in what came to be called Goldstone's theorem, which appeared in a 1962 paper by Jeffrey Goldstone, Abdus Salam, and Steven Weinberg.

In 1964, the construction of a relativistic, gauge-invariant theory with a massive force particle was achieved in a paper by Englert and Brout, and, a month later, independently in two papers by Higgs. Their work relied on spontaneous symmetry breaking and circumvented the difficulty posed by Goldstone's theorem. It also introduced a new fundamental particle and an associated field pervading all of space-time. Not only the three heavy force carriers of the electroweak theory but also the quarks and leptons acquire their mass by interacting with this field, with their masses proportional to the intensity of the interaction. The field can be pictured as a viscous medium that selectively resists the motion of other particles through it. The particle and associated field have come to be called the Higgs particle or boson and the Higgs field, respectively, although they are also a consequence of the work of Englert and Brout.

Incorporating this work, Weinberg and Salam, in 1967 and 1968, respectively, presented a gauge theory of the electroweak interaction based on the same symmetry as Glashow's earlier attempt. However, the theory did not gain widespread acceptance until 1972, when Gerard 't Hooft and Martinus Veltman proved that all gauge theories are renormalizable. In 1973, David Gross, Frank Wilczek, and David Politzer presented a gauge theory for the strong interactions. The theory of elementary particles in which matter is constructed from the quarks and leptons and interacts through the gauge theories of the electroweak and strong interactions is called the standard model. Over the years it has been verified with great precision, but one piece, the detection of the Higgs boson, remained incomplete. This was a major objective of the construction of the Large Hadron Collider (LHC), probably the largest and most complex machine ever built, and was finally achieved in 2012.

For background information *see* ELECTROWEAK INTERACTION; ELEMENTARY PARTICLE; FUNDAMENTAL

INTERACTIONS; GAUGE THEORY; HIGGS BOSON; LEPTON; QUANTUM CHROMODYNAMICS; QUANTUM ELECTRODYNAMICS; QUANTUM FIELD THEORY; QUANTUM MECHANICS; QUARKS; STANDARD MODEL; STRONG NUCLEAR INTERACTIONS; SYMMETRY BREAKING; UNCERTAINTY PRINCIPLE; WEAK NUCLEAR INTERACTIONS in the McGraw-Hill Encyclopedia of Science & Technology.

Physiology or medicine. The prize in physiology or medicine was awarded jointly to James E. Rothman of Yale University in New Haven, Connecticut, United States, Randy W. Schekman of the University of California at Berkeley, United States, and Thomas C. Südhof of Stanford University in Stanford, California, United States, for their discoveries of the machinery regulating vesicle traffic, which is a major transport system in complex cells (including human cells).

Cells are the microscopic functional and structural units of all living organisms. Their survival and healthy function depend on the production, use, and export of various molecules. As such, the transport system inside a cell that directs specific molecules to where they are needed must be highly organized and controlled.

Molecules manufactured by a cell can include proteins, hormones, neurotransmitters, and other chemical signals; for example, the hormone insulin is produced by beta cells of the pancreas and then released into the blood. Because of the large size of such molecules, however, the majority cannot diffuse directly through cell membranes. Instead, cells move molecules from one side of a membrane barrier to the other by loading them into small membrane-wrapped containers. These containers or packages are called vesicles, and they are formed by membrane budding from organelles such as the plasma membrane, the endoplasmic reticulum, and the Golgi apparatus. The vesicles, once loaded, deliver their molecular cargo to locations inside or outside cells at specific moments. The exact nature of this system for cargo organization and transport has long eluded scientists. The 2013 Nobel award recognizes the tremendous work that led to the discovery of the molecular principles that govern how the cargo in vesicles is delivered and transported from one compartment to another within cells and how the vesicles enter and leave the cells.

The three recipients of the 2013 Nobel Prize played distinct roles in pinpointing the mechanism of cell vesicle trafficking and transport. Schekman elucidated the genes required for vesicle traffic. Rothman discovered the protein machinery that permits vesicles to deliver their cargo by fusing with their targets. Südhof determined which signals are needed to instruct the vesicles to release their cargo. These researchers' further investigations revealed how disturbances in this transport system can have harmful effects and contribute to various conditions and disorders (including neurological diseases, diabetes, and immunological dysfunctions).

In the 1970s, Schekman began to analyze the genetic basis of how the cell (specifically, the yeast cell) organizes its transport system. Using genetic techniques, he was able to identify certain yeast cells in which vesicles accumulated because of a defective transport mechanism. Later, his studies exposed the mutated genes that were the cause for this condition and identified three classes of genes that regulate components of the cell's transport system.

In the 1980s and 1990s, Rothman initiated his research into vesicular transport in mammalian cells. He was able to recognize a protein complex that allowed vesicles to attach to and fuse with their specific target membranes. He also showed that the same mechanism acts both inside a cell and when a vesicle binds to the outer membrane of a cell to release its cargo.

The research of Schekman and Rothman intersected with the discovery that some of the transport-related genes in yeast also coded for the transport-related proteins identified in mammals. This finding highlighted that the cellular transport system likely had an ancient evolutionary origin.

Südhof was interested in determining how nerve cells in the brain communicate with one another. In the 1990s, he determined that the trafficking system that enables neurotransmitters to be released from vesicles that fuse with the outer membrane of nerve cells is controlled by calcium ion–sensitive proteins. In revealing the exact proteins that were involved in nerve-cell signaling, he was able to show how the contents of vesicles can be released in a precise way and at a precise time.

The groundbreaking research into the cell transport process is important from a biochemical and biomolecular point of view. However, it is also important with regard to cell physiology. The proper functioning of both the cell transport system and the delivery of its vesicular cargo is critical for a variety of physiological processes in which vesicle fusion must be controlled precisely. These processes include neurotransmitter signaling in the brain and the release of hormones and immune factors. If any step or stage of the vesicular transport system is defective, then physiological diseases or conditions may result, including serious neurological, hormonal, and immunological disorders.

For background information *see* CELL (BIOLOGY); CELL BIOLOGY; CELL MEMBRANES; CELL ORGANIZATION; CYTOPLASM; ENDOCYTOSIS; ENDOPLASMIC RETICULUM; GOLGI APPARATUS; LYSOSOME-RELATED ORGANELLES; NEUROBIOLOGY; PROTEIN; SIGNAL TRANSDUCTION in the McGraw-Hill Encyclopedia of Science & Technology.

Contributors

Contributors

The affiliation of each Yearbook contributor is given, followed by the title of his or her article. An article title with the notation "coauthored" indicates that two or more authors jointly prepared an article or section.

A

Abney, Carter W. *Department of Chemistry, University of North Carolina, Chapel Hill.* METAL-ORGANIC FRAMEWORKS—coauthored.

Acevedo-Whitehouse, Dr. Karina. *Institute of Zoology, Zoological Society of London, United Kingdom; and Unit for Basic and Applied Microbiology, School of Natural Sciences, Autonomous University of Querétaro, México.* RESPONSES TO ACUTE SUN EXPOSURE IN LARGE WHALES—coauthored.

Aguilera, Prof. Anna. *Department of Computer Science, Universidad de Carabobo, Valencia, Venezuela.* TRUSTED SYSTEMS—coauthored.

Alahari, Dr. Navin. *Grand Accélérateur National d'Ions Lourds (GANIL), Caen, France.* GAMMA-RAY SPECTROSCOPY OF NEUTRON-RICH FISSION FRAGMENTS—coauthored.

Allen-Vercoe, Dr. Emma. *Department of Molecular and Cellular Biology, University of Guelph, Ontario, Canada.* HUMAN MICROBIOME AND DISEASE.

Almkvist, Dr. Gunnar. *Department of Chemistry, Swedish University of Agricultural Sciences, Uppsala, Sweden.* VASA: THE STATE OF DETERIORATION—coauthored.

Arasi, Dr. Stefania. *Department of Pediatrics, University of Messina, Italy.* ORAL IMMUNOTHERAPY—coauthored.

Argue, Dr. Debbie. *School of Archaeology and Anthropology, Australian National University, Acton, Canberra, Australian Capital Territory, Australia.* HOMO FLORESIENSIS: FURTHER INSIGHTS.

Athienitis, Prof. Andreas K. *Department of Building, Civil and Environmental Engineering, Concordia University, Montreal, Quebec, Canada.* SMART NET-ZERO ENERGY BUILDINGS.

Atsumi, Dr. Shota. *Department of Chemistry, University of California, Davis.* BIOSYNTHESIS OF FUELS—coauthored.

Aubet, Dr. Natalie R. *Department of Earth and Atmospheric Sciences, University of Alberta, Edmonton, Canada.* EARLIEST EVIDENCE OF BILATERIANS—coauthored.

B

Baharav, Dr. Zachi. *Corning West Technology Center, Corning, Inc., Palo Alto, California.* TOUCH-SCREEN DISPLAY.

Barnes, Nathan. *L'Garde, Inc., Tustin, California.* SOLAR SAILING.

Beatty, J. Kelly. *Senior Contributing Editor, Sky & Telescope Magazine, Cambridge, Massachusetts.* MARS SCIENCE LABORATORY.

Benjamin, Dr. Tavya G. R. *Department of Chemistry, Biochemistry and Physics, The University of Tampa, Florida.* MOLECULAR GADOLINIUM COMPLEXES FOR MAGNETIC RESONANCE IMAGING—coauthored.

Bennett, Dr. George N. *Department of Biochemistry and Cell Biology, Rice University, Houston, Texas.* METABOLIC ENGINEERING OF BIOCHEMICAL PATHWAYS—coauthored.

Bindi, Dr. Luca. *Dipartimento di Scienze della Terra, Università di Firenze, Italy.* NATURAL QUASICRYSTALS—coauthored.

Birch-Machin, Prof. Mark. *Dermatological Sciences, Institute of Cellular Medicine, Newcastle University, United Kingdom.* RESPONSES TO ACUTE SUN EXPOSURE IN LARGE WHALES—coauthored.

Blanton, Dr. Michael. *Department of Physics, New York University, New York.* SLOAN DIGITAL SKY SURVEY: NEW INSTRUMENTS AND PROJECTS.

Bogdanove, Dr. Adam J. *Department of Plant Pathology and Plant-Microbe Biology, Cornell University, Ithaca, New York; and Department of Plant Pathology and Microbiology, Iowa State University, Ames.* TAL EFFECTORS—coauthored.

Boon, Prof. Elizabeth M. *Department of Chemistry, Stony Brook University, New York.* BIOLOGICAL RELEVANCE OF METAL COMPLEXES OF NITRIC OXIDE—coauthored.

Boothby, Erica J. *Department of Psychology, Yale University, New Haven, Connecticut.* PROSOCIAL BEHAVIOR—coauthored.

Bowman, Amy. *Institute of Cellular Medicine, Newcastle University, United Kingdom.* RESPONSES TO ACUTE SUN EXPOSURE IN LARGE WHALES—coauthored.

Brooks, Raina D. *Student Services Contractor at U.S. Environmental Protection Agency, Research Triangle Park, North Carolina.* MINING INTERNET SEARCH AND SOCIAL MEDIA FOR EPIDEMIOLOGY; PERSONAL CHEMICAL EXPOSURE INFORMATICS—both coauthored.

Brown, Dr. Gilbert M. *Chemical Sciences Division, Oak Ridge National Laboratory, Oak Ridge, Tennessee.* ALUMINUM-BASED BATTERY TECHNOLOGIES.

Burdette, Graham. *School of Aerospace Engineering, Georgia Institute of Technology, Atlanta.* MEASUREMENT OF AIRCRAFT FUEL EFFICIENCY—coauthored.

Burhans, Mr. Bryan. *President and Chief Executive Officer, The American Chestnut Foundation, Asheville, North Carolina.* RESTORATION OF THE AMERICAN CHESTNUT TREE—coauthored.

C

Cahill, Dr. John Daniel. *Department of Psychiatry, Yale University School of Medicine, New Haven, Connecticut.* KETAMINE AND DEPRESSION.

Caldeira, João M. L. P. *Institute for Telecommunications, University of Beira Interior, Department of Informatics, Covilhã, Portugal.* BODY AREA NETWORKS FOR HEALTH CARE—coauthored.

Caminiti, Dr. Lucia. *Department of Pediatrics, University of Messina, Italy.* ORAL IMMUNOTHERAPY—coauthored.

Canelón, Prof. Rodolfo. *Department of Systems, Universidad Centroccidental Lisandro Alvarado, Barquisimeto, Venezuela.* TRUSTED SYSTEMS—coauthored.

Chan, Nelson. *Transportation Sustainability Research Center, University of California, Berkeley.* ECODRIVING—coauthored.

Chang, Dr. Daniel T. *U.S. Environmental Protection Agency, National Exposure Research Laboratory, Research Triangle Park, North Carolina.* BIOMARKERS: KEY TO EXPOSURE RECONSTRUCTION; DATA-MINING AND INFORMATICS APPROACHES FOR ENVIRONMENTAL CONTAMINANTS; PERSONAL CHEMICAL EXPOSURE INFORMATICS—all coauthored.

Clark, Dr. Alex M. *Molecular Materials Informatics, Montreal, Quebec, Canada.* MOBILE MODELING IN THE MOLECULAR SCIENCES—coauthored.

Clark, Dr. Margaret S. *Department of Psychology, Yale University, New Haven, Connecticut.* PROSOCIAL BEHAVIOR—coauthored.

Cohen, Dr. Debbie L. *Renal, Electrolyte and Hypertension Division, Department of Medicine, University of Pennsylvania, Philadelphia.* RENAL DENERVATION AS THERAPY FOR HYPERTENSION—coauthored.

Csonka, Steven. *Executive Director, Commercial Aviation Alternative Fuels Initiative (CAAFI), Lebanon, Ohio.* DROP-IN ALTERNATIVE JET FUEL.

D

Dai, Chunhui. *Department of Chemistry, Boston University, Massachusetts.* VISIBLE-LIGHT-ASSISTED SYNTHESIS—coauthored.

Dancey, Dr. Clinton L. *Department of Mechanical Engineering, Virginia Polytechnic Institute and State University, Blacksburg.* PARTICLE MOVEMENT SUBJECT TO A FLUCTUATING FLUID FORCE—coauthored.

Dary, Dr. Curtis C. *U.S. Environmental Protection Agency, National Exposure Research Laboratory, Research Triangle Park, North Carolina.* PERSONAL CHEMICAL EXPOSURE INFORMATICS—coauthored.

de Gouvêa, Dr. André. *Department of Physics and Astronomy, Northwestern University, Evanston, Illinois.* INTENSITY FRONTIER OF PARTICLE AND NUCLEAR PHYSICS

Demianski, Prof. Marek. *Department of Astronomy, Williams College, Williamstown, Massachusetts.* PLANCK MISSION.

Diplas, Prof. Panayiotis. *P.C. Rossin Professor and Chair, Fritz Engineering Laboratory, Department of Civil and Environmental Engineering, Lehigh University, Bethlehem, Pennsylvania.* PARTICLE MOVEMENT SUBJECT TO A FLUCTUATING FLUID FORCE—coauthored.

Domínguez-Rodrigo, Dr. Manuel. *Department of Prehistory, School of Geography and History, Complutense University of Madrid, Spain.* OLDUVAI GORGE.

Dorcas, Dr. Michael E. *Department of Biology, Davidson College, North Carolina.* EFFECTS OF INVASIVE BURMESE PYTHONS IN EVERGLADES NATIONAL PARK—coauthored.

Doyle, Erin L. *Department of Plant Pathology and Microbiology, Iowa State University, Ames.* TAL EFFECTORS—coauthored.

Draayer, Prof. Jerry P. *Department of Physics and Astronomy, Louisiana State University, Baton Rouge.* SYMMETRY-ADAPTED NO-CORE SHELL MODEL—coauthored.

Dytrych, Dr. Tomas. *Department of Physics and Astronomy, Louisiana State University, Baton Rouge.* SYMMETRY-ADAPTED NO-CORE SHELL MODEL—coauthored.

E

Ebrahimian, Ed. *Director of the City of Los Angeles Bureau of Street Lighting, California.* LED ROADWAY LIGHTING: THE LOS ANGELES CONVERSION PROJECT.

Edwards, Ryan. *North Carolina State University, Raleigh.* MINING INTERNET SEARCH AND SOCIAL MEDIA FOR EPIDEMIOLOGY—coauthored.

Egeghy, Dr. Peter P. *U.S. Environmental Protection Agency, National Exposure Research Laboratory, Research Triangle Park, North Carolina.* DATA-MINING AND INFORMATICS APPROACHES FOR ENVIRONMENTAL CONTAMINANTS—coauthored.

Ekins, Dr. Sean. *Collaborations in Chemistry, Fuquay Varina, North Carolina.* MOBILE MODELING IN THE MOLECULAR SCIENCES—coauthored.

Engel, Dr. Isaac. *Department of Developmental Immunology, La Jolla Institute for Allergy and Immunology, California.* NATURAL KILLER T CELLS—coauthored.

F

Fainman, Prof. Yeshaiahu S. *Principal Investigator, Ultrafast and Nanoscale Optics Group, Department of Electrical and Computer Engineering, University of California, San Diego, La Jolla.* PLASMONICS—coauthored.

Farnham, Dr. Peggy J. *Department of Biochemistry and Molecular Biology, Norris Comprehensive Cancer Center, University of Southern California, Los Angeles.* ENCODE PROJECT.

Forment, Dr. Josep Vicent. *Gurdon Institute and Department of Biochemistry, University of Cambridge, United Kingdom.* CHROMOTHRIPSIS.

Fortágh, Prof. Dr. József. *Physics Institute, University of Tübingen, Germany.* ATOMS IN MICROTRAPS.

Freake, Dr. Michael. *Department of Natural Sciences and Mathematics, Lee University, Cleveland, Tennessee.* HELLBENDER SALAMANDERS.

G

Gallop, Prof. John. *Quantum Detection Group, National Physical Laboratory, Teddington, Middlesex, United Kingdom.* CIRCUIT CAVITY ELECTROMECHANICS IN THE STRONG-COUPLING REGIME—coauthored.

Gendron, Dr. Diane. *Centro Interdisciplinario de Ciencias Marinas, Instituto Politécnico Nacional, La Paz, México.* RESPONSES TO ACUTE SUN EXPOSURE IN LARGE WHALES—coauthored.

Ghovanloo, Dr. Maysam. *GT-Bionics Laboratory, School of Electrical and Computer Engineering, Georgia Institute of Technology, Atlanta.* TONGUE DRIVE SYSTEM.

Gingras, Dr. Murray K. *Department of Earth and Atmospheric Sciences, University of Alberta, Edmonton, Canada.* EARLIEST EVIDENCE OF BILATERIANS—coauthored.

Gogtay, Dr. Nitin. *Child Psychiatry Branch, National Institute of Mental Health, National Institutes of Health, Bethesda, Maryland.* CORTICAL GRAY MATTER CHANGES IN CHILDHOOD-ONSET SCHIZOPHRENIA—coauthored.

Goldsmith, Dr. Michael-Rock. *U.S. Environmental Protection Agency, National Exposure Research Laboratory, Research Triangle Park, North Carolina.* BIOMARKERS: KEY TO EXPOSURE RECONSTRUCTION; DATA-MINING AND INFORMATICS APPROACHES FOR ENVIRONMENTAL CONTAMINANTS; MINING INTERNET SEARCH AND SOCIAL MEDIA FOR EPIDEMIOLOGY; MOBILE MODELING IN THE MOLECULAR SCIENCES; PERSONAL CHEMICAL EXPOSURE INFORMATICS—all coauthored.

Grigoriev, Dr. Igor V. *United States Department of Energy Joint Genome Institute, Walnut Creek, California.* FUTURE OF FUNGAL GENOMICS FOR ENERGY AND THE ENVIRONMENT.

Griswold, Dr. Charles E. *Schlinger Curator of Arachnology, Department of Entomology, California Academy of Sciences, San Francisco.* NEW SPIDER: TROGLORAPTOR MARCHINGTONI.

Grulke, Dr. Christopher M. *U.S. Environmental Protection Agency, National Exposure Research Laboratory, Research Triangle Park, North Carolina.* DATA-MINING AND INFORMATICS APPROACHES FOR ENVIRONMENTAL CONTAMINANTS; MINING INTERNET SEARCH AND SOCIAL MEDIA FOR EPIDEMIOLOGY; MOBILE MODELING IN THE MOLECULAR SCIENCES; PERSONAL CHEMICAL EXPOSURE INFORMATICS—all coauthored.

Gupta, Dr. Pranshu. *Department of Computing and Information Sciences, Kansas State University, Manhattan.* GREEN CLOUD ARCHITECTURE—coauthored.

H

Hao, Prof. Ling. *Quantum Detection Group, National Physical Laboratory, Teddington, Middlesex, United Kingdom.* CIRCUIT CAVITY ELECTROMECHANICS IN THE STRONG-COUPLING REGIME—coauthored.

Harley, Dr. John P. *Department of Biological Sciences, Eastern Kentucky University, Richmond.* FUNGAL MENINGITIS OUTBREAK.

Hebard, Dr. Frederick V. *Chief Scientist, The American Chestnut Foundation, Meadowview Research Farms, Meadowview, Virginia.* RESTORATION OF THE AMERICAN CHESTNUT TREE—coauthored.

Heikenfeld, Dr. Jason. *Novel Devices Laboratory, University of Cincinnati, Ohio.* COLOR ELECTRONIC PAPER.

Hejnol, Dr. Andreas. *Sars International Centre for Marine Molecular Biology, University of Bergen, Norway.* PRIAPULIDA (PENIS WORMS): IMPLICATIONS OF EMBRYONIC DEVELOPMENT—coauthored.

Henshilwood, Dr. Christopher. *Department of Archeology, History, Cultural Studies and Religion, University of Bergen, Norway.* ORIGINS OF SYMBOLIC BEHAVIOR.

Hidalgo, Dr. José A. *Law and Psychiatry Service, Massachusetts General Hospital, Boston.* NEUROSCIENCE IN THE JUDICIAL SYSTEM—coauthored.

Higham, Dr. James P. *Center for the Study of Human Origins, Department of Anthropology, New York University.* PRIMATE VISUAL SIGNALS.

Hohensee, Dr. Michael A. *Department of Physics, University of California, Berkeley.* ATOM INTERFEROMETRY—coauthored.

Hua, Prof. Hong. *College of Optical Sciences, University of Arizona, Tucson.* FREEFORM OPTICAL SURFACES.

Huan, Dr. Yonghong. *Renal, Electrolyte and Hypertension Division, Department of Medicine, University of Pennsylvania, Philadelphia.* RENAL DENERVATION AS THERAPY FOR HYPERTENSION—coauthored.

Hutcheson, Don, *HutchColor, LLC, Washington, New Jersey.* RGB WORKFLOW.

I

Ibach, Dr. Rebecca E. *Forest Products Laboratory, USDA Forest Service, Madison, Wisconsin.* STRENGTH LOSS IN DECAYED WOOD—coauthored.

Ingersoll, Dr. Daniel T. *Director of Research Collaborations, NuScale Power, LLC, Corvallis, Oregon.* SMALL MODULAR REACTORS.

Isaacs, Dr. Kristin. *U.S. Environmental Protection Agency, National Exposure Research Laboratory, Research Triangle Park, North Carolina.* MINING INTERNET SEARCH AND SOCIAL MEDIA FOR EPIDEMIOLOGY—coauthored.

J

Janecek, Dr. Julie D. *Department of Neurology, Medical College of Wisconsin, Milwaukee.* SPORTS AND BRAIN INJURY—coauthored.

K

Kibenge, Dr. Frederick S. B. *Department of Pathology and Microbiology, Atlantic Veterinary College, University of Prince Edward Island, Charlottetown, Canada.* INFECTIOUS SALMON ANEMIA.

Kimmel, Dr. Alan R. *Laboratory of Cellular and Developmental Biology, National Institute of Diabetes and Digestive and Kidney Diseases, National Institutes of Health, Bethesda, Maryland.* PERILIPINS: PRIMARY REGULATORS OF CELLULAR LIPID STORAGE—coauthored.

Kirby, Dr. Michelle. *School of Aerospace Engineering, Georgia Institute of Technology, Atlanta.* MEASUREMENT OF AIRCRAFT FUEL EFFICIENCY—coauthored.

Kirkpatrick, Prof. Michael S. *Department of Computer Science, James Madison University, Harrisonburg, Virginia.* ACCESS CONTROL MODELS.

Klein, Dr. Gabriel. *Department of Surgery, Health Sciences Center, Stony Brook Medicine, New York.* BARIATRIC SURGERY FOR OBESITY—coauthored.

Knell, Dr. Robert J. *School of Biological and Chemical Sciences, Queen Mary University of London, United Kingdom.* RESPONSES TO ACUTE SUN EXPOSURE IN LARGE WHALES—coauthored.

Koch, Dr. Sarah. *Benjamin Peirce Assistant Professor, Department of Mathematics, Harvard University, Cambridge, Massachusetts.* COMPLEX DYNAMICS.

Konhauser, Dr. Kurt O. *Department of Earth and Atmospheric Sciences, University of Alberta, Edmonton, Canada.* EARLIEST EVIDENCE OF BILATERIANS—coauthored.

Kreitman, Dr. Martin. *Department of Ecology and Evolution, Biological Sciences Collegiate Division, University of Chicago, Illinois.* ENHANCERS IN DEVELOPMENT AND EVOLUTION—coauthored.

Kronenberg, Dr. Mitchell. *Department of Developmental Immunology, La Jolla Institute for Allergy and Immunology, California.* NATURAL KILLER T CELLS—coauthored.

L

Lan, Dr. Shau-Yu. *Department of Physics, University of California, Berkeley.* ATOM INTERFEROMETRY—coauthored.

Launey, Dr. Kristina D. *Department of Physics and Astronomy, Louisiana State University, Baton Rouge.* SYMMETRY-ADAPTED NO-CORE SHELL MODEL—coauthored.

Lebow, Dr. Patricia K. *Forest Products Laboratory, USDA Forest Service, Madison, Wisconsin.* STRENGTH LOSS IN DECAYED WOOD—coauthored.

Li, Ai. *Research Chemist, Boral Industries Inc., San Antonio, Texas.* NEW GENERATION OF CONCRETES—coauthored.

Li, Prof. Guo-Qiang. *College of Civil Engineering, Tongji University, Shanghai, China.* APPLICATION AND RESEARCH OF HIGH-STRENGTH CONSTRUCTIONAL STEEL—coauthored.

Lim, Dr. Dongwook. *School of Aerospace Engineering, Georgia Institute of Technology, Atlanta.* MEASUREMENT OF AIRCRAFT FUEL EFFICIENCY—coauthored.

Lin, Prof. Wenbin. *Department of Chemistry, The University of Chicago, Illinois.* METAL-ORGANIC FRAMEWORKS—coauthored.

Lisch, Dr. Damon. *Department of Plant and Microbial Biology, University of California, Berkeley.* TRANSPOSABLE ELEMENTS IN PLANTS.

Lui, Dr. Eric M. *Department of Civil & Environmental Engineering, Syracuse University, New York.* APPLICATION OF SHAPE MEMORY ALLOYS IN EARTHQUAKE-RESISTANT DESIGN—coauthored.

Lundberg, Dr. Daniel. *Department of Chemistry, Swedish University of Agricultural Sciences, Uppsala, Sweden.* VASA: THE STATE OF DETERIORATION—coauthored.

Lundsten, Lonny. *Senior Research Technician, Monterey Bay Aquarium Research Institute, Moss Landing, California.* CARNIVOROUS DEMOSPONGE BIOLOGY.

M

Ma, Dr. Lin. *Department of Aerospace and Ocean Engineering, Virginia Polytechnic Institute and State University, Blacksburg.* MODERN METHODS OF FLOW VISUALIZATION.

MacGorman, Dr. Donald R. *NOAA/National Severe Storms Laboratory, Norman, Oklahoma.* THE ELECTRICAL NATURE OF THUNDERSTORMS.

Major, Dr. Robert J. *Department of Biology, Indiana University of Pennsylvania.* HEART REGENERATION.

Malis, Dr. Oana. *Department of Physics, Purdue University, West Lafayette, Indiana.* QUANTUM CASCADE LASERS.

Martin, Dr. Elliot. *Transportation Sustainability Research Center, University of California, Berkeley.* ECODRIVING—coauthored.

Martín-Durán, Dr. José M. *Sars International Centre for Marine Molecular Biology, University of Bergen, Norway.* PRIAPULIDA (PENIS WORMS): IMPLICATIONS OF EMBRYONIC DEVELOPMENT—coauthored.

Martinez, Dr. Carlos A. *Department of Ecology and Evolution, University of Chicago, Illinois.* ENHANCERS IN DEVELOPMENT AND EVOLUTION—coauthored.

Martinez-Levasseur, Dr. Laura M. *Department of Biology, Trent University, Peterborough, Ontario, Canada.* RESPONSES TO ACUTE SUN EXPOSURE IN LARGE WHALES—coauthored.

Mata-Toledo, Dr. Ramon A. *Professor of Computer Science, James Madison University, Harrisonburg, Virginia.* GREEN CLOUD ARCHITECTURE—coauthored.

McCrea, Dr. Michael A. *Professor and Director of Brain Injury Research, Departments of Neurosurgery and Neurology, Medical College of Wisconsin, Milwaukee.* SPORTS AND BRAIN INJURY—coauthored.

McKesson, Chris B. *Department of Naval Architecture and Marine Engineering, University of New Orleans, Louisiana.* WAKE-WASH PREDICTION.

Meier-Augenstein, Prof. Wolfram. *Stable Isotope Unit at The James Hutton Institute, Dundee, United Kingdom.* FORENSIC ISOTOPE ANALYSIS.

Mitchell-Blackwood, Dr. Jade. *College of Engineering, Michigan State University, East Lansing.* DATA-MINING AND INFORMATICS APPROACHES FOR ENVIRONMENTAL CONTAMINANTS—coauthored.

Moreno, Dr. Pablo. *Synova, S.A., Ecublens, Switzerland.* LASER MICROJET TECHNOLOGY—coauthored.

Morris, Craig. *Redtree Development Inc., Fernie, British Columbia, Canada.* MOBILE MODELING IN THE MOLECULAR SCIENCES—coauthored.

Müller, Dr. Holger. *Department of Physics, University of California, Berkeley.* ATOM INTERFEROMETRY—coauthored.

Muralidharan, Dr. Sandhya. *Department of Chemistry, Stony Brook University, New York.* BIOLOGICAL RELEVANCE OF METAL COMPLEXES OF NITRIC OXIDE—coauthored.

Muzzio, Prof. Fernando J. *Department of Chemical and Biochemical Engineering, Rutgers, The State University of New Jersey, Piscataway.* POWDER MIXING—coauthored.

N

Nam, Dr. Taewoo. *School of Aerospace Engineering, Georgia Institute of Technology, Atlanta.* MEASUREMENT OF AIRCRAFT FUEL EFFICIENCY—coauthored.

Nelson, Dr. Lindsay D. *Department of Neurology, Medical College of Wisconsin, Milwaukee.* SPORTS AND BRAIN INJURY—coauthored.

Nilsson, Dr. Thomas. *Department of Wood Science, Swedish University of Agricultural Sciences, Uppsala, Sweden.* TUNNELING BACTERIA AND TUNNELING OF WOOD CELL WALLS—coauthored.

Noël, Dr. Agnès. *Laboratory of Tumor and Development Biology, Groupe Interdisciplinaire de Génoprotéomique Appliqué-Cancer (GIGA-Cancer), University of Liège, Belgium.* LYMPHANGIOGENESIS—coauthored.

Nozzi, Dr. Nicole E. *Department of Chemistry, University of California, Davis.* BIOSYNTHESIS OF FUELS—coauthored.

O

O'Brien, Kevin T. *Complex and Adaptive Systems Laboratory, University College Dublin, Ireland.* PEPDUCINS—coauthored.

Oinas-Kukkonen, Dr. Harri. *Department of Information Processing Science, University of Oulu, Finland.* PERSUASIVE TECHNOLOGY.

Osorio, Dr. Juan G. *Department of Chemical and Biochemical Engineering, Rutgers, The State University of New Jersey, Piscataway.* POWDER MIXING—coauthored.

O'Toole, Dr. Edel A. *Centre for Cutaneous Research, Blizard Institute of Cell and Molecular Science, Barts and the London School of Medicine and Dentistry, Queen Mary University of London, United Kingdom.* RESPONSES TO ACUTE SUN EXPOSURE IN LARGE WHALES—coauthored.

Otsuka, Prof. Hideyuki. *Institute for Materials Chemistry and Engineering, Kyushu University, Fukuoka, Japan.* SELF-HEALING POLYMERS.

P

Pajno, Dr. Giovanni B. *Department of Pediatrics, Allergy Unit, University of Messina, Italy.* ORAL IMMUNOTHERAPY—coauthored.

Pang, Dr. Lin. *Ultrafast and Nanoscale Optics Group, Department of Electrical and Computer Engineering, University of California, San Diego, La Jolla.* PLASMONICS—coauthored.

Paonni, Matteo. *Joint Research Centre of the European Commission, Institute for the Protection and Security of the Citizen, Ispra, Italy.* ALTERNATIVE SATELLITE NAVIGATION SYSTEMS.

Pask, Dr. Andrew J. *Department of Molecular and Cellular Biology, University of Connecticut, Storrs.* KANGAROO GENOME.

Paupert, Dr. Jenny. *Laboratory of Tumor and Development Biology, Groupe Interdisciplinaire de Génoprotéomique Appliqué-Cancer (GIGA-Cancer), University of Liège, Belgium.* LYMPHANGIOGENESIS—coauthored.

Pecoits, Dr. Ernesto. *Department of Earth and Atmospheric Sciences, University of Alberta, Edmonton, Canada.* Earliest evidence of bilaterians—coauthored.

Peredo, Dr. Andrew. *Department of Surgery, Health Sciences Center, Stony Brook Medicine, New York.* Bariatric surgery for obesity—coauthored.

Phillips, Dr. Martin. *U.S. Environmental Protection Agency, National Exposure Research Laboratory, Research Triangle Park, North Carolina.* Biomarkers: key to exposure reconstruction—coauthored.

Pierce, Dr. Marcia M. *Department of Biological Sciences, Eastern Kentucky University, Richmond.* "Cruise ship" virus: new vaccine; Sewage water reclamation.

Platt, Dr. Donald. *Micro Aerospace Solutions, Inc., Melbourne, Florida.* Space flight, 2012.

Ploetz, Dr. Randy C. *Department of Plant Pathology, Tropical Research and Education Center, Institute of Food and Agricultural Sciences, University of Florida, Homestead.* Panama disease of bananas.

Porter, Dr. Glenn. *School of Science & Health, University of Western Sydney, Penrith, New South Wales, Australia.* Forensic photography.

Prevedouros, Prof. Panos D. *Department of Civil and Environmental Engineering, University of Hawaii at Manoa, Honolulu, Hawaii.* Integrated process for traffic project evaluation and decision making—coauthored.

Pryor, Dr. Aurora D. *Department of Surgery, Health Sciences Center, Stony Brook Medicine, New York.* Bariatric surgery for obesity—coauthored.

Pujanauski, Dr. Lindsey. *Integrated Department of Immunology, University of Colorado School of Medicine and National Jewish Health, Denver.* Broadly neutralizing antibodies—coauthored.

Purdy, Dr. Thomas P. *JILA, Boulder, Colorado, and Department of Physics, University of Colorado, Boulder.* Quantum uncertainty in macroscopic measurements.

R

Raymond, Dr. Carol Anne. *Jet Propulsion Laboratory, California Institute of Technology, Pasadena.* Dawn's asteroid exploration; Evolution of asteroid 4 Vesta—both coauthored.

Reich, Madeline. *Fuquay-Varina High School, Fuquay-Varina, North Carolina.* Mining Internet search and social media for epidemiology—coauthored.

Rejmund, Dr. Maurycy. *Grand Accélérateur National d'Ions Lourds (GANIL), Caen, France.* Gamma-ray spectroscopy of neutron-rich fission fragments—coauthored.

Retallack, Dr. Gregory J. *Department of Geological Sciences, University of Oregon, Eugene.* Origin of grasslands.

Richerzhagen, Dr. Bernold. *Synova, S.A., Ecublens, Switzerland.* Laser Microjet technology—coauthored.

Roberts, Dr. Mallory S. E. *Eureka Scientific, Inc., New York.* Black widow pulsars.

Robinson, Dr. Terry E. *Department of Psychology, University of Michigan, Ann Arbor.* Incentive-sensitization disease model of addiction—coauthored.

Rodrigues, Prof. Joel J. P. C. *Institute for Telecommunications, University of Beira Interior, Department of Informatics, Covilhã, Portugal.* Body area networks for health care—coauthored.

Rowell, Dr. Roger M. *Professor Emeritus, Department of Biological Systems Engineering, University of Wisconsin, Madison.* Fire retardant treatment of wood.

Russell, Prof. Christopher T. *Institute of Geophysics and Planetary Physics and the Department of Earth and Space Sciences, University of California, Los Angeles.* Dawn's asteroid exploration; Evolution of asteroid 4 Vesta—both coauthored.

Rutter, Dr. Jared. *Department of Biochemistry, University of Utah, Salt Lake City.* Mitochondrial pyruvate carrier.

S

San, Dr. Ka-Yiu. *Department of Bioengineering, Rice University, Houston, Texas.* Metabolic engineering of biochemical pathways—coauthored.

Sari, Prof. Hikmet. *Telecommunications Department, Supélec, Gif sur Yvette, France.* Channel equalization.

Sato, Dr. Yuki. *Rowland Institute, Harvard University, Cambridge, Massachusetts.* Manipulation of heat flow.

Scherrer, Prof. Philip H. *Department of Physics, Stanford University, Stanford, California.* Solar dynamics observatory.

Schouten, Dr. Ronald. *Law and Psychiatry Service, Massachusetts General Hospital, Boston.* Neuroscience in the judicial system—coauthored.

Shaheen, Dr. Susan. *Transportation Sustainability Research Center, University of California, Berkeley.* Ecodriving—coauthored.

Shen, Dr. Lin. *Department of Civil and Environmental Engineering, University of Hawaii at Manoa, Honolulu, Hawaii.* New generation of concretes—coauthored.

Shields, Dr. Denis C. *Department of Clinical Bioinformatics, Conway Institute of Biomolecular and Biomedical Research, University College Dublin, Ireland.* Pepducins—coauthored.

Shors, Dr. Teri. *Department of Biology and Microbiology, University of Wisconsin–Oshkosh.* Hantavirus outbreak.

Singer, Dr. Bryan F. *Department of Psychology, University of Michigan, Ann Arbor.* Incentive-sensitization disease model of addiction—coauthored.

Singh, Dr. Adya P. *Department of Wood Science and Technology, Kyungpook National University, Daegu, Republic of Korea.* TUNNELING BACTERIA AND TUNNELING OF WOOD CELL WALLS—coauthored.

Singh, Dr. Manuraj. *Centre for Cutaneous Research, Blizard Institute of Cell and Molecular Science, Barts and the London School of Medicine and Dentistry, Queen Mary University of London, United Kingdom.* RESPONSES TO ACUTE SUN EXPOSURE IN LARGE WHALES—coauthored.

Snow, Dr. Paul. *Department of Physics, University of Bath, Claverton Down, Bath, Somerset, United Kingdom.* HYPERSONIC SPECTROSCOPY FOR MATERIALS CHARACTERIZATION.

Sobus, Dr. Jon. *U.S. Environmental Protection Agency, National Exposure Research Laboratory, Research Triangle Park, North Carolina.* BIOMARKERS: KEY TO EXPOSURE RECONSTRUCTION—coauthored.

Stanton, Dr. Anthony P. *Teaching Professor and Director, Graphic Media Management, Tepper School of Business, Carnegie Mellon University, Pittsburgh, Pennsylvania.* HEADS-UP DISPLAYS.

Steinhardt, Prof. Paul J. *Princeton Center for Theoretical Science and the Department of Physics, Princeton University, New Jersey.* NATURAL QUASICRYSTALS—coauthored.

Stephenson, Prof. Corey. *Department of Chemistry, University of Michigan, Ann Arbor.* VISIBLE-LIGHT-ASSISTED SYNTHESIS—coauthored.

Sun, Dr. Yadong. *School of Earth and Environment, University of Leeds, United Kingdom.* ANCIENT LETHAL HOTHOUSE—coauthored.

Sztalryd, Dr. Carole. *Department of Medicine, University of Maryland School of Medicine, Baltimore.* PERILIPINS: PRIMARY REGULATORS OF CELLULAR LIPID STORAGE—coauthored.

T

Tan, Dr. Yumei. *U.S. Environmental Protection Agency, National Exposure Research Laboratory, Research Triangle Park, North Carolina.* BIOMARKERS: KEY TO EXPOSURE RECONSTRUCTION; DATA-MINING AND INFORMATICS APPROACHES FOR ENVIRONMENTAL CONTAMINANTS; PERSONAL CHEMICAL EXPOSURE INFORMATICS—all coauthored.

Tang, Dr. Man-Chung. *Chairman of the Board, T.Y. Lin International, San Francisco, California.* PARTIALLY CABLE-SUPPORTED GIRDER BRIDGE.

Tang, Wenke. *Department of Civil & Environmental Engineering, Syracuse University, New York.* APPLICATION OF SHAPE MEMORY ALLOYS IN EARTHQUAKE-RESISTANT DESIGN—coauthored.

Torres, Dr. Raul M. *Integrated Department of Immunology, University of Colorado School of Medicine and National Jewish Health, Denver.* BROADLY NEUTRALIZING ANTIBODIES—coauthored.

Turnbull, Dr. Laura. *Department of Geography, Durham University, United Kingdom.* ECOHYDROLOGY.

V

Vallero, Dr. Daniel A. *U.S. Environmental Protection Agency, National Exposure Research Laboratory, Research Triangle Park, North Carolina.* PERSONAL CHEMICAL EXPOSURE INFORMATICS—coauthored.

Venkatesh, Dr. Bala. *Academic Director, Centre for Urban Energy, Ryerson University, Toronto, Ontario, Canada.* FEED-IN TARIFF—coauthored.

Vyas, Dr. Nora S. *Child Psychiatry Branch, National Institute of Mental Health, National Institutes of Health, Bethesda, Maryland.* CORTICAL GRAY MATTER CHANGES IN CHILDHOOD-ONSET SCHIZOPHRENIA—coauthored.

W

Waikel, Patricia A. *Department of Biological Sciences, Broward College, Fort Lauderdale, Florida.* NEW PLANKTONIC SYMBIOSIS FOUND IN THE OCEAN.

Wang, Dr. Yan-Bo. *College of Civil Engineering, Tongji University, Shanghai, China.* APPLICATION AND RESEARCH OF HIGH-STRENGTH CONSTRUCTIONAL STEEL—coauthored.

Wasser, Dr. Solomon P. *Department of Evolutionary and Environmental Biology, Institute of Evolution, University of Haifa, Mount Carmel, Israel.* HEALTH BENEFITS OF EDIBLE AND MEDICINAL MUSHROOMS.

Watkins, Dr. Christopher B. *Department of Horticulture, Cornell University, Ithaca, New York.* POSTHARVEST TREATMENTS OF FRUIT.

Webb, Prof. William. *Neul Ltd., Cambridge, United Kingdom.* WHITE SPACE.

Werner, Dr. Eric J. *Department of Chemistry, Biochemistry and Physics, The University of Tampa, Florida.* MOLECULAR GADOLINIUM COMPLEXES FOR MAGNETIC RESONANCE IMAGING—coauthored.

Wignall, Prof. Paul B. *School of Earth and Environment, University of Leeds, United Kingdom.* ANCIENT LETHAL HOTHOUSE—coauthored.

Wildman, Dr. Derek E. *Center for Molecular Medicine and Genetics, Wayne State University School of Medicine, Detroit, Michigan.* BONOBO GENOME.

Wilkins, Katherine E. *Department of Plant Pathology and Plant-Microbe Biology, Cornell University, Ithaca, New York.* TAL EFFECTORS—coauthored.

Williams, Dr. Antony J. *Royal Society of Chemistry, Wake Forest, North Carolina.* MOBILE MODELING IN THE MOLECULAR SCIENCES—coauthored.

Willson, Dr. John D. *Department of Biological Sciences, University of Arkansas, Fayetteville.* EFFECTS OF INVASIVE BURMESE PYTHONS IN EVERGLADES NATIONAL PARK—coauthored.

X

Xu Landén, Dr. Ning. *Molecular Dermatology Research Group, Unit of Dermatology and Venereology, Department of Medicine, Karolinska Institutet, Stockholm, Sweden.* MicroRNA biogenesis pathway.

Y

Yang, Rachel Lan Chung. *Centre for Urban Energy, Ryerson University, Toronto, Ontario, Canada.* Feed-in tariff—coauthored.

Yanoviak, Andrew Charles. *Environmental Systems Planning and Design Consultants, Honolulu, Hawaii.* Masdar, sustainable desert city.

Yu, Dr. Xin Alyx. *Department of Civil and Environmental Engineering, University of Hawaii at Manoa, Honolulu, Hawaii.* Integrated process for traffic project evaluation and decision making—coauthored.

Z

Zhu, Dr. Yu-Xian. *State Key Laboratory of Protein and Plant Gene Research, College of Life Sciences, Peking University, Beijing, China.* Regulation of cotton lint growth.

Index

Index

Asterisks indicate page references to article titles.